New Perspectives on

Microsoft® Office Access® 2007

Premium Video Edition

Comprehensive

What is the Microsoft Business Certification Program?

The Microsoft Business Certification Program enables candidates to show that they have something exceptional to offer – proven expertise in Microsoft Office programs. The two certification tracks allow candidates to choose how they want to exhibit their skills, either through validating skills within a specific Microsoft product or taking their knowledge to the next level and combining Microsoft programs to show that they can apply multiple skill sets to complete more complex office tasks. Recognized by businesses and schools around the world, over 3 million certifications have been obtained in over 100 different countries. The Microsoft Business Certification Program is the only Microsoft-approved certification program of its kind.

What is the Microsoft Certified Application Specialist Certification?

 The Microsoft Certified Application Specialist Certification exams focus on validating specific skill sets within each of the Microsoft® Office system programs. The candidate can choose which exam(s) they want to take according to which skills they want to validate. The available Application Specialist exams include:

- Using Windows Vista™
- Using Microsoft® Office Word 2007
- Using Microsoft® Office Excel® 2007
- Using Microsoft® Office PowerPoint® 2007
- Using Microsoft® Office Access 2007
- Using Microsoft® Office Outlook® 2007

What is the Microsoft Certified Application Professional Certification?

 The Microsoft Certified Application Professional Certification exams focus on a candidate's ability to use the 2007 Microsoft® Office system to accomplish industry-agnostic functions, for example Budget Analysis and Forecasting, or Content Management and Collaboration. The available Application Professional exams currently include:

- Organizational Support
- Creating and Managing Presentations
- Content Management and Collaboration
- Budget Analysis and Forecasting

What do the Microsoft Business Certification Vendor of Approved Courseware logos represent?

The logos validate that the courseware has been approved by the Microsoft® Business Certification Vendor program and that these courses cover objectives that will be included in the relevant exam. It also means that after utilizing this courseware, you may be prepared to pass the exams required to become a Microsoft Certified Application Specialist or Microsoft Certified Application Professional.

For more information:

To learn more about Microsoft Certified Application Specialist or Professional exams, visit
www.microsoft.com/learning/msbc.

To learn about other Microsoft Certified Application Specialist approved courseware from Course Technology, visit
www.course.com.

*The availability of Microsoft Certified Application exams varies by Microsoft Office program, program version and language. Visit www.microsoft.com/learning for exam availability.

Microsoft, the Office Logo, Outlook, and PowerPoint are either registered trademarks or trademarks of Microsoft Corporation in the United States and/or other countries. The Microsoft Certified Application Specialist and Microsoft Certified Application Professional Logos are used under license from Microsoft Corporation.

New Perspectives on

Microsoft® Office Access® 2007

Premium Video Edition

Comprehensive

Joseph J. Adamski

Grand Valley State University

Kathleen T. Finnegan

COURSE TECHNOLOGY
CENGAGE Learning™

Australia • Brazil • Japan • Korea • Mexico • Singapore • Spain • United Kingdom • United States

COURSE TECHNOLOGY
CENGAGE Learning™

New Perspectives on Microsoft Office Access 2007—Comprehensive, Premium Video Edition

Vice President, Publisher: Nicole Jones Pinard

Executive Editor: Marie L. Lee

Associate Acquisitions Editor: Brandi Shailer

Senior Product Manager: Kathy Finnegan

Product Manager: Leigh Hefferon

Associate Product Manager: Julia Leroux-Lindsey

Editorial Assistant: Zina Kresin

Director of Marketing: Cheryl Costantini

Senior Marketing Manager: Ryan DeGrote

Marketing Coordinator: Kristen Panciocco

Developmental Editor: Jessica Evans

Senior Content Project Manager:
    Jennifer Goguen McGrail

Content Project Manager: Matthew Hutchinson

Composition: GEX Publishing Services

Text Designer: Steve Deschene

Art Director: Marissa Falco

Cover Designer: Elizabeth Paquin

Cover Art: Bill Brown

For product information and technology assistance, contact us at
Cengage Learning Customer & Sales Support, 1-800-354-9706

For permission to use material from this text or product, submit all requests online at **cengage.com/permissions**
Further permissions questions can be emailed to
permissionrequest@cengage.com

Some of the product names and company names used in this book have been used for identification purposes only and may be trademarks or registered trademarks of their respective manufacturers and sellers.

Microsoft and the Office logo are either registered trademarks or trademarks of Microsoft Corporation in the United States and/or other countries. Course Technology, Cengage Learning is an independent entity from the Microsoft Corporation, and not affiliated with Microsoft in any manner.

Disclaimer: Any fictional data related to persons or companies or URLs used throughout this book is intended for instructional purposes only. At the time this book was printed, any such data was fictional and not belonging to any real persons or companies.

ISBN-13: 978-0-538-47528-0

ISBN-10: 0-538-47528-5

Course Technology
20 Channel Center Street
Boston, Massachusetts 02210
USA

Cengage Learning is a leading provider of customized learning solutions with office locations around the globe, including Singapore, the United Kingdom, Australia, Mexico, Brazil, and Japan. Locate your local office at:
international.cengage.com/global

Cengage Learning products are represented in Canada by Nelson Education, Ltd.

To learn more about Course Technology, visit **www.cengage.com/coursetechnology**
To learn more about Cengage Learning, visit **www.cengage.com**

Purchase any of our products at your local college store or at our preferred online store **www.CengageBrain.com**

Printed in the United States of America
1 2 3 4 5 6 7 8 9 14 13 12 11 10

Preface

The New Perspectives Series' critical-thinking, problem-solving approach is the ideal way to prepare students to transcend point-and-click skills and take advantage of all that Microsoft Office 2007 has to offer.

In developing the New Perspectives Series for Microsoft Office 2007, our goal was to create books that give students the software concepts and practical skills they need to succeed beyond the classroom. We've updated our proven case-based pedagogy with more practical content to make learning skills more meaningful to students.

With the New Perspectives Series, students understand *why* they are learning *what* they are learning, and are fully prepared to apply their skills to real-life situations.

About This Book

"I really love the Margin Tips, which add 'tricks of the trade' to students' skills package. In addition, the Reality Check exercises provide for practical application of students' knowledge. I can't wait to use them in the classroom."

—Terry Morse Colucci Institute of Technology, Inc.

This book provides thorough, hands-on coverage of Microsoft Office Access 2007, and includes the following:

- *New with this Edition:* A Video Companion offering a suite of videos that illustrate the most important and challenging Access 2007 concepts and skills; **look for the ⊙ icon in the Table of Contents to see which topics have associated videos**
- *New with this Edition:* An Appendix presenting the basics of the new Microsoft Windows 7 operating system
- Complete instruction on Access 2007 basics, including creating and maintaining a database, querying a database, and creating forms and reports
- Expanded and in-depth coverage of higher level skills, including creating advanced queries, enhancing table design, creating custom forms and reports, integrating Access with other programs, automating tasks with macros, expanding Access with Visual Basic for Applications, and managing and securing a database
- A solid and complete presentation of important database concepts, including database design, field properties, table relationships, join types, splitting a database, object dependencies, normalization, and Access naming conventions
- Certification requirements for the Microsoft Certified Application Specialist exam, "Using Microsoft® Office Access 2007"

System Requirements

This book assumes a typical installation of Microsoft Office Access 2007 and Microsoft Windows Vista Ultimate with the Aero feature turned off (or Windows Vista Home Premium or Business edition). Note that you can also complete the tutorials in this book using Windows XP; you will notice only minor differences if you are using Windows XP. Refer to the tutorial "Getting Started with Microsoft Office 2007" for Tips noting these differences. The browser used in this book for any steps that require a browser is Internet Explorer 7.

The New Perspectives Approach

Context

Each tutorial begins with a problem presented in a "real-world" case that is meaningful to students. The case sets the scene to help students understand what they will do in the tutorial.

Hands-on Approach

Each tutorial is divided into manageable sessions that combine reading and hands-on, step-by-step work. Colorful screenshots help guide students through the steps. **Trouble?** tips anticipate common mistakes or problems to help students stay on track and continue with the tutorial.

InSight

InSight Boxes

New for Office 2007! InSight boxes offer expert advice and best practices to help students better understand how to work with the software. With the information provided in the InSight boxes, students achieve a deeper understanding of the concepts behind the software features and skills.

Tip

Margin Tips

New for Office 2007! Margin Tips provide helpful hints and shortcuts for more efficient use of the software. The Tips appear in the margin at key points throughout each tutorial, giving students extra information when and where they need it.

Reality Check

Reality Checks

New for Office 2007! Comprehensive, open-ended Reality Check exercises give students the opportunity to practice skills by creating practical, real-world documents, such as resumes and budgets, which they are likely to use in their everyday lives at school, home, or work.

Review

In New Perspectives, retention is a key component to learning. At the end of each session, a series of Quick Check questions helps students test their understanding of the concepts before moving on. Each tutorial also contains an end-of-tutorial summary and a list of key terms for further reinforcement.

Apply

Assessment

Engaging and challenging Review Assignments and Case Problems have always been a hallmark feature of the New Perspectives Series. Colorful icons and brief descriptions accompany the exercises, making it easy to understand, at a glance, both the goal and level of challenge a particular assignment holds.

Reference Window

Task Reference

Reference

While contextual learning is excellent for retention, there are times when students will want a high-level understanding of how to accomplish a task. Within each tutorial, Reference Windows appear before a set of steps to provide a succinct summary and preview of how to perform a task. In addition, a complete Task Reference at the back of the book provides quick access to information on how to carry out common tasks. Finally, each book includes a combination Glossary/Index to promote easy reference of material.

Brief
Introductory
Comprehensive

Our Complete System of Instruction

Coverage To Meet Your Needs

Whether you're looking for just a small amount of coverage or enough to fill a semester-long class, we can provide you with a textbook that meets your needs.

- Brief books typically cover the essential skills in just 2 to 4 tutorials.
- Introductory books build and expand on those skills and contain an average of 5 to 8 tutorials.
- Comprehensive books are great for a full-semester class, and contain 9 to 12+ tutorials.

So if the book you're holding does not provide the right amount of coverage for you, there's probably another offering available. Go to our Web site or contact your Course Technology sales representative to find out what else we offer.

Student Online Companion

This book has an accompanying online companion Web site designed to enhance learning. This Web site, www.course.com/np/office2007, includes:

- Internet Assignments for selected tutorials
- Student Data Files
- PowerPoint presentations

COURSECASTS

CourseCasts – Learning on the Go. Always available…always relevant.

Want to keep up with the latest technology trends relevant to you? Visit our site to find a library of podcasts, CourseCasts, featuring a "CourseCast of the Week," and download them to your mp3 player at http://coursecasts.course.com.

Our fast-paced world is driven by technology. You know because you're an active participant—always on the go, always keeping up with technological trends, and always learning new ways to embrace technology to power your life.

Ken Baldauf, host of CourseCasts, is a faculty member of the Florida State University Computer Science Department where he is responsible for teaching technology classes to thousands of FSU students each year. Ken is an expert in the latest technology trends; he gathers and sorts through the most pertinent news and information for CourseCasts so your students can spend their time enjoying technology, rather than trying to figure it out. Open or close your lecture with a discussion based on the latest CourseCast.

Visit us at http://coursecasts.course.com to learn on the go!

SAM: Skills Assessment Manager

SAM 2007 is designed to help bring students from the classroom to the real world. It allows students to train and test on important computer skills in an active, hands-on environment.

SAM's easy-to-use system includes powerful interactive exams, training, and projects on the most commonly used Microsoft Office applications. SAM simulates the Office 2007 application environment, allowing students to demonstrate their knowledge and think through the skills by performing real-world tasks, such as bolding text or setting up slide transitions. Add in live-in-the-application projects, and students are on their way to truly learning and applying skills to business-centric documents.

Designed to be used with the New Perspectives Series, SAM includes handy page references, so students can print helpful study guides that match the New Perspectives textbooks used in class. For instructors, SAM also includes robust scheduling and reporting features.

Instructor Resources

We offer more than just a book. We have all the tools you need to enhance your lectures, check students' work, and generate exams in a new, easier-to-use and completely revised package. This book's Instructor's Manual, ExamView testbank, PowerPoint presentations, data files, solution files, figure files, and a sample syllabus are all available on a single CD-ROM or for downloading at http://www.cengage.com/coursetechnology.

Content for Online Learning

Course Technology has partnered with the leading distance learning solution providers and class-management platforms today. To access this material, visit www.cengage.com/webtutor and search for your title. Instructor resources include the following: additional case projects, sample syllabi, PowerPoint presentations, and more. For students to access this material, they must have purchased a WebTutor PIN-code specific to this title and your campus platform. The resources for students might include (based on instructor preferences): topic reviews, review questions, practice tests, and more. For additional information, please contact your sales representative.

Acknowledgments

Our sincere thanks to the following reviewers for their helpful feedback and valuable insights: Steve Belville, Bryant & Stratton College; Bashar Elkhatib, Grantham University; Diane M. Larson, Indiana University Northwest; Ryan Murphy, Sinclair Community College; Diane Perreault, California State University, Sacramento; Debi Revelle, Sanford-Brown College; Lynne Stuhr, Trident Technical College; and Robert Van Cleave, Laramie County Community College. Many thanks to all the Course Technology staff, especially Kristina Matthews for her leadership, dedication, and good humor; Brandi Henson, for ensuring the quality and timely delivery of the supplements that accompany this text; Leigh Robbins, for her support throughout the development of this text; and Matthew Hutchinson, for his excellent management of the production process. Thanks as well to the following Manuscript Quality Assurance staff members for their diligent efforts in ensuring the quality and accuracy of this text: Christian Kunciw, MQA Project Leader; and John Freitas, Serge Palladino, Danielle Shaw, Marianne Snow, Teresa Storch, and Susan Whalen, MQA Testers. Many thanks to Lisa Ruffolo and Holly Ben-Joseph for their special contributions to this book. To Jen Goguen McGrail, more thanks than can be expressed for her exceptional work and tireless efforts in all matters related to the production of this text and the entire New Perspectives Series. To Jessica Evans, Developmental Editor, very special thanks for her outstanding editorial skills, incredible attention to detail, going above and beyond more times than I can recall, and for her friendship and "can-do" attitude that helped us overcome many hurdles to complete this text. Finally, I'm extremely grateful to Joe Adamski for his expertise, guidance, patience, and above all, friendship.

This book is dedicated with love to my parents, Ed and Mary Curran, for all their support and encouragement throughout the years; and to my two amazing sons, Connor and Devon, who demonstrated such patience and true "endurance" (go Blue Team!) during the many long hours I worked on this text; you both make me very proud.
–Kathleen T. Finnegan

Thank you to all the people who contributed to the challenge of completing of this book, with special thanks to Kathy Finnegan for her writing and friendship and for all the support she gives me in my writing; to Jessica Evans for her positive personality and influences, unlimited talents, friendship, and considerable contributions to the book; and to my wife, Judy, for everything.
–Joseph J. Adamski

Brief Contents

Access—Level III Tutorials

The ▶ icon next to a topic in the Table of Contents indicates the topic has an associated video available on the Video Companion.

Table of Contents

Access Level I Tutorials

Tutorial 1 Creating a Database
Creating a Database to Contain Customer, Contract, and Invoice Data . . . .*AC 1*

Tutorial 6 Using Form Tools and Creating Custom Forms
Creating Forms for Entering and Maintaining Contract and Invoice Data . . . .*AC 263*

Tutorial 7 Creating Custom Reports
Creating Reports with Information
About Contracts and Invoices ....*AC 333*

Tutorial 10 Automating Tasks with Macros
Creating a User Interface for the Holland Database

Tutorial 11 Using and Writing Visual Basic for Applications Code

Creating VBA Code for the Holland Database User Interface

Appendix A Introduction to Microsoft Windows 7

Exploring the Basics of Microsoft Windows 7 . . . . . .WIN7 3

Objectives

- Develop file management strategies
- Explore files and folders
- Create, name, copy, move, and delete folders
- Name, copy, move, and delete files
- Work with compressed files

Managing Your Files

Creating and Working with Files and Folders in Windows Vista

Case | Distance Learning Company

The Distance Learning Company specializes in distance-learning courses for people who want to participate in college-level classes to work toward a degree or for personal enrichment. Distance learning is formalized education that typically takes place using a computer and the Internet, replacing normal classroom interaction with modern communications technology. The company's goal is to help students gain new skills and stay competitive in the job market. The head of the Customer Service Department, Shannon Connell, interacts with the Distance Learning Company's clients on the phone and from her computer. Shannon, like all other employees, is required to learn the basics of managing files on her computer.

In this tutorial, you'll work with Shannon to devise a strategy for managing files. You'll learn how Windows Vista organizes files and folders, and you'll examine Windows Vista file management tools. You'll create folders and organize files within them. You'll also explore options for working with compressed files.

Starting Data Files

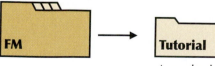

FM → Tutorial	Review	Case1
Agenda.docx	Billing.xlsx	Inv Feb.xlsx
Holiday.bmp	Car Plan.xlsx	Inv Jan.xlsx
Members.htm	Commissions.xlsx	Inv March.xlsx
New Logo.bmp	Contracts.xlsx	Painting-Agenda.docx
Proposal.docx	Customers.xlsx	Painting-Eval.docx
Resume.docx	Loan.docx	Painting-Manual.docx
Stationery.bmp	Photos.pptx	Paris.jpg
Vinca.jpg	Speech.wav	Still Life.jpg
	Water lilies.jpg	

Organizing Files and Folders

Knowing how to save, locate, and organize computer files makes you more productive when you are working with a computer. A **file**, often referred to as a **document**, is a collection of data that has a name and is stored on a computer. After you create a file, you can open it, edit its contents, print it, and save it again—usually using the same program you used to create it. You organize files by storing them in **folders**, which are containers for your files. You need to organize files so that you can find them easily and work efficiently.

A file cabinet is a common metaphor for computer file organization. A computer is like a file cabinet that has two or more drawers—each drawer is a storage device, or **disk**. Each disk contains folders that hold documents, or files. To make it easy to retrieve files, you arrange them logically into folders. For example, one folder might contain financial data, another might contain your creative work, and another could contain information you're collecting for an upcoming vacation.

A computer can store folders and files on different types of disks, ranging from removable media—such as **USB drives** (also called USB flash drives), **compact discs (CDs)**, and **digital video discs (DVDs)**—to **hard disks**, or fixed disks, which are permanently stored on a computer. Hard disks are the most popular type of computer storage because they can contain many gigabytes of data and are economical.

To have your computer access a removable disk, you must insert the disk into a **drive**, which is a computer device that can retrieve and sometimes record data on a disk. See Figure 1. A hard disk is already contained in a drive, so you don't need to insert it each time you use the computer.

Figure 1 Comparing drives and disks

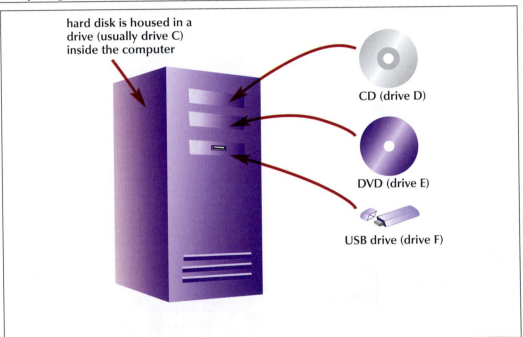

A computer distinguishes one drive from another by assigning each a drive letter. The hard disk is usually assigned to drive C. The remaining drives can have any other letters, but are usually assigned in the order that the drives were installed on the computer—so your USB drive might be drive D or drive F. Most contemporary computers have ports for more than one USB drive.

Understanding the Need for Organizing Files and Folders

Windows Vista stores thousands of files in many folders on the hard disk of your computer. These are system files that Windows Vista needs to display the desktop, use drives, and perform other operating system tasks. To ensure system stability and find files quickly, Windows Vista organizes the folders and files in a hierarchy, or **file system**. At the top of the hierarchy, Windows Vista stores folders and important files that it needs when you turn on the computer. This location is called the **root directory**, and is usually drive C (the hard disk). The term "root" refers to another popular metaphor for visualizing a file system—an upside-down tree, which reflects the file hierarchy that Windows Vista uses. In Figure 2, the tree trunk corresponds to the root directory, the branches to the folders, and the leaves to the files.

Windows file hierarchy   Figure 2

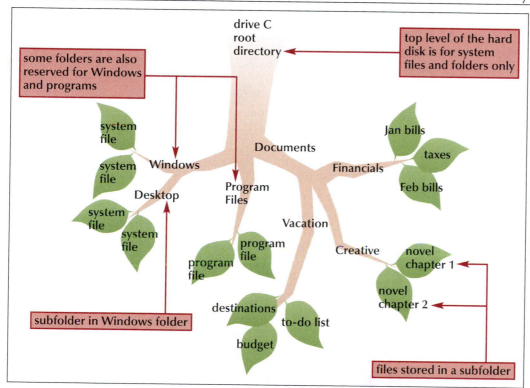

Note that some folders contain other folders. An effectively organized computer contains a few folders in the root directory, and those folders contain other folders, also called **subfolders**.

The root directory, or top level, of the hard disk is for system files and folders only—you should not store your own work here because it could interfere with Windows or a program. (If you are working in a computer lab, you might not be allowed to access the root directory.)

Do not delete or move any files or folders from the root directory of the hard disk—doing so could mean that you cannot run or start the computer. In fact, you should not reorganize or change any folder that contains installed software because Windows Vista expects to find the files for specific programs within certain folders. If you reorganize or change these folders, Windows Vista cannot locate and start the programs stored in that folder. Likewise, you should not make changes to the folder that contains the Windows Vista operating system (usually named Windows or Winnt).

Because the top level of the hard disk is off-limits for your files—the ones that you create, open, and save on the hard disk—you must store your files in subfolders. If you are working on your own computer, you should store your files within the Documents folder. If you are working in a computer lab, you will probably use a different location that your instructor specifies. If you simply store all your files in one folder, however, you will soon have trouble finding the files you want. Instead, you should create folders within a main folder to separate files in a way that makes sense for you.

Likewise, if you store most of your files on removable media, such as USB drives, you need to organize those files into folders and subfolders. Before you start creating folders, whether on a hard disk or removable disk, you should plan the organization you will use.

Developing Strategies for Organizing Files and Folders

The type of disk you use to store files determines how you organize those files. Figure 3 shows how you could organize your files on a hard disk if you were taking a full semester of distance-learning classes. To duplicate this organization, you would open the main folder for your documents, create four folders—one each for the Basic Accounting, Computer Concepts, Management Skills II, and Professional Writing courses—and then store the writing assignments you complete in the Professional Writing folder.

| Figure 3 | Organizing folders and files on a hard disk |

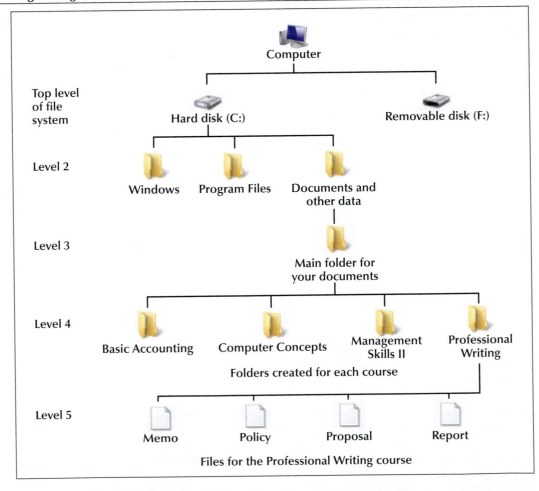

If you store your files on removable media, such as a USB drive or rewritable CD, you can use a simpler organization because you do not have to account for system files. In general, the larger the medium, the more levels of folders you should use because large media can store more files, and, therefore, need better organization. For example, you could organize your files on a 128-MB USB drive. In the top level of the USB drive, you could create folders for each general category of documents you store—one each for Courses, Creative, Financials, and Vacation. The Courses folder could then include one folder for each course, and each of those folders could contain the appropriate files.

If you work on two computers, such as one computer at an office or school and another computer at home, you can duplicate the folders you use on both computers to simplify transferring files from one computer to another. For example, if you have four folders in your Documents folder on your work computer, you would create these same four folders on your removable media as well as in the Documents folder of your home computer. If you change a file on the hard disk of your home computer, you can copy the most recent version of the file to the corresponding folder on your removable media so that it is available when you are at work. You also then have a **backup**, or duplicate copy, of important files that you need.

Planning Your Organization

Now that you've explored the basics of organizing files on a computer, you can plan the organization of your files for this book by writing in your answers to the following questions:

1. How do you obtain the files for this book (on a USB drive from your instructor, for example)?_____

_____

2. On what drive do you store your files for this book (drive A, C, D, for example)?

_____

3. Do you use a particular folder on this drive? If so, which folder do you use?_____

_____

4. Is this folder contained within another folder? If so, what is the name of that main folder?_____

5. On what type of disk or drive do you save your files for this book (hard disk, USB drive, CD, or network drive, for example)?_____

If you cannot answer any of these questions, ask your instructor for help.

Exploring Files and Folders

Windows Vista provides two tools for exploring the files and folders on your computer—Windows Explorer and the Computer window. Both display the contents of your computer, using icons to represent drives, folders, and files. However, by default, each presents a slightly different view of your computer. **Windows Explorer** shows the files, folders, and drives on your computer, making it easy to navigate, or move from one location to another within the file hierarchy. The **Computer** window shows the drives on your computer and makes it easy to perform system tasks, such as viewing system information. Most of the time, you use one of these tools to open a **folder window** that displays the files and subfolders in a folder.

The Windows Explorer and Computer windows are divided into two sections, called **panes**. The left pane is the **Navigation pane**. It contains a **Favorite Links list**, which can provide quick access to the folders you use often, and a **Folders list**, which shows the hierarchy of the folders and other locations on your computer. The right pane lists the contents of these folders and other locations. If you select a folder in the left pane, for example, the files stored in that folder appear in the right pane.

> **Tip**
>
> The term "folder window" refers to any window that displays the contents of a folder, including the Computer, Windows Explorer, and Recycle Bin windows. In all of these windows, you can use the same techniques to display folders and their contents, navigate your computer, and work with files.

If the Folders list showed all the folders on your computer at once, it could be a very long list. Instead, you open drives and folders only when you want to see what they contain. If a folder contains subfolders, an expand icon ▷ appears to the left of the folder icon. (The same is true for drives.) To view the folders contained in an object, you click the expand icon. A collapse icon ◢ then appears next to the folder icon; click the collapse icon to hide the folder's subfolders. To view the files contained in a folder, you click the folder icon, and the files appear in the right pane. See Figure 4.

| Figure 4 | Viewing folder contents in Windows Explorer |

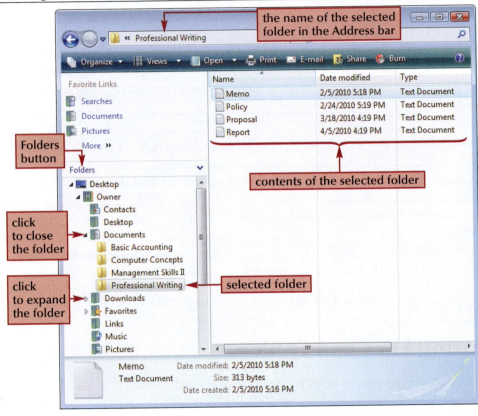

Using the Folders list helps you navigate your computer and orients you to your current location. As you move, copy, delete, and perform other tasks with the files in the right pane of a folder window, you can refer to the Folders list to see how your changes affect the overall organization.

Both Windows Explorer and the Computer window let you view, organize, and access the drives, folders, and files on your computer. In addition to using the Folders list, you can navigate your computer in other ways:

- **Opening drives and folders in the right pane**: To view the contents of a drive or folder, double-click the drive or folder icon in the right pane of a folder window.
- **Using the Address bar**: Use the Address bar to navigate to a different folder. The Address bar displays your current folder as a series of locations separated by arrows. Click a folder name or an arrow button to navigate to a different location.

Tip

To display or hide the Folders list in a folder window, click the Folders button in the Navigation pane.

- **Clicking the Back, Forward, and Recent Pages buttons**: Use the Back, Forward, and Recent Pages buttons to navigate to other folders you have already opened. After you change folders, use the Back button to return to the original folder or click the Recent Pages button to navigate to a location you've visited recently.
- **Using the Search box**: To find a file or folder stored in the current folder or its subfolders, type a word or phrase in the Search box. The search begins as soon as you start typing. Windows finds files based on text in the filename, text within the file, and other characteristics of the file, such as tags (descriptive words or phrases you add to your files) or the author.

These navigation controls are available in Windows Explorer, Computer, and other folder windows, including many dialog boxes. In fact, all of these folder windows share common tools. By default, when you first open Computer, it shows all the drives available on your computer, whereas Windows Explorer shows the folders on your computer. However, by changing a single setting, you can make the two windows interchangeable. If you open the Folders list in Computer, you have the same setup as Windows Explorer. Likewise, if you close the Folders list in the Windows Explorer window, you have the same setup as in the Computer window.

Shannon prefers to use Windows Explorer to manage her files. You'll use Windows Explorer to manage files in the rest of this tutorial.

Using Windows Explorer

Windows Vista also provides a folder for your documents—your **personal folder**, which is designed to store the files and folders you work with regularly and is labeled with the name you use to log on to Windows Vista, such as Shannon. On your own computer, this is where you can keep your data files—the memos, videos, graphics, music, and other files that you create, edit, and manipulate in a program. Windows Vista provides a few built-in folders in your personal folder, including Music (for songs and other music files), Pictures (for photos and other image files), and Documents (for text, spreadsheets, presentations, and other files you create). If you are working in a computer lab, you might not have a personal folder or be able to access the Documents folder, or you might have a personal folder or be able to store files there only temporarily because that folder is emptied every night. Instead, you might permanently store your Data Files on removable media or in a different folder on your computer or network.

When you start Windows Explorer from the All Programs menu, it opens to the Documents folder by default. If you cannot access the Documents folder, the screens you see as you perform the following steps will differ. However, you can still perform the steps accurately.

To examine the organization of your computer using Windows Explorer:

▶ 1. Click the **Start** button 🟦 on the taskbar, click **All Programs**, click **Accessories**, and then click **Windows Explorer**. The Windows Explorer window opens.

▶ 2. Scroll the Folders list, point to the **Folders list**, and then click the **expand** icon ▷ next to the Computer icon. The drives and other useful locations on your computer appear under the Computer icon, as shown in Figure 5. The contents of your computer will differ.

Figure 5   **Viewing the contents of your computer**

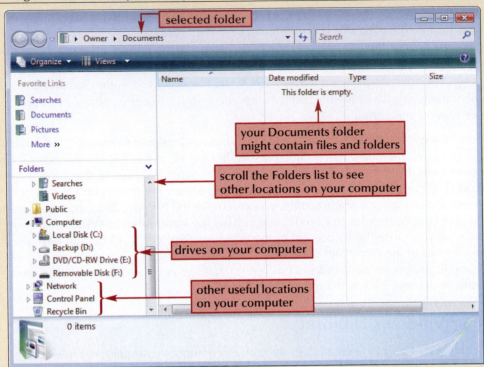

3. Click the **expand** icon ▷ next to the Local Disk (C:) icon. The contents of your hard disk appear under the Local Disk (C:) icon.

   Trouble? If you do not have permission to access drive C, skip Step 3 and read but do not perform the remaining steps.

   Documents is still the selected folder. To view the contents of an object in the right pane, you can click the object's icon in the Folders list.

4. If necessary, scroll up the list, and then click the **Public** folder in the Folders list. Its contents appear in the right pane. Public is a built-in Windows Vista folder that contains folders any user can access on this computer.

Navigating to Your Data Files

The **file path** is a notation that indicates a file's location on your computer. The file path leads you through the Windows file system to your file. For example, the Holiday file is stored in the Tutorial subfolder of the FM folder. If you are working on a USB drive, for example, the path to this file might be as follows:

F:\FM\Tutorial\Holiday.bmp

This path has four parts, and each part is separated by a backslash (\ ):

- **F**: The drive name; for example, drive F might be the name for the USB drive. If this file were stored on the hard disk, the drive name would be C.
- **FM**: The top-level folder on drive F.
- **Tutorial**: A subfolder in the FM folder.
- **Holiday.bmp**: The full filename with the file extension.

If someone tells you to find the file F:\FM\Tutorial\Holiday.bmp, you know you must navigate to your USB drive, open the FM folder, and then open the Tutorial folder to find the Holiday file. By default, the Address bar includes arrow buttons instead of back-slashes when displaying a path. To navigate to a different folder in the FM folder, for example, you can click the arrow button to right of FM in the Address bar, and then click the folder name.

You can use Windows Explorer to navigate to the Data Files you need for the rest of this tutorial. Refer to the information you provided in the "Planning Your Organization" section and note the drive on your system that contains your Data Files. In the following steps, this is drive F, a USB drive. If necessary, substitute the appropriate drive on your system when you perform the steps.

To navigate to your Data Files:

▶ **1.** Make sure your computer can access your Data Files for this tutorial. For example, if you are using a USB drive, insert the drive into the USB port.

   Trouble? If you don't have the Data Files, you need to get them before you can proceed. Your instructor will either give you the Data Files or ask you to obtain them from a specified location (such as a network drive). In either case, be sure that you make a backup copy of your Data Files before you start using them, so that the original files will be available on your copied disk in case you need to start over because of an error or problem. If you have any questions about the Data Files, see your instructor or technical support person for assistance.

▶ **2.** In the Windows Explorer window, click the **expand** icon ▷ next to the drive containing your Data Files, such as Removable Disk (F:). A list of the folders on that drive appears.

▶ **3.** If the list of folders does not include the FM folder, continue clicking the **expand** icon ▷ to navigate to the folder that contains the FM folder.

▶ **4.** Click the **expand** icon ▷ next to the FM folder, and then click the **FM** folder. Its contents appear in the Folders list and in the right pane of the Windows Explorer window. The FM folder contains the Case1, Review, and Tutorial folders, as shown in Figure 6. The other folders on your system might vary.

Figure 6 Navigating to the FM folder

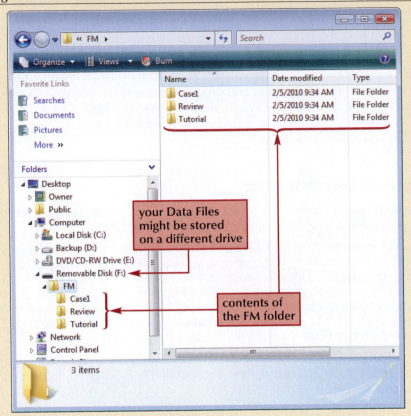

5. In the left pane, click the **Tutorial** folder. The files it contains appear in the right pane. You want to view them as a list.

6. Click the **Views button arrow** on the toolbar, and then click **List**. The files appear in List view in the Windows Explorer window. See Figure 7.

Figure 7 Files in the Tutorial folder in List view

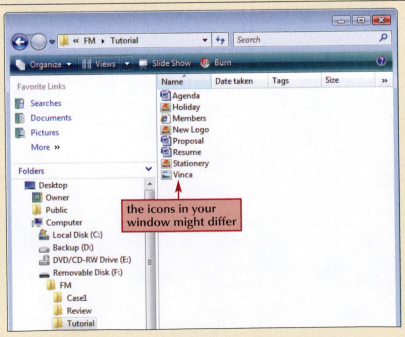

The file icons in your window depend on the programs installed on your computer, so they might be different from the ones shown in Figure 7.

Working with Folders and Files

After you devise a plan for storing your files, you are ready to get organized by creating folders that will hold your files. For this tutorial, you create folders in the Tutorial folder. When you are working on your own computer, you usually create folders within the Documents folder in your personal folder.

Examine the files shown in Figure 7 again and determine which files seem to belong together. Holiday, New Logo, and Vinca are all graphics files containing pictures or photos. The Resume and Stationery files were created for a summer job hunt. The other files were created for a neighborhood association to update a playground.

One way to organize these files is to create three folders—one for graphics, one for the job hunt files, and another for the playground files. When you create a folder, you give it a name, preferably one that describes its contents. A folder name can have up to 255 characters, except / \ : * ? " < > or |. Considering these conventions, you could create three folders as follows:

- **Graphics folder**: Holiday, New Logo, and Vinca files
- **Job Hunt folder**: Resume and Stationery files
- **Playground folder**: Agenda, Proposal, and Members files

Guidelines for Creating Folders | InSight

- **Keep folder names short and familiar**: Long filenames can be cut off in a folder window, so use names that are short but clear. Choose names that will be meaningful later, such as project names or course numbers.
- **Develop standards for naming folders**: Use a consistent naming scheme that is clear to you, such as one that uses a project name as the name of the main folder, and includes step numbers in each subfolder name, such as 01Plan, 02Approvals, 03Prelim, and so on.
- **Create subfolders to organize files**: If a file listing in a folder window is so long that you must scroll the window, consider organizing those files into subfolders.

Creating Folders

You've already seen folder icons in the windows you've examined. Now, you'll create folders in the Tutorial folder using the Windows Explorer toolbar.

Creating a Folder | Reference Window

- In the left pane, click the drive or folder where you want to create a folder.
- Click the Organize button on the toolbar, and then click New Folder (*or* right-click a blank area in the folder window, point to New, and then click Folder).
- Type a name for the folder, and then press the Enter key.

Next you will create three folders in your Tutorial folder. The Windows Explorer window should show the contents of the Tutorial folder in List view.

To create folders in a folder window:

► 1. Click the **Organize** button on the toolbar, and then click **New Folder**. A folder icon with the label "New Folder" appears in the right pane. See Figure 8.

| Figure 8 | Creating a folder in the Tutorial folder |

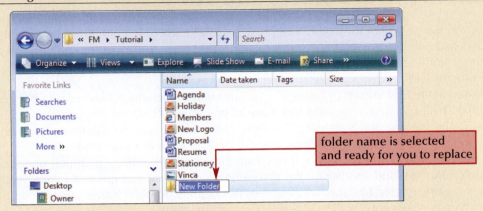

Trouble? If the "New Folder" name is not selected, right-click the new folder, click Rename, and then continue with Step 2.

Windows Vista uses "New Folder" as a placeholder, and selects the text so that you can replace it with the name you want.

► 2. Type **Graphics** as the folder name, and then press the **Enter** key. The new folder is named "Graphics" and is the selected item in the right pane.

You are ready to create a second folder. This time, you'll use a shortcut menu to create a folder.

► 3. Right-click a blank area near the Graphics folder, point to **New** on the shortcut menu, and then click **Folder**. A folder icon with the label "New Folder" appears in the right pane with the "New Folder" text selected.

► 4. Type **Job Hunt** as the name of the new folder, and then press the **Enter** key.

► 5. Using the toolbar or the shortcut menu, create a folder named **Playground**. The Tutorial folder contains three new subfolders.

Moving and Copying Files and Folders

If you want to place a file into a folder from another location, you can either move the file or copy it. **Moving** a file removes it from its current location and places it in a new location you specify. **Copying** places the file in both locations. Windows Vista provides several techniques for moving and copying files. The same principles apply to folders—you can move and copy folders using a variety of methods.

| Reference Window | **Moving a File or Folder** |

- Right-click and drag the file or folder you want to move to the destination folder.
- Click Move Here on the shortcut menu.

or

- Right-click the file or folder you want to move, and then click Cut on the shortcut menu.
- Navigate to and right-click the destination folder, and then click Paste on the shortcut menu.

Next, you'll move the Agenda, Proposal, and Members files to the Playground folder.

To move a file using the right mouse button:

1. Point to the **Agenda** file in the right pane, and then press and hold the *right* mouse button.

2. With the right mouse button still pressed down, drag the **Agenda** file to the **Playground** folder. When a "Move to Playground" ScreenTip appears, release the button. A shortcut menu opens.

3. With the left mouse button, click **Move Here** on the shortcut menu. The Agenda file is removed from the main Tutorial folder and stored in the Playground subfolder.

   Trouble? If you release the mouse button before dragging the Agenda file to the Playground folder, the shortcut menu opens, letting you move the file to a different folder. Press the Esc key to close the shortcut menu without moving the file, and then repeat Steps 1 through 3.

4. In the right pane, double-click the **Playground** folder. The Agenda file is in the Playground folder.

5. In the left pane, click the **Tutorial** folder to see its contents. The Tutorial folder no longer contains the Agenda file.

The advantage of moving a file or folder by dragging with the right mouse button is that you can efficiently complete your work with one action. However, this technique requires polished mouse skills so that you can drag the file comfortably. Another way to move files and folders is to use the **Clipboard**, a temporary storage area for files and information that you have copied or moved from one place and plan to use somewhere else. You can select a file and use the Cut or Copy commands to temporarily store the file on the Clipboard, and then use the Paste command to insert the file elsewhere. Although using the Clipboard takes more steps, some users find it easier than dragging with the right mouse button.

You'll move the Resume file to the Job Hunt folder next.

To move files using the Clipboard:

1. Right-click the **Resume** file, and then click **Cut** on the shortcut menu. Although the file icon is still displayed in the folder window, Windows Vista removes the Resume file from the Tutorial folder and stores it on the Clipboard.

2. In the Folders list, right-click the **Job Hunt** folder, and then click **Paste** on the shortcut menu. Windows Vista pastes the Resume file from the Clipboard to the Job Hunt folder. The Resume file icon no longer appears in the folder window.

3. In the Folders list, click the **Job Hunt** folder to view its contents in the right pane. The Job Hunt folder now contains the Resume file.

   You'll move the Stationery file from the Tutorial folder to the Job Hunt folder.

4. Click the **Back** button ⬅ on the Address bar to return to the Tutorial folder, right-click the **Stationery** file in the folder window, and then click **Cut** on the shortcut menu.

5. Right-click the **Job Hunt** folder, and then click **Paste** on the shortcut menu.

> **6.** Click the **Back** button ◀ on the Address bar to return to view the contents of the Job Hunt folder. It now contains the Resume and Stationery files. See Figure 9.

Figure 9 | **Moving files**

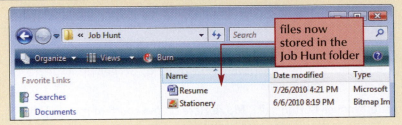

> **7.** Click the **Forward** button ▶ to return to the Tutorial folder.

Tip

To use keyboard shortcuts to move files, click the file you want to move, press Ctrl+X to cut the file, navigate to a new location, and then press Ctrl+V to paste the file.

You can also copy a file using the same techniques as when you move a file—by dragging with the right mouse button or by using the Clipboard. You can copy more than one file at the same time by selecting all the files you want to copy, and then clicking them as a group. To select files that are listed together in a window, click the first file in the list, hold down the Shift key, click the last file in the list, and then release the Shift key. To select files that are not listed together, click one file, hold down the Ctrl key, click the other files, and then release the Ctrl key.

Reference Window | **Copying a File or Folder**

- Right-click and drag the file or folder you want to copy to the destination folder.
- Click Copy Here on the shortcut menu.

or

- Right-click the file or folder you want to copy, and then click Copy on the shortcut menu.
- Navigate to the destination folder.
- Right-click a blank area of the destination folder window, and then click Paste on the shortcut menu.

You'll copy the three graphics files from the Tutorial folder to the Graphics folder now.

To copy files using the shortcut menu:

> **1.** In the Tutorial window, click the **Holiday** file.

> **2.** Hold down the **Ctrl** key, click the **New Logo** file, click the **Vinca** file, and then release the **Ctrl** key. Three files are selected in the Tutorial window.

Tip

It's easiest to select multiple files in List view or Details view.

> **3.** Right-click a selected file, and then click **Copy** on the shortcut menu.

> **4.** In the right pane, double-click the **Graphics** folder to open it.

> **5.** Right-click a blank area in the right pane, and then click **Paste** on the shortcut menu. Windows Vista copies the three files to the Graphics folder.

> **6.** Switch to List view, if necessary.

Now that you are familiar with two ways to copy files, you can use the technique you prefer to copy the Proposal and Members files to the Playground folder.

To copy the two files:

▶ **1.** In the Graphics folder window, click the **Back** button ⬅ on the toolbar to return to the Tutorial folder.

▶ **2.** Use any technique you've learned to copy the **Proposal** and **Members** files from the Tutorial folder to the Playground folder.

You can move and copy folders in the same way that you move and copy files. When you do, you move or copy all the files contained in the folder.

Naming and Renaming Files

As you work with files, pay attention to **filenames**—they provide important information about the file, including its contents and purpose. A filename such as Car Sales.docx has three parts:

- **Main part of the filename**: The name you provide when you create a file, and the name you associate with a file
- **Dot**: The period (.) that separates the main part of the filename from the file extension
- **File extension**: Usually three or four characters that follow the dot in the filename

The main part of a filename can have up to 260 characters—this gives you plenty of room to name your file accurately enough so that you'll know the contents of the file just by looking at the filename. You can use spaces and certain punctuation symbols in your filenames. Like folder names, however, filenames cannot contain the symbols \ / ? : * " < > | because these characters have special meaning in Windows Vista.

A filename might display an **extension**—three or more characters following a dot—that identifies the file's type and indicates the program in which the file was created. For example, in the filename Car Sales.docx, the extension "docx" identifies the file as one created by Microsoft Office Word 2007, a word-processing program. You might also have a file called Car Sales.xlsx—the "xlsx" extension identifies the file as one created in Microsoft Office Excel 2007, a spreadsheet program. Though the main parts of these filenames are identical, their extensions distinguish them as different files. You usually do not need to add extensions to your filenames because the program that you use to create the file adds the file extension automatically. Also, although Windows Vista keeps track of extensions, not all computers are set to display them.

Be sure to give your files and folders meaningful names that help you remember their purpose and contents. You can easily rename a file or folder by using the Rename command on the file's shortcut menu.

Guidelines for Naming Files	InSight

The following are a few suggestions for naming your files:

- **Use common names**: Avoid cryptic names that might make sense now, but could cause confusion later, such as nonstandard abbreviations or imprecise names like Stuff08.
- **Don't change the file extension**: When renaming a file, don't change the file extension. If you do, Windows might not be able to find a program that can open it.
- **Find a comfortable balance between too short and too long**: Use filenames that are long enough to be meaningful, but short enough to read easily on the screen.

Next, you'll rename the Agenda file to give it a more descriptive name.

To rename the Agenda file:

▶ **1.** In the Tutorial folder window, double-click the **Playground** folder to open it.

▶ **2.** Right-click the **Agenda** file, and then click **Rename** on the shortcut menu. The filename is highlighted and a box appears around it.

▶ **3.** Type **Meeting Agenda**, and then press the **Enter** key. The file now appears with the new name.

Trouble? If you make a mistake while typing and you haven't pressed the Enter key yet, press the Backspace key until you delete the mistake, and then complete Step 3. If you've already pressed the Enter key, repeat Steps 1 through 3 to rename the file again.

Trouble? If your computer is set to display file extensions, a message might appear asking if you are sure you want to change the file extension. Click the No button, right-click the Agenda file, click Rename on the shortcut menu, type "Meeting Agenda.docx", and then press the Enter key.

All the files in the Tutorial folder are now stored in appropriate subfolders. You can streamline the organization of the Tutorial folder by deleting the files you no longer need.

Deleting Files and Folders

Tip

To retrieve a deleted file from the hard disk, double-click the Recycle Bin, right-click the file you want to retrieve, and then click Restore.

You should periodically delete files and folders you no longer need so that your main folders and disks don't get cluttered. In the Computer window or Windows Explorer, you delete a file or folder by deleting its icon. Be careful when you delete a folder, because you also delete all the files it contains. When you delete a file from a hard disk, Windows Vista removes the filename from the folder, but stores the file contents in the Recycle Bin. The **Recycle Bin** is an area on your hard disk that holds deleted files until you remove them permanently; an icon on the desktop allows you easy access to the Recycle Bin. If you change your mind and want to retrieve a file deleted from your hard disk, you can use the Recycle Bin to recover it or return it to its original location. However, after you empty the Recycle Bin, you can no longer recover the files that were in it.

When you delete a file from removable media, it does not go into the Recycle Bin. Instead, it is deleted as soon as its icon disappears—and you cannot recover it.

Shannon reminds you that because you copied the Holiday, New Logo, Proposal, Members, and Vinca files to the Graphics and Playground folders, you can safely delete the original files in the Tutorial folder. As with moving, copying, and renaming files and folders, you can delete a file or folder in many ways, including using a shortcut menu.

To delete files in the Tutorial folder:

▶ **1.** Use any technique you've learned to navigate to and open the **Tutorial** folder.

▶ **2.** Click **Holiday** (the first file in the file list), hold down the **Shift** key, click **Vinca** (the last file in the file list), and then release the **Shift** key. All the files in the Tutorial folder are now selected. None of the subfolders should be selected.

▶ **3.** Right-click the selected files, and then click **Delete** on the shortcut menu. Windows Vista asks if you're sure you want to delete these files.

▶ **4.** Click the **Yes** button.

So far, you've moved, copied, renamed, and deleted files, but you haven't viewed any of their contents. To view file contents, you can preview or open the file. When you double-click a file in a folder window, Windows Vista starts the appropriate program and opens the file. To preview the file contents, you can select the file in a folder window, and then open the Preview pane by clicking the Organize button, pointing to Layout, and then clicking Preview Pane.

Working with Compressed Files

If you transfer files from one location to another, such as from your hard disk to a removable disk or vice versa, or from one computer to another via e-mail, you can store the files in a **compressed (zipped) folder** so that they take up less disk space. You can then transfer the files more quickly. When you create a compressed folder, Windows Vista displays a zipper on the folder icon.

You compress a folder so that the files it contains use less space on the disk. Compare two folders—a folder named Pictures that contains about 8.6 MB of files and a compressed folder containing the same files, but requiring only 6.5 MB of disk space. In this case, the compressed files use about 25 percent less disk space than the uncompressed files.

You can create a compressed folder using the Compressed (zipped) Folder command on the New submenu of the shortcut menu in a folder window. Then, you can compress files or other folders by dragging them into the compressed folder. You can open files directly from a compressed folder, although you cannot modify the file. To edit and save a compressed file, you must extract it first. When you **extract** a file, you create an uncompressed copy of the file and folder in a folder you specify. The original file remains in the compressed folder.

If a different compression program has been installed on your computer, such as WinZip or PKZIP, the Compressed (zipped) Folder command might not appear on the New submenu. Instead, it might be replaced by the name of your compression program. In this case, refer to your compression program's Help system for instructions on working with compressed files.

Shannon suggests you compress the files and folders in the Tutorial folder so that you can more quickly transfer them to another location.

To compress the folders and files in the Tutorial folder:

▶ **1.** If necessary, navigate to the Tutorial folder.

▶ **2.** Right-click a blank area of the right pane, point to **New** on the shortcut menu, and then click **Compressed (zipped) Folder**. A new compressed folder with a zipper icon appears in the Tutorial window. See Figure 10. Your window might appear in a different view.

Creating a compressed folder   **Figure 10**

Trouble? If the Compressed (zipped) Folder command does not appear on the New submenu, a different compression program is probably installed on your computer. Click a blank area of the Tutorial window to close the shortcut menu, and then read but do not perform the remaining steps.

▶ **3.** Type **Final Files**, and then press the **Enter** key. Windows Vista names the compressed folder in the Tutorial folder.

4. Click the **Graphics** folder, hold down the **Shift** key, click the **Playground** folder in the right pane, and then release the **Shift** key. Three folders are selected in the Tutorial window.

5. Drag the three folders to the **Final Files** compressed folder. Windows Vista copies the files to the folder, compressing them to save space.

You open a compressed folder by double-clicking it. You can then move and copy files and folders in a compressed folder, although you cannot rename them. When you extract files, Windows Vista uncompresses and copies them to a location that you specify, preserving the files in their folders as appropriate.

To extract the compressed files:

1. Right-click the **Final Files** compressed folder, and then click **Extract All** on the shortcut menu. The Extract Compressed (Zipped) Folders dialog box opens.

2. Press the **End** key to deselect the path in the text box, press the **Backspace** key as many times as necessary to delete "Final Files," and then type **Extracted**. The final three parts of the path in the text box should be "\FM\Tutorial\Extracted." See Figure 11.

| Figure 11 | Extracting compressed files |

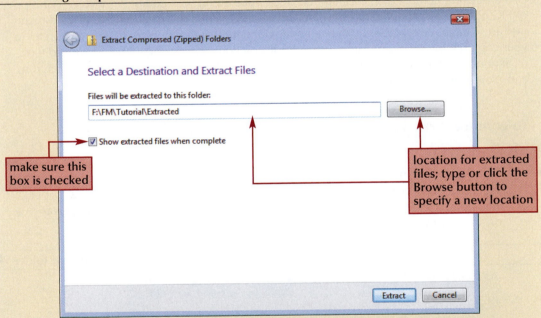

3. Make sure the **Show extracted files when complete** check box is checked, and then click the **Extract** button. The Extracted folder opens, showing the Graphics, Job Hunt, and Playground folders.

4. Open each folder to make sure it contains the files you worked with in this tutorial.

5. Close all open windows.

Quick Check | Review

1. What do you call a named collection of data stored on a disk?
2. Name two types of removable media for storing files.
3. The letter C is typically used for the _____ drive of a computer.
4. What are the two tools that Windows Vista provides for exploring the files and folders on your computer?
5. What is the notation you can use to indicate a file's location on your computer?
6. True or False: The advantage of moving a file or folder by dragging with the right mouse button is that you can efficiently complete your work with one action.
7. What part of a filename indicates the file type and program that created it?
8. Is a file deleted from a compressed folder when you extract it?

Tutorial Summary | Review

In this tutorial, you examined Windows Vista file organization, noting that you need to organize files and folders to work efficiently. You learned about typical file management strategies, including how to organize files and folders by creating folders, moving and copying files, and renaming and deleting files. You also learned how to copy files to a compressed (zipped) folder, and then extract files from a compressed folder.

Key Terms

backup	extract	move
Clipboard	Favorite Links list	Navigation pane
compact disc (CD)	file	pane
compressed (zipped) folder	file path	personal folder
Computer	file system	Recycle Bin
copy	filename	root directory
disk	folder	subfolder
document	folder window	USB drive
drive	Folders list	Windows Explorer
extension	hard disk	

| Practice | **Review Assignments** |

Practice the skills you learned in the tutorial.

Data Files needed for the Review Assignments: Billing.xlsx, Car Plan.xlsx, Commissions.xlsx, Contracts.xlsx, Customers.xlsx, Loan.docx, Photos.pptx, Speech.wav, Water lilies.jpg

Complete the following steps, recording your answers to any questions:

1. Use the Computer window or Windows Explorer as necessary to record the following information:
   - Where are you supposed to store the files you use in the Review Assignments for this tutorial?
   - Describe the method you will use to navigate to the location where you save your files for this book.
   - Do you need to follow any special guidelines or conventions when naming the files you save for this book? For example, should all the filenames start with your course number or tutorial number? If so, describe the conventions.
   - When you are instructed to open a file for this book, what location are you supposed to use?
   - Describe the method you will use to navigate to this location.

2. Use the Computer window or Windows Explorer to navigate to and open the FM\Review folder provided with your Data Files.

3. Examine the nine files in the Review folder included with your Data Files, and then answer the following questions:
   - How will you organize these files?
   - What folders will you create?
   - Which files will you store in these folders?
   - Will you use any built-in Windows folders? If so, which ones? For which files?

4. In the Review folder, create three folders: Business, Finances, and Project.

5. Move the **Billing**, **Commissions**, **Contracts**, and **Customers** files from the Review folder to the Business folder.

6. Move the **Car Plan** and **Loan** files to the Finances folder.

7. Copy the remaining files to the Project folder.

8. Delete the files in the Review folder (do *not* delete any folders).

9. Rename the **Speech** file in the Project folder to **Ask Not**.

10. Create a compressed (zipped) folder in the Review folder named **Final Review** that contains all the files and folders in the Review folder.

11. Extract the contents of the Final Review files folder to a new folder named **Extracted**. (*Hint:* The file path will end with "\FM\Review\Extracted.")

12. Locate all copies of the **Loan** file in the subfolders of the Review folder. In which locations did you find this file?

13. Close all open windows.

14. Submit the results of the preceding steps to your instructor, either in printed or electronic form, as requested.

Apply	**Case Problem 1**

Use the skills you learned in the tutorial to manage files and folders for an arts organization.

Data Files needed for this Case Problem: Inv Feb.xlsx, Inv Jan.xlsx, Inv March.xlsx, Painting–Agenda.docx, Painting–Eval.docx, Painting–Manual.docx, Paris.jpg, Still Life.jpg

Jefferson Street Fine Arts Center Rae Wysnewski owns the Jefferson Street Fine Arts Center (JSFAC) in Pittsburgh, and offers classes and gallery, studio, and practice space for aspiring and fledgling artists, musicians, and dancers. Rae opened JSFAC two years ago, and this year the center has a record enrollment in its classes. She hires you to teach a painting class and to show her how to manage her files on her new Windows Vista computer. Complete the following steps:

1. In the FM\Case1 folder in your Data Files, create two folders: Invoices and Painting Class.
2. Move the **Inv Jan**, **Inv Feb**, and **Inv March** files from the Case1 folder to the Invoices folder.
3. Rename the three files in the Invoices folder to remove "Inv" from each name.
4. Move the three text documents from the Case1 folder to the Painting Class folder. Rename the three documents, using shorter but still descriptive names.
5. Copy the remaining files to the Painting Class folder.
6. Switch to Details view, if necessary, and then answer the following questions:
   a. What is the largest file in the Painting Class folder?
   b. How many files in the Painting Class folder are JPEG images?
7. Delete the **Paris** and **Still Life** files from the Case1 folder.
8. Open the Recycle Bin folder by double-clicking the Recycle Bin icon on the desktop. Do the Paris and Still Life files appear in the Recycle Bin folder? Explain why or why not. Close the Recycle Bin window.
9. Copy the Painting Class folder to the Case1 folder. The duplicate folder appears as "Painting Class – Copy." Rename the Painting Class – Copy folder as **Graphics**.
10. Delete the text files from the Graphics folder.
11. Delete the **Paris** and **Still Life** files from the Painting Class folder.
12. Close all open windows, and then submit the results of the preceding steps to your instructor, either in printed or electronic form, as requested.

Challenge	**Case Problem 2**

Extend what you've learned to discover other methods of managing files for a social service organization.

There are no Data Files needed for this Case Problem.

First Call Outreach Victor Crillo is the director of a social service organization named First Call Outreach in Toledo, Ohio. Its mission is to connect people who need help from local and state agencies to the appropriate service. Victor has a dedicated staff, but they are all relatively new to Windows Vista. In particular, they have trouble finding files that they have saved on their hard disks. He asks you to demonstrate how to find files in Windows Vista. Complete the following:

⊕ EXPLORE

1. Windows Vista Help and Support includes topics that explain how to search for files on a disk without looking through all the folders. Click the Start button, click Help and Support, and then use one of the following methods to locate topics on searching for files.
   • In the Windows Help and Support window, click the Windows Basics icon. Click the Working with files and folders link. In the "In this article" list, clicking Finding your files.

- In the Windows Help and Support window, click the Table of Contents icon. (If necessary, click the Home icon first, and then click the Table of Contents icon.) the Files and folders link, and then click Working with files and folders. In the "In this article" list, click Finding your files.
- In the Search Help box, type **searching for files**, and then press the Enter key. Click the Find a file or folder link. In the article, click the Show all link.

EXPLORE   2. Read the topic and click any See also or For more information links in the topic, if necessary, to provide the following information:

     a. Where is the Search box located?

     b. Do you need to type the entire filename to find the file?

     c. Name three file characteristics you can use as search options.

EXPLORE   3. Use the Windows Vista Help and Support window to locate topics related to managing files and folders. Write out two procedures for working with files and folders that were not covered in the tutorial.

   4. Submit the results of the preceding steps to your instructor, either in printed or electronic form, as requested.

Assess | SAM Assessment and Training

If you have a SAM user profile, you may have access to hands-on instruction, practice, and assessment of the skills covered in this tutorial. Log in to your SAM account (**http://sam2007.course.com**) to launch any assigned training activities or exams that relate to the skills covered in this tutorial.

Review | Quick Check Answers

1. file
2. USB drives, CDs, and DVDs
3. hard disk
4. Windows Explorer and the Computer window
5. file path
6. True
7. extension
8. No

Ending Data Files

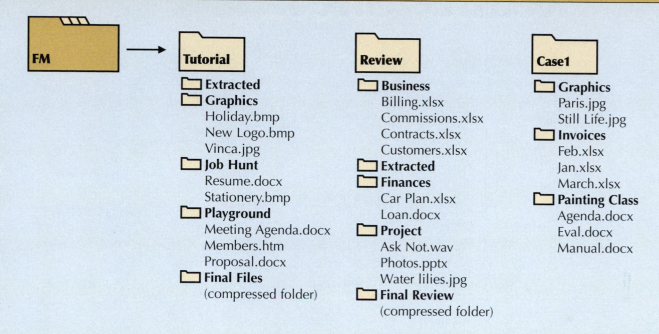

FM →

Tutorial
- 📁 **Extracted**
- 📁 **Graphics**
  - Holiday.bmp
  - New Logo.bmp
  - Vinca.jpg
- 📁 **Job Hunt**
  - Resume.docx
  - Stationery.bmp
- 📁 **Playground**
  - Meeting Agenda.docx
  - Members.htm
  - Proposal.docx
- 📁 **Final Files**
  - (compressed folder)

Review
- 📁 **Business**
  - Billing.xlsx
  - Commissions.xlsx
  - Contracts.xlsx
  - Customers.xlsx
- 📁 **Extracted**
- 📁 **Finances**
  - Car Plan.xlsx
  - Loan.docx
- 📁 **Project**
  - Ask Not.wav
  - Photos.pptx
  - Water lilies.jpg
- 📁 **Final Review**
  - (compressed folder)

Case1
- 📁 **Graphics**
  - Paris.jpg
  - Still Life.jpg
- 📁 **Invoices**
  - Feb.xlsx
  - Jan.xlsx
  - March.xlsx
- 📁 **Painting Class**
  - Agenda.docx
  - Eval.docx
  - Manual.docx

Reality Check

Now that you have reviewed the fundamentals of managing files, organize the files and folders you use for course work or for other projects on your own computer. Be sure to follow the guidelines presented in this tutorial for developing an organization strategy, creating folders, naming files, and moving, copying, deleting, and compressing files. To manage your own files, complete the following tasks:

1. Use a program such as Word or Notepad to create a plan for organizing your files. List the types of files you work with, and then determine whether you want to store them on your hard disk or on removable media. Then sketch the folders and subfolders you will use to manage these files. If you choose a hard disk as your storage medium, make sure you plan to store your work files and folders in a subfolder of the Documents folder.

2. Use Windows Explorer or the Computer window to navigate to your files. Determine which tool you prefer for managing files, if you have a preference.

3. Create or rename the main folders you want to use for your files. Then create or rename the subfolders you will use.

4. Move and copy files to the appropriate folders according to your plan, and rename and delete files as necessary.

5. Create a backup copy of your work files by creating a compressed file and then copying the compressed file to a removable disk, such as a USB flash drive.

6. Submit your finished plan to your instructor, either in printed or electronic form, as requested.

Objectives

- Explore the programs that comprise Microsoft Office
- Start programs and switch between them
- Explore common window elements
- Minimize, maximize, and restore windows
- Use the Ribbon, tabs, and buttons
- Use the contextual tabs, Mini toolbar, and shortcut menus
- Save, close, and open a file
- Use the Help system
- Print a file
- Exit programs

Getting Started with Microsoft Office 2007

Preparing a Meeting Agenda

Case | Recycled Palette

Recycled Palette, a company in Oregon founded by Ean Nogella in 2006, sells 100 percent recycled latex paint to both individuals and businesses in the area. The high-quality recycled paint is filtered to industry standards and tested for performance and environmental safety. The paint is available in both 1 gallon cans and 5 gallon pails, and comes in colors ranging from white to shades of brown, blue, green, and red. The demand for affordable recycled paint has been growing each year. Ean and all his employees use Microsoft Office 2007, which provides everyone in the company with the power and flexibility to store a variety of information, create consistent files, and share data. In this tutorial, you'll review how the company's employees use Microsoft Office 2007.

Starting Data Files

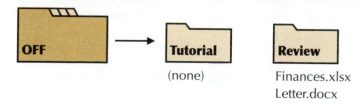

OFF → Tutorial
(none)

Review
Finances.xlsx
Letter.docx

Exploring Microsoft Office 2007

Microsoft Office 2007, or **Office**, is a collection of Microsoft programs. Office is available in many suites, each of which contains a different combination of these programs. For example, the Professional suite includes Word, Excel, PowerPoint, Access, Outlook, and Publisher. Other suites are available and can include more or fewer programs (for additional information about the available suites, go to the Microsoft Web site). Each Office program contains valuable tools to help you accomplish many tasks, such as composing reports, analyzing data, preparing presentations, compiling information, sending e-mail, and planning schedules.

Microsoft Office Word 2007, or **Word**, is a computer program you use to enter, edit, and format text. The files you create in Word are called **documents**, although many people use the term *document* to refer to any file created on a computer. Word, often called a word processing program, offers many special features that help you compose and update all types of documents, ranging from letters and newsletters to reports, brochures, faxes, and even books—all in attractive and readable formats. You can also use Word to create, insert, and position figures, tables, and other graphics to enhance the look of your documents. For example, the Recycled Palette employees create business letters using Word.

Microsoft Office Excel 2007, or **Excel**, is a computer program you use to enter, calculate, analyze, and present numerical data. You can do some of this in Word with tables, but Excel provides many more tools for recording and formatting numbers as well as performing calculations. The graphics capabilities in Excel also enable you to display data visually. You might, for example, generate a pie chart or a bar chart to help people quickly see the significance of and the connections between information. The files you create in Excel are called **workbooks** (commonly referred to as spreadsheets), and Excel is often called a spreadsheet program. The Recycled Palette accounting department uses a line chart in an Excel workbook to visually track the company's financial performance.

Microsoft Office Access 2007, or **Access**, is a computer program used to enter, maintain, and retrieve related information (or data) in a format known as a database. The files you create in Access are called **databases**, and Access is often referred to as a database or relational database program. With Access, you can create forms to make data entry easier, and you can create professional reports to improve the readability of your data. The Recycled Palette operations department tracks the company's inventory in a table in an Access database.

Microsoft Office PowerPoint 2007, or **PowerPoint**, is a computer program you use to create a collection of slides that can contain text, charts, pictures, sound, movies, multimedia, and so on. The files you create in PowerPoint are called **presentations**, and PowerPoint is often called a presentation graphics program. You can show these presentations on your computer monitor, project them onto a screen as a slide show, print them, share them over the Internet, or display them on the World Wide Web. You can also use PowerPoint to generate presentation-related documents such as audience handouts, outlines, and speakers' notes. The Recycled Palette marketing department has created an effective slide presentation with PowerPoint to promote its paints to a wider audience.

Microsoft Office Outlook 2007, or **Outlook**, is a computer program you use to send, receive, and organize e-mail; plan your schedule; arrange meetings; organize contacts; create a to-do list; and jot down notes. You can also use Outlook to print schedules, task lists, phone directories, and other documents. Outlook is often referred to as an information management program. The Recycled Palette staff use Outlook to send and receive e-mail, plan their schedules, and create to-do lists.

Although each Office program individually is a strong tool, their potential is even greater when used together.

Integrating Office Programs

One of the main advantages of Office is **integration**, the ability to share information between programs. Integration ensures consistency and accuracy, and it saves time because you don't have to reenter the same information in several Office programs. The staff at Recycled Palette uses the integration features of Office daily, including the following examples:

- The accounting department created an Excel bar chart on the previous two years' fourth-quarter results, which they inserted into the quarterly financial report created in Word. They included a hyperlink in the Word report that employees can click to open the Excel workbook and view the original data.
- The operations department included an Excel pie chart of sales percentages by paint colors on a PowerPoint slide, which is part of a presentation to stockholders.
- The marketing department produced a mailing to promote its recycled paints to local contractors and designers by combining a form letter created in Word with an Access database that stores the names and addresses of these potential customers.
- A sales representative wrote a letter in Word about an upcoming promotion for new customers and merged the letter with an Outlook contact list containing the names and addresses of prospective customers.

These are just a few examples of how you can take information from one Office program and integrate it with another.

Starting Office Programs

You can start any Office program by clicking the Start button on the Windows taskbar, and then selecting the program you want from the All Programs menu. As soon as the program starts, you can immediately begin to create new files or work with existing ones. If an Office program appears in the most frequently used programs list on the left side of the Start menu, you can click the program name to start the program.

Starting Office Programs | Reference Window

- Click the Start button on the taskbar.
- Click All Programs.
- Click Microsoft Office.
- Click the name of the program you want to start.

or

- Click the name of the program you want to start in the most frequently used programs list on the left side of the Start menu.

You'll start Excel using the Start button.

To start Excel and open a new, blank workbook:

▶ 1. Make sure your computer is on and the Windows desktop appears on your screen.

   Trouble? If your screen varies slightly from those shown in the figures, your computer might be set up differently. The figures in this book were created while running Windows Vista with the Aero feature turned off, but how your screen looks depends on the version of Windows you are using, the background settings, and so forth.

Windows XP Tip

The Start button is the green button with the word "start" on it, located at the bottom left of the taskbar.

2. Click the **Start** button on the taskbar, and then click **All Programs** to display the All Programs menu.

3. Click **Microsoft Office** on the All Programs list, and then point to **Microsoft Office Excel 2007**. Depending on how your computer is set up, your desktop and menu might contain different icons and commands.

   Trouble? If you don't see Microsoft Office on the All Programs list, click Microsoft Office Excel 2007 on the All Programs list. If you still don't see Microsoft Office Excel 2007, ask your instructor or technical support person for help.

4. Click **Microsoft Office Excel 2007**. Excel starts, and a new, blank workbook opens. See Figure 1.

Figure 1 New, blank Excel workbook

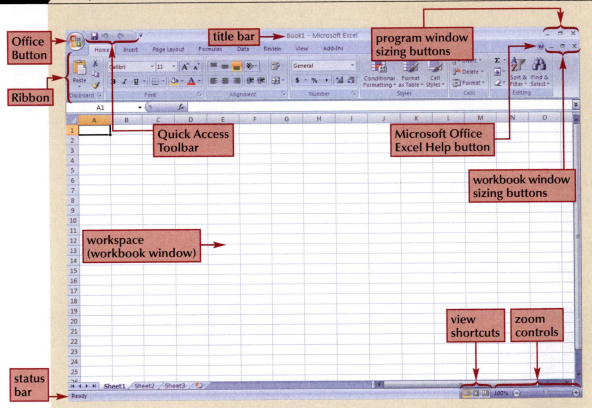

Trouble? If the Excel window doesn't fill your entire screen, the window is not maximized, or expanded to its full size. You'll maximize the window shortly.

You can have more than one Office program open at once. You'll use this same method to start Word and open a new, blank document.

To start Word and open a new, blank document:

1. Click the **Start** button on the taskbar, click **All Programs** to display the All Programs list, and then click **Microsoft Office**.

   Trouble? If you don't see Microsoft Office on the All Programs list, click Microsoft Office Word 2007 on the All Programs list. If you still don't see Microsoft Office Word 2007, ask your instructor or technical support person for help.

2. Click **Microsoft Office Word 2007**. Word starts, and a new, blank document opens. See Figure 2.

New, blank document in Word | Figure 2

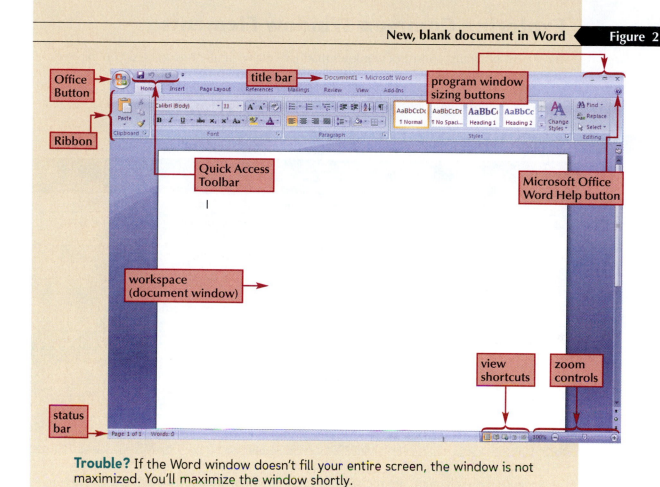

Trouble? If the Word window doesn't fill your entire screen, the window is not maximized. You'll maximize the window shortly.

Switching Between Open Programs and Files

Two programs are running at the same time—Excel and Word. The taskbar contains buttons for both programs. When you have two or more programs running or two files within the same program open, you can use the taskbar buttons to switch from one program or file to another. The button for the active program or file is darker. The employees at Recycled Palette often work in several programs at once.

To switch between Word and Excel files:

▶ 1. Click the **Microsoft Excel – Book1** button on the taskbar. The active program switches from Word to Excel. See Figure 3.

Excel and Word programs opened simultaneously | Figure 3

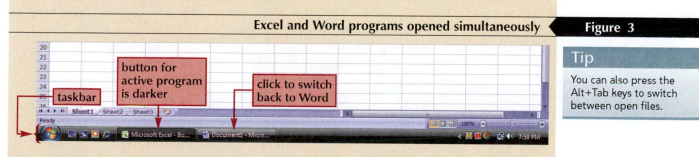

Tip

You can also press the Alt+Tab keys to switch between open files.

▶ 2. Click the **Document1 – Microsoft Word** button on the taskbar to return to Word.

Exploring Common Window Elements

The Office programs consist of windows that have many similar features. As you can see in Figures 1 and 2, many of the elements in both the Excel program window and the Word program window are the same. In fact, all the Office programs have these same elements. Figure 4 describes some of the most common window elements.

Figure 4 ➤ **Common window elements**

Element	Description
Office Button	Provides access to document-level features and program settings
Quick Access Toolbar	Provides one-click access to commonly used commands, such as Save, Undo, and Repeat
Title bar	Contains the name of the open file, the program name, and the sizing buttons
Sizing buttons	Resize and close the program window or the workspace
Ribbon	Provides access to the main set of commands organized by task into tabs and groups
Microsoft Office Help button	Opens the Help window for that program
Workspace	Displays the file you are working on (Word document, Excel workbook, Access database, or PowerPoint slide)
Status bar	Provides information about the program, open file, or current task as well as the view shortcuts and zoom controls
View shortcuts	Change how a file is displayed in the workspace
Zoom controls	Magnify or shrink the content displayed in the workspace

Because these elements are the same in each program, after you've learned one program, it's easy to learn the others. The next sections explore these common features.

Resizing the Program Window and Workspace

There are three different sizing buttons. The Minimize button ▬ , which is the left button, hides a window so that only its program button is visible on the taskbar. The middle button changes name and function depending on the status of the window—the Maximize button ▢ expands the window to the full screen size or to the program window size, and the Restore Down button ◰ returns the window to a predefined size. The Close button ✖ , on the right, exits the program or closes the file. Excel has two sets of sizing buttons. The top set controls the program window and the lower set controls the workspace. The workspace sizing buttons look and function in exactly the same way as the program window sizing buttons, except the button names change to Minimize Window and Restore Window when the workspace is maximized.

Most often, you'll want to maximize the program window and workspace to take advantage of the full screen size you have available. If you have several files open, you might want to restore down their windows so that you can see more than one window at a time, or you might want to minimize programs or files you are not working on at the moment. You'll try minimizing, maximizing, and restoring down windows and workspaces now.

To resize windows and workspaces:

▶ **1.** Click the **Minimize** button ▬ on the Word title bar. The Word program window reduces to a taskbar button. The Excel program window is visible again.

▶ **2.** If necessary, click the **Maximize** button ◻ on the Excel title bar. The Excel program window expands to fill the screen.

▶ **3.** Click the **Restore Window** button ▭ in the lower set of Excel sizing buttons. The workspace is resized and is now smaller than the full program window. See Figure 5.

Resized Excel window and workspace ◁ **Figure 5**

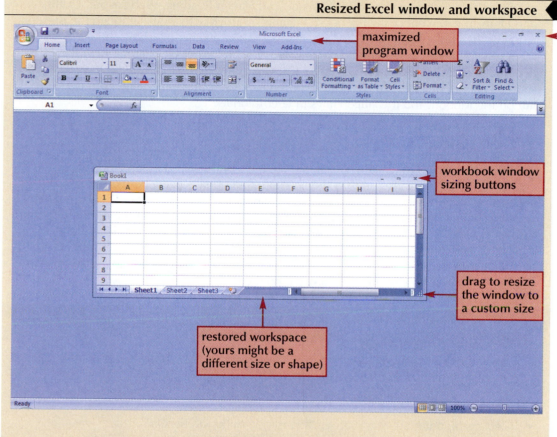

maximized program window

program window sizing buttons

workbook window sizing buttons

drag to resize the window to a custom size

restored workspace (yours might be a different size or shape)

▶ **4.** Click the **Maximize** button ◻ on the Excel workbook window title bar. The Excel workspace expands to fill the program window.

▶ **5.** Click the **Document1 - Microsoft Word** button on the taskbar. The Word program window returns to its previous size.

▶ **6.** If necessary, click the **Maximize** button ◻ on the Word title bar. The Word program window expands to fill the screen.

The sizing buttons give you the flexibility to arrange the program and file windows on your screen to best fit your needs.

Getting Information from the Status Bar

The **status bar** at the bottom of the program window provides information about the open file and current task or selection. It also has buttons and other controls for working with the file and its content. The status bar buttons and information displays are specific to the individual programs. For example, the Excel status bar displays summary information about a selected range of numbers (such as their sum or average), whereas the Word status bar shows the current page number and total number of words in a document. The right side of the status bar includes buttons that enable you to switch the workspace view in Word, Excel, PowerPoint, and Access as well as zoom the workspace in Word, Excel, and PowerPoint. You can customize the status bar to display other information or hide the **default** (original or preset) information.

Switching Views

Each program has a variety of views, or ways to display the file in the workspace. For example, Word has five views: Print Layout, Full Screen Reading, Web Layout, Outline, and Draft. The content of the file doesn't change from view to view, although the presentation of the content will. In Word, for example, Page Layout view shows how a document would appear as the printed page, whereas Web Layout view shows how the document would appear as a Web page. You can quickly switch between views using the shortcuts at the right side of the status bar. You can also change the view from the View tab on the Ribbon. You'll change views in later tutorials.

Zooming the Workspace

Zooming is a way to magnify or shrink the file content displayed in the workspace. You can zoom in to get a closer look at the content of an open document, worksheet, or slide, or you can zoom out to see more of the content at a smaller size. There are several ways to change the zoom percentage. You can use the Zoom slider at the right of the status bar to quickly change the zoom percentage. You can click the Zoom level button to the left of the Zoom slider in the status bar to open the Zoom dialog box and select a specific zoom percentage or size based on your file. You can also change the zoom settings using the Zoom group in the View tab on the Ribbon.

Reference Window | **Zooming the Workspace**

- Click the Zoom Out or Zoom In button on the status bar (or drag the Zoom slider button left or right) to the desired zoom percentage.

or

- Click the Zoom level button on the status bar.
- Select the appropriate zoom setting, and then click the OK button.

or

- Click the View tab on the Ribbon, and then in the Zoom group, click the zoom setting you want.

The figures shown in these tutorials are zoomed to enhance readability. You'll zoom the Word and Excel workspaces.

To zoom the Word and Excel workspaces:

► **1.** On the Zoom slider on the Word status bar, drag the **slider button** to the left until the Zoom percentage is **10%**. The document reduces to its smallest size, which makes the entire page visible but unreadable. See Figure 6.

Word document zoomed to 10% | Figure 6

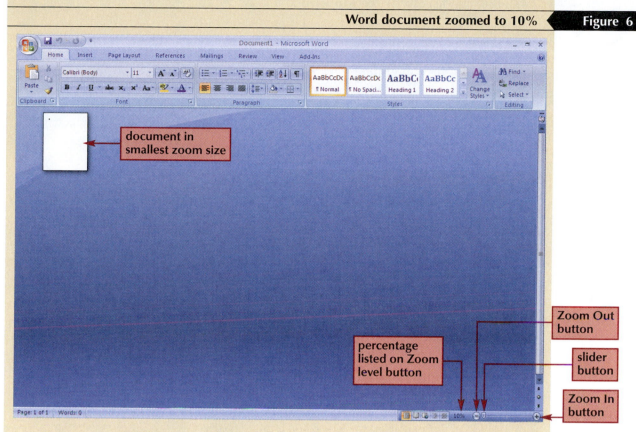

document in smallest zoom size

Zoom Out button

percentage listed on Zoom level button

slider button

Zoom In button

You'll zoom the document so its page width fills the workspace.

2. Click the **Zoom level** button `10%` on the Word status bar. The Zoom dialog box opens. See Figure 7.

Zoom dialog box | Figure 7

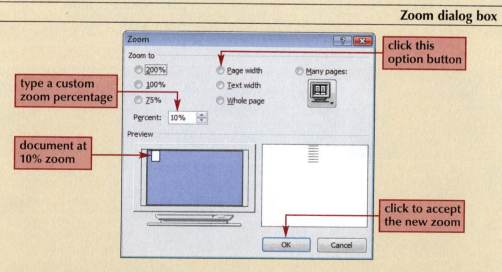

click this option button

type a custom zoom percentage

document at 10% zoom

click to accept the new zoom

3. Click the **Page width** option button, and then click the **OK** button. The Word document magnifies to its page width to match the rest of the Word figures shown in these tutorials.

Now, you'll zoom the workbook to 120%.

▶ 4. Click the **Microsoft Excel – Book1** button on the taskbar. The Excel program window is displayed.

▶ 5. Click the **Zoom In** button ⊕ on the status bar two times. The workspace magnifies to 120%. This is the zoom percentage that matches the rest of the Excel figures shown in these tutorials.

▶ 6. Click the **Document1 – Microsoft Word** button on the taskbar. The Word program window is displayed.

Using the Ribbon

The **Ribbon** at the top of the program window just below the title bar is the main set of commands that you click to execute tasks. The Ribbon is organized into tabs. Each **tab** has commands related to particular activities. For example, in Word, the Insert tab on the Ribbon provides access to all the commands for adding objects such as shapes, pages, tables, illustrations, text, and symbols to a document. Although the tabs differ from program to program, the first tab in each program, called the Home tab, contains the commands for the most frequently performed activities, including cutting and pasting, changing fonts, and using editing tools. In addition, the Insert, Review, View, and Add-Ins tabs appear on the Ribbon in all the Office programs except Access, although the commands they include might differ from program to program. Other tabs are program specific, such as the Design tab in PowerPoint and the Datasheet tab in Access.

To use the Ribbon tabs:

▶ 1. In Word, point to the **Insert** tab on the Ribbon. The Insert tab is highlighted, though the Home tab with the options for using the Clipboard and formatting text remains visible.

▶ 2. Click the **Insert** tab. The Ribbon displays the Insert tab, which provides access to all the options for adding objects such as shapes, pages, tables, illustrations, text, and symbols to a document. See Figure 8.

Figure 8   Insert tab on the Ribbon

Tip

To view more workspace, you can reduce the Ribbon to a single line by double-clicking any tab on the Ribbon. Double-click any tab again to redisplay the full Ribbon.

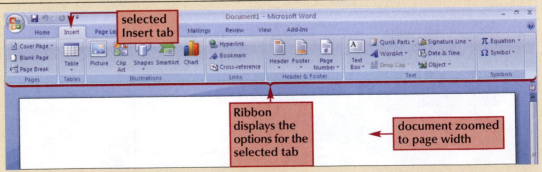

▶ 3. Click the **Home** tab on the Ribbon. The Ribbon displays the Home options.

Clicking Button Icons

Each **button**, or icon, on the tabs provides one-click access to a command. Most buttons are labeled so that you can easily find the command you need. For the most part, when you click a button, something happens in your file. If you want to repeat that action, you click the button again. Buttons for related commands are organized on a tab in **groups**. For example, the Clipboard group on the Home tab includes the Cut, Copy, Paste, and Format Painter buttons—the commands for moving or copying text, objects, and formatting.

Buttons can be toggle switches: one click turns on the feature and the next click turns off the feature. While the feature is on, the button remains colored or highlighted to remind you that it is active. For example, in Word, the Show/Hide button on the Home tab in the Paragraph group displays the nonprinting screen characters when toggled on and hides them when toggled off.

Some buttons have two parts: a button that accesses a command and an arrow that opens a menu of all the commands available for that task. For example, the Paste button on the Home tab includes the default Paste command and an arrow that opens the menu of all the Paste commands—Paste, Paste Special, and Paste as Hyperlink. To select a command on the menu, you click the button arrow and then click the command on the menu.

The buttons and groups change based on your monitor size, your screen resolution, and the size of the program window. With smaller monitors, lower screen resolutions, and reduced program windows, buttons can appear as icons without labels and a group can be condensed into a button that you click to display the group options. The figures in these tutorials were created using a screen resolution of 1024 × 768 and, unless otherwise specified, the program and workspace windows are maximized. If you are using a different screen resolution or window size, the button icons on the Ribbon might show more or fewer button names, and some groups might be condensed into buttons.

You'll type text in the Word document, and then use the buttons on the Ribbon.

To use buttons on the Ribbon:

1. Type **Recycled Palette**, and then press the **Enter** key. The text appears in the first line of the document and the insertion point moves to the second line.

   Trouble? If you make a typing error, press the Backspace key to delete the incorrect letters, and then retype the text.

2. In the Paragraph group on the Home tab, click the **Show/Hide** button ¶ . The nonprinting screen characters appear in the document, and the Show/Hide button remains toggled on. See Figure 9.

   Trouble? If the nonprinting characters are removed from your screen, the Show/Hide button ¶ was already selected. Repeat Step 2 to show the nonprinting screen characters.

Button toggled on | **Figure 9**

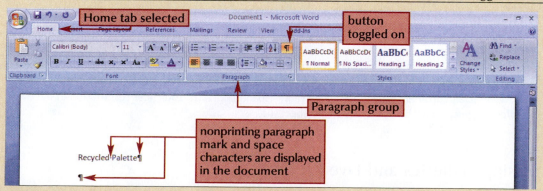

3. Drag to select all the text in the first line of the document (but not the paragraph mark).

4. In the Clipboard group on the Home tab, click the **Copy** button . The selected text is copied to the Clipboard.

5. Press the ↓ key. The text is deselected and the insertion point moves to the second line in the document.

6. In the Clipboard group on the Home tab, point to the top part of the **Paste** button. Both parts of the Paste button are highlighted, but the icon at top is darker to indicate it will be clicked if you press the mouse button.

7. Point to the **Paste button arrow**. The button arrow is now darker.

8. Click the **Paste button arrow**. A menu of paste commands opens. See Figure 10. To select one of the commands on the list, you click it.

Figure 10 | **Two-part Paste button**

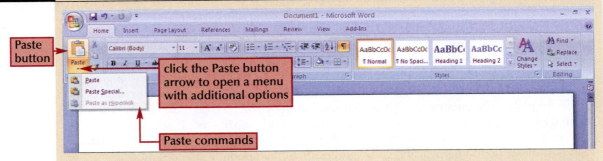

Paste button

click the Paste button arrow to open a menu with additional options

Paste commands

9. Click **Paste**. The menu closes, and the text is duplicated in the second line of the document.

As you can see, you can quickly access commands and turn features on and off with the buttons on the Ribbon.

InSight | **Using Keyboard Shortcuts and Key Tips**

Keyboard shortcuts can help you work faster and more efficiently. A **keyboard shortcut** is a key or combination of keys you press to access a tool or perform a command. To quickly access options on the Ribbon, the Quick Access Toolbar, and the Office Button without removing your hands from the keyboard:

1. Press the Alt key. Key Tips appear that list the keyboard shortcut for each Ribbon tab, each Quick Access Toolbar button, and the Office Button.
2. Press the key for the tab or button you want to use. An action is performed or Key Tips appear for the buttons on the selected tab or the commands for the selected button.
3. Continue to press the appropriate key listed in the Key Tip until the action you want is performed.

You can also use keyboard shortcuts to perform specific commands. For example, Ctrl+S is the keyboard shortcut for the Save command (you hold down the Ctrl key while you press the S key). This type of keyboard shortcut appears in ScreenTips next to the command's name. Not all commands have this type of keyboard shortcut. Identical commands in each Office program use the same keyboard shortcut.

Using Galleries and Live Preview

A button can also open a **gallery**, which is a grid or menu that shows a visual representation of the options available for that command. For example, the Bullet Library gallery in Word shows an icon of each bullet style you can select. Some galleries include a More button that you click to expand the gallery to see all the options in it. When you hover the pointer over an option in a gallery, **Live Preview** shows the results you would achieve in your file if you clicked that option. To continue the bullets example, when you hover over a bullet style in the Bullet Library gallery, the current paragraph or selected text previews that bullet style. By moving the pointer from option to option, you can quickly see the text set with different bullet styles; you can then select the style that works best for your needs.

To use a gallery and Live Preview:

▶ **1.** In the Paragraph group on the Home tab, click the **Bullets button arrow** ⊞ ▾. The Bullet Library gallery opens.

▶ **2.** Point to the **check mark bullet** style. Live Preview shows the selected bullet style in your document, so you can determine if you like that bullet style. See Figure 11.

Live Preview of bullet style ◀ **Figure 11**

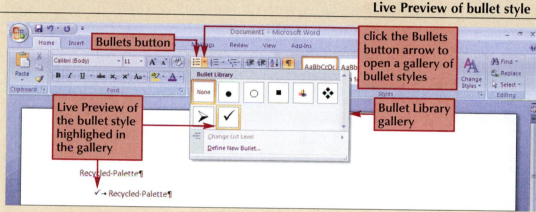

▶ **3.** Place the pointer over each of the remaining bullet styles and preview them in your document.

You don't want to add bullets to your document right now, so you'll close the Bullet Library gallery and deselect the Bullets button.

▶ **4.** Press the **Esc** key on the keyboard. The Bullet Library gallery closes and the Bullets button is deselected.

▶ **5.** Press the **Backspace** key on the keyboard to delete the text "Recycled Palette" on the second line.

Galleries and Live Preview let you quickly see how your file will be affected by a selection.

Opening Dialog Boxes and Task Panes

The button to the right of the group names is the **Dialog Box Launcher**, which you click to open a task pane or dialog box that provides more advanced functionality for that group of tasks. A **task pane** is a window that helps you navigate through a complex task or feature. For example, the Clipboard task pane allows you to paste some or all of the items that have been cut or copied from any Office program during the current work session and the Research task pane allows you to search a variety of reference resources from within a file. A **dialog box** is a window from which you enter or choose settings for how you want to perform a task. For example, the Page Setup dialog box in Word contains options for how you want a document to look. Some dialog boxes organize related information into tabs, and related options and settings are organized into groups, just as they are on the Ribbon. You select settings in a dialog box using option buttons, check boxes, text boxes, lists, and other controls to collect information about how you want to perform a task.

In Excel, you'll use the Dialog Box Launcher for the Page Setup group to open the Page Setup dialog box.

To open the Page Setup dialog box using the Dialog Box Launcher:

▶ 1. Click the **Microsoft Excel – Book1** button on the taskbar to switch from Word to Excel.

▶ 2. Click the **Page Layout** tab on the Ribbon.

▶ 3. In the Page Setup group, click the **Dialog Box Launcher**, which is the small button to the right of the Page Setup group name. The Page Setup dialog box opens with the Page tab displayed. See Figure 12.

Figure 12 | **Page tab in the Page Setup dialog box**

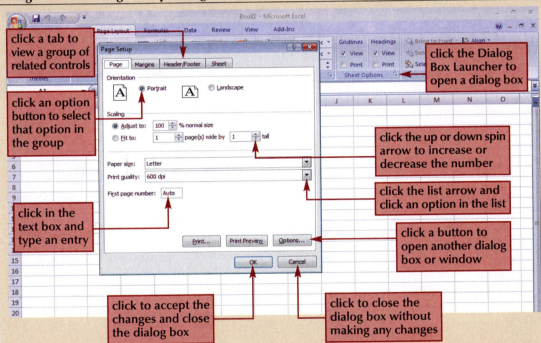

click a tab to view a group of related controls

click the Dialog Box Launcher to open a dialog box

click an option button to select that option in the group

click the up or down spin arrow to increase or decrease the number

click the list arrow and click an option in the list

click in the text box and type an entry

click a button to open another dialog box or window

click to accept the changes and close the dialog box

click to close the dialog box without making any changes

▶ 4. Click the **Landscape** option button. The workbook's page orientation changes to a page wider than it is long.

▶ 5. Click the **Sheet** tab. The dialog box displays options related to the worksheet. You can click a check box to turn an option on (checked) or off (unchecked). You can check more than one check box in a group, whereas you can select only one option button in a group.

▶ 6. In the Print group, click the **Gridlines** check box and the **Row and column headings** check box. Check marks appear in both check boxes, indicating that these options are selected.

You don't want to change the page setup right now, so you'll close the dialog box.

▶ 7. Click the **Cancel** button. The dialog box closes without making any changes to the page setup.

Using Contextual Tools

Some tabs, toolbars, and menus come into view as you work. Because these tools become available only as you might need them, the workspace on your screen remains more open and less cluttered. However, tools that appear and disappear as you work can be distracting and take some getting used to.

Displaying Contextual Tabs

Any object that you can select in a file has a related contextual tab. An **object** is anything that appears on your screen that can be selected and manipulated as a whole, such as a table, a picture, a text box, a shape, a chart, WordArt, an equation, a diagram, a header, or a footer. A **contextual tab** is a Ribbon tab that contains commands related to the selected object so you can manipulate, edit, and format that object. Contextual tabs appear to the right of the standard Ribbon tabs just below a title label. For example, Figure 13 shows the Table Tools contextual tabs that appear when you select a table in a Word document. Although the contextual tabs appear only when you select an object, they function in the same way as standard tabs on the Ribbon. Contextual tabs disappear when you click elsewhere on the screen and deselect the object. Contextual tabs can also appear as you switch views. You'll use contextual tabs in later tutorials.

Table Tools contextual tabs — Figure 13

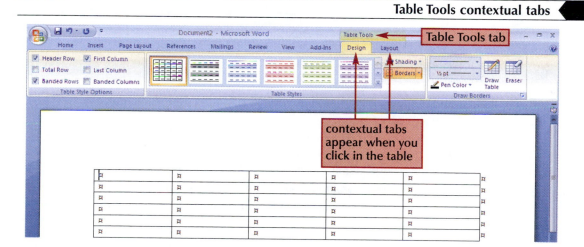

Accessing the Mini Toolbar

The **Mini toolbar** is a toolbar that appears next to the pointer whenever you select text, and it contains buttons for the most commonly used formatting commands, such as font, font size, styles, color, alignment, and indents that may appear in different groups or tabs on the Ribbon. The Mini toolbar buttons differ in each program. A transparent version of the Mini toolbar appears immediately after you select text. When you move the pointer over the Mini toolbar, it comes into full view so you can click the appropriate formatting button or buttons. The Mini toolbar disappears if you move the pointer away from the toolbar, press a key, or press a mouse button. The Mini toolbar can help you format your text faster, but initially you might find that the toolbar disappears unexpectedly. All the commands on the Mini toolbar are also available on the Ribbon. Be aware that Live Preview of selected styles does not work in the Mini toolbar.

You'll use the Mini toolbar to format text you enter in the workbook.

Tip

You can turn off the Mini toolbar and Live Preview in Word, Excel, and PowerPoint. Click the Office Button, click the Options button at the bottom of the Office menu, uncheck the first two check boxes in the Popular category, and then click the OK button.

To use the Mini toolbar to format text:

1. If necessary, click cell **A1** (the rectangle in the upper-left corner of the worksheet).

2. Type **Budget**. The text appears in the cell.

3. Press the **Enter** key. The text is entered in cell A1 and cell A2 is selected.

4. Type **2008**, and then press the **Enter** key. The year is entered in cell A2 and cell A3 is selected.

   You'll use the Mini toolbar to make the word in cell A1 boldface.

5. Double-click cell **A1** to place the insertion point in the cell. Now you can select the text you typed.

6. Double-click **Budget** in cell A1. The selected text appears white in a black background, and the transparent Mini toolbar appears directly above the selected text. See Figure 14.

Figure 14	Transparent Mini toolbar

7. Move the pointer over the Mini toolbar. The Mini toolbar is now completely visible, and you can click buttons.

   Trouble? If the Mini toolbar disappears, you probably moved the pointer to another area of the worksheet. To redisplay the Mini toolbar, repeat Steps 5 through 7, being careful to move the pointer directly over the Mini toolbar in Step 7.

8. Click the **Bold** button **B** on the Mini toolbar. The text in cell A1 is bold and the Mini toolbar remains visible so you can continue formatting the selected text. See Figure 15.

Figure 15	Mini toolbar with the Bold button selected

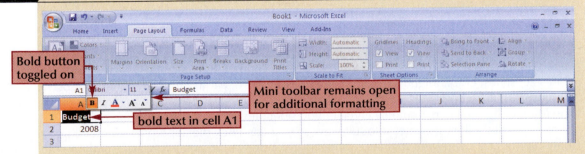

You don't want to make any other changes, so you'll close the Mini toolbar.

9. Press the **Enter** key. The Mini toolbar disappears and cell A2 is selected.

Tip

You can redisplay the Mini toolbar if it disappears by right-clicking the selected text.

Opening Shortcut Menus

A **shortcut menu** is a list of commands related to a selection that opens when you click the right mouse button. Each shortcut menu provides access to the commands you'll most likely want to use with the object or selection you right-click. The shortcut menu includes commands that perform actions, commands that open dialog boxes, and galleries of options that provide Live Preview. The Mini toolbar also opens when you right-click. If you click a button on the Mini toolbar, the rest of the shortcut menu closes while the Mini toolbar remains open so you can continue formatting the selection. Using a shortcut menu provides quick access to the commands you need without having to access the tabs on the Ribbon. For example, you can right-click selected text to open a shortcut menu with a Mini toolbar, text-related commands, such as Cut, Copy, and Paste, as well as other program-specific commands.

You'll use a shortcut menu in Excel to delete the content you entered in cell A1.

To use a shortcut menu to delete content:

▶ 1. Right-click cell **A1**. A shortcut menu opens, listing commands related to common tasks you'd perform in a cell, along with a Mini toolbar. See Figure 16.

Shortcut menu with Mini toolbar ◄ Figure 16

Mini toolbar appears above the shortcut menu

click a command with ellipsis to open a dialog box

click a command to perform an action

point to an arrow to open a submenu of additional options

shortcut menu

You'll use the Clear Contents command to delete the bold text from cell A1.

▶ 2. Click **Clear Contents** on the shortcut menu. The shortcut menu closes, the Mini toolbar disappears, and the formatted text is removed from cell A1.

You'll use the Clear Contents command again to delete the year from cell A2.

▶ 3. Right-click cell **A2**, and then click **Clear Contents** on the shortcut menu. The year is removed from cell A2.

Shortcut menus enable you to quickly access commands that you're most likely to need in the context of the task you're performing.

Tip

Press the Esc key to close an open menu, shortcut menu, list, gallery, and so forth without selecting an option.

Working with Files

The most common tasks you perform in any Office program are to create, open, save, and close files. The processes for these tasks are basically the same in all the Office programs. In addition, there are several methods for performing most tasks in Office. This flexibility enables you to use Office in a way that best fits how you like to work.

The **Office Button** provides access to document-level features, such as creating new files, opening existing files, saving files, printing files, and closing files, as well as the most common program options, called **application settings**. The **Quick Access Toolbar** is a collection of buttons that provide one-click access to commonly used commands, such as Save, Undo, and Repeat.

To begin working in a program, you need to create a new file or open an existing file. When you start Word, Excel, or PowerPoint, the program opens along with a blank file—ready for you to begin working on a new document, workbook, or presentation. When you start Access, the Getting Started with Microsoft Access window opens, displaying options for creating a new database or opening an existing one.

Ean has asked you to continue working on the agenda for the stockholder meeting. You already started typing in the document that opened when you started Word. Next, you will enter more text in the Word document.

Tip

You can add buttons you use frequently to the Quick Access Toolbar. Click the Customize Quick Access Toolbar button, and then click a button name on the menu.

To enter text in the Word document:

▶ **1.** Click the **Document1 – Microsoft Word** button on the taskbar to activate the Word program window.

▶ **2.** Type **Meeting Agenda** on the second line of the document, and then press the **Enter** key. The text you typed appears in the document.

   Trouble? If you make a typing error, press the Backspace key to delete the incorrect letters, and then retype the text.

Saving a File

As you create and modify Office files, your work is stored only in the computer's temporary memory, not on a hard disk. If you were to exit the programs without saving, turn off your computer, or experience a power failure, your work would be lost. To prevent losing work, save your file to a disk frequently—at least every 10 minutes. You can save files to the hard disk located inside your computer, a floppy disk, an external hard drive, a network storage drive, or a portable storage disk, such as a USB flash drive.

Reference Window | **Saving a File**

To save a file the first time or with a new name or location:
- Click the Office Button, and then click Save As (or for an unnamed file, click the Save button on the Quick Access Toolbar or click the Office Button, and then click Save).
- In the Save As dialog box, navigate to the location where you want to save the file.
- Type a descriptive title in the File name box, and then click the Save button.

To resave a named file to the same location:
- Click the Save button on the Quick Access Toolbar (or click the Office Button, and then click Save).

The first time you save a file, you need to name it. This **filename** includes a descriptive title you select and a file extension assigned by Office. You should choose a descriptive title that accurately reflects the content of the document, workbook, presentation, or database, such as "Shipping Options Letter" or "Fourth Quarter Financial Analysis." Your descriptive title can include uppercase and lowercase letters, numbers, hyphens, and spaces in any combination, but not the following special characters: ? " / \ < > * | and :. Each filename ends with a **file extension**, a period followed by several characters that Office adds to your descriptive title to identify the program in which that file was created. The default file extensions for Office 2007 are .docx for Word, .xlsx for Excel, .pptx for PowerPoint, and .accdb for Access. Filenames (the descriptive title and the file extension) can include a maximum of 255 characters. You might see file extensions depending on how Windows is set up on your computer. The figures in these tutorials do not show file extensions.

You also need to decide where to save the file—on which disk and in what folder. A **folder** is a container for your files. Just as you organize paper documents within folders stored in a filing cabinet, you can organize your files within folders stored on your computer's hard disk or a removable disk, such as a USB flash drive. Store each file in a logical location that you will remember whenever you want to use the file again. The default storage location for Office files is the Documents folder; you can create additional storage folders within that folder or navigate to a new storage location.

You can navigate the Save As dialog box by clicking a folder or location on your computer in the Navigation pane along the left side of the dialog box, and then double-clicking folders in the file list until you display the storage location you want. You can also navigate to a storage location with the Address bar, which displays the current file path. Each location in the file path has a corresponding arrow that you can click to quickly select a folder within that location. For example, you can click the Documents arrow in the Address bar to open a list of all the folders in the Documents folder, and then click the folder you want to open. If you want to return to a specific spot in the file hierarchy, you click that folder name in the Address bar. The Back and Forward buttons let you quickly move between folders.

> **Tip**
>
> Office adds the correct file extension when you save a file. Do not type one in the descriptive title, or you will create a duplicate (such as Meeting Agenda. docx.docx).

> **Windows XP Tip**
>
> The default storage location for Office files is the My Documents folder.

Saving and Using Files with Earlier Versions of Office | InSight

The default file types in Office 2007 are different from those used in earlier versions. This means that someone using Office 2003 or earlier cannot open files created in Office 2007. Files you want to share with earlier Office users must be saved in the earlier formats, which use the following extensions: .doc for Word, .xls for Excel, .mdb for Access, and .ppt for PowerPoint. To save a file in an earlier format, open the Save As dialog box, click the Save as type list arrow, and then click the appropriate 97-2003 format. A compatibility checker reports which Office 2007 features or elements are not supported by the earlier version of Office, and you can choose to remove them before saving. You can use Office 2007 to open and work with files created in earlier versions of Office. You can then save the file in its current format or update it to the Office 2007 format.

The lines of text you typed are not yet saved on disk. You'll do that now.

Windows XP Tip

To navigate to a location in the Save As dialog box, you use the Save in arrow.

To save a file for the first time:

▶ 1. Click the **Save** button 🔲 on the Quick Access Toolbar. The Save As dialog box opens because you have not yet saved the file and need to specify a storage location and filename. The default location is set to the Documents folder, and the first few words of the first line appear in the File name box as a suggested title.

▶ 2. In the Navigation pane, click the link for the location that contains your Data Files, if necessary.

Trouble? If you don't have the starting Data Files, you need to get them before you can proceed. Your instructor will either give you the Data Files or ask you to obtain them from a specified location (such as a network drive). In either case, make a backup copy of the Data Files before you start so that you will have the original files available in case you need to start over. If you have any questions about the Data Files, see your instructor or technical support person for assistance.

▶ 3. Double-click the **OFF** folder in the file list, and then double-click the **Tutorial** folder. This is the location where you want to save the document.

Next, you'll enter a more descriptive title for the filename.

▶ 4. Type **Meeting Agenda** in the File name box. See Figure 17.

| Figure 17 | Completed Save As dialog box |

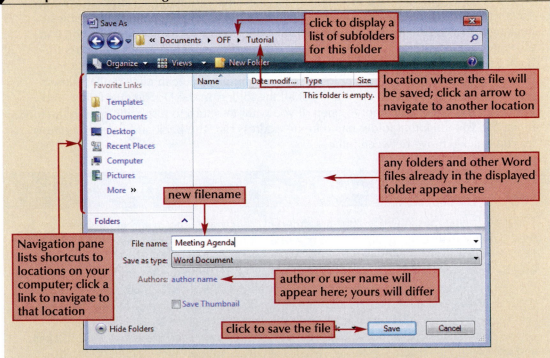

Trouble? If the .docx file extension appears after the filename, your computer is configured to show file extensions. Continue with Step 5.

▶ 5. Click the **Save** button. The Save As dialog box closes, and the name of your file appears in the title bar.

The saved file includes everything in the document at the time you last saved it. Any new edits or additions you make to the document exist only in the computer's memory and are not saved in the file on the disk. As you work, remember to save frequently so that the file is updated to reflect the latest content of the document.

Because you already named the document and selected a storage location, the Save As dialog box doesn't open whenever you save the document again. If you want to save a copy of the file with a different filename or to a different location, you reopen the Save As dialog box by clicking the Office Button, and then clicking Save As. The previous version of the file remains on your disk as well.

You need to add your name to the agenda. Then, you'll save your changes.

To modify and save the Word document:

▶ 1. Type your name, and then press the **Enter** key. The text you typed appears on the next line.

▶ 2. Click the **Save** button 🔲 on the Quick Access Toolbar to save your changes.

Closing a File

Although you can keep multiple files open at one time, you should close any file you are no longer working on to conserve system resources as well as to ensure that you don't inadvertently make changes to the file. You can close a file by clicking the Office Button and then clicking the Close command. If that's the only file open for the program, the program window remains open and no file appears in the window. You can also close a file by clicking the Close button in the upper-right corner of the title bar or double-clicking the Office Button. If that's the only file open for the program, the program also closes.

As a standard practice, you should save your file before closing it. However, Office has an added safeguard: If you attempt to close a file without saving your changes, a dialog box opens, asking whether you want to save the file. Click the Yes button to save the changes to the file before closing the file and program. Click the No button to close the file and program without saving changes. Click the Cancel button to return to the program window without saving changes or closing the file and program. This feature helps to ensure that you always save the most current version of any file.

You'll add the date to the agenda. Then, you'll attempt to close it without saving.

To modify and close the Word document:

▶ 1. Type today's date, and then press the **Enter** key. The text you typed appears below your name in the document.

▶ 2. In the upper-left corner of the program window, click the **Office Button** 🔴. A menu opens with commands for creating new files, opening existing files, saving files, printing files, and closing files.

▶ 3. Click **Close**. A dialog box opens, asking whether you want to save the changes you made to the document.

▶ 4. Click the **Yes** button. The current version of the document is saved to the file, and then the document closes. Word is still running.

After you have a program open, you can create additional new files for the open program or you can open previously created and saved files.

Opening a File

When you want to open a blank document, workbook, presentation, or database, you create a new file. When you want to work on a previously created file, you must first open it. Opening a file transfers a copy of the file from the storage disk (either a hard disk or a portable disk) to the computer's memory and displays it on your screen. The file is then in your computer's memory and on the disk.

Reference Window | **Opening an Existing File or Creating a New File**

- Click the Office Button, and then click Open.
- In the Open dialog box, navigate to the storage location of the file you want to open.
- Click the filename of the file you want to open.
- Click the Open button.

or

- Click the Office Button, and then click a filename in the Recent Documents list.

or

- Click the Office Button, and then click New.
- In the New dialog box, click Blank Document, Blank Workbook, Blank Presentation, or Blank Database (depending on the program).
- Click the Create button.

Ean asks you to print the agenda. To do that, you'll reopen the file.

To open the existing Word document:

▶ 1. Click the **Office Button** 🟠, and then click **Open**. The Open dialog box, which works similarly to the Save As dialog box, opens.

▶ 2. Use the Navigation pane or the Address bar to navigate to the **OFF\Tutorial** folder included with your Data Files. This is the location where you saved the agenda document.

▶ 3. Click **Meeting Agenda** in the file list. See Figure 18.

Figure 18 ▶ **Open dialog box**

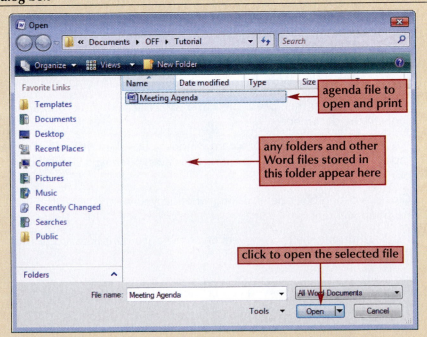

▶ 4. Click the **Open** button. The agenda file opens in the Word program window.

Next, you'll use Help to get information about printing files in Word.

Getting Help

If you don't know how to perform a task or want more information about a feature, you can turn to Office itself for information on how to use it. This information, referred to simply as **Help**, is like a huge encyclopedia available from your desktop. You can get Help in ScreenTips, from the Help window, and in Microsoft Office Online.

Viewing ScreenTips

ScreenTips are a fast and simple method you can use to get help about objects you see on the screen. A **ScreenTip** is a box with the button's name, its keyboard shortcut if it has one, a description of the command's function, and, in some cases, a link to more information. Just position the mouse pointer over a button or object to view its ScreenTip. If a link to more information appears in the ScreenTip, press the F1 key while the ScreenTip is displayed to open the Help window with the appropriate topic displayed.

To view ScreenTips:

1. Point to the **Microsoft Office Word Help** button. The ScreenTip shows the button's name, its keyboard shortcut, and a brief explanation of the button. See Figure 19.

Figure 19 ScreenTip for the Help button

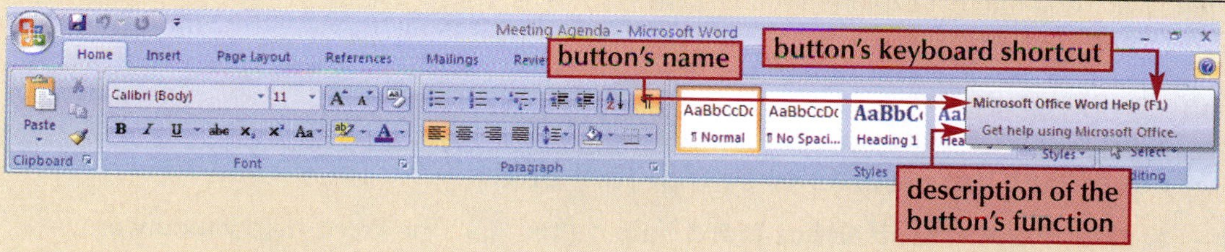

2. Point to other buttons on the Ribbon to display their ScreenTips.

Using the Help Window

For more detailed information, you can use the **Help window** to access all the Help topics, templates, and training installed on your computer with Office and available on Microsoft Office Online. **Microsoft Office Online** is a Web site maintained by Microsoft that provides access to the latest information and additional Help resources. For example, you can access current Help topics, templates of predesigned files, and training for Office. To connect to Microsoft Office Online, you need Internet access on your computer. Otherwise, you see only those topics stored locally.

Reference Window | **Getting Help**

- Click the Microsoft Office Help button (the button name depends on the Office program).
- Type a keyword or phrase in the "Type words to search for" box, and then click the Search button.
- Click a Help topic in the search results list.
- Read the information in the Help window. For more information, click other topics or links.
- Click the Close button on the Help window title bar.

You open the Help window by clicking the Microsoft Office Help button [icon] located below the sizing buttons in every Office program. Each program has its own Help window from which you can find information about all the Office commands and features as well as step-by-step instructions for using them. You can search for information in the Help window using the "Type words to search for" box and the Table of Contents pane.

The "Type words to search for" box enables you to search the Help system using keywords or phrases. You type a specific word or phrase about a task you want to perform or a topic you need help with, and then click the Search button to search the Help system. A list of Help topics related to the keyword or phrase you entered appears in the Help window. If your computer is connected to the Internet, your search results come from Microsoft Office Online rather than only the Help topics stored locally on your computer. You can click a link to open a Help topic with step-by-step instructions that will guide you through a specific procedure and/or provide explanations of difficult concepts in clear, easy-to-understand language. For example, if you type "format cell" in the Excel Help window, a list of Help topics related to the words you typed appears in the Help window. You can navigate through the topics you've viewed using the buttons on the Help window toolbar. These buttons—including Back, Forward, Stop, Refresh, Home, and Print—are the same as those in the Microsoft Internet Explorer Web browser.

You'll use the "Type words to search for" box in the Help window to obtain more information about printing a document in Word.

To use the "Type words to search for" box:

▶ **1.** Click the **Microsoft Office Word Help** button [icon] . The Word Help window opens.

▶ **2.** Click the **Type words to search for** box, if necessary, and then type **print document**. You can set where you want to search.

▶ **3.** Click the **Search button arrow**. The Search menu shows the online and local content available.

4. If your computer is connected to the Internet, click **All Word** in the Content from Office Online list. If your computer is not connected to the Internet, click **Word Help** in the Content from this computer list.

5. Click the **Search** button. The Help window displays a list of topics related to your keywords. See Figure 20.

Search results displaying Help topics | Figure 20

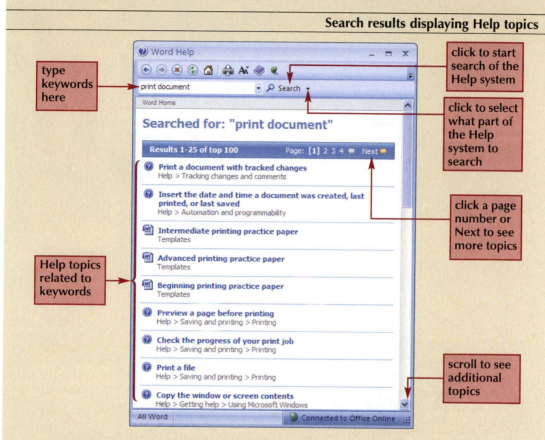

type keywords here

click to start search of the Help system

click to select what part of the Help system to search

click a page number or Next to see more topics

Help topics related to keywords

scroll to see additional topics

Trouble? If your search results list differs from the one shown in Figure 20, your computer is not connected to the Internet or Microsoft has updated the list of available Help topics since this book was published. Continue with Step 6.

6. Scroll through the list to review the Help topics.

7. Click **Print a file**. The Help topic is displayed in the Help window so you can learn more about how to print a document. See Figure 21.

Figure 21 ▸ **Print a file Help topic**

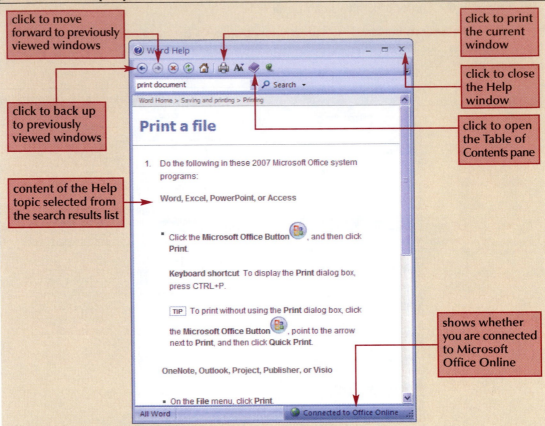

click to move forward to previously viewed windows

click to print the current window

click to back up to previously viewed windows

click to close the Help window

click to open the Table of Contents pane

content of the Help topic selected from the search results list

shows whether you are connected to Microsoft Office Online

Trouble? If you don't see the Print a file Help topic on page 1, its current location might be on another page. Click the Next link to move to the next page, and then scroll down to find the Print a file topic, repeating to search additional pages until you locate the topic.

▸ **8.** Read the information.

Another way to find information in the Help system is to use the Table of Contents pane. The Show Table of Contents button on the Help window toolbar opens a pane that displays a list of the Help system content organized by subjects and topics, similar to a book's table of contents. You click main subject links to display related topic links. You click a topic link to display that Help topic in the Help window. You'll use the Table of Contents to find information about getting help in Office.

To use the Help window table of contents:

▸ **1.** Click the **Show Table of Contents** button 📖 on the Help window toolbar. The Table of Contents pane opens on the left side of the Help window.

▸ **2.** Click **Getting help** in the Table of Contents pane, scrolling up if necessary. The Getting help "book" opens, listing the topics related to that subject.

▸ **3.** Click the **Work with the Help window** topic, and then click the **Maximize** button 🗖 on the title bar. The Help topic is displayed in the maximized Help window, and you can read the text to learn more about the various ways to obtain help in Word. See Figure 22.

Table of Contents pane in the Help window | Figure 22

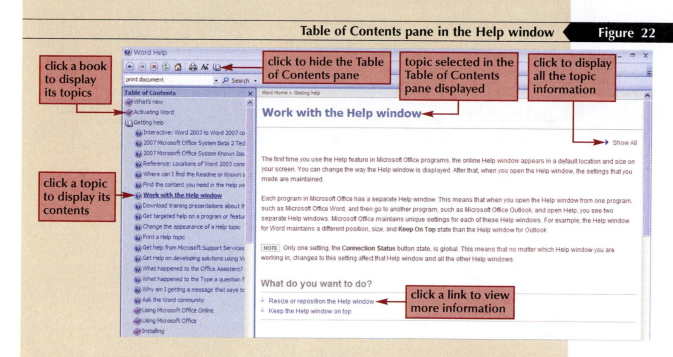

Trouble? If your search results list differs from the one shown in Figure 22, your computer is not connected to the Internet or Microsoft has updated the list of available Help topics since this book was published. Continue with Step 4.

4. Click **Using Microsoft Office Online** in the Table of Contents pane, click the **Get online Help, templates, training, and additional content** topic to display information about that topic, and then read the information.

5. Click the links within this topic and read the information.

6. Click the **Close** button ⊠ on the Help window title bar to close the window.

Printing a File

At times, you'll want a paper copy of your Office file. The first time you print during each session at the computer, you should use the Print command to open the Print dialog box so you can verify or adjust the printing settings. You can select a printer, the number of copies to print, the portion of the file to print, and so forth; the printing settings vary slightly from program to program. If you want to use the same default settings for subsequent print jobs, you can use the Quick Print button to print without opening the dialog box.

Printing a File	Reference Window

- Click the Office Button, and then click Print.
- Verify the print settings in the Print dialog box.
- Click the OK button.

or

- Click the Office Button, point to Print, and then click Quick Print.

Now that you know how to print, you'll print the agenda for Ean.

To print the Word document:

1. Make sure your printer is turned on and contains paper.

2. Click the **Office Button** 🔘, and then click **Print**. The Print dialog box opens. See Figure 23.

Figure 23 Print dialog box

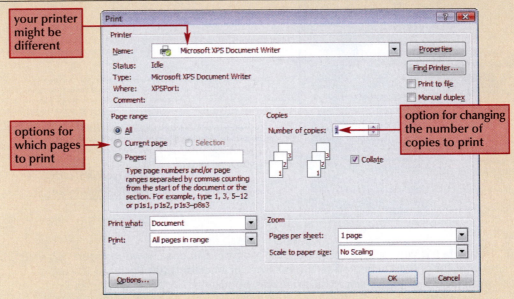

your printer might be different

options for which pages to print

option for changing the number of copies to print

Trouble? If a menu of Print commands opens, you clicked the Print button arrow on the two-part Print button. Click Print on the menu to open the Print dialog box.

3. Verify that the correct printer appears in the Name box in the Printer group. If necessary, click the **Name** arrow, and then click the correct printer from the list of available printers.

4. Verify that **1** appears in the Number of copies box.

5. Click the **OK** button to print the document.

Trouble? If the document does not print, see your instructor or technical support person for help.

Exiting Programs

When you finish working with a program, you should exit it. As with many other aspects of Office, you can exit programs with a button or a command. You'll use both methods to exit Word and Excel. You can use the Exit command to exit a program and close an open file in one step. If you haven't saved the final version of the open file, a dialog box opens, asking whether you want to save your changes. Clicking the Yes button saves the open file, closes the file, and then exits the program.

To exit the Word and Excel programs:

1. Click the **Close** button ☒ on the Word title bar to exit Word. The Word document closes and the Word program exits. The Excel window is visible again.

Trouble? If a dialog box opens, asking if you want to save the document, you might have inadvertently made a change to the document. Click the No button.

▶ **2.** Click the **Office Button** 🔘, and then click **Exit Excel**. A dialog box opens, asking whether you want to save the changes you made to the workbook. If you click the Yes button, the Save As dialog box opens and Excel exits after you finish saving the workbook. This time, you don't want to save the workbook.

▶ **3.** Click the **No** button. The workbook closes without saving a copy, and the Excel program exits.

Exiting programs after you are done using them keeps your Windows desktop uncluttered for the next person using the computer, frees up your system's resources, and prevents data from being lost accidentally.

Quick Check | Review

1. What Office program would be best to use to create a budget?
2. How do you start an Office program?
3. Explain the difference between Save and Save As.
4. How do you open an existing Office file?
5. What happens if you open a file, make edits, and then attempt to close the file or exit the program without saving the current version of the file?
6. What are two ways to get Help in Office?

Tutorial Summary | Review

You have learned how to use features common to all the programs included in Microsoft Office 2007, including starting and exiting programs; resizing windows; using the Ribbon, dialog boxes, shortcut menus, and the Mini toolbar; opening, closing, and printing files; and getting Help.

Key Terms

Access	Help window	Office Button
application settings	integration	Outlook
button	keyboard shortcut	PowerPoint
contextual tab	Live Preview	presentation
database	Microsoft Office 2007	Quick Access Toolbar
default	Microsoft Office Access 2007	Ribbon
dialog box	Microsoft Office Excel 2007	ScreenTip
Dialog Box Launcher	Microsoft Office Online	shortcut menu
document	Microsoft Office	status bar
Excel	Outlook 2007	tab
file extension	Microsoft Office	task pane
filename	PowerPoint 2007	Word
folder	Microsoft Office Word 2007	workbook
gallery	Mini toolbar	zoom
group	object	
Help	Office	

Practice | **Review Assignments**

Practice the skills you learned in the tutorial.

Data Files needed for the Review Assignments: Finances.xlsx, Letter.docx

You need to prepare for an upcoming meeting at Recycled Palette. You'll open and print documents for the presentation. Complete the following:

1. Start PowerPoint.
2. Use the Help window to search Office Online for the PowerPoint demo "Demo: Up to Speed with PowerPoint 2007." (*Hint:* Use "demo" as the keyword to search for, and make sure you search All PowerPoint in the Content from Office Online list. If you are not connected to the Internet, continue with Step 3.) Open the Demo topic, and then click the Play Demo link to view it. Close Internet Explorer and the Help window when you're done.
3. Start Excel.
4. Switch to the PowerPoint window using the taskbar, and then close the presentation but leave open the PowerPoint program. (*Hint:* Click the Office Button and then click Close.)
5. Open a new, blank PowerPoint presentation from the New Presentation dialog box.
6. Close the PowerPoint presentation and program using the Close button on the PowerPoint title bar; do not save changes if asked.
7. Open the **Finances** workbook located in the OFF\Review folder included with your Data Files.
8. Use the Save As command to save the workbook as **Recycled Palette Finances** in the OFF\Review folder.
9. Type your name, press the Enter key to insert your name at the top of the worksheet, and then save the workbook.
10. Print one copy of the worksheet using the Print button on the Office Button menu.
11. Exit Excel using the Office Button.
12. Start Word, and then open the **Letter** document located in the OFF\Review folder included with your Data Files.
13. Use the Save As command to save the document with the filename **Recycled Palette Letter** in the OFF\Review folder.
14. Press and hold the Ctrl key, press the End key, and then release both keys to move the insertion point to the end of the letter, and then type your name.
15. Use the Save button on the Quick Access Toolbar to save the change to the Recycled Palette Letter document.
16. Print one copy of the document, and then close the document.
17. Exit the Word program using the Close button on the title bar.

| Assess | **SAM Assessment and Training** |

If you have a SAM user profile, you may have access to hands-on instruction, practice, and assessment of the skills covered in this tutorial. Log in to your SAM account (**http://sam2007.course.com**) to launch any assigned training activities or exams that relate to the skills covered in this tutorial.

| Review | **Quick Check Answers** |

1. Excel
2. Click the Start button on the taskbar, click All Programs, click Microsoft Office, and then click the name of the program you want to open.
3. Save updates a file to reflect its latest contents using its current filename and location. Save As enables you to change the filename and storage location of a file.
4. Click the Office Button, and then click Open.
5. A dialog box opens asking whether you want to save the changes to the file.
6. Two of the following: ScreenTips, Help window, Microsoft Office Online

Ending Data Files

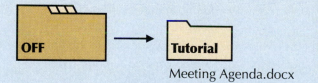

OFF → **Tutorial**

Meeting Agenda.docx

Review

Recycled Palette Finances.xlsx
Recycled Palette Letter.docx

Reality Check

At home, school, or work, you probably complete many types of tasks, such as writing letters and balancing a checkbook, on a regular basis. You can use Microsoft Office to streamline many of these tasks.

Note: Please be sure *not* to include any personal information of a sensitive nature in the documents you create to be submitted to your instructor for this exercise. Later on, you can update the documents with such information for your own personal use.

1. Start Word, and open a new document, if necessary.
2. In the document, type a list of all the personal, work, and/or school tasks you do on a regular basis.
3. For each task, identify the type of Office file (document, workbook, presentation, or database) you would create to complete that task. For example, you would create a Word document to write a letter.
4. For each file, identify the Office program you would use to create that file, and explain why you would use that program. For example, Word is the best program to use to create a document for a letter.
5. Save the document with an appropriate filename in an appropriate folder location.
6. Use a Web browser to visit the Microsoft Web site at *www.microsoft.com* and research the different Office 2007 suites available. Determine which suite includes all the programs you need to complete the tasks on your list.
7. At the end of the task list you created in your Word document, type which Office suite you decided on and a brief explanation of why you chose that suite. Then save the document.
8. Double-click the Home tab on the Ribbon to minimize the Ribbon to show only the tab names and extend the workspace area. At the end of the Word document, type your opinion of whether minimizing the Ribbon is a helpful feature. When you're done, double-click the Home tab to display the full Ribbon.
9. Print the finished document, and then submit it to your instructor.

Objectives

Session 1.1
- Define the terms field, record, table, relational database, primary key, and foreign key
- Create a blank database
- Identify the components of the Microsoft Access window
- Create and save a table in Datasheet view
- Enter field names and records in a table datasheet
- Open a table using the Navigation Pane

Session 1.2
- Open an Access database
- Copy and paste records from another Access database
- Navigate a table datasheet
- Create and navigate a simple query
- Create and navigate a simple form
- Create, preview, navigate, and print a simple report
- Learn how to manage a database by compacting, backing up, and restoring a database

Creating a Database

Creating a Database to Contain Customer, Contract, and Invoice Data

Case | Belmont Landscapes

Soon after graduating with a degree in Landscape Architecture from nearby Michigan State University, Oren Belmont returned to his hometown of Holland, on the shores of Lake Michigan. There, Oren worked for a local firm that provided basic landscaping services to residential customers. After several years, Oren started his own landscape architecture firm, Belmont Landscapes, which specializes in landscape designs for residential and commercial customers and numerous public agencies.

Belmont Landscapes provides a wide range of services—from site analyses and feasibility studies, to drafting and administering construction documents—for projects of various scales. Oren and his staff depend on computers to help manage all aspects of the firm's operations, including financial and information management. Several months ago the company upgraded to Microsoft Windows and **Microsoft Office Access 2007** (or simply **Access**), a computer program used to enter, maintain, and retrieve related data in a format known as a database. Oren and his staff want to use Access to maintain such data as information about customers, contracts, and invoices. He asks for your help in creating the necessary Access database.

Starting Data Files

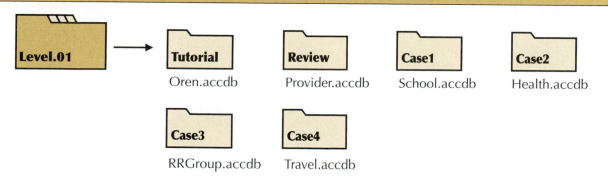

Level.01 → Tutorial
Oren.accdb

Review
Provider.accdb

Case1
School.accdb

Case2
Health.accdb

Case3
RRGroup.accdb

Case4
Travel.accdb

Session 1.1

Introduction to Database Concepts

Before you begin using Access to create the database for Oren, you need to understand a few key terms and concepts associated with databases.

Organizing Data

Data is a valuable resource to any business. At Belmont Landscapes, for example, important data includes customers' names and addresses and contract amounts and dates. Organizing, storing, maintaining, retrieving, and sorting this type of data are critical activities that enable a business to find and use information effectively. Before storing data on a computer, however, you must organize the data.

Your first step in organizing data is to identify the individual fields. A **field** is a single characteristic or attribute of a person, place, object, event, or idea. For example, some of the many fields that Belmont Landscapes tracks are customer ID, first name, last name, company name, address, phone number, contract amount, contract signing date, and contract type.

Next, you group related fields together into tables. A **table** is a collection of fields that describe a person, place, object, event, or idea. Figure 1-1 shows an example of a Customer table that contains four fields named Customer ID, First Name, Last Name, and Phone.

Figure 1-1 ▶ **Data organization for a table of customers**

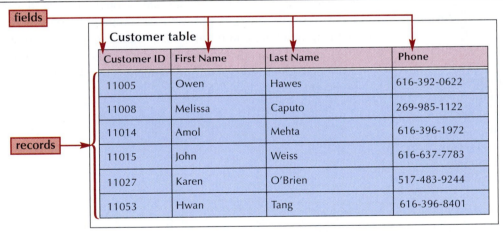

The specific value, or content, of a field is called the **field value**. In Figure 1-1, the first set of field values for Customer ID, First Name, Last Name, and Phone are, respectively: 11005; Owen; Hawes; and 616-392-0622. This set of field values is called a **record**. In the Customer table, the data for each customer is stored as a separate record. Figure 1-1 shows six records; each row of field values is a record.

Databases and Relationships

A collection of related tables is called a **database**, or a **relational database**. In this tutorial, you will create the database for Belmont Landscapes and a table named Contract to store data about contracts. In Tutorial 2, you will create two more tables, named Customer and Invoice, to store related information about customers and their invoices.

As Oren and his staff use the database that you will create, they will need to access information about customers and their contracts. To obtain this information, you must have a way to connect records in the Customer table to records in the Contract table. You connect the records in the separate tables through a **common field** that appears in both tables.

In the sample database shown in Figure 1-2, each record in the Customer table has a field named Customer ID, which is also a field in the Contract table. For example, Owen Hawes is the first customer in the Customer table and has a Customer ID field value of 11005. This same Customer ID field value, 11005, appears in three records in the Contract table. Therefore, Owen Hawes is the customer with these three contracts.

Database relationship between tables for customers and contracts ◄ **Figure 1-2**

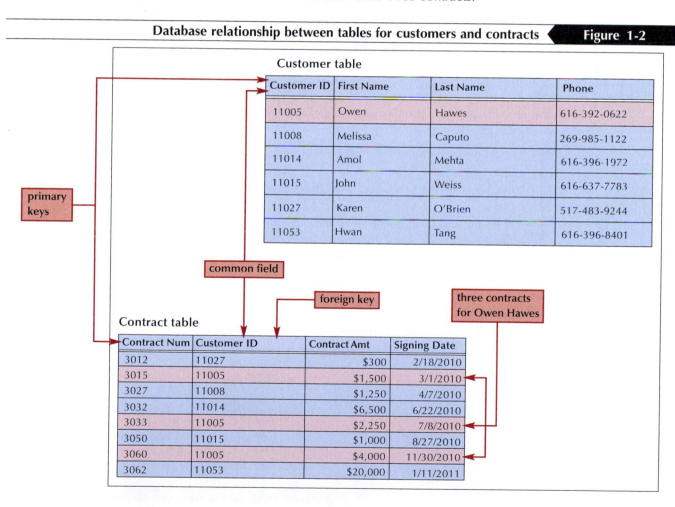

Customer table

Customer ID	First Name	Last Name	Phone
11005	Owen	Hawes	616-392-0622
11008	Melissa	Caputo	269-985-1122
11014	Amol	Mehta	616-396-1972
11015	John	Weiss	616-637-7783
11027	Karen	O'Brien	517-483-9244
11053	Hwan	Tang	616-396-8401

primary keys

common field

foreign key

three contracts for Owen Hawes

Contract table

Contract Num	Customer ID	Contract Amt	Signing Date
3012	11027	$300	2/18/2010
3015	11005	$1,500	3/1/2010
3027	11008	$1,250	4/7/2010
3032	11014	$6,500	6/22/2010
3033	11005	$2,250	7/8/2010
3050	11015	$1,000	8/27/2010
3060	11005	$4,000	11/30/2010
3062	11053	$20,000	1/11/2011

Each Customer ID value in the Customer table must be unique so that you can distinguish one customer from another. These unique Customer ID values also identify each customer's specific contracts in the Contract table. The Customer ID field is referred to as the primary key of the Customer table. A **primary key** is a field, or a collection of fields, whose values uniquely identify each record in a table. No two records can contain the same value for the primary key field. In the Contract table, the Contract Num field is the primary key because Belmont Landscapes assigns each contract a unique contract number.

When you include the primary key from one table as a field in a second table to form a relationship between the two tables, it is called a **foreign key** in the second table, as shown in Figure 1-2. For example, Customer ID is the primary key in the Customer table and a foreign key in the Contract table. Although the primary key Customer ID contains unique values in the Customer table, the same field as a foreign key in the Contract table does not necessarily contain unique values. The Customer ID value 11005, for example, appears three times in the Contract table because Owen Hawes has three contracts. Each foreign key value, however, must match one of the field values for the primary key in the other table. In the example shown in Figure 1-2, each Customer ID value in the Contract table must match a Customer ID value in the Customer table. The two tables are related, enabling users to connect the facts about customers with the facts about their contracts.

Relational Database Management Systems

To manage its databases, a company purchases a database management system. A **database management system (DBMS)** is a software program that lets you create databases and then manipulate data in them. Most of today's database management systems, including Access, are called relational database management systems. In a **relational database management system**, data is organized as a collection of tables. As stated earlier, a relationship between two tables in a relational DBMS is formed through a common field.

A relational DBMS controls the storage of databases on disk and facilitates the creation, manipulation, and reporting of data, as illustrated in Figure 1-3. Specifically, a relational DBMS provides the following functions:

- It allows you to create database structures containing fields, tables, and table relationships.
- It lets you easily add new records, change field values in existing records, and delete records.
- It contains a built-in query language, which lets you obtain immediate answers to the questions you ask about your data.
- It contains a built-in report generator, which lets you produce professional-looking, formatted reports from your data.
- It protects databases through security, control, and recovery facilities.

Figure 1-3   **Relational database management system**

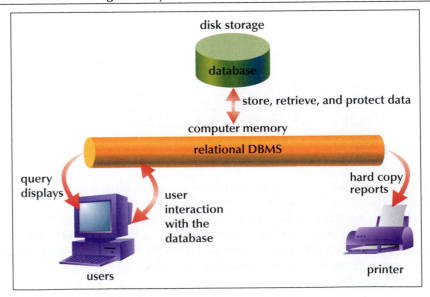

A company such as Belmont Landscapes benefits from a relational DBMS because it allows users working in different groups to share the same data. More than one user can enter data into a database, and more than one user can retrieve and analyze data that other users entered. For example, the database for Belmont Landscapes will contain only one copy of the Contract table, and all employees will use it to meet their specific requests for contract information.

Finally, unlike other software programs, such as spreadsheet programs, a DBMS can handle massive amounts of data and can be used to create relationships among multiple tables. Each Access database, for example, can be up to two gigabytes in size, can contain up to 32,768 objects (tables, queries, forms, and so on), and can have up to 255 people using the database at the same time. For instructional purposes, the databases you will create and work with throughout this text contain a relatively small number of records compared to most databases you would encounter outside the classroom, which likely contain tables with very large numbers of records.

Creating a Database

Now that you've learned some database terms and concepts, you're ready to start Access and create the Belmont database for Oren.

To start Access:

1. Click the **Start** button on the taskbar, click **All Programs**, click **Microsoft Office**, and then click **Microsoft Office Access 2007**. The Getting Started with Microsoft Office Access page opens. See Figure 1-4.

    Trouble? If you don't see the Microsoft Office Access 2007 option on the Microsoft Office submenu, look for it on a different submenu or as an option on the All Programs menu. If you still cannot find the Microsoft Office Access 2007 option, ask your instructor or technical support person for help.

Getting Started with Microsoft Office Access page   Figure 1-4

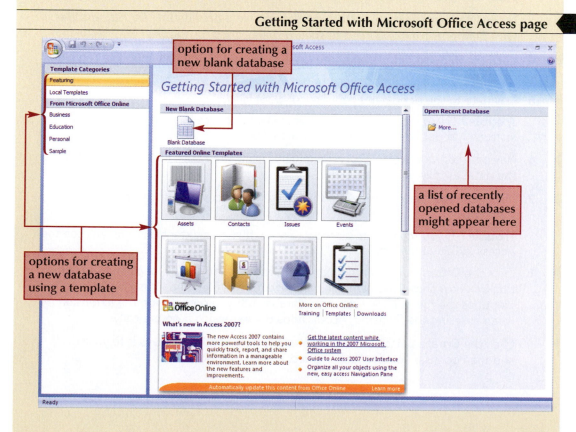

Trouble? If the Microsoft Access program window on your computer is not maximized, click the Maximize button 🗖 on the program window title bar.

The Getting Started with Microsoft Office Access page contains options for creating a new database, opening an existing database, or viewing content from Microsoft Office Online. You can create a new database that does not contain any data or objects by using the Blank Database option. If the database you need to create contains objects that match the ones found in common databases, such as ones that store data about contacts or events, you can use a template that Access installs (listed in the "Template Categories" section on the left side of the page) or download a template from Microsoft Office Online (listed in the "Featured Online Templates" section in the middle of the page). A **template** is a predesigned database that includes professionally designed tables, reports, and other database objects that can make it quick and easy for you to create a database.

In this case, the templates provided do not match Oren's needs for the Belmont Landscapes database, so you need to create a new database from scratch. To do this, you will use the Blank Database option on the Getting Started page.

To create the new Belmont database:

1. Make sure you have created your copy of the Access Data Files, and that your computer can access them.

   Trouble? If you don't have the starting Data Files, you need to get them before you can proceed. Your instructor will either give you the Data Files or ask you to obtain them from a specified location (such as a network drive). In either case, make a backup copy of the Data Files before you start so that you will have the original files available in case you need to start over. If you have any questions about the Data Files, see your instructor or technical support person for assistance.

2. Click the **Blank Database** option in the center of the page. The right section of the page changes to display options for creating a blank database.

3. In the File Name text box, select the default name provided by Access, and then type **Belmont**. Next you need to specify the location for the file.

4. Click the **Browse** button 📂 to the right of the File Name text box. The File New Database dialog box opens.

5. Navigate to the drive that contains your Data Files.

   Trouble? If you do not know where your Data Files are located, consult with your instructor about where to save your Data Files.

6. Navigate to the **Level.01\Tutorial** folder. This is the folder in which you will store the database file you create.

7. Make sure the "Save as type" text box displays "Microsoft Office Access 2007 Databases."

   Trouble? If your computer is set up to show filename extensions, you will see the Access 2007 filename extension ".accdb" in this text box as well.

8. Click the **OK** button. You return to the Getting Started page, and the File Name text box now shows the name Belmont.accdb. The filename extension ".accdb" identifies the file as an Access 2007 database. If you do not type the extension when entering the filename, Access adds the extension automatically.

9. Click the **Create** button. Access creates the new database, saves it to your disk, and then opens an empty table named Table1. See Figure 1-5.

Microsoft Access window   **Figure 1-5**

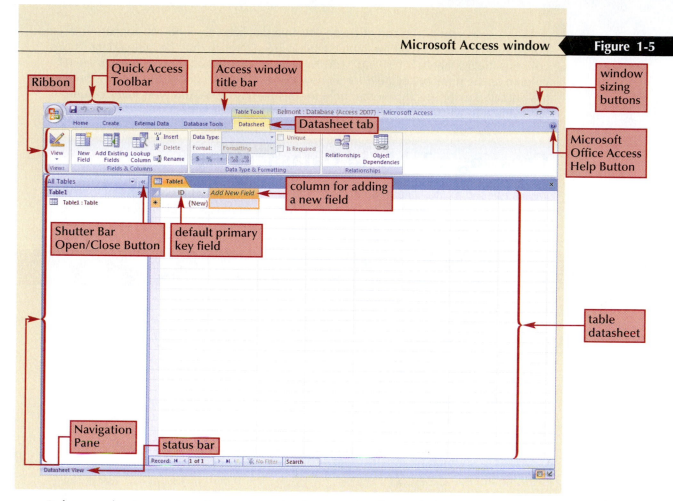

Before you begin entering data, you need to become familiar with the components of the Microsoft Access window.

Exploring the Microsoft Access Window

The **Microsoft Access window** (or simply the **Access window**) is the program window that appears when you create a new database or open an existing database. Most of the Access window components—including the title bar, window sizing buttons, Help button, Quick Access Toolbar, Ribbon, tabs, and status bar—are the same as the components in other Microsoft Office 2007 programs.

The new blank table that Access created is displayed in **Datasheet view**, which shows a table's contents as a **datasheet** in rows and columns, similar to a table that you create in Word or an Excel spreadsheet. Each row will be a separate record in the table, and each column will contain the field values for one field in the table. Because you are in Datasheet view, the Datasheet tab is the active tab on the Ribbon. The status bar also indicates the current view.

The **Navigation Pane** is the area on the left side of the window that lists all the objects (tables, reports, and so on) in the database, and it is the main control center for opening and working with database objects. Currently, the Navigation Pane lists only the new table you are in the process of creating, which is named "Table1" by default. You will give the table a more meaningful name as part of creating it. Notice the Shutter Bar Open/Close Button at the top-right of the Navigation Pane (see Figure 1-5). You can use this button to close and open the pane. Depending on the size of your database table, you might want to close the Navigation Pane so that you have more room on the screen to view the table's contents.

When you open tables and other objects in a database, their names appear on tabbed documents. Currently, only the Table1 table is open. Notice that the table contains two columns (fields) labeled "ID" and "Add New Field." By default, Access creates the **ID column** as the primary key field for all new tables. You can choose to keep this field as the primary key or specify another field for this purpose. The **Add New Field column** is the column in which you create the first new field for your table.

Creating a Table in Datasheet View

Tables contain all the data in a database and are the fundamental objects for your work in Access. There are different ways to create a table in Access, including entering the fields and records for a table directly in Datasheet view.

Reference Window	**Creating a Table in Datasheet View**

- Click the Create tab on the Ribbon.
- In the Tables group, click the Table button.
- Accept the default ID primary key field with the AutoNumber data type, or rename the field and change its data type, if necessary.
- Double-click the Add New Field column heading, and then type the name for the field you are adding to the table.
- Press the Tab key or the Enter key.
- Add all the fields to your table by typing the field names in the column headings and pressing the Tab key or the Enter key to move to the next column.
- In the first row below the field names, enter the value for each field in the first record, pressing the Tab key or the Enter key to move from field to field.
- After entering the value for the last field in the first record, press the Tab key or the Enter key to move to the next row, and then enter the values for the next record. Continue this process until you have entered all the records for the table.
- Click the Save button on the Quick Access Toolbar, enter a name for the table, and then click the OK button.

For Belmont Landscapes, Oren needs to track information about the company's contracts with its customers. He asks you to create the Contract table according to the plan shown in Figure 1-6.

Figure 1-6	Plan for the Contract table

Field	Purpose
Contract Num	Unique number assigned to each contract; will serve as the table's primary key
Customer ID	Unique number assigned to each customer; common field that will be a foreign key to connect to the Customer table
Contract Amt	Dollar amount for the full contract
Signing Date	Date on which the customer signed the contract
Contract Type	Brief description of the contract

As shown in Oren's plan, he wants to store data about contracts in five fields, including fields to contain the amount of each contract, when it was signed, and the type of contract. These are the most important aspects of a contract and, therefore, must be tracked. Also, notice that the Contract Num field will be the primary key for the table; each contract at Belmont Landscapes has a unique contract number, so this field is the logical choice for the primary key. Finally, the Customer ID field is needed in the Contract table as a foreign key to tie the information about contracts to customers. The data about customers and their invoices will be stored in separate tables, which you will create in Tutorial 2.

Notice the name of each field in Figure 1-6. You need to name each field, table, and other object in an Access database.

Guidelines for Naming Fields | InSight

Keep the following guidelines in mind when you name fields:

- A field name can consist of up to 64 characters, including letters, numbers, spaces, and special characters, except for a period (.), exclamation mark (!), accent grave (`), and square brackets ([ ]).
- A field name cannot begin with a space.
- Capitalize the first letter of each word in the field name so it is clear which words are part of the name.
- Use concise field names that are easy to remember and reference, and that won't take up a lot of space in the table datasheet.
- Use standard abbreviations, such as Num for Number, Amt for Amount, and Qty for Quantity.
- Give fields descriptive names so that you can easily identify them when you view or edit records.
- Different DBMSs and some organizations have specific rules for naming fields. For example, many experienced database users do not include spaces in field names for ease of use when working with fields and other objects to perform more complex tasks, such as programming.

Renaming the Default Primary Key Field

As noted earlier, Access provides the ID field as a default primary key for a new table you create in Datasheet view. Recall that a primary key is a field, or a collection of fields, whose values uniquely identify each record in a table. However, according to Oren's plan, the Contract Num field should be the primary key for the Contract table. You'll begin by renaming the default ID field to create the Contract Num field.

To rename the ID field to the Contract Num field:

▶ 1. Right-click the **ID** column heading to display the shortcut menu, and then click **Rename Column**. The column heading ID is selected, so that whatever text you type next will replace it.

▶ 2. Type **Contract Num** and then press the **Enter** key. The column heading changes to Contract Num and the insertion point moves to the row below the heading. See Figure 1-7.

Trouble? Your instructor might ask you to omit spaces in field names as you create the tables in this book so your table designs will conform to standard field naming conventions. If so, your field names will not match the ones shown in the figures exactly, but this discrepancy will not cause problems.

Figure 1-7 ID field renamed to Contract Num

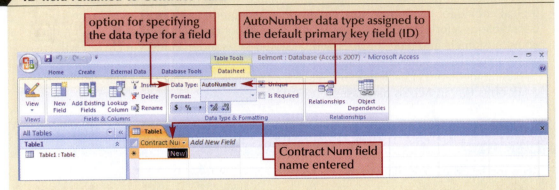

Trouble? If you make a mistake when typing the field name, use the Backspace key to delete characters to the left of the insertion point or the Delete key to delete characters to the right of the insertion point. Then type the correct text. To correct a field name by replacing it entirely, press the Esc key, and then type the correct text.

Trouble? The entire field name "Contract Num" might not be visible on your screen. You'll learn how to resize columns to display the full field names later in this tutorial.

You have renamed the default primary key field, ID, to Contract Num. However, the Contract Num field still maintains the characteristics of the ID field, including its data type. Your next task is to change the data type of this field.

Changing the Data Type of the Default Primary Key Field

Notice the Data Type & Formatting group on the Datasheet tab. One of the options available in this group is the Data Type option (see Figure 1-7). Each field in an Access table must be assigned a data type. The **data type** determines what field values you can enter for the field. In this case, the AutoNumber data type is displayed. Access assigns the AutoNumber data type to the default ID primary key field because the **AutoNumber** data type automatically inserts a unique number in this field for every record. Therefore, it can serve as the primary key for any table you create.

Contract numbers at Belmont Landscapes are specific, four-digit numbers, so the AutoNumber data type is not appropriate for the Contract Num field, which is the new primary key field in the table you are creating. A better choice is the **Text** data type, which allows field values containing letters, digits, and other characters, and which is appropriate for identifying numbers, such as contract numbers, that are never used in calculations. So, Oren asks you to change the data type for the Contract Num field from AutoNumber to Text.

To change the data type for the Contract Num field:

► 1. Make sure that the Contract Num column is selected (the column heading should have an orange background).

   Trouble? If the background color of the Contract Num column heading is not orange, click the Contract Num column to select it.

► 2. In the Data Type & Formatting group on the Datasheet tab, click the **Data Type arrow**, and then click **Text**. The Contract Num field is now a Text field. See Figure 1-8.

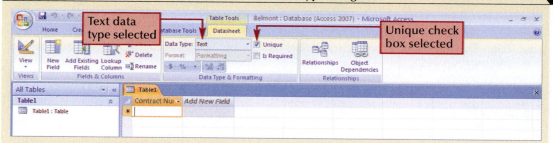

Text data type assigned to the Contract Num field ◄ **Figure 1-8**

Note the Unique check box in the Data Type & Formatting group. This check box is selected because the Contract Num field assumed the characteristics of the default primary key field, ID, including the fact that each value in the field must be unique. No two records in the Contract table will be allowed to have the same value in the Contract Num field.

With the Contract Num field created and established as the primary key, you can now enter the field names for the rest of the fields in the Contract table. (In Tutorial 2, you'll learn more about the different data types in Access and how to work with them.)

Entering Field Names

When you create a table in Datasheet view, you type the field names as the column headings, and enter the field values for each record in a row. Oren requests that you enter eight records in the Contract table, as shown in Figure 1-9.

Contract table records ◄ **Figure 1-9**

Contract Num	Customer ID	Contract Amt	Signing Date	Contract Type
3011	11001	$4,000	2/9/2010	Residential landscape plan
3026	11038	$165,000	3/11/2010	Landscape plans for large-scale housing development
3012	11027	$300	2/18/2010	Consultation for backyard, residential
3015	11005	$1,500	3/1/2010	Schematic plan for backyard, residential
3022	11043	$22,000	4/14/2010	Landscape design for two entrances
3017	11012	$2,250	3/1/2010	Peer plan review for town
3023	11070	$39,000	3/22/2010	Renovation of large multifamily housing open space
3021	11040	$28,000	5/3/2010	Landscape plans for multifamily housing site

To enter the rest of the field names for the Contract table:

▶ **1.** Double-click the column heading **Add New Field**. The insertion point replaces the text "Add New Field" in the column heading and is ready for you to type the field name for the second field in the table.

▶ **2.** Type **Customer ID**. Notice that the field name is displayed in italics while you type, signifying this is a new field name you are entering. See Figure 1-10.

Figure 1-10 | **Customer ID field name entered in column heading**

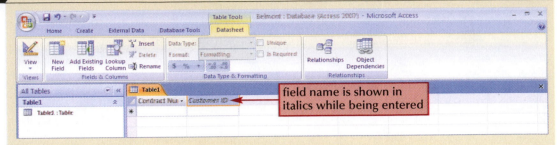

3. Press the **Tab** key. The insertion point moves to the next column and is ready for you to enter the next field name.

4. Type **Contract Amt** and then press the **Tab** key. Like the Contract Num field name, the Contract Amt field name might not be completely visible. You will resize all the columns to fully display the field names after you finish entering them.

5. Type **Signing Date**, press the **Tab** key, type **Contract Type**, and then press the **Tab** key. The datasheet now contains the five fields for the Contract table.

   Several of the field names are not completely visible, so you need to resize the datasheet columns.

6. Place the pointer on the vertical line between the Contract Num and Customer ID field names until the pointer changes to a ↔ shape.

7. Double-click the pointer. The Contract Num column is resized and now displays the full field name.

   Trouble? If you click the arrow immediately to the right of the Contract Num column heading by mistake, a menu will open. Simply click the arrow again to close the menu, and then repeat Steps 6 and 7.

8. Double-click the ↔ pointer on the vertical line to the right of the Customer ID, Contract Amt, Signing Date, and Contract Type column headings to resize the columns in the datasheet. Your datasheet should now look like the one shown in Figure 1-11.

Figure 1-11 | **Table with field names entered**

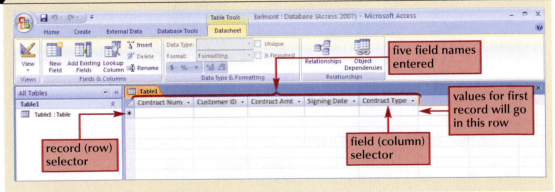

As noted earlier, Datasheet view shows a table's contents in rows (records) and columns (fields). Each column is headed by a field name inside a field selector, and each row has a record selector to its left (see Figure 1-11). Clicking a **field selector** or a **record selector** selects that entire column or row (respectively), which you then can manipulate. A field selector is also called a **column selector**, and a record selector is also called a **row selector**.

With the field names in place, you can now enter the records for the Contract table (see Figure 1-9).

Entering Records

To enter records in a table datasheet, you type the field values below the column headings for the fields. As shown in Figure 1-11, the first record you enter will go in the first row below the field names.

To enter the first record for the Contract table:

▶ **1.** Click in the first row for the Contract Num field, type **3011** (the Contract Num field value for the first record), and then press the **Tab** key. Access adds the field value and moves the insertion point to the right, in the Customer ID column. See Figure 1-12.

First field value entered ◀ | **Figure 1-12**

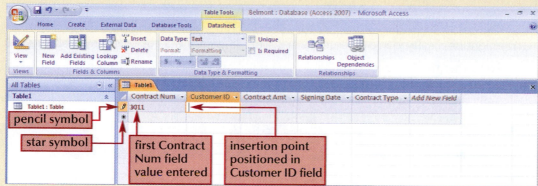

Trouble? If you make a mistake when typing a value, use the Backspace key to delete characters to the left of the insertion point or the Delete key to delete characters to the right of the insertion point. Then type the correct value. To correct a value by replacing it entirely, press the Esc key, and then type the correct value.

Notice the pencil symbol that appears in the row selector for the new record. The **pencil symbol** indicates that the record is being edited. Also notice the star symbol that appears in the row selector for the second row. The **star symbol** identifies the second row as the next row available for a new record.

▶ **2.** Type **11001** (the Customer ID field value for the first record), and then press the **Tab** key. Access enters the field value and moves the insertion point to the Contract Amt column.

▶ **3.** Type **$4,000** (the Contract Amt field value for the first record), and then press the **Tab** key. Notice that Access formats the field value with two decimal places, displaying it as "$4,000.00" even though you did not enter the value this way. You'll learn more about formatting field values later in this text.

Trouble? If Access does not change the value $4,000 to $4,000.00 when you press the Tab key and go to the next field, click the Contract Amt field value, click the Data Type arrow in the Data Type & Formatting group, and then click Currency in the list. Press the Tab key and continue with Step 4.

▶ **4.** Type **2/9/2010** (the Signing Date field value for the first record), and then press the **Tab** key.

Trouble? If your date value is left-aligned in the column after you press the Tab key and go to the next field, instead of right-aligned, click the Signing Date field value, click the Data Type arrow in the Data Type & Formatting group, and then click Date/Time in the list. Press the Tab key and continue with Step 5.

▶ **5.** Type **Residential landscape plan** (the Contract Type field value for the first record), and then press the **Tab** key. The first record is entered into the table, and the insertion point is positioned in the Contract Num field for the second record. The table is now ready for you to enter the second record. See Figure 1-13.

Figure 1-13 | **Datasheet with first record entered**

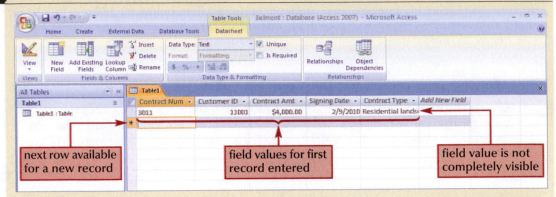

Trouble? Depending on your Windows date setting, your Signing Date field values might be displayed in a different format. This difference will not cause any problems.

Note that the Contract Type field value is not completely displayed. Again, you'll resize the columns, as necessary, after you enter all the data.

InSight | **Understanding How Access Interprets Values Entered**

When you create a table by entering field names and records directly into the table in Datasheet view, Access automatically assigns each field a data type based on the field values you enter. Access also formats the field values accordingly. For example, when you entered the value "$4,000" for the first record in the Contract Amt field, Access interpreted the value as a currency value because you typed a dollar sign and comma in the value. Likewise, when you entered the value "2/9/2010" in the Signing Date field, Access interpreted the value as a date value. After you've entered the first record in this way, Access will continue to format the field values for subsequent records, making data entry easier for you. So, as you continue to enter Contract Amt field values, you don't have to type the dollar sign or comma every time; Access will insert them automatically for you because it "knows" that the Contract Amt field contains currency values. Similarly, as you continue to enter Signing Date field values, you don't have to type the complete year "2010" but can instead type only the final two digits, "10," and Access will automatically insert the full four digits for each year.

As you enter field values in a datasheet, you should verify that Access is assigning them the data type you plan to use. If Access does not correctly interpret the field values you enter, you can easily assign the correct data type using the Data Type option in the Data Type & Formatting group on the Datasheet tab.

Now you can enter the remaining seven records in the Contract table.

To enter the remaining records in the Contract table:

1. Referring to Figure 1-9, enter the values for records 2 through 8, pressing the **Tab** key to move from field to field and to the next row for a new record. Keep in mind that you do not have to type the dollar sign or comma in the Contract Amt values, because Access will add them automatically; also, you can type just the final two digits of the year in the Signing Date values, and Access will display the full four digits in each year value.

Tip

You can also press the Enter key instead of the Tab key to move from one field to another, and to the next row.

Trouble? If you enter a value in the wrong field by mistake, such as entering a Contract Type field value in the Contract Amt field, a menu will open with options for addressing the problem. If this happens, choose the "Enter new value" option on the menu. You'll return to the field with the incorrect value highlighted, which you can then replace by typing the correct value.

To see more of the table datasheet and the full field values, you'll close the Navigation Pane and resize the Contract Type column.

▶ **2.** Click the **Shutter Bar Open/Close Button** « at the top of the Navigation Pane. The Navigation Pane closes, and the window displays the complete table datasheet.

▶ **3.** Place the pointer on the vertical line to the right of the Contract Type field name until the pointer changes to a ↔ shape, and then double-click the pointer. All the Contract Type field values are now fully displayed. See Figure 1-14.

Datasheet with eight records entered | **Figure 1-14**

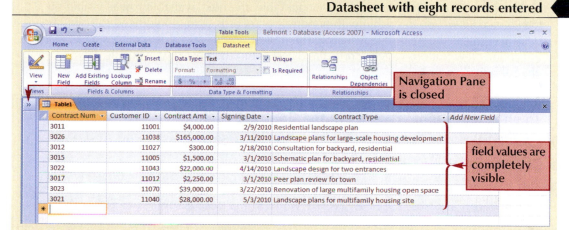

Trouble? If any of the field values on your screen do not match those shown in the figure, you can correct a field value by clicking to position the insertion point in the value, and then using the Backspace key or Delete key to delete incorrect text. Then type the correct text and press the Enter key.

Saving a Table

After you add fields and records to a table, you need to save the table's design. The records you enter are immediately stored in the database as soon as you enter them; however, the table's design—the field names and characteristics of the fields themselves—are not saved until you save the table. When you save a new table for the first time, you should give it a name that best identifies the information it contains. Like a field name, a table name can be up to 64 characters long, including spaces.

Saving a Table | Reference Window

- Click the Save button on the Quick Access Toolbar. The Save As dialog box opens.
- In the Table Name text box, type the name for the table.
- Click the OK button.

Now you need to save the table and give it the name "Contract."

Tip

You can also choose the Save option from the Office menu to save and name a new table.

To save and name the Contract table:

▶ 1. Click the **Save** button 🖫 on the Quick Access Toolbar. The Save As dialog box opens.

▶ 2. With the default name Table1 selected in the Table Name text box, type **Contract**, and then click the **OK** button. The tab for the table now displays the name "Contract," and the Contract table design is saved in the Belmont database.

Notice that after you saved and named the Contract table, Access reordered the records in the table so that they appear in order by the values in the Contract Num field, because it is the primary key. If you compare your screen to Figure 1-9, which shows the records in the order you entered them, you'll see that the current screen shows the records in order by the Contract Num field values.

Oren asks you to add two more records to the Contract table. When you add a record to an existing table, you must enter the new record in the next row available for a new record; you cannot insert a row between existing records for the new record. In a table with just a few records, such as the Contract table, the next available row is visible on the screen. However, in a table with hundreds of records, you would need to scroll the datasheet to see the next row available. The easiest way to add a new record to a table is to use the New button, which scrolls the datasheet to the next row available so you can enter the new record.

To enter additional records in the Contract table:

▶ 1. Click in the first record's Contract Num field value (3011) to make it the current record.

▶ 2. Click the **Home** tab on the Ribbon.

▶ 3. In the Records group, click the **New** button. The insertion point is positioned in the next row available for a new record, which in this case is row 9. See Figure 1-15.

Figure 1-15 ▶ **Entering a new record**

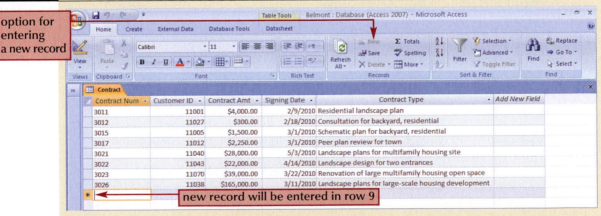

option for entering a new record

new record will be entered in row 9

▶ 4. With the insertion point in the Contract Num field for the new record, type **3020**, and then press the **Tab** key.

▶ 5. Complete the entry of this record by entering each value shown below, pressing the Tab key to move from field to field:

Customer ID =   **11055**
Contract Amt =   **6500**
Signing Date =   **2/19/10**
Contract Type =   **Landscape design for restaurant**

6. Enter the values for the next new record, as follows:

Contract Num =   **3025**
Customer ID =   **11083**
Contract Amt =   **15500**
Signing Date =   **3/25/10**
Contract Type =   **Landscape renovation for plaza**

Your datasheet should now look like the one shown in Figure 1-16.

Datasheet with additional records entered ◄ Figure 1-16

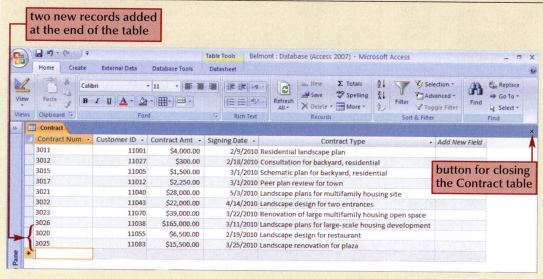

The new records you added appear at the end of the table, and are not in the correct primary key order. For example, Contract Num 3020 should be the fifth record in the table, placed between Contract Num 3017 and Contract Num 3021. When you add records to a table datasheet, they appear at the end of the table. The records are not displayed in primary key order until you close and reopen the table, or switch between views.

7. Click the **Close 'Contract'** button [X] on the table window bar (see Figure 1-16 for the location of this button). The table closes, and the main portion of the Access window is now blank because no database object is currently open.

Opening a Table

Any table you create and save is listed in the Navigation Pane. You open a table, or any Access object (query, form, report), by simply double-clicking the object name in the Navigation Pane. Next, you'll open the Contract table so you can see the order of all the records you've entered.

To open the Contract table:

1. On the Navigation Pane, click the **Shutter Bar Open/Close Button** [»] to open the pane. Note that the Contract table is listed.

2. Double-click **Contract : Table** to open the table in Datasheet view. See Figure 1-17.

Figure 1-17 | **Table with 10 records entered and displayed in primary key order**

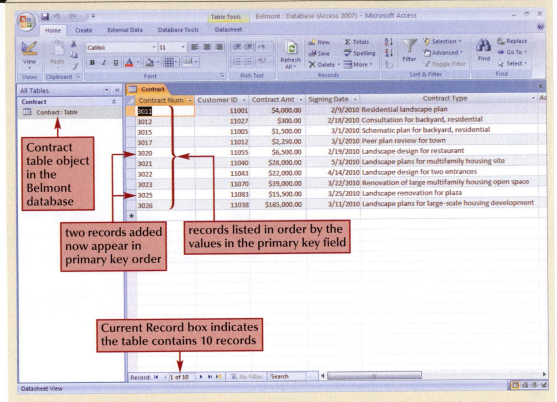

The two records you added, with Contract Num field values of 3020 and 3025, now appear in the correct primary key order. The table now contains a total of 10 records, as indicated by the Current Record box at the bottom of the datasheet. The **Current Record box** displays the number of the current record as well as the total number of records in the table.

▶ 3. If you are not continuing on to Session 1.2, click the **Close** button ⊠ on the program window title bar. Access closes the Contract table and the Belmont database, and then the Access program closes.

Saving a Database | InSight

Notice the Save button on the Quick Access Toolbar. Unlike the Save buttons in other Office programs, this Save button does not save the active document (database) to your disk. Instead, you use the Save button to save the design of an Access object, such as a table (as you saw earlier), or to save datasheet format changes, such as resizing columns. Access does not have a button or option you can use to save the active database. Similarly, you cannot use the Save As option on the Office menu to save the active database file with a new name, as you can with other Office programs.

Access saves changes to the active database to your disk automatically when you change or add a record or close the database. If your database is stored on a removable medium, such as a USB drive, you should never remove the drive while the database file is open. If you do, Access will encounter problems when it tries to save the database, which might damage the database.

Now that you've become familiar with database concepts and Access, and created the Belmont database and the Contract table, Oren wants you to add more records to the table and work with the data stored in it to create database objects including a query, form, and report. You will complete these tasks in Session 1.2.

Session 1.1 Quick Check | Review

1. A(n) _____ is a single characteristic of a person, place, object, event, or idea.
2. You connect the records in two separate tables through a(n) _____ that appears in both tables.
3. The _____ , whose values uniquely identify each record in a table, is called a(n) _____ when it is placed in a second table to form a relationship between the two tables.
4. The _____ is the area of the Access window that lists all the objects in a database, and it is the main control center for opening and working with database objects.
5. Which field does Access create, by default, as the primary key field for all new datasheets?
6. What does a pencil symbol at the beginning of a record represent? A star symbol?
7. Explain how the saving process in Access is different from saving in other Office programs.

Session 1.2

Copying Records from Another Access Database

When you created the Contract table, you entered records directly into the table datasheet. There are many other ways to enter records in a table, including copying and pasting records from a table in the same database or in a different database. To use this method, however, the tables must have the same structure—that is, the tables must contain the same fields, with the same design and characteristics, in the same order.

Oren has already created a table named Agreement that contains additional records with contract data. The Agreement table is contained in a database named "Oren" located in the Level.01\Tutorial folder included with your Data Files. The Agreement table has the same table structure as the Contract table you created. Your next task is to copy the records from the Agreement table and paste them into your Contract table. To do so, you need to open the Oren database.

Reference Window | **Opening a Database**

- Start Access and display the Getting Started with Microsoft Office Access page.
- Click the More option to display the Open dialog box.
- Navigate to the database file you want to open, and then click the file.
- Click the Open button.

To copy the records from the Agreement table:

▶ **1.** If you took a break after the previous session, make sure that the Belmont database is open, and the Contract table is open in Datasheet view.

▶ **2.** In the Navigation Pane, click the **Shutter Bar Open/Close Button** « to close the pane (if necessary) and display more of the table datasheet.

To open a second database, you need to start Access again.

▶ **3.** Click the **Start** button 🔵 on the taskbar, click **All Programs**, click **Microsoft Office**, and then click **Microsoft Office Access 2007**. The Getting Started with Microsoft Office Access page opens.

To open an existing database, you use the More option in the Open Recent Database section on the right side of the page.

▶ **4.** Click **More** to display the Open dialog box.

▶ **5.** Navigate to the drive that contains your Data Files.

▶ **6.** Navigate to the **Level.01\Tutorial** folder, click the database file named **Oren**, and then click the **Open** button. The Oren database opens in a second Access window. Note that the database contains only one object, the Agreement table.

Trouble? A Security Warning might appear below the Ribbon; this warning cautions you about opening databases that could contain content that might harm your computer. Because the Oren database does not contain objects that could be harmful, you can open it safely. Click the Options button next to the Security Warning. In the dialog box that opens, click the "Enable this content" option button, and then click the OK button.

▶ **7.** In the Navigation Pane, double-click **Agreement : Table** to open the Agreement table in Datasheet view. The table contains 55 records and the same five fields, with the same characteristics, as the fields in the Contract table. See Figure 1-18.

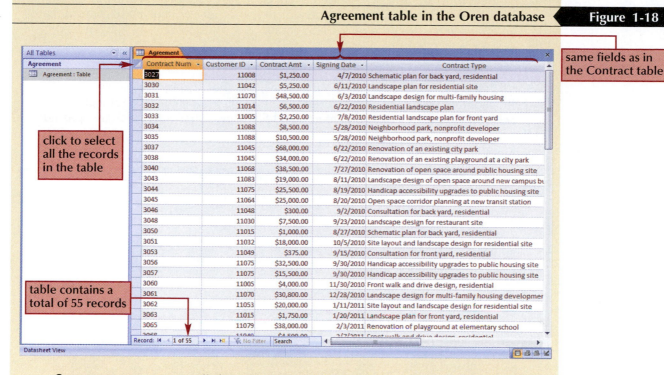

Agreement table in the Oren database   Figure 1-18

Oren wants you to copy all the records in the Agreement table. You can select all the records by clicking the **datasheet selector**, which is the box to the left of the first field name in the table datasheet (see Figure 1-18).

▶ **8.** Click the datasheet selector to the left of the Contract Num field. Access selects all the records in the table.

▶ **9.** In the Clipboard group on the Home tab, click the **Copy** button. All the records are copied to the Clipboard.

▶ **10.** Click the **Close 'Agreement'** button ☓ on the table window bar. A dialog box opens asking if you want to save the data you copied to the Clipboard.

▶ **11.** Click the **Yes** button in the dialog box. The dialog box closes, and then the table closes.

▶ **12.** Click the **Close** button ☓ on the Access window title bar to close the Oren database and the second Access program window.

With the records copied to the Clipboard, you can now paste them into the Contract table.

To paste the records into the Contract table:

▶ **1.** With the Belmont database's Contract table open in Datasheet view, position the pointer on the row selector for row 11, the next row available for a new record, until the pointer changes to a ➚ shape, and then click to select the row.

Trouble? If you have difficulty displaying the correct pointer shape, click in an empty area of the table datasheet to establish the window as the active window. Then repeat Step 1.

> **2.** In the Clipboard group on the Home tab, click the **Paste** button. The pasted records are added to the table, and a dialog box opens asking you to confirm that you want to paste all the records (55 total).
>
> **Trouble?** If the Paste button isn't active, click the pointer on the row selector for row 11, making sure the entire row is selected, and then repeat Step 2.
>
> **3.** Click the **Yes** button. The dialog box closes, and the pasted records are highlighted. See Figure 1-19. Notice that the table now contains a total of 65 records—10 records that you entered and 55 records that you copied and pasted.

Figure 1-19	Contract table after copying and pasting records

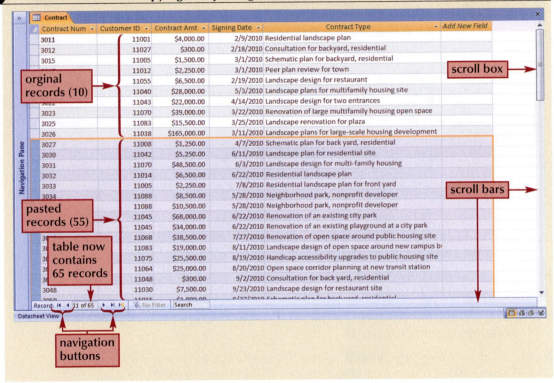

Navigating a Datasheet

The Contract table now contains 65 records, but only some of the records are visible on the screen. To view fields or records not currently visible in the datasheet, you can use the horizontal and vertical scroll bars shown in Figure 1-19 to navigate the data. The **navigation buttons**, also shown in Figure 1-19, provide another way to move vertically through the records. The Current Record box appears between the two sets of navigation buttons and displays the number of the current record as well as the total number of records in the table. Figure 1-20 shows which record becomes the current record when you click each navigation button. Note the New (blank) record button, which works in the same way as the New button on the Home tab you used earlier to enter a new record in the table.

Navigation Button	Record Selected	Navigation Button	Record Selected
◄	First record	►|	Last record
◄	Previous record	►✳	New (blank) record
►	Next record		

Oren suggests that you use the various navigation techniques to move through the Contract table and become familiar with its contents.

To navigate the Contract datasheet:

► **1.** Click in the first record's Contract Num field value (3011). The Current Record box shows that record 1 is the current record.

► **2.** Click the **Next record** navigation button ►. The second record is now high-lighted, which identifies it as the current record. Also, notice that the second record's value for the Contract Num field is selected, and the Current Record box displays "2 of 65" to indicate that the second record is the current record.

► **3.** Click the **Last record** navigation button ►|. The last record in the table, record 65, is now the current record.

► **4.** Drag the scroll box in the vertical scroll bar (see Figure 1-19) up to the top of the bar. Notice that record 65 is still the current record, as indicated in the Current Record box. Dragging the scroll box changes the display of the table datasheet, but does not change the current record.

► **5.** Drag the scroll box in the vertical scroll bar back down so that you can see the end of the table and the current record (record 65).

► **6.** Click the **Previous record** navigation button ◄. Record 64 is now the current record.

► **7.** Click the **First record** navigation button |◄. The first record is now the current record.

Tip

You can make a field the current field by clicking anywhere within the column for that field.

The Contract table now contains all the data about the customer contracts for Belmont Landscapes. To better understand how to work with this data, Oren asks you to create simple objects for the other main types of database objects—queries, forms, and reports.

Creating a Simple Query

A **query** is a question you ask about the data stored in a database. In response to a query, Access displays the specific records and fields that answer your question. When you create a query, you tell Access which fields you need and what criteria Access should use to select the records. Then Access displays only the information you want, so you don't have to navigate through the entire database for the information. In the Contract table, for example, Oren might create a query to display only those records for contracts that were signed in a specific month. Even though a query can display table information in a different way, the information still exists in the table as it was originally entered.

Oren wants to focus on the amount of each contract and the contract type. He doesn't want the list to include all the fields in the Contract table (such as Customer ID and Signing Date). To produce this list for Oren, you need to create a query based on the Contract table.

You can design your own queries or use an Access Query Wizard, which guides you through the steps to create a query. The **Simple Query Wizard** allows you to select records and fields quickly, and is an appropriate choice for producing the contract list Oren wants.

To start the Simple Query Wizard:

1. Click the **Create** tab on the Ribbon. The Create tab provides options for creating database objects—tables, forms, reports, queries, and so on. See Figure 1-21.

| Figure 1-21 | Create tab on the Ribbon |

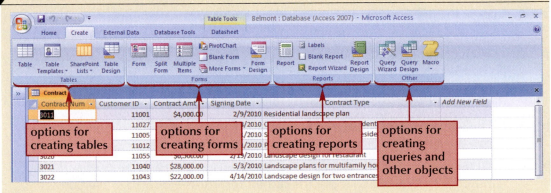

2. In the Other group on the Create tab, click the **Query Wizard** button. The New Query dialog box opens.

3. Make sure **Simple Query Wizard** is selected, and then click the **OK** button. The first Simple Query Wizard dialog box opens. See Figure 1-22.

| Figure 1-22 | First Simple Query Wizard dialog box |

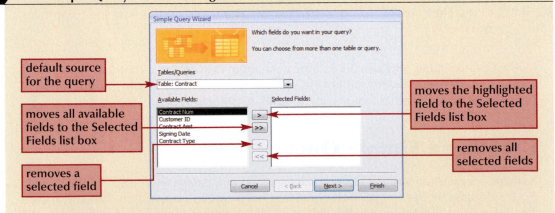

Because the Contract table is the only object in the Belmont database, it is listed in the Tables/Queries box by default. If the database contained more objects, you could click the Tables/Queries arrow and choose another table or a query as the basis for the new query you are creating. The Available Fields list box lists all the fields in the Contract table.

You need to select fields from the Available Fields list box to include them in the query. To select fields one at a time, click a field and then click the > button. The selected field moves from the Available Fields list box on the left to the Selected Fields list box on the right. To select all the fields, click the >> button. If you change your mind or make a mistake, you can remove a field by clicking it in the Selected Fields list box and then clicking the < button. To remove all selected fields, click the << button.

Each Simple Query Wizard dialog box contains buttons on the bottom that allow you to move to the previous dialog box (Back button), move to the next dialog box (Next button), or cancel the creation process (Cancel button). You can also finish creating the object (Finish button) and accept the wizard's defaults for the remaining options.

Oren wants his list to include data from only the following fields: Contract Num, Contract Amt, and Contract Type. You need to select these fields to include them in the query.

To create the query using the Simple Query Wizard:

▶ 1. Click **Contract Num** in the Available Fields list box to select the field (if necessary), and then click the > button. The Contract Num field moves to the Selected Fields list box.

▶ 2. Repeat Step 1 for the fields **Contract Amt** and **Contract Type**, and then click the **Next** button. The second Simple Query Wizard dialog box opens and asks if you want a detail or summary query. This dialog box opens when the values in one of the fields selected for the query could be used in calculations—in this case, the Contract Amt field. Oren wants to see every field of every record and does not want to perform summary calculations on the Contract Amt field values, so you need to create a detail query.

▶ 3. Make sure the **Detail** option button is selected, and then click the **Next** button. The third, and final, Simple Query Wizard dialog box opens and asks you to choose a name (title) for your query. Access suggests the name "Contract Query" because the query you are creating is based on the Contract table. You'll change the suggested name to "Contract List."

▶ 4. Click at the end of the suggested name, use the **Backspace** key to delete the word "Query," and then type **List**. Now you can view the query results.

▶ 5. Click the **Finish** button to complete the query. Access displays the query results in Datasheet view, on a new tab named "Contract List." A query datasheet is similar to a table datasheet, showing fields in columns and records in rows—but only for those fields and records you want to see, as determined by the query specifications you select.

▶ 6. Place the pointer on the vertical line to the right of the Contract Type field name until the pointer changes to a ⟷ shape, and then double-click the pointer. All the Contract Type field values are now fully displayed. See Figure 1-23.

Tip

You can also double-click a field to move it from the Available Fields list box to the Selected Fields list box.

Figure 1-23 | **Query results**

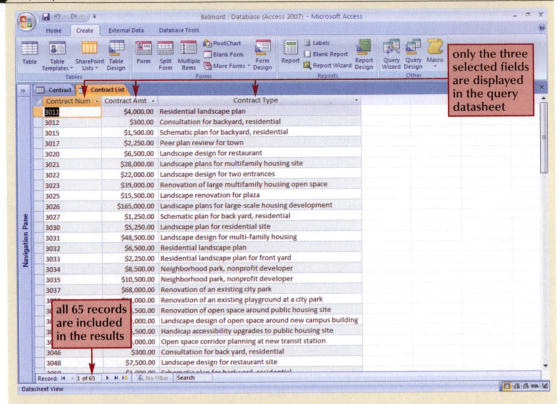

The Contract List query datasheet displays the three selected fields for each record in the Contract table. The fields are shown in the order you selected them in the Simple Query Wizard, from left to right. The records are listed in order by the primary key field, Contract Num. Even though the datasheet displays only the three fields you chose for the query, the Contract table still includes all the fields for all records.

Notice that the navigation buttons are located at the bottom of the window. You navigate a query datasheet in the same way that you navigate a table datasheet.

▶ 7. Click the **Last record** navigation button ▶️. The last record in the query datasheet is now the current record.

▶ 8. Click the **Previous record** navigation button ◀. Record 64 in the query datasheet is now the current record.

▶ 9. Click the **First record** navigation button ◀️. The first record is now the current record.

▶ 10. Click the **Close 'Contract List'** button ❌ on the table window bar. A dialog box opens asking if you want to save the changes to the layout of the query. This dialog box opens because you resized the Contract Type column.

▶ 11. Click the **Yes** button to save the query layout changes and close the query.

The query results are not stored in the database; however, the query design is stored as part of the database with the name you specified. You can re-create the query results at any time by opening the query again. You'll learn more about creating and working with queries in Tutorial 3.

Next, Oren asks you to create a form for the Contract table so that Belmont Landscapes employees can use the form to enter and work with data in the table easily.

Creating a Simple Form

A **form** is an object you use to enter, edit, and view records in a database. Although you can perform these same functions with tables and queries, forms can present data in many customized and useful ways. In Access, there are many different ways to create a form. You can design your own forms, use the Form Wizard (which guides you through the process of creating a form), or use the Form tool to create a simple form with one mouse click. The **Form tool** creates a form containing all the fields in the table or other database object on which you're basing the form.

Oren wants a form for the Contract table that shows all the fields for one record at a time, with fields listed one below another in a column. This type of form will make it easier for his staff to focus on all the data for a particular contract. You'll use the Form tool to create this form quickly and easily.

To create the form using the Form tool:

▶ 1. Make sure the Contract table is still open in Datasheet view. The table or other database object you're using as the basis for the form must either be open or selected in the Navigation Pane when you use the Form tool.

Trouble? If the Contract table is not open, click the Shutter Bar Open/Close Button ⟩⟩ to open the Navigation Pane. Then double-click Contract : Table to open the Contract table in Datasheet view. Click the Shutter Bar Open/Close Button ⟨⟨ again to close the pane.

▶ 2. In the Forms group on the Create tab, click the **Form** button. The Form tool creates a simple form showing every field in the Contract table and places it on a tab named "Contract." Access assigns the name "Contract" because the form is based on the Contract table. See Figure 1-24.

Form created by the Form tool   **Figure 1-24**

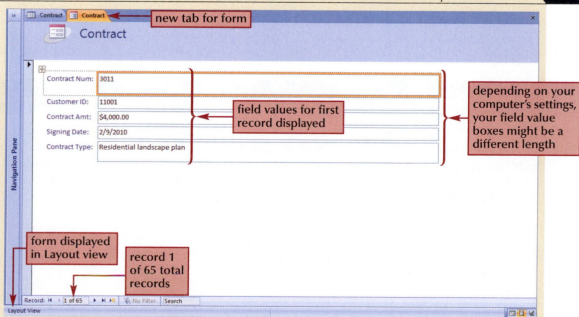

The form displays one record at a time in the Contract table, providing another view of the data that is stored in the table and allowing you to focus on the values for one record. Access displays the field values for the first record in the table and selects the first field value (Contract Num) by placing a border around the value. Each field name appears on a separate line and on the same line as its field value, which appears in a box to the right. Depending on your computer's settings, the field value boxes in your form might be shorter or longer than those shown in the figure. As indicated in the status bar, the form is displayed in Layout view. In **Layout view**, you can make design changes to the form while it is displaying data, so that you can see the effects of the changes you make immediately.

To view and maintain data using a form, you must know how to move from field to field and from record to record. Notice that the form contains navigation buttons, similar to those available in Datasheet view, which you can use to display different records in the form. You'll use these now to navigate the form; then you'll save and close the form.

To navigate, save, and close the form:

1. Click the **Next record** navigation button ▶. The form now displays the values for the second record in the Contract table.

2. Click the **Last record** navigation button ▶| to move to the last record in the table. The form displays the information for contract number 3110.

3. Click the **Previous record** navigation button ◀ to move to record 64.

4. Click the **First record** navigation button |◀ to return to the first record in the Contract table.

   Next, you'll save the form with the name "Contract Data" in the Belmont database. Then the form will be available for later use.

5. Click the **Save** button 🖫 on the Quick Access Toolbar. The Save As dialog box opens.

6. In the Form Name text box, click at the end of the highlighted word "Contract," press the **spacebar**, type **Data**, and then press the **Enter** key. Access saves the form as Contract Data in the Belmont database and closes the dialog box. The tab containing the form now displays the name "Contract Data."

7. Click the **Close 'Contract Data'** button ✖ on the form window bar to close the form.

| InSight | **Saving Database Objects** |

In general, it is best to save a database object—query, form, or report—only if you anticipate using the object frequently or if it is time consuming to create, because these objects use storage space on your disk. For example, a form you create with the Form tool would most likely not be saved, since you can re-create it easily with one mouse click. (However, for the purposes of this text, you need to save the objects you create.)

After attending a staff meeting, Oren returns with another request. He would like to see the information in the Contract table presented in a more readable format. You'll help Oren by creating a report.

Creating a Simple Report

A **report** is a formatted printout (or screen display) of the contents of one or more tables in a database. As with forms, you can design your own reports, use a Report Wizard to guide you through the steps of creating a report, or use the Report tool to create a simple report with one mouse click.

To produce the report for Oren, you'll use the Report tool, which is similar to the Form tool you used earlier to create the Contract Data form. The **Report tool** places all the fields from a selected table (or query) on a report, making it the quickest way to create a report.

To create the report using the Report tool:

1. With the Contract table open in Datasheet view, click the **Create** tab on the Ribbon.

2. In the Reports group on the Create tab, click the **Report** button. The Report tool creates a simple report showing every field in the Contract table and places it on a tab named "Contract." Again, Access assigns this name because the object you created (the report) is based on the Contract table. See Figure 1-25.

Report created by the Report tool   **Figure 1-25**

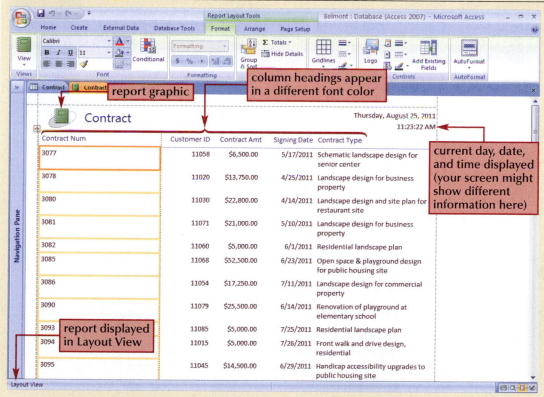

The report shows each field in a column, with the field values for each record in a row, similar to a datasheet. However, the report offers a more visually appealing format for the data, with the column headings in a different color and a line separating them from the records, a graphic of a report at the top left, and the current day, date, and time at the top right. The report is displayed in Layout view, which doesn't show how many pages there are in the report. To see this, you need to switch to Print Preview.

To view the report in Print Preview:

▶ **1.** In the Views group on the Report Layout Tools Format tab, click the **View button arrow**, and then click **Print Preview**. The first page of the report is displayed in Print Preview. See Figure 1-26.

Figure 1-26   **First page of the report in Print Preview**

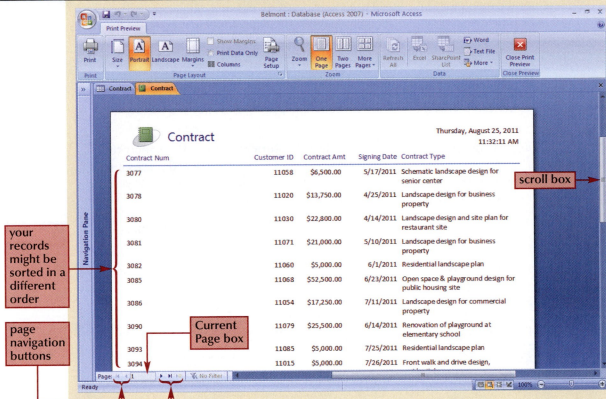

Print Preview shows exactly how the report will look when printed. Notice that Print Preview provides page navigation buttons at the bottom of the window, similar to the navigation buttons you've used to move through records in a table, query, and form.

▶ **2.** Click the **Next Page** navigation button ▶. The second page of the report is displayed in Print Preview.

▶ **3.** Click the **Last Page** navigation button ▶| to move to the last page of the report.

▶ **4.** Drag the scroll box in the vertical scroll bar (see Figure 1-26) down until the bottom of the report page is displayed. The notation "Page 3 of 3" appears at the bottom of the page, indicating that you are on page 3 out of a total of 3 pages in the report. See Figure 1-27.

Viewing the last page of the report ◄ Figure 1-27

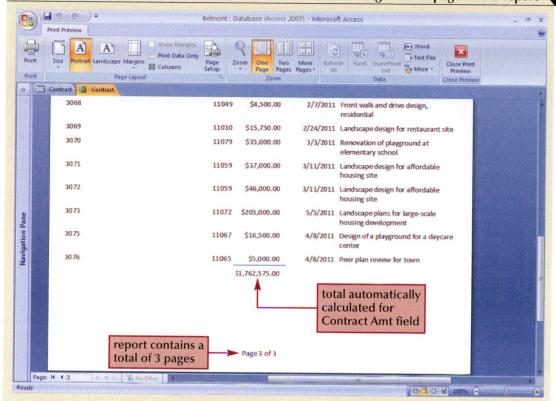

Trouble? Depending on the printer you are using, your report might have more or fewer pages, and some of the pages might be blank. If so, don't worry. Different printers format reports in different ways, sometimes affecting the total number of pages and the number of records printed per page.

Notice the total amount shown at the end of the report for the Contract Amt field. The Report tool calculated this amount and displayed it on the report. Often, you want to include such information as summaries and totals in a report; in this case, the Report tool generated it for you automatically.

► **5.** Click the **First Page** navigation button ⏮ to return to the first page of the report, and then drag the scroll box in the vertical scroll bar back up so that the top of the report is displayed.

Next you'll save the report as "Contract Details," and then close it.

► **6.** Click the **Save** button 💾 on the Quick Access Toolbar. The Save As dialog box opens.

► **7.** In the Report Name text box, click at the end of the highlighted word "Contract," press the **spacebar**, type **Details**, and then press the **Enter** key. Access saves the report as Contract Details in the Belmont database and closes the dialog box. The tab containing the report now displays the name "Contract Details."

Printing a Report

After creating a report, you typically print it to distribute it to others who need to view the report's contents. You use the Print command available from the Office menu to print a report.

| Reference Window | **Printing a Report** |

- Open the report in any view, or select the report in the Navigation Pane.
- To print the report with the default print settings, click the Office Button, point to Print, and then click Quick Print.

or

- To display the Print dialog box and select the options you want for printing the report, click the Office Button, point to Print, and then click Print (or, if the report is displayed in Print Preview, click the Print button in the Print group on the Print Preview tab).

Oren asks you to print the entire report, so you'll use the Quick Print option available from the Office Button menu.

Note: To complete the following steps, your computer must be connected to a printer.

To print the report:

▶ 1. Click the **Office Button** (🔘), point to **Print**, and then click **Quick Print**. The report prints with the default print settings.

Trouble? If your report did not print, make sure that your computer is connected to a printer, and that the printer is turned on and ready to print. Then repeat Step 1.

▶ 2. Click the **Close 'Contract Details'** button ⊠ on the report window bar to close the report.

▶ 3. Click the **Close 'Contract'** button ⊠ on the table window bar to close the Contract table.

You can also use the Print dialog box to print other database objects, such as table and query datasheets. Most often, these objects are used for viewing and entering data, and reports are used for printing the data in a database.

Viewing Objects in the Navigation Pane

The Belmont database now contains four objects—the Contract table, the Contract List query, the Contract Data form, and the Contract Details report. You can view and work with these objects in the Navigation Pane.

To view the objects in the Belmont database:

▶ 1. Click the **Shutter Bar Open/Close Button** ⧉ on the Navigation Pane to open the pane. See Figure 1-28.

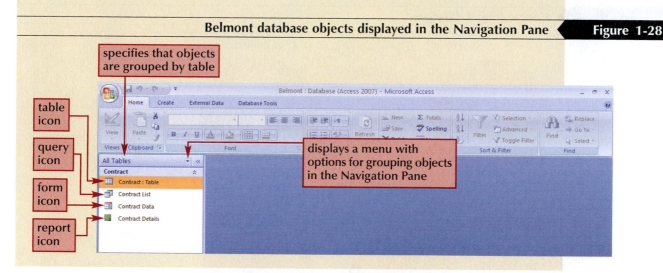

Belmont database objects displayed in the Navigation Pane ◄ Figure 1-28

The Navigation Pane currently displays the default view, **All Tables**, which groups objects according to the tables in the database. Note the bar containing the word "Contract" in the pane; this bar is a heading for the Contract table, which is the only table in the Belmont database. Below the bar, all the objects related to the Contract table, including the table itself, are listed. Each database object—the Contract table, the Contract List query, the Contract Data form, and the Contract Details report—has a unique icon to its left to indicate the type of object. This makes it easy for you to identify the objects and choose which one you want to open and work with.

The arrow on the All Tables bar displays a menu with options for various ways to group and display objects in the Navigation Pane. As you continue to build the Belmont database and add more objects to it in later tutorials, you'll learn how to use the options in this menu.

Managing a Database

One of the main tasks involved in working with database software is managing your databases and the data they contain. By managing your databases, you can ensure that they operate in the most efficient way, that the data they contain is secure, and that you can work with the data effectively. Some of the activities involved in database management include compacting and repairing a database and backing up and restoring a database.

Compacting and Repairing a Database

Whenever you open an Access database and work in it, the size of the database increases. Further, when you delete records and when you delete or replace database objects—such as queries, forms, and reports—the space that had been occupied on the disk by the deleted or replaced records or objects does not automatically become available for other records or objects. To make the space available, you must compact the database. **Compacting** a database rearranges the data and objects in a database to decrease its file size, thereby making more space available on your disk and letting you open and close the database more quickly. Figure 1-29 illustrates the compacting process.

Figure 1-29 | **Compacting a database**

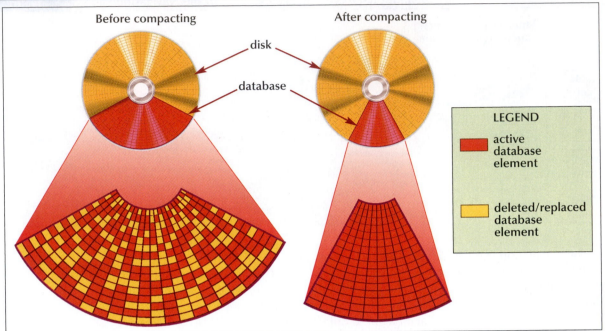

When you compact a database, Access repairs the database at the same time. In many cases, Access detects that a database is damaged when you try to open it and gives you the option to compact and repair it at that time. For example, the data in your database might become damaged, or corrupted, if you exit the Access program suddenly by turning off your computer. If you think your database might be damaged because it is behaving unpredictably, you can use the "Compact and Repair Database" option to fix it.

Reference Window | **Compacting and Repairing a Database**

- Make sure the database file you want to compact and repair is open.
- Click the Office Button, point to Manage, and then click Compact and Repair Database.

Access also allows you to set an option for your database file so that every time you close the database, it will be compacted automatically. The Compact on Close option is available in the Current Database section of the Access Options dialog box, which you open by clicking the Office Button and then clicking the Access Options button. By default, the Compact on Close option is off.

Next, you'll compact the Belmont database manually using the Compact and Repair Database option. This will make the database a much smaller and more manageable size. After compacting the database, you'll close it.

To compact and repair the Belmont database:

▶ 1. Click the **Office Button** 🔘, and then point to **Manage**.

   Trouble? Check with your instructor before selecting the option to compact and repair the database. If your instructor tells you not to select this option, click the Exit Access button on the Office menu.

▶ 2. Click **Compact and Repair Database**. Although nothing visible happens on screen, Access compacts the Belmont database, making it smaller, and repairs it at the same time.

▶ 3. Click the **Close** button ❎ on the program window title bar. Access closes the Belmont database. Then the Access program window closes.

Backing Up and Restoring a Database

Backing up a database is the process of making a copy of the database file to protect your database against loss or damage. Experienced database users make it a habit to back up a database before they work with it for the first time, keeping the original data intact, and to make frequent backups while continuing to work with a database. Most users back up their databases on tapes, USB drives, recordable CDs or DVDs, or hard disks. Also, it is recommended to store the backup copy in a different location from the original. For example, if the original database is stored on a USB drive, you should not store the backup copy on the same USB drive. If you lose the drive, the original database and its backup copy would both be lost.

The Back Up Database command enables you to back up your database file from within the Access program, while you are working on your database. To use this option, you click the Office Button, point to the Manage option, and then choose Back Up Database. In the resulting Save As dialog box, Access provides a default filename for the backup copy that consists of the same filename as the database you are backing up (for example, "Belmont") plus the current date. This filenaming system makes it easy for you to keep track of your database backups and when they were created.

To restore a backup database file, you simply copy the backup from the drive on which it is stored to your hard drive, or whatever device you use to work in Access, and start working with the restored database file. If the original database file and the backup copy have the same name, restoring the backup copy might replace the original. If you want to save the original file, rename it before you restore the backup copy. To ensure that the restored database has the most current data, you should update the restored database with any changes made to the original between the time it became damaged or lost and the time you created the backup copy. (You will not actually back up the Belmont database in this tutorial.)

With the Contract table in place, you can continue to build the Belmont database so that Oren and his staff members can use it to store, manipulate, and retrieve important data for Belmont Landscapes. In the following tutorials, you'll help Oren complete and maintain the database, and you'll use it to meet the specific information needs of the firm's employees.

Review | **Session 1.2 Quick Check**

1. True or False: You can copy records from any Access database table and paste them in another table.
2. A(n) _____ is a question you ask about the data stored in a database.
3. The quickest way to create a form is to use the _____ .
4. To see the total number of pages in a report and navigate through the report pages, you need to display the report in _____ .
5. In the Navigation Pane, each database object has a unique _____ to its left that identifies the object's type.
6. _____ a database rearranges the data and objects in a database to decrease its file size.
7. _____ a database is the process of making a copy of the database file to protect the database against loss or damage.

Review | **Tutorial Summary**

In this tutorial, you learned the basic concepts associated with databases, including how data is organized in a database and the functions of a relational database management system. You also learned how to create a new blank database, and how to create a table in Datasheet view by entering field names and records. You learned the function of the primary key and its role in the design of a table. To complete the table, you copied and pasted records from another Access database table with the same design. You used the Simple Query Wizard to display only certain fields and their values. Using the Form tool and the Report tool, you learned how to create simple forms and reports quickly in order to view and work with the data stored in a table in different ways. Finally, you were introduced to some of the important tasks involved in managing a database, including compacting and backing up a database.

Key Terms

Access	Datasheet view	query
Access window	field	record
Add New Field column	field selector	record selector
All Tables (view)	field value	relational database
AutoNumber	foreign key	relational database manage-
backing up	form	ment system
column selector	Form tool	report
common field	ID column	Report tool
compacting	Layout view	row selector
Current Record box	Microsoft Access window	Simple Query Wizard
data type	Microsoft Office Access 2007	star symbol
database	navigation buttons	table
database management	Navigation Pane	template
system (DBMS)	pencil symbol	Text (data type)
datasheet	primary key	
datasheet selector	Print Preview	

Practice | Review Assignments

Take time to practice the skills you learned in the tutorial using the same case scenario.

Data File needed for the Review Assignments: Provider.accdb

In the Review Assignments, you'll create a new database to contain information about the suppliers that Belmont Landscapes works with on its landscape design projects. Complete the following steps:

1. Create a new blank database named **Supplier**, and save it in the Level.01\Review folder provided with your Data Files.
2. In Datasheet view for the Table1 table, rename the default ID primary key field to **Company ID**. Change the data type of the Company ID field to Text.
3. Add the following 10 fields to the new table in the order shown: **Company Name**, **Product Type**, **Address**, **City**, **State**, **Zip**, **Phone**, **Contact First Name**, **Contact Last Name**, and **Initial Contact Date**. Resize the columns as necessary so that the complete field names are displayed. Save the table as **Company**.
4. Enter the records shown in Figure 1-30 in the Company table. As you enter the field values for the first record, use the Data Type option in the Data Type & Formatting group on the Datasheet tab to confirm that all the fields use the Text data type, except for the Zip field (which should have the Number data type) and the Initial Contact Date field (which should have the Date/Time data type). If necessary, make any changes so the fields have the correct data types.

Figure 1-30

Company ID	Company Name	Product Type	Address	City	State	Zip	Phone	Contact First Name	Contact Last Name	Initial Contact Date
AND225	Anderson OnSite	Site furnishings	200 Lincoln Dr	Kalamazoo	MI	49007	269-337-9266	Matt	Anderson	6/3/2009
HOL292	Holland Nursery	Plants	380 W 20th St	Holland	MI	49424	616-396-9330	Brenda	Ehlert	9/2/2010
BES327	Best Paving	Pavers	780 N Main St	Rockford	MI	49341	616-866-6364	Shirley	Hauser	2/14/2010
MID312	Midwest Lighting	Outdoor lighting	435 Central Dr	Battle Creek	MI	49014	269-979-3970	Weston	Caldwell	5/15/2009
BAC200	Backyard Structures	Play equipment	105 E 8th St	Holland	MI	49423	616-396-3989	Alan	Bastian	4/15/2009

5. Oren created a database named Provider that contains a Business table with supplier data. The Company table you created has the same design as the Business table. Copy all the records from the **Business** table in the **Provider** database (located in the Level.01\Review folder provided with your Data Files) to the end of the Company table in the Supplier database.
6. Resize all the columns in the datasheet so that all the field values are completely displayed, and then save the Company table.
7. Close the Company table, and then use the Navigation Pane to reopen it. Note that the records are displayed in primary key order.
8. Use the Simple Query Wizard to create a query that includes the Company Name, Product Type, Contact First Name, Contact Last Name, and Phone fields (in that order) from the Company table. Name the query **Company List**, and then close the query.
9. Use the Form tool to create a form for the Company table. Save the form as **Company Info**, and then close it.

10. Use the Report tool to create a report based on the Company table. Save the report as **Company Details**, and then close it.
11. Close the Company table, and then compact and repair the Supplier database.
12. Close the Supplier database.

| Apply | **Case Problem 1** |

Use the skills you learned in the tutorial to create a database for a small music school.

Data File needed for this Case Problem: School.accdb

Pine Hill Music School   After giving private piano lessons from her home for several years, Yuka Koyama founded the Pine Hill Music School in Portland, Oregon. Because of her popularity as a music teacher, Yuka attracted top-notch students, and her school quickly established a reputation for excellence. During the past two years, other qualified teachers have joined Yuka to offer instruction in voice, violin, cello, guitar, percussion, and other instruments. As her school continues to grow, Yuka wants to use Access to keep track of information about students, teachers, and contracts. You'll help Yuka create and maintain an Access database to store data about her school. Complete the following:

1. Create a new blank database named **Pinehill**, and save it in the Level.01\Case1 folder provided with your Data Files.
2. In Datasheet view for the Table1 table, rename the default primary key ID field to **Teacher ID**. Change the data type of the Teacher ID field to Text.
3. Add the following five fields to the new table in the order shown: **First Name**, **Last Name**, **Degree**, **School**, and **Hire Date**. Save the table as **Teacher**.
4. Enter the records shown in Figure 1-31 in the Teacher table. As you enter the field values for the first record, use the Data Type option in the Data Type & Formatting group on the Datasheet tab to confirm that all the fields use the Text data type, except for the Hire Date field, which should have the Date/Time data type. If necessary, make any changes so the fields have the correct data types.

Figure 1-31

Teacher ID	First Name	Last Name	Degree	School	Hire Date
13-1100	Yuka	Koyama	MM	Pacific University	1/13/2009
17-1798	Richard	Jacobson	PhD	Pacific University	1/15/2009
55-5310	Annamaria	Romano	BA	Lewis & Clark College	4/21/2009
22-0102	Andre	Dvorak	BM	University of Portland	3/3/2009
34-4506	Marilyn	Schwartz	BM	University of Portland	5/1/2009

5. Yuka created a database named School that contains a Faculty table with teacher data. The Teacher table you created has the same design as the Faculty table. Copy all the records from the **Faculty** table in the **School** database (located in the Level.01\Case1 folder provided with your Data Files) to the end of the Teacher table in the Pinehill database.
6. Resize all the columns in the datasheet so that all the field values are completely displayed, and then save the Teacher table.
7. Close the Teacher table, and then use the Navigation Pane to reopen it. Note that the records are displayed in primary key order.

8. Use the Simple Query Wizard to create a query that includes the First Name, Last Name, and Hire Date fields (in that order) from the Teacher table. Name the query **Start Date**, and then close the query.

9. Use the Form tool to create a form for the Teacher table. Save the form as **Teacher Info**, and then close it.

10. Use the Report tool to create a report based on the Teacher table. Save the report as **Teacher List**, print the report (only if asked by your instructor to do so), and then close it.

11. Close the Teacher table, and then compact and repair the Pinehill database.

12. Close the Pinehill database.

| Apply | Case Problem 2 |

Apply what you learned in the tutorial to create a database for a new business in the health and fitness industry.

Data File needed for this Case Problem: Health.accdb

Parkhurst Health & Fitness Center After many years working in various corporate settings, Martha Parkhurst decided to turn her lifelong interest in health and fitness into a new business venture and opened the Parkhurst Health & Fitness Center in Richmond, Virginia. In addition to providing the usual fitness classes and weight training facilities, the center also offers specialized programs designed to meet the needs of athletes—both young and old—who participate in certain sports or physical activities. Martha's goal in establishing such programs is twofold: to help athletes gain a competitive edge through customized training, and to ensure the health and safety of all participants through proper exercises and physical preparation. Martha wants to use Access to maintain information about the members who have joined the center and the types of programs offered. She needs your help in creating this database. Complete the following:

1. Create a new blank database named **Fitness**, and save it in the Level.01\Case2 folder provided with your Data Files.

2. In Datasheet view for the Table1 table, rename the default primary key ID field to **Program ID**. Change the data type of the Program ID field to Text.

3. Add the following three fields to the new table in the order shown: **Program Type**, **Monthly Fee**, and **Physical Required**. Resize the columns as necessary so that the complete field names are displayed. Save the table as **Program**.

4. Enter the records shown in Figure 1-32 in the Program table. As you enter the field values for the first record, use the Data Type option in the Data Type & Formatting group on the Datasheet tab to confirm that all the fields use the Text data type, except for the Monthly Fee field, which should have the Currency data type. If necessary, make any changes so the fields have the correct data types.

Figure 1-32

Program ID	Program Type	Monthly Fee	Physical Required
201	Junior Full (ages 13-17)	$35.00	Yes
202	Junior Limited (ages 13-17)	$25.00	Yes
203	Young Adult Full (ages 18-25)	$45.00	No
204	Young Adult Limited (ages 18-25)	$30.00	No

5. Martha created a database named Health that contains a Class table with program data. The Program table you created has the same design as the Class table. Copy all the records from the **Class** table in the **Health** database (located in the Level.01\Case2 folder provided with your Data Files) to the end of the Program table in the Fitness database.

6. Resize all the columns in the datasheet so that all the field values are completely displayed, and then save the Program table.

7. Use the Simple Query Wizard to create a query that includes all the fields from the Program table. In the second Simple Query Wizard dialog box, select the Detail option. Resize the columns in the query datasheet so that all the field values are completely displayed, save the query as **Program Data**, and then close the query.

8. Use the Form tool to create a form for the Program table. Save the form as **Program Info**, and then close it.

9. Use the Report tool to create a report based on the Program table. Save the report as **Program List**, print the report (only if asked by your instructor to do so), and then close it.

10. Close the Program table, and then compact and repair the Fitness database.

11. Close the Fitness database.

Challenge	Case Problem 3

Use what you've learned, and expand your skills, to create a database containing information about an agency that recycles household goods.

Data File needed for this Case Problem: RRGroup.accdb

Rossi Recycling Group   The Rossi Recycling Group is a not-for-profit agency in Salina, Kansas that provides recycled household goods to needy people and families at no charge. Residents of Salina and surrounding communities donate cash and goods, such as appliances, furniture, and tools, to the Rossi Recycling Group. The group's volunteers then coordinate with local human services agencies to distribute the goods to those in need. The Rossi Recycling Group was established by Mary and Tom Rossi, who live on the outskirts of Salina on a small farm. Mary and Tom organize the volunteers to collect the goods and store the collected items in their barn for distribution. Tom wants to create an Access database to keep track of information about donors, their donations, and the human services agencies. Complete the following:

1. Create a new blank database named **Rossi**, and then save it in the Level.01\Case3 folder provided with your Data Files.

2. In Datasheet view for the Table1 table, rename the default primary key ID field to **Donor ID**. Change the data type of the Donor ID field to Text.

3. Add the following four fields to the new table in the order shown: **Title**, **First Name**, **Last Name**, and **Phone**. Resize the columns as necessary so that the complete field names are displayed. Save the table as **Donor**.

4. Enter the records shown in Figure 1-33 in the Donor table. As you enter the field values for the first record, use the Data Type option in the Data Type & Formatting group on the Datasheet tab to confirm that all the fields use the Text data type. If necessary, make any changes so the fields have the correct data types.

Figure 1-33

Donor ID	Title	First Name	Last Name	Phone
36012	Mr.	Joel	Martinson	785-823-9275
36016	Mr.	Doug	Showers	620-793-8477
36001	Mrs.	Janis	Fendrick	785-452-8736
36020	Mrs.	JoAnn	Randolph	785-309-6540
36019	Ms.	Connie	Springen	785-452-1178

5. Tom created a database named RRGroup that contains a Contributors table with data about donors. The Donor table you created has the same design as the Contributors table. Copy all the records from the **Contributors** table in the **RRGroup** database (located in the Level.01\Case3 folder provided with your Data Files) to the end of the Donor table in the Rossi database.

6. Resize all the columns in the datasheet so that all the field values are completely displayed, and then save the Donor table.

7. Close the Donor table, and then use the Navigation Pane to reopen it. Note that the records are displayed in primary key order.

EXPLORE 8. Use the Simple Query Wizard to create a query that includes all the fields in the Donor table *except* the Title field. (*Hint*: Use the >> and < buttons to select the necessary fields.) Save the query using the name **Donor Phone List**.

EXPLORE 9. The query results are displayed in order by the Donor ID field values. You can specify a different order by sorting the query. Display the Home tab. Then, click the insertion point anywhere within the Last Name column to make it the current field. In the Sort & Filter group on the Home tab, click the Ascending button. The records are now listed in order by the values in the Last Name field. Save and close the query.

EXPLORE 10. Use the Form tool to create a form for the Donor table. In the new form, navigate to record 8, and then print the form *for the current record only*. (*Hint*: You must use the Print dialog box in order to print only the current record. Click the Office Button, point to Print, and then click Print to open the Print dialog box. Click the Selected Record(s) option button and then click the OK button to print the current record.) Save the form as **Donor Info**, and then close it.

11. Use the Report tool to create a report based on the Donor table. Save the report as **Donor List**. Print the report (only if asked by your instructor to do so), and then close it.

12. Close the Donor table, and then compact and repair the Rossi database.

13. Close the Rossi database.

Challenge | Case Problem 4

Work with the skills you've learned, and explore some new skills, to create a database for a luxury rental company.

Data File needed for this Case Problem: Travel.accdb

GEM Ultimate Vacations As guests of a friend, Griffin and Emma MacElroy spent two weeks at a magnificent villa in the south of France. This unforgettable experience stayed with them upon returning to their home in a suburb of Chicago, Illinois. As a result, they decided to open their own agency, GEM Ultimate Vacations, which specializes in locating and booking luxury rental properties, primarily in Europe. Recently, Griffin and Emma expanded their business to include properties in Africa as well. From the beginning, Griffin and Emma used computers to help them manage all aspects of their business. They recently installed Access and now would like you to create a database to store information about guests, properties, and reservations. Complete the following:

1. Create a new blank database named **GEM**, and then save it in the Level.01\Case4 folder provided with your Data Files.

2. In Datasheet view for the Table1 table, rename the default primary key ID field to **Guest ID**. Change the data type of the Guest ID field to Text.

3. Add the following eight fields to the new table in the order shown: **Guest First Name**, **Guest Last Name**, **Address**, **City**, **State/Prov**, **Postal Code**, **Country**, and **Phone**. Resize the columns as necessary so that the complete field names are displayed. Save the table as **Guest**.

⊕ EXPLORE 4. Enter the records shown in Figure 1-34 in the Guest table. As you enter the field values for the first record, use the Data Type option in the Data Type & Formatting group on the Datasheet tab to confirm that all the fields use the Text data type, except for the Postal Code field, which should have the Number data type. If necessary, make any changes so the fields have the correct data types. When you type the Postal Code value for the fourth record, Access will open an error menu because you entered letters into a field that is formatted with the Number data type, which stores numbers that will be used in calculations. Because the postal codes will not be used in calculations, choose the option on the menu to convert the data in this column to the Text data type to continue.

Figure 1-34

Guest ID	Guest First Name	Guest Last Name	Address	City	State/Prov	Postal Code	Country	Phone
201	Michael	Miskowsky	153 Summer Ave	Evanston	IL	60201	USA	847-623-0975
203	Tom	Davis	5003 Wilson Blvd	Chicago	IL	60603	USA	312-897-4515
206	Li	Zhu	6509 Great Rd	Gary	IN	46401	USA	219-655-8109
202	Ingrid	Gorman	207 Riverside Dr West	Windsor	ON	N9A 5K4	Canada	519-977-8577
205	Richard	Nelson	34 Settlers Dr	Tinley Park	IL	60477	USA	708-292-4441

5. Emma created a database named Travel that contains a Client table with data about guests. The Guest table you created has the same design as the Client table. Copy all the records from the **Client** table in the **Travel** database (located in the Level.01\Case4 folder provided with your Data Files) to the end of the Guest table in the GEM database.

6. Resize all the columns in the datasheet so that all the field values are completely displayed, and then save the Guest table.

7. Close the Guest table, and then use the Navigation Pane to reopen it. Note that the records are displayed in primary key order.

8. Use the Simple Query Wizard to create a query that includes the following fields from the Guest table, in the order shown: Guest ID, Guest Last Name, Guest First Name, City, and Phone. Name the query **Guest Data**.

⊕ EXPLORE 9. The query results are displayed in order by the Guest ID field values. You can specify a different order by sorting the query. Display the Home tab. Then, click the insertion point anywhere within the Guest Last Name column to make it the current field. In the Sort & Filter group on the Home tab, click the Ascending button. The records are now listed in order by the values in the Guest Last Name field. Save and close the query.

⊕ **EXPLORE**

10. Use the Form tool to create a form for the Guest table. In the new form, navigate to record 12, and then print the form *for the current record only*. (*Hint:* You must use the Print dialog box in order to print only the current record. Click the Office Button, point to Print, and then click Print to open the Print dialog box. Click the Selected Record(s) option button and then click the OK button to print the current record.) Save the form as **Guest Info**, and then close it.

11. Use the Report tool to create a report based on the Guest table. Save the report as **Guest List**.

⊕ **EXPLORE**

12. Display the report in Print Preview. Use the Two Pages button in the Zoom group on the Print Preview tab to view both pages of the report at the same time. Use the Landscape button in the Page Layout group to change the orientation of the report to landscape. Print the report (only if asked by your instructor to do so), and then close it.

13. Close the Guest table, and then compact and repair the GEM database.

14. Close the GEM database.

Research	**Internet Assignments**

Use the Internet to find and work with data related to the topics presented in this tutorial.

The purpose of the Internet Assignments is to challenge you to find information on the Internet that you can use to work effectively with this software. The actual assignments are updated and maintained on the Course Technology Web site. Log on to the Internet and use your Web browser to go to the Student Online Companion for New Perspectives Office 2007 at **www.course.com/np/office2007**. Then navigate to the Internet Assignments for this tutorial.

Assess	**SAM Assessment and Training**

If you have a SAM user profile, you may have access to hands-on instruction, practice, and assessment of the skills covered in this tutorial. Log in to your SAM account (**http://sam2007.course.com**) to launch any assigned training activities or exams that relate to the skills covered in this tutorial.

Review	**Quick Check Answers**

Session 1.1

1. field
2. common field
3. primary key; foreign key
4. Navigation Pane
5. ID field
6. the record being edited; the next row available for a new record
7. Access saves changes to the active database to disk automatically, when a record is changed or added and when you close the database. You use the Save button in Access only to save changes to the design of an object, such as a table, or to the format of a datasheet—not to save the database file.

Session 1.2

1. False; to copy and paste records from one table to another, the tables must have the same structure—that is, the tables must contain the same fields, with the same characteristics, in the same order.
2. query
3. Form tool
4. Print Preview
5. icon
6. Compacting
7. Backing up

Ending Data Files

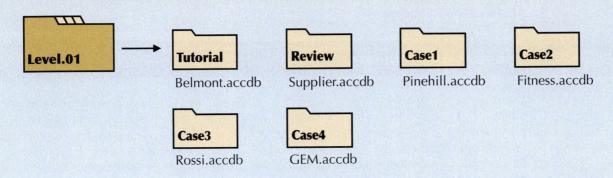

Objectives

Session 2.1
- Learn the guidelines for designing databases and setting field properties
- View and modify field data types and formatting
- Create a table in Design view
- Define fields and specify a table's primary key
- Modify the structure of a table

Session 2.2
- Import data from an Excel worksheet
- Create a table by importing an existing table structure
- Delete, rename, and move fields
- Add data to a table by importing a text file
- Define a relationship between two tables

Building a Database and Defining Table Relationships

Creating the Invoice and Customer Tables

Case | Belmont Landscapes

The Belmont database currently contains one table, the Contract table. Oren also wants to track information about the firm's customers, both residential and commercial, and the invoices sent to customers for services provided by Belmont Landscapes. This information includes such items as each customer's name and address and the invoice amount and invoice date.

In this tutorial, you'll create two new tables in the Belmont database—Invoice and Customer—to contain the data Oren wants to track. You will use two different methods for creating the tables, and learn how to modify the fields. After adding records to the tables, you will define the necessary relationships between the tables in the Belmont database to relate the tables, enabling Oren and his staff to work with the data more efficiently.

Starting Data Files

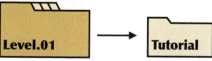

Level.01 → **Tutorial**

Belmont.accdb (*cont.*)
Customer.txt
Invoices.xlsx
Sarah.accdb

Review

Goods.xlsx
Supplier.accdb (*cont.*)

Case1

Lessons.xlsx
Music.accdb
Pinehill.accdb (*cont.*)
Student.txt

Case2

Center.xlsx
Fitness.accdb (*cont.*)

Case3

Agency.txt
Gifts.xlsx
Recycle.accdb
Rossi.accdb (*cont.*)

Case4

Bookings.txt
GEM.accdb (*cont.*)
Overseas.accdb

Session 2.1

Guidelines for Designing Databases

A database management system can be a useful tool, but only if you first carefully design the database so that it meets the needs of its users. In database design, you determine the fields, tables, and relationships needed to satisfy the data and processing requirements. When you design a database, you should follow these guidelines:

- **Identify all the fields needed to produce the required information.** For example, Oren needs information about contracts, invoices, and customers. Figure 2-1 shows the fields that satisfy these information requirements.

Figure 2-1	Oren's data requirements

Contract Num	Contract Amt
Customer ID	Signing Date
Company	Invoice Date
First Name	Contract Type
Last Name	Phone
Address	Invoice Paid
City	Invoice Num
State	Invoice Amt
Zip	

- **Organize each piece of data into its smallest useful part.** For example, Oren could store each customer's complete name in one field called Customer Name instead of using two fields called First Name and Last Name, as shown in Figure 2-1. However, doing so would make it more difficult to work with the data. If Oren wanted to view the records in alphabetical order by last name, he wouldn't be able to do so with field values such as "Tom Cotter" and "Ray Yost" stored in a Customer Name field. He could do so with field values such as "Cotter" and "Yost" stored separately in a Last Name field.
- **Group related fields into tables.** For example, Oren grouped the fields related to contracts into the Contract table, which you created in Tutorial 1. The fields related to invoices are grouped into the Invoice table, and the fields related to customers are grouped into the Customer table. Figure 2-2 shows the fields grouped into all three tables for the Belmont database.

Figure 2-2	Oren's fields grouped into tables

Contract table	Invoice table	Customer table
Contract Num	Invoice Num	Customer ID
Customer ID	Contract Num	Company
Contract Amt	Invoice Amt	First Name
Signing Date	Invoice Date	Last Name
Contract Type	Invoice Paid	Phone
		Address
		City
		State
		Zip

- **Determine each table's primary key.** Recall that a primary key uniquely identifies each record in a table. Although a primary key is not mandatory in Access, it's a good idea to include one in each table. Without a primary key, selecting the exact record that you want can be a problem. For some tables, one of the fields, such as a Social Security or credit card number, naturally serves the function of a primary key. For other tables, two or more fields might be needed to function as the primary key. In these cases, the primary key is called a **composite key**. For example, a school grade table would use a combination of student number and course code to serve as the primary key. For a third category of tables, no single field or combination of fields can uniquely identify a record in a table. In these cases, you need to add a field whose sole purpose is to serve as the table's primary key. For Oren's tables, Contract Num is the primary key for the Contract table, Invoice Num is the primary key for the Invoice table, and Customer ID is the primary key for the Customer table.

- **Include a common field in related tables.** You use the common field to connect one table logically with another table. For example, Oren's Contract and Customer tables include the Customer ID field as a common field. Recall that when you include the primary key from one table as a field in a second table to form a relationship, the field is called a foreign key in the second table; therefore, the Customer ID field is a foreign key in the Contract table. With this common field, Oren can find all contracts for a particular customer; he can use the Customer ID value for a customer and search the Contract table for all records with that Customer ID value. Likewise, he can determine which customer has a particular contract by searching the Customer table to find the one record with the same Customer ID value as the corresponding value in the Contract table. Similarly, the Contract Num field is a common field, serving as the primary key in the Contract table and a foreign key in the Invoice table.

- **Avoid data redundancy.** When you store the same data in more than one place, **data redundancy** occurs. With the exception of common fields to connect tables, you should avoid redundancy because it wastes storage space and can cause inconsistencies. An inconsistency would exist, for example, if you type a field value one way in one table and a different way in the same table or in a second table. Figure 2-3, which contains portions of potential data stored in the Customer and Contract tables, shows an example of incorrect database design that has data redundancy in the Contract table. In Figure 2-3, the Company field in the Contract table is redundant, and one value for this field was entered incorrectly, in three different ways.

| Figure 2-3 | Incorrect database design with data redundancy |

Customer table

Customer ID	Company	First Name	Last Name
11067	Blossom Day Care Center	Christina	Garrett
11068	Grand Rapids Housing Authority	Jessica	Ropiak
11070	Legacy Companies, LTD.	Michael	Faraci
11071	Blue Star Mini Golf	Vanetta	Walker
11072	Sierra Investment Company	Rodrigo	Valencia

data redundancy

Contract table

Contract Num	Customer ID	Company	Contract Amt	Signing Date
3023	11070	Legacy Company	$39,000.00	3/22/2010
3040	11068	Grand Rapids Housing Authority	$38,500.00	7/27/2010
3042	11070	Legacies Co. Limited	$48,500.00	6/3/2010
3073	11072	Sierra Investment Company	$205,000.00	5/5/2011
3081	11071	Blue Star Mini Golf	$21,000.00	5/10/2011
3085	11070	Legacy Corp. Ltd	$30,800.00	12/28/2010
3099	11067	Blossom Day Care Center	$6,500.00	7/25/2011

inconsistent data

- **Determine the properties of each field.** You need to identify the **properties**, or characteristics, of each field so that the DBMS knows how to store, display, and process the field values. These properties include the field's name, maximum number of characters or digits, description, valid values, and other field characteristics. You will learn more about field properties later in this tutorial.

The Invoice and Customer tables you need to create will contain the fields shown in Figure 2-2. Before you create these new tables in the Belmont database, you first need to learn some guidelines for setting field properties.

Guidelines for Setting Field Properties

As just noted, the last step of database design is to determine which values to assign to the properties, such as the name and data type, of each field. When you select or enter a value for a property, you **set** the property. Access has rules for naming fields, choosing data types, and setting other properties for fields.

Naming Fields and Objects

You must name each field, table, and other object in an Access database. Access then stores these items in the database, using the names you supply. It's best to choose a field or object name that describes the purpose or contents of the field or object so that later you can easily remember what the name represents. For example, the three tables in the Belmont database will be named Contract, Invoice, and Customer, because these names suggest their contents. Note that a table or query name must be unique within a database. A field name must be unique within a table, but it can be used again in another table. Refer to the "Guidelines for Naming Fields" InSight box in Tutorial 1 for a reminder of these guidelines, which apply to naming all database objects.

Assigning Field Data Types

Each field must have a data type, which is either assigned automatically by Access or specifically by the table designer. The **data type** determines what field values you can enter for the field and what other properties the field will have. For example, the Invoice table will include an Invoice Date field, which will store date values, so you will assign the Date/Time data type to this field. Then Access will allow you to enter and manipulate only dates or times as values in the Invoice Date field.

Figure 2-4 lists the data types available in Access, describes the field values allowed for each data type, explains when you should use each data type, and indicates the field size of each data type.

Data types for fields ◁ **Figure 2-4**

Data Type	Description	Field Size
Text	Allows field values containing letters, digits, spaces, and special characters. Use for names, addresses, descriptions, and fields containing digits that are not used in calculations.	0 to 255 characters; default is 255
Memo	Allows field values containing letters, digits, spaces, and special characters. Use for long comments and explanations.	1 to 65,535 characters; exact size is determined by entry
Number	Allows positive and negative numbers as field values. Numbers can contain digits, a decimal point, commas, a plus sign, and a minus sign. Use for fields that will be used in calculations, except those involving money.	1 to 15 digits
Date/Time	Allows field values containing valid dates and times from January 1, 100 to December 31, 9999. Dates can be entered in month/day/year format, several other date formats, or a variety of time formats, such as 10:35 PM. You can perform calculations on dates and times, and you can sort them. For example, you can determine the number of days between two dates.	8 bytes
Currency	Allows field values similar to those for the Number data type, but is used for storing monetary values. Unlike calculations with Number data type decimal values, calculations performed with the Currency data type are not subject to round-off error.	Accurate to 15 digits on the left side of the decimal point and to 4 digits on the right side
AutoNumber	Consists of integer values created automatically by Access each time you create a new record. You can specify sequential numbering or random numbering, which guarantees a unique field value, so that such a field can serve as a table's primary key.	9 digits
Yes/No	Limits field values to yes and no, on and off, or true and false. Use for fields that indicate the presence or absence of a condition, such as whether an order has been filled or whether an invoice has been paid.	1 character
OLE Object	Allows field values that are created in other Microsoft Windows programs as objects, such as spreadsheets and word-processing documents. These objects can be linked or embedded. Each field value is limited to a single file.	1 gigabyte maximum; exact size depends on object size
Hyperlink	Consists of text used as a hyperlink address, which can have up to four parts: the text that appears in a field or control; the path to a file or page; a location within the file or page; and text displayed as a ScreenTip.	Up to 65,535 characters total for the four parts of the Hyperlink data type
Attachment	Allows field values with one or more attached files, such as images, videos, documents, charts, and other supported files, similar to e-mail attachments. Provides greater flexibility than the OLE Object data type and uses storage space more efficiently.	2 gigabytes maximum; individual attached files cannot exceed 256 MB
Lookup Wizard	Creates a field that lets you look up a value in another table or in a predefined list of values.	Same size as the primary key field used to perform the lookup

Setting Field Sizes

The **Field Size property** defines a field value's maximum storage size for Text, Number, and AutoNumber fields only. The other data types have no Field Size property because their storage size is either a fixed, predetermined amount or is determined automatically by the field value itself, as shown in Figure 2-4. A Text field has a default field size of 255 characters; you can also set its field size by entering a number from 0 to 255. For example, the First Name and Last Name fields in the Customer table will be Text fields with a size of 20 characters and 25 characters, respectively. These field sizes will accommodate the values that will be entered in each of these fields.

InSight	**Understanding the Field Size Property for Number Fields**

When you use the Number data type to define a field, you should set the field's Field Size property based on the largest value that you expect to store in that field. Access processes smaller data sizes faster, using less memory, so you can optimize your database's performance and its storage space by selecting the correct field size for each field. Field Size property settings for Number fields are as follows:

- **Byte:** Stores whole numbers (numbers with no fractions) from 0 to 255 in one byte
- **Integer:** Stores whole numbers from −32,768 to 32,767 in two bytes
- **Long Integer** (default)**:** Stores whole numbers from −2,147,483,648 to 2,147,483,647 in four bytes
- **Single:** Stores positive and negative numbers to precisely seven decimal places and uses four bytes
- **Double:** Stores positive and negative numbers to precisely 15 decimal places and uses eight bytes
- **Replication ID:** Establishes a unique identifier for replication of tables, records, and other objects in databases created using Access 2003 and earlier versions and uses 16 bytes
- **Decimal:** Stores positive and negative numbers to precisely 28 decimal places and uses 12 bytes

For example, it would be wasteful to use the Long Integer field size for a Number field that will store only whole numbers ranging from 0 to 255, because the Long Integer field size uses four bytes of storage space. A better choice would be the Byte field size, which uses one byte of storage space to store the same values.

In Tutorial 1, you created the Belmont database and the Contract table. Access assigned the data types and field formatting for the fields you created in the Contract table based on the data you entered into each field in Datasheet view. Oren suggests that you view the data types and formatting of the fields in the Contract table to determine if you need to modify any of them to better store and format the data they contain.

Viewing and Modifying Field Data Types and Formatting

When you create a table in Datasheet view, such as the Contract table, you enter field (column) headings and field values in the rows below the headings. Access then determines what data type to assign to each field based on the values you enter for the field. If the values entered do not provide enough information for Access to "guess" the data type, the default type assigned is the Text data type.

Now, you'll open the Contract table in the Belmont database to view the data type and formatting for each field in Datasheet view.

To view the data type and formatting of the Contract table's fields:

▶ **1.** Start Access and open the **Belmont** database you created in Tutorial 1. This database file should be located in the Level.01\Tutorial folder provided with your Data Files.

   Trouble? If the Security Warning is displayed below the Ribbon, click the Options button next to the Security Warning. In the dialog box that opens, click the "Enable this content" option button, and then click the OK button.

▶ **2.** In the Navigation Pane, double-click **Contract : Table** to open the Contract table in Datasheet view.

▶ **3.** On the Navigation Pane, click the **Shutter Bar Open/Close Button** ≪ to close the pane and view more of the table datasheet.

   You can view the data type and some properties for each field using the Datasheet tab.

▶ **4.** Click in the first field value for the **Contract Num** field to make it the current field, and then click the **Datasheet** tab on the Ribbon. The Data Type option in the Data Type & Formatting group indicates that the current field, Contract Num, has the Text data type. In Tutorial 1, you changed the data type for this field to Text after you created this field by renaming the default primary key ID field.

▶ **5.** Press the **Tab** key to move to the Customer ID field and make it the active field. This field has the Number data type. See Figure 2-5.

Data type for the Customer ID field ◀ **Figure 2-5**

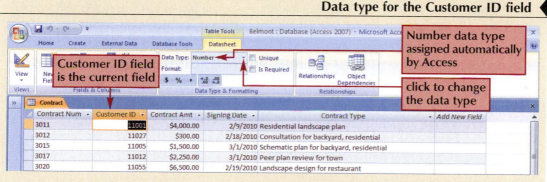

Access automatically assigned the Number data type to the Customer ID field when you created the Contract table in Tutorial 1. Because you entered numeric values in the field, such as 11001, Access determined that the field should be a Number field. However, the Number data type is best used for fields that will be used in mathematical calculations (except those involving money), or for numeric values that require a high degree of accuracy. The Customer ID field values will not be used in calculations; therefore, the Text data type is a better choice for this field.

Changing the Data Type of a Field in Datasheet View

As you learned in Tutorial 1, you can easily change the data type for a field in Datasheet view. Next, you'll change the data type of the Customer ID field to Text.

To change the data type of the Customer ID field:

▶ **1.** Make sure the Customer ID field is still the active field.

▶ **2.** In the Data Type & Formatting group on the Datasheet tab, click the **Data Type arrow**, and then click **Text**. The Customer ID field is now a Text field. See Figure 2-6.

Figure 2-6   **Customer ID field data type changed to Text**

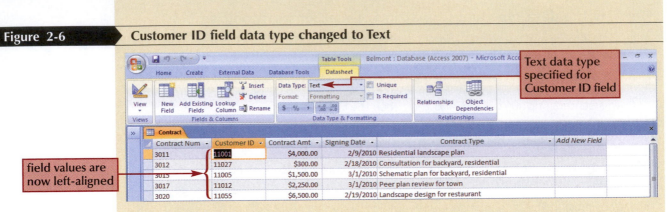

Notice that the values in the Customer ID field now appear left-aligned within their boxes, as opposed to their previous right-aligned format (see Figure 2-5). In Access, values for Text fields are left-aligned, and values for Number, Date/Time, and Currency fields are right-aligned.

The next field in the Contract table, Contract Amt, contains dollar values representing the total amount of each Belmont Landscapes contract. Oren knows that these dollar amounts will never contain cents, because the contracts are drawn up in whole amounts only; therefore, the two decimal places currently shown for the values are unnecessary. Furthermore, Oren feels that the dollar signs clutter the datasheet and are also unnecessary. He asks you to modify the format of the Contract Amt field to remove the dollar signs and decimal places.

Changing the Format of a Field in Datasheet View

The Data Type & Formatting group on the Datasheet tab allows you to modify some formatting for certain field types. When you format a field, you change the way data is displayed, but not the actual values stored in the table. Next, you'll use the options provided to modify the format of the Contract Amt field. You'll also check the format of the Signing Date field and modify it, if necessary.

To modify the format of the Contract Amt and Signing Date fields:

▶ 1. With the Customer ID field still active, press the **Tab** key to move to the Contract Amt field. The options in the Data Type & Formatting group indicate that this field has the Currency data type and the Currency format. See Figure 2-7.

Figure 2-7   **Contract Amt field with the Currency data type**

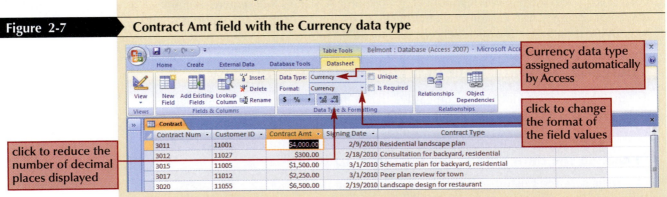

When you first entered the field values for the Contract Amt field in Tutorial 1, you included the dollar sign and commas; therefore, Access determined that this field should have the Currency data type, which is correct. The Currency format specifies that the values appear with dollar signs and two decimal places. You need to change this format to the Standard format, which does not contain dollar signs.

2. In the Data Type & Formatting group, click the **Format arrow**, and then click **Standard**. The dollar signs are removed, but the two decimal places are still displayed.

3. In the Data Type & Formatting group, click the **Decrease Decimals** button .00→.0 . Access decreases the decimal places by one, and the values now display only one decimal place.

4. Click the **Decrease Decimals** button .00→.0 again to remove the second decimal place and the decimal point. The Contract Amt field values are now displayed without dollar signs or decimal places. See Figure 2-8.

Contract Amt field values after modifying the format | Figure 2-8

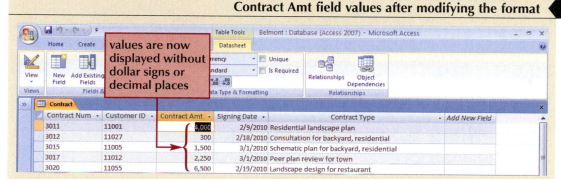

5. Press the **Tab** key to move to the Signing Date field. The Data Type option shows that this field is a Date/Time field. In Tutorial 1, when you entered date values in this field, Access automatically assigned the Date/Time data type to the field.

   By default, Access assigns the General Date format to Date/Time fields. This format includes settings for date or time values, or a combination of date and time values. However, Oren wants only date values to appear in the Signing Date field, so he asks you to specify the Short Date format for the field.

6. In the Data Type & Formatting group, click the **Format arrow**, and then click **Short Date**. See Figure 2-9.

Signing Date field after modifying the format | Figure 2-9

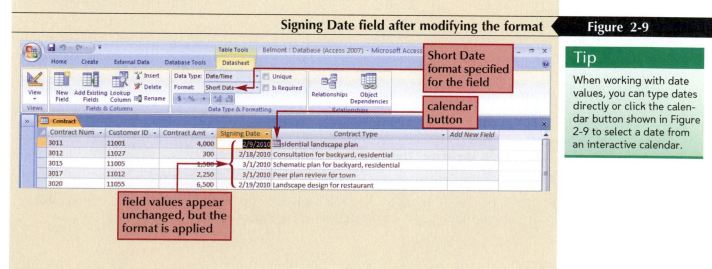

Tip

When working with date values, you can type dates directly or click the calendar button shown in Figure 2-9 to select a date from an interactive calendar.

Although no change is apparent in the worksheet—the Signing Date field values already appear with the Short Date setting (for example, 2/9/2010), as part of the default format—the field now has the Short Date format applied to it. This ensures that only date field values, and not time or date/time values, are displayed in the field.

7. Press the **Tab** key to move to the Contract Type field. Notice that Access assigned the Text data type to this field, which is correct because this field stores values with fewer than 255 characters.

Each of the three Text fields in this table—Contract Num, Customer ID, and Contract Type—has the default field size of 255. To change the field size, you need to work in Design view. You'll change the field sizes for these fields later in this session, after you learn more about Design view. For now, you can close the Contract table.

To close the Contract table:

1. Click the **Close 'Contract'** button ☒ on the table window bar.

According to his plan for the Belmont database, Oren wants to track information about the invoices the firm sends to its customers. Next, you'll create the Invoice table for Oren—this time, working directly in Design view.

Creating a Table in Design View

Creating a table in Design view involves entering the field names and defining the properties for the fields, specifying a primary key for the table, and then saving the table structure.

Oren documented the design for the new Invoice table by listing each field's name, data type, size (if applicable), and description, as shown in Figure 2-10.

Figure 2-10 **Design for the Invoice table**

Field Name	Data Type	Field Size	Description	Other
Invoice Num	Text	4	Primary key	
Contract Num	Text	4	Foreign key	
Invoice Amt	Currency			Format = Currency
				Decimal Places = 2
Invoice Date	Date/Time			Format = mm/dd/yyyy
Invoice Paid	Yes/No			

You will use Oren's design as a guide for creating the Invoice table in the Belmont database.

To begin creating the Invoice table:

1. Click the **Create** tab on the Ribbon.

2. In the Tables group on the Create tab, click the **Table Design** button. A new table named Table1 opens in Design view. See Figure 2-11.

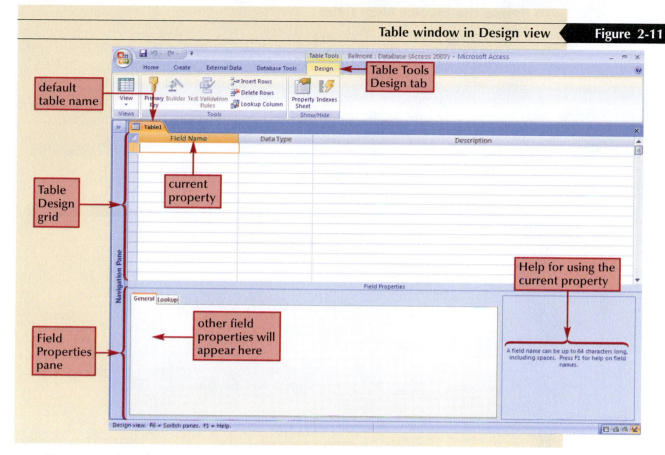

Table window in Design view Figure 2-11

You use **Design view** to define or modify a table structure or the properties of the fields in a table.

Defining Fields

Initially, the default table name, Table1, appears on the tab for the new table, and the insertion point is located in the first row's Field Name box. The purpose or characteristics of the current property (Field Name, in this case) appear in the Field Properties pane. You can display more complete Help information about the current property by pressing the **F1 key**.

You enter values for the Field Name, Data Type, and Description field properties in the **Table Design grid**. You select values for all other field properties, most of which are optional, in the **Field Properties pane**. These other properties will appear when you move to the first row's Data Type box.

Defining a Field in Design View	Reference Window

- In the Field Name box, type the name for the field, and then press the Tab key.
- Accept the default Text data type, or click the arrow and select a different data type for the field. Press the Tab key.
- Enter an optional description for the field, if necessary.
- Use the Field Properties pane to type or select other field properties, as appropriate.

The first field you need to define is the Invoice Num field. This field will be the primary key for the Invoice table.

To define the Invoice Num field:

▶ 1. Type **Invoice Num** in the first row's Field Name box, and then press the **Tab** key to advance to the Data Type box. The default data type, Text, appears highlighted in the Data Type box, which now also contains an arrow, and the field properties for a Text field appear in the Field Properties pane. See Figure 2-12.

| Figure 2-12 | Table window after entering the first field name |

Tip

You can also press the Enter key to move from one property to the next in the Table Design grid.

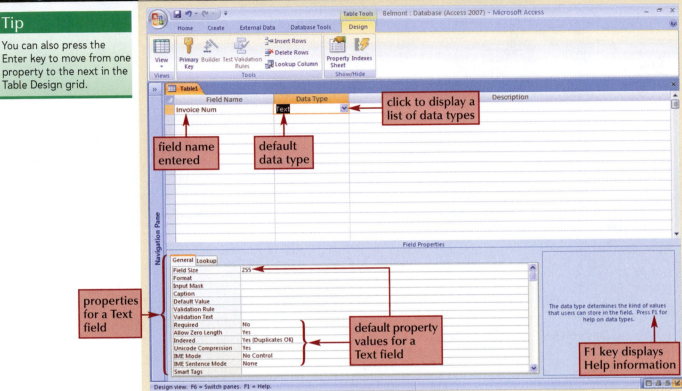

Notice that the right side of the Field Properties pane now provides an explanation for the current property, Data Type. You can display Help information about the current property by pressing the F1 key.

Trouble? If you make a typing error, you can correct it by clicking to position the insertion point, and then using either the Backspace key to delete characters to the left of the insertion point or the Delete key to delete characters to the right of the insertion point. Then type the correct text.

Because the Invoice Num field values will not be used in calculations, you will accept the default Text data type for the field.

▶ 2. Press the **Tab** key to accept Text as the data type and to advance to the Description box.

Next you'll enter the Description property value as "Primary key." You can use the **Description property** to enter an optional description for a field to explain its purpose or usage. A field's Description property can be up to 255 characters long, and its value appears on the status bar when you view the table datasheet. Note that specifying "Primary key" for the Description property does *not* establish the current field as the primary key; you use a button on the Ribbon to specify the primary key in Design view, which you will do later in this session.

▶ 3. Type **Primary key** in the Description box.

Notice the Field Size property for the field. The default setting of 255 for Text fields is displayed. You need to change this number to 4 because all invoice numbers at Belmont Landscapes contain only four digits.

▶ **4.** Double-click the number **255** in the Field Size property box to select it, and then type **4**. The definition of the first field is complete. See Figure 2-13.

Invoice Num field defined **Figure 2-13**

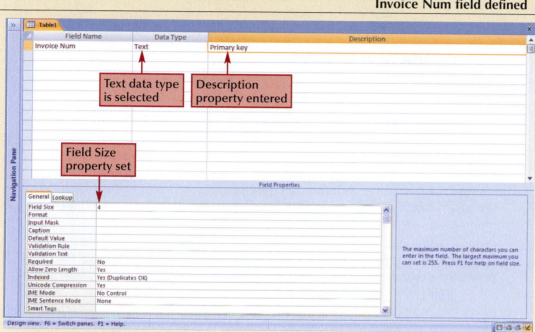

Oren's Invoice table design (Figure 2-10) shows Contract Num as the second field. Because Oren and other staff members want to relate information about invoices to the contract data in the Contract table, the Invoice table must include the Contract Num field, which is the Contract table's primary key. Recall that when you include the primary key from one table as a field in a second table to connect the two tables, the field is a foreign key in the second table. The field must be defined in the same way in both tables.

Next, you will define Contract Num as a Text field with a Field Size of 4. Later in this session, you will change the Field Size of the Contract Num field in the Contract table to 4 so that the field definition is the same in both tables.

To define the Contract Num field:

▶ **1.** In the Table Design grid, click in the second row's Field Name box, type **Contract Num** in the box, and then press the **Tab** key to advance to the Data Type box.

▶ **2.** Press the **Tab** key to accept Text as the field's data type. Because the Contract Num field is a foreign key to the Contract table, you'll enter "Foreign key" in the Description property to help users of the database understand the purpose of this field.

▶ **3.** Type **Foreign key** in the Description box.

Next, you'll change the Field Size property to 4. When defining the fields in a table, you can move between the Table Design grid and the Field Properties pane of the Table window by pressing the **F6** key.

▶ **4.** Press the **F6** key to move to the Field Properties pane. The current entry for the Field Size property, 255, is highlighted.

▶ **5.** Type **4** to set the Field Size property. You have completed the definition of the second field.

The third field in the Invoice table is the Invoice Amt field, which will display currency values, similar to the Contract Amt field in the Contract table. However, for this field, Oren wants the values to appear with two decimal places, because invoice amounts might include cents. He also wants the values to include dollar signs, so that the values will be formatted as currency when they are printed in reports sent to customers.

To define the Invoice Amt field:

▶ **1.** Click in the third row's Field Name box, type **Invoice Amt** in the box, and then press the **Tab** key to advance to the Data Type box.

▶ **2.** Click the **Data Type** arrow, click **Currency** in the list box, and then press the **Tab** key to advance to the Description box.

According to Oren's design (Figure 2-10), you do not need to enter a description for this field. If you've assigned a descriptive field name and the field does not fulfill a special function (such as primary key), you usually do not enter a value for the optional Description property. Invoice Amt is a field that does not require a value for its Description property.

Oren wants the Invoice Amt field values to be displayed with two decimal places, even if he decides to change the format for this field later. The **Decimal Places property** specifies the number of decimal places that are displayed to the right of the decimal point.

▶ **3.** In the Field Properties pane, click the **Decimal Places** box to position the insertion point there. An arrow appears on the right side of the Decimal Places box. When you position the insertion point or select text in many Access boxes, Access displays an arrow, which you can click to display a list box with options.

▶ **4.** Click the **Decimal Places** arrow, and then click **2** in the list box to specify two decimal places for the Invoice Amt field values. The definition of the third field is now complete. See Figure 2-14.

Figure 2-14 ▶ **Table window after defining the first three fields**

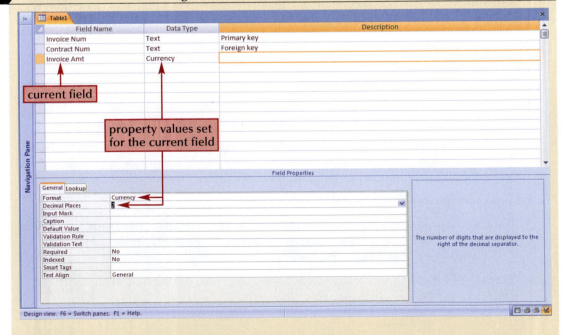

The next field you'll define in the Invoice table is Invoice Date. This field will contain the dates on which invoices are generated for Belmont Landscapes customers. When Belmont Landscapes first draws up contracts with its customers, the firm establishes invoice dates based on the different phases of the projects. For long-term projects with multiple phases, some of these dates are months or years in the future. You'll define the Invoice Date field using the Date/Time data type. Also, according to Oren's design (Figure 2-10), the date values should be displayed in the format mm/dd/yyyy, which is a two-digit month, a two-digit day, and a four-digit year.

To define the Invoice Date field:

1. Click in the fourth row's Field Name box, type **Invoice Date**, and then press the **Tab** key to advance to the Data Type box.

   You can select a value from the Data Type list box as you did for the Invoice Amt field. Alternately, you can type the property value in the box or type just the first character of the property value.

2. Type **d**. The value in the fourth row's Data Type box changes to "date/Time," with the letters "ate/Time" highlighted. See Figure 2-15.

Selecting a value for the Data Type property   Figure 2-15

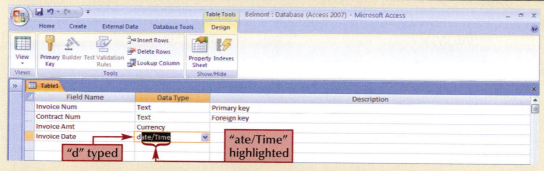

3. Press the **Tab** key to advance to the Description box. Note that Access changes the value for the Data Type property to "Date/Time."

   Oren wants the values in the Invoice Date field to be displayed in a format showing the month, the day, and a four-digit year, as in the following example: 03/11/2010. You use the Format property to control the display of a field value.

4. In the Field Properties pane, click the right side of the **Format** box to display the list of predefined formats for Date/Time fields. As noted in the right side of the Field Properties pane, you can either choose a predefined format or enter a custom format.

   Trouble? If you see an arrow instead of a list of predefined formats, click the arrow to display the list.

   None of the predefined formats matches the exact layout Oren wants for the Invoice Date values. Therefore, you need to create a custom date format. Figure 2-16 shows some of the symbols available for custom date and time formats.

Figure 2-16 **Symbols for some custom date formats**

Symbol	Description
/	date separator
d	day of the month in one or two numeric digits, as needed (1 to 31)
dd	day of the month in two numeric digits (01 to 31)
ddd	first three letters of the weekday (Sun to Sat)
dddd	full name of the weekday (Sunday to Saturday)
w	day of the week (1 to 7)
ww	week of the year (1 to 53)
m	month of the year in one or two numeric digits, as needed (1 to 12)
mm	month of the year in two numeric digits (01 to 12)
mmm	first three letters of the month (Jan to Dec)
mmmm	full name of the month (January to December)
yy	last two digits of the year (01 to 99)
yyyy	full year (0100 to 9999)

Oren wants the dates to be displayed with a two-digit month (mm), a two-digit day (dd), and a four-digit year (yyyy). You'll enter this custom format now.

▶ **5.** Click the **Format** arrow to close the list of predefined formats, and then type **mm/dd/yyyy** in the Format property box. See Figure 2-17.

Figure 2-17 **Specifying the custom date format**

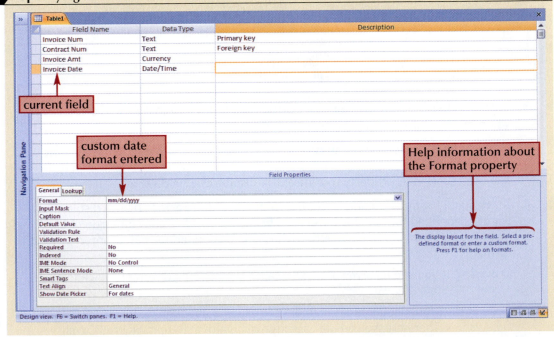

The fifth, and final, field to be defined in the Invoice table is Invoice Paid. This field will be a Yes/No field to indicate the payment status of each invoice record stored in the Invoice table.

To define the Invoice Paid field:

▶ **1.** Click in the fifth row's Field Name box, type **Invoice Paid**, and then press the **Tab** key to advance to the Data Type box.

▶ **2.** Type **y**. Access completes the data type as "yes/No."

▶ **3.** Press the **Tab** key to select the Yes/No data type and move to the Description box.

According to Oren's table design (see Figure 2-10), the Invoice Paid field does not have a description, so you've finished defining the fields for the Invoice table. Next, you need to specify the primary key for the table.

Specifying the Primary Key

As you learned in Tutorial 1, the primary key for a table uniquely identifies each record in a table.

Understanding the Importance of the Primary Key	InSight

Although Access does not require a table to have a primary key, including a primary key offers several advantages:

- A primary key uniquely identifies each record in a table.
- Access does not allow duplicate values in the primary key field. For example, if a record already exists in the Contract table with a Contract Num value of 3020, Access prevents you from adding another record with this same value in the Contract Num field. Preventing duplicate values ensures the uniqueness of the primary key field.
- When a primary key has been specified, Access forces you to enter a value for the primary key field in every record in the table. This is known as **entity integrity**. If you do not enter a value for a field, you have actually given the field a **null value**. You cannot give a null value to the primary key field because entity integrity prevents Access from accepting and processing that record.
- Access stores records on disk as you enter them. You can enter records in any order, but Access displays them by default in order by the field values of the primary key. If you enter records in no specific order, you are ensured that you will later be able to work with them in a more meaningful, primary key sequence.
- Access responds faster to your requests for specific records based on the primary key.

According to Oren's design, you need to specify Invoice Num as the primary key for the Invoice table. You can do so while the table is in Design view.

Specifying a Primary Key in Design View	Reference Window

- In the Table window in Design view, click in the row for the field you've chosen to be the primary key. If the primary key will consist of two or more fields, click the row selector for the first field, press and hold down the Ctrl key, and then click the row selector for each additional primary key field.
- In the Tools group on the Table Tools Design tab, click the Primary Key button.

To specify Invoice Num as the primary key:

▶ **1.** Click in the row for the Invoice Num field to make it the current field.

▶ **2.** In the Tools group on the Table Tools Design tab, click the **Primary Key** button. A key symbol appears in the row selector for the first row, indicating that the Invoice Num field is the table's primary key. See Figure 2-18.

Figure 2-18 **Invoice Num field selected as the primary key**

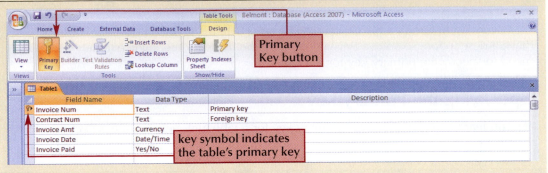

The Primary Key button works as a toggle; you can click it to remove the key symbol from the selected field if you want to specify a different field as the primary key.

You've defined the fields for the Invoice table and specified its primary key, so you can now save the table structure.

Saving the Table Structure

The last step in creating a table is to name the table and save the table's structure. When you save a table structure, the table is stored in the database file (in this case, the Belmont database file). Once the table is saved, you can use it to enter data in the table. According to Oren's plan, you need to save the table you've defined as "Invoice."

To name and save the Invoice table:

► 1. Click the **Save** button 🔲 on the Quick Access Toolbar. The Save As dialog box opens.

► 2. Type **Invoice** in the Table Name text box, and then press the **Enter** key. Access saves the table with the name Invoice in the Belmont database. Notice that the tab for the table now displays the name "Invoice" instead of Table1.

Modifying the Structure of an Access Table

Even a well-designed table might need to be modified. Access allows you to modify a table's structure in Design view: you can change the order of fields, add and delete fields, and change field properties.

After meeting with Sarah Fisher, the office manager at Belmont Landscapes, and reviewing the structure of the Invoice table, Oren has changes he wants you to make to the table. First, he wants the Invoice Amt field to be moved so that it appears right before the Invoice Paid field. Then, he wants you to add a new Text field, named Invoice Item, to the table to include information about what the invoice is for, such as schematic landscape plans, construction documents, and so on. Oren would like the Invoice Item field to be inserted between the Invoice Date and Invoice Amt fields.

Moving a Field

To move a field, you use the mouse to drag it to a new location in the Table window in Design view. Next, you'll move the Invoice Amt field so that it is before the Invoice Paid field.

To move the Invoice Amt field:

▸ **1.** Position the pointer on the row selector for the Invoice Amt field until the pointer changes to a ➡ shape.

▸ **2.** Click the **row selector** to select the entire Invoice Amt row.

▸ **3.** Place the pointer on the row selector for the Invoice Amt field, click the ⬚ pointer, and then drag the ⬚ pointer to the row selector for the Invoice Paid field. See Figure 2-19.

Moving the Invoice Amt field in the table structure — **Figure 2-19**

▸ **4.** Release the mouse button. Access moves the Invoice Amt field between the Invoice Date and Invoice Paid fields in the table structure.

Trouble? If the Invoice Amt field did not move, repeat Steps 1 through 4, making sure you hold down the mouse button during the drag operation.

Adding a Field

Next, you need to add the Invoice Item field to the table structure between the Invoice Date and Invoice Amt fields. To add a new field between existing fields, you must insert a row. You begin by selecting the field that will be below the new field you want to insert.

Adding a Field Between Two Existing Fields | Reference Window

- In the Table window in Design view, select the row for the field above which you want to add a new field.
- In the Tools group on the Table Tools Design tab, click the Insert Rows button.
- Define the new field by entering the field name, data type, optional description, and any property specifications.

To add the Invoice Item field to the Invoice table:

▸ **1.** Click in the Field Name box for the Invoice Amt field. You need to establish this field as the current field so that the row for the new record will be inserted above this field.

▸ **2.** In the Tools group on the Table Tools Design tab, click the **Insert Rows** button. Access adds a new, blank row between the Invoice Date and Invoice Amt fields. The insertion point is positioned in the Field Name box for the new row, ready for you to type the name for the new field. See Figure 2-20.

Figure 2-20 **Table structure after inserting a row**

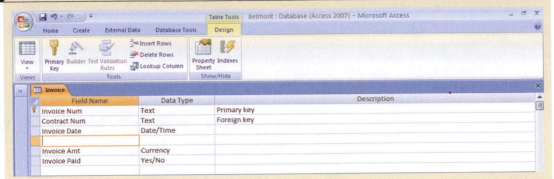

You'll define the Invoice Item field in the new row of the Invoice table. This field will be a Text field with a Field Size of 40.

▶ 3. Type **Invoice Item**, press the **Tab** key to move to the Data Type property, and then press the **Tab** key again to accept the default Text data type and to move to the Description property.

▶ 4. Press the **F6** key to move to the Field Size property and to select the default field size, and then type **40**. The definition of the new field is complete. See Figure 2-21.

Figure 2-21 **Invoice Item field added to the Invoice table**

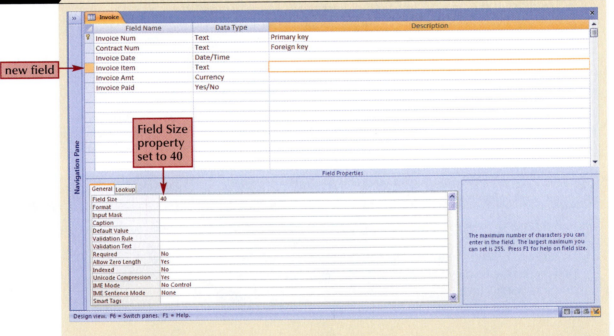

▶ 5. Click the **Save** button on the Quick Access Toolbar to save the changes to the Invoice table structure.

Changing Field Properties

With the Invoice table design complete, you can now go back and modify the Field Size property for the three Text fields in the Contract table. Recall that each of these fields still has the default field size of 255, which is too large for the data contained in these fields.

To modify the Field Size property of the Contract table's Text fields:

▶ 1. Click the **Close 'Invoice'** button ☒ on the table window bar to close the Invoice table.

▶ 2. On the Navigation Pane, click the **Shutter Bar Open/Close Button** ⏩ to open the pane. Notice that the Invoice table is listed below the bar containing the word "Invoice." Because the Navigation Pane is set to All Tables view, the pane organizes objects by table and displays each table name in its own bar. See Figure 2-22.

Navigation Pane with two tables ◀ Figure 2-22

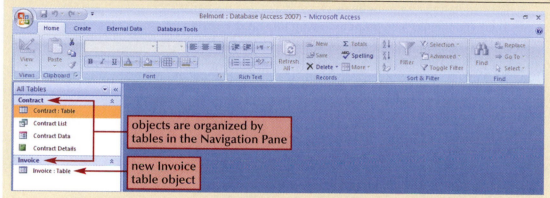

objects are organized by tables in the Navigation Pane

new Invoice table object

▶ 3. Double-click **Contract : Table** to open the Contract table in Datasheet view. To change the Field Size property, you need to display the table in Design view.

▶ 4. In the Views group on the Home tab, click the **View** button. The table is displayed in Design view with the Contract Num field selected. You need to change the Field Size property for this field to 4, because each contract number at Belmont Landscapes consists of four digits.

▶ 5. Press the **F6** key to move to and select the default setting of 255 for the Field Size property, and then type **4**.

Next you need to set the Customer ID Field Size property to 5, because each Customer ID number at Belmont Landscapes consists of five digits.

▶ 6. Click in the **Customer ID** Field Name box to make this the active field, press the **F6** key, and then type **5**.

Finally, for the Contract Type field, you will set the Field Size property to 75. This size can accommodate the values for the Contract Type field, some of which are lengthy.

▶ 7. Click in the **Contract Type** Field Name box, press the **F6** key, and then type **75**. Now you can save the modified table.

▶ 8. Click the **Save** button 🖫 on the Quick Access Toolbar. A dialog box opens informing you that some data may be lost because you decreased the field sizes. Because you know that all of the values in the Contract Num, Customer ID, and Contract Type fields include fewer characters than the new Field Size properties that you set for each field, you can ignore this message.

▶ 9. Click the **Yes** button, and then close the Contract table.

▶ 10. If you are not continuing to Session 2.2, click the **Close** button ☒ on the program window title bar. Access closes the Belmont database, and then the Access program closes.

You have created the Invoice table and made modifications to its design. In the next session, you'll add records to the Invoice table and create the new Customer table in the Belmont database.

Review	**Session 2.1 Quick Check**

1. What guidelines should you follow when designing a database?
2. What is the purpose of the Data Type property for a field?
3. For which three types of fields can you assign a field size?
4. The default Field Size property setting for a Text field is _____ .
5. In Design view, which key do you press to move from the Table Design grid to the Field Properties pane?
6. A(n) _____ value, which results when you do not enter a value for a field, is not permitted for a primary key.

Session 2.2

Adding Records to a New Table

The Invoice table design is complete. Now, Oren would like you to add records to the table so it will contain the invoice data for Belmont Landscapes. You add records to a table in Datasheet view as you did in Tutorial 1, by typing the field values in the rows below the column headings for the fields. You'll begin by entering the records shown in Figure 2-23.

Figure 2-23	Records to be added to the Invoice table

Invoice Num	Contract Num	Invoice Date	Invoice Item	Invoice Amt	Invoice Paid
2011	3011	03/23/2010	Schematic Plan	$1,500.00	Yes
2031	3020	04/19/2010	Schematic Plan	$1,500.00	Yes
2073	3023	09/21/2012	Construction Observation	$10,000.00	No
2062	3026	09/12/2011	Permitting	$10,000.00	No

To add the first record to the Invoice table:

▶ 1. If you took a break after the previous session, make sure that the **Belmont** database is open, and the Navigation Pane is open.

▶ 2. In the Navigation Pane, double-click **Invoice : Table** to open the Invoice table in Datasheet view.

▶ 3. Close the Navigation Pane, and then use the ✥ pointer to resize each column so that the field names are completely visible.

▶ 4. In the Invoice Num field, type **2011**, press the **Tab** key, type **3011** in the Contract Num field, and then press the **Tab** key.

Next you need to enter the Invoice Date field value. Recall that you specified a custom date format, mm/dd/yyyy, for this field. You do not need to type each digit; for example, you can type just "3" instead of "03" for the month, and you can type "10" instead of "2010" for the year. Access will display the full value according to the custom date format.

5. Type **3/23/10**, press the **Tab** key, type **Schematic Plan** in the Invoice Item field, and then press the **Tab** key. Notice that Access displays the date "03/23/2010" in the Invoice Date field.

Next you need to enter the Invoice Amt value for the first record. This is a Currency field with the Currency format and two decimal places specified. Because of the field's set properties, you do not need to type the dollar sign, comma, or zeroes for the decimal places; Access will display these items automatically for you.

6. Type **1500** and then press the **Tab** key. Access displays the value as "$1,500.00."

The last field in the table, Invoice Paid, is a Yes/No field. Notice the check box displayed in the field. By default, the value for any Yes/No field is "No"; therefore, the check box is initially empty. For Yes/No fields with check boxes, you press the Tab key to leave the check box unchecked, and you press the spacebar to insert a check mark in the check box. For the record you are entering in the Invoice table, the invoice has been paid, so you need to insert a check mark in the check box.

7. Press the **spacebar** to insert a check mark, and then press the **Tab** key. The values for the first record are entered. See Figure 2-24.

First record entered in the Invoice table ◄ **Figure 2-24**

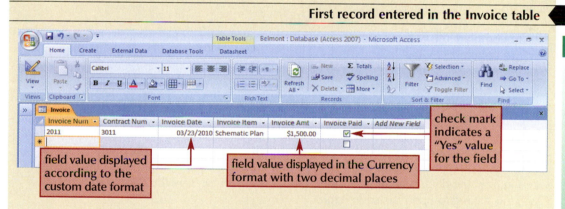

field value displayed according to the custom date format

field value displayed in the Currency format with two decimal places

check mark indicates a "Yes" value for the field

Tip

The spacebar works as a toggle for check boxes in Yes/No fields; you press the spacebar to insert a check mark in an empty check box and to remove an existing check mark. You can also change a check box to select it or deselect it by clicking it with the mouse.

Now you can add the remaining three records. As you do, you'll learn a shortcut for inserting the value from the same field in the previous record.

To add the next three records to the Invoice table:

1. Refer to Figure 2-23 and enter the values for the second record's Invoice Num, Contract Num, and Invoice Date fields.

Notice the value for the second record's Invoice Item field, "Schematic Plan." This value is the exact same value as this field in the first record. You can quickly insert the value from the same field in the previous record using the **Ctrl + '** (apostrophe) keyboard shortcut.

2. In the Invoice Item field, press the **Ctrl + '** keys. Access inserts the value "Schematic Plan" in the Invoice Item field for the second record.

3. Press the **Tab** key to move to the Invoice Amt field. Again, the value you need to enter for this field—$1,500.00—is the same as the value for this field in the previous record. So, you can use the keyboard shortcut again.

4. In the Invoice Amt field, press the **Ctrl + '** keys. Access inserts the value $1,500.00 in the Invoice Amt field for the second record.

5. Press the **Tab** key to move to the Invoice Paid field, press the **spacebar** to insert a check mark in the check box, and then press the **Tab** key. The second record is entered in the Invoice table.

> **6.** Refer to Figure 2-23 to enter the values for the third and fourth records, using the Ctrl + ' keys to enter the fourth record's Invoice Amt value. Also, for both records, the invoices have not been paid. Therefore, be sure to press the Tab key to leave the Invoice Paid field values unchecked (signifying "No").

> **7.** Resize the columns, as necessary, so that all field values are completely visible. Your table should look like the one in Figure 2-25.

| Figure 2-25 | Invoice table with four records added |

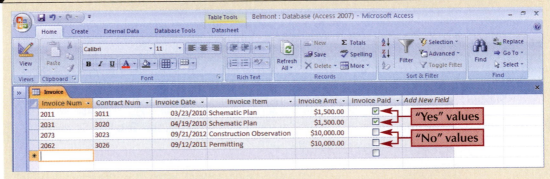

To complete the entry of records in the Invoice table, you'll use a method that allows you to import the data.

Importing Data from an Excel Worksheet

Often, the data you want to add to an Access table exists in another file, such as a Word document or an Excel workbook. You can bring the data from other files into Access in different ways. For example, you can copy and paste the data from an open file, or you can **import** the data, which is a process that allows you to copy the data from a source without having to open the source file.

Oren had been using Excel to track invoice data for Belmont Landscapes and already created a worksheet, named "Invoices," containing this data. You'll import this Excel worksheet into your Invoice table to complete the entry of data in the table. To use the import method, the columns in the Excel worksheet must match the names and data types of the fields in the Access table. The Invoices worksheet contains the following columns: Invoice Num, Contract Num, Invoice Date, Invoice Item, Invoice Amt, and Invoice Paid. These column headings match the fields names in the Invoice table exactly, so you can import the data. Before you import data into a table, you need to close the table.

To import the Invoices worksheet into the Invoice table:

> **1.** Click the **Close 'Invoice'** button ☒ on the table window bar to close the Invoice table. A dialog box opens asking if you want to save the changes to the table layout. This dialog box opens because you resized the table columns.

> **2.** Click the **Yes** button in the dialog box.

> **Trouble?** If your instructor has asked you to omit spaces in field names in the tables you create, including the Invoice table, you'll first need to modify the Invoices.xlsx Excel file to remove the spaces in the column headings (for example, change "Invoice Num" to "InvoiceNum") before you import the worksheet in the following steps. The column headings in the Excel worksheet must match the field names in the Access table in order for the import process to work correctly. If your field names match those shown in the text, then you do not have to modify the Excel file and can proceed with these steps. See your instructor if you have any questions about the field names in your Access tables.

> **3.** Click the **External Data** tab on the Ribbon.

> **4.** In the Import group on the External Data tab, click the **Excel** button (with the ScreenTip "Import Excel spreadsheet"). The Get External Data - Excel Spreadsheet dialog box opens. See Figure 2-26.

Get External Data - Excel Spreadsheet dialog box | **Figure 2-26**

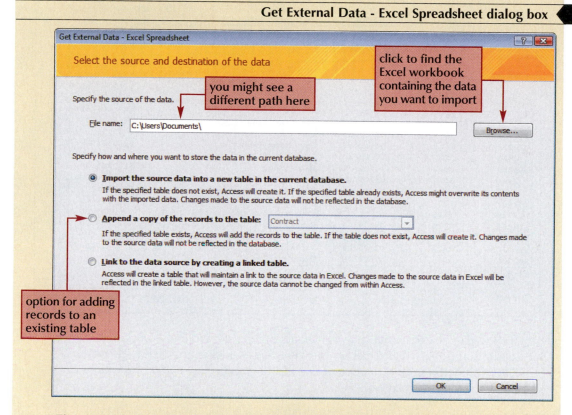

The dialog box provides options for importing the entire worksheet as a new table in the current database, adding the data from the worksheet to an existing table, or linking the data in the worksheet to the table. You need to add, or append, the worksheet data to the Invoice table.

> **5.** Click the **Browse** button. The File Open dialog box opens. The Excel workbook file is named "Invoices" and is located in the Level.01\Tutorial folder provided with your Data Files.

> **6.** Navigate to the **Level.01\Tutorial** folder, where your starting Data Files are stored, and then double-click the **Invoices** Excel file. You return to the dialog box.

> **7.** Click the **Append a copy of the records to the table** option button. The list box to the right of this option becomes active. Next, you need to select the table to which you want to add the data.

> **8.** Click the **arrow** on the list box, and then click **Invoice**.

> **9.** Click the **OK** button. The first Import Spreadsheet Wizard dialog box opens. See Figure 2-27.

Figure 2-27 | **First Import Spreadsheet Wizard dialog box**

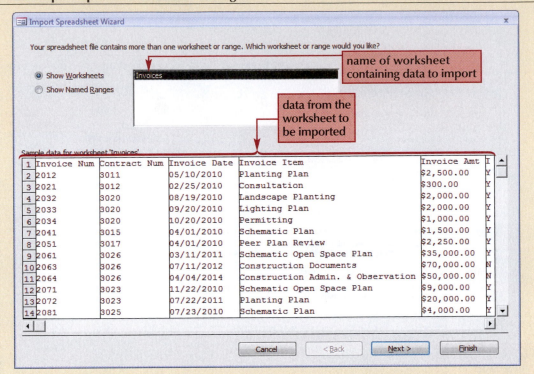

The dialog box shows all the worksheets in the selected Excel workbook. In this case, the Invoices workbook contains only one worksheet, which is also named "Invoices." The bottom section of the dialog box displays some of the data contained in the selected worksheet.

▶ **10.** Click the **Next** button. The second Import Spreadsheet Wizard dialog box opens and indicates that the column headings from the Invoices worksheet will be used as field names in the table.

▶ **11.** Click the **Next** button. The third, and final, Import Spreadsheet Wizard dialog box opens. Notice that the Import to Table text box shows that the data from the spreadsheet will be imported into the Invoice table.

▶ **12.** Click the **Finish** button. A dialog box opens asking if you want to save the import steps. If you needed to repeat this same import procedure many times, it would be a good idea to save the steps for the procedure. However, you don't need to save these steps because you'll be importing the data only this one time. Once the data is in the Access table, Oren will no longer use Excel to track invoice data.

▶ **13.** Click the **Close** button in the dialog box to close it without saving the steps.

The data from the Invoices worksheet has been added to the Invoice table. Next, you'll open the table to view the new records.

To open the Invoice table and view the imported data:

▶ **1.** Open the Navigation Pane, and then double-click **Invoice : Table** to open the table in Datasheet view.

2. Resize the Invoice Item column so that all field values are fully displayed. Notice that the table now contains a total of 176 records—four records you entered plus 172 records imported from the Invoices worksheet. The records are displayed in primary key order by the values in the Invoice Num field. See Figure 2-28.

Invoice table after importing data from Excel | Figure 2-28

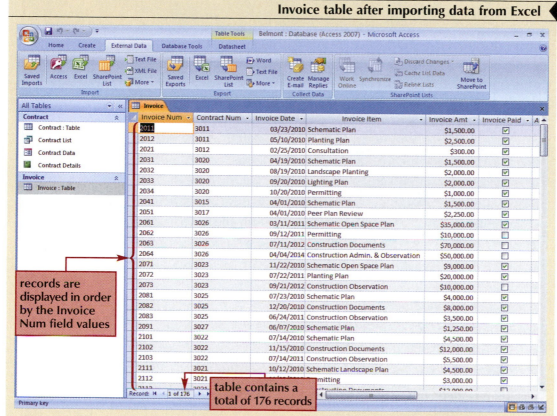

3. Save and close the Invoice table, and then close the Navigation Pane.

Two of the tables—Contract and Invoice—are now complete. According to Oren's plan for the Belmont database, you need to create a third table, named "Customer," to track data about Belmont Landscapes' residential and commercial customers. You'll use a different method to create this table.

Creating a Table by Importing an Existing Table Structure

If another Access database contains a table—or even just the design, or structure, of a table—that you want to include in your database, you can easily import the table and any records it contains or import only the table structure into your database.

Oren documented the design for the new Customer table by listing each field's name, data type, size (if applicable), and description, as shown in Figure 2-29. Note that each field in the Customer table will be a Text field, and the Customer ID field will be the table's primary key.

Figure 2-29 ▶ **Design for the Customer table**

Field Name	Data Type	Field Size	Description
Customer ID	Text	5	Primary key
Company	Text	50	
Last Name	Text	25	Contact's last name
First Name	Text	20	Contact's first name
Phone	Text	14	
Address	Text	35	
City	Text	25	
State	Text	2	
Zip	Text	10	
E-mail Address	Text	50	

Sarah already created an Access database containing a Customer table design. She never entered any records into the table because she wasn't sure if the table design was correct. After reviewing the table design, both Sarah and Oren agree that it contains many of the fields Oren wants to track, but that some changes are needed. Therefore, you can import the table structure in Sarah's database to create the Customer table in the Belmont database, and then modify it to produce the final table structure Oren wants.

To create the Customer table by importing the structure of another table:

▶ **1.** Make sure the **External Data** tab is the active tab on the Ribbon.

▶ **2.** In the Import group, click the **Access** button. The Get External Data - Access Database dialog box opens. This dialog box is similar to the one you used earlier when importing the Excel spreadsheet.

▶ **3.** Click the **Browse** button. The File Open dialog box opens. The Access database file from which you need to import the table structure is named "Sarah" and is located in the Level.01\Tutorial folder provided with your Data Files.

▶ **4.** Navigate to the **Level.01\Tutorial** folder, where your starting Data Files are stored, and then double-click the **Sarah** database file. You return to the dialog box.

▶ **5.** Make sure the **Import tables, queries, forms, reports, macros, and modules into the current database** option button is selected, and then click the **OK** button. The Import Objects dialog box opens. The dialog box contains tabs for importing all the different types of Access database objects—tables, queries, forms, and so on. The Tables tab is the current tab.

▶ **6.** Click the **Options** button in the dialog box to see all the options for importing tables. See Figure 2-30.

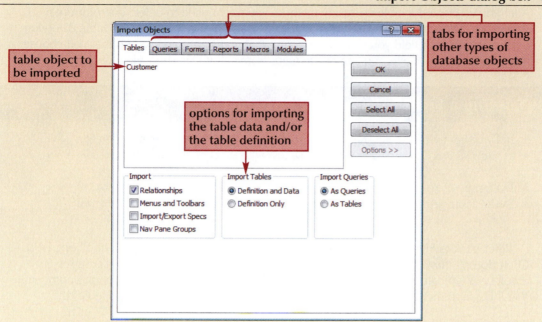

Import Objects dialog box   Figure 2-30

Note the Import Tables section of the dialog box, which contains options for importing the definition and data—that is, the structure of the table and any records contained in the table—or the definition only. You need to import only the structure of the Customer table Sarah created.

▶ **7.** On the Tables tab, click **Customer** to select this table.

▶ **8.** In the Import Tables section of the dialog box, click the **Definition Only** option button, and then click the **OK** button. Access creates the Customer table in the Belmont database using the structure of the Customer table in the Sarah database, and opens a dialog box asking if you want to save the import steps.

▶ **9.** Click the **Close** button to close the dialog box without saving the import steps.

▶ **10.** Open the Navigation Pane and note that the Customer table is listed.

▶ **11.** Double-click **Customer : Table** to open the table, and then close the Navigation Pane. See Figure 2-31.

Imported Customer table in Datasheet view   Figure 2-31

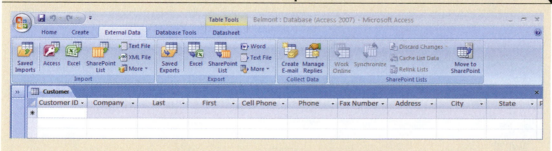

The Customer table opens in Datasheet view. The table contains no records.

The table structure you imported contains more fields than Oren wants to include in the Customer table (see Figure 2-29). Also, he wants to rename and reorder some of the fields. You'll begin to modify the table structure by deleting fields.

Deleting Fields from a Table Structure

After you've created a table using any method, you might need to delete one or more fields. When you delete a field, you also delete all the values for the field from the table. Therefore, before you delete a field you should make sure that you want to do so and that you choose the correct field to delete. You can delete fields from either Datasheet view or Design view.

Reference Window | **Deleting a Field from a Table Structure**

- In Datasheet view, select the column heading for the field you want to delete.
- In the Fields & Columns group on the Datasheet tab, click the Delete button.

or

- In Design view, click in the Field Name box for the field you want to delete.
- In the Tools group on the Table Tools Design tab, click the Delete Rows button.

Refer back to Figure 2-29. Notice that Oren's design does not specify a Cell Phone field. Oren doesn't think it's necessary to track customers' cell phone numbers because his employees typically contact customers using either their home or business phone numbers. You'll begin to modify the Customer table sturcture by deleting the Cell Phone field.

To delete the Cell Phone field from the table in Datasheet view:

▶ **1.** Click the **Datasheet** tab on the Ribbon.

▶ **2.** Click the **Cell Phone** column heading to select the Cell Phone field.

▶ **3.** In the Fields & Columns group on the Datasheet tab, click the **Delete** button. The Cell Phone field is removed.

You can also delete fields from a table structure in Design view. You'll switch to Design view to delete the rest of the unnecessary fields.

To delete the fields in Design view:

▶ **1.** In the Views group on the Datasheet tab, click the **View** button. The Customer table opens in Design view. See Figure 2-32.

Figure 2-32 ▶ **Customer table in Design view**

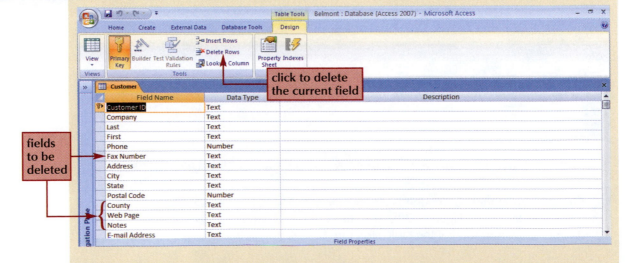

> **2.** Click in the **Fax Number** Field Name box to make it the current field.

> **3.** In the Tools group on the Table Tools Design tab, click the **Delete Rows** button. The Fax Number field is removed from the Customer table structure.
>
> You'll delete the County, Web Page, and Notes fields next. Instead of deleting these fields individually, you'll use the pointer to select them and then delete them at the same time.

> **4.** Click and hold down the mouse button on the row selector for the **County** field, and then drag the mouse to select the **Web Page** and **Notes** fields.

> **5.** Release the mouse button. The rows for the three fields are selected.

> **6.** In the Tools group on the Table Tools Design tab, click the **Delete Rows** button. See Figure 2-33.

Customer table after deleting fields | Figure 2-33

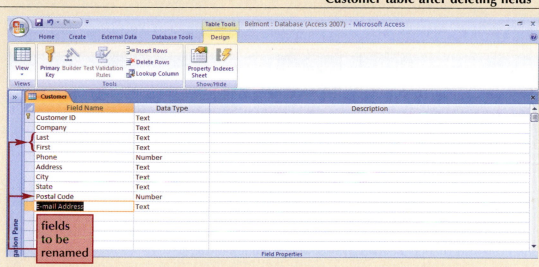

Renaming Fields in Design View

To match Oren's design for the Customer table, you need to rename several fields. In Tutorial 1, you renamed the default primary key field, ID, in Datasheet view. You can also rename fields in Design view by simply editing the names in the Table Design grid.

To rename the fields in Design view:

> **1.** Click to position the insertion point to the right of the word **Last** in the third row's Field Name box, press the **spacebar**, and then type **Name**. The name of the third field is now Last Name.

> **2.** Click to position the insertion point to the right of the word **First** in the fourth row's Field Name box, press the **spacebar**, and then type **Name**. The name of the fourth field is now First Name.
>
> You can also select an entire field name and then type new text to replace it.
>
> **3.** In the ninth field's Field Name box, drag to select the text **Postal Code**, and then type **Zip**. The text you type replaces the original text. See Figure 2-34.

Figure 2-34 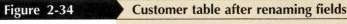 Customer table after renaming fields

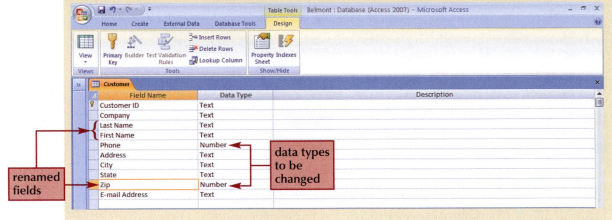

Changing the Data Type for Fields in Design View

According to Oren's plan, all of the fields in the Customer table should be Text fields. The table structure you imported specifies the Number data type for the Phone and the Zip fields. In Tutorial 1, you used an option in Datasheet view to change a field's data type. You can also change the data type for a field in Design view.

To change the data type of the fields in Design view:

> **1.** Click the right side of the **Data Type** box for the Phone field to display the list of data types.
>
> **2.** Click **Text** in the list. The Phone field is now a Text field. Note that, by default, the Field Size property is set to 255. According to Oren's plan, the Phone field should have a Field Size property of 14. You'll make this change next.
>
> **3.** Press the **F6** key to move to and select the default Field Size property, and then type **14**.
>
> **4.** Click the right side of the **Data Type** box for the Zip field, and then click **Text** in the list. The Zip field is now a Text field. According to Oren's plan, you need to change the Field Size property to 10.
>
> **5.** Press the **F6** key to move to and select the default Field Size property, and then type **10**.

Finally, Oren would like descriptions entered for the Customer ID, Last Name, and First Name fields. You'll enter those now.

To enter the Description property values:

▶ **1.** Click in the Description box for the Customer ID field, and then type **Primary key**.

▶ **2.** Press the ↓ key to move to the Description property for the Company field. After you press the ↓ key, a Property Update Options button ⚡ appears near the Description box for the Company field. When you change a field's property in Design view, you can use this button to update the corresponding property on forms and reports that include the field you've modified. For example, if the Belmont database included a form that contained the Customer ID field, you could choose to **propagate**, or update, the modified Description property in the form by clicking the Property Update Options button, and then choosing the option to make the update everywhere the field is used. The text on the Property Update Options button varies depending on the task; in this case, if you click the button, the option is "Update Status Bar Text everywhere Customer ID is used."

Because the Belmont database does not include any forms or reports that are based on the Customer table, you do not need to update the properties, so you can ignore the button for now.

▶ **3.** Press the ↓ key to move to the Description box for the Last Name field, and then type **Contact's last name**.

▶ **4.** Press the ↓ key to move to the Description box for the First Name field, and then type **Contact's first name**. See Figure 2-35.

Customer table after changing data types and entering descriptions ◀ **Figure 2-35**

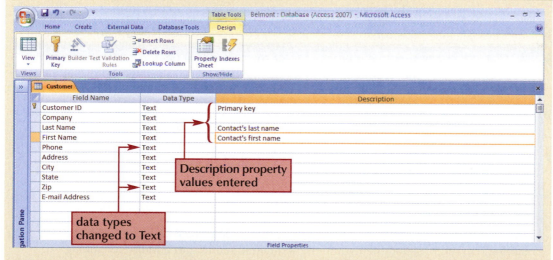

▶ **5.** Click the **Save** button 💾 on the Quick Access Toolbar to save your changes to the Customer table.

▶ **6.** In the Views group on the Table Tools Design tab, click the **View** button to display the table in Datasheet view. See Figure 2-36.

Figure 2-36

Modified Customer table in Datasheet view

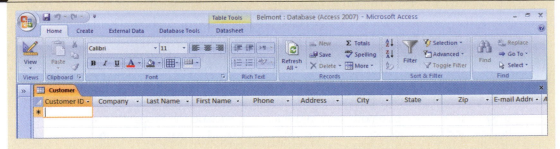

After viewing the Customer table datasheet, Oren decides that he would like the First Name field to appear before the Last Name field. Earlier in this tutorial, when you created the Invoice table, you learned how to change the order of fields in Design view. Although you can reorder fields in Datasheet view by dragging a field's column heading to a new location, doing so rearranges only the *display* of the table's fields; the table structure is not changed. To move a field, you must display the table in Design view.

To move the Last Name field to follow the First Name field:

1. In the Views group on the Datasheet tab, click the **View** button. The Customer table opens in Design view.

2. Position the pointer on the row selector for the Last Name field until the pointer changes to a ➡ shape.

3. Click the **row selector** to select the entire row for the Last Name field.

4. Place the pointer on the row selector for the Last Name field, click the ⬇ pointer, and then drag the ⬇ pointer down to the line below the row selector for the First Name field.

5. Release the mouse button. The Last Name field now appears below the First Name field in the table structure.

6. Click the **Save** button 🖫 on the Quick Access Toolbar to save the change to the Customer table design.

7. Display the table in Datasheet view.

With the Customer table design set, you can now enter records in it. You'll begin by entering two records, and then you'll use a different method to add the remaining records.

To add two records to the Customer table:

1. Enter the following values for the fields in the first record (these values are for a residential customer with no company name):

   Customer ID = **11001**
   Company = [do not enter a value; leave blank]
   First Name = **Sharon**
   Last Name = **Maloney**
   Phone = **616-866-3901**
   Address = **49 Blackstone Dr**
   City = **Rockford**

State = **MI**
Zip = **49341**
E-mail Address = **smaloney2@milocal123.com**

2. Enter the following values for the fields in the second record, for a commercial customer:

Customer ID = **11012**
Company = **Grand Rapids Engineering Dept.**
First Name = **Anthony**
Last Name = **Rodriguez**
Phone = **616-454-9801**
Address = **225 Summer St**
City = **Grand Rapids**
State = **MI**
Zip = **49503**
E-mail Address = **arod24@gred11.gov**

3. Close the Customer table.

Before Belmont Landscapes decided to store data using Access, Sarah managed the company's customer data in a different system. She exported that data into a text file and asks you to import it into the new Customer table. You can import the data contained in this text file to add the remaining records to the Customer table.

Adding Data to a Table by Importing a Text File

There are many ways to import data into an Access database. So far, you've learned how to add data to an Access table by importing an Excel spreadsheet, and you've created a new table by importing the structure of an existing table. You can also import data contained in text files.

To complete the entry of records in the Customer table, you'll import the data contained in Sarah's text file. The file is named Customer.txt and is located in the Level.01\Tutorial folder provided with your Data Files.

To import the data contained in the Customer.txt file:

1. Click the **External Data** tab on the Ribbon.

2. In the Import group, click the **Text File** button (with the ScreenTip "Import text file"). The Get External Data - Text File dialog box opens. This dialog box is similar to the one you used earlier when importing the Excel spreadsheet and the Access table structure.

3. Click the **Browse** button. The File Open dialog box opens.

4. Navigate to the **Level.01\Tutorial** folder, where your starting Data Files are stored, and then double-click the **Customer** text file. You return to the dialog box.

5. Click the **Append a copy of the records to the table** option button. The list box to the right of this option becomes active. Next, you need to select the table to which you want to add the data.

6. Click the **arrow** on the list box, and then click **Customer**.

▶ 7. Click the **OK** button. The first Import Text Wizard dialog box opens. The dialog box indicates that the data to be imported is in a "Delimited" format. A **delimited** text file is one in which fields of data are separated by a character such as a comma or a tab. In this case, the dialog box shows that data is separated by the comma character in the text file.

▶ 8. Make sure the **Delimited** option button is selected in the dialog box, and then click the **Next** button. The second Import Text Wizard dialog box opens. See Figure 2-37.

Figure 2-37 ▶ **Second Import Text Wizard dialog box**

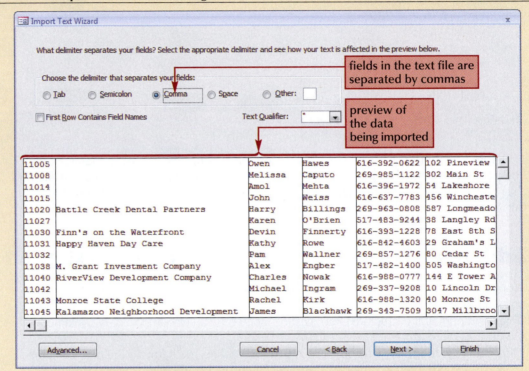

This dialog box asks you to confirm the delimiter character that separates the fields in the text file you're importing. Access detects that the comma character is used in the Customer text file and selects this option. The bottom area of the dialog box gives you a preview of the data you're importing.

▶ 9. Make sure the **Comma** option button is selected, and then click the **Next** button. The third, and final, Import Text Wizard dialog box opens. Notice that the Import to Table text box shows that the data from the text file will be imported into the Customer table.

▶ 10. Click the **Finish** button. A dialog box opens asking if you want to save the import steps. You'll only import the customer data once, so you can close the dialog box without saving the import steps.

▶ 11. Click the **Close** button in the dialog box to close it without saving the import steps.

Oren asks you to open the Customer table in Datasheet view so he can see the results of importing the text file.

To view the Customer table datasheet:

▶ **1.** Open the Navigation Pane, and then double-click **Customer : Table** to open the Customer table in Datasheet view. The Customer table contains a total of 40 records.

▶ **2.** Close the Navigation Pane.

Next, you need to resize all the columns in the datasheet, both to make sure all the field values are fully displayed and to reduce the width of any fields that are wider than the values they contain, such as the Zip field. When you resize a column by double-clicking the pointer on the column dividing line, you are sizing the column to its **best fit**—that is, so the column is just wide enough to display the longest visible value in the column, including the field name.

▶ **3.** Resize all the columns to their best fit, scrolling the table datasheet as necessary. When finished, scroll back to display the first fields in the table. See Figure 2-38.

Customer table after importing data from the text file ◀ **Figure 2-38**

Tip

When you resize a column to its best fit, only the visible field values are affected. You must scroll down the datasheet to make sure all field values for the entire column are fully displayed, resizing as you scroll, if necessary.

▶ **4.** Save and close the Customer table, and then open the Navigation Pane.

The Belmont database now contains three tables—Contract, Invoice, and Customer—and the tables contain all the necessary records. Your final task is to complete the database design by defining the necessary relationships between its tables.

Defining Table Relationships

One of the most powerful features of a relational database management system is its ability to define relationships between tables. You use a common field to relate one table to another. The process of relating tables is often called performing a **join**. When you join tables that have a common field, you can extract data from them as if they were one larger table. For example, you can join the Customer and Contract tables by using the Customer ID field in both tables as the common field. Then you can use a query, form, or report to extract selected data from each table, even though the data is contained in two separate tables, as shown in Figure 2-39. In the Customer Contracts query shown in Figure 2-39, the Customer ID, Company, First Name, and Last Name columns are fields from the Customer table, and the Contract Num and Contract Amt columns are fields from the Contract table. The joining of records is based on the common field of Customer ID. The Customer and Contract tables have a type of relationship called a one-to-many relationship.

Figure 2-39 **One-to-many relationship and sample query**

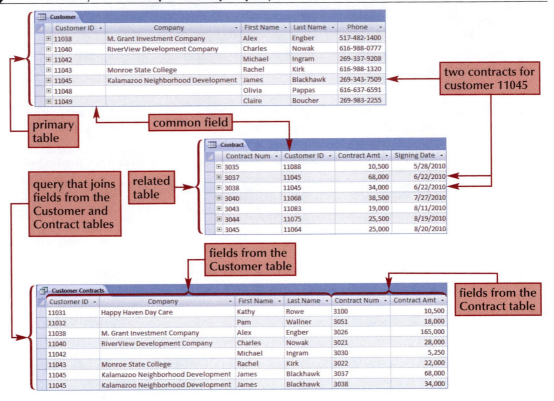

One-to-Many Relationships

A **one-to-many relationship** exists between two tables when one record in the first table matches zero, one, or many records in the second table, and when one record in the second table matches at most one record in the first table. For example, as shown in Figure 2-39, customer 11045 has two contracts in the Contract table. Other customers have one or more contracts. Every contract has a single matching customer.

Access refers to the two tables that form a relationship as the primary table and the related table. The **primary table** is the "one" table in a one-to-many relationship; in Figure 2-39, the Customer table is the primary table because there is only one customer for each contract. The **related table** is the "many" table; in Figure 2-39, the Contract table is the related table because a customer can have zero, one, or many contracts.

Because related data is stored in two tables, inconsistencies between the tables can occur. Consider the following scenarios:

- Oren adds a record to the Contract table for a new customer, Taylor McNulty, using Customer ID 12050. Oren did not first add the new customer's information to the Customer table, so this contract does not have a matching record in the Customer table. The data is inconsistent, and the contract record is considered to be an **orphaned record**.
- Oren changes the Customer ID in the Customer table for Kalamazoo Neighborhood Development from 11045 to 12090. Because there is no customer 11045 in the Customer table, this change creates two orphaned records in the Contract table, and the database is inconsistent.

- Oren deletes the record for Kalamazoo Neighborhood Development, customer 11045, from the Customer table because this customer no longer does business with Belmont Landscapes. The database is again inconsistent; two records for customer 11045 in the Contract table have no matching record in the Customer table.

You can avoid these problems by specifying referential integrity between tables when you define their relationships.

Referential Integrity

Referential integrity is a set of rules that Access enforces to maintain consistency between related tables when you update data in a database. Specifically, the referential integrity rules are as follows:

- When you add a record to a related table, a matching record must already exist in the primary table, thereby preventing the possibility of orphaned records.
- If you attempt to change the value of the primary key in the primary table, Access prevents this change if matching records exist in a related table. However, if you choose the **cascade updates option**, Access permits the change in value to the primary key and changes the appropriate foreign key values in the related table, thereby eliminating the possibility of inconsistent data.
- When you attempt to delete a record in the primary table, Access prevents the deletion if matching records exist in a related table. However, if you choose the **cascade deletes option**, Access deletes the record in the primary table and also deletes all records in related tables that have matching foreign key values.

Understanding the Cascade Deletes Option	InSight

Although there are advantages to using the cascade deletes option for enforcing referential integrity, its use does present risks as well. You should rarely select the cascade deletes option, because setting this option might cause you to inadvertently delete records you did not intend to delete. It is best to use other methods for deleting records that give you more control over the deletion process.

Now you'll define a one-to-many relationship between the Customer (primary) and Contract (related) tables. You will also define a one-to-many relationship between the Contract (primary) table and the Invoice (related) table.

Defining a Relationship Between Two Tables

When two tables have a common field, you can define a relationship between them in the Relationships window. The **Relationships window** illustrates the relationships among a database's tables. Using this window, you can view or change existing relationships, define new relationships between tables, and rearrange the layout of the tables in the window.

You need to open the Relationships window and define the relationship between the Customer and Contract tables. You'll define a one-to-many relationship between the two tables, with Customer as the primary table and Contract as the related table, and with Customer ID as the common field (the primary key in the Customer table and a foreign key in the Contract table). You'll also define a one-to-many relationship between the Contract and Invoice tables, with Contract as the primary table and Invoice as the related table, and with Contract Num as the common field (the primary key in the Contract table and a foreign key in the Invoice table).

To define the one-to-many relationship between the Customer and Contract tables:

1. Click the **Database Tools** tab on the Ribbon.

2. In the Show/Hide group on the Database Tools tab, click the **Relationships** button. The Show Table dialog box opens. See Figure 2-40.

Figure 2-40 **Show Table dialog box**

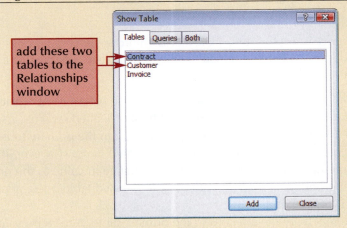

You must add each table participating in a relationship to the Relationships window. Because the Customer table is the primary table in the relationship, you'll add it first.

Tip

You can also double-click a table name in the Show Table dialog box to add it to the Relationships window.

3. Click **Customer**, and then click the **Add** button. The Customer table is added to the Relationships window.

4. Click **Contract**, and then click the **Add** button. The Contract table is added to the Relationships window.

5. Click the **Close** button in the Show Table dialog box to close it.

When you add a table to the Relationships window, the fields in the table appear in a **field list**. So that you can view all the fields and complete field names, you'll resize the Customer table field list.

6. Use the ⬍ pointer to drag the bottom of the Customer table field list to lengthen it until the vertical scroll bar disappears and all the fields are visible. See Figure 2-41.

Figure 2-41 **Field list boxes for the two tables**

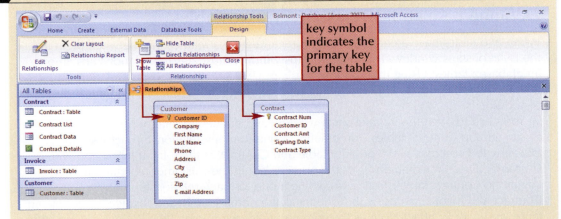

Notice that the key symbol appears next to the Customer ID field in the Customer table field list and next to the Contract Num field in the Contract table field list to indicate that these fields are the primary key fields for their respective tables.

To form the relationship between the two tables, you drag the common field of Customer ID from the primary table to the related table. Then Access opens the Edit Relationships dialog box, in which you select the relationship options for the two tables.

▶ 7. Click **Customer ID** in the Customer field list, and then drag it to **Customer ID** in the Contract field list. When you release the mouse button, the Edit Relationships dialog box opens. See Figure 2-42.

Edit Relationships dialog box ◀ Figure 2-42

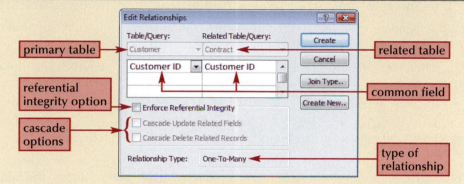

The primary table, related table, and common field appear at the top of the dialog box. The relationship type, One-To-Many, appears at the bottom of the dialog box. When you click the Enforce Referential Integrity check box, the two cascade options become available. If you select the Cascade Update Related Fields option, Access will update the appropriate foreign key values in the related table when you change a primary key value in the primary table. You will not select the Cascade Delete Related Records option, because doing so could cause you to delete records that you do not want to delete; this option is rarely selected.

▶ 8. Click the **Enforce Referential Integrity** check box, and then click the **Cascade Update Related Fields** check box.

▶ 9. Click the **Create** button to define the one-to-many relationship between the two tables and to close the dialog box. The completed relationship appears in the Relationships window. See Figure 2-43.

Defined relationship in the Relationships window ◀ Figure 2-43

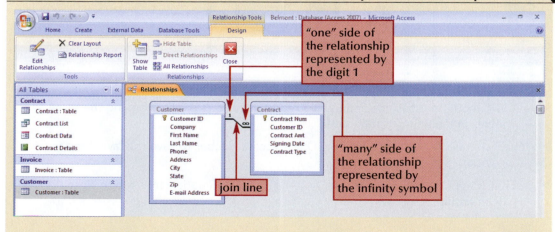

The **join line** connects the Customer ID fields, which are common to the two tables. The common field joins the two tables, which have a one-to-many relationship. The "one" side of the relationship has the digit 1 at its end, and the "many" side of the relationship has the infinity symbol at its end. The two tables are still separate tables, but you can use the data in them as if they were one table.

Now you need to define the one-to-many relationship between the Contract and Invoice tables. In this relationship, Contract is the primary ("one") table because there is at most one contract for each invoice. Invoice is the related ("many") table because there are zero, one, or many invoices set up for each contract, depending on how many project phases are involved for each contract.

To define the relationship between the Contract and Invoice tables:

▶ **1.** In the Relationships group on the Relationship Tools Design tab, click the **Show Table** button. The Show Table dialog box opens.

▶ **2.** Click **Invoice** in the list of tables, click the **Add** button, and then click the **Close** button to close the Show Table dialog box. The Invoice table's field list appears in the Relationships window to the right of the Contract table's field list.

Because the Contract table is the primary table in this relationship, you need to drag the Contract Num field from the Contract field list to the Invoice field list.

▶ **3.** Click and drag the **Contract Num** field in the Contract field list to the **Contract Num** field in the Invoice field list. When you release the mouse button, the Edit Relationships dialog box opens.

▶ **4.** Click the **Enforce Referential Integrity** check box, and then click the **Cascade Update Related Fields** check box.

▶ **5.** Click the **Create** button to define the one-to-many relationship between the two tables and close the dialog box. The completed relationship appears in the Relationships window. See Figure 2-44.

Figure 2-44	Both relationships defined

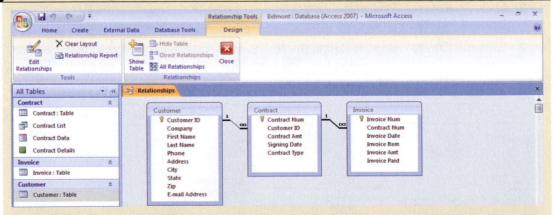

With both relationships defined, you have connected the data among the three tables in the Belmont database.

▶ **6.** Click the **Save** button 🔲 on the Quick Access Toolbar to save the layout in the Relationships window.

▶ **7.** Click the **Close 'Relationships'** button ⊠ on the Relationships tab to close the Relationships window.

▶ 8. Click the **Office Button** 🔘, point to **Manage**, and then click **Compact and Repair Database**. Access compacts the Belmont database.

▶ 9. Click the **Close** button ❎ on the program window title bar. Access closes the Belmont database and then the Access program window closes.

Session 2.2 Quick Check | Review

1. To insert a check mark in an empty check box for a Yes/No field, you press the
   _____ .

2. What is the keyboard shortcut for inserting the value from the same field in the previous record into the current record?

3. _____ data is a process that allows you to copy the data from a source without having to open the source file.

4. What is the effect of deleting a field from a table structure?

5. A(n) _____ text file is one in which fields of data are separated by a character such as a comma or a tab.

6. The _____ is the "one" table in a one-to-many relationship, and the _____ is the "many" table in the relationship.

7. _____ is a set of rules that Access enforces to maintain consistency between related tables when you update data in a database.

Tutorial Summary | Review

In this tutorial, you learned some important guidelines for designing databases and tables and for setting field properties. You put these guidelines into practice by creating two tables—one in Design view, and another by importing the structure of an existing table. You worked in Design view to define fields, set properties, specify a table's primary key, and modify a table's structure. To complete the first table, you imported data from an Excel worksheet into the table. After creating the second table, you deleted, renamed, and moved fields in the table structure. To complete the second table, you imported data from a text file into the table. This tutorial also presented one of the most important database concepts—defining table relationships. You learned how to define a one-to-many relationship between two tables in a database and how to enforce referential integrity as part of the relationship.

Key Terms

best fit	Double	one-to-many relationship
Byte	entity integrity	orphaned record
cascade deletes option	F1 key	primary table
cascade updates option	F6 key	propagate
composite key	field list	properties
Ctrl + '	Field Properties pane	referential integrity
data redundancy	Field Size property	related table
data type	import	Relationships window
Decimal	Integer	Replication ID
Decimal Places property	join	set (a property)
delimited	join line	Single
Description property	Long Integer	Table Design grid
Design view	null value	

| **Review Assignments**

Practice the skills you learned in the tutorial using the same case scenario.

Data Files needed for the Review Assignments: Supplier.accdb *(cont. from Tutorial 1)* **and Goods.xlsx**

In addition to tracking information about the suppliers Belmont Landscapes works with, Oren also wants to track information about their products. He asks you to create a new table in the Supplier database by completing the following:

1. Open the **Supplier** database located in the Level.01\Review folder provided with your Data Files, and then open the **Company** table in Design view.
2. Enter **Primary key** for the Company ID field's Description property.
3. Change the Data Type property for the Zip field to Text.
4. Change the Format property for the Initial Contact Date field to Short Date. Do not propagate the field property changes.
5. Change the Field Size property for each Text field in the table, as follows:
   Company ID = **6**
   Company Name = **50**
   Product Type = **40**
   Address = **35**
   City = **25**
   State = **2**
   Zip = **10**
   Phone = **14**
   Contact First Name = **20**
   Contact Last Name = **25**
6. Save and close the Company table. Click the Yes button when a message appears indicating some data might be lost.
7. Create a new table in Design view, using the table design shown in Figure 2-45.

Figure 2-45

Field Name	Data Type	Description	Field Size	Other
Product ID	Text	Primary key	4	
Company ID	Text	Foreign key	6	
Product Type	Text		35	
Price	Currency			Format = Standard
				Decimal Places = 2
Color	Text		15	
Size	Text		15	
Material	Text		30	
Weight in Lbs	Number		Single	
Discount Offered	Yes/No			

8. Make sure Product ID is specified as the primary key, and then save the table as **Product**.
9. Modify the table structure by adding a new field named **Unit** (Text field, Field Size: 15) between the Price and Color fields. Move the Size field so that it follows the Material field.
10. Enter the records shown in Figure 2-46 in the Product table. When finished, close the Product table.

Figure 2-46

Product ID	Company ID	Product Type	Price	Unit	Color	Material	Size	Weight in Lbs	Discount Offered
5306	GEN359	Pine mulch	23.35	Cubic yard	Dark brown	Softwoods-pine			Y
5013	HOL207	Small bench	712.00	Each	Green	Steel and cast iron	8 x 2 feet	266	N

11. Use the Import Spreadsheet Wizard to add data to the Product table. The data you need to import is contained in the Goods workbook, which is an Excel file located in the Level.01\Review folder provided with your Data Files.
    a. Specify the Goods workbook as the source of the data.
    b. Select the option for appending the data.
    c. Select Product as the table.
    d. In the Import Spreadsheet Wizard dialog boxes, choose the Goods worksheet, make sure Access uses column headings as field names, and import to the Product table. Do not save the import steps.

12. Open the **Product** table and resize all columns to their best fit. Then save and close the Product table.

13. Define a one-to-many relationship between the primary Company table and the related Product table. Select the referential integrity option and the cascade updates option for the relationship.

14. Save the changes to the Relationships window, compact and repair the Supplier database, and then close the database.

| Apply | **Case Problem 1** |

Use the skills you learned in the tutorial to create and modify tables containing data for a small music school.

Data Files needed for this Case Problem: Pinehill.accdb (*cont. from Tutorial 1*), Music.accdb, Lessons.xlsx, and Student.txt

Pine Hill Music School   Yuka Koyama uses the Pinehill database to maintain information about the students, teachers, and contracts for her music school. Yuka asks you to help her build the database by updating one table and creating two new tables. Complete the following:

1. Open the **Pinehill** database located in the Level.01\Case1 folder provided with your Data Files.

2. Open the **Teacher** table, and set field properties as shown in Figure 2-47.

Figure 2-47

Field Name	Data Type	Description	Field Size	Format
Teacher ID	Text	Primary key	7	
First Name	Text		20	
Last Name	Text		25	
Degree	Text		3	
School	Text		50	
Hire Date	Date/Time			Short Date

3. Add a new field as the last field in the Teacher table with the field name **Takes Beginners** and the Yes/No data type.

4. Save the Teacher table. Click the Yes button when a message appears indicating some data might be lost.

5. In the datasheet, resize the Takes Beginners field to best fit, and then specify that the following teachers can take beginners: Schwartz, Romano, Eberle, Norris, Tanaka, Culbertson, and Mueller.

6. Save and close the Teacher table.

7. Yuka created a table named Student in the Music database that is located in the Level.01\Case1 folder provided with your Data Files. Import the structure of the Student table in the Music database into a new table named Student in the Pinehill database. Do not save the import steps.

8. Delete the following fields from the **Student** table: Company, E-mail Address, Business Phone, Fax Number, and Notes.

9. Add two fields to the end of the Student table: **Birth Date** (Date/Time data type) and **Gender** (Text data type).

10. Rename the primary key field, ID, to **Student ID**, and change its data type to Text. Save the Student table.

11. Move the Last Name field so it follows the First Name field.

12. Modify the design of the Student table so that it matches the design in Figure 2-48, including the revised field names. Do not propagate the field property changes.

Figure 2-48

Field Name	Data Type	Description	Field Size
Student ID	Text	Primary key	7
First Name	Text		20
Last Name	Text		25
Address	Text		35
City	Text		25
State	Text		2
Zip	Text		10
Phone	Text		14
Birth Date	Date/Time		Short Date
Gender	Text	F(emale), M(ale)	1

13. Save your changes to the table design, add the records shown in Figure 2-49 to the Student table, and then close the Student table.

Figure 2-49

Student ID	First Name	Last Name	Address	City	State	Zip	Phone	Birth Date	Gender
APP7509	Sam	Applegate	15675 SW Greens Way	Portland	OR	97224	503-968-2245	10/10/1993	M
BAR7544	Andrea	Barreau	7660 SW 135th Ave	Beaverton	OR	97008	503-579-2227	11/28/1996	F

14. Yuka exported the student data that she was maintaining in another computer system to a text file, and she asks you to add this data to the Student table. The data you need to import is contained in the Student text file (located in the Level.01\Case1 folder provided with your Data Files).

   a. Specify the Student text file as the source of the data.

   b. Select the option for appending the data to the table.

   c. Select Student as the table.

   d. In the Import Text Wizard dialog boxes, choose the option to import delimited data, to use a comma delimiter, and to import the data into the Student table. Do not save the import steps.

15. Open the Student table, resize all the columns in the datasheet to their best fit, and then save and close the table.

16. Create a new table in Design view, using the table design shown in Figure 2-50.

Figure 2-50

Field Name	Data Type	Description	Field Size	Other Properties
Contract ID	Text	Primary key	4	
Student ID	Text	Foreign key	7	
Teacher ID	Text	Foreign key	7	
Contract Start Date	Date/Time		Short Date	
Contract End Date	Date/Time		Short Date	
Lesson Type	Text		25	
Lesson Length	Number	30 or 60 minutes	Integer	
Lesson Monthly Cost	Currency			Format: Currency Decimal Places: 0
Monthly Rental Cost	Currency	Monthly rental charge for instrument		Format: Currency Decimal Places: 0

17. Specify Contract ID as the primary key, save the table using the name **Contract**, and then close the table.

18. Use the Import Spreadsheet Wizard to add data to the Contract table. The data you need to import is contained in the Lessons workbook, which is an Excel file located in the Level.01\Case1 folder provided with your Data Files.
    a. Specify the Lessons workbook as the source of the data.
    b. Select the option for appending the data to the table.
    c. Select Contract as the table.
    d. In the Import Spreadsheet Wizard dialog boxes, choose the Sheet1 worksheet, and import to the Contract table. Do not save the import steps.

19. Open the **Contract** table and add the records shown in Figure 2-51. (*Hint*: Use the New button on the Home tab to add a new record.)

Figure 2-51

Contract ID	Student ID	Teacher ID	Contract Start Date	Contract End Date	Lesson Type	Lesson Length	Lesson Monthly Cost	Monthly Rental Cost
3176	VAR7527	91-0178	3/21/2010	3/21/2011	Violin	30	$140	$35
3179	MCE7551	70-4490	6/1/2010	6/1/2011	Guitar	60	$200	$0

20. Resize all the columns in the datasheet to their best fit, and then save and close the Contract table.

21. Define the one-to-many relationships between the database tables as follows: between the primary Student table and the related Contract table, and between the primary Teacher table and the related Contract table. Select the referential integrity option and the cascade updates option for each relationship.

22. Save the changes to the Relationships window, compact and repair the Pinehill database, and then close the database.

| Challenge | **Case Problem 2** |

Challenge yourself by using the Import Spreadsheet Wizard to create a new table to store data about fitness center members.

Data Files needed for this Case Problem: Fitness.accdb (*cont. from Tutorial 1*) and Center.xlsx

Parkhurst Health & Fitness Center   Martha Parkhurst uses the Fitness database to track information about members who join the center and the program in which each member is enrolled. She asks you to help her maintain this database. Complete the following:

1. Open the **Fitness** database located in the Level.01\Case2 folder provided with your Data Files.

2. Open the **Program** table, and change the following field properties:

   Program ID: Type **Primary key** for the description, and change the field size to **3**.

   Monthly Fee: Change the Format property to Standard.

   Physical Required: Change the data type to Yes/No.

3. Save and close the Program table. Click the Yes button when a message appears indicating some data might be lost.

⊕**EXPLORE**   4. Use the Import Spreadsheet Wizard to create a table in the Fitness database. As the source of the data, specify the Center workbook, located in the Level.01\Case2 folder provided with your Data Files. Select the option to import the source data into a new table in the current database, and then click the OK button.

⊕**EXPLORE**   5. Complete the Import Spreadsheet Wizard as follows:

   a. Select Sheet1 as the worksheet you want to import.

   b. Accept the option specifying that the first row contains column headings.

   c. Accept the field options the wizard suggests, and do not skip any fields.

   d. Choose Member ID as your own primary key.

   e. Import the data to a table named **Member**, and do not save your import steps.

6. Open the **Member** table, and then delete the Initiation Fee Waived field.

7. Modify the design of the Member table so that it matches the design shown in Figure 2-52, including the field names and their order. (*Hint:* For Text fields, delete any formats specified in the Format property boxes.) Do not propagate the field property changes.

Figure 2-52

Field Name	Data Type	Description	Field Size	Other Properties
Member ID	Text	Primary key	4	
Program ID	Text	Foreign key	3	
First Name	Text		18	
Last Name	Text		18	
Street	Text		30	
City	Text		24	
State	Text		2	
Zip	Text		10	
Phone	Text		14	
Date Joined	Date/Time			Format: Short Date
Expiration Date	Date/Time	Date when membership expires		Format: Short Date
Membership Status	Text	Active, Inactive, or On Hold	8	

⊕ **EXPLORE**

8. Open the Access Help window and enter **default value** as the search text. Select the Help article titled "Set default values for fields or controls," and then select "Set a default value for a table field." Read that section of the Help article, and then scroll down and examine the examples of default values. Set the Default Value property for the Membership Status field to **"Active"** (including the quotation marks). Close the Access Help window.

9. Save the Member table. Click the Yes button when a message appears indicating some data might be lost.

10. Add the records shown in Figure 2-53 to the Member table. (*Hint*: Use the New button on the Home tab to add a new record.)

Figure 2-53

Member ID	Program ID	First Name	Last Name	Street	City	State	Zip	Phone	Date Joined	Expiration Date	Membership Status
1170	210	Ed	Curran	25 Fairway Drive	Bon Air	VA	23235	804-323-6824	6/3/2010	12/3/2010	Active
1172	206	Tung	Lin	40 Green Boulevard	Richmond	VA	23220	804-674-0227	11/16/2010	11/16/2011	Active

11. Resize all the columns in the datasheet to their best fit, and then save and close the table.

12. Define a one-to-many relationship between the primary Program table and the related Member table. Select the referential integrity option and the cascade updates option for this relationship.

13. Save the changes to the Relationships window, compact and repair the Fitness database, and then close the database.

Apply | **Case Problem 3**

Use the skills you learned in the tutorial to create and modify tables containing data for a not-for-profit agency that recycles household goods.

Data Files needed for this Case Problem: Agency.txt, Rossi.accdb (*cont. from Tutorial 1*), **Gifts.xlsx, and Recycle.accdb**

Rossi Recycling Group Tom Rossi uses the Rossi database to maintain information about the donors, agencies, and donations to his not-for-profit agency. Tom asks you to help him maintain the database by updating one table and creating two new ones. Complete the following:

1. Open the **Rossi** database located in the Level.01\Case3 folder provided with your Data Files.

2. Open the **Donor** table. For the Donor ID field, add **Primary key** as the description and set the Field Size property to **5**. Set the Field Size properties for the remaining fields as follows:

   Title: **4**

   First Name: **20**

   Last Name: **25**

   Phone: **14**

3. Save and close the Donor table. Click the Yes button when a message appears indicating some data might be lost.

4. Tom created a table named Agency in the Recycle database that is located in the Level.01\Case3 folder provided with your Data Files. Import the structure of the Agency table in the Recycle database into a new table named Agency in the Rossi database. Do not save the import steps.

5. Delete the following fields from the Agency table: Fax Number, Mobile Phone, E-mail Address, and Notes.
6. Rename the ID field to **Agency ID**, and change its data type to Text. Make sure Agency ID is the primary key.
7. Modify the design of the Agency table so that it matches the design shown in Figure 2-54, including the field names and their order. Do not propagate the field property changes.

Figure 2-54

Field Name	Data Type	Description	Field Size
Agency ID	Text	Primary key	3
Agency Name	Text		40
Contact First Name	Text		20
Contact Last Name	Text		25
Address	Text		30
City	Text		24
State	Text		2
Zip	Text		10
Phone	Text		14

8. Save your changes to the table design, add the records shown in Figure 2-55 to the Agency table, and then close the Agency table.

Figure 2-55

Agency ID	Agency Name	Contact First Name	Contact Last Name	Address	City	State	Zip	Phone
K64	Community Development	Jerri	Clarkson	223 Penn Ave	Salina	KS	67401	785-309-3351
K82	SeniorCare Program	Todd	Groverman	718 N Walnut	McPherson	KS	67460	620-241-3668

9. Tom exported the student data that he was maintaining in another computer system to a text file, and he asks you to add this data to the Agency table. The data you need to import is contained in the Agency text file (located in the Level.01\Case3 folder provided with your Data Files).
   a. Specify the Agency text file as the source of the data.
   b. Select the option for appending the data to the table.
   c. Select Agency as the table.
   d. In the Import Text Wizard dialog boxes, choose the option to import delimited data, to use a comma delimiter, and to import the data into the Agency table. Do not save the import steps.
10. Resize all the columns in the datasheet to their best fit, and then save and close the table.
11. Use Design view to create a table using the table design shown in Figure 2-56.

Figure 2-56

Field Name	Data Type	Description	Field Size	Other Properties
Donation ID	Text	Primary key	4	
Donor ID	Text	Foreign key	5	
Agency ID	Text	Foreign key	3	
Donation Date	Date/TIme			Format: Short Date
Donation Description	Text		50	
Donation Value	Currency	Cash amount donated or estimated value of goods donated		Format: Currency Decimal Places: 2
Pickup Required	Yes/No			

12. Specify Donation ID as the primary key, save the table as **Donation**, and then close the table.

13. Use the Import Spreadsheet Wizard to add data to the Donation table. The data you need to import is contained in the Gifts workbook, which is an Excel file located in the Level.01\Case3 folder provided with your Data Files.
    a. Specify the Gifts workbook as the source of the data.
    b. Select the option for appending the data to the table.
    c. Select Donation as the table.
    d. In the Import Spreadsheet Wizard dialog boxes, choose the Sheet1 worksheet, and import to the Donation table. Do not save the import steps.

14. Open the **Donation** table, and add the records shown in Figure 2-57. Whenever possible, use a keyboard shortcut to insert the same value as in the previous record.

Figure 2-57

Donation ID	Donor ID	Agency ID	Donation Date	Donation Description	Donation Value	Pickup Required
2117	36012	K82	2/20/2010	Cash	$50.00	No
2122	36016	N33	3/22/2010	Cash	$35.00	No

15. Resize all the columns in the datasheet to their best fit, and then save and close the table.

16. Define the one-to-many relationships between the database tables as follows: between the primary Donor table and the related Donation table, and between the primary Agency table and the related Donation table. Select the referential integrity option and the cascade updates option for each relationship.

17. Save the changes to the Relationships window, compact and repair the Rossi database, and then close the database.

| Challenge | Case Problem 4 |

Work with the skills you've learned, and explore some new skills, to create a database for a luxury rental company.

Data Files needed for this Case Problem: Bookings.txt, GEM.accdb *(cont. from Tutorial 1)*, and Overseas.accdb

GEM Ultimate Vacations Griffin and Emma MacElroy use the GEM database to track the data about the services they provide to the clients who book luxury vacations through their agency. They ask you to help them maintain this database. Complete the following:

1. Open the **GEM** database located in the Level.01\Case4 folder provided with your Data Files.

2. Open the **Guest** table. Add **Primary key** as the description for the Guest ID field and change its Field Size property to **3**. Change the Field Size property for the following fields:
   Guest First Name: **20**
   Guest Last Name: **25**
   Address: **32**
   City: **24**
   State/Prov: **2**
   Postal Code: **10**
   Country: **15**
   Phone: **14**

3. Save and close the Guest table. Click the Yes button when a message appears indicating some data might be lost.

EXPLORE
4. Open the Access Help window and enter **import table** as the search text. Select the Help article titled "Import or link to data in another Access database," and then select "Import data from another Access database." Read the steps in the "Import the data" section of the Help article. Close the Access Help window, click the External Data tab on the Ribbon, and then click the Access button (with the ScreenTip "Import Access database") in the Import group.

EXPLORE
5. Import the Rentals table structure and data from the Overseas database into a new table in the GEM database as follows:
   a. As the source of the data, specify the Overseas database, located in the Level.01\Case4 folder provided with your Data Files.
   b. Select the option button to import tables, queries, forms, reports, macros, and modules into the current database, and then click the OK button.
   c. In the Import Objects dialog box, click Rentals, click the Options button, and then make sure that the correct option is selected to import the table's data and structure.
   d. Do not save your import steps.

EXPLORE
6. Right-click the Rentals table in the Navigation Pane, click Rename on the shortcut menu, and then enter **Property** as the new name for this table.

7. In the Property table, delete the VIP Program field, and then move the Property Type field so that it appears between the Sleeps and Description fields.

8. Make sure that the Property ID field is the table's primary key. Change the data type of the Property ID field to Text with a Field Size property of **4**.

9. Resize all the columns in the datasheet to their best fit, and then save and close the table.

10. Use Design view to create a table using the table design shown in Figure 2-58.

Figure 2-58

Field Name	Data Type	Description	Field Size	Other Properties
Reservation ID	Text	Primary key	3	
Guest ID	Text	Foreign key	3	
Property ID	Text	Foreign key	4	
Start Date	Date/Time			
End Date	Date/Time			
People	Number	Number of people in the party	Integer	
Rental Rate	Currency	Rate per day; includes any discounts or promotions		Format: Currency Decimal Places: 0

11. Specify Reservation ID as the primary key, and then save the table as **Reservation**.

✦ EXPLORE
12. Open the Access Help window and enter **custom date format** as the search text. Select the Help article titled "Enter a date or time value," and then scroll down and read the "Custom Date/Time format reference" section. Change the Format property of the Start Date and End Date fields to a custom format that displays dates in a format similar to 11/23/10. Save and close the Reservation table, and then close the Access Help window.

13. Griffin exported the reservation data that he was maintaining in another computer system to a text file, and he asks you to add this data to the Reservation table. The data you need to import is contained in the Bookings text file (located in the Level.01\Case4 folder provided with your Data Files).

    a. Specify the Bookings text file as the source of the data.

    b. Select the option for appending the data to the table.

    c. Select Reservation as the table.

    d. In the Import Text Wizard dialog boxes, choose the option to import delimited data, to use a comma delimiter, and to import the data into the Reservation table. Do not save the import steps.

14. Resize all the columns in the datasheet to their best fit, and then save and close the table.

15. Define the one-to-many relationships between the database tables as follows: between the primary Guest table and the related Reservation table, and between the primary Property table and the related Reservation table. Select the referential integrity option and the cascade updates option for each relationship.

16. Save the changes to the Relationships window, compact and repair the GEM database, and then close the database.

Research | **Internet Assignments**

Use the Internet to find and work with data related to the topics presented in this tutorial.

The purpose of the Internet Assignments is to challenge you to find information on the Internet that you can use to work effectively with this software. The actual assignments are updated and maintained on the Course Technology Web site. Log on to the Internet and use your Web browser to go to the Student Online Companion for New Perspectives Office 2007 at **www.course.com/np/office2007**. Then navigate to the Internet Assignments for this tutorial.

Review | **Quick Check Answers**

Session 2.1

1. Identify all the fields needed to produce the required information, organize each piece of data into its smallest useful part, group related fields into tables, determine each table's primary key, include a common field in related tables, avoid data redundancy, and determine the properties of each field.
2. The Data Type property determines what field values you can enter into the field and what other properties the field will have.
3. Text, Number, and AutoNumber fields
4. 255
5. F6
6. null

Session 2.2

1. spacebar
2. Ctrl + '
3. Importing
4. The field and all its values are removed from the table.
5. delimited
6. primary table; related table
7. Referential integrity

Ending Data Files

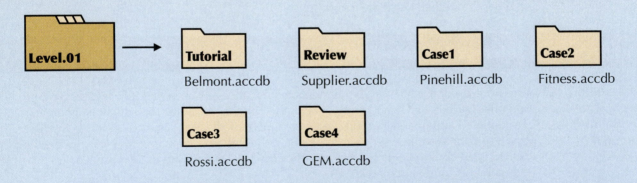

Level.01 → Tutorial — Belmont.accdb

Review — Supplier.accdb

Case1 — Pinehill.accdb

Case2 — Fitness.accdb

Case3 — Rossi.accdb

Case4 — GEM.accdb

Objectives

Session 3.1
- Find, modify, and delete records in a table
- Learn how to use the Query window in Design view
- Create, run, and save queries
- Update data using a query datasheet
- Create a query based on multiple tables
- Sort data in a query
- Filter data in a query

Session 3.2
- Specify an exact match condition in a query
- Change the font size and alternating row color in a datasheet
- Use a comparison operator in a query to match a range of values
- Use the And and Or logical operators in queries
- Create and format a calculated field in a query
- Perform calculations in a query using aggregate functions and record group calculations
- Change the display of database objects in the Navigation Pane

Maintaining and Querying a Database

Updating and Retrieving Information About Customers, Contracts, and Invoices

Case | Belmont Landscapes

At a recent meeting, Oren Belmont and his staff discussed the importance of maintaining accurate information about the firm's customers, contracts, and invoices, and regularly monitoring the business activities of Belmont Landscapes. For example, Sarah Fisher and the office staff need to make sure they have up-to-date contact information, such as phone numbers and e-mail addresses, for all the firm's customers. They also must monitor the invoice activity to ensure that invoices are paid on time and in full. Taylor Sico, the marketing manager at Belmont Landscapes, and her marketing staff track customer activity to develop new strategies for promoting the services provided by Belmont Landscapes. In addition, Oren is interested in analyzing other aspects of the business related to contracts and finances. You can satisfy all these informational needs for Belmont Landscapes by updating data in the Belmont database and by creating and using queries that retrieve information from the database.

Starting Data Files

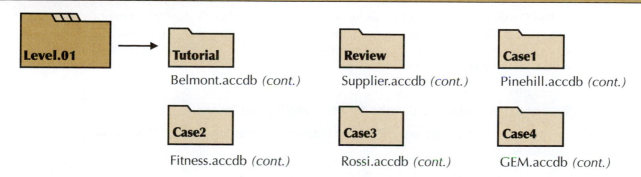

Level.01 → Tutorial
Belmont.accdb *(cont.)*

Review
Supplier.accdb *(cont.)*

Case1
Pinehill.accdb *(cont.)*

Case2
Fitness.accdb *(cont.)*

Case3
Rossi.accdb *(cont.)*

Case4
GEM.accdb *(cont.)*

Session 3.1

Updating a Database

Updating, or **maintaining**, a database is the process of adding, modifying, and deleting records in database tables to keep them current and accurate. After reviewing the data in the Belmont database, Sarah identified some changes that need to be made to the data. She would like you to modify the field values in one record in the Customer table, and then delete a record in the Contract table.

Modifying Records

To modify the field values in a record, you must first make the record the current record. Then you position the insertion point in the field value to make minor changes or select the field value to replace it entirely. In Tutorial 1, you used the mouse with the scroll bars and the navigation buttons to navigate the records in a datasheet. You can also use keystroke combinations and the F2 key to navigate a datasheet and to select field values. The **F2 key** is a toggle that you use to switch between navigation mode and editing mode:

- In **navigation mode**, Access selects an entire field value. If you type while you are in navigation mode, your typed entry replaces the highlighted field value.
- In **editing mode**, you can insert or delete characters in a field value based on the location of the insertion point.

Figure 3-1 shows some of the navigation mode and editing mode keystroke techniques.

Figure 3-1	Navigation mode and editing mode keystroke techniques

Press	To Move the Selection in Navigation Mode	To Move the Insertion Point in Editing Mode
←	Left one field value at a time	Left one character at a time
→	Right one field value at a time	Right one character at a time
Home	Left to the first field value in the record	To the left of the first character in the field value
End	Right to the last field value in the record	To the right of the last character in the field value
↑ or ↓	Up or down one record at a time	Up or down one record at a time and switch to navigation mode
Tab or Enter	Right one field value at a time	Right one field value at a time and switch to navigation mode
Ctrl+Home	To the first field value in the first record	To the left of the first character in the field value
Ctrl+End	To the last field value in the last record	To the right of the last character in the field value

The Customer table record Sarah wants you to change is for Walker Investment Company, one of Belmont Landscapes' commercial customers. The company recently moved its office from Grand Rapids to Battle Creek, so you need to update the Customer table record with the new address and phone information.

To open the Belmont database and modify the record:

1. Start Access and open the **Belmont** database located in the Level.01\Tutorial folder.

Trouble? If the Security Warning is displayed below the Ribbon, click the Options button next to the Security Warning. In the dialog box that opens, click the "Enable this content" option button, and then click the OK button.

2. Open the **Customer** table in Datasheet view. The first value for the Customer ID field (11001) is highlighted, indicating that the table is in navigation mode.

   The record you need to modify is near the end of the table and has a Customer ID field value of 11087.

3. Press the **Ctrl+End** keys. Access displays records from the end of the table and selects the last field value in the last record, record 40. This field value is for the E-mail Address field.

4. Press the **Home** key. The first field value in the last record is now selected. This field value is for the Customer ID field.

5. Press the ↑ key. The Customer ID field value for the previous record (Customer ID 11087) is selected. This record is the one you need to change.

6. Press the **Tab** key four times to move to the Phone field and select its field value, type **269-963-0190**, press the **Tab** key, type **1752 S Main St**, press the **Tab** key, type **Battle Creek**, press the **Tab** key twice, type **49014**, and then press the **Tab** key. The changes to the record are complete. See Figure 3-2.

Table after changing field values in a record   Figure 3-2

7. Close the Customer table.

The next update Sarah asks you to make is to delete a record in the Contract table. The customer who signed Contract Num 3101 owns a chain of small restaurants and had planned to renovate the landscaping at each restaurant site. His plans have changed for one of these sites, and he has cancelled the contract. When you are maintaining database tables, you first need to find the data to change.

Finding Data in a Table

Access provides options you can use to locate specific field values in a table. Instead of scrolling the Contract table datasheet to find the contract that you need to delete—the record for contract number 3101—you can use the Find command to find the record. The **Find command** allows you to search a table or query datasheet, or a form, to locate a specific field value or part of a field value. This feature is particularly useful when searching a table that contains a large number of records.

To search for the record in the Contract table:

1. Open the **Contract** table in Datasheet view. The first field value for the Contract Num field (3011) is selected. You need to search the Contract Num field to find the record containing the Contract Num field value 3101, so the insertion point is already correctly positioned in the field you want to search.

2. In the Find group on the Home tab, click the **Find** button. The Find and Replace dialog box opens. See Figure 3-3.

Figure 3-3 ▶ **Find and Replace dialog box**

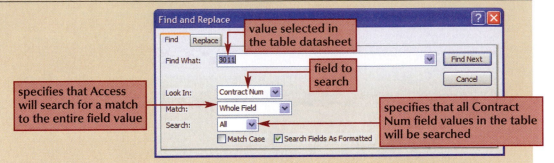

The field value 3011 appears in the Find What text box because this value is selected in the table datasheet. Also, the Contract Num field is displayed in the Look In list box because it is the current field. The Match list box indicates that the Find command will match the whole field value, which is correct for your search. You also can choose to search for only part of a field value, such as when you need to find all contract numbers that start with a certain value. The Search list box indicates that all the records in the table will be searched for the value you want to find. You also can choose to search up or down from the currently selected record.

Trouble? Some of the settings in your dialog box might be different from those shown in Figure 3-3, depending on the last search performed on the computer you're using. If so, change the settings so that they match those in the figure.

3. Make sure the value 3011 is selected in the Find What text box, type **3101** to replace the selected value, and then click the **Find Next** button. Access moves to and selects the field value you specified.

4. Click the **Cancel** button to close the Find and Replace dialog box.

Deleting Records

To delete a record, you need to select the record in Datasheet view, and then delete it using the Delete button in the Records group on the Home tab, or the Delete Record option on the shortcut menu.

Reference Window | **Deleting a Record**

- With the table in Datasheet view, click the row selector for the record you want to delete.
- In the Records group on the Home tab, click the Delete button (or right-click the row selector for the record, and then click Delete Record on the shortcut menu).
- In the dialog box asking you to confirm the deletion, click the Yes button.

Now that you have found the record with Contract Num 3101, you can delete it. To delete a record, you must first select the entire row for the record.

To delete the record:

1. Click the row selector for the record containing the Contract Num field value **3101**, which should still be highlighted. The entire row is selected.

▶ **2.** In the Records group on the Home tab, click the **Delete** button. A dialog box opens and indicates that you cannot delete the record. The dialog box indicates that the Invoice table contains records that are related to Contract Num 3101 and, therefore, you cannot delete the record in the Contract table. Recall that you defined a one-to-many relationship between the Contract and Invoice tables and enforced referential integrity. When you try to delete a record in the primary table (Contract), Access prevents the deletion if matching records exist in the related table (Invoice). This protection helps to maintain the integrity of the data in the database.

To delete the record in the Contract table, you first must delete the related records in the Invoice table.

▶ **3.** Click the **OK** button in the dialog box to close it. Notice the plus sign that appears at the beginning of each record in the Contract table. The **plus sign** indicates that the records have related records in another table—in this case, the Invoice table.

▶ **4.** Scroll the table window down until you see the rest of the records in the table, so that you have room to view the related records for the contract record.

▶ **5.** Click the **plus sign** next to Contract Num 3101. Access displays the four related records from the Invoice table for this contract. The plus sign changes to a minus sign for the current record when its related records are displayed. See Figure 3-4.

Related records from the Invoice table in the subdatasheet ◀ **Figure 3-4**

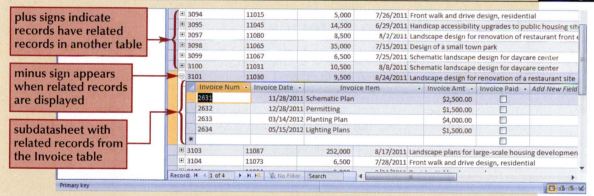

The related records from the Invoice table are displayed in a **subdatasheet**. When you first open a table that is the primary table in a one-to-many relationship, the subdatasheet containing the records from the related table is not displayed. You need to click the plus sign, also called the **expand indicator**, to display the related records in the subdatasheet. When the subdatasheet is open you can navigate and update it, just as you can using a table datasheet.

You need to delete the records in the Invoice table that are related to Contract Num 3101 so you can then delete this contract record. The four Invoice table records are for invoices set up to be paid for future phases of the contract, which has now been cancelled. You could open the Invoice table and find the related records. However, an easier way to delete the related records for Contract Num 3101 is to delete them from the subdatasheet. The records will be deleted from the Invoice table automatically.

▶ **6.** Click and hold the mouse button on the row selector for the first Invoice table record in the subdatasheet, drag the pointer down to select all four records, and then release the mouse button. With the four records selected, you can delete them all at the same time.

▶ **7.** In the Records group on the Home tab, click the **Delete** button. Access opens a dialog box asking you to confirm the deletion of four records. Because the deletion of a record is permanent and cannot be undone, Access prompts you to make sure that you want to delete the records.

▶ **8.** Click the **Yes** button to confirm the deletion and close the dialog box. The records are removed from the Invoice table, and the subdatasheet is now empty.

▶ **9.** Click the **minus sign** next to Contract Num 3101 to close the subdatasheet.

Now that you have deleted all the related records in the Invoice table, you can delete the record for Contract Num 3101. You will use the shortcut menu to delete the record.

▶ **10.** Right-click the row selector for the record for Contract Num **3101**. Access selects the record and displays the shortcut menu.

▶ **11.** Click **Delete Record** on the shortcut menu, and then click the **Yes** button in the dialog box to confirm the deletion. The record is deleted from the table.

▶ **12.** Close the Contract table.

You have finished updating the Belmont database by modifying and deleting records. Next, you'll retrieve specific data from the database to meet various requests for information about Belmont Landscapes.

Introduction to Queries

As you learned in Tutorial 1, a query is a question you ask about data stored in a database. For example, Oren might create a query to find records in the Customer table for only those customers located in a specific city. When you create a query, you tell Access which fields you need and what criteria Access should use to select the records. Access provides powerful query capabilities that allow you to do the following:

• Display selected fields and records from a table.
• Sort records.
• Perform calculations.
• Generate data for forms, reports, and other queries.
• Update data in the tables in a database.
• Find and display data from two or more tables.

Most questions about data are generalized queries in which you specify the fields and records you want Access to select. These common requests for information, such as "Which customers are located in Kalamazoo?" or "How many invoices have been paid?" are called **select queries**. The answer to a select query is returned in the form of a datasheet. The result of a query is also referred to as a **recordset**, because the query produces a set of records that answers your question.

More specialized, technical queries, such as finding duplicate records in a table, are best formulated using a Query Wizard. A **Query Wizard** prompts you for information by asking a series of questions and then creates the appropriate query based on your answers. In Tutorial 1, you used the Simple Query Wizard to display only some of the fields in the Contract table; Access provides other Query Wizards for more complex queries. For common, informational queries, it is easier for you to design your own query than to use a Query Wizard.

Taylor wants you to create a query to display the customer ID, company, first name, last name, city, and e-mail address for each record in the Customer table. Her marketing staff needs this information to complete an e-mail campaign advertising a special promotion being offered to Belmont Landscapes' customers. You'll open the Query window in Design view to create the query for Taylor.

Query Window

You use the Query window in Design view to create a query. In Design view, you specify the data you want to view by constructing a query by example. When you use **query by example** (**QBE**), you give Access an example of the information you are requesting. Access then retrieves the information that precisely matches your example.

For Taylor's query, you need to display data from the Customer table.

To open the Query window in Design view:

▶ **1.** Close the Navigation Pane so that more of the workspace is displayed.

▶ **2.** Click the **Create** tab on the Ribbon. Access displays the options for creating different database objects.

▶ **3.** In the Other group on the Create tab, click the **Query Design** button. The Show Table dialog box opens on the Query window in Design view. See Figure 3-5.

Show Table dialog box　　　　　**Figure 3-5**

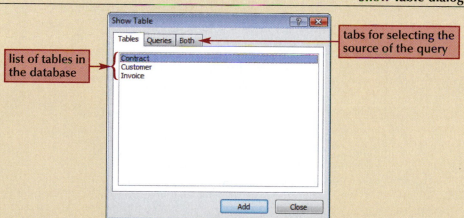

tabs for selecting the source of the query

list of tables in the database

The Show Table dialog box lists all the tables in the Belmont database. You can choose to base a query on one or more tables, on other queries, or on a combination of tables and queries. The query you are creating will retrieve data from the Customer table, so you need to add this table to the Query window.

▶ **4.** Click **Customer** in the Tables list box, click the **Add** button, and then click the **Close** button. Access places the Customer table's field list in the Query window and closes the Show Table dialog box. See Figure 3-6.

Figure 3-6   Select query in Design view

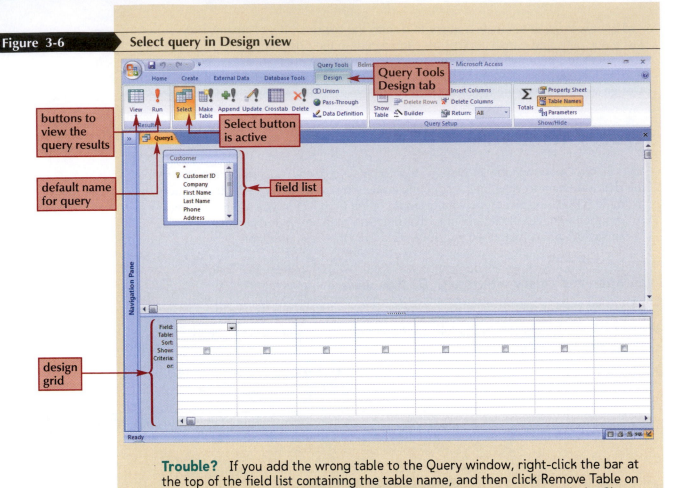

> **Trouble?**   If you add the wrong table to the Query window, right-click the bar at the top of the field list containing the table name, and then click Remove Table on the shortcut menu. To add the correct table to the Query window, click the Show Table button in the Query Setup group on the Query Tools Design tab to redisplay the Show Table dialog box, and then repeat Step 4.

In Design view, the Ribbon displays the Query Tools Design tab, with options for creating and running different types of queries. In the Query Type group on the Query Tools Design tab, notice that the Select button is active; this indicates that you are creating a select query, which is the default type of query. The default query name (Query1) is displayed on the tab for the query. You'll change the default query name to a more meaningful one later when you save the query.

The top portion of the Query window in Design view contains the field list (or lists) for the table(s) used in the query, and the bottom portion contains the design grid. Each **field list** contains the fields for the table(s) you are querying. The table name appears at the top of the list box, and the fields are listed in the order in which they appear in the table. Notice that the primary key for the table is identified by the key symbol. You can scroll the field list to see more fields, or you can expand the field list box by dragging its borders to display all the fields and the complete field names. In the **design grid**, you include the fields and record selection criteria for the information you want to see. Each column in the design grid contains specifications about a field you will use in the query. You can choose a single field for your query by double-clicking the field name to place it in the next available design grid column.

Tip

You can also use the mouse to drag a field name from the field list to a column in the design grid.

When you are constructing a query, you can see the query results at any time by clicking the View button or the Run button in the Results group on the Query Tools Design tab. In response, Access displays the query datasheet (or recordset), which contains the set of fields and records that results from answering, or **running**, the query. The order of the fields in the query datasheet is the same as the order of the fields in the design grid.

Comparing Methods for Adding All Fields to the Design Grid | InSight

If the query you are creating includes every field from the specified table, you can use one of the following three methods to transfer all the fields from the field list to the design grid:

- Click and drag each field individually from the field list to the design grid. Use this method if you want the fields in your query to appear in an order that is different from the order in the field list.
- Double-click the asterisk at the top of the field list. Access places the table name followed by a period and an asterisk (as in "Customer.*") in the design grid, which signifies that the order of the fields is the same in the query as it is in the field list. Use this method if you don't need to sort the query or specify conditions for the records you want to select. The advantage of using this method is that you do not need to change the query if you add or delete fields from the underlying table structure. Such changes are reflected automatically in the query.
- Double-click the field list title bar to highlight all the fields, and then click and drag one of the highlighted fields to the design grid. Access places each field in a separate column and arranges the fields in the order in which they appear in the field list. Use this method when you need to sort your query or include record selection criteria.

Now you'll create and run Taylor's query to display selected fields from the Customer table.

Creating and Running a Query

The default table datasheet displays all the fields in the table in the same order as they appear in the table. In contrast, a query datasheet can display selected fields from a table, and the order of the fields can be different from that of the table, enabling those viewing the query results to see only the information they need and in the order they want.

Taylor wants the Customer ID, Company, First Name, Last Name, City, and E-mail Address fields from the Customer table to appear in the query results. You'll add each of these fields to the design grid. First you'll resize the Customer table field list to display all of the fields.

To select the fields for the query, and then run the query:

1. Position the pointer on the bottom border of the Customer field list until the pointer changes to a ↕ shape, and then click and drag the pointer down until the vertical scroll bar in the field list disappears and all fields in the Customer table are displayed.

2. In the Customer field list, double-click **Customer ID** to place the field in the design grid's first column Field text box. See Figure 3-7.

Figure 3-7 | **Field added to the design grid**

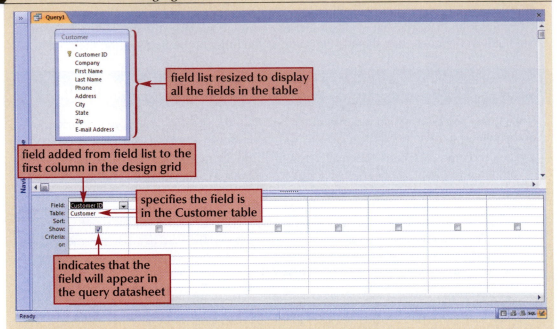

In the design grid's first column, the field name Customer ID appears in the Field text box, the table name Customer appears in the Table text box, and the check mark in the Show check box indicates that the field will be displayed in the datasheet when you run the query. Sometimes you might not want to display a field and its values in the query results. For example, if you are creating a query to list all customers located in Lansing, and you assign the name "Lansing Customers" to the query, you do not need to include the City field value for each record in the query results—the query design only lists customers with the City field value of "Lansing." Even if you choose not to include a field in the display of the query results, you can still use the field as part of the query to select specific records or to specify a particular sequence for the records in the datasheet.

►　**3.** Double-click **Company** in the Customer field list. Access adds this field to the second column in the design grid.

►　**4.** Repeat Step 3 for the **First Name**, **Last Name**, **City**, and **E-mail Address** fields to add these fields to the design grid in that order.

　　　Trouble? If you double-click the wrong field and accidentally add it to the design grid, you can remove the field from the grid. Select the field's column by clicking the pointer ↓ on the field selector, which is the thin bar above the Field text box, for the field you want to delete, and then press the Delete key (or in the Query Setup group on the Query Tools Design tab, click the Delete Columns button).

　　　Having selected the fields for Taylor's query, you can now run the query.

►　**5.** In the Results group on the Query Tools Design tab, click the **Run** button. Access runs the query and displays the results in Datasheet view. See Figure 3-8.

Datasheet displayed after running the query   Figure 3-8

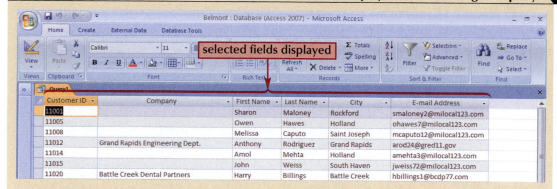

The six fields you added to the design grid appear in the datasheet, and the records are displayed in primary key sequence by Customer ID. Access selected a total of 40 records for display in the datasheet. Taylor asks you to save the query as "Customer E-mail" so that she can easily retrieve the same data again.

▶ **6.** Click the **Save** button 🖫 on the Quick Access toolbar. The Save As dialog box opens.

▶ **7.** Type **Customer E-mail** in the Query Name text box, and then press the **Enter** key. Access saves the query with the specified name in the Belmont database and displays the name on the tab for the query.

Query Datasheet vs. Table Datasheet   InSight

Although a query datasheet looks just like a table datasheet and appears in Datasheet view, a query datasheet is temporary, and its contents are based on the criteria you establish in the design grid. In contrast, a table datasheet shows the permanent data in a table. However, you can update data while viewing a query datasheet, just as you can when working in a table datasheet or form.

When viewing the query results, Taylor noticed that the contact person for the River-View Development Company is incorrect. Charles Nowak recently retired from his position, and she asks you to update the record with the first name, last name, and e-mail address of the new contact.

Updating Data Using a Query

Although a query datasheet is temporary and its contents are based on the criteria in the query design grid, you can update the data in a table using a query datasheet. In this case, Taylor has changes she wants you to make to a record in the Customer table. Instead of making the changes in the table datasheet, you can make them in the Customer E-mail query datasheet because the query is based on the Customer table. The underlying Customer table will be updated with the changes you make.

To update data using the Customer E-mail query datasheet:

▶ **1.** Locate the record with Customer ID 11040, RiverView Development Company (record 13 in the datasheet).

▶ **2.** In the First Name field for this record, double-click **Charles** to select the name, and then type **Susan**.

▶ **3.** Press the **Tab** key to move to and select the value in the Last Name field, and then type **Darcy**.

▶ **4.** Press the **Tab** key twice to move to and select the value in the E-mail Address field, type **sdarcy33@rvdc3.com**, and then press the **Tab** key.

▶ **5.** Close the Customer E-mail query, and then open the Navigation Pane. Note that the Customer E-mail query is listed in the Customer section of the Navigation Pane.

Now you'll check the Customer table to verify that the changes you made in the query datasheet were also made in the Customer table.

▶ **6.** Open the **Customer** table in Datasheet view, and then close the Navigation Pane.

▶ **7.** For the record with Customer ID 11040 (record 13), use the **Tab** key to move through the field values. Notice that the changes you made in the query datasheet to the First Name, Last Name, and E-mail Address field values were made to the record in the Customer table.

▶ **8.** Close the Customer table.

Sarah also wants to view specific information in the Belmont database. She would like to review the contract signing dates and amounts for customers while also viewing certain contact information for the customers. So, she needs to see data from both the Customer table and the Contract table at the same time.

Creating a Multitable Query

A multitable query is a query based on more than one table. If you want to create a query that retrieves data from multiple tables, the tables must have a common field. In Tutorial 2, you established a relationship between the Customer (primary) and Contract (related) tables based on the common Customer ID field that exists in both tables, so you can now create a query to display data from both tables at the same time. Specifically, Sarah wants to view the values in the City, Company, First Name, and Last Name fields from the Customer table and the Signing Date and Contract Amt fields from the Contract table.

To create the query using the Customer and Contract tables:

▶ **1.** Click the **Create** tab on the Ribbon.

▶ **2.** In the Other group on the Create tab, click the **Query Design** button. Access opens the Show Table dialog box. You need to add the Customer and Contract tables to the Query window.

▶ **3.** Click **Customer** in the Tables list box, click the **Add** button, click **Contract**, click the **Add** button, and then click the **Close** button. The Customer and Contract field lists appear in the Query window, and the Show Table dialog box closes.

▶ **4.** Use the ↕ pointer to resize the Customer field list so that all the fields in the table are displayed.

The one-to-many relationship between the two tables is shown in the Query window, in the same way that Access indicates a relationship between two tables in the Relationships window. Note that the join line is thick at both ends; this signifies that you selected the option to enforce referential integrity. If you had not selected this option, the join line would be thin at both ends and neither the "1" nor the infinity symbol would appear, even though the tables have a one-to-many relationship.

You need to place the City, Company, First Name, and Last Name fields (in that order) from the Customer field list into the design grid, and then place the Signing Date and Contract Amt fields from the Contract field list into the design grid. This is the order in which Sarah wants to view the fields in the query results.

▶ 5. In the Customer field list, double-click **City** to place this field in the design grid's first column Field text box.

▶ 6. Repeat Step 5 to add the **Company**, **First Name**, and **Last Name** fields from the Customer table to the second through fourth columns of the design grid.

▶ 7. Repeat Step 5 to add the **Signing Date** and **Contract Amt** fields (in that order) from the Contract table to the fifth and sixth columns of the design grid. The query specifications are complete, so you can now run the query.

▶ 8. In the Results group on the Query Tools Design tab, click the **Run** button. Access runs the query and displays the results in Datasheet view. See Figure 3-9.

Datasheet for query based on the Customer and Contract tables ◀ Figure 3-9

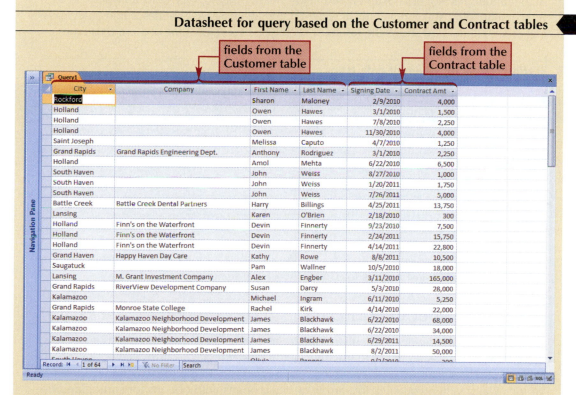

Only the six selected fields from the Customer and Contract tables appear in the datasheet. The records are displayed in order according to the values in the Customer ID field, because it is the primary key field in the primary table, even though this field is not included in the query datasheet.

Sarah plans on frequently tracking the data retrieved by the query, so she asks you to save the query as "Customer Contracts."

▶ 9. Click the **Save** button 🖫 on the Quick Access Toolbar. The Save As dialog box opens.

▶ 10. Type **Customer Contracts** in the Query Name text box, and then press the **Enter** key. Access saves the query and displays its name on the query tab.

Sarah decides she wants the records displayed in alphabetical order by city. Because the query displays data in order by the field values in the Customer ID field, which is the primary key for the Customer table, you need to sort the records by the City field to display the data in the order Sarah wants.

Sorting Data in a Query

Sorting is the process of rearranging records in a specified order or sequence. Sometimes you might need to sort data before displaying or printing it to meet a specific request. For example, Sarah might want to review contract information arranged by the Signing Date field because she needs to know which months are the busiest for Belmont Landscapes in terms of signings. On the other hand, Oren might want to view contract information arranged by the Contract Amt field, because he monitors the financial aspects of the business.

When you sort data in a query, you do not change the sequence of the records in the underlying tables. Only the records in the query datasheet are rearranged according to your specifications.

To sort records, you must select the **sort field**, which is the field used to determine the order of records in the datasheet. In this case, Sarah wants the data sorted by city, so you need to specify City as the sort field. Sort fields can be Text, Number, Date/Time, Currency, AutoNumber, Yes/No, or Lookup Wizard fields, but not Memo, OLE object, Hyperlink, or Attachment fields. You sort records in either ascending (increasing) or descending (decreasing) order. Figure 3-10 shows the results of each type of sort for some of these data types.

Figure 3-10	Sorting results for different data types

Data Type	Ascending Sort Results	Descending Sort Results
Text	A to Z	Z to A
Number	lowest to highest numeric value	highest to lowest numeric value
Date/Time	oldest to most recent date	most recent to oldest date
Currency	lowest to highest numeric value	highest to lowest numeric value
AutoNumber	lowest to highest numeric value	highest to lowest numeric value
Yes/No	yes (check mark in check box) then no values	no then yes values

Access provides several methods for sorting data in a table or query datasheet and in a form. One of the easiest ways is to use the AutoFilter feature for a field.

Using AutoFilter to Sort Data

As you've probably noticed when working in Datasheet view for a table or query, each column heading has an arrow to the right of the field name. This arrow gives you access to the **AutoFilter** feature, which enables you to quickly sort and display field values in various ways. When you click this arrow, a menu opens with options for sorting and displaying field values. The first two options on the menu enable you to sort the values in the current field in ascending or descending order. Unless you save the datasheet or form after you've sorted the records, the rearrangement of records is temporary.

Next, you'll use an AutoFilter to sort the Customer Contracts query results by the City field.

Tip

You can also use the Ascending and Descending buttons in the Sort & Filter group on the Home tab to quickly sort records based on the currently selected field in a datasheet.

To sort the records using an AutoFilter:

▶ **1.** Click the arrow on the City column heading to display the AutoFilter menu. See Figure 3-11.

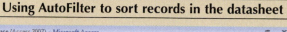

Using AutoFilter to sort records in the datasheet ◄ **Figure 3-11**

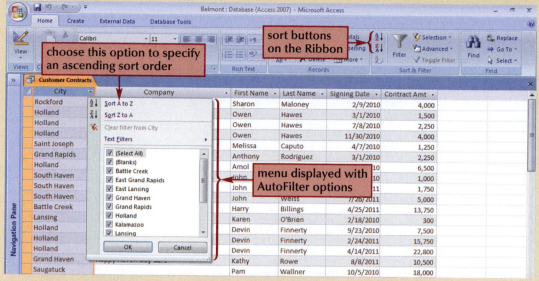

Sarah wants the data sorted in ascending order by the values in the City field, so you need to select the first option in the menu.

▶ **2.** Click **Sort A to Z**. The records are rearranged in ascending alphabetical order by city. A small, upward-pointing arrow appears on the right side of the City column heading. This arrow indicates that the values in the field have been sorted in ascending order. If you used the same method to sort the field values in descending order, a small downward-pointing arrow would appear there.

After viewing the query results, Sarah decides that she would also like to see the records arranged by the values in the Contract Amt field, so that she can identify the contracts with the largest amounts. She still wants the records to be arranged by the city field values as well. To produce the results Sarah wants, you need to sort using two fields.

Sorting Multiple Fields in Design View

Sort fields can be unique or nonunique. A sort field is **unique** if the value in the sort field for each record is different. The Customer ID field in the Customer table is an example of a unique sort field because each customer record has a different value in this primary key field. A sort field is **nonunique** if more than one record can have the same value for the sort field. For example, the City field in the Customer table is a nonunique sort field because more than one record can have the same City value.

When the sort field is nonunique, records with the same sort field value are grouped together, but they are not sorted in a specific order within the group. To arrange these grouped records in a specific order, you can specify a **secondary sort field**, which is a second field that determines the order of records that are already sorted by the **primary sort field** (the first sort field specified).

Access lets you select up to 10 different sort fields. When you use the buttons on the Ribbon to sort by more than one field, the sort fields must be in adjacent columns in the datasheet. (Note that you cannot use an AutoFilter to sort on more than one field. This method works for a single field only.) You can specify only one type of sort—either

> **Tip**
>
> The primary sort field is *not* the same as a table's primary key field. A table has at most one primary key, which must be unique, whereas any field in a table can serve as a primary sort field.

ascending or descending—for the selected columns in the datasheet. You highlight the adjacent columns, and Access sorts first by the first column and then by each remaining highlighted column in order from left to right.

Sarah wants the records sorted first by the City field values, as they currently are, and then by the Contract Amt field values. The two fields are in the correct left-to-right order in the query datasheet, but they are not adjacent, so you cannot use the Ascending and Descending buttons on the Ribbon to sort them. You could move the City field to the left of the Contract Amt field in the query datasheet, but both columns would be sorted with the same sort order. This is not what Sarah wants—she wants the City field values sorted in ascending order so that they are in the correct alphabetical order, for ease of reference; and she wants the Contract Amt field values to be sorted in descending order, so that she can focus on the contracts with the largest amounts. To sort the City and Contract Amt fields with different sort orders, you must specify the sort fields in Design view.

In the Query window in Design view, Access first uses the sort field that is leftmost in the design grid. Therefore, you must arrange the fields you want to sort from left to right in the design grid, with the primary sort field being the leftmost. In Design view, multiple sort fields do not have to be adjacent to each other, as they do in Datasheet view; however, they must be in the correct left-to-right order.

Reference Window | **Sorting a Query Datasheet**

- In the query datasheet, click the arrow on the column heading for the field you want to sort.
- In the menu that opens, click Sort A to Z for an ascending sort, or click Sort Z to A for a descending sort.

or

- In the query datasheet, select the column or adjacent columns on which you want to sort.
- In the Sort & Filter group on the Home tab, click the Ascending button or the Descending button.

or

- In Design view, position the fields serving as sort fields from left to right.
- Click the right side of the Sort text box for the field you want to sort, and then click Ascending or Descending for the sort order.

To achieve the results Sarah wants, you need to modify the query in Design view to specify the sort order for the two fields.

To select the two sort fields in Design view:

Tip

In Design view, the sort fields do not have to be adjacent, and fields that are not sorted can appear between the sort fields.

1. In the Views group on the Home tab, click the **View** button to open the query in Design view. The fields are currently in the correct left-to-right order in the design grid, so you only need to specify the sort order for the two fields.

   First, you need to specify an ascending sort order for the City field. Even though the records are already sorted by the values in this field, you need to modify the query so that this sort order, and the sort order you will specify for the Contract Amt field, are part of the query's design. Any time the query is run, the records will be sorted according to these specifications.

2. Click the right side of the **City Sort** text box to display the arrow and the sort options, and then click **Ascending**. You've selected an ascending sort order for the City field, which will be the primary sort field. The City field is a Text field, and an ascending sort order will display the field values in alphabetical order.

3. Click the right side of the **Contract Amt Sort** text box, click **Descending**, and then click in one of the empty text boxes to the right of the Contract Amt field to deselect the setting. You've selected a descending sort order for the Contract Amt field, which will be the secondary sort field, because it appears to the right of the primary sort field (City) in the design grid. The Contract Amt field is a Currency field, and a descending sort order will display the field values with the highest amounts first. See Figure 3-12.

Selecting two sort fields in Design view | Figure 3-12

You have finished your query changes, so now you can run the query and then save the modified query with the same query name.

4. In the Results group on the Query Tools Design tab, click the **Run** button. Access runs the query and displays the query datasheet. The records appear in ascending order, based on the values of the City field. Within groups of records with the same City field value, the records appear in descending order by the values of the Contract Amt field. See Figure 3-13.

Datasheet sorted on two fields | Figure 3-13

primary sort field						secondary sort field	records grouped by City are shown in descending order by Contract Amt

Customer Contracts

City	Company	First Name	Last Name	Signing Date	Contract Amt
Battle Creek	Walker Investment Company	Nancy	Belanger	8/17/2011	252,000
Battle Creek	Battle Creek Dental Partners	Harry	Billings	4/25/2011	13,750
Battle Creek	Fox and Hound Grille	Steve	Gorski	2/19/2010	6,500
East Grand Rapids	Dept. of Neighborhood Development	Sarah	Russell	8/25/2011	38,000
East Grand Rapids	Dept. of Neighborhood Development	Sarah	Russell	2/3/2011	38,000
East Grand Rapids	Dept. of Neighborhood Development	Sarah	Russell	3/3/2011	35,000
East Grand Rapids	Dept. of Neighborhood Development	Sarah	Russell	6/14/2011	25,500
East Grand Rapids		Jerome	Smith	6/1/2011	5,000
East Lansing	Hopedale State College	John	Williams	8/11/2010	19,000
East Lansing	Hopedale State College	John	Williams	3/25/2010	15,500
Grand Haven	Happy Haven Day Care	Kathy	Rowe	8/8/2011	10,500
Grand Rapids	Grand Rapids Housing Authority	Jessica	Ropiak	6/23/2011	52,500
Grand Rapids	Legacy Companies, LTD.	Michael	Faraci	6/3/2010	48,500
Grand Rapids	G.R. Neighborhood Development Corp.	Matthew	Fraser	3/11/2011	46,000
Grand Rapids	G.R. Neighborhood Development Corp.	Matthew	Fraser	8/18/2011	41,000
Grand Rapids	Legacy Companies, LTD.	Michael	Faraci	3/22/2010	39,000
Grand Rapids	Grand Rapids Housing Authority	Jessica	Ropiak	7/27/2010	38,500
Grand Rapids	G.R. Neighborhood Development Corp.	Matthew	Fraser	3/11/2011	37,000
Grand Rapids	Legacy Companies, LTD.	Michael	Faraci	12/28/2010	30,800
Grand Rapids	RiverView Development Company	Susan	Darcy	5/3/2010	28,000
Grand Rapids	Monroe State College	Rachel	Kirk	4/14/2010	22,000
Grand Rapids	Weston Community Parks Foundation	Sam	Kervin	5/28/2010	10,500
Grand Rapids	Weston Community Parks Foundation	Sam	Kervin	5/28/2010	8,500
Grand Rapids	Grand Rapids Engineering Dept.	Anthony	Rodriguez	3/1/2010	2,250
Holland	Town of Holland	Amber	Ward	7/15/2011	35,000

Record: 1 of 64 — No Filter — Search

When you save the query, all of your design changes—including the selection of the sort fields—are saved with the query. The next time Sarah runs the query, the records will appear sorted by the primary and secondary sort fields.

5. Click the **Save** button 🖫 on the Quick Access Toolbar to save the revised Customer Contracts query.

Sarah knows that Belmont Landscapes has seen an increase in business recently for customers located in the city of Grand Rapids. She would like to focus briefly on the information for customers in that city only. Furthermore, she is interested in knowing how many contracts were signed in March, because this month has sometimes been a slow month for Belmont Landscapes in terms of contract signings. Selecting only the records with a City field value of "Grand Rapids" and a Signing Date field value beginning with "3" (for the month of March) is a temporary change that Sarah wants in the datasheet, so you do not need to switch to Design view and change the query. Instead, you can apply a filter.

Filtering Data

A **filter** is a set of restrictions you place on the records in an open datasheet or form to *temporarily* isolate a subset of the records. A filter lets you view different subsets of displayed records so that you can focus on only the data you need. Unless you save a query or form with a filter applied, an applied filter is not available the next time you run the query or open the form.

The simplest technique for filtering records is Filter By Selection. **Filter By Selection** lets you select all or part of a field value in a datasheet or form, and then display only those records that contain the selected value in the field. You can also use the AutoFilter feature to filter records. When you click the arrow on a column heading, the menu that opens provides options for filtering the display based on a field value or the selected part of a field value. Another technique for filtering records is to use **Filter By Form**, which changes your datasheet to display blank fields. Then you can select a value using the arrow that appears when you click any blank field to apply a filter that selects only those records containing that value.

Reference Window | Using Filter By Selection

- In the datasheet or form, select part of the field value that will be the basis for the filter; or, if the filter will be based on the entire field value, click anywhere within the field value.
- In the Sort & Filter group on the Home tab, click the Selection button, and then click the type of filter you want to apply.

For Sarah's request, you need to select a City field value of Grand Rapids, and then use Filter By Selection to display only those query records with this value. Then you will filter the records further by selecting only those records with a Signing Date value that begins with "3" (for March).

To display the records using Filter By Selection:

▶ **1.** In the query datasheet, locate the first occurrence of a City field containing the value **Grand Rapids**, and then click anywhere within that field value.

▶ **2.** In the Sort & Filter group on the Home tab, click the **Selection** button. A menu opens with options for the type of filter to apply. See Figure 3-14.

Using Filter By Selection | **Figure 3-14**

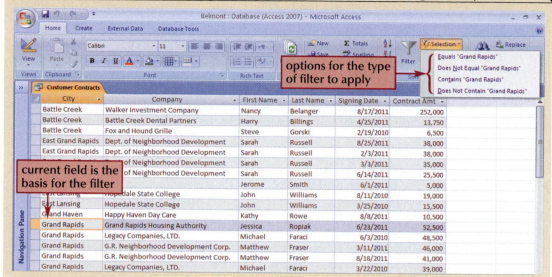

The menu provides options for displaying only those records with a City field value that equals the selected value (in this case, Grand Rapids); does not equal the value; contains the value somewhere within the field; or does not contain the value somewhere within the field. You want to display all the records whose City field value equals Grand Rapids.

3. In the Selection menu, click **Equals "Grand Rapids"**. Access displays the filtered results. Only the 13 records that have a City field value of "Grand Rapids" appear in the datasheet. See Figure 3-15.

Datasheet after applying the filter | **Figure 3-15**

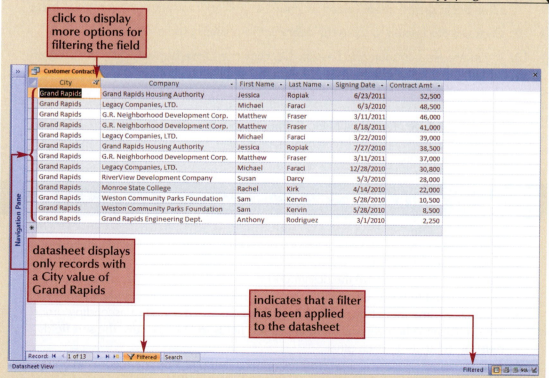

On the status bar, the button labeled "Filtered" to the right of the navigation buttons and the notation "Filtered" both indicate that a filter has been applied to the datasheet. Also, notice that the Toggle Filter button in the Sort & Filter group on the Home tab is active; you can click this button (or the Filtered button next to the navigation buttons) to toggle between the filtered and nonfiltered displays of the query datasheet. The City field also has a filtered icon to the right of the field name; you can click this icon to display additional options for filtering the field.

Next, Sarah wants to view only those records with a Signing Date value in the month of March to focus on the contracts signed in that month for customers located in Grand Rapids. So, you need to apply an additional filter to the datasheet.

4. In any Signing Date field value beginning with the number "3" (for the month of March), select only the first digit **3**.

5. In the Sort & Filter group on the Home tab, click the **Selection** button. Notice that three filters are available based on your selection: to display only those records with a Signing Date field value that begins with 3; to display only those records with a Signing Date field value that does not begin with 3; or to display only those records with a Signing Date field value that is between two dates. If you choose the between option, a dialog box opens, in which you enter the date values that you want to use.

6. Click **Begins With 3** in the Selection menu. The second filter is applied to the query datasheet, which now shows only the four records for customers located in Grand Rapids who signed contracts in the month of March.

Now you can redisplay all the query records by clicking the Toggle Filter button, which you use to switch between the filtered and nonfiltered displays.

7. In the Sort & Filter group on the Home tab, click the **Toggle Filter** button. Access redisplays all the records in the query datasheet.

8. Close the Customer Contracts query. Access asks if you want to save your changes to the design of the query—in this case, the filtered display, which is still available through the Toggle Filter button. Sarah does not want the query saved with the filter because she doesn't need to view the filtered information on a regular basis.

9. Click the **No** button to close the query without saving the changes.

10. If you are not continuing to Session 3.2, click the **Close** button ☒ on the program window title bar. Access closes the Belmont database, and then the Access program closes.

The queries you've created will help Belmont Landscapes employees retrieve just the information they want to view. In the next session, you'll continue to create queries to meet their information needs.

Review | **Session 3.1 Quick Check**

1. In Datasheet view, what is the difference between navigation mode and editing mode?
2. What is a select query?
3. Describe the field list and the design grid in the Query window in Design view.
4. How are a table datasheet and a query datasheet similar? How are they different?
5. For a Date/Time field, how do the records appear when sorted in ascending order?
6. True or False: When you define multiple sort fields in Design view, the sort fields must be adjacent to each other.
7. A(n) _____ is a set of restrictions you place on the records in an open datasheet or form to isolate a subset of records temporarily.

Session 3.2

Defining Record Selection Criteria for Queries

Oren wants to display customer and contract information for all customers who live in Holland, Oren's hometown. He is planning to do a special local promotion for Holland customers, because Belmont Landscapes is located there, and Oren wants to increase his firm's presence in the community. For this request, you could create a query to select the correct fields and all records in the Customer and Contract tables, select a City field value of Holland in the query datasheet, and then click the Selection button and choose the appropriate filter option to filter the query results and display the information for only those customers in Holland. However, a faster way of displaying the data Oren needs is to create a query that displays the selected fields and only those records in the Customer and Contract tables that satisfy a condition.

Just as you can display selected fields from a database in a query datasheet, you can display selected records. To tell Access which records you want to select, you must specify a condition as part of the query. A **condition** is a criterion, or rule, that determines which records are selected. To define a condition for a field, you place the condition in the field's Criteria text box in the design grid.

A condition usually consists of an operator, often a comparison operator, and a value. A **comparison operator** asks Access to compare the value in a database field to the condition value and to select all the records for which the relationship is true. For example, the condition >50000 for the Contract Amt field selects all records in the Contract table with Contract Amt field values greater than $50,000. Figure 3-16 shows the Access comparison operators.

Access comparison operators **Figure 3-16**

Operator	Meaning	Example
=	equal to (optional; default operator)	="Hall"
<	less than	<#1/1/99#
<=	less than or equal to	<=100
>	greater than	>"C400"
>=	greater than or equal to	>=18.75
<>	not equal to	<>"Hall"
Between ... And ...	between two values (inclusive)	Between 50 And 325
In ()	in a list of values	In ("Hall", "Seeger")
Like	matches a pattern that includes wildcards	Like "706*"

Specifying an Exact Match

For Oren's request, you need to create a query that will display only those records in the Customer table with the value Holland in the City field. This type of condition is called an **exact match** because the value in the specified field must match the condition exactly in order for the record to be included in the query results. You'll create the query in Design view.

To create the query in Design view:

▶ 1. If you took a break after the previous session, make sure that the Belmont database is open in the Access program window and that the Navigation Pane is closed.

▶ 2. Click the **Create** tab on the Ribbon.

▶ 3. In the Other group on the Create tab, click the **Query Design** button. The Show Table dialog box opens. You need to add the Customer and Contract tables to the Query window.

▶ 4. Click **Customer** in the Tables list box, click the **Add** button, click **Contract**, click the **Add** button, and then click the **Close** button.

▶ 5. Use the ↕ pointer to resize the Customer field list so that all the fields are displayed.

▶ 6. Add the following fields from the Customer table to the design grid in the order shown: **Company**, **First Name**, **Last Name**, **Phone**, **Address**, **City**, and **E-mail Address**.

Oren also wants information from the Contract table included in the query results.

▶ 7. Add the following fields from the Contract table to the design grid in the order shown: **Contract Num**, **Contract Amt**, **Signing Date**, and **Contract Type**. See Figure 3-17.

Figure 3-17	Query in Design view

The field lists for the Customer and Contract tables appear in the top portion of the window, and the join line indicating a one-to-many relationship connects the two tables. The fields you selected appear in the design grid; to see all of the fields, you need to scroll to the right using the horizontal scroll bar.

To display the information Oren wants, you need to enter the condition for the City field in its Criteria text box. Oren wants to display only those records with a City field value of Holland.

To enter the exact match condition, and then save and run the query:

▶ 1. Click the **City Criteria** text box, type **Holland**, and then press the **Enter** key. The condition changes to "Holland".

Access automatically enclosed the condition you typed in quotation marks. You must enclose Text values in quotation marks when using them as selection criteria. If you omit the quotation marks, however, Access will include them automatically.

2. Click the **Save** button 🖫 on the Quick Access Toolbar to open the Save As dialog box.

3. Type **Holland Customers** in the Query Name text box, and then press the **Enter** key. Access saves the query with the specified name and displays the name on the query tab.

4. In the Results group on the Query Tools Design tab, click the **Run** button. Access runs the query and displays the selected field values for only those records with a City field value of Holland. A total of 12 records are selected and displayed in the datasheet. See Figure 3-18.

Datasheet displaying selected fields and records — Figure 3-18

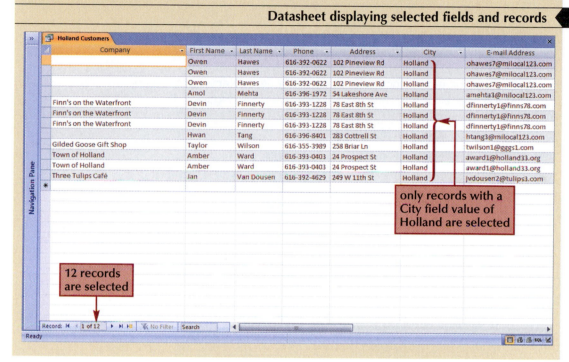

Oren realizes that it's not necessary to include the City field values in the query results. The name of the query, Holland Customers, indicates that the query design includes all customers that are located in Holland, so the City field values are unnecessary and repetitive. Also, he decides that he would prefer the query datasheet to show the fields from the Contract table first, followed by the Customer table fields. You need to modify the query to produce the results Oren wants.

Modifying a Query

After you create a query and view the results, you might need to make changes to the query if the results are not what you expected or want to view. First, Oren asks you to modify the Holland Customers query to remove the City field values from the query results.

To remove the display of the City field values:

1. In the Views group on the Home tab, click the **View** button. The Holland Customers query opens in Design view.

    You need to keep the City field as part of the query design, because it contains the defined condition for the query. You only need to remove the display of the field's values from the query results.

> **2.** Click the **City Show** check box to remove the check mark. The query will still find only those records with the value Holland in the City field, but the query results will not display these field values.

Next, you need to change the order of the fields in the query so that the contract information is listed first.

To move the fields from the Contract table before the fields from the Customer table:

> **1.** Scroll the design grid to the right until the remaining fields in the query design are visible. You need to move the Contract Num field so it becomes the first field in the query design.

> **2.** Position the pointer on the Contract Num field selector until the pointer changes to a ↓ shape, and then click to select the field. See Figure 3-19.

Figure 3-19	Selected Contract Num field

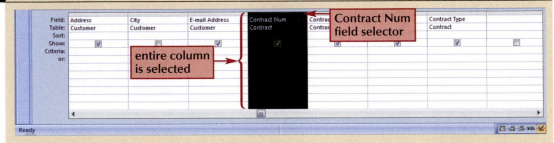

> **3.** Position the pointer on the Contract Num field selector, and then click and drag the pointer to the left, allowing the design grid to scroll back to the left, until the vertical line to the left of the Company field is highlighted. See Figure 3-20.

Figure 3-20	Dragging the field in the design grid

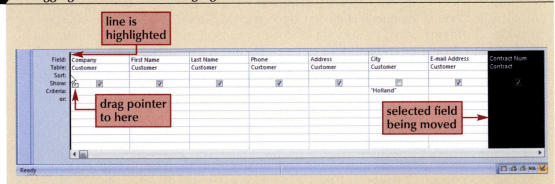

> **4.** Release the mouse button. The Contract Num field moves to the left of the Company field.

> You can also select and move multiple fields at once.

> **5.** Scroll back to the right to view the remaining fields in the design grid. Now you need to select and move the Contract Amt, Signing Date, and Contract Type fields so that they follow the Contract Num field in the query design. To select multiple fields, you simply click and drag the mouse over the field selectors for the fields you want.

6. Click and hold the pointer ↓ on the Contract Amt field selector, drag the pointer to the right to select the Signing Date and Contract Type fields, and then release the mouse button. All three fields are now selected. See Figure 3-21.

Multiple fields selected to be moved ◄ **Figure 3-21**

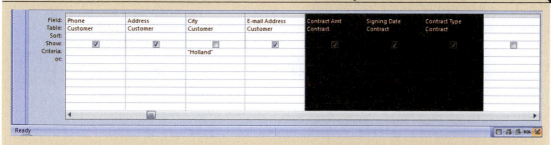

7. Position the pointer ⌖ anywhere near the top of the three selected fields, and then click and drag the pointer to the left until the vertical line to the right of the Contract Num field is highlighted.

8. Release the mouse button. The four fields from the Contract table are now the first four fields in the query design.

   You have finished making the modifications to the query Oren requested, so you can now run the query.

9. In the Results group on the Query Tools Design tab, click the **Run** button. Access displays the results of the modified query. See Figure 3-22.

Results of modified query ◄ **Figure 3-22**

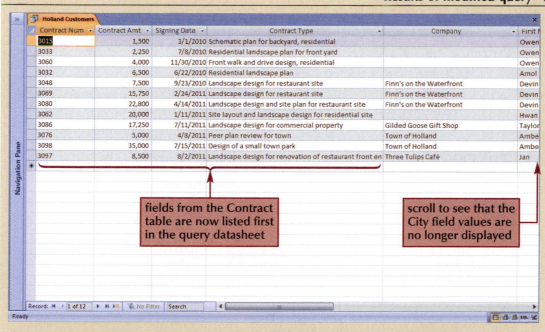

Note that the City field values are no longer displayed in the query results (you need to scroll the datasheet to the right to verify this).

Oren would like to see more fields and records on the screen at one time. He asks you to change the datasheet's font size, and then to resize all the columns to their best fit.

Changing a Datasheet's Appearance

You can change the characteristics of a datasheet, including the font type and size of text in the datasheet, to improve its appearance or readability. As you learned in earlier tutorials, you can also resize the datasheet columns to view more columns on the screen at the same time. You'll change the font size from the default 11 points to 9, and then resize the datasheet columns.

To change the font size and resize the columns in the datasheet:

▶ **1.** In the Font group on the Home tab, click the **Font Size** arrow, and then click **9**. The font size for the entire datasheet changes to 9 points.

Next, you need to resize the columns to their best fit, so that each column is just wide enough to fit the longest value in the column. Instead of resizing each column individually, you'll use the datasheet selector to select all the columns and resize them at the same time.

▶ **2.** Click the **datasheet selector**, which is the box to the left of the Contract Num field name. All the columns in the datasheet are highlighted, indicating they are selected.

▶ **3.** Position the pointer ✛ at the right edge of any column in the datasheet, and then double-click the pointer. All the columns visible on the screen are resized to their best fit. Because only the visible columns are resized, you must scroll the datasheet to the right to make sure all field values for the entire column are fully displayed, resizing as you scroll, if necessary.

▶ **4.** Scroll the datasheet to the right and verify that all columns were resized to their best fit. If necessary, resize any individual column that might not have been resized to best fit the data it contains.

▶ **5.** Scroll to the left, if necessary, so that the Contract Num field is visible, and then click any field value in the Contract Num column to make it the current field. More columns are now visible in the datasheet.

Changing the Background Color of Datasheet Rows

By default, the rows in a datasheet are displayed with alternating background colors of white and light gray to distinguish one row from another, making it easier to view and read the contents of a datasheet. The default white/gray alternate scheme provides a subtle color difference between the rows. You can change the background color for datasheet rows to something more noticeable using the **Alternate Fill/Back Color button** in the Font group. Oren suggests that you change the row colors of the query datasheet to see the effect of using this feature.

To change the background color of the datasheet rows:

▶ **1.** In the Font group on the Home tab, click the arrow on the **Alternate Fill/Back Color** button ▦ ▾ to display the gallery of color choices. See Figure 3-23.

Gallery of color choices for alternate fill color — Figure 3-23

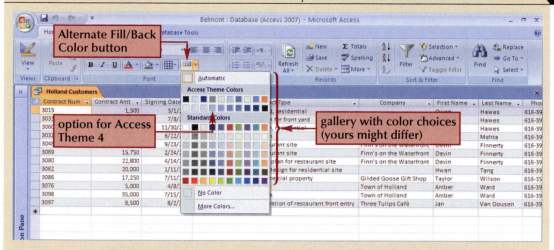

The Access Theme Colors palette provides colors from Access themes, so that your datasheet's color scheme matches the default used for the Access program. The Standard Colors palette provides many standard color choices. You might also see a Recent Colors palette, with colors that you have recently used in a datasheet. On the menu, you could also choose the No Color option, which sets each row's background to white; or the More Colors option, which creates a custom color. You'll use one of the theme colors.

Tip

The name of the color appears in a ScreenTip when you point to a color in the gallery.

▶ **2.** In the Access Theme Colors palette, click the color box for **Access Theme 4** (second row, fourth color box). The alternating background color is applied to the query datasheet. See Figure 3-24.

Datasheet formatted with new fill color — Figure 3-24

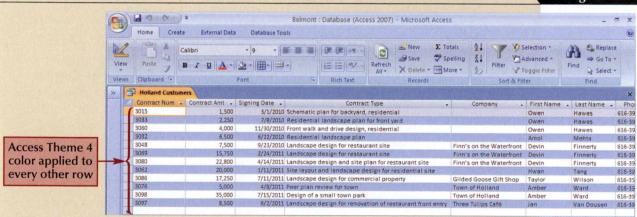

Every other row in the datasheet uses the Access Theme 4 background color. Oren likes how the datasheet looks with this color scheme, so he asks you to save the query.

▶ **3.** Save and close the Holland Customers query.

After viewing the query results, Oren decides that he would like to see the same fields, but only for those records with a Contract Amt field value equal to or greater than $25,000. He is interested to know which Belmont Landscapes customers in all cities and towns have signed the largest contracts, so that he can follow up with these customers personally. To create the query that will produce the results Oren wants, you need to use a comparison operator to match a range of values—in this case, any Contract Amt value greater than or equal to $25,000.

Using a Comparison Operator to Match a Range of Values

Once you create and save a query, you can double-click the query name in the Navigation Pane to run the query again. You can then click the View button to change its design. You can also use an existing query as the basis for creating another query. Because the design of the query you need to create next is similar to the Holland Customers query, you will copy, paste, and rename this query to create the new query. Using this approach keeps the Holland Customers query intact.

To create the new query by copying the Holland Customers query:

1. Open the Navigation Pane. Note that the Holland Customers query is listed below both the Contract and Customer groups, because the query is based on data from both tables.

   You need to use the shortcut menu to copy the Holland Customers query and paste it in the Navigation Pane; then you'll give the copied query a different name. To do so, you could copy either instance of the Holland Customers query in the Navigation Pane.

2. In the Customer group on the Navigation Pane, right-click **Holland Customers** to select it and display the shortcut menu.

3. Click **Copy** on the shortcut menu.

4. Right-click the empty area of the Navigation Pane, and then click **Paste** on the shortcut menu. The Paste As dialog box opens with the text "Copy Of Holland Customers" in the Query Name text box. Because Oren wants the new query to show the contracts with the largest amounts, you'll name the new query "Large Contract Amounts."

5. Type **Large Contract Amounts** in the Query Name text box, and then press the **Enter** key. The new query appears in both the Contract and Customer groups in the Navigation Pane.

6. In the Customer group on the Navigation Pane, double-click the **Large Contract Amounts** query to open, or run, the query. Notice that all the design changes you made to the original Holland Customers query—decreasing the font size, resizing all the columns, and applying the new alternating background row color—were saved with the query.

7. Close the Navigation Pane.

Next, you need to open the query in Design view and modify its design to produce the results Oren wants—to display only those records with Contract Amt field values that are greater than or equal to $25,000.

To modify the design of the new query:

1. In the Views group on the Home tab, click the **View** button to display the query in Design view.

2. Click the **Contract Amt Criteria** text box, type **>=25000**, and then press the **Tab** key. See Figure 3-25.

Criteria entered for Contract Amt field | Figure 3-25

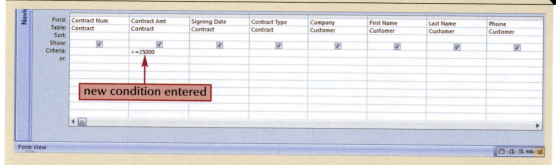

Trouble? If you receive an error message saying that you entered an expression containing invalid syntax, you might have typed a comma in the amount "25000" or a dollar sign. Commas and dollar signs are not allowed in selection criteria. Delete the comma and/or dollar sign from the Contract Amt Criteria box, and then press the Tab key.

The condition specifies that a record will be selected only if its Contract Amt field value is $25,000 or greater. Before you run the query, you need to delete the condition for the City field. Recall that the City field is part of the query, but its values are not displayed in the query results. When you modified the query to remove the City field values from the query results, Access moved the field to the end of the design grid. So, you need to locate the City field, delete its condition, specify that the City field values should be included in the query results, and then move the field back to its original position following the Address field.

3. Press the **Tab** key eight times until the condition for the City field is highlighted, and then press the **Delete** key. The condition for the City field is removed.

4. Click the **Show** check box for the City field to insert a check mark so that the field values will be displayed in the query results.

5. Use the ⬇ pointer to select the City field, drag the selected field to the right of the Address field, and then click in an empty box to deselect the City field. See Figure 3-26.

Design grid after moving City field | Figure 3-26

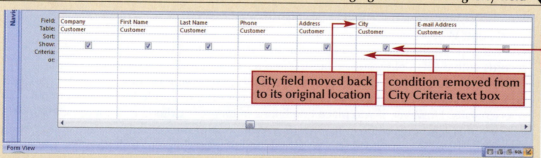

6. In the Results group on the Query Tools Design tab, click the **Run** button. Access runs the query and displays the selected fields for only those records with a Contract Amt field value of greater than or equal to $25,000. A total of 23 records are selected. See Figure 3-27.

Figure 3-27   ▶   **Running the modified query**

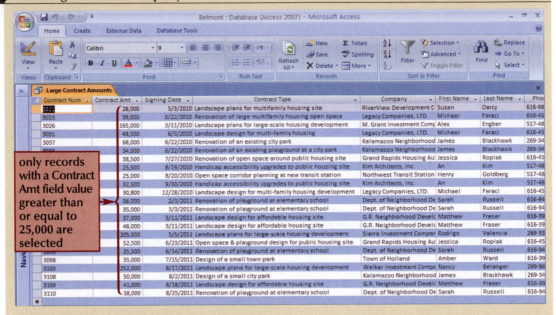

only records with a Contract Amt field value greater than or equal to 25,000 are selected

The City field values are also included in the query datasheet; you need to scroll the datasheet to the right to view them.

7. Save and close the Large Contract Amounts query.

Oren recently hired Steve Barry as a new consultant at Belmont Landscapes. Steve will focus primarily on customers located in Lansing. To help Steve prioritize his site visits in Lansing, Oren asks you to provide him with a list of all customers in Lansing who have signed contracts with values greater than $25,000. To produce this list, you need to create a query containing two conditions—one for the city and another for the contract amount.

Defining Multiple Selection Criteria for Queries

Multiple conditions require you to use **logical operators** to combine two or more conditions. When you want a record selected only if two or more conditions are met, you need to use the **And logical operator**. In this case, Oren wants to see only those records with a City field value of Lansing *and* a Contract Amt field value greater than $25,000. If you place conditions in separate fields in the *same* Criteria row of the design grid, all conditions in that row must be met in order for a record to be included in the query results. However, if you place conditions in *different* Criteria rows, a record will be selected if at least one of the conditions is met. If none of the conditions are met, Access does not select the record. When you place conditions in different Criteria rows, you are using the **Or logical operator**. Figure 3-28 illustrates the difference between the And and Or logical operators.

Logical operators And and Or for multiple selection criteria ◀ Figure 3-28

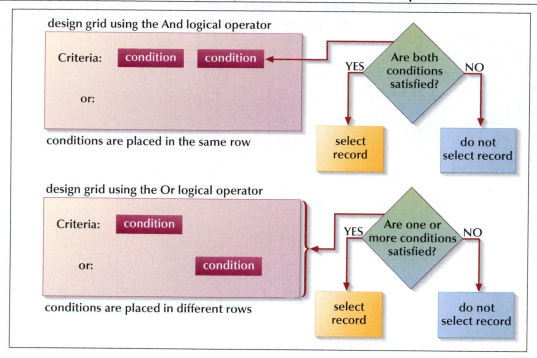

The And Logical Operator

To create the query for Oren, you need to use the And logical operator to show only the records for customers located in Lansing *and* with a contract amount greater than $25,000. You'll create a new query based on both the Customer and Contract tables to produce the necessary results. In the query design, both conditions you specify will appear in the same Criteria row; therefore, the query will select records only if both conditions are met.

To create a new query using the And logical operator:

▶ **1.** Click the **Create** tab on the Ribbon.

▶ **2.** In the Other group on the Create tab, click the **Query Design** button.

▶ **3.** Add the **Customer** and **Contract** tables to the Query window, and then close the Show Table dialog box. Resize the Customer field list to display all the field names.

▶ **4.** Add the following fields from the Customer field list to the design grid in the order shown: **Company**, **First Name**, **Last Name**, **Phone**, and **City**.

▶ **5.** Add the **Contract Amt** and **Signing Date** fields from the Contract table to the design grid.

   Now you need to enter the two conditions for the query.

▶ **6.** Click the **City Criteria** text box, and then type **Lansing**.

▶ **7.** Press the **Tab** key to move to the **Contract Amt Criteria** text box, type **>25000**, and then press the **Tab** key. See Figure 3-29.

Figure 3-29 Query to find customers in Lansing with large contracts

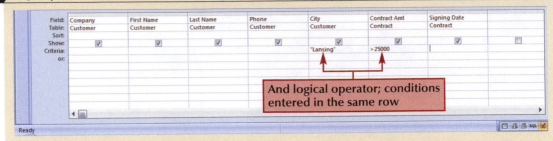

8. **Run** the query. Access displays only those records that meet both conditions: a City field value of Lansing and a Contract Amt field value greater than $25,000. Three records are selected, for two different customers. See Figure 3-30.

Figure 3-30 Results of query using the And logical operator

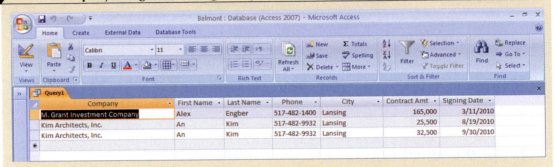

9. Click the **Save** button on the Quick Access Toolbar, and then save the query as **Key Lansing Customers**.

10. Close the query. When Steve begins working at Belmont Landscapes, he can run this query to see which customers in Lansing he should contact first.

Next, Oren and Taylor meet to discuss strategies for increasing business for Belmont Landscapes. They are interested in knowing which customers signed contracts for small amounts—less than $10,000—or which contracts were signed in the first two months of 2011, because business seemed unusually slow during those months. They want to use this information for two reasons: (1) to target specific customers who signed smaller contracts with Belmont Landscapes, to determine if these customers might have additional landscaping needs; and (2) to analyze the number and type of contracts signed during these slow months so they can develop strategies for increasing contract signings in the future. To help with their planning, Oren and Taylor have asked you to produce a list of all contracts with amounts less than $10,000 or that were signed between 1/1/2011 and 3/1/2011. To create this query, you need to use the Or logical operator.

The Or Logical Operator

To create the query that Oren and Taylor requested, your query must select a record when either one of two conditions is satisfied or when both conditions are satisfied. That is, a record is selected if the Contract Amt field value is less than $10,000 *or* if the Signing Date field value is between 1/1/2011 and 3/1/2011 *or* if both conditions are met. You will enter the condition for the Contract Amt field in the Criteria row and the condition for the Signing Date field in the "or" criteria row, thereby using the Or logical operator.

To display the information Oren and Taylor want to view, you'll create a new query containing the First Name, Last Name, Company, and City fields from the Customer table (in that order); and the Contract Amt, Signing Date, and Contract Type fields from the Contract table. Then you'll specify the conditions using the Or logical operator.

To create a new query using the Or logical operator:

1. Click the **Create** tab on the Ribbon and then, in the Other group, click the **Query Design** button.

2. Add the **Customer** and **Contract** tables to the Query window, close the Show Table dialog box, and then resize the Customer field list.

3. Add the following fields from the Customer table to the design grid in the order shown: **First Name**, **Last Name**, **Company**, and **City**.

4. Add the following fields from the Contract table to the design grid in the order shown: **Contract Amt**, **Signing Date**, and **Contract Type**.

   Now you need to specify the first condition, <10000, in the Contract Amt field.

5. Click the **Contract Amt Criteria** text box, type **<10000** and then press the **Tab** key.

   Because you want records selected if either of the conditions for the Contract Amt or Signing Date fields is satisfied, you must enter the condition for the Signing Date field in the "or" row of the design grid. To specify the date period for the query, you'll use the Between operator.

6. Press the **↓** key, type **Between 1/1/2011 And 3/1/2011** in the "or" text box for Signing Date, and then press the **Tab** key.

   To view the entire condition for the Signing Date field, you'll resize this field's column in the design grid.

7. Place the pointer on the vertical line to the right of the Signing Date field selector until the pointer changes to a ✛ shape, and then double-click to widen the column. The condition in the Signing Date field is now fully displayed. Note that Access automatically places number signs around the date values in the condition to distinguish the date values from the operators. See Figure 3-31.

Query window with the Or logical operator Figure 3-31

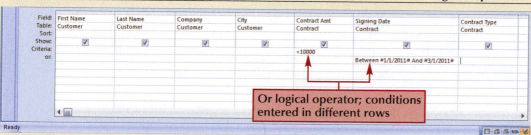

Oren wants the list displayed in descending order by Signing Date, to better analyze the data.

8. Click the right side of the **Signing Date Sort** text box, and then click **Descending**.

▶ **9.** Run the query. Access displays only those records that meet either condition: a Contract Amt field value less than $10,000 or a Signing Date field value between 1/1/2011 and 3/1/2011. Access also selects records that meet both conditions. A total of 29 records are selected. The records in the query datasheet appear in descending order based on the values in the Signing Date field. See Figure 3-32.

Figure 3-32 | **Results of query using the Or logical operator**

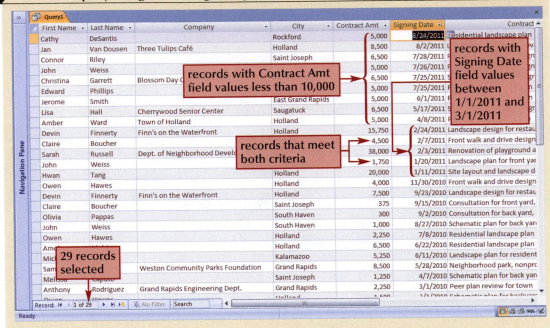

▶ **10.** Save the query as **Small Contracts Or Winter Signings**, and then close it.

InSight | **Understanding the Results of Using And vs. Or**

When you use the And logical operator to define multiple selection criteria in a query, you *narrow* the results produced by the query, because a record must meet more than one condition to be included in the results. When you use the Or logical operator, you *broaden* the results produced by the query, because a record must meet only one of the conditions to be included in the results. This is an important distinction to keep in mind when you include multiple selection criteria in queries, so that the queries you create will produce the results you want.

Next, Oren turns his attention to some financial aspects of his business. He wants to use the Belmont database to perform calculations. He is considering imposing a 3% late fee on unpaid invoices and wants to know exactly what the late fee charges would be, should he decide to institute such a policy in the future. To produce the information for Oren, you need to create a calculated field.

Creating a Calculated Field

In addition to using queries to retrieve, sort, and filter data in a database, you can use a query to perform calculations. To perform a calculation, you define an **expression** containing a combination of database fields, constants, and operators. For numeric expressions, the data types of the database fields must be Number, Currency, or Date/Time; the constants are numbers such as .03 (for the 3% late fee); and the operators can be arithmetic operators (+ – * /) or other specialized operators. In complex expressions, you can enclose calculations in parentheses to indicate which one should be performed first. In expressions without parentheses, Access calculates in the following order of precedence: multiplication and division before addition and subtraction. When operators have equal precedence, Access calculates them in order from left to right.

To perform a calculation in a query, you add a calculated field to the query. A **calculated field** is a field that displays the results of an expression. A calculated field appears in a query datasheet or in a form or report; however, it does not exist in a database. When you run a query that contains a calculated field, Access evaluates the expression defined by the calculated field and displays the resulting value in the query datasheet, form, or report.

To enter an expression for a calculated field, you can type it directly in a Field text box in the design grid. Alternately, you can open the Zoom box or Expression Builder and use either one to enter the expression. The **Zoom box** is a dialog box that you can use to enter text, expressions, or other values. To use the Zoom box, however, you must know all the parts of the expression you want to create. **Expression Builder** is an Access tool that makes it easy for you to create an expression; it contains a box for entering the expression, buttons for common operators, and one or more lists of expression elements, such as table and field names. Unlike a Field text box, which is too small to show an entire expression at one time, the Zoom box and Expression Builder are large enough to display lengthy expressions. In most cases, Expression Builder provides the easiest way to enter expressions, because you don't have to know all the parts of the expression; you can choose the necessary elements from the Expression Builder dialog box.

> **Tip**
>
> If your field names include spaces in the names, as in the fields "First Name" and "Last Name," you must enclose the names in brackets when using them in an expression.

Using Expression Builder | Reference Window

- Open the query in Design view.
- In the design grid, position the insertion point in the Field text box of the field for which you want to create an expression.
- In the Query Setup group on the Query Tools Design tab, click the Builder button.
- Use the expression elements and common operators to build the expression, or type the expression directly.
- Click the OK button.

To produce the information Oren wants, you need to create a new query based on the Invoice table and, in the query, create a calculated field that will multiply each Invoice Amt field value by .03 to calculate the proposed 3% late fee.

To create the new query that will include the calculated field:

▶ **1.** Click the **Create** tab on the Ribbon and then, in the Other group, click the **Query Design** button.

Oren wants to see data from both the Contract and Invoice tables, so you need to add these two tables to the Query window.

▶ **2.** Add the **Contract** and **Invoice** tables to the Query window, and then close the Show Table dialog box. The field lists appear in the Query window, and the one-to-many relationship between the Contract (primary) and Invoice (related) tables is displayed.

▶ **3.** Add the following fields to the design grid in the order given: **Contract Num** and **Contract Amt** from the Contract table; and **Invoice Item**, **Invoice Paid**, and **Invoice Amt** from the Invoice table.

Oren is interested in viewing data for unpaid invoices only, because a late fee would apply only to them, so you need to enter the necessary condition for the Invoice Paid field. Recall that Invoice Paid is a Yes/No field. The condition you need to enter is the word "No" in the Criteria text box for this field, so that Access will retrieve the records for unpaid invoices only.

▶ **4.** In the **Invoice Paid Criteria** text box, type **No** and then press the **Tab** key.

The query name you'll use will indicate that the data is for unpaid invoices, so you don't need to include the Invoice Paid values in the query results.

▶ **5.** Click the **Invoice Paid Show** check box to remove the check mark.

▶ **6.** Save the query with the name **Unpaid Invoices With Late Fees**.

Now you can use the Expression Builder to create the calculated field for the Invoice Amt field.

To create the calculated field:

▶ **1.** Click the blank Field text box to the right of the Invoice Amt field. This field will contain the calculated field values.

▶ **2.** In the Query Setup group on the Query Tools Design tab, click the **Builder** button. The Expression Builder dialog box opens.

The center pane in the dialog box lists the fields from the query so you can include them in the expression. You can use the common operators and expression elements to help you build an expression.

The expression for the calculated field will multiply the Invoice Amt field values by the numeric constant .03 (which represents a 3% late fee). To include a field in the expression, you select the field and then click the Paste button in the dialog box. To include a numeric constant, you simply type the constant in the expression.

▶ **3.** Click **Invoice Amt** in the field list, and then click the **Paste** button in the dialog box. The field name appears in the expression box, within brackets.

To include the multiplication operator in the expression, you click the asterisk (*) button. Note that you do not include spaces between the elements in an expression.

▶ **4.** Click the ***** button in the row of common operators, and then type **.03**. You have finished entering the expression. See Figure 3-33.

Completed expression for the calculated field | **Figure 3-33**

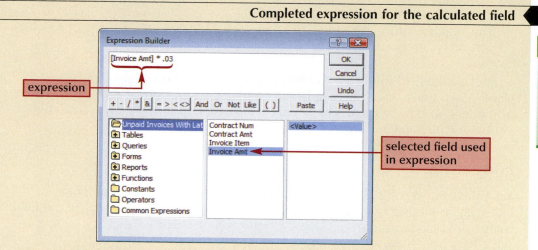

expression

selected field used in expression

Tip

You can also type an expression directly into the expression box, instead of clicking field names, operators, and so on.

▶ **5.** Click the **OK** button. Access closes the Expression Builder dialog box and adds the expression to the design grid in the Field text box for the calculated field.

Next, you need to specify a name for the calculated field as it will appear in the query results.

▶ **6.** Press the **Home** key to position the insertion point to the left of the expression.

You'll enter the name Late Fee, which is descriptive of the field's contents; then you'll run the query. To separate the calculated field name from the expression, you must type a colon between them.

▶ **7.** Type **Late Fee:**. *Make sure you include the colon following the field name.*

▶ **8.** Run the query. Access displays the query datasheet, which contains the specified fields and the calculated field with the name "Late Fee." See Figure 3-34.

Datasheet displaying the calculated field | **Figure 3-34**

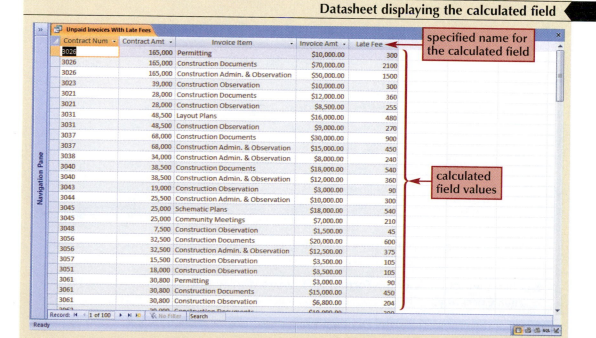

specified name for the calculated field

calculated field values

Trouble? If the calculated field name does not appear correctly, as shown in Figure 3-34, you might not have included the required colon. Switch to Design view, resize the column in the design grid that contains the calculated field to best fit, and then change your expression to Late Fee: [Invoice Amt]*0.03 and repeat Step 8.

The Late Fee field values are currently displayed without dollar signs and decimal places. Oren wants these values to be displayed in the same format as the Invoice Amt field values, in case he decides to produce a report for customers showing both the invoice amounts and any imposed late fees.

Formatting a Calculated Field

You can specify a particular format for a calculated field, just as you can for any field, by modifying its properties. Next, you'll change the format of the Late Fee calculated field so that all values appear in the Currency format with two decimal places.

To format the calculated field:

1. Switch to Design view.

2. Right-click the **Late Fee** calculated field in the design grid to open the shortcut menu, and then click **Properties**. The Property Sheet for the calculated field opens on the right side of the window. See Figure 3-35.

Figure 3-35 Property Sheet for the calculated field

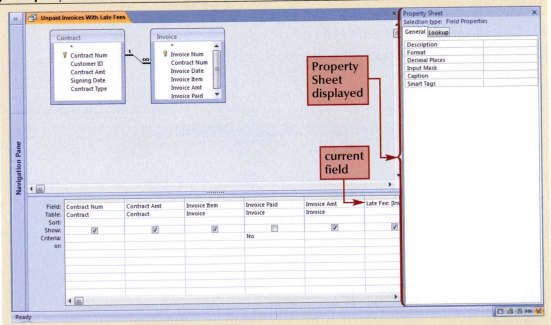

You need to change the Format property to Currency and the Decimal Places property to 2.

3. Click the right side of the **Format** text box to display the list of formats, and then click **Currency**.

4. Click the right side of the **Decimal Places** text box, and then click **2**.

5. Close the Property Sheet for the calculated field, and then run the query. The amounts in the Late Fee calculated field are now displayed with dollar signs and two decimal places.
6. Save and close the Unpaid Invoices With Late Fees query.

Creating Calculated Fields | InSight

Values that are produced by calculated fields should not be stored as separate fields in a database table. If you store the results of a calculated field in a table and the data produced by the calculated field becomes outdated, you would have to update the records in the table datasheet with the current data. It is best to create a query that includes a calculated field to perform the calculation you want. Then, every time you open the query, the calculation is performed and the resulting query datasheet reflects the most current data.

Oren wants to prepare a report on a regular basis that includes a summary of information about the contract amounts for Belmont Landscapes. He would like to know the minimum, average, and maximum contract amounts. He asks you to determine these statistics from data in the Contract table.

Using Aggregate Functions

You can calculate statistical information, such as totals and averages, on the records displayed in a table datasheet or selected by a query. To do this, you use the Access aggregate functions. **Aggregate functions** perform arithmetic operations on selected records in a database. Figure 3-36 lists the most frequently used aggregate functions.

Frequently used aggregate functions **Figure 3-36**

Aggregate Function	Determines	Data Types Supported
Average	Average of the field values for the selected records	AutoNumber, Currency, Date/Time, Number
Count	Number of records selected	AutoNumber, Currency, Date/Time, Memo, Number, OLE Object, Text, Yes/No
Maximum	Highest field value for the selected records	AutoNumber, Currency, Date/Time, Number, Text
Minimum	Lowest field value for the selected records	AutoNumber, Currency, Date/Time, Number, Text
Sum	Total of the field values for the selected records	AutoNumber, Currency, Date/Time, Number

Working with Aggregate Functions Using the Totals Row

If you want to quickly perform a calculation using an aggregate function in a table or query datasheet, you can use the Totals button on the Home tab. When you click this button, a row labeled "Total" appears at the end of the datasheet. You can then choose one of the aggregate functions for a field in the datasheet, and the results of the calculation will be displayed in the Total row for that field.

Oren is interested to know the total amount of all contracts for the company. You can quickly display this amount using the Sum function in the Total row in the Contract table datasheet.

To display the total amount of all contracts in the Contract table:

▶ 1. Open the Navigation Pane, open the **Contract** table in Datasheet view, and then close the Navigation Pane.

▶ 2. In the Records group on the Home tab, click the **Totals** button. Access adds a row with the label "Total" to the end of the datasheet.

▶ 3. Scroll to the end of the datasheet to view the Total row. You want to display the sum of all the values in the Contract Amt field.

▶ 4. Click the **Contract Amt** field in the Total row. An arrow appears on the left side of the field.

▶ 5. Click the **arrow** to display the menu of aggregate functions. See Figure 3-37.

| Figure 3-37 | Using aggregate functions in the Total row |

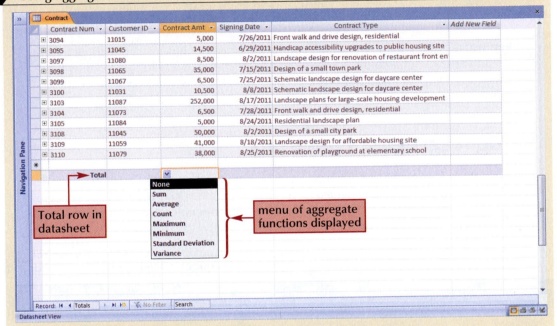

6. Click **Sum** in the menu. Access adds all the values in the Contract Amt field and displays the total 1,753,075 in the Total row for the field.

Oren doesn't want to change the Contract table to always display this total. You can remove the Total row by clicking the Totals button again; this button works as a toggle to switch between the display of the Total row and the results of any calculations in the row, and the display of the datasheet without this row.

▶ 7. In the Records group on the Home tab, click the **Totals** button. Access removes the Total row from the datasheet.

▶ 8. Close the Contract table without saving the changes.

For Oren's report, he wants to know the minimum, average, and maximum contract amounts for the company. To produce this information for Oren, you need to use aggregate functions in a query.

Creating Queries with Aggregate Functions

Aggregate functions operate on the records that meet a query's selection criteria. You specify an aggregate function for a specific field, and the appropriate operation applies to that field's values for the selected records.

To display the minimum, average, and maximum of all the contract amounts in the Contract table, you will use the Minimum, Average, and Maximum aggregate functions for the Contract Amt field.

To calculate the minimum, average, and maximum of all contract amounts:

▶ **1.** Create a new query in Design view, add the **Contract** table to the Query window, and then close the Show Table dialog box.

To perform the three calculations on the Contract Amt field, you need to add the field to the design grid three times.

▶ **2.** Double-click **Contract Amt** in the Contract field list three times to add three copies of the field to the design grid.

You need to select an aggregate function for each Contract Amt field. When you click the Totals button in the Show/Hide group on the Query Tools Design tab, a row labeled "Total" is added to the design grid. The Total row provides a list of the aggregate functions that you can select.

▶ **3.** In the Show/Hide group on the Query Tools Design tab, click the **Totals** button. A new row labeled "Total" appears between the Table and Sort rows in the design grid. The default entry for each field in the Total row is the Group By operator, which you will learn about later in this tutorial. See Figure 3-38.

Total row inserted in the design grid ◀ **Figure 3-38**

In the Total row, you specify the aggregate function you want to use for a field.

▶ **4.** Click the right side of the first column's **Total** text box, and then click **Min**. This field will calculate the minimum amount of all the Contract Amt field values.

When you run the query, Access automatically will assign a datasheet column name of "MinOfContract Amt" for this field. You can change the datasheet column name to a more descriptive or readable name by entering the name you want in the Field text box. However, you must also keep the field name Contract Amt in the Field text box, because it identifies the field whose values will be calculated. The Field text box will contain the datasheet column name you specify followed by the field name (Contract Amt) with a colon separating the two names.

5. Click to the left of Contract Amt in the first column's Field text box, and then type **Minimum Contract Amt:**. *Be sure that you type the colon following the name.*

6. Click the right side of the second column's **Total** text box, and then click **Avg**. This field will calculate the average of all the Contract Amt field values.

7. Click to the left of Contract Amt in the second column's Field text box, and then type **Average Contract Amt:**.

8. Click the right side of the third column's **Total** text box, and then click **Max**. This field will calculate the maximum amount of all the Contract Amt field values.

9. Click to the left of Contract Amt in the third column's Field text box, and then type **Maximum Contract Amt:**.

10. Run the query. Access displays one record containing the three aggregate function values. The single row of summary statistics represents calculations based on all the records selected for the query—in this case, all 64 records in the Contract table.

11. Resize all columns to their best fit so that the column names are fully displayed, and then click the field value in the first column. See Figure 3-39.

| Figure 3-39 | Result of the query using aggregate functions |

12. Save the query as **Contract Amt Statistics**.

Oren also wants his report to include the same contract amount statistics (minimum, average, and maximum) grouped by city.

Using Record Group Calculations

In addition to calculating statistical information on all or selected records in selected tables, you can calculate statistics for groups of records. For example, you can determine the number of customers in each city or the average contract amount by city.

To create a query for Oren's latest request, you can modify the current query by adding the City field and assigning the Group By operator to it. The **Group By operator** divides the selected records into groups based on the values in the specified field. Those records with the same value for the field are grouped together, and the datasheet displays one record for each group. Aggregate functions, which appear in the other columns of the design grid, provide statistical information for each group.

You need to modify the current query to add the Group By operator to the City field from the Customer table. This will display the statistical information grouped by city for all the records in the query datasheet. To create the new query, you will save the Contract Amt Statistics query with a new name, keeping the original query intact, and then modify the new query.

To create a new query with the Group By operator:

1. Display the **Contract Amt Statistics** query in Design view.

2. Click the **Office Button** 🔘, point to **Save As**, and then click **Save Object As**. The Save As dialog box opens, indicating that you are saving a copy of the Contract Amt Statistics query as a new query.

3. Type **Contract Amt Statistics By City** to replace the highlighted name, and then press the **Enter** key. The new query is saved with the name you specified.

   You need to add the City field to the query. This field is in the Customer table. To include another table in an existing query, you open the Show Table dialog box.

4. In the Query Setup group on the Query Tools Design tab, click the **Show Table** button to open the Show Table dialog box.

5. Add the **Customer** table to the Query window, close the Show Table dialog box, and then resize the Customer field list.

6. Drag the **City** field from the Customer field list to the first column in the design grid. When you release the mouse button, the City field appears in the design grid's first column, and the existing fields shift to the right. Group By, the default option in the Total row, appears for the City field.

7. Run the query. Access displays 12 records—one for each City group. Each record contains the City field value for the group and the three aggregate function values. The summary statistics represent calculations based on the 64 records in the Contract table. See Figure 3-40.

Aggregate functions grouped by City ◆ **Figure 3-40**

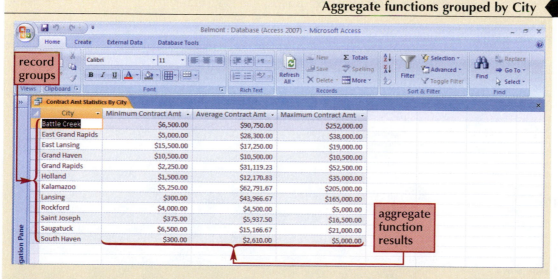

8. Save and close the query.

9. Open the Navigation Pane.

You have created and saved many queries in the Belmont database. The Navigation Pane provides options for opening and managing the queries you've created, as well as the other objects in the database, such as tables, forms, and reports.

Working with the Navigation Pane

As noted in Tutorial 1, the Navigation Pane is the main area for working with the objects in a database. As you continue to create objects in your database, you might want to display and work with them in different ways. The Navigation Pane provides options for grouping database objects in various ways to suit your needs. For example, you might want to view only the queries created for a certain table or all the query objects in the database.

The Navigation Pane divides database objects into categories, and each category contain groups. The groups contain one or more objects. The default category is **Tables and Related Views**, which arranges objects by tables, and the default group is **All Tables**, which includes all tables in the database in the list. You can also choose to display the objects for a specific table only.

The default group name, All Tables, appears at the top of the Navigation Pane. Currently, each table in the Belmont database—Contract, Invoice, and Customer—is displayed in a bar, and the objects related to each table are listed below the table name. Some objects appear more than once. As noted earlier, when an object is based on more than one table, that object appears in the group for each table. For example, the Holland Customers query is based on both the Contract and Customer tables, so it is listed in the group for both tables.

To group objects differently, you can select another category by using the Navigation Pane menu. You'll try this next.

Tip

You can hide the display of a group's objects by clicking the bar for the group; click the bar again to expand the group and display its objects.

To group objects differently in the Navigation Pane:

▶ 1. At the top of the Navigation Pane, click the **All Tables** bar. A menu is displayed for choosing different categories and groups. See Figure 3-41.

Figure 3-41 ▶ **Navigation Pane menu**

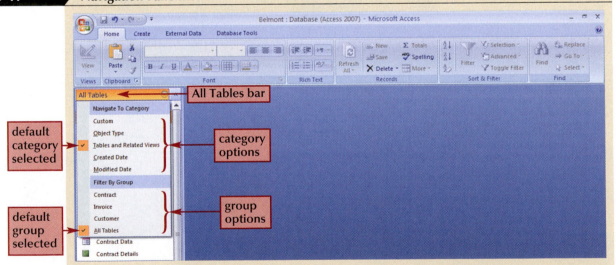

The top section of the menu provides the options for choosing a different category. The Tables and Related Views category has a check mark next to it, signifying that it is the currently selected category. The lower section of the menu provides options for choosing a different group; these options might change depending on the selected category.

2. In the top section of the menu, click **Object Type**. The Navigation Pane is now grouped into categories of object types—tables, queries, forms, and reports. See Figure 3-42.

Database objects grouped by type in the Navigation Pane   **Figure 3-42**

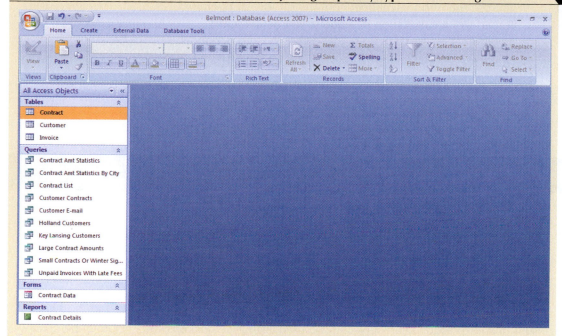

Trouble? If your Navigation Pane doesn't show all the object types, click the bar at the top of the pane to open the Navigation Pane menu, and then click All Access Objects.

You can also select a different group for a category display.

3. Click the **All Access Objects** bar to display the Navigation Pane menu, and then click **Queries**. The Navigation Pane now shows only the query objects in the database.

4. Click the **Queries** bar, and then click **Tables and Related Views** to return to the default display of the Navigation Pane.

5. Compact and repair the Belmont database, and then close Access.

The default Tables and Related Views category is a predefined category. You can also create custom categories to group objects in the way that best suits how you want to manage your database objects. As you continue to build a database and the list of objects grows, creating a custom category can help you to work more efficiently with the objects in the database.

The queries you've created and saved will help Oren, Taylor, Sarah, and others to monitor and analyze the business activity of Belmont Landscapes and its customers. Now any staff member can run the queries at any time, modify them as needed, or use them as the basis for designing new queries to meet additional information requirements.

| Review | | **Session 3.2 Quick Check** |

1. A(n) _____ is a criterion, or rule, that determines which records are selected for a query datasheet.
2. In the design grid, where do you place the conditions for two different fields when you use the And logical operator? The Or logical operator?
3. To perform a calculation in a query, you define a(n) _____ containing a combination of database fields, constants, and operators.
4. How does a calculated field differ from a table field?
5. What is an aggregate function?
6. The _____ operator divides selected records into groups based on the values in a field.
7. What is the default category for the display of objects in the Navigation Pane?

| Review | | **Tutorial Summary** |

In this tutorial, you learned how to maintain a database by finding specific data, modifying values in records, and deleting records. You also learned how to create queries in Design view, based on one or more tables, and how to run and save queries. You learned different methods for sorting and filtering data to view records in a particular order. Using record selection criteria, you specified an exact match in a query, used a comparison operator to match a range of values, and used the And and Or logical operators to meet various requests for data retrieval. You also created a calculated field in the Expression Builder dialog box to display the results of an expression in a query, and you used aggregate functions and the Group By operator to calculate and display statistical information in a query. Finally, you learned how to change the display and grouping of database objects in the Navigation Pane.

Key Terms

aggregate function
All Tables
Alternate Fill/Back Color
    button
And logical operator
AutoFilter
calculated field
comparison operator
condition
datasheet selector
design grid
editing mode
exact match
expand indicator
expression

Expression Builder
F2 key
field list
filter
Filter By Form
Filter By Selection
Find command
Group By operator
logical operator
maintain (a database)
navigation mode
nonunique sort field
Or logical operator
plus sign
primary sort field

query by example (QBE)
Query Wizard
recordset
run (a query)
secondary sort field
select query
sort
sort field
subdatasheet
Tables and Related Views
unique sort field
update (a database)
Zoom box

Practice	**Review Assignments**

Build on what you learned in the tutorial by practicing those skills using the same case scenario.

Data File needed for the Review Assignments: Supplier.accdb *(cont. from Tutorial 2)*

Oren asks you to update some information in the Supplier database and also to retrieve specific information from the database. Complete the following:

1. Open the **Supplier** database located in the Level.01\Review folder provided with your Data Files.

2. Open the **Company** table, and then change the following field values for the record with the Company ID MID312: Address to **2250 E Riverview St**, Phone to **269-979-0700**, Contact First Name to **Aimee**, and Contact Last Name to **Gigandet**. Close the table.

3. Open the **Product** table, find the record with Product ID 5318, and then delete the record. Close the table.

4. Create a query based on the Company table. Include the following fields, in the order shown, in the query: Company Name, Contact First Name, Contact Last Name, Phone, and Initial Contact Date. Sort the query in ascending order based on the Company Name. Save the query as **Contact List**, and then run the query.

5. Use the Contact List query datasheet to update the Company table by changing the Phone field value for Genesis Garden Center to **616-456-1783**.

6. Change the alternate background color for the rows in the Contact List query datasheet to Light Label Text, and then save and close the query.

7. Use Design view to create a query based on the Company and Product tables. Select the Company Name and City fields from the Company table, and the Product Type, Price, Unit, and Discount Offered fields from the Product table. Sort the query results in descending order based on the Price. Select only those records with a City field value of Holland, but do not display the City field values in the query results. Save the query as **Holland Companies**, and then run the query. Resize all columns in the datasheet, if necessary, and then save and close the query.

8. Use Design view to create a query that lists all products that cost more than $5,000 and are not eligible for a discount. Display the following fields from the Product table in the query results: Product ID, Product Type, Price, Unit, and Weight in Lbs. (*Hint*: The Discount Offered field is a Yes/No field that should not appear in the query results.) Save the query as **High Prices No Discount**, run the query, and then close it.

9. Use Design view to create a query that lists companies located in Grand Rapids or products that cost less than $1,000. Include the Company Name, City, Contact First Name, and Contact Last Name fields from the Company table; and the Product Type, Price, and Discount Offered fields from the Product table. Save the query as **Grand Rapids Or Low Prices**, run the query, and then close it.

10. Use Design view to create a query that lists only those products that are eligible for a discount, along with a 5% discount amount based on the current price. Include the following fields from the Product table in the query: Product ID, Product Type, and Price. (*Hint:* The Discount Offered field is a Yes/No field that should not appear in the query results.) Display the discount in a calculated field named **Discount** that determines a 5% discount based on the Price field values. Display the results in descending order by Price. Save the query as **Prices With Discount Amounts**, and then run the query.

11. Modify the format of the Discount field in the Prices With Discount Amounts query so that it uses the Standard format and two decimal places. Run the query, resize all columns in the datasheet to best fit, and then save and close the query.

12. Create a query that calculates the lowest, highest, and average prices for all products using the field names **Lowest Price**, **Highest Price**, and **Average Price**, respectively. Run the query, resize all columns in the datasheet to best fit, save the query as **Price Statistics**, and then close it.

13. In the Navigation Pane, copy the Price Statistics query, and then rename the copied query as **Price Statistics By Company**.

14. Modify the Price Statistics By Company query so that the records are grouped by the Company Name field in the Company table. Company Name should appear as the first field in the query datasheet. Save and run the query, and then close it.

15. Change the Navigation Pane so that it displays all objects grouped by object type.

16. Compact and repair the Supplier database, and then close it.

Apply	**Case Problem 1**

Use the skills you learned in the tutorial to update records and create queries in a database for a small music school.

Data File needed for this Case Problem: Pinehill.accdb *(cont. from Tutorial 2)*

Pine Hill Music School After reviewing the Pinehill database, Yuka Koyama wants to modify some records and then view specific information about the students, teachers, and contracts for her music school. She asks you to update and then query the Pinehill database to perform these tasks. Complete the following:

1. Open the **Pinehill** database located in the Level.01\Case1 folder provided with your Data Files.

2. In the **Teacher** table, change the following information for the record with Teacher ID 55-5310: Degree is **BM** and Hire Date is **3/12/2009**. Close the table.

3. In the **Student** table, find the record with the Student ID HAV7535, and then delete the related record in the subdatasheet for this student. Delete the record for Student ID HAV7535, and then close the Student table.

4. Create a query based on the Student table that includes the Last Name, First Name, and Phone fields, in that order. Save the query as **Student Phone List**, and then run the query.

5. In the results of the Student Phone List query, change the phone number for Andrea Barreau to **503-579-2277**. Close the query.

6. Use Design view to create a query based on the Teacher and Contract tables. Display the Last Name field from the Teacher table, and the Student ID, Contract End Date, Lesson Type, Lesson Length, and Lesson Monthly Cost fields, in that order, from the Contract table. Sort in ascending order first on the teacher's last name, and then in ascending order by the Student ID. Save the query as **Lessons By Teacher**, and then run it.

7. Use the Office Button to save the Lessons By Teacher query as **Current Lessons**.

8. Modify the Current Lessons query to display all contracts that end on or after 7/1/2010. Save your changes, and then run the query.

9. Save the Current Lessons query as **Current Guitar Lessons**.

10. Modify the Current Guitar Lessons query to display only those records for guitar lesson contracts that end on or after 7/1/2010. Do not include the Lesson Type field values in the query results. Run and save the query.

11. In the Current Guitar Lessons query datasheet, calculate the total monthly amount for current guitar lessons.

12. Change the alternate background color for the rows in the Current Guitar Lessons query datasheet to Light Label Text and the font size to 12. Resize all columns in the datasheet to fit the data, and then save and close the query.

13. Change the Navigation Pane so that it displays all objects grouped by object type.

14. Compact and repair the Pinehill database, and then close it.

| Create | **Case Problem 2** |

Follow the steps provided and use the figures as guides to create queries for a health and fitness center.

Data File needed for this Case Problem: Fitness.accdb (*cont. from Tutorial 2*)

Parkhurst Health & Fitness Center Martha Parkhurst needs to change a few records in the Fitness database, and analyze the records for members enrolled in different programs at the fitness center. To help her perform these tasks, you'll update the Fitness database and create queries to answer her questions. Complete the following:

1. Open the **Fitness** database located in the Level.01\Case2 folder provided with your Data Files.

2. In the **Member** table, find the record for Member ID 1158, and then change the Street value to **89 Mockingbird Lane** and the Phone to **804-751-1847**. Close the table.

3. In the **Program** table, find the record for Program ID 205. In the subdatasheet, delete the related record from the Member table. Then delete the record for Program ID 205 in the Program table. Close the table.

4. Use Design view to create a query that lists members who are required to have physical examinations. In the query results, display the First Name, Last Name, and Date Joined fields from the Member table, and the Monthly Fee field from the Program table. Sort the records in descending order by the Date Joined. Select records only for members required to take a physical. (*Hint:* The Physical Required field is a Yes/No field.) Save the query as **Physicals Needed**, and then run the query.

5. Use the Physicals Needed query datasheet to update the Member table by changing the Date Joined value for Ed Curran to **10/18/2010**.

6. Use the Physicals Needed query datasheet to display the total Monthly Fee for the selected members. Save and close the query.

7. Use Design view to create a query that lists the Member ID, First Name, Last Name, Date Joined, Program Type, and Monthly Fee fields for members who joined the fitness center between June 1 and June 30, 2010. Save the query as **June Members**, run the query, and then close it.

8. Create and save the query to produce the results shown in Figure 3-43. Close the query when you are finished.

Figure 3-43

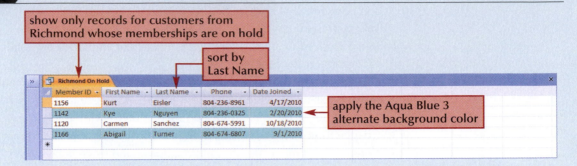

show only records for customers from Richmond whose memberships are on hold

sort by Last Name

apply the Aqua Blue 3 alternate background color

EXPLORE   9. Create and save the query to produce the results shown in Figure 3-44. Close the query when you are finished.

Figure 3-44

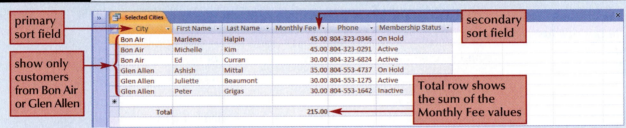

primary sort field

secondary sort field

show only customers from Bon Air or Glen Allen

Total row shows the sum of the Monthly Fee values

EXPLORE   10. Create and save the query to produce results that display statistics for the Monthly Fee field, as shown in Figure 3-45. Close the query when you are finished.

Figure 3-45

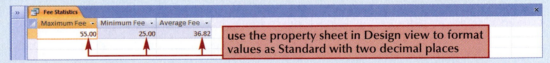

use the property sheet in Design view to format values as Standard with two decimal places

11. In the Navigation Pane, copy the Fee Statistics query and rename the copied query as **Fee Statistics By City**.

12. Modify the Fee Statistics By City query to display the same statistics grouped by City, with City appearing as the first field. (*Hint:* Add the Member table to the query.) Run the query, and then save and close it.

13. Change the Navigation Pane so that it displays all objects grouped by object type.

14. Compact and repair the Fitness database, and then close it.

| Challenge | **Case Problem 3** |

Work with the skills you've learned, and explore some new skills, to create queries for a not-for-profit agency that recycles household goods.

Data File needed for this Case Problem: Rossi.accdb (cont. from Tutorial 2)

Rossi Recycling Group   Tom Rossi needs to modify some records in the Rossi database, and then he wants to find specific information about the donors, agencies, and donations to his not-for-profit agency. Tom asks you to help him update the database and create queries. Complete the following:

1. Open the **Rossi** database located in the Level.01\Case3 folder provided with your Data Files.

2. In the **Donor** table, delete the record with a Donor ID of 36065. (*Hint:* Delete the related record first.) Close the table.

3. Create a query based on the Agency table that includes the Agency Name, Contact First Name, Contact Last Name, and City fields, in that order. Save the query as **Agencies By City**, and then run it.

4. Modify the Agencies By City query so that it sorts records in ascending order first by City and then by Agency Name. Save and run the query.

5. In the Agencies By City query datasheet, change the contact for the Community Development agency to **Beth Dayton**. Close the query.

6. Use Design view to create a query that displays the Donor ID, First Name, Last Name, Donation Description, and Donation Value for all donations over $50. Sort the query in ascending order by Donation Value. Save the query as **Large Donations**, and then run the query.

7. Save the Large Donations query as **Large Cash Donations**.

<img id="explore-icon" /> EXPLORE   8. Modify the Large Cash Donations query to display only those records with donations valuing more than $50 in cash. Use the query datasheet to calculate the average large cash donation. Save and close the query.

9. Use Design view to create a query that displays the Agency ID, Donation ID, Donation Date, and Donation Description fields. Save the query as **Senior Donations**, and then run the query.

10. Filter the results of the Senior Donations query datasheet to display records for all donations to the SeniorCare Program (Agency ID K82).

<img id="explore-icon2" /> EXPLORE   11. Format the datasheet of the Senior Donations query so that it does not display gridlines, uses an alternate background color for rows of Green 2, and displays a font size of 12. (*Hint*: Use the Gridlines button on the Home tab to select a gridlines option.) Resize the columns to display the complete field names and values. Save your changes.

12. Save the Senior Donations query as **Computer Or Youth Donations**.

13. Modify the Computer Or Youth Donations query to display donations of computer equipment or those to the After School Youth agency (Agency ID Y68). Sort the records in ascending order first by Donation Description and then by Agency ID. Run, save, and then close the query.

<img id="explore-icon3" /> EXPLORE   14. Use Design view to create a query that displays the Donor ID, Agency Name, Donation Description, and Donation Value fields for all donations that require a pickup. (*Hint:* The Pickup Required field is a Yes/No field.) Create a calculated field named **Net Donation** that displays the results of subtracting $8.75 from the Donation Value field values. Display the results in ascending order by Donation Value. Save the query as **Donations After Pickup Charge**, and then run it. Modify the query to format the calculated field as Currency with two Decimal Places. Run the query and resize the columns in the datasheet to their best fit. Save and close the query.

<img id="explore-icon4" /> EXPLORE   15. Use the **Donation** table to display the sum, average, and count of the Donation Value field for all donations. Then complete the following:

    a. Specify column names of **Total Donations**, **Average Donation**, and **Number of Donations**.

    b. Save the query as **Donation Statistics**, and then run it.

    c. Modify the field properties so that the values in the Total Donations and Average Donation columns display two decimal places and the Standard format. Run the query and resize the columns in the datasheet to their best fit. Save and close the query.

d. In the Navigation Pane, create a copy of the Donation Statistics query named **Donation Statistics By Agency**.

e. Modify the Donation Statistics By Agency query to display the sum, average, and count of the Donation Value field for all donations grouped by Agency Name, with Agency Name appearing as the first field. (*Hint*: Add the Agency table to the query.) Sort the records in descending order by Total Donations. Save, run, and then close the query.

16. Change the Navigation Pane so that it displays only queries. (*Hint:* Display the objects by type, and then select Queries in the Filter by Group section of the Navigation Pane menu.)

17. Compact and repair the Rossi database, and then close it.

| Challenge | **Case Problem 4** |

Work with the skills you've learned, and explore some new skills, to create queries for a luxury rental company.

Data File needed for this Case Problem: GEM.accdb *(cont. from Tutorial 2)*

GEM Ultimate Vacations   Griffin and Emma MacElroy want to modify some records, and then analyze data about their clients and the luxury properties they rent. You offer to help them update and query the GEM database. Complete the following:

1. Open the **GEM** database located in the Level.01\Case4 folder provided with your Data Files.

2. In the **Guest** table, delete the record with a Guest ID of 224, and then close the table.

3. Create a query based on the Property table that includes the Property Name, Location, Country, Nightly Rate, and Property Type fields, in that order. Sort in ascending order based on the Nightly Rate field values. Save the query as **Properties By Rate**, and then run the query.

⊕ EXPLORE
4. In the results of the Properties By Rate query, change the nightly rate for the Hartfield Country Manor property to $2,500, and then use the datasheet to display the number of properties and the average nightly rate. Save and close the query.

5. Create a query that displays the Guest Last Name, City, State/Prov, Reservation ID, Start Date, and End Date fields. Save the query as **Guest Trip Dates**, and then run the query. Change the alternate background color of the rows in the query datasheet to Access Theme 2. In Datasheet view, use an AutoFilter to sort the query results from oldest to newest Start Date. Save and close the query.

6. Create a query that displays the Guest Last Name, City, Reservation ID, People, Start Date, and End Date fields for all guests from Illinois (IL). Sort the query in ascending order by City. Save the query as **Illinois Guests**, run it, and then close the query.

⊕ EXPLORE
7. Create a query that displays the Guest Last Name, City, Reservation ID, Start Date, and Property ID fields for all guests who are not from Illinois or who are renting a property starting in the month of June 2010. Sort the query in descending order by Start Date. Save the query as **Out Of State Or June**, and then run the query.

8. Save the Out Of State Or June query as **Out Of State And June**.

9. Modify the Out Of State And June query to select all clients who are not from Illinois and who are renting a property beginning in the month of June 2010. Sort the query in ascending order by Start Date. Run the query, and then save and close it.

10. Create a query that displays the Reservation ID, Start Date, End Date, Property ID, Property Name, People, and Rental Rate fields for all reservations. Add a field to the query named **Cost Per Person** that displays the results of dividing the Rental Rate field values by the People field values. Display the results in descending order by Cost Per Person. Save the query as **Rental Cost** and then run it. Modify the query by setting the following properties for the Cost Per Person field: Format set to Currency and Decimal Places set to 2. Run the query, resize all datasheet columns to their best fit, and then save your changes.

11. Save the Rental Cost query as **Top Rental Cost**.

EXPLORE 12. Open the Access Help window and use **top values query** as the search text. Select the Help article titled "Find the records with the top or bottom values in a group or field," and then read the "Find the records that contain top or bottom values" section. Close the Access Help window. Modify the Top Rental Cost query in Design view to display only the top five values for the Cost Per Person field. (*Hint:* Use the Return list box in the Query Setup group on the Query Tools Design tab.) Save, run, and then close the query.

EXPLORE 13. Use the Reservation table to determine the minimum, average, and maximum Rental Rate values for all reservations. Then complete the following:

    a. Specify column names of **Lowest Rate**, **Average Rate**, and **Highest Rate**.

    b. Save the query as **Rate Statistics**, and then run the query.

    c. In Design view, use the property sheet for each column to format the results with the Standard format and two decimal places.

    d. Run the query, resize all the datasheet columns to their best fit, save your changes, and then close the query.

    e. Create a copy of the Rate Statistics query named **Rate Statistics By Country**.

    f. Revise the Rate Statistics By Country query to display the rate statistics grouped by Country of the property, with Country appearing as the first field. Save your changes and then run and close the query.

14. Change the view of the Navigation Pane to show all Access objects grouped by object type.

15. Compact and repair the GEM database, and then close it.

Research | **Internet Assignments**

Use the Internet to find and work with data related to the topics presented in this tutorial.

The purpose of the Internet Assignments is to challenge you to find information on the Internet that you can use to work effectively with this software. The actual assignments are updated and maintained on the Course Technology Web site. Log on to the Internet and use your Web browser to go to the Student Online Companion for New Perspectives Office 2007 at **www.course.com/np/office2007**. Then navigate to the Internet Assignments for this tutorial.

Assess | **SAM Assessment and Training**

If you have a SAM user profile, you may have access to hands-on instruction, practice, and assessment of the skills covered in this tutorial. Log in to your SAM account (**http://sam2007.course.com**) to launch any assigned training activities or exams that relate to the skills covered in this tutorial.

Session 3.1

1. In navigation mode, the entire field value is selected, and anything you type replaces the field value; in editing mode, you can insert or delete characters in a field value based on the location of the insertion point.
2. A select query is a general query in which you specify the fields and records you want Access to select.
3. The field list contains the table name at the top of the list box and the table's fields listed in the order in which they appear in the table; the design grid displays columns that contain specifications about a field you will use in the query.
4. A table datasheet and a query datasheet look the same, appearing in Datasheet view, and can be used to update data in a database. A table datasheet shows the permanent data in a table, whereas a query datasheet is temporary and its contents are based on the criteria you establish in the design grid.
5. oldest to most recent date
6. False
7. filter

Session 3.2

1. condition
2. in the same Criteria row; in different Criteria rows
3. expression
4. A calculated field appears in a query datasheet, form, or report but does not exist in a database, as does a table field.
5. a function that performs an arithmetic operation on selected records in a database
6. Group By
7. Tables and Related Views

Ending Data Files

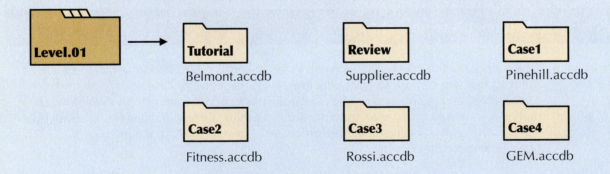

Level.01 →

Tutorial
Belmont.accdb

Review
Supplier.accdb

Case1
Pinehill.accdb

Case2
Fitness.accdb

Case3
Rossi.accdb

Case4
GEM.accdb

Objectives

Session 4.1
- Create a form using the Form Wizard
- Modify a form's design in Layout view
- Change a form's AutoFormat
- Add a picture to a form
- Change the color, line type, and position of items on a form
- Navigate a form and find data using a form
- Maintain table data using a form
- Preview and print selected form records

Session 4.2
- Create a form with a main form and a subform
- Create a report using the Report Wizard
- Modify a report's design in Layout view
- Move and resize fields in a report
- Insert a picture in a report
- Change the font color of a report title
- Use conditional formatting in a report
- Preview and print a report

Creating Forms and Reports

Creating a Customer Data Form, a Customer Contracts Form, and a Customers and Contracts Report

Case | Belmont Landscapes

Oren Belmont wants to continue enhancing the Belmont database to make it easier for his staff to enter, locate, and maintain data. In particular, he wants the database to include a form based on the Customer table to make it easier for employees to enter and change data about the firm's customers. He also wants the database to include a form that shows data from both the Customer and Contract tables at the same time. This form will show the contract information for each customer along with the corresponding customer data, providing a complete picture of Belmont Landscapes' customers and their contracts.

In addition, Taylor Sico would like the database to include a formatted report of customer and contract data so that employees will have printed output when completing market analyses and planning strategies for selling Belmont Landscapes' services to customers. She wants the information to be formatted in a professional manner, to make the report appealing and easy to use.

Starting Data Files

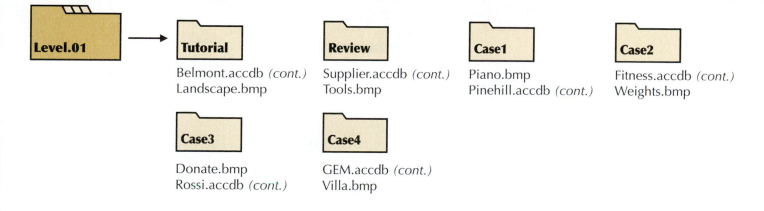

Level.01 →

Tutorial
Belmont.accdb *(cont.)*
Landscape.bmp

Review
Supplier.accdb *(cont.)*
Tools.bmp

Case1
Piano.bmp
Pinehill.accdb *(cont.)*

Case2
Fitness.accdb *(cont.)*
Weights.bmp

Case3
Donate.bmp
Rossi.accdb *(cont.)*

Case4
GEM.accdb *(cont.)*
Villa.bmp

Session 4.1

Creating a Form Using the Form Wizard

As you learned in Tutorial 1, a form is an object you use to enter, edit, and view records in a database. You can design your own forms or have Access create them for you automatically. In Tutorial 1, you used the Form tool to create the Contract Data form in the Belmont database. Recall that the Form tool creates a form automatically, using all the fields in the selected table or query.

Oren asks you to create a new form that his staff can use to view and maintain data in the Customer table. To create the form for the Customer table, you'll use the Form Wizard. The **Form Wizard** allows you to choose some or all of the fields in the selected table or query, choose fields from other tables and queries, and display the selected fields in any order on the form. You can also apply an existing style to the form to format its appearance quickly.

To open the Belmont database and start the Form Wizard:

▶ 1. Start Access and open the **Belmont** database located in the Level.01\Tutorial folder.

Trouble? If the Security Warning is displayed below the Ribbon, click the Options button next to the Security Warning. In the dialog box that opens, click the "Enable this content" option button, and then click the OK button.

▶ 2. If necessary, open the Navigation Pane. To create a form based on a table or query, you can select the table or query in the Navigation Pane first, or you can select it using the Form Wizard.

▶ 3. In the Navigation Pane, click **Customer : Table** to select the Customer table as the basis for the new form.

▶ 4. Click the **Create** tab on the Ribbon. The Forms group on the Create tab provides options for creating various types of forms and designing your own forms.

▶ 5. In the Forms group, click the **More Forms** button, and then click **Form Wizard**. The first Form Wizard dialog box opens. See Figure 4-1.

| Figure 4-1 | **First Form Wizard dialog box** |

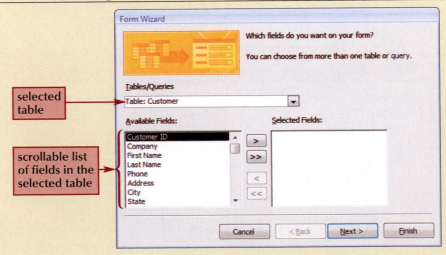

selected table

scrollable list of fields in the selected table

Because you selected the Customer table in the Navigation Pane before starting the Form Wizard, this table is selected in the Tables/Queries list box, and the fields for the Customer table are listed in the Available Fields list box.

Oren wants the form to display all the fields in the Customer table, but in a different order. He would like the Phone field to appear at the bottom of the form so that it stands out, making it easier for someone who needs to call customers to use the form and quickly identify the phone number for a customer.

To create the form using the Form Wizard:

1. Click the >> button to move all the fields to the Selected Fields list box. Next, you need to remove the Phone field, and then add it back as the last selected field so that it will appear at the bottom of the form.

2. In the Selected Fields list box, click the **Phone** field, and then click the < button to move the field back to the Available Fields list box.

   To add the Phone field to the end of the form, you need to highlight the last field in the list, and then move the Phone field back to the Selected Fields list box.

3. In the Selected Fields list box, click the **E-mail Address** field.

4. With the Phone field selected in the Available Fields list box, click the > button to move the Phone field to the end of the Selected Fields list box.

5. Click the **Next** button to display the second Form Wizard dialog box, in which you select a layout for the form. See Figure 4-2.

Choosing a layout for the form ◀ **Figure 4-2**

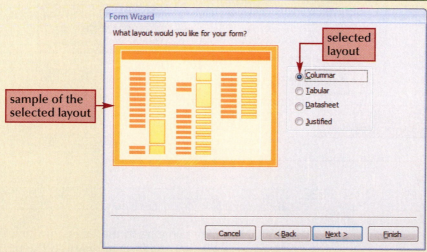

The layout choices are Columnar, Tabular, Datasheet, and Justified. A sample of the selected layout appears on the left side of the dialog box.

6. Click each of the option buttons and review the corresponding sample layout.

   The Tabular and Datasheet layouts display the fields from multiple records at one time, whereas the Columnar and Justified layouts display the fields from one record at a time. Oren thinks the Columnar layout is the appropriate arrangement for displaying and updating data in the table, so that anyone using the form can focus on just one customer record at a time.

▶ **7.** Click the **Columnar** option button (if necessary), and then click the **Next** button. Access displays the third Form Wizard dialog box, in which you choose a style for the form. A sample of the selected style appears in the box on the left. If you choose a style, which is called an **AutoFormat**, and decide you'd prefer a different one after the form is created, you can change it.

▶ **8.** Scroll through the list of styles and click a few of them to review the corresponding sample. Oren likes the Office style and asks you to use it for the form.

▶ **9.** Click **Office** in the list of styles, and then click the **Next** button. Access displays the final Form Wizard dialog box and shows the Customer table's name as the default form name. "Customer" is also the default title that will appear on the tab for the form.

You'll use "Customer Data" as the form name and, because you don't need to change the form's design at this point, you'll display the form.

▶ **10.** Click the insertion point to the right of Customer in the text box, press the **spacebar**, type **Data**, and then click the **Finish** button.

▶ **11.** Close the Navigation Pane to display more of the form window. The completed form is opened in Form view. See Figure 4-3.

Figure 4-3   **Customer Data form in Form view**

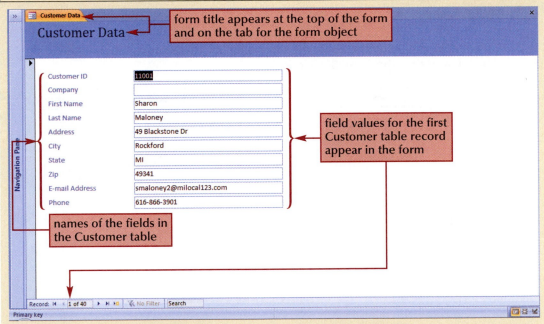

You use Form view to view, enter, and maintain data in the table on which the form is based. Notice that the title you specified for the form appears on the tab for the form object and as a title on the form itself. The Columnar layout you selected places the names of the fields in the Customer table in a column on the left of the form, and the corresponding field values in boxes on the right. The form currently displays the field values for the first record in the Customer table.

After viewing the form, Oren decides that he doesn't like the form's style. The font color of the field names is somewhat light, making the names a bit difficult to read. Also, he wants the colors used in the form to reflect the landscaping business. He also suggests adding a graphic to the form, for visual interest, and perhaps modifying other form elements, such as the color of certain text, the type of line used for the text boxes, and so on. You can make all of these changes working with the form in Layout view.

Modifying a Form's Design in Layout View

After you create a form, you might need to modify its design to improve its appearance or to make the form easier to use. **Layout view** allows you to modify many aspects of a form's layout and design. In Layout view, you see the form as it appears in Form view, but you can still modify the form's design; in Form view, you cannot make any design changes. Because you can see the form and its data while you are modifying the form, Layout view makes it easy for you to see the results of any design changes you make. You can continue to make changes, undo modifications, and rework the design in Layout view to achieve the look you want for the form.

The first modification you'll make to the Customer Data form is to change its AutoFormat.

> **Tip**
>
> Some form design changes require you to switch to Design view, which gives you a more detailed view of the form's structure.

Changing a Form's AutoFormat

You can change a form's appearance by choosing a different AutoFormat for the form. As you learned when you created the Customer Data form, an AutoFormat is a predefined style for a form (or report). The AutoFormats available for a form are the ones you saw when you selected the form's style using the Form Wizard. To change an AutoFormat, you first need to switch to Layout view.

Changing a Form's AutoFormat | Reference Window

- Display the form in Layout view.
- In the AutoFormat group on the Form Layout Tools Format tab, click the More button.
- In the displayed gallery, click the AutoFormat you want to apply; or, click AutoFormat Wizard to open the AutoFormat dialog box, click the name of the AutoFormat you want to apply, and then click the OK button.

To change the AutoFormat for the Customer Data form:

▶ 1. In the Views group on the Home tab, click the **View** button. The form is displayed in Layout view. See Figure 4-4.

Figure 4-4 | **Form displayed in Layout view**

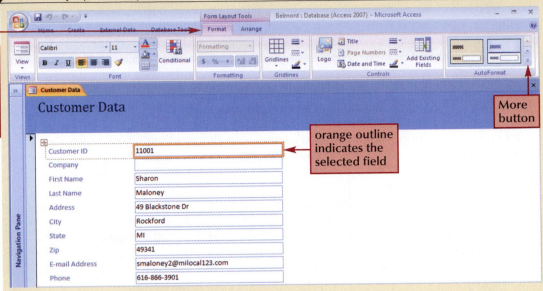

Form Layout Tools Format tab displays options for changing the form's appearance

orange outline indicates the selected field

More button

Trouble? If the Field List or Property Sheet opens on the right side of your window, click the Close button ⊠ to close it.

You can use Layout view to modify an existing form. In Layout view, an orange outline identifies the currently selected object on the form; in this case, the first field, Customer ID, is selected. You need to change the AutoFormat for the Customer Data form.

▶ 2. In the AutoFormat group on the Form Layout Tools Format tab, click the **More** button (see Figure 4-4 for the location of this button). A gallery opens showing the available AutoFormats for the form. See Figure 4-5.

Figure 4-5 | **Gallery of AutoFormats displayed**

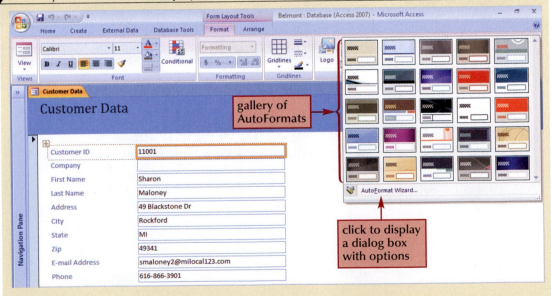

gallery of AutoFormats

click to display a dialog box with options

You can point to each option in the gallery to see its ScreenTip; or choose the Auto-Format Wizard option to open a dialog box and view a sample form with each AutoFormat applied.

▶ **3.** Click **AutoFormat Wizard** at the bottom of the gallery. The AutoFormat dialog box opens. Each form AutoFormat is listed on the left, and a sample of the selected AutoFormat appears on the right.

▶ **4.** Scroll the list and click several form AutoFormats to view their samples.

Oren decides that he prefers the Foundry AutoFormat, because its field names and field values are easier to read. Also, the earth tone colors provided by the AutoFormat are more reflective of the landscaping business.

▶ **5.** Click **Foundry** in the Form AutoFormats list box, and then click the **OK** button. The AutoFormat dialog box closes, and the Form window in Layout view shows the new AutoFormat.

> **Tip**
>
> You can also click an Auto-Format in the gallery to apply it directly to the form, without opening the AutoFormat dialog box.

Oren is pleased with the form's new style. Next, he asks you to add a picture to the form for visual interest. The picture, which is included on various stationery items for Belmont Landscapes—business cards, flyers, and so on—is a small graphic of a piece of landscaping equipment. You'll add this picture to the form.

Adding a Picture to a Form

A picture is one of many controls you can add and modify on a form. A **control** is an item on a form, report, or other database object that you can manipulate to modify the object's appearance. The controls you can add and modify in Layout view for a form are available in the Controls group on the Form Layout Tools Format tab. The picture you need to add is contained in a file named Landscape.bmp, which is located in the Level.01\Tutorial folder provided with your Data Files.

To add the picture to the form:

▶ **1.** Make sure the form is still displayed in Layout view.

▶ **2.** In the Controls group on the Form Layout Tools Format tab, click the **Logo** button. The Insert Picture dialog box opens.

▶ **3.** Navigate to the **Level.01\Tutorial** folder provided with your Data Files, click the **Landscape** filename, and then click the **OK** button. The picture appears as a selected object on top of the form's title.

▶ **4.** Use the ⬚ pointer to move the picture to the right of the Customer Data form title, and then click in a blank area on the main form (to the right of the field values) to deselect the picture. See Figure 4-6.

Figure 4-6 **Form with new AutoFormat applied and picture added**

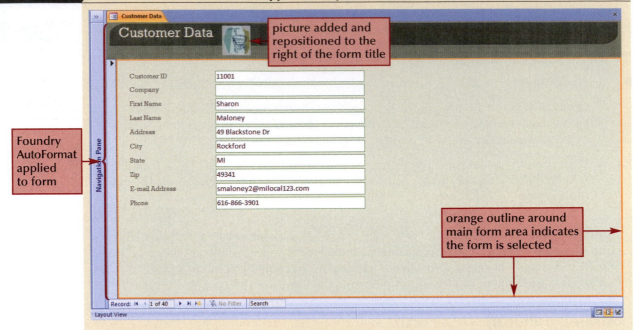

Trouble? Don't be concerned if your picture is not in the exact location as the one shown in Figure 4-6. Just make sure the picture is not blocking any part of the form title, and appears to the right of the form title and above the main part of the form.

The addition of the picture to the form provides more color and visual interest. Next, Oren asks you to change the color of the form title to a light blue so that it will coordinate better with the picture next to the title.

Changing the Color of the Form Title

The Font group on the Form Layout Tools Format tab provides many options you can use to change the appearance of text on a form. For example, you can bold, italicize, and underline text; change the font, font color, and font size; and change the alignment of text. Next, you'll change the color of the title "Customer Data" on the form to a light blue.

To change the color of the form's title text:

1. Click anywhere in the title **Customer Data** at the top of the form (not on the form tab). An orange outline appears around the words to indicate the text is selected.

   Trouble? If a white box with the insertion point appears at the location of the title, you most likely double-clicked the title by mistake and changed to editing mode. Press the Esc key to move out of editing mode. The title should now be selected and you can continue to Step 2.

2. In the Font group on the Form Layout Tools Format tab, click the arrow on the **Font Color** button [A ·] to display the gallery of available colors. The gallery provides colors for Access themes and standard colors, as well as an option for creating a custom color.

3. In the Access Theme Colors palette, place the pointer over the fourth color box in the second row of boxes. The ScreenTip indicates this is the Access Theme 4 color.

> **4.** Click the color box for **Access Theme 4**.

> **5.** Click in a blank area of the main form to deselect the title text. The light blue color is applied to the form title, tying it to the picture on the form. See Figure 4-7.

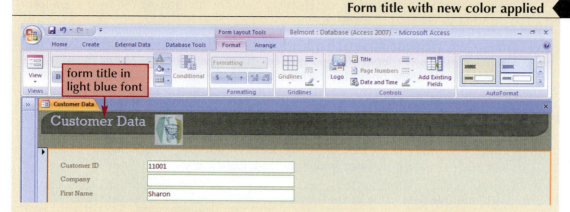

You have made a couple of changes to the form, and should save it now.

> **6.** Click the **Save** button on the Quick Access Toolbar to save the modified form.

Oren suggests a different type of line for the boxes that contain the field values. He thinks the solid line currently used on the form somewhat overshadows the field values within the boxes, and that a more subtle type of line might look better and make the field values easier to read.

Changing the Type of Line on a Form

A line on a form, such as the box around each field value, is another type of control that you can modify in Layout view. The Controls group provides options for changing the thickness, type, and color of any line on a form. Next, you'll change the type of line for the boxes around the field values on the Customer Data form.

To change the type of line for the field value boxes:

> **1.** Click the field value **11001** for the Customer ID field. An orange outline appears around the box to indicate it is selected. The field value is also selected, and its appearance can be modified. See Figure 4-8.

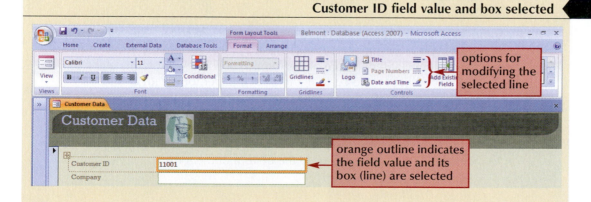

2. In the Controls group on the Form Layout Tools Format tab, click the **Line Type** button , and then point to each option in the gallery of line types to see the ScreenTip for each type of line.

3. Click the **Dots** option (fourth line type option in the gallery), and then click in a blank area of the main form to deselect the box. The box around the field value for Customer ID changes to a dotted line.

   Oren thinks the dotted line type is much better and makes the field value easier to see. He asks you to change the line type for the rest of the boxes on the form. To do so, you can select the remaining boxes and apply the new line type to them all at the same time.

4. Click the field value box for the **Company** field (the box is currently empty), press and hold the **Shift** key, click each of the remaining field value boxes, and then release the **Shift** key. All the field value boxes except the first one should be selected; each box is outlined in orange to indicate it is selected. See Figure 4-9.

Figure 4-9	Form with multiple field value boxes selected

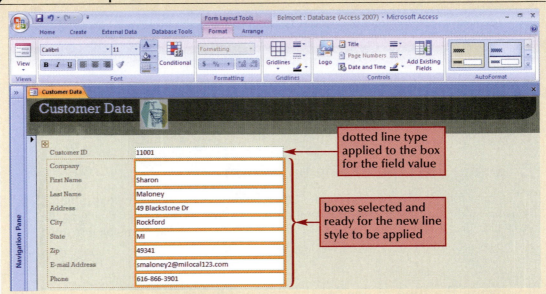

5. In the Controls group on the Form Layout Tools Format tab, click the **Line Type** button , and then click the **Dots** option.

6. Click in a blank area of the main form to deselect the field value boxes. The line type for each box is now dotted.

Oren approves of all the formatting changes you have made so far. After viewing the form and considering how his employees will use it, he realizes that the E-mail Address field should be positioned at the bottom of the form. When a new customer signs a contract with Belmont Landscapes, the customer fills out a paper form with contact information. On this paper form, the customer's e-mail address is the final piece of information provided. Because Oren's employees will enter customer information into the Customer table based on the paper forms customers fill out, the design and layout of the Customer Data form should match the paper form, for ease of data entry. Therefore, Oren asks you to move the E-mail Address field to the bottom of the form.

Moving a Field in Layout View

In Layout view, you can reposition fields on a form to improve the form's appearance or make it easier to use. You move a field by selecting it and then dragging it to a new location on the form. When you move a field, both the field name and the box for the field value are repositioned.

To move the E-mail Address field to the bottom of the form:

▶ 1. Click the field value box for the **E-mail Address** field. An orange outline appears around the field value box, and a thin dotted line appears around the field name. This indicates both are selected.

▶ 2. Place the pointer over the selected field until it changes to ⊹⊹.

▶ 3. Click and drag the pointer down until an orange line appears below the Phone field. This indicates the new location for the field you are moving. See Figure 4-10.

Moving the E-mail Address field ◀ **Figure 4-10**

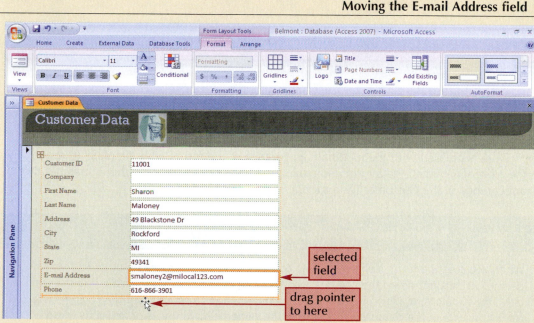

▶ 4. Release the mouse button, and then click in a blank area of the main form to deselect the field. The E-mail Address field is now positioned below the Phone field at the bottom of the form.

▶ 5. Click the **Save** button ⊟ on the Quick Access Toolbar to save the form.

▶ 6. In the Views group on the Form Layout Tools Format tab, click the **View** button to display the form in Form view. See Figure 4-11.

Figure 4-11   **Modified form displayed in Form view**

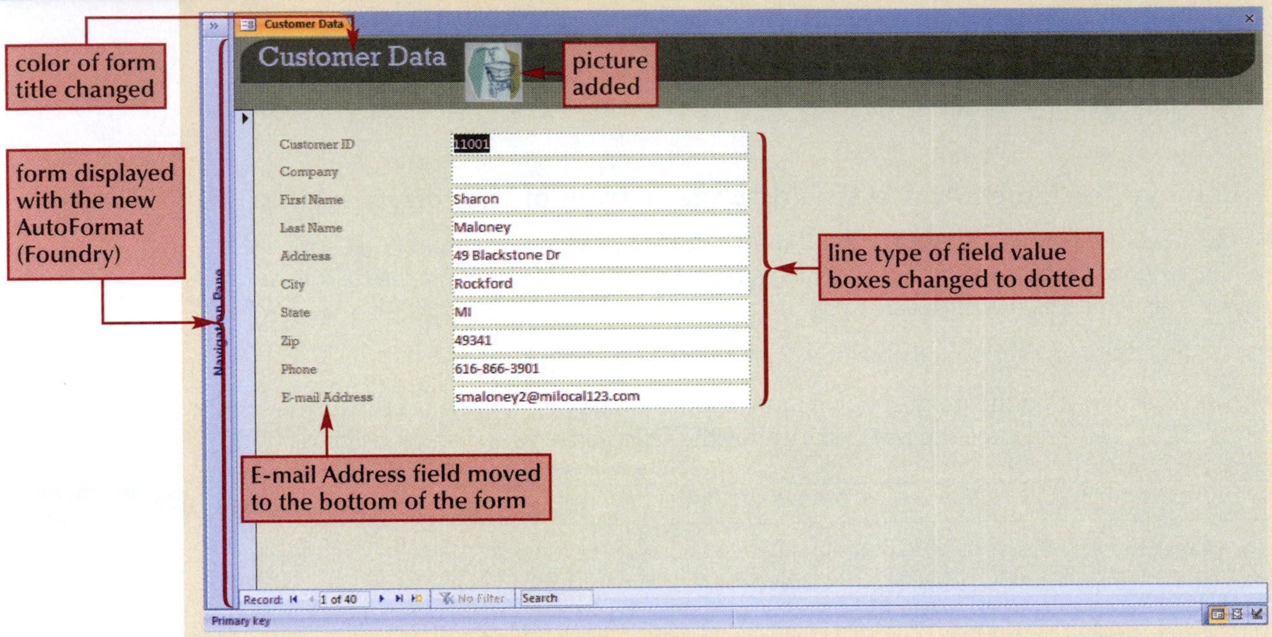

color of form title changed

picture added

form displayed with the new AutoFormat (Foundry)

line type of field value boxes changed to dotted

E-mail Address field moved to the bottom of the form

Trouble? If the E-mail Address field value is selected in your form, you might not have clicked a blank area of the main form as instructed in Step 4. If so, double-click the Customer ID field value to select it.

Oren is pleased with the modified appearance of the form. Later, he plans to revise the existing Contract Data form and make the same changes to it, so that it matches the appearance of the Customer Data form.

InSight | **Understanding the Importance of Form Design**

When you create a form, it's important to consider how the form will be used, so that its design will accommodate the needs of people using the form to view, enter, and maintain data. For example, if a form in a database mimics a paper form that users will enter data from, the form in the database should have the same fields in the same order as those on the paper form. This will enable users to easily tab from one field to the next in the database form to enter the necessary information from the paper form. Also, it's important to include a meaningful title on the form to identify its purpose, and to enhance the appearance of the form. A form that is visually appealing makes working with the database more user-friendly and can improve the readability of the form, thereby helping to prevent errors in data entry. Finally, be sure to use a consistent design for all the forms in your database. Users will expect to see similar elements—titles, pictures, styles, and so on—in each form contained in a database. A mix of form styles and elements among the forms in a database could cause confusion and lead to problems when working with the forms.

Navigating a Form

Oren wants to use the Customer Data form to view some data in the Customer table. As you saw earlier, you use Layout view to modify the appearance of a form. To view, navigate, and change data using a form, you need to display the form in Form view. As you learned in Tutorial 1, you navigate a form in the same way that you navigate a table datasheet. Also, the navigation mode and editing mode keystroke techniques you used with datasheets in Tutorial 3 are the same when navigating a form.

The Customer Data form is already displayed in Form view, so you can use it to navigate through the fields and records of the Customer table.

To navigate the Customer Data form:

1. Press the **Tab** key twice to move to the First Name field value, and then press the **End** key to move to the E-mail Address field.

2. Press the **Home** key to move back to the Customer ID field value. The first record in the Customer table still appears in the form.

3. Press the **Ctrl+End** keys to move to the E-mail Address field for record 40, which is the last record in the table. The record number for the current record appears in the Current Record box between the navigation buttons at the bottom of the form.

4. Click the **Previous record** navigation button ◀ to move to the E-mail Address field in record 39.

5. Press the ↑ key twice to move to the Zip field in record 39.

6. Click the insertion point between the numbers "7" and "5" in the Address field value to switch to editing mode, press the **Home** key to move the insertion point to the beginning of the field value, and then press the **End** key to move the insertion point to the end of the field value.

7. Click the **First record** navigation button ◀◀ to move to the Address field value in the first record. The entire field value is highlighted because you have switched from editing mode to navigation mode.

8. Click the **Next record** navigation button ▶ to move to the Address field value in record 2, the next record.

Next, Oren asks you to display the record for the Three Tulips Café, one of Belmont Landscapes' customers. The paper form containing the original contact information for this customer was damaged. Oren recently contacted the owner of the café and obtained all the customer information again. Now Oren wants to view the data for this customer in the Customer table to make sure it is correct.

Finding Data Using a Form

As you learned in Tutorial 3, the Find command lets you search for data in a form or datasheet so you can display only those records you want to view. You choose a field to serve as the basis for the search by making that field the current field, and then you enter the value you want Access to match in the Find and Replace dialog box.

Finding Data in a Form or Datasheet

- Open the form or datasheet, and then make the field you want to search the current field.
- In the Find group on the Home tab, click the Find button to open the Find and Replace dialog box.
- In the Find What text box, type the field value you want to find.
- Complete the remaining options, as necessary, to specify the type of search to conduct.
- Click the Find Next button to begin the search.
- Click the Find Next button to continue searching for the next match.
- Click the Cancel button to stop the search operation.

You need to find the record for the Three Tulips Café. Oren doesn't recall the Customer ID value for this customer, so you'll base the search on the Company field name.

To find the record using the Customer Data form:

▶ 1. Click in the **Company** field value (which is empty for the current record) to establish Company as the current field. This is the field you need to search.

Instead of searching for the entire company name, Three Tulips Café, you can search for a record that contains part of the name anywhere in the Company field value. Performing a partial search such as this is often easier than matching the entire field value and is useful when you don't know or can't remember the entire field value.

▶ 2. In the Find group on the Home tab, click the **Find** button. The Find and Replace dialog box opens. The Look In box shows that the Company field will be searched. You'll search for records that contain the word "tulips" in the company name.

▶ 3. In the Find What text box, type **tulips**. Note that you do not have to enter the word as "Tulips" with a capital letter "T" because the Match Case option is not selected in the Find and Replace dialog box. Access will find any record containing the word "tulips" with any combination of uppercase and lowercase letters.

▶ 4. Click the **Match** arrow to display the list of matching options, and then click **Any Part of Field**. Access will find any record that contains the word "tulips" in any part of the Company field.

▶ 5. Move the Find and Replace dialog box by dragging its title bar so that you can see both the dialog box and the form at the same time. See Figure 4-12.

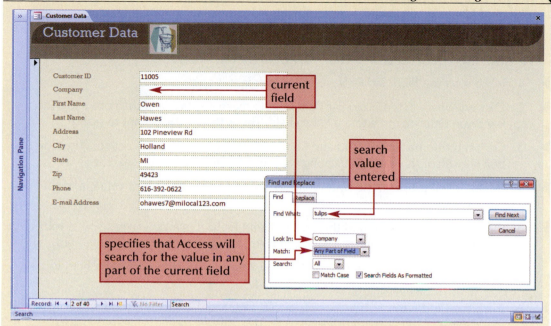

Finding data using the form — Figure 4-12

6. Click the **Find Next** button. The Customer Data form now displays record 35, which is the record for the Three Tulips Café (Customer ID 11080). The word "Tulips" is selected in the Company field value because you searched for this word. Oren reviews the information for the record and determines it is correct.

The search value you enter can be an exact value or it can include wildcard characters. A **wildcard character** is a placeholder you use when you know only part of a value or when you want to start or end with a specific character or match a certain pattern. Figure 4-13 shows the wildcard characters you can use when finding data.

Wildcard characters — Figure 4-13

Wildcard Character	Purpose	Example
*	Match any number of characters. It can be used as the first and/or last character in the character string.	th* finds the, that, this, therefore, and so on
?	Match any single alphabetic character.	a?t finds act, aft, ant, apt, and art
[]	Match any single character within the brackets.	a[fr]t finds aft and art but not act, ant, and apt
!	Match any character not within brackets.	a[!fr]t finds act, ant, and apt but not aft and art
-	Match any one of a range of characters. The range must be in ascending order (a to z, not z to a).	a[d-p]t finds aft, ant, and apt but not act and art
#	Match any single numeric character.	#72 finds 072, 172, 272, 372, and so on

Next, Oren wants to view the customer records for any customers with phone numbers beginning with the area code 517. He is curious to know how many customers are in cities serviced by that area code, and what the cities are. You could search for any field containing the digits 517 in any part of the field, but this search would also find records with the digits 517 in any part of the phone number. To find only those records with the 517 area code, you'll use the * wildcard character.

To find the records using the * wildcard character:

▶ **1.** Make sure the Find and Replace dialog box is still open.

▶ **2.** Click anywhere in the Customer Data form to make it active, and then press the **Tab** key seven times to move to the Phone field. This is the field you want to search.

▶ **3.** Click the title bar of the Find and Replace dialog box to make it active. The Look In box now displays Phone, indicating that the Phone field will be searched.

▶ **4.** Double-click **tulips** in the Find What text box to select the entire value, and then type **517***.

▶ **5.** Click the **Match** arrow, and then click **Whole Field**. Because you're using a wild-card character in the search value, you want Access to search the whole field.

With the settings you've entered, Access will find records in which any field value in the Phone field begins with the digits 517.

▶ **6.** Click the **Find Next** button. Access displays record 36, which is the first record found for a customer with the area code 517. This customer is located in East Lansing. Notice that the search process started from the point of the previously displayed record in the form, which was record 35.

▶ **7.** Click the **Find Next** button. Access displays record 8, which is the next record found for a customer with the area code 517. This customer is located in Lansing. Notice that the search process cycles back through the beginning of the records in the underlying table.

▶ **8.** Click the **Find Next** button. Access displays record 12, the third record found; this customer is also located in Lansing.

▶ **9.** Click the **Find Next** button. Access displays record 25 for another customer located in Lansing, with the area code 517.

▶ **10.** Click the **Find Next** button. Access displays record 33 for another customer located in Lansing.

▶ **11.** Click the **Find Next** button. Access displays a dialog box informing you that the search is finished.

▶ **12.** Click the **OK** button to close the dialog box. Oren notes that all customers with an area code of 517 are located in either Lansing or East Lansing.

▶ **13.** Click the **Cancel** button to close the Find and Replace dialog box.

Oren has identified some updates he wants you to make to the Customer table. You'll use the Customer Data form to update the data in the Customer table.

Maintaining Table Data Using a Form

Maintaining data using a form is often easier than using a datasheet, because you can concentrate on all the changes required to a single record at one time. In Form view, you can edit the field values for a specific record, delete a record from the underlying table, or add a new record to the table. You already know how to navigate a form and find specific records. Now you'll use the Customer Data form to make the changes Oren wants to the Customer table.

First, you'll update the record for the Cherrywood Senior Center. The center has a new contact person with a new phone number and e-mail address, so you need to update the First Name, Last Name, Phone, and E-mail Address fields for this customer. Oren happens to know that the Cherrywood Senior Center is record 22 in the Customer table. If you know the number of the record you want to view, you can enter the number in the Current Record box to move to that record.

To change the record using the Customer Data form:

▶ **1.** Select **33** in the Current Record box at the bottom of the form, type **22**, and then press the **Enter** key. Record 22 (Cherrywood Senior Center) is now the current record.

You need to update the values in the First Name, Last Name, Phone, and E-mail Address fields with the information for the new contact person at the center, Dan Lewis.

▶ **2.** In the First Name field value box, double-click **Lisa** to select the entry, and then type **Dan**.

▶ **3.** Press the **Tab** key to move to and select the field value in the Last Name field, and then type **Lewis**.

▶ **4.** Click the insertion point at the end of the field value for the Phone field, press the **Backspace** key three times, and then type **890**. The Phone field value is now 269-857-1890.

▶ **5.** Click the insertion point before the first character in the E-mail Address field, press the **Delete** key seven times to delete the characters before the @ symbol, and then type **dlewis4**. The E-mail Address field value is now dlewis4@csc77.com. The updates to the record are complete. See Figure 4-14.

Tip

Note that the pencil symbol appears in the upper-left corner of the form, indicating that the form is in editing mode.

Customer record after changing field values | Figure 4-14

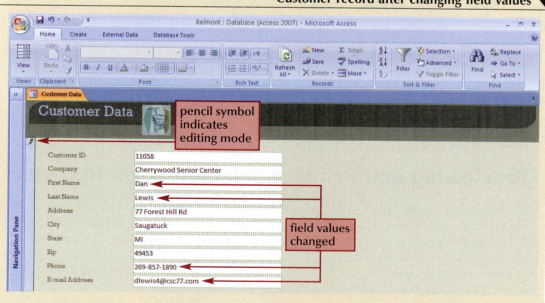

Next, Oren asks you to add a record for a new customer. The customer has not yet returned a signed contract, but Oren expects to receive the contract soon and wants to be sure the Customer table is updated first with the new customer record. You'll use the Customer Data form to add the new record.

To add the new record using the Customer Data form:

▶ **1.** In the Records group on the Home tab, click the **New** button. Record 41, the next available new record, becomes the current record. All field value boxes are empty, and the insertion point is positioned in the field value box for Customer ID.

▶ **2.** Refer to Figure 4-15 and enter the value shown for each field. Press the **Tab** key to move from field to field.

Figure 4-15	Completed form for the new record

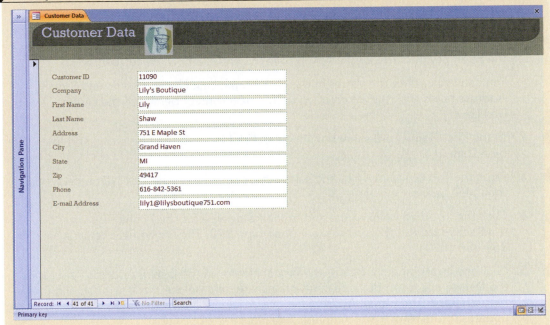

Trouble? Compare your screen with Figure 4-15. If any field value is incorrect, correct it now, using the methods described earlier for editing field values.

▶ **3.** After entering the value for the E-mail Address field, press the **Tab** key. Record 42, the next available new record, becomes the current record, and the record for Customer ID 11090 is saved in the Customer table.

Oren would like a printed copy of the record for the new customer only. He wants to give the printout to a staff member as a reminder to look for the new contract for this customer when it comes in.

Previewing and Printing Selected Form Records

Access prints as many form records as can fit on a printed page. If only part of a form record fits on the bottom of a page, the remainder of the record prints on the next page. Access allows you to print all pages or a range of pages. In addition, you can print the currently selected form record.

Before printing record 41, the record for Lily's Boutique, you'll preview the form record to see how it will look when printed.

To preview the form and print the data for record 41:

▶ **1.** Click the **Previous record** navigation button ◀ to redisplay record 41.

2. Click the **Office Button** 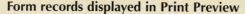, point to **Print**, and then click **Print Preview**. The Print Preview window opens, showing the form records for the Customer table. Notice that each record appears in its own form. See Figure 4-16.

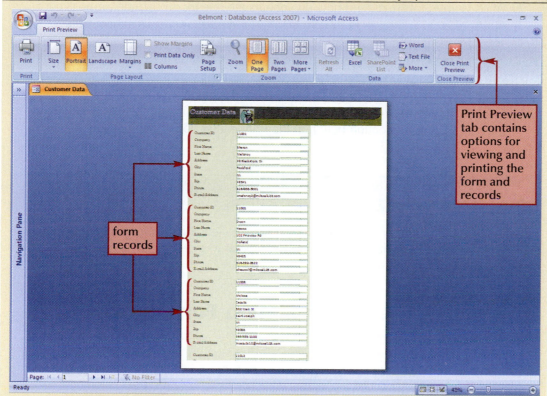

Print Preview tab contains options for viewing and printing the form and records

form records

If you clicked the Print button now, all the records for the table would be printed, beginning with the first record.

3. In the Close Preview group on the Print Preview tab, click the **Close Print Preview** button. You return to the form in Form view.

The record that you need to print (for Lily's Boutique) is currently displayed in the form. To print selected records, you use the Print dialog box.

4. Click the **Office Button** 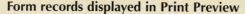, point to **Print**, and then click **Print**. The Print dialog box opens.

5. Click the **Selected Record(s)** option button to print the current form record (record 41).

   Trouble? Check with your instructor to be sure you should print the form; then continue to the next step. If you should not print the form, click the Cancel button, and then skip to Step 7.

6. Click the **OK** button to close the dialog box and to print the selected record.

7. Close the Customer Data form.

8. If you are not continuing to Session 4.2, click the **Close** button ☒ on the program window title bar. Access closes the Belmont database, and then the Access program closes.

The Customer Data form will enable Oren and his staff to enter and maintain data easily in the Customer table. In the next session, you'll create another form for working with data in both the Customer and Contract tables at the same time. You'll also create a report showing data from both tables.

Review | **Session 4.1 Quick Check**

1. Describe the difference between creating a form using the Form tool and creating a form using the Form Wizard.
2. What is an AutoFormat, and how do you change one for an existing form?
3. A(n) _____ is an item on a form, report, or other database object that you can manipulate to modify the object's appearance.
4. Which table record is displayed in a form when you press the Ctrl+End keys while you are in navigation mode?
5. Which wildcard character matches any single alphabetic character?
6. To print only the current record displayed in a form, you need to select the _____ option button in the Print dialog box.

Session 4.2

Oren would like you to create a form so that he can view the data for each customer and the customer's contracts at the same time. The type of form you need to create will include a main form and a subform.

Creating a Form with a Main Form and a Subform

To create a form based on two tables, you must first define a relationship between the two tables. In Tutorial 2, you defined a one-to-many relationship between the Customer (primary) and Contract (related) tables, so you can now create a form based on both tables.

When you create a form containing data from two tables that have a one-to-many relationship, you actually create a **main form** for data from the primary table and a **subform** for data from the related table. Access uses the defined relationship between the tables to join them automatically through the common field that exists in both tables.

Oren and his staff will use the form when contacting customers about their contracts. The main form will contain the customer ID, company name (if any), first and last names, phone number, and e-mail address for each customer. The subform will contain the information about the contracts for each customer.

You'll use the Form Wizard to create the form.

To create the form using the Form Wizard:

1. If you took a break after the previous session, make sure that the Belmont database is open and the Navigation Pane is closed.

2. Click the **Create** tab on the Ribbon.

3. In the Forms group on the Create tab, click the **More Forms** button, and then click **Form Wizard**. The first Form Wizard dialog box opens.

When creating a form based on two tables, you first choose the primary table and select the fields you want to include in the main form; then you choose the related table and select fields from it for the subform.

4. If necessary, click the **Tables/Queries** arrow, and then click **Table: Customer**.

   Oren wants the form to include only the Customer ID, Company, First Name, Last Name, Phone, and E-mail Address fields from the Customer table.

5. Click **Customer ID** in the Available Fields list box (if necessary), and then click the ⟩ button to move the field to the Selected Fields list box.

6. Repeat Step 5 for the **Company**, **First Name**, **Last Name**, **Phone**, and **E-mail Address** fields.

   The Customer ID field will appear in the main form, so you do not have to include it in the subform. Otherwise, Oren wants the subform to include all the fields from the Contract table.

7. Click the **Tables/Queries** arrow, scroll the list up, and then click **Table: Contract**. The fields from the Contract table appear in the Available Fields list box. The quickest way to add the fields you want to include is to move all the fields to the Selected Fields list box, and then to remove the only field you don't want to include (Customer ID).

8. Click the ⟩⟩ button to move all the fields in the Contract table to the Selected Fields list box.

9. Click **Contract.Customer ID** in the Selected Fields list box, and then click the ⟨ button to move the field back to the Available Fields list box.

10. Click the **Next** button. The next Form Wizard dialog box opens. See Figure 4-17.

Choosing a format for the main form and subform ◀ **Figure 4-17**

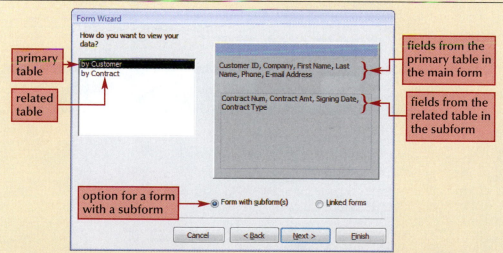

In this dialog box, the list box on the left shows the order in which you will view the selected data: first by data from the primary Customer table, and then by data from the related Contract table. The form will be displayed as shown on the right side of the dialog box, with the fields from the Customer table at the top in the main form, and the fields from the Contract table at the bottom in the subform. The selected "Form with subform(s)" option button specifies a main form with a subform. The Linked forms option creates a form structure in which only the main form fields are displayed. A button with the subform's name on it appears on the main form; you can click this button to display the associated subform records.

The default options shown in Figure 4-17 are correct for creating a form with Customer data in the main form and Contract data in the subform.

To finish creating the form:

1. Click the **Next** button. The next Form Wizard dialog box opens, in which you choose the subform layout.

   The Tabular layout displays subform fields as a table, whereas the Datasheet layout displays subform fields as a table datasheet. The layout choice is a matter of personal preference. You'll use the Datasheet layout.

2. Click the **Datasheet** option button (if necessary), and then click the **Next** button. The next Form Wizard dialog box opens, in which you choose the form's style (AutoFormat).

   Oren wants all forms in the Belmont database to have the same style, so you will choose Foundry, which is the same AutoFormat you applied to the Customer Data form.

3. Click **Foundry** (if necessary), and then click the **Next** button. The next Form Wizard dialog box opens, in which you choose names for the main form and the subform.

   You will use the name "Customer Contracts" for the main form and the name "Contract Subform" for the subform.

4. Click the insertion point to the right of the last letter in the Form text box, press the **spacebar**, and then type **Contracts**. The main form name is now Customer Contracts. The Contract Subform name is already set.

5. Click the **Finish** button. After a few moments, the completed form opens in Form view. Next, you'll resize the columns in the subform to their best fit.

6. Double-click the pointer ✛ at the right edge of each column in the subform. The columns are resized to their best fit. See Figure 4-18.

Figure 4-18   **Main form with subform in Form view**

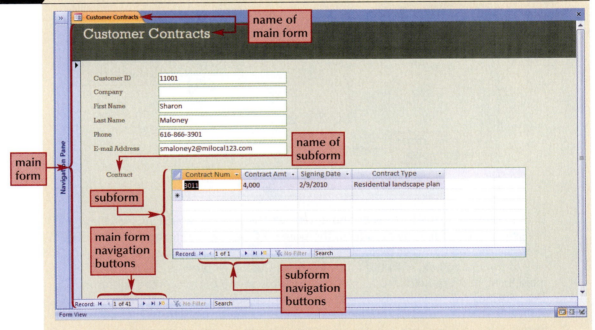

In the main form, Access displays the fields from the first record in the Customer table in a columnar format. The records in the main form appear in primary key order by Customer ID. Customer ID 11001 has one related record in the Contract table; this record, for Contract Num 3011, is shown in the subform datasheet. The main form name, "Customer Contracts," appears as the form's title and on the form object tab. The name of the subform appears to the left of the subform. Note that only the word "Contract" and not the complete name "Contract Subform" appears on the form. Access displays only the table name for the subform itself, but displays the complete name of the object, "Contract Subform," when you view and work with objects in the Navigation Pane. The subform designation is necessary in a list of database objects, so that you can distinguish the Contract subform from other objects, such as the Contract table; but the subform designation is not needed in the Customer Contracts form. Only the table name is required to identify the table containing the records in the subform.

The form includes two sets of navigation buttons. You use the top set of navigation buttons to select records from the related table in the subform, and you use the set of navigation buttons at the bottom of the form window to select records from the primary table in the main form.

You'll use the navigation buttons to view different records.

To navigate to different main form and subform records:

1. In the main form, click the **Last record** navigation button ⏭. Record 41 in the Customer table (for Lily's Boutique) becomes the current record in the main form. The subform shows that this customer currently has no contracts; recall that you just entered this customer record in the Customer table. Oren can use the subform to enter the information for this customer's contract when he receives it, and that information will be updated in the Contract table.

2. In the main form, click the **Previous record** navigation button ◀. Record 40 in the Customer table (for Weston Community Parks Foundation) becomes the current record in the main form. The subform shows that this customer has two contracts.

3. In the main form, select **40** in the Current Record box, type **34**, and then press the **Enter** key. Record 34 in the Customer table (for Dept. of Neighborhood Development) becomes the current record in the main form. The subform shows that this customer has four contracts.

4. Double-click the pointer ✛ at the right edge of the Contract Type column in the subform so that the complete values for this field are visible.

5. In the subform, click the **Last record** navigation button ⏭. Record 4 in the Contract table becomes the current record in the subform.

6. Save and close the Customer Contracts form.

> **Tip**
>
> As you move through the form/subform, notice that some field values in the subform are not completely visible. You can resize any subform field to its best fit to fully display the field values.

You've finished your work for Oren on the forms in the Belmont database. Next, Taylor Sico asks you to create a report that she can use to prepare a new advertising campaign.

Creating a Report Using the Report Wizard

As you learned in Tutorial 1, a report is a formatted printout of the contents of one or more tables or queries in a database. In Access, you can create your own reports or use the Report Wizard to create them for you. Like the Form Wizard, the **Report Wizard** asks you a series of questions and then creates a report based on your answers. Whether you use the Report Wizard or design your own report, you can change the report's design after you create it.

InSight	**Creating a Report Based on a Query**

You can create a report based on one or more tables or queries. When you use a query as the basis for a report, you can use criteria and other query tools to retrieve only the information you want to examine in the report. Experienced Access users often create a query just so they can create a report based on that query. When thinking about the type of report you want to create, consider creating a query first and basing the report on the query, to produce the exact results you want to see in the report.

Taylor wants you to create a report that includes selected data from the Customer table and all the data from the Contract table for each customer. Taylor has sketched a design of the report she wants (Figure 4-19). Like the Customer Contracts form you just created, which includes a main form and a subform, the report will be based on both tables, which are joined in a one-to-many relationship through the common Customer ID field. As shown in the sketch in Figure 4-19, the selected customer data from the primary Customer table includes the customer ID, company, first name, last name, city, and phone number. Below the data for each customer, the report will include the signing date, contract number, contract amount, and contract type from the related Contract table. The set of field values for each contract is called a **detail record**.

Figure 4-19	**Report sketch for the Customers and Contracts report**

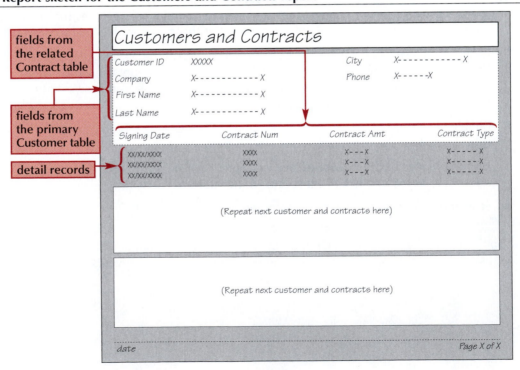

You'll use the Report Wizard to create the report according to Taylor's sketch.

To start the Report Wizard and select the fields to include in the report:

1. Click the **Create** tab on the Ribbon.

2. In the Reports group on the Create tab, click the **Report Wizard** button. The first Report Wizard dialog box opens.

   As was the case when you created the form with a subform, initially you can choose only one table or query to be the data source for the report. Then you can include data from other tables or queries. You will select the primary Customer table first.

3. If necessary, click the **Tables/Queries** arrow, and then click **Table: Customer**.

   In the first Report Wizard dialog box, you select fields in the order you want them to appear on the report. Taylor wants the Customer ID, Company, First Name, Last Name, City, and Phone fields from the Customer table to appear on the report, in that order.

4. Click **Customer ID** in the Available Fields list box (if necessary), and then click the `>` button. The field moves to the Selected Fields list box.

5. Repeat Step 4 to add the **Company**, **First Name**, **Last Name**, **City**, and **Phone** fields to the report.

6. Click the **Tables/Queries** arrow, and then scroll the list up and click **Table: Contract**. The fields from the Contract table appear in the Available Fields list box.

   The Customer ID field will appear on the report with the customer data, so you do not have to include it in the detail records for each contract. Otherwise, Taylor wants all the fields from the Contract table to be included in the report.

7. Click the `>>` button to move all the fields from the Available Fields list box to the Selected Fields list box.

8. Click **Contract.Customer ID** in the Selected Fields list box, click the `<` button to move the selected field back to the Available Fields list box, and then click the **Next** button. The second Report Wizard dialog box opens. See Figure 4-20.

Choosing a grouped or ungrouped report ◀ Figure 4-20

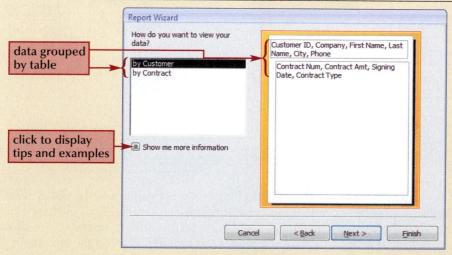

data grouped by table

click to display tips and examples

Tip

You can display tips for creating reports and examples of reports by clicking the "Show me more information" button.

You can choose to arrange the selected data grouped by table, which is the default, or ungrouped. For a **grouped report**, the data from a record in the primary table appears as a group, followed on subsequent lines of the report by the joined records from the related table. For the report you are creating, data from a record in the Customer table appears in a group, followed by the related records for each customer from the Contract table. An example of an ungrouped report would be a report of records from the Customer and Contract tables in order by Contract Num. Each contract and its associated customer data would appear together on one or more lines of the report; the data would not be grouped by table.

The default options shown on your screen are correct for the report Taylor wants, so you can continue responding to the Report Wizard questions.

To finish creating the report using the Report Wizard:

▶ 1. Click the **Next** button. The next Report Wizard dialog box opens, in which you choose additional grouping levels.

Two grouping levels are shown: one for a customer's data, and the other for a customer's contracts. Grouping levels are useful for reports with multiple levels, such as those containing monthly, quarterly, and annual totals, or for those containing city and country groups. Taylor's report contains no further grouping levels, so you can accept the default options.

▶ 2. Click the **Next** button. The next Report Wizard dialog box opens, in which you choose the sort order for the detail records. See Figure 4-21.

Figure 4-21 ▷ **Choosing the sort order for detail records**

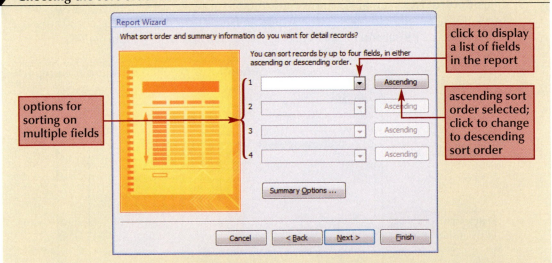

The records from the Contract table for a customer represent the detail records for Taylor's report. She wants these records to appear in increasing, or ascending, order by the value in the Signing Date field, so that the contracts will be shown in chronological order. The Ascending option is already selected by default. To change to descending order, you click this button, which acts as a toggle between the two sort orders. Also, you can sort on multiple fields, as you can with queries.

3. Click the arrow on the first list box, click **Signing Date**, and then click the **Next** button. The next Report Wizard dialog box opens, in which you choose a layout and page orientation for the report. See Figure 4-22.

Choosing the report layout **Figure 4-22**

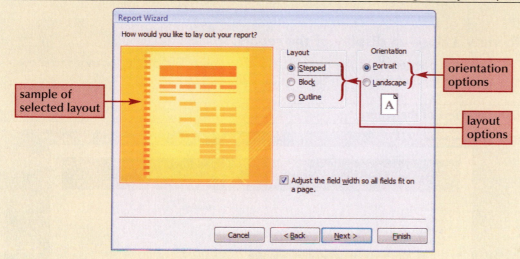

4. Click each layout option and examine each sample that appears.

   You'll use the Outline layout option because it resembles the layout shown in Taylor's sketch. Also, because there are few fields in the Contract table, the information will fit in portrait orientation, so you will accept the default page orientation.

5. Click the **Outline** option button, and then click the **Next** button. The next Report Wizard dialog box opens, in which you choose a style for the report.

   A sample of the selected style, or AutoFormat, appears in the box on the left. You can always choose a different AutoFormat after you create the report. For consistency with the form objects you created, you'll choose the Foundry AutoFormat.

6. Click **Foundry** (if necessary), and then click the **Next** button. The final Report Wizard dialog box opens, in which you choose a report name, which also serves as the printed title on the report.

   According to Taylor's sketch, the report title you need to specify is "Customers and Contracts." However, for consistency with how other objects are named in the database, you'll specify the name "Customers And Contracts," with each word capitalized. Later, you'll change the report title so that it appears with the word "and," per Taylor's sketch.

7. In the text box for the title, enter the title **Customers And Contracts** and then click the **Finish** button. The Report Wizard creates the report based on your answers and saves it as an object in the Belmont database. Then Access opens the report in Print Preview.

   To view the entire page, you need to change the Zoom setting.

8. In the Zoom group on the Print Preview tab, click the arrow for the **Zoom** button, and then click **Fit to Window**. The first page of the report is displayed in Print Preview.

When a report is displayed in Print Preview, you can use the pointer to toggle between a full-page display and a close-up display of the report. Taylor asks you to check the report to see if any adjustments need to be made. For example, some of the field titles or values might not be displayed completely, or you might need to move fields to enhance the report's appearance. You need to view a close-up display of the report.

To view a close-up display of the report:

▶ 1. Click the pointer 🔍 at the top center of the report. The display changes to show a close-up view of the report. See Figure 4-23.

Figure 4-23	Close-up view of the report

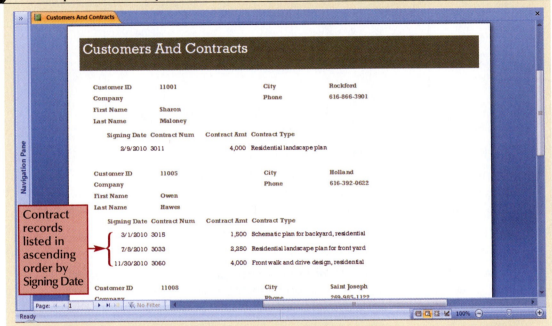

Contract records listed in ascending order by Signing Date

Trouble? Depending on your computer settings, the shading and colors used in your report might look different. This difference should not cause any problems.

The detail records for the Contract table fields appear in ascending order based on the values in the Signing Date field. Because the Signing Date field is used as the basis for sorting records, it appears as the first field in this section, even though you selected the fields in the order in which they appear in the Contract table.

All of the text in this portion of the report is displayed completely and is legible. However, you should check the entire report because some field values are longer than others and might not be fully displayed.

▶ 2. Use the vertical scroll bar to scroll to the bottom of the first page, checking the text in the report as you scroll. Notice the current date and page number at the bottom of the first page of the report; these elements were included by the Report Wizard as part of the report's design. The first page is fine; now you need to check the second page.

▶ 3. Click the **Next Page** navigation button ▶ to move to page 2 of the report.

▶ 4. Use the vertical scroll bar to scroll back up the page and check the field values. All are displayed completely.

▶ 5. Click the **Next Page** navigation button ▶ to move to page 3 of the report. Notice that the Company field value for the RiverView Development Company (Customer ID 11040) is not completely displayed.

▶ **6.** Continue to scroll through the pages of the report. Note that several Company field values are too long to fit within the space provided and are not fully displayed. Otherwise, all other text in the report is displayed correctly.

To fix the display of the Company field values, you first need to move the City and Phone fields to the right to provide more space for the company names. Then, you need to widen the space for the Company field values so that the complete values are displayed. The changes you need to make can be done in Layout view for the report. Also in Layout view, you can fix the report title so that it reads "Customers and Contracts."

Modifying a Report's Design in Layout View

Similar to Layout view for forms, Layout view for reports enables you to make modifications to the report's design. Many of the same options—such as those for changing the AutoFormat and changing the color of text and lines—are provided in Layout view for reports. Before moving and resizing the necessary fields, you'll fix the name of the report title to change the word "And" to "and" so that the title matches Taylor's sketch.

To edit the report title:

▶ **1.** Click the **Layout View** button ▣, which is located at the bottom right of the report window in Print Preview, on the status bar. The report is displayed in Layout view.

   Trouble? If the Field List or Property Sheet opens on the right side of your wndow, click the Close button ✕ to close it.

▶ **2.** Click the **Customers And Contracts** report title. An orange outline appears around the title, indicating it is selected.

▶ **3.** Click the title again to switch to editing mode. The title now appears in a white box, and the insertion point appears at the location you clicked.

▶ **4.** Click to the right of the letter "A" in "And," press the **Backspace** key, and then type **a**.

▶ **5.** Press the **Enter** key. The title of the report is now "Customers and Contracts." Notice that the name of the report object in the database is still "Customers And Contracts," as shown on the tab for the report.

Moving a Field on a Report in Layout View

Working in Layout view, you can reposition fields to improve the appearance of the report or to address the problem of some field values not being completely displayed. In the Customers And Contracts report, you need to make space for the longer Company field values by moving the City and Phone fields to the right. To make sure all the Company field values will fit, you should make any adjustments based on the longest company name—Kalamazoo Neighborhood Development.

To move the City and Phone fields:

▶ 1. Use the vertical scroll bar to scroll the report until the record for Customer ID 11045, Kalamazoo Neighborhood Development, is displayed.

   To select and move multiple fields, you use the Shift key.

▶ 2. Click the **City** field name for Customer ID 11045, press and hold the **Shift** key, and then click the **Phone** field name for the same record. Both fields are selected and can be moved. See Figure 4-24.

Figure 4-24	Fields selected and ready to be moved

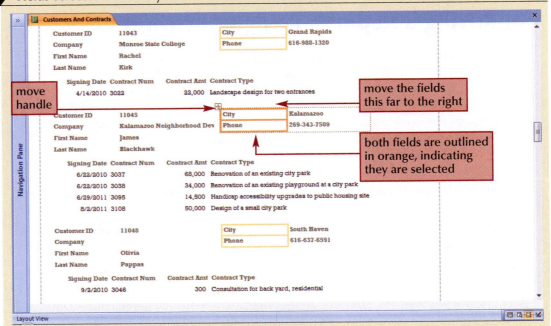

Notice the small box with two double-arrowed lines that is above the top-left corner of the selected fields. This box is called the **move handle**; you use it to reposition selected fields on a report or other database object.

▶ 3. Position the pointer on the move handle for the selected fields, and then drag them to the right. As you drag, black outlines indicate the location of both the field names and the field values.

▶ 4. Release the mouse when the left edge of the field names is approximately aligned with the beginning of the word "two" in the Contract Type field value above (see Figure 4-24). The City and Phone fields are now positioned farther to the right. Note that *all* City and Phone fields for the entire report have been moved, not just those for the current record. See Figure 4-25.

Report after moving fields | Figure 4-25

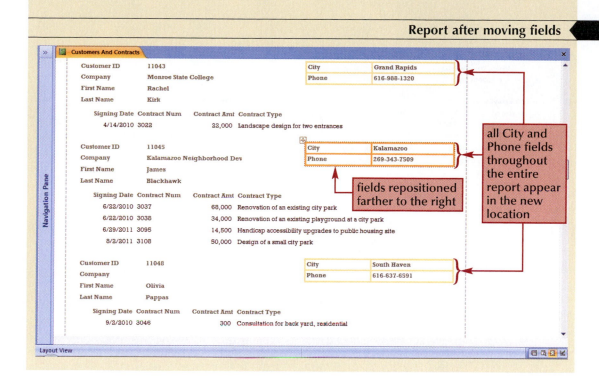

Resizing a Field on a Report in Layout View

With the City and Phone fields in the new location, there is more room on the report to display the full Company field values. Your next task is to resize the Company field value box so that the longest value (Kalamazoo Neighborhood Development) is fully displayed. This will ensure that all other company names will be completely visible in the report as well.

To widen the field value for the Company field:

▶ **1.** Click the field value **Kalamazoo Neighborhood Development** for Customer ID 11045. An orange outline appears around the field value, indicating it is selected.

▶ **2.** Position the pointer on the right side of the orange box until the pointer changes to a ↔ shape.

▶ **3.** Click and drag the ↔ pointer to the right until the right edge of the Company field value box is aligned approximately with the "e" in the word "design" in the Contract Type field value above it, and the complete field value is displayed. The field values for all fields in this section of the main report—Customer ID, Company, First Name, and Last Name—are resized as well. See Figure 4-26.

Trouble? When you release the mouse button after resizing the field, the screen might scroll to another location. If this happens, scroll your screen so that it matches Figure 4-26.

Figure 4-26 **Report after resizing fields**

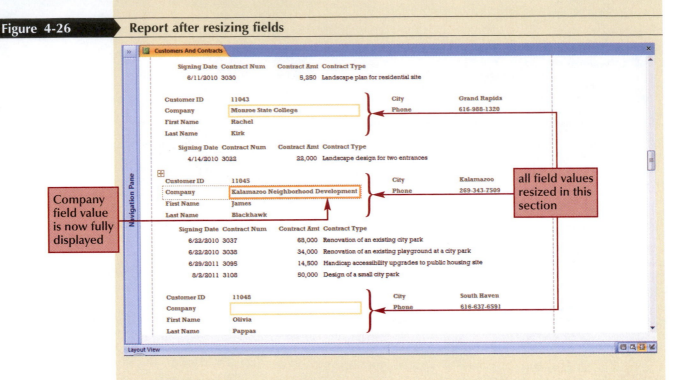

Even though you needed to increase the width of the Company field only, it's not a problem that all the other field values in this part of the report were also resized. With the City and Phone fields moved to the right, the report can accommodate the wider field values throughout.

Earlier, when meeting with Oren, Taylor viewed and worked with the Customer Data form. She likes how the picture looks on the form, and she likes the blue color applied to the form's title. She asks you to insert the same picture on the Customers And Contracts report, and to change the color of the report title to the same blue color used on the form.

Inserting a Picture in a Report and Changing the Font Color

You can add a picture to a report for visual interest or to identify a particular section of the report. You can also change the color of text on the report to enhance its appearance. Because Taylor plans to print the report using a color printer, she asks you to include a picture in the report and change the report title color to blue.

To insert the picture and change the color of the title in the report:

▶ 1. Press the **Ctrl+Home** keys to scroll to the top of the report.

▶ 2. Make sure the **Report Layout Tools Format** tab is selected on the Ribbon. Notice that the options provided in the Controls group for reports are the same as those you worked with for forms.

▶ 3. In the Controls group, click the **Logo** button.

▶ 4. Navigate to the **Level.01\Tutorial** folder, and then double-click the **Landscape** file. The picture is inserted in the top-left corner of the report, partially covering the report title.

▶ 5. Use the pointer to move the picture to the right of the report title.

Now you can change the color of the report title.

6. Click the title **Customers and Contracts** to select it. An orange outline surrounds the words, indicating they are selected.

7. In the Font group on the Report Layout Tools Format tab, click the arrow for the **Font Color** button A ▾ , and then click the color box for **Access Theme 4**. The color is applied to the report title. See Figure 4-27.

Report after adding the picture and changing the title font color   **Figure 4-27**

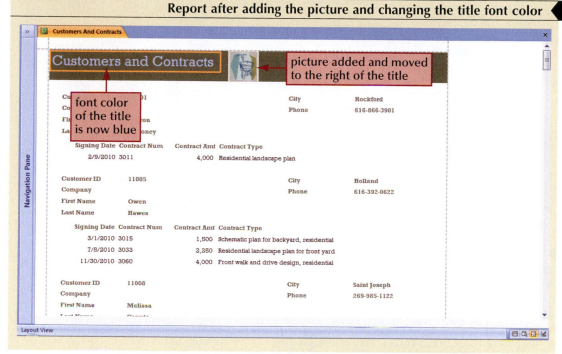

Taylor is pleased with the report's appearance, and shows it to Oren. He also approves of the report's contents and design, but has one final suggestion to enhance the report. He'd like to draw attention to the contract amounts that are greater than $25,000 by formatting them with a bold, red font. Because Oren doesn't want all the contract amounts to appear in this font, you need to use conditional formatting.

Using Conditional Formatting in a Report

Conditional formatting in a report (or form) is special formatting applied to certain field values depending on one or more conditions—similar to criteria you establish for queries. If a field value meets the condition or conditions you specify, the formatting is applied to the value.

Oren would like the Customers And Contracts report to show any contract amount that is greater than $25,000 in a bold, red font. This formatting will help to highlight the more significant contracts for Belmont Landscapes.

To apply conditional formatting to the Contract Amt field in the report:

1. Click the first Contract Amt field value, **4,000**, for Contract Num 3011. An orange outline appears around the field value, and a dotted line appears down the column for the field value throughout the entire report. Because you selected a value in the Contract Num column, the conditional formatting you specify next will affect only the values in this column. You must select a field *value*, and not the field *name*, before applying a conditional format.

2. In the Font group on the Report Layout Tools Format tab, click the **Conditional** button. The Conditional Formatting dialog box opens. See Figure 4-28.

Figure 4-28
Conditional Formatting dialog box

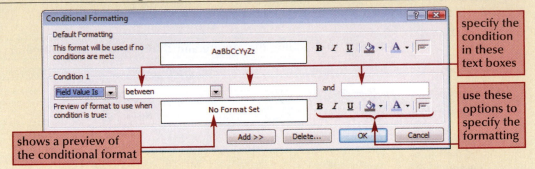

specify the condition in these text boxes

use these options to specify the formatting

shows a preview of the conditional format

The Default Formatting section at the top of the dialog box shows how text that does not meet the condition will be formatted in the report. In the Condition 1 section of the dialog box, you enter the specifications for the condition in the text boxes provided. Then, you use the formatting buttons to determine how text in the report should be formatted when the condition is met. The preview box shows how the text will look with the conditional formatting.

3. In the Condition 1 section of the dialog box, click the arrow for the box containing the word "between," and then click **greater than**. Oren wants only those contract amounts greater than $25,000 to be formatted.

The options available in this box include the operators you used when establishing criteria in a query. For example, if you wanted to apply conditional formatting to only those field values that are equal to a specific value, you would choose the "equal to" option in the list.

4. Press the **Tab** key to move to the text box, and then type **25000**.

5. In the Condition 1 section, click the arrow for the **Font/Fore Color** button ⃞ᴬ⃔, and then click the first color box in the last row (the dark red color).

6. In the Condition 1 section, click the **Bold** button ⃞**B**. The specifications for the conditional formatting are complete. See Figure 4-29.

Figure 4-29
Conditional formatting set for the Contract Amt field

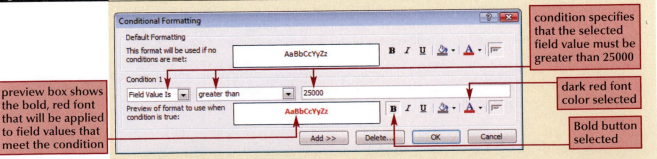

condition specifies that the selected field value must be greater than 25000

dark red font color selected

preview box shows the bold, red font that will be applied to field values that meet the condition

Bold button selected

7. Click the **OK** button. The dialog box closes, and the conditional format is applied to the Contract Amt field values.

To get a better view of the report and the formatting changes, you'll switch to Print Preview.

8. In the Views group on the Report Layout Tools Format tab, click the arrow for the **View** button, and then click **Print Preview**. The report appears in Print Preview.

9. Move to page 7 of the report and scroll down the window. Notice the conditional formatting applied to the Contract Amt field values that are greater than $25,000. See Figure 4-30.

Viewing the finished report in Print Preview | Figure 4-30

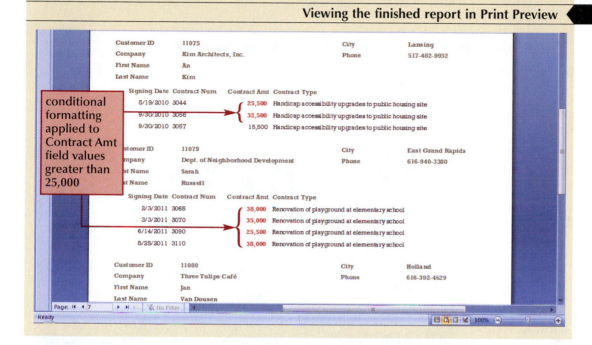

The Importance of Previewing Reports | InSight

When you create a report, it is a good idea to display the report in Print Preview repeatedly as you continue to develop the report. Doing so will give you a chance to find any formatting problems or other issues so that you can make any necessary corrections before printing the report. It is particularly important to preview a report after you've made changes to its design to ensure that the changes you made have not created new problems with the report's format. Before printing any report, you should preview it so you can determine where the pages will break, and make any necessary adjustments so that the final printed output looks exactly the way you want it to.

The report is now complete. You'll print just the first page of the report so that Oren and Taylor can view the final results and share the report design with other staff members before printing the entire report. (*Note:* Check with your instructor first to be sure you should complete the following printing steps.)

To print page 1 of the report:

1. In the Print group on the Print Preview tab, click the **Print** button. The Print dialog box opens.

2. In the Print Range section, click the **Pages** option button. The insertion point now appears in the From text box so that you can specify the range of pages to print.

3. Type **1** in the From text box, press the **Tab** key to move to the To text box, and then type **1**. These settings specify that only page 1 of the report will be printed.

4. Click the **OK** button. The Print dialog box closes, and the first page of the report is printed.

5. Save and close the Customers And Contracts report.

You've created many different objects in the Belmont database. Before you close it and exit Access, you'll open the Navigation Pane to view all the objects in the database.

To view the Belmont database objects in the Navigation Pane:

1. Open the Navigation Pane and scroll up, if necessary, to display the top of the pane. See Figure 4-31.

Figure 4-31   Belmont database objects in the Navigation Pane

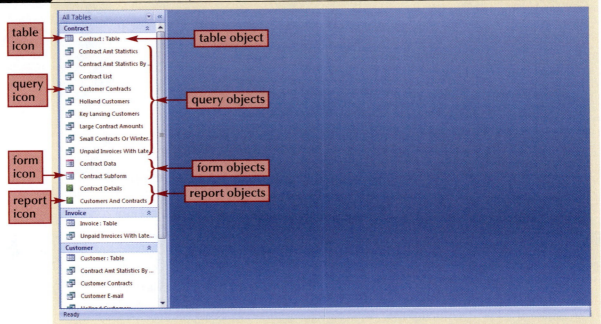

The Navigation Pane displays the objects grouped by table. Within each table group, the table itself is listed first, followed by any queries, forms, and reports you created based on the table. Each object is identified with a unique icon to help you distinguish objects with similar names or the same names. Objects you created based on more than one table appear in the list of objects for both tables. For example, note that the Customer Contracts query object is listed for both the Contract table and the Customer table because its design is based on both tables.

2. Scroll down to the bottom of the Navigation Pane. Notice the Customer Contracts form in the Customer table list. This is the form you created containing a main form based on the Customer table and a subform based on the Contract table. The Contract Subform object is listed with the Contract table. Also, note that the database contains a query object with the same name, "Customer Contracts." The icons in the Navigation Pane help you to distinguish the Customer Contracts query (listed for both the Customer and Contract tables) from the Customer Contracts report.

3. Compact and repair the Belmont database, and then close Access.

Oren is satisfied that the forms you created—the Customer Data form and the Customer Contracts form—will make it easier to enter, view, and update data in the Belmont database. The Customers And Contracts report presents important information about Belmont Landscapes' customers in an attractive and professional format, which will help Taylor and other staff members in their marketing efforts.

Session 4.2 Quick Check | Review

1. In a form that contains a main form and a subform, what data is displayed in the main form and what data is displayed in the subform?
2. Describe how you use the navigation buttons to move through a form containing a main form and a subform.
3. When you create a report based on two tables that are joined in a one-to-many relationship, the field values for the records from the related table are called the _____ records.
4. True or False: To move a field to another location on a report, you first need to display the report in Design view.
5. When working in Layout view for a report, which key do you press and hold down so that you can click to select multiple fields?
6. _____ in a report (or form) is special formatting applied to certain field values depending on one or more conditions.

Tutorial Summary | Review

In this tutorial, you learned how to create a form using the Form Wizard and how to modify the form's design in Layout view by changing the form's AutoFormat, adding a picture, changing the font color of the form's title, changing the type of line around field values on the form, and moving a field on the form. You also used the form's navigation buttons and various keyboard techniques to navigate through the records in a form. You used the Find command to locate specific form records, and included wildcard characters to search for records by specifying only a partial field value. In addition, you maintained table data using a form, and previewed and printed selected form records. With the one-to-many relationship already established between the necessary tables, you were able to create a form with a main form and a subform to display data from both tables at the same time. You also used the Report Wizard to create a report displaying data from two related tables. Working in Layout view, you modified the report by moving and resizing fields, and you enhanced the report by adding a picture and changing the font color of the report title. Finally, you learned how to apply conditional formatting to certain field values in the report to format them differently from other text in the report.

Key Terms

AutoFormat	Form Wizard	move handle
conditional formatting	grouped report	Report Wizard
control	Layout view	subform
detail record	main form	wildcard character

Practice	Review Assignments

Practice the skills you learned in the tutorial using the same case scenario.

Data Files needed for the Review Assignments: Supplier.accdb (*cont. from Tutorial 3*) **and Tools.bmp**

Oren asks you to enhance the Supplier database with forms and reports. Complete the following:

1. Open the **Supplier** database located in the Level.01\Review folder provided with your Data Files.

2. Use the Form Wizard to create a form based on the **Product** table. Select all fields for the form, the Columnar layout, and the Office style, and specify the title **Product Data** for the form.

3. In the Product Data form, change the AutoFormat to Foundry.

4. Insert the Tools picture, which is located in the Level.01\Review folder provided with your Data Files, in the Product Data form. Move the picture just to the right of the Product Data form title.

5. Change the font color of the Product Data form title to Green 3.

6. Change the type of line displayed around the Tools picture to Transparent.

7. Use the Product Data form to update the Product table as follows:

    a. Use the Find command to search for "wall" in the Product Type field and then display the record for a retaining wall (Product ID 5227). Change the Price in this record to **11.45** and the Discount Offered to **Yes**.

    b. Add a new record with the following field values, leaving the Color, Material, and Weight in Lbs fields blank:
    Product ID: **5630**
    Company ID: **GEN359**
    Product Type: **Annual**
    Price: **2.70**
    Unit: **Each**
    Color: [do not enter a value]
    Material: [do not enter a value]
    Size: **1 quart**
    Weight in Lbs: [do not enter a value]
    Discount Offered: **Yes**

    c. Save and close the form.

8. Use the Form Wizard to create a form containing a main form and a subform. Select all fields except Product Type from the Company table for the main form, and select Product ID, Product Type, Price, Unit, and Color—in that order—from the Product table for the subform. Use the Datasheet layout and the Foundry style. Specify the title **Companies And Products** for the main form and **Product Subform** for the subform.

9. Change the form title text to **Companies and Products**.

10. Resize all columns in the subform to their best fit, working left to right. Navigate through each record in the main form to make sure all the field values in the subform are completely displayed. Save and close the form.

11. Use the Report Wizard to create a report based on the primary Company table and the related Product table. Select the Company ID, Company Name, Contact First Name, Contact Last Name, and City fields—in that order—from the Company table and the Product ID, Product Type, Price, and Unit fields from the Product table. Sort the detail records in ascending order by Product ID. Choose the Stepped layout, Landscape orientation, and the Foundry style. Specify the title **Products By Company** for the report.

12. Change the report title text to **Products by Company**.

13. Resize the controls in the Products By Company report as follows, scrolling the report in Layout view to make sure your changes apply to all field values as necessary:

   a. Resize the Company ID field so that its left edge aligns with the left edge of the report. Also resize this field to its best fit.

   b. Resize the remaining column widths as necessary to fit the longest name or value they contain.

14. Insert the Tools picture, which is located in the Level.01\Review folder provided with your Data Files, in the **Products By Company** report. Position the picture just to the right of the Products by Company title so that its top edge is just below the top border of the report.

15. Apply conditional formatting so that the City field values equal to Lansing appear as dark red and bold.

16. Preview each page of the report, verifying that all the fields fit on the page. If necessary, return to Layout view and make changes so the report prints within the margins of the page and so that all field names and values are completely displayed.

17. Save the report, print its first page (only if asked by your instructor to do so), and then close the report.

18. Compact and repair the Supplier database, and then close it.

| Apply | **Case Problem 1** |

Use the skills you learned in the tutorial to create forms and a report to work with and display data about music school classes.

Data Files needed for this Case Problem: Pinehill.accdb *(cont. from Tutorial 3)* **and Piano.bmp**

Pine Hill Music School   Yuka Koyama wants to use the Pinehill database to track and view information about the classes her music school offers. She asks you to create the necessary forms and a report to help her manage this data. Complete the following:

1. Open the **Pinehill** database located in the Level.01\Case1 folder provided with your Data Files.

2. Use the Form Wizard to create a form based on the Student table. Select all the fields for the form, the Columnar layout, and the Office style. Specify the title **Student Data** for the form.

3. Change the AutoFormat for the Student Data form to Technic.

4. Use the Find command to display the record for Jeff Tealey, and then change the Address field value for this record to **304 Forest Ave**.

5. Use the Student Data form to add a new record to the Student table with the following field values:
   Student ID: **NEL7584**
   First Name: **Kayla**
   Last Name: **Nelson**
   Address: **15540 Belleview Dr**
   City: **Portland**
   State: **OR**
   Zip: **97229**
   Phone: **541-563-3156**
   Birth Date: **10/13/2000**
   Gender: **F**

6. Save and close the Student Data form.

7. Use the Form Wizard to create a form containing a main form and a subform. Select all the fields from the Teacher table for the main form, and select the Contract ID, Student ID, and Lesson Type fields from the Contract table for the subform. Use the Datasheet layout and the Technic style. Specify the title **Contracts By Teacher** for the main form and the title **Contract Subform** for the subform.

8. Change the form title text for the main form to **Contracts by Teacher**, and change the font color of the title to Access Theme 2.

9. Change the type of line bordering the field values in the main form to Dots.

10. Save and close the Contracts By Teacher form.

11. Use the Report Wizard to create a report based on the primary Student table and the related Contract table. Select the Student ID, First Name, Last Name, and Phone fields from the Student table, and select all fields from the Contract table except Student ID and Contract Start Date. Sort the detail records in ascending order by Contract ID. Choose the Stepped layout, Landscape orientation, and the Technic style. Specify the title **Student Contracts** for the report.

12. Resize the fields in the report so that the field names and values are completely displayed and the report fits completely within the margins of the page. (*Hint:* Switch to Print Preview to determine whether all of the fields fit on the page.)

13. Insert the Piano picture, which is located in the Level.01\Case1 folder provided with your Data Files, in the Student Contracts report. Position the picture to the right of the Student Contracts report title so that its top edge is just below the top edge of the report.

14. Apply conditional formatting so that Contract End Date values that occur earlier than 1/1/2011 appear as bold and green (last row, sixth column in the gallery).

15. Preview the report to confirm that it is formatted correctly. If necessary, return to Layout view and make changes so the report prints within the margins of the page and so that all field names and values are completely displayed. When you are finished, save the report, print its first page (only if asked by your instructor to do so), and then close the report.

16. Compact and repair the Pinehill database, and then close it.

Challenge | Case Problem 2

Challenge yourself by creating and working with a form and report for a fitness center.

Data Files needed for this Case Problem: Fitness.accdb (*cont. from Tutorial 3*) and Weights.bmp

Parkhurst Health & Fitness Center   Martha Parkhurst is using the Fitness database to track and analyze the business activity of the fitness center members and their programs. To make her work easier, you'll create a form and report in the Fitness database. Complete the following:

1. Open the **Fitness** database located in the Level.01\Case2 folder provided with your Data Files.

⊕ **EXPLORE**

2. Use the Form Wizard to create a form containing a main form and a subform. Select all the fields from the Program table for the main form, and select the Member ID, First Name, Last Name, and Phone fields from the Member table for the subform. Use the Tabular layout and the Office style. Specify the title **Program Members** for the main form and the title **Member Subform** for the subform.

⊕ **EXPLORE**

3. Change the AutoFormat of the Member Subform to Northwind. (*Hint:* Close the Program Members form, and then open the Member Subform. Change the AutoFormat of the subform, and then save and close the subform.)

4. In the Program Members form, change the AutoFormat to Origin. Change the font color of the main form title to Access Theme 3, and change the line type of the field boxes in the main form to Solid.

5. Save the Program Members form, navigate to the second record in the subform for the first main record, and then change the Phone field value to **804-553-7986**.

6. Navigate to the ninth record in the main form, and then change the Last Name field value for the fourth record in the subform to **Larsen**. Close the form.

⊕ **EXPLORE**

7. Use the Report Wizard to create a report based on the primary Program table and the related Member table. Select all fields except Physical Required from the Program table, and then select the following fields from the Member table: Member ID, First Name, Last Name, City, Phone, and Date Joined. In the third Report Wizard dialog box, specify the City field as an additional grouping level. Sort the detail records by Date Joined in *descending* order. Choose the Block layout, Landscape orientation, and the Office style for the report. Specify the title **Programs And Members** for the report.

8. Revise the report title text to **Programs and Members**.

9. Change the report's AutoFormat to Origin.

10. Resize the fields as necessary so that all the field names and values are completely displayed within the margins of the report.

11. Insert the Weights picture, which is located in the Level.01\Case2 folder provided with your Data Files, in the report. Move the picture just to the right of the Programs and Members title.

⊕ **EXPLORE**

12. Open the Access Help window and use **resize an image in a report** as the search text. Select the Help article titled "Modify, edit, or change a report," select the section titled "Modify your report in Layout view," select the topic titled "Add or modify a logo or other image," and then read the "Resize a control that contains a logo or other image" section. Verify that the Weights picture is still selected, and then resize it to about 75 percent of its original height. Close the Access Help window.

13. Apply conditional formatting so that all City field values equal to Ashland are formatted as bold and dark blue-green (sixth row, ninth column in the gallery).

14. Preview the report to confirm that it is formatted correctly. Save the report, print its first page (only if asked by your instructor to do so), and then close the report.

15. Compact and repair the Fitness database, and then close it.

| Challenge | **Case Problem 3** |

Work with the skills you've learned, and explore some new skills, to create forms and a report for a not-for-profit agency.

Data Files needed for this Case Problem: Rossi.accdb *(cont. from Tutorial 3)* **and Donate.bmp**

Rossi Recycling Group   Tom Rossi wants to work with and display data about the donations made to the Rossi Recycling Group. You'll help him by creating forms and a report in the Rossi database. Complete the following:

1. Open the **Rossi** database located in the Level.01\Case3 folder provided with your Data Files.

2. Use the Form Wizard to create a form based on the Donation table. Select all the fields for the form, the Columnar layout, and the Median style. Specify the title **Donation Info** for the form.

⊕ EXPLORE   3. Use the Donation Info form to update the Donation table as follows:

    a. Use the Find command to search for the record that contains "tools" in the Donation Description field. Display the record for Power tools, and then change the Donation Value to **565**.

    b. Add a new record with the following values:

       Donation ID: **2219**

       Donor ID: **36077**

       Agency ID: **W22**

       Donation Date: **12/21/2010**

       Donation Description: **Toys**

       Donation Value: **45**

       Pickup Required: **No**

    c. Find the record with Donation ID 2150, and then delete it. (*Hint:* Select the record by clicking the record selector—the bar with a right-pointing triangle to the left of the form—and then click the Delete button in the Records group on the Home tab. When asked to confirm the deletion, click the Yes button.)

4. Change the AutoFormat of the Donation Info form to Verve, and then change the font color of the form title to Maroon 3.

⊕ EXPLORE   5. With the title text selected, drag the right title border to resize the title to fit on one line. Save and close the form.

⊕ EXPLORE   6. Use the Form Wizard to create a form containing a main form and a subform. Select all the fields from the Donor table for the main form, and select the Donation ID, Agency ID, Donation Date, Donation Description, and Donation Value fields from the Donation table for the subform. Use the Tabular layout and the Verve style. Specify the name **Donors And Donations** for the main form and the title **Donation Subform** for the subform.

7. Revise the title text in the main form to **Donors and Donations**.

8. Use the appropriate wildcard character to find all records with a Phone value that begins with the area code 316. Change the record with the Phone field value of 316-282-2226 to **316-282-2556**. Save and close the form.

EXPLORE

9. Use the Report Wizard to create a report based on the primary Agency table and the related Donation table. Select the Agency Name and Phone fields from the Agency table, and select all fields except Agency ID and Pickup Required from the Donation table. In the third Report Wizard dialog box, select Donor ID as an additional grouping level. Sort the detail records in *descending* order by Donation Value. Choose the Stepped layout, Portrait orientation, and the Verve style. Specify the name **Agencies And Donations** for the report.

10. Revise the report title text to **Agencies and Donations**.

11. Resize the fields as necessary so that all the field names and values are completely displayed on the page.

12. Insert the Donate picture, which is located in the Level.01\Case3 folder provided with your Data Files, in the report. Move the picture just to the right of the Agencies and Donations report title.

EXPLORE

13. Change the fill color of the Donate picture to Transparent. (*Hint:* Select the picture, click the arrow for the Fill/Back Color button in the Font group on the Format tab, and then click Transparent.) Change the line type of the picture border to Transparent.

EXPLORE

14. Open the Access Help window and use **add gridlines to a report** as the search text. Select the Help article titled "Modify, edit, or change a report," select the topic titled "Modify your report in Layout view," and then select and read the "Add gridlines" section. Display Horizontal gridlines for the fields from the Agency table. (*Hint:* Click an Agency Name or Phone field value, and then select a gridline option.) Close the Access Help window.

15. Apply conditional formatting so that any Donation Value greater than or equal to $200 is formatted using a bold, blue-green (top row, ninth column in the gallery) font.

16. Preview the report to confirm that it is formatted correctly. If necessary, return to Layout view and make changes so the report prints within the margins of the page and so that all field names and values are completely displayed. When you are finished, save the report, print its first page (only if asked by your instructor to do so), and then close the report.

17. Change the Navigation Pane so it displays all objects grouped by object type.

18. Compact and repair the Rossi database, and then close it.

*With the figures pro-
vided as guides, create
a form and a report to
display and manage
data for a luxury rental
agency.*

| Create | **Case Problem 4** |

Data Files needed for this Case Problem: GEM.accdb *(cont. from Tutorial 3)* **and
Villa.bmp**

GEM Ultimate Vacations   Griffin and Emma MacElroy want to use the GEM database to
track and analyze data about their clients and the luxury properties they rent. You'll help
them by creating forms and reports to meet this goal. Complete the following:

1. Open the **GEM** database located in the Level.01\Case4 folder provided with your
Data Files.

◆ **EXPLORE**

2. Create the form shown in Figure 4-32.

Figure 4-32

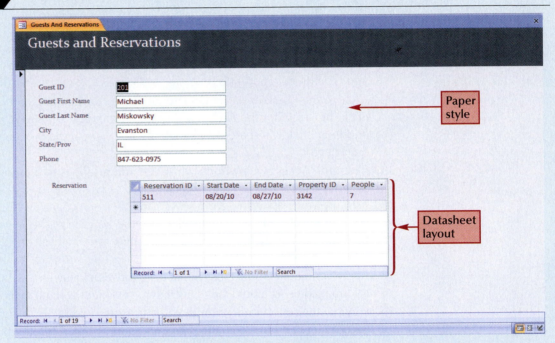

(*Hints:* To resize the subform to display all five fields, use the same technique you
use to resize any form control: click the subform control to select it, and then drag
the border. Widen the subform to display most of the fields in the subform, resize all
columns in the subform to their best fit, and then adjust the size of the subform
again.)

3. Using the form you just created, navigate to the second record in the subform for the
third main record, and then change the People field value to **7**.

4. Use the Find command to move to the record for Kelly Skolnik, and then change the
End Date field value for Reservation ID 507 to **5/22/10**.

5. Use the appropriate wildcard character to find all records with a Phone value that
begins with the area code 630. Change the Phone field value of 630-442-4831 to
630-442-5943. Save and close the form.

◆ **EXPLORE**

6. Use the Report Wizard to create the report shown in Figure 4-33.

Figure 4-33

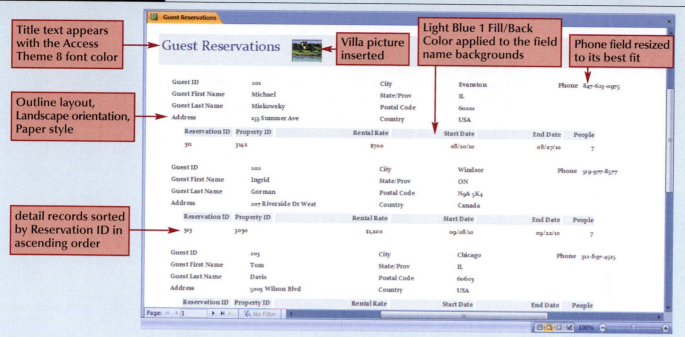

Title text appears with the Access Theme 8 font color

Villa picture inserted

Light Blue 1 Fill/Back Color applied to the field name backgrounds

Phone field resized to its best fit

Outline layout, Landscape orientation, Paper style

detail records sorted by Reservation ID in ascending order

(*Hint*: To display the Light Blue 1 background color with the field names from the Reservation table, press and hold down the Shift key and click to select the six field names, and then apply the Light Blue 1 Fill/Back Color.)

7. Apply conditional formatting so that all People field values greater than 7 are formatted as bold and aqua blue (top row, ninth column in the gallery).

 EXPLORE

8. Preview the report so you see two pages at once. (*Hint*: Use a button on the Print Preview tab.) Print page 1 of the report (only if asked by your instructor to do so).

9. Save and close the report, compact and repair the GEM database, and then close it.

Research | Internet Assignments

Use the Internet to find and work with data related to the topics presented in this tutorial.

The purpose of the Internet Assignments is to challenge you to find information on the Internet that you can use to work effectively with this software. The actual assignments are updated and maintained on the Course Technology Web site. Log on to the Internet and use your Web browser to go to the Student Online Companion for New Perspectives Office 2007 at **www.course.com/np/office2007**. Then navigate to the Internet Assignments for this tutorial.

Assess | SAM Assessment and Training

If you have a SAM user profile, you may have access to hands-on instruction, practice, and assessment of the skills covered in this tutorial. Log in to your SAM account (**http://sam2007.course.com**) to launch any assigned training activities or exams that relate to the skills covered in this tutorial.

Review | **Quick Check Answers**

Session 4.1

1. The Form tool creates a form automatically using all the fields in the selected table or query; the Form Wizard allows you to choose some or all of the fields in the selected table or query, choose fields from other tables and queries, and display fields in any order on the form.
2. An AutoFormat is a predefined style for a form (or report). To change a form's Auto-Format, display the form in Layout view, click the More button in the AutoFormat group on the Form Layout Tools Format tab, and then click the AutoFormat you want to apply in the gallery displayed, or click AutoFormat Wizard to open the AutoFormat dialog box and select the AutoFormat you want to apply.
3. control
4. the last record in the table
5. the question mark (?)
6. Selected Record(s)

Session 4.2

1. The main form displays the data from the primary table, and the subform displays the data from the related table.
2. You use the top set of navigation buttons to select and move through records from the related table in the subform, and the bottom set to select and move through records from the primary table in the main form.
3. detail
4. False
5. Shift
6. Conditional formatting

Ending Data Files

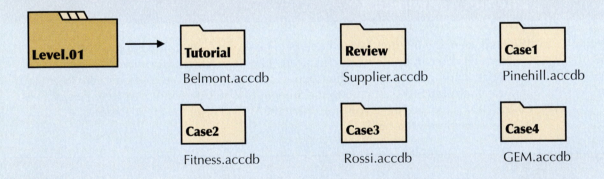

Level.01 → Tutorial
Belmont.accdb

Review
Supplier.accdb

Case1
Pinehill.accdb

Case2
Fitness.accdb

Case3
Rossi.accdb

Case4
GEM.accdb

Reality Check

The Microsoft Access program is widely used in corporations to track business data, but it can also be a valuable tool to use to track data in your personal life. For example, you might want to create an Access database to track information about items in a personal collection, such as CDs, DVDs, or books; items related to a hobby, such as coin or stamp collecting, travel, or family history; or items related to sports teams, theater clubs, or other organizations to which you might belong. In this exercise, you'll use Access to create a database that will contain information of your choice, using the Access skills and features presented in Tutorials 1 through 4.

Using Templates

The Access program includes templates for creating databases and tables. A **database template** is a database containing predefined tables, queries, forms, and reports. A **table template** is a template containing predefined fields. Using a database or table template can save you time and effort in the creation process. For example, if the fields available in one of the table templates Access offers are similar to the data you want to track, you can use the table template to quickly create a table with the fields and field properties already created and set for you. You can then modify the table, as necessary, to suit your needs. Before you begin to create your own database, review the following steps for using database and table templates.

To create a database using a database template:

1. On the Getting Started with Microsoft Office Access page, click the appropriate link in the Template Categories pane; or click a link in the From Microsoft Office Online pane; or click one of the templates in the Featured Online Templates section in the middle of the page.
2. Specify the name for your database and a location in which to save the database file.
3. Click the Create button (or the Download button if you are using an Office Online template).
4. Use the resulting database objects to enter, modify, or delete data or database objects.

To create a table using a table template:

1. With your database file open, click the Create tab on the Ribbon.
2. In the Tables group, click the Table Templates button. A gallery opens listing the different table templates provided with Access.
3. Click the template you want to use.
4. Modify the resulting table as needed, by adding or deleting fields, changing field properties, and so on.

You can decide to use a database and/or table template for the following exercise if the templates fit the data you want to track. Note, however, that you still need to create the additional database objects indicated in the following steps—tables, queries, forms, and reports—to complete the exercise successfully.

Note: Please be sure *not* to include any personal information of a sensitive nature in the database you create to be submitted to your instructor for this exercise. Later on, you can update the data in your database with such information for your own personal use.

1. Create a new Access database to contain personal data you want to track.

2. Create two or three tables in the database that can be joined through one-to-many relationships.

3. Define the properties for each field in each table. Make sure you include a mix of data types for the fields (for example, do not include only Text fields in each table).

4. Specify a primary key for each table.

5. Define the necessary one-to-many relationships between the tables in the database with referential integrity enforced.

6. Enter 20 to 30 records in each table. If appropriate, you can import the data for a table from another source, such as an Excel spreadsheet or a text file.

7. Create 5 to 10 queries based on single tables and multiple tables. Be sure that some of the queries you create include some or all of the following: exact match conditions, comparison operators, and logical operators.

8. For some of the queries, use various sorting and filtering techniques to display the query results in various ways. Save these queries with the sort and/or filter applied.

9. If possible, and depending on the data you are tracking, create at least one calculated field in one of the queries.

10. If possible, and depending on the data you are tracking, use aggregate functions to produce summary statistics based on the data in at least one of your tables.

11. Create at least one form for each table in your database. Enhance each form's appearance with pictures, AutoFormats, line colors, and so on.

12. Create at least one form with a main form and subform based on related tables in your database. Enhance the form's appearance as appropriate.

13. Create at least one report based on each table in your database. Enhance each report's appearance with pictures, AutoFormats, color, and so on.

14. Apply conditional formatting to the values in at least one of your reports.

15. Submit your completed database to your instructor as requested. Include printouts of any database objects, such as reports, if required.

Objectives

Creating Advanced Queries and Enhancing Table Design

Making the Panorama Database Easier to Use

Case | Belmont Landscapes

After graduating with a university degree in Landscape Architecture and then working for a firm that provides basic landscape services to residential customers, Oren Belmont started his own landscape architecture firm in Holland, Michigan. Belmont Landscapes specializes in landscape designs for residential and commercial customers and numerous public agencies. The firm provides a wide range of services—from site analyses and feasibility studies, to drafting and administering construction documents—for projects of various scales. Oren's company developed the Panorama database of customer, contract, and invoice data; and the employees use Microsoft Office Access 2007 (or simply Access) to manage it. The Panorama database contains tables, queries, forms, and reports that Sarah Fisher, office manager, and Taylor Sico, marketing manager, use to track customers and their landscape projects.

Oren, Sarah, and Taylor are interested in taking better advantage of the power of Access to make the database easier to use and to create more sophisticated queries. For example, Taylor wants to obtain lists of employers in certain cities, and Sarah needs a summarized list of invoice amounts by city. Sarah wants to change the design of the Customer and Contract tables. In this tutorial, you'll modify and customize the Panorama database to satisfy these requirements.

Starting Data Files

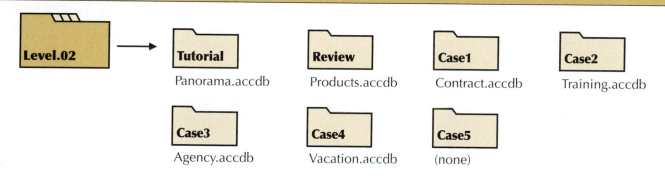

Level.02	→	Tutorial	Review	Case1	Case2
		Panorama.accdb	Products.accdb	Contract.accdb	Training.accdb

Case3	Case4	Case5
Agency.accdb	Vacation.accdb	(none)

Session 5.1

Reviewing the Panorama Database

Tip

Read the Microsoft Access Naming Conventions section in the appendix titled "Relational Databases and Database Design" for more information about naming conventions.

Sarah and her staff had no previous database experience when they created the Panorama database using the wizards and other easy-to-use Access tools. As business continued to grow at Belmont Landscapes, Sarah convinced Oren that they needed to hire a computer expert to further enhance the Panorama database, and they hired Lucia Perez, who has a business information systems degree and nine years of experience developing database systems. Lucia spent a few days reviewing the Panorama database, and she decided to implement simple naming standards for the objects and field names in the database to make her future work easier.

Before implementing the enhancements for Sarah and Taylor, you'll review the naming changes Lucia made to the object and field names in the Panorama database.

To review the object naming standards in the Panorama database:

▶ 1. Make sure you have created your copy of the Access Data Files, and that your computer can access them.

Trouble? If you don't have the Access Data Files, you need to get them before you can proceed. Your instructor will either give you the Data Files or ask you to obtain them from a specified location (such as a network drive). In either case, make a backup copy of the Data Files before you start so that you will have the original files available in case you need to start over. If you have any questions about the Data Files, see your instructor or technical support person for assistance.

▶ 2. Start Access, and then open the **Panorama** database in the Level.02\Tutorial folder provided with your Data Files.

Trouble? If the Security Warning is displayed below the Ribbon, click the Options button next to the Security Warning. In the dialog box that opens, click the "Enable this content" option button, and then click the OK button.

The Navigation Pane displays the objects grouped by object type, as shown in Figure 5-1. Lucia added prefix tags to the object names—a tbl prefix tag for tables, a qry prefix tag for queries, a frm prefix tag for forms, and a rpt prefix tag for reports. Using object prefix tags, you can readily identify the object type, even when the objects have the same base name—for instance, tblContract, frmContract, and rptContract. In addition, Lucia removed spaces from the object names based on her experience with other database management systems, such as SQL Server and Oracle, that do not permit spaces in object and field names. If Belmont Landscapes needs to upscale to one of these other database management systems in the future, Lucia will have to do less work to make the transition.

Panorama database objects on the Navigation Pane | Figure 5-1

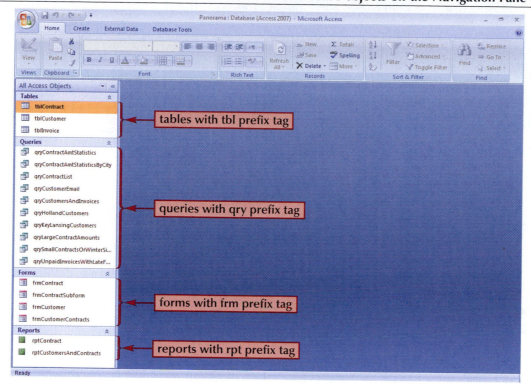

Next, you'll review the naming changes Lucia made to the tables by opening the tblContract table in Datasheet view and then in Design view.

To review the field naming standards in the tblContract table:

▶ **1.** In the Tables group on the Navigation Page, double-click **tblContract** to open the tblContract table in Datasheet view.

Notice that each column heading name contains spaces. You need to review the table in Design view to see Lucia's changes.

▶ **2.** In the Views group on the Home tab, click the **View** button. The table is displayed in Design view with the ContractNum field selected. See Figure 5-2.

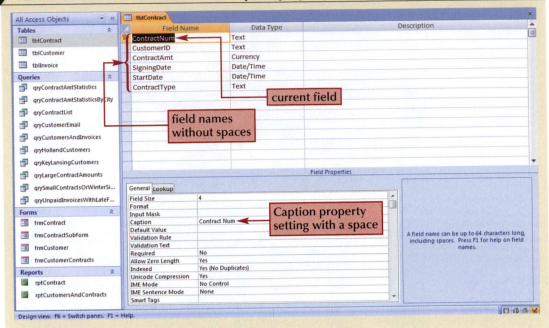

Notice that Lucia removed the spaces from each of the six field names. If the field names do not contain spaces, why do the column headings in Datasheet view contain spaces? Lucia set the Caption property for the ContractNum field to Contract Num, and she set the Caption property for the other five fields in a similar way. The **Caption property** for a field specifies its column heading value in datasheets and its label value in forms and reports. If you don't set the Caption property, Access uses the field name as the default column heading name and the default label name. Using the Caption property, you can use field names without spaces as a standard, while providing the users with more readable names on their queries, forms, and reports.

Now that you've reviewed Lucia's database changes, you'll create the queries that Sarah and Taylor need.

Using a Pattern Match in a Query

You are already familiar with queries that use an exact match or a range of values (for example, queries that use the >= or < comparison operators) to select records. Access provides many other operators for creating select queries. These operators let you create more complicated queries that are difficult or impossible to create with exact match or range of values selection criteria.

Sarah and Taylor created a list of questions they want to answer using the Panorama database:

- Which customers have the 616 area code?
- What is the customer information for customers located in Holland, Rockford, or Saugatuck?
- What is the customer information for all customers *except* those located in Holland, Rockford, or Saugatuck?
- What is the customer and contract information for contracts that have values of less than $10,000 or that were signed during the winter *and* are located in Grand Rapids or East Grand Rapids?

- What are the names of Belmont Landscapes' customers? The customer name is either the company name for nonresidential customers or the last and first names for residential customers.
- What is the customer information for customers in a particular city? For this query, the user needs to be able to specify the city.

Next, you will create the queries necessary to answer these questions. Taylor wants to view the records for all customers located in the 616 area code. She plans to travel to this area next week and wants to contact customers ahead of time to schedule appointments. To answer Taylor's question, you can create a query that uses a pattern match. A **pattern match** selects records with a value for the designated field that matches the pattern of the simple condition value, in this case, customers with the 616 area code. You do this using the Like comparison operator.

The **Like comparison operator** selects records by matching field values to a specific pattern that includes one or more of these wildcard characters: asterisk (*), question mark (?), and number symbol (#). The asterisk represents any string of characters, the question mark represents any single character, and the number symbol represents any single digit. Using a pattern match is similar to using an exact match, except that a pattern match includes wildcard characters.

To create the query, you must first place the tblCustomer table field list in the Query window in Design view.

To create the new query in Design view:

1. Close the **tblContract** table, and then click the **Shutter Bar Open/Close Button** « at the top of the Navigation Pane to close it.

2. Click the **Create** tab on the Ribbon and then, in the Other group on the Create tab, click the **Query Design** button. Access opens the Show Table dialog box on top of the Query window in Design view.

3. Click **tblCustomer** in the Tables list box, click the **Add** button, and then click the **Close** button. Access places the tblCustomer table field list in the Query window and closes the Show Table dialog box.

4. Double-click the **title bar** of the tblCustomer field list to highlight all the fields, and then drag the highlighted fields to the first column's Field text box in the design grid. Access places each field in a separate column in the design grid, in the same order that the fields appear in the table. See Figure 5-3.

Tip

You can also double-click a table name to add the table's field list to the Query window.

Figure 5-3 | **Adding the fields for the pattern match query**

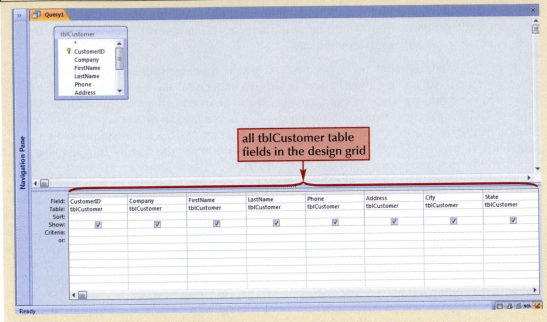

Trouble? If tblCustomer.* appears in the first column's Field text box, you dragged the * from the field list instead of the highlighted fields. Press the Delete key, and then repeat Step 4.

Now you will enter the pattern match condition Like "616*" for the Phone field. Access will select records with a Phone field value of 616 in positions one through three. The asterisk wildcard character specifies that any characters can appear in the remaining positions of the field value.

To specify records that match the specified pattern:

▶ **1.** Click the **Phone Criteria** text box, and then type **Like "616*"**. See Figure 5-4.

Figure 5-4 | **Record selection based on matching a specific pattern**

Tip

If you omit the Like operator, Access automatically adds it when you run the query.

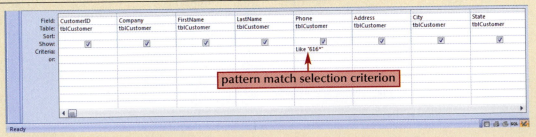

Now you can save the query.

▶ **2.** Click the **Save** button 🔲 on the Quick Access Toolbar to open the Save As dialog box.

▶ **3.** Type **qry616AreaCode** in the Query Name text box, and then press the **Enter** key. Access saves the query with the specified name and displays the name on the query tab.

▶ **4.** In the Results group on the Query Tools Design tab, click the **Run** button. The query results display the 24 records with the area code 616 in the Phone field. See Figure 5-5.

tblCustomer table records for area code 616 | Figure 5-5

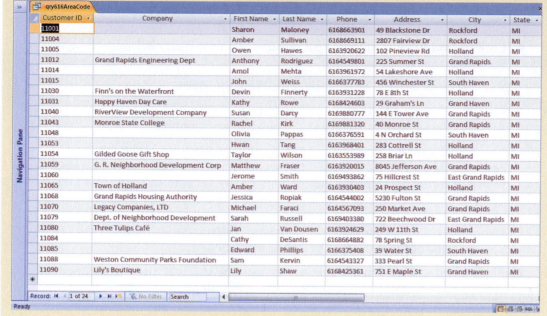

Customer ID	Company	First Name	Last Name	Phone	Address	City	State
11001		Sharon	Maloney	6168663901	49 Blackstone Dr	Rockford	MI
11004		Amber	Sullivan	6168669111	2807 Fairview Dr	Rockford	MI
11005		Owen	Hawes	6163920622	102 Pineview Rd	Holland	MI
11012	Grand Rapids Engineering Dept	Anthony	Rodriguez	6164549801	225 Summer St	Grand Rapids	MI
11014		Amol	Mehta	6163961972	54 Lakeshore Ave	Holland	MI
11015		John	Weiss	6166377783	456 Winchester St	South Haven	MI
11030	Finn's on the Waterfront	Devin	Finnerty	6163931228	78 E 8th St	Holland	MI
11031	Happy Haven Day Care	Kathy	Rowe	6168424603	29 Graham's Ln	Grand Haven	MI
11040	RiverView Development Company	Susan	Darcy	6169880777	144 E Tower Ave	Grand Rapids	MI
11043	Monroe State College	Rachel	Kirk	6169881320	40 Monroe St	Grand Rapids	MI
11048		Olivia	Pappas	6166376591	4 N Orchard St	South Haven	MI
11053		Hwan	Tang	6163968401	283 Cottrell St	Holland	MI
11054	Gilded Goose Gift Shop	Taylor	Wilson	6163553989	258 Briar Ln	Holland	MI
11059	G. R. Neighborhood Development Corp	Matthew	Fraser	6163920015	8045 Jefferson Ave	Grand Rapids	MI
11060		Jerome	Smith	6169493862	75 Hillcrest St	East Grand Rapids	MI
11065	Town of Holland	Amber	Ward	6163930403	24 Prospect St	Holland	MI
11068	Grand Rapids Housing Authority	Jessica	Ropiak	6164544002	5230 Fulton St	Grand Rapids	MI
11070	Legacy Companies, LTD	Michael	Faraci	6164567093	250 Market Ave	Grand Rapids	MI
11079	Dept. of Neighborhood Development	Sarah	Russell	6169403380	722 Beechwood Dr	East Grand Rapids	MI
11080	Three Tulips Café	Jan	Van Dousen	6163924629	249 W 11th St	Holland	MI
11084		Cathy	DeSantis	6168664882	78 Spring St	Rockford	MI
11085		Edward	Phillips	6166375408	39 Water St	South Haven	MI
11088	Weston Community Parks Foundation	Sam	Kervin	6164543327	333 Pearl St	Grand Rapids	MI
11090	Lily's Boutique	Lily	Shaw	6168425361	751 E Maple St	Grand Haven	MI

Record: 1 of 24   No Filter   Search

Ready

Note that Lucia removed the hyphens from the Phone field values; for example, 6168663901 in the first record used to be 616-866-3901. You'll modify the Phone field later in this tutorial to format its values with hyphens.

5. Close the qry616AreaCode query.

Next, Sarah asks you to create a query that displays information about customers in Holland, Rockford, or Saugatuck. She wants a printout of the customer data for her administrative aide, who will contact these customers. To produce the results Sarah wants, you'll create a query using a list-of-values match.

Using a List-of-Values Match in a Query

A **list-of-values match** selects records whose value for the designated field matches one of two or more simple condition values. You could accomplish this by including several Or conditions in the design grid, but the In comparison operator provides an easier and clearer way to do this. The **In comparison operator** lets you define a condition with a list of two or more values for a field. If a record's field value matches one value from the list of defined values, then Access selects and includes that record in the query results.

To display the information Sarah requested, you want to select records if their City field value equals Holland, Rockford, or Saugatuck. These are the values you will use with the In comparison operator. Sarah wants the query to contain the same data as the qry616AreaCode query, so you'll make a copy of that query and modify it.

To create the query using a list-of-values match:

1. Open the Navigation Pane, then in the Queries group on the Navigation Page, right-click **qry616AreaCode**, and then click **Copy** on the shortcut menu.

2. In the Clipboard group on the Home tab, click the **Paste** button, type **qryHollandRockfordSaugatuckCustomers** in the Query Name text box, and then press the **Enter** key.

To modify the copied query, you need to open it in Design view.

3. In the Queries group on the Navigation Pane, right-click **qryHollandRockfordSaugatuckCustomers** to select it and display the shortcut menu.

4. Click **Design View** on the shortcut menu to open the query in Design view, and then close the Navigation Pane.

You need to delete the existing condition from the Phone field.

5. Click the **Phone Criteria** text box, press the **F2** key to highlight the entire condition, and then press the **Delete** key to remove the condition.

Now you can enter the criteria for the new query using the In comparison operator. When you use this operator, you must enclose the list of values you want to match within parentheses and separate the values with commas. In addition, for fields defined using the Text data type, you enclose each value in quotation marks, although Access adds the quotation marks if you omit them. When using the In comparison operator for fields defined using the Number or Currency data type, you don't enclose the values in quotation marks.

6. Right-click the **City Criteria** text box to open the shortcut menu, click **Zoom** to open the Zoom dialog box, and then type **In ("Holland","Rockford", "Saugatuck")**. See Figure 5-6.

Figure 5-6 ▶ **Record selection based on matching field values to a list of values**

Tip

After clicking in a text box, you can also open the Zoom dialog box for that text box by holding down the Shift key and pressing the F2 key.

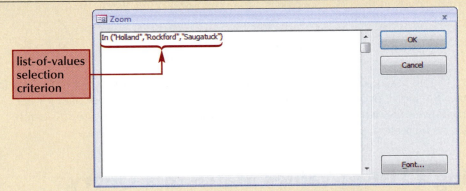

7. Click the **OK** button to close the Zoom dialog box, and then save and run the query. Access displays the recordset, which shows the 13 records with Holland, Rockford, or Saugatuck in the City field.

8. Close the query.

Sarah asks her assistant to contact Belmont Landscapes customers who are not in Holland, Rockford, and Saugatuck. You can provide Sarah with this information by creating a query with the Not logical operator.

Using the Not Operator in a Query

The **Not logical operator** negates a criterion or selects records for which the designated field does not match the criterion. For example, if you enter Not "Holland" in the Criteria text box for the City field, the query results show records that do not have the City field value Holland, that is, records of all customers not located in Holland.

To create Sarah's query, you will combine the Not logical operator with the In comparison operator to select customers whose City field value is not in the list ("Holland", "Rockford","Saugatuck"). The qryHollandRockfordSaugatuckCustomers query has the fields that Sarah needs to see in the query results. Sarah doesn't need to keep the qryHollandRockfordSaugatuckCustomers query, so you'll rename and then modify the query.

To create the query using the Not logical operator:

▶ 1. Open the Navigation Pane, then in the Queries group on the Navigation Page, right-click **qryHollandRockfordSaugatuckCustomers**, and then click **Rename** on the shortcut menu.

▶ 2. Position the insertion point after "qry," type **Non**, and then press the **Enter** key. The query name is now qryNonHollandRockfordSaugatuckCustomers.

▶ 3. Open the **qryNonHollandRockfordSaugatuckCustomers** query in Design view, and then close the Navigation Pane.

   You need to change the existing condition in the City field to add the Not logical operator.

▶ 4. Click the **City Criteria** text box, open the Zoom dialog box, click at the beginning of the expression, type **Not**, and then press the **spacebar**. See Figure 5-7.

> **Tip**
>
> You can rename any object type, including tables, in the Navigation Pane using the Rename command on the shortcut menu.

Record selection based on not matching a list of values ◀ Figure 5-7

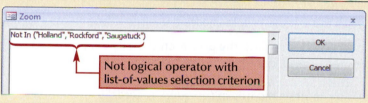

▶ 5. Click the **OK** button, and then save and run the query. The recordset displays only those records with a City field value that is not Holland, Rockford, or Saugatuck. The recordset includes a total of 29 customer records.

▶ 6. Scroll down the datasheet to make sure that no Holland or Rockford or Saugatuck customers appear in your results.

   Now you can close and delete the query, because Sarah does not need to run this query again.

▶ 7. Close the query, and then open the Navigation Pane.

▶ 8. Right-click **qryNonHollandRockfordSaugatuckCustomers**, click **Delete** on the shortcut menu, and then click the **Yes** button when asked to confirm the query deletion. The query is permanently deleted from the database.

> **Tip**
>
> You can delete any object type, including tables, in the Navigation Pane using the Delete command on the shortcut menu.

You now are ready to answer Taylor's question about Grand Rapids or East Grand Rapids customers that signed contracts for less than $10,000 or that signed contracts during the winter.

Using an AutoFilter to Filter Data

Taylor wants to view the customer last and first names, company names, cities, contract amounts, signing dates, and contract types for customers in Grand Rapids or East Grand Rapids that have signed contracts for less than $10,000 or that signed contracts during the winter. The qrySmallContractsOrWinterSignings query contains the same fields Taylor wants to view. This query also uses the Or logical operator to select records if the ContractAmt field value is less than $10,000 or if the SigningDate field value is between 1/1/2011 and 3/1/2011. These are two of the conditions needed to answer Taylor's question. You could modify the qrySmallContractsOrWinterSignings query in Design view to further restrict the records selected to customers located only in Grand Rapids and East Grand Rapids. However, you can use the AutoFilter feature to choose the city restrictions faster and more flexibly. You previously used the AutoFilter feature to sort records, and you previously used Filter By Form and Filter By Selection to filter records. Now you'll show Taylor how to use the AutoFilter feature to filter records.

To filter the records using an AutoFilter:

1. Open the **qrySmallContractsOrWinterSignings** query in Design view, and then close the Navigation Pane.

   The *<10000* condition for the ContractAmt field selects records whose contract amounts are less than $10,000, and the *Between #1/1/2011# And #3/1/2011#* condition for the SigningDate field selects records whose contracts were signed during the first two months of 2011. Because the conditions are in two different rows, the query uses the Or logical operator. If you wanted to answer Taylor's question in Design view, you would add a condition for the City field, using either the Or logical operator—*"Grand Rapids" Or "East Grand Rapids"*—or the In comparison operator—*In ("Grand Rapids","East Grand Rapids")*. You'd place this condition for the City field in both the Criteria row and in the or row. The query recordset would include a record only if both conditions in either row are satisfied.

   Instead, you'll show Taylor how to choose the information she wants using an AutoFilter.

2. Run the query, and then click the **arrow** on the City column heading to display the AutoFilter menu. See Figure 5-8.

| Figure 5-8 | Using an AutoFilter to filter records in the query recordset |

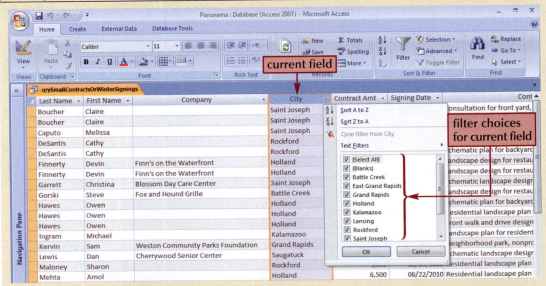

The AutoFilter menu lists all City field values that appear in the recordset. A check mark next to an entry indicates that records with that City field value appear in the recordset. To filter for selected City field values, you uncheck the cities you don't want selected and leave checked the cities you do want selected. You can click the "(Select All)" check box to select or deselect all field values. The "(Blanks)" entry includes null values when checked and excludes null values when unchecked. (Recall that a null field value is the absence of a value for the field.)

3. Click the **(Select All)** check box to deselect all check boxes, click the **East Grand Rapids** check box, and then click the **Grand Rapids** check box.

   The two check boxes indicate that the AutoFilter will include only East Grand Rapids and Grand Rapids City field values.

4. Click the **OK** button. Access displays the four records for customers in East Grand Rapids and Grand Rapids with small contract amounts or with winter signing dates. See Figure 5-9.

Using an AutoFilter to filter records in the query recordset ◄ Figure 5-9

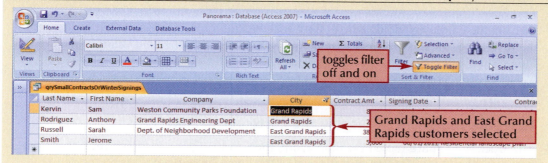

You click the Toggle Filter button in the Sort & Filter group on the Home tab to remove the current filter and display all records in the query. If you click the Toggle Filter button a second time, you reapply the filter.

5. In the Sort & Filter group on the Home tab, click the **Toggle Filter** button. Access removes the filter, and all 31 records appear in the recordset.

6. Click the **Toggle Filter** button. Access applies the City filter, displaying the four records for customers in East Grand Rapids and Grand Rapids.

   Taylor knows how to use the AutoFilter feature and has the information she needs. You can close the query without saving your query design changes.

7. Close the query without saving the query design changes.

Sarah wants to view all fields from the tblCustomer table, along with the customer name. The customer name is either the company name for nonresidential customers or the last and first names for residential customers.

Assigning a Conditional Value to a Calculated Field

Records for residential customers have nonnull FirstName and LastName field values and null Company field values in the tblCustomer table, while records for all other customers have nonnull values for all three fields. Sarah wants to view records from the tblCustomer table in order by the Company field value, if it's nonnull, and at the same time in order by the LastName and then FirstName field values, if the Company field value is null. To produce the information for Sarah, you need to create a query that includes all fields from the tblCustomer table and then add a calculated field that will display the customer name—either the Company field value or the LastName and FirstName field values, separated by a comma and a space.

To combine the LastName and FirstName fields, you'll use the expression *LastName & ", " & FirstName*. The **& (ampersand) operator** is a concatenation operator that joins text expressions. If the LastName field value is Maloney and the FirstName field value is Sharon, for example, the result of the expression is *Maloney, Sharon*.

To display the correct customer value, you'll use the IIf function. The **IIf (Immediate If) function** assigns one value to a calculated field or control if a condition is true, and a second value if the condition is false. The IIf function has three parts: a condition that is true or false, the result when the condition is true, and the result when the condition is false. Each part of the IIf function is separated by a comma. The condition you'll use is *IsNull(Company)*. The **IsNull function** tests a field value or an expression for a null value; if the field value or expression is null, the result is true; otherwise, the result is false. The expression *IsNull(Company)* is true when the Company field value is null, and is false when the Company field value is not null.

For the calculated field, you'll enter *IIf(IsNull(Company),LastName & ", " & FirstName,Company)*. You interpret this expression as: If the Company field value is null, then set the calculated field value to the concatenation of the LastName field value and the text string ", " and the FirstName field value. If the Company field value is not null, then set the calculated field value to the Company field value.

Now you are ready to create Sarah's query to display the customer name.

To create the query to display the customer name:

▶ 1. Click the **Create** tab on the Ribbon and then, in the Other group on the Create tab, click the **Query Design** button to open the Show Table dialog box on top of the Query window in Design view.

▶ 2. Click **tblCustomer** in the Tables list box, click the **Add** button, and then click the **Close** button to place the tblCustomer table field list in the Query window and close the Show Table dialog box.

Sarah wants all fields from the tblCustomer table to appear in the query recordset and the new calculated field to appear in the first column.

▶ 3. Double-click the **title bar** of the tblCustomer field list to highlight all the fields, and then drag the highlighted fields to the second column's Field text box in the design grid. Access places each field in a separate column in the design grid starting with the second column in the design grid, in the same order that the fields appear in the table.

Trouble? If you accidentally drag the highlighted fields to the first column in the design grid, click the CustomerID Field text box, and then click the Insert Columns button in the Query Setup group on the Query Tools Design tab. Continue with Step 4.

▶ 4. Right-click the blank Field text box to the left of the CustomerID field, and then click **Build** on the shortcut menu to open the Expression Builder dialog box.

Sarah wants to use "Customer" as the name of the calculated field, so you'll type that name, followed by a colon, and then you'll choose the IIf function.

▶ 5. Type **Customer:** and then press the **spacebar**. Be sure you type the colon following Customer.

▶ 6. Double-click **Functions** in the left column, click **Built-In Functions** in the left column, scroll down the middle column and click **Program Flow**, click **IIf** in the right column, and then click the **Paste** button. Access adds the IIf function with four placeholders to the right of the calculated field name in the expression box. See Figure 5-10.

Tip

After clicking in a text box, you can also open the Expression Builder dialog box for that text box by holding down the Ctrl key and pressing the F2 key.

Pasted IIf function for the calculated field ◄ **Figure 5-10**

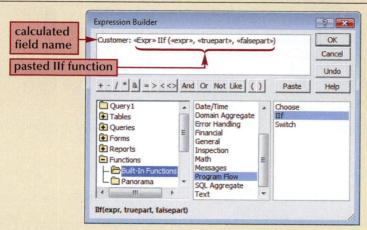

The expression you will create does not need the leftmost placeholder, <<Expr>>, so you'll delete it. You'll replace the second placeholder (<<expr>>) with the condition using the IsNull function, the third placeholder (<<truepart>>) with the expression using the & operator, and the fourth placeholder (<<falsepart>>) with the Company field name.

▶ 7. Click **<<Expr>>** in the expression box, and then press the **Delete** key to delete the first placeholder.

▶ 8. Click **<<expr>>** in the expression box, click **Inspection** in the middle column, click **IsNull** in the right column, click the **Paste** button, click **<<varexpr>>** in the expression box, and then type **Company**. You've completed the entry of the condition in the IIf function. See Figure 5-11.

After entering the condition for the calculated field's IIf function ◄ **Figure 5-11**

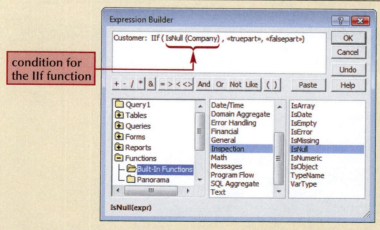

Instead of typing the field name of Company in the previous step, you could have double-clicked Tables in the left column, clicked tblCustomer, and then pasted Company.

Now you'll replace the fourth placeholder and then the third placeholder.

▶ 9. Click **<<falsepart>>** and then type **Company**.

▶ 10. Click **<<truepart>>**, and then type **LastName & ", " & FirstName** to finish creating the calculated field. Be sure you type a space after the comma within the quotation marks. See Figure 5-12.

Figure 5-12 The completed calculated field

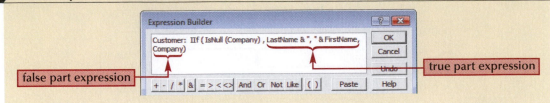

Sarah wants the query sorted in ascending order by the Customer calculated field.

To sort, save, and run the query:

▶ 1. Click the **OK** button in the Expression Builder dialog box to close it.

▶ 2. Click the right side of the **Customer Sort** text box to display the sort order options, and then click **Ascending**. The query will display the records in alphabetical order based on the Customer field values.

The calculated field name of Customer consists of a single word, so you do not need to set the Caption property for it. However, you'll review the properties for the calculated field by opening the property sheet for it.

▶ 3. In the Show/Hide group on the Query Tools Design tab, click the **Property Sheet** button. The property sheet opens and displays the properties for the Customer calculated field. See Figure 5-13.

Figure 5-13 Property sheet for the Customer calculated field

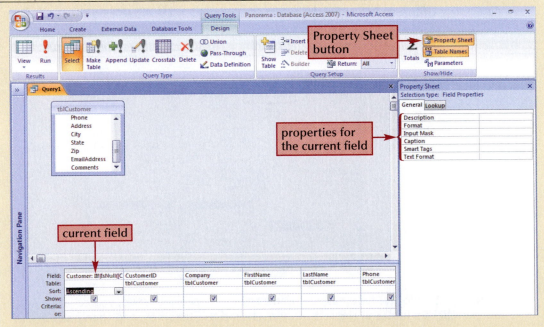

Among the properties for the calculated field, which is the current field, is the Caption property. Leaving the Caption property set to null means that the column name for the calculated field in the query recordset will be Customer, which is the calculated field name. The Property Sheet button is a toggle, so you'll click it again to close the property sheet.

▶ 4. Click the **Property Sheet** button to close the property sheet.

5. Save the query as **qryCustomersByName**, run the query, and then resize the Customer column to its best fit. Access displays all records from the tblCustomer table in alphabetical order by the Customer field. See Figure 5-14.

Completed query displaying the Customer calculated field **Figure 5-14**

the customer name is the same as the nonnull Company values

the customer name is the concatenation of the LastName, FirstName for null Company values

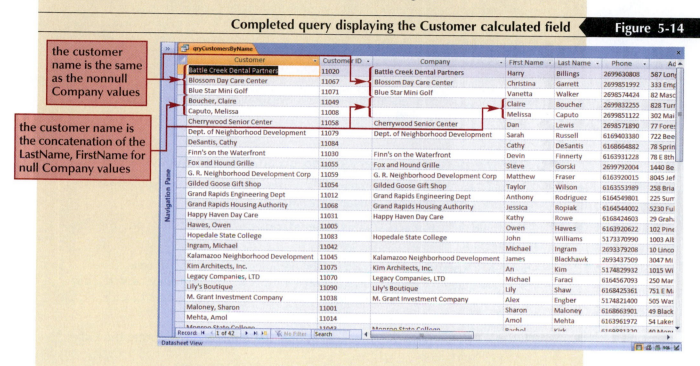

6. Save and close the query.

You are now ready to create the query to satisfy Sarah's request for information about customers in a particular city.

Creating a Parameter Query

Sarah's next request is for records in the qryCustomersByName query for customers in a particular city. For this query, she wants to specify the city, such as Battle Creek or Holland, when she executes the query.

To create this query, you will copy, rename, and modify the qryCustomersByName query. You could create a simple condition using an exact match for the City field, but you would need to change it in Design view every time you run the query. Alternatively, Sarah or a member of her staff could filter the qryCustomersByName query for the city records they want to view. Instead, you will create a parameter query. A **parameter query** displays a dialog box that prompts the user to enter one or more criteria values when the query is run. In this case, you want to create a query that prompts for the city and selects only those customer records with that City field value from the table. You will enter the prompt in the Criteria text box for the City field. When Access runs the query, it will open a dialog box and prompt you to enter the city. Access then creates the query results, just as if you had changed the criteria in Design view.

Reference Window | **Creating a Parameter Query**

- Create a select query that includes all fields to appear in the query results. Also choose the sort fields and set the criteria that do not change when you run the query.
- Decide which fields to use as prompts when the query runs. In the Criteria text box for each of these fields, type the prompt you want to appear in a message box when you run the query, and enclose the prompt in brackets.

Now you can copy and rename the qryCustomersByName query, and then change its design to create the parameter query.

To create the parameter query based on an existing query:

1. Open the Navigation Pane, copy and then paste the qryCustomersByName query, renaming it **qryCustomersByNameParameter**.

2. Open the **qryCustomersByNameParameter** query in Design view, and then close the Navigation Pane.

   Next, you must enter the criteria for the parameter query. In this case, Sarah wants the query to prompt users to enter the city for the customer records they want to view. So, you need to enter the prompt in the Criteria text box for the City field. Brackets must enclose the text of the prompt.

3. Click the **City Criteria** text box, type **[Enter the city:]** and then press the **Enter** key. See Figure 5-15.

Figure 5-15 | Specifying the prompt for the parameter query

prompt text enclosed in brackets

4. Save and run the query. Access displays a dialog box prompting you for the name of the city. See Figure 5-16.

Figure 5-16 | Enter Parameter Value dialog box

The bracketed text you specified in the Criteria text box of the City field appears above a text box, in which you must type a City field value. Sarah wants to see all customers in Holland.

5. Type **Holland**, press the **Enter** key, and then scroll to the right, if necessary, to display the City field values. The recordset displays the data for the seven customers in Holland. See Figure 5-17.

Results of the parameter query ◄ **Figure 5-17**

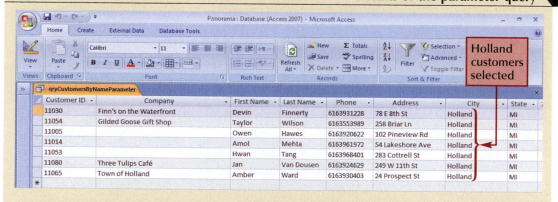

Sarah asks what happens if she doesn't enter a value in the dialog box when she runs the qryCustomersByNameParameter query. You can run the query again to show Sarah the answer to her question.

6. Switch to Design view, and then run the query. The Enter Parameter Value dialog box opens.

If you click the OK button or press the Enter key, you'll run the parameter query without entering a value for the City field criterion.

7. Click the **OK** button. Access displays no records in the query results.

When you run the parameter query and enter Holland in the dialog box, Access runs the query the same way as if you had entered *"Holland"* in the City Criteria text box in the design grid by displaying all Holland customer records. When you do not enter a value in the dialog box, Access runs the query the same way as if you had entered *null* in the City Criteria text box. Because none of the records has a null City field value, Access displays no records. Sarah asks if there's a way to display records for a selected City field value when she enters its value in the dialog box and to display all records when she doesn't enter a value.

| InSight | | **Creating a More Flexible Parameter Query** |

Most users want parameter queries to display the records that match their entered parameter value or to display all records when they don't enter a parameter value. To provide this functionality, you can change the Criteria text box in the design grid for the specified column. For example, you could change an entry for a City field from *[Enter the city:]* to *Like [Enter the city:] & "*"*. That is, you can prefix the Like operator to the original criterion and concatenate the criterion to a wildcard character. When you run the parameter query with this new entry, Access will display one of the following recordsets:

- If you enter a specific City field value in the dialog box, such as Saugatuck, the entry is the same as *Like "Saugatuck" & "*"*, which becomes *Like "Saugatuck*"* after the concatenation operation. That is, Access selects all records whose City field values have Saugatuck in the first nine positions and any characters in the remaining positions. If the table on which the query is based contains records with City field values of Saugatuck, Access displays only those records. However, if the table on which the query is based also contains records with City field values of Saugatuck City, then Access would display both the Saugatuck and the Saugatuck City records.
- If you enter a letter in the dialog box, such as S, the entry is the same as *Like "S*"*, and the recordset displays all records with City field values that begin with the letter S.
- If you enter no value in the dialog box, the entry is the same as *Like Null & "*"*, which becomes *Like "*"* after the concatenation operation, and the recordset displays all records.

Now you'll modify the parameter query to satisfy Sarah's request and test the new version of the query.

To modify and test the parameter query:

1. Switch to Design view.

2. Click the **City Criteria** text box, and then open the Zoom dialog box.

    You'll use the Zoom dialog box to modify the value in the City Criteria text box.

3. Click to the left of the expression in the Zoom dialog box, type **Like**, press the **spacebar**, press the **End** key, press the **spacebar**, and then type **& "*"**. See Figure 5-18.

| Figure 5-18 | Modified City Criteria value in the Zoom dialog box |

Now you can test the modified parameter query.

4. Click the **OK** button to close the Zoom dialog box, save your query design changes, and then run the query.

    First, you'll test the query to display customers in Saugatuck.

5. Type **Saugatuck**, and then press the **Enter** key. The recordset displays the data for the three customers in Saugatuck.

    Now you'll test the query without entering a value when prompted.

6. Switch to Design view, run the query, and then click the **OK** button. The recordset displays all 42 original records from the tblCustomer table.

Finally, you'll test the query and enter S in the dialog box.

▶ 7. Switch to Design view, run the query, type **S**, and then press the **Enter** key. The recordset displays the 10 records for customers in Saint Joseph, Saugatuck, and South Haven.

▶ 8. Close the query.

▶ 9. If you are not continuing on to the next session, close the Panorama database, and then exit Access, clicking the **Yes** button if you are prompted to confirm that you want to exit Access and to empty the Clipboard.

The queries you created will make the Panorama database easier to use. In the next session, you will create a top values query and use query wizards to create three additional queries.

Session 5.1 Quick Check | Review

1. You use the _____ property to specify how a field name appears in datasheet column headings and in form and report labels.
2. Which comparison operator selects records based on a specific pattern?
3. What is the purpose of the asterisk (*) in a pattern match query?
4. When do you use the In comparison operator?
5. How do you negate a selection criterion?
6. The _____ function returns one of two values based on whether the condition being tested is true or false.
7. When do you use a parameter query?

Session 5.2

Creating a Crosstab Query

Oren wants to analyze his company's invoices by city, so he can view the paid and unpaid contract amounts for all customers located in each city. He asks you to create a crosstab query using the Crosstab Query Wizard to provide the information he needs.

A **crosstab query** performs aggregate function calculations on the values of one database field and displays the results in a spreadsheet format. Recall that an aggregate function performs an arithmetic operation on selected records in a database. Figure 5-19 lists the aggregate functions you can use in a crosstab query. A crosstab query can also display one additional aggregate function value that summarizes the set of values in each row. The crosstab query uses one or more fields for the row headings on the left and one field for the column headings at the top.

Figure 5-19 ▶ **Aggregate functions used in crosstab queries**

Aggregate Function	Definition
Avg	Average of the field values
Count	Number of the nonnull field values
First	First field value
Last	Last field value
Max	Highest field value
Min	Lowest field value
StDev	Standard deviation of the field values
Sum	Total of the field values
Var	Variance of the field values

Figure 5-20 shows two query recordsets—the top recordset (qryCustomersAndInvoices) is from a select query and the bottom recordset (qryCitiesAndInvoicesCrosstab) is from a crosstab query based on the select query.

Figure 5-20 ▶ **Comparing a select query to a crosstab query**

qryCustomersAndInvoices						
Customer ID	Company	First Name	Last Name	City	Invoice Amt	Invoice Paid
11001		Sharon	Maloney	Rockford	$1,500.00	✓
11001		Sharon	Maloney	Rockford	$2,500.00	✓
11027		Karen	O'Brien	Lansing	$300.00	✓
11005		Owen	Hawes	Holland	$1,500.00	✓
11012	Grand Rapids Engineerin	Anthony	Rodriguez	Grand Rapids	$2,250.00	✓
11055	Fox and Hound Grille	Steve	Gorski	Battle Creek	$1,500.00	✓
11055	Fox and Hound Grille	Steve	Gorski	Battle Creek	$2,000.00	✓
11055	Fox and Hound Grille	Steve	Gorski	Battle Creek	$2,000.00	✓
11055	Fox and Hound Grille	Steve	Gorski	Battle Creek	$1,000.00	✓
11040	RiverView Development Company	Susan	Darcy	Grand Rapids	$4,500.00	✓
11040	RiverView Development Company	Susan	Darcy	Grand Rapids	$3,000.00	✓
11040	RiverView Development Company	Susan	Darcy	Grand Rapids	$12,000.00	☐
11040	RiverView Development Company	Susan	Darcy	Grand Rapids	$8,500.00	☐
11043	Monroe State College	Rachel	Kirk	Grand Rapids	$4,500.00	✓
11043	Monroe State College	Rachel	Kirk	Grand Rapids	$12,000.00	✓
11043	Monroe State College	Rachel	Kirk	Grand Rapids	$5,500.00	✓
11070	Legacy Companies, LTD	Michael	Faraci	Grand Rapids	$9,000.00	✓
11070	Legacy Companies, LTD	Michael	Faraci	Grand Rapids	$20,000.00	✓
11070	Legacy Companies, LTD	Michael	Faraci	Grand Rapids	$10,000.00	☐
11083	Hopedale State College	John	Williams	East Lansing	$4,000.00	✓
11083	Hopedale State College	John	Williams	East Lansing	$8,000.00	✓
11083	Hopedale State College	John	Williams	East Lansing	$3,500.00	✓
11038	M. Grant Investment Company	Alex	Engber	Lansing	$35,000.00	✓
11038	M. Grant Investment Company	Alex	Engber	Lansing	$10,000.00	☐
11038	M. Grant Investment Company	Alex	Engber	Lansing	$70,000.00	☐

individual Lansing records

Lansing records with paid invoices

Lansing records with unpaid invoices

Comparing a select query to a crosstab query (continued) ◄ Figure 5-20

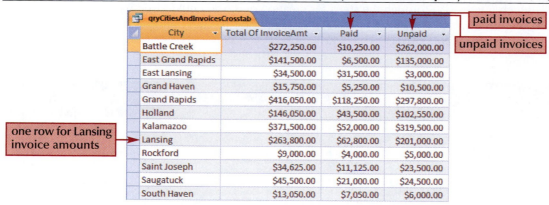

paid invoices

unpaid invoices

one row for Lansing invoice amounts

City	Total Of InvoiceAmt	Paid	Unpaid
Battle Creek	$272,250.00	$10,250.00	$262,000.00
East Grand Rapids	$141,500.00	$6,500.00	$135,000.00
East Lansing	$34,500.00	$31,500.00	$3,000.00
Grand Haven	$15,750.00	$5,250.00	$10,500.00
Grand Rapids	$416,050.00	$118,250.00	$297,800.00
Holland	$146,050.00	$43,500.00	$102,550.00
Kalamazoo	$371,500.00	$52,000.00	$319,500.00
Lansing	$263,800.00	$62,800.00	$201,000.00
Rockford	$9,000.00	$4,000.00	$5,000.00
Saint Joseph	$34,625.00	$11,125.00	$23,500.00
Saugatuck	$45,500.00	$21,000.00	$24,500.00
South Haven	$13,050.00	$7,050.00	$6,000.00

The qryCustomersAndInvoices query, a select query, joins the tblCustomer, tblContract, and tblInvoice tables to display selected data from those tables for all invoices. The qryCitiesAndInvoicesCrosstab query, a crosstab query, uses the qryCustomersAndInvoices query as its source query and displays one row for each unique City field value. The City column in the crosstab query identifies each row. The crosstab query uses the Sum aggregate function on the InvoiceAmt field to produce the displayed values in the Paid and Unpaid columns for each City row. An entry in the Total Of InvoiceAmt column represents the total of the Paid and Unpaid values for the City field value in that row.

Select Queries versus Crosstab Queries | InSight

A select query displays several records—one for each row selected by the select query—while a crosstab query displays only one summarized record for each unique field value. If you want to analyze the records in a query to see the big picture, you would start with a crosstab query, identify which field values to analyze further, and then look in detail at the select query for specific field values. Both select and crosstab queries serve as valuable tools in tracking and analyzing a company's business, and you should use each type of query in the appropriate situation.

When you create a query in Design view or with a wizard, Access automatically constructs an equivalent SQL statement and saves only the SQL statement version of the query. **SQL (Structured Query Language)** is a standard language used in querying, updating, and managing relational databases. If you learn SQL for one relational DBMS, it's a relatively easy task to begin using SQL for other relational DBMSs. However, differences exist between DBMSs in their versions of SQL, somewhat like having different dialects in English, and in what additions they make to SQL. The SQL statement equivalent that Access creates for a crosstab query is one such SQL-language addition. If you need to convert an Access database to SQL-Server, Oracle, or another DBMS, you should know that your crosstab queries most likely will not work in these other databases.

Tip

Microsoft Office Access Help provides more information on creating a crosstab query without using a wizard.

The quickest way to create a crosstab query is to use the **Crosstab Query Wizard**, which guides you through the steps for creating one. You could also change a select query to a crosstab query in Design view using the Crosstab button in the Query Type group on the Query Tools Design tab.

Reference Window | **Using the Crosstab Query Wizard**

- In the Other group on the Create tab, click the Query Wizard button.
- In the New Query dialog box, click Crosstab Query Wizard, and then click the OK button.
- Complete the Wizard dialog boxes to select the table or query on which to base the crosstab query, select the row heading field (or fields), select the column heading field, select the calculation field and its aggregate function, and enter a name for the crosstab query.

The crosstab query you will create, which is similar to the one shown in Figure 5-20, has the following characteristics:

- The qryCustomersAndInvoices query in the Panorama database is the basis for the new crosstab query. The base query includes the CustomerID, Company, FirstName, LastName, City, InvoiceAmt, and InvoicePaid fields.
- The City field is the leftmost column in the crosstab query and identifies each crosstab query row.
- The values from the InvoicePaid field, which is a Yes/No field, identify the rightmost columns of the crosstab query.
- The crosstab query applies the Sum aggregate function to the InvoiceAmt field values and displays the resulting total values in the Paid and Unpaid columns of the query results.
- The grand total of the InvoiceAmt field values appears for each row in a column with the heading Total Of InvoiceAmt.

You are now ready to create the crosstab query for Oren.

To start the Crosstab Query Wizard:

1. If you took a break after the previous session, make sure that the Panorama database is open and the Navigation Pane is closed.

   Trouble? If the Security Warning is displayed below the Ribbon, click the Options button next to the Security Warning. In the dialog box that opens, click the "Enable this content" option button, and then click the OK button.

2. Click the **Create** tab on the Ribbon and then, in the Other group on the Create tab, click the **Query Wizard** button. The New Query dialog box opens.

3. Click **Crosstab Query Wizard**, and then click the **OK** button. The first Crosstab Query Wizard dialog box opens.

You'll now use the Crosstab Query Wizard to create the crosstab query for Oren.

To finish the Crosstab Query Wizard:

1. Click the **Queries** option button in the View section to display the list of queries in the Panorama database, and then click **Query: qryCustomersAndInvoices**. See Figure 5-21.

Choosing the query for the crosstab query | **Figure 5-21**

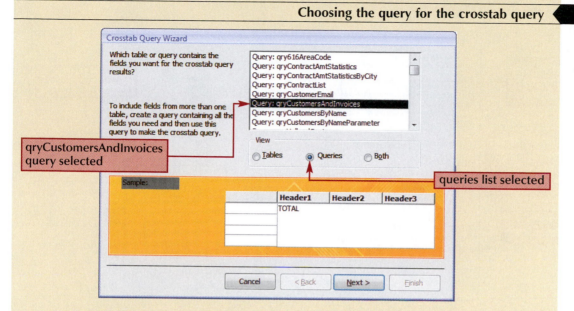

> 2. Click the **Next** button to open the next Crosstab Query Wizard dialog box, in which you choose the field (or fields) for the row headings. Because Oren wants the crosstab query to display one row for each unique City field value, you will select that field for the row headings.

> 3. In the Available Fields list box, click **City**, and then click the ⟩ button to move the City field to the Selected Fields list box.

> 4. Click the **Next** button to open the next Crosstab Query Wizard dialog box, in which you select the field values that will serve as column headings. Oren wants to see the paid and unpaid total invoice amounts, so you need to select the InvoicePaid field for the column headings.

> 5. Click **InvoicePaid** in the list box, and then click the **Next** button.

> In the Crosstab Query Wizard dialog box that appears next, you choose the field that will be calculated for each row and column intersection and the function to use for the calculation. The results of the calculation will appear in the row and column intersections in the query results. Oren needs to calculate the sum of the InvoiceAmt field value for each row and column intersection.

> 6. Click **InvoiceAmt** in the Fields list box, click **Sum** in the Functions list box, and then make sure that the **Yes, include row sums** check box is checked. The "Yes, include row sums" option creates a column showing the overall totals for the values in each row of the query recordset. See Figure 5-22.

Tip

When you select a field, Access changes the sample crosstab query in the dialog box to illustrate your choice.

Figure 5-22 | **Completed crosstab query design**

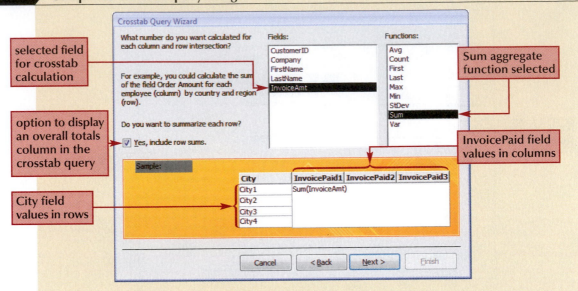

> **7.** Click the **Next** button to open the final Crosstab Query Wizard dialog box, in which you choose the query name.

> **8.** Click in the text box, delete the underscore character so that the query name is qryCustomersAndInvoicesCrosstab, be sure the option button for viewing the query is selected, and then click the **Finish** button. Access saves the crosstab query, and then displays the query recordset.

> **9.** Resize all the columns in the query recordset to their best fit, and then click the City field value in the first row (**Battle Creek**). See Figure 5-23.

Figure 5-23 | **Crosstab query recordset**

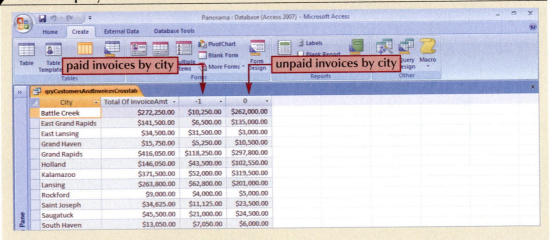

The query recordset contains one row for each City field value. The Total Of InvoiceAmt column shows the total invoice amount for the customers in each city. The columns labeled -1 and 0 show the total paid (-1 column) and unpaid (0 column) invoice amounts for customers in each city. Because the InvoicePaid field is a Yes/No field, by default, Access displays field values in datasheets, forms, and reports in a check box (either checked or unchecked), but stores a checked value in the database as a -1 and an unchecked value as a zero. Instead of displaying check boxes, the crosstab query displays the stored values as column headings.

Oren wants you to change the column headings of -1 to Paid and of zero to Unpaid. You'll use the IIf function to change the column headings, using the expression *IIf (InvoicePaid,"Paid","Unpaid")*—if the InvoicePaid field value is true (because it's a Yes/No field or a True/False field), or is checked, use Paid as the column heading; otherwise, use Unpaid as the column heading.

Tip

Because the InvoicePaid field is a Yes/No field, the condition *InvoicePaid* is the same as the condition *InvoicePaid = -1*, which uses a comparison operator and a value. For all data types except Yes/No fields, you must use a comparison operator in a condition.

To change the crosstab query column headings:

▶ **1.** Click the **Home** tab on the Ribbon, and then switch to Design view. The design grid has four entries. See Figure 5-24.

Crosstab query in the design grid ◣ **Figure 5-24**

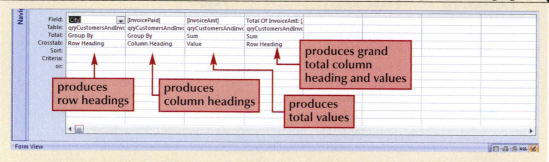

From left to right, the City entry produces the row headings in the crosstab query, the InvoicePaid entry produces the column headings, the InvoiceAmt entry produces the totals in each row/column intersection, and the Total Of InvoiceAmt entry produces the row total column heading and total values. Each field name is enclosed in brackets.

You need to replace the Field text box value in the second column with the IIf function expression to change the -1 and zero column headings to Paid and Unpaid. You can type the expression directly in the text box, use Expression Builder to create the expression, or type the expression in the Zoom dialog box. You'll use the last method.

▶ **2.** Click the **InvoicePaid Field** text box, and then open the Zoom dialog box.

▶ **3.** Delete the highlighted expression, and then type **IIf (InvoicePaid,"Paid", "Unpaid")** in the Zoom dialog box. See Figure 5-25.

IIf function for the crosstab query column headings ◣ **Figure 5-25**

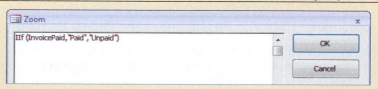

▶ **4.** Click the **OK** button, and then save and run the query. Access displays the complete crosstab query with Paid and Unpaid as column headings.

You can now close the completed query.

▶ **5.** Close the query, and then open the Navigation Pane.

In the Navigation Pane, Access displays objects alphabetically by object type with tables appearing first and then queries, forms, and reports. Access displays some types of queries separately from select queries; for example, crosstab queries appear before select queries. Access uses unique icons to represent different types of queries. The crosstab query icon appears in the Queries list to the left of the qryCustomersAndInvoicesCrosstab query. This icon looks different from the icon that appears to the left of the other queries, which are all select queries.

Next, Oren wants to identify any contracts that have the same start dates as other contracts, because these are the ones that might have potential scheduling difficulties. To find the information Oren needs, you'll create a find duplicates query.

Creating a Find Duplicates Query

A **find duplicates query** is a select query that finds duplicate records in a table or query. You can create this type of query using the **Find Duplicates Query Wizard**. A find duplicates query searches for duplicate values based on the fields you select as you answer the Wizard's questions. For example, you might want to display all employers that have the same name, all students who have the same phone number, or all products that have the same description. Using this type of query, you can locate duplicates to avert potential problems (for example, you might have inadvertently assigned two different numbers to the same product), or you can eliminate duplicates that cost money (for example, you could send just one advertising brochure to all customers having the same address).

You can meet Oren's request by using the Find Duplicates Query Wizard to display records for contracts that have the same start dates in the tblContract table.

Reference Window | **Using the Find Duplicates Query Wizard**

- In the Other group on the Create tab, click the Query Wizard button.
- Click Find Duplicates Query Wizard, and then click the OK button.
- Complete the Wizard dialog boxes to select the table or query on which to base the query, select the field (or fields) to check for duplicate values, select the additional fields to include in the query results, enter a name for the query, and then click the Finish button.

You'll use the Find Duplicates Query Wizard to create and run a new query to display duplicate start dates in the tblContract table.

To create the query using the Find Duplicates Query Wizard:

▶ 1. Close the Navigation Pane, click the **Create** tab on the Ribbon and then, in the Other group on the Create tab, click the **Query Wizard** button to open the New Query dialog box.

▶ 2. Click **Find Duplicates Query Wizard**, and then click the **OK** button. The first Find Duplicates Query Wizard dialog box opens. In this dialog box, you select the table or query on which to base the new query. You'll use the tblContract table.

▶ 3. Click **Table: tblContract** (if necessary), and then click the **Next** button. Access opens the next Find Duplicates Query Wizard dialog box, in which you choose the fields you want to check for duplicate values.

4. In the Available fields list box, click **StartDate**, click the ⟦ > ⟧ button to select the StartDate field as the field to check for duplicate values, and then click the **Next** button. In the next Find Duplicates Query Wizard dialog box, you select the additional fields you want displayed in the query results.

Oren wants all remaining fields to be included in the query results.

5. Click the ⟦ >> ⟧ button to move all fields from the Available fields list box to the Additional query fields list box, and then click the **Next** button. Access opens the final Find Duplicates Query Wizard dialog box, in which you enter a name for the query. You'll use qryDuplicateContractStartDates as the query name.

6. Type **qryDuplicateContractStartDates** in the text box, be sure the option button for viewing the results is selected, and then click the **Finish** button. Access saves the query, and then displays the 10 records for contracts with duplicate start dates. See Figure 5-26.

Query recordset for contracts with the same start dates ◀ **Figure 5-26**

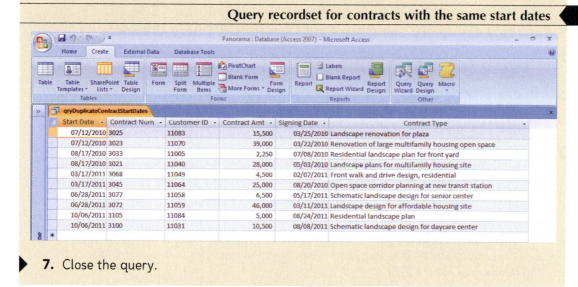

7. Close the query.

Oren now asks you to find the records for customers with no contracts. These are customers who had contracts in the past, but who have chosen not to sign a contract with Belmont Landscapes in the past year. Oren wants to contact these customers to see if there are any services that the company might be able to furnish. To provide Oren with this information, you need to create a find unmatched query.

Creating a Find Unmatched Query

A **find unmatched query** is a select query that finds all records in a table or query that have no related records in a second table or query. For example, you could display all customers who have not signed recent contracts or all students who are not currently enrolled in classes. Such a query provides information for Oren to solicit business from the inactive customers and for a school administrator to contact the students to find out their future educational plans. You can use the **Find Unmatched Query Wizard** to create this type of query.

Reference Window | **Using the Find Unmatched Query Wizard**

- In the Other group on the Create tab, click the Query Wizard button.
- Click Find Unmatched Query Wizard, and then click the OK button.
- Complete the Wizard dialog boxes to select the table or query on which to base the new query, select the table or query that contains the related records, specify the common field in each table or query, select the additional fields to include in the query results, enter a name for the query, and then click the Finish button.

Oren wants to know which customers have no open contracts. These customers are inactive, and he will contact them to determine their interest in doing further business with Belmont Landscapes. To create a list of inactive customers, you'll use the Find Unmatched Query Wizard to display only those records from the tblCustomer table with no matching CustomerID field value in the tblContract table.

To create the query using the Find Unmatched Query Wizard:

▶ 1. In the Other group on the Create tab, click the **Query Wizard** button to open the New Query dialog box.

▶ 2. Click **Find Unmatched Query Wizard**, and then click the **OK** button. The first Find Unmatched Query Wizard dialog box opens. In this dialog box, you select the table or query on which to base the new query. You'll use the qryCustomersByName query.

▶ 3. Click the **Queries** option button in the View section to display the list of queries, click **Query: qryCustomersByName** in the list box to select this query, and then click the **Next** button to open the next Find Unmatched Query Wizard dialog box, in which you choose the table that contains the related records. You'll select the tblContract table.

▶ 4. Click **Table: tblContract** in the list box (if necessary), and then click the **Next** button to open the next dialog box, in which you choose the common field for both tables. See Figure 5-27.

| **Figure 5-27** | **Selecting the common field** |

Tip

If the two objects you selected for the find unmatched query have a one-to-many relationship defined in the Relationships window, the Matching fields box will join the two correct fields automatically.

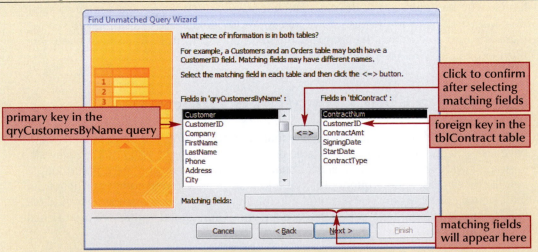

The common field between the query and the table is the CustomerID field. You need to click the common field in each list box, and then click the symbol between the two list boxes to join the two objects. The Matching fields box then will display CustomerID <=> CustomerID to indicate the joining of the two matching fields.

5. Click **CustomerID** in the Fields in 'qryCustomersByName' list box, click **CustomerID** in the Fields in 'tblContract' list box, click the $<=>$ button to connect the two selected fields, and then click the **Next** button to open the next Find Unmatched Query Wizard dialog box, in which you choose the fields you want to see in the query recordset. Oren wants the query recordset to display all available fields.

6. Click the $>>$ button to to move all fields from the Available fields list box to the Selected fields list box, and then click the **Next** button to open the final dialog box, in which you enter the query name.

7. Type **qryInactiveCustomers**, be sure the option button for viewing the results is selected, and then click the **Finish** button. Access saves the query and then displays two records in the query recordset. See Figure 5-28.

Query recordset displaying customers without contracts ◄ Figure 5-28

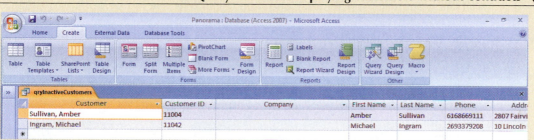

The query recordset includes information for the two inactive customers. Oren will use this information to contact these customers to see if they have any current or future landscaping needs.

8. Close the query.

Next, Oren wants Taylor to contact those customers who have the highest contract amounts to make sure that Belmont Landscapes is providing satisfactory service. To display the information Taylor needs, you will create a top values query.

Creating a Top Values Query

Whenever a query displays a large group of records, you might want to limit the number to a more manageable size by displaying, for example, just the first 10 records. The **Top Values property** for a query lets you limit the number of records in the query results. For the Top Values property, you can click one of the preset values from a list, or enter either an integer (such as 15, to display the first 15 records) or a percentage (such as 20%, to display the first fifth of the records) to find a specific number of records.

Suppose you have a select query that displays 45 records. If you want the query recordset to show only the first five records, you can change the query by entering a Top Values property value of either 5 or 10%. If the query contains a sort and the last record that Access can display is one of two or more records with the same value for the primary sort field, Access displays all records with that matching key value.

Taylor wants to view the same data that appears in the qryLargeContractAmounts query for customers with the highest 25% contract amounts. You will modify the query and then use the Top Values property to produce this information for Taylor.

To set the Top Values property for the query:

1. Open the Navigation Pane, open the **qryLargeContractAmounts** in Datasheet view, and then close the Navigation Pane. Access displays 22 records, all with ContractAmt field values greater than $25,000, sorted in descending order by the ContractAmt field.

2. Click the **Home** tab, and then switch to Design view.

3. In the Query Setup group on the Query Tools Design tab, click the **Return** arrow (with the ScreenTip "Top Values"), and then click **25%**. See Figure 5-29.

Figure 5-29	Creating the top values query

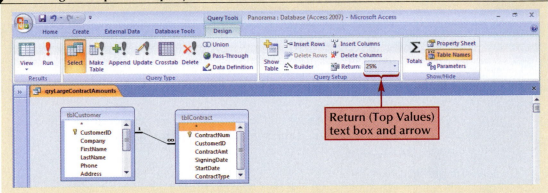

If the number or percentage of records you want to select, such as 15 or 20%, doesn't appear in the Top Values list, you can type the number or percentage in the Return text box.

4. Run the query. Access displays six records in the query recordset; these records represent the customers with the highest 25% contract amounts (25% of the original 22 records). See Figure 5-30.

Figure 5-30	Top values query recordset

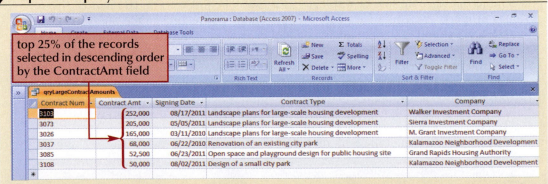

Because Taylor won't need to run this query again, you won't save it.

5. Close the query without saving it.

6. If you are not continuing on to the next session, close the Panorama database, and then exit Access, clicking the **Yes** button if you are prompted to confirm that you want to exit Access and to empty the Clipboard.

Oren and Taylor will use the information provided by the queries you created to analyze the business and to contact customers. In the next session, you will enhance the tblCustomer and tblContract tables.

Session 5.2 Quick Check | Review

1. What is the purpose of a crosstab query?
2. What are the four query wizards you can use to create a new query?
3. What is a find duplicates query?
4. What does a find unmatched query do?
5. What happens when you set a query's Top Values property?
6. What happens if you set a query's Top Values property to 2 and the first five records have the same value for the primary sort field?

Session 5.3

Creating a Lookup Field

The tblContract table in the Panorama database contains information about the contracts Belmont Landscapes has signed with its customers. Sarah wants to make entering data in the table easier for her staff. In particular, data entry is easier if they do not need to remember the correct CustomerID field values for each customer. Because the tblCustomer and tblContract tables have a one-to-many relationship, Sarah asks you to change the tblContract table's CustomerID field, which is a foreign key to the tblCustomer table, to a lookup field. A **lookup field** lets the user select a value from a list of possible values. For the CustomerID field, the user will be able to select a customer's ID number from the list of customer names in the qryCustomersByName query rather than having to remember the correct CustomerID field value. Access will store the CustomerID in the tblContract table, but both the customer name and the CustomerID field value will appear in Datasheet view when entering or changing a CustomerID field value. This arrangement makes entering and changing CustomerID field values easier for the user and guarantees that the CustomerID field value is valid. You use a **Lookup Wizard field** in Access to create a lookup field in a table.

Sarah asks you to change the CustomerID field in the tblContract table to a lookup field. You begin by opening the Panorama database and then opening the tblContract table in Design view.

To change the CustomerID field to a lookup field:

1. If you took a break after the previous session, make sure that the Panorama database is open.

   Trouble? If the Security Warning is displayed below the Ribbon, click the Options button next to the Security Warning. In the dialog box that opens, click the "Enable this content" option button, and then click the OK button.

2. If necessary, open the Navigation Pane, and then open the **tblContract** table in Design view.

▶ **3.** Click the right side of the **Data Type** text box for the CustomerID field to display the list of data types, and then click **Lookup Wizard**. A message box appears, warning you to delete the relationship between the tblCustomer and tblContract tables if you want to make the CustomerID field a lookup field. See Figure 5-31.

| Figure 5-31 | Warning message for an existing table relationship |

Tip

When you click or select text in many Access text boxes, Access displays an arrow, which you can click to display a list box with options. You can display the arrow and the list box simultaneously if you click the text box near its right side.

Access will use the lookup field to form the one-to-many relationship between the tblCustomer and tblContract tables, so you don't need the relationship you previously defined between the two tables.

▶ **4.** Click the **OK** button, close the tblContract table, and then click the **No** button when asked if you want to save the table design changes.

▶ **5.** Click the **Database Tools** tab on the Ribbon, and then, in the Show/Hide group on the Database Tools tab, click the **Relationships** button to open the Relationships window.

▶ **6.** Right-click the join line between the tblCustomer and tblContract tables, click **Delete**, and then click the **Yes** button to confirm the deletion.

Trouble? If the Delete command does not appear on the shortcut menu, click a blank area in the Relationships window to close the shortcut menu, and then repeat Step 6.

▶ **7.** Close the Relationships window.

Now you can resume changing the CustomerID field to a lookup field.

To finish changing the CustomerID field to a lookup field:

▶ **1.** Open the **tblContract** table in Design view.

▶ **2.** Click the right side of the **Data Type** text box for the CustomerID field, and then click **Lookup Wizard**. The first Lookup Wizard dialog box opens.

This dialog box lets you specify a list of allowed values for the CustomerID field in a record in the tblContract table. You can specify a table or query from which users select the value, or you can enter a new list of values. You want the CustomerID values to come from the qryCustomersByName query.

▶ **3.** Make sure the option for looking up the values in a table or query is selected, and then click the **Next** button to display the next Lookup Wizard dialog box.

▶ **4.** Click the **Queries** option button in the View section to display the list of queries, click **Query: qryCustomersByName**, and then click the **Next** button to display the next Lookup Wizard dialog box. See Figure 5-32.

Selecting the lookup fields ◄ **Figure 5-32**

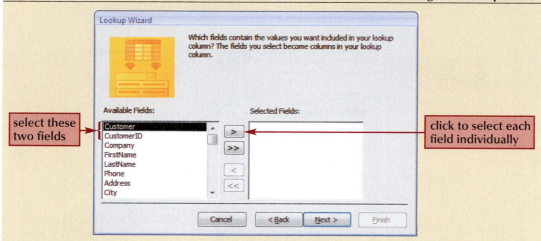

This dialog box lets you select the lookup fields from the qryCustomersByName query. You need to select the CustomerID field because it's the common field that links the query and the tblContract table. You also must select the Customer field because Sarah wants the user to be able to select from a list of customer names when entering a new contract record or changing an existing CustomerID field value.

5. Click **Customer** (if necessary), click the ⟩ button to move the Customer field to the Selected Fields list box, click **CustomerID** (if necessary), click the ⟩ button to move the CustomerID field to the Selected Fields list box, and then click the **Next** button to display the next Lookup Wizard dialog box. This dialog box lets you choose a sort order for the list box entries. Sarah wants the entries to appear in ascending Customer order. Note that ascending is the default sort order.

6. Click the **1** arrow, click **Customer**, and then click the **Next** button to open the next dialog box.

   In this dialog box, you can adjust the widths of the lookup columns. Note that when you resize a column to its best fit, Access resizes the column so that the widest column heading and the visible field values fit the column width. However, some field values that aren't visible in this dialog box might be wider than the column width, so you must scroll down the column to make sure you don't have to repeat the column resizing.

7. Click the **Customer** column selector, press and hold down the **Shift** key, click the **CustomerID** column selector to select both columns, release the **Shift** key, and then place the pointer on the right edge of the CustomerID field column heading. When the pointer changes to a ↔ shape, double-click to resize the columns to their best fits, and then scroll down the columns, and repeat the resizing as necessary. When you are finished, press **Ctrl + Home** to scroll back to the top of the Customer column. See Figure 5-33.

Figure 5-33 | **Adjusting the widths of lookup columns**

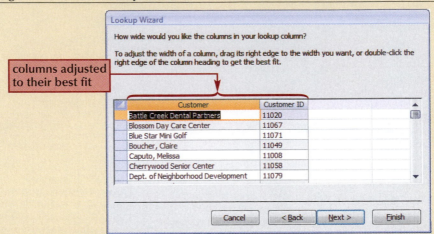

8. Click the **Next** button.

   In the dialog box that appears next, you select the field you want to store in the table. You'll store the CustomerID field in the tblContract table, because it's the foreign key to the tblCustomer table.

9. Click **CustomerID** in the Available Fields list box, and then click the **Next** button.

   In the dialog box that appears next, you specify the field name for the lookup field. Because you'll be storing the CustomerID field in the table, you'll accept the default field name, CustomerID.

10. Click the **Finish** button, and then save the table.

    The Data Type value for the CustomerID field is still Text because this field contains text data. However, when you update the field, Access uses the CustomerID field value to look up and display in the tblContract table datasheet both the Customer and CustomerID field values from the qryCustomersByName query.

In reviewing contracts recently, Sarah noticed that the CustomerID field value stored in the tblContract table for contract number 3030 is incorrect. She asks you to test the new lookup field to select the correct code. To do so, you need to switch to Datasheet view.

To change the CustomerID field value:

1. Switch to Datasheet view, and then resize the **CustomerID** column to its best fit.

   Notice that the Customer ID column displays Customer field values, even though it's the CustomerID field values that are stored in the table.

2. For Contract Num 3030, click **Lily's Boutique** in the Customer ID column, and then click the **arrow** to display the list of Customer and CustomerID field values from the qryCustomersByName query. See Figure 5-34.

List of Customer and CustomerID field values | Figure 5-34

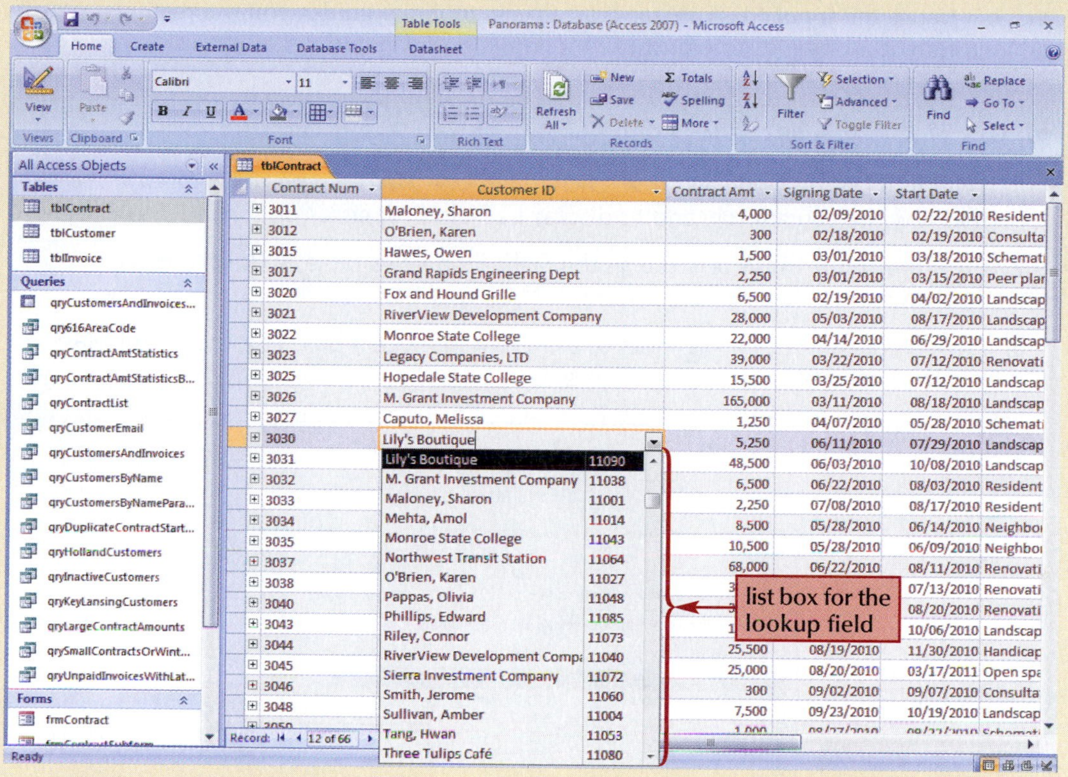

The customer for contract 3030 is Michael Ingram, so you need to select his entry in the list box to change the CustomerID field value.

3. Scroll up the list box, and then click **Ingram, Michael** to select that value to display in the datasheet and to store the CustomerID field value of 11042 in the table. The list box closes and "Ingram, Michael" appears in the Customer ID text box.

4. Save and close the tblContract table.

Sarah wants you to make changes to the design of the tblCustomer table, so you'll open the table in preparation for the changes.

5. Open the **tblCustomer** table in Datasheet view, and then close the Navigation Pane.

Sarah asks you to change the appearance of the Phone field in the tblCustomer table to a standard telephone number format.

Using the Input Mask Wizard

The Phone field in the tblCustomer table is a 10-digit number that's difficult to read because it appears with none of the special formatting characters usually associated with a telephone number. For example, the Phone field value for Sharon Maloney, which appears as 6168663901, would be more readable in any of the following formats: 616-866-3901, 616.866.3901, 616/866-3901, or (616) 866-3901. Sarah asks you to use the (616) 866-3901 style for the Phone field.

Sarah wants the parentheses and hyphens to appear as literal display characters whenever users enter Phone field values. A **literal display character** is a special character that automatically appears in specific positions of a field value; users don't need to type literal display characters. To include these characters, you need to create an **input mask**, a pre-defined format used to enter and display data in a field. An easy way to create an input mask is to use the **Input Mask Wizard**, an Access tool that guides you in creating a pre-defined format for a field. You must use the Input Mask Wizard in Design view.

To use the Input Mask Wizard for the Phone field:

▶ 1. Switch to Design view, and then click the **Phone Field Name** text box to make that row the current row and to display its Field Properties options.

▶ 2. Click the **Input Mask** text box in the Field Properties pane. A Build button ... appears to the right of the Input Mask text box.

▶ 3. Click the **Build** button ... next to the Input Mask text box. The first Input Mask Wizard dialog box opens. See Figure 5-35.

Figure 5-35 ▶ Input Mask Wizard dialog box

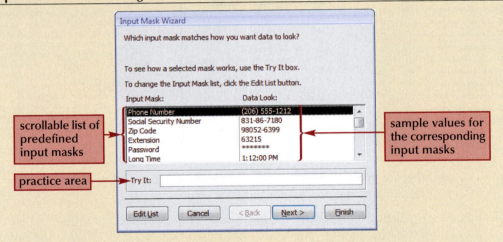

You can scroll the Input Mask list box, select the input mask you want, and then enter representative values to practice using the input mask.

▶ 4. If necessary, click **Phone Number** in the Input Mask list box to select it.

▶ 5. Click the far left side of the **Try It** text box. (___) ___-____ appears in the Try It text box. As you type a phone number, Access replaces the underscores, which are placeholder characters.

   Trouble? If your insertion point is not immediately to the right of the left parenthesis, press the ← key until it is.

▶ 6. Type **9876543210** to practice entering a sample phone number. The input mask formats the typed value as (987) 654-3210.

▶ 7. Click the **Next** button. The next Input Mask Wizard dialog box opens. In it, you can change the input mask and placeholder character. Because you can change an input mask easily after the Input Mask Wizard finishes, you'll accept all wizard defaults.

▶ 8. Click the **Finish** button. The Input Mask Wizard creates the phone number input mask, placing it in the Input Mask text box for the Phone field. See Figure 5-36.

Phone number input mask created by the Input Mask Wizard — Figure 5-36

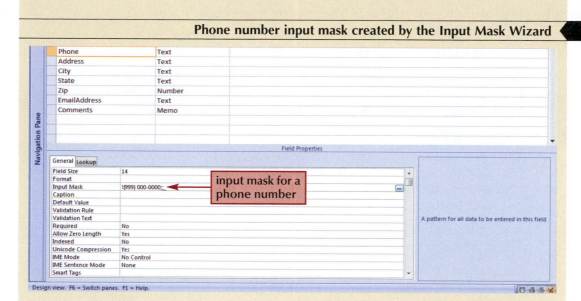

The characters used in a field's input mask restrict the data you can enter in the field, as shown in Figure 5-37. Other characters, such as the left and right parenthesis in the phone number input mask, that appear in an input mask are literal display characters.

Input mask characters — Figure 5-37

Input Mask Character	Description
0	Digit only must be entered. Entry is required.
9	Digit or space can be entered. Entry is optional.
#	Digit, space, or a plus or minus sign can be entered. Entry is optional.
L	Letter only must be entered. Entry is required.
?	Letter only can be entered. Entry is optional.
A	Letter or digit must be entered. Entry is required.
a	Letter or digit can be entered. Entry is optional.
&	Any character or a space must be entered. Entry is required.
C	Any character or a space can be entered. Entry is optional.
>	All characters that follow are displayed in uppercase.
<	All characters that follow are displayed in lowercase.
"	Enclosed characters treated as literal display characters.
\	Following character treated as a literal display character. This is the same as enclosing a single character in quotation marks.
!	Input mask is displayed from right to left, rather than the default of left to right. Characters typed into the mask always fill in from left to right.
;;	The character between the first and second semicolon determines whether to store in the database the literal display characters. If left blank or a value of 1, do not store the literal display characters. If a value of 0, store the literal display characters. The character following the second semicolon is the placeholder character that will appear in the displayed input mask.

Sarah wants to view the Phone field with the default input mask before you change it for her.

To view and change the input mask for the Phone field:

1. Save the table, and then switch to Datasheet view. The Phone field values now have the format specified by the input mask.

   Sarah decides that she would prefer to omit the parentheses around the area codes and use only hyphens as separators in the displayed Phone field values, so you'll change the input mask in Design view.

2. Switch to Design view.

   The input mask changed from !(999) 000-0000;;_ to !\(999") "000\-0000;;_. The backslash character (\) causes the character that follows it to appear as a literal display character. Characters enclosed in quotation marks also appear as literal display characters. (See Figure 5-37.)

3. Change the input mask to **999\-000\-0000;;_** in the Input Mask text box for the Phone field, and then press the **Tab** key.

   Because you've modified a field property, the Property Update Options button appears to the left of the Input Mask property.

4. Click the **Property Update Options** button, and then click **Update Input Mask everywhere Phone is used**. The Update Properties dialog box opens. See Figure 5-38.

Tip

If you omit the backslashes preceding the hyphens, Access will automatically insert them when you press the Tab key. However, Access doesn't add backslashes automatically for other literal display characters, such as periods and slashes, so it's best to always include the backslashes.

| Figure 5-38 | Update Properties dialog box |

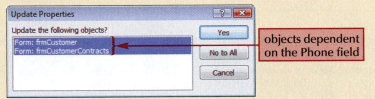

objects dependent on the Phone field

Because the frmCustomer and frmCustomerContracts forms display Phone field values from the tblCustomer table, Access will automatically change the Phone field's Input Mask property in these objects to your new input mask. This capability to update field properties in objects automatically when you modify a table field property is called **property propagation**. Although the Update Properties dialog box displays no queries, property propagation also does occur with queries automatically. Property propagation is limited to field properties such as the Decimal Places, Description, Format, and Input Mask properties.

5. Click the **Yes** button, save the table, and then switch to Datasheet view. The Phone field values now have the format Sarah requested. See Figure 5-39.

| Figure 5-39 | After changing the Phone field input mask |

Because Sarah wants her staff to store only standard 10-digit U.S. phone numbers for customers, the input mask you've created will enforce the standard entry and display format that Sarah desires.

Understanding When to Use Input Masks | InSight

An input mask is appropriate for a field only if all field values have a consistent format. For example, you can use an input mask with hyphens as literal display characters to store U.S. phone numbers in a consistent format of 987-654-3210. However, a multinational company would not be able to use an input mask to store phone numbers from all countries, because international phone numbers do not have a consistent format. For another example, U.S. zip codes have a consistent format, and you could use an input mask of 00000#9999 to enter and display U.S. zip codes such as 98765 and 98765-4321, but you could not use an input mask if you need to store and display foreign postal codes in the same field. If you need to store and display phone numbers, zip/postal codes, and other fields in a variety of formats, it's best to define them as Text fields without an input mask and let users enter field values and the literal display characters.

After the change to the Phone field's input mask, Access gave you the option to update, selectively and automatically, the Phone field's Input Mask property in other objects in the database. Sarah asks if there's an easy way to determine which objects are affected by changes made to other objects. To show Sarah how to determine the dependencies among objects in an Access database, you'll open the Object Dependencies pane.

Identifying Object Dependencies

An **object dependency** exists between two objects when a change to the properties of data in one object affects the properties of data in the other object. Dependencies between Access objects (tables, queries, forms, and so on) can occur in various ways. For example, the tblContract and tblInvoice tables are dependent on each other because they have a one-to-many relationship. As another example, because the tblContract table uses the qryCustomersByName query to obtain the Customer field to display along with the CustomerID field, these two tables have a dependency. Any query, form, or other object that uses fields from the tblCustomer table is dependent on the tblCustomer table. Any form or report that uses fields from a query is directly dependent on the query and is indirectly dependent on the tables that provide the data to the query. Large databases contain hundreds of objects, so it would be useful to have a way to view the dependencies among objects easily before you attempt to delete or modify an object. The **Object Dependencies pane** displays a collapsible list of the dependencies among the objects in an Access database; you click the list's expand indicators to show or hide different levels of dependencies. Next, you'll open the Object Dependencies pane to show Sarah the object dependencies in the Panorama database.

To open and use the Object Dependencies pane:

▶ **1.** Click the **Database Tools** tab on the Ribbon, and then, in the Show/Hide group, click the **Object Dependencies** button to open the Object Dependencies pane, and then drag the left edge of the pane to the left until the horizontal scroll bar at the bottom of the pane disappears. See Figure 5-40.

Figure 5-40 After opening the Object Dependencies pane

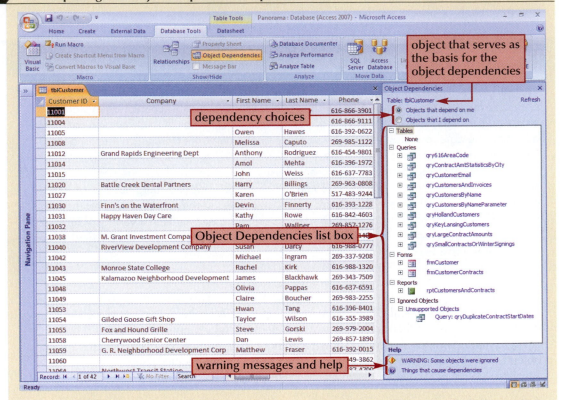

Trouble? If the "Objects that depend on me" option button is not selected, click the option button to select it.

The Object Dependencies list box displays the objects that depend on the tblCustomer table, the object name that appears at the top of the pane. If you change the design of the tblCustomer table, the change might affect objects in the list box. Changing a property for a field in the tblCustomer table that's also used by another listed object affects that other object. If the other object does not use the field you are changing, that other object is not affected.

Objects listed in the Ignored Objects portion of the pane might, or might not, have an object dependency with the tblCustomer table, and you'd have to review them yourself. The Help section at the bottom of the pane displays links for further information about object dependencies.

▶ 2. Click the **frmCustomer** link in the Object Dependencies pane. The frmCustomer form opens in Design view. All the fields in the form are fields from the tblCustomer table, which is why the form has an object dependency with the table.

▶ 3. Switch to Form view for the frmCustomer form. Note that the Phone field values are displayed using the input mask you applied to the field in the tblCustomer table. This change propagated from the table to the form.

▶ 4. Close the frmCustomer form, open the **tblContract** table in Datasheet view, and then click the **Refresh** link near the top of the Object Dependencies pane. The Object Dependencies list box now displays the objects that depend on the tblContract table.

▶ 5. Click the **Objects that I depend on** option button near the top of the pane to view the objects that affect the tblContract table.

▶ **6.** Click the **expand indicator** ⊞ for the qryCustomersByName query in the Object Dependencies pane. The list expands to display all the tblCustomer table, which is another table that the query depends upon.

▶ **7.** Close the tblContract table, close the Object Dependencies pane, and then close the Navigation Pane.

Sarah now better understands object dependencies and how to identify them by using the Object Dependencies pane.

Defining Data Validation Rules

Sarah wants to limit the entry of Zip field values in the tblCustomer table to Michigan zip codes because Belmont Landscapes customers are located only in Michigan. In addition, Sarah wants to make sure that a SigningDate field value entered in a tblContract table record is chronologically earlier than the StartDate field value in the same record. She's concerned that typing errors might produce incorrect query results and cause other problems. To provide these data-entry capabilities, you'll set field validation properties for the Zip field in the tblCustomer table and set table validation properties in the tblContract table.

Defining Field Validation Rules

To prevent a user from entering an incorrect value in the Zip field, you can create a **field validation rule** that verifies a field value by comparing it to a constant or a set of constants. You create a field validation rule by setting the Validation Rule and the Validation Text field properties. The **Validation Rule property** value specifies the valid values that users can enter in a field. The **Validation Text property** value will be displayed in a dialog box if the user enters an invalid value (in this case, a value other than a Michigan zip code). After you set these two Zip field properties in the tblCustomer table, Access will prevent users from entering an invalid Zip field value in the tblCustomer table and in all current and future queries and forms that include the Zip field.

You'll now set the Validation Rule and Validation Text properties for the Zip field in the tblCustomer table. Michigan zip codes must be between 48000 and 49999.

To create and test a field validation rule for the Zip field:

▶ **1.** Switch to Design view for the tblCustomer table, and then click the **Zip Field Name** text box to make that row the current row.

To make sure that the only values entered in the Zip field are between 48000 and 49999, you'll specify a range of valid values in the Validation Rule text box. The Zip field is a Number field, so you can use this numeric range test.

▶ **2.** In the Field Properties pane, click the **Validation Rule** text box, type **>=48000 And <=49999**, and then press the **Tab** key.

Instead of using the range of values test, you could also use the equivalent *Between 48000 And 49999.*

You can set the Validation Text property to a value that appears in a dialog box that opens if a user enters a value not listed in the Validation Rule text box.

▶ **3.** Type **Michigan zip codes must be between 48000 and 49999** in the Validation Text text box. See Figure 5-41.

> **Tip**
>
> Using the numeric range test with a Text field isn't allowed; you'll get an error message. Also, enclosing the numbers in quotation marks for a Text field range test will eliminate the error message but will yield unpredictable results.

Figure 5-41 **Validation properties for the Zip field**

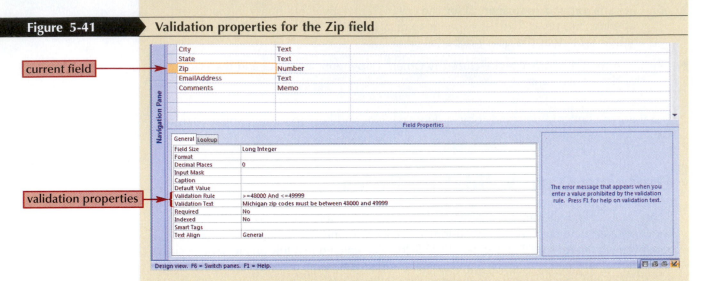

You can now save the table design changes and then test the validation properties.

▶ **4.** Save the table, and then click the **Yes** button when asked if you want to test the existing Zip field values in the tblCustomer table against the new validation rule.

Access tests the existing records in the tblCustomer table against the validation rule. If any record violates the rule, you are prompted to continue testing or to revert to the previous Validation Rule property setting. Next, you'll test the validation rule.

▶ **5.** Switch to Datasheet view, and then scroll the table to the right until the Zip field is visible.

▶ **6.** Double-click **49341** in the first row's Zip field text box, type **54321**, and then press the **Tab** key. A dialog box opens containing the message "Michigan zip codes must be between 48000 and 49999," which is the Validation Text property setting you created in Step 3.

▶ **7.** Click the **OK** button, and then press the **Esc** key. The first row's Zip field value again has its original value, 49341.

▶ **8.** Close the tblCustomer table.

Now that you've finished entering the field validation rule for the Zip field in the tblCustomer table, you'll enter the table validation rule for the date fields in the tblContract table.

Defining Table Validation Rules

To make sure that a user enters a SigningDate field value in the tblContract table that is chronologically earlier than the record's StartDate field value, you can create a **table validation rule** that compares one field value in a table record to another field value in the same record to verify their relative accuracy. Once again, you'll use the Validation Rule and Validation Text properties, but this time you'll set these properties for the table instead of for an individual field.

You'll now set the Validation Rule and Validation Text properties to compare the SigningDate and StartDate field values in the tblContract table.

To create and test a table validation rule in the tblContract table:

1. Open the Navigation Pane, open the **tblContract** table in Design view, and then, in the Show/Hide group on the Table Tools Design tab, click the **Property Sheet** button to open the property sheet for the table.

   To make sure that each SigningDate field value is chronologically earlier than, or less than, each StartDate field value, you'll compare the two field values in the Validation Rule text box.

2. In the property sheet, click the **Validation Rule** text box, type **[SigningDate]<[StartDate]**, and then press the **Tab** key.

3. Type **The signing date must be earlier than the start date** in the Validation Text text box. See Figure 5-42.

Tip

Make sure you type the brackets to enclose the field names. If you omit the brackets, Access automatically inserts quotation marks around the field names, in effect treating the field names as field values, and the table validation rule will not work correctly.

Setting table validation properties ◄ **Figure 5-42**

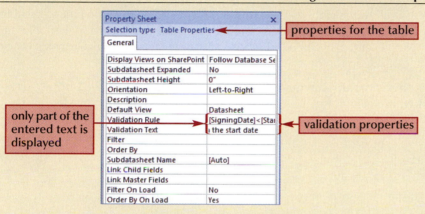

You can now test the validation properties.

4. Close the property sheet, save the table, and then click the **Yes** button when asked if you want to test the existing dates in the tblContract table against the new validation rule.

5. Close the Navigation Pane, switch to Datasheet view, click the Signing Date column value in the first record, click the **date picker** icon to the right of the date, click **27** in the calendar control to change the date to 2/27/2010, press the **Tab** key to advance to the Start Date column, and then press the **Tab** key two more times to complete your changes to the record. A dialog box opens containing the message "The signing date must be earlier than the start date," which is the Validation Text property setting you entered in Step 3.

   Unlike field validation rule violations, which Access detects immediately after you finish your field entry and advance to another field, Access detects table validation rule violations when you finish all changes to the current record and advance to another record.

6. Click the **OK** button, and then press the **Esc** key to undo your change to the Signing Date column value.

7. Close the tblContract table.

Based on a request from Sarah, Lucia added a Memo field to the tblCustomer table, and now you'll review Lucia's work.

Working with Memo Fields

You use a Memo field for long comments and explanations. Text fields are limited to 255 characters, but Memo fields can hold up to 65,535 characters. In addition, Text fields limit you to plain text with no special formatting, but you can define Memo fields either to store plain text similar to Text fields or to store rich text, which you can selectively format with options such as bold, italic, and different fonts and colors.

You'll review the Memo field, named Comments, that Lucia added to the tblCustomer table.

To review the Memo field in the tblCustomer table:

1. Open the Navigation Pane, open the **tblCustomer** table in Datasheet view, and then close the Navigation Pane.

   If you scroll to the right to view the Comments field, you'll no longer be able to identify which customer applies to a row because the Company, First Name, and Last Name columns will be hidden. You'll freeze those three columns so they remain visible in the datasheet as you scroll to the right.

2. Click the **Company** column selector, press and hold down the **Shift** key, click the **Last Name** column selector, and then release the **Shift** key to select the Company, First Name, and Last Name columns.

3. In the Records group on the Home tab, click the **More** button, and then click **Freeze**. The three selected columns shift to the left and are now the three leftmost columns in the datasheet.

4. Scroll to the right until you see the Comments column. Notice that the Company, First Name, and Last Name columns, the three leftmost columns, remain visible. See Figure 5-43.

Figure 5-43 | **Freezing three datasheet columns**

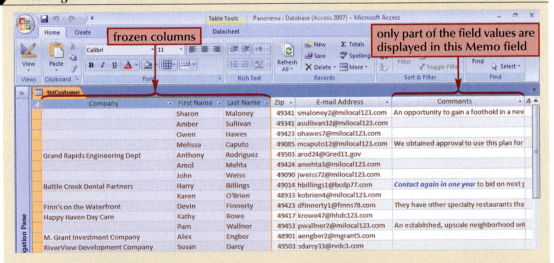

The Comments column is a Memo field that Belmont Landscapes staff members use to store notes, explanations, and other commentary about the customer. Notice that the Comments field value for Battle Creek Dental Partners displays rich text, using a bold, italic, and blue font. The Comments field values are partially hidden because the datasheet column is not wide enough. You'll view the first record's Comments field value in the Zoom dialog box.

▶ **5.** Click the **Comments** text box for the first record, hold down the **Shift** key, press the **F2** key, and then release the **Shift** key. The Zoom dialog box displays the entire Comments field value.

▶ **6.** Click the **OK** button to close the Zoom dialog box.

Table Datasheet Row and Column Resizing for Memo Fields | InSight

For Memo fields that contain many characters, you can widen the column to view more of its contents by dragging the right edge of the field's column selector to the right or by using the Column Width command when you click the More button in the Records group on the Home tab. However, increasing the column width reduces the number of other columns you can view at the same time. Further, for Memo fields containing thousands of characters, you can't widen the column enough to be able to view the entire contents of the field at one time across the width of the screen. Therefore, increasing the column width of a Memo field seldom makes sense.

Alternatively, you can increase the row height of a datasheet by dragging the bottom edge of a row selector down or by using the Row Height command when you click the More button in the Records group on the Home tab. Increasing the row height causes the text in a Memo field to wrap to the next line, so that you can view multiple lines at one time. Once again, however, for Memo fields containing thousands of characters, you can't increase the row height enough to ensure viewing the entire contents of the field at one time on screen. In addition, you'd view fewer records at one time, and the row height setting for a table propagates to all queries that have an object dependency with the table. Thus, you shouldn't increase the row height of a table datasheet to accommodate a Memo field.

What is the best way to view the contents of Memo fields that contain a large number of characters? It is best to use the Zoom dialog box in a datasheet, or to use a large scrollable text box on a form.

Now you'll review the property settings for the Comments field Lucia added to the tblCustomer table.

To review the property settings of the Memo field:

▶ **1.** Save the table, switch to Design view, click the **Comments Field Name** text box to make that row the current row, and then scroll to the bottom of the list of properties in the Field Properties pane.

▶ **2.** Click the **Text Format** text box in the Field Properties pane, and then click its **arrow**. The list of available text formats appears in the list box. See Figure 5-44.

Figure 5-44 **Viewing the properties for a Memo field**

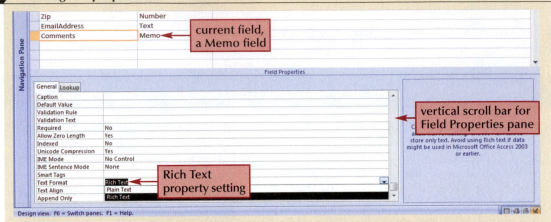

Lucia set the **Text Format property** to Rich Text, which lets you format the datasheet field contents using the options in the Font group on the Home tab. The default Text Format property setting for a Memo field is Plain Text, which doesn't allow text formatting.

▶ **3.** Click the **arrow** on the Text Format text box to close the list, and then click the **Append Only** text box.

The **Append Only property**, which appears at the bottom of the list of properties, tracks the changes that you make to a Memo field. The default setting of No lets you edit the Memo field value in a normal way. Setting this property to Yes also lets you edit the Memo field value in a normal way but, additionally, causes Access to keep a historical record of all versions of the Memo field value. You can view each version of the field value, along with a date and time stamp of when each version change occurred.

You've finished your review of the Memo field, so you can close the table.

▶ **4.** Close the tblCustomer table.

When employees at Belmont Landscapes open the Panorama database, a Security Warning appears below the Ribbon, and they must "enable this content" in the database before beginning their work. Sarah asks if you can eliminate this extra step when employees open the database.

Designating a Trusted Folder

A database is a file, and files can contain malicious instructions that can damage other files on your computer or files on other computers on your network. Unless you take special steps, Access treats every database as a potential threat to your computer. One such special step is to designate a folder as a trusted folder. A **trusted folder** is a folder on a drive or network that you designate as trusted and where you place databases you know are safe. When you open a database located in a trusted folder, Access treats it as a safe file and no longer displays a Security Warning. You can also place files used with other Microsoft Office programs, such as Word documents and Excel workbooks, in a trusted folder to eliminate warnings when you open them.

Because the Panorama database does not contain harmful instructions, you'll set up a trusted folder in which to store it to eliminate the Security Warning when a user opens the database.

To designate a trusted folder:

▶ **1.** Click the **Office Button** 🔘, and then click the **Access Options** button. The Access Options dialog box opens.

▶ **2.** In the left section of the dialog box, click **Trust Center**, click the **Trust Center Settings** button in the window on the right to open the Trust Center dialog box, and then in the left section, click **Trusted Locations**. The trusted locations for your installation of Access and other options are displayed on the right. See Figure 5-45.

Designating a trusted folder ◂ **Figure 5-45**

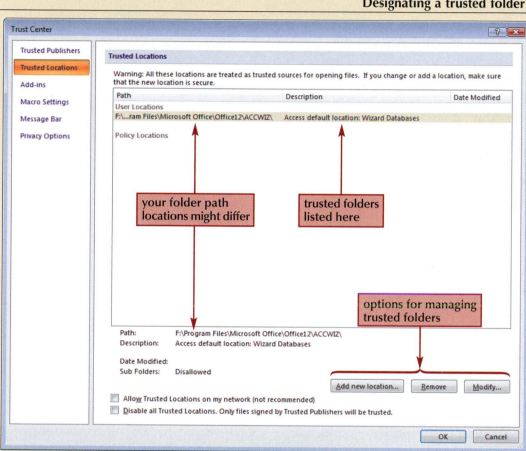

Existing trusted locations appear in the list at the top; and options to add, remove, and modify trusted locations appear at the bottom.

Trouble? Check with your instructor before adding a new trusted location. If your instructor tells you not to select this option, skip to Step 5.

▶ **3.** Click the **Add new location** button to open the Microsoft Office Trusted Location dialog box, click the **Browse** button, navigate to the Level.02\Tutorial folder where your Data Files are stored, and then click the **OK** button.

You can also choose to designate subfolders of the selected location as trusted locations, but you won't select this option.

▶ **4.** Click the **OK** button. Access adds the Level.02\Tutorial folder to the list of trusted locations.

▶ **5.** Click the **OK** button to close the Trust Center dialog box, and then click the **OK** button to close the Access Options dialog box.

To show Sarah that adding the trusted location eliminates the Security Warning, you need to close and then open the database. You've created several queries and completed several table design changes, so you should compact and repair the Panorama database when you reopen it. Lucia doesn't use the Compact on Close option with the Panorama database, because it's possible to lose the database if there's a computer malfunction when the Compact on Close operation runs. As a precaution, you'll make a backup copy of the database before you reopen it. Making frequent backup copies of your critical files safeguards your data from hardware and software malfunctions, which can occur at any time.

To copy, open, and compact and repair the Panorama database:

▶ 1. Click the **Office Button** 📋, and then click **Close Database** to close the Panorama database.

▶ 2. Make a backup copy of the Panorama database, preferably to a USB drive or other external medium, using a filename of Copy of Panorama_date, where *date* is the current date in the format 2010_02_15, for example, if you made the backup on February 15, 2010.

Tip

The date the database was last opened appears below the filename in the Open Recent Database pane.

▶ 3. Make sure the Access window is the active window, and then click **C:\Level.02\ ... \Panorama** in the Open Recent Database pane of the Getting Started window. The database opens, and no Security Warning appears below the Ribbon because the database is located in the trusted location you designated.

   Next, you'll compact and repair the database.

▶ 4. Click the **Office Button** 📋, point to **Manage**, and then click **Compact and Repair Database**.

   You've finished the work requested by Belmont Landscapes, so you can close the database and exit Access.

▶ 5. Close the Panorama database and then exit Access, clicking the **Yes** button if you are prompted to confirm that you want to exit Access and empty the Clipboard.

You've completed the table design changes to the Panorama database that will make working with it easier and more accurate.

Review | Session 5.3 Quick Check

1. What is a lookup field?
2. A(n) _____ is a predefined format you use to enter and display data in a field.
3. What is property propagation?
4. Define the Validation Rule property, and give an example of when you would use it.
5. Define the Validation Text property, and give an example of when you would use it.
6. Setting a Memo field's Text Format property to _____ lets you format its contents.
7. A(n) _____ folder is a location in which you can place safe databases.

In this tutorial, you built on your earlier work with simple queries by learning how to use pattern and list-of-values matches, the Not operator, the & operator, and the IIf function. You also learned how to create parameter, crosstab, find duplicates, find unmatched, and top values queries. You enhanced the design of tables by creating lookup fields and input masks and by defining field and table validation rules. You also learned how to identify object dependencies, work with Memo fields, and designate trusted folders.

Key Terms

& (ampersand) operator
Append Only property
Caption property
crosstab query
Crosstab Query Wizard
field validation rule
find duplicates query
Find Duplicates Query
  Wizard
find unmatched query
Find Unmatched Query
  Wizard
IIf (Immediate If) function

In comparison operator
input mask
Input Mask Wizard
IsNull function
Like comparison operator
list-of-values match
literal display character
lookup field
Lookup Wizard field
Not logical operator
Object Dependencies pane
object dependency

parameter query
pattern match
property propagation
SQL (Structured Query
  Language)
table validation rule
Text Format property
Top Values property
trusted folder
Validation Rule property
Validation Text property

Practice	Review Assignments

Practice the skills you learned in the tutorial using the same case scenario.

Data File needed for the Review Assignments: Products.accdb

In the Review Assignments, you'll create several new queries and enhance the table design in a database that contains information about the suppliers that Belmont Landscapes works with on its landscape design projects. Complete the following steps:

1. Open the **Products** database, which is located in the Level.02\Review folder provided with your Data Files.

2. Modify the first record in the **tblCompany** table datasheet by changing the ContactFirstName and ContactLastName field values to your first and last names. Close the table.

3. Create a query to find all records in the tblCompany table in which the City field value starts with the letter H. Display all fields in the query recordset, and sort in ascending order by CompanyName. Save the query as **qryHSelectedCities**, run the query, and then close it.

4. Make a copy of the qryHSelectedCities query using the new name **qryOtherSelectedCities**. Modify the new query to find all records in the tblCompany table in which the City field values are not Lansing, Rockford, or Zeeland. Save and run the query, and then close it.

5. Create a query to find all records from the tblProduct table in which the Color field value is Black, White, or Grey. Use a list-of-values match for the selection criteria. Display all fields in the query recordset, and sort in descending order by Price. Save the query as **qrySelectedColors**, run the query, and then close it.

6. Create a query to display all records from the tblCompany table, selecting the CompanyName, City, and Phone fields, and sorting in ascending order by CompanyName. Add a calculated field named **ContactName** as the first column that concatenates the ContactFirstName, a space, and the ContactLastName. Set the Caption property for the ContactName field to **Contact Name**. Save the query as **qryCompanyContacts**, run the query, resize the Contact Name column to its best fit, and then save and close the query.

7. Create a parameter query to select the tblProduct table records for a Color field value that the user specifies. If the user doesn't enter a Color field value, select all records from the table. Display the ProductType, Price, Color, and DiscountOffered fields in the query recordset, sorting in ascending order by Price. Save the query as **qryColorParameter**. Run the query and enter no value as the Color field value, and then run the query again and enter **Wood** as the Color field value. Close the query.

8. Create a find duplicates query based on the tblProduct table. Select ProductType as the field that might contain duplicates, and select the ProductID, CompanyID, Price, and DiscountOffered fields as additional fields in the query recordset. Save the query as **qryDuplicateProductTypes**, run the query, and then close it.

9. Create a find unmatched query that finds all records in the tblCompany table for which there is no matching record in the tblProduct table. Display the CompanyID, CompanyName, City, Phone, ContactFirstName, and ContactLastName fields from the tblCompany table in the query recordset. Save the query as **qryCompaniesWithoutMatchingProducts**, run the query, and then close it.

10. Make a copy of the qryPricesWithDiscountAmounts query using the new name **qryTopPricesWithDiscountAmounts**. Modify the new query to use the Top Values property to select the top 25% of records. Save and run the query, and then close it.

11. In the **tblProduct** table, change the CompanyID field to a lookup field. Select the CompanyName and CompanyID fields from the tblCompany table, sort in ascending order by the CompanyName field, do not hide the key column, make sure the Company Name column is the leftmost column, resize the lookup columns to their best fit, select CompanyID as the field to store in the table, and accept the default label for the lookup column. View the tblProduct table datasheet, resize the Company ID column to its best fit, test the lookup field without changing a value permanently, and then save and close the table.

12. Use the Input Mask Wizard to add an input mask to the Phone field in the **tblCompany** table. The ending input mask should use periods as separators, as in 987.654.3210 with only the last seven digits required; do not store the literal display characters if you are asked to do so. Update the Input Mask property everywhere the Phone field is used. Test the input mask by typing over an existing Phone field value, being sure not to change the value by pressing the Esc key after you type the last digit in the Phone field.

13. Add a Memo field named **CompanyComments** as the last field in the tblCompany table. Set the Caption property to **Company Comments** and the Text Format property to Rich Text. In the table datasheet, resize the new column to its best fit, and then add your city and state in bold, italic font to the Memo field in the first record. Save and close the tblCompany datasheet.

14. Designate the Level.02\Review folder as a trusted folder. (*Note:* Check with your instructor before adding a new trusted location.)

15. Close the Products database without exiting Access, make a backup copy of the database, open the **Products** database, compact and repair the database, close the database, and then exit Access.

Apply	**Case Problem 1**

Use the skills you learned in the tutorial to work with the data contained in a database for a small music school.

Data File needed for this Case Problem: Contract.accdb

Pine Hill Music School   Yuka Koyama owns and runs the Pine Hill Music School in Portland, Oregon. She and the qualified teachers who work for her offer instruction in voice, violin, cello, guitar, percussion, and other instruments. Yuka created an Access database named Contract to store data about students, teachers, and contracts. You'll help Yuka create several new queries and make design changes to the tables. Complete the following:

1. Open the **Contract** database, which is located in the Level.02\Case1 folder provided with your Data Files.

2. Change the first record in the **tblStudent** table datasheet so the First Name and Last Name columns contain your first and last names. Close the table.

3. Create a query to find all records in the tblStudent table in which the Phone field value begins with 541. Display the FirstName, LastName, City, and Phone fields in the query recordset; and sort in ascending order by LastName. Save the query as **qry541AreaCodes**, run the query, and then close it.

4. Make a copy of the qryCurrentLessons query using the new name **qrySelectedLessons**. Modify the new query to delete the existing condition for the ContractEndDate field and to include a list-of-values criterion that finds all records in which the LessonType field value is Cello, Flute, or Violin. Save and run the query, and then close it.

5. Create a query to find all records in the tblStudent table in which the City field value is not equal to Portland. Display the FirstName, LastName, City, and Phone fields in the query recordset; and sort in ascending order by City. Save the query as **qryNonPortland**, run the query, and then close it.

6. Create a query to display all records from the tblTeacher table, selecting all fields, and sorting in ascending order by LastName and then in ascending order by FirstName. Add a calculated field named **TeacherName** as the second column that concatenates FirstName, a space, and LastName for each teacher. Set the Caption property for the TeacherName field to **Teacher Name**. Do not display the FirstName and LastName fields in the query recordset. Save the query as **qryTeacherNames**, run the query, resize the Teacher Name column to its best fit, and then save and close the query.

7. Create a parameter query to select the tblContract table records for a LessonType field value that the user specifies. If the user doesn't enter a LessonType field value, select all records from the table. Include all fields from the tblContract table in the query recordset. Save the query as **qryLessonTypeParameter**. Run the query and enter no value as the LessonType field value, and then run the query again and enter **Guitar** as the LessonType field value. Close the query.

⊕ EXPLORE

8. Create a crosstab query based on the tblContract table. Use the LessonType field values for the row headings, the LessonLength field values for the column headings, and the count of the ContractID field values as the summarized value, and include row sums. Save the query as **qryLessonTypeCrosstab**. Change the column heading for the row sum column to **Total Number of Lessons**, and change the column headings for the [LessonLength] columns to **Number of 30-Minute Lessons** and **Number of 60-Minute Lessons**. Resize the columns in the query recordset to their best fit, and then save and close the query.

9. Create a find duplicates query based on the tblContract table. Select StudentID and LessonType as the fields that might contain duplicates, and select all other fields in the table as additional fields in the query recordset. Save the query as **qryMultipleLessonsForStudents**, run the query, and then close it.

10. Create a find unmatched query that finds all records in the tblStudent table for which there is no matching record in the tblContract table. Display all fields from the tblStudent table in the query recordset. Save the query as **qryStudentsWithoutContracts**, run the query, and then close it.

11. In the **tblContract** table, change the TeacherID field data type to Lookup Wizard. Select the TeacherName and TeacherID fields from the qryTeacherNames query, sort in ascending order by TeacherName, resize the lookup columns to their best fit, select TeacherID as the field to store in the table, and accept the default label for the lookup column. View the tblContract table datasheet, resize the TeacherID column to its best fit, and then save and close the table.

12. Use the Input Mask Wizard to add an input mask to the Phone field in the **tblStudent** table. The ending input mask should use periods as separators, as in 987.654.3210 with only the last seven digits required; do not store the literal display characters if you are asked to do so. Update the Input Mask property everywhere the Phone field is used. Test the input mask by typing over an existing Phone field value, being sure not to change the value permanently by pressing the Esc key after you type the last digit in the Phone field.

13. Define a field validation rule for the Gender field in the tblStudent table. Acceptable field values for the Gender field are M or F. Use the message "Gender values must be M or F" to notify a user who enters an invalid Gender field value. Save your table changes, test the field validation rule for the Gender field, making sure any tested field values are the same as they were before your testing, and then close the table.

14. Define a table validation rule for the **tblContract** table to verify that ContractStartDate field values precede ContractEndDate field values in time. Use an appropriate validation message. Save your table changes, test the table validation rule, making sure any tested field values are the same as they were before your testing, and then close the table.

15. Designate the Level.02\Case1 folder as a trusted folder. (*Note:* Check with your instructor before adding a new trusted location.)

16. Close the Contract database without exiting Access, make a backup copy of the database, open the **Contract** database, compact and repair the database, close the database, and then exit Access.

| Apply | Case Problem 2 |

Apply what you learned in the tutorial to work with the data for a new business in the health and fitness industry.

Data File needed for this Case Problem: Training.accdb

Parkhurst Health & Fitness Center Martha Parkhurst owns and operates the Parkhurst Health & Fitness Center in Richmond, Virginia. The center offers the usual weight training equipment and fitness classes and also offers specialized programs designed to meet the needs of athletes who participate in certain sports or physical activities. Martha created the Training database to maintain information about the members who have joined the center and the types of programs offered. To make the database easier to use, Martha wants you to create several queries and to make changes to its table design. Complete the following steps:

1. Open the **Training** database, which is located in the Level.02\Case2 folder provided with your Data Files.

2. Modify the first record in the **tblMember** table datasheet by changing the First Name and Last Name column values to your first and last names. Close the table.

3. Create a query to find all records in the tblProgram table in which the MonthlyFee field value is 20, 30, or 40. Use a list-of-values match for the selection criterion, and include all fields from the table in the query recordset. Sort the query in descending order by the ProgramID field. Save the query as **qrySelectedPrograms**, run the query, and then close it.

4. Make a copy of the qrySelectedPrograms query using the new name **qrySelectedProgramsModified**. Modify the new query to find all records in the tblProgram table in which the MonthlyFee field value is not 20, 30, or 40. Save and run the query, and then close it.

5. Create a query to display all records from the tblMember table, selecting the LastName, FirstName, Street, and Phone fields, and sorting in ascending order by LastName and then in ascending order by FirstName. Add a calculated field named **MemberName** as the first column that concatenates FirstName, a space, and LastName. Set the Caption property for the MemberName field to **Member Name**. Do not display the FirstName and LastName fields in the query recordset. Create a second calculated field named **CityLine**, inserting it between the Street and Phone fields. The CityLine field concatenates City, a space, State, two spaces, and Zip. Set the Caption property for the CityLine field to **City Line**. Save the query as **qryMemberNames**, run the query, resize all columns to their best fit, and then save and close the query.

⊕ EXPLORE   6. Create a query to display all matching records from the tblProgram and tblMember tables, selecting the ProgramType and MonthlyFee fields from the tblProgram table, and the FirstName and LastName fields from the tblMember table. Add a calculated field named **MonthlyFeeStatus** as the last column that equals Active if the MembershipStatus field is equal to Active and equals Not Active otherwise. Set the Caption property for the calculated field to **Monthly Fee Status**. Save the query as **qryMonthlyFeeStatus**, run the query, resize all columns to their best fit, and then save and close the query.

7. Make a copy of the qryRichmondOnHold query using the new name **qryRichmondAndChesterActive**. Modify the new query to select all records in which the City field value is Richmond or Chester and the MembershipStatus field value is Active. Save and run the query, and then close the query.

8. Create a parameter query to select the tblMember table records for a City field value that the user specifies. If the user doesn't enter a City field value, select all records from the table. Display all fields from the tblMember table in the query recordset. Save the query as **qryMemberCityParameter**. Run the query and enter no value as the City field value, and then run the query again and enter **Ashland** as the City field value. Close the query.

9. Create a crosstab query based on the qryMonthlyFeeStatus query. Use the ProgramType field values for the row headings, the MonthlyFeeStatus field values for the column headings, the sum of the MonthlyFee field values as the summarized value, and include row sums. Save the query as **qryMonthlyFeeCrosstab**, resize the columns in the query recordset to their best fit, and then save and close the query.

10. Create a find duplicates query based on the tblMember table. Select ExpirationDate as the field that might contain duplicates, and select all other fields in the table as additional fields in the query recordset. Save the query as **qryDuplicateMemberExpirationDates**, run the query, and then close it.

11. Create a find unmatched query that finds all records in the tblProgram table for which there is no matching record in the tblMember table. Select all fields from the tblProgram table. Save the query as **qryProgramsWithoutMembers**, run the query, and then close it.

12. Create a new query based on the tblMember table. Display the FirstName, LastName, Phone, ExpirationDate, MembershipStatus, and ProgramID fields in the query recordset. Sort in ascending order by the ExpirationDate field, and then use the Top Values property to select the top 25% of records. Save the query as **qryUpcomingExpirations**, run the query, and then close it.

⊕ EXPLORE   13. Use the Input Mask Wizard to add an input mask to the JoinDate field in the **tblMember** table. Select the Short Date input mask, and then modify the default Short Date input mask by changing the two slashes to dashes. Next type **mm-dd-yyyy** in the Format property text box for the JoinDate field to specify the date format. Test the input mask by typing over an existing Join Date column value, being certain not to change the value by pressing the Esc key after you type the last digit in the Join Date column. Finally, repeat the same procedure to add the same input mask and Format property setting to the ExpirationDate field, and then save and close the table.

14. Define a field validation rule for the MonthlyFee field in the **tblProgram** table. Acceptable field values for the MonthlyFee field are values between 15 and 55. Enter the message **Value must be between 15 and 55, inclusive** so it appears if a user enters an invalid MonthlyFee field value. Save your table changes and then test the field validation rule for the MonthlyFee field; be certain the field values are the same as they were before your testing.

15. Define a table validation rule for the **tblMember** table to verify that JoinDate field values precede ExpirationDate field values in time. Use an appropriate validation message. Save your table changes, test the table validation rule, making sure any tested field values are the same as they were before your testing.

16. Add a Memo field named **MemberComments** as the last field in the tblMember table. Set the Caption property to **Member Comments** and the Text Format property to Rich Text. In the table datasheet, resize the new column to its best fit, and then add a comment in the Memo field in the first record about the types of physical activities you pursue, formatting the text with blue, italic font. Save your table changes, and then close the table.

17. Designate the Level.02\Case2 folder as a trusted folder. (*Note:* Check with your instructor before adding a new trusted location.)

18. Close the Training database without exiting Access, make a backup copy of the database, open the **Training** database, compact and repair the database, close the database, and then exit Access.

| Challenge | **Case Problem 3** |

Apply the skills you've learned, and explore some new skills, to work with a database that contains data about an agency that recycles household goods.

Data File needed for this Case Problem: Agency.accdb

Rossi Recycling Group   The Rossi Recycling Group is a not-for-profit agency in Salina, Kansas that provides recycled household goods to needy people and families at no charge. Residents of Salina and surrounding communities donate cash and goods, such as appliances, furniture, and tools, to the Rossi Recycling Group. The group's volunteers then coordinate with local human services agencies to distribute the goods to those in need. The Rossi Recycling Group was established by Mary and Tom Rossi, who live on the outskirts of Salina on a small farm. Mary and Tom organize the volunteers to collect the goods and store the collected items in their barn for distribution. Tom has created an Access database to keep track of information about donors, their donations, and the human services agencies. He wants you to create several queries and to make changes to the table design of the database. To do so, you'll complete the following steps:

1. Open the **Agency** database, which is located in the Level.02\Case3 folder provided with your Data Files.

2. Modify the first record in the **tblDonor** table datasheet by changing the Title, First Name, and Last Name column values to your title and name. Close the table.

3. Create a query to find all records in the tblDonation table in which the AgencyID field value starts with either the letter R or the letter W. Display all fields in the query recordset, and sort in descending order by DonationValue. Save the query as **qryROrWAgencyDonations**, run the query, and then close it.

4. Make a copy of the qryAgenciesByCity query using the new name **qryNonSalinaAgencies**. Modify the new query to select all records in which the City field value is not Salina. Save and run the query, and then close it.

EXPLORE

5. The existing qryDonationsAfterPickupCharge query displays the DonorID, AgencyName, DonationDescription, and DonationValue fields for all donations that require a pickup, along with the NetDonation calculated field that displays the results of subtracting $8.75 from the DonationValue field value. Make a copy of the qryDonationsAfterPickupCharge query using the new name **qryNetDonations**. Modify the new query to select *all* records, to display the PickupRequired field, and to sort only in descending order by NetDonation. Also, change the NetDonation calculated field to subtract the delivery charge of $8.75 from the DonationField value when a pickup is required and to otherwise use the DonationValue field value. Save and run the query, and then close it.

6. Create a query to display all records from the tblAgency table, selecting all the fields except the ContactFirstName and ContactLastName fields, and sorting in ascending order by AgencyName. Add a calculated field named **ContactName** as the third column that concatenates ContactFirstName, a space, and ContactLastName. Set the Caption property for the ContactName field to **Contact Name**. Save the query as **qryAgencyContactNames**, run the query, resize the new column to its best fit, and then save and close the query.

7. Create a parameter query to select the tblDonation table records for a DonationDesc (donation description) field value that the user specifies. If the user doesn't enter a DonationDesc field value, select all records from the table. Display all fields from the tblDonation table in the query recordset, and sort in ascending order by DonationValue. Save the query as **qryDonationDescParameter**. Run the query and enter no value as the DonationDesc field value, and then run the query again and enter **Cash** as the DonationDesc field value. Close the query.

EXPLORE

8. Create a crosstab query based on the qryNetDonations query. Use the AgencyName field values for the row headings, the PickupRequired field values for the column headings, and the sum of the NetDonation field values as the summarized value, and include row sums. Save the query as **qryNetDonationsCrosstab**. Change the column headings for the two rightmost columns to **No Pickup** and **Pickup Required**. Change the format of the displayed values to Standard with two decimal places. Resize the columns in the query recordset to their best fit, and then save and close the query.

9. Create a find duplicates query based on the qryNetDonations query. Select DonorID and AgencyName as the fields that might contain duplicates, and select the remaining fields in the query as additional fields in the query recordset. Save the query as **qryMultipleDonorDonations**, run the query, and then close it.

10. Create a find unmatched query that finds all records in the tblDonor table for which there is no matching record in the tblDonation table. Select all fields from the tblDonor table in the query recordset. Save the query as **qryDonorsWithoutDonations**, run the query, and then close it.

EXPLORE

11. Make a copy of the qryNetDonations query using the new name **qryTopNetDonations**. Modify the new query by using the Top Values property to select the top 40% of the records. Save and run the query, and then close the query.

12. Use the Input Mask Wizard to add an input mask to the Phone field in the **tblDonor** table. The ending input mask should use hyphens as separators, as in 987-654-3210, with only the last seven digits required; do not store the literal display characters if you are asked to do so. Update the Input Mask property everywhere the Phone field is used. Test the input mask by typing over an existing Phone field value, being sure not to change the value permanently by pressing the Esc key after you type the last digit in the Phone field. Close the table.

13. Designate the Level.02\Case3 folder as a trusted folder. (*Note:* Check with your instructor before adding a new trusted location.)

14. Close the Agency database without exiting Access, make a backup copy of the database, open the **Agency** database, compact and repair the database, close the database, and then exit Access.

| Challenge | **Case Problem 4** |

Apply the skills you've learned, and explore some new skills, to work with the data for a luxury property rental company.

Data File needed for this Case Problem: Vacation.accdb

GEM Ultimate Vacations Griffin and Emma MacElroy own and operate their own agency, GEM Ultimate Vacations, which specializes in locating and booking luxury rental properties in Europe and Africa. To track their guests, properties, and reservations, they created the Vacation database. Griffin and Emma want you to create several queries and to make changes to the table design. To do so, you'll complete the following steps:

1. Open the **Vacation** database, which is located in the Level.02\Case4 folder provided with your Data Files.

2. Modify the first record in the **tblGuest** table datasheet by changing the First Name and Last Name column values to your first and last names.

3. Create a query to find all records in the tblProperty table in which the PropertyName field value starts with the word Chateau. Display all fields except the Description field in the query recordset. Save the query as **qryChateauProperties**, run the query, and then close it.

4. Make a copy of the qryChateauProperties query using the new name **qryNonChateauProperties**. Modify the new query to find all records in the tblProperty table in which the PropertyName field value starts with a word other than Chateau, and sort in ascending order by PropertyName. Save and run the query, and then close it.

5. Create a query to find all records in the tblGuest table in which the City field value is Aurora, Chicago, or Crown Point. Use a list-of-values match for the selection criterion, and display all fields from the tblGuest table in the query recordset. Save the query as **qrySelectedGuests**, run the query, and then close it.

⊕ EXPLORE
6. Create a query to select all records from the tblProperty table with nightly rates of $1,700 or $2,000 in France or Italy. Display all fields except the Description field in the query recordset. Save the query as **qryFranceItalySelectedProperties**, run the query, and then close it.

7. Create a parameter query to select the tblProperty table records for a Country field value that the user specifies. If the user doesn't enter a Country field value, select all records from the table. Display all fields from the tblProperty table in the query recordset, and sort in ascending order by PropertyName. Save the query as **qryCountryParameter**. Run the query and enter no value as the Country field value, and then run the query again and enter **Scotland** as the Country field value. Close the query.

8. Create a query that contains all records from the tblGuest table and all matching records from the tblReservation table. Display all fields from the tblGuest table and all fields except GuestID from the tblReservation table. Save the query as **qryGuestsAndReservations**, run the query, and then close it. Create a crosstab query based on the qryGuestsAndReservations query. Use the City field values for the row headings, the People field values for the column headings, and the sum of the RentalRate field as the summarized value, and include row sums. Save the query as **qryReservationsCrosstab**, resize the columns in the query recordset to their best fit, and then save and close the query.

9. Create a find duplicates query based on the tblProperty table. Select Location and Country as the fields that might contain duplicates, and select the remaining fields in the table as additional fields in the query recordset. Save the query as **qryDuplicateLocations**, run the query, and then close it.

10. Create a find unmatched query that finds all records in the tblGuest table for which there is no matching record in the tblReservation table. Display the GuestFirstName, GuestLastName, City, and Phone fields from the tblGuest table in the query recordset. Save the query as **qryGuestsWithoutReservations**, run the query, and then close it.

EXPLORE 11. Modify the **qryTopRentalCost** query to use the Top Values property to select the top 30% of the records. Save and run the query, and then close it.

12. In the **tblReservation** table, change the PropertyID field data type to Lookup Wizard. Select the PropertyID, PropertyName, and Location fields from the tblProperty table, sort in ascending order by PropertyName, do not hide the key column, resize the lookup columns to their best fit, select PropertyID as the field to store in the table, and accept the default label for the look up column. View the tblReservation datasheet, resize the PropertyID column to its best fit, test the lookup field without changing a field value permanently, and then close the table.

EXPLORE 13. Open the **tblGuest** table in Design view. Change the StateProv field data type to Lookup Wizard using a list of values that you enter. In the Lookup Wizard dialog box, create two columns and type the following pairs of values: **Illinois** and **IL**, **Indiana** and **IN**, and **Ontario** and **ON**. Resize the lookup columns to their best fit, select Col2 as the field to store in the table, and accept the default label for the lookup column. View the tblGuest table datasheet, resize the lookup column to its best fit, test the lookup field without changing permanently field values, and then save and close the table.

EXPLORE 14. Define a field validation rule for the Bedrooms field in the **tblProperty** table. Acceptable field values for the Bedrooms field are values between 3 and 25, including those two values. Display the message **Value must be between 3 and 25** when a user enters an invalid Bedrooms field value. Save your table changes and then test the field validation rule for the Bedrooms field; be certain the field values are the same as they were before your testing.

15. Define a table validation rule for the **tblReservation** table to verify that StartDate field values precede EndDate field values in time. Use an appropriate validation message. Save your table changes, test the table validation rule, making sure any tested field values are the same as they were before your testing, and then close the table.

16. Designate the Level.02\Case4 folder as a trusted folder. (*Note:* Check with your instructor before adding a new trusted location.)

17. Close the Vacation database without exiting Access, make a backup copy of the database, open the **Vacation** database, compact and repair the database, close the database, and then exit Access.

| Create | | Case Problem 5 |

Work with the skills you've learned, and explore some new skills, to create a database for an Internet service provider.

There are no Data Files needed for this Case Problem.

Always Connected Everyday   Chris and Pat Dixon own and manage Always Connected Everyday (ACE), a successful Internet service provider (ISP) in your area. ACE provides Internet access to residential and business customers and offers a variety of access plans, from dial-up and DSL to wireless. Figure 5-46 shows the pricing options for the access plans ACE offers.

Figure 5-46

Access Plan	Monthly	Annually	Setup Fee
Dial-up limited	$9.95		
Dial-up no e-mail	$14.95	$149.50	
Dial-up unlimited	$19.95	$199.50	
DSL pro	$29.95		$69.00
DSL turbo	$49.95		$69.00
DSL business	$89.95		$129.00
Wireless city economy	$39.95		$99.00
Wireless city basic	$49.95		$99.00
Wireless city advanced	$64.95		$109.00
Wireless city business	$99.95		$199.00
Wireless rural basic	$59.95		$109.00

Dial-up plans are available in all communities served by ACE, and DSL and wireless access are limited by a customer's proximity to DSL phone lines or wireless towers. Within each type of service—dial-up, DSL, and wireless—ACE offers low-cost plans with either slower access speeds or fewer capabilities and more expensive plans with either higher access speeds or greater service and features.

Chris and Pat need you to create a database to track their plans, customers, and service calls. The process of creating a complete database—including all fields, tables, relationships, queries, forms, and other database objects—for ACE is an enormous undertaking. You will start with just a few database components, and then you will create additional objects and functionality in subsequent tutorials.

Complete the following steps to create the database and its initial objects:

1. Read the appendix titled "Relational Databases and Database Design" at the end of this book.
2. If you are not familiar with ISPs, use your Web browser to find out more about them, so that you know common terminology and offerings.
3. The initial database structure includes the following tables and fields:
    a. The **tblAccessPlan** table includes the fields shown in Figure 5-46, along with a primary key field, which you can define as an AutoNumber field.
    b. The **tblCustomer** table includes a unique customer account number; an optional company name; and first name, last name, address, city, state, zip, phone, access plan ID (foreign key), next billing date, and e-mail address for the customer; and the customer's user ID and password for accessing ACE's Web site.

4. Building on Step 3, for each field, determine and set its attributes, such as data type, field size, and validation rules.

5. Create the database structure using Access. Use the database name **ACE**, and save the database in the Level.02\Case5 folder provided with your Data Files. Create the tables with their fields, following the naming standards used in this tutorial. Be sure to set each field's properties correctly, including the Caption property. Select a primary key for each table, use an input mask for one field, and then define the relationships between the tables.

6. For each table, create a form that you'll use to view, add, edit, and delete records in that table.

7. For tables with one-to-many relationships, create a form with a main form for the primary table and a subform for the related table.

8. Design test data for each table in the database. Your tblCustomer table should contain at least 15 records. Make sure your test data covers common situations. For example, your test data should include at least two access plans with multiple customers using the plans; at least two access plans with no customers using it; multiple cities, phone prefixes, and next billing dates; residential customers with no company names; and commercial customers with company names and the first and last names of the company's contact. Use your first and last names for the first record in the tblCustomer table.

9. Add the test data to your tables using the forms you created in Steps 6 and 7.

10. Open each table datasheet, and resize all datasheet columns to their best fit.

11. For the foreign key field in the tblCustomer table, change the field's data type to Lookup Wizard, including both the foreign key and its description as lookup columns. If necessary, resize the lookup column in the table datasheet.

12. Create a query named **qryCustomerNames** that contains all the fields from the tblCustomer table. Add a calculated field named **CustomerName** as the first column that is either the company name or the concatenation of the last name, a comma, a space, and the first name; set its Caption property to **Customer Name**. Sort in ascending order by CustomerName.

13. Create one parameter query, one crosstab query, and one find unmatched query, and save them using appropriate object names.

14. Designate the Level.02\Case5 folder as a trusted folder. (*Note:* Check with your instructor before adding a new trusted location.)

15. Close the ACE database without exiting Access, make a backup copy of the database, open the **ACE** database, compact and repair the database, close the database, and then exit Access.

Research	**Internet Assignments**

Use the Internet to find and work with data related to the topics presented in this tutorial.

The purpose of the Internet Assignments is to challenge you to find information on the Internet that you can use to work effectively with this software. The actual assignments are updated and maintained on the Course Technology Web site. Log on to the Internet and use your Web browser to go to the Student Online Companion for New Perspectives Office 2007 at **www.course.com/np/office2007**. Then navigate to the Internet Assignments for this tutorial.

Review | **Quick Check Answers**

Session 5.1

1. Caption
2. Like
3. a wildcard that represents any string of characters in a pattern match query
4. to define a condition with two or more values
5. Use the Not logical operator to negate a condition.
6. IIf (or Immediate If)
7. when you want to prompt the user to enter the selection criterion when the query runs

Session 5.2

1. It performs aggregate function calculations on the values of one database field and displays the results in a spreadsheet format.
2. Simple Query Wizard, Crosstab Query Wizard, Find Duplicates Query Wizard, Find Unmatched Query Wizard
3. It finds duplicate records in a table or query based on the values in one or more fields.
4. It finds all records in a table or query that have no related records in a second table or query.
5. You limit the number of records displayed in the query results.
6. Access displays the first five records.

Session 5.3

1. A field that lets you select a value from a list of possible values
2. input mask
3. an Access feature that updates control properties in objects when you modify table field properties
4. A property that specifies the valid values that users can enter in a field. You could use this property to specify that users can enter only positive numeric values in a numeric field.
5. A property value that appears in a dialog box if a user violates the field's validation rule. You could display the message "Must be a positive integer" if the user enters a value less than or equal to zero.
6. Rich Text
7. Trusted

Ending Data Files

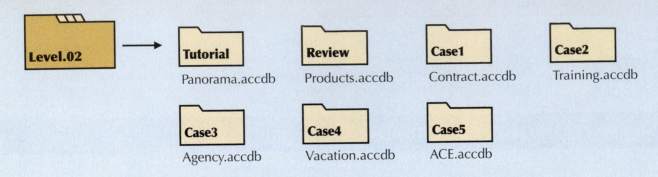

Level.02 → Tutorial
Panorama.accdb

Review
Products.accdb

Case1
Contract.accdb

Case2
Training.accdb

Case3
Agency.accdb

Case4
Vacation.accdb

Case5
ACE.accdb

Objectives

Session 6.1
- Change a lookup field to a Text field
- View and print database documentation
- Create datasheet, multiple items, and split forms
- Modify a form and anchor form controls in Layout view

Session 6.2
- Plan, design, and create a custom form in Design view and in Layout view
- Select, move, align, resize, delete, and rename controls in a form
- Add a combo box to a form
- Add form headers and footers to a form

Session 6.3
- Add a combo box to a form to find records
- Add a subform to a form
- Add calculated controls to a form and a subform
- Change the tab order in a form
- Improve the appearance of a form

Using Form Tools and Creating Custom Forms

Creating Forms for Entering and Maintaining Contract and Invoice Data

Case | Belmont Landscapes

Oren Belmont hired Lucia Perez to enhance the Panorama database, and she initially concentrated on standardizing the table design and creating queries for Belmont Landscapes. Sarah Fisher and her staff created a few forms before Lucia's hiring, and Lucia's next priority is to work with Sarah to create new forms that will be more useful and easier to use.

In this tutorial, you will create new forms for Belmont Landscapes. In creating the forms, you will use many Access form customization features, such as adding controls and a subform to a form, using combo boxes and calculated controls, and adding color and special effects to a form. These features will make it easier for Sarah and her staff to interact with the Panorama database.

Starting Data Files

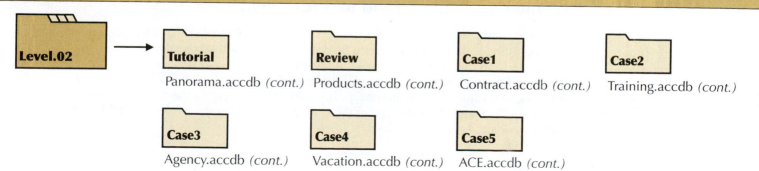

Level.02 → Tutorial
Panorama.accdb *(cont.)*

Review
Products.accdb *(cont.)*

Case1
Contract.accdb *(cont.)*

Case2
Training.accdb *(cont.)*

Case3
Agency.accdb *(cont.)*

Case4
Vacation.accdb *(cont.)*

Case5
ACE.accdb *(cont.)*

Session 6.1

Designing Forms

You've used wizards to create forms, and you've modified a form's design in Layout view to create a custom form. To create a **custom form**, you can modify an existing form in Layout view or in Design view, or you can design and create a form from scratch in Layout view or in Design view. You can design a custom form to match a paper form, to display some fields side by side and others top to bottom, to highlight certain sections with color, or to add visual effects. Whether you want to create a simple or complex custom form, planning the form's content and appearance is always your first step.

InSight	**Form Design Guidelines**

When you plan a form, you should keep in mind the following form design guidelines:
- Use forms to perform all database updates, because forms provide better readability and control than do table and query recordsets.
- Determine the fields and record source needed for each form. A form's **Record Source property** specifies the table or query that provides the fields for the form.
- Group related fields and position them in a meaningful, logical order.
- If users will refer to a source document while working with the form, design the form to match the source document closely.
- Identify each field value with a label that names the field, and align field values and labels for readability.
- Size the width of each text box to fully display the values it contains and also to provide a visual clue to users about the length of those values.
- Display calculated fields in a distinctive way, and prevent users from changing and updating them.
- Use default values, list boxes, and other form controls whenever possible to reduce user errors by minimizing keystrokes and limiting entries. A **control** is an item, such as a text box or command button, that you place in a form or report.
- Use colors, fonts, and graphics sparingly to keep the form uncluttered and to keep the focus on the data.
- Use a consistent style for all forms in a database.

Sarah and her staff had created a few forms and made table design changes before learning about proper form design guidelines. The guidelines recommend performing all database updates using forms. As a result, Belmont Landscapes won't use table or query datasheets to update the database, and Sarah asks if she should reconsider any of the table design changes you made to the Panorama database in the previous tutorial.

Changing a Lookup Field to a Text Field

The input mask and validation rule changes are important table design changes, but setting the CustomerID field to a lookup field in the tblContract table is an unnecessary change. A form combo box provides the same capability in a clearer, more flexible way. A **combo box** is a control that provides the features of a text box and a list box; it lets you choose a value from the list or type an entry. Before creating the new forms for Sarah, you'll change the data type of the CustomerID field in the tblContract table from a Lookup Wizard field to a Text field.

To change the data type of the CustomerID field:

▶ 1. Start Access, and then open the **Panorama** database in the Level.02\Tutorial folder provided with your Data Files.

Trouble? If the Security Warning is displayed below the Ribbon, either the Panorama database is not located in the Level.02\Tutorial folder or you did not designate that folder as a trusted folder. Make sure you opened the database in the Level.02\Tutorial folder, and make sure that it's a trusted folder.

▶ 2. Open the Navigation Pane, open the **tblContract** table in Design view, and then close the Navigation Pane.

▶ 3. Click the Field Name box for the CustomerID field, and then click the **Lookup** tab in the Field Properties pane. The Field Properties pane now displays the lookup properties for the CustomerID field. See Figure 6-1.

Tip

You can press the F11 key to open or close the Navigation Pane.

Lookup properties for the CustomerID field — Figure 6-1

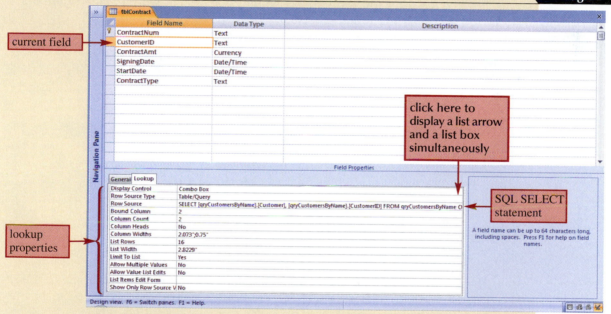

Notice the **Row Source property**, which specifies the data source for a control in a form or report or for a field in a table or query. The Row Source property is usually set to a table name, a query name, or an SQL statement. For the CustomerID field, the Row Source property is set to an SQL SELECT statement. You'll learn more about SQL later in the text.

To remove the lookup feature for the CustomerID field, you need to change the **Display Control property**, which specifies the default control used to display a field, from Combo Box to Text Box.

▶ 4. Click the right side of the **Display Control** property box, and then click **Text Box**. All the lookup properties in the Field Properties pane disappear, and the CustomerID field changes back to a Text field without lookup properties.

▶ 5. Click the **General** tab in the Field Properties pane and notice that the properties for a Text field still apply to the CustomerID field.

> **6.** Save the table, switch to Datasheet view, resize the Customer ID column to its best fit, and then click one of the **CustomerID** text boxes. An arrow does not appear in the CustomerID text box because the field is no longer a lookup field.

> **7.** Save the table, and then close the tblContract table.

Before you could change the CustomerID field in the tblContract table to a lookup field in the previous tutorial, you had to delete the one-to-many relationship between the tblCustomer and tblContract tables. Now that you've changed the data type of the CustomerID field back to a Text field, you'll view the table relationships to make sure that the tables in the Panorama database are related correctly.

To view the table relationships in the Relationships window:

> **1.** On the Ribbon, click the **Database Tools** tab, and then in the Show/Hide group, click the **Relationships** button to open the Relationships window. See Figure 6-2.

Figure 6-2	Panorama database tables in the Relationships window

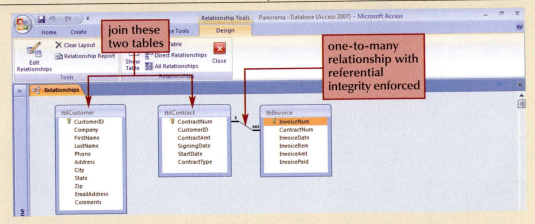

The primary tblContract table and the related tblInvoice table have a one-to-many relationship with referential integrity enforced. You need to establish a similar one-to-many relationship between the tblCustomer and tblContract tables.

> **2.** Click **CustomerID** in the tblCustomer field list, drag it to **CustomerID** in the tblContract field list, and then release the mouse button to open the Edit Relationships dialog box.

> **3.** Click the **Enforce Referential Integrity** check box, click the **Cascade Update Related Fields** check box, and then click the **Create** button to define the one-to-many relationship between the two tables and to close the dialog box. The join line connecting the tblCustomer and tblContract tables indicates the type of relationship (one-to-many) with referential integrity enforced (bold join line).

Sarah asks you to print a copy of the database relationships to use as a reference, and she asks if other Access documentation is available.

Printing Database Relationships and Using the Documenter

You can print the Relationships window to document the fields, tables, and relationships in a database. You can also use the **Documenter**, another Access tool, to create detailed documentation of all, or selected, objects in a database. For each selected object, the Documenter lets you print documentation, such as the object's properties and relationships, and the fields used by the object and their properties. You can use the documentation to help you understand an object and to help you plan changes to that object.

Using the Documenter
Reference Window

- Start Access and open the database you want to document.
- In the Analyze group on the Database Tools tab, click the Database Documenter button.
- Select the object(s) you want to document.
- If necessary, click the Options button to select specific documentation options for the selected object(s), and then click the OK button.
- Click the OK button, print the documentation, and then close the Object Definition window.

Next, you'll print the Relationships window and use the Documenter to create documentation for the tblContract table. Sarah will show her staff the tblContract table documentation as a sample of the information that the Documenter provides.

To print the Relationships window and use the Documenter:

1. In the Tools group on the Design tab, click the **Relationship Report** button to open the Relationships for Panorama report in Print Preview. See Figure 6-3.

Relationships for Panorama report · Figure 6-3

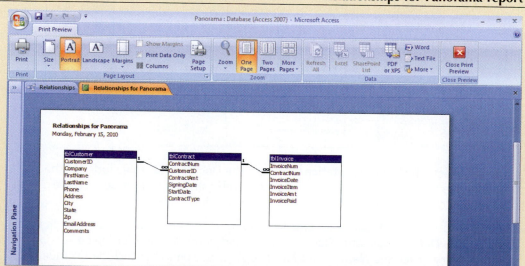

2. In the Print group on the Print Preview tab, click the **Print** button, select your printer in the Name text box, and then click the **OK** button. Access prints the Relationships for Panorama report.

▶ **3.** Click the **Close 'Relationships for Panorama'** button ⊠ on the Relationships for Panorama tab to close the window. A dialog box opens and asks if you want to save the report. Because you can easily create the report at any time, you won't save it.

▶ **4.** Click the **No** button to close the report without saving changes, and then close the Relationships window.

Now you'll use the Documenter to create detailed documentation for the tblContract table as a sample to show Sarah.

▶ **5.** On the Ribbon, click the **Database Tools** tab. In the Analyze group, click the **Database Documenter** button, and then click the **Tables** tab (if necessary) in the Documenter dialog box. See Figure 6-4.

| Figure 6-4 | Documenter dialog box |

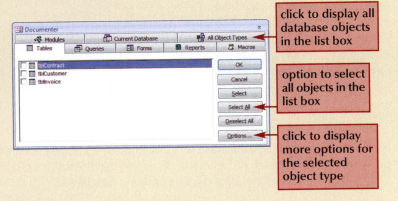

click to display all database objects in the list box

option to select all objects in the list box

click to display more options for the selected object type

▶ **6.** Click the **tblContract** check box, and then click the **Options** button. The Print Table Definition dialog box opens. See Figure 6-5.

| Figure 6-5 | Print Table Definition dialog box |

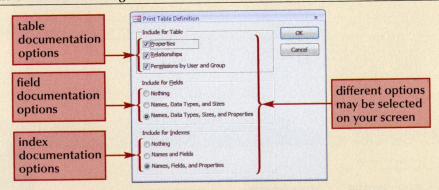

table documentation options

field documentation options

index documentation options

different options may be selected on your screen

You select which documentation you want the Documenter to include for the selected table, its fields, and its indexes. Sarah asks you to include all table documentation and the second options for fields and for indexes.

▶ **7.** Make sure all check boxes are checked in the Include for Table section, click the **Names, Data Types, and Sizes** option button in the Include for Fields section (if necessary), click the **Names and Fields** option button in the Include for Indexes section (if necessary), click the **OK** button, and then click the **OK** button. The Documenter dialog box closes and the Object Definition report opens in Print Preview.

▶ **8.** In the Zoom group on the Print Preview tab, click the arrow on the **Zoom** button, and then click **Zoom 100%**.

When you need to view more of the horizontal contents of an open object, you can close the Navigation Pane. You can also minimize the Ribbon when you want to view more of the vertical contents of an open object. To minimize the Ribbon, double-click any tab on the Ribbon, or right-click a tab and then click Minimize the Ribbon. To restore the Ribbon, double-click any tab on the Ribbon, or right-click a tab and then click Minimize the Ribbon (it's a toggle option).

▶ **9.** Double-click the **Print Preview** tab on the Ribbon to minimize the Ribbon, and then scroll down the report so you can see the date at the top of the window. See Figure 6-6.

Tip

After minimizing the Ribbon, if you click, instead of double-click, any tab on the Ribbon, the full Ribbon appears and then minimizes again as soon as you click anywhere outside the Ribbon.

Object Definition report for the tblContract table ◀ **Figure 6-6**

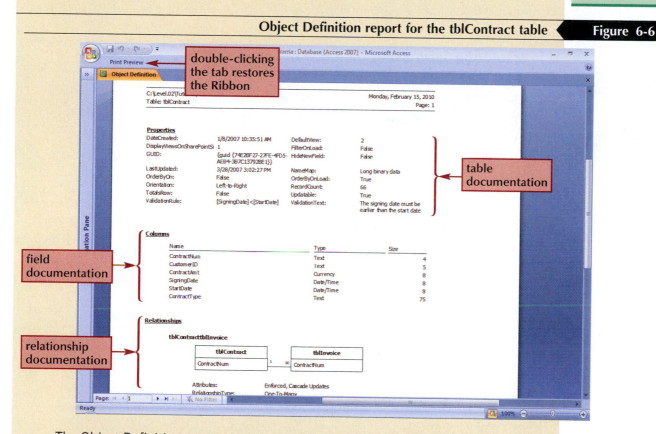

The Object Definition report displays table, field, and relationship documentation for the tblContract table.

▶ **10.** Scroll down the Object Definition report to view the remaining information in the documentation, print the documentation if your instructor asks you to do so, and then close the Object Definition report. Notice that the Navigation Pane is closed and the Ribbon is minimized.

Sarah and her staff will review the printout of the Relationships window and the documentation about the tblContract table and decide if they need to view additional documentation. Next, you'll create new forms for Sarah and her staff.

Creating Forms Using Form Tools

The Panorama database currently contains four forms: the frmContract form was created using the Form tool, the frmCustomer form was created using the Form Wizard, and the frmCustomerContracts main form and its frmContractSubform subform were created using the Form Wizard. Only the frmCustomer form is a custom form. Design changes that were made to the frmCustomer form in Layout view include changing its AutoFormat, changing its form title color and its line type, adding a picture, and moving a field.

Sarah wants to view the forms that can be created using other types of form tools, so she can determine if any of the forms would be helpful to her when updating the database.

Creating a Form Using the Datasheet Tool

The **Datasheet tool** creates a form in a datasheet format that contains all the fields in the source table or query. You'll use the Datasheet tool to create a form based on the tblContract table.

Tip

When you use the Datasheet tool, the record source (either a table or query) for the form must either be open or selected in the Navigation Pane.

To create the form using the Datasheet tool:

1. Open the Navigation Pane, and then click **tblContract** (if necessary) in the Navigation Pane.

2. Double-click the **Create** tab on the Ribbon to restore the Ribbon and to display the Create tab.

3. In the Forms group, click the **More Forms** button, and then click **Datasheet**. The Datasheet tool creates a form showing every field in the tblContract table in a datasheet format. See Figure 6-7.

Figure 6-7 **Form created by the Datasheet tool**

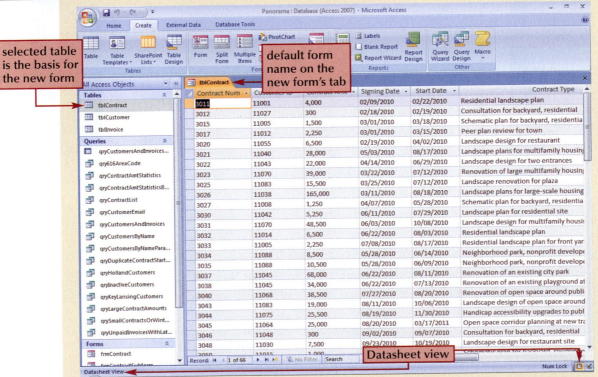

The new form displays all the records and fields from the tblContract table in Datasheet view and in the same format as a table or query recordset displayed in Datasheet view. "Datasheet View" appears on the status bar, as do two view icons, one for Datasheet view and the other for Design view. The form name, tblContract, is the same name as the table used as the basis for the form, but you should change the name when you save the form.

When working with forms, you view and update data in Form view, you view and make simple design changes in Layout view, and you make simple and complex design changes in Design view. For the form created with the Datasheet tool, you'll check the available view options.

Tip

Each table and query in a database must have a unique name. Although you could name a form or report the same as a table or query, it would cause confusion. Fortunately, using object name prefixes prevents this confusing practice.

▶ **4.** Click the **Home** tab on the Ribbon.

▶ **5.** In the Views group, click the arrow on the **View** button. See Figure 6-8.

View options for a form created by the Datasheet tool ◀ **Figure 6-8**

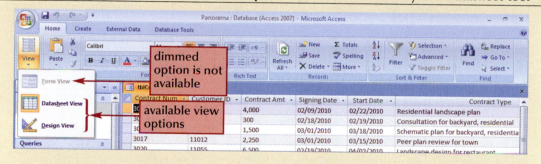

Form view is dimmed, which means that it's unavailable for this form type, and Layout view is not an option in the list. Datasheet view allows you to view and update data, and Design view is the only other view option for this form.

Sarah and her staff don't have a need for a form with a datasheet format, so you won't save it.

▶ **6.** Click the arrow on the **View** button to close the menu, and then close the form without saving it.

Next, you'll show Sarah a form created using the Multiple Items tool.

Creating a Form Using the Mulitple Items Tool

The **Multiple Items tool** creates a customizable form that displays multiple records from a source table or query in a datasheet format. You'll use the Multiple Items tool to create a form based on the tblContract table.

To create the form using the Multiple Items tool:

▶ **1.** Make sure that the tblContract table is selected in the Navigation Pane, and then click the **Create** tab on the Ribbon.

▶ **2.** In the Forms group, click the **Multiple Items** button. The Multiple Items tool creates a form showing every field in the tblContract table and opens the form in Layout view. See Figure 6-9.

Figure 6-9 | **Form created by the Multiple Items tool**

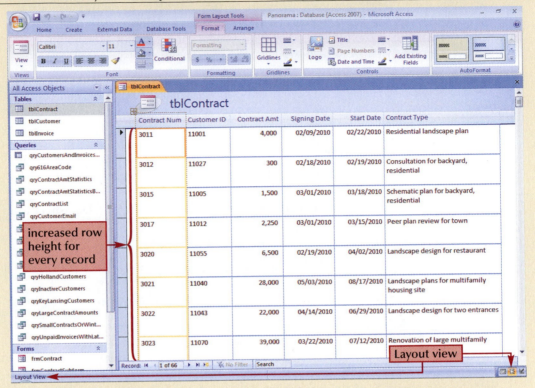

The new form displays all the records and fields from the tblContract table in a format similar to a datasheet, but the row height for every record is increased compared to a standard datasheet. Unlike a form created by the Datasheet tool, which has only Datasheet view and Design view available, a Multiple Items form is a standard form that can be displayed in Form view, Layout view, and Design view, as indicated by the buttons on the right side of the status bar.

For the form created with the Multiple Items tool, you'll check the available view options.

▶ 3. In the Views group, click the arrow on the **View** button. Form view, Layout view, and Design view are the available views for this form. See Figure 6-10.

Figure 6-10 | **View options for a form created by the Multiple Items tool**

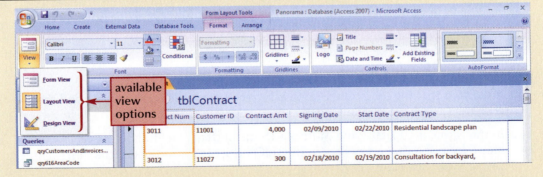

Sarah thinks this new form could be more useful than the form created by the Datasheet tool, but she doesn't have an immediate need for the form, so you won't save it.

4. Click the arrow on the **View** button to close the menu, and then close the form without saving it.

The final form tool you'll show Sarah is the Split Form tool.

Creating a Form Using the Split Form Tool

The **Split Form tool** creates a customizable form that displays the data in a form in both Form view and Datasheet view at the same time. The two views are synchronized with each other at all times. Selecting a field in one view selects the same field in the other view. You can add, change, or delete data from either view. Typically, you'd use Datasheet view to locate a record, and then use Form view to update the record. You'll use the Split Form tool to create a form based on the tblContract table.

To create the form using the Split Form tool:

1. Make sure that the tblContract table is selected in the Navigation Pane, and then click the **Create** tab on the Ribbon.

2. In the Forms group, click the **Split Form** button, and then close the Navigation Pane. The Split Form tool creates a split form that opens in Layout view and displays a form with the contents of the first record in the tblContract table on the top and a datasheet of the first several records in the tblContract table on the bottom. See Figure 6-11.

Form created by the Split Form tool ◄ **Figure 6-11**

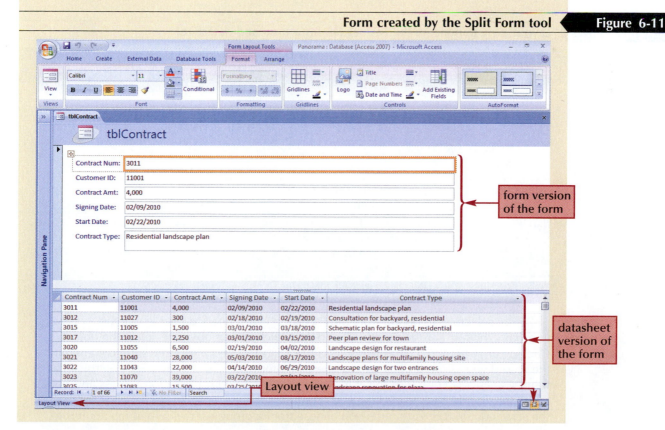

In Layout view, you can make layout and design changes to the form and layout changes to the datasheet. Sarah thinks the split form will be a useful addition to the

Panorama database, and she wants you to show her the types of design modifications that are possible with a split form.

Modifying a Split Form in Layout View

You use the Format tab on the Ribbon, as shown in Figure 6-12, to modify the format and appearance of a split form and all other form types.

Figure 6-12 | Layout view options on the Format tab

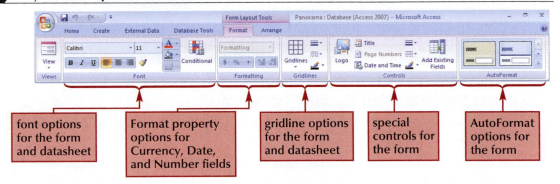

For a split form, some options on the Format tab apply to the form or the datasheet, other options apply to only the form, and the Add Existing Fields in the Controls group applies to both the form and the datasheet at the same time, as described in Figure 6-13.

Figure 6-13 | Layout view options on the Format tab for a form and datasheet

Group	Form Is Active	Datasheet Is Active
Font	Selected option applied to the selected labels and text boxes.	Selected option applied to every field value in the datasheet.
Formatting	Selected option applied to the selected text box, which must be a Currency, Date, or Number field.	Selected option applied to every field value in the active column, which must be a Currency, Date, or Number field.
Gridlines	Selected option applied to every label and text box in the form.	Only the options in the Gridlines list apply to the entire datasheet.
Controls	All options applied only to the form, except for the Add Existing Fields button, which applies to both the form and the datasheet.	Options do not apply in a datasheet, except for the Add Existing Fields button, which applies to both the form and the datasheet.
AutoFormat	Selected choice applied only to the form.	Not available.

Before selecting an option from the Format tab, you need to decide whether you want to modify the form or the datasheet, and then click in that object to select the object. Clicking anywhere in a datasheet selects the datasheet and also selects the column and the record you clicked. Clicking anywhere in a form selects the form. For controls in a form, you click a control to select it. To select several controls in a form, press and hold down the Shift key while clicking each control; a thicker, colored border appears around the selected controls. An option you choose from a group on the Format tab applies to all selected controls.

In previous tutorials, you've shown Sarah how to use some of the form modification options on the Format tab, and you'll use other options on this tab later in this tutorial, so you won't show her any Format tab options now. Instead, you'll show her some options on the Arrange tab. For a split form, options on the Arrange tab apply only to the form and do not apply to the datasheet.

To modify the form in Layout view:

▶ **1.** Click the **Arrange** tab on the Ribbon.

The form's label and text box controls for the fields from the tblContract table are grouped in a control layout. A **control layout** is a set of controls grouped together in a form or report, so that you can manipulate the set as a single control. For example, you can move and resize all the controls in a control layout as a group—moving or resizing one control in the control layout moves or resizes all controls in the control layout. You also can rearrange fields and their attached labels within the control layout.

All the text boxes in the control layout are the same width. The first five text boxes—from the ContractNum text box to the StartDate text box—are much wider than necessary. However, if you reduce the width of any text box in a control layout, all text boxes in the control layout are also resized. Sarah wants you to reduce the width of the first five text boxes and to move and resize the ContractType label and text box.

▶ **2.** Click the **layout selector** ⊞, which is located at the top-left corner of the Contract Num label, to select the entire control layout. An orange outline, which identifies the controls that you've selected, appears around the labels and text boxes in the form. See Figure 6-14.

Control layout selected in the form — Figure 6-14

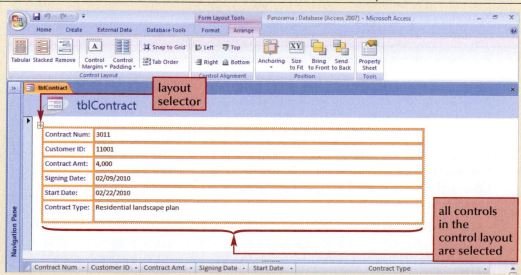

Next, you'll resize the text boxes in the control layout.

▶ **3.** Click the **ContractNum** text box (the text box that contains the value 3011) to deselect the control layout and select the ContractNum text box, hold down the **Shift** key, click each of the five text boxes below the ContractNum text box, and then release the **Shift** key to select all six text boxes in the control layout. When you resize one of the text boxes, all six selected text boxes will be resized equally.

> **4.** Position the pointer on the right edge of the SigningDate text box until the pointer changes to a ↔ shape, click and drag to the left until the right edge is just to the right of the SigningDate field value, and then release the mouse button. You've resized all six text boxes. See Figure 6-15.

Figure 6-15 **After resizing the text boxes in the control layout**

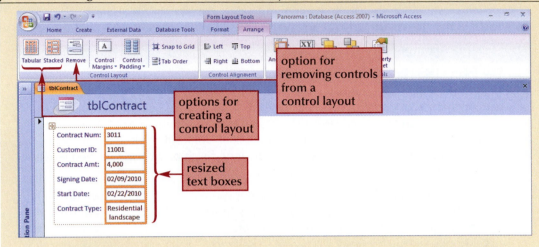

Trouble? If you resize the text boxes too far to the left, number signs appear inside the SigningDate and StartDate text boxes. Drag the right edge of the text boxes slightly to the right and repeat the process until the date values are visible inside the text boxes.

The control layout for the form is a **stacked layout**, which arranges text box controls vertically with a label to the left of each control; you click the Stacked button in the Control Layout group to place selected controls in a stacked layout. You can also choose a **tabular layout**, which arranges text box controls in a datasheet format with labels above each column; you click the Tabular button in the Control Layout group to place selected controls in a tabular layout.

You can now remove the ContractType text box and its label from the stacked layout, move the two controls, and then resize the text box.

> **5.** Click the **ContractType** text box, and then in the Control Layout group, click the **Remove** button. An orange outline appears around the ContractType text box and its label, indicating that the two controls have been removed from the stacked layout.

> **6.** Make sure that the ContractType text box and its label are selected, and then drag the two controls up and to the right until their tops are aligned with the top of the ContractNum controls. See Figure 6-16. (*Note:* You will resize the ContractType text box in the next step.)

> **7.** Click the **ContractType** text box so that it's the only selected control, and then drag the right edge of the control to the right and the bottom edge of the control down to the positions shown in Figure 6-16.

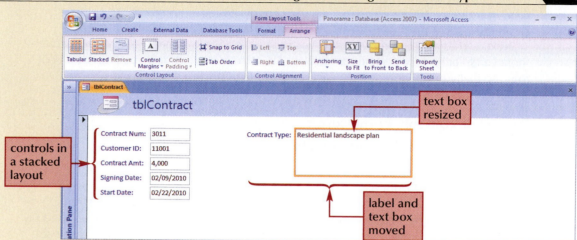

After moving and resizing the ContractType controls | Figure 6-16

Trouble? It won't cause any problems if the two ContractType controls on your screen are in slightly different positions than the ones shown in the figure or your ContractType text box is not exactly the same size.

You do not usually need to change the default settings for the **Control Margins property**, which controls the spacing around the text inside a control, and the **Control Padding property**, which controls the spacing around the outside of a control. However, you'll show Sarah the effects of changing these properties.

8. Click one of the controls in the stacked layout, click the **layout selector** ⊞ to select all controls in the stacked layout, click the **Control Margins** button in the Control Layout group, and then click **Medium**. The text inside the stacked layout controls moves down and to the right.

9. Click the **Control Margins** button, click **Wide** and observe the effect of this setting on the text inside the controls, click the **Control Margins** button, click **None** and observe the effect of this setting, click the **Control Margins** button, and then click **Narrow**. Narrow is the default setting for the Control Margins property.

Narrow is also the default setting for the Control Padding property.

10. In the Control Layout group, click the **Control Padding** button, click **Medium** and observe the change to the spacing around the controls, and then repeat for the other settings of this property, making sure you set the property to **Narrow** as your final step.

Next, you'll show Sarah how to anchor controls.

Anchoring Controls in a Form

You can design attractive forms that use the screen dimensions effectively when all the users of a database have the same sized monitors and use the same screen resolution. How do you design attractive forms when users have a variety of monitor sizes and screen resolutions? If you design a form to fit on large monitors using high screen resolutions, then only a portion of the controls in the form fit on smaller monitors with lower resolutions, forcing users to scroll the form. If you design a form to fit on small monitors with low screen resolutions, then the form is displayed on larger monitors in a small area in the upper-left corner of the screen, making the form look unattractively cramped. As a compromise, you can anchor the controls in the form. The **Anchor property** for a control automatically resizes the control and places the control in the same relative position on the screen as the screen size and resolution change. Unfortunately, when you use the Anchor property, Access doesn't scale the control's font size to match the screen size and resolution.

Next, you'll show Sarah how to anchor controls in a form. Because all monitors at Belmont Landscapes are the same size and use the same resolution, first you'll save the split form, so that you can demonstrate anchoring and then discard those changes to the form.

To anchor controls in the form:

▶ 1. Save the form as **frmContractSplit**.

You can't anchor individual controls in a control layout; you can only anchor the entire control layout as a group. You've already removed the ContractType controls from the stacked layout, so you can anchor them separately from the stacked layout. You'll remove the SigningDate and StartDate controls from the stacked layout, so you'll have three sets of controls to anchor—the stacked layout is one set, the ContractType controls are in the second set, and the SigningDate and StartDate controls make up the third set.

▶ 2. Use **Shift + Click** to select the **SigningDate** and **StartDate** text boxes, and then click the **Remove** button in the Control Layout group to remove these two controls and their labels from the stacked layout.

First, you'll anchor the selected SigningDate and StartDate controls.

▶ 3. In the Position group on the Arrange tab, click the **Anchoring** button to open the Anchoring gallery. See Figure 6-17.

Figure 6-17	Displaying the Anchoring gallery

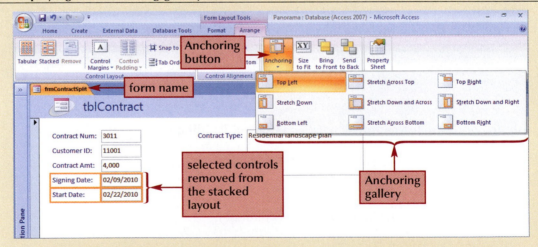

Four of the nine options in the Anchoring gallery fix the position of the selected controls in the top left (the default setting), bottom left, top right, or bottom right positions in the form. If other controls block the corner positions for controls you're anchoring for the first time, the new controls are positioned in relation to the blocking controls. The other five anchoring options resize, or stretch, and position the selected controls.

You'll anchor the SigningDate and StartDate controls in the bottom left and the ContractType controls in the top right.

▶ 4. Click **Bottom Left** in the Anchoring gallery, click the **ContractType** text box, click the **Anchoring** button, and then click **Top Right**. The SigningDate and StartDate controls shifted down, and the ContractType controls shifted to the right.

Next, you'll open the Navigation Pane, and then increase the height of the form to simulate the effect of a larger screen for the form.

▶ 5. Open the Navigation Pane. The two sets of controls on the left shift to the right, because the horizontal dimensions of the form decreased from the left, and these two sets of controls are anchored to the left in the form. The ContractType controls remain in the same position in the form.

▶ 6. Position the pointer on the border between the form and the datasheet until the pointer changes to a ✚ shape, and then drag down until you see only the column headings and the first row in the datasheet. The bottom set of controls shifts down, because it's anchored to the bottom, and the two sets of controls at the top remain in the same positions in the form. See Figure 6-18.

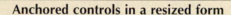
Anchored controls in a resized form   Figure 6-18

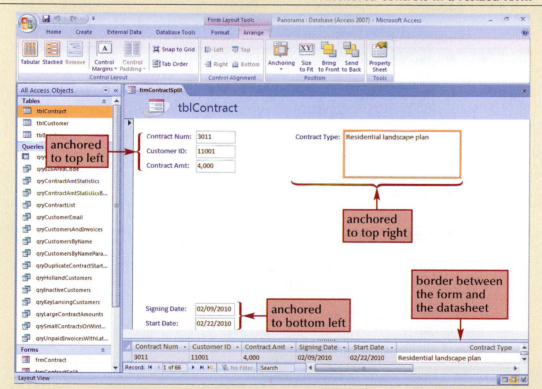

Finally, you'll show Sarah one of the anchoring options that resizes the ContractType text box as the form dimensions change.

▶ 7. Click the **ContractType** text box, click the **Anchoring** button, and then click **Stretch Down and Right**. Because the ContractType text box is already anchored to the top right, it can't stretch any more to the right, but it does stretch down to increase the height of the text box.

▶ 8. Position the pointer on the border between the form and the datasheet until the pointer changes to a ✚ shape, and then drag up until you can see several rows in the datasheet. The bottom set of controls shifts up, and the bottom edge of the ContractType text box shifts up, reducing its height.

> You've finished showing Sarah Layout view changes to the split form, so you can close the form without saving the anchoring changes.
>
> ▶ **9.** Close the frmContractSplit form without saving your design changes.
>
> ▶ **10.** If you are not continuing on to the next session, close the Panorama database, and then exit Access.

You've used form wizards and form tools to create forms, and you've modified forms in Layout view. In the next session, you will continue your work with forms, concentrating on the techniques, tools, and options available in Design view.

Review | **Session 6.1 Quick Check**

1. According to the form design guidelines, which object(s) should you use to perform all database updates?
2. The _____ property specifies the data source for a control in a form or report or for a field in a table or query.
3. What is the Documenter?
4. What is the Multiple Items tool?
5. What is a split form?
6. The _____ property for a control automatically resizes the control and places the control in the same relative position on the screen as the screen's size and resolution change.

Session 6.2

Planning and Designing a Custom Form

Sarah needs a form to enter and view information about Belmont Landscapes' contracts and their related invoices. She wants the information in a single form, and she asks Lucia to design a form for her review.

After several discussions with Sarah and her staff, Lucia prepared a paper design for a custom form to display a contract and its related invoices. Lucia then used her paper design to create the form shown in Figure 6-19.

Lucia's design for the custom form   Figure 6-19

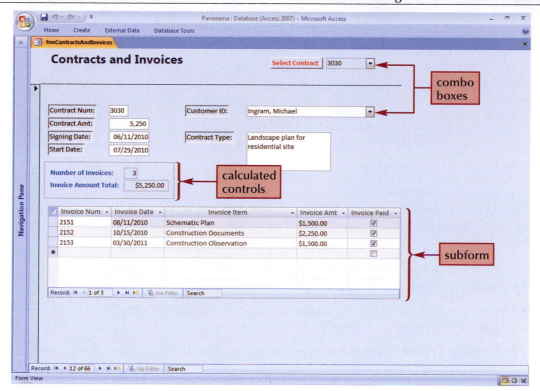

Notice that the top of the form displays a title and a combo box to select a contract record. Below these items are six field values with identifying labels from the tblContract table; these fields are the ContractNum, ContractAmt, SigningDate, StartDate, CustomerID, and ContractType fields. The CustomerID field is displayed in a combo box and the other field values are displayed in text boxes. The tblInvoice table fields appear in a subform, a separate form contained within another form. Unlike the tblContract table data, which displays identifying labels to the left of the field values in text boxes, the tblInvoice table data is displayed in datasheet format with identifying column headings above the field values. Finally, Number of Invoices and Invoice Amount Total in the main form display calculated controls based on the content of the subform.

Creating a Custom Form in Design View

To create Lucia's custom form, you could use the Form Wizard to create a basic version of the form and then customize it in Layout and Design views. However, to create Lucia's form, you would need to make many modifications to a basic form created by a wizard, so you will create the form directly in Design view. Creating forms in Design view is easy once you've done one form, and Design view allows you more control, precision, and options than creating forms in Layout view. You'll also find that you'll create forms more productively if you switch between Design view and Layout view, because some design modifications are easier to make in one of the two views than in the other view.

The Form Window in Design View

You use the Form window in Design view to create and modify forms. To create the custom form based on Lucia's design, you'll create a blank form, add the fields from the tblContract and tblInvoice tables, and then add other controls and make other form modifications.

Reference Window | Creating a Form in Design View

- Click the Create tab on the Ribbon.
- In the Forms group, click the Blank Form button.
- Click the Design View button on the status bar.
- Make sure the Field List pane is open, and then add the required fields to the form.
- Add other required controls to the form.
- Modify the size, position, and other properties as necessary for the fields and other controls in the form.
- Save the form.

The form you'll create will be a bound form. A **bound form** is a form that has a table or query as its record source. You use bound forms for maintaining and displaying table data. **Unbound forms** are forms that do not have a record source and are usually used for forms that help users navigate among the objects in a database. Now you'll create a blank bound form based on the tblContract table.

To create a blank form in Design view:

▶ **1.** If you took a break after the previous session, make sure that the Panorama database is open and the Navigation Pane is open.

▶ **2.** Click the **Create** tab on the Ribbon and then, in the Forms group on the Create tab, click the **Blank Form** button. Access opens the Form window in Layout view.

▶ **3.** Click the **Design View** button ⬚ on the status bar to switch to Design view, and then close the Navigation Pane. See Figure 6-20.

Figure 6-20 Blank form in Design view

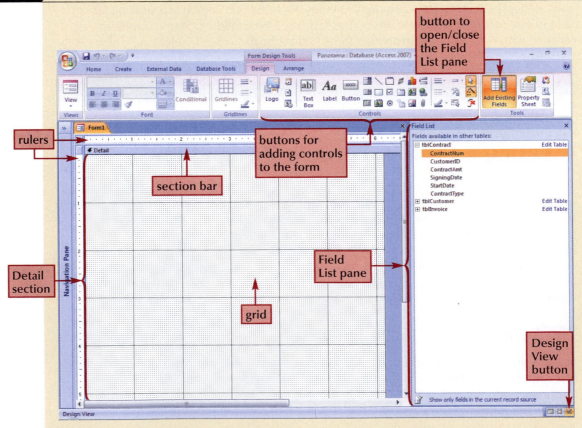

Trouble? If the Field List pane displays the "No fields available to be added to the current view" message, click the "Show all tables" link to display the tables in the Panorama database, and then click the plus sign next to tblContract in the Field List pane to display the fields in the table.

Trouble? If the tblContract table in the Field List pane is not expanded to show the fields in the table, click the plus sign next to tblContract to display the fields.

Design view contains the tools necessary to create a custom form. You create the form by placing controls in the blank form. You can place three kinds of controls in a form:

- A **bound control** is connected, or bound, to a field in the database based on the record source, or the underlying table or query. You use bound controls to display and maintain table field values.
- An **unbound control** is not connected to a field in the database. You use unbound controls to display text, such as a form title or instructions; to display lines, rectangles, and other objects; or to display graphics and pictures created using other software programs. An unbound control that displays text is called a **label**.
- A **calculated control** displays a value that is the result of an expression. The expression usually contains one or more fields, and the calculated control is recalculated each time any value in the expression changes.

To create a bound control, you add fields from the Field List pane to the Form window, and position the bound controls where you want them to appear in the form. To place other controls in a form or a report, you use the buttons in the Controls group on the Design tab; ScreenTips are available for each control in the Controls group. The buttons in the Controls group let you add to the form controls such as lines, rectangles, images, buttons, check boxes, and list boxes.

Design view for a form contains a **Detail section**, which is a rectangular area consisting of a grid with a section bar above the grid. You click the **section bar** to select the section in preparation for setting properties for the entire section. The **grid** consists of the area with dotted and solid lines that help you position controls precisely in a form. In the Detail section, you place bound controls, unbound controls, and calculated controls for your form. You can change the size of the Detail section by dragging its edges.

Rulers at the top and left edges of the Detail section define the horizontal and vertical dimensions of the form and serve as guides for placing controls in a form.

Your first task is to add bound controls to the Detail section for the six fields from the tblContract table.

Adding Fields to a Form

When you add a bound control to a form, Access adds a text box and, to its left, an attached label. The text box displays a field value from the record source. The attached label displays either the Caption property value for the field, if the Caption property value has been set, or the field name. To create a bound control, you first display the Field List pane by clicking the Add Existing Fields button in the Tools group on the Design tab. Then you double-click a field in the Field List pane to add the bound control to the Detail section. You can also drag a field from the Field List pane to the Detail section.

Next, you'll add bound controls to the Detail section for the six fields in the Field List pane. The Field List pane displays the three tables in the Panorama database, and the six fields in the tblContract table.

To add bound controls from the tblContract table to the grid:

▶ 1. Double-click **ContractNum** in the Field List pane. Access adds a bound control in the Detail section of the form, removes the tblCustomer and tblInvoice tables from the "Fields available for this view" section of the Field List pane, and places the two tables in the "Fields available in related tables" section of the Field List pane.

▶ 2. Repeat Step 1 for the **ContractAmt**, **SigningDate**, **StartDate**, **CustomerID**, and **ContractType** fields, in this order, in the Field List pane. Six bound controls—one for each of the six fields in the Field List pane—have been added in the Detail section of the form. See Figure 6-21.

Figure 6-21	Adding text boxes and attached labels as bound controls to a form

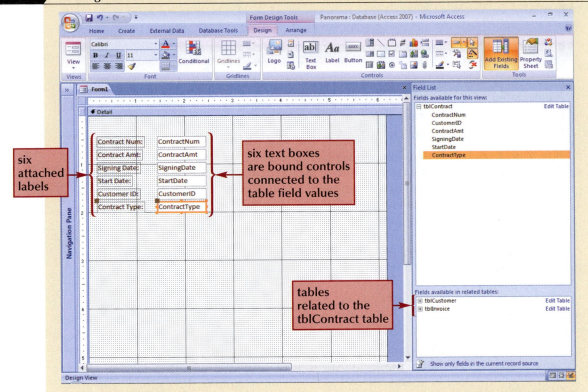

You should periodically save your work as you create a form, so you'll now save the form.

▶ 3. Click the **Save** button on the Quick Access Toolbar. The Save As dialog box opens.

▶ 4. With the default name Form1 selected in the Form Name text box, type **frmContractsAndInvoices**, and then press the **Enter** key. The tab for the form now displays the form name, and the form design is saved in the Panorama database.

You've added the fields you need to the grid, so you can close the Field List pane.

▶ 5. In the Tools group on the Design tab, click the **Add Existing Fields** button to close the Field List pane.

Creating and modifying a form in Design view might seem awkward at first. With practice you will become comfortable working with custom forms.

To design a form productively, you should keep in mind the following suggestions:

- You can click the Undo button one or more times immediately after you make one or more errors or make undesired form adjustments.
- You should back up your database frequently, especially before you create new objects or customize existing objects. If you run into difficulty, you can revert to your most recent backup copy of the database.
- You should save your form after you've completed a portion of your work successfully and before you need to perform steps you've never done before. If you're not satisfied with subsequent steps, close the form without saving the changes you made since your last save, and then open the form and perform the steps again.
- You can always close the form, make a copy of the form in the Navigation Pane, and practice with the copy.
- Adding controls, setting properties, and performing other tasks in Access in the correct way should work all the time with consistent results, but in rare instances, you might find a feature doesn't work properly. If a feature you've used succesfully doesn't work suddenly, you should save your work, close the database, make a backup copy of the database, open the database, and then compact and repair the database. Performing a compact and repair resolves most of these types of problems.

Compare your form's Detail section with Sarah's design, and notice that you need to move the ContractType bound control up and to the right. To do so, you must select and move the bound control.

Selecting, Moving, and Aligning Controls

Six text boxes now appear in the form's Detail section, one below the other. Each text box is a bound control connected to a field in the underlying table. Each text box has an attached label to its left. Each text box and attached label pair is a control in the form, and each individual text box is also a control in the form, as is each individual label. When you select a control, the control becomes outlined in orange, and eight squares, called handles, appear on its four corners and at the midpoints of its four edges. The larger handle in a control's upper-left corner is its **move handle**, which you use to move the control. You use the other seven handles, called **sizing handles**, to resize the control. When you work in Design view, controls you place in the form do not become part of a control layout, so you can individually select, move, resize, and otherwise manipulate one control without also changing the other controls. However, at any time you can select a group of controls and place them in a control layout—either a stacked layout or a tabular layout.

Selecting and Moving Controls

- Click the control to select it. To select several controls at once, press and hold down the Shift key while clicking each control. Handles appear around all selected controls.
- To move a single selected control, drag the control's move handle, which is the handle in the upper-left corner, to its new position.
- To move a group of selected controls, point to any selected control until the pointer changes to a move pointer, and then drag the group of selected controls to its new position.
- To move selected controls in small increments, press the appropriate arrow key.
- To move selected controls to the next nearest grid dot, hold down the Ctrl key and press the appropriate arrow key.

Based on Lucia's design for the custom form, you must select the ContractType bound control and move it up and to the right in the Detail section. The ContractType bound control consists of a field-value text box, labeled ContractType, and an attached label, labeled Contract Type, to its left.

To select the ContractType bound control:

▸ 1. If necessary, click the **ContractType** text box to select it. Move handles, which are the larger handles, appear on the upper-left corners of the selected text box control and its attached label. Sizing handles also appear, but only on the text box. See Figure 6-22.

Figure 6-22 Selecting the ContractType bound control

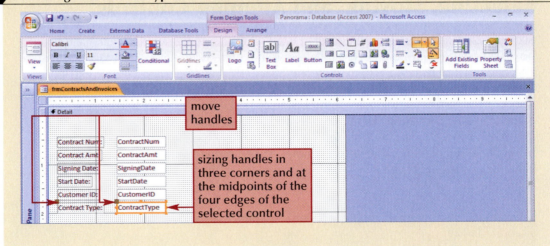

You can move a text box and its attached label together. To move them, place the pointer anywhere on the border of the text box, but not on a move handle or a sizing handle. When the pointer changes to a ⬆ shape, you can drag the text box and its attached label to the new location. As you move a control, an outline of the control moves on the rulers to indicate the current position of the control as you drag it. To move a group of selected controls, point to any selected control until the pointer changes to a ⬆ shape, and then drag the group of selected controls to its new position. You can move controls with more precision when you use the arrow keys instead of the mouse. To move selected controls in small increments, press the appropriate arrow key. To move selected controls to the next nearest grid dot, hold down the Ctrl key and press the appropriate arrow key.

You can also move either a text box or its label individually. If you want to move the text box but not its label, for example, place the pointer on the text box's move handle. When the pointer changes to a ⬆ shape, drag the text box to the new location. You use the label's move handle in a similar way to move only the label.

You'll now arrange the controls to match Lucia's design.

To move the ContractType bound control:

▸ 1. Position the pointer on one of the edges of the ContractType text box, but not on a move handle or a sizing handle. When the pointer changes to a ⬆ shape, drag the control to the right until the left edge of the highlight on the horizontal ruler is at the 3-inch mark, drag the control up until the top of the highlight on the vertical ruler is just below the top of the SigningDate bound control, and then release the mouse button. See Figure 6-23.

After moving the ContractType bound control ◀ **Figure 6-23**

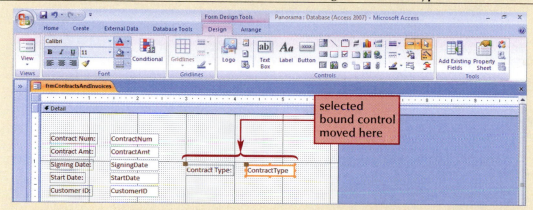

Trouble? If you need to make major adjustments to the placement of the ContractType bound control, click the Undo button on the Quick Access Toolbar one or more times until the bound control is back to its starting position, and then repeat Step 1. If you need to make minor adjustments to the placement of the ContractType bound control, use the arrow keys.

Now you need to align the ContractType and SigningDate bound controls on their top edges. If you've selected a column of controls, you can align the left edges or the right edges of the controls. If you've selected a row of controls, you can align the top edges or the bottom edges of the controls. A fifth alignment option, To Grid, aligns selected controls with the dots in the grid. You can find the five alignment options on the Arrange tab of the Ribbon or on the shortcut menu. You'll use the shortcut menu to align the two bound controls. Then you'll save the modified form and review your work in Form view.

To align the ContractType and SigningDate bound controls:

▸ 1. Make sure the ContractType bound control is selected, hold down the **Shift** key, click the **Contract Type** label, click the **SigningDate** text box, click the **Signing Date** label, and then release the **Shift** key. This action selects the four controls; each selected control has an orange border.

▸ 2. Right-click one of the selected controls, point to **Align** on the shortcut menu, and then click **Top**. The four selected controls are aligned on their top edges. See Figure 6-24.

Figure 6-24 | **After top-aligning four controls in the Detail section**

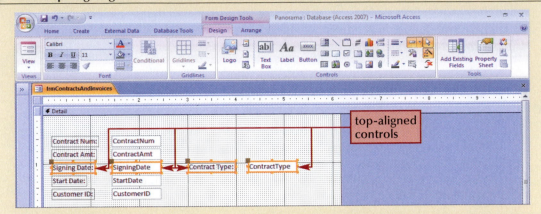

As you create a form, you should periodically save your modifications to the form and review your progress in Form view.

3. Save your form design changes, and then switch to Form view. See Figure 6-25.

Figure 6-25 | **Form displayed in Form view**

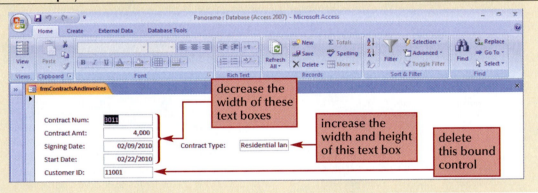

The value in the ContractType text box is not fully displayed, so you need to increase the size of the text box. The widths of the other four text boxes are wider than necessary, so you'll reduce their widths. Also, the CustomerID bound control consists of a label and a text box, but the plan for the form shows a combo box for the CustomerID positioned above the ContractType bound control. You'll delete the CustomerID bound control in preparation for adding it to the form as a combo box.

Resizing and Deleting Controls

A selected control displays seven sizing handles: four at the midpoints on each edge of the control and one at each corner except the upper-left corner. Recall that the upper-left corner displays the move handle. Positioning the pointer over a sizing handle changes the pointer to a two-headed arrow; the directions in which the arrows point indicate in which direction you can resize the selected control. When you drag a sizing handle, you resize the control. As you resize the control, a thin line appears inside the sizing handle to guide you in completing the task accurately, as do the outlines that appear on the horizontal and vertical rulers.

Resizing a Control | Reference Window

- Click the control to select it and display the sizing handles.
- Place the pointer over the sizing handle you want, and then drag the edge of the control until it is the size you want.
- To resize selected controls in small increments, hold down the Shift key and press the appropriate arrow key. This technique applies the resizing to the right edge and the bottom edge of the control.

You'll begin by deleting the CustomerID bound control. Then you'll resize the ContractType text box, which is too narrow and too short to display ContractType field values. Then you'll resize the remaining four text boxes to reduce their widths.

To delete a bound control and resize the text boxes:

1. Switch to Design view, click an unused portion of the grid to deselect all controls, and then click the **CustomerID** text box to select it.

2. Right-click the **CustomerID** text box to open the shortcut menu, and then click **Delete**. The label and the text box for the CustomerID bound control are deleted.

3. Click the **ContractType** text box to select it.

4. Place the pointer on the middle-right handle of the ContractType text box. When the pointer changes to a ↔ shape, drag the right border horizontally to the right to the 6-inch mark on the horizontal ruler.

5. Place the pointer on the middle-bottom handle of the ContractType text box. When the pointer changes to a ↕ shape, drag the bottom border down to the 1.75-inch mark on the vertical ruler. See Figure 6-26.

> **Tip**
>
> If you want to delete a label but not its associated text box, right-click the label, and then click Delete on the shortcut menu.

After resizing the ContractType text box ◀ Figure 6-26

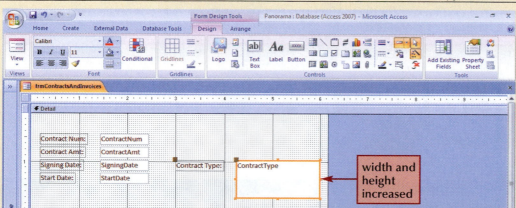

Resizing controls in Design view is a trial-and-error process, in which you resize a control in Design view, switch to Form view to observe the effect of the resizing, switch back to Design view to make further refinements to the control's size, and continue until the control is sized correctly. It's easier to resize controls in Layout view, because you can see actual field values while you resize the controls. You'll resize the other four text boxes in Layout view.

6. Switch to Layout view, and then click the **ContractNum** text box (if necessary) to select it.

7. Position the pointer on the right edge of the **ContractNum** text box. When the pointer changes to a ↔ shape, drag the right border horizontally to the left until the text box is slightly wider than the field value it contains. See Figure 6-27.

   The sizes of the ContractAmt, SigningDate, and StartDate text boxes will look fine if you reduce them to have the same widths, so you'll select all three text boxes and resize them as a group.

Tip

If you select a control by mistake, hold down the Shift key, and then click the selected control to deselect it.

8. Select the **ContractAmt**, **SigningDate**, and **StartDate** text boxes.

9. Position the pointer on the right edge of any of the three selected controls. When the pointer changes to a ↔ shape, drag the right border horizontally to the left until the SigningDate and StartDate text boxes are slightly wider than the field values they contain. See Figure 6-27.

Figure 6-27 | **After resizing text boxes in Layout view**

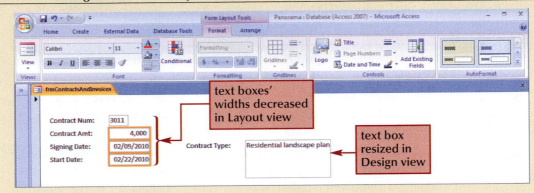

Trouble? If you resized the text boxes too far to the left, number signs will be displayed inside the SigningDate and StartDate text boxes. Drag the right edge of the text boxes slightly to the right and repeat the process until the date values are visible inside the text boxes.

10. Navigate through the first several records to make sure the five text boxes are sized properly to display the full field values. If any text box is too small, select the text box and increase its width the appropriate amount.

11. Save your form design changes, switch to Design view, and then deselect all controls by clicking in an unused portion of the grid.

InSight | **Making Form Design Modifications**

When you design forms and other objects, you'll find it helpful to switch frequently between Design view and Layout view. Some form modifications are easier to make in Layout view, other form modifications are easier to make in Design view, and still other form modifications can be made only in Design view. You should check your progress frequently in either Layout view or Form view, and you should save your modifications after completing a set of changes successfully.

Recall that you removed the lookup feature from the CustomerID field because a combo box provides the same lookup capability in a form. Next, you'll add a combo box for the CustomerID field to the custom form.

Adding a Combo Box to a Form

The tblCustomer and tblContract tables are related in a one-to-many relationship. The CustomerID field in the tblContract table is a foreign key to the tblCustomer table, and you can use a combo box in the custom form to view and maintain CustomerID field values more easily and accurately than using a text box. Recall that a combo box is a control that provides the features of a text box and a list box; you can choose a value from the list or type an entry.

You use the **Combo Box tool** in Design view to add a combo box to a form. If you want help when adding the combo box, you can select one of the Access Control Wizards. A **Control Wizard** asks a series of questions and then uses your answers to create a control in a form or report. Access offers Control Wizards for the Combo Box, List Box, Option Group, Command Button, Subform/Subreport, and other control tools.

You will use the Combo Box Wizard to add a combo box to the form for the CustomerID field.

To add a combo box to the form:

▶ 1. In the Controls group on the Design tab, make sure the Use Control Wizards button 🔸 is selected.

▶ 2. In the Controls group on the Design tab, click the **Combo Box** button 🔲 (with the ScreenTip "Combo Box (Form Control)"). After you click the Combo Box tool or most other tools in the Controls group, nothing happens until you move the pointer over the form. When you move the pointer over the form, the pointer changes to a shape that is unique for the tool with a plus symbol in its upper-left corner. You position the plus symbol in the location where you want to place the upper-left corner of the control.

You'll place the combo box near the top of the form above the ContractType bound control, and then position it more precisely after you've finished the wizard.

▶ 3. Position the + portion of the pointer three grid dots from the top of the grid and at the 4-inch mark on the horizontal ruler, and then click the mouse button. Access places a combo box control in the form and opens the first Combo Box Wizard dialog box.

You can use an existing table or query as the source for a new combo box or type the values for the combo box. In this case, you'll use the qryCustomersByName query as the basis for the new combo box. This query includes the Customer calculated field, whose value equals the Company field value, if it's nonnull, or the concatenation of the LastName and FirstName field values in all other cases.

▶ 4. Click the **I want the combo box to look up the values in a table or query** option button (if necessary), click the **Next** button to open the next Combo Box Wizard dialog box, click the **Queries** option button in the View group, click **Query: qryCustomersByName**, and then click the **Next** button. Access opens the third Combo Box Wizard dialog box. This dialog box lets you select the fields from the query to appear as columns in the combo box. You'll select the first two fields.

▶   **5.** Double-click **Customer** to move this field to the Selected Fields list box, double-click **CustomerID**, and then click the **Next** button. This dialog box lets you choose a sort order for the combo box entries. Sarah wants the entries to appear in ascending Customer order.

▶   **6.** Click the **arrow** for the first list box, click **Customer**, and then click the **Next** button to open the next Combo Box Wizard dialog box.

▶   **7.** Resize the columns to their best fit, scrolling down the columns to make sure all values are visible and resizing again if they're not, and then click the **Next** button.

   In this dialog box, you select the foreign key, which is the CustomerID field.

▶   **8.** Click **CustomerID** and then click the **Next** button.

   In this dialog box, you specify the field in the tblContract table where you will store the selected CustomerID value from the combo box. You'll store the value in the CustomerID field in the tblContract table.

▶   **9.** Click the **Store that value in this field** option button, click its **arrow**, click **CustomerID**, and then click the **Next** button.

   Trouble? If CustomerID doesn't appear in the list, click the Cancel button, press the Delete key to delete the combo box, click the Add Existing Fields button in the Tools group on the Ribbon, double-click CustomerID in the Field List pane, press the Delete key to delete CustomerID, close the Field List pane, and then repeat Steps 1-9.

   In this dialog box, you specify the name for the combo box control. You'll use the field name of CustomerID.

▶   **10.** Type **CustomerID** and then click the **Finish** button. The completed CustomerID combo box appears in the form.

You need to position and resize the combo box control, but first you'll change the text for the attached label from CustomerID to Customer ID with a terminating colon to match the format used for other label controls in the form. To change the text for a label control, you set the control's **Caption property** value.

Reference Window | Changing a Label's Caption

- Right-click the label to select it and to display the shortcut menu, and then click Properties to display the property sheet.
- If necessary, click the All tab to display the All page in the property sheet.
- Edit the existing text in the Caption text box; or click the Caption text box and press the F2 key to select the current value, and then type a new caption.
- In the Tools group on the Design tab, click the Property Sheet button to close the property sheet.

Next, you'll change the text that appears in the combo box label.

To set the Caption property value for the Customer ID label:

1. Right-click the **Customer ID** label, which is the control to the left of the CustomerID text box, to select it and to display the shortcut menu, and then click **Properties** on the shortcut menu. The property sheet for the Customer ID label opens.

2. If necessary, click the **All** tab to display all properties for the selected Customer ID label.

   Trouble? If the Selection type entry below the Property Sheet title bar is not "Label," then you selected the wrong control in Step 1. Click the Customer ID label to change to the property sheet for this control.

3. Click before the "ID" in the Caption text box, press the **spacebar**, press the **End** key, type a colon, and then press the **Tab** key to move to the next property in the property sheet. The Caption property value should now be Customer ID: and the label for the CustomerID bound control now displays Customer ID:. See Figure 6-28.

Tip

After selecting a control, you can press the F4 key to open and close the property sheet for the control.

Tip

After you've set a property value, you won't see the effects of the new setting until you select another property in the property sheet, select another control in the form, or close the property sheet.

CustomerID combo box added to the form | **Figure 6-28**

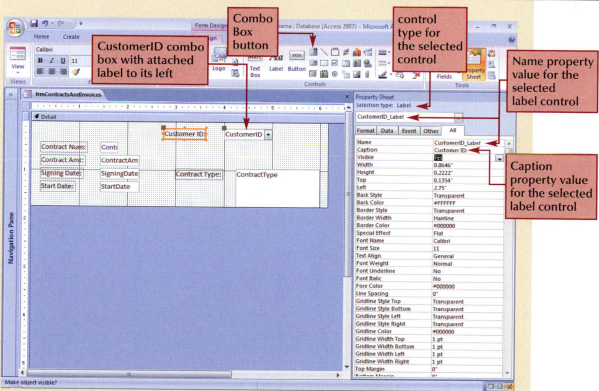

Trouble? Some property values in your property sheet, such as the Width and Top property values, might differ if your label's position slightly differs from the label position used as the basis for Figure 6-28. These differences cause no problems.

Tip

You should always check that the Selection type entry is the correct control type and the Control list box displays the correct name for the control whose properties you are changing.

The Selection type entry, which is the line below the property sheet title bar, displays the control type (Label in this case) for the selected control. Below the Selection type entry in the property sheet is the Control list box, which you can use to select another control in the form and then change its properties in the property sheet. Or you can simply click the control to change to its properties in the property sheet. The first property in the property sheet, the **Name property**, is the property that specifies the name of a control, section, or object (CustomerID_Label in this case). The Name property value is the same as the value displayed in the Control list box. For bound controls, the Name property value matches the field name. For unbound controls, Access sets the Name property to the control type (for example, Label) followed by a number (for example, Label2). For unbound controls, you can set the Name property to another, more meaningful value at any time.

▶ 4. Close the property sheet, and then save your design changes.

Now that you've added the combo box to the form, you can view the form in Layout view, and then position the combo box and its attached label and resize the combo box. You'll need to view the form in Form view to determine any fine-tuning necessary for the width of the combo box.

To view and modify the combo box in Layout view:

▶ 1. Switch to Layout view to view the form, and then click the **CustomerID** combo box, hold down the **Shift** key, click the **Customer ID** label, and then release the **Shift** key to select both controls.

First, you'll align the CustomerID combo box and its label with the ContractType and ContractNum bound controls. You'll move the selected controls to the right of the Contract Type label, align the Customer ID and Contract Type labels on their left edges, align the CustomerID and ContractType controls on their left edges, and then align the bottom edges of the combo box and its label with the bottom edges of the ContractNum bound control.

▶ 2. Drag the selected controls to the right until the Customer ID label is approximately one inch to the right of the Contract Type label, making sure the two controls remain above the ContractNum bound control.

▶ 3. Select the **Customer ID** label and the **Contract Type** label, click the **Arrange** tab on the Ribbon, and then in the Control Alignment group on the Arrange tab, click the **Left** button. The selected controls are aligned on their left edges.

▶ 4. Repeat Step 3 to align the **CustomerID** combo box and the **ContractType** text boxes on their left edges.

▶ 5. Select the **Contract Num** label, **ContractNum** text box, **Customer ID** label, and **CustomerID** combo box, and then in the Control Alignment group on the Arrange tab, click the **Bottom** button. The four selected controls are aligned on their bottom edges.

▶ 6. Switch to Form view, and then click the **CustomerID** arrow to open the control's list box. See Figure 6-29.

CustomerID combo box in Form view | **Figure 6-29**

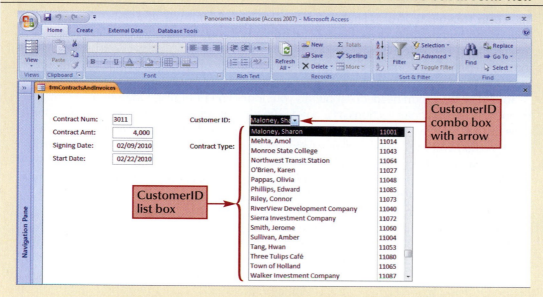

You need to widen the CustomerID combo box, so that the widest customer value in the list is displayed in the combo box. You can widen the combo box in Layout view or in Design view. Because Layout view displays live data, you'll use Layout view instead of Design view to make this change because you can determine the proper width more accurately in Layout view.

7. Switch to Layout view, and then navigate to record 16. Weston Community Parks Foundation, which is the customer value for this record, is the widest value that is displayed in the combo box. You want to widen the combo box, so that the value in record 16 is completely visible.

8. Make sure that only the combo box is selected, and then pointing to the right edge, widen the combo box until the entire customer value is visible. See Figure 6-30.

After resizing the CustomerID combo box in Layout view | **Figure 6-30**

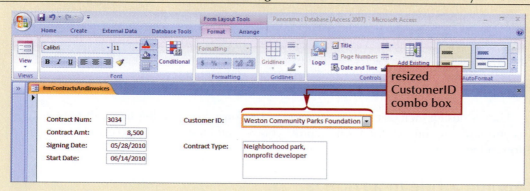

Now you'll add the title to the top of the form.

Using Form Headers and Form Footers

The **Form Header** and **Form Footer sections** let you add titles, instructions, command buttons, and other controls to the top and bottom of your form, respectively. Controls placed in the Form Header or Form Footer sections remain on the screen whenever the form is displayed in Form view or Layout view; they do not change when the contents of the Detail section change as you navigate from one record to another record.

To add either a form header or footer to your form, you must first add both the Form Header and Form Footer sections as a pair to the form. If your form needs one of these sections but not the other, you can remove a section by setting its height to zero, which is the same method you would use to remove any form section. You can also prevent a section from appearing in Form view or in Print Preview by setting its Visible property to No. The **Visible property** determines if Access displays a control or section. Set the Visible property to Yes to display the control or section, and set the Visible property to No to hide it.

You can add the Form Header and Form Footer sections as a pair to a form either directly or indirectly. The direct way to add these sections is to click the Form Header/ Footer button in the Show/Hide group on the Arrange tab. This direct method is available only in Design view. The indirect way to add the Form Header and Form Footer sections in Layout view or Design view is to use one of these four buttons in the Controls group on the Design tab: the Logo button, the Title button, the Page Numbers button (Insert Page Number button in Design view), or the Date and Time button (Date & Time button in Design view). Clicking any of these four buttons causes Access to add the Form Header and Form Footer sections to the form and to place an appropriate control in the Form Header section. If you use the indirect method in Layout view, Access sets the Form Footer section's height to zero. In Design view, the indirect method creates a nonzero height Form Footer section. Note that the Page Numbers button is dimmed, and thus inactive, in Layout view. Many forms contain a title and possibly a picture, but forms rarely display a page number or the date and time, so an inactive Page Numbers button is not a problem, especially because you can add page numbers in Design view.

Tip

If you've set the Form Footer section's height to zero or set its Visible property to No and a future form design change makes adding controls to the Form Footer section necessary, you can restore the section by using the pointer to drag its bottom edge back down or by setting its Visible property to Yes.

Reference Window | Adding and Removing Form Header and Form Footer Sections

- In Design view, click the Form Header/Footer button in the Show/Hide group on the Arrange tab.

or

- In Layout view or Design view, click a button in the Controls group to add a logo, title, page numbers, or date and time to the form.
- To remove a Form Header or Form Footer section, drag its bottom edge up until the section area disappears or set the section's Visible property to No.

Lucia's design includes a title at the top of the form. Because the title will not change as you navigate through the form records, you will add the title to the Form Header section in the form.

Adding a Title to a Form

You'll add the title to Sarah's form in Layout view. When you add the title to the form in Layout view, Access adds the Form Header section to the form and places the title in the Form Header section. At the same time, Access adds the Page Footer section to the form and sets its height to zero.

To add a title to the form:

▸ **1.** In the Controls group on the Format tab, click the **Title** button. Access adds the title to the form, displaying it in the upper-left corner of the form and using the form name as the title.

You need to change the title. Because the title is already selected, you can type over or edit the selected title.

▸ **2.** Press the **Home** key to move to the start of the title, press the **Delete** key three times to delete the first three characters, click before the word "And," press the **spacebar**, type the letter **a**, press the **Delete** key, press the → key twice, press the **spacebar**, and then press the **Enter** key. You've changed the title to Contracts and Invoices. See Figure 6-31.

Title placed in the Form Header section ◂ **Figure 6-31**

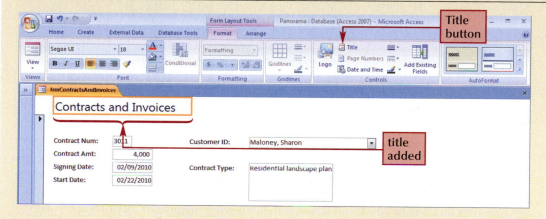

Sarah wants the title to be prominent in the form. The title is already a larger font size than the font used for the form's labels and text boxes, so you'll change the title's font weight to bold to increase its prominence.

▸ **3.** Make sure the title control is still selected, and then in the Font group on the Format tab, click the **Bold** button **B**. The title is displayed in 18-point, bold text.

It is not obvious in Layout view that the title is displayed in the Form Header section, so you'll view the form design in Design view.

▸ **4.** Switch to Design view, and then save your design changes. The title is displayed in the Form Header section. See Figure 6-32.

Tip

Keep in mind that a form's total height includes the heights of the Form Header, Detail, and Form Footer sections. If you set the form's total height to more than the screen size, users will need to use scroll bars to view the content of your form, which is less productive for users and isn't good form design.

Figure 6-32 ▶ **Form Header and Form Footer sections in Design view**

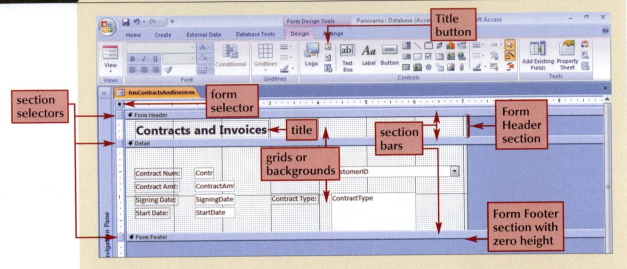

5. If you are not continuing on to the next session, close the Panorama database, and then exit Access.

The form now contains a Form Header section that displays the title, a Detail section that displays the bound controls and combo box, and a Form Footer section that is set to a height of zero. Each section consists of a **section selector** and a section bar, either of which you can click to select and set properties for the entire section, and a grid or background, which is where you place controls that you want display in the form. The **form selector** is the selector at the intersection of the horizontal and vertical rulers; you click the form selector when you want to select the form and set its properties. The vertical ruler is segmented into sections for the Form Header section, the Detail section, and the Form Footer section.

So far, you've added controls to the form and modified the controls by selecting, moving, aligning, resizing, and deleting them. You've added and modified a combo box and added a title in the Form Header section. In the next session, you will continue your work with the custom form by adding a combo box to find records, adding a subform, adding calculated controls, changing form and section properties, and changing control properties.

| Review | **Session 6.2 Quick Check** |

1. What is a bound form, and when do you use bound forms?
2. What is the difference between a bound control and an unbound control?
3. The _____ consists of the dotted and solid lines that appear in the Detail section to help you position controls precisely in a form.
4. The handle in a selected object's upper-left corner is the _____ handle.
5. How do you move a selected text box and its label at the same time?
6. How do you resize a control?
7. A(n) _____ control provides the features of a text box and a list box.
8. How do you change a label's caption?
9. What is the Form Header section?

Session 6.3

Adding a Combo Box to Find Records

Most combo boxes, such as the CustomerID combo box, are used to display and update data. You can also use combo boxes to find records. You will add a combo box to the Form Header section to find a specific record in the tblContract table to display in the form.

Adding a Combo Box to Find Records	Reference Window

- Open the property sheet for the form in Design view, make sure the record source is a table or query, and then close the property sheet.
- In the Controls section on the Design tab, click the Combo Box button, and then click the position in the form where you want to place the control.
- Click the third option button (Find a record on my form based on the value I selected in my combo box) in the first Combo Box Wizard dialog box, and then complete the remaining Combo Box Wizard dialog boxes.

You can use the Combo Box Wizard to add a combo box to find records in a form. However, the Combo Box Wizard provides this find option only if the form's record source is a table or query. You'll view the property sheet for the form to view the Record Source property, and you'll change the property setting, if necessary.

To add a combo box to find records to the form:

▶ **1.** If you took a break after the previous session, make sure that the Panorama database is open, the frmContractsAndInvoices form is open in Design view, and the Navigation Pane is closed.

▶ **2.** Click the **form selector** (located to the left of the horizontal ruler) to select the form, open the property sheet, and then click the **All** tab (if necessary). The property sheet displays the properties for the form. See Figure 6-33.

Property sheet settings for the form ◀ Figure 6-33

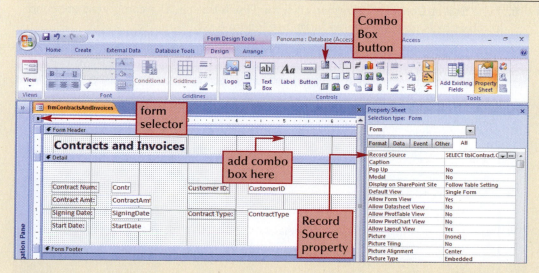

The Record Source property is set to an SQL SELECT statement. You need to change the Record Source property to a table or query, or the Combo Box Wizard will not present you with the option to find records in a form. You'll change the Record Source property to the tblContract table, because this table is the record source for all the bound controls you added to the Detail section.

▶ 3. Click the **Record Source** text box, press the **F2** key to select the entire property setting, type **tblContract**, and then close the property sheet.

You'll now use the Combo Box Wizard to add a combo box to the form's Form Header section to find a record in the tblContract table to display in the form.

▶ 4. In the Controls group on the Design tab, click the **Combo Box** button 📇 (with the ScreenTip "Combo Box (Form Control)"), position the + portion of the pointer at the top of the Form Header section and at the 5-inch mark on the horizontal ruler (see Figure 6-33), and then click the mouse button. Access places a combo box control in the form and opens the first Combo Box Wizard dialog box.

The dialog box now displays a third option to "Find a record on my form based on the value I selected in my combo box," which you'll use for this combo box. You choose the first option, which you used for the CustomerID combo box, when you want to select a value from a list of foreign key values from an existing table or query. You choose the second option when you want users to select a value from a short fixed list of values that don't change. For example, if Belmont Landscapes wanted to include a field in the tblCustomer table to classify each customer, you could use a combo box with this second option to display a list of values such as Residential, Commercial, Nonprofit, and Government.

▶ 5. Click the **Find a record on my form based on the value I selected in my combo box** option button, and then click the **Next** button to open the next dialog box. This dialog box lets you select the fields from the tblContract table to appear as columns in the combo box. You'll select the first field.

▶ 6. Double-click **ContractNum** to move this field to the Selected Fields list box, and then click the **Next** button.

▶ 7. The column is already resized properly, so click the **Next** button.

In this dialog box, you specify the name for the combo box's label. You'll use Select Contract as the label.

▶ 8. Type **Select Contract**, and then click the **Finish** button. The completed unbound combo box is displayed in the form. See Figure 6-34.

Figure 6-34 | **Unbound combo box added to the form**

You'll align the right edges of the two combo boxes, move the attached label close to the combo box, and then align the bottoms of the combo box and its attached label with the bottom of the title in the Form Header section.

▶ 9. Deselect all controls, select the two combo boxes (one in the Form Header section and the other in the Detail section), right-click one of the selected controls, point to **Align**, and then click **Right**. The two combo boxes are aligned on their right edges.

▶ 10. Click the **Select Contract** label, point to the label's move handle, and then drag the label to the right until it is two grid dots to the left of the combo box.

▶ 11. Select the combo box in the Form Header section, the **Select Contract** label, and the title, right-click one of the selected controls, point to **Align**, click **Bottom**, and then click the **Select Contract** label. The three controls are aligned on their bottom edges. See Figure 6-35.

After aligning the combo box and its label   ◀   **Figure 6-35**

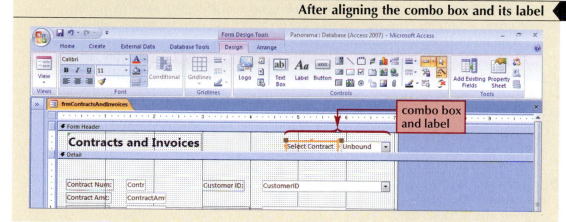

You'll save your form changes and view the new combo box in Form view.

To find contract records using the combo box:

▶ 1. Save the form design changes, and then switch to Form view.

▶ 2. Click the **Select Contract** combo box arrow to open the combo box's list box. See Figure 6-36.

Displaying the combo box's list of contract numbers   ◀   **Figure 6-36**

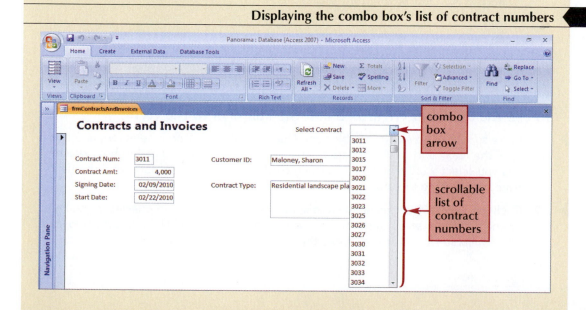

> **3.** Scroll down the list, and then click **3073**. The current record changes from record 1 to record 41, which is the record for contract number 3073.

The form design is very plain at this point with no color, special effects, or visual contrast among the controls. Before making the form more attractive and useful, you'll add the remaining controls to the form: a subform and two calculated controls.

Adding a Subform to a Form

Lucia's design for the form includes a subform that displays the related invoices for the displayed contract. The form you've been creating is the main form for records from the primary tblContract table (the "one" side of the one-to-many relationship), and the subform will display records from the related tblInvoice table (the "many" side of the one-to-many relationship). You use the **Subform/Subreport tool** in Design view to add a subform to a form. You can add the subform on your own, or you can get help adding the subform by using the SubForm Wizard.

You will use the SubForm Wizard to add the subform for the Invoice table records to the bottom of the form. First, you'll increase the height of the Detail section to make room for the subform.

To add the subform to the form:

> **1.** Switch to Design view.

Tip

When you increase a section's height, you might need to go slightly beyond the desired ending position to expose the vertical ruler measurement, and then decrease the height back to the correct position.

> **2.** Place the pointer on the bottom edge of the Detail section. When the pointer changes to a ╪ shape, drag the section's edge down until it is at the 4-inch mark on the vertical ruler.

> **3.** In the Controls group on the Design tab, make sure the Use Control Wizards tool 📐 is selected.

> **4.** In the Controls group on the Design tab, click the **Subform/Subreport** button 📧.

> **5.** Position the + portion of the pointer in the Detail section at the 2.5-inch mark on the vertical ruler and at the 1-inch mark on the horizontal ruler, and then click the mouse button. Access places a subform control in the form's Detail section and opens the first SubForm Wizard dialog box.

You can use a table or query, or an existing form as the record source for a subform. In this case, you'll use the related tblInvoice table as the record source for a new subform.

To use the SubForm Wizard to add the subform to the form:

> **1.** Make sure the Use existing Tables and Queries option button is selected, and then click the **Next** button. Access opens the next SubForm Wizard dialog box, which lets you select a table or query as the record source for the subform and the fields from the selected table or query.

> **2.** Click the **Tables/Queries** arrow to display the list of tables and queries in the Panorama database, scroll to the top of the list box, and then click **Table: tblInvoice**. The Available Fields list box shows the fields in the tblInvoice table.

Lucia's form design includes all fields from the tblInvoice table in the subform, except the ContractNum field, which is already placed in the Detail section of the form from the tblContract table.

▶ 3. Click the >> button to move all available fields to the Selected Fields list box, click **ContractNum** in the Selected Fields list box, click the < button, and then click the **Next** button to open the next SubForm Wizard dialog box. See Figure 6-37.

Selecting the linking field ◀ Figure 6-37

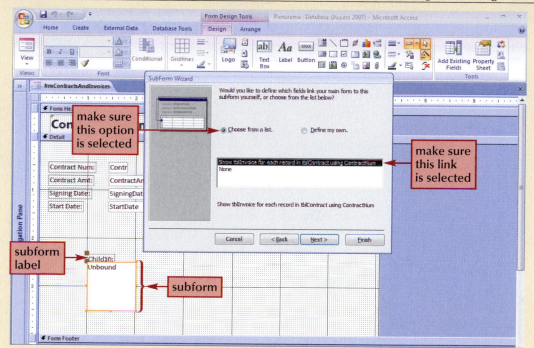

In this dialog box, you select the link between the primary tblContract table and the related tblInvoice table. The common field in the two tables, ContractNum, links the tables. Access uses the ContractNum field to display a record in the main form, which displays data from the primary tblContract table, and to select and display the related records for that contract in the subform, which displays data from the related tblInvoice table.

▶ 4. Make sure the Choose from a list option button is selected and that the first link is highlighted, and then click the **Next** button. The next SubForm Wizard dialog box lets you specify a name for the subform.

▶ 5. Type **frmInvoiceSubform** and then click the **Finish** button. Access increases the height and width of the subform in the form. The subform is where the related tblInvoice records will appear. The subform label appears above the subform and displays the subform name.

▶ 6. Deselect all controls, save your form changes, switch to Form view, and then click the **ContractNum** text box to deselect the value. See Figure 6-38.

Figure 6-38 **Viewing the subform in Form view**

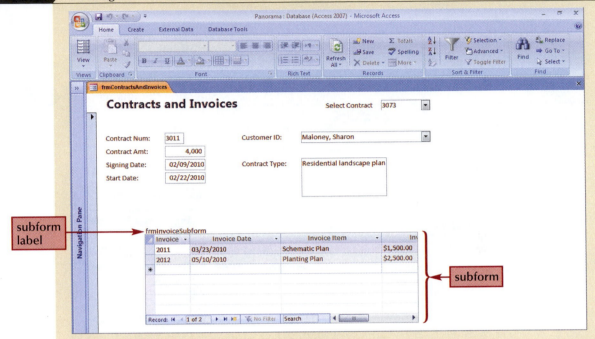

The subform displays the two invoices related to the first contract record for contract number 3011.

Trouble? If the size of the columns in your datasheet differs or the position of your subform is different, don't worry. You'll resize all columns to their best fit and move the subform later.

After viewing the form, Sarah identifies some modifications she wants you to make. The subform is not properly sized and the columns in the subform are not sized to their best fit. She wants you to resize the subform and its columns, so that all columns in the subform are entirely visible. Also, she asks you to delete the subform label, because the label is unnecessary for identifying the subform contents. You'll switch to Design view to make these changes.

To modify the subform's design:

▶ **1.** Switch to Design view. Notice that in Design view, the subform data does not appear in a datasheet format as it does in Form view. That difference causes no problem; you can ignore it.

First, you'll delete the subform label.

▶ **2.** Deselect all controls, right-click the subform label to open the shortcut menu (make sure no other controls have handles), and then click **Cut**.

Next, you'll open the subform in another window, and then resize the columns to their best fit in Datasheet view.

3. Move the pointer to the edge of the subform border, click the border's edge to select the subform (an orange border and handles appear on the subform's border when the subform is selected), position the pointer on the border and right-click the border when the pointer changes to a ⛶ shape, and then click **Subform in New Window** on the shortcut menu. The subform opens in Design view. You'll switch to Datasheet view to resize the columns to their best fit.

4. Switch to Datasheet view, and then resize all columns to their best fit, scrolling down the datasheet to resize the Invoice Item column again, as necessary.

5. Save your design changes, and then close the frmInvoiceSubform form.

   Trouble? If the subform in the frmContractsAndInvoices form appears to be blank after you close the frmInvoiceSubform, don't worry. This is a temporary effect; the subform's controls do still exist.

   Next, you'll move and resize the subform in Layout view, where you can more easily observe the effects of your changes.

6. Switch to Layout view, click the edge of the subform to select it, hold down the **Shift** key, click the **Start Date** label, and then release the **Shift** key. The subform and the Start Date label are selected, and you'll align the two controls on their left edges.

7. Click the **Arrange** tab on the Ribbon, and then in the Control Alignment group on the Arrange tab, click **Left**. The two controls are aligned on their left edges.

   Next, you'll widen the subform on its right side.

8. Hold down the **Shift** key, click the **Start Date** label to deselect it, release the **Shift** key, leaving only the subform selected, and then drag the right edge of the subform to the right until all five datasheet columns are fully visible. See Figure 6-39.

After moving and resizing the subform in Layout view | Figure 6-39

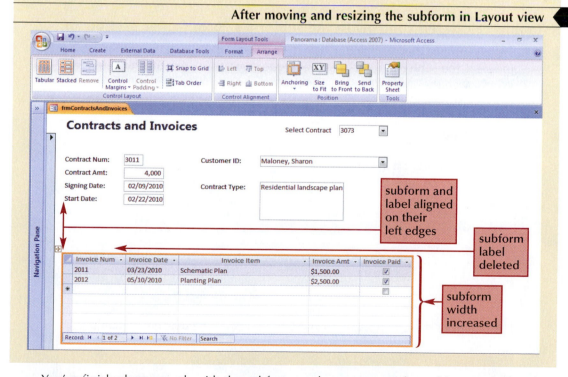

You've finished your work with the subform, and now you need to add two calculated controls to the main form. The first calculated control will display the number of invoices displayed in the subform, and the other will display the total of the invoice amounts displayed in the subform.

Displaying a Subform's Calculated Controls in the Main Form

For the invoices displayed in the subform, Lucia's form design includes calculated controls in the main form for the number of invoices and for the total of the invoice amounts for the related records displayed in the subform. To display these calculated controls in a form or report, you use the Count and Sum functions. The **Count function** determines the number of occurrences of an expression, and its general format as a control in a form or report is =Count(*expression*). The **Sum function** calculates the total of an expression, and its general format as a control in a form or report is =Sum(*expression*). The invoices and invoice amounts are displayed in the subform's Detail section, so you'll need to place calculated controls for the number of invoices and the total invoice amounts in the subform's Form Footer section. However, your design has these two calculated controls displayed in the main form, not in the subform. Fortunately, the subform appears in Datasheet view, and Form Headers and Footers do not appear in Datasheet view, so the subform's calculated controls will not appear in the subform. Although the calculated controls are not displayed in the subform, the calculations occur, and you can add calculated controls in the main form that reference the subform's calculated controls and display these values.

Adding Calculated Controls to a Subform's Form Footer Section

First, you'll open the subform in Design view in another window and add the calculated controls to the subform's Form Footer section.

To add calculated controls to the subform's Form Footer section:

1. Save your form design changes, switch to Design view, click the subform border to select the subform, right-click the border, and then click **Subform in New Window** on the shortcut menu. The subform opens in Design view. See Figure 6-40.

Figure 6-40 Subform in Design view

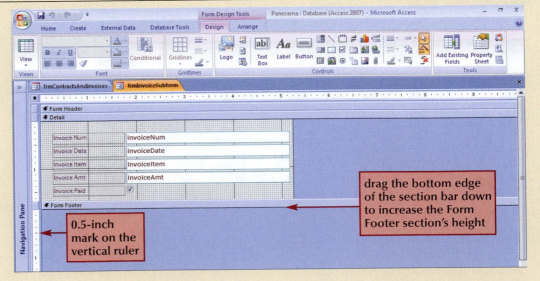

drag the bottom edge of the section bar down to increase the Form Footer section's height

0.5-inch mark on the vertical ruler

The subform's Detail section contains the tblInvoice table fields. As a subform in the main form, the fields appear as a datasheet even though the fields do not appear that way in Design view. The heights of the subform's Form Header and Form Footer sections are zero, meaning that these sections have been removed from the subform. You'll increase the height of the Form Footer section so that you can add the two calculated controls to the section.

▶ **2.** Place the pointer at the bottom edge of the Form Footer section bar. When the pointer changes to a ✛ shape, drag the bottom edge of the section down to the 0.5-inch mark on the vertical ruler.

Now you'll add the first calculated control to the Form Footer section. To create the text box for the calculated control, you use the **Text Box tool** in the Controls group on the Design tab. Because the Form Footer section is not displayed in a datasheet, you do not need to position the control precisely.

▶ **3.** In the Controls group on the Design tab, click the **Text Box** button.

▶ **4.** Position the + portion of the pointer near the top of the Form Footer section and at the 1-inch mark on the horizontal ruler, and then click the mouse button. Access places a text box control and an attached label control to its left in the Form Footer section.

Next, you'll set the Name and Control Source properties for the text box. Recall that the Name property specifies the name of an object or control. Later, when you add the calculated control in the main form, you'll reference the subform's calculated control value by using its Name property value. The **Control Source property** specifies the source of the data that appears in the control; the Control Source property setting can be either a field name or an expression. You precede expressions with an equal sign to distinguish them from field names, which do not have an equal sign.

▶ **5.** Open the property sheet for the text box in the Form Footer section (the word "Unbound" is displayed inside the text box), click the **All** tab (if necessary), select the entry in the Name text box, type **txtInvoiceAmtSum** in the Name text box, press the **Tab** key, type **=Sum(InvoiceAmt)** in the Control Source text box, and then press the **Tab** key. See Figure 6-41.

Setting properties for the subform calculated control ◆ **Figure 6-41**

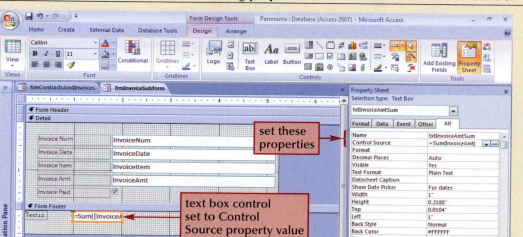

The calculated control's Name property setting (txtInvoiceAmtSum) follows a common naming convention: txt is a prefix tag to identify the control type (a text box), InvoiceAmt is the name for the related field, and Sum is a suffix tag to identify the control as a summary control.

You've finished creating the first calculated control, and now you'll create the other calculated control.

▶ **6.** Repeat Steps 3 through 5, positioning the + portion of the pointer near the top of the Form Footer section and at the 4-inch mark on the horizontal ruler, setting the Name property value to **txtInvoiceNumCount**, and setting the Control Source property value to **=Count(InvoiceNum)**.

When you use the Count function, you are counting the number of displayed records—in this case, the number of records displayed in the subform. Instead of using InvoiceNum as the expression for the Count function, you could use any of the other fields displayed in the subform.

You've finished creating the subform's calculated controls, so you can close the property sheet, save your subform design changes, and return to the main form.

▶ **7.** Close the property sheet, save your subform changes, and then close the subform. You return to Design view for the main form.

Next, you'll add two calculated controls in the main form to display the values of the two calculated controls from the subform.

Adding Calculated Controls to a Main Form

The subform's calculated controls now contain a count of the number of invoices and a total of the invoice amounts. You need to add two calculated controls in the main form that reference the values in the subform's calculated controls. Because it's easy to make a typing mistake with these references, you'll use Expression Builder to set the Control Source property for the two main form calculated controls.

To add a calculated control to the main form's Detail section:

▶ **1.** In the Controls group on the Design tab, click the **Text Box** button, and then add the text box and its attached label in the Detail section, clicking the + portion of the pointer at the 2-inch mark on the horizontal ruler and the 2-inch mark on the vertical ruler. Don't be concerned about positioning the control precisely, because you'll resize and move the label and text box later.

▶ **2.** Select the label and open the property sheet, set its Caption property to **Number of Invoices:**, right-click an edge of the label to open the shortcut menu, point to **Size**, and then click **To Fit**. Don't be concerned if the label now overlaps the text box.

You'll use Expression Builder to set the Control Source property for the text box.

▶ **3.** Click the text box (the word "Unbound" is displayed inside the text box) to select it, click the **Control Source** text box in the property sheet, and then click the property's **Build** button ⎡...⎤ to open Expression Builder.

▶ **4.** Double-click **frmContractsAndInvoices** in the left column, click **frmInvoiceSubform** in the left column, scroll down the middle column, click **txtInvoiceNumCount** in the middle column, and then click the **Paste** button. See Figure 6-42.

Text box control's expression in the Expression Builder dialog box   Figure 6-42

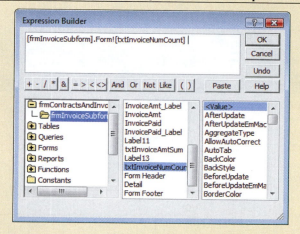

Access changed the pasted txtInvoiceNumCount to [frmInvoiceSubform].Form!
[txtInvoiceNumCount]. This expression asks Access to display the value of the
txtInvoiceNumCount control that is located in the frmInvoiceSubform form, which
is a form object.

You need to add an equal sign to the start of the expression.

5. Press the **Home** key, click the **=** button in the row of operators to the left of the
Paste button, and then click the **OK** button. Access closes the Expression Builder
dialog box and sets the Control Source property.

Next, you'll add a second text box to the main form, set the Caption property for
the label, and use Expression Builder to set the text box's Control Source property.

6. Repeat Steps 1 through 3 to add a text box to the main form, clicking the + portion of
the pointer at the 5-inch mark on the horizontal ruler and the 2-inch mark on the vertical ruler, and setting the label's Caption property to **Invoice Amount Total:**.

7. With the Expression Builder dialog box open for the new text box, click the **=** button to
insert an equal sign in the large text box, double-click **frmContractsAndInvoices** in
the left column, click **frmInvoiceSubform** in the left column, scroll down the middle
column, click **txtInvoiceAmtSum** in the middle column, and then click the **Paste**
button. Access changed the pasted txtInvoiceAmtSum to the expression
[frmInvoiceSubform].Form![txtInvoiceAmtSum].

Next, you'll save your form changes and view the form in Layout view.

8. Close the Expression Builder dialog box, close the property sheet, save your form
changes, and then switch to Layout view. See Figure 6-43.

Figure 6-43 | After adding two calculated controls

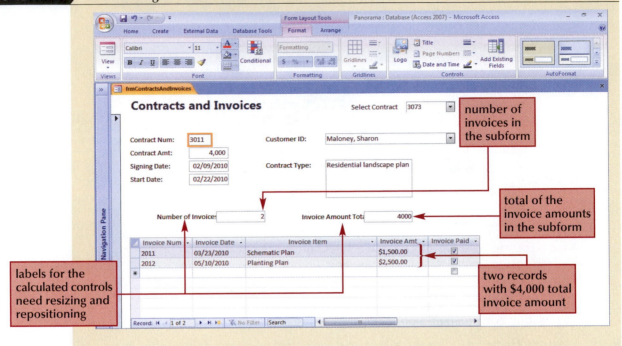

Next, you need to resize, move, and format the two calculated controls and their attached labels.

Resizing, Moving, and Formatting Calculated Controls

In addition to resizing and repositioning the two calculated controls and their attached labels, you need to change the format of the rightmost calculated control to Currency and to set the following properties for both calculated controls:

- Set the Tab Stop property to a value of No. The **Tab Stop property** specifies whether users can use the Tab key to move to a control on a form. If the Tab Stop property is set to No, users can't tab to the control.
- Set the ControlTip Text property to a value of "Calculated total number of invoices for this contract" for the leftmost calculated control and "Calculated invoice total for this contract" for the rightmost calculated control. The **ControlTip Text property** specifies the text that appears in a ScreenTip when users hold the mouse pointer over a control on a form.

InSight | **Setting Properties in the Property Sheet**

You can set many properties in the property sheet by typing a value in the property's text box, by selecting a value from the property's list box, or by double-clicking the property name. If you need to set a property by typing a long text entry, you can open the Zoom dialog box and type the entry in the dialog box. You can also use Expression Builder to help you enter expressions.

Now you'll resize, move, and format the calculated controls and their attached labels, and you'll set other properties for the calculated controls.

To modify the calculated controls and their attached labels:

1. Right-click the rightmost calculated control, click **Properties** on the shortcut menu to open the property sheet, click the **All** tab in the property sheet (if necessary), set the Format property to **Currency**, and then close the property sheet. The value displayed in the calculated control changes from 4000 to $4,000.00.

   Now you'll resize the calculated controls, adjust the positions of each label and text box pair with respect to each other, and then move the controls into their final positions in the form.

2. Individually, reduce the widths of the two calculated controls. See Figure 6-44.

3. Click the **Number of Invoices** label, use the arrow keys to move the label into position next to its related calculated control, repeat the process for the **Invoice Amount Total** label and its related calculated control, and then deselect all controls. See Figure 6-44.

After modifying the calculated controls and their labels Figure 6-44

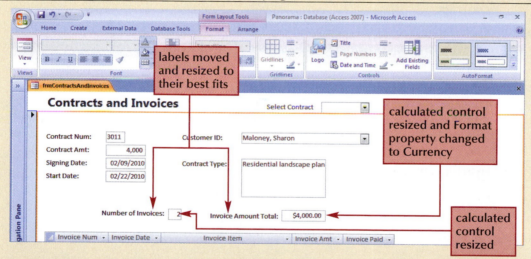

4. Use **Shift + Click** to select the **Start Date** label and the **Number of Invoices** label, click the **Arrange** tab on the Ribbon, click the **Left** button in the Control Alignment group to align the labels on their left edges, press the **Shift** key, click the **Start Date** label to deselect it, release the **Shift** key, and then move the **Number of Invoices** label up to the position shown in Figure 6-45.

5. Select the **Number of Invoices** label and its related calculated control, and then in the Control Alignment group, click the **Top** button to align the two controls on their top edges.

6. Repeat Steps 4 and 5 for the **Invoice Amount Total** label and its related calculated control. See Figure 6-45.

7. Move the bottom calculated control to the left to the position shown in Figure 6-45, align the two calculated controls on their left edges, and then deselect all controls.

Figure 6-45 ▶ After moving and aligning the calculated controls and their labels

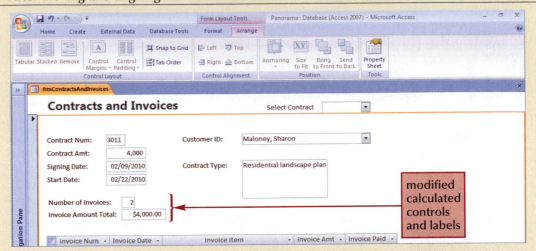

8. Right-click the bottom calculated control, click **Properties** on the shortcut menu, click the **Other** tab in the property sheet, set the Tab Stop property to **No**, and then set the ControlTip Text property to **Calculated invoice total for this contract**.

9. Click the top calculated control, set the Tab Stop property to **No**, set the ControlTip Text property to **Calculated total number of invoices for this contract**, close the property sheet, save your form design changes, and then switch to Form view.

10. Click the **Number of Invoices** text box, position the pointer on the Number of Invoices text box to display its ScreenTip, click the **Invoice Amount Total** text box, and then position the pointer on the Invoice Amount Total text box to display its ScreenTip. See Figure 6-46.

Figure 6-46 ▶ Displaying a control's ScreenTip

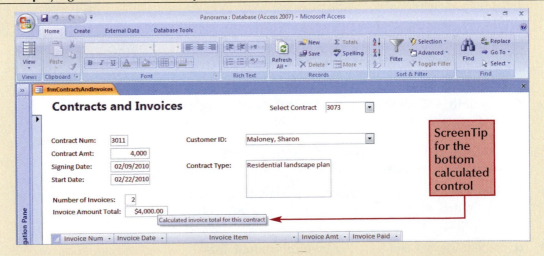

Trouble? Do not be concerned if the ScreenTips do not display on your screen.

Sarah asks you to verify that users can't update the calculated controls in the main form and that users will tab in the correct order through the controls in the form.

Changing the Tab Order in a Form

Pressing the Tab key in Form view moves the focus from one control to another. **Focus** refers to the control that is currently active and awaiting user action; focus also refers to the object and record that is currently active. The order in which you move from control to control, or change the focus, in a form when you press the Tab key is called the **tab order**. Sarah wants to verify that the tab order in the main form is top-to-bottom, left-to-right. First, you'll verify that users can't update the calculated controls.

To test the calculated controls and modify the tab order:

▶ 1. Select **2** in the Number of Invoices text box, and then press the **8** key. The Number of Invoices value remains at 2, and a message is displayed on the status bar. See Figure 6-47.

After attempting to update a calculated control ◀ **Figure 6-47**

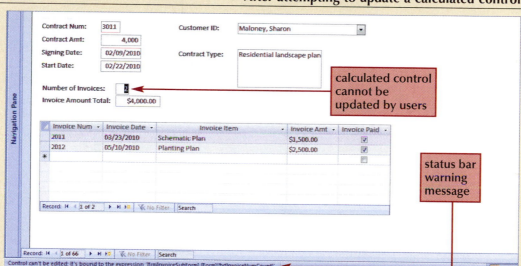

The status bar message warns you that you can't update, or edit, the calculated control because it's bound to an expression. The calculated control in the main form changes in value only when the value of the expression changes.

▶ 2. Click the **Invoice Amount Total** text box, and then press any key. The value remains unchanged, and a message displays on the status bar, because you cannot edit a calculated control.

Next, you'll determine the tab order of the fields in the main form. Sarah wants the tab order to be down and then across.

▶ 3. Select **3011** in the ContractNum text box, press the **Tab** key to advance to the ContractAmt text box, and then press the **Tab** key five more times to advance to the SigningDate, StartDate, ContractType, CustomerID text boxes, in order, and then to the subform.

You tab through the text boxes in a main form before tabbing through the fields in a subform. In the main form, tabbing bypasses the two calculated controls because you set their Tab Stop property to No, and you bypass the Select Contract combo box because it's an unbound control. Also, you tab through only the text boxes in a form, not the labels.

The tab order Sarah wants for the text boxes in the main form (top-to-bottom, left-to-right) is correct for the first four text boxes (ContractNum, ContractAmt, SigningDate, and StartDate text boxes). Then you should tab from the StartDate text box to the CustomerID text box and finally to the ContractType text box, but tabbing is reversed for the last two text boxes. The default tab order doesn't match the order Sarah wants, so you'll change the tab order. You can change the tab order in Layout view or in Design view.

▶ 4. Switch to Design view, click the **Arrange** tab on the Ribbon, and then in the Control Layout group on the Arrange tab, click the **Tab Order** button. The Tab Order dialog box opens. See Figure 6-48.

Figure 6-48 ▶ **Changing the tab order for the main form**

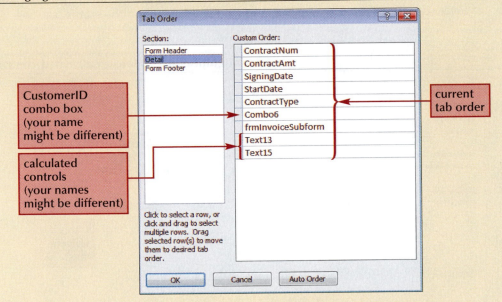

Because you did not set the Name property for the combo box control and the calculated controls, Access assigned their names: Combo6 (your name might be different) for the CustomerID combo box, Text13 (your name might be different) for the Number of Invoices calculated control, and Text15 (your name might be different) for the Invoice Amount Total calculated control. The Auto Order button lets you create a left-to-right, top-to-bottom tab order automatically, which is not the order Sarah wants. You need to move the Combo6 entry above the ContractType entry.

▶ 5. Click the **row selector** to the left of Combo6, and then drag the row selector above the ContractType entry. The entries are now correct in the correct order.

▶ 6. Click the **OK** button, save your form design changes, switch to Form view, and then tab through the controls in the main form to make sure the tab order is correct.

Trouble? If the tab order is incorrect, switch to Design view, click the Arrange tab on the Ribbon, click Tab Order in the Control Layout group, move appropriate entries in the Tab Order dialog box, and then repeat Step 6.

You've finished adding controls to the form, but the form is plain looking and lacks visual clues for the different controls in the form. You'll complete the form by making it more attractive and easier for Sarah and her staff to use.

Improving a Form's Appearance

The frmContractsAndInvoices form has four distinct areas: the Form Header section containing the title and the Select Contract combo box, the six bound controls in the Detail section, the two calculated controls in the Detail section, and the subform in the Detail section. To visually separate these four areas, you'll increase the height of the Form Header section, add a horizontal line at the bottom of the Form Header section, and draw a rectangle around the calculated controls.

Adding a Line to a Form

You can use lines in a form to improve the form's readability, to group related information, or to underline important values. You use the **Line tool** in Design view to add a line to a form or report.

Adding a Line to a Form or Report | Reference Window

- Display the form or report in Design view.
- In the Controls group on the Design tab, click the Line button.
- Position the pointer where you want the line to begin.
- Drag the pointer to the position for the end of the line, and then release the mouse button. If you want to ensure that you draw a straight horizontal or vertical line, hold down the Shift key before and during the drag operation.
- To make small adjustments to the line length, select the line, hold down the Shift key, and then press an arrow key. To make small adjustments in the placement of a line, select the line, hold down the Ctrl key, and then press an arrow key.

You will add a horizontal line to the Form Header section to separate the controls in the this section from the controls in the Detail section.

To add a line to the form:

1. Switch to Design view, and then drag down the bottom of the Form Header section to the 1-inch mark on the vertical ruler to make room to draw a horizontal line at the bottom of the Form Header section.

2. In the Controls group on the Design tab, click the **Line** button ⬛.

3. Position the pointer's plus symbol (+) at the left edge of the Form Header section and at the 0.75-inch mark on the vertical ruler.

4. Hold down the **Shift** key, drag a horizontal line from left to right, so the end of the line aligns with the right edge of the grid in the Form Header section, release the mouse button, and then release the **Shift** key. See Figure 6-49.

Figure 6-49 ▶ Adding a line to the form

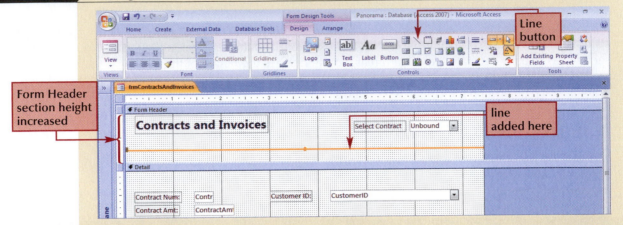

Trouble? If the line is not straight or not positioned correctly, click the Undo button on the Quick Access Toolbar, and then repeat Steps 2 through 4. If the line is not the correct length, hold down the Shift key, and press one or more of the arrow keys until the line's length is the same as that of the line shown in Figure 6-49.

▶ **5.** Drag up the bottom of the Form Header section to just below the line at the 0.75-inch mark on the vertical ruler.

▶ **6.** Save your form design changes.

Next, you'll add a Rectangle around the calculated controls in the Detail section.

Adding a Rectangle to a Form

You can use a rectangle in a form to group related controls and to separate the group from other controls. You use the **Rectangle tool** in Design view to add a rectangle to a form or report.

Reference Window | **Adding a Rectangle to a Form or Report**

- Display the form or report in Design view.
- In the Controls group on the Design tab, click the Rectangle button.
- Click in the form or report to create a default-sized rectangle, or drag a rectangle in the position and size you want.

You will add a rectangle to the Detail section around the calculated controls and their labels to separate them from the subform and from the other controls in the Detail section.

To add a rectangle to the form:

▶ **1.** In the Controls group on the Design tab, click the **Rectangle** button ▢.

▶ **2.** Position the pointer's plus symbol (+) approximately two grid dots above and two grid dots to the left of the Number of Invoices label.

3. Drag a rectangle down and to the right until all four sides of the rectangle are approximately two grid dots from the two calculated controls and their labels. See Figure 6-50.

Adding a rectangle to the form ◄ Figure 6-50

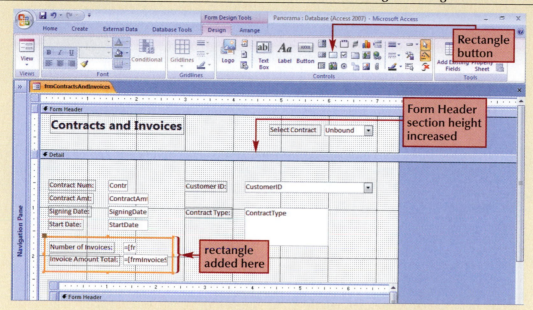

Trouble? If the rectangle is not sized or positioned correctly, use the sizing handles to adjust its size and the move handle to adjust its position.

Next, you'll set the thickness of the rectangle's lines.

4. In the Controls group on the Design tab, click the **Line Thickness** button ≡▾, click the line with the ScreenTip **2 pt** in the list, and then deselect the control.

Next, you'll add color and visual effects to the controls in the Detail and Form Header sections.

Modifying the Visual Effects of the Controls in a Form

Distinguishing one group of controls in a form from other groups is an important visual cue to the users of the form. For example, users should be able to distinguish the bound controls in the form from the calculated controls and from the Select Contract control in the Form Header section. You'll now modify the controls in the form to provide these visual cues. You'll start by setting font properties for the calculated control's labels.

To modify the controls in the form:

1. Select the **Number of Invoices** label and the **Invoice Amount Total** label; in the Font group on the Design tab, click the arrow for the **Font Color** button A; click the **Blue** color (row 7, column 8) in the Standard Colors palette; and then in the Font group on the Design tab, click the **Bold** button B. The labels' captions now use a bold, blue font.

Next, you'll set properties for the Select Contract label in the Form Header section.

> **Tip**
>
> Using one of the available AutoFormats is always an option for improving the appearance of a form, but an AutoFormat doesn't provide the control you can achieve by setting properties in Design view and in Layout view.

2. Select the **Select Contract** label in the Form Header section, set the label's color to **Red** (row 7, column 2 in the Standard Colors palette), and then set the font style to bold.

Next, you'll set the label's Special Effect property to a raised effect. The **Special Effect property** specifies the type of special effect applied to a control in a form or report. The choices for this property are Flat, Raised, Sunken, Etched, Shadowed, and Chiseled.

3. In the Controls group on the Design tab, click the arrow for the **Special Effect** button ▭, and then click **Special Effect: Raised**. The label now has a raised special effect, and the label's caption now uses a bold, red font.

Next, you'll set the Special Effect property for the bound control labels to a sunken effect.

4. Select the **Contract Num** label, **Contract Amt** label, **Signing Date** label, **Start Date** label, **Customer ID** label, and **Contract Type** label, set the controls' Special Effect property to **Special Effect: Sunken**, and then deselect all controls.

Trouble? If setting the Sunken effect does not work, repeat Step 4 and set the selected controls' Special Effect property to Special Effect: Shadowed, and then repeat Step 4 and set the selected controls' Special Effect property to Special Effect: Sunken.

Finally, you'll set the background color of the Form Header section, the Detail section, the Select Contract combo box, and the two calculated controls. You can use the **Fill/Back Color button** in the Font group on the Design tab to change the background color of a control, section, or object (form or report).

5. Click the Form Header's section bar, and in the Font group on the Design tab, click the arrow for the **Fill/Back Color** button 🎨; and then click the **Access Theme 2** color (row 2, column 2) in the Access Theme Colors palette. The Form Header's background color changes to the Access Theme 2 color.

6. Click the Detail section's section bar, and in the Font Group on the Design tab, click the **Fill/Back Color** button to change the Detail section's background color to the **Access Theme 2** color.

7. Select the **Select Contract** combo box, **Number of Invoices** text box, and the **Invoice Amount Total** text box, set the selected controls' background color to the **Access Theme 2** color, and then deselect all controls by clicking to the right of the Detail section's grid. See Figure 6-51.

Completed custom form in Design view | Figure 6-51

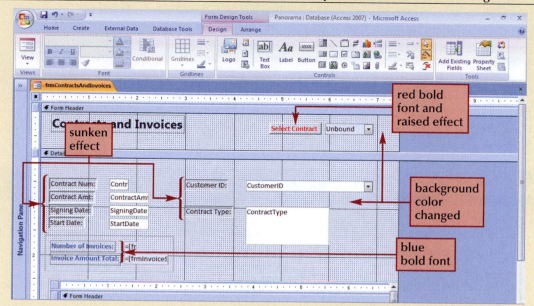

8. Switch to Form view, and then click the **ContractNum** text box to deselect the value. See Figure 6-52.

Completed custom form in Form view | Figure 6-52

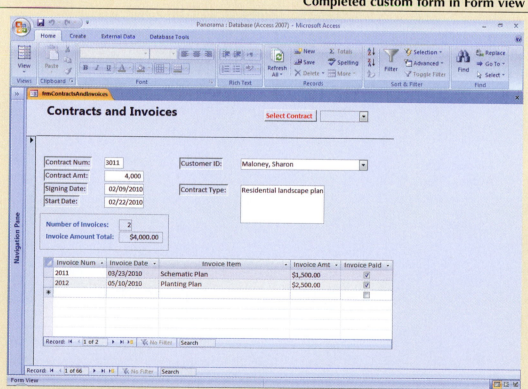

Trouble? Depending on which control has the focus in the form, the CustomerID combo box's background color might be white or it might be the background color of the Detail section.

▶ **9.** Test the form by tabbing from field to field, navigating from record to record, and using the Select Contract combo box to find records, making sure you don't change any field values and observing that the calculated controls display the correct values.

You've completed the custom form.

▶ **10.** Save your form design changes, close the form, close the Panorama database, make a backup copy of the database, open the **Panorama** database, compact and repair the database, close the database, and then exit Access.

The custom form you created will make it easier for Sarah and her staff to work with contract and invoice data in the Panorama database.

Review	**Session 6.3 Quick Check**

1. To create a combo box to find records in a form with the Combo Box Wizard, the form's record source must be a(n) _____ .

2. You use the _____ tool to add a subform to a form.

3. To calculate subtotals and overall totals in a form or report, you use the _____ function.

4. The Control Source property setting can be either a(n) _____ or a(n) _____ .

5. Explain the difference between the Tab Stop property and tab order.

6. What is focus?

7. The _____ property has settings such as Raised and Sunken.

Tutorial Summary | Review

In this tutorial, you examined general form design guidelines and learned how to use them in planning a custom form. You learned how to change a lookup field back to a Text field, to print database relationships, and to use the Documenter. You created a datasheet form, a multiple items form, and a split form, and you modified a form in Layout view. After creating a blank bound form, you learned how to add bound controls to a form, and how to select, move, align, resize, delete, and rename controls. You also learned how to add and delete form headers and footers, how to add a combo box to display and update a field and a combo box to find records, how to add a subform to a form, how to add calculated controls to a subform and a main form, and how to change the tab order in a form. Finally, you learned how to improve the visual appearance of a form.

Key Terms

Anchor property
bound control
bound form
calculated control
Caption property
combo box
Combo Box tool
control
control layout
Control Margins property
Control Padding property
Control Source property
Control Wizard
ControlTip Text property
Count function
custom form
Datasheet tool

Detail section
Display Control property
Documenter
Fill/Back Color button
focus
Form Footer section
Form Header section
form selector
grid
label
Line tool
move handle
Multiple Items tool
Name property
Record Source property
Rectangle tool
Row Source property

rulers
section bar
section selector
sizing handle
Special Effect property
Split Form tool
stacked layout
Subform/Subreport tool
Sum function
tab order
Tab Stop property
tabular layout
Text Box tool
unbound control
unbound form
Visible property

Practice	Review Assignments

Practice the skills you learned in the tutorial using the same case scenario.

Data File needed for the Review Assignments: Products.accdb (*cont. from Tutorial 5*)

Sarah wants you to create several forms, including a custom form that displays and updates companies and the products they offer. You'll do so by completing the following:

1. Open the **Products** database located in the Level.02\Review folder provided with your Data Files.

2. Remove the lookup feature from the CompanyID field in the **tblProduct** table, and resize the Company ID column to its best fit.

3. Edit the relationship between the primary tblCompany and related tblProduct tables to enforce referential integrity and to cascade update related fields. Create the relationship report, and then save the report as **rptRelationshipsForProducts**.

4. Use the Documenter to document the qryContactList query. Select all query options; use the Names, Data Types, and Sizes option for fields; and use the Names and Fields option for indexes. Print the report produced by the Documenter.

5. Use the Datasheet tool to create a form based on the tblProduct table, and then save the form as **frmProductDatasheet**.

6. Use the Multiple Items tool to create a form based on the qryCompanyList query, and then save the form as **frmCompanyListMultipleItems**.

7. Use the Split Form tool to create a split form based on the tblProduct table, and then make the following changes to the form in Layout view.
   a. Remove the Unit control from the stacked layout, and then anchor it to the bottom left.
   b. Remove the five controls in the right column from the stacked layout, and then anchor the group to the bottom right.
   c. Remove the ProductType and Price controls from the stacked layout, move them to the top right, and then anchor them to the top right.
   d. Reduce the widths of the ProductID and CompanyID text boxes to a reasonable size.
   e. Save the modifiied form as **frmProductSplitForm**.

8. Use Figure 6-53 and the following steps to create a custom form named **frmCompaniesWithProducts** based on the tblCompany and tblProduct tables.

Figure 6-53

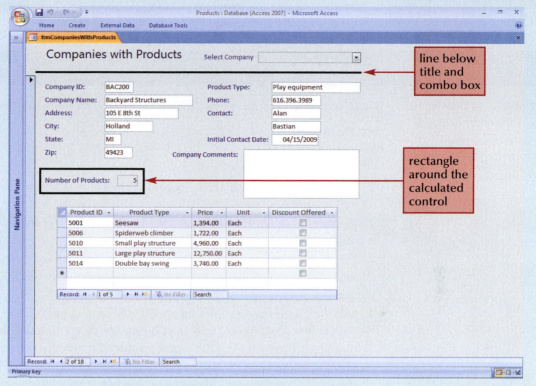

a. Place the fields from the tblCompany table at the top of the Detail section. Delete the Contact Last Name label and change the caption for the Contact First Name label to **Contact:**.

b. Move the fields into two columns in the Detail section, resizing and aligning controls, as necessary.

c. Add the title in the Form Header section.

d. Make sure the form's Record Source property is set to tblCompany, and then add a combo box in the Form Header section to find CompanyName field values. In the wizard steps, select the CompanyName and CompanyID fields, and hide the key column. Resize and move the control.

e. Add a subform based on the tblProduct table, include only the fields shown in Figure 6-53, link with CompanyID, name the subform **frmPartialProductSubform**, delete the subform label, and resize the columns in the subform to their best fit and resize and position the subform.

f. Add a calculated control that displays the number of products displayed in the subform. Set the calculated control's Tab Stop property to No, and the ControlTip Text property to **Calculated number of products**.

g. Add a line in the Form Header section, and add a rectangle around the calculated control and its label, setting the line thickness of both controls to the line style with the ScreenTip 3 pt.

h. Use the Dark Label Text font (row 1, column 3 in the Access Theme Colors palette) for all labels, and use the Background fill color (row 1, column 5 in the Access Theme Colors palette) for the sections, the calculated control, and the Select Company combo box.

i. Make sure the tab order is top-to-bottom, left-to-right for the main form text boxes.

9. Close the Products database without exiting Access, make a backup copy of the database, open the **Products** database, compact and repair the database, close the database, and then exit Access.

Challenge	**Case Problem 1**

Apply the skills you learned in the tutorial to create a custom form for a small music school.

Data File needed for this Case Problem: Contract.accdb (*cont. from Tutorial 5*)

Pine Hill Music School   Yuka wants you to create several forms, including a custom form that displays and updates the school's music contracts with students. You'll do so by completing the following:

1. Open the **Contract** database located in the Level.02\Case1 folder provided with your Data Files.

2. Remove the lookup feature from the TeacherID field in the **tblContract** table, and then resize the Teacher ID column to its best fit.

3. Define a one-to-many relationship between the primary tblTeacher table and the related tblContract table. Select the referential integrity option and the cascade updates option for this relationship.

4. Use the Documenter to document the tblContract table. Select all table options; use the Names, Data Types, and Sizes option for fields; and use the Names and Fields option for indexes. Print the report produced by the Documenter.

5. Use the Multiple Items tool to create a form based on the qryLessonsByTeacher query, change the title to **Lessons by Teacher**, and then save the form as **frmLessonsByTeacherMultipleItems**.

6. Use the Split Form tool to create a split form based on the qryLessonsByTeacher query, and then make the following changes to the form in Layout view.
   a. Reduce the widths of all six text boxes to a reasonable size.
   b. Remove the LessonType, LessonLength, and MonthlyLessonCost controls from the stacked layout, move these three controls to the right and then to the top of the form, and then anchor them to the top right.
   c. Select the MonthlyLessonCost control and its label, and then anchor them to the bottom right.
   d. Remove the ContractEndDate control from the stacked layout, and then anchor the control to the bottom left.
   e. Change the title to **Lessons by Teacher**, and then save the modifiied form as **frmLessonsByTeacherSplitForm**.

7. Use Figure 6-54 and the following steps to create a custom form named **frmContract** based on the tblContract table.

Figure 6-54

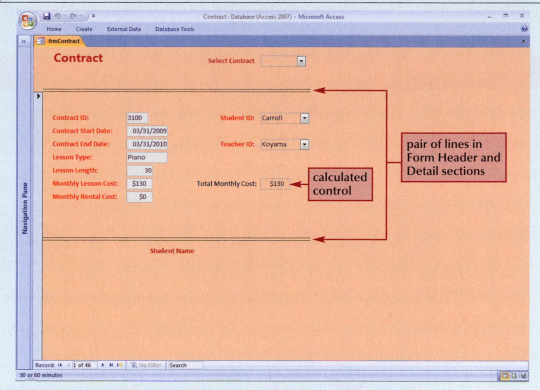

a. For the StudentID combo box, select the LastName, FirstName, and StudentID fields, in order; and sort in ascending order by the LastName field and then by the FirstName field.

b. For the TeacherID combo box, select the LastName, FirstName, and TeacherID fields, in order; and sort in ascending order by the LastName field and then by the FirstName field.

c. Make sure the form's Record Source property is set to tblContract, and then add a combo box in the Form Header section to find ContractID field values.

⊕ EXPLORE

d. Add a calculated control that displays the total of the MonthlyLessonCost and MonthlyRentalCost fields. Set the calculated control's Tab Stop property to No and format the values as currency with no decimal places.

⊕ EXPLORE

e. Add a line in the Form Header section, add a second line below it, and then add a second pair of lines near the bottom of the Detail section. Set the line thickness of all lines to the line setting with the ScreenTip 1 pt.

⊕ EXPLORE

f. Use the Label tool to add your name below the pair of lines at the bottom of the Detail section.

g. For the labels in the Details section, except for the Total Monthly Cost label and the label displaying your name, use the Red font (row 7, column 2 in the Standard Colors palette).

h. For the title, the Select Contract label, and the label displaying your name, use the Dark Red font (row 7, column 1 in the Standard Colors palette).

i. For the background color of the bound controls in the Detail section, use the Background fill color (row 1, column 5 in the Access Theme Colors palette). For the background fill color of the sections, the calculated control, and the Select Contract combo box, use the Brown 3 color (row 4, column 10 in the Standard Colors palette).

j. Make sure the tab order is top-to-bottom, left-to-right for the main form text boxes.

8. Close the Contract database without exiting Access, make a backup copy of the database, open the **Contract** database, compact and repair the database, close the database, and then exit Access.

| Create | **Case Problem 2** |

Use the skills you learned in the tutorial to work with the data for a health and fitness center and to create a custom form.

Data File needed for this Case Problem: Training.accdb (*cont. from Tutorial 5*)

Parkhurst Health & Fitness Center   Martha Parkhurst wants you to create several forms, including two custom forms that display and update data in the Training database. You'll do so by completing the following:

1. Open the **Training** database located in the Level.02\Case2 folder provided with your Data Files.
2. Use the Documenter to document the qryMemberNames query. Select all query options; use the Names, Data Types, and Sizes option for fields; and use the Names and Fields option for indexes. Print the first page of the report produced by the Documenter.
3. Use the Datasheet tool to create a form based on the tblProgram table, and then save the form as **frmProgramDatasheet**.

⊕ EXPLORE

4. Create a custom form based on the qryUpcomingExpirations query. Display all fields from the query in the form. Create your own design for the form. Add a label to the bottom of the Detail section that contains your first and last names. Change the label's font so that your name appears in bold, blue text. Change the ExpirationDate text box format so that the field value displays in bold, red text. Save the form as **frmUpcomingExpirations**.
5. Use Figure 6-55 and the following steps to create a custom form named **frmProgramsAndMembers** based on the tblProgram and tblMember tables.

Figure 6-55

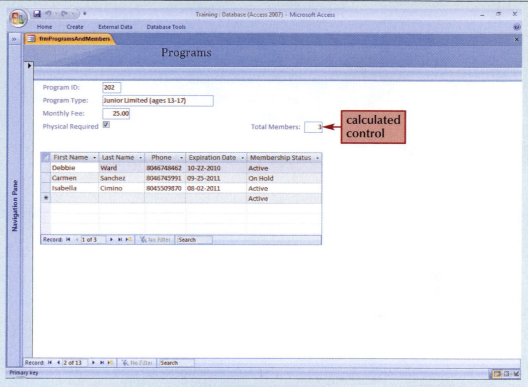

a. Selected fields from the **tblMember** table appear in a subform named **frmProgramMemberSubform**.

b. The calculated control displays the total number of records that appear in the subform. Set the calculated control's ControlTip Text property to **Total number of members in this program**. Set the calculated control's Tab Stop property to No.

c. Apply an appropriate AutoFormat to the form.

d. View the completed form.

6. Close the Training database without exiting Access, make a backup copy of the database, open the **Training** database, compact and repair the database, close the database, and then exit Access.

| Create | **Case Problem 3** |

Use the skills you learned in the tutorial to create forms for a recycling agency.

Data File needed for this Case Problem: Agency.accdb (*cont. from Tutorial 5*)

Rossi Recycling Group   Mary Rossi asks you to create several forms, including a custom form for the Agency database so that she can better track donations for the agency. You'll do so by completing the following:

1. Open the **Agency** database located in the Level.02\Case3 folder provided with your Data Files.

2. Use the Documenter to document the tblDonor table. Select all table options; use the Names, Data Types, and Sizes option for fields; and use the Names and Fields option for indexes. Print the report produced by the Documenter.

3. Use the Multiple Items tool to create a form based on the qryDonorPhoneList query, change the title to **Donor Phone List**, and then save the form as **frmDonorPhoneListMultipleItems**.

4. Use the Split Form tool to create a split form based on the tblDonor table, and then make the following changes to the form in Layout view.

   a. Reduce the widths of all five text boxes to a reasonable size.

   b. Remove the FirstName, LastName, and Phone controls from the stacked layout, move them to the top right, and then anchor them to the top right.

   c. Change the title to **Donor**, and then save the modifiied form as **frmDonorSplitForm**.

5. Use Figure 6-56 and the following steps to create a custom form named **frmDonorDonations** based on the tblDonor and tblDonation tables.

Figure 6-56

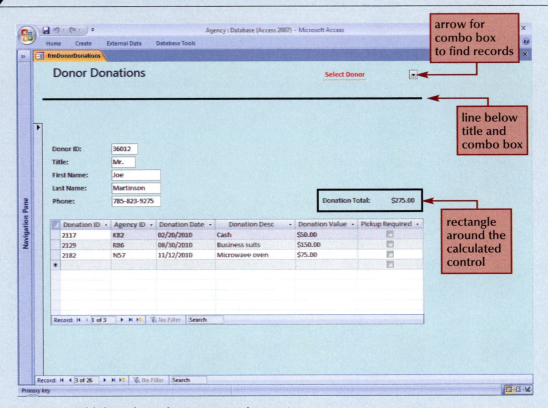

   a. Add the title in the Form Header section.

   b. Make sure the form's Record Source property is set to tblDonor, and then add a combo box in the Form Header section to find DonorID field values. In the wizard steps, select the DonorID field. Format the label using a bold, Red font (row 7, column 2 in the Standard Colors palette) and the Chiseled special effect.

   c. Add a subform based on the tblDonation table, name the subform **frmDonorDonationSubform**, delete the subform label, and resize the columns in the subform to their best fit and resize and position the subform.

EXPLORE

    d. Add a calculated control that displays the total of the DonationValue field displayed in the subform with the Currency format. Set the calculated control's Tab Stop property to No, and the Border Style property to Transparent.

    e. Add a line in the Form Header section, and add a rectangle around the calculated control and its label, setting the line thickness of both controls to the line style with the ScreenTip 3 pt.

    f. Use the background color Aqua Blue 2 (row 3, column 9 in the Standard Colors palette) for the sections, the calculated control, and the Select Donor combo box.

    g. Make sure the tab order is top-to-bottom for the main form text boxes.

6. Close the Agency database without exiting Access, make a backup copy of the database, open the **Agency** database, compact and repair the database, close the database, and then exit Access.

Create	**Case Problem 4**

Use the skills you learned in the tutorial to create forms for a luxury property rental company.

Data File needed for this Case Problem: Vacation.accdb (*cont. from Tutorial 5*)

GEM Ultimate Vacations   Griffin and Emma MacElroy want you to create several forms, including a custom form that displays and updates guest and reservation data in the Vacation database. You'll do so by completing the following:

1. Open the **Vacation** database located in the Level.02\Case4 folder provided with your Data Files.

2. Remove the lookup feature from the PropertyID field in the **tblReservation** table.

3. Edit the relationship between the primary tblProperty and related tblReservation tables to enforce referential integrity and to cascade update related fields. Create the relationship report, and then save the report as **rptRelationshipsForVacation**.

4. Use the Documenter to document the qryIllinoisGuests query. Select all query options; use the Names, Data Types, and Sizes option for fields; and use the Nothing option for indexes. Print the report produced by the Documenter.

5. Use the Datasheet tool to create a form based on the qryGuestTripDates query, and then save the form as **frmGuestTripDates**.

EXPLORE   6. Create a custom form based on the qryRentalCost query. Display all fields in the form. Use your own design for the form, but use the title **Reserved Trips** in the Form Header section, and use the Label tool to add your name to the Form Header section. Save the form as **frmRentalCost**.

7. Use Figure 6-57 and the following steps to create a custom form named **frmGuestsWithReservations** based on the tblGuest and tblReservation tables.

Figure 6-57

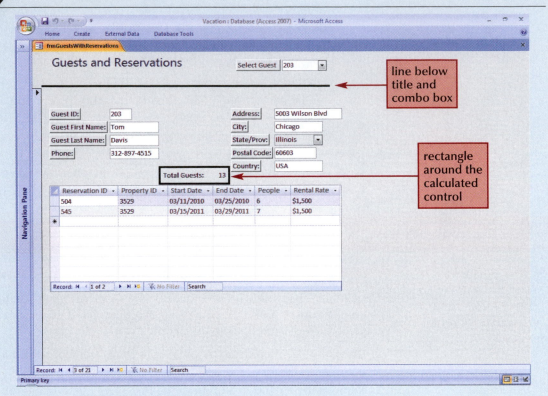

a. Add the title in the Form Header section.

b. Make sure the form's Record Source property is set to tblGuest and then add a combo box in the Form Header section to find GuestID field values.

c. Add a subform based on the tblReservation table, name the subform **frmGuestAndReservationSubform**, delete the subform label, and resize the columns in the subform to their best fit and resize and position the subform.

d. Add a calculated control that displays the total of the People field displayed in the subform. Set the calculated control's Tab Stop property to No, and set the label's and calculated control's Border Style property to Transparent.

e. Add a line in the Form Header section, and add a rectangle around the calculated control and its label, setting the line thickness of both controls to the line style with the ScreenTip 3 pt.

f. Use the Background fill color (row 1, column 5 in the Access Theme Colors palette) for the sections and the calculated control.

g. Use the Raised special effect for the labels in the Detail section and the Form Header section.

h. Make sure the tab order is top-to-bottom and left-to-right for the main form text boxes.

8. Close the Vacation database without exiting Access, make a backup copy of the database, open the **Vacation** database, compact and repair the database, close the database, and then exit Access.

| Create | **Case Problem 5** |

Use the skills you learned in this tutorial to work with the data for an Internet service provider.

Data File needed for this Case Problem: ACE.accdb (*cont. from Tutorial 5*)

Always Connected Everyday   Chris and Pat Dixon want you to create several forms, including a custom form that displays and updates data in the ACE database. You'll do so by completing the following:

1. Open the **ACE** database located in the Level.02\Case5 folder provided with your Data Files.
2. In Tutorial 5, you created a lookup field in the tblCustomer table. Remove the lookup feature from this field.
3. Make sure that the table relationship enforces referential integrity and cascade updates related fields. Create the relationship report, and then save the report as **rptRelationshipsForACE**.
4. Use the Documenter to document one of your forms. Select all form options and use the Names option for sections and controls. Print the report produced by the Documenter.
5. In Tutorial 5, you created forms to display and update the data in the ACE database. Review these forms, and develop a consistent design strategy that you'll use to customize all the forms. Your design strategy should include the use of combo boxes for foreign keys and for searching, calculated controls, and visual effects.
6. Using your form design strategy, customize all the forms in the ACE database.
7. Close the ACE database without exiting Access, make a backup copy of the database, open the **ACE** database, compact and repair the database, close the database, and then exit Access.

| Research | **Internet Assignments** |

Use the Internet to find and work with data related to the topics presented in this tutorial.

The purpose of the Internet Assignments is to challenge you to find information on the Internet that you can use to work effectively with this software. The actual assignments are updated and maintained on the Course Technology Web site. Log on to the Internet and use your Web browser to go to the Student Online Companion for New Perspectives Office 2007 at **www.course.com/np/office2007**. Then navigate to the Internet Assignments for this tutorial.

| Assess | **SAM Assessment and Training** |

If you have a SAM user profile, you may have access to hands-on instruction, practice, and assessment of the skills covered in this tutorial. Log in to your SAM account (**http://sam2007.course.com**) to launch any assigned training activities or exams that relate to the skills covered in this tutorial.

| Review | **Quick Check Answers** |

Session 6.1

1. forms
2. Row Source
3. An Access tool that creates detailed documentation of the objects in a database.

4. A form tool that creates a customizable form that displays multiple records from a source table or query in a datasheet format.

5. A form that displays a form's data in Form view and Datasheet view at the same time; the views are synchronized with each other at all times.

6. Anchor

Session 6.2

1. A bound form has a table or query as its record source, and is used to maintain and display table data.

2. A bound control is connected to a field in the database; an unbound control is not.

3. grid

4. move

5. Click the text box to select it, position the pointer anywhere on the border of the text box (but not on a move or sizing handle), and then drag the text box and its attached label.

6. Select the control, position the pointer on a sizing handle, and then drag the pointer in the appropriate direction until it is the desired size.

7. combo box

8. Right-click the label, click Properties on the shortcut menu, click the All tab, and then change the entry in the Caption text box.

9. The Form Header section lets you add titles, instructions, command buttons, and other controls to the top of a form. This section of the form does not change as you navigate through the records.

Session 6.3

1. table or query

2. Subform/Subreport

3. Sum

4. field name, expression

5. The Tab Stop property specifies whether users can use the Tab key to move to a control on a form. Tab order is the order in which you move from control to control, or change the focus, in a form when you press the Tab key.

6. Focus refers to the control that is currently active and awaiting user action; focus also refers to the object and record that is currently active.

7. Special Effect

Ending Data Files

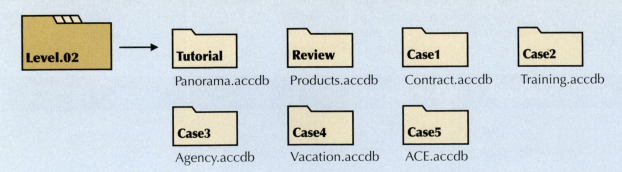

Level.02 → Tutorial   Review   Case1   Case2

Panorama.accdb   Products.accdb   Contract.accdb   Training.accdb

Case3   Case4   Case5

Agency.accdb   Vacation.accdb   ACE.accdb

Objectives

Session 7.1
- View, filter, and copy report information in Report view
- Modify a report in Layout view
- Modify a report in Design view

Session 7.2
- Design and create a custom report
- Sort and group data in a report
- Add, move, resize, and align controls in a report
- Add lines to a report
- Hide duplicate values in a report

Session 7.3
- Add the date, page numbers, and title to a report
- Create and modify mailing labels

Creating Custom Reports

Creating Reports with Information About Contracts and Invoices

Case | Belmont Landscapes

At a recent staff meeting, Sarah Fisher indicated that she would like to make some changes to an existing report in the database. She also requested a new report that she can use to produce a printed list of all invoices for all contracts.

In this tutorial, you will modify an existing report and create the new report for Sarah. In modifying and building these reports, you will use many Access report customization features, including grouping data, calculating totals, and adding lines to separate report sections. These features will enhance Sarah's reports and make them easier to read and use.

Starting Data Files

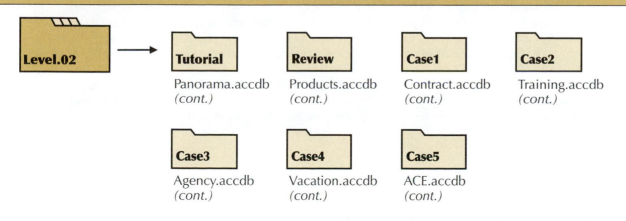

Level.02 → Tutorial
Panorama.accdb
(cont.)

Review
Products.accdb
(cont.)

Case1
Contract.accdb
(cont.)

Case2
Training.accdb
(cont.)

Case3
Agency.accdb
(cont.)

Case4
Vacation.accdb
(cont.)

Case5
ACE.accdb
(cont.)

Session 7.1

Customizing Existing Reports

A report is a formatted printout (or screen display) of the contents of one or more tables in a database. Although you can format and print data using datasheets, queries, and forms, reports offer greater flexibility and provide a more professional, readable appearance. For example, the staff at Belmont Landscapes can create reports from the database for billing statements and mailing labels, but they could not use datasheets, queries, and forms for the same purposes.

Before Lucia Perez joined Belmont Landscapes to enhance the Panorama database, Sarah Fisher and her staff created two reports. Sarah used the Report tool to create the rptContract report and the Report Wizard to create the rptCustomersAndContracts report. One of Sarah's staff members modified the rptCustomersAndContracts report in Layout view by modifying the title, moving and resizing fields, changing the font color of field names, inserting a picture, and using conditional formatting to format values in the ContractAmt field that exceed $25,000 in a red font. The rptCustomersAndContracts report is an example of a custom report. When you modify a report created by the Report tool or the Report Wizard in Layout view or in Design view, or when you create a report from scratch in Layout view or in Design view, you produce a **custom report**. You need to produce a custom report whenever the Report tool or the Report Wizard cannot automatically create the specific report you need, or when you need to fine-tune an existing report to fix formatting problems or to add controls and special features.

Sarah asks Lucia to review the rptContract report, make improvements to it, and demonstrate features that Sarah's staff can use when working with reports.

Viewing a Report in Report View

You can view reports on screen in Print Preview, Layout view, Design view, and Report view. You've already viewed and worked with reports in Print Preview and Layout view, and you'll find that making modifications in Design view for reports is similar to making changes in Design view for forms. **Report view** provides an interactive view of a report. You can use Report view to view the contents of a report and to apply a filter to the data in a report. You can also copy selected portions of the report to the Clipboard and use the selected data in another program.

InSight	Choosing the View to Use for a Report

You can view a report on screen using Report view, Print Preview, Layout view, or Design view. Which view you choose depends on what you intend to do with the report and its data.

- Use Report view when you want to filter the report data before printing a report, or when you want to copy a selected portion of a report.
- Use Print Preview when you want to see what a report will look like when it is printed. Print Preview is the only view in which you can navigate the pages of a report, zoom in or out, and view a **multiple-column report**, which is a report that prints the same collection of field values in two or more sets across the page.
- Use Layout view when you want to modify a report while seeing actual report data.
- Use Design view when you want to fine-tune a report's design, or when you want to add lines, rectangles, and other controls that are available only in Design view.

You'll open the rptContract report in Report view and show Sarah how she can interact with the report in this view.

To interact with the rptContract report in Report view:

▶ 1. Start Access, and then open the **Panorama** database in the Level.02\Tutorial folder provided with your Data Files.

Trouble? If the Security Warning is displayed below the Ribbon, either the Panorama database is not located in the Level.02\Tutorial folder or you did not designate that folder as a trusted folder. Make sure you opened the database in the Level.02\Tutorial folder, and make sure that it's a trusted folder.

▶ 2. Open the Navigation Pane, scroll down the Navigation Pane (if necessary), right-click **rptContract**, click **Open** on the shortcut menu, and then close the Navigation Pane. The rptContract report opens in Report view and the Navigation Pane closes. See Figure 7-1.

> **Tip**
>
> Double-clicking a report name in the Navigation Pane opens the report in Report view.

Report displayed in Report view | **Figure 7-1**

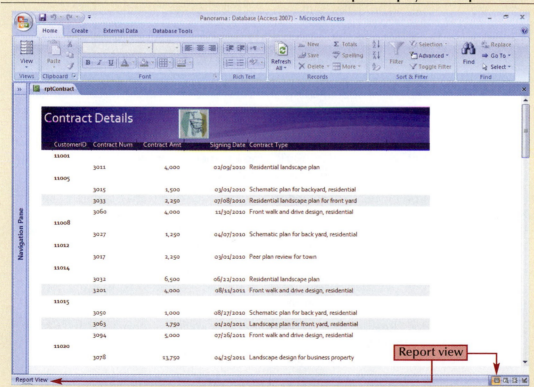

In Report view, you can view the live version of the report prior to printing it, just as you can do in Print Preview. Unlike Print Preview, you can apply filters to the report before printing it. You'll show Sarah how to apply filters to the rptContract report.

▶ 3. In the first report detail line for Contract Num 3011, right-click **Residential landscape plan** in the Contract Type column to open the shortcut menu, and then point to **Text Filters**. A submenu of filter options for the Text field opens. See Figure 7-2.

Figure 7-2 **Filter options for a Text field in Report view**

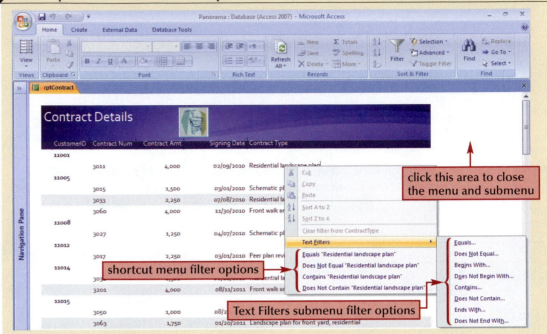

The filter options that appear on the shortcut menu depend on the selected field's data type and the selected value. Because you clicked the ContractType field value without selecting a portion of the value, the shortcut menu displays filter options—various conditions using the value "Residential landscape plan"—for the entire ContractType field value. You'll close the menus and select a portion of the ContractNum field value to show Sarah a different way of filtering the report.

▶ 4. Click an unused portion of the window (see Figure 7-2) to close the menus, and in the report detail line for Contract Num 3011, double-click **Residential** in the Contract Type column to select it, right-click **Residential**, and then point to **Text Filters** on the shortcut menu. The filter options now apply to the selected text.

Notice that the filter options on the shortcut menu include options such as "Begins With" and "Does Not Begin With," because the text you selected is at the beginning of the field value in the Contract Type column.

▶ 5. Click **Contains "Residential"** on the shortcut menu. The report content changes to display only those contracts that contain the word "residential" in the Contract Type column.

▶ 6. Double-click the word **residential** in the Contract Type column for the report detail line for Contract Num 3015 to select it, right-click **residential** to open the shortcut menu, and then point to **Text Filters**. The filter options on the shortcut menu now include the "Ends With" and "Does Not End With" options, because the text you selected is at the end of the field value in the Contract Type column.

Sarah wants to view only those contracts whose Contract Type column equals "residential landscape plan."

▶ 7. Click an unused portion of the window to close the menus, and in the report detail line for Contract Num 3011, right-click **Residential landscape plan** in the Contract Type column, and then click **Equals "Residential landscape plan"** on the shortcut menu. Only the five contracts that contain the selected phrase are displayed in the report. See Figure 7-3.

Filter applied to the report in Report view **Figure 7-3**

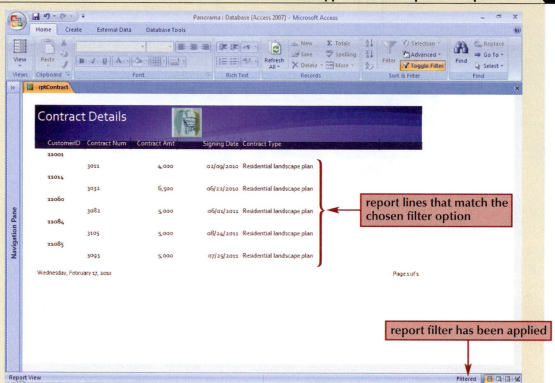

report lines that match the chosen filter option

report filter has been applied

Sarah can print the filtered report, or she can select the entire filtered report or a portion of the filtered report. Then she can copy the selection to the Clipboard and paste it into another program, such as a Word document or an Excel spreadsheet. You'll show Sarah how to copy the entire filtered report to the Clipboard.

8. Click to the left of the Contract Details title at the top of the report (but don't click in the Navigation Pane), drag down to the bottom of the report, release the mouse button to select the entire report, and then in the Clipboard group on the Home tab, point to the **Copy** button. See Figure 7-4.

Tip

To select a portion of the report instead of the entire report, click to the left of the top of the selection and drag down to the bottom of the selection.

Figure 7-4 | After selecting the entire report in Report view

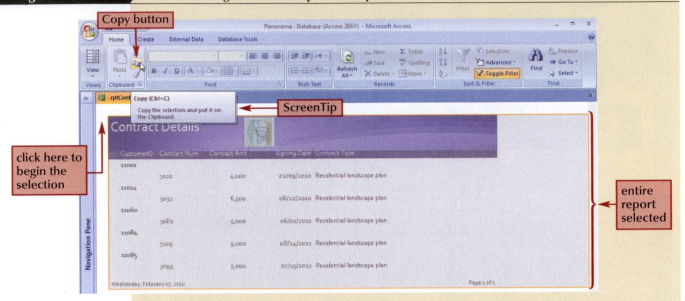

If you needed to copy the selection to the Clipboard, you would click the Copy button (see Figure 7-4). Sarah doesn't need to copy the selection, so you'll show her how to remove the filter from the report.

▶ 9. Click to the left of the Contract Details title at the top of the report to select the top portion of the report and to deselect the rest of the report, right-click **Residential landscape plan** in any report detail line in the Contract Type column, and then click **Clear filter from ContractType**. Access removes the filter and displays the complete report.

▶ 10. Scroll down the report, and notice that some field values in the Contract Type column are not fully displayed and that no grand total of the ContractAmt field values is displayed at the end of the report.

Sarah wants you to enlarge the Contract Type column in the rptContract report so that all field values are fully displayed. She also wants you to insert a space in the CustomerID column heading, remove the report's AutoFormat, format the ContractAmt field values using the Currency format, and add a grand total of the ContractAmt field values. These changes will make the report more useful for Sarah.

Enhancing and Correcting Reports Created by the Report Tool and the Report Wizard | InSight

Creating a report using the Report tool or the Report Wizard can save time, but you should review the report to determine if you need to make any of the following types of common enhancements and corrections:

- Change the report title from the report object name (with an rpt prefix and no spaces) to one that has meaning to the users.
- Reduce the widths of the date and page number controls, and move the controls so that they are not printed on a separate page.
- Review the report in Print Preview and, if the report displays excess pages, adjust the page margins and the placement of controls.
- Verify that all controls are large enough to fully display their values.

Modifying a Report in Layout View

You can make all the report changes Sarah wants in Layout view. Modifying a report in Layout view is similar to modifying a form in Layout view.

To view the report in Layout view:

1. On the status bar, click the **Layout View** button ⊞, and then scroll to the top of the report (if necessary). See Figure 7-5.

Viewing the report in Layout view | Figure 7-5

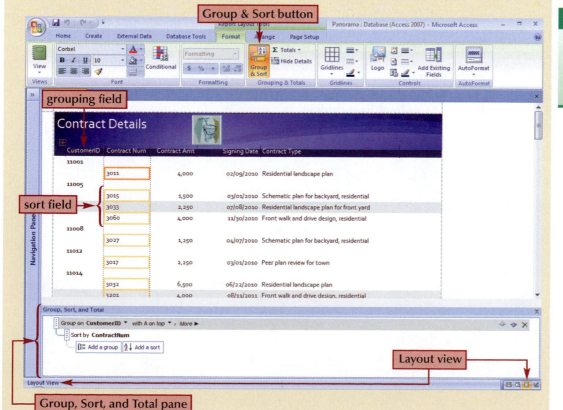

Tip

You can also switch views by right-clicking the object tab, and then clicking the view option on the shortcut menu.

Trouble? If the Group, Sort, and Total pane is not open at the bottom of the screen, click the Group & Sort button in the Grouping & Totals group on the Format tab.

Tip

You can click the Group & Sort button in the Grouping & Totals group to open and close the Group, Sort, and Total pane.

Because the rptContract report has a grouping field and a sort field, the Group & Sort button is selected, and the Group, Sort, and Total pane is open at the bottom of the screen. In the **Group, Sort, and Total pane**, you can modify the report's grouping fields and sort fields, and the report calculations for the groups. A **grouping field** is a report sort field that includes a Group Header section before a group of records having the same sort field value and a Group Footer section after the group of records. A **Group Header section** usually displays the group name and the sort field value for the group. A **Group Footer section** usually displays subtotals or counts for the records in that group. The rptContract report's grouping field is the CustomerID field, which is displayed in a Group Header section that precedes the set of contracts for the customer; the grouping field does not have a Group Footer section. The ContractNum field is a secondary sort key, as shown in the Group, Sort, and Total pane.

Because you don't need to change the grouping or sort fields for the report, you'll close the pane and then make Sarah's modifications to the report.

To modify the report in Layout view:

 ▶ **1.** In the Grouping & Totals group on the Format tab, click the **Group & Sort** button to close the Group, Sort, and Total pane.

First, you'll increase the height of the Contract Type column.

 ▶ **2.** Scroll down the report to CustomerID 11083, which has the longest field value in the Contract Type column, click the **ContractType** field value for ContractNum 3043, move the pointer to the bottom edge of the selected value, and when the pointer changes to a ↕ shape, drag down the bottom edge to increase the height to display two lines. See Figure 7-6. After you make a resizing adjustment to the control, the portion of the report you're using as a basis for the resizing might move off the screen, and you might have to scroll back to it.

Figure 7-6 ▶ After resizing the Contract Type column

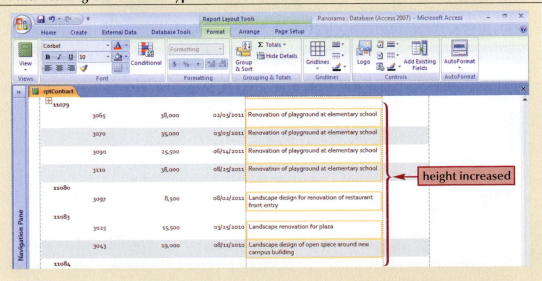

Next, you'll change the format of the field values in the Contract Amt column to Currency.

3. Right-click any value in the Contract Amt column to open the shortcut menu, click **Properties** to open the property sheet, set the Format property to **Currency**, and then close the property sheet.

When Lucia made her initial modifications to the tables, queries, forms, and reports in the Panorama database, she failed to change the first column heading in the rptContract report to Customer ID (with a space) when she modified the report. Although Lucia had set the Caption property for the CustomerID field in the tblContract table to Customer ID before she modified the rptContract report, Caption property changes do not propagate to existing forms and reports. However, a Caption property setting propagates to all new forms and reports.

4. Scroll to the top of the report (if necessary), double-click the **CustomerID** column heading, insert a space before "ID," and then press the **Enter** key.

Sarah intends to print the rptContract report periodically in the future, and she finds the AutoFormat at the beginning of the report distracting and unnecessary in a printed report. You'll remove the AutoFormat from the report.

5. In the AutoFormat group on the Format tab, click the **AutoFormat** button to open the AutoFormat gallery, and then click the **None** button (row 3, column 4). The AutoFormat gallery closes, and the AutoFormat is removed from the report. See Figure 7-7.

After removing the AutoFormat from the report **Figure 7-7**

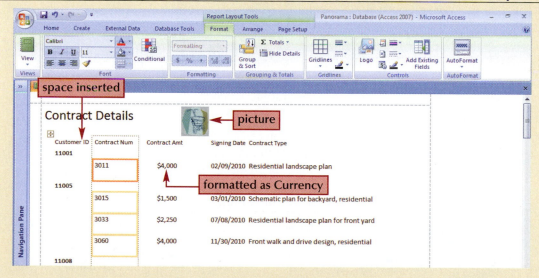

Sarah notes that the picture at the top of the report isn't needed now that you've removed the AutoFormat, so you'll delete it.

6. Right-click the picture at the top of the report to open the shortcut menu, and then click **Delete** to remove the picture.

Removing the AutoFormat also removed the alternate background color setting in the detailed contract lines, and Sarah wants you to restore this feature.

7. Click to the left of **3011** in the Contract Num column to select the detail lines, click the arrow on the **Alternate Fill/Back Color** button to display the gallery of available colors, and then in the Access Theme Colors palette, click the **Background** color (row 1, column 5). The Background color is applied to alternate detail lines in the report.

Sarah's last change to the report is to add a grand total of the ContractAmt field values. First, you must select the Contract Amt column or one of the values in the column.

▶ 8. In the detail line for ContractNum 3011, click **$4,000** in the Contract Amt column, and then in the Grouping & Totals group on the Format tab, click the **Totals** button to display the Totals menu. See Figure 7-8.

Figure 7-8 Displaying options on the Totals menu

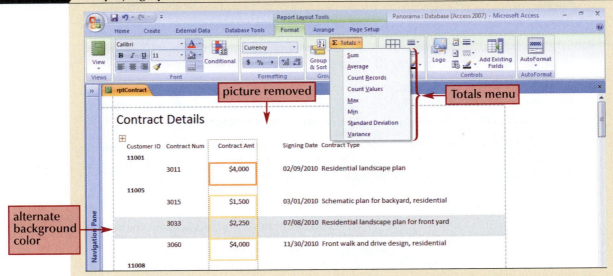

You select one of the eight aggregate functions on the Totals menu to summarize values in the selected column. To calculate and display the grand total contract amount, you'll select the Sum aggregate function.

▶ 9. Click **Sum** on the Totals menu, and then scroll to the bottom of the report. The grand total of the ContractAmt field values ($1,758,075) is displayed at the end of the report, as are subtotals for each group of contracts for each CustomerID field value ($19,000 for the last customer). See Figure 7-9.

Figure 7-9 After adding subtotals and a grand total of the ContractAmt field values

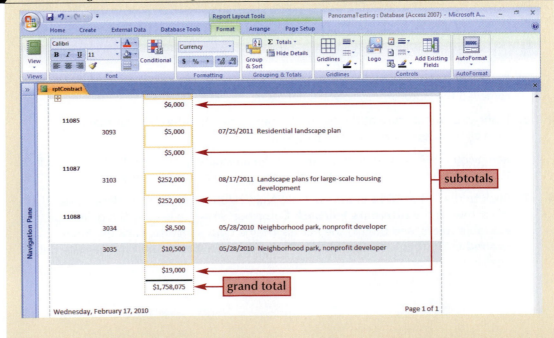

When you use an aggregate function in Layout view, Access adds the results of the function to the end of the report and adds subtotals for each grouping field. Because each customer has few contracts, Sarah asks you to remove the subtotals from the report.

▶ **10.** Right-click the **$19,000** subtotal to open the shortcut menu, click **Delete** to remove the subtotals, and then scroll to the end of the report. Although you deleted the subtotals, the grand total still appears at the end of the report.

Sarah wants to review the rptContract report in Print Preview.

▶ **11.** Save your report changes, switch to Print Preview, and then scroll through the report, ending on the last page of the report.

You can use the Zoom control on the status bar to zoom in or out the report view in 10% increments (click the Zoom In or Zoom Out buttons) or in variable increments (drag the Zoom slider control).

▶ **12.** Click the **Zoom In** button ⊕ on the status bar to increase the zoom percentage to 110%. See Figure 7-10.

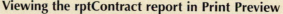

Viewing the rptContract report in Print Preview | **Figure 7-10**

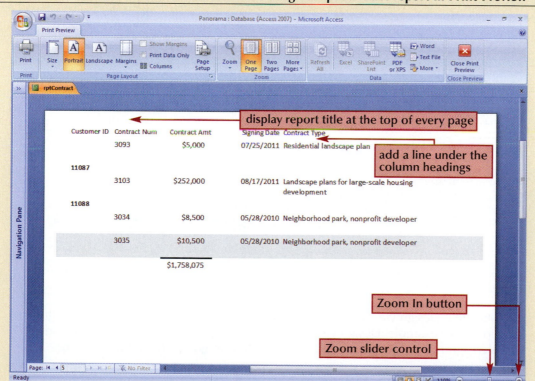

Trouble? Depending on the printer you are using, the last page of your report might differ. If so, don't worry. Different printers format reports in different ways, sometimes affecting the total number of pages and the number of records printed per page.

Sarah identifies two additional modifications she wants you to make to the report. She wants you to add a line below the column heading labels to separate them from the following detail report lines, and she wants the report title to be displayed at the top of every page, not just on the first page of the report.

Modifying a Report in Design View

Unlike the modifications you made to the report in Layout view, you can't use Layout view for Sarah's two new modifications. You must make these modifications in Design view. Design view for reports is similar to Design view for forms, which you used in Tutorial 6 to customize forms.

To view the report in Design view:

▶ 1. Switch to display the report in Design view. See Figure 7-11.

Figure 7-11 | **rptContract report in Design view**

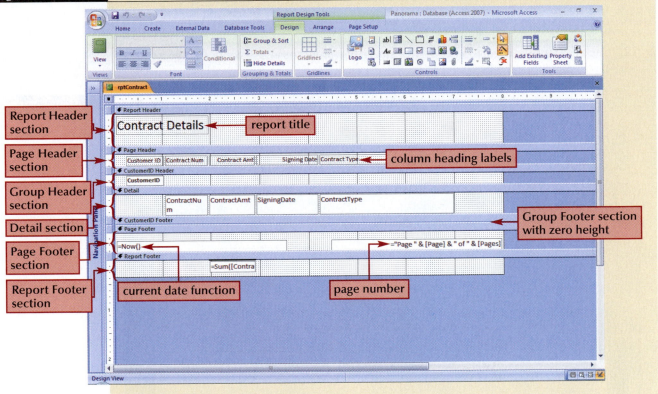

Notice that Design view for a report has most of the same components as Design view for a form. For example, Design view for forms and reports includes horizontal and vertical rulers, grids in each section, and similar buttons in groups on the Design tab.

Design view for the rptContract report displays seven sections: the Report Header section contains the report title, the Page Header section contains column heading labels, the Group Header section (CustomerID Header) contains the CustomerID grouping field, the Detail section contains the bound controls to display the field values for each record in the record source (tblContract), the Group Footer section (CustomerID Footer) has zero height and isn't displayed in the report, the Page Footer section contains the current date and the page number, and the Report Footer section contains a horizontal line above the Sum function for the grand total of the ContactAmt field values.

Each Access report can have the seven different sections described in Figure 7-12.

Access report sections — **Figure 7-12**

Report Section	Description
Report Header	Appears once at the beginning of a report. Use it for report titles, company logos, report introductions, and cover pages.
Page Header	Appears at the top of each page of a report. Use it for column headings, report titles, page numbers, and report dates. If your report has a Report Header section, it precedes the first Page Header section.
Group Header	Appears before each group of records that has the same sort field value. Use it to print the group name and the field value that all records in the group have in common. A report can have up to 10 grouping levels.
Detail	Appears once for each record in the underlying table or query. Use it to print selected fields from the table or query and to print calculated values.
Group Footer	Appears after each group of records that has the same sort field value. It is usually used to print totals for the group.
Report Footer	Appears once at the end of the report. Use it for report totals and other summary information.
Page Footer	Appears at the bottom of each page of a report. Use it for page numbers and brief explanations of symbols or abbreviations. If your report has a Report Footer section, it precedes the Page Footer section on the last page of the report.

You don't have to include all seven sections in a report. When you design a report, you determine which sections to include and what information to place in each section. Figure 7-13 shows a sample report produced from the Panorama database; it includes all seven sections.

Figure 7-13 — **Sample report showing the seven sections of a report**

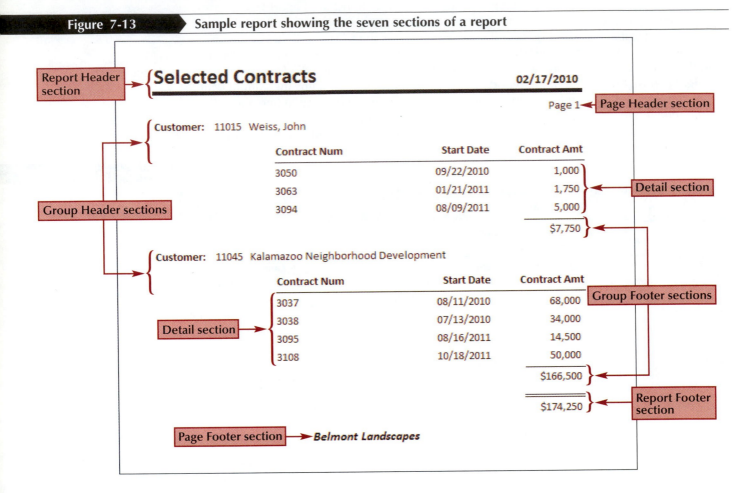

The Report tool used six of the seven report sections to create the rptContract report for Sarah. To make Sarah's changes to the report, you need to increase the height of the Page Header section, move the column heading labels down in the section, add a line under the column heading labels, cut the report title from the Report Header section and paste it in the Page Header section, move the report title, and then resize the Report Header and Page Header sections.

To modify the report in Design view:

► **1.** Place the pointer on the bottom edge of the Page Header section. When the pointer changes to a ✛ shape, drag the section's edge down until it is at the 1-inch mark on the vertical ruler.

Before you can move the column heading labels down in the Page Header section, you need to remove them and their related text boxes from the tabular layout. Recall that a tabular layout is a control layout arranged in a datasheet format. If you don't remove all the controls from the tabular layout before moving the labels, some of the controls that remain in the tabular layout might shift position or undergo unintended property changes.

► **2.** Use **Shift + Click** to select all five labels in the Page Header section, the **CustomerID** text box in the CustomerID Header section, the four text boxes in the Detail section, and the grand total text box in the Report Footer section, and then click the **Arrange** tab on the Ribbon. See Figure 7-14.

Labels and text boxes selected | **Figure 7-14**

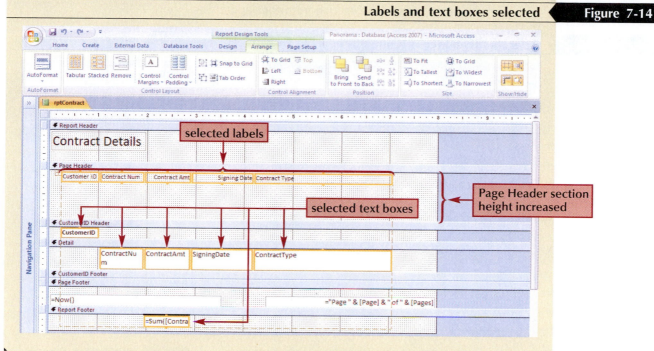

3. In the Control Layout group on the Arrange tab, click the **Remove** button to remove all selected controls from the tabular layout.

4. Use **Shift + Click** to deselect the **CustomerID** text box in the CustomerID Header section, the four text boxes in the Detail section, and the grand total text box in the Report Footer section, leaving only the five labels selected, and then use the ↓ key to move the labels down in the Page Header section until the tops of the labels are at the 0.625-inch mark on the vertical ruler.

   Next, you'll add a line under the labels.

5. Click to the right of the grid in the Page Header section to deselect all controls, click the **Design** tab on the Ribbon, and then in the Controls group on the Design tab, click the **Line** button ◹ .

6. Position the pointer's plus symbol (+) at the lower-left corner of the Customer ID label in the Page Header section, hold down the **Shift** key, drag a horizontal line from left to right, so the end of the line aligns with the right edge of "Contract Type" in the Contract Type label box, release the mouse button, and then release the **Shift** key.

7. In the Controls group on the Design tab, click the **Line Thickness** button ≡▾ , click the line with the ScreenTip **1 pt** in the list, and then deselect the control.

8. Reduce the height of the Page Header section by dragging the bottom of the section up until it touches the bottom of the line you just added.

   Finally, you'll cut the report title from the Report Header section and paste it in the Page Header section, and then remove the Report Header section.

9. Right-click the report title in the Report Header section to open the shortcut menu, click **Cut** to delete the control and place it on the Clipboard, right-click the **Page Header** section bar to select that section and open the shortcut menu, and then click **Paste**. The report title is pasted in the upper-left corner of the Page Header section.

Tip

If you want to make sure you draw a straight horizontal or vertical line, press the Shift key before you start drawing the line and release the Shift key after you've created it.

10. Drag the bottom of the Report Header section all the way up to the Report Header section bar to remove the section from the report. See Figure 7-15.

Figure 7-15   **After modifying the rptContract report in Design view**

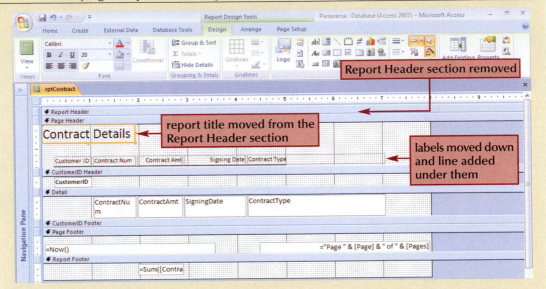

11. Save your report changes, switch to Print Preview, and then scroll through the report, ending on the last page of the report. See Figure 7-16.

Figure 7-16   **The modified rptContract report in Print Preview**

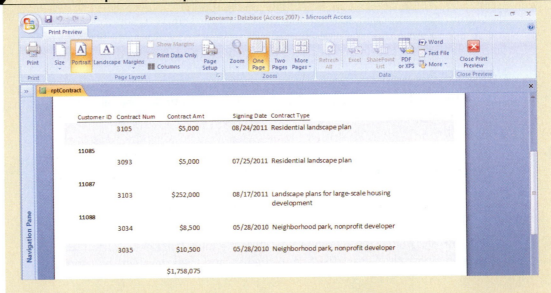

12. Close the report.

13. If you are not continuing on to the next session, close the Panorama database, and then exit Access.

Now that you have completed the changes to the rptContract report, you'll create a custom report for Sarah in the next session.

Session 7.1 Quick Check | Review

1. What is a custom report?
2. You can view a report in Report view. What other actions can you perform in Report view?
3. What is a grouping field?
4. Describe the seven sections of an Access report.

Session 7.2

Designing a Custom Report

Before you create a custom report, you should first plan the report's contents and appearance.

Guidelines for Designing a Report | InSight

When you plan a report, you should keep in mind the following report design guidelines:

- Determine the purpose of and record source for the report. Recall that the record source is a table or query that provides the fields for a form or report. If the report displays detailed information (a **detail report**), such as a list of all contracts, then the report will display fields from the record source in the Detail section. If the report displays only summary information (a **summary report**), such as total contracts by city, then no detailed information appears; only grand totals and possibly subtotals appear based on calculations using fields from the record source.
- Determine the sort order for the information in the report.
- Identify any grouping fields in the report.

At the same time you are designing a report, you should keep in mind the following report formatting guidelines:

- Balance the report's attractiveness against its readability and economy. Keep in mind that an attractive, readable two-page report is more economical than a report of three pages or more. Unlike forms, which usually display one record at a time in the main form, reports display multiple records. Instead of arranging fields vertically as you do in a form, you usually position fields horizontally across the page in a report. Typically, you single space the detail lines in a report. At the same time, make sure to include enough white space between columns so the values do not overlap or run together.
- Group related fields and position them in a meaningful, logical order. For example, position identifying fields, such as names and codes, on the left. Group together all location fields, such as street and city, and position them in their customary order.
- Identify each column of field values with a column heading label that names the field.
- Include the report title, page number, and date on every page of the report.
- Identify the end of a report either by displaying grand totals or an end-of-report message.
- Use few colors, fonts, and graphics to keep the report uncluttered and to keep the focus on the information.
- Use a consistent style for all reports in a database.

After working with Sarah and her staff to determine their requirements for a new report, Lucia prepared a paper design for a custom report to display invoices grouped by invoice item. Lucia then used her paper design to create the report shown in Figure 7-17.

Figure 7-17 **Lucia's design for the custom report**

The custom report will list the records for all invoices and will contain five sections:

- The Page Header section contains the report title ("Invoices by Item") centered between the current date on the left and the page number on the right. A horizontal line separates the column heading labels from the rest of the report page. From your work with the Report tool and the Report Wizard, you know that, by default, Access places the report title in the Report Header section and the date and page number in the Page Footer section. Sarah prefers the date, report title, and page number to appear at the top of each page, so you need to place this information in the custom report's Page Header section.
- The InvoiceItem field value from the tblInvoice table is displayed in a Group Header section.
- The Detail section contains the InvoiceDate, InvoiceAmt, and InvoicePaid field values from the tblInvoice table; the ContractType field value from the tblContract table; the City field value from the tblCustomer table; and the Customer calculated field value from the qryCustomersByName query. The detail records are sorted in ascending value by the InvoiceDate field.
- A subtotal of the InvoiceAmt field values is displayed below a line in the a Group Footer section.
- The grand total of the InvoiceAmt field values is displayed below a double line in the Report Footer section.

Before you start creating the custom report, you need to create a query that'll serve as the record source for the report.

Creating a Query for a Custom Report

The data for a report or form can come from a single table, from a single query based on one or more tables, or from multiple tables and/or queries. Sarah's report will contain data from the tblInvoice, tblContract, and tblCustomer tables, and from the qryCustomersByName query. You'll use the Simple Query Wizard to create a query to retrieve all the data required for the custom report and to serve as the report's record source.

Tip

For reports and forms that use data from multiple tables and/or queries, you should create a query to serve as the record source. If the report or form requirements change, you can easily add fields, including calculated fields, to the query.

To create the query using the Simple Query Wizard:

1. If you took a break after the previous session, make sure that the Panorama database is open and the Navigation Pane is closed.

2. Click the **Create** tab on the Ribbon, in the Other group on the Create tab, click the **Query Wizard** button, make sure **Simple Query Wizard** is selected, and then click the **OK** button. The first Simple Query Wizard dialog box opens.

   You need to select fields from the tblInvoice, tblContract, and tblCustomer tables, and from the qryCustomersByName query, in that order.

3. Make sure **Table: tblInvoice** is selected in the Tables/Queries box, and then move the **InvoiceItem**, **InvoiceDate**, **InvoiceAmt**, and **InvoicePaid** fields, in that order, to the Selected Fields list box.

4. Select **Table: tblContract** in the Tables/Queries box, and then move the **ContractType** field to the Selected Fields list box.

5. Select **Table: tblCustomer** in the Tables/Queries box, and then move the **City** field to the Selected Fields list box.

6. Select **Query: qryCustomersByName** in the Tables/Queries box, move the **Customer** calculated field to the Selected Fields list box, and then click the **Next** button.

7. Make sure the **Detail (shows every field of every record)** option button is selected, and then click the **Next** button to open the final Simple Query Wizard dialog box.

   After entering the query name and creating the query, you'll need to set the sort fields for the query.

8. Change the query name to **qryInvoicesByItem**, click the **Modify the query design** option button, and then click the **Finish** button.

   The InvoiceItem field will be a grouping field, which means it's the primary sort field, and the InvoiceDate field is the secondary sort field.

9. Set the InvoiceItem Sort text box to **Ascending**, set the InvoiceDate Sort text box to **Ascending**, save your query changes, and then click below the field lists and above the design grid to deselect all values. The completed query contains seven fields from three tables and one query and has two sort fields, the InvoiceItem primary sort field and the InvoiceDate secondary sort field. See Figure 7-18.

Figure 7-18	Finished qryInvoicesByItem query in Design view

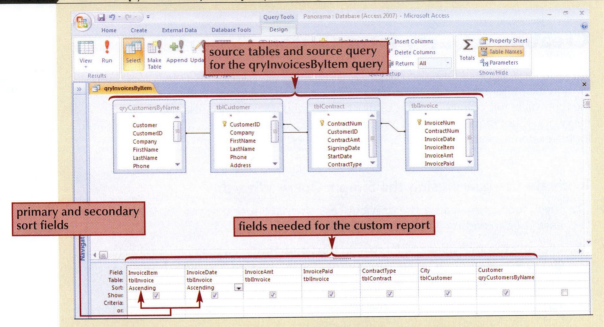

Trouble? After you've finished creating the query and close it, if you later open the query in Design view, you'll see the thicker join lines with referential integrity enforced connecting the tblCustomer and tblContract table field lists and the tblContract and tblInvoice table field lists.

Before closing the query, you'll run it to view the query recordset.

▶ **10.** Run the query, which displays 172 records, and then close the query.

You'll use the qryInvoicesByItem query as the record source for Lucia's custom report.

Creating a Custom Report

You could use the Report Wizard to create the report and then modify it to match the report design. However, because you need to customize several components of the report, you will create a custom report in Layout view, and then switch between Layout and Design view to fine-tune the report. As the first step to creating the report, you need to display a blank report in Layout view.

Reference Window	**Creating a Blank Report in Layout View**

- Click the Create tab on the Ribbon.
- In the Reports group on the Create tab, click the Blank Report button to open a blank report in Layout view.

Making Report Design Modifications | InSight

You perform operations in Layout and Design views for reports the same as you perform operations in these views for forms. These operations become easier with practice. Remember to use the Undo button, back up your database frequently, save your report changes frequently, work from a copy of the report for complicated design changes, and compact and repair the database on a regular basis. You can also display the report in Print Preview at any time to view your progress on the report.

The record source for the report will the qryInvoicesByItem query. You'll set the record source after you create a blank report in Layout view.

To create a blank report and add bound controls in Layout view:

▶ 1. Click the **Create** tab on the Ribbon, and then in the Reports group on the Create tab, click the **Blank Report** button. A new report opens in Layout view. In addition, the Field List pane and the Group, Sort, and Total pane open. See Figure 7-19.

Blank report in Layout view ◀ Figure 7-19

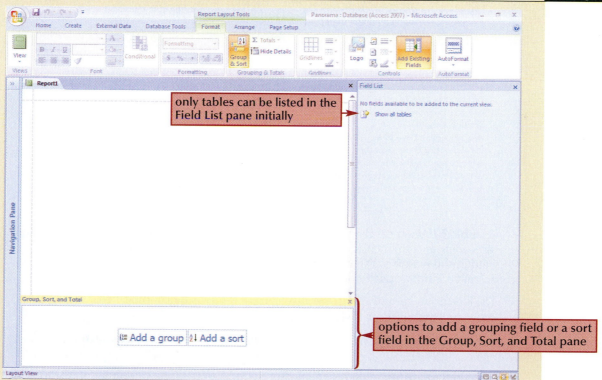

only tables can be listed in the Field List pane initially

options to add a grouping field or a sort field in the Group, Sort, and Total pane

Trouble? If the Group, Sort, and Total pane is not open on your screen, click the Group & Sort button in the Grouping & Totals group on the Format tab.

▶ 2. Click the **Arrange** tab on the Ribbon, and then in the Tools group on the Arrange tab, click the **Property Sheet** button to open the property sheet for the report.

▶ 3. In the property sheet, click the **Record Source** arrow, click **qryInvoicesByItem**, and then close the property sheet.

4. Click the **Format** tab on the Ribbon, and then in the Controls group on the Format tab, click the **Add Existing Fields** button to open the Field List pane. The Field List pane displays the seven fields in the qryInvoicesByItem query, which is the record source for the report.

Referring to Lucia's report design, you'll add six of the seven fields to the report in a tabular layout, which is the default control layout when you add fields to a report in Layout view.

5. Double-click **InvoiceDate** in the Field List pane, and then in order, double-click **Customer**, **City**, **ContractType**, **InvoiceAmt**, and **InvoicePaid** in the Field List pane. The six bound controls are displayed in a tabular layout in the report. See Figure 7-20.

Figure 7-20 | **After adding fields to the report in Layout view**

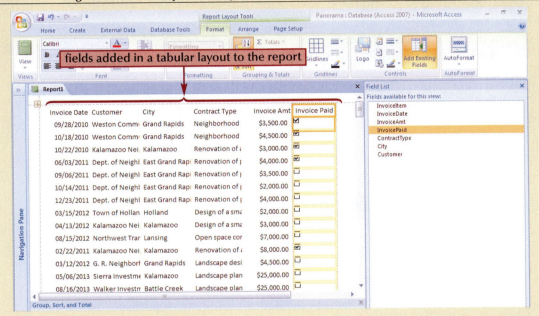

Trouble? If you add the wrong field to the report, right-click the field in the tabular layout, and then click Delete on the shortcut menu to delete it. If you add a field in the wrong order, click the field in the tabular layout, and then drag it to its correct columnar position.

You'll add the seventh field, the InvoiceItem field, as a grouping field, so you are done working with the Field List pane.

6. Close the Field List pane, and then save the report as **rptInvoicesByItem**.

Next, you'll adjust the column widths in Layout view, and then fine-tune the adjustments and the spacing between columns later in Design view. Also, because the Invoice Amt and Invoice Paid columns are adjacent, you can change the rightmost column heading to Paid without losing any meaning and to save space.

To resize and rename columns in Layout view:

1. Click **Customer** to select the column, and then drag the right edge of the control to increase its width. See Figure 7-21.

2. Repeat Step 1 to increase the width of the **City** column and the **Contract Type** column. See Figure 7-21.

3. Double-click **Invoice Paid** in the rightmost column, delete **Invoice** and the following space, and then press the **Enter** key.

4. Drag the right edge of the **Paid** control to the left to decrease the column's width. See Figure 7-21.

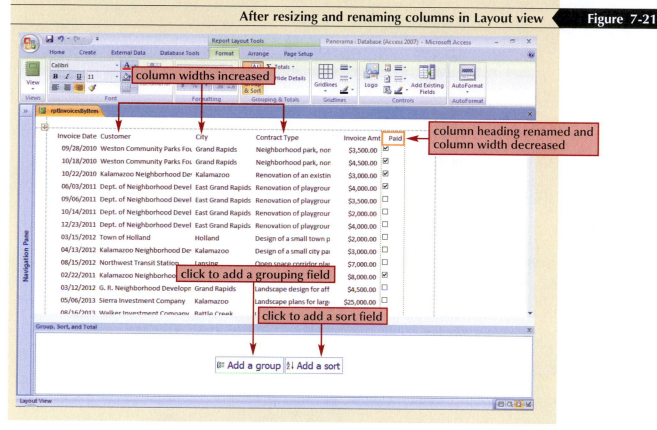

According to Lucia's plan for the report (see Figure 7-17), the InvoiceItem field is a grouping field that is displayed in a Group Header section. Subtotals for the InvoiceAmt field are displayed in a Group Footer section for each InvoiceItem field value.

Sorting and Grouping Data in a Report

Access lets you organize records in a report by sorting them using one or more sort fields. Each sort field can also be a grouping field. If you specify a sort field as a grouping field, you can include a Group Header section and a Group Footer section for the group. A Group Header section typically includes the name of the group, and a Group Footer section typically includes a count or subtotal for records in that group. Some reports have a Group Header section but not a Group Footer section, some reports have a Group Footer section but not a Group Header section, and some reports have both sections or have neither section.

You use the Group, Sort, and Total pane to select sort fields and grouping fields for a report. Each report can have up to 10 sort fields, and any of its sort fields can also be grouping fields.

Reference Window | **Sorting and Grouping Data in a Report**

- Display the report in Layout or Design view.
- If necessary, click the Group & Sort button in the Grouping & Totals group on the Format tab in Layout view or the Design tab in Design view to display the Group, Sort, and Total pane.
- To select a grouping field, click the Add a group button in the Group, Sort, and Total pane, and then click the grouping field in the list. To set additional properties for the grouping field, click the More button on the grouping field band.
- To select a sort field that is not a grouping field, click the Add a sort button in the Group, Sort, and Total pane, and then click the sort field in the list. To set additional properties for the sort field, click the More button on the sort field band.

In Lucia's report design, the InvoiceItem field is a grouping field, and the InvoiceDate field is a sort field. The InvoiceItem field value is displayed in a Group Header section, but not its label. The sum of the InvoiceAmt field values is displayed in the Group Footer section for the InvoiceItem grouping field. Next, you'll select the grouping field and the sort field and set their properties.

To select and set the properties for the grouping field and the sort field:

1. In the Group, Sort, and Total pane, click the **Add a group** button, and then click **InvoiceItem** in the list. Access adds a Group Header section to the report with InvoiceItem as the grouping field, and adds a group band in the Group, Sort, and Total pane. See Figure 7-22.

Figure 7-22 | **After selecting InvoiceItem as a grouping field in Layout view**

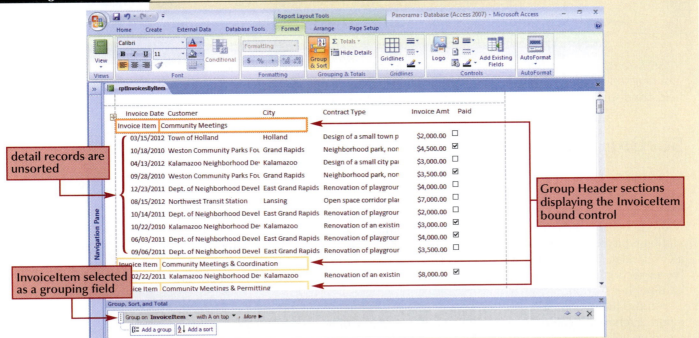

detail records are unsorted

Group Header sections displaying the InvoiceItem bound control

InvoiceItem selected as a grouping field

InvoiceItem is now a bound control in the report in a Group Header section that displays a field value text box and its attached label. The group band in the Group, Sort, and Total pane contains the name of the grouping field (InvoiceItem), the sort order ("with A on top" to indicate ascending), and the More option, which you click to display more options for the grouping field. You can click the "with A on top" arrow to change to descending sort order ("with Z on top").

Notice that the detail records are unsorted, and Lucia's design specifies an ascending sort on the InvoiceDate field. Next, you'll select this field as a secondary sort field; the InvoiceItem grouping field is the primary sort field.

▶ **2.** In the Group, Sort, and Total pane, click the **Add a sort** button, and then click **InvoiceDate** in the list. Access displays the detail records in ascending InvoiceDate order, and adds a sort band for the InvoiceDate field in the Group, Sort, and Total pane.

Next, you'll display all the options for the InvoiceItem grouping field, and set grouping options as shown in Lucia's report design.

▶ **3.** Click ⁝ to the left of the group band to select it, and then click **More** to expand the band and display all group options. See Figure 7-23.

After expanding the group band ◀ Figure 7-23

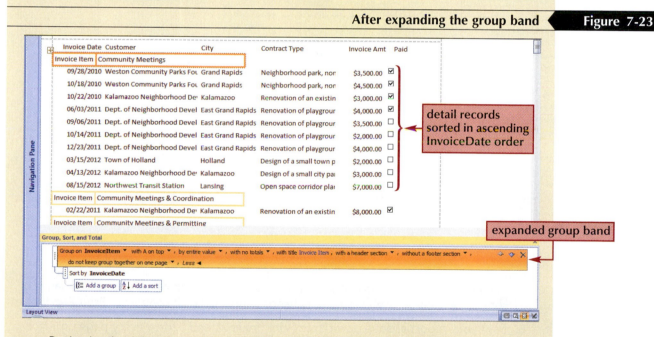

Reviewing Lucia's report design (see Figure 7-17), you need to delete the InvoiceItem label, add a Group Footer section, add a grand total and subtotals for the InvoiceAmt field values to the Group Footer section, and set the Keep Together property. The **Keep Together property** prints a group header on a page only if there is enough room on the page to print the first detail record for the group; otherwise, the group header prints at the top of the next page.

4. In the "with title Invoice Item" option, click the **Invoice Item** link to open the Zoom dialog box, press the **Delete** key to delete the expression, and then click the **OK** button. The Invoice Item label is deleted from the report, and the option in the group band changes to "with title click to add."

5. Click the **do not keep group together on one page** arrow, and then click **keep header and first record together on one page**.

6. Click the **without a footer section** arrow, and then click **with a footer section**. Access adds a Group Footer section for the InvoiceItem grouping field, but the report doesn't display this new section until you add controls to it.

7. Click the **with no totals** arrow to open the Totals menu, click the **Total On** arrow, click **InvoiceAmt**, make sure **Sum** is selected in the Type box, click the **Show Grand Total** check box, click the **Show in group footer** check box, and then click an empty area of the group band to close the menu. Access adds InvoiceAmt subtotals to the report. See Figure 7-24.

Figure 7-24 ▸ **After setting properties in the group band**

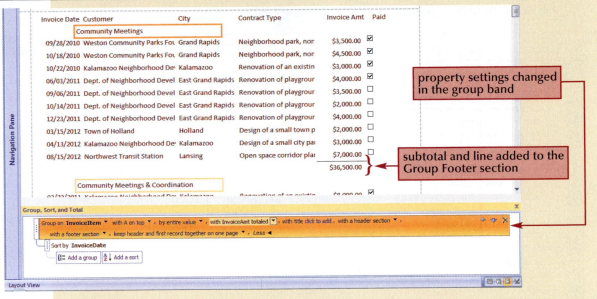

Similar to the sound form design strategy you followed in the previous tutorial, you should frequently save your report changes and review the report in Print Preview.

8. Save your report changes, switch to Print Preview, and review every page until you reach the end of the report—noticing in particular the details of the report format and the effects of the Keep Together property. See Figure 7-25.

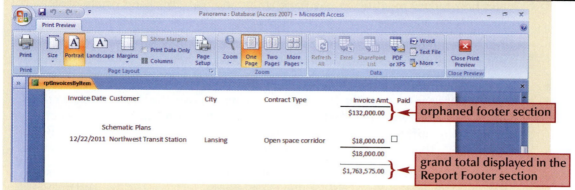

Last page of the custom report in Print Preview ◄ Figure 7-25

Trouble? Depending on the printer you are using, the last page of your report might differ.

The grand total of the InvoiceAmt field values is displayed at the end of the report. Also, as shown in Figure 7-25, it's possible for subtotals, which you added to the Group Footer section, to appear in an orphaned footer section. An **orphaned footer section** appears by itself at the top of a page, and the detail lines for the section appear on the previous page. When you set the Keep Together property for the grouping field, you set it to keep the group and the first detail record together on one page to prevent an **orphaned header section**, which is a section that appears by itself at the bottom of a page. To prevent both types of orphaned sections, you'll set the Keep Together property to keep the whole group together on one page.

In addition, you need to fine-tune the sizes of the text boxes in the Detail section, adjust the spacing between columns, and make other adjustments to the current content of the report design before adding a report title, the date, and page numbers to the Page Header section. You'll make most of these report design changes in Design view.

Working with Controls in Design View

Compared to Layout view, Design view gives you greater control over the placement and sizing of controls, and lets you add and manipulate many more controls, but at the expense of not being able to see live data in the controls to guide you as you make changes.

You'll switch to Design view to move and resize controls in the report.

To move and resize controls in the report:

► **1.** Switch to Design view. The report has five sections: the Page Header section contains the six column heading labels, the InvoiceItem Header section (a Group Header section) contains the InvoiceItem text box, the Detail section contains the six bound controls, the InvoiceItem Footer section (a Group Footer section) contains a line and the subtotal text box, and the Report Footer section contains a line and the grand total text box.

The Group, Sort, and Total pane is still open, so first you'll change the Keep Together property setting.

2. In the Group, Sort, and Total pane, click ⋮ to the left of the group band to select it, click **More** to expand the band and display all group options, click the **keep header and first record together on one page** arrow, and then click **keep whole group together on one page**, and then close the Group, Sort, and Total pane.

You'll start improving the report by moving the InvoiceItem text box to the left in the InvoiceItem Header section and setting its font to bold.

3. Select the **InvoiceItem** text box in the InvoiceItem Header section and the **InvoiceDate** text box in the Detail section, align the two selected controls on their left edges, hold down the **Shift** key, click the **InvoiceDate** text box to deselect it, release the **Shift** key, and then in the Font group on the Design tab, click the **Bold** button **B**. The InvoiceItem text box is displayed as bold text.

The report width is 8 inches, and Sarah will want to print the report on standard 8.5" × 11" paper, so you'll change the page orientation to landscape, and set the left and right margin widths to 1.5 inches each.

4. Click the **Page Setup** tab on the Ribbon, and in the Page Layout group on the Page Setup tab, click the **Page Setup** button to open the Page Setup dialog box, click the **Page** tab, click the **Landscape** option button, click the **Print Options** tab, set the Top and Bottom margin properties to **0.7** and the Left and Right margin properties to **1.5**, and then click the **OK** button.

The text boxes in the Detail section are crowded together with little space between them. Your reports shouldn't have too much space between columns, but reports are easier to read when the columns are separated more than they are in the rptInvoicesByItem report. Sometimes the amount of spacing is dictated by the users of the report, but mostly it's the report designer's choice to make. First, you'll remove the Paid label and the InvoicePaid text box from the tabular layout, resize them, and move them to the right.

5. Select the **Paid** label in the Page Header section and the **InvoicePaid** text box (it contains a check box) in the Detail section, right-click one of the selected controls to open the shortcut menu, point to **Layout**, click **Remove** to remove both controls from the tabular layout, deselect the **InvoicePaid** text box, right-click an edge of the **Paid** label to open the shortcut menu, point to **Size**, click **To Fit**, and then move the label to the right until its right edge is at the 8-inch mark on the horizontal ruler.

6. Click the **InvoicePaid** text box in the Detail section, decrease its width until it's slightly wider than the check box inside it, and then move it to the right until the check box is centered under the Paid label. See Figure 7-26.

To move the remaining bound controls, you first need to remove them from the tabular layout.

7. Select the **InvoiceAmt** text box and the other three controls in that column, right-click the **InvoiceAmt** text box, point to **Layout** on the shortcut menu, click **Remove**, deselect all controls except the **Invoice Amt** label in the Page Header section, right-click the **Invoice Amt** label, point to **Size** on the shortcut menu, click **To Fit**, select all controls in the column, right-click one of the selected controls, point to **Align** on the shortcut menu, click **Right**, and then move the selected controls to the right. See Figure 7-26.

8. Refer to Figure 7-26 and repeat Step 7 for the **ContractType**, **City**, and **Customer** bound controls, in that order, but do not align the bound controls on their right edges. See Figure 7-26.

After resizing and moving controls in Design view | Figure 7-26

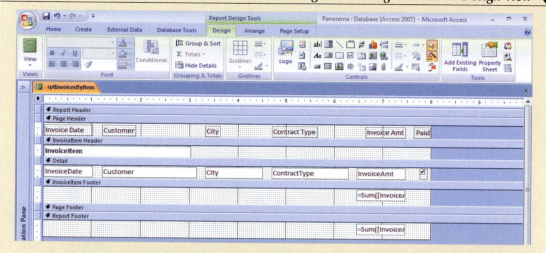

You resized the Customer and ContractType text boxes in Layout view, but you did not resize them wide enough to display the entire field value in all cases. For the Customer and ContractType text boxes, you'll set their Can Grow property to Yes. The **Can Grow property**, when set to Yes, expands a text box vertically to fit the field value when the report is printed, previewed, or viewed in Layout and Report views.

▶ 9. Select the **Customer** and **ContractType** text boxes in the Detail section, open the property sheet, click the **Format** tab in the property sheet, scroll down the property sheet, set the Can Grow property to **Yes** (if necessary), close the property sheet, and then save your report changes.

▶ 10. Switch to Print Preview, and review every page of the report, ending on the last page of the report. See Figure 7-27.

Reviewing the report changes in Print Preview | Figure 7-27

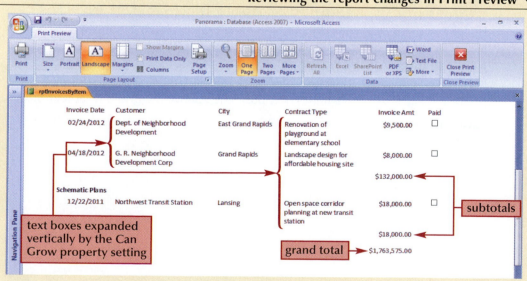

The groups stay together on one page, except for the Schematic Plan group, which has too many lines to fit on one page. The Can Grow property correctly expands the height of the Customer and ContractType text boxes. Also, the lines that were displayed above the subtotals and grand total are no longer displayed. You'll add those lines back in the report.

Adding Lines to a Report

You've used the Line tool to add lines to a form. You can also use the Line tool to add lines to a report, and you'll use the Line tool to add a single line above the subtotal control and a double line above the grand total control.

You'll switch to Design view to add the lines to the report.

To add lines to the report:

1. Switch to Design view.

2. In the Controls group on the Design tab, click the **Line** button ⬎, position the pointer's plus symbol (+) at the upper-left corner of the subtotal text box in the InvoiceItem Footer section, hold down the **Shift** key, drag a horizontal line from left to right, so the end of the line aligns with the upper-right corner of the subtotal text box, release the mouse button, and then release the **Shift** key.

3. Click the **grand total** text box in the Report Footer section, and then press the ↓ key four times to move the control down slightly in the section, and then deselect all controls.

4. In the Controls group on the Design tab, click the **Line** button ⬎, position the pointer's plus symbol (+) at the grid dot just above the upper-left corner of the grand total text box in the Report Footer section, hold down the **Shift** key, drag a horizontal line from left to right, so the end of the line aligns with the right edge of the grand total text box, release the mouse button, and then release the **Shift** key.

   Next, you'll copy and paste the line in the Report Footer section, and then align the copied line into position.

5. Right-click the selected line in the Report Footer section, and then click **Copy** on the shortcut menu.

6. Right-click the Report Footer section bar, and then click **Paste** on the shortcut menu. A copy of the line is pasted in the upper-left corner of the Report Footer section.

7. Press the ↓ key twice to move the copied line down slightly in the section, hold down the **Shift** key, click the original line in the Report Footer section to select both lines, release the **Shift** key, right-click the copied line, point to **Align**, and then click **Right**. A double line is now positioned above the grand total text box.

8. Save your report changes, switch to Print Preview, and then navigate to the last page of the report. See Figure 7-28.

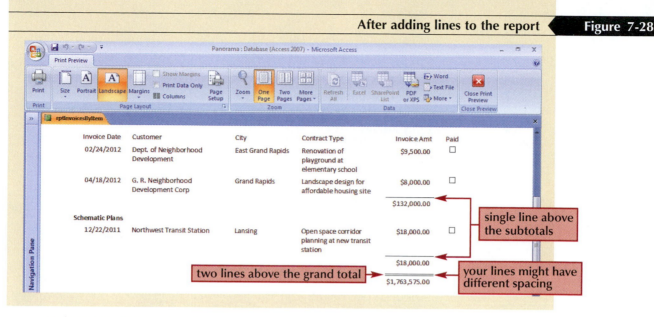

After adding lines to the report — Figure 7-28

For the rptInvoicesByItem report, the InvoiceDate field is a sort field. Two or more consecutive detail report lines can have the same InvoiceDate field value. In these cases, Sarah wants the InvoiceDate field value printed for the first detail line but not for subsequent detail lines because she believes it makes the printed information easier to read.

Hiding Duplicate Values in a Report

You use the **Hide Duplicates property** to hide a control in a report when the control's value is the same as that of the preceding record in the group.

Hiding Duplicate Values in a Report | Reference Window

- Display the report in Layout or Design view.
- Open the property sheet for the field whose duplicate values you want to hide, set the Hide Duplicates property to Yes, and then close the property sheet.

Your next design change to the report is to hide duplicate InvoiceDate field values in the Detail section. This change will make the report easier to read.

To hide the duplicate InvoiceDate field values:

1. Switch to Design view, and then click below the Report Footer section to deselect all controls.

2. Open the property sheet for the **InvoiceDate** text box in the Detail section.

3. Click the **All** tab (if necessary), click the right side of the **Hide Duplicates** text box, and then click **Yes**. See Figure 7-29.

Tip

For properties in the property sheet that offer a list of choices, you can double-click the property name to cycle through the options in the list.

Figure 7-29 ▶ **Hiding duplicate field values**

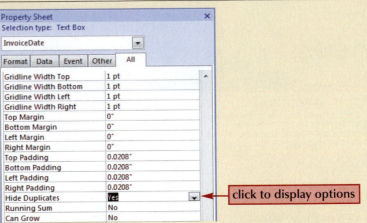

4. Close the property sheet, save your report changes, switch to Print Preview, navigate to the last page of the report, and then navigate back one page (if necessary) until you see the two invoice records for 08/25/2011. The InvoiceDate value is hidden for the second of the two consecutive records with a 08/25/2011 date. See Figure 7-30.

Figure 7-30 ▶ **Report in Print Preview with hidden duplicate values**

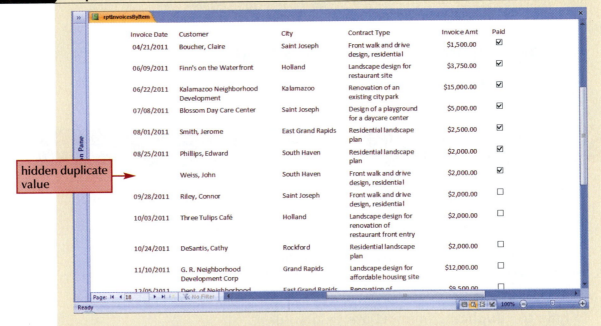

5. If you are not continuing on to the next session, close the Panorama database, and then exit Access.

You have completed the Detail section of the custom report. In the next session, you will complete the custom report according to Lucia's design by adding controls to the Page Header section.

Session 7.2 Quick Check | Review

1. What is a detail report? a summary report?
2. The _____ property prints a group header on a page only if there is enough room on the page to print the first detail record for the group; otherwise, the group header prints at the top of the next page.
3. A(n) _____ section appears by itself at the top of a page, and the detail lines for the section appear on the previous page.
4. The _____ property, when set to Yes, expands a text box vertically to fit the field value when a report is printed, previewed, or viewed in Layout and Report views.
5. Why might you want to hide duplicate values in a report?

Session 7.3

Adding the Date to a Report

According to Lucia's design, the rptInvoicesByItem report includes the date in the Page Header section, along with the report title, the page number, the column heading labels, and a line under the labels.

Placing the Report Title, Date, and Page Number in the Page Header Section | InSight

When you use the Report tool or the Report Wizard to create a report, the report title is displayed in the Report Header section and the page number is displayed in the Page Footer section. However, the date (and time) is displayed in the Report Header section when you use the Report tool and in the Page Footer section when you use the Report Wizard. Because you should create reports that display controls in consistent positions, you have to move the date control for reports created by the Report tool or by the Report Wizard so the date is displayed in the same section for all reports.

Although company standards vary, a common report standard places the report title, date, and page number on the same line in the Page Header section. Using one line saves vertical space in the report compared to placing some controls in the Page Header section and others in the Page Footer section. Placing the report title in the Page Header section, instead of in the Report Header section, allows users to identify the report title on any page without having to turn to the first page.

To add the date to a report, you can click the Date & Time button in the Controls group on the Ribbon, and Access will insert the Date function in a text box without an attached label at the right edge of the Report Header section. The **Date function** returns the current date. The format of the Date function is =Date(). The equal sign (=) indicates that what follows it is an expression; *Date* is the name of the function; and the empty set of parentheses indicates a function rather than simple text.

Adding the Date and Time to a Report

- Display the report in Layout or Design view.
- In the Controls group on the Design tab in Design view, or on the Format tab in Layout view, click the Date & Time button to open the Date and Time dialog box.
- To display the date, click the Include Date check box, and then click one of the three date option buttons.
- To display the time, click the Include Time check box, and then click one of the three time option buttons.
- Click the OK button.

According to Lucia's design for the report, the date appears at the left edge of the Page Header section, so you'll need to add the date to the report, and then cut the date from the Report Header section and paste it into the Page Header section.

To add the date to the Page Header section:

▶ **1.** If you took a break after the previous session, make sure that the Panorama database is open, that the rptInvoicesByItem report is open in Print Preview, and that the Navigation Pane is closed.

You can add the current date in Layout or Design view. Because you can't cut and paste controls between sections in Layout view, you'll add the date in Design view. First, you'll move the column heading labels down in the Page Header section to make room for the controls you'll be adding above them.

▶ **2.** Switch to Design view, increase the height of the Page Header section until the bottom edge of the section is at the 1-inch mark on the vertical ruler, select all six labels in the Page Header section, and then use the ↓ key to move the labels down until the tops of the labels are at the 0.5-inch mark on the vertical ruler.

Lucia's report design has a horizontal line under the labels that you'll add next.

▶ **3.** In the Controls group on the Design tab, click the **Line** button ◳ , position the pointer's plus symbol (+) at the lower-left corner of the Invoice Date label in the Page Header section, hold down the **Shift** key, drag a horizontal line from left to right so the end of the line aligns with the right edge of the Paid label, release the mouse button, and then release the **Shift** key.

▶ **4.** Reduce the height of the Page Header section by dragging the bottom of the section up until it touches the bottom of the line you just added.

▶ **5.** In the Controls group on the Design tab, click the **Date & Time** button ▦ to open the Date and Time dialog box, make sure the **Include Date** check box is checked and the **Include Time** check box is unchecked, and then click the third date option button. See Figure 7-31.

◄ **Figure 7-31**

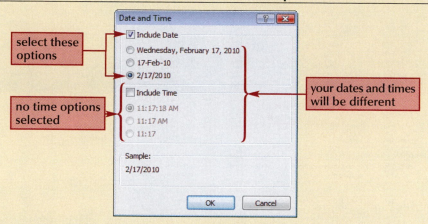

select these options

no time options selected

your dates and times will be different

6. Click the **OK** button. The Date function is added to the Report Header section. See Figure 7-32.

Date function added to the Report Header section ◄ **Figure 7-32**

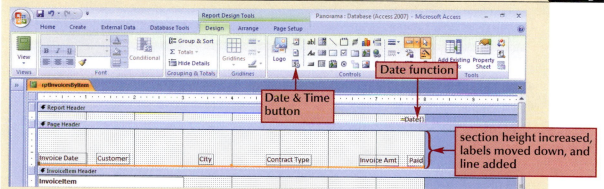

Date & Time button

Date function

section height increased, labels moved down, and line added

The default size for the Date function text box must accommodate long dates and long times, so the text box is much wider than needed for the date that'll appear in the custom report. You'll decrease its width before moving it to the Page Header section.

7. Click the **Date function** text box, decrease its width from the left to one inch total, right-click an edge of the Date function text box to open the shortcut menu, click **Cut** to delete the control, right-click the **Page Header** section bar to select that section and open the shortcut menu, and then click **Paste**. The Date function text box is pasted in the upper-left corner of the Page Header section.

8. Save your report changes, and then switch to Print Preview to view the date in the Page Header section. See Figure 7-33.

Tip

When you print, preview, or view the report in Report or Layout view, the current date is displayed instead of the Date function that appears in the text box in Design view.

Figure 7-33 | Viewing the date in Print Preview

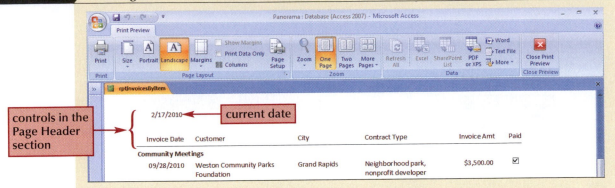

Trouble? Your year might appear with two digits instead of four digits as shown in Figure 7-33. Your date format might also differ, depending on your computer's date settings. These differences do not cause any problems.

You'll left-align the date in the text box in Design view.

▶ 9. Switch to Design view, make sure the Date function text box is selected, and then in the Font group on the Design tab, click the **Align Text Left** button 🔲.

You are now ready to add page numbers to the Page Header section.

Adding Page Numbers to a Report

You can display page numbers in a report by including an expression in the Page Header or Page Footer section. You can click the Insert Page Number button in the Controls group in Layout or Design view to add a page number expression to a report. The inserted page number expression automatically displays the correct page number on each page of a report.

Lucia's design shows the page number displayed on the right side of the Page Header section, on the same line with the date.

To add page numbers in the Page Header section:

▶ 1. In the Controls group on the Design tab, click the **Insert Page Number** button 🔳. The Page Numbers dialog box opens.

You use the Format options to specify the format of the page number. Sarah wants page numbers to appear as Page 1, Page 2, and so on. This is the Page N format option. You use the Position options to place the page numbers at the top of the page in the Page Header section or at the bottom of the page in the Page Footer section. Lucia's design shows page numbers at the top of the page.

▶ **2.** Make sure that the **Page N** option button in the Format section and that the **Top of Page [Header]** option button in the Position section are both selected.

The report design shows page numbers at the right side of the page. You can specify this placement in the Alignment list box.

▶ **3.** Click the **Alignment** arrow, and then click **Right**.

▶ **4.** Make sure the **Show Number on First Page** check box is checked, so the page number prints on the first page and all other pages as well. See Figure 7-34.

Completed Page Numbers dialog box ◀ Figure 7-34

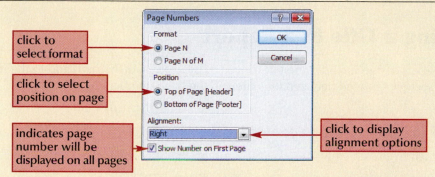

click to select format

click to select position on page

indicates page number will be displayed on all pages

click to display alignment options

▶ **5.** Click the **OK** button. The text box shown in Figure 7-35 appears in the upper-right corner of the Page Header section. The expression =*"Page " & [Page]* in the text box means that the printed report will show the word "Page" followed by a space and the page number.

Page number expression added to the Page Header section ◀ Figure 7-35

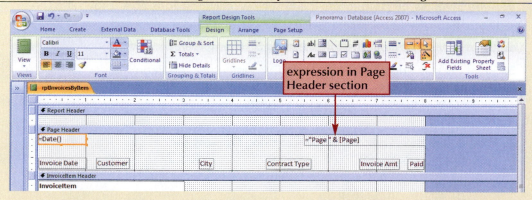

expression in Page Header section

The page number text box is much wider than needed for the page number expression that'll appear in the custom report. You'll decrease its width and right-align it.

▶ **6.** Click the **Page Number** text box, decrease its width from the left to one inch total, and then in the Font group on the Design tab, click the **Align Text Right** button ≣.

▶ **7.** Save your report changes, and then switch to Print Preview. See Figure 7-36.

Figure 7-36   **Date and page number in the Page Header section**

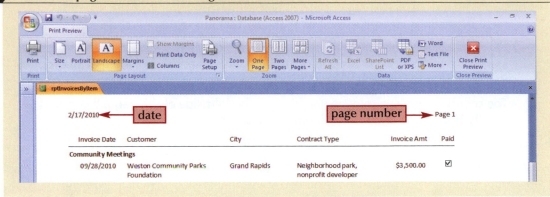

Now you are ready to add the title to the Page Header section.

Adding a Title to a Report

Lucia's report design includes the title "Invoices by Item," which you'll add to the Page Header section centered between the date and the page number.

To add the title to the Page Header section:

▶ 1. Switch to Design view.

▶ 2. In the Controls group on the Design tab, click the **Title** button [image]. The title "rptInvoicesByItem," which is name of the report object, appears in the Report Header section in 18-point font.

   To match Lucia's design, you need to change the title, set its font size to 14 points, move it to the Page Header section, and then resize the Report Header section to zero height. The title is selected, so typing the new title will replace the current title.

▶ 3. Type **Invoices by Item**, press the **Enter** key, click the **Font Size** arrow, and then click **14**.

▶ 4. Right-click an edge of the title, point to **Size**, and then click **To Fit**.

▶ 5. Right-click an edge of the title, click **Cut**, right-click the **Page Header** section bar, and then click **Paste**. The title is pasted in the upper-left corner of the Page Header section, and the Error Checking Options button [image] appears to the right of the report title.

▶ 6. Position the pointer on the **Error Checking Options** button [image]. A ScreenTip is displayed and describes the potential error. See Figure 7-37.

Pasted report title in the Page Header section   **Figure 7-37**

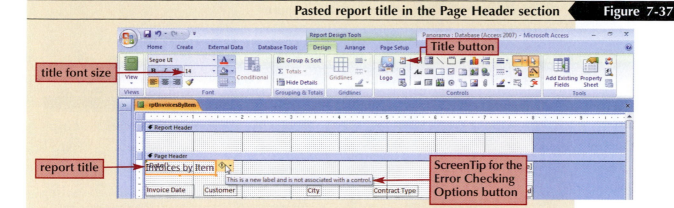

The ScreenTip indicates that the report title, which is a label control, is not associated with any bound or calculated control. Because you don't want a label that contains a report title to be associated with another control, you can ignore this potential error.

7. Click the **Error Checking Options** button ⟨⬦⟩, and then click **Ignore Error**.

The report title is still selected, so you can move it so that it's centered between the date and the page number. Because the report title is positioned on top of the date control, there's a chance you might inadvertently also select the date control when you try to drag the report title into position, so you should use the → key to move the report title.

8. Move the report title control to the right until it's centered between the date and page number controls.

Finally, you'll align the date, report title, and page number controls on their bottom edges.

9. Select the date, report title, and page number controls in the Page Header section, right-click one of the selected controls, point to **Align**, and then click **Bottom**.

10. Drag the bottom edge of the Report Header section up all the way to the Report Header section bar to remove the section from the report, and then save your report changes. You completed the design of the custom report. See Figure 7-38.

Figure 7-38 **Completed design of the rptInvoicesByItem report**

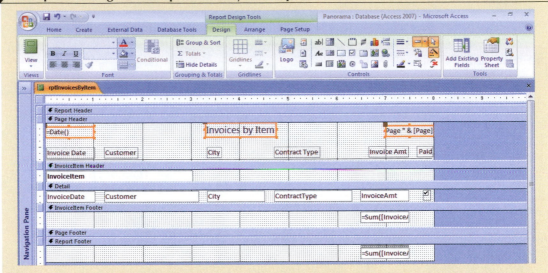

> **11.** Switch to Print Preview to review the completed report, and then navigate to the last page of the report. See Figure 7-39.

Figure 7-39 **Completed rptInvoicesByItem report in Print Preview**

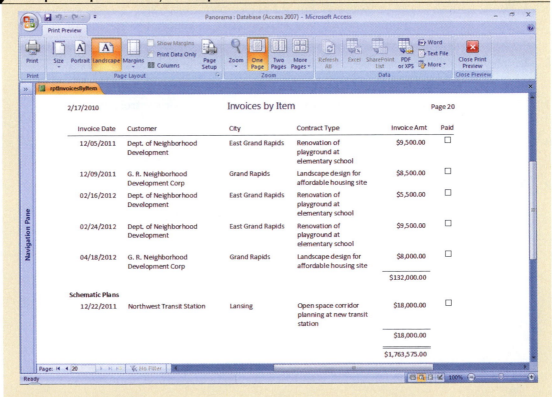

> **12.** Close the report.

Next, Sarah wants you to create mailing labels that can be used to address materials to Belmont Landscapes' customers.

Creating Mailing Labels

Sarah needs a set of mailing labels printed for all customers so she can mail a marketing brochure and other materials to them. The tblCustomer table contains the name and address information that will serve as the record source for the labels. Each mailing label will have the same format: first name and last name on the first line; company name (if it exists for the customer) on the second line; address on the third line; and city, state, and zip code on the fourth line.

You could create a custom report to produce the mailing labels, but using the Label Wizard is an easier and faster way to produce them. The **Label Wizard** provides templates for hundreds of standard label formats, each of which is uniquely identified by a label manufacturer's name and number. These templates specify the dimensions and arrangement of labels on each page. Standard label formats can have between one and five labels across a page; the number of labels printed on a single page also varies. Sarah's mailing labels are Avery number C2163; each sheet has 12 1.5-inch by 3.9-inch labels arranged in two columns and six rows on the page.

Creating Mailing Labels and Other Labels | Reference Window

- In the Navigation Pane, click the table or query that'll serve as the record source for the labels.
- In the Reports group on the Create tab, click the Labels button to start the Label Wizard and open its first dialog box.
- Select the label manufacturer and its product number, and then click the Next button.
- Select the label font, color, and style, and then click the Next button.
- Construct the label content by selecting the fields from the record source and specifying their placement and spacing on the label, and then click the Next button.
- Select one or more optional sort fields, click the Next button, specify the report name, and then click the Finish button.

You'll use the Label Wizard to create a report to produce mailing labels for all customers.

To use the Label Wizard to create the mailing label report:

1. Open the Navigation Pane, click **tblCustomer** to make it the current object that'll serve as the record source for the labels, close the Navigation Pane, and then click the **Create** tab on the Ribbon.

2. In the Reports group on the Create tab, click the **Labels** button. The first Label Wizard dialog box opens and asks you to select the standard or custom label you'll use.

3. Make sure that the **English** option button is selected in the Unit of Measure section, that the **Sheet feed** option button is selected in the Label Type section, and that **Avery** is selected in the Filter by manufacturer list box, and then click **C2163** in the Product number list box. See Figure 7-40.

Figure 7-40 | **Selecting a standard label**

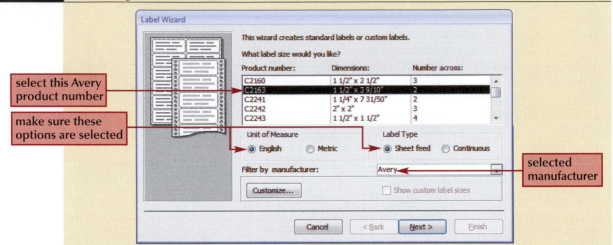

Tip

If your label manufacturer or its labels do not appear in the list box, you can create your own custom format for them.

Because the labels are already filtered for the Avery manufacturer, the top list box shows the Avery product number, dimensions, and number of labels across the page for each of its standard label formats. You can display the dimensions in the list in either inches or millimeters by choosing the appropriate option in the Unit of Measure section. You can also specify in the Label Type section whether the labels are on individual sheets or are continuous forms.

▶ **4.** Click the **Next** button to open the second Label Wizard dialog box, in which you choose font specifications for the labels.

Sarah wants the labels to use 10-point Arial with a medium font weight and without italics or underlines. The font weight determines how light or dark the characters will print; you can choose from nine values ranging from thin to heavy.

▶ **5.** If necessary, select **Arial** for the font name, **10** for the font size, and **Medium** for the font weight; make sure the Italic and the Underline check boxes are not checked and that black is the text color; and then click the **Next** button to open the third Label Wizard dialog box, from which you select the data to appear on the labels.

Sarah wants the mailing labels to print the FirstName and LastName fields on the first line; the Company field on the second line; the Address field on the third line; and the City, State, and Zip fields on the fourth line. One space will separate the FirstName and LastName fields, the City and State fields, and the State and Zip fields.

Tip

If a Company field value is null in the second line, Access moves up the third and fourth lines when you print or preview the label report to eliminate the blank line on the label.

▶ **6.** Click **FirstName** in the Available fields list box, click the `>` button to move the field to the Prototype label box, press the **spacebar**, click **LastName** in the Available fields list box (if necessary), and then click the `>` button (see Figure 7-41). The braces around the field names in the Prototype label box indicate that the name represents a field rather than text that you entered.

Trouble? If you select the wrong field or type the wrong text, highlight the incorrect item in the Prototype label box, press the Delete key to remove the item, and then select the correct field or type the correct text.

▶ **7.** Press the **Enter** key to move to the next line in the Prototype label box, and then use Figure 7-41 to complete the entries in the Prototype label box. Make sure you press the **spacebar** after selecting the City field and the State field.

Completed label prototype ◀ **Figure 7-41**

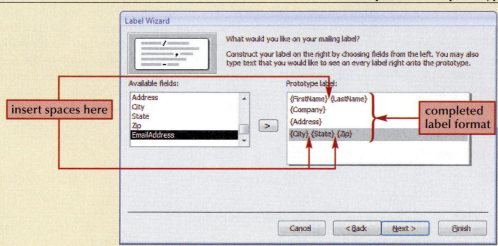

Tip

As you select fields from the Available fields list box or type text for the label, the Prototype label box shows the format for the label.

▶ 8. Click the **Next** button to open the fourth Label Wizard dialog box, in which you choose the sort fields for the labels.

Sarah wants Zip to be the primary sort field and LastName to be the secondary sort field.

▶ 9. Select the **Zip** field as the primary sort field, select the **LastName** field as the secondary sort field, and then click the **Next** button to open the last Label Wizard dialog box, in which you enter a name for the report.

▶ 10. Change the report name to **rptCustomerMailingLabels**, and then click the **Finish** button. Access saves the report as rptCustomerMailingLabels and then opens the first page of the report in Print Preview. Note that two columns of labels appear across the page. See Figure 7-42.

Previewing the label content and sequence ◀ **Figure 7-42**

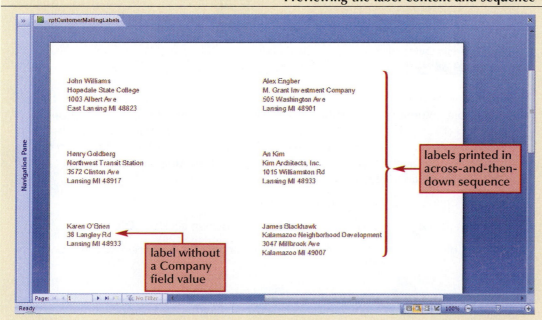

The rptCustomerMailingLabels report is a multiple-column report. The labels will be printed in ascending order by zip code and then in ascending order by last name. The first label will be printed in the upper-left corner on the first page, the second label will be printed to its right, the third label will be printed under the first label, and so on. This style of multiple-column report is the across-and-then-down layout. Instead, Sarah wants the labels to print with the "down, then across" layout—the first label is printed, the second label is printed under the first, and so on. After the bottom label in the first column is printed, the next label is printed at the top of the second column. The "down, then across" layout is also called **newspaper-style columns**, or **snaking columns**.

To change the layout of the mailing label report:

▶ 1. Switch to Design view. The Detail section, the only section in the report, is sized for a single label.

First, you'll change the layout to snaking columns.

▶ 2. Click the **Page Setup** tab on the Ribbon, click the **Page Setup** button in the Page Layout group, and then click the **Columns** tab. The Page Setup dialog box displays the Columns options for the report. See Figure 7-43.

| **Figure 7-43** | **Column options in the Page Setup dialog box** |

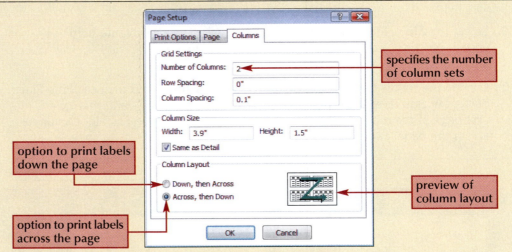

The Columns options in the Page Setup dialog box let you change the properties of a multiple-column report. In the Grid Settings section, you specify the number of column sets and the row and column spacing between the column sets. In the Column Size section, you specify the width and height of each column set. In the Column Layout section, you select between the "down, then across" and the "across, then down" layouts.

You can now change the layout for the labels.

▶ 3. Click the **Down, then Across** option button, and then click the **OK** button.

You've finished the report changes, so you can now save and preview the report.

Tip

When you select a label using a manufacturer's name and product code, the options in the Grid Settings and Column Size sections are set for you automatically based on your selection.

▶ **4.** Save your report design changes, and then switch to Print Preview. The labels appear in the snaking-columns layout.

You've finished all work on Sarah's reports.

▶ **5.** Close the report, close the Panorama database, make a backup copy of the database, open the **Panorama** database, compact and repair the database, close the database, and then exit Access.

Sarah is very pleased with the modified report and the two new reports, which will provide her with improved information and help expedite her written communications with customers.

Session 7.3 Quick Check | Review

1. What is the function and its format to print the current date in a report?
2. How do you insert a page number in the Page Header section?
3. Clicking the Title button in the Controls group on the Design tab adds a report title to the _____ section.
4. What is a multiple-column report?

Tutorial Summary | Review

In this tutorial, you viewed a report created by the Report tool in Report view, filtered and copied information in the report, and customized the report in Layout view and Design view. You then examined general report design guidelines, learned how to use the guidelines in planning a custom report, and created a query to serve as the record source for the report. In creating the custom report, you sorted and grouped data; added fields and modified report controls; added lines; and added the date, page numbers, and a title. Finally, you created mailing labels.

Key Terms

Can Grow property	Group, Sort, and Total pane	newspaper-style columns
custom report	grouping field	orphaned footer section
Date function	Hide Duplicates property	orphaned header section
detail report	Keep Together property	Report view
Group Footer section	Label Wizard	snaking columns
Group Header section	multiple-column report	summary report

| Practice | **Review Assignments** |

Practice the skills you learned in the tutorial using the same case scenario.

Data File needed for the Review Assignments: Products.accdb (*cont. from Tutorial 6*)

Sarah wants you to create a custom report for the Products database that prints all companies and the products they offer. She also wants you to customize an existing report. You will perform the tasks for Sarah by completing the following steps:

1. Open the **Products** database located in the Level.02\Review folder provided with your Data Files.
2. Modify the **rptProductsByCompany** report. Figure 7-44 shows a sample of the last page of the completed report. Refer to the figure as you modify the report.

Figure 7-44

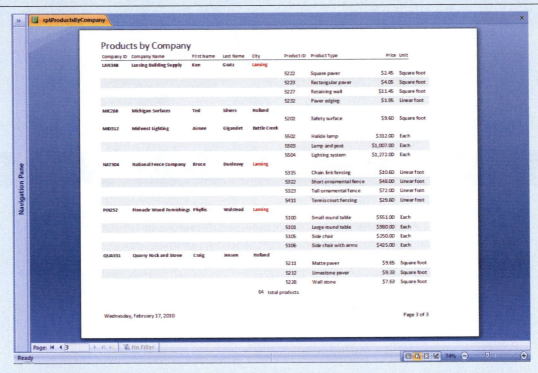

a. Change the Caption property for the report so that it matches the report name.
b. To fit the report on three pages, you might have to change Page Setup properties and reduce the width of the report in Design view after moving the page number to the left.
c. Use the Label tool in the Controls group on the Ribbon to add a label that contains the text **total products** to the right of the count of the total number of products displayed in the Report Footer section.

3. After you've completed and saved your modifications to the rptProductsByCompany report, filter the report in Report view, selecting all records that contain the word "soil" in the ProductType field. Copy the entire filtered report and paste it into a new Word document. Save the document as **rptProductsByCompanyCopy** in the Level.02\Review folder provided with your Data Files. Close Word, and then close the report without saving changes.

4. Create a query that displays the ProductType and CompanyName fields from the tblCompany table, and the ProductType, Price, and Unit fields from the tblProduct table. Sort in ascending order by the first three fields in the query, and then save the query as **qryCompanyProducts**.

5. Create a custom report based on the qryCompanyProducts query. Figure 7-45 shows a sample of the last page of the completed report. Refer to the figure as you create the report.

Figure 7-45

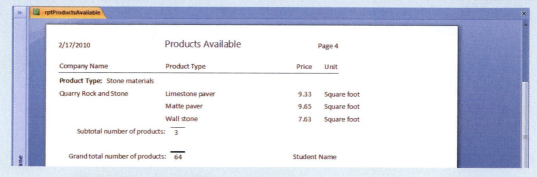

a. Save the report as **rptProductsAvailable**.
b. The ProductType field (from the tblCompany table) is a grouping field.
c. Hide duplicate values for the CompanyName field.
d. Use the Label tool in the Controls group on the Ribbon to add labels for the subtotals, the grand total, and your name.
e. Keep the whole group together on one page.

6. Create a mailing label report according to the following instructions:
a. Use the tblCompany table as the record source.
b. Use Avery C2160 labels, and use the default font and color.
c. For the prototype label, add the ContactFirstName, a space, and ContactLastName on the first line; the CompanyName on the second line; the Address on the third line; and the City, a space, State, a space, and Zip on the fourth line.
d. Sort by Zip and then by CompanyName, and then enter the report name **rptCompanyMailingLabels**.

7. Close the Products database without exiting Access, make a backup copy of the database, open the **Products** database, compact and repair the database, close the database, and then exit Access.

| Create | **Case Problem 1** |

Use the skills you learned in the tutorial to create reports for a music school.

Data File needed for this Case Problem: Contract.accdb (*cont. from Tutorial 6*)

Pine Hill Music School   Yuka wants you to modify an existing report and to create a custom report and mailing labels for the Contract database. You'll do so by completing the following:

1. Open the **Contract** database located in the Level.02\Case1 folder provided with your Data Files.
2. Modify the **rptStudentContracts** report. Figure 7-46 shows a sample of the last page of the completed report. Refer to the figure as you modify the report.

Figure 7-46

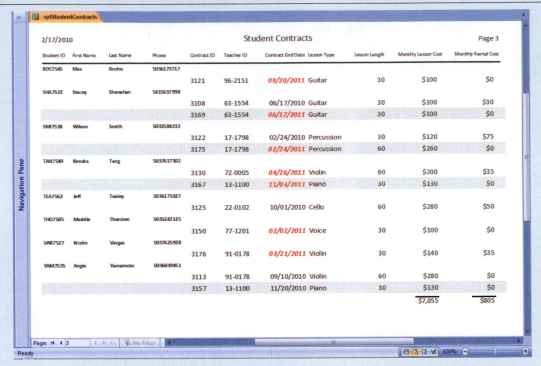

a. Change the conditional formatting rule for the ContractEndDate field to display the date in red, bold, italic font when the date is more recent than 1/1/2011.

b. Add controls to the last page of the report that calculate the total monthly lesson cost and total monthly rental cost below the correct columns.

3. Create a query that displays the LastName and FirstName fields from the tblTeacher table, the LessonType field from the tblContract table, the FirstName and LastName fields from the tblStudent table, and the MonthlyLessonCost and MonthlyRentalCost fields from the tblContract table. Sort in ascending order by the first three fields in the query, and then save the query as **qryTeacherLessons**.

4. Create a custom report based on the qryTeacherLessons query. Figure 7-47 shows a sample of the last page of the completed report. Refer to the figure as you create the report.

Figure 7-47

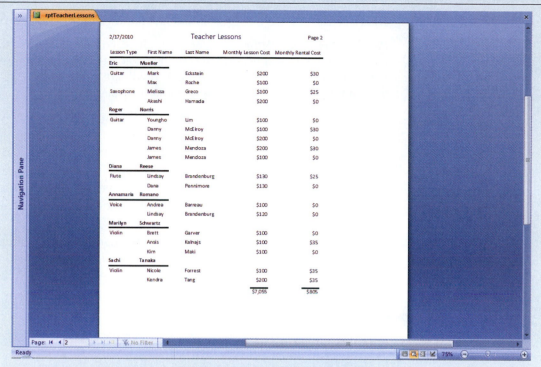

a. Save the report as **rptTeacherLessons**.

b. The LastName field (from the tblTeacher table) is a grouping field.

c. The LessonType field is a sort field, and the LastName field (from the tblStudent table) is a sort field.

d. Hide duplicate values for the LessonType field.

e. Add the FirstName field (from the tblTeacher table) to the Group Header section, and then delete its attached label.

5. Create a mailing label report according to the following instructions:

a. Use the tblStudent table as the record source.

⊕ EXPLORE

b. Use Avery C2160 labels, use a larger font size and a heavier font weight, and use the other default font and color options.

c. For the prototype label, place FirstName, a space, and LastName on the first line; Address on the second line; and City, a space, State, a space, and Zip on the third line.

d. Sort by Zip and then by LastName, and then enter the report name **rptStudentMailingLabels**.

e. Change the mailing label layout to snaking columns.

6. Close the Contract database without exiting Access, make a backup copy of the database, open the **Contract** database, compact and repair the database, close the database, and then exit Access.

Apply | **Case Problem 2**

Apply what you learned in the tutorial to create a report and labels for a health and fitness center.

Data File needed for this Case Problem: Training.accdb (*cont. from Tutorial 6*)

Parkhurst Health & Fitness Center   Martha Parkhurst wants you to create a custom report and mailing labels for the Training database. The custom report will be based on the results of a query you will create. You will create the query, the custom report, and the mailing labels by completing the following steps:

1. Open the **Training** database located in the Level.02\Case2 folder provided with your Data Files.
2. Create a query that displays the ProgramID, ProgramType, and MonthlyFee fields from the tblProgram table, and the MembershipStatus, FirstName, and LastName fields from the tblMember table. Sort in ascending order by the ProgramID, MembershipStatus, and LastName fields, and then save the query as **qryProgramMembership**.
3. Create a custom report based on the qryProgramMembership query. Figure 7-48 shows a sample of the last page of the completed report. Refer to the figure as you create the report.

Figure 7-48

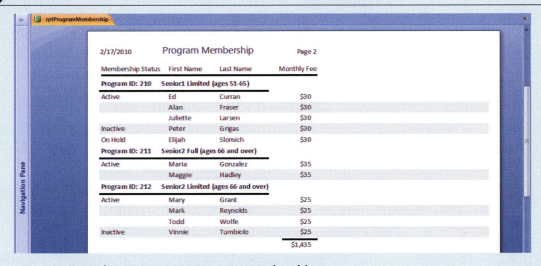

a. Save the report as **rptProgramMembership**.
b. The ProgramID field is a grouping field.
c. The MembershipStatus field is a sort field, and the LastName field is a sort field.
d. Hide duplicate values for the MembershipStatus field.
e. Add the ProgramType field to the Group Header section, and then delete its attached label.
4. Use the following instructions to create the mailing labels:
a. Use the tblMember table as the record source for the mailing labels.
b. Use Avery C2160 labels, and use the default font and color.
c. For the prototype label, place FirstName, a space, and LastName on the first line; Street on the second line; and City, a space, State, a space, and Zip on the third line.
d. Sort by Zip and then by LastName, and then type the report name **rptMemberLabels**.
5. Close the Training database with out exiting Access, make a backup copy of the database, open the **Training** database, compact and repair the database, close the database, and then exit Access.

Apply | **Case Problem 3**

Apply what you learned in the tutorial to create a report and labels for a recycling agency.

Data File needed for this Case Problem: Agency.accdb (*cont. from Tutorial 6*)

Rossi Recycling Group Mary Rossi asks you to create a custom report for the Agency database so that she can better track donations made by donors and to create mailing labels. You'll do so by completing the following:

1. Open the **Agency** database located in the Level.02\Case3 folder provided with your Data Files.
2. Create a query that displays the DonationDesc, DonationDate, and DonationValue fields from the tblDonation table, and the FirstName and LastName fields from the tblDonor table. Sort in ascending order by the DonationDesc, DonationDate, and LastName fields, and then save the query as **qryDonorDonations**.
3. Create a custom report based on the qryDonorDonations query. Figure 7-49 shows a sample of the last page of the completed report. Refer to the figure as you create the report.

Figure 7-49

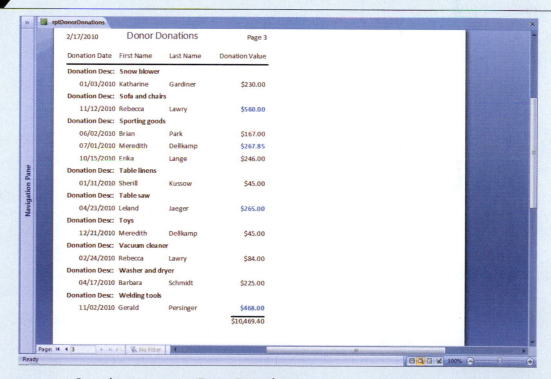

a. Save the report as **rptDonorDonations**.
b. The DonationDesc field is a grouping field.
c. The DonationDate field is a sort field, and the LastName field is a sort field.
d. Hide duplicate values for the DonationDate field.
e. Create a conditional formatting rule for the DonationValue field to display the value in blue, bold font when the amount is more than $250.

4. After you've created and saved the rptDonorDonations report, filter the report in Report view, selecting all records whose LastName field value is "Park." Copy the entire filtered report and paste it into a new Word document. Save the document as **rptDonorDonationsCopy**. Close Word, and then close the report without saving it.

5. Use the following instructions to create the mailing labels:
   a. Use the tblAgency table as the record source for the mailing labels.
   b. Use Avery C2160 labels, and use the default font and color.
   c. For the prototype label, place ContactFirstName, a space, and ContactLastName on the first line; AgencyName on the second line; Address on the third line; and City, a space, State, a space, and Zip on the fourth line.
   d. Sort by Zip and then by ContactLastName, and then type the report name **rptAgencyLabels**.
   e. Change the mailing label layout to snaking columns.

6. Close the Agency database without exiting Access, make a backup copy of the database, open the **Agency** database, compact and repair the database, close the database, and then exit Access.

| Create | **Case Problem 4** |

Use the skills you've learned in this tutorial to create a report and labels for a luxury property rental company.

Data File needed for this Case Problem: Vacation.accdb (*cont. from Tutorial 6*)

GEM Ultimate Vacations Griffin and Emma MacElroy want you to create a custom report and mailing labels for the Vacation database. You will create the custom report and the mailing labels by completing the following steps:

1. Open the **Vacation** database located in the Level.02\Case4 folder provided with your Data Files.

2. Create a query that displays the PropertyName and Country fields from the tblProperty table, the StateProv field from the tblGuest table, and the StartDate, EndDate, and People fields from the tblReservation table. Sort in ascending order by the PropertyName, StateProv, and StartDate fields, and then save the query as **qryPropertyReservations**.

3. Create a custom report based on the qryPropertyReservations query. Figure 7-50 shows a sample of the last page of the completed report. Refer to the figure as you create the report.

| Figure 7-50 |

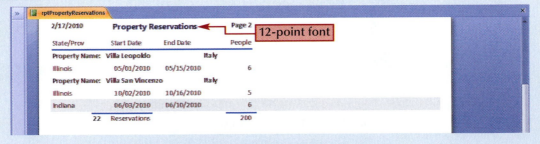

a. Save the report as **rptPropertyReservations**.
b. The PropertyName field is a grouping field.
c. The StateProv field is a sort field, and the StartDate field is a sort field.
d. Hide duplicate values for the StateProv field.

e. Add the Country field to the Group Header section.

4. Use the following instructions to create the mailing labels:
   a. Use the tblGuest table as the record source for the mailing labels.
   b. Use Avery C2163 labels, with the default font and color settings. (*Hint*: Be certain the English option button is selected in the Unit of Measure section.)
   c. For the prototype label, place GuestFirstName, a space, and GuestLastName on the first line; Address on the second line; City, a space, StateProv, a space, and PostalCode on the third line; and Country on the fourth line.
   d. Sort by PostalCode, then by GuestLastName, and then enter the report name **rptGuestLabels**.
   e. Change the mailing label layout to snaking columns.

⊕ EXPLORE

5. Make a copy of the rptPropertyReservations report. For the copy use the name **rptPropertyReservationsSummary**. Read Access Help to find out how to create a summary report. Modify the rptPropertyReservationsSummary report as follows:
   a. Delete the column heading labels, move up the line in the Page Header section to just below the remaining controls, and then reduce the height of the section.
   b. Add subtotals for the number of reservations and number of people.
   c. Change the report to a summary report.

6. Close the Vacation database without exiting Access, make a backup copy of the database, open the **Vacation** database, compact and repair the database, close the database, and then exit Access.

| Create | **Case Problem 5** |

Work with the skills you've learned in the tutorial to create a report and labels for an Internet service provider.

Data File needed for this Case Problem: ACE.accdb (*cont. from Tutorial 6*)

Always Connected Everyday Chris and Pat Dixon want you to create a custom report and mailing labels for the ACE database. You'll do so by completing the following:

1. Open the **ACE** database located in the Level.02\Case5 folder provided with your Data Files.
2. Create a query to serve as the record source for the custom report shown in Figure 7-51, and then save the query as **qryAccessPlanCustomers**.
3. Create a custom report based on the qryAccessPlanCustomers query. Figure 7-51 shows a sample of the completed report. Refer to the figure as you create the report. Save the report as **rptAccessPlanCustomers**.

Figure 7-51

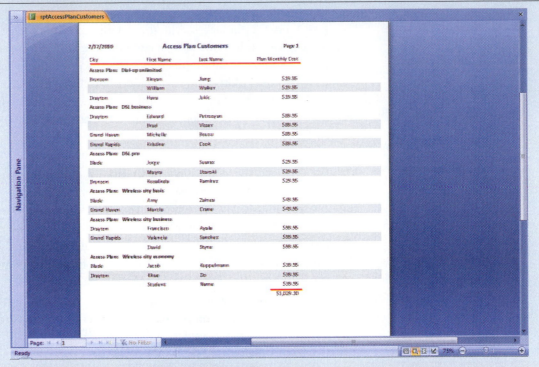

4. After you've created the rptAccessPlanCustomers report, filter the report in Report view, selecting all records that contain a specific value in the city field. Copy the entire filtered report and paste it into a new Word document. Save the document as **rptAccessPlanCustomersCopy**.

5. Use the tblCustomer table as the record source for the mailing labels. Choose appropriate options in the Label Wizard, change the mailing label layout to snaking columns, and save the report as **rptCustomerLabels**.

6. Close the ACE database without exiting Access, make a backup copy of the database, open the **ACE** database, compact and repair the database, close the database, and then exit Access.

Use the Internet to find and work with data related to the topics presented in this tutorial.

The purpose of the Internet Assignments is to challenge you to find information on the Internet that you can use to work effectively with this software. The actual assignments are updated and maintained on the Course Technology Web site. Log on to the Internet and use your Web browser to go to the Student Online Companion for New Perspectives Office 2007 at **www.course.com/np/office2007**. Then navigate to the Internet Assignments for this tutorial.

| Assess | **SAM Assessment and Training** |

If you have a SAM user profile, you may have access to hands-on instruction, practice, and assessment of the skills covered in this tutorial. Log in to your SAM account (**http://sam2007.course.com**) to launch any assigned training activities or exams that relate to the skills covered in this tutorial.

Review | Quick Check Answers

Session 7.1

1. A custom report is a report created by the Report tool or the Report Wizard and that you modify in Layout or Design view, or a report you create from scratch in Layout or Design view.
2. You can apply a filter or you can copy selected portions of the report to the Clipboard.
3. A report sort field that includes a Group Header section before a group of records having the same sort field value and that includes a Group Footer section after the group of records.
4. The Report Header section appears once at the beginning of a report. The Page Header section appears at the top of each page of a report. The Group Header section appears once at the beginning of a new group of records. The Detail section appears once for each record in the underlying table or query. The Group Footer section appears once at the end of a group of records. The Report Footer section appears once at the end of a report. The Page Footer section appears at the bottom of each page of a report.

Session 7.2

1. A detail report is a report that displays fields from the record source in the Detail section. A summary report is a report that displays only summary information, such as grand totals and subtotals.
2. Keep Together
3. orphaned footer
4. Can Grow
5. Hiding duplicate values makes a report easier to read; duplicate values clutter the report.

Session 7.3

1. =Date()
2. Click the Insert Page Number button in the Controls group in Layout or Design view; specify the format, position, and alignment of the page number; and then click the OK button.
3. Report Header
4. A multiple-column report prints the same collection of data in two or more sets across the page.

Ending Data Files

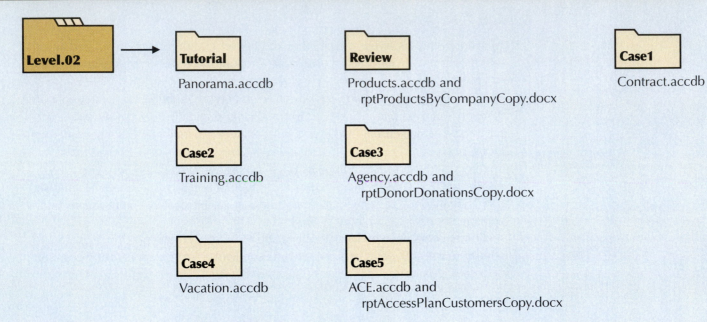

Level.02 →

Tutorial
Panorama.accdb

Review
Products.accdb and
rptProductsByCompanyCopy.docx

Case1
Contract.accdb

Case2
Training.accdb

Case3
Agency.accdb and
rptDonorDonationsCopy.docx

Case4
Vacation.accdb

Case5
ACE.accdb and
rptAccessPlanCustomersCopy.docx

Objectives

Sharing, Integrating, and Analyzing Data

Importing, Exporting, Linking, and Analyzing Data in the Panorama Database

Case | Belmont Landscapes

Oren Belmont, Sarah Fisher, and Taylor Sico are pleased with the design and contents of the Panorama database. Oren feels that other employees would benefit from gaining access to the Panorama database and by sharing data among the different programs employees use. Oren and Sarah would also like to be able to analyze the data in the database.

In this tutorial, you will show Oren and Sarah how to import, export, link, and embed data. You will also introduce them to the charting, PivotTable, and PivotChart features of Access.

Starting Data Files

Level.02 → **Tutorial**

BelmLogo.gif
BelmTemp.htm
Panorama.accdb *(cont.)*
Products.xlsx
tblCustomerBilling.csv
tblProspect.xml

Review

Ads.xlsx
BelmLogo.gif
BelmTemp.htm
Payables.csv
Products.accdb *(cont.)*
tblPayments.xml

Case1

Contract.accdb *(cont.)*
Instrument.csv
Room.xlsx

Case2

CreditCard.xml
ParkLogo.gif
ParkTemp.htm
Schedule.xlsx
Training.accdb *(cont.)*

Case3

Agency.accdb *(cont.)*
Facility.csv

Case4

Personnel.xlsx
Vacation.accdb *(cont.)*
Works.xml

Case5

ACE.accdb *(cont.)*

Session 8.1

Using the Web

The **Internet** is a worldwide collection of millions of interconnected computers and computer networks that share resources. The **World Wide Web** (or the **Web**) is a vast collection of digital documents available on the Internet. Each digital document on the Web is called a **Web page**, each computer on which an individual or company stores Web pages for access on the Internet is called a **Web server**, and each computer requesting a Web page from a Web server is called a **Web client**. Each Web page is assigned an Internet address, which is also called a **Uniform Resource Locator** (**URL**); the URL identifies where the Web page is stored—the location of the Web server and the name and location of the Web page on the server. For example, http://www.course.com/catalog/default.html is a URL that identifies the Web server (www.course.com), the location path (catalog) on the Web server, and the Web page name (default.html). The beginning of the URL (http) specifies the **Hypertext Transfer Protocol** (**HTTP**), which is the data communication method used by Web clients and Web servers to exchange data over the Internet. To view a Web page, you use a computer program called a **Web browser**, such as Microsoft Internet Explorer or Mozilla Firefox. After you start a Web browser, you enter the Web page's URL. The Web browser uses the URL to find and retrieve the Web page, and then displays it on your computer screen.

Each Web page is a text document that contains the necessary codes, called **tags**, that the Web browser interprets to position and format the text in the Web page. A Web page can also contain tags for links to audio files to be played, to graphics and animations to be displayed on the screen, and to other files, which are sent along with the Web page by the Web server. A Web page can also contain tags for **hyperlinks**, which connect Web pages to other Web pages or Web sites or to a location in the same Web page. When you click hyperlink text, the linked page opens. Hyperlinks connect Web pages throughout the Internet.

Web pages are usually created using a programming language called **Hypertext Markup Language** (**HTML**). You can create a Web page by typing all the necessary HTML tags into a text document, called an **HTML document**, and saving the document with the .htm or .html file extension. You can also use a program, such as ColdFusion or Adobe Dreamweaver, to create the HTML documents for Web pages without needing to learn HTML. Many programs, including Access, have built-in tools that convert and export objects, such as tables and queries, to HTML documents.

Tip

An intranet is an internal company network that uses software tools and languages, such as HTML, that typically are used on the Internet and the Web. The company that manages or owns the intranet restricts access to it by using passwords.

Exporting an Access Query to an HTML Document

Oren wants to display the customer contact data in the qryCustomersByName query on the company's intranet so that all employees working in the office are able to access it. To store the data on the company's intranet, you'll create a Web page version of the qryCustomersByName query.

Creating the necessary HTML document to provide Oren with the information he wants is not as difficult as it might appear at first. You can use Access to export the query and convert it to an HTML document automatically.

Exporting an Access Query to an HTML Document | Reference Window

- In the Navigation Pane, right-click the object (table, query, form, or report) you want to export, point to Export on the shortcut menu, and then click HTML Document.

or

- In the Navigation Pane, click the object (table, query, form, or report) you want to export, click the External Data tab on the Ribbon, click the More button in the Export group on the External Data tab, and then click HTML Document.
- Enter the filename in the File name text box of the Export - HTML Document dialog box, click the Browse button, select the location where you want to save the file, and then click the Save button.
- Click the Export data with formatting and layout check box to retain most formatting and layout information, check the other two check boxes, as necessary, and then click the OK button.
- If using a template, click the Select a HTML Template check box in the HTML Output Options dialog box, click the Browse button, select the location for the template, click the template filename, and then click the OK button.
- Click the OK button.
- Click the Close button to close the Export - HTML Document dialog box.

To complete the following steps, you need to use Access and a Web browser. The steps in this tutorial are written for Internet Explorer, the Web browser used at Belmont Landscapes. If you use another browser, the steps you need to complete might be slightly different.

You'll export the qryCustomersByName query as an HTML document.

To export the qryCustomersByName query as an HTML document:

▶ 1. Start Access, and then open the **Panorama** database in the Level.02\Tutorial folder provided with your Data Files.

▶ 2. Open the Navigation Pane (if necessary), right-click **qryCustomersByName** to display the shortcut menu, point to **Export**, and then click **HTML Document**. The Export - HTML Document dialog box opens.

▶ 3. Select the text in the File name text box, and then type **Customers by Name**. See Figure 8-1.

Figure 8-1 Export - HTML Document dialog box

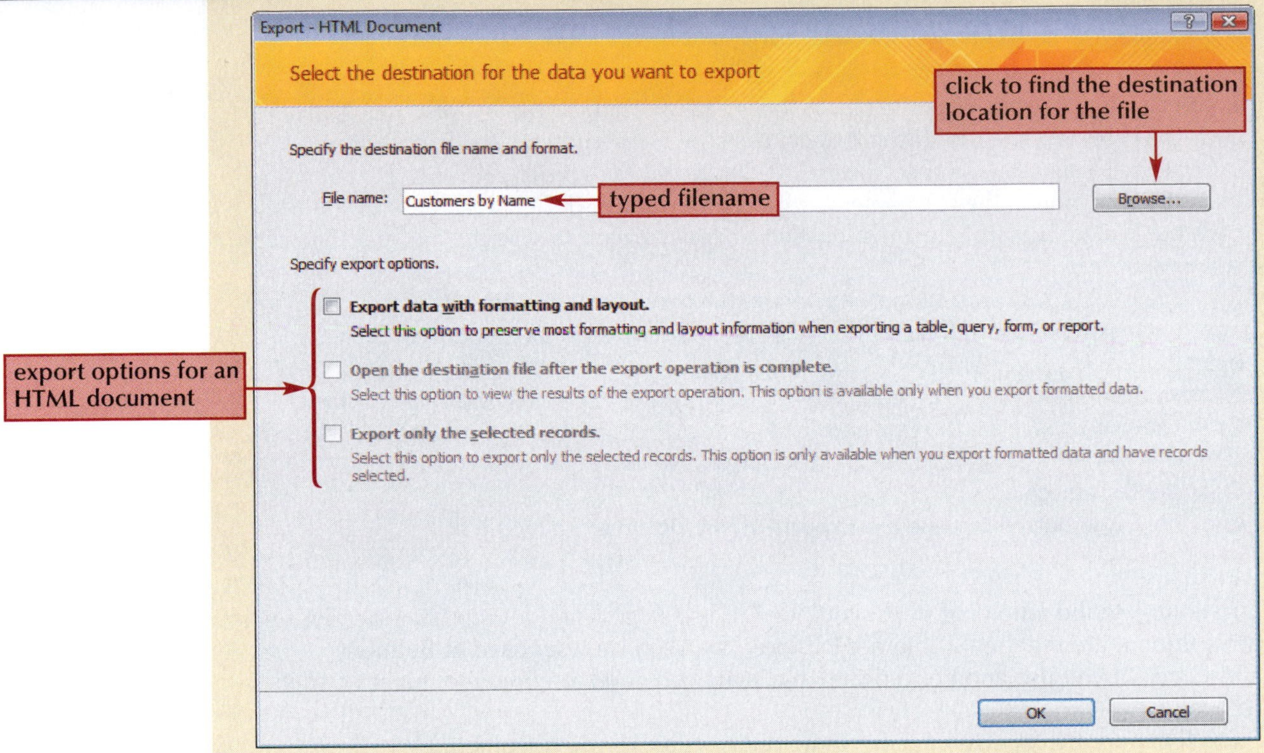

Tip

You should always select the "Export data with formatting and layout" option. Not selecting this option results in an HTML document that's poorly formatted and difficult to read.

The dialog box provides options for exporting the data with formatting and layout, opening the exported file after the export operation is complete, and exporting selected records from the source object (available only when you selected records in an object instead of the object on the Navigation Pane). You need to select the option for exporting the data with formatting and layout and the destination location for the exported file.

4. Click the **Export data with formatting and layout** check box, click the **Browse** button, navigate to and open the **Level.02\Tutorial** folder, and then click the **Save** button in the File Save dialog box. The File Save dialog box closes, and the File name text box displays the path to your Data Files and the filename Customers by Name.html.

5. Click the **OK** button. The Export - HTML Document dialog box closes and the HTML Output Options dialog box opens.

   This dialog box lets you specify an HTML template or use the default format when saving the object. An **HTML template** is a file that contains HTML instructions for creating a Web page with both text and graphics, together with special instructions that tell Access where to place the Access data in the Web page. Lucia used a text-editing program to create an HTML template named BelmTemp that you'll use to create the Customers by Name HTML document. The template will automatically insert a Belmont Landscapes logo in all Web pages created with it. You need to locate Lucia's template file in your Data Files.

6. If necessary, click the **Select a HTML Template** check box to select it.

7. Click the **Browse** button to open the HTML Template to Use dialog box, navigate to and open the **Level.02\Tutorial** folder, click **BelmTemp**, and then click the **OK** button. Access closes the HTML Template to Use dialog box, returns to the HTML Output Options dialog box, and displays the location and filename for the HTML template. See Figure 8-2.

HTML Output Options dialog box ◄ **Figure 8-2**

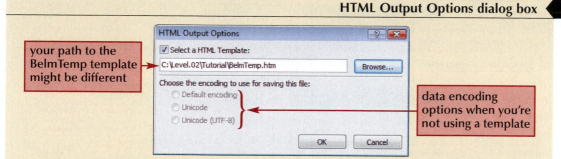

Trouble? If BelmTemp does not appear in the Level.02\Tutorial folder when you open the HTML Template to Use dialog box, click the Cancel button to return to the HTML Output Options dialog box so you can specify the template filename manually. In the HTML Template text box, type the full path to the BelmTemp.htm file in the Level.02\Tutorial folder—for example, C:\Level.02\Tutorial\BelmTemp.htm.

8. Click the **OK** button. The HTML Output Options dialog box closes, the HTML document named Customers by Name is saved in the Level.02\Tutorial folder, and the Export - HTML Document dialog box asks if you want to save the export steps. You won't save these export steps.

9. Click the **Close** button in the dialog box to close it without saving the steps.

Now you can view the Web page.

Viewing an HTML Document Using Internet Explorer

Oren asks to see the Web page you created. You can view the HTML document that you created using any Web browser. You'll view it using Internet Explorer.

To view the qryCustomersByName query Web page:

1. Open Windows Explorer, and then navigate to and open the **Level.02\Tutorial** folder, which is where you saved the exported HTML document.

2. Right-click **Customers by Name** in the file list to open the shortcut menu, click **Open With**, click **Internet Explorer** in the list of programs in the Open With dialog box, and then click the **OK** button. Internet Explorer starts and opens the Customers by Name Web page. See Figure 8-3.

Figure 8-3   **qryCustomersByName query in the Internet Explorer window**

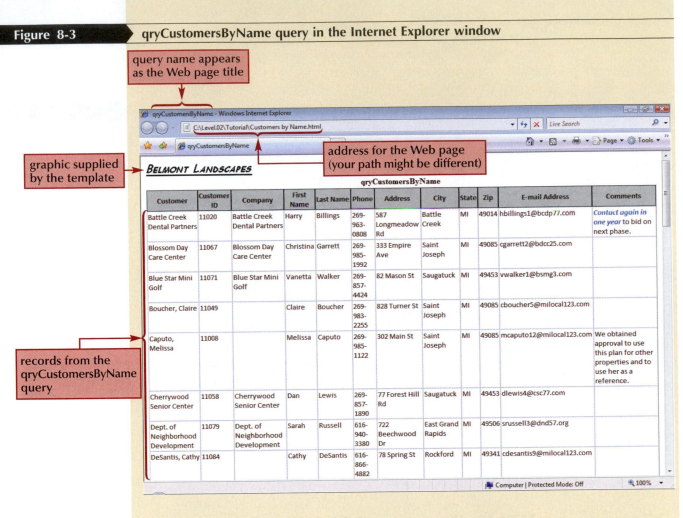

query name appears
as the Web page title

graphic supplied
by the template

address for the Web page
(your path might be different)

records from the
qryCustomersByName
query

Trouble? If Internet Explorer does not appear in the program list but another Web browser does appear, click the name of that browser. When you use another Web browser, your screens might look slightly different from the screen shown in the figure.

Changes that employees make to the Panorama database will not appear in the Customers by Name Web page that you created because it is a **static Web page**—that is, it reflects the state of the qryCustomersByName query in the Panorama database at the time you created it. If data in the qryCustomersByName query changes, you will need to export the query as an HTML document again.

Because this static Web page is not linked to the qryCustomersByName query on which it is based, you cannot use your browser to make changes to its data. Before closing the Customers by Name Web page, you'll try to change one of its field values.

To attempt to change a field value, and then close the browser:

1. Double-click **MI** in the State column for the first record (Battle Creek Dental Partners), and then type **NY**. The value of MI remains highlighted and unchanged, because the Customers by Name Web page is a static page.

2. Click the **Close** button [X] on the Internet Explorer window title bar to close it and to return to Windows Explorer.

3. Click the **Close** button ❎ on the Windows Explorer window title bar to close it and to return to Access.

Trouble? If the Access window is not active on your screen, click the Microsoft Access program button on the taskbar.

Sarah has a file containing customer billing addresses that she needs to add to the Panorama database. Instead of typing these billing addresses into new records, she asks you to import the data into the Panorama database.

Importing a CSV File as an Access Table

For most customers, the Address, City, State, and Zip fields in the tblCustomer table identify both the customer's location and billing address, which is where Belmont Landscapes sends the customer's invoices. In a few cases, however, the billing address is different from the location address; in addition, the company name used for billing purposes might be different from the company name stored in the tblCustomer table. Sarah has been maintaining an Excel workbook containing customer billing data, and she's exported the data to a CSV file. A **CSV (comma-separated values) file** is a text file in which commas separate values, and each line is a record containing the same number of values in the same positions.

Access can import data from a CSV file directly into a database table. Sarah's CSV file is named tblCustomerBilling, and you'll import it as a table with the same name into the Panorama database.

Importing a CSV File as an Access Table | Reference Window

- Click the External Data tab on the Ribbon.
- In the Import group on the External Data tab, click the Text File button to open the Get External Data - Text File dialog box.
- Click the Browse button in the dialog box, navigate to the location where the file to import is stored, click the filename, and then click the Open button.
- Click the Import the source data into a new table in the current database option button, and then click the OK button.
- In the Import Text Wizard dialog box, click the Delimited option button, and then click the Next button.
- Make sure the Comma option button is selected. If appropriate, click the First Row Contains Field Names check box to select it, and then click the Next button.
- For each field, select the column, type its field name, and select its data type, and then click the Next button.
- Choose the appropriate option button to let Access create a primary key, to choose your own primary key, or to avoid setting a primary key, click the Next button, type the table name, and then click the Finish button.

Now you will import the tblCustomerBilling.csv file as an Access database table.

To import the CSV file as an Access table:

1. Click the **External Data** tab on the Ribbon, and then in the Import group on the External Data tab, click the **Text File** button (with the ScreenTip "Import text file") to open the Get External Data - Text File dialog box.

2. Click the **Browse** button, navigate to and open the **Level.02\Tutorial** folder, click **tblCustomerBilling**, click the **Open** button, and then click the **Import the source data into a new table in the current database** option button. The selected path and filename appears in the File name text box. See Figure 8-4.

Figure 8-4 **Get External Data - Text File dialog box**

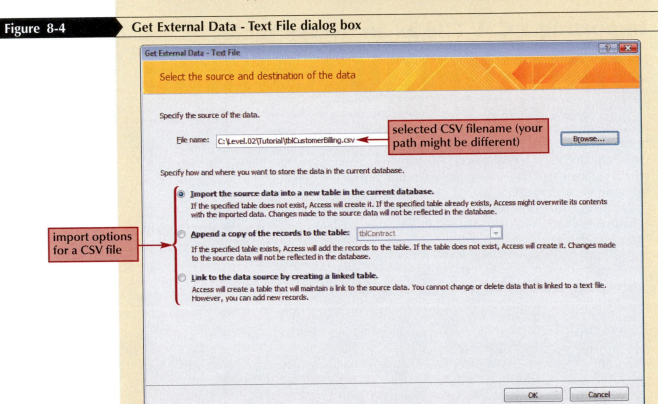

The dialog box provides options for importing the data into a new table in the database, appending a copy of the data to an existing table in the database, and linking to the source data. In the future, Sarah wants to maintain the customer billing data in the Panorama database, instead of using her Excel workbook, so you'll import the data into a new table.

3. Click the **OK** button to open the first Import Text Wizard dialog box, in which you designate how to identify the separation between field values in each line in the source data. The choices are the use of commas, tabs, or another character to separate, or delimit, the values, or the use of fixed width columns with spaces between each column. The wizard has correctly identified that values are delimited by commas.

4. Click the **Next** button to open the second Import Text Wizard dialog box, in which you verify the delimiter for values in each line. See Figure 8-5.

Verifying the delimiter for values in the CSV file 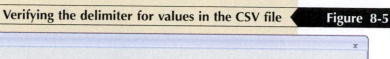 Figure 8-5

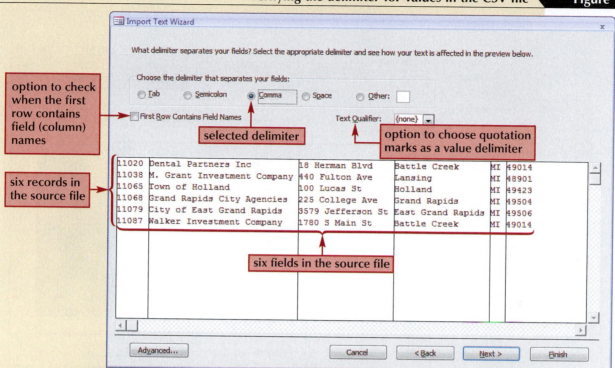

The CSV source file contains six records with six fields in each record. A comma serves as the delimiter for values in each line, so the Comma option button is selected. The first row in the source file contains the first record, not field names, so the First Row Contains Field Names check box is not checked. If the source file uses either single quotation marks or double quotation marks to enclose values, you would click the Text Qualifier arrow to choose the appropriate option.

5. Click the **Next** button to open the third Import Text Wizard dialog box, in which you enter the field name and set other properties for the imported fields. You will import all fields from the source file and use the default data type and indexed settings for each field.

6. Type **CustomerID** in the Field Name text box, and then click **Field2** in the table list. CustomerID (partially hidden) is the heading for the first column in the table list, and the second column is selected.

7. Repeat Step 6 for the rightmost five columns, typing **BillingCompany**, **BillingAddress**, **BillingCity**, **BillingState**, and **BillingZip** in the Field Name text box. See Figure 8-6.

Figure 8-6 After setting field names for the six fields in the source file

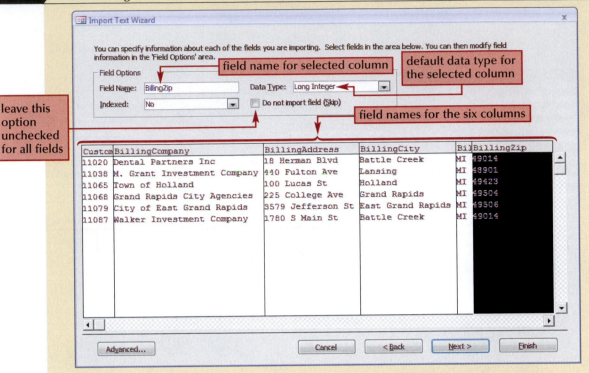

8. Click the **Next** button to open the fourth Import Text Wizard dialog box, in which you select the primary key for the imported table. CustomerID, the first column, will be the primary key.

9. Click the **Choose my own primary key** option button, make sure **CustomerID** appears in the list box for the option, click the **Next** button, click the **I would like a wizard to analyze my table after importing the data** check box, and then click the **Finish** button. An Import Text Wizard dialog box opens asking if you want to analyze the table.

After importing data and creating a new table, you can use the Import Text Wizard to analyze the imported table. When you choose this option, you start the Table Analyzer.

Analyzing a Table with the Table Analyzer

Tip

Read the Normalization section in the appendix titled "Relational Databases and Database Design" for more information about normalization and third normal form.

The **Table Analyzer** analyzes a single table and, if necessary, splits it into two or more tables that are in third normal form. The Table Analyzer looks for redundant data in the table. When the Table Analyzer encounters redundant data, it removes redundant fields from the table and then places the redundant fields in new tables.

To use the Table Analyzer to analyze the imported table:

1. Click the **Yes** button to close the dialog box and to open the first Table Analyzer Wizard dialog box. The diagram and explanation in this dialog box describe the problem when duplicate data is stored in a table.

2. Click the first **Show me an example** button, read the explanation, close the example box, click the second **Show me an example** button, read the explanation, close the example box, and then click the **Next** button to open the second Table Analyzer Wizard dialog box. The diagram and explanation in this dialog box describe how the Table Analyzer solves the duplicate data problem.

3. Click the first **Show me an example** button, read the explanation, close the example box, click the second **Show me an example** button, read the explanation, close the example box, and then click the **Next** button to open the third Table Analyzer Wizard dialog box. In this dialog box, you choose whether to let the wizard decide which fields go in what tables, if the table is not already normalized. You'll let the wizard decide.

4. Make sure the **Yes, let the wizard decide** option button is selected, and then click the **Next** button. A message box informs you that the wizard does not recommend splitting the table because the table is normalized and does not contain redundant data.

5. Click the **Cancel** button to close the message box, exit the wizard, and return to the Get External Data - Text File dialog box, in which you are asked if you want to save the import steps. You don't need to save these steps because you're importing the data only this one time.

6. Click the **Close** button to close the dialog box.

Tip

You can start the Table Analyzer directly by clicking the Database Tools tab, and then clicking the Analyze Table button in the Analyze group.

The TblCustomerBilling table is now listed in the Tables section in the Navigation Pane. You'll rename the table to change the initial letter to lowercase, and then open the table to verify the import results.

To rename and open the imported TblCustomerBilling table:

1. Right-click **TblCustomerBilling** in the Navigation Pane, click **Rename**, press the **Home** key, press the **Delete** key, type the letter **t**, and then press the **Enter** key to change the table name to tblCustomerBilling.

2. Double-click **tblCustomerBilling** in the Navigation Pane to open the table datasheet, resize all columns to their best fit, and then click **11020** in the first row in the CustomerID column to deselect all values. See Figure 8-7.

Imported tblCustomerBilling table datasheet ◄ **Figure 8-7**

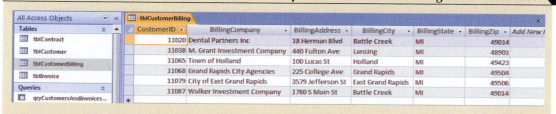

CustomerID	BillingCompany	BillingAddress	BillingCity	BillingState	BillingZip	Add New F
11020	Dental Partners Inc	18 Herman Blvd	Battle Creek	MI	49014	
11038	M. Grant Investment Company	440 Fulton Ave	Lansing	MI	48901	
11065	Town of Holland	100 Lucas St	Holland	MI	49423	
11068	Grand Rapids City Agencies	225 College Ave	Grand Rapids	MI	49504	
11079	City of East Grand Rapids	3579 Jefferson St	East Grand Rapids	MI	49506	
11087	Walker Investment Company	1780 S Main St	Battle Creek	MI	49014	

3. Save and close the table.

Sarah has some additional data that she wants to import into the Panorama database. The data is stored in XML format.

Using XML

Belmont Landscapes has contacts in the building trade industry and gets customer leads from builders when they sell new homes. One of the builders has several prospective customers available to Sarah in an XML document, which she wants to add to the Panorama database. **XML** (**Extensible Markup Language**) is a programming language that is similar in format to HTML, but is more customizable and suited to the exchange of data between different programs. Unlike HTML, which uses a fixed set of tags to describe the appearance of a Web page, developers can customize XML to describe the data it contains and how that data should be structured.

Importing an XML File as an Access Table

Access can import data from an XML file directly into a database table. Sarah's XML file is named tblProspect, and you'll import it as a table with the same name into the Panorama database.

Reference Window | **Importing an XML File as an Access Table**

- Click the External Data tab on the Ribbon.
- In the Import group on the External Data tab, click the XML File button to open the Get External Data - XML File dialog box.
- Click the Browse button, navigate to the location for the XML file, click the XML filename, and then click the Open button.
- Click the OK button in the Get External Data - XML File dialog box, click the table name in the Import XML dialog box, click the appropriate option button in the Import Options section, and then click the OK button.
- Click the Close button.

or

- If you need to save the import steps, click the Save import steps check box, enter a name for the saved steps in the Save as text box, and then click the Save Import button.

Now you will import the tblProspect.xml document as an Access database table.

To import the XML document as an Access table:

▶ 1. Click the **External Data** tab on the Ribbon (if necessary), and then in the Import group on the External Data tab, click the **XML File** button (with the ScreenTip "Import XML file"). The Get External Data - XML File dialog box opens.

▶ 2. Click the **Browse** button, navigate to and open the **Level.02\Tutorial** folder, click **tblProspect**, and then click the **Open** button. The selected path and filename now appear in the File name text box.

▶ 3. Click the **OK** button. The Import XML dialog box opens. See Figure 8-8.

Import XML dialog box   Figure 8-8

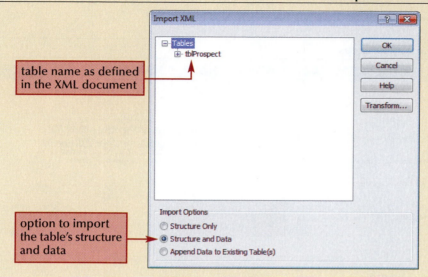

table name as defined in the XML document

option to import the table's structure and data

From the XML file, you can import only the table structure to a new table, import the table structure and data to a new table, or append the data in the XML file to an existing table. You'll import the table structure and data to a new table named tblProspect.

4. Make sure the **Structure and Data** option button is selected, click **tblProspect** in the list box, and then click the **OK** button. The Import XML dialog box closes, and the last Get External Data - XML File dialog box is displayed.

Before reviewing the imported table, you'll save the import steps.

Saving and Running Import Specifications

If you need to repeat the same import procedure many times, you can save the steps for the procedure and expedite future imports by running the saved import steps without using a wizard. Because the builder intends to send Sarah additional lists of prospective customers in the future, you'll save the import steps for Sarah.

To save and run the XML file import steps:

▶ 1. Click the **Save import steps** check box. The dialog box expands to display additional options for the save operation. See Figure 8-9.

Figure 8-9 | **Saving the import steps**

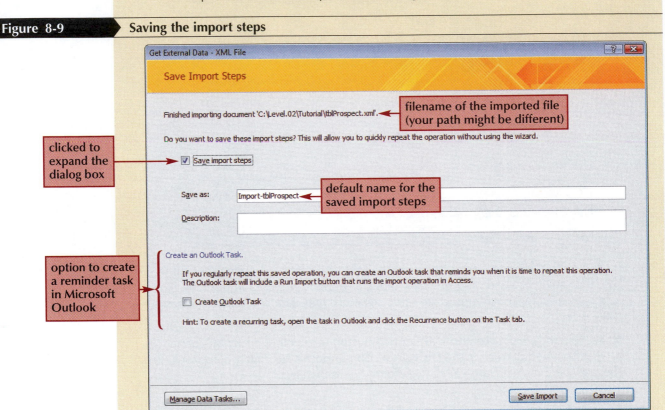

In the expanded dialog box, you can accept the default name for the saved import steps or choose one that you create, and you can enter an optional description. If the import will occur on a set schedule, you can also create a reminder task in Microsoft Outlook. You'll accept the default name for the saved steps, and you won't enter a description or schedule an Outlook task.

▶ 2. Click the **Save Import** button. The import steps are saved as Import-tblProspect, the Get External Data - XML File dialog box closes, the tblProspect file is imported to the Panorama database, and the table is now listed in the Navigation Pane.

You'll now show Sarah how she can run the saved steps when she receives customer prospects from the builder in the future.

▶ 3. In the Import group on the External Data tab, click the **Saved Imports** button. The Manage Data Tasks dialog box opens. See Figure 8-10.

Manage Data Tasks dialog box   Figure 8-10

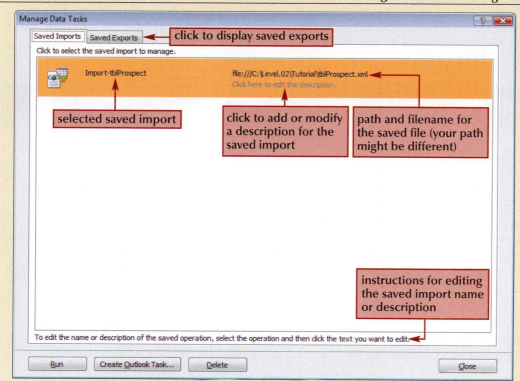

In this dialog box, you can change the saved import name, add or change its description, create an Outlook task for the saved import, run a saved import, or delete a saved import. You can also manage any saved export by clicking the Saved Exports tab. You'll add a description for the saved procedure and review the list of saved exports.

▶ 4. Click the **Click here to edit the description** link to open an editing box, type **Builder's XML file of customer prospects**, click an unused portion of the orange selection band to close the editing box and accept the typed description, and then click the **Saved Exports** tab. You have not saved any export steps, so no saved exports are displayed.

▶ 5. Click the **Close** button to close the Manage Data Tasks dialog box.

▶ 6. Double-click the **tblProspect** table in the Navigation Pane to open the table datasheet, close the Navigation Pane, resize all columns to their best fit, and then click **12001** in the first row in the CustomerID column to deselect all values. See Figure 8-11.

Imported tblProspect table datasheet   Figure 8-11

▶ 7. Save and close the table.

Sarah next asks you to export the tblInvoice table as an XML file.

Exporting an Access Table as an XML File

Belmont Landscapes uses an accounting package that accepts the data in XML files as input for making accounting entries. Sarah wants to test this capability by exporting the tblInvoice table as an XML file and giving the XML file to the company's accounting manager for testing with the accounting package.

Reference Window | Exporting an Access Table as an XML File

- Right-click the object (table, query, form, or report) in the Navigation Pane, point to Export, and then click XML File.

or

- Click the object (table, query, form, or report) in the Navigation Pane. In the Export group on the External Data tab, click the More button, and then click XML File.
- Click the Browse button in the Export - XML File dialog box, navigate to the location where you will save the XML file, and then click the Save button.
- Click the OK button in the dialog box, select the options in the Export XML dialog box or click the More Options button and select the options in the expanded Export XML dialog box, and then click the OK button.
- Click the Close button.

or

- If you need to save the export steps, click the Save export steps check box, enter a name for the saved steps in the Save as text box, and then click the Save Export button.

InSight | Importing and Exporting Data

You've imported data from an Excel workbook and a text file (TXT extension) in Tutorial 2 and from a text file (CSV extension) and an XML file in this tutorial. Additional Access options include importing an object from another Access database, importing data from other databases (ODBC databases such as SQL Server, dBASE, and Paradox), and importing a Lotus 1-2-3 file, an HTML document, an Outlook folder, or a SharePoint list.

In addition to exporting Access objects as an XML file or an HTML document, Access includes options for exporting data to another Access database, other databases (ODBC database, dBASE, or Paradox), an Excel workbook, a Lotus 1-2-3 file, a text file, a Word document, or a SharePoint list. You can also "export" table or query data to Word's mail merge feature, or export a report to a snapshot file (SNP extension) so you can view it with the Microsoft Snapshot Viewer available from the Microsoft Download Center.

Also available from the Microsoft Download Center is the Microsoft Save as PDF or XPS add-in that you can download and install to export and save objects as PDF or XPS files. Installing this download adds a "PDF or XPS" button in the Export group on the External Data tab. PDF (Portable Document Format) and XPS (XML Paper Specification) are file formats that render reports and other objects in a form viewable on any computer using the free Adobe Reader program for PDF files and an XPS reader program, such as Windows Presentation Foundation, for XPS files.

The steps you follow for all import and export options work similar to the import and export steps you've used in this tutorial and in Tutorial 2. For example, to save an object as an XPS file, right-click the name of the object you want to export in the Navigation Pane, point to Export on the shortcut menu, click PDF or XPS, navigate to the folder where you want to store the file, click the Save as type arrow, click XPS Document, click the Publish button, and then click the Close button.

You can now export the tblInvoice table as an XML file.

To export the tblInvoice table as an XML file:

▶ 1. Open the Navigation Pane, right-click **tblInvoice** in the Navigation Pane, point to **Export** on the shortcut menu, and then click **XML File**. The Export - XML File dialog box opens.

▶ 2. Click the **Browse** button, navigate to and open the **Level.02\Tutorial** folder, and then click the **Save** button. The selected path and filename now appears in the File name text box in the Export - XML File dialog box.

▶ 3. Click the **OK** button. The Export XML dialog box opens.

Clicking the More Options button in the Export XML dialog box expands the dialog box and lets you view and change detailed options for exporting a database object to an XML file.

▶ 4. Click the **More Options** button to reveal detailed export options in the Export XML dialog box. See Figure 8-12.

Data tab in the Export XML dialog box ◀ Figure 8-12

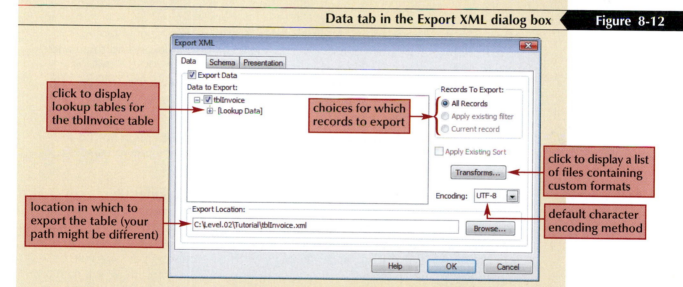

click to display lookup tables for the tblInvoice table

choices for which records to export

click to display a list of files containing custom formats

location in which to export the table (your path might be different)

default character encoding method

The Export Data check box, the Export Location text box, and the Records To Export option group display the selections you made in the previous step. You're exporting all records from the tblInvoice table, including the data in the records and the structure of the table, to the tblInvoice.xml file in the Level.02\Tutorial folder. The encoding option determines how characters will be represented in the exported XML file. The encoding choices are UTF-8, which uses 8 bits to represent each character, and UTF-16, which uses 16 bits to represent each character. You can also click the Transforms button if you have a special file that contains instructions for changing the exported data.

The accounting package doesn't have a transform file and requires the default encoding, but Sarah wants to review the tables that contain lookup data.

▶ 5. Click the **plus box** to the left of [Lookup Data]. The tblContract table contains lookup data because it's the primary table in the one-to-many relationship with the related tblInvoice table. The accounting package requirements don't include any lookup data from the tblContract table, so make sure the tblContract check box is not checked.

The Data tab settings are correct, so you'll verify the Schema tab settings.

6. Click the **Schema** tab. See Figure 8-13.

Figure 8-13 **Schema tab in the Export XML dialog box**

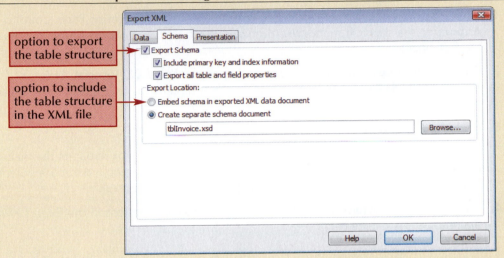

option to export
the table structure

option to include
the table structure
in the XML file

Along with the data from the tblInvoice table, you'll be exporting its table structure, including information about the table's primary key, indexes, and table and
field properties. You can include this information in a separate **XSD** (**XML
Structure Definition**) file, or you can embed the information in the XML file. The
accounting package expects a single XML file, so you'll embed the structure information in the XML file.

7. Click the **Embed schema in exported XML data document** option button to
select that option and to dim the "Create separate schema document" text box,
and then click the **Presentation** tab.

The Presentation tab options let you export a separate **XSL** (**Extensible
Stylesheet Language**) file containing the format specifications for the tblInvoice
table data. Unlike HTML, XML provides no screen formatting information. An XSL
file provides formatting instructions so that a browser or another program can display the data in the XML file in a readable way. The accounting package will
import the tblInvoice table data directly into its computer program, which contains
its own formatting instructions, so you will not export an XSL file.

8. Make sure that the **Export Presentation (HTML 4.0 Sample XSL)** check box is
not checked, and then click the **OK** button. Access closes the Export XML dialog
box, exports the data in the tblInvoice table as an XML file in the Level.02\Tutorial
folder, and returns you to the final Export - XML File dialog box.

Sarah plans to make further tests exporting the tblInvoice table as an XML file, so
you'll save the export steps.

Saving and Running Export Specifications

Saving the steps to export the tblInvoice table as an XML file will save time and eliminate
errors when Sarah repeats the export procedure. You'll save the export steps and then
show Sarah how to run the saved export steps.

To save and run the XML file export steps:

▶ **1.** Click the **Save export steps** check box. The dialog box expands to display additional options for the save operation.

The expanded dialog box has the same options you saw earlier when you saved the XML import steps. You'll enter a description, and you won't create an Outlook task because Sarah will be running the saved export steps on an as needed basis.

▶ **2.** In the Description text box, type **XML file accounting entries from the tblInvoice table**. See Figure 8-14.

Saving the export steps ◀ | Figure 8-14

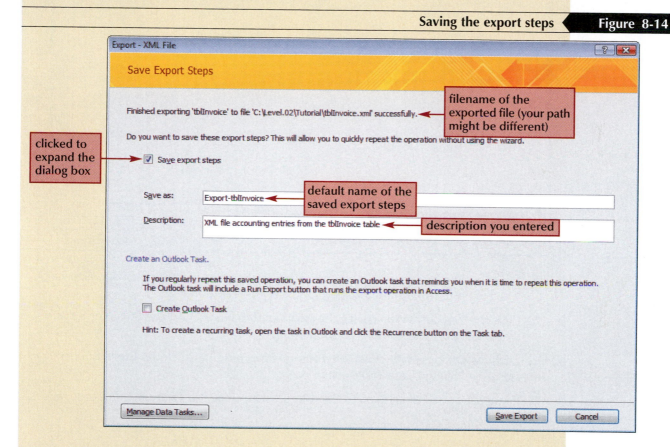

▶ **3.** Click the **Save Export** button. The export steps are saved as Export-tblInvoice, the Export - XML File dialog box closes, and the tblInvoice table is exported as an XML file named tblInvoice.

You'll now show Sarah how she can to run the saved steps.

▶ **4.** Click the **External Data** tab on the Ribbon (if necessary), and in the Export group on the External Data tab, click the **Saved Exports** button. The Manage Data Tasks dialog box opens. See Figure 8-15.

Figure 8-15 | Manage Data Tasks dialog box

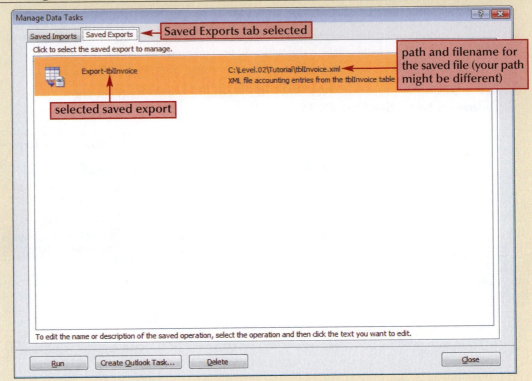

5. Click the **Run** button. The saved procedure runs, and a message box opens, asking if you want to replace the existing XML file you created earlier.

6. Click the **Yes** button to replace the existing XML file. A message box informs you that the export was completed successfully.

7. Click the **OK** button to close the message box, and then click the **Close** button to close the Manage Data Tasks dialog box.

8. If you are not continuing on to the next session, close the Panorama database, and then exit Access.

You've imported and exported data, analyzed a table's design, and saved and run import and export specifications. In the next session, you will analyze data by working with a chart, PivotTable, PivotChart, and linked data, and you will add a tab control to a form.

Review | **Session 8.1 Quick Check**

1. What is the World Wide Web, and what do you use to view the information it provides?
2. What is a hyperlink?
3. What is HTML?
4. What is an HTML template?
5. What is a static Web page?
6. What is a CSV file?
7. What is the Table Analyzer?
8. _____ is a programming language that describes data and its structure.

Session 8.2

Creating a Multi-page Form Using a Tab Control

You can create a multi-page form in two ways: use the **Page Break tool** to insert a page break control in the form, or use the **Tab Control tool** to insert a control that's called a tab control. If you insert a page break control in a form, users can move between the form pages by pressing the Page Up and Page Down keys. If you use a tab control, the control appears with tabs at the top, with one tab for each page. Users can switch between pages by clicking the tabs.

Sarah wants to include a tab control with two pages in the frmContractsAndInvoices form. The first page of the tab control will contain the frmInvoiceSubform subform that is currently positioned at the bottom of the frmContractsAndInvoices form. The second page of the tab control will contain a chart showing the invoice amounts for the invoices associated with the displayed contract.

To expedite placing the subform in the tab control, you'll cut the subform from the form, add the tab control, and then paste the subform into the left tab on the tab control. You need to perform these steps in Design view.

To add the tab control to the form:

▶ **1.** If you took a break after the previous session, make sure that the Panorama database is open and the Navigation Pane is open.

▶ **2.** Open the **frmContractsAndInvoices** form in Design view, and then close the Navigation Pane.

▶ **3.** Right-click the top edge of the subform control to open the shortcut menu, and then click **Cut** to delete the subform control and place it on the Clipboard.

   Trouble? If you do not see Subform in New Window as one of the options on the shortcut menu, you did not click the top edge of the subform control correctly. Right-click the top edge of the subform control until you see this option on the shortcut menu, and then repeat Step 3.

▶ **4.** In the Controls group on the Design tab, click the **Tab Control** button 🖳.

▶ **5.** Position the + portion of the pointer in the Detail section three grid dots from the left edge of the grid and at the 2.5-inch mark on the vertical ruler, and then click the mouse button. Access places a tab control with two pages in the form.

▶ **6.** Right-click the left tab, and then click **Paste** on the shortcut menu. The subform is pasted in the tab control. See Figure 8-16.

Figure 8-16 | Subform on the tab control in the Detail section

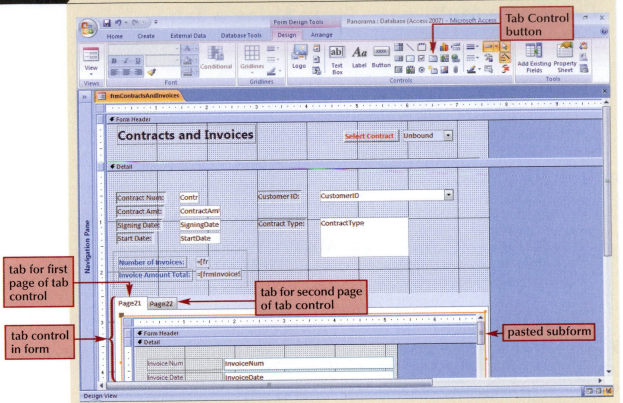

7. Save your form design changes, switch to Form view, and then click **3011** in the ContractNum text box to deselect all controls. The left tab, which represents the first page in the tab control, is the active tab. See Figure 8-17.

Figure 8-17 | Subform on the tab control in Form view

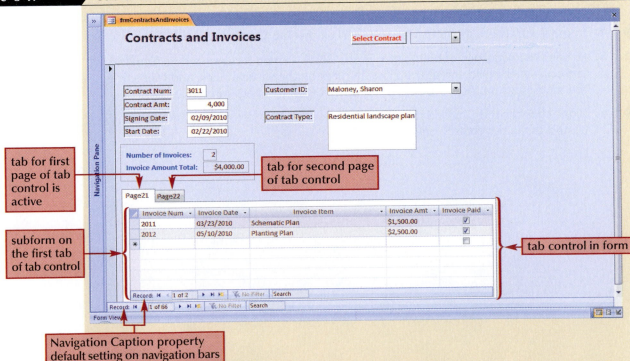

The subform is now displayed on the first page of the tab control and its design is the same as it was before you cut and pasted it to the tab control.

▶ **8.** Click the right tab of the tab control to display the second page, which is empty because you haven't added any controls to it yet.

After viewing the form in Form view, Sarah asks you to edit the labels for the tabs in the tab control, so they indicate the contents of each page. Also, Sarah's staff finds the two sets of navigation buttons confusing—they waste time determining which set of navigation buttons applies to the subform and which to the main form. You'll set the Navigation Caption property for the main form and the subform. The **Navigation Caption property** lets you change the navigation label from the word "Record" to another value. Because the main form displays data about contracts and the subform displays data about invoices, you'll change the Navigation Caption property for the main form to "Contract" and for the subform to "Invoice."

To change the captions for the tabs and the navigation buttons:

▶ **1.** Switch to Design view.

▶ **2.** Click the **form selector** for the main form to select the form control in the main form, open the property sheet to display the properties for the selected form control, click the **Navigation Caption** text box, and then type **Contract**. See Figure 8-18.

Setting the Navigation Caption property for the main form ◀ **Figure 8-18**

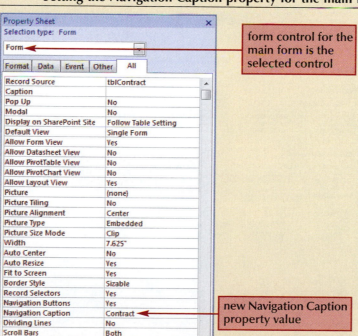

form control for the main form is the selected control

new Navigation Caption property value

▶ **3.** Click the **form selector** for the subform to select the subform, click the **form selector** for the subform again to select the form control in the subform and display the properties for the selected form control, click the **Navigation Caption** text box, and then type **Invoice**. Navigation buttons don't appear in Design view, so you won't see the effects of the Navigation Caption property settings until you switch to Form view.

▶ **4.** Click the left tab in the subform to select it, and then type **Invoice Data** in the Caption text box on the property sheet. See Figure 8-19.

Figure 8-19 **Setting the Caption property for the left tab**

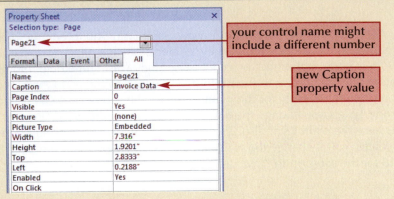

your control name might include a different number

new Caption property value

▶ **5.** Click the right tab in the subform to select it, type **Invoice Chart** in the Caption text box, and then close the property sheet.

▶ **6.** Save your form design changes, switch to Form view, and then click **3011** in the ContractNum text box to deselect all controls. The tabs and the navigation buttons now display the new caption values. See Figure 8-20.

Figure 8-20 **Subform on the tab control in Form view**

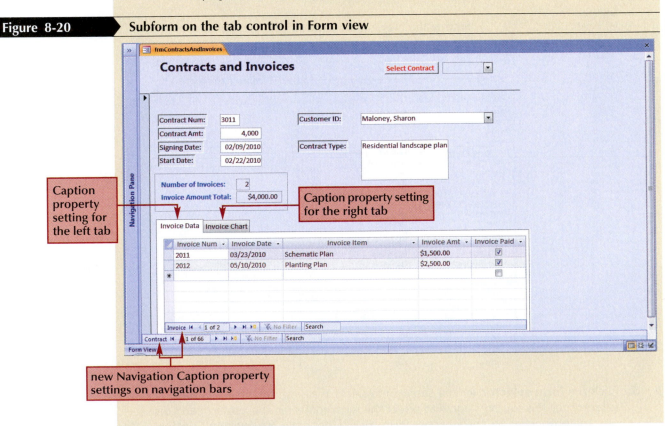

Caption property setting for the left tab

Caption property setting for the right tab

new Navigation Caption property settings on navigation bars

Sarah wants you to add a simple chart to the second page of the tab control.

Integrating Access with Other Programs

When you create a form or report in Access, you include more than just the data from the record source table or query. You've added controls such as lines, rectangles, tab controls, and graphics in your forms and reports to improve their appearance and usability. You can also add charts, drawings, and other objects to your forms and reports, but Access doesn't have the capability to create them. Instead, you create these other objects using other programs and then place them in a form or report using the appropriate integration method.

When you integrate information between programs, the program containing the original information, or object, is called the **source program**, and the program in which you place the information created by the source program is called the **destination program**. Access offers three ways for you to integrate objects created by other programs.

- **Importing**. When you import an object, you include the contents of a file in a new table or append it to an existing table, or you include the contents of the file in a form, report, or field. For example, in Tutorial 2 you added a picture to a form, or imported it into the form, and in this tutorial you imported CSV and XML files as new tables in the Panorama database. The imported picture is a file with a .bmp extension that was created by a graphics program, and the CSV and XML files were created by other programs. Once an object is imported, it has no relation to the program in which it was created. Any changes made to the object using the source program are not reflected in the imported objects.
- **Embedding**. When you embed an object in a form, report, or field, you preserve its connection to the source program, which enables you to edit the object, if necessary, using the features of the source program. Any changes you make to the object are reflected only in the form, report, or field in which it is embedded; the changes do not affect the original object in the file from which it was embedded. Likewise, if you start the source program outside Access and make any changes to the original object, these changes are not reflected in the embedded object.
- **Linking**. When you link an object to a form, report, or field, you include a connection in the destination program to the original file maintained by the source program; you do not store data from the file in the destination program. Any changes you made to the original file using the source program are reflected in the linked file version in the destination program.

InSight | **Importing, Embedding, and Linking Data**

How do you decide which method to use when you need to use data stored in another format in Access? You import a file as a new table or append the records in the file to an existing table when you intend to use Access to maintain the data and no longer need an updated version of the data with the source program. You link to the data when the source program will continue to maintain the data in the file, and you need to use an updated version of the file at all times in the destination program. When linking to the data, you can also maintain the data using the destination program, and the source program will always use the updated version of the file.

For objects in forms or reports, you import an object (such as a picture) when you want a copy of the object in your form or report and you don't intend to make any changes to the object. You embed or link an object when you want a copy of the object in your form or report and you intend to edit the object using the source program in the future. You embed the object when you do not want your edits to the object in the destination program to affect any other copies of the object used by other programs. You link the object when you want your edits to the object in the destination program to affect the object used by other programs.

Sarah wants you to embed a chart on the second page of the tab control.

Embedding a Chart in a Form

The Chart Wizard in Access helps you to embed a chart in a form or report. The chart is actually created by another program, Microsoft Graph, but the Chart Wizard does the work of embedding the chart. After embeddng the chart in a form or report, you can edit it using the Microsoft Graph program.

Reference Window | **Embedding a Chart in a Form**

- In the Controls group on the Design tab in Design view, click the Insert Chart button.
- Position the + portion of the pointer where you want to position the upper-left corner of the chart, and then click the mouse button to start the Chart Wizard.
- Select the record source, fields, and chart type.
- Edit the chart contents, and select the fields that link the object and chart, if necessary.
- Enter a chart title, select whether to include a legend, and then click the Finish button.

The tblInvoice table contains the information needed for the chart Sarah wants you to include in the form's right tab in the tab control.

To add a chart in the tab control and start the Chart Wizard:

1. Switch to Design view, and then click the **Invoice Chart** tab on the tab control, if necessary.

2. In the Controls group on the Design tab, click the **Insert Chart** button 📊 , and then move the pointer to the tab control. When the pointer is inside the tab control, the rectangular portion of the tab control you can use to place controls is filled in black.

3. Position the + portion of the pointer in the upper-left corner of the black portion of the tab control, and then click the mouse button. Access places a chart control in the form and opens the first Chart Wizard dialog box, in which you select the record source for the chart.

Sarah wants the chart to provide her staff with a simple visual display of the relative proportions of the invoice amounts for the invoices for the currently displayed contract. You'll use the tblInvoice table as the record source for the chart and select the InvoiceDate and InvoiceAmt fields as the fields to use in the chart.

To create the chart with the Chart Wizard:

1. Click **Table: tblInvoice** in the list box, and then click the **Next** button to display the second Chart Wizard dialog box.

2. Select the **InvoiceDate** and the **InvoiceAmt** fields, and then click the **Next** button to display the third Chart Wizard dialog box, in which you choose the chart type.

3. Click the **Pie Chart** button (row 4, column 1) to select the pie chart as the chart type to use for Sarah's chart. See Figure 8-21.

Selecting the chart type   Figure 8-21

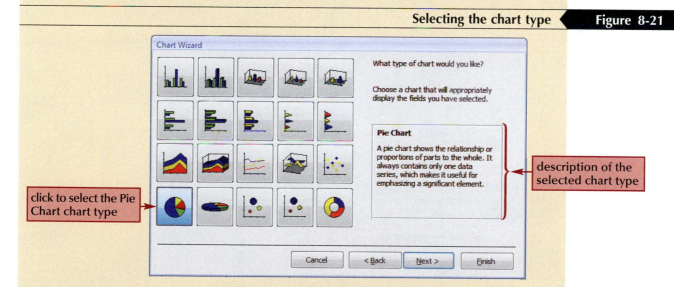

click to select the Pie Chart chart type

description of the selected chart type

4. Click the **Next** button to display the next Chart Wizard dialog box, in which you preview the chart and modify the data and its placement in the chart. Because visualizing the chart from the displayed preview is difficult, you'll use the default layout based on the two selected fields. You can easily modify the chart after you create it.

Tip

The box on the right displays a brief description of the selected chart type.

Tip

The record source for a primary main form must have a one-to-many relationship to the record source for a related subform or chart. The subform or chart object has its Link Master Fields property set to the primary key in the record source to the main form. Its Link Child Fields property is set to the foreign key in the record source to the subform or chart.

▶ 5. Click the **Next** button to display the next Chart Wizard dialog box, in which you choose the fields that link records in the main form, which uses the tblContract table as its record source, to records in the chart, which uses the tblInvoice table as its record source. ContractNum is the common field linking these two tables, and you can use that field as the linking field even though you didn't select it as a field for the chart.

▶ 6. Click the **Next** button to display the final dialog box, in which you enter the title that will appear at the top of the chart and choose whether to include a legend in the chart.

▶ 7. Type **Invoices for this Contract**, make sure the **Yes, display a legend** option button is selected, and then click the **Finish** button. The completed chart appears in the tab control.

You'll view the form in Form view, where it's easier to assess the chart's appearance.

▶ 8. Save your form design changes, switch to Form view, navigate to record 5 in the main form, notice the four contracts displayed in the subform, click the **Invoice Chart** tab to display the chart, and then scroll down the form (if necessary). See Figure 8-22.

Figure 8-22   ▶   **Embedded chart in Form view**

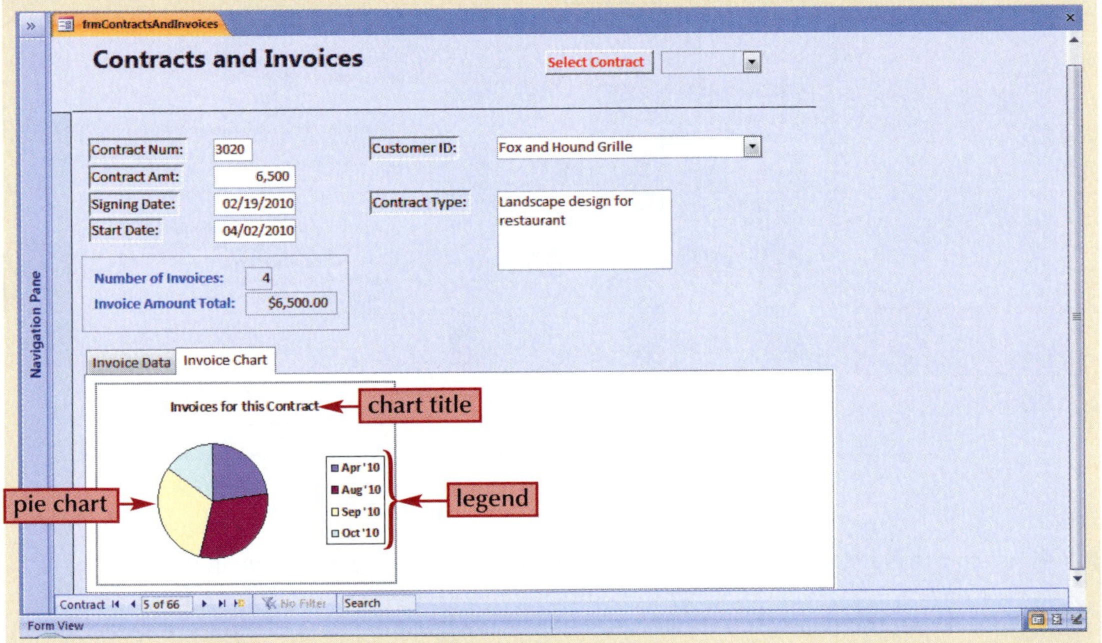

After viewing the chart, Sarah decides it needs some modifications. She wants you to change the chart type from a pie chart to a bar chart, remove the legend, and modify the chart's background color. You'll make these changes by switching to Design view, and then you'll start Microsoft Graph so you can edit the chart.

To edit the chart using Microsoft Graph:

▶ **1.** Switch to Design view, right-click an edge of the chart object to open the shortcut menu, point to **Chart Object**, and then click **Open**. Microsoft Graph starts and displays the chart. See Figure 8-23.

Editing the chart with Microsoft Graph **Figure 8-23**

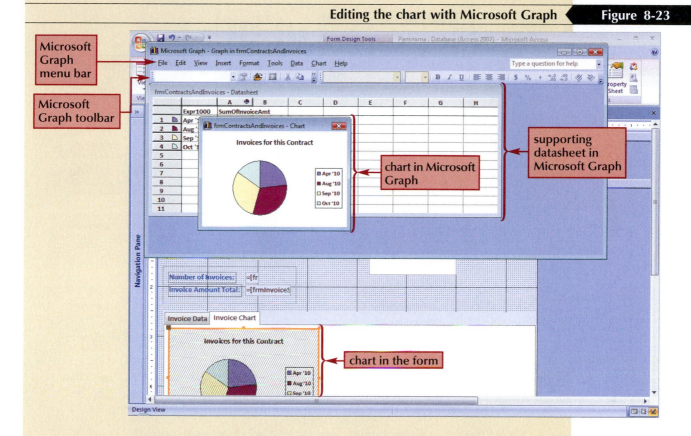

Microsoft Graph is the source program that the Chart Wizard used to create the chart. Because the chart was embedded in the form, editing the chart object starts Graph and allows you to edit the chart using the Graph menu bar and toolbar. In addition to displaying the selected chart, the Graph window displays a datasheet, which contains the data on which the chart is based. You'll now make Sarah's chart changes using Graph.

▶ **2.** Click **Chart** on the Graph menu bar, click **Chart Type** to open the Chart Type dialog box, and then click **Column** in the Chart type list box to display the types of column charts. See Figure 8-24.

Figure 8-24   Chart Type dialog box

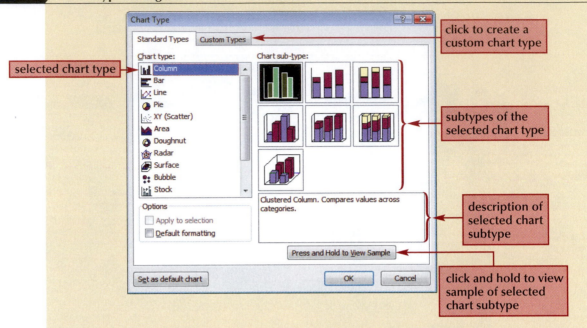

The Column chart is the selected chart type, and the Clustered Column chart is the default chart subtype (row 1, column 1). A description of the selected chart subtype appears below the chart subtypes. You can create a custom chart by clicking the Custom Types tab. If you click and hold down the Press and Hold to View Sample button, you'll see a sample of the selected subtype.

3. Click the **Press and Hold to View Sample** button to view a sample of the chart, release the mouse button, and then click the **OK** button to close the dialog box and change the chart to a column chart in the Graph window and in the form.

4. Click **Chart** on the Graph menu bar, click **Chart Options** to open the Chart Options dialog box, click the **Legend** tab to display the chart's legend options, click the **Show legend** check box to clear it, and then click the **OK** button. The legend is removed from the chart object in the Graph window and in the form.

   To change the color or other properties of a chart control—the chart background (or chart area), axes, labels to the left of the y-axis, labels below the x-axis, or data markers (columnar bars for a column chart)—you need to double-click the control.

5. In the Graph window, double-click one of the blue data markers inside the chart to open the Format Data Series dialog box, and then click the orange box (row 2, column 2) in the color palette in the Area section. See Figure 8-25.

Tip

A data marker is a bar, dot, segment, or other symbol that represents a single data value.

Format Data Series dialog box | Figure 8-25

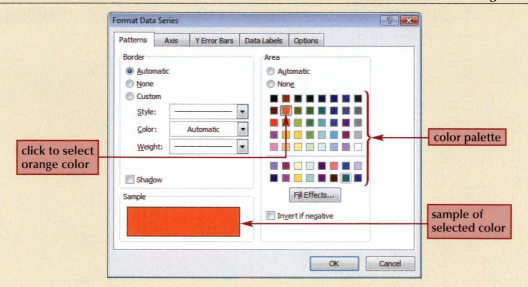

The sample color in the dialog box changes to orange to match the selected color in the color palette.

▶ 6. Click the **OK** button to close the dialog box and to change the color of the data markers in the chart in the Graph window and in the form to orange.

▶ 7. In the Graph window, double-click the white chart background to open the Format Chart Area dialog box, click the light orange box (row 5, column 2) in the color palette in the Area section, and then click the **OK** button. The background color changes to light orange in the chart in the Graph window and in the form.

▶ 8. Click **File** on the Graph menu bar, and then click **Exit & Return to frmContractsAndInvoices** to exit Graph and return to the form.

▶ 9. Save your form design changes, switch to Form view, navigate to record 5 in the main form, click the **Invoice Chart** tab to display the chart, and then scroll down the form (if necessary). See Figure 8-26.

Figure 8-26 | Completed chart in Form view

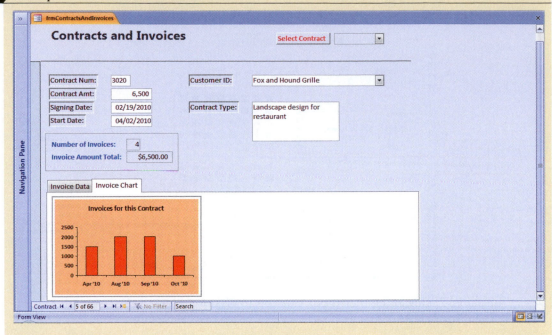

10. Close the form.

Sarah wants to know if Access has other charting and data analysis tools. You'll show her how to create a PivotTable and a PivotChart.

Creating and Using a PivotTable

Sarah wants to be able to analyze Belmont Landscapes' business in a flexible way. You can use PivotTables to provide the flexible analysis that Sarah needs. A **PivotTable** is an interactive table that lets you analyze data dynamically. You can use a PivotTable to view and organize data from a database, look for summary or detail information, and dynamically change the contents and organization of the table. Figure 8-27 shows a PivotTable.

Sample PivotTable | Figure 8-27

A PivotTable contains the following basic components:

- The **detail area**, consisting of a **detail field** and **detail values**, provides details or totals from a database table or query. In Figure 8-27, the detail field is the InvoiceAmt field from the tblInvoice table, and the detail values are the InvoiceAmt field values.

- The **row area**, consisting of a **row field** and **row field items**, provides row groupings in the PivotTable. In Figure 8-27, the row field is the City field from the tblCustomer table, and the row field items are the City field values.

- The **column area**, consisting of a **column field** and **column field items**, provides column groupings in the PivotTable. In Figure 8-27, the column field is the InvoicePaid field from the tblInvoice table, and the column field items are the InvoicePaid field values.

- The **filter area**, consisting of a **filter field** and **filter field items**, lets you restrict which data appears in the PivotTable. In Figure 8-27, the filter field is the InvoiceDate field from the tblInvoice table, and the filter field item is "All" dates, which means that all InvoiceDate field values are represented in the PivotTable.

- All the PivotTable areas—detail area, row area, column area, and filter area—can have multiple fields with multiple field items.

When you work with PivotTables, you use another program, the **Office PivotTable Component**, which is one of the **Office Web Components** that are part of Office 2007. Therefore, you can use PivotTables with other programs such as Excel. You can create PivotTables with Access tables and queries; the PivotTable view with these Access objects provides this capability.

Creating a PivotTable

Sarah wants to analyze invoice amounts by city and by invoice date in various ways. You'll create a PivotTable using the qryInvoicesByItem query to let her perform this analysis.

To create a PivotTable using a query:

▶ **1.** Open the Navigation Pane, open the **qryInvoicesByItem** query datasheet to display the 172 records in the query, close the Navigation Pane, right-click the **qryInvoicesByItem** tab, and then click **PivotTable View** to switch to PivotTable view. See Figure 8-28.

Figure 8-28   **PivotTable view for the qryInvoicesByItem query**

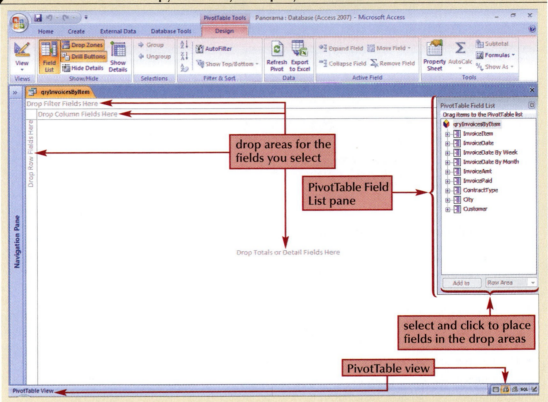

To create a PivotTable, you click a field in the PivotTable Field List pane to select it, and then drag it to one of the four drop areas—row, column, filter, or totals/detail—or click the Add to button at the bottom of the PivotTable Field List pane after selecting one of the four drop areas in the list to the right of the Add to button.

Sarah wants to use the InvoicePaid field as the column field, the City field as the row field, the InvoiceDate field as the filter field, and the InvoiceAmt field as the detail field.

▶ **2.** Click **InvoicePaid** in the PivotTable Field List pane, click the **arrow** on the list box to the right of the Add to button in the PivotTable Field List pane, click **Column Area** in the list, and then click the **Add to** button. Access places the InvoicePaid field and its field values in the column drop area.

▶ **3.** Repeat Step 2 to add the **City** field to the row drop area, the **InvoiceDate** field to the filter drop area, and the **InvoiceAmt** field to the totals or detail drop area. The four selected fields are bold in the PivotTable Field List pane and appear as components in the PivotTable. See Figure 8-29.

After adding the four fields to the PivotTable | **Figure 8-29**

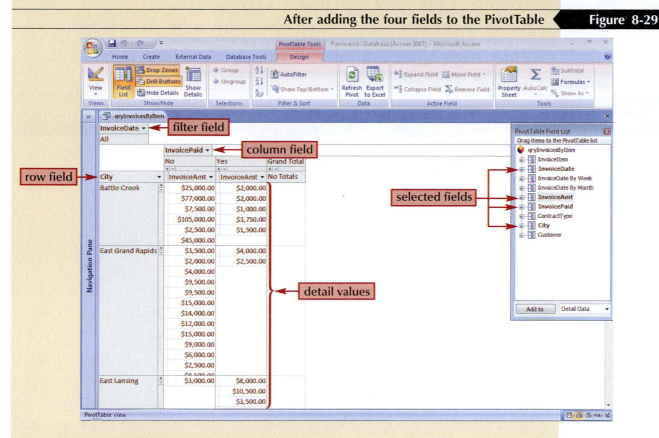

The PivotTable displays all the InvoiceAmt field values from the source query organized by city and invoice status (unpaid or paid).

4. Close the PivotTable Field List pane.

Sarah can filter the PivotTable using one or more of the four selected fields. She can also add total fields and hide the detail values in the PivotTable.

Filtering and Summarizing Data in a PivotTable

A **total field** summarizes values from a source field. For example, Sarah can add subtotals and a grand total of the InvoiceAmt field values to the PivotTable. You'll show Sarah how to filter data in the PivotTable and how to add subtotals by city and a grand total for the InvoiceAmt field values.

To filter data and add a total field in a PivotTable:

▶ 1. Click the **City** arrow, click the **All** check box to clear all the selections, click the **East Lansing** check box, click the **Lansing** check box, click the **Rockford** check box, and then click the **OK** button. Access applies the City filter and display total invoice amounts for the three selected cities. See Figure 8-30.

Figure 8-30	Filtering data by city

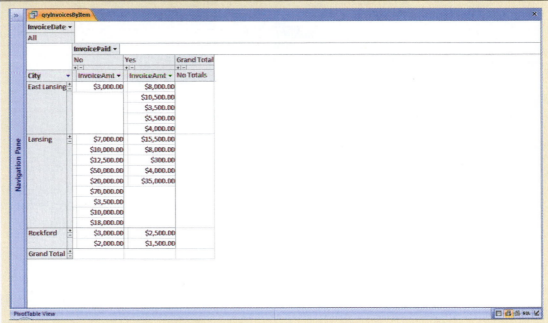

The applied City filter displays all the InvoiceAmt field values from the source query for the cities of East Lansing, Lansing, and Rockford.

▶ 2. Click one of the **InvoiceAmt** column heading labels; in the Tools group on the Design tab, click the **AutoCalc** button, click **Sum**, and then click to the right of the PivotTable to deselect all values. Access adds a new row for each city in the PivotTable that displays the city's InvoiceAmt total and a new row at the bottom of the PivotTable that displays the grand total for the displayed InvoiceAmt values. See Figure 8-31.

After adding the total field to the PivotTable ◀ **Figure 8-31**

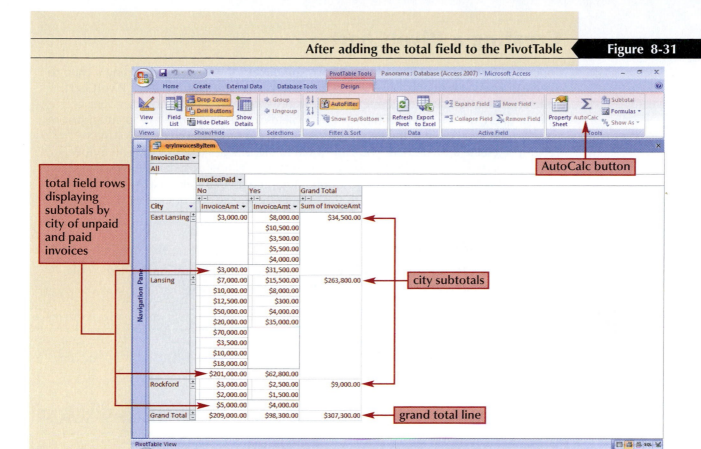

total field rows displaying subtotals by city of unpaid and paid invoices

AutoCalc button

city subtotals

grand total line

▶ **3.** In the Show/Hide group on the Design tab, click the **Hide Details** button. Access hides the detail lines and displays only the subtotal and grand total lines in the PivotTable. See Figure 8-32.

Subtotals and grand total displayed in the PivotTable ◀ **Figure 8-32**

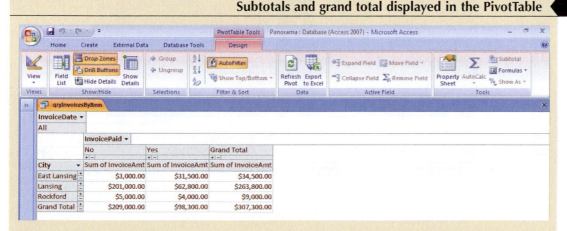

▶ **4.** In the Show/Hide group on the Design tab, click the **Show Details** button. Access shows the detail lines and the subtotal and grand total lines in the PivotTable for the cities of East Lansing, Lansing, and Rockford.

Sarah asks if you can display the filtered PivotTable data in a chart. You'll switch to PivotChart view to satisfy Sarah's request.

Creating a PivotChart

Office 2007 provides the **Office PivotChart Component** to assist you in adding a chart to a table or query. Using the Office PivotChart Component, you can create a **PivotChart**, an interactive chart that provides capabilities similar to a PivotTable. You can open a table or query, switch to PivotChart view, add fields to the PivotChart's drop areas, just as you did when you created the PivotTable, and then filter the data in the PivotChart. When you create a PivotChart, you can switch to PivotTable view to view and further filter the charted data in a PivotTable. Likewise, after creating a PivotTable, you can switch to PivotChart view to view and further filter the tabular data in a PivotChart.

You'll switch to PivotChart view to show Sarah the PivotChart of the PivotTable data.

To switch to PivotChart view:

▶ **1.** Right-click the **qryInvoicesByItem** tab, and then click **PivotChart View** on the shortcut menu to switch to PivotChart view. See Figure 8-33.

Figure 8-33 Filtered PivotTable data in a PivotChart

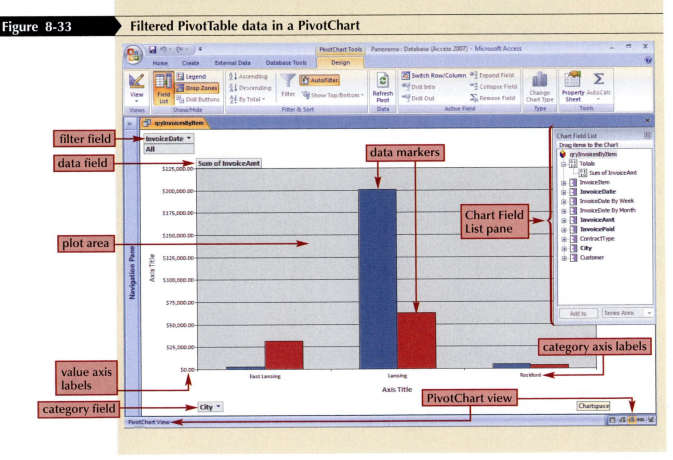

A PivotChart contains the following basic components:

• The **plot area** provides a background for the data markers and gridlines. A **data marker** is a bar, dot, segment, or other symbol that represents a single data value. The **data field**, which is the Sum of InvoiceAmt field in Figure 8-33, identifies which values the data markers represent and identifies each value displayed as a **value axis label**. Each **gridline**, which appears in Figure 8-33 as one of the horizontal lines in the plot area, makes it easier to see the values represented by the data markers.

- The **category field** identifies each value that's displayed as a **category axis label**; each category axis label identifies an individual data marker. In Figure 8-33, the City field is the category field; East Lansing, Lansing, and Rockford are the category axis labels. The data markers show the total unpaid and paid InvoiceAmt field values for each city.
- The **filter field** lets you restrict which data appears in the PivotChart. In Figure 8-33, the filter field is the InvoiceDate field. The "All" value below InvoiceDate indicates that no filter has been applied to the filter field.
- The **series field** identifies the data markers' subdivisions or splits. In Figure 8-33, the InvoicePaid field is the series field, and each pair of data markers represent the two values for the InvoicePaid field. (The series field is not visible in Figure 8-33) The left data marker represents unpaid invoices, and the right data marker represents paid invoices. An optional **legend** provides a list of the series field values and how these values are indicated on the data markers. (Figure 8-33 does not include a legend.)

Next, you'll show Sarah how to modify the PivotChart.

To modify the PivotChart:

▶ 1. Close the Chart Field List pane. The InvoicePaid field, which is the series field for the PivotChart, is now visible to the right of the PivotChart.

▶ 2. In the Show/Hide group on the Design tab, click the **Legend** button. A legend is displayed below the InvoicePaid field and indicates that the blue bars represent unpaid invoices (No value) and the red bars represent paid invoices (Yes value).

Sarah wants to change the City filter to display data for Grand Rapids, Holland, Kalamazoo, and Lansing.

▶ 3. Click the **City** arrow, click the **East Lansing** check box to clear it, click the **Rockford** check box to clear it, click the **Grand Rapids** check box to select it, click the **Holland** check box to select it, click the **Kalamazoo** check box to select it, and then click the **OK** button. Access applies the City filter, displays total invoice amounts for the four selected cities, and changes the scale of the vertical axis and its value axis labels. See Figure 8-34.

Figure 8-34 | **After changing the City filter and displaying the legend**

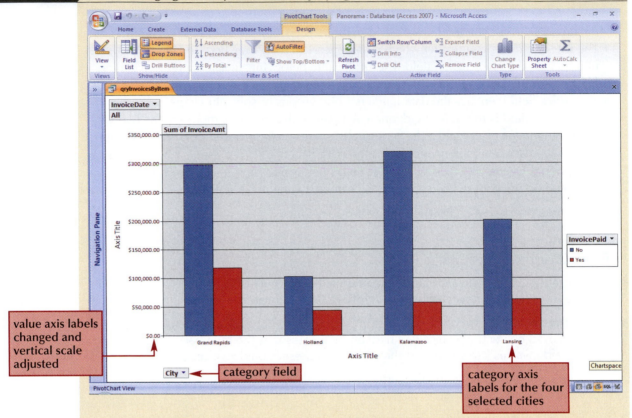

value axis labels changed and vertical scale adjusted

category field

category axis labels for the four selected cities

Sarah wants to change the PivotChart from a column chart to a bar chart to take advantage of the screen width, and she wants to change the colors of the data markers.

▶ **4.** Click in the white portion of the chart (if necessary) to deselect any chart control, and then in the Type group on the Design tab, click the **Change Chart Type** button, click **Bar** in the left list, and then click the **Clustered Bar** chart (row 1, column 1) in the right list. The chart changes from a clustered column chart to a clustered bar chart.

▶ **5.** In the chart, click the red data marker for Lansing, hold down the **Shift** key, click the red data marker for Lansing a second time, and then release the **Shift** key. All red data markers are now selected, and any property change you make in the Properties dialog box will apply to all four red data markers.

▶ **6.** Click the **Border/Fill** tab in the Properties dialog box, click the **Fill Color** arrow, and then click the **DodgerBlue** color (row 3, column 4) in the color palette. The four selected data markers change to the selected DodgerBlue color. See Figure 8-35.

▶ **7.** Repeat Steps 5-6, selecting the other four data markers (the lower data marker in each set), and clicking the **Tomato** color (row 8, column 13), and then click the **Fill Color** arrow to display the color palette. The four selected data markers change to the Tomato color. See Figure 8-35.

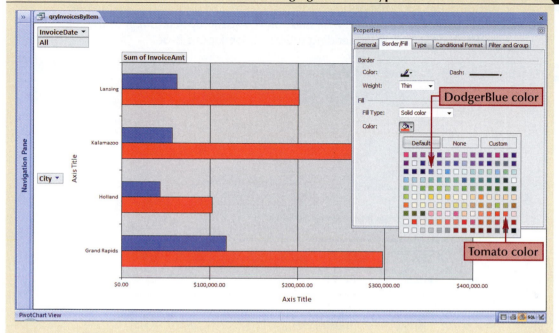

After changing the chart type and data marker colors — Figure 8-35

8. Close the Properties dialog box, save your PivotTable and PivotChart changes, and then close the query.

9. Open the Navigation Pane, open the **qryInvoicesByItem** query datasheet to display the 172 records in the query, switch to PivotChart view to display the saved PivotChart, switch to PivotTable view to display the saved PivotTable, and then close the query.

Sarah's staff maintains an Excel worksheet that tracks the products Belmont Landscapes has used for its landscaping projects. Sarah want to use the product data in the Panorama database.

Linking Data from an Excel Worksheet

Sarah's staff has extensive experience working with Excel and prefers to maintain the data in the Products worksheet using Excel. However, Sarah needs to reference the products data in the Panorama database, and the data she's referencing must always be the current version of the worksheet data. Importing the Excel worksheet data as an Access table would provide Sarah with data that's quickly out of date unless she repeats the import steps each time the data in the Excel worksheet changes. Because Sarah doesn't need to update the products data in the Panorama database, you'll link to the worksheet from the database. When the staff changes the Products worksheet, the changes will be reflected automatically in the linked version of the table in the database. At the same time, Sarah won't be able to update the products data from the Panorama database, which ensures that only the staff members responsible for maintaining the Excel worksheet can update the data.

You'll now link to the data in the Excel worksheet.

To link to the data in the Excel worksheet:

1. Click the **External Data** tab on the Ribbon, and then in the Import group on the External Data tab, click the **Excel** button (with the ScreenTip "Import Excel spreadsheet"). The Get External Data - Excel Spreadsheet dialog box opens.

> **2.** Click the **Browse** button, navigate to and open the **Level.02\Tutorial** folder, click **Products**, click the **Open** button, and then click the **Link to the data source by creating a linked table** option button. The selected path and filename now appear in the File name text box, and you've set the option to link to the data instead of importing or appending the data. See Figure 8-36.

Figure 8-36 | Linking to data in an Excel worksheet

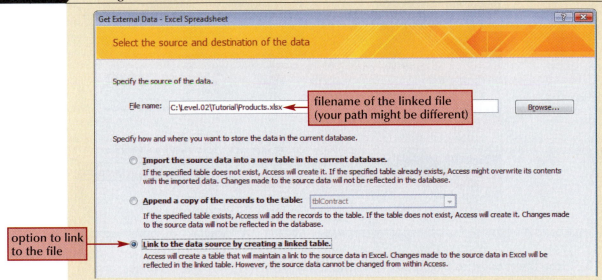

> **3.** Click the **OK** button. The Link Spreadsheet Wizard dialog box opens. See Figure 8-37.

Figure 8-37 | Linking to data in an Excel worksheet

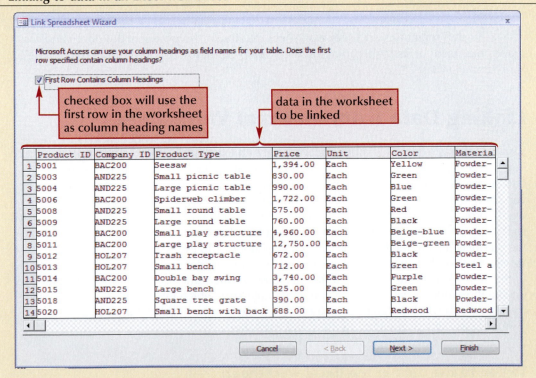

The first row in the worksheet contains column heading names, and each row in the worksheet represents the data about a single product.

4. Click the **Next** button to open the next Link Spreadsheet Wizard dialog box, in which you choose a name for the linked table. You'll use the default table name tblProduct.

5. Click the **Finish** button. A message box informs you that you've created a linking table to the Excel worksheet file.

6. Click the **OK** button to close the message box and complete the linking steps. The tblProduct table now appears in the Navigation Pane. The icon to the left of the table name 🔗 identifies the table as a linked table.

You can open and view the tblProduct table and use fields from the linked table in queries, forms, and reports, but you can't update the products data using the Panorama database. You can update the products data only from the Excel worksheet.

Next, you'll show Sarah how the worksheet and the linked table interact.

To update the Excel worksheet and view the data in the linked table:

1. Open Windows Explorer, navigate to and open the **Level.02\Tutorial** folder, right-click **Products**, click **Open With** on the shortcut menu, click **Microsoft Office Excel**, and then click the **OK** button. The Products workbook opens and displays the tblProduct worksheet.

2. Click the **Microsoft Office Access** program button on the taskbar to switch to the Panorama database, and then open the **tblProduct** datasheet. The fields and records in the tblProduct table display the same data as the Excel worksheet.

3. Select **Yellow** in the first record's Color column, and then type **G**. A warning sound chimes, the message "This Recordset is not updateable" is displayed on the status bar, and the value is not changed.

4. Click the **Microsoft Excel** program button on the taskbar to switch to the Products workbook, select **Yellow** in cell F2, type **Green**, and then press the **Enter** key. The value in cell F2 changes from Yellow to Green.

5. Click the **Microsoft Office Access** program button on the taskbar to switch to the Panorama database. The first row's Color field value is now Green, because this is the newly changed value in the Excel worksheet.

You've completed your work for Sarah and her staff.

6. Close the table.

7. Click the **Microsoft Excel** program button on the taskbar to switch to the Products workbook, save your worksheet change, and then exit Excel.

8. Close the Panorama database, make a backup copy of the database, open the **Panorama** database, compact and repair the database, close the database, and then exit Access.

Knowing how to create charts, PivotTables, and PivotCharts and how to link to data maintained by other programs will make it easier for Sarah and her staff to anlayze their operations and to work efficiently in managing data.

Tip

If Excel has the worksheet open at the same time Access is displaying the linked file's data, you must close the table in Access before closing the worksheet in Excel, or Access will display error values in the linked file.

Review | Session 8.2 Quick Check

1. The _____ property lets you change the navigation label from the word "Record" to another value.
2. When you use the Microsoft Graph program to create and change charts in a form or report, you must _____ the chart.
3. What is a PivotTable?
4. Within a PivotTable you can choose fields form the field list to be a column field, a row field, a detail field, or a(n) _____ field.
5. In a PivotChart, the _____ field identifies which values are shown as value axis labels.
6. You can show/hide a legend for the _____ field in a PivotChart.

Review | Tutorial Summary

In this tutorial, you learned how to share and integrate data. You exported an Access query to an HTML document and then used a Web browser to view the document. You imported a CSV file as an Access table, imported and exported XML files, used the Table Analyzer, and saved and executed import and export specifications. Then you created a multi-page form using a tab control, embedded a chart in one of the tab control's pages, and modified the chart. Finally, you created and modified a PivotTable and a PivotChart and linked data from an Excel worksheet.

Key Terms

category axis label
category field
column area
column field
column field items
CSV (comma-separated values) file
data field
data marker
destination program
detail area
detail field
detail values
embedding
filter area
filter field
filter field items
gridline
HTML document
HTML template
hyperlink

Hypertext Markup Language (HTML)
Hypertext Transfer Protocol (HTTP)
importing
Internet
legend
linking
Navigation Caption property
Office PivotChart Component
Office PivotTable Component
Office Web Component
Page Break tool
PivotChart
PivotTable
plot area
row area
row field
row field items
series field
source program

static Web page
Tab Control tool
Table Analyzer
tag
total field
Uniform Resource Locator (URL)
value axis label
Web
Web browser
Web client
Web page
Web server
World Wide Web
XML (Extensible Markup Language)
XSD (XML Structure Definition)
XSL (Extensible Stylesheet Language)

Practice | Review Assignments

Practice the skills you learned in the tutorial using the same case scenario.

Data Files needed for the Review Assignments: Ads.xlsx, BelmLogo.gif, BelmTemp.htm, Payables.csv, Products.accdb (*cont. from Tutorial 7*), and tblPayments.xml

Sarah wants you to integrate the data in the Products database with other programs and she wants to be able to analyze the data in the database. You'll help her achieve these goals by completing the following:

1. Open the **Products** database located in the Level.02\Review folder provided with your Data Files.
2. Export the qryCompanyList query as an HTML document to the Level.02\Review folder, using the HTML template file named BelmTemp, which is located in the Level.02\Review folder, and saving the file as **qryCompanyList**. Do not save the export steps.
3. Import the CSV file named Payables, which is located in the Level.02\Review folder, as a new table in the database. Choose your own primary key, name the table **tblPayables**, run the Table Analyzer, and record the Table Analyzer's recommendation. Do not save the import steps.
4. Import the XML file named tblPayments, which is located in the Level.02\Review folder, as a new table named **tblPayments** in the database. Save the import steps.
5. Export the tblCompany table as an XML file named **tblCompany** to the Level.02\Review folder; do not create a separate XSD file. Save the export steps.
6. Link to the Ads workbook, which is located in the Level.02\Review folder, using **tblAd** as the table name. Change the cost of the flyer for Ad Num 5 to **$300**.
7. Modify the **frmCompaniesWithProducts** form in the following ways:
   a. Add a tab control to the bottom of the Detail section, and place the existing subform on the first page of the tab control.
   b. Change the caption for the left tab to **Product Data** and for the right tab to **Product Chart**.
   c. Change the caption for the main form's navigation buttons to **Company** and for the subform's navigation buttons to **Product**.
   d. Add a chart to the second page of the tab control. Use the tblProduct table as the record source, select the ProductType, Price, and Unit fields, use the 3-D Column Chart type, include a legend, and use **Products Offered** as the chart title.
   e. Change the chart to a Clustered Column chart, and change the blue colored data marker to pink.
8. Open the **tblPayments** table and create a PivotTable with PaymentAmt as the detail field, PaymentDate as the column field, CompanyID as the row field, and PaymentID as the filter field.
9. Switch to PivotChart view. Filter the CompanyID field, selecting BAC200, BEL273, and CHE802, select PaymentAmt as the data field, display the legend, and then save the table.
10. Close the Products database without exiting Access, make a backup copy of the database, open the **Products** database, compact and repair the database, close the database, and then exit Access.

| Apply | | Case Problem 1 |

Apply the skills you learned in the tutorial to import and export data and create charts for a music school.

Data Files needed for this Case Problem: Contract.accdb (*cont. from Tutorial 7*), **Instrument.csv, and Room.xlsx**

Pine Hill Music School   Yuka wants you to integrate the data in the Contract database with other programs, and she wants to be able to analyze the data in the database. You'll help her achieve these goals by completing the following:

1. Open the **Contract** database located in the Level.02\Case1 folder provided with your Data Files.

⊕ EXPLORE

2. Export the rptTeacherLessons report as an HTML document to the Level.02\Case1 folder; do not use a template or save the export steps. Use your Web browser to open the **rptTeacherLessons** HTML document. Then scroll to the bottom of the page; use the First, Previous, Next, and Last links to navigate through the document.

3. Import the CSV file named Instrument, which is located in the Level.02\Case1 folder, as a new table in the database. Choose your own primary key, name the table **tblInstrument**, run the Table Analyzer, and record the Table Analyzer's recommendation, but do not accept the recommendation. Do not save the import steps.

4. Export the tblTeacher table as an XML file named **tblTeacher** to the Level.02\Case1 folder; do not create a separate XSD file. Save the export steps.

5. Link to the Room workbook, which is located in the Level.02\Case1 folder, using **tblRoom** as the table name. Add a new record to the Room workbook as follows: Room Num **5**, Rental Cost **$25**, and Type **Private**.

6. Open the qryLessonsByTeacher query, and create a PivotTable with MonthlyLessonCost as the detail field, LessonType as the column field, LastName as the row field, and LessonLength as the filter field. Filter the LessonType field, selecting Guitar, Piano, and Saxophone. Add subtotals and a grand total for the MonthlyLessonCost field values.

7. Switch to PivotChart view. Display the legend (if necessary), change the color of the Saxophone data markers to yellow, and then save the query.

8. Close the Contract database without exiting Access, make a backup copy of the database, open the **Contract** database, compact and repair the database, close the database, and then exit Access.

| Apply | | Case Problem 2 |

Use the skills you learned in the tutorial to analyze the data for a health and fitness center.

Data Files needed for this Case Problem: CreditCard.xml, ParkLogo.gif, ParkTemp.htm, Schedule.xlsx, and Training.accdb (*cont. from Tutorial 7*)

Parkhurst Health & Fitness Center   Martha Parkhurst wants you to integrate the data in the Training database with other programs, and she wants to be able to analyze the data in the database. You'll help her achieve these goals by completing the following:

1. Open the **Training** database located in the Level.02\Case2 folder provided with your Data Files.

2. Export the qryPhysicalsNeeded query as an HTML document to the Level.02\Case2 folder, using the HTML template file named ParkTemp, which is located in the Level.02\Case2 folder, and saving the file as **qryPhysicalsNeeded**. Save the export steps.

EXPLORE

3. Export the rptProgramMembership report as an HTML document to the Level.02\Case2 folder; do not use a template or save the export steps. Use your Web browser to open the **rptProgramMembership** HTML document. Then scroll to the bottom of the page; use the First, Previous, Next, and Last links to navigate through the document.

4. Import the XML file named CreditCard, which is located in the Level.02\Case2 folder, as a new table named **tblCreditCard**. Save the import steps.

5. Export the tblProgram table as an XML file named **tblProgram** to the Level.02\Case2 folder; do not create a separate XSD file. Save the export steps.

6. Link to the Schedule workbook, which is located in the Level.02\Case2 folder, using **tblSchedule** as the table name. For ClassID 301, change the ClassDay value to **F**.

7. Modify the **frmProgramsAndMembers** form in the following ways:
   a. Add a tab control to the bottom of the Detail section, and place the existing subform on the first page of the tab control.
   b. Change the caption for the left tab to **Member Data** and for the right tab to **Member Chart**.
   c. Change the caption for the main form's navigation buttons to **Program** and for the subform's navigation buttons to **Member**.
   d. Add a chart to the second page of the tab control. Use the tblMember table as the record source, select the ProgramID and MembershipStatus fields, use the Clustered Column chart type, include a legend, and use **Membership Status** as the chart title.
   e. Change the color of the right data marker (or the middle data marker, depending on whether you see two or three data markers) to red.

8. Open the **qryMonthlyFeeStatus** query and create a PivotTable with MonthlyFee as the detail field, MonthlyFeeStatus as the column field, LastName as the row field, and ProgramType as the filter field. Add subtotals and a grand total of the MonthlyFee values, hide the details, and filter the ProgramType field to display only programs for juniors.

9. Switch to PivotChart view for the qryMonthlyFeeStatus query. Change the chart type to Clustered Bar, display the legend, change the data markers to colors of your choice, and then save the query.

10. Close the Training database without exiting Access, make a backup copy of the database, open the **Training** database, compact and repair the database, close the database, and then exit Access.

Challenge | Case Problem 3

Use the skills you learned in the tutorial to integrate and analyze data about an agency that recycles household goods.

Data Files needed for this Case Problem: Agency.accdb (*cont. from Tutorial 7*) and Facility.csv

Rossi Recycling Group   Mary Rossi wants you to integrate the data in the Agency database with other programs, and she wants to be able to analyze the data in the database. You'll help her achieve these goals by completing the following:

1. Open the **Agency** database located in the Level.02\Case3 folder provided with your Data Files.

2. Export the qryNetDonationsCrosstab query as an HTML document to the Level.02\Case3 folder; do not use a template. Save the file as **qryNetDonationsCrosstab**. Save the export steps.

EXPLORE   3. Export the frmDonationInfo form as an HTML document to the Level.02\Case3 folder; do not use a template or save the export steps. Use your Web browser to open the **frmDonationInfo** HTML document and review its contents.

EXPLORE   4. Import the CSV file named Facility, which is located in the Level.02\Case3 folder, as a new table in the database. Choose your own primary key, name the table **tblTemporary**, and run the Table Analyzer. Accept the Table Analyzer's recommendations, rename the tables as **tblStorage** and **tblFacility**, make sure each table has the correct primary key, and let the Table Analzyer create a query. Do not save the import steps. Review the tblTemporary query, review the tblTemporary table (it might be named tblTemporary_OLD), and then review the tblStorage and tblFacility tables.

5. Export the tblDonation table as an XML file named **tblDonation** to the Level.02\Case3 folder; do not create a separate XSD file. Save the export steps.

6. Modify the **frmDonorDonations** form in the following ways:
    a. Add a tab control to the bottom of the Detail section, and place the existing subform on the first page of the tab control.
    b. Change the caption for the left tab to **Donation Data** and for the right tab to **Donation Chart**.
    c. Change the caption for the main form's navigation buttons to **Donor** and for the subform's navigation buttons to **Donation**.
    d. Add a chart to the second page of the tab control. Use the tblDonation table as the record source; select the AgencyID, DonationValue, PickupRequired, and DonationDate fields; use the 3-D Column Chart type; include a legend; and use **Donations by Agency** as the chart title.
    e. Change the chart to a Clustered Bar chart, and change the color of the maroon data marker to red.

7. Open the **qryNetDonations** query and create a PivotTable with NetDonation as the detail field, AgencyName as the column field, DonationDesc as the row field, and PickupRequired as the filter field. Filter the DonationDesc field to display only cash donations.

8. Switch to PivotChart view. Select NetDonation as the data field, filter the AgencyName by removing the first five agencies, leaving the data for five agencies in the chart, display the legend, change the chart type to Clustered Bar, and then save the query.

9. Close the Agency database without exiting Access, make a backup copy of the database, open the **Agency** database, compact and repair the database, close the database, and then exit Access.

Apply | Case Problem 4

Use the skills you learned in the tutorial to analyze the data for a luxury property rental company.

Data Files needed for this Case Problem: Personnel.xlsx, Vacation.accdb (*cont. from Tutorial 7*), and Works.xml

GEM Ultimate Vacations   Griffin and Emma MacElroy want you to integrate the data in the Vacation database with other programs, and they want to be able to analyze the data in the database. You'll help them achieve these goals by completing the following:

1. Open the **Vacation** database located in the Level.02\Case4 folder provided with your Data Files.

2. Export the qryPropertiesByRate query as an HTML document to the Level.02\Case4 folder; do not use a template. Save the file as **qryPropertiesByRate**. Save the export steps.

3. Import the XML file named Works, which is located in the Level.02\Case4 folder, as a new table in the database named **tblWorks**. Save the import steps.

4. Export the qryPropertyReservations query as an XML file named **qryPropertyReservations** to the Level.02\Case4 folder; do not create a separate XSD file. Save the export steps.

5. Link to the Personnel workbook, which is located in the Level.02\Case4 folder, using **tblPersonnel** as the table name. Change the name in the fourth record from Edward Leary to **Marie Leary**.

6. Modify the **frmGuestsWithReservations** form in the following ways:
   a. Add a tab control to the bottom of the Detail section, and place the existing subform on the first page of the tab control.
   b. Change the caption for the left tab to **Reservation Data** and for the right tab to **Reservation Chart**.
   c. Change the caption for the main form's navigation buttons to **Guest** and for the subform's navigation buttons to **Reservation**.
   d. Add a chart to the second page of the tab control. Use the tblReservation table as the record source, select the StartDate, PropertyID, and RentalRate fields, use the Column Chart chart type, include a legend, and use **Reservations** as the chart title.

7. Open the **qryGuestsAndReservations** query, and create a PivotTable with RentalRate as the detail field, StateProv as the column field, the Quarters component of the StartDate By Month entry in the PivotTable Field List as the row field, and PropertyID as the filter field. Add subtotals and a grand total of the RentalRate field, and then hide the details.

8. Switch to PivotChart view. Display the legend, change the green color to yellow, and then save the query.

9. Close the Vacation database without exiting Access, make a backup copy of the database, open the **Vacation** database, compact and repair the database, close the database, and then exit Access.

| Create | **Case Problem 5** |

Use the skills you learned in this tutorial to integrate and analyze the data for an Internet service provider.

Data File needed for this Case Problem: ACE.accdb (*cont. from Tutorial 7*)

Always Connected Everyday Chris and Pat Aquino want you to integrate the data in the ACE database with other programs, and they want to be able to analyze the data in the database. You'll help them achieve these goals by completing the following:

1. Open the **ACE** database located in the Level.02\Case5 folder provided with your Data Files.

2. Export the tblAccessPlan table as an HTML document to the Level.02\Case5 folder; do not use a template or save the import steps. Save the file as **tblAccessPlan**.

⊕ EXPLORE

3. Export the rptAccessPlanCustomers report as an HTML document to the Level.02\Case5 folder; do not use a template or save the export steps. Use your Web browser to open and review the HTML document.

4. Export the tblCustomer table as an XML file named **tblCustomer** to the Level.02\Case5 folder; do not create a separate XSD file. Save the export steps.

5. Modify one of the existing forms or create a new form so that the form uses a tab control. Change the caption for the navigation buttons, and set the captions for the tab labels.

6. For one of the existing queries (or create a new query), create a PivotTable, add subtotals and a grand total, apply a filter, and hide details. In PivotChart view, display the legend and make any other appropriate changes.

7. Close the ACE database without exiting Access, make a backup copy of the database, open the **ACE** database, compact and repair the database, close the database, and then exit Access.

Research | **Internet Assignments**

Use the Internet to find and work with data related to the topics presented in this tutorial.

The purpose of the Internet Assignments is to challenge you to find information on the Internet that you can use to work effectively with this software. The actual assignments are updated and maintained on the Course Technology Web site. Log on to the Internet and use your Web browser to go to the Student Online Companion for New Perspectives Office 2007 at **www.course.com/np/office2007**. Then navigate to the Internet Assignments for this tutorial.

Assess | **SAM Assessment and Training**

If you have a SAM user profile, you may have access to hands-on instruction, practice, and assessment of the skills covered in this tutorial. Log in to your SAM account (**http://sam2007.course.com**) to launch any assigned training activities or exams that relate to the skills covered in this tutorial.

Review | **Quick Check Answers**

Session 8.1

1. a vast collection of digital documents available on the Internet; Web browser
2. links one Web page to another Web page or Web site, or to another location in the same Web page
3. language used to create most Web pages
4. An HTML template is a file that contains HTML instructions for creating a Web page with both text and graphics, together with special instructions that tell Access where to place the Access data in the page.
5. shows the state of the database at the time the page was created; any subsequent changes made to the database object, such as updates to field values in records, are not reflected in a static Web page
6. a text file in which commas separate values, and each line is a record containing the same number of values in the same positions
7. an Access tool that analyzes a single table and, if necessary, splits it into two or more tables that are in third normal form
8. XML (Extensible Markup Language)

Session 8.2

1. Navigation Caption
2. embed
3. an interactive table that lets you analyze data dynamically
4. filter
5. data
6. series

Ending Data Files

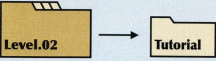

Tutorial

Customers by Name.html
Panorama.accdb
Products.xlsx
tblInvoice.xml

Review

Ads.xlsx
Products.accdb
qryCompanyList.html
tblCompany.xml

Case1

Contract.accdb
Room.xlsx
rptTeacherLessons.html
rptTeacherLessonsPage2.html
tblTeacher.xml

Case2

qryPhysicalsNeeded.html
rptProgramMembership.html
rptProgramMembershipPage2.html
Schedule.xlsx
tblProgram.xml
Training.accdb

Case3

Agency.accdb
frmDonationInfo.html
qryNetDonationsCrosstab.html
tblDonation.xml

Case4

Personnel.xlsx
qryPropertiesByRate.html
qryPropertyReservations.xml
Vacation.accdb

Case5

ACE.accdb
rptAccessPlanCustomers.html
tblAccessPlan.html
tblCustomer.xml

Reality Check

You interact with databases whenever you place an order on the Internet, check out at a retail store or restaurant, verify your bank account balance, or register for classes. Most businesses use databases, and you can also use databases to track data in your personal life. Examples of personal database use include tracking personal collections, such as DVDs or books; hobby data, such as family histories or antiques; or items related to sports teams, theater clubs, or other organizations to which you might belong. In this exercise, you'll use Access to create a database that will contain information of your choice, using the Access skills and features you've learned in Tutorials 5 through 8.

Note: Please be sure *not* to include any personal information of a sensitive nature in the database you create to be submitted to your instructor for this exercise. Later on, you can update the data in your database with such information for your own personal use.

1. Create a new Access database to contain personal data you want to track. (If you completed Tutorials 1-4 of this book and the Reality Check at the end of Tutorial 4, you can use and enhance the database you've already created, and you can skip this step.) The database must include two or more tables that you can join through one-to-many relationships. Define the properties for each field in each table. Make sure you include a mix of data types for the fields (for example, do not include only Text fields in each table). Specify a primary key for each table, define the table relationships and enforce referential integrity, and enter records in each table.

2. Create queries that include at least the following: pattern query match, list-of-values match, parameter, crosstab, find duplicates, find unmatched, and the use of a conditional value in a calculated field.

3. For one or more fields, apply an input mask and specify field validation rules.

4. Create a split form and modify the form.

5. Create a custom form that uses at least the following: combo box for a lookup, combo box to find records, subform, lines and rectangles, and a tab control. Add one or more calculated controls to the main form based on the subform's calculated control(s), and add a chart, if appropriate. Check the main form's tab order, and improve the form's appearance.

6. Create a custom report that uses at least the following: grouping field, sort field(s), lines, and rectangles. Hide duplicates, and add the date, page numbers, and a report title.

7. Export two or more objects in different formats, and save the step specifications.

8. Create a PivotTable and PivotChart for one of the tables or queries.

9. Designate a trusted folder, backup the database, and compact and repair it.

10. Submit your completed database to your instructor as requested. Include printouts of any database objects, if required.

Objectives

Session 9.1
- Create an action query to create a table
- Create action queries to append, delete, and update data

Session 9.2
- Define many-to-many and one-to-one relationships between tables
- Learn about joining tables
- Join a table using a self-join
- View and create indexes for tables

Using Action Queries and Advanced Table Relationships

Enhancing User Interaction with the Holland Database

Case | Belmont Landscapes

After graduating with a university degree in Landscape Architecture and then working for a firm that provides basic landscape services to residential customers, Oren Belmont started his own landscape architecture firm in Holland, Michigan. Belmont Landscapes specializes in landscape designs for residential and commercial customers and numerous public agencies. The firm provides a wide range of services—from site analyses and feasibility studies, to drafting and administering construction documents—for projects of various scales. Oren's company developed the Holland database of customer, contract, invoice, employee, and assignment data; and the employees use Microsoft Office Access 2007 (or simply Access) to manage it. Lucia Perez, the company's database expert and developer, has been enhancing the Holland database containing tables, queries, forms, and reports that Sarah Fisher, office manager, and Taylor Sico, marketing manager, use to track customers and their landscape projects. Oren, Sarah, and Taylor have asked you to continuing enhancing the database by creating some advanced queries and integrating more tables into the database.

Starting Data Files

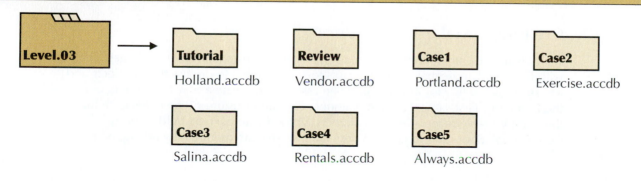

Level.03 →	Tutorial	Review	Case1	Case2
	Holland.accdb	Vendor.accdb	Portland.accdb	Exercise.accdb

	Case3	Case4	Case5
	Salina.accdb	Rentals.accdb	Always.accdb

Session 9.1

Action Queries

Tip

Because action queries modify many records in a table at a time, you should first create a select query that chooses the records you need to update. After you confirm that the query works correctly, you can convert it to an action query.

Queries can do more than display answers to the questions you ask; they can also perform actions on the data in your database. An **action query** is a query that adds, changes, or deletes multiple table records at a time. For example, Sarah can use an action query to delete all paid invoices from the previous year. Access provides four types of action queries: the make-table query, the append query, the delete query, and the update query.

A **make-table query** creates a new table by copying records from one or more existing tables. The new table can be an exact copy of the records in an existing table, a subset of the fields and records in an existing table, or a combination of the fields and records from two or more tables. Access does not delete the selected fields and records from the existing tables. You can use make-table queries, for example, to create backup copies of tables or to create customized tables for others to use. The new table reflects data at a point in time; future changes made to the original (existing) tables will not be reflected in the new table. You need to run the make-table query periodically if you want the newly created table to contain current data.

An **append query** adds records from existing tables or queries to the end of another table. For an append query, you choose the fields you want to append from one or more tables or queries; the selected data remains in the original tables. Usually you append records to history tables. A **history table** contains data that is no longer needed for current processing but that you might need to reference in the future.

A **delete query** deletes a group of records matching the criteria you specify from one or more tables. You choose which records you want to delete by entering selection criteria. Deleting records removes them permanently from the database.

InSight	**Appending to History Tables and Deleting the Original Records**

Tables containing data about cleared checks, former employees, inactive customers, and obsolete products are examples of history tables. Because the records you append to a history table are no longer needed for current processing in the original table, you can delete the records from the original table after you append the records to the history table. Before deleting the data from the original table, be sure to verify that you appended the correct records. When you delete data, the deletion is permanent.

An **update query** changes selected field values from selected records in one or more tables. You choose the fields and records you want to change by entering the selection criteria and the update rules. You can use update queries, for example, to increase the salaries of selected employee groups by a specified percentage or to change the billing dates of selected customers from one date to another. Update queries are particularly valuable in performing multiple updates to large tables.

Creating a Make-Table Query

Taylor wants to call all commercial customers. These customers have the largest contracts with Belmont Landscapes, and she wants to contact them to discuss their projects and assess the possibility for further work. She asks you to create a new table containing the Company, FirstName, LastName, Phone, City, and CustomerType fields from the tblCustomer table records for all customers whose CustomerType field value is Commercial. She wants to create a new table so she can modify it by adding notes that she will take when she calls the commercial customers. By creating a new table, Taylor won't need to worry about disrupting or changing the data in any existing tables or in any objects on which those existing tables are based.

You can create the new table for Taylor by using a make-table query that uses fields from the tblCustomer table in the Holland database. When you run a make-table query, you create a new table. The records in the new table are based on the records in the query's underlying tables. The fields in the new table will have the same data type and field size of the fields in the query's underlying tables. The new table does not preserve the primary key designation or field properties such as the format or lookup properties.

Creating a Make-Table Query | Reference Window

- Create a select query with the necessary fields and selection criteria.
- In the Results group on the Design tab on the Ribbon, click the Run button to preview the results.
- Switch to Design view to make any necessary changes to the query. When the query is correct, click the Make Table button in the Query Type group on the Design tab.
- In the Make Table dialog box, type the new table name in the Table Name list box. Make sure the Current Database option button is selected to include the new table in the current database, or click the Another Database option button and enter the database name in the File Name text box. Then click the OK button.
- Click the Run button, and then click the Yes button to confirm the creation of the new table.

Now you can create the new table using a make-table query. You'll base the make-table query on the tblCustomer table to enter the fields and records that Taylor wants in the new table.

To create and run the select query based on the tblCustomer table:

1. Make sure you have created your copy of the Access Data Files, and that your computer can access them.

   Trouble? If you don't have the Access Data Files, you need to get them before you can proceed. Your instructor will either give you the Data Files or ask you to obtain them from a specified location (such as a network drive). In either case, make a backup copy of the Data Files before you start so that you will have the original files available in case you need to start over. If you have any questions about the Data Files, see your instructor or technical support person for assistance.

2. Start Access, open the **Holland** database in the Level.03\Tutorial folder provided with your Data Files, click the **Options** button next to the Security Warning, and in the dialog box that opens, click the **Enable this content** option button, and then click the **OK** button.

   You can eliminate the Security Warning by designating the Level.03\Tutorial folder as a trusted folder.

3. Click the **Office Button** , and then click the **Access Options** button to open the Access Options dialog box.

4. In the left section of the dialog box, click **Trust Center**, click the **Trust Center Settings** button in the pane on the right to open the Trust Center dialog box, and then in the left pane click **Trusted Locations**. The trusted locations for your installation of Access and other options are displayed on the right.

Trouble? Check with your instructor before adding a new trusted location. If your instructor tells you not to select this option, skip to Step 6.

5. Click the **Add new location** button to open the Microsoft Office Trusted Location dialog box, click the **Browse** button, navigate to the **Level.03\Tutorial** folder where your Data Files are stored, click the **OK** button, click the **OK** button to add the Level.03\Tutorial folder to the list of trusted locations, click the **OK** button to close the Trust Center dialog box, and then click the **OK** button to close the Access Options dialog box.

6. Click the **Create** tab on the Ribbon and then, in the Other group on the Create tab, click the **Query Design** button. Access opens the Show Table dialog box on top of the Query window in Design view.

7. Click **tblCustomer** in the Tables list box, click the **Add** button, and then click the **Close** button. Access places the tblCustomer table field list in the Query window and closes the Show Table dialog box.

8. Drag down the bottom of the tblCustomer field list to display all its fields, double-click **Company**, double-click **FirstName**, double-click **LastName**, double-click **Phone**, double-click **City**, and then double-click **CustomerType** to add these six fields to the design grid.

   Next, you'll enter the CustomerType field's selection criterion of Commercial.

9. Click the **CustomerType** Criteria text box, type **Commercial**, and then press the **Tab** key. The condition changes to "Commercial". See Figure 9-1.

Figure 9-1	Select query on which to base the make-table query

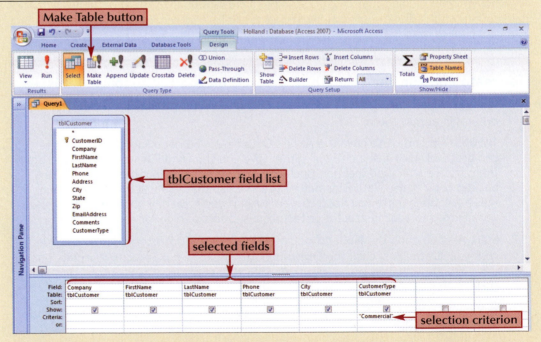

You've completed the select query, so now you can run it to make sure the record-set contains the data Taylor needs.

10. Run the query. The query recordset shows the 14 records for commercial customers.

Now that you have the correct select query, you can change the query to a make-table query.

To change the query type, and then run and save the make-table query:

▶ **1.** Switch to Design view, and then in the Query Type group on the Design tab on the Ribbon, click the **Make Table** button. Access opens the Make Table dialog box, in which you enter the name of the new table and designate the database to be used to store the table. See Figure 9-2.

Make Table dialog box ◀ Figure 9-2

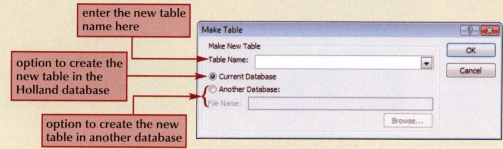

enter the new table name here

option to create the new table in the Holland database

option to create the new table in another database

▶ **2.** In the Table Name list box, type **tblContactCustomer**, make sure the **Current Database** option button is selected so that the new table will be added to the Holland database, and then click the **OK** button.

Now that you have created and tested the query, you can run it to create the tblContactCustomer table. After you run the query, you can save it, and then you can view the new table.

▶ **3.** Run the query. Access opens a dialog box indicating that you are about to paste 14 rows into a new table. Because you are running an action query, which alters the contents of the database, Access gives you the opportunity to cancel the operation, if necessary, or to confirm it.

▶ **4.** Click the **Yes** button. Access closes the dialog box, runs the make-table query to create the tblContactCustomer table and continues displaying the query in Design view.

▶ **5.** Save the query as **qryContactCustomerMakeTable**, close the query, and then open the Navigation Pane. The qryContactCustomerMakeTable query appears in the Queries list with a special icon indicating that it is a make-table query. See Figure 9-3.

Figure 9-3 **Query type icons in the Navigation Pane**

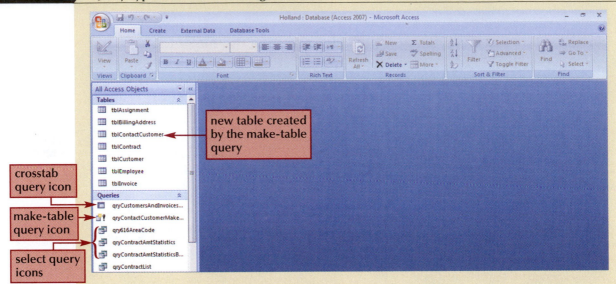

new table created by the make-table query

crosstab query icon

make-table query icon

select query icons

You can now open the tblContactCustomer table to view the results of the make-table query.

▶ **6.** Open the **tblContactCustomer** table in Datasheet view, resize all datasheet columns to their best fit, and then click the first row's **Company** field value to deselect all values. See Figure 9-4.

Figure 9-4 **tblContactCustomer table datasheet**

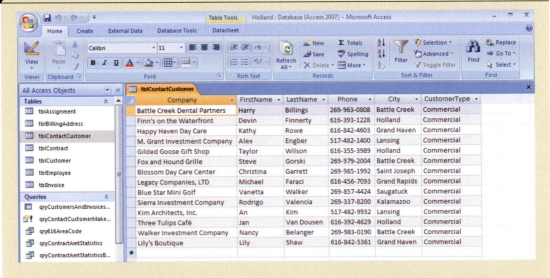

The tblContactCustomer table includes the Company, FirstName, LastName, Phone, City, and CustomerType fields for commercial customers.

▶ **7.** Save your datasheet changes, and then close the table.

Taylor can now make any necessary changes to the tblContactCustomer table records when she contacts customers without affecting the tblCustomer table in the Holland database.

Creating an Append Query

Taylor has decided to expand the list of customers that she will call to include public housing customers, which also have large contracts with Belmont Landscapes. She asks you to add these new records to the tblContactCustomer table. You could make this change by modifying the selection criterion in the qryContactCustomerMakeTable query to select customers with CustomerType field values of Public Housing. If you ran this modified query, however, you would overwrite the existing tblContactCustomer table with a new table. If Taylor had made any changes to the existing tblContactCustomer table records, creating a new table would overwrite these changes, as well.

Instead, you will modify the qryContactCustomerMakeTable query to select only public housing customers and change the query to an append query. When you run this new query, the selected records will be appended to the records in the existing tblContactCustomer table.

Creating an Append Query | Reference Window

- Create a select query with the necessary fields and selection criteria.
- In the Results group on the Design tab on the Ribbon, click the Run button to preview the results.
- Switch to Design view to make any necessary changes to the query. When the query is correct, click the Append button in the Query Type group on the Design tab.
- In the Append dialog box, select the table name in the Table Name list box. Make sure the Current Database option button is selected to include the new table in the current database, or click the Another Database option button and enter the database name in the File Name text box. Then click the OK button. Access replaces the Show row in the design grid with the Append To row.
- Click the Run button, and then click the Yes button to confirm the appending the records to the table.

You can now modify the qryContactCustomerMakeTable query to create the append query you'll use to include the additional customer data Taylor wants in the tblContactCustomer table.

To create the append query:

▶ 1. Open the **qryContactCustomerMakeTable** query in Design view.

   You'll change the selection criterion to "Public Housing."

▶ 2. Click the **CustomerType Criteria** text box, press the **F2** key to highlight the entire condition, type **Public Housing**, and then press the ↓ key. The condition changes to "Public Housing". See Figure 9-5.

Figure 9-5

Changing the selection criterion

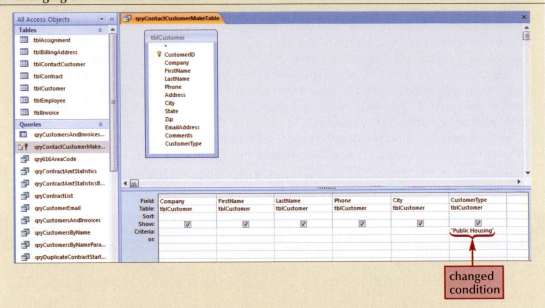

changed condition

Before you can run the query to append the records to the tblContactCustomer table, you have to change the query type to an append query. It is always a good idea to test an action query before you run it, so you will first change the query type to a select query and run it to make sure the correct records are selected. Then you will change the query type to an append query and run it to append the new records to the tblContactCustomer table.

▶ **3.** In the Query Type group on the Design tab on the Ribbon, click the **Select** button.

▶ **4.** Run the query. The query recordset shows the two records for public housing customers.

These two records are the additional records you will append to the tblContactCustomer table. Now that the results show that the query is correct, you can change the query type to an append query.

▶ **5.** Switch to Design view, and then in the Query Type group on the Design tab, click the **Append** button. Access opens the Append dialog box, in which you select the name of the new table to which you want to append the data and designate the database to be used to store the table.

▶ **6.** Make sure **tblContactCustomer** appears in the Table Name text box and that the **Current Database** option button is selected, and then click the **OK** button. Access replaces the Show row in the design grid with the Append To row. See Figure 9-6.

After changing the query type to an append query Figure 9-6

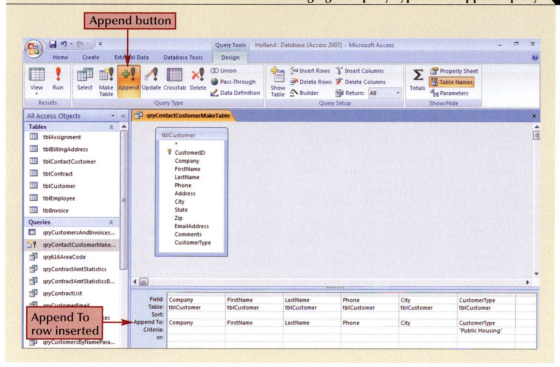

The Append To row in the design grid identifies the fields that the query will append to the designated table. The Company, FirstName, LastName, Phone, City, and CustomerType fields are selected and will be appended to the tblContactCustomer table, which already contains these same six fields for commercial customers.

You can now run and then save the append query.

To run and save the append query:

▶ 1. Run the query. Access opens a dialog box warning you that you are about to append two rows.

▶ 2. Click the **Yes** button to acknowledge the warning. Access closes the dialog box, runs the append query, adds the two records to the tblContactCustomer table, and continues displaying the Query window in Design view.

▶ 3. Click the **Office Button** 🔘, point to **Save As**, and then click **Save Object As** to open the Save As dialog box.

▶ 4. Change the entry in the Save text box to **qryContactCustomerAppend**, and then click the **OK** button. Access saves the query with the new name, which now appears in the Navigation Pane with a special icon that identifies the query as an append query.

▶ 5. Close the query.

Next, you'll open the tblContactCustomer table to make sure that the two records were appended to the table.

▶ 6. Open the **tblContactCustomer** table datasheet, and then click the first row's **Company** field value to deselect all values. See Figure 9-7.

> **Tip**
>
> You can arrange the records in a different order by sorting the records using the Ascending button or the Descending button in the Sort & Filter group on the Home tab on the Ribbon and then saving the table.

Figure 9-7 **tblContactCustomer table datasheet after appending records**

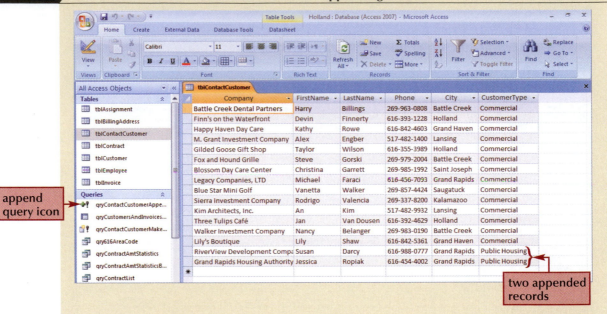

The new records have been added to the tblContactCustomer table. Because the tblContactCustomer table does not have a primary key, the new records appear at the end of the table.

7. Close the table.

Creating a Delete Query

Taylor has contacted all the customers in the tblContactCustomer table that are located in the city of Holland. She asks you to delete these records from the tblContactCustomer table so that the table contains only those records for customers she has not yet contacted. You can either delete the table records individually or create a delete query to remove them all at once.

Reference Window | **Creating a Delete Query**

- Create a select query with the necessary fields and selection criteria.
- In the Results group on the Design tab on the Ribbon, click the Run button to preview the results.
- Switch to Design view to make any necessary changes to the query. When the query is correct, click the Delete button in the Query Type group on the Design tab. Access replaces the Show and Sort rows in the design grid with the Delete row.
- Click the Run button, and then click the Yes button to confirm deleting the records.

You'll create a delete query to delete the Holland customers in the tblContactCustomer table. First, you'll create a select query to choose the correct records and run the query to verify you're selecting the correct records. Then you'll change the query to a delete query and run it.

To create the delete query:

▶ 1. Click the **Create** tab on the Ribbon and then, in the Other group on the Create tab, click the **Query Design** button, add the **tblContactCustomer** table field list to the Query window, and then close the Show Table dialog box.

▶ 2. Double-click the title bar of the tblContactCustomer field list to select all the fields in the table, drag the pointer from the highlighted area of the field list to the design grid's first column Field text box, and then release the mouse button. Access adds all the fields to the design grid.

▶ 3. Click the **City Criteria** text box, type **Holland**, and then press the **Tab** key. Access changes the criterion to "Holland" and will select only the records with a City field value of Holland when you run the query.

▶ 4. Run the query, and then click the first row's **Company** field value to deselect all values. The query results display the three records with City field values of Holland. The select query is correct. See Figure 9-8.

Three records to be deleted ◀ Figure 9-8

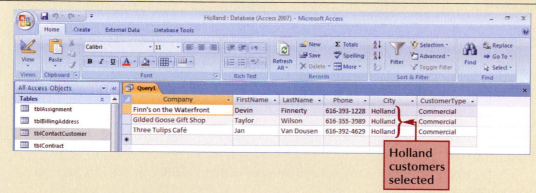

Trouble? If your query did not select the correct three records, switch to Design view, correct the selection criterion, and then run the query again.

Now that you have verified that the correct records are selected, you can change the query to a delete query.

▶ 5. Switch to Design view, and then in the Query Type group on the Design tab, click the **Delete** button. In the design grid, Access replaces the Sort and Show rows with the Delete row. See Figure 9-9.

Figure 9-9 **Design view for the delete query**

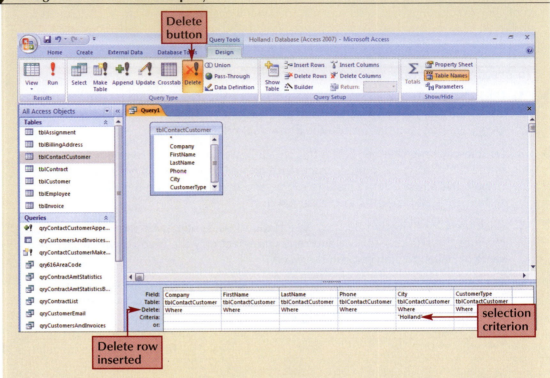

6. Run the query. Access opens a dialog box warning that you are about to delete three rows.

7. Click the **Yes** button to close the dialog box and run the delete query. Access deletes the three records in the tblContactCustomer table and continues to display the Query window in Design view. Because you'll need to run this query only once, you won't save it.

8. Close the query, and then click the **No** button when Access asks if you want to save it.

   You can now open the tblContactCustomer table to verify that the records have been deleted.

9. Open the **tblContactCustomer** table in Datasheet view, and then click the first row's **Company** field value to deselect all values. The table contains 13 records, and the Holland records were correctly deleted. See Figure 9-10.

tblContactCustomer table after deleting three records   **Figure 9-10**

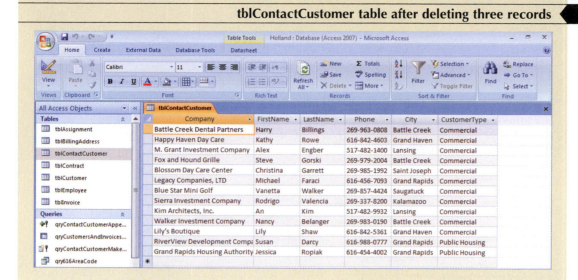

Taylor wants you to add a field named ContactComments to the tblContactCustomer table in which she can keep notes about the calls she makes. You can add the field to the tblContactCustomer table without affecting the objects in the Holland database because the table was created only to meet Taylor's specific need to contact commercial and public housing customers.

To add the new ContactComments field to the tblContactCustomer table:

▶ **1.** Switch to Design view.

You'll set the new field's data type to Memo, so that Taylor is not limited to 255 characters of data in the field, which would be the case with the Text data type.

▶ **2.** Click the **Field Name** text box below the **CustomerType** field, type **ContactComments**, press the **Tab** key, type the letter **m**, and then press the **Tab** key to select the Memo data type.

▶ **3.** Press the **F6** key to position the insertion point in the Format property in the Field Properties pane, press the **Tab** key, and then type **Contact Comments** in the Caption text box. You've completed adding the ContactComments field to the table. See Figure 9-11.

Figure 9-11 **ContactComments field added to the tblContactCustomer table**

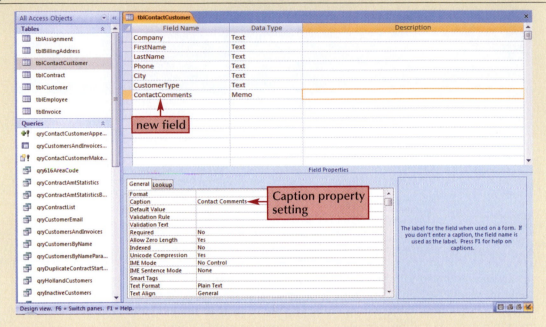

> **4.** Save your table structure changes, and then close the table.

Taylor has contacted the commercial and public housing customers in Grand Rapids and Grand Haven, and she wants to update the ContactComments field in the tblContactCustomer table with the same comments for all Grand Rapids and Grand Haven records. She could type the comments in the ContactComments field for one of the records, and then copy and paste the comments to the other records. However, performing these steps takes time and could result in updating a wrong record or missing one of the records. Instead, you'll create an update query.

Creating an Update Query

Recall that an update query changes selected field values and records in one or more tables.

Now you can create an update query to update the ContactComments field in the tblContactCustomer table for records with City field values of Grand Haven or Grand Rapids.

To create the update query:

1. Click the **Create** tab on the Ribbon and then, in the Other group on the Create tab, click the **Query Design** button, add the **tblContactCustomer** table field list to the Query window, and then close the Show Table dialog box.

   You will select the City and ContactComments fields for the query results. The City field lets you select records for customers in particular cities. The ContactComments field is the field Taylor needs to update.

2. In the tblContactCustomer field list, double-click **City** and **ContactComments** to add these fields to the design grid, scrolling down the field list as necessary.

3. Click the **City Criteria** text box, type **Grand Rapids**, press the ↓ key, and then type **Grand Haven** in the or text box. Access will select a record only if the City field value is Grand Rapids or Grand Haven.

4. Run the query. The query recordset displays five records, each one with a City field value of Grand Rapids or Grand Haven. The select query is correct.

   Now that you have verified that the correct records are selected, you can change the query to an update query.

5. Switch to Design view, and then in the Query Type group on the Design tab on the Ribbon, click the **Update** button. In the design grid, Access replaces the Sort and Show rows with the Update To row.

   You tell Access how you want to change a field value for the selected records by entering an expression in the field's Update To text box. An expression is a calculation resulting in a single value. You can type a simple expression directly into the Update To text box.

6. Click the **ContactComments Update To** text box, type **"Called in May. Contact again in July."** (be sure to type the quotation marks), and then drag the right edge of the ContactComments column to the right to display the entire expression value. See Figure 9-12.

> **Tip**
>
> If you need help creating a complicated expression, you can create it using Expression Builder, or if the expression is lengthy, you can use the Zoom dialog box.

Updating the ContactComments field ◄ **Figure 9-12**

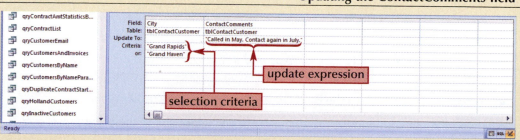

> **Tip**
>
> When a text expression includes quotation marks, you need to type the quotation marks twice. For example, you would enter the expression This is a "text" expression as "This is a ""text"" expression".

7. Run the query. Access opens a dialog box warning you that you are about to update five rows in the tblContactCustomer table.

8. Click the **Yes** button to close the dialog box and run the update query. Access updates the ContactComments field values for customers in Grand Rapids or Grand Haven and leaves the Query window in Design view open.

   You are finished updating the tblContactCustomer table, so you can close the query without saving it.

9. Close the query, and then click the **No** button when Access asks if you want to save it.

Now you can view the tblContactCustomer table to see the results of the update operation.

To view the updated tblContactCustomer table:

▶ 1. Open the **tblContactCustomer** table in Datasheet view, close the Navigation Pane, resize the **Contact Comments** column to its best fit, and then click the first row's **Company** field value to deselect all values. The ContactComments field values for customers in Grand Rapids or Grand Haven have been updated correctly. See Figure 9-13.

Figure 9-13 | tblContactCustomer table with updated ContactComments field values

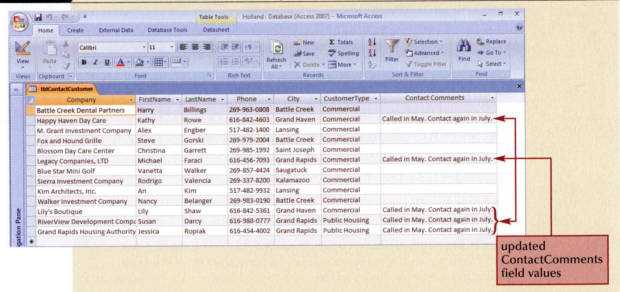

updated ContactComments field values

▶ 2. Save your table datasheet changes, close the table, and then open the Navigation Pane.

Because you saved the make-table and append queries after you ran them, you'll delete them now.

▶ 3. Right-click **qryContactCustomerAppend** in the Queries list, click **Delete** on the shortcut menu, and then click the **Yes** button to confirm the deletion.

▶ 4. Repeat Step 3 to delete the **qryContactCustomerMakeTable** query.

▶ 5. If you are not continuing on to the next session, close the Holland database, and then exit Access.

Tip

If you create and run an action query, save it, and accidentally run it again, you might update tables in unintended ways. Therefore, after you've run an action query, you usually shouldn't save it in your database.

Taylor can now use action queries in her future work with the Holland database. In the next session, you'll learn about the different types of relationships you can create between tables, and view and create indexes to increase a database's efficiency.

Review | **Session 9.1 Quick Check**

1. What is an action query?
2. What precautions should you take before running an action query?
3. What is the difference between a make-table query and an append query?

4. What does a delete query do?
5. What does an update query do?
6. How does the design grid change when you create an update query?

Session 9.2

Relationships Between Database Tables

As you learned in previous tutorials, a one-to-many relationship (abbreviated as 1:M) exists between two tables when each record in the primary table matches zero, one, or more records in the related table, and when each record in the related table matches at most one record in the primary table. For example, Figure 9-14 shows a one-to-many relationship between portions of the tblCustomer and tblContract tables and also shows a sample query based on the two tables. (Most examples in this session use portions of tables for illustrative purposes.) Customer 11065 has two contracts, customers 11038 and 11087 have one contract, and customer 11004 has zero contracts. The first four contracts each have a single matching customer based on the CustomerID foreign key values. The fifth contract with a ContractNum value of 3110 has a null CustomerID foreign key value. Permitted foreign key values are governed by referential integrity, which is the rule that requires each nonnull foreign key value to match a primary key value in the primary table.

One-to-many relationship and sample query

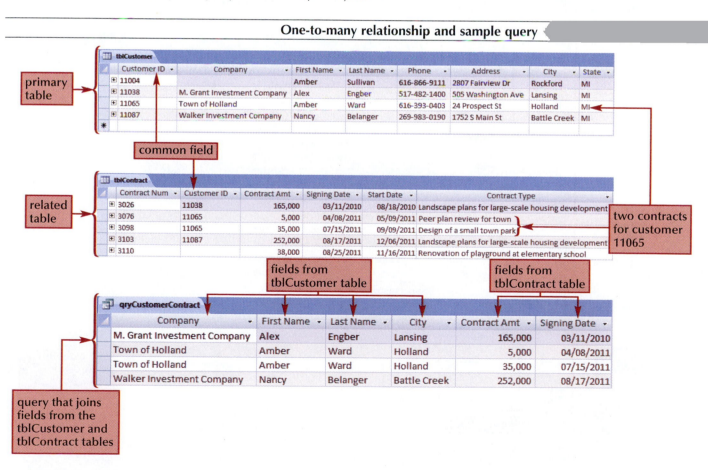

You use the common field, the Customer ID column, to form the one-to-many relationship between the tblCustomer and tblContract tables. When you join the two tables based on Customer ID column values, you can extract data from them as if they are one larger table. For example, you can join the tblCustomer and tblContract tables to create the qryCustomerContract query shown in Figure 9-14. In the qryCustomerContract query, the Company, First Name, Last Name, and City columns are from the tblCustomer table, and the Contract Amt and Signing Date columns are from the tblContract table.

In addition to one-to-many relationships between tables, you can also relate tables through many-to-many and one-to-one relationships.

Many-to-Many Relationships

A **many-to-many relationship** (abbreviated as **M:N**) exists between two tables when each record in the first table matches many records in the second table, and each record in the second table matches many records in the first table.

In the Holland database, the tblInvoice table contains one record for each invoice billed for work performed by Belmont Landscapes' employees, and the tblEmployee table contains one record for each Belmont Landscapes' employee performing work billed to invoices. Because an invoice can represent work performed by many employees, and each employee can work on many invoiced projects, the tblInvoice and tblEmployee tables have a many-to-many relationship, as shown in Figure 9-15.

| Figure 9-15 | tblInvoice and tblEmployee tables with a M:N relationship using the tblAssignment table |

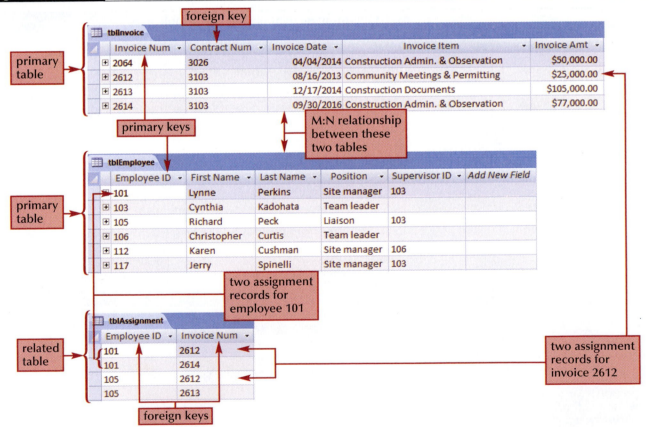

When you have a many-to-many relationship between two tables, you must create a third table and form one-to-many relationships between the two original primary tables and the new related table. For instance, the tblAssignment table, shown in Figure 9-15, exists only because the tblInvoice and tblEmployee tables have a many-to-many relationship. Each record in the tblAssignment table contains two foreign keys: the Employee ID column is a foreign key that allows you to join the tblEmployee table to the tblAssignment table; and the Invoice Num column is a foreign key that allows you to join the tblInvoice table to the tblAssignment table. For example, the first record in the tblAssignment table represents Community Meetings & Permitting work for InvoiceNum 2612 that was performed by Lynne Perkins with EmployeeID 101. Lynne Perkins, who has EmployeeID 101, appears in two records in the tblAssignment table that represent work she performed for invoices 2612 and 2614. Also, InvoiceNum 2612 appears in two tblAssignment table records, each for a different employee: Lynne Perkins and Richard Peck. The primary key of the tblAssignment table is a composite key, consisting of the combination of the Employee ID and Invoice Num columns. Each pair of values in this primary key is unique.

Many-to-Many Relationships | InSight

Although one-to-many relationships are the most common type of table relationship, many-to-many relationships occur frequently, and most databases have one or more many-to-many relationships. For example, in a college database, a student takes more than one class, and each class has more than one student enrolled; a course has many prerequisites and can be the prerequisite to many courses. In a pharmacy database, a medication is prescribed to many customers, and a customer can take many medications. In an airline database, a flight has many passengers, and a passenger can take many flights. In a publisher database, an author writes many books, and a book can have multiple authors. In a manufacturing database, a manufactured product consists of many parts, and a part can be a component in many manufactured products. In a film database, a movie has many actors, and each actor appears in many movies.

Common one-to-many relationships can turn into many-to-many relationships when circumstances change. For example, a department in an organzation has many employees, and an employee usually works in a single department. However, an instructor can have a joint appointment to two departments, and some companies hire employees and split their time between two departments. You must carefully analzye each situation and design your table relationships to handle the requirements.

When you join tables that have a many-to-many relationship, you can extract data from them as if they were one larger table. For example, you can join the tblInvoice and tblEmployee tables to create the qryInvoiceEmployee query shown in Figure 9-16.

Query recordset produced by joining tables having an M:N relationship   Figure 9-16

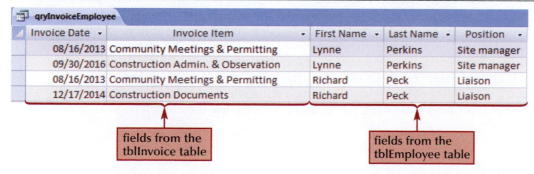

fields from the tblInvoice table

fields from the tblEmployee table

In the tblAssignment table, the Employee ID column joins the tblEmployee and tblAssignment tables, and the Invoice Num column joins the tblInvoice and tblAssignment tables. In the qryInvoiceEmployee query, the Invoice Date and Invoice Item columns are from the tblInvoice table, and the First Name, Last Name, and Position columns are from the tblEmployee table. The first record in the query recordset shows data from the second record in the tblInvoice table, joined with data from the matching first record in the tblEmployee table. These two records are joined through the third record in the tblAssignment table.

One-to-One Relationships

A **one-to-one relationship** (abbreviated as **1:1**) exists between two tables when each record in the first table matches at most one record in the second table, and each record in the second table matches at most one record in the first table. Most relationships between tables are either one-to-many or many-to-many; the primary use for one-to-one relationships is as entity subtypes. An **entity subtype** is a table whose primary key is a foreign key to a second table and whose fields are additional fields for the second table. For example, the tblCustomer table and the tblBillingAddress table, which is an entity subtype, have a one-to-one relationship, as shown in Figure 9-17.

| Figure 9-17 | tblCustomer and tblBillingAddress tables with a 1:1 relationship |

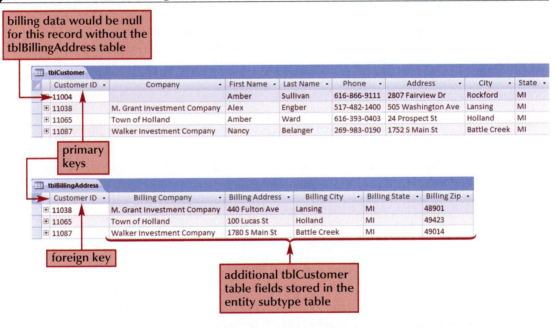

For most customers, the Address, City, State, and Zip fields in the tblCustomer table identify both the customer's location and billing address, which is where Belmont Landscapes sends the customer's invoices. In a few cases, however, the billing address is different from the location address; additionally, the customer name used for billing purposes might be different from the customer name in the tblCustomer table. There are two ways to handle these two sets of names and addresses. The first way is to add the BillingCompany, BillingAddress, BillingCity, BillingState, and BillingZip fields to the tblCustomer table. For those customers having a different billing name and address, you'd store the appropriate values in these billing fields. For those customers having identical location and billing names and addresses, leave these billing fields null.

As shown in Figure 9-17, the second way to handle the two sets of addresses is to create the entity subtype named tblBillingAddress. In the tblBillingAddress table, CustomerID, which is the primary key, is also a foreign key to the tblCustomer table. A record appears in the tblBillingAddress table only for those customers having a different billing name and address.

When you join tables that have a one-to-one relationship, you can extract data from them as if they were one larger table. For example, you can join the tblCustomer and tblBillingAddress tables to create the qryBillingAddressData query shown in Figure 9-18.

Query results produced by joining tables having a 1:1 relationship **Figure 9-18**

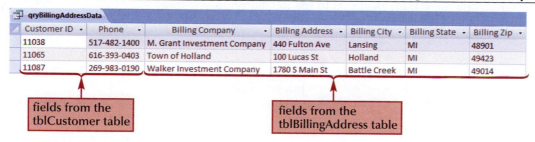

fields from the
tblCustomer table

fields from the
tblBillingAddress table

The Customer ID column joins the tblCustomer and tblBillingAddress tables. In the query, the Customer ID and Phone columns are from the tblCustomer table; and the Billing Company, Billing Address, Billing City, Billing State, and Billing Zip columns are from the tblBillingAddress table. Only the three customers that have records in the tblBillingAddress table—because they have different billing addresses—appear in the qryBillingAddressData query recordset.

Next, you'll define a many-to-many relationship between the tblInvoice and tblEmployee tables, and a one-to-one relationship between the tblCustomer and tblBillingAddress tables.

Defining M:N and 1:1 Relationships Between Tables

Similar to how you defined one-to-many relationships in earlier tutorials, you define many-to-many and one-to-one relationships in the Relationships window. First, you'll open the Relationships window and define the many-to-many relationship between the tblInvoice and tblEmployee tables. You'll define a one-to-many relationship between the tblInvoice and tblAssignment tables, with tblInvoice as the primary table, tblAssignment as the related table, and InvoiceNum as the common field (the primary key in the tblInvoice table and a foreign key in the tblAssignment table). Next, you'll define a one-to-many relationship between the tblEmployee and tblAssignment tables, with tblEmployee as the primary table, tblAssignment as the related table, and EmployeeID as the common field (the primary key in the tblEmployee table and a foreign key in the tblAssignment table).

To define a many-to-many relationship between the tblInvoice and tblEmployee tables:

▶ **1.** If you took a break after the previous session, make sure that the Holland database is open and the Navigation Pane is open.

▶ **2.** Close the Navigation Pane, click the **Database Tools** tab on the Ribbon, and then in the Show/Hide group on the Database Tools tab, click the **Relationships** button to open the Relationships window.

3. In the Relationships group on the Design tab, click the **Show Table** button to open the Show Table dialog box, double-click **tblAssignment** to add the tblAssignment field list to the Relationships window, double-click **tblBillingAddress** to add the tblBillingAddress field list to the Relationships window, double-click **tblEmployee** to add the tblEmployee field list to the Relationships window, and then close the Show Table dialog box.

4. Drag the tblBillingAddress field list title bar to the left until the tblBillingAddress field list is positioned as shown in Figure 9-19, and then position the field lists for the tblEmployee and tblAssignment tables as shown in Figure 9-19.

Figure 9-19 | **After adding three table field lists to the Relationships window**

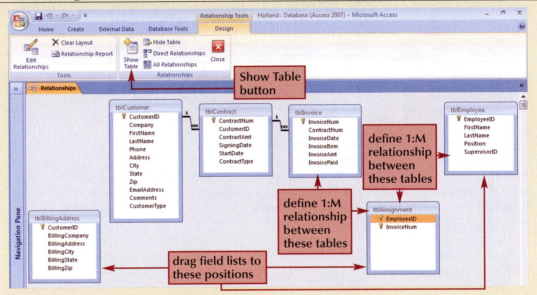

First, you'll define the one-to-many relationship between the tblInvoice and tblAssignment tables.

5. Click **InvoiceNum** in the tblInvoice field list, and drag it to **InvoiceNum** in the tblAssignment field list. When you release the mouse button, the Edit Relationships dialog box opens.

The primary table, related table, and common field appear at the top of the dialog box. The type of relationship, One-To-Many, appears at the bottom of the dialog box. When you click the Enforce Referential Integrity check box, the two cascade options become available. If you select the Cascade Update Related Fields option, Access will change the appropriate foreign key values in the related table when you change a primary key value in the primary table. If you select the Cascade Delete Related Records option, when you delete a record in the primary table, Access will delete all records in the related table that have a matching foreign key value. As you did in earlier tutorials, you'll enforce referential integrity and cascade updates to related fields, but you won't cascade deletions to related records.

6. Click the **Enforce Referential Integrity** check box, and then click the **Cascade Update Related Fields** check box. You have now selected all the necessary relationship options.

▶ **7.** Click the **Create** button to close the dialog box and define the one-to-many relationship between the two tables. The completed relationship appears in the Relationships window.

▶ **8.** Repeat Steps 5 through 7 to define the one-to-many relationship between the primary tblEmployee table and the related tblAssignment table, using EmployeeID as the common field. See Figure 9-20.

M:N relationship defined between the tblInvoice and tblEmployee tables ◀ Figure 9-20

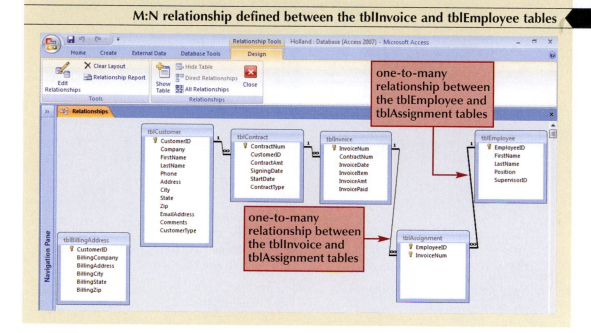

Now you'll define a one-to-one relationship between the tblCustomer and tblBillingAddress tables.

To define a one-to-one relationship between the tblCustomer and tblBillingAddress tables:

▶ **1.** Click **CustomerID** in the tblCustomer field list, and drag it to **CustomerID** in the tblBillingAddress field list. When you release the mouse button, the Edit Relationships dialog box opens.

The primary table, related table, and common field appear at the top of the dialog box. The type of relationship, One-To-One, appears at the bottom of the dialog box.

▶ **2.** Click the **Enforce Referential Integrity** check box, click the **Cascade Update Related Fields** check box, and then click the **Create** button to define the one-to-one relationship between the two tables and close the dialog box. The completed relationship appears in the Relationships window. See Figure 9-21.

Figure 9-21 **1:1 relationship defined between the tblCustomer and tblBillingAddress tables**

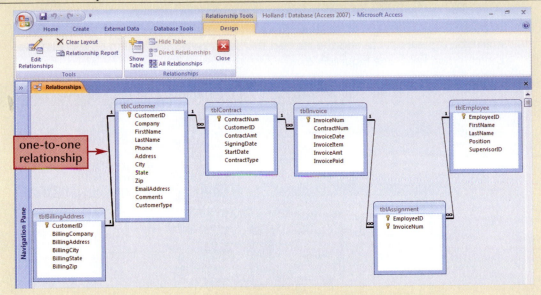

Both sides of the relationship have the digit 1 at the ends of their join lines to indicate a one-to-one relationship between the two tables. The thick join line indicates that you've chosen to enforce referential integrity in the relationship.

3. Save your relationship changes.

The tblEmployee table contains data about the workers at Belmont Landscapes who work directly on landscaping projects and whose efforts on the projects are billed to customer invoices. Sarah asks you to create a select query to display the employees in the tblEmployee table and their supervisors. The select query you'll create will require a special join using the tblEmployee table.

Joining Tables

The design of the Holland database includes a one-to-many relationship between the tblCustomer and tblContract tables using CustomerID as the common field, which allows you to join the two tables to create a query based on data from both tables. The type of join you have used so far is an inner join. Two other types of joins are the outer join and the self-join.

Inner and Outer Joins

An **inner join** is a join in which the DBMS selects records from two tables only when the records have the same value in the common field that links the tables. For example, in a database containing a table of student information and a table of class information, an inner join would show all student records that have a matching class record and all class records that have a matching student record. In the Holland database, CustomerID is the common field for the tblCustomer and tblContract tables. As shown in Figure 9-22, the results of a query based on an inner join of these two tables include only those records that have a matching CustomerID value. The record in the tblCustomer table with a Customer ID column value of 11004 is not included in the query recordset, because it fails to match a record with the same Customer ID column value in the tblContract table. (That customer has no current contracts.) Also, the record in the tblContract table with a

Contract Num column value of 3110 is not included in the query recordset, because it has a null Customer ID column value. (Perhaps the clerk entering the contract in the Holland database wasn't sure which customer signed that contract and left the field value null.) Because primary key values can't be null, records with null foreign key values do not appear in a query recordset based on an inner join. You usually use an inner join whenever you perform a query based on more than one table; it is the default join you have used to this point.

Example of an inner join ◄ **Figure 9-22**

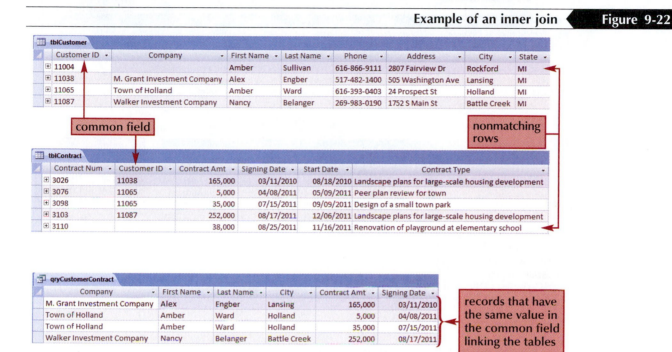

An **outer join** is a join in which the DBMS selects all records from one table and only those records from a second table that have matching common field values. For example, in a database containing a student table and a class table, an outer join would show all students whether or not the students are enrolled in a class, and another outer join would show all classes whether or not there are any students enrolled in them. In the Holland database, you would use this kind of join if you wanted to see, for example, all records from the tblCustomer table and also all matching records from the tblContract table. Figure 9-23 shows an outer join for the tblCustomer and tblContract tables. All records from the tblCustomer table appear in the query recordset, along with only matching records from the tblContract table. Notice that the first record from the tblCustomer table for Amber Sullivan appears even though it does not match a record in the tblContract table. The record in the tblContract table with ContractNum 3110 does not appear in the query recordset, however, because it does not match a record in the tblCustomer table.

Figure 9-23 | **Example of an outer join**

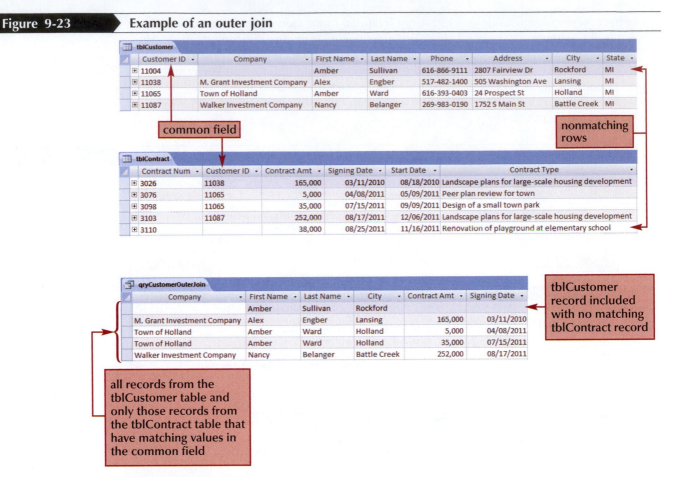

Another example of an outer join using the tblCustomer and tblContract tables is shown in Figure 9-24. All records from the tblContract table appear in the query record-set, even the Contract Num 3110 record that does not match a record in the tblCustomer table. The Amber Sullivan record from the tblCustomer table does not appear in the query recordset, however, because it does not match a record in the tblContract table.

Another example of an outer join | Figure 9-24

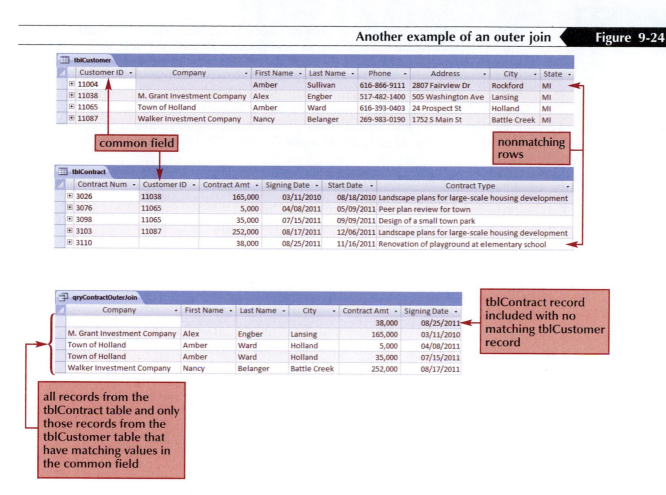

tblCustomer

Customer ID	Company	First Name	Last Name	Phone	Address	City	State
⊞ 11004		Amber	Sullivan	616-866-9111	2807 Fairview Dr	Rockford	MI
⊞ 11038	M. Grant Investment Company	Alex	Engber	517-482-1400	505 Washington Ave	Lansing	MI
⊞ 11065	Town of Holland	Amber	Ward	616-393-0403	24 Prospect St	Holland	MI
⊞ 11087	Walker Investment Company	Nancy	Belanger	269-983-0190	1752 S Main St	Battle Creek	MI

common field

nonmatching rows

tblContract

Contract Num	Customer ID	Contract Amt	Signing Date	Start Date	Contract Type
⊞ 3026	11038	165,000	03/11/2010	08/18/2010	Landscape plans for large-scale housing development
⊞ 3076	11065	5,000	04/08/2011	05/09/2011	Peer plan review for town
⊞ 3098	11065	35,000	07/15/2011	09/09/2011	Design of a small town park
⊞ 3103	11087	252,000	08/17/2011	12/06/2011	Landscape plans for large-scale housing development
⊞ 3110		38,000	08/25/2011	11/16/2011	Renovation of playground at elementary school

qryContractOuterJoin

Company	First Name	Last Name	City	Contract Amt	Signing Date
				38,000	08/25/2011
M. Grant Investment Company	Alex	Engber	Lansing	165,000	03/11/2010
Town of Holland	Amber	Ward	Holland	5,000	04/08/2011
Town of Holland	Amber	Ward	Holland	35,000	07/15/2011
Walker Investment Company	Nancy	Belanger	Battle Creek	252,000	08/17/2011

tblContract record included with no matching tblCustomer record

all records from the tblContract table and only those records from the tblCustomer table that have matching values in the common field

Inner joins are the default join type, but you can change the join type between two tables to be an outer join. You'll show Sarah how she can view the join type between the tblCustomer and tblContract tables and how she would change the default join type.

To view the join type between the tblCustomer and tblContract tables:

1. Right-click the join line between the tblCustomer and tblContract tables, and then click **Edit Relationship** on the shortcut menu to open the Edit Relationships dialog box.

   Trouble? If right-clicking the join line does not work, click the join line, and then click the Edit Relationships button in the Tools group on the Design tab on the Ribbon.

2. Click the **Join Type** button in the dialog box to open the Join Properties dialog box. See Figure 9-25.

Join Properties dialog box | Figure 9-25

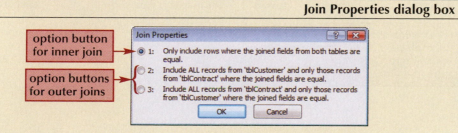

option button for inner join

option buttons for outer joins

Join Properties

- ◉ 1: Only include rows where the joined fields from both tables are equal.
- ○ 2: Include ALL records from 'tblCustomer' and only those records from 'tblContract' where the joined fields are equal.
- ○ 3: Include ALL records from 'tblContract' and only those records from 'tblCustomer' where the joined fields are equal.

OK   Cancel

Tip

When you change the join type between two tables in the Relationships window, every new query based on the two tables uses the join type you selected in the Join Properties dialog box. Existing queries based on the two tables continue to use the join type that was in effect at the time you created the query.

In the Join Properties dialog box, the first option button is selected, indicating that the join type between the tblCustomer and tblContract tables is an inner join. You would click the second or third option button to establish an outer join between the two tables. You'd select the second option when you want to select all records from the tblCustomer table and any matching records from the tblContract table based on the CustomerID common field. You'd select the third option when you want to select all records from the tblContract table and any matching records from the tblCustomer table based on the CustomerID common field.

Sarah wants to continue to use an inner join for all queries based on the tblCustomer and tblContract tables.

3. Click the **Cancel** button to close the Join Properties dialog box without making any changes, click the **Cancel** button to close the Edit Relationships dialog box without making any changes, and then close the Relationships window.

Self-Joins

A table can also be joined with itself; this join is called a **self-join**. A self-join can be either an inner or outer join. For example, you would use this kind of join if you wanted to see records from the tblEmployee table together with information about each employee's supervisor. Figure 9-26 shows a self-join for the tblEmployee table. In this case, the self-join is an inner join because records appear in the query results only if the SupervisorID field value matches a EmployeeID field value. To create this self-join, you would add two copies of the tblEmployee table to the Query window in Design view, and then join the SupervisorID field of one tblEmployee table to the EmployeeID field of the other tblEmployee table.

Figure 9-26   **Example of a self-join**

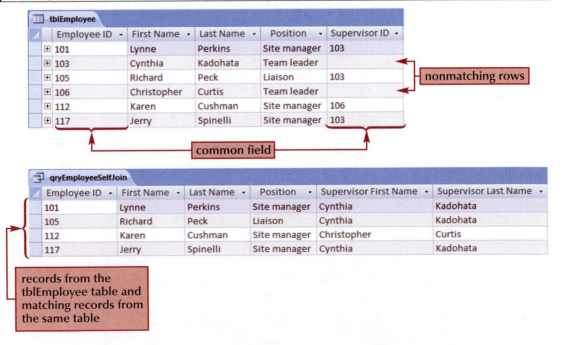

In Figure 9-26, the query results show the record for each employee in the tblEmployee table and the supervisor for that employee. The supervisor information also comes from the tblEmployee table through the SupervisorID field. The table join for the query is an inner join, so only employees with nonnull SupervisorID field values appear in the query recordset.

To create a select query to display the employees in the tblEmployee table and their supervisors, you need to create a self-join.

Creating a Self-Join

You need to create a query to display the employees and their supervisors in the tblEmployee table. This query requires a self-join. To create the self-join, you need to add two copies of the tblEmployee field list to the Query window in Design view, and then add a join line from the EmployeeID field in one field list to the SupervisorID field in the other. The SupervisorID field is a foreign key that matches the primary key field EmployeeID. You can then create a query to display employee information from one copy of the table and supervisor information from the other copy of the table.

Creating a Self-Join | Reference Window

- Click the Create tab on the Ribbon.
- In the Other group on the Create tab, click the Query Design button.
- In the Show Table dialog box, double-click the table for the self-join, double-click the table a second time, and the click the Close button.
- Click and drag the primary key field from one field list to the foreign key field in the other field list.
- Right-click the join line between the two tables, and then click Join Properties on the shortcut menu to open the Join Properties dialog box.
- Click the first option button to select an inner join, or click the second option button or the third option button to select an outer join, and then click the OK button.
- Select the fields, specify the selection criteria, select the sort options, and set other properties as appropriate for the query.

Now you'll create the self-join query to display employees and their supervisors.

To create the self-join query:

1. Click the **Create** tab on the Ribbon, and then in the Other group on the Create tab on the Ribbon, click the **Query Design** button to open the Show Table dialog box on top of the Query window in Design view.

2. Double-click **tblEmployee** to add the tblEmployee field list to the Query window.

3. Double-click **tblEmployee** again to add a second copy of the tblEmployee field list to the Query window, and then click the **Close** button. Access identifies the left field list as tblEmployee and the right field list as tblEmployee_1 to distinguish the two copies of the table.

   You will now create a join between the two copies of the tblEmployee table by linking the EmployeeID field in the tblEmployee field list to the SupervisorID field in the tblEmployee_1 field list. The SupervisorID field is a foreign key that matches the primary key field EmployeeID.

Tip

If you add the wrong table to a query or change a query design so that it no longer needs a table you've added previously, right-click the field list in the Query window and then click Remove Table on the shortcut menu to remove the table from the query.

▶ **4.** Click and drag the **EmployeeID** field from the tblEmployee field list to the **SupervisorID** field in the tblEmployee_1 field list. Access adds a join line between the two fields. You can verify that this is an inner join query by opening the Join Properties dialog box.

▶ **5.** Right-click the join line between the two tables, click **Join Properties** on the shortcut menu to open the Join Properties dialog box, and then click **tblEmployee** in the Left Table Name text box to deselect all controls. See Figure 9-27.

Figure 9-27 Join Properties dialog box

The first option button is selected, indicating that this is an inner join. Because the inner join is correct, you can cancel the dialog box and then add the necessary fields in the design grid.

▶ **6.** Click the **Cancel** button, and then double-click the following fields (in order) from the tblEmployee_1 field list: **EmployeeID**, **FirstName**, **LastName**, and **Position**.

▶ **7.** Double-click the following fields (in order) from the tblEmployee field list: **FirstName** and **LastName**.

▶ **8.** Run the query, and then click the first row's **Employee ID** field value to deselect all values. Access displays the query recordset in increasing EmployeeID order with six fields and 12 records. See Figure 9-28.

Figure 9-28 Initial self-join on the tblEmployee table

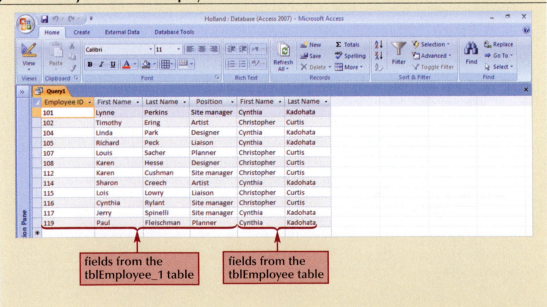

The query recordset displays all employees and their supervisors with the exception of the records for Cynthia Kadohata and Christopher Curtis, because their records contain null SupervisorID field values. (They are supervisors of the other employees and do not have assigned supervisors.) Remember that an inner join doesn't display records from the second table unless it contains a matching value in the common field. In the tblEmployee_1 table, the SupervisorID field values for Cynthia Kadohata and Christopher Curtis are null, so the inner join doesn't select their records in the tblEmployee table.

Trouble? If your query results do not match Figure 9-28, switch to Design view, and review the preceding steps to make any necessary corrections to your query design. Then run the query again.

Access displays 12 of the 14 records from the tblEmployee table. The records for Cynthia Kadohata and Christopher Curtis have null SupervisorID field values; therefore, their records are not displayed. Two column names in the query recordset are "First Name," and two column names are "Last Name." Sarah asks you to rename the two rightmost columns so that the query recordset will be easier to read. After you set the Caption property for the two rightmost fields, the column names in the query recordset will be, from left to right, Employee ID, First Name, Last Name, Position, Supervisor First Name, and Supervisor Last Name.

To set the Caption property for two query fields:

1. Switch to Design view.

2. Click the sixth column's Field text box, in the Show/Hide group on the Design tab on the Ribbon, click the **Property Sheet** button, and then set the Caption property to **Supervisor Last Name**.

3. Click the fifth column's Field text box, and then set the Caption property to **Supervisor First Name**.

4. Close the property sheet, save the query as **qryEmployeeSupervisors**, run the query, resize all columns to their best fits, and then click the first row's **Employee ID** field value to deselect all values. The query recordset displays the new names for the fifth and sixth columns. See Figure 9-29.

Final self-join on the tblEmployee table | **Figure 9-29**

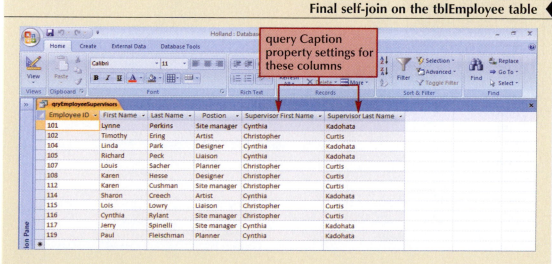

5. Save and close the query.

Sarah asks you if her staff's work will take longer as the Holland database grows in size with the addition of more table records. Specifically, she wants to know if queries will take longer to run. You tell her that using indexes will help make her queries run faster.

Using Indexes for Table Fields

Suppose you need to find all the pages in a book that discuss a specific topic. The fastest, most accurate way to perform your search is to look up the topic in the book's index. In a similar fashion, you can create indexes for fields in a table, so that Access can quickly locate all the records in a table that contain specific values for one or more fields. An **index** is a list that relates field values to the records that contain those field values.

Access automatically creates and maintains an index for a table's primary key. For example, the tblInvoice table in the Holland database includes an index for the InvoiceNum field, which is the table's primary key. Conceptually, as shown in Figure 9-30, Access identifies each record in the tblInvoice table by its record number, and the InvoiceNum index has two columns. The first column contains an InvoiceNum value, and the second column contains the record number in the tblInvoice table for that InvoiceNum value. For instance, InvoiceNum 2063 in the index has a record number value of 4; and record number 4 in the tblInvoice table contains the data for InvoiceNum 2063.

Figure 9-30   **tblInvoice table with index for the InvoiceNum field**

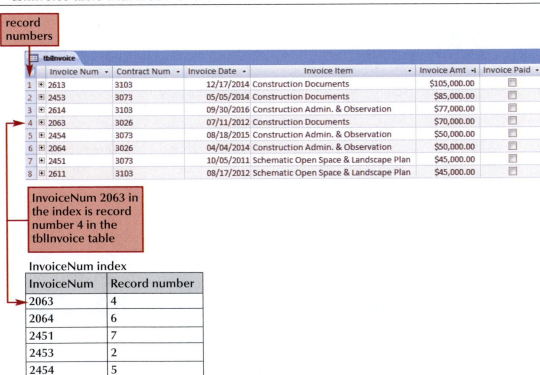

record numbers

tblInvoice

	Invoice Num	Contract Num	Invoice Date	Invoice Item	Invoice Amt	Invoice Paid
1	2613	3103	12/17/2014	Construction Documents	$105,000.00	
2	2453	3073	05/05/2014	Construction Documents	$85,000.00	
3	2614	3103	09/30/2016	Construction Admin. & Observation	$77,000.00	
4	2063	3026	07/11/2012	Construction Documents	$70,000.00	
5	2454	3073	08/18/2015	Construction Admin. & Observation	$50,000.00	
6	2064	3026	04/04/2014	Construction Admin. & Observation	$50,000.00	
7	2451	3073	10/05/2011	Schematic Open Space & Landscape Plan	$45,000.00	
8	2611	3103	08/17/2012	Schematic Open Space & Landscape Plan	$45,000.00	

InvoiceNum 2063 in the index is record number 4 in the tblInvoice table

InvoiceNum index

InvoiceNum	Record number
2063	4
2064	6
2451	7
2453	2
2454	5
2611	8
2613	1
2614	3

Because InvoiceNum values in the tblInvoice table are unique, each row in the InvoiceNum index has a single record number. When you or Access create indexes for non-primary-key fields, however, the indexes may contain multiple record numbers in a row. Figure 9-31 illustrates a ContractNum index for the tblInvoice table. Because ContractNum is a foreign key in the tblInvoice table (a contract can have many invoices), each ContractNum entry in the index can be associated with many record numbers in the tblInvoice table. For instance, ContractNum 3026 in the index has record number values of 4 and 6, and record numbers 4 and 6 in the tblInvoice table contain the invoice data for ContractNum 3026.

tblInvoice table with index for the ContractNum field   Figure 9-31

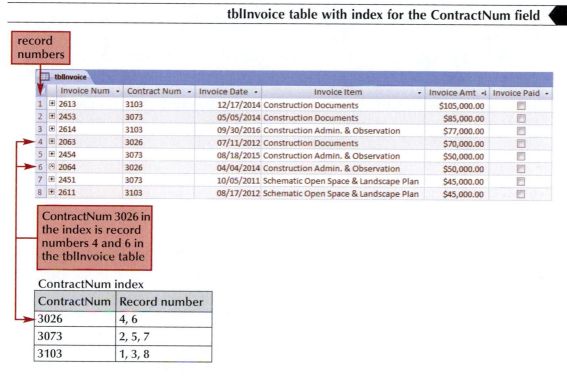

record numbers

ContractNum 3026 in the index is record numbers 4 and 6 in the tblInvoice table

ContractNum index

ContractNum	Record number
3026	4, 6
3073	2, 5, 7
3103	1, 3, 8

If an index exists for the ContractNum field in the tblInvoice table, queries that use ContractNum as a sort field or as a selection criterion will run faster.

InSight | **Tradeoffs of Using Indexes**

With small tables, the increased speed associated with indexes is not readily apparent. In practice, tables with hundreds of thousands or millions of records are common. In such cases, the increase in speed is dramatic. In fact, without indexes, many database operations in large tables would not be practical, because they would take too long to complete. Why the speed difference in these cases? To sort or select records from a large table without an index, Access must make numerous accesses to disk storage to retrieve table records, because the entire table can't fit in computer memory. In contrast, indexes are usually small enough to fit completely in computer memory, and Access sorts and selects records based on indexes with minimal need to access disk storage. Because accessing disk storage is very slow and performing operations in computer memory is very fast, using indexes in large tables is faster.

The speed advantage of using an index must be weighed against two disadvantages: the index adds disk storage requirements to the database, and it takes time to update the index as you add and delete records. Except for primary key indexes, you can add and delete indexes at any time. Thus, you can add an index if you think searching and querying would be faster as the number of records in the database increases. You can also delete an existing index if you later deem it to be unnecessary.

Viewing Existing Indexes

You can view the existing indexes for a table by opening the table in Design view.

Reference Window | **Viewing a Table's Existing Indexes**

- Open the table in Design view.
- To view an index for a single field, click the field, and then view the Indexed property in the Field Properties pane.
- To view all the indexes for a table or to view an index consisting of multiple fields, click the Indexes button in the Show/Hide group on the Design tab on the Ribbon.

Sarah wants to view the indexes for the tblAssignment table.

To view the indexes for the tblAssignment table:

1. Open the Navigation Pane, and then open the **tblAssignment** table in Design view.

2. In the Show/Hide group on the Design tab on the Ribbon, click the **Indexes** button to open the Indexes: tblAssignment dialog box, and then click **PrimaryKey** in the Index Name text box to deselect all values. See Figure 9-32.

Indexes for the tblAssignment table   Figure 9-32

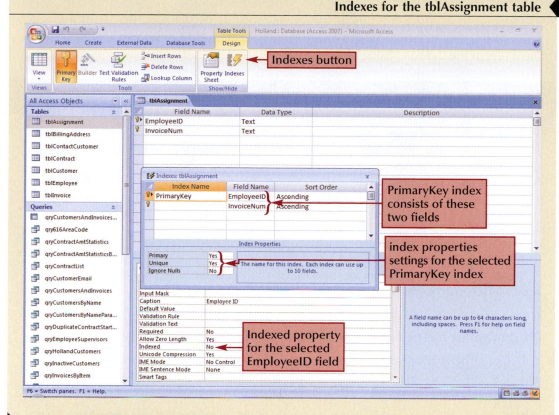

3. Close the Indexes: tblAssignment dialog box, and then close the table.

Because the EmployeeID field was selected when you opened the Indexes dialog box, the properties in the Field Properties pane pertained to this field. In particular, the Indexed property value of No for the EmployeeID field specifies there's no index for this field.

In the Indexes: tblAssignment dialog box, the properties in the Index Properties pane apply to the selected PrimaryKey index, which consists of the table's composite key of the EmployeeID and InvoiceNum fields. Because InvoiceNum in the dialog box's second row does not have an Index Name property value, both EmployeeID and InvoiceNum make up the PrimaryKey index. Access automatically created the PrimaryKey index when the table was created and the EmployeeID and InvoiceNum fields were designated as the table's composite key. The properties for the PrimaryKey index indicate that this index is the primary key index (Primary property setting of Yes), and that values in this index must be unique (Unique property setting of Yes)—that is, each EmployeeID and InvoiceNum pair of field values must be unique. The Ignore Nulls property setting of No means that records with null values for the EmployeeID field or InvoiceNum field are included in the index, but this setting is ignored because the Yes setting for the Primary property doesn't allow either field to have a null value.

Over the past few weeks, Sarah's staff has been monitoring the performance of the Holland database by timing how long it takes to run queries. She wants her staff to let her know if the performance changes over the next several days if she creates an index for the City field in the tblCustomer table. Many queries use the City field as a sort field or selection criterion, and adding an index might speed up those queries.

Creating an Index

You can create an index for a single field in the Indexes dialog box or by setting its Indexed property in Design view. However, for a multiple-field index, you must create the index in the Indexes dialog box.

Reference Window | **Creating an Index**

- Open the table in Design view.
- To create an index for a single field, click the field, and then set the Indexed property in the Field Properties pane.
- To create an index consisting of multiple fields, click the Indexes button in the Show/Hide group on the Design tab on the Ribbon, enter a name for the index in the Index Name text box, select the fields in the Field Name text box, and then set other properties as necessary for the index.

Next, you'll create an index for the City field in the tblCustomer table by setting the field's Indexed property.

To create an index for the City field in the tblCustomer table:

1. Open the **tblCustomer** table in Design view, and then in the Show/Hide group on the Design tab on the Ribbon, click the **Indexes** button to open the Indexes: tblCustomer dialog box.

2. Drag the title bar of the dialog box to the right, click the **tblCustomer** tab to make the Table window the active window, and then click **City** in the Field Name column to make it the current field. See Figure 9-33.

Figure 9-33 | Indexes for the tblCustomer table

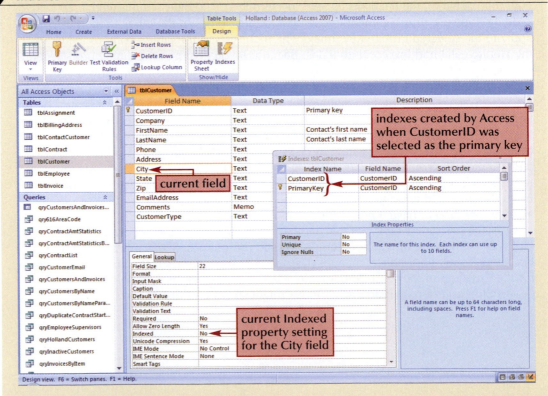

Access created two indexes when CustomerID was selected as the primary key: the PrimaryKey index and the CustomerID index. No other indexes exist for the tblCustomer table. You'll create an index for the City field allowing duplicates because the same City field value can appear in many records in the tblCustomer table.

3. Click the right side of the **Indexed** property in the Field Properties pane, click **Yes (Duplicates OK)**, and then click the **Indexed** property text box to deselect the value. An index for the City field is created with duplicate values allowed. Setting the Indexed property automatically created the City index in the Indexes: tblCustomer dialog box. See Figure 9-34.

After creating the City index | Figure 9-34

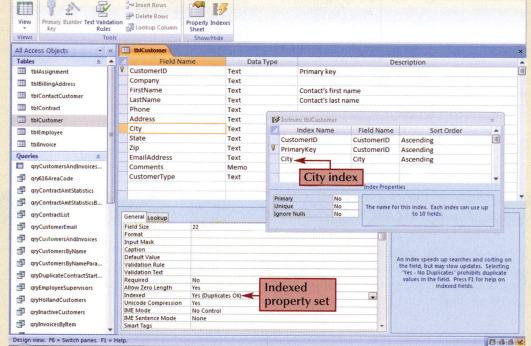

4. Close the dialog box, save your table design changes, and then close the table.

5. Close the Holland database, make a backup copy of the database, open the **Holland** database, compact and repair the database, close the database, and then exit Access.

The work you completed with table relationships, table and query joins, and indexes will make it much easier for Sarah and her staff to enter, retrieve, and view information in the Holland database.

1. What are the three types of relationships you can define between tables?
2. What is an entity subtype?
3. What is the difference between an inner join and an outer join?
4. What is a self-join?
5. What is an index?
6. Figure 9-35 lists the field names from two tables: tblDepartment and tblEmployee.

Figure 9-35

tblDepartment	tblEmployee
DepartmentID	EmployeeSSN
DepartmentName	EmployeeName
PhoneNumber	DepartmentID
	Salary
	SupervisorSSN

  a. What is the primary key for each table?
  b. What type of relationship exists between the two tables?
  c. Is an inner join possible between the two tables? If so, give one example of an inner join.
  d. Is an outer join possible between the two tables? If so, give one example of an outer join.
  e. Is a self-join possible for one of the two tables? If so, give one example of a self-join.

Review | **Tutorial Summary**

In this tutorial, you created action queries, including make-table, append, delete, and update queries. You learned about one-to-many, many-to-many, and one-to-one relationships, and inner joins, outer joins, and self-joins, and you defined table relationships and created a self-join. Finally, you viewed and created indexes.

Key Terms

action query	index	one-to-one relationship (1:1)
append query	inner join	outer join
delete query	make-table query	self-join
entity subtype	many-to-many	update query
history table	relationship (M:N)	

Practice	Review Assignments

Practice the skills you learned in the tutorial using the same case scenario.

Data File needed for the Review Assignments: Vendor.accdb

The Vendor database contains data about Belmont Landscapes' suppliers and their products, and the invoices from the suppliers and the payments made by Belmont Landscapes to the suppliers. The database also contains queries, forms, and reports. Sarah wants you to define relationships between the tables and to create some new queries for her. To help with these requests, complete the following steps:

1. Open the **Vendor** database located in the Level.03\Review folder provided with your Data Files.

2. Designate the Level.03\Review folder as a trusted folder. (*Note:* Check with your instructor before adding a new trusted location.)

3. Modify the first record in the **tblCompany** table datasheet by changing the ContactFirstName and ContactLastName field values to your first and last names. Close the table.

4. Define a many-to-many relationship between the tblInvoice and tblPayment tables, using the tblInvoicePayment table as the related table. Define a one-to-one relationship between the primary tblCompany table and the related tblCompanyCreditLine table. Select the referential integrity option and the cascade updates option for the relationships.

5. Create a make-table query based on the tblProduct table, selecting the ProductID, CompanyID, ProductType, Price, Unit, Material, and DiscountOffered fields, and selecting only those records that contain the word **steel** anywhere in the Material field value. Use **tblProductSpecial** as the new table name, and store the table in the current database. Run the query, and then close the query without saving it.

6. Create an append query based on the tblProduct table, selecting the ProductID, CompanyID, ProductType, Price, Unit, Material, and DiscountOffered fields and selecting only those records that contain the word **iron** anywhere in the Material field value. Append the records to the tblProductSpecial table, run the query, and then close the query without saving it.

7. Suppliers are offering a 10% discount off the regular price for all products in the tblProductSpecial table. Create an update query to select all records in the tblProductSpecial table, decrease the Price field values by 10%, run the query, and then close the query without saving it. (*Hint*: Use the expression **0.9*[Price]**.)

8. Create a delete query that deletes all records in the tblProductSpecial table in which the ProductType field value starts with the word **small**. Run the query, and then close the query without saving it. Open the tblProductSpecial table, resize all columns to their best fit, and then save and close the table.

9. Create an outer join between the tblCompany and tblInvoice tables, selecting all records from the tblCompany table and any matching records from the tblInvoice table. Display the CompanyName, City, Phone, ContactFirstName, and ContactLastName from the tblCustomer table, and the InvoiceDate and InvoiceAmt fields from the tblInvoice table. Save the query as **qryCustomerInvoiceOuterJoin**, and then run and close the query.

10. Open the **tblProductSpecial** table in Design view, specify the primary key, add an index for the CompanyID field, allowing duplicates, and then save and close the table.

11. Close the Vendor database without exiting Access, make a backup copy of the database, open the **Vendor** database, compact and repair the database, close the database, and then exit Access.

| Apply | **Case Problem 1** |

Apply the skills you learned in the tutorial to create action queries to manage the data for a small music school.

Data File needed for this Case Problem: Portland.accdb

Pine Hill Music School   Yuka Koyama owns and runs the Pine Hill Music School in Portland, Oregon. She and the qualified teachers who work for her offer instruction in voice, violin, cello, guitar, percussion, and other instruments. Yuka created an Access database named Portland to store data about students, teachers, contracts, instruments, and credit cards. The tblStudent table contains data about the students taking lessons, the tblTeacher table contains data about the lesson instructors, the tblCreditCard table contains data about the credit cards used to pay the monthly fees for lessons, the tblContract table contains data about the student contracts, the tblInstrument table contains data about the instruments students can rent, and the tblInstrumentContract table contains data about the contracts that have instrument rental agreements. Yuka asks you to define table relationships and create some new queries for her. To do so, complete the following steps:

1. Open the **Portland** database located in the Level.03\Case1 folder provided with your Data Files.
2. Designate the Level.03\Case1 folder as a trusted folder. (*Note:* Check with your instructor before adding a new trusted location.)
3. Change the first record in the **tblStudent** table datasheet so the First Name and Last Name columns contain your first and last names. Close the table.
4. Define a many-to-many relationship between the tblContract and tblInstrument tables, using the tblInstrumentContract table as the related table. Define a one-to-one relationship between the primary tblStudent table and the related tblCreditCard table. Select the referential integrity option and the cascade updates option for the relationships.
5. Create a make-table query based on the qryLessonsByTeacher query, selecting all fields from the query and only those records where the LessonType field value is **Cello**, **Piano**, **Violin**, or **Voice**. Use **tblSpecialLesson** as the new table name, and store the table in the current database. Run the query, and then close the query without saving it.
6. Create an append query based on the qryLessonsByTeacher query, selecting all fields and selecting only those records where the LessonType field value is **Guitar**. Append the records to the tblSpecialLesson table, run the query, and then close the query without saving it.
7. Create an update query to select all records in the tblSpecialLesson table where the LessonLength field value is **60**, changing the field value to **55**. Run the query, and then close the query without saving it.
8. Create a delete query that deletes all records in the tblSpecialLesson table in which the ContractEndDate field value is less than **7/1/2010**. Run the query, and then close the query without saving it. Open the **tblSpecialLesson** table, resize all columns to their best fit, and then save and close the table.
9. Create an outer join between the tblStudent and tblCreditCard tables, selecting all records from the tblStudent table and any matching records from the tblCreditCard table. Display the StudentID, FirstName, and LastName fields from the tblStudent table, and the FirstName, LastName, and CreditRelationship fields from the tblCreditCard table. Change the column names for the FirstName and LastName fields from the tblCreditCard table to **Credit First Name** and **Credit Last Name**. Save the query as **qryStudentCreditCardOuterJoin**, run the query, resize all columns to their best fit, and then save and close the query.

EXPLORE

10. Create a self-join based on the tblTeacher table with the TeacherID field as the primary key and the Coordinator field as the foreign key. Select the TeacherID, FirstName, LastName, and HireDate fields from the related table (the table that has the Coordinator field connected to the join line), and the FirstName and LastName fields from the primary table. The column names in the query recordset should be **Teacher ID**, **First Name**, **Last Name**, **Hire Date**, **Coordinator First Name**, and **Coordinator Last Name**, respectively. Use an outer join on the related table. Run the query, resize all columns to their best fit, save the query as **qryTeacherSelfJoin**, and then close the query.

11. Open the **tblSpecialLesson** table in Design view, add an index for the StudentID field, allowing duplicates, and adding an index for the LessonType field, allowing duplicates, and then save and close the table.

12. Close the Portland database without exiting Access, make a backup copy of the database, open the **Portland** database, compact and repair the database, close the database, and then exit Access.

Apply	**Case Problem 2**

Apply what you learned in the tutorial to manage the data for a new business in the health and fitness industry.

Data File needed for this Case Problem: Exercise.accdb

Parkhurst Health & Fitness Center   Martha Parkhurst owns and operates the Parkhurst Health & Fitness Center in Richmond, Virginia. The center offers the usual weight training equipment and fitness classes and offers specialized programs designed to meet the needs of athletes who participate in certain sports or physical activities. Martha created the Exercise database to maintain information about the members who have joined the center and the types of programs and classes the center offers. The tblClass table contains data about members and the scheduled classes they take, the tblCreditCard table contains data about members' credit cards, the tblMember table contains data about members, the tblProgram table contains data about training programs offered to members, and the tblSchedule table contains data about each scheduled class. The database also contains several other objects, including queries, forms, and reports. Martha wants you to define a many-to-many relationship between the tblMember and tblSchedule tables, create a one-to-one relationship between the tblMember and tblCreditCard tables, and create several new queries. To do so, complete the following steps:

1. Open the **Exercise** database located in the Level.03\Case2 folder provided with your Data Files.

2. Designate the Level.03\Case2 folder as a trusted folder. (*Note:* Check with your instructor before adding a new trusted location.)

3. Modify the first record in the **tblMember** table datasheet by changing the First Name and Last Name column values to your first and last names. Close the table.

4. Define a many-to-many relationship between the tblMember and tblSchedule tables, using the tblClass table as the related table. Define a one-to-one relationship between the primary tblMember table and the related tblCreditCard table. Select the referential integrity option and the cascade updates option for the relationships.

5. Create a make-table query based on the tblMember table, selecting all fields from the table except the Street, City, and State fields, and only those records where the MembershipStatus field value is **On Hold**. Use **tblSpecialMember** as the new table name, and store the table in the current database. Run the query, and then close the query without saving it.

6. Create an append query based on the tblMember table, selecting all fields from the table except the Street, City, and State fields, and selecting only those records where the MembershipStatus field value is **Inactive**. Append the records to the tblSpecialMember table, run the query, and then close the query without saving it.

7. Create an update query to select all records in the tblSpecialMember table in which the Zip field value is **23058**, changing the MemberComments field value to **Create a special program**. Run the query, and then close the query without saving it.

8. Create a delete query that deletes all records in the tblSpecialMember table where the ProgramID field value equals **207**. Run the query, and then close the query without saving it. Open the tblSpecialMember table, resize all columns to their best fit, and then save and close the table.

9. Create an outer join between the tblMember and tblCreditCard tables, selecting all records from the tblMember table and any matching records from the tblCreditCard table. Display all fields from the tblMember table, and the CardNum and ExpDate fields from the tblCreditCard table. Save the query as **qryMemberCreditCardOuterJoin**, and then run and close the query.

10. Add an index named JoinDate to the **tblMember** table, using the default property settings, delete the ProgramID index, and then save and close the table.

11. Close the Exercise database without exiting Access, make a backup copy of the database, open the **Exercise** database, compact and repair the database, close the database, and then exit Access.

Apply	**Case Problem 3**

Apply what you learned in the tutorial to manage a database that contains data about an agency that recycles household goods

Data File needed for this Case Problem: Salina.accdb

Rossi Recycling Group   The Rossi Recycling Group is a not-for-profit agency in Salina, Kansas that provides recycled household goods to needy people and families at no charge. Residents of Salina and surrounding communities donate cash and goods, such as appliances, furniture, and tools, to the Rossi Recycling Group. The group's volunteers then coordinate with local human services agencies to distribute the goods to those in need. The Rossi Recycling Group was established by Mary and Tom Rossi, who live on the outskirts of Salina on a small farm. Mary and Tom organize the volunteers to collect the goods and store the collected items in their barn for distribution. Tom has created an Access database to keep track of information about donors, their donations, and the human services agencies. The tblDonor table contains data about people who donate cash or goods, the tblAgency table contains data about the human services agencies, the tblDonation table contains data about the donations people make, the tblFacility table contains data about the buildings used to temporarily store donated goods, the tblStorage table contains data about the storage locations in the facilities, and the tblDonationStorage table contains data about the location of stored goods. The database also contains other objects, such as queries, forms, and reports. Tom wants you to define table relationships and create several new queries. To do so, you'll complete the following steps:

1. Open the **Salina** database located in the Level.03\Case3 folder provided with your Data Files.

2. Designate the Level.03\Case3 folder as a trusted folder. (*Note:* Check with your instructor before adding a new trusted location.)

3. Modify the first record in the **tblDonor** table datasheet by changing the Title, First Name, and Last Name column values to your title and name. Close the table.

4. Define a one-to-many relationship between the primary tblFacility table and the related tblStorage table. Define a many-to-many relationship between the tblDonation and tblStorage tables, using the tblDonationStorage table as the related table. Select the referential integrity option and the cascade updates option for the relationships.

5. Create a make-table query based on the tblDonation table, selecting all fields from the table and only those records where the DonationDesc field value is **Cash**. Use **tblSpecialDonation** as the new table name, and store the table in the current database. Run the query, and then close the query without saving it.

6. Create an append query based on the tblDonation table, selecting all fields from the table and selecting only those records where the DonationDesc field value is **Computer equipment**. Append the records to the **tblSpecialDonation** table, run the query, and then close the query without saving it.

7. Create an update query to select all records in the tblSpecialDonation table in which the AgencyID field value equals **Y68**, changing the AgencyID field value to **N57**. Run the query, and then close the query without saving it.

8. Create a delete query that deletes all records in the **tblSpecialDonation** table in which the DonationValue field value is less than **$50**. Run the query, and then close the query without saving it. Open the **tblSpecialDonation** table, resize all columns to their best fit, and then save and close the table.

9. Create an outer join between the tblAgency and tblDonation tables, selecting all records from the tblAgency table and any matching records from the tblDonation table. Display the AgencyID and AgencyName fields from the tblAgency table, and the DonationID, DonationDate, and DonationValue fields from the tblDonation table. Save the query as **qryAgencyDonationOuterJoin**, and then run and close the query.

10. Add an index named City to the **tblAgency** table, using the default property settings, delete the AgencyID index, and then save and close the table.

11. Close the Salina database without exiting Access, make a backup copy of the database, open the **Salina** database, compact and repair the database, close the database, and then exit Access.

Apply | Case Problem 4

Apply what you learned in the tutorial to manage the data for a luxury property rental company.

Data File needed for this Case Problem: Rentals.accdb

GEM Ultimate Vacations   Griffin and Emma MacElroy own and operate their own agency, GEM Ultimate Vacations, which specializes in locating and booking luxury rental properties in Europe and Africa. To track their guests, properties, and reservations, they created the Rentals database. The tblReservation table contains data about scheduled vacations by their client guests, the tblGuest table contains data about guests, the tblProperty table contains data about the available luxury rental properties, the tblPersonnel table contains data about the people who manage the properties, and the tblWorks table contains data about the management personnel assigned to each property. The database also contains several other objects, including queries, forms, and reports. Griffin and Emma want you to define a many-to-many relationship between the tblProperty and tblPersonnel tables, and to create several new queries. To do so, complete the following steps:

1. Open the **Rentals** database located in the Level.03\Case4 folder provided with your Data Files.

2. Designate the Level.03\Case4 folder as a trusted folder. (*Note:* Check with your instructor before adding a new trusted location.)

3. Modify the first record in the **tblGuest** table datasheet by changing the First Name and Last Name column values to your first and last names.

4. Define a many-to-many relationship between the tblProperty and tblPersonnel tables, using the tblWorks table as the related table. Select the referential integrity option and the cascade updates option for the relationships.

5. Create a make-table query based on the tblGuest and tblReservation tables, selecting the GuestFirstName, GuestLastName, and City fields from the tblGuest table and the StartDate, EndDate, and RentalRate fields from the tblReservation table. Select those records with a City field value of **Chicago**. Save the table as **tblSelectedReservation** in the current database. Run the query, and then close the query without saving it.

6. Create an append query based on the tblGuest and tblReservation tables, selecting the GuestFirstName, GuestLastName, and City fields from the tblGuest table and the StartDate, EndDate, and RentalRate fields from the tblReservation table. Select those records with a City field value of **Aurora** or **Evanston**, and append the selected records to the tblSelectedReservation table. Run the query, and then close the query without saving it.

7. Create a delete query that deletes all records from the tblSelectedReservation table in which the RentalRate field value is less than **$1,000**. Run the query, and then close the query without saving it. Open the **tblSelectedReservation** table, resize all columns to their best fit, and then save and close the table.

8. Create an outer join between the tblGuest and tblReservation tables, selecting all records from the tblGuest table and any matching records from the tblReservation table. Display the GuestFirstName, GuestLastName, and City fields from the tblGuest table, and the PropertyID and RentalRate fields from the tblReservation table. Save the query as **qryGuestReservationOuterJoin**, and then run and close the query.

⊕ EXPLORE
9. Create a self-join based on the tblPersonnel table with the PersonID field as the primary key and Manager as the foreign key. Select the PersonID, FirstName, and LastName fields from the related table (the table that has the Manager field connected to the join line), and the PersonID, FirstName, and LastName fields from the primary table. The column names in the query recordset should be **Person ID**, **First Name**, **Last Name**, **Manager ID**, **Manager First Name**, and **Manager Last Name**, respectively. Use an inner join. Run the query, resize all columns to their best fit, save the query as **qryPersonnelSelfJoin**, and then close the query.

⊕ EXPLORE
10. Add an index named **Location** to the **tblGuest** table that consists of the StateProv and City fields and uses the default property settings, delete the PostalCode index, and then save and close the table.

11. Close the Rentals database without exiting Access, make a backup copy of the database, open the **Rentals** database, compact and repair the database, close the database, and then exit Access.

| Create | **| Case Problem 5** |

Work with the skills you've learned, and explore some new skills, to manage and update a database for an Internet service provider.

Data File needed for this Case Problem: Always.accdb

Always Connected Everyday Chris and Pat Dixon own and manage Always Connected Everyday (ACE), a successful Internet service provider (ISP) in your area. ACE provides Internet access to residential and business customers and offers a variety of access plans, from dial-up and DSL to wireless. Within each type of service—dial-up, DSL, and wireless—ACE offers low-cost plans with either slower access speeds or fewer capabilities and more expensive plans with either higher access speeds or greater service and features.

To keep track of their business, Chris and Pat have developed the Always database. The database has two tables: the tblAccessPlan table contains data about the plans they offer commercial and residential customers, and the tblCustomer contains data about their customers. The database also contains several queries, forms, and reports.

Chris and Pat want you to add two new tables to the database to keep track of their business's service calls. Also, they want you to define a many-to-many relationship and to create several new queries. To help them with their requests, complete the following steps.

1. Open the **Always** database located in the Level.03\Case5 folder provided with your Data Files.
2. Designate the Level.03\Case5 folder as a trusted folder. (*Note:* Check with your instructor before adding a new trusted location.)
3. Use your first and last names for the first record in the **tblCustomer** table.
4. Create the following tables:
   a. The **tblService** table includes a unique service ID (AutoNumber data type), a service description, and a service rate (Currency data type).
   b. The **tblServiceCall** table includes a unique service call ID (AutoNumber data type), the customer account number, service ID, and service date.
5. Define a many-to-many relationship between the tblCustomer and tblService tables, using the tblServiceCall table as the related table. Select the referential integrity option and the cascade updates option for the relationships.
6. Design test data for the tblService and tblServiceCall tables, and then add the test data to the tables. Your tblService table should contain at least 10 records, and your tblServiceCall table should contain at least 12 records.
7. Create a make-table query based on the tblCustomer table, selecting the CustomerAcctNum, CompanyName, FirstName, LastName, City, and AccessPlanID fields from the table. Select those records with a City field value of **Blade** or **Drayton**. Save the table as **tblSelectedCustomer** in the current database. Run the query, and then close the query without saving it.
8. Create an append query based on the tblCustomer table, selecting the CustomerAcctNum, CompanyName, FirstName, LastName, City, and AccessPlanID fields from the table. Select those records with a City field value of **Brunson**, and append the selected records to the tblSelectedCustomer table. Run the query, and then close the query without saving it.
9. Create an update query to select all records in the tblSelectedCustomer table in which the AccessPlanID field value equals **4**, changing the AccessPlanID field value to **5**. Run the query, and then close the query without saving it.

10. Create a delete query that deletes all records from the tblSelectedCustomer table in which the AccessPlanID field value equals **7**. Run the query, and then close the query without saving it. Open the **tblSelectedCustomer** table, resize all columns to their best fit, and then save and close the table.

11. Create an outer join between the tblAccessPlan and tblCustomer tables, selecting all records from the tblAccessPlan table and any matching records from the tblCustomer table. Display the AccessPlanID, AccessPlan, and PlanMonthlyCost fields from the tblAccessPlan table, and the CompanyName, FirstName, and LastName fields from the tblCustomer table. Save the query as **qryPlanCustomerOuterJoin**, and then run and close the query.

⊕ **EXPLORE** 12. Add an index named **Zip** to the **tblCustomer** table, using the default property settings, delete the UserID index, and then save and close the table.

13. Close the Always database without exiting Access, make a backup copy of the database, open the **Always** database, compact and repair the database, close the database, and then exit Access.

| **Research** | **Internet Assignments** |

Use the Internet to find and work with data related to the topics presented in this tutorial.

The purpose of the Internet Assignments is to challenge you to find information on the Internet that you can use to work effectively with this software. The actual assignments are updated and maintained on the Course Technology Web site. Log on to the Internet and use your Web browser to go to the Student Online Companion for New Perspectives Office 2007 at **www.course.com/np/office2007**. Then navigate to the Internet Assignments for this tutorial.

| **Assess** | **SAM Assessment and Training** |

If you have a SAM user profile, you may have access to hands-on instruction, practice, and assessment of the skills covered in this tutorial. Log in to your SAM account (**http://sam2007.course.com**) to launch any assigned training activities or exams that relate to the skills covered in this tutorial.

Review | Quick Check Answers

Session 9.1

1. a query that adds, changes, or deletes multiple table records at a time
2. You should preview the results before running an action query to confirm that the correct records are selected. You do this by creating a select query version of the query.
3. A make-table query creates a new table from one or more existing tables. An append query adds records from existing tables or queries to the end of another table.
4. deletes a group of records from one or more tables based on one or more conditions
5. changes selected field values from selected records in one or more tables based on a condition
6. Access replaces the Show and Sort rows in the design grid with the Update To row.

Session 9.2

1. one-to-many (1:M), many-to-many (M:N), one-to-one (1:1)
2. a table whose primary key is a foreign key to a second table and whose fields are additional fields for the second table
3. An inner join selects records from two tables when they have matching values in the common field(s). An outer join selects all records from one table and records from a second table whose common field value(s) match records in the first table.
4. a join between a table and itself
5. a list that relates field values to the records that contain those field values
6. a. The primary key for the tblDepartment table is DepartmentID, and the primary key for the tblEmployee table is EmployeeSSN.
   b. There is a one-to-many relationship between the primary tblDepartment table and the related tblEmployee table.
   c. Yes, an inner join is possible based on the common field of DepartmentID. One example of an inner join is a list of all employees, including the EmployeeName, EmployeeSSN, and DepartmentName fields, in alphabetical order by EmployeeName.
   d. Yes, an outer join is possible. One example of an outer join is a list that shows all records from the tblDepartment table and their employees, even those departments without any employees currently assigned.
   e. Yes, a self-join is possible using the tblEmployee table. The SupervisorSSN field is a foreign key that matches the primary key field EmployeeSSN, so you could list all employees and the supervisor name for each employee.

Ending Data Files

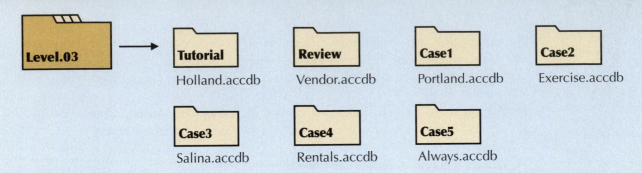

Level.03 → Tutorial
Holland.accdb

Review
Vendor.accdb

Case1
Portland.accdb

Case2
Exercise.accdb

Case3
Salina.accdb

Case4
Rentals.accdb

Case5
Always.accdb

Objectives

Session 10.1
- Design a switchboard and dialog box for a graphical user interface
- Run and add actions to macros
- Single step a macro
- Create a macro

Session 10.2
- Add a macro to a macro group
- Add a command button to a form
- Attach a macro to a command button
- Create a dialog box form
- Add a list box to a form
- Use an SQL statement to fill a list box with object names

Session 10.3
- Create a macro group
- Use the Switchboard Manager to create a switchboard
- Modify a switchboard

Automating Tasks with Macros

Creating a User Interface for the Holland Database

Case | Belmont Landscapes

At a recent office automation conference, Lucia Perez, the database developer for Belmont Landscapes, saw several database applications developed by database designers. The designers' applications used several advanced Access features to automate and control how a user interacts with Access. These features allowed the designers to create a custom user interface for a database. This interface made it much easier for inexperienced users to access the database, and it minimized the chance that an unauthorized user could change the design of any database objects.

Lucia would like to implement a similar user interface for the Holland database. She would like the interface to display a list of available forms, reports, and queries in the database that the user can select by clicking a command button or selecting from a list of choices. This interface will make it much easier for Belmont Landscapes' employees to use the Holland database, and it will reduce the chance that they will make undesirable changes to the design of the database objects.

Starting Data Files

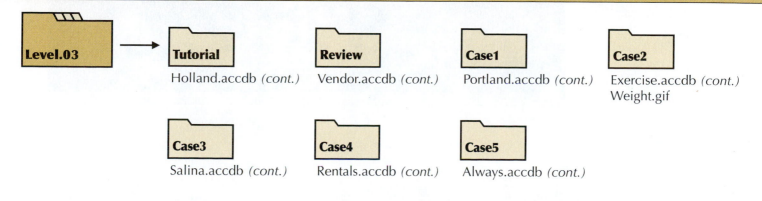

Level.03 → Tutorial — Holland.accdb *(cont.)*

Review — Vendor.accdb *(cont.)*

Case1 — Portland.accdb *(cont.)*

Case2 — Exercise.accdb *(cont.)* Weight.gif

Case3 — Salina.accdb *(cont.)*

Case4 — Rentals.accdb *(cont.)*

Case5 — Always.accdb *(cont.)*

Session 10.1

Implementing a Graphical User Interface

A **user interface** is what you see and use when you communicate with a computer program. All the programs developed for today's popular operating environments, such as Microsoft Windows, provide graphical user interfaces. A **graphical user interface** (**GUI**) (pronounced "gooey") displays windows, dialog boxes, command buttons, other controls, and graphical pictures, called icons, that you use to communicate with a program. All Microsoft Windows programs use a similar visual interface, so once you learn one program, you can easily learn another. Overall, a GUI benefits a user by simplifying work, improving productivity, and decreasing errors.

Lucia wants to provide an easier way to work with the Holland database. The type of user interface you need for working with a database is called a switchboard.

Switchboards

A **switchboard** is a form that appears when you open a database and that provides controlled access to the database's forms, reports, and queries. When a user opens the database, Access opens a switchboard from which the user can choose an option. When you create a switchboard, you are essentially creating a new interface, and it's up to you to decide what options you want to give the user. Figure 10-1 shows the finished Holland switchboard, which you will begin in this tutorial and finish in Tutorial 12.

Figure 10-1 | Holland switchboard

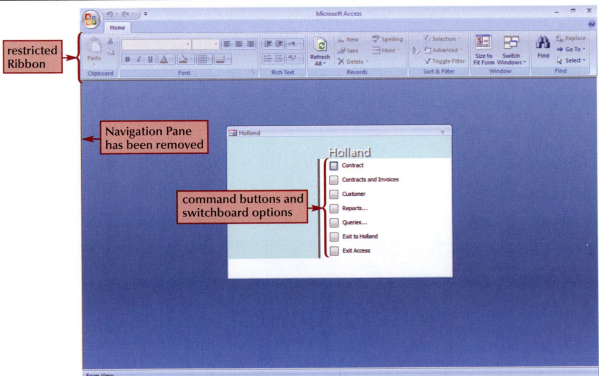

A typical switchboard provides the following items:

- Command buttons provide access to all the options available to the user. In the switch-board shown in Figure 10-1, for example, you can click a command button to open one of three forms (Contract, Contracts and Invoices, or Customer), to open another switchboard with report options, to open a list of available queries, to close the switch-board and leave the Holland database open, or to exit Access. When a selected form, query list, or report switchboard is closed, Access redisplays the Holland switchboard shown in Figure 10-1, so the user can choose the next option. In other words, the user starts and ends with the switchboard and navigates between options from the Holland switchboard.
- A restricted Ribbon contains only selected options on the Home tab that a user needs for manipulating data; there are no options for changing the database design.
- The Navigation Pane has been removed. Users can open only those objects that appear as options on the switchboard.
- Text boxes and pictures can be used to provide identification and visual appeal. Including a few attractively designed pictures and text boxes can help users understand the switchboard's functions. Keep in mind, however, that too many graphics can be confusing or distracting.

Using a Switchboard | InSight

A switchboard provides an attractive presentation for a user interface, but there are two more important reasons to use a switchboard. First, a switchboard lets you customize the organization of the user interface so you can make it easier for users to access commonly used objects quickly or restrict users to specific objects. Second, a switchboard prevents users from changing the design of tables, forms, queries, reports, and other objects. By removing the Navigation Pane and using a restricted Ribbon, you limit users to only those database features that you want them to use and prevent them from inadvertently or purposely changing the design of the objects in the database.

The Reports and Queries command buttons on the Holland switchboard include ellipses after the button names. These ellipses signify that a dialog box containing additional options opens when you click these command buttons. To display the list of available reports, you will create the Reports switchboard shown in Figure 10-2, which is similar in appearance to the Holland switchboard.

Reports switchboard | Figure 10-2

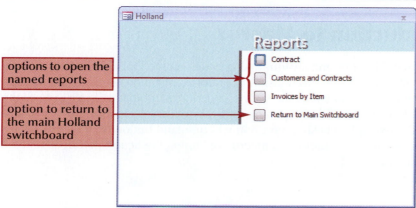

options to open the named reports

option to return to the main Holland switchboard

Because they are used frequently, the Reports switchboard contains command buttons to open the Contract, Customers and Contracts, and Invoices by Item reports. The switchboard also has a command button to return to the Holland switchboard, which is the main switchboard.

To display the list of available queries, you will create a custom dialog box.

Dialog Boxes

A **custom dialog box** is a form that resembles a dialog box, both in appearance and function. You use a custom dialog box to ask for user input, selection, or confirmation before an action is performed, such as running a query or printing a query datasheet. Figure 10-3 shows the finished Queries dialog box that you will create later in this tutorial for the Holland database user interface.

| Figure 10-3 | Queries dialog box |

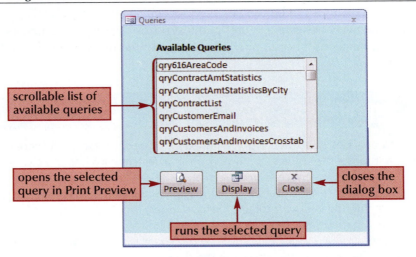

You will add a list box, which displays the queries available for selection, to the dialog box. You will also add three command buttons. A **command button** is a control on a form that starts an action, or a set of actions, when you click it. An **action** is an instruction to Access to perform an operation, such as opening a form or displaying a query in Print Preview. Command buttons can contain text, standard pictures available from Access, or pictures you supply, to indicate their functions. Clicking the Close command button in the dialog box returns you to the Holland switchboard. Clicking the Preview command button opens the selected query in Print Preview. Clicking the Display command button opens the selected query in Datasheet view.

Introduction to Macros

The command buttons and custom dialog boxes on the Holland switchboard gain their power from macros—and from Visual Basic for Applications code. A **macro** is an action, or a set of actions, that you want Access to perform automatically for you. Macros automate repetitive tasks, such as opening forms, printing selected form records, and running queries. For example, clicking the Contract command button on the Holland switchboard causes Access to perform a macro containing the action that opens the frmContract form.

Deciding When to Use Macros and VBA | InSight

Access lets you automate most tasks using either macros or **Visual Basic for Applications (VBA)**, the programming language for Microsoft Office programs. As a beginner, you will find it easier to use macros than to create programs using VBA. With macros, you simply select a series of actions from a list to create a macro that does what you want it to do. To use VBA, you need to understand the VBA command language well enough to be able to write your own code. VBA does provide advantages over using macros, such as better error-handling capabilities and making your application easier to change. Macros, however, are useful for small applications and for simple tasks, such as opening and closing objects. Additionally, you cannot use VBA to assign actions to a specific key or key combination or to open an application in a special way. For these types of actions, you must use macros.

When you use Access, over 50 actions are available; Figure 10-4 shows several frequently used Access actions.

Frequently used Access actions | **Figure 10-4**

Action	Description
Beep	Produces a beep tone through the computer's speakers
Close	Closes the specified window, or the active window if none is specified
FindRecord	Finds the first record, or the next record if the action is used again, that meets the specified criteria
Maximize	Maximizes the active window
MsgBox	Displays a message box containing a warning or informational message
OpenForm	Opens a form in Datasheet view, Design view, Form view, or Print Preview
Quit	Exits Microsoft Access
Restore	Restores a maximized or minimized window to its previous size
RunMacro	Runs a macro
SendKeys	Sends keystrokes to Microsoft Access or another active program

Running a Macro

Before you begin creating the Holland switchboard and its supporting macros, you'll run an existing macro, named mcrOpenContractForm, that Lucia created after she returned from the conference. You can reference and run a macro from within a form or report, or you can run an existing macro directly.

Tip

The prefix tag used to identify the macro object type is *mcr*. Read the Naming Conventions section in the appendix titled "Relational Databases and Database Design" for more information about naming conventions.

Directly Running an Existing Macro

- In the Macro window, click the Run button in the Tools group on the Design tab on the Ribbon.

or

- In the Macro group on the Database Tools tab on the Ribbon, click the Run Macro button, select the macro name in the Macro Name list box in the Run Macro dialog box, and then click the OK button.

or

- In the Macros group in the Navigation Pane, right-click the macro name, and then click Run on the shortcut menu.

You'll use the shortcut menu to run the mcrOpenContractForm macro.

To run the mcrOpenContractForm macro:

▶ 1. Start Access, and then open the **Holland** database in the Level.03\Tutorial folder provided with your Data Files.

   Trouble? If the Security Warning is displayed below the Ribbon, either the Holland database is not located in the Level.03\Tutorial folder or you did not designate that folder as a trusted folder. Make sure you opened the database in the Level.03\Tutorial folder, and make sure that it's a trusted folder.

▶ 2. Make sure the Navigation Pane is open, scroll down the Navigation Pane (if necessary), right-click **mcrOpenContractForm** in the Macros group, and then click **Run** on the shortcut menu. A message box opens. See Figure 10-5.

Figure 10-5 | **Using a macro action to open a message box**

Opening the message box is the first action Lucia added to the mcrOpenContractForm macro. A **message box** is a special type of dialog box that contains a message and a command button but no options. The message box remains on the screen until you click the OK button. This message box specifies that the next macro action will open the frmContract form. When you click the OK button, the message box closes, and the macro resumes with the next action. Lucia added this message box and other message boxes to the macro so that she could more easily observe the other actions. In most situations, you don't include message boxes between steps as Lucia did in this macro.

▶ 3. Click the **OK** button. The next two actions in the mcrOpenContractForm macro are performed: the frmContract form opens, and the second message box opens. See Figure 10-6.

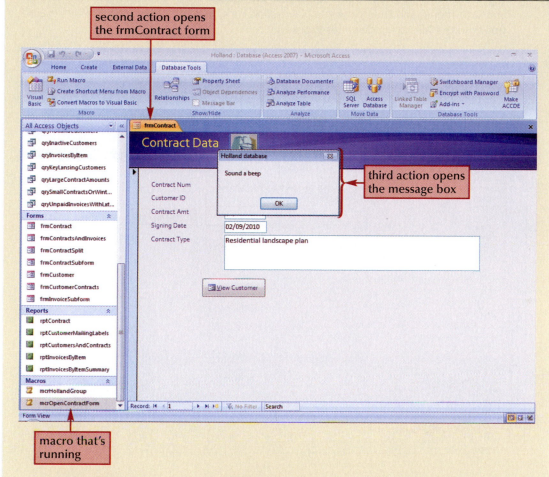

Second and third actions in the mcrOpenContractForm macro ◄ **Figure 10-6**

4. Click the **OK** button. A beep sounds, and the third message box opens. These are the fourth and fifth actions in the mcrOpenContractForm macro.

   Trouble? If your computer doesn't have speakers, you won't hear the beep sound. If you do hear the beep, its sound varies depending on your computer and its settings.

5. Click the **OK** button, and then drag the message title bar to the right so you can view the values in the form's text boxes. The frmContract form now displays record 17 for contract number 3035. These are the sixth and seventh actions in the mcrOpenContractForm macro.

6. Click the **OK** button. The frmContract form closes, and the mcrOpenContractForm macro ends.

Lucia suggests that you add some actions to the mcrOpenContractForm macro to learn about the Macro window and how to modify an existing macro.

Adding Actions to a Macro

To modify the mcrOpenContractForm macro, you need to open the macro in the Macro window.

To open the Macro window:

▶ 1. Right-click **mcrOpenContractForm** in the Navigation Pane, click **Design View** on the shortcut menu, and then close the Navigation Pane. The mcrOpenContractForm macro opens in the Macro window. See Figure 10-7.

Figure 10-7 | **Macro window**

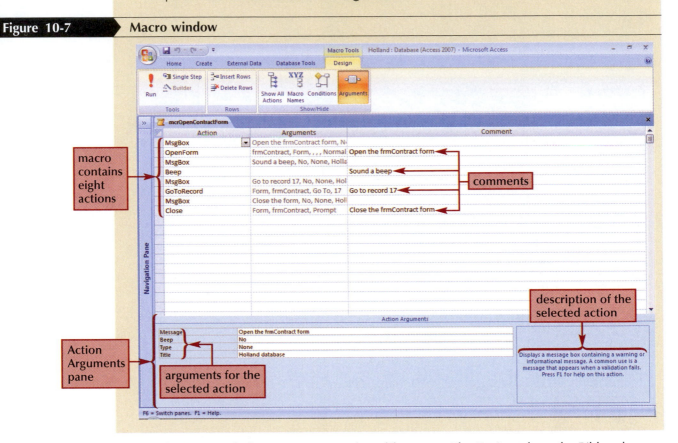

In the **Macro window**, you create and modify macros. The Design tab on the Ribbon has options that are specifically related to macros. The Macro window also includes an **Action column**, in which you select the actions you want Access to perform, an **Arguments column**, which displays the argument settings for the action, and a **Comment column**, in which you enter optional comments to document the specific actions. You usually don't enter comments for actions that are self-descriptive.

The first MsgBox action is the current action. Access documents the current action in the Action Arguments pane of the Macro window on the right; pressing the F1 key displays more detailed documentation about the action. On the left, Access lists the arguments associated with the current action. **Arguments** are additional facts Access needs to execute an action. The action for opening a message box, for example, needs the wording of the message to be displayed and the title bar's name as arguments.

You'll add two actions, the MsgBox and FindRecord actions, to the mcrOpenContractForm macro between the GoToRecord and the last MsgBox actions. For the FindRecord action, you'll find the record for ContractNum 3040. You use the **FindRecord action** to find the first record, or the next record if the action is used again, that meets the criteria specified by the FindRecord arguments.

The **MsgBox action** opens a message box and displays a warning or informational message. The macro containing a MsgBox action does not proceed to the next action until you click the OK button, so when you add this action to the mcrOpenContractForm macro, you'll have as much time as you need to read and react to the message box.

The MsgBox action requires four arguments: Message, Beep, Type, and Title, described as follows:

- Message contains the text that will appear in the message box when it is displayed.
- Beep is a Yes/No argument that specifies whether a beep will sound when the message box is opened.
- Type determines which icon, if any, appears in the message box to signify the critical level of the message. The icon choices are None (no icon), Critical (white X in a red ball), Warning? (white question mark in a blue balloon), Warning! (black exclamation point in a yellow triangle), and Information (white letter "I" in a blue balloon).
- Title contains the title that will appear in the message box title bar.

You'll now add the MsgBox and FindRecord actions to the mcrOpenContractForm macro.

To add two actions to the mcrOpenContractForm macro:

1. Right-click the **row selector** for the last MsgBox action, which is the seventh action, and then click **Insert Rows** on the shortcut menu. Access adds a new, blank row between the GoToRecord and MsgBox actions.

   Because you'll be adding two actions, you need to insert a second blank row.

2. Repeat Step 1 to add a second blank row.

   You'll add the MsgBox action to the first blank row.

3. Click the right side of the first blank row's **Action** box to display the list of actions, scroll down the list, and then click **MsgBox**. The list closes, MsgBox becomes the new action, four arguments for this action appear in the Action Arguments pane, and the two argument settings appear in the Arguments column.

   You'll enter values for the Message and Title arguments, change the Beep argument value from Yes to No, and retain the default Type argument value of None. The description appearing on the right side of the Action Arguments pane changes as you select different action arguments on the left. The description is a brief explanation of the current action argument. If you need a more detailed explanation, press the F1 key to open the Microsoft Office Access Help window and a page related to the current action argument. You can also use Help to learn about specific actions and their arguments, and about macros in general.

4. Press the **F6** key to move the insertion point to the Message box in the Action Arguments pane, type **Find contract 3040**, press the **Tab** key, click the **Beep** arrow, click **No**, press the **Tab** key twice, and then type **Holland database** in the Title box. See Figure 10-8.

Figure 10-8 After adding the MsgBox action

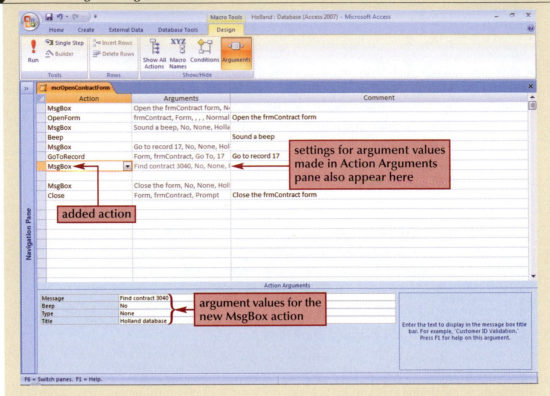

You'll now add the FindRecord action in the next row's Action column.

▶ **5.** Click the right side of the **Action** box for the second blank row you inserted, and then click **FindRecord** in the list. The FindRecord action has seven arguments in the Action Arguments pane.

You need to type a comment and to set the Find What argument to a value of 3040. You'll accept the defaults for the other action arguments.

▶ **6.** Press the **Tab** key twice, type **Find contract 3040** in the Comments box, press the **F6** key to move the insertion point to the **Find What** box, and then type **3040**.

When you create complicated macros with many actions, you'll find it useful to run through a macro one step at a time.

Single Stepping a Macro

Single stepping executes a macro one action at a time, pausing between actions. You use single stepping to make sure you have placed actions in the right order and with the correct arguments. If you have problems with a macro, you can use single stepping to find the cause of the problems and to determine their proper corrections. The Single Step button in the Tools group on the Design tab on the Ribbon is a toggle you use to turn single stepping on and off. Once you turn on single stepping, it stays on for all macros until you turn it off.

Single Stepping a Macro | Reference Window

- In the Macro window, click the Single Step button in the Tools group on the Design tab on the Ribbon.
- Click the Run button in the Tools group on the Design tab on the Ribbon.
- In the Macro Single Step dialog box, click the Step button to execute the next action, click the Stop All Macros button to stop the macro, or click the Continue button to execute all remaining actions in the macro and turn off single stepping.

To get a clearer view of the effects of the actions in the mcrOpenContractForm macro, you can single step through it. First, you need to save your macro changes.

To save the macro changes and then single step through it:

1. Click the **Save** button 🖫 on the Quick Access Toolbar to save your macro design changes.

2. Click the **Single Step** button in the Tools group on the Design tab to turn on single stepping.

3. Click the **Run** button in the Tools group on the Design tab. The Macro Single Step dialog box opens. See Figure 10-9.

Macro Single Step dialog box ◀ Figure 10-9

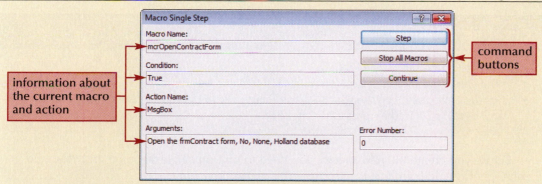

Trouble? If the first message box opens instead of the Macro Single Step dialog box, then you turned off single stepping in Step 2 when you clicked the button. Click the OK buttons to run the macro, and then repeat Steps 2 and 3.

When you single step through a macro, Access opens the Macro Single Step dialog box before performing each action. This dialog box shows the macro's name and the action's condition, name, and arguments. The action will be executed or not executed, depending on whether the condition is true or false. The three command buttons let you step through the macro one action at a time, stop all remaining macros and return to the Macro window, or continue by executing all remaining actions without pausing. If you click the Continue button, you also turn off single stepping.

4. Click the **Step** button. Access runs the first action (MsgBox). Because the MsgBox action pauses the macro, the Macro Single Step dialog box remains hidden until you click the OK button in the message box.

5. Click the **OK** button to close the message box. The Macro Single Step dialog box shows the macro's second action (OpenForm).

▶ 6. Click the **Step** button. Access runs the second action by opening the frmContract form and shows the macro's third action (MsgBox) in the Macro Single Step dialog box.

▶ 7. Click the **Step** button five more times, and click the **OK** button two more times, making sure you read the Macro Single Step dialog box carefully and observe the actions that occur. At this point, the message box you added is open (Find contract 3040), and record 17 is the current record in the frmContract form.

▶ 8. Click the **OK** button, and then click the **Step** button. The FindRecord action runs, record 20 for ContractNum 3040 is now the current record in the frmContract form, and the Macro Single Step dialog box shows the macro's last MsgBox action.

▶ 9. Click the **Step** button two more times, and click the **OK** button once. The Macro Single Step dialog box closes automatically after the last macro action is completed; the last macro action closes the frmContract form.

Lucia suggests you complete your practice with macros by creating a new macro and adding an action to a macro by dragging an object from the Navigation Pane.

Creating a Macro

You use the Macro window to create and modify macros. To create the new macro, you'll create a blank macro and then add the actions to it.

Reference Window | **Creating a Macro**

- Click the Create tab on the Ribbon.
- In the Other group on the Create tab, click the Macro button.
- Click the Save button on the Quick Access Toolbar, type the macro name in the Macro Name text box, and then press the Enter key.

Before you create the new macro, you need to turn off single stepping and close the mcrOpenContractForm macro.

To turn off single stepping and close the mcrOpenContractForm macro:

▶ 1. Click the **Single Step** button in the Tools group on the Design tab to turn off single stepping.

▶ 2. Click the **Close 'mcrOpenContractForm'** button ☒ to close the macro.

You'll create a practice macro named mcrOpenCustomerForm; this macro will contain actions to open and close the frmCustomer form.

To create the mcrOpenCustomerForm macro:

▶ 1. Click the **Create** tab on the Ribbon.

▶ 2. In the Other group on the Create tab, click the **Macro** button. The Macro window opens.

Because you can save a macro at any time, you'll save the blank macro immediately and name it mcrOpenCustomerForm.

▶ **3.** Click the **Save** button 🖫 on the Quick Access Toolbar. The Save As dialog box opens.

▶ **4.** Type **mcrOpenCustomerForm** in the Macro Name text box, and then press the **Enter** key.

Adding Actions by Dragging

Another way to add an action to a macro is by dragging an object from the Navigation Pane to a new row in the Macro window. When you do this, Access adds the appropriate action and specifies its default argument values. Figure 10-10 describes the effect of dragging each of the six Access objects to a new row in the Macro window. For example, dragging a table creates an OpenTable action that opens the table in Datasheet view and permits editing or updating. To use this dragging technique, be sure that the Macro window and Navigation Pane are both open.

Actions created by dragging objects from the Navigation Pane   Figure 10-10

Object Dragged	Action Created	Arguments and Their Default Values
Table	OpenTable	View: Datasheet Data Mode: Edit
Query	OpenQuery	View: Datasheet Data Mode: Edit
Form	OpenForm	View: Form Filter Name: none Where Condition: none Data Mode: none Window Mode: Normal
Report	OpenReport	View: Print Filter Name: none Where Condition: none Window Mode: Normal
Macro	RunMacro	Repeat Count: none Repeat Expression: none
Module	OpenModule	Procedure Name: none

Creating an Action by Dragging | Reference Window

- Make sure the Macro window and the Navigation Pane are open.
- Drag an object from the Navigation Pane to an Action box in the Macro window. Access adds the appropriate macro action and sets its arguments to their default values.

Next, you'll use the dragging technique to add actions that open and close the frmCustomer form.

To add actions using the dragging method:

▶ **1.** Open the Navigation Pane.

▶ **2.** Drag **frmCustomer** from the Forms list in the Navigation Pane to the first row's **Action** box in the Macro window. Access adds the OpenForm action for the frmCustomer form and sets the action arguments to their default values.

▶ **3.** Click the first row's **Comment** box, and then type **Open the frmCustomer form** in the Comment box.

Next, you'll add the MsgBox action so that you'll be able to see the opened frmCustomer form before you close it. You'll use the default values for the Beep and Type arguments.

▶ **4.** Press the **Tab** key, click the **Action** arrow, scroll down the list, and then click **MsgBox**.

▶ **5.** Press the **F6** key, type **Close the frmCustomer form** in the Message box, press the **Tab** key three times, and then type **Holland database** in the Title box.

You'll select Close as the final action in the mcrOpenCustomerForm macro, and set its arguments by dragging the frmCustomer form from the Navigation Pane to the Object Name box in the Action Arguments pane of the Macro window.

▶ **6.** Click the right side of the third row's **Action** box, click **Close**, press the **Tab** key twice, and then type **Close the frmCustomer form** in the Comment box.

▶ **7.** Drag **frmCustomer** from the Forms list in the Navigation Pane to the **Object Name** box in the Action Arguments pane of the Macro window. When you release the mouse button in the Object Name box, Access automatically sets the Object Type argument to Form and the Object Name argument to frmCustomer. See Figure 10-11.

| Figure 10-11 | Macro window with action arguments set by dragging |

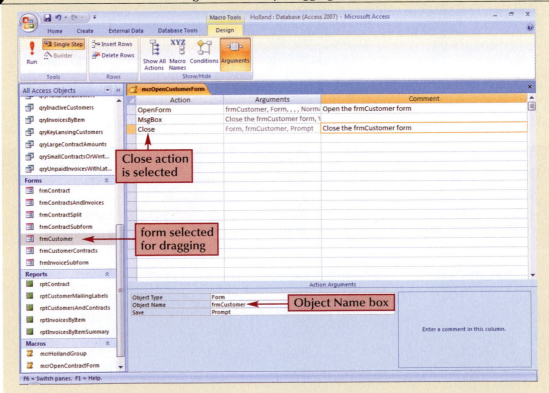

The macro is now completed, so you'll run it to be sure it is correct.

To run the mcrOpenCustomerForm macro:

1. Click the **Run** button in the Tools group on the Design tab on the Ribbon, and then click the **Yes** button to save the modified macro. Access runs the first two macro actions by opening the message box after opening the frmCustomer form. See Figure 10-12.

First two mcrOpenCustomerForm macro actions ◄ **Figure 10-12**

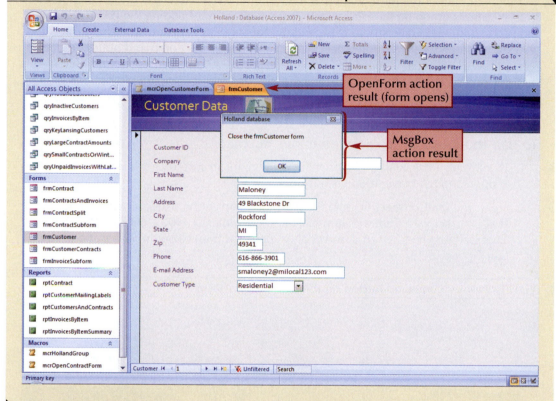

2. Click the **OK** button in the message box. Access closes the message box, and then runs the last macro action by closing the frmCustomer form.

3. Close the macro.

4. If you are not continuing on to the next session, close the Holland database, and then exit Access.

You've completed your initial work with macros. In the next session, you'll use a macro attached to a command button, and then you'll add a command button with an attached macro to the frmContractsAndInvoices form.

Session 10.1 Quick Check | Review

1. Define a switchboard and provide two reasons for using one.
2. What is a macro?
3. What is an action argument?
4. What does the MsgBox action do?
5. What are you trying to accomplish when you single step through a macro?

Session 10.2

Using a Command Button with an Attached Macro

Lucia created a macro that she associated with, or attached to, a command button on the frmContract form that you opened in Session 10.1. In Session 10.1, you learned how to create a macro with actions that open and close forms, find records, and open message boxes. You can also add a command button to a form to execute a set of actions. To add a command button to a form, you open the form in Design view and use the Button tool in the Controls group on the Design tab on the Ribbon. After adding the command button to the form and while still in Design view, you attach the macro with the desired actions to the command button. Then, when a user clicks the command button, the macro's actions are executed. Lucia asks you to use the View Customer command button on the frmContract form to see how the macro attaches to the command button, and then to view the macro.

To use the View Customer command button:

▶ 1. If you took a break after the previous session, make sure that the Holland database is open and the Navigation Pane is open.

▶ 2. Open the **frmContract** form in Form view to display the frmContract form for the first contract with ContractNum 3011 and CustomerID 11001, click **3011** in the ContractNum text box to deselect all values, and then close the Navigation Pane. See Figure 10-13.

| Figure 10-13 | View Customer command button on the frmContract form |

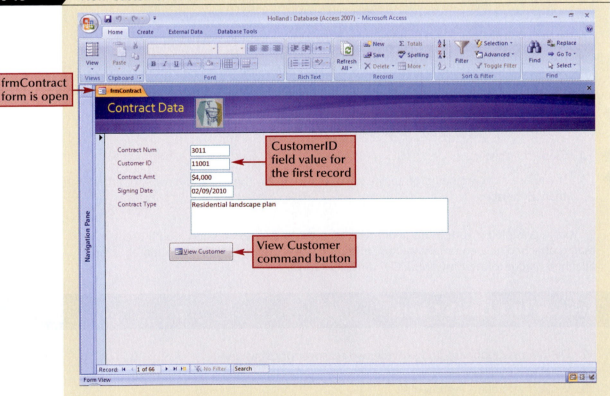

3. Click the **View Customer** command button, and then click **11001** in the CustomerID text box to deselect all values. The frmContract form remains open, and the frmCustomer form opens for CustomerID 11001. The frmCustomer form is the active form. See Figure 10-14.

After opening the frmCustomer form with the View Customer command button Figure 10-14

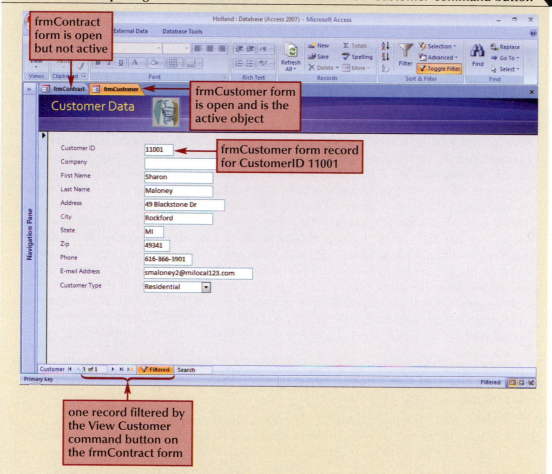

frmContract form is open but not active

frmCustomer form is open and is the active object

frmCustomer form record for CustomerID 11001

one record filtered by the View Customer command button on the frmContract form

Clicking the View Customer command button triggered an attached macro that opened the frmCustomer form. The record displayed in the frmCustomer form is for the customer (CustomerID 11001) that signed the contract displayed in the frmContract form. The text "Customer 1 of 1 (Filtered)" that appears around the navigation buttons in the frmCustomer form indicates that you can view only the record for CustomerID 11001 in the frmCustomer form at this point.

4. Close the frmCustomer form, click the **Next record** navigation button ▶ to move to record 2 in the frmContract form for ContractNum 3012 and CustomerID 11027, and then click the **View Customer** command button. The frmCustomer form opens for CustomerID 11027.

5. Close the frmCustomer form. The frmContract form is now the active object.

Clicking the View Customer command button is an event, and the opening of the frmCustomer form is controlled by setting an event property.

Events

An **event** is a state, condition, or occurrence detectable by Access. For example, events occur when you click a command button on a form, when you use the mouse to position the pointer on a form, or when you press a key to choose an option. In your work with Access, you've initiated hundreds of events on forms, controls, records, and reports without any special effort. For example, three form events are: Open, which occurs when you open a form; Activate, which occurs when the form becomes the active window; and Close, which occurs when you close a form and the form is removed from the screen. Each event has an associated event property. An **event property** specifies how an object responds when an event occurs. For example, each form has OnOpen, OnActivate, and OnClose event properties associated with Open, Activate, and Close events, respectively.

Event properties appear in the property sheet when you create forms and reports. Unlike most properties you've used previously in property sheets, event properties do not have an initial value. If an event property contains no value, it means the event property has not been set. In this case Access takes no *special action* when the associated event occurs. For example, if a form's OnOpen event property is not set and you open the form, then the Open event occurs (the form opens), and no *special action* occurs beyond the opening of the form. You can set an event property value to a macro name, and Access will execute the macro when the event occurs. For example, you could write a macro that automatically selects a particular field in a form when you open it. You can also create a group of statements using VBA code and set the event property value to the name of that group of statements. Access will then execute the group of statements, or **procedure**, when the event occurs. Such a procedure is called an **event procedure**.

When you clicked the View Customer command button on the frmContract form, the Click event occurred and triggered an attached macro. The View Customer command button contains an OnClick event property setting, which you will examine next.

To view the OnClick event property setting for the View Customer command button:

1. Switch to Design view, right-click the **View Customer** command button, click **Properties** on the shortcut menu to open the property sheet for the command button, and then click the **Event** tab (if necessary) in the property sheet.

2. Right-click the **On Click** box, click **Zoom** on the shortcut menu to open the Zoom dialog box, and then click to the right of the selected text to deselect it. See Figure 10-15.

Figure 10-15 | **Macro attached to the OnClick event property**

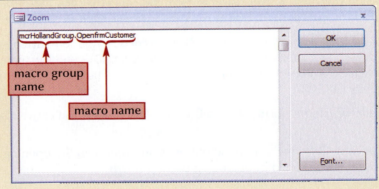

The OnClick event property value shown in the Zoom dialog box is *mcrHollandGroup.*
OpenfrmCustomer. This is an example of a reference to a macro in a macro group.

Macro Groups

Instead of creating several separate macros, you can combine them into a macro group.
A **macro group** is a macro that contains other macros. Macro groups allow you to con-
solidate related macros and to manage large numbers of macros. For the OnClick event
property value shown in Figure 10-15, mcrHollandGroup is the macro group name, and
OpenfrmCustomer is the macro name. A period separates the two names. When you
click the View Customer command button on the frmContract form, Access processes
the actions contained in the OpenfrmCustomer macro, which is located in the
mcrHollandGroup macro group.

You'll now close the Zoom dialog box, and then open the Macro window from the
property sheet.

To open the mcrHollandGroup macro in the Macro window:

▶ 1. Click the **Cancel** button in the Zoom dialog box to close it. The OnClick event property value is selected in the property sheet for the selected View Customer command button (named cmdViewCustomer, where *cmd* is a prefix tag to identify a
command button control), and the On Click box contains an arrow and Build button
to its right. See Figure 10-16.

| OnClick event property value for the View Customer command button | Figure 10-16 |

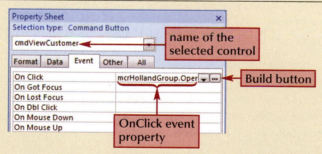

You click the On Click arrow if you want to change the current macro to a different
macro, and you click the Build button if you want to use the Macro window to view
or change the existing macro. The Build button is also called the **Macro Builder**
when you use it to work with macros.

▶ 2. Click the **Build** button [...] to the right of the On Click box, and then click the first
row's Macro Name column value to deselect all values. The Macro window opens
and displays the mcrHollandGroup macro. See Figure 10-17.

Figure 10-17 ▸ **Macro window displaying the mcrHollandGroup macro**

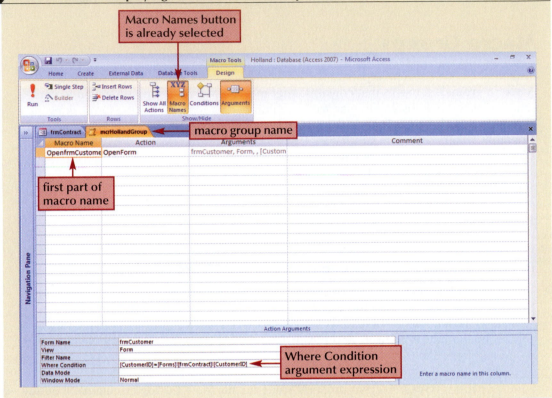

The **Macro Name column** in the Macro window lets you distinguish individual macros in a macro group. Each individual macro is identified by name in the Macro Name column. If a macro contains several actions, you leave the Macro Name column blank for actions added after the first one. To display or hide the Macro Name column, you click the Macro Names button in the Show/Hide group on the Design tab.

The OpenfrmCustomer macro consists of a single action, OpenForm, which opens the frmCustomer form (the Form Name argument value is frmCustomer). The other OpenForm action arguments are as follows:

- The **View argument** specifies the window view in which to open the object. For forms, you can specify Form, Design, Print Preview, Datasheet, PivotTable, PivotChart, or Layout view.

- The **Filter Name argument** specifies the name of a query, or a filter that was saved as a query, that will be used to sort or filter the object's records.

- The **Where Condition argument** specifies an expression or SQL statement that will be used to select records to display in the form. You'll learn more about SQL statements later in this tutorial.

- The **Data Mode argument** specifies the form's data-entry options. Allowable settings for this argument are Add (users can add new records but can't change or delete existing records), Edit (users can change and delete existing records and can add new records), and Read Only (users can only view records). Edit is the default setting, if you don't select an argument value.

- The **Window Mode argument** specifies the form's window characteristics. Allowable settings for this argument are Normal (the form opens as it normally would from the Navigation Pane), Hidden (the form opens but is not visible), Icon (the form opens minimized as a small title bar at the bottom of the screen), and Dialog (the form opens as a dialog box). Normal is the default setting.

The Where Condition argument value in Figure 10-17 specifies which record appears in the frmCustomer form when you open the form by clicking the View Customer button. The Where Condition argument value contains the expression *[CustomerID]=[Forms]! [frmContract]![CustomerID]*. In simple terms, the expression asks Access to find the record in the frmCustomer form with the same CustomerID as the current record in the frmContract form. The expression, however, is complex. The OpenForm action in the macro opens the frmCustomer form; the value *[CustomerID]* to the left of the equals sign determines which record will be displayed in the frmCustomer form. What is this CustomerID value? It's the same as (equals sign) the CustomerID that appears in the current frmContract form record (*[Forms]![frmContract]![CustomerID]* to the right of the equals sign). To the right of the equals sign, *[Forms]* identifies the object collection, such as forms or queries. Next, *[frmContract]* identifies the name of the specific object within the object collection—in this case, frmContract. Finally, *[CustomerID]* identifies the specific control within the specified object—in this case, the CustomerID field in the frmContract form.

Now that you've seen a macro that's attached to a command button, Lucia asks you to add a command button to the frmContractsAndInvoices form, and then to attach a new macro to the command button. Users want to be able to print the current record in the frmContractsAndInvoices form by clicking a command button on the form. Because the Macro window is already open for the mcrHollandGroup macro group, you'll add the new macro to it.

Adding a Macro to a Macro Group

To print the contents of a form's current record, normally you have to click the Office Button, point to Print, click Print, click Selected Record(s), and then click the OK button—a process that takes five steps and several seconds. Instead of following this process, you can create a command button on a form and a macro that prints the contents of a form's current record, and then attach the macro to the command button on the form. To print the form's current record, you'd simply click the command button.

First, you'll add a macro to the mcrHollandGroup macro group. You'll use the SelectObject and RunCommand actions for the new macro. The **SelectObject action** selects a specified object so that you can run an action that applies to the object. The **RunCommand action** selects and runs a command on the Ribbon or on the Office Button menu. The specific argument you'll use with the RunCommand action is the **PrintSelection argument**, which prints the selected form record. You'll use the macro name PrintSelectedRecord when you add it to the mcrHollandGroup macro group, so that the macro's function is obvious.

Reference Window | **Adding a Macro to a Macro Group**

- Open the macro group in the Macro window. (For a macro group, the Macro Names button is already selected.)
- Type the macro name in the Macro Name column, select the action in the Action column, type an optional comment in the Comment column, and then use the Action Arguments pane to set the macro's arguments.
- If the macro consists of more than one action, enter the remaining actions in the rows immediately following the first macro action. Leave the Macro Name column blank for each additional action.
- Save the macro group.

You'll now add the PrintSelectedRecord macro to the mcrHollandGroup macro group.

To add the PrintSelectedRecord macro to the mcrHollandGroup macro group:

▶ 1. Click the second row's **Macro Name** box, type **PrintSelectedRecord**, press the **Tab** key, click the **Action** arrow, scroll down the list, click **SelectObject**, press the **Tab** key twice, and then type **Print selected record** in the Comment column.

You need to set the Object Type and Object Name arguments.

Tip

You can also type the first few letters of the action until the full action name appears and then press the Tab key to select the action.

▶ 2. Press the **F6** key to switch to the Action Arguments pane, type **f** to select Form as the Object Type argument entry, press the **Tab** key, click the **Object Name** arrow, click **frmContractsAndInvoices** in the Object Name list, and then click the Object Name box to deselect all values. You've completed the first action. See Figure 10-18.

Figure 10-18 ▶ **Adding a new macro to a macro group**

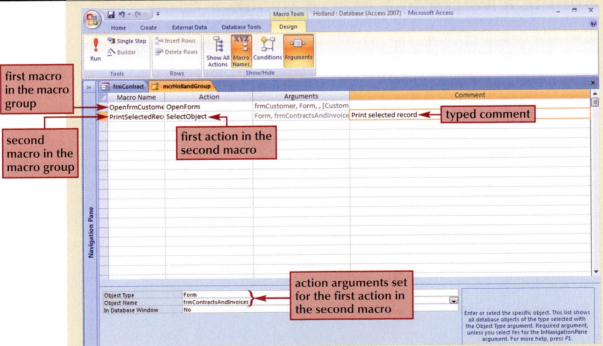

The SelectObject action selects the frmContractsAndInvoices form as the object to which the next action, the RunCommand action, will apply.

3. Click the right side of the third row's **Action** box, scroll down the list, click **RunCommand**, press the **F6** key to switch to the Action Arguments pane, click the **Command** arrow, scroll down the list, and then click **PrintSelection**.

You'll add a third action, the SelectObject action, to the macro to return control back to the frmContractsAndInvoices form after printing the selected record.

4. Click the right side of the fourth row's **Action** box, scroll down the list, click **SelectObject**, press the **F6** key to switch to the Action Arguments pane, set the Object Type argument to **Form**, set the Object Name argument to **frmContractsAndInvoices**, and then click the **Object Name** box to deselect all values. You've finished adding the three actions to the PrintSelectedRecord macro. See Figure 10-19.

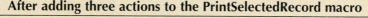

After adding three actions to the PrintSelectedRecord macro   Figure 10-19

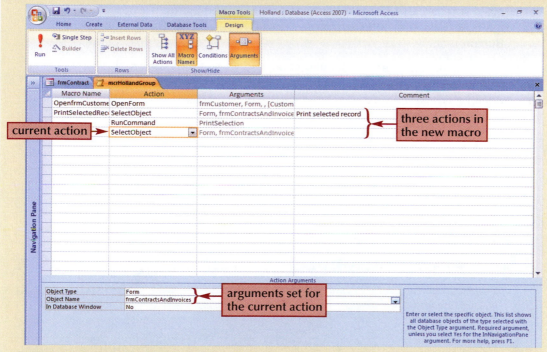

5. Save your macro design changes, and then close the macro. The frmContract form is the active object.

Because you've finished working with the frmContract form, you'll close the property sheet and the form.

6. Close the property sheet, and then close the form.

Next, you'll add a command button to the frmContractsAndInvoices form. After you attach the PrintSelectedRecord macro to the command button, you'll be able to click the command button to print the current frmContractsAndInvoices form record.

Adding a Command Button to a Form

In Design view for a form, you use the Button tool in the Controls group on the Design tab to add a command button to a form. If the Use Control Wizards tool is selected when you click the Button tool, the Command Button Wizard guides you through the process of adding the command button. Instead, you'll add the command button directly to the frmContractsAndInvoices form without using the wizard. Then you'll set the command button's properties using its property sheet.

To add a command button to the frmContractsAndInvoices form:

1. Open the Navigation Pane, open the **frmContractsAndInvoices** form in Design view, and then close the Navigation Pane.

2. Make sure the **Use Control Wizards** tool in the Controls group on the Design tab is not selected, and then in the Controls group on the Design tab, click the **Button** tool.

3. Move the pointer over the Detail section, and when the pointer's plus symbol (+) is positioned in the Detail section at the 5-inch mark on the horizontal ruler and the 2-inch mark on the vertical ruler, click the mouse button. Access adds a command button to the form. See Figure 10-20.

Figure 10-20	After adding a command button to the frmContractsAndInvoices form

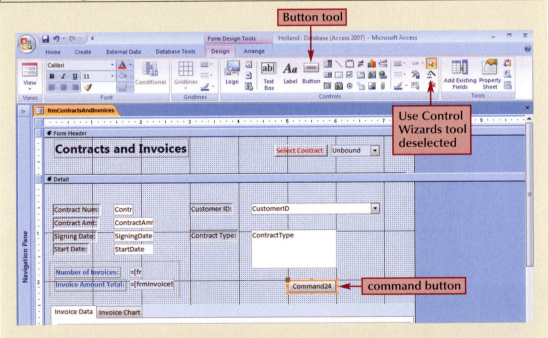

Trouble? If the Command Button Wizard dialog box opens, click the Cancel button to close it, and then click the Use Control Wizards tool in the Controls group on the Design tab to deselect it.

Trouble? The command button on your screen might show a different number in its label, depending on how you completed the previous steps. This difference will not affect the command button or macro. Just continue with the tutorial.

You can now attach the PrintSelectedRecord macro to the command button.

Attaching a Macro to a Command Button

You created the PrintSelectedRecord macro and added the command button to the frmContractsAndInvoices form. You'll attach the macro to the command button's OnClick property so that the macro is executed when the command button is clicked.

> **To attach the PrintSelectedRecord macro to the command button:**
>
> ▶ **1.** Make sure the command button is selected, and in the Tools group on the Design tab, click the **Property Sheet** button to open the property sheet, and then if necessary click the **Event** tab in the property sheet.
>
> ▶ **2.** Click the **On Click** arrow in the property sheet to display the macros list, and then click **mcrHollandGroup.PrintSelectedRecord**.
>
> **Trouble?** If your property sheet isn't wide enough to display the macro names, drag the left edge of the property sheet to the left to widen it.
>
> You can change the text that appears on the command button (also known as the command button's label or caption) by changing its Caption property, you can replace the text with a picture by setting its Picture property, or you can include both text and a picture. Lucia wants you to place a picture of a printer on the command button and to display text on the command button.
>
> ▶ **3.** Click the **Format** tab in the property sheet, click the **Picture** box, and then click the **Build** button [...] that appears next to the Picture box. The Picture Builder dialog box opens. See Figure 10-21.

Picture Builder dialog box ◀ **Figure 10-21**

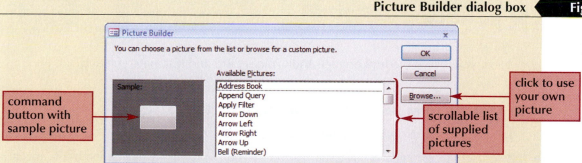

The Picture Builder dialog box contains an alphabetical list of pictures supplied with Access. You can scroll the list and select one of the pictures, or you can click the Browse button to select your own picture. When you select a picture, a sample of the picture appears on the command button in the Sample box on the left.

▶ **4.** Scroll down the Available Pictures list box, and then click **Printer**. A printer picture appears on the command button in the Sample box.

▶ **5.** Click the **OK** button. The Picture Builder dialog box closes, and the printer picture appears on the command button in the form.

▶ **6.** Click the **Caption** box in the property sheet, press the **F2** key to select the Caption property value, and then type **Print selected record**.

The **Picture Caption Arrangement property** specifies how a command button's Caption property value is arranged in relation to the picture placed on the command button. The choices are No Picture Caption, General, Top, Bottom, Left, and Right.

7. Click the **Picture Caption Arrangement** arrow, click **Bottom**, and then close the property sheet.

The command button is not tall enough or wide enough to display the picture and caption, so you'll resize it.

8. Use the middle-bottom sizing handle and the middle-right sizing handle to increase the width and height of the command button so it looks like the one shown in Figure 10-22.

Figure 10-22	Completed command button with displayed picture and caption

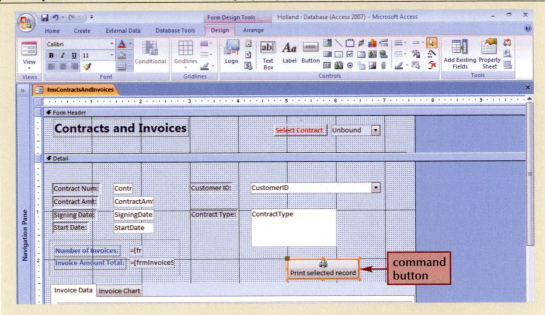

Next, you'll save the frmContractsAndInvoices form and test the command button.

To save the form and test the command button:

1. Save your form design changes, and then switch to Form view.

2. Click the **Last record** navigation button ▶| on the Contract navigation bar to move to the last contract record for ContractNum 3201.

3. Click the **Print selected record** command button on the form to open the Print dialog box, and then click the **OK** button to print the last contract record.

4. Close the form.

You've now completed your initial work with macros. Next, you'll start to develop the user interface for the Holland database. You'll create the dialog box to display the queries in the Holland database, use an SQL statement to select the values for the list box, and then add command buttons and a list box to the dialog box.

Creating the Queries Dialog Box Form

To create the user interface for the Holland database, you need to create the Holland and Reports switchboards and the Queries dialog box. First, you'll create the dialog box shown in Figure 10-23.

Queries dialog box form | Figure 10-23

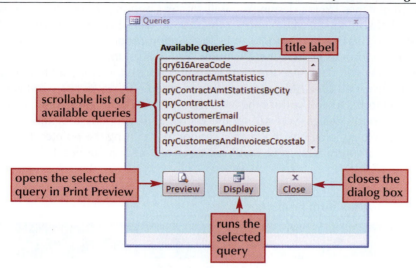

The Queries dialog box is actually a form that you will create. You'll add a label, a list box, and three command buttons to the form, and you'll enter an SQL statement that will provide the contents of the list box. (SQL is a language used with relational databases.) Sarah's staff will use the dialog box as follows:

- Scroll the list box until the desired query name is visible.
- Click the query name, and then click the command button with the Print Preview icon and the Preview caption to open the query in Print Preview. Alternatively, double-click the query name to open the query in Print Preview.
- Click the query name, and then click the command button with the Datasheet icon and the Display caption to display the query results.
- Click the Close button to close the dialog box and return to the Holland switchboard.

To create the Queries dialog box, you'll begin by creating a blank form. Because none of the form controls need data from a table or query (an SQL statement will supply the list box with its values), you will create an unbound form, or one that does not use a table or query as its source.

To create and save the frmQueriesDialogBox form:

▸ **1.** Click the **Create** tab on the Ribbon, and then in the Forms group on the Create tab, click the **Blank Form** button. Access opens the Form window in Layout view and opens the Field List pane.

▸ **2.** Close the Field List pane, and then click the **Design View** button 🖾 on the status bar to switch to Design view.

▸ **3.** Click the **Save** button 🖫 on the Quick Access Toolbar, type **frmQueriesDialogBox** in the Form Name text box, and then press the **Enter** key.

Before adding any controls to the form, you need to set the overall form properties so that the form matches Lucia's design. You will set the Caption property to Queries, which is the value that will appear in the form's title bar. You will also set the Shortcut Menu, Record Selectors, Navigation Buttons, and Close Button properties to No, because Lucia doesn't want the form to include these features. You will set the Auto Resize property to No so that Access will not resize the form when it is opened, thereby maintaining a consistent form size for all users. Also, Lucia wants to disable other Access windows until the user closes the form, so you will set the Modal property to Yes. Finally, after you have completed the form's design, you will set the Border Style property to Dialog so that the form will look like a dialog box that a user cannot resize using the pointer. Figure 10-24 shows the form property settings you will use to create the frmQueriesDialogBox form for Lucia.

Figure 10-24 ▶ **frmQueriesDialogBox form properties**

Property	Setting	Function
Auto Resize	No	Opens a form using the last saved size
Border Style	Dialog	Prevents a user from resizing the form
Caption	Queries	Value that appears in the form's title bar
Close Button	No	Disables the display of the Close button in the form's title bar
Modal	Yes	Disables other Access windows until a user closes the form
Navigation Buttons	No	Disables the display of navigation buttons on the bottom of the form
Record Selectors	No	Disables the display of a record selector on the left side of the form
Shortcut Menu	No	Disables the display of the shortcut menu if a user right-clicks the form

InSight | **Tabbed Documents Versus Overlapping Windows**

The default Access object window style is **tabbed documents**, which displays a single window with open objects organized with tabs; you click a tab to switch to the display of an open object. All open objects are the same size, no matter how much data they contain. Using tabbed documents is efficient for developing a database, but most professionally developed databases use overlapping windows for open objects instead of tabbed documents. **Overlapping windows** display each open object in a separate window that you can size to fit the displayed data and that you can arrange on the screen to overlap other open objects.

You'll change the window style to overlapping windows, and then you'll use the property sheet to set the form properties shown in Figure 10-24.

To change to overlapping windows and set the properties for the unbound form:

1. Click the **Office Button** 🔘, and then click the **Access Options** button. The Access Options dialog box opens.

2. In the left section of the dialog box, click **Current Database**, click the **Overlapping Windows** option button in the Application Options section, and then click the **OK** button. A message box opens advising you that you must close and reopen the database for the specified option to take effect.

3. Click the **OK** button, close the Holland database, open the **Holland** database, open the Navigation Pane, open the **frmQueriesDialogBox** in Design view, and then close the Navigation Pane. The frmQueriesDialogBox opens as an overlapping window instead of as a tabbed document. See Figure 10-25.

After changing the database to overlapping windows **Figure 10-25**

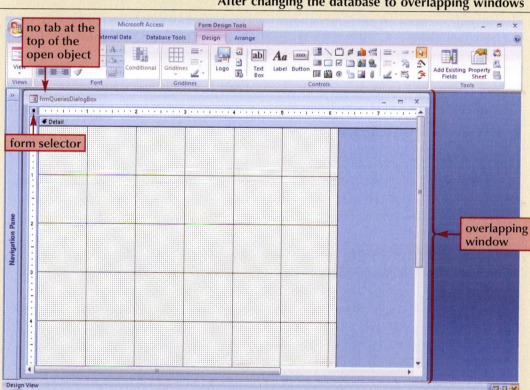

Trouble? If your form is sized differently from the one shown in Figure 10-25, resize your form until it matches the one in the figure.

Now you'll set the form properties for the unbound form.

4. Right-click the **form selector**, which is the box immediately to the left of the horizontal ruler in the Form window (see Figure 10-25), and the click **Properties** on the shortcut menu to open the form's property sheet.

5. If necessary, click the **Format** tab in the property sheet to display the Format page of the property sheet.

   You can now set the Caption property for the form. The Caption property value will appear in the title bar when the form is displayed.

▶ **6.** Click the **Caption** box, and then type **Queries**.

Next, you'll set the Record Selectors property so that a record selector will not be displayed on the left side of the form. Because the form does not display any records, there's no need to include a record selector.

▶ **7.** Double-click **Yes** in the Record Selectors box to change the property setting from Yes to No.

You'll now set the remaining form properties.

▶ **8.** Scrolling as necessary, set the Navigation Buttons property to **No**, set the Auto Resize property to **No**, set the Close Button property to **No**, click the **Other** tab in the property sheet, set the Modal property to **Yes**, and then set the Shortcut Menu property to **No**.

▶ **9.** Close the property sheet, and then save your form design changes.

Now that you have set the form's properties, you can add a label and a list box to it. The label will identify the list box for the user, and the list box will display the list of queries in the Holland database. You will not use the Control Wizards tool for the list box, because you'll be using an SQL statement to provide the query names for the list box.

Adding a List Box to a Form

A **list box** is a control that displays a list of values. The list box in the frmQueriesDialogBox form will display the list of queries that the user can preview or view. Clicking the name of a query selects it, and then the user can click one of the command buttons to preview or view the query. Double-clicking a query name in the list box will open the query in Print Preview.

Reference Window | **Adding a List Box to a Form**

- Switch to Design view, if necessary.
- If necessary, click the Use Control Wizards button in the Controls group on the Design tab to deselect it.
- Click the List Box tool in the Controls group on the Design tab.
- Position the pointer's plus symbol where you want the place the upper-left corner of the list box, and then click the mouse button.
- If you use the List Box Wizard (the Use Control Wizards button is selected), complete the dialog boxes to choose the source of the list, select the fields to appear in the list box, size the columns, select the field that will provide the data for the field in the main form, choose to remember the value for later use or store it in a field, and then enter the value to appear in the list box label.
- If you do not use the List Box Wizard, set the Row Source property and size the list box.

First, you'll add the label "Available Queries" to the form. Then you'll add the list box to display the list of queries in the database.

To add the label to the form:

1. In the Controls group on the Design tab on the Ribbon, click the **Label** tool.

2. Position the pointer in the Detail section; when the pointer's plus symbol is positioned at the 0.5-inch mark on the horizontal ruler and the 0.25-inch mark on the vertical ruler, click the mouse button. A small label box containing an insertion point opens in the form.

3. Type **Available Queries** and then press the **Enter** key.

   Lucia wants the label to stand out more, so you'll make the label bold, and then resize the label box.

4. In the Font group on the Design tab, click the **Bold** button **B**, right-click the label box to open the shortcut menu, point to **Size**, and then click **To Fit**.

Now you can add the list box to the form.

To add the list box to the form:

1. Make sure the **Use Control Wizards** tool ▨ in the Controls group on the Design tab is not selected, and then in the Controls group on the Design tab, click the **List Box** tool ▤ .

2. Move the pointer over the Detail section, and when the pointer's plus symbol (+) is positioned in the row of grid dots below the left edge of the Available Queries label box, click the mouse button. Access adds a list box to the form. See Figure 10-26.

Form design after adding the label and the list box   ◀ Figure 10-26

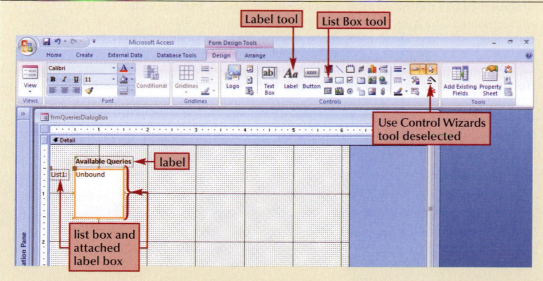

Trouble? If your list box is sized or positioned differently, resize it or move it until it matches the list box shown in Figure 10-26.

You can now save the form and then check your progress by switching to Form view.

3. Save your form design changes, and then switch to Form view. See Figure 10-27.

Figure 10-27 **frmQueriesDialogBox form displayed in Form view**

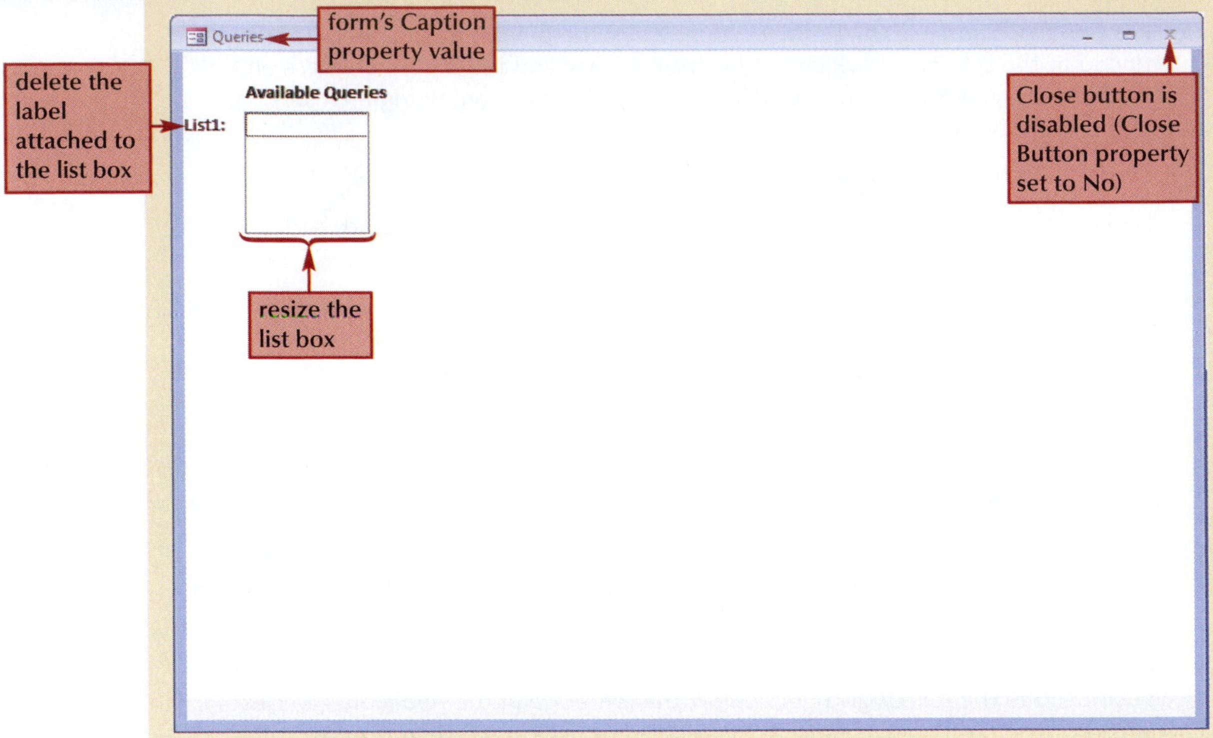

After viewing the form, Lucia asks you to make two changes to it. Because the form already includes the label "Available Queries," the label attached to the list box is unnecessary. Lucia asks you to delete this label. She'd also like you to resize the list box by making it wider so that it will accommodate the list of queries better.

To delete the label attached to the list box and resize the list box:

▶ **1.** Switch to Design view.

▶ **2.** Right-click the label attached to the list box to open the shortcut menu, and then click **Cut** to delete it.

▶ **3.** Click the list box to select it.

▶ **4.** Use the middle-right sizing handle to drag the right border of the list box to the 3-inch mark on the horizontal ruler, and then save your form design changes.

You now can enter the SQL statement that will provide the query names for the list box.

Using SQL

SQL (Structured Query Language) is a standard language used in querying, updating, and managing relational databases. Every full-featured relational DBMS has its own version of the current standard SQL. If you learn SQL for one relational DBMS, it's a relatively easy task to begin using SQL for other relational DBMSs. When you work with two or more relational DBMSs, which is the case in most companies, you'll learn that few differences exist among the various SQL versions.

Much of what Access accomplishes behind the scenes is done with SQL. Whenever you create a query, for example, Access automatically constructs an equivalent SQL statement. When you save a query, Access saves the SQL statement version of the query.

Viewing an SQL Statement for a Query

When you are working in Design view or viewing a query recordset, you can see the SQL statement that is equivalent to your query by switching to SQL view.

Viewing an SQL Statement for a Query | Reference Window

- Open the query in Datasheet view or Design view.
- Click the SQL View button on the status bar, or right-click the query tab (or title bar) and click SQL View on the shortcut menu, or click the View arrow in the Views group on the Ribbon and click SQL View.

Next, you'll examine the SQL statements that are equivalent to two existing queries: qryContractList and qryCustomersAndInvoices.

To view the SQL statement for the qryContractList query:

▶ **1.** Open the Navigation Pane, open the **qryContractList** query datasheet, and then close the Navigation Pane. The query displays 66 records from the tblContract table. The columns displayed are Contract Num, Contract Amt, and Contract Type.

▶ **2.** Right-click the **qryContractList** title bar to open the shortcut menu, click **SQL View** to open the SQL window, and then click an unused portion of the SQL window to deselect the SQL statement. See Figure 10-28.

SQL window for the qryContractList query | Figure 10-28

Trouble? The SQL statement might look different on your screen if your window is sized differently from the window shown in Figure 10-28.

SQL uses the **SELECT statement** to define what data it retrieves from a database and how it presents the data. For the work you've done so far, the options on the Ribbon, in dialog boxes, and on the property sheet have sufficed. If you learn SQL to the point where you can use it efficiently, you will be able to enter your own SELECT and other SQL statements in the SQL window. If you work with more complicated databases, you might find that you need the extra power of the SQL language to implement your database strategies fully.

The rules that SQL uses to construct a statement similar to the SELECT statement shown in Figure 10-28 are summarized as follows:

- The basic form of an SQL SELECT statement is: SELECT-FROM-WHERE-ORDER BY. After SELECT, list the fields you want to display. After FROM, list the tables used in the query. After WHERE, list the selection criteria. After ORDER BY, list the sort fields.
- If a field name includes a space or special symbol, enclose the field name in brackets. Because the Holland database does not use field names with spaces or special symbols, you don't have to enclose its field names in brackets. However, if you used a database that had field names such as *Contract Type*, then you would use [Contract Type] in an SQL statement.
- Precede a field name with the name of its table by connecting the table name to the field name with a period. For example, you would enter the ContractNum field in the tblContract table as *tblContract.ContractNum*.
- Separate field names and table names by commas, and end the statement with a semicolon.

The SQL statement shown in Figure 10-28 selects the ContractNum, ContractAmt, and ContractType fields from the tblContract table; the records are sorted in ascending order by the ContractNum field. The SQL statement does not contain a WHERE clause so all records are included in the recordset.

You can enter or change SQL statements directly in the SQL window. If you enter an SQL statement and then switch to Design view, you will see its equivalent in the design grid.

Next, you'll examine the SQL statement for the qryCustomersAndInvoices query.

To view the SQL statement for the qryCustomersAndInvoices query:

1. Close the qryContractList query, open the Navigation Pane, open the **qryCustomersAndInvoices** query in Design view, and then close the Navigation Pane. The query selects data from the tblCustomer, tblContract, and tblInvoice tables and does not sort the records. The fields included in the query design are CustomerID, Company, FirstName, LastName, City, InvoiceAmt, and InvoicePaid.

2. In the Results group on the Design tab, click the **View** arrow, click **SQL View** to open the SQL window, and then click an unused portion of the SQL window to deselect the SQL statement. See Figure 10-29.

Figure 10-29 | SQL window for the qryCustomersAndInvoices query

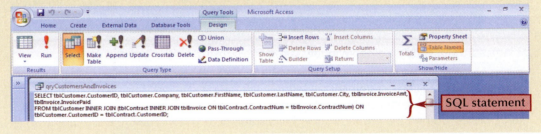

The SELECT statement for this query is similar to the one shown in Figure 10-28, except for the INNER JOIN clause. The INNER JOIN clause selects records from the two tables only when the records have the same value in the common field that links the tables. The syntax for this clause is to type INNER JOIN between the two table names, followed by ON, and then followed by the names of the fields serving as the common field, connected by an equals sign. (Access uses the ON clause here instead of the standard SQL WHERE clause.)

The SQL SELECT statements mirror the query options you viewed in Design view. In effect, every choice you make in Design view is reflected as part of the SQL SELECT statement. Viewing the SQL statements generated from queries that you design is an effective way to begin learning SQL. Also, if you select an SQL keyword, such as SELECT or ORDER BY, in the SQL window and press the F1 key, Access displays context-sensitive Help for that keyword.

To close the query and return to the frmQueriesDialogBox form:

▶ **1.** Close the query. The frmQueriesDialogBox form is now the active object and is open in Design view.

You now can enter the SQL statement that will provide the query names for the list box.

Using an SQL Statement for a List Box

You'll use a SELECT statement to retrieve the list of query names from one of the Access system tables. **System tables** are special tables maintained by Access that store information about the characteristics of a database and about the structure of the objects in a database. Although system tables do not appear in the Database window's Tables list box, you can retrieve information from system tables using SELECT statements. One of the system tables, the **MSysObjects table**, keeps track of the names, types, and other characteristics of every object in a database. The Name and Type fields are the two MSysObjects table fields you'll use in the SELECT statement. The Name field contains a query name when the Type field value is 5, as shown in Figure 10-30.

MSysObjects table Type field values ◀ **Figure 10-30**

Object Type	Type Field Value in MSysObjects Table
Table	1
Query	5
Form	-32768
Report	-32764
Macro	-32766
Module	-32761

Access creates its own queries to handle many tasks for you; each of these queries has a name that begins with the tilde (~) character. Because you want to exclude these special system queries from the list box, you'll also need to use the Left function in your SELECT statement. The **Left function** provides the first character(s) in a text string. The format of the Left function is Left(text string, number of characters). You'll use Left([Name],1) to retrieve the first character of the Name field. To include only those queries whose names do not begin with the ~ character, you'll use the expression

Left([Name],1)<>"~". In this expression, the <> operator is the not equal operator. Access interprets this expression as "the first character of the Name field does not equal the ~ character." Figure 10-31 shows the Zoom dialog box, which contains the complete SELECT statement that you will use to select the list of query names.

Figure 10-31   **SELECT statement for the list box**

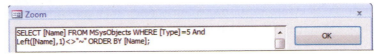

The **Row Source property** specifies the data source, such as a table, a query, or an SQL statement, to a list box and to other controls, so you'll enter the SELECT statement as the value for the list box's Row Source property.

To set the Row Source property for the list box:

1. Right-click the list box to open the shortcut menu, click **Properties** to open the property sheet, and then click the **Data** tab (if necessary).

2. Right-click the **Row Source** box to open the shortcut menu, and then click **Zoom**. The Zoom dialog box opens.

3. Type **SELECT [Name] FROM MSysObjects WHERE [Type]=5 And Left([Name],1)<>"~" ORDER BY [Name];** in the Zoom dialog box (be sure to type the semicolon at the end of the statement), and then click the **OK** button.

4. Close the property sheet, save your form design changes, and then switch to Form view. The queries in the database now appear in alphabetical order in the list box. See Figure 10-32.

Figure 10-32   **Completed list box**

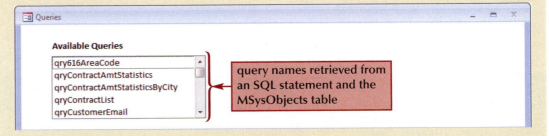

Trouble? If a syntax-error message appears, click the OK button, switch to Design view, right-click the list box, click Properties, right-click the Row Source box, and then click Zoom. Correct the SELECT statement until it's the same as the statement shown in Figure 10-31, click the OK button, and then repeat Step 4.

You can now add command buttons to the form.

Adding Command Buttons to a Form

First, you will add the Preview command button to the form. You can add a command button to a form by placing the button directly on the form or by using the Use Control Wizards tool. If you use the Use Control Wizards tool, you can attach a standard Access action (such as opening a specific query or closing a window) or a macro to the button.

You cannot use a standard Access action for this command button, because the query to be opened will depend on the query the user has selected in the list box. Instead, you will add the command button to the form now and attach VBA code to it in Tutorial 11. First, you'll increase the height of the list box.

To add the Preview command button to the form:

1. Switch to Design view, click the list box to select it, and then use the middle-bottom sizing handle to drag the bottom border down to the 2-inch mark on the vertical ruler.

2. Make sure the **Use Control Wizards** tool ⬆ in the Controls group on the Design tab is deselected, and then in the Controls group on the Design tab, click the **Button** tool.

3. Position the pointer in the Detail section; when the pointer's plus symbol is positioned at the 2.25-inch mark on the vertical ruler and one grid dot from the left edge of the list box, click the mouse button. Access adds a command button to the form.

4. If necessary, open the property sheet for the command button.

   You can now change the default text that appears on the command button to the word "Preview" and add the Print Preview picture.

5. Click the **Format** tab (if necessary), set the Caption property to **Preview**, click the **Picture** box, and then click the **Build** button ⌗ to the right of the Picture box. The Picture Builder dialog box opens.

6. Scroll down the Available Pictures list box, and then click **Preview**. A Print Preview picture appears on the command button in the Sample box.

7. Click the **OK** button to close the Picture Builder dialog box and to place the Print Preview picture on the command button.

8. Click the **Picture Caption Arrangement** box and then click its arrow, click **Bottom**, and then close the property sheet.

9. Use the middle-bottom sizing handle and the middle-right sizing handle to increase the height and decrease the width of the command button, and then deselect the command button. See Figure 10-33.

Figure 10-33 After adding the Preview command button to the form

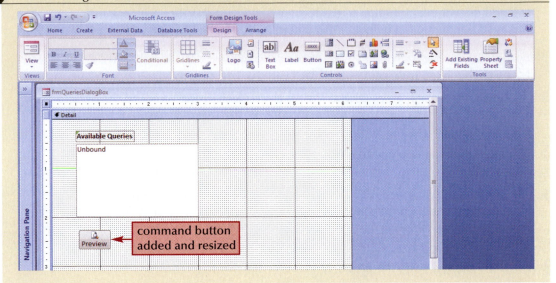

Instead of repeating the steps to add the command button for viewing a query record-set, you can copy the first command button and paste it in the Detail section. After moving the copied button into position, you can change the text and picture on it.

To add the Display command button to the form:

▶ **1.** Right-click the **Preview** command button, and then click **Copy** on the shortcut menu.

▶ **2.** Right-click the **Detail** section bar, and then click **Paste** on the shortcut menu. Access adds a copy of the command button in the upper-left corner of the Detail section.

▶ **3.** Move the new command button into position to the right of the original command button, and then deselect all controls. See Figure 10-34.

After adding and repositioning a copy of the command button   Figure 10-34

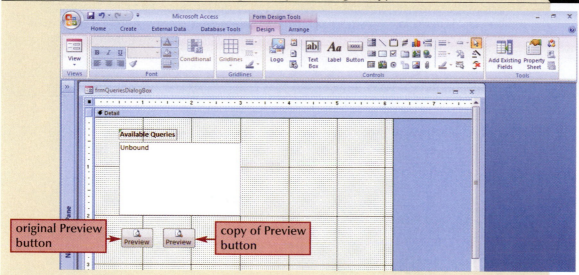

original Preview button

copy of Preview button

▶ **4.** Open the property sheet for the new command button, set the Caption property to **Display**, and then set the Picture property to the **MS Access Query**.

▶ **5.** Close the property sheet, and then save your form design changes.

You can now add the final command button using control wizards. The Close button will close the dialog box when the user clicks it.

Adding a Command Button to a Form Using Control Wizards | Reference Window

- If necessary, click the Use Control Wizards tool in the Controls group on the Design tab so that it is selected.
- Click the Button tool in the Controls group on the Design tab.
- Position the pointer's plus symbol where you want to place the upper-left corner of the command button, and then click the mouse button.
- Complete the Command Button Wizard dialog boxes to select the action category and the action for the command button, enter the text to display on the command button or select a picture for the button, and then enter a name for the button.

To define the Close button, you'll use the Control Wizards tool, because the tool automatically attaches the correct macro (for closing the frmQueriesDialogBox form) to the command button.

To add the Close command button to the form using the Control Wizards tool:

▶ **1.** Click the **Use Control Wizards** tool 🔧 in the Controls group on the Design tab to select it.

> **Tip**
>
> Standard operations, such as opening and closing forms, are good candidates for using the Control Wizards tool when you add command buttons to forms.

> 2. Click the **Button** tool in the Controls group on the Design tab, position the pointer's plus symbol at the 2.25-inch mark on the vertical ruler and approximately five grid dots to the right of the Display command button, and then click the mouse button. Access adds a command button to the form and opens the first Command Button Wizard dialog box. The sample box shows how the command button will appear. See Figure 10-35.

Figure 10-35 | First Command Button Wizard dialog box

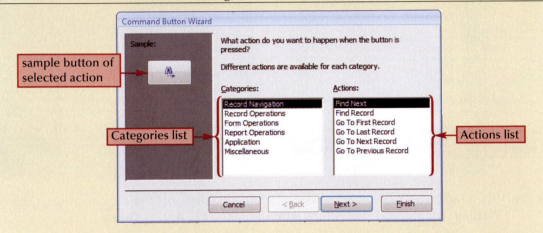

You'll now select the command that will be attached to the command button. The dialog box form must close when the user clicks the Close button, so you'll select the Close Form action in the Form Operations category for this button.

> 3. Click **Form Operations** in the Categories list box, click **Close Form** in the Actions list box, and then click the **Next** button. Access opens the next Command Button Wizard dialog box, in which you specify the text or picture you want to appear on the button. In this case, Lucia wants the button to display the word "Close" and a Close Window picture. You'll specify the picture now and set the Caption property after the wizard ends.

> 4. Click the **Show All Pictures** check box, scroll the **Picture** list box, and then click **Close Window**. A sample of the Close Window picture appears in the Sample box. See Figure 10-36.

Figure 10-36 | Specifying the picture on the Close command button

> 5. Click the **Next** button to open the next Command Button Wizard dialog box, in which you enter a name for the button.

6. Type **cmdClose** in the text box, and then click the **Finish** button. Access closes the final Command Button Wizard dialog box and displays the Close Window picture on the new command button on the form.

7. Open the property sheet for the new button, click the **Format** tab (if necessary), set the Caption property to **Close**, set the Picture Caption Arrangement property to **Bottom**, and then press the **Tab** key.

8. Use the middle-right sizing handle to widen the Close command button. See Figure 10-37.

Completed Close command button ◄ **Figure 10-37**

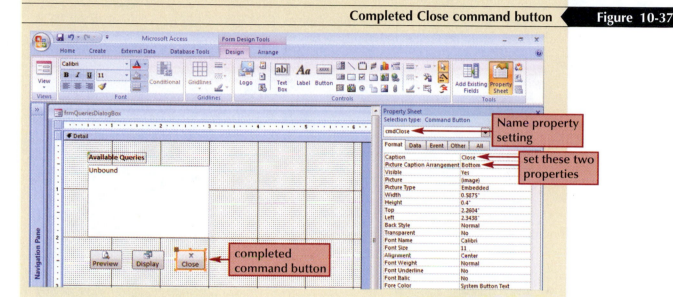

In the next tutorial, you will create the VBA code for the Preview and Display command buttons. This code will define what Access should do when a user clicks each button. The VBA code you will create must refer to the list box control. It is a good idea to give meaningful names to controls on your forms so you can identify them later, so you will enter the name lstQueryList for the list box control, where *lst* is a prefix tag to identify a list box control.

To set the Name property for the list box:

1. Click the list box to make it the active control.

2. Click the **All** tab in the property sheet, select the value in the Name box, type **lstQueryList** in the Name box, and then close the property sheet.

You've completed your work with the list box and command buttons for now, so you'll finish your initial work with the frmQueriesDialogBox form by modifying some of its properties.

Modifying Form Properties

Next, you'll resize and position the form and set the form's Border Style property to Dialog, according to Lucia's design.

To resize and position the form, and then set form properties:

▶ **1.** Drag the right edge of the form's Detail section to the 3.5-inch mark on the horizontal ruler, and then scroll down the form and drag the bottom edge of the form's Detail section to the 3-inch mark on the vertical ruler.

▶ **2.** Switch to Form view, and then position and resize the Queries form until it is in approximately the same position and it is approximately the same size as the form shown in Figure 10-38.

Figure 10-38 **Resized and repositioned form**

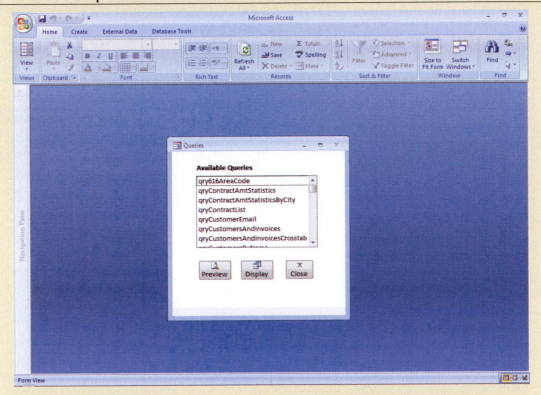

▶ **3.** Save your form layout changes, and then switch to Design view.

You'll now set the form's Border Style property to Dialog, which will prevent a user from resizing the form.

▶ **4.** Right-click the **form selector** to open the shortcut menu, click **Properties** to display the property sheet, and then click the **All** tab (if necessary).

▶ **5.** Click the right side of the **Border Style** text box, click **Dialog**, and then close the property sheet.

The form's background color and the list box's background color are white, and the form would look better with light-colored backgrounds for these controls.

▶ **6.** Click the Detail section's section bar, and in the Font group on the Design tab, click the arrow for the **Fill/Back Color** button ; and then click the **Aqua Blue 2** color (row 3, column 9) in the Standard Colors palette. The Detail section's background color changes to the Aqua Blue 2 color.

7. Click the list box, and in the Font group on the Design tab, click the arrow for the **Fill/Back Color** button; and then click the **Aqua Blue 1** color (row 2, column 9) in the Standard Colors palette. The list box's background color changes to the Aqua Blue 1 color.

8. Save your form design changes, and then switch to Form view to display the completed form. See Figure 10-39.

Completed form　Figure 10-39

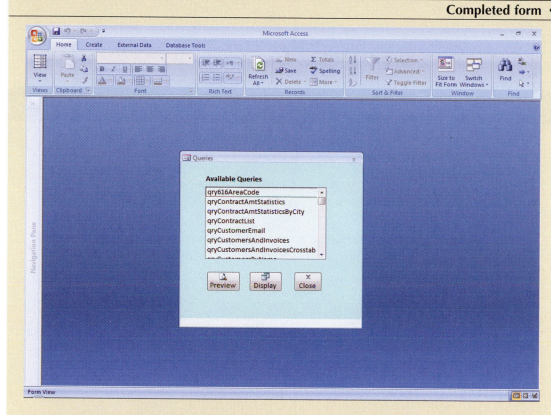

Trouble? If the form is not the correct size or if scroll bars appear on the form, switch to Design view and set the form's Border Style property to Sizable. Switch back to Form view and resize the form. Save the form changes, switch to Design view, set the form's Border Style property to Dialog, and then save the form again and switch to Form view.

You'll now test the work you've completed for the frmQueriesDialogBox form.

Testing the Dialog Box Form

After creating a custom form, you should test the form in Form view. For the frmQueriesDialogBox form, clicking the Preview command button, clicking the Display command button, or double-clicking a query name in the list box will have no effect, because you have not yet added the VBA code for these actions. However, you can click these controls to make sure they have no effect, and you can click the Close button to close the form.

To test the form's design:

▶ **1.** Double-click any query name in the Available Queries list, click the **Preview** button, and then click the **Display** button to verify that using these controls does not initiate any further action.

▶ **2.** Click the **Close** button to close the form.

▶ **3.** If you are not continuing on to the next session, close the Holland database, and then exit Access.

You've completed the initial work on the frmQueriesDialogBox form. In the next session, you'll create the switchboard pages and their macros.

Review | **Session 10.2 Quick Check**

1. What is an event property?
2. What is a macro group?
3. What is the purpose of the Where Condition argument for the OpenForm action?
4. What is a list box control?
5. What are system tables?
6. How do you change the picture on a command button?
7. What is the purpose of setting a form's Border Style property value to Dialog?

Session 10.3

Reviewing the Holland Database Switchboard Requirements

Recall that a switchboard is a form that provides controlled access to a database's forms, queries, reports, and other objects. You need to create the switchboard form that will serve as the primary user interface for the Holland database. Figure 10-40 shows the finished Holland switchboard form that you will create.

Figure 10-40   ▶   **Holland switchboard form**

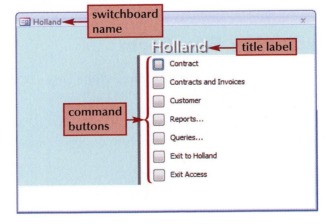

Lucia has the following design specifications for the Holland switchboard:

- The form will not include Minimize, Restore, or Close buttons, scroll bars, navigation buttons, or a record selector.
- The user cannot resize the form.
- "Holland" will appear in the form's title bar and will be the form's title. The form title will have a shadowed special effect applied to it.
- The command buttons will have the same sizes.
- Macros will be attached to the Exit to Holland and Exit Access command buttons to specify the actions that Access should take when each button is clicked.

You'll also create the Reports switchboard, which will look similar to the Holland switchboard. The Reports switchboard will have four command buttons: one to open the rptContract report, a second to open the rptCustomersAndContracts report, a third to open the rptInvoicesByItem report, and a fourth to return to the Holland switchboard.

Your first step in creating the switchboard forms is to create the macros you need to attach to the command buttons on the switchboard forms.

Creating the Macro Group for the Switchboard

You'll create the macros for the switchboards in a macro group. The Macro Name column in the Macro window lets you distinguish macros in a macro group. Because a macro can contain many actions, the macro name tells Access where the macro begins. First, you'll name one macro and list the actions for it. Then you'll name the second macro, and list the actions for it, and so on. You can define the macros in any order, and you can group as many macros as you want in the Macro window.

Creating a Macro Group | Reference Window

- Click the Create tab on the Ribbon.
- In the Other group on the Create tab, click the Macro button.
- In the Show/Hide group on the Design tab, click the Macro Names button.
- Enter the macros in the macro group by entering each macro name in the Macro Name column and the corresponding action(s) in the Action column. Enter comments as needed in the Comment column, and set arguments as needed in the Action Arguments pane.
- Click the Save button on the Quick Access Toolbar, enter the macro group name in the Macro Name text box, and then click the OK button.

You will use the name mcrSwitchboardMacros for the macro group, so it will be easy to locate the macro group containing the macros for the switchboard. You'll create two macros in the macro group: one to close the switchboard and return control to the Access window, and the other macro to close the switchboard and exit Access. You will not use macros for other command buttons on the Holland switchboard nor for the command buttons on the Reports switchboard. After you create the macro group, you'll use the Switchboard Manager to create the Holland and Reports switchboards and to provide the features needed for the other command buttons on these two switchboards. The **Switchboard Manager** is an Access tool that helps you create and customize a switchboard.

You'll now create the mcrSwitchboardMacros macro group for the two command buttons on the Holland switchboard form that use macros. First, you'll start a new macro, and then you'll enter the two macros—ExitAccess and ExitToHolland.

To create the macro group:

▶ 1. If you took a break after the previous session, make sure that the Holland database is open and the Navigation Pane is closed.

▶ 2. Click the **Create** tab on the Ribbon, and then in the Other group on the Create tab, click the **Macro** button. The Macro window opens.

▶ 3. In the Show/Hide group on the Design tab, click the **Macro Names** button. Access adds the Macro Name column to the left of the Action column.

Next, you'll add the ExitAccess macro and its two actions: the Close action to close the Switchboard form and the Quit action to exit Access.

▶ 4. Type **ExitAccess**, press the **Tab** key, click the **Action** arrow, click **Close**, press the **Tab** key twice, and then type **Close the Switchboard form and exit Access**.

You need to specify the arguments for the Close action. In the Object Type box, you specify the type of object to close, in this case, a form. In the Object Name box, you specify which object to close. Even though you haven't created the Switchboard form yet, you can specify it as the object to close.

▶ 5. In the Action Arguments pane, click the right side of the **Object Type** box, click **Form**, press the **Tab** key, and then type **Switchboard** in the Object Name box. You've completed the first action for the first macro.

Next, you'll define the second action for this macro, which will exit the Access program.

▶ 6. Click the right side of the second row's **Action** box, scroll through the list, and then click **Quit**. You've completed the first macro, which contains two actions: the first to close the Switchboard form and the second to exit Access. These two actions will occur in sequence when a user clicks the Exit Access command button on the Switchboard form.

Next, you'll define the second macro, ExitToHolland, which will close the Switchboard form.

▶ 7. Click the third row's **Macro Name** box, type **ExitToHolland**, press the **Tab** key, click the **Action** arrow, click **Close**, press the **Tab** key twice, and then type **Close the Switchboard form and return to the Access window**.

▶ 8. In the Action Arguments pane, click the right side of the **Object Type** box, click **Form**, press the **Tab** key, and then type **Switchboard** in the Object Name box. You've completed the first and only action for the second macro.

▶ 9. Save the macro as **mcrSwitchboardMacros**. See Figure 10-41.

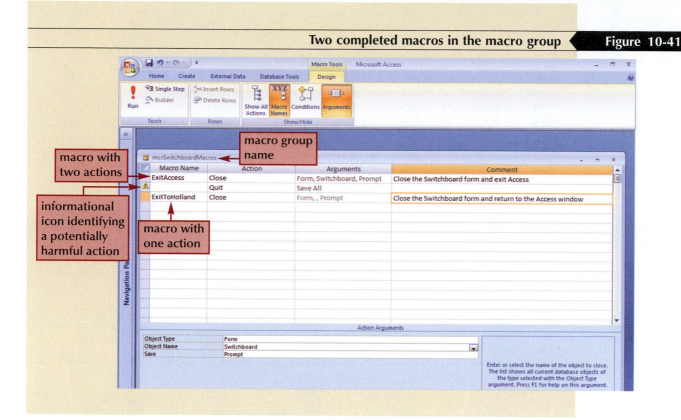

Two completed macros in the macro group — Figure 10-41

The macro name, which appears in the Macro window title bar, is mcrSwitchboardMacros. mcrSwitchboardMacros is also the name of the macro group, because the mcrSwitchboardMacros macro contains more than one macro. The first macro in the macro group is ExitAccess, and the second macro in the macro group is ExitToHolland. A macro in a macro group starts in the row containing the macro name and continues until the next macro name or a blank row.

When Access executes the ExitAccess macro, it runs the Close action, it runs the Quit action, and then the macro ends. The ExitToHolland macro begins with the Close action and ends when it reaches the end of the macro group.

Now that you've defined the two macros that will execute the necessary actions for two command buttons on the switchboard, you can create the form for the switchboard.

Creating a Switchboard

To create the switchboard, you'll use the Access Switchboard Manager. When you use the Switchboard Manager, you specify the command buttons that will appear on the switchboard. For each button, you identify the command to execute when its button is clicked. The Switchboard Manager automatically attaches the command to the OnClick property for that command button; this property specifies the action to take when the command button is clicked. Some commands require one or more arguments, which you can specify as well. When you complete the switchboard design, the Switchboard Manager creates a form for your switchboard with the default name Switchboard. The Switchboard Manager also creates a table, named **Switchboard Items**, which contains records describing the command buttons on the switchboard.

Tip

The Switchboard Manager creates and maintains the Switchboard Items table. Do not change any data in the Switchboard Items table or the name of the Switchboard form, or your Switchboard form will no longer work properly.

The Switchboard Manager allows you to create only one Switchboard form for a database, but the switchboard can contain many pages. You can designate only one of the switchboard pages as the default page. The **default page**, or **main page**, is the switchboard page that will appear when you open the Switchboard form. You can place command buttons on the default page to open other switchboard pages.

You will use the Switchboard Manager to create the Switchboard form for the Holland database. Review the design of the form shown in Figure 10-40. As you use the Switchboard Manager to create the form, you'll place the appropriate command buttons on the switchboard and associate the two macros from the mcrSwitchboardMacros macro group with two buttons on the Holland switchboard and select other actions for the other buttons from choices provided by the Switchboard Manager.

InSight	The Navigation Pane as a Replacement for a Switchboard

As an alternative to switchboards, you can customize the Navigation Pane to display the objects that the users of the database need to access. You can create a custom category, which would be comparable to a switchboard's default page, and display just that category in the Navigation Pane. After you create the custom category, you can create groups for the new category and place into each group the objects that fit the group. For example, you could create a Reports group and a Forms group and place in the groups the report and form objects you want your users to be able to access. To create custom categories and groups, right-click the bar at the top of the Navigation Pane, and then click Navigation Options on the shortcut menu to open the Navigation Options dialog box. To add a new category, click the Add Item button. After creating a new category, click the category name, and then click the Add Group button to add a group to the category. To add objects to a group, click the bar at the top of the Navigation Pane to open the menu, and then drag the objects from the Unassigned Objects group to the group.

The Holland switchboard shown in Figure 10-40 will be the default page. You'll create a second switchboard page for the Reports switchboard. As shown in Figure 10-42, this switchboard page will contain command buttons to print a choice of three reports and to return to the default page.

Figure 10-42	Reports switchboard as a second switchboard page

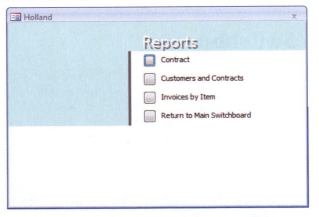

First, you'll create the Switchboard form and two switchboard pages.

To create the Switchboard form with two pages:

▶ 1. Close the macro, click the **Database Tools** tab on the Ribbon, and then in the Database Tools group on the Database Tools tab, click the **Switchboard Manager** button. Access opens a dialog box asking if you want to create a switchboard.

▶ 2. Click the **Yes** button. The Switchboard Manager dialog box opens. See Figure 10-43.

Switchboard Manager dialog box ◀ **Figure 10-43**

The Switchboard Manager has created the Main Switchboard page, which is the default page. You use the Switchboard Manager dialog box to add new pages, to edit and delete existing pages, or to change the default page. You will add a new page next.

▶ 3. Click the **New** button. The Create New dialog box opens.

▶ 4. Type **Reports** in the Switchboard Page Name text box, and then click the **OK** button. The Create New dialog box closes, and the Switchboard Pages list box now shows the original default page and the new Reports page.

Next, you'll edit the default page to changes its name to Holland.

▶ 5. Make sure the **Main Switchboard (Default)** page is selected, and then click the **Edit** button. The Edit Switchboard Page dialog box opens on top of the Switchboard Manager dialog box. This dialog box lets you edit the name of the selected switchboard page and add command buttons to the page.

▶ 6. Select the current entry in the **Switchboard Name** text box, and then type **Holland**. See Figure 10-44.

Edit Switchboard Page dialog box ◀ **Figure 10-44**

new name of the switchboard page

place command button labels here

Adding Command Buttons to a Switchboard Page

You can now add the command buttons for each macro in the mcrSwitchboardMacros macro group. Each command button will carry out the actions in its associated macro or its chosen action from the Switchboard Manager when the command button is clicked.

To add command buttons to the switchboard page:

▶ 1. Click the **New** button in the Edit Switchboard Page dialog box. The Edit Switchboard Item dialog box opens.

  The first button you will add is the Contract button, which will open the frmContract form.

▶ 2. Type **Contract** in the Text text box. This text will appear to the right of the command button on the form.

  Next, you need to specify the command that will be executed when the user clicks the button. In this case, you want Access to run the OpenForm action to open the frmContract form.

▶ 3. Click the **Command** arrow, click **Open Form in Edit Mode**, click the **Form** arrow, click **frmContract**, and then click the Form text box to deselect the value. The first command button definition is now completed. See Figure 10-45.

Figure 10-45 | Edit Switchboard Item dialog box

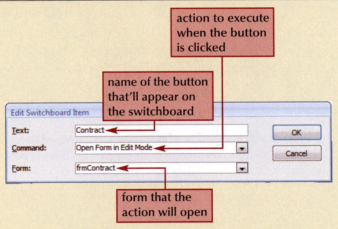

action to execute when the button is clicked

name of the button that'll appear on the switchboard

form that the action will open

▶ 4. Click the **OK** button. The Edit Switchboard Item dialog box closes, and the Switchboard Manager returns to the Edit Switchboard Page dialog box. Notice that the Items on this Switchboard list now shows the Contract label for the first command button on the Switchboard form.

  Three of the next four command buttons on the Holland switchboard page also open forms, so you'll add these three buttons to the page.

▶ 5. Repeat Steps 1 through 4 to define the **Contracts and Invoices** command button to open the **frmContractsAndInvoices** form, repeat Steps 1 through 4 to define the **Customer** command button to open the **frmCustomer** form, and then repeat Steps 1 through 4 to define the **Queries...** command button (be sure to type the ellipsis in the button name) to open the **frmQueriesDialogBox** form.

The next two command buttons (Exit to Holland and Exit Access) on the Holland switchboard page have associated macros in the mcrSwitchboardMacros macro group. Next, you'll add these two command buttons to the switchboard.

To add two command buttons that use macros to the switchboard page:

▶ **1.** Click the **New** button in the Edit Switchboard Page dialog box. The Edit Switchboard Item dialog box opens.

▶ **2.** Type **Exit to Holland** in the Text text box.

Next, you need to specify the command that will be executed when the user clicks the button. In this case, you want Access to run the ExitToHolland macro, which closes the Switchboard form. This macro is a macro in the mcrSwitchboardMacros macro group.

▶ **3.** Click the **Command** arrow, click **Run Macro**, click the **Macro** arrow, click **mcrSwitchboardMacros.ExitToHolland**, and then click the Macro text box to deselect the value. The Exit to Holland command button definition is now completed. See Figure 10-46.

Defining a switchboard command button that uses a macro ◀ **Figure 10-46**

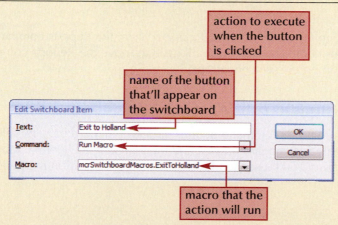

action to execute when the button is clicked

name of the button that'll appear on the switchboard

macro that the action will run

▶ **4.** Click the **OK** button. The Edit Switchboard Item dialog box closes, and the Switchboard Manager returns to the Edit Switchboard Page dialog box.

▶ **5.** Repeat Steps 1 through 4 to define the **Exit Access** command button to run the **ExitAccess** macro in the mcrSwitchboardMacros macro group. The switchboard's default page contains six command buttons. See Figure 10-47.

Six command buttons added to the default switchboard page ◀ **Figure 10-47**

command buttons added to the switchboard page will appear in this order

Trouble? Compare your Edit Switchboard Page dialog box with the one shown in Figure 10-47. If any of your command buttons are incorrect, click the button name and then click the Edit button. Make the necessary changes and then click the OK button to return to the Edit Switchboard Page dialog box.

The Holland switchboard page is completed, except for the Reports command button. You'll add this command button next.

To add the Reports command button to the switchboard page:

▶ 1. Click the **New** button in the Edit Switchboard Page dialog box. The Edit Switchboard Item dialog box opens.

▶ 2. Type **Reports...** in the Text text box. Be sure to type the ellipsis in the command button name.

   You'll use the default command, Go to Switchboard, which allows you to change from one switchboard page to another page.

▶ 3. Click the **Switchboard** arrow, and then click **Reports**.

▶ 4. Click the **OK** button. The switchboard design for the Holland switchboard page now contains all the necessary command buttons.

In Lucia's design for the Holland switchboard page, the Reports command button precedes the Queries command button. You'll need to move the Reports command button to its correct position on the switchboard page.

Moving Command Buttons on a Switchboard Page

You can delete and move command buttons on a switchboard page by selecting an entry in the Items on this Switchboard list box and then clicking the Delete, Move Up, or Move Down buttons. You'll use the Move Up button to reposition the Reports command button.

To reposition the Reports command button:

▶ 1. Click **Reports...** in the Items on this Switchboard list, and then click the **Move Up** button. The Reports... entry moves up one position in the list and remains selected. See Figure 10-48.

Moving a command button   Figure 10-48

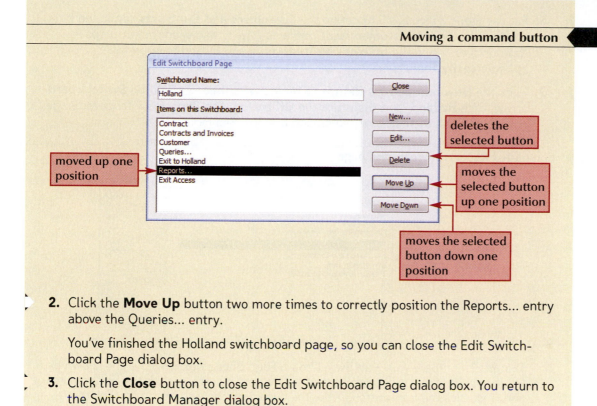

2. Click the **Move Up** button two more times to correctly position the Reports... entry above the Queries... entry.

> You've finished the Holland switchboard page, so you can close the Edit Switchboard Page dialog box.

3. Click the **Close** button to close the Edit Switchboard Page dialog box. You return to the Switchboard Manager dialog box.

Next, you'll add the command buttons to the Reports switchboard page.

Adding Command Buttons to a Second Switchboard Page

You've already used the Open Form in Edit Mode, Run Macro, and Go to Switchboard options in the Edit Switchboard Item dialog box. The other Command text box options in this dialog box that you can use are: Open Form in Add Mode, Open Report, Design Application, Exit Application, and Run Code. For the Reports switchboard page, you'll use the Open Report option for the first three command buttons (Contract, Customers and Contracts, and Invoices by Item) and the Go to Switchboard option for the Return to Main Switchboard command button.

To add command buttons to the Reports switchboard page:

1. Click **Reports** in the Switchboard Pages list, and then click the **Edit** button. The Edit Switchboard Page dialog box opens on top of the Switchboard Manager dialog box.

2. Click the **New** button. The Edit Switchboard Item dialog box opens.

3. Type **Contract** in the Text text box.

4. Click the **Command** arrow, and then click **Open Report**. The third text box in the Edit Switchboard Item dialog box now displays the label "Report." In this text box, you specify the report to open when the button is clicked. When you click the Report arrow, you see a list of all the reports in the database.

5. Click the **Report** arrow, click **rptContract**, and then click the **OK** button.

6. Repeat Steps 2 through 5 to define the **Customers and Contracts** command button to open the **rptCustomersAndContracts** report, and then repeat Steps 2 through 5 to define the **Invoices by Item** command button to open the **rptInvoicesByItem** report.

7. Click the **New** button, type **Return to Main Switchboard**, click the **Switchboard** arrow, click **Holland**, and then click the **OK** button. The Reports switchboard page now contains all the necessary command buttons. See Figure 10-49.

| Figure 10-49 | Completed Reports switchboard page |

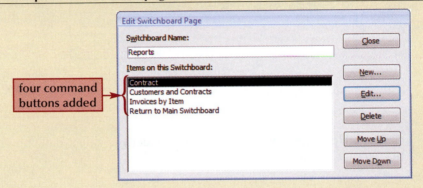

Trouble? Compare your Edit Switchboard Page dialog box with the one shown in Figure 10-49. If any of your command buttons are incorrect, click the button name and then click the Edit button. Make the necessary changes and then click the OK button to return to the Edit Switchboard Page dialog box.

Viewing and Testing a Switchboard

You are finished using the Switchboard Manager, so you can now exit it and view the new switchboard.

To exit the Switchboard Manager and view the Switchboard form:

1. Click the **Close** button to close the Edit Switchboard Page dialog box.

2. Click the **Close** button to close the Switchboard Manager dialog box and return to the Access window.

3. Open the Navigation Pane, open the **Switchboard** form in Form view, and then close the Navigation Pane. See Figure 10-50.

Switchboard form in Form view ◄ Figure 10-50

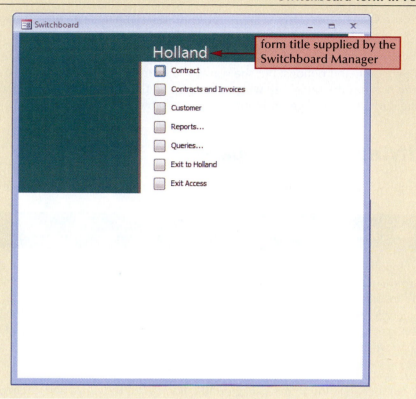

form title supplied by the Switchboard Manager

The Switchboard form contains the seven command buttons you defined for the Holland switchboard page using the Switchboard Manager. Each command button has an attached label displaying the command button name. The form title "Holland" appears in white text in a label control above the command buttons; the Switchboard Manager automatically created this label on the form. Behind the Holland label is another copy of the Holland label displaying the text in gray letters, creating a shadowed effect. The Switchboard Manager also added the large green areas on the switchboard, which are green rectangle objects.

Overall, Lucia is pleased with the appearance of the Switchboard form, but there are some changes she would like you to make. Before you make these changes, you will test some of the command buttons to make sure that they work properly.

To test the command buttons:

▶ **1.** Click the **Contract** command button. Access opens the frmContract form in Form view and displays the first form record.

▶ **2.** Close the form to return to the Holland switchboard.

▶ **3.** Click the **Reports** command button. Access replaces the Holland switchboard page with the Reports switchboard page.

▶ **4.** Click the **Invoices by Item** command button. Access opens the rptInvoicesByItem report in Report view.

▶ **5.** Close the report to return to the Reports switchboard page.

▶ **6.** Click the **Return to Main Switchboard** command button to replace the Reports switchboard page with the Holland switchboard page.

▶ **7.** Click the **Queries** command button. Access opens the frmQueriesDialogBox form in Form view.

▶ **8.** Click the **Close** command button to return to the Holland switchboard page.

Lucia wants you to make some changes to the design of the switchboard. She likes the layout of the command buttons, but she wants you to resize the form and make sure that the form always has the same size when it appears on the screen. She also wants you to change the dark green background form color to a lighter color.

Modifying a Switchboard

Because the switchboard is a form, you can make Lucia's changes in Design view.

InSight	**Modifying the Switchboard Form**

When you modify the design of the Switchboard form, you must be careful not to make any changes to the command buttons that would affect the actions and macros associated with them. You should only make these types of changes using the Switchboard Manager. If you were to change the definitions of any of the command buttons in Design view, the Switchboard Manager would not be able to make the necessary updates to its table, and the switchboard would not function correctly.

Next, you'll change the form's background color, resize the form, and change form properties so that users can't change the form's size.

To change the Switchboard form properties:

▶ **1.** Switch to Design view.

▶ **2.** In the Form Header section, click the dark green rectangle, and in the Font group on the Design tab, click the arrow for the **Fill/Back Color** button 🖌; and then click the **Aqua Blue 2** color (row 3, column 9) in the Standard Colors palette. The Form Header section's background color changes to the Aqua Blue 2 color.

▶ **3.** On the left side of the Detail section, click the dark green rectangle, and then click the **Fill/Back Color** button 🖌. The rectangle in the Detail section changes to the Aqua Blue 2 color.

▶ **4.** Switch to Form view, and then position and resize the form until it is in approximately the same position and it is approximately the same size as the form shown in Figure 10-51.

Modified Switchboard form in Form view ◢ **Figure 10-51**

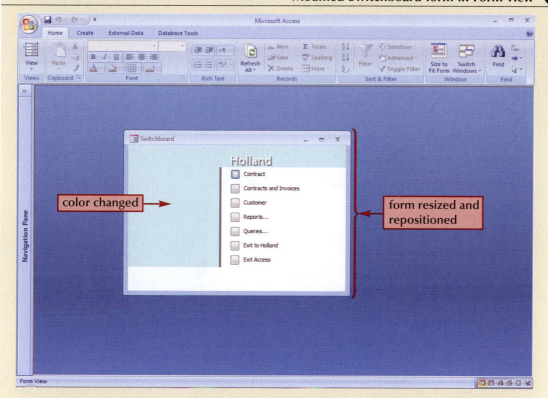

5. Save your form layout changes, and then switch to Design view.

6. Right-click the **form selector** to open the shortcut menu, click **Properties** to display the property sheet for the form, and then click the **All** tab (if necessary).

First, you'll set the form's Caption property to Holland, and then you'll set the Auto Resize property to No so that Access will not resize the form when it is opened.

7. Double-click **Switchboard** in the Caption box, type **Holland**, and then double-click **Yes** in the Auto Resize text box to change this property setting to No.

Next, you'll set the Border Style property to Dialog to prevent users from resizing the form.

8. Click the right side of the **Border Style** box, and then click **Dialog**.

Setting the Close Button property to No disables the Close button on the form's title bar. You'll disable this button, because Lucia wants users to close the form by clicking the Exit to Holland or Exit Access command buttons.

9. Double-click **Yes** in the Close Button text box to change the property setting to No.

10. Close the property sheet, save your form design changes, and then close the form.

Lucia wants to view the modified switchboard, so you'll open the switchboard in Form view.

To view the switchboard:

▶ **1.** Open the Navigation Pane, open the **Switchboard** form in Form view, and then close the Navigation Pane. See Figure 10-52.

Figure 10-52 **Finished Switchboard form in Form view**

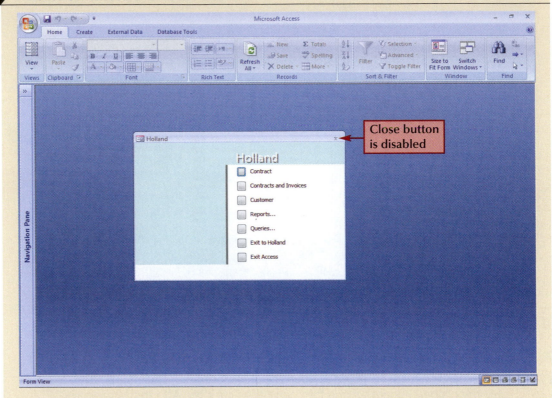

▶ **2.** Click the **Exit to Holland** button. Access closes the switchboard and returns to the Access window.

▶ **3.** Close the Holland database, make a backup copy of the database, open the **Holland** database, compact and repair the database, close the database, and then exit Access.

Lucia's design for the Holland database user interface also includes a restricted Ribbon and has the Navigation Pane removed from the screen. In Tutorial 12, you'll add these features to the switchboard, and in Tutorial 11 you'll create the necessary VBA code for the frmQueriesDialogBox form command buttons.

Review | **Session 10.3 Quick Check**

1. How do you determine the beginning and end of a macro in a macro group?

2. What is the Switchboard Manager?

3. Which macro action you used in creating the Switchboard form is considered to be potentially harmful and identifed as being an untrusted action?

4. To which property does the Switchboard Manager automatically assign commands for each command button?

5. How do you specify that a form is a dialog box?

Tutorial Summary | Review

In this tutorial, you worked with macros by running a macro, adding actions to a macro, single stepping a macro, creating a macro group, adding actions to a macro group, and attaching macros to command buttons. You also created a dialog box by adding a list box to a form, using an SQL statement to provide the source data for the list box, adding command buttons, and modifying form properties. Finally, you created a switchboard with two pages, attached macros to the command buttons on the switchboard, and modified the switchboard by setting properties for the form.

Key Terms

action
Action column
argument
Arguments column
command button
Comment column
custom dialog box
Data Mode argument
default page
event
event procedure
event property
Filter Name argument
FindRecord action
graphical user
    interface (GUI)
Left function
list box

macro
Macro Builder
macro group
Macro Name column
Macro window
main page
message box
MsgBox action
MSysObjects table
overlapping window
Picture Caption Arrange-
    ment property
PrintSelection argument
procedure
Row Source property
RunCommand action
SELECT statement

SelectObject action
single stepping
SQL (Structured Query
    Language)
switchboard
Switchboard Items
Switchboard Manager
system table
tabbed document
user interface
View argument
Visual Basic for
    Applications (VBA)
Where Condition
    argument
Window Mode argument

| Practice | **Review Assignments** |

Practice the skills you learned in the tutorial using the same case scenario.

Data File needed for the Review Assignments: Vendor.accdb *(cont. from Tutorial 9)*

Lucia wants you to create a switchboard interface for the Vendor database. To help with this request, complete the following steps:

1. Open the **Vendor** database located in the Level.03\Review folder provided with your Data Files.

2. Change the database's window style to overlapping windows.

3. Design and create a form named **frmReportsDialogBox** that has the following components and characteristics:

   a. Use the text **Print Reports** in the form's title bar.

   b. A list box with a Name property value of **lstReportList** displays all the report names contained in the Vendor database. To place the report names in the list box, use an SQL SELECT statement to retrieve the report names from the MSysObjects table, and display the reports in report name order. Delete the label attached to the list box, and widen the list box to approximately two inches.

   c. Use the heading **Reports Available**, formatted with a 12-point, bold font, above the list box.

   d. Two command buttons appear below the list box. The left command button displays the Preview icon above the word **Preview**, and the right command button displays the Close Window icon above the word **Close**. Double-clicking a report name has the same effect as selecting a report name in the list box and clicking the left command button. Both events cause Access to display the selected report in Print Preview. (You will add the VBA code for these events in the next tutorial. For now, double-clicking or clicking should cause no action to occur.) Clicking the Close command button causes Access to close the dialog box.

   e. Set the form's background color to Maroon 3 in the Standard Colors palette and the list box's background color to Maroon 2, resize the form's Detail section in Design view, resize the form in Form view, and then set form properties that are appropriate for a dialog box.

4. Create a macro group named **mcrSwitchboardMacros** that contains macros to be used with two of the command buttons in the switchboard you'll create in the next step. The two macros perform these actions: close the switchboard, and close the switchboard and exit Access.

5. Design and create a Switchboard form named **Switchboard**. Use Figure 10-53 and the following descriptions as a guide to create the switchboard.

Figure 10-53

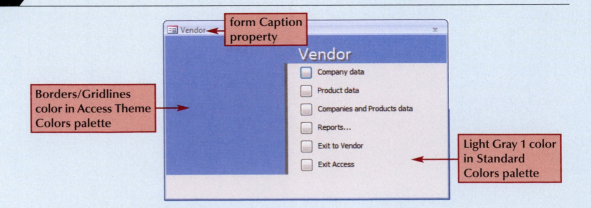

a. Use the Switchboard Manager to create the switchboard. Place the command buttons on the form; the last two command buttons should use the macros in the **mcrSwitchboardMacros** macro group. The first four command buttons should open the frmCompanyInfo form in edit mode, open the frmProductData form in edit mode, open the frmCompaniesWithProducts form in edit mode, and open the frmReportsDialogBox form in edit mode.

b. Set the background colors for the switchboard, as shown in Figure 10-53, delete the Form Footer section, resize the switchboard in Form view, and then set form properties that are appropriate for a switchboard.

6. Save the Switchboard form, and then test the command buttons and the frmReportsDialogBox form to make sure that your switchboard items work correctly. If necessary, return to the Switchboard Manager and make any corrections.

7. Close the Vendor database without exiting Access, make a backup copy of the database, open the **Vendor** database, compact and repair the database, close the database, and then exit Access.

Apply | Case Problem 1

Use the skills you learned in the tutorial to create a new user interface for music school's database.

Data File needed for this Case Problem: Portland.accdb (*cont. from Tutorial 9*)

Pine Hill Music School Yuka Koyama wants the Portland database to include an easy-to-use switchboard interface. To help Yuka with her request, complete the following steps:

1. Open the **Portland** database located in the Level.03\Case1 folder provided with your Data Files.

2. Change the database's window style to overlapping windows.

3. Design and create a form named **frmQueriesDialogBox**. Use Figure 10-54 and the following descriptions as a guide to create the form.

Figure 10-54

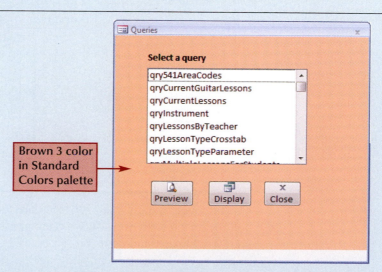

Brown 3 color in Standard Colors palette

a. Use the text **Queries** in the form's title bar.

   b. A list box with a Name property value of **lstQueryList** displays all the query names contained in the Portland database, excluding those queries that start with a "~" character. To place the query names in the list box, use an SQL SELECT statement to retrieve the query names from the MSysObjects table, and display the queries in query name order. Delete the label attached to the list box, and widen the list box to approximately 2.5 inches.

   c. Use the heading **Select a query**, formatted with a 12-point, bold font, above the list box.

   d. Three command buttons appear below the list box. The left command button displays the Preview icon above the word **Preview**, the middle command button displays the MS Access Query icon above the word **Display**, and the right command button displays the Close Window icon above the word **Close**. Double-clicking a query name has the same effect as selecting a query name in the list box and clicking the middle command button. Both events cause Access to display the query datasheet for the selected query. Clicking the left command button opens the selected query in Print Preview. (You will add the VBA code for these events in the next tutorial. For now, double-clicking or clicking should cause no action to occur.) Clicking the Close command button causes Access to close the dialog box.

   e. Set the form's background color to Brown 3 in the Standard Colors palette, resize the form's Detail section in Design view, resize the form in Form view, and then set form properties that are appropriate for a dialog box.

4. Create a macro group named **mcrSwitchboardMacros** that contains macros to be used with two of the command buttons in the switchboard you'll create in the next step. The two macros perform these actions: close the switchboard, and close the switchboard and exit Access.

5. Design and create a Switchboard form named **Switchboard**. Use Figure 10-55 and the following descriptions as a guide to create the switchboard.

Figure 10-55

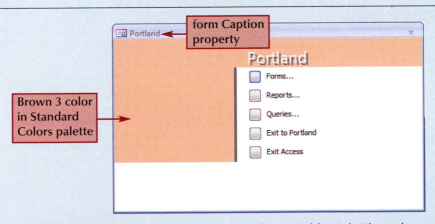

   a. Use the Switchboard Manager to create the switchboard. Place the command buttons on the form; the last two command buttons should use the macros in the **mcrSwitchboardMacros** macro group. The first three command buttons should switch to the Forms switchboard page, switch to the Reports switchboard page, and open the frmQueriesDialogBox form in edit mode.

   b. The Forms switchboard page should open the frmStudentData form in edit mode, open the frmTeacherInfo form in edit mode, open the frmContract form in edit mode, and return to the main switchboard.

c. The Reports switchboard page should have four options to open each of the four reports and a fifth option to return to the main switchboard.

d. Set the background color for the switchboard, as shown in Figure 10-55, delete the Form Footer section, resize the switchboard in Form view, and then set form properties that are appropriate for a switchboard.

6. Save the Switchboard form, and then test the command buttons on the main switchboard page, the other switchboard pages, and the frmQueriesDialogBox form to make sure that your switchboard items work correctly. If necessary, return to the Switchboard Manager and make any corrections.

7. Close the Portland database without exiting Access, make a backup copy of the database, open the **Portland** database, compact and repair the database, close the database, and then exit Access.

| Challenge | **Case Problem 2** |

Use the skills you learned, and explore some new skills, to create a new user interface for a fitness center's database.

Data Files needed for this Case Problem: Exercise.accdb (cont. from Tutorial 9) and Weight.gif

Parkhurst Health & Fitness Center To make the Exercise database easier to use, Martha Parkhurst wants you to create a switchboard interface for it. To help Martha with her request, complete the following steps:

1. Open the **Exercise** database located in the Level.03\Case2 folder provided with your Data Files.

2. Change the database's window style to overlapping windows.

⊕ **EXPLORE**
3. Create a macro group named **mcrSwitchboardMacros** that contains macros to be used with three of the command buttons in the switchboard you'll create in the next step. The three macros perform these actions: open the qryMonthlyFeeCrosstab query, close the switchboard, and close the switchboard and exit Access.

4. Design and create a Switchboard form named **Switchboard**. Use Figure 10-56 and the following descriptions as a guide to create the switchboard.

Figure 10-56

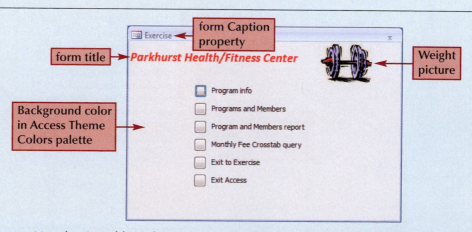

a. Use the Switchboard Manager to create the switchboard. Place the command buttons on the form; the last three command buttons should use the macros in the mcrSwitchboardMacros macro group. The first three command buttons should open the frmProgramInfo form in edit mode, open the frmProgramsAndMembers form in edit mode, and open the rptProgramAndMembers report.

⊕ **EXPLORE**

    b. Delete the colored rectangles created by the Switchboard Manager, and add a label with the form title of **Parkhurst Health/Fitness Center** in 14-point, bold, italic, red text. (*Hint*: Set the Visible property to No for the two form title labels created by the Switchboard Manager.)

⊕ **EXPLORE**

    c. Add the Weight picture from the Level.03\Case2 folder to the form. (*Hint:* Use the Image button in the Controls group on the Design tab.)

    d. Set the background color for the switchboard, as shown in Figure 10-56, delete the Form Footer section, resize the switchboard in Form view, and then set form properties that are appropriate for a switchboard.

5. Save the Switchboard form, and then test the command buttons on the main switchboard page to make sure that your switchboard items work correctly. If necessary, return to the Switchboard Manager and make any corrections.

6. Close the Exercise database without exiting Access, make a backup copy of the database, open the **Exercise** database, compact and repair the database, close the database, and then exit Access.

Apply	**Case Problem 3**

Apply what you learned in the tutorial to create a new user interface for an agency that recycles household goods.

Data File needed for this Case Problem: Salina.accdb (*cont. from Tutorial 9*)

Rossi Recycling Group   Mary and Tom Rossi want the Salina database to include an easy-to-use switchboard interface. To help them with their request, complete the following steps:

1. Open the **Salina** database located in the Level.03\Case3 folder provided with your Data Files.

2. Change the database's window style to overlapping windows.

3. Design and create a form named **frmQueriesDialogBox**. Use Figure 10-57 and the following descriptions as a guide to create the form:

Figure 10-57

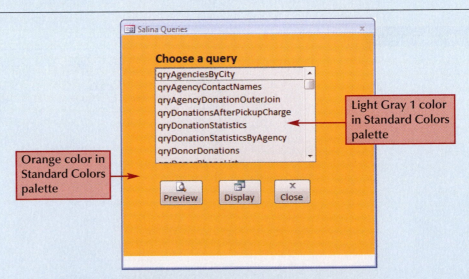

    a. Use the text **Salina Queries** in the form's title bar.

b. A list box with a Name property value of **lstQueryList** displays all the query names contained in the Salina database, excluding those queries that start with a "~" character. To place the query names in the list box, use an SQL SELECT statement to retrieve the query names from the MSysObjects table, and display the queries in query name order. Delete the label attached to the list box, and widen the list box to approximately 2.5 inches.

c. Use the heading **Choose a query**, formatted with a 14-point, bold font above the list box.

d. Three command buttons appear below the list box. The left command button displays the Preview icon above the word **Preview**, the middle command button displays the MS Access Query icon above the word **Display**, and the right command button displays the Close Window icon above the word **Close**. Double-clicking a query name has the same effect as selecting a query name in the list box and clicking the middle command button. Both events cause Access to display the query datasheet for the selected query. Clicking the left command button opens the selected query in Print Preview. (You will add the VBA code for these events in the next tutorial. For now, double-clicking or clicking should cause no action to occur.) Clicking the Close command button causes Access to close the dialog box.

e. Set the form's background color and the list box's background color, resize the form's Detail section in Design view, resize the form in Form view, and then set form properties that are appropriate for a dialog box.

4. Create a macro group named **mcrSwitchboardMacros** that contains macros to be used with two of the command buttons on the switchboard you'll create in the next step. The two macros perform these actions: close the switchboard, and close the switchboard and exit Access.

5. Design and create a Switchboard form named **Switchboard**. Use Figure 10-58 and the following descriptions as a guide to create the switchboard.

Figure 10-58

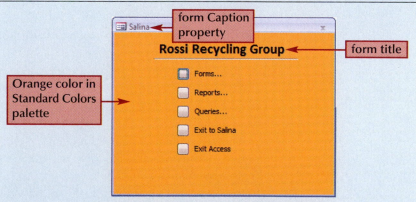

a. Use the Switchboard Manager to create the switchboard. Place the command buttons on the form; the last two command buttons should use the macros in the mcrSwitchboardMacros macro group. The first three command buttons should switch to the Forms switchboard page, switch to the Reports switchboard page, and open the frmQueriesDialogBox form in edit mode.

b. The Forms switchboard page should open the frmDonorDonations form in edit mode, open the frmDonorInfo form in edit mode, open the frmDonationInfo form in edit mode, and return to the main switchboard.

c. The Reports switchboard page should open the rptDonorDonations report, open the rptAgenciesAndDonations report, open the rptDonorDonationsSummary report, and return to the main switchboard.

⊕ EXPLORE

d. Delete the colored rectangles created by the Switchboard Manager, and add a label with the form title of **Rossi Recycling Group** in 16-point, bold text. (*Hint*: Set the Visible property to No for the two form title labels created by the Switchboard Manager.)

e. Draw a rectangle around the label box, and apply the Chiseled special effect to the rectangle.

f. Set the background color for the switchboard, as shown in Figure 10-58, delete the Form Footer section, resize the switchboard in Form view, and then set form properties that are appropriate for a switchboard.

6. Save the Switchboard form, and then test the command buttons on the main switchboard page, the other switchboard pages, and the frmQueriesDialogBox form to make sure that your switchboard items work correctly. If necessary, return to the Switchboard Manager and make any corrections.

7. Close the Salina database without exiting Access, make a backup copy of the database, open the **Salina** database, compact and repair the database, close the database, and then exit Access.

| Create | **Case Problem 4** |

Apply what you learned in the tutorial to create a new user interface for the database of a luxury property rental company.

Data File needed for this Case Problem: Rentals.accdb (*cont. from Tutorial 9*)

GEM Ultimate˚ Vacations   Griffin and Emma MacElroy want you to create a user-friendly interface, including a switchboard and dialog boxes, for the Rentals database. To help them with their request, complete the following steps:

1. Open the **Rentals** database located in the Level.03\Case4 folder provided with your Data Files.

2. Change the database's window style to overlapping windows.

3. Design and create a form named **frmQueriesDialogBox** that has the following components and characteristics:

a. Use the title **Queries** in the form's title bar.

b. A list box with a Name property value of **lstQueryList** displays all the query names contained in the Rentals database, excluding those queries that start with a "~" character. To place the query names in the list box, use an SQL SELECT statement to retrieve the query names from the MSysObjects table, and display the queries in query name order. Delete the label attached to the list box, and widen the list box to approximately two inches.

c. Use the heading **Queries Available**, formatted with an 11-point, bold font, above the list box.

d. Two command buttons appear below the list box. The left command button displays the MS Access Query icon below the word **Display**, and the right command button displays the Close Window icon below the word **Close**. Double-clicking a query name has the same effect as selecting a query name in the list box and clicking the left command button. Both events cause Access to display the query datasheet for the selected query. (You will add the VBA code for these events in the next tutorial. For now, double-clicking or clicking should cause no action to occur.) Clicking the Close command button causes Access to close the dialog box.

    e. Set the form's background color to Light Gray 1 in the Standard Colors palette, set the list box's background color to Aqua Blue 1 in the Standard Colors palette, resize the form's Detail section in Design view, resize the form in Form view, and then set form properties that are appropriate for a dialog box.

4. Create a copy of the frmQueriesDialogBox form and name it **frmReportsDialogBox**. Make the following modifications to the frmReportsDialogBox form:

    a. Change the text that appears in the title bar to **Reports**.

    b. Change the SQL SELECT statement to retrieve the report names from the MSysObjects table.

    c. Change the text that appears as a heading above the list box to **Reports Available**.

    d. Change the left command button to display the Preview icon below the word **Preview**.

    e. Change the Name property value of the list box to **lstReportList**.

 EXPLORE

    f. If necessary, resize the form's Detail section in Design view, resize the form in Form view, and then set form properties that are appropriate for a dialog box. (*Hint*: You have to change some of the form properties that are appropriate for a dialog box before resizing the form.)

5. Create a macro group named **mcrExitSwitchboard** that contains macros to be used with two of the command buttons in the switchboard you'll create in the next step. The two macros perform these actions: close the switchboard, and close the switchboard and exit Access.

6. Design and create a Switchboard form named **Switchboard**. Use Figure 10-59 and the following descriptions as a guide to create the switchboard.

Figure 10-59

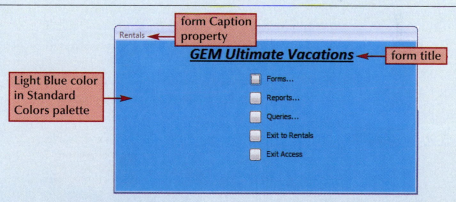

    a. Use the Switchboard Manager to create the switchboard. The switchboard should have two pages. Use **Rentals** as the main switchboard page name, and **Forms** as the second switchboard page name.

    b. Place the command buttons on the form; the last two command buttons should use the macros in the mcrExitSwitchboard macro group. The first three command buttons should switch to the Forms switchboard page, open the frmReportsDialogBox form in edit mode, and open the frmQueriesDialogBox form in edit mode.

    c. The Forms switchboard page should open the frmGuestInfo form in edit mode, open the frmGuestsWithReservations form in edit mode, open the frmRentalCost form in edit mode, and return to the main switchboard.

✦ EXPLORE

d. Delete the colored rectangles created by the Switchboard Manager, and add a label with the form title of **GEM Ultimate Vacations** in 18-point, bold, italic, and underlined text. (*Hint*: Set the Visible property to No for the two form title labels created by the Switchboard Manager.)

e. Set the background color for the switchboard, as shown in Figure 10-59, delete the Form Footer section, resize the switchboard in Form view, and then set form properties that are appropriate for a switchboard.

7. Save the Switchboard form, and then test the command buttons on the main switchboard page, the other switchboard pages, and the dialog box forms to make sure that your switchboard items work correctly. If necessary, return to the Switchboard Manager and make any corrections.

8. Close the Rentals database without exiting Access, make a backup copy of the database, open the **Rentals** database, compact and repair the database, close the database, and then exit Access.

| Create | **Case Problem 5** |

Work with the skills you've learned, and explore some new skills, to create a user interface for an Internet service provider.

Data File needed for this Case Problem: Always.accdb (*cont. from Tutorial 9*)

Always Connected Everyday   Chris and Pat Dixon want you to create a user-friendly switchboard interface for the Always database. To help them with their request, complete the following steps:

1. Open the **Always** database located in the Level.03\Case5 folder provided with your Data Files.

2. Change the database's window style to overlapping windows.

3. Create a macro group named **mcrExitSwitchboard** that contains macros to be used with two of the command buttons on the switchboard you'll create in the next step. The two macros perform these actions: close the switchboard, and close the switchboard and exit Access.

4. Design and create a Switchboard form named **Switchboard**. Use Figure 10-60 and the following descriptions as a guide to create the switchboard.

Figure 10-60

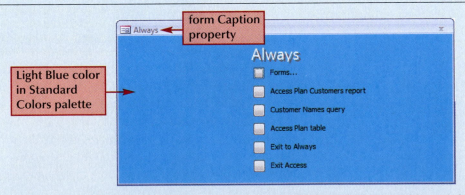

a. Use the Switchboard Manager to create the switchboard. The switchboard should have two pages. Use **Always** as the main switchboard page name, and **Forms** as the second switchboard page name. Add to the Forms switchboard page the command buttons shown in Figure 10-61.

Figure 10-61

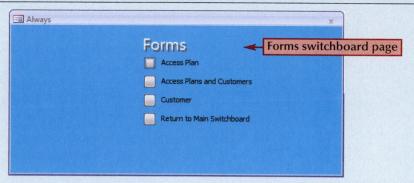

Forms switchboard page

EXPLORE

b. Place the command buttons on the Always switchboard page; the last two command buttons should use the macros in the mcrExitSwitchboard macro group. The first four command buttons should switch to the Forms switchboard page, open the rptAccessPlanCustomers report, open the qryCustomerNames query, and open the tblAccessPlan table. Modify the mcrExitSwitchboard macro group by adding macros to open the query and the table.

c. Delete the colored rectangles created by the Switchboard Manager, set the background color for the switchboard, as shown in Figure 10-60, delete the Form Footer section, resize the switchboard in Form view, and then set form properties that are appropriate for a switchboard.

5. Save the Switchboard form, and then test the command buttons on the switchboard pages to make sure that your switchboard items work correctly. If necessary, return to the Switchboard Manager and make any corrections.

6. Close the Always database without exiting Access, make a backup copy of the database, open the **Always** database, compact and repair the database, close the database, and then exit Access.

Research | **Internet Assignments**

Use the Internet to find and work with data related to the topics presented in this tutorial.

The purpose of the Internet Assignments is to challenge you to find information on the Internet that you can use to work effectively with this software. The actual assignments are updated and maintained on the Course Technology Web site. Log on to the Internet and use your Web browser to go to the Student Online Companion for New Perspectives Office 2007 at **www.course.com/np/office2007**. Then navigate to the Internet Assignments for this tutorial.

Assess | **SAM Assessment and Training**

If you have a SAM user profile, you may have access to hands-on instruction, practice, and assessment of the skills covered in this tutorial. Log in to your SAM account (**http://sam2007.course.com**) to launch any assigned training activities or exams that relate to the skills covered in this tutorial.

Review | Quick Check Answers

Session 10.1

1. A form that appears when you open a database and that provides controlled access to the database's forms, queries, and reports. It lets you customize the organization of the user interface, and prevents users from changing the design of objects.
2. an action, or a set of actions, that you want Access to perform automatically
3. An action argument provides additional facts Access needs to execute an action.
4. opens a message box that remains on the screen until you click the OK button
5. Single stepping executes a macro one action at a time, pausing between actions. Use single stepping to make sure you have placed actions in the right order and with the right arguments, thereby ensuring that the macro works correctly.

Session 10.2

1. An event property specifies how an object responds when an event occurs.
2. a macro that contains other macros
3. specifies which record to display in the form
4. a control that displays a list of values
5. special tables maintained by Access that store information about the characteristics of a database and about the structure of its objects
6. In Design view, open the property sheet for the command button. Click the All tab in the property sheet, click the Picture box, and then click the Build button. Select the picture using the Picture Builder dialog box, and then click the OK button.
7. Users will not be able to resize the form.

Session 10.3

1. The beginning of each macro in a macro group has an entry in the Macro Name column of the Macro window; subsequent actions in the macro do not have entries in this column. The macro ends with the start of a new macro or at the end of the macro group, whichever comes first.
2. an Access tool that helps you create and customize a switchboard
3. Quit
4. OnClick
5. Open the form in Design view, open the form's property sheet, and then set the Border Style property to Dialog

Ending Data Files

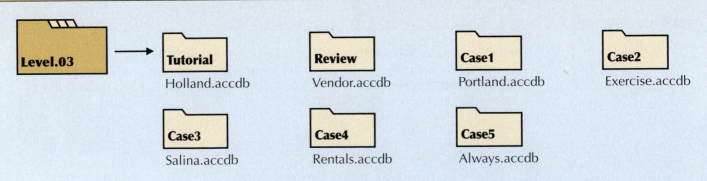

Objectives

Session 11.1
- Learn about Function procedures (functions), Sub procedures (subroutines), and modules
- Review and modify an existing subroutine in an event procedure
- Create a function in a standard module

Session 11.2
- Create event procedures
- Compile and test functions, subroutines, and event procedures

Session 11.3
- Hide text and change display colors
- Create event procedures for a dialog box

Using and Writing Visual Basic for Applications Code

Creating VBA Code for the Holland Database User Interface

Case | Belmont Landscapes

Lucia Perez and Sarah Fisher review your progress in developing the graphical user interface for the Holland database. So far, you have created the switchboard that contains command buttons for opening forms, opening a new switchboard page containing command buttons for opening reports, displaying a dialog box with a list of available queries, exiting the switchboard, and exiting the switchboard and Access. You also have created a macro group that contains the macros attached to command buttons on the switchboard.

You'll continue developing the user interface for the Holland database by modifying the frmQueriesDialogBox form so that its command buttons carry out the appropriate operations. You'll also modify the frmCustomerContracts, frmCustomer, and frmContractsAndInvoices forms to make data entry easier and to highlight important information on them. To make these modifications, you will write Visual Basic for Applications code to perform the necessary operations, and then you will attach the code to the appropriate event properties for the buttons and forms.

Starting Data Files

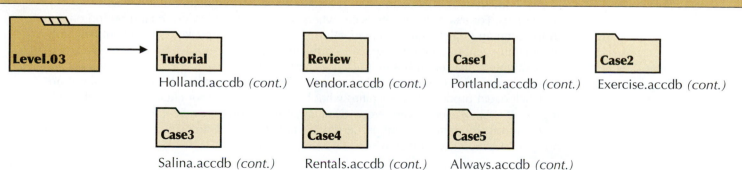

Level.03 → Tutorial
Holland.accdb *(cont.)*

Review
Vendor.accdb *(cont.)*

Case1
Portland.accdb *(cont.)*

Case2
Exercise.accdb *(cont.)*

Case3
Salina.accdb *(cont.)*

Case4
Rentals.accdb *(cont.)*

Case5
Always.accdb *(cont.)*

Session 11.1

Introduction to Visual Basic for Applications

Your next task in the development of the graphical user interface for the Holland database is to refine it further by adding a procedure to ensure proper capitalization of data entered using the frmCustomer form. Sarah wants to make sure that all values entered in this form's State field will be stored in the tblCustomer table using uppercase letters. She asks you to modify the form so that it will automatically convert any lowercase letters entered in the State field to uppercase. To accomplish this objective, you will use Visual Basic for Applications.

Visual Basic for Applications (VBA) is the programming language provided with Access and other Office programs. VBA has a common syntax and a set of common features for all Microsoft Office programs, but it also has features that are unique for each Microsoft Office program due to each program's different structure and components. For example, because Access has fields, tables, queries, forms, other objects, tab controls, subforms, and other controls that are unique to Access, VBA for Access has features that support these components. In contrast, because Microsoft Excel does not have these same Access components, VBA for Excel does not support them, but VBA for Excel does support cells, ranges, and worksheets—three of the basic structures of Excel. The fundamental VBA skills you learn for one of the Microsoft Office programs transfer to any other Microsoft Office program, but to become proficient with VBA in another program, you first need to master its unique aspects.

When you use a programming language, such as VBA, you write a set of instructions to direct the computer to perform specific operations in a specific order, similar to writing a set of instructions for a recipe or an instruction manual. The process of writing instructions in a programming language is called **coding**. You write the VBA instructions, each of which is called a **statement**, to respond to an event that occurs with an object or control in a database. A language such as VBA is, therefore, called both an **event-driven language**—an event in the database triggers a set of instruction—and an **object-oriented language**—each set of instructions operates on objects in the database. Your experience with macros, which are also event-driven and object-oriented, should facilitate your learning of VBA. Although you must use macros if you need to assign actions to a specific keyboard key or key combination, or if you need to open a database in a special way, you can use VBA for everything else you can do with macros. VBA provides advantages over using macros, such as better error-handling features and easier updating capabilities. You can also use VBA in situations that macros do not handle, such as creating your own set of statements to perform special calculations, verifying a field value based on the value of another field or set of fields, or dynamically changing the color of a form control when a user enters or views a specific field value.

Events

Recall from Tutorial 10 that an event is a state, condition, or action that Access recognizes. For example, events occur when you click a field or command button on a form, open an object, change a field value in a form, or press a key. Each event has an associated event property that specifies how an object responds when an event occurs. For example, each report has an OnOpen event property that specifies what happens when a user opens the report and triggers the Open event, and each form control has an OnClick event property that specifies what happens when a user clicks the control and triggers the Click event. Event properties appear in the property sheet for forms, reports, and controls. By default, event properties are not set to an initial value, which means that no special action takes place when the event occurs.

In Tutorial 10, you set event property values to macro names and Access executed the macros when those events occurred. You can also create a group of statements using VBA code and set an event property value to the name of that group of statements. Access then executes the group of statements, or procedure, when the event occurs. Such a procedure is called an event procedure. Access has over 60 events and associated event properties. Figure 11-1 describes some frequently used Access events. Each event (such as the AfterUpdate event) has an associated event property (AfterUpdate) and event procedure (ContractNum_AfterUpdate for the AfterUpdate event procedure for the ContractNum control).

Frequently used Access events   **Figure 11-1**

Event	Description
AfterUpdate	Occurs after changed data in a control or a record is updated
BeforeUpdate	Occurs before changed data in a control or a record is updated
Click	Occurs when a user presses and then releases a mouse button over a control in a form
Current	Occurs when the focus moves to a record, making it the current record, or when a form is refreshed or requeried
DblClick	Occurs when a user presses and releases the left mouse button twice over a control in a form within the double-click time limit
Delete	Occurs when a user performs some action, such as pressing the Delete key, to delete a record, but before the record is actually deleted
GotFocus	Occurs when a form or a form control receives the focus
Load	Occurs when a form is opened and its records are displayed
MouseDown	Occurs when a user presses a mouse button
NoData	Occurs after Access formats a report for printing that has no data (the report is bound to an empty recordset), but before the report is printed. Use this event to cancel the printing of a blank report.
Open	Occurs when a form is opened, but before the first record is displayed. For reports, the event occurs before a report is previewed or printed.

Procedures

When you work with VBA, you code a group of statements to perform a set of operations or calculate a value, and then you attach the group of statements to the event property of an object. Access then executes (or runs or **calls**) these statements every time the event occurs for that object or control. Each group of statements is called a procedure. The two types of procedures are Function procedures and Sub procedures.

A **Function procedure**, or **function**, performs operations, returns a value, accepts input values, and can be used in expressions (recall that an expression is a calculation resulting in a single value). For example, some of the Holland database queries use built-in Access functions, such as Sum, Count, and Avg, to calculate a sum, a record count, or an average. To meet Sarah's request, you will create a function named CapAll by entering the appropriate VBA statements. The CapAll function will accept the value entered in a field text box—in this case, the State field—as an input value, capitalize all characters of the field value, and then return the changed field value to be stored in the database and displayed in the field text box.

A **Sub procedure**, or **subroutine**, performs operations and accepts input values, but does not return a value and cannot be used in expressions. Most Access procedures are subroutines because you need the procedures to perform a series of actions or operations in response to an event. Later in this tutorial, you will create a subroutine that displays a message in the frmContractsAndInvoices form only when the contract start date is earlier than a specified date.

Modules

You store a group of related procedures together in an object called a **module**. Figure 11-2 shows the structure of a typical module.

Figure 11-2   **Structure of a VBA module and its procedures**

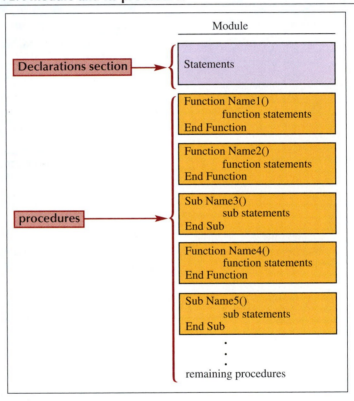

Each module starts with a **Declarations section**, which contains statements that apply to all procedures in the module. One or more procedures, which follow the Declarations section and which can be a mixture of functions and subroutines, constitute the rest of the module. The two basic types of modules are standard modules and class modules.

A **standard module** is a database object that is stored in memory with other database objects (queries, forms, and so on) when you open the database. You can use the procedures in a database's standard modules from anywhere in the database—even from procedures in other modules. A procedure that more than one object can use is called a **public procedure**. For example, the CapAll procedure that you will create capitalizes all letters in the value passed to it. Although you are creating this procedure specifically to work with State field values, you will place it in a standard module and make it public. You could then use the CapAll procedure for any object in the database. All standard modules are listed under the Modules bar in the Navigation Pane.

A **class module** is usually associated with a particular form or report. When you create the first event procedure for a form or report, Access automatically creates an associated form or report class module. When you add additional event procedures to the form or report, Access adds them to the class module for that form or report. Each event procedure in a class module is a **local procedure**, or a **private procedure**, which means that only the form or report for which the class module was created can use the event procedure.

Using an Existing Procedure

Before creating the CapAll procedure for Sarah, you'll use an existing procedure that Lucia created in the class module for the frmCustomerContracts form. Sarah has assigned Cynthia, a staff supervisor, and her team to work with Holland customers and Christopher, another staff supervisor, and his team to work with Grand Rapids customers. The procedure in the class module for the frmCustomerContracts form displays Cynthia's name in blue in a text box to the right of the Zip field text box for Holland customers and Christophers's name in red for Grand Rapids customers. For customers in other cities, the text box is made invisible.

You'll navigate the frmCustomerContracts form to observe the effects of the procedure.

To navigate a form that uses a VBA procedure:

▶ 1. Start Access, and then open the **Holland** database in the Level.03\Tutorial folder provided with your Data Files.

▶ 2. Open the Navigation Pane (if necessary), open the **frmCustomerContracts** form in Form view, and then close the Navigation Pane. For the first record for Sharon Maloney, no value is displayed to the right of the Zip field text box because the City field value is neither Grand Rapids nor Holland.

▶ 3. Select the record number **1** in the Current Record box between the Customer navigation buttons, type **3**, press the **Enter** key, and then click the **CustomerID** text box to deselect all values. The frmCustomerContracts form displays record 3 for Owen Hawes. Because he is a Holland customer, "Cynthia" appears in a blue font to the right of the Zip field text box. See Figure 11-3.

Figure 11-3

Using an existing VBA procedure

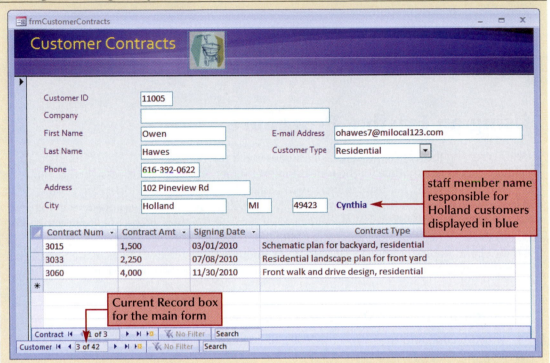

4. Click the **Customer Next record** navigation button ▶ twice to display record 5 for Grand Rapids Engineering Dept, which is a Grand Rapids customer. "Christopher" appears in a red font to the right of the Zip field text box.

Sarah asks you to change the red color for the display of "Christopher" to black so that it doesn't appear to be a warning and so it blends in better with the form.

Displaying an Event Procedure

The VBA procedure that controls the display of the staff member's name and its color for each record is in the class module for the frmCustomerContracts form. Access processes the statements in the procedure when you open the frmCustomerContracts form and also when the focus leaves one record and moves to another. Because the **Current event** occurs when a form opens and when the focus moves to another record, the VBA procedure is associated as an event procedure with the form's **OnCurrent property**.

To change the color of the display of "Christopher" from red to black, you'll modify the event procedure for the form's OnCurrent property. First, you'll switch to Design view, and then you'll display the event procedure.

To display the event procedure for the form's OnCurrent property:

1. Switch to Design view.

2. Right-click the **form selector** to display the shortcut menu, and then click **Properties** to open the property sheet for the form.

3. Click the **Event** tab (if necessary) to display the Event page of the property sheet, and then click the **On Current** box. See Figure 11-4.

Event properties for the frmCustomerContracts form | Figure 11-4

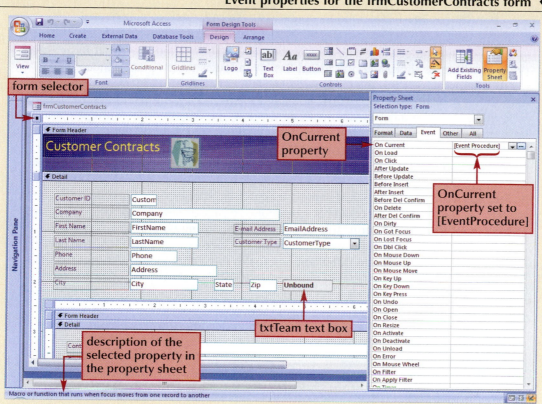

Trouble? The subform on your screen might appear in a white box with "frmContractSubform" inside the box. This is not an error and does not affect your results.

The OnCurrent property is set to [Event Procedure], indicating that Access calls a VBA procedure when the Current event occurs. You'll click the Build button to display the procedure.

4. Click the **Build** button to the right of the On Current box. The Code window opens in the Visual Basic window. See Figure 11-5.

Code window in the Visual Basic window | Figure 11-5

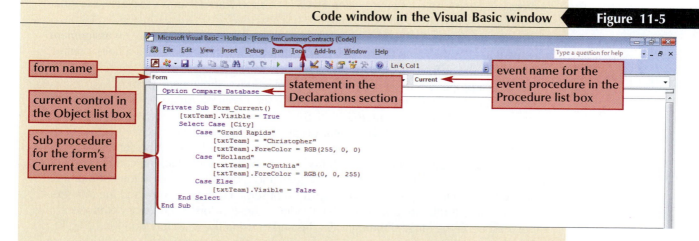

Trouble? If other windows appear in your Visual Basic window, click their Close buttons to close them.

Trouble? If your Code window opens in a restored window, maximize it.

The program you use to create and modify VBA code is called the **Visual Basic Editor** (**VBE**, or **editor** for short), and the **Visual Basic window** is the program window that opens when you use VBE. The **Code window** is the window in which you create, modify, and display specific VBA procedures. You can have as many Code windows open as you have modules in the database. In the Code window, the Object list box (the upper-left list box) indicates the current control (Form), and the Procedure list box (the upper-right list box) indicates the event name (Current) for the event procedure you are viewing.

All event procedures are subroutines. A horizontal line visually separates each procedure in the Code window. Each subroutine begins with a **Sub statement** and ends with an **End Sub statement**. The Sub statement includes the **scope** of the procedure (private or public), the name of the procedure (for example, Form_Current, which means the Current event for the form control), and an opening and closing parenthesis.

Notice the Option Compare statement in the Declarations section above the horizontal line. The **Option Compare statement** designates the technique Access uses to compare and sort text data. The default method "Database," as shown in Figure 11-5, means that Access compares and sorts letters in normal alphabetical order, using the language settings specified for Access running on your computer.

The remaining statements in the Form_Current procedure shown in Figure 11-5 use only two controls in the form: the City field from the tblCustomer table; and txtTeam, which is the text box control that displays "Cynthia" or "Christopher" when it's visible. Based on the City field value, the statements in the procedure do the following:

- If the City field value is "Grand Rapids," then set txtTeam to "Christopher" and set its font color to red.
- If the City field value is "Holland," then set txtTeam to "Cynthia" and set its font color to blue.
- If the City field has any other value, then hide the txtTeam control.

The statements from the *Select Case [City]* statement to the *End Select* statement are an example of a control structure. A **control structure** is a set of VBA statements that work together as a unit. The **Case control structure** is a conditional control structure; it evaluates an expression—the value of the City field, in this case—and then performs one of several alternative actions based on the resulting value (or condition) of the evaluated expression. Each Case statement, such as *Case "Grand Rapids"* and *Case Else*, designates the start of an alternative set of actions.

Statements such as *[txtTeam] = "Christopher"* are assignment statements. An **assignment statement** assigns the value of an expression—Christopher, in this case—to a field, control, or property—the txtTeam control, in this case.

Because a property is associated with a control, you use the general form of *ControlName.PropertyName* to specify a property for a control. An assignment statement such as *[txtTeam].ForeColor = RGB(255, 0, 0)*, for example, assigns a value to the txtTeam's ForeColor property. A control's **ForeColor property** determines the control's foreground, or font, color. The expression in this assignment statement uses a built-in VBA function named RGB. The **RGB function** returns an RGB (red, green, blue) color value, indicating the relative intensity of red (first value), green (second value), and blue (third value) in the color of a property for a control. Figure 11-6 displays a list of some common colors and the red, green, and blue values for the RGB function that produces those colors. Each color component value must be in the range 0 through 255. Instead of using the RGB function for the eight colors shown in Figure 11-6, you can use one of the VBA constants (vbBlack, vbBlue, vbCyan, vbGreen, vbMagenta, vbRed, vbWhite, or vbYellow). A **VBA constant** is a predefined memory location that is initialized to a value that doesn't change. For example, *[txtTeam].ForeColor = vbRed* and *[txtTeam].ForeColor = RGB(255, 0, 0)* both set the color of the txtTeam control to red. You must use the RGB function when you want colors that differ from the eight colors shown in Figure 11-6.

RGB function values for some common colors ◄ **Figure 11-6**

Color	Red Value	Green Value	Blue Value	VBA Constant
Black	0	0	0	vbBlack
Blue	0	0	255	vbBlue
Cyan	0	255	255	vbCyan
Green	0	255	0	vbGreen
Magenta	255	0	255	vbMagenta
Red	255	0	0	vbRed
White	255	255	255	vbWhite
Yellow	255	255	0	vbYellow

The Visible property determines when Access displays a control. Access displays a control when its Visible property is True, and hides the control when its Visible property is False. The *[txtTeam].Visible = True* statement, which Access processes before the *Select Case [City]* statement, displays the txtTeam control. Because Sarah doesn't want the txtTeam control to appear for cities other than Grand Rapids and Holland, the *[txtTeam].Visible = False* statement hides the txtTeam control when the City field value doesn't equal one of the two cities.

Modifying an Event Procedure

Because Sarah wants you to change the red color for the display of "Christopher" to black, with a RGB function value of (0, 0, 0), you'll modify the first set of RGB function values in the event procedure. Then you'll close the Visual Basic window and save and test your modifications.

To modify, save, and test the event procedure:

▶ **1.** Double-click **255** in the first RGB function, and then type **0**. The RGB function is now RGB (0, 0, 0).

▶ **2.** Click the **Save** button 🔲 on the Standard toolbar to save your change, and then click the **Close** button ❎ on the Visual Basic window title bar to close it and return to the Form window in Design view.

▶ **3.** Close the property sheet, save your form design changes, and then switch to Form view.

▶ **4.** Navigate to record 5 for Grand Rapids Engineering Dept. The text "Christopher" displays in black to the right of the Zip field value. Your modification to the event procedure was completed successfully.

▶ **5.** Close the frmCustomerContracts form.

You've completed your modifications to the event procedure. Next, you'll create the CapAll function.

Creating Functions in a Standard Module

Sarah wants you to create a VBA procedure for the frmCustomer form that will automatically convert the values entered in the State field to uppercase. That is, if a user enters "mi" as the state, the procedure should automatically convert it to "MI". Sarah feels that this function will make data entry easier and reduce the number of data-entry errors. Users might not always be consistent about capitalizing entries in the State field, and using this procedure to capitalize entries will ensure consistency.

To accomplish this change, you will first create a simple function, named CapAll, that accepts a **string** (text) input value and returns that string with all letters converted to uppercase. You create the function by typing the statements in the Module window. Then you will create an event procedure that calls the CapAll function whenever the user enters a value in the State field using the frmCustomer form.

Whenever a user enters or changes a field value in a control or in a form and changes the focus to another control or record, Access automatically triggers the **AfterUpdate event**, which, by default, simply accepts the new or changed entry. However, you can set the AfterUpdate event property of a control to a specific event procedure in order to have something else happen when a user enters or changes the field value. In this case, you need to set the State field's AfterUpdate event property to [Event Procedure], and then code an event procedure to call the CapAll function. Calling the CapAll function will cause the entry in the State field to be converted to uppercase letters before storing it in the database.

You will use the CapAll function with the frmCustomer form, so you could add it to the class module for that form. Adding the function to the class module for the frmCustomer form would make it a private function; that is, you could not use it in other forms or database objects. Because you might use the CapAll function in other forms in the Holland database, you'll instead place the CapAll function in a new standard module named basHollandProcedures (*bas* is a standard prefix for modules). Generally, when you enter a procedure in a standard module, it is public, and you can use it in event procedures for any object in the database.

To create a new standard module, you'll begin by opening the Code window.

Reference Window | **Creating a New Standard Module**

- Click the Create tab on the Ribbon.
- In the Other group on the Create tab, click the arrow on the New Object button (with the ScreenTip "New Object: Macro," "New Object: Module," or "New Object: Class Module," depending on which option was last chosen), and then click Module.

You'll now create a new standard module.

To create a new standard module:

1. Click the **Create** tab on the Ribbon.

2. In the Other section on the Create tab, click the arrow on the **New Object** button, and then click **Module** in the list. A new Code window opens in the Visual Basic window. See Figure 11-7.

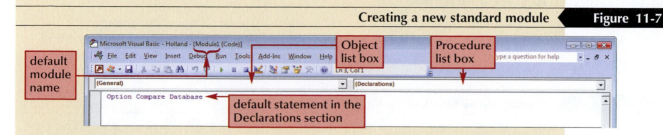

Creating a new standard module | Figure 11-7

Trouble? If other windows appear in your Visual Basic window, click their Close buttons to close them.

In the Code window for the new standard module, the Procedure list box displays the Declarations section as the current procedure in the module. Access automatically includes the Option Compare statement in the Declarations section of a new module. The CapAll function is a simple function that does not require additional statements in the Declarations section.

Creating a Function

Each function begins with a **Function statement** and ends with an **End Function statement**. Access visually separates each procedure in the Code window with a horizontal line. You can view a procedure's statements by selecting the procedure name from the Procedure list box.

The CapAll function begins with the statement *Function CapAll(FValue)*. CapAll is the function name and FValue is used as a placeholder for the input value in the function definition. When the user enters a value for the State field in the frmCustomer form, that value will be passed to the CapAll function and substituted for FValue in the function definition. A placeholder like FValue is called a **parameter**. The value passed to the function and used in place of the parameter when the function is executed is called an **argument**. In other words, the value passed to the function is the argument, which is assigned to the parameter named FValue.

You'll enter the CapAll function in the Code window and then test it. Then you'll attach it to an event procedure for the frmCustomer form. You now can start entering the CapAll function.

To start a new function:

▶ **1.** With the insertion point two lines below the Option Compare statement, type **Function CapAll(FValue)** and then press the **Enter** key. The editor displays a horizontal line that visually separates the new function from the Declarations section. See Figure 11-8.

Figure 11-8 **Starting a new function**

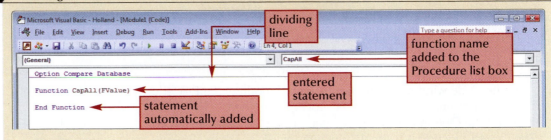

The function name CapAll now appears in the Procedure list box. The editor automatically added the End Function statement and moved the insertion point to the beginning of the blank line between the Function and End Function statements, where you will enter the procedure statements. The editor displays the reserved words Function and End Function in blue. The function name and the parameter name appear in black.

The CapAll function will consist of a single executable assignment statement that you will place between the Function and End Function statements. You'll enter the following assignment statement: *CapAll = UCase(FValue)*. The value of the expression, which is UCase(FValue), will be assigned to the function, which is CapAll.

The expression in the assignment statement uses a built-in Access function named UCase. The **UCase function** accepts a single string argument as input, converts the value of the argument to uppercase letters, and then returns the converted value. The assignment statement assigns the converted value to the CapAll function. Figure 11-9 illustrates this process.

Figure 11-9 **Evaluation of the assignment statement**

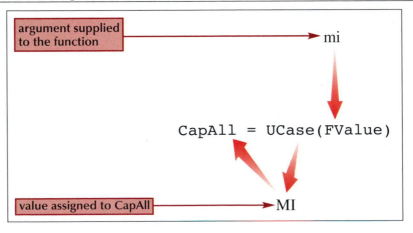

Before entering the assignment statement, you will add a comment line to explain the procedure's purpose. You can include comments anywhere in a VBA procedure to describe what the procedure or a statement does to make it easier for you and other programmers to identify the purpose of statements in your code. You begin a comment with the word Rem (for "Remark") or with a single quotation mark ('). VBA ignores anything following the word Rem or the single quotation mark on a single line.

> **Tip**
>
> Because VBA ignores the contents of comments, you can include spaces, special characters, and mixed-case letters in your comments.

Commenting and Indenting VBA Code | InSight

Different people can use different approaches to solving a problem, so you should use comments in a VBA procedure to explain the purpose of the procedure and to clarify any complicated programming logic used. Most companies have documentaion standards that specify the types of comments that should be included in each procedure. These standards typically require comments that identify the name of the orginal creator of the procedure, the purpose of the procedure, and a history of changes made to the procedure by whom and for what purpose.

VBA does not require statements to be indented in procedures. However, all experienced programmers indent statements to make procedures easier to read and maintain. Pressing the Tab key once indents the line four spaces to the right, which is a sufficient amount of indentation, and pressing the Shift + Tab key combination or the Backspace key once moves the insertion point four spaces to the left. As an example of indenting statements, you left align Select Case and End Select statements to clearly show the start and end of the Case control structure, and indent the statements between them four spaces.

To add a comment and statement to the function:

1. Press the **Tab** key.

2. Type **'Capitalize all letters of a field value** and then press the **Enter** key. Notice that the editor displays the comment in green and indents the new line. After entering the comment line, you can enter the assignment statement, which is the executable statement in the function that performs the actual conversion of the argument to uppercase.

3. Type **CapAll = UCase(**. The editor provides assistance as you enter the statement. After you type UCase and the opening parenthesis, the editor displays a Quick Info banner with a reminder that UCase accepts a single string argument. See Figure 11-10.

> **Tip**
>
> The editor displays a similar Quick Info banner after you type CapAll and press the spacebar; you should ignore this banner because its reminder is incorrect.

Entering the CapAll function in the Code window ◀ Figure 11-10

Trouble? If the Quick Info banner does not open, click Tools on the menu bar, click Options, click the Editor tab, click the Auto Quick Info check box to select it, and then click the OK button.

You'll now finish typing the assignment statement.

> **4.** Type **FValue)** to finish the assignment statement.
>
> The editor scans each statement for errors when you press the Enter key or change the focus to another statement. Because the function is complete and you want the editor to scan the line you just entered for errors, you must move the insertion point to another line.
>
> **5.** Press the ↓ key to move the insertion point to the next line. Because Access finds no errors, the insertion point continues to blink on the last line.

You have finished entering the function, so you'll save it before continuing with your work.

Saving a Function

When you click the Save button in the Visual Basic window, the editor saves the module and its procedures. If you are entering a long procedure, it's a good idea to save your work periodically.

> **To save the module:**
>
> **1.** Click the **Save** button 🖫 on the Standard toolbar, type **basHollandProcedures** in the Module Name text box, and then press the **Enter** key. The editor saves the module and places the new module name in the title bar.

Before making the changes to the frmCustomer form so that the CapAll function automatically acts on every entry in the State field, you can test the function using the Immediate window.

Testing a Procedure in the Immediate Window

When you finish entering a VBA statement, the editor checks the statement to make sure its syntax is correct. Although you may have entered all procedure statements with the correct syntax, the procedure may still contain logic errors. A **logic error** occurs when the procedure produces incorrect results. For example, the CapAll function would have a logic error if you typed mi and the function changed it to mI, Mi, or anything other than the correct result of MI. Even the simplest procedure can contain errors. Be sure to test each procedure thoroughly to ensure that it does exactly what you expect it to do in all situations.

When working in the Code window, you can use the **Immediate window** to test VBA procedures without changing any data in the database. In the Immediate window, you can enter different values to test the procedure you just entered. To test a procedure, type the *Print* keyword or a question mark (?), followed by the procedure name and the value you want to test in parentheses. For example, to test the CapAll function in the Immediate window using the test word mi, type *?CapAll("mi")* and then press the Enter key. Access executes the function and prints the value returned by the function (you expect it to return MI). Note that you must enclose a string of characters within quotation marks in the test statement.

| Reference Window

Testing a Procedure in the Immediate Window

- In the Code window, click View on the menu bar, and then click Immediate Window to open the Immediate window.
- Type a question mark (?), the procedure name, and the procedure's arguments in parentheses. If the argument contains a string of characters, enclose the value in quotation marks.
- Press the Enter key and verify the displayed answer.

Now you can use the Immediate window to test the CapAll function.

To test the CapAll function in the Immediate window:

1. Click **View** on the menu bar, and then click **Immediate Window**. The editor opens the Immediate window across the bottom of the screen and places the insertion point inside the window.

   The Immediate window allows you to run individual lines of VBA code for **debugging** (testing). You will use the Immediate window to test the CapAll function.

2. Type **?CapAll("mi")** and then press the **Enter** key. The editor executes the function and prints the function result, MI, on the next line. See Figure 11-11.

CapAll function executed in the Immediate window ◄ **Figure 11-11**

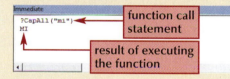

Trouble? If Access displays a dialog box with an error message, click the OK button in the dialog box, correct the error in the Immediate window, and then press the Enter key. If the function does not produce the correct output (MI), correct the CapAll function statements in the Code window, save your changes, click a blank line in the Immediate window, and then repeat Step 2.

To test the CapAll function further, you could enter several other test values, retyping the entire statement each time. Instead, you'll select the current test value, type another value, and then press the Enter key.

3. Double-click the characters **mi** in the first line of the Immediate window.

4. Type **mI** and then press the **Enter** key. The editor executes the function and prints the function result, MI, on the next line.

5. Repeat Steps 3 and 4 two more times, using **Mi** and then **MI** as the test values. The editor prints the correct values, MI and MI.

6. Click the **Close** button ⊠ on the Immediate window title bar to close it, and then click the **Close** button ⊠ on the Visual Basic window title bar to return to the Access window.

7. If you are not continuing on to the next session, close the Holland database, and then exit Access.

Your initial test of the CapAll function is successful. In the next session, you'll modify the frmCustomer form to call the CapAll function for the State field.

1. Why is Visual Basic for Applications called an event-driven, object-oriented language?
2. What is an event procedure?
3. What are the differences between a Function procedure and a Sub procedure?
4. What are the two different types of modules?
5. The _____ of a procedure is either private or public.
6. What can you accomplish in the Immediate window?

Session 11.2

Creating an Event Procedure

Recall that when you add a procedure to a form or report, Access automatically creates a class module for that form or report. Each of these procedures is called an event procedure; Access runs a procedure when a specific event occurs.

Now that you have created the CapAll function as a public procedure in the standard module named basHollandProcedures, you can create an event procedure for the frmCustomer form to call the CapAll function for the State field's AfterUpdate event. Whenever a user enters or changes a State field value, the AfterUpdate event occurs and Access will run your event procedure.

What exactly happens when Access calls a procedure? There is an interaction between the calling statement and the function statements as represented by a series of steps. Figure 11-12 shows the process for the CapAll procedure.

| **Figure 11-12** | **Process of executing a function** |

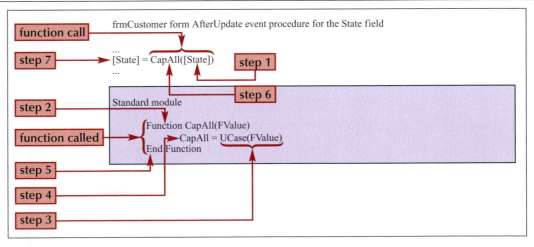

The steps in Figure 11-12 are numbered in the order in which they occur as Access processes the statement and the function. Access goes through the following steps:

- Step 1. The call to the function CapAll passes the value of the argument [State]. This is the value of the State field that is entered or changed by the user.
- Step 2. The function CapAll begins, and the parameter FValue receives the value of [State].
- Step 3. FValue is changed to uppercase.
- Step 4. The value of CapAll is set equal to the result of Step 3.
- Step 5. The function CapAll ends.
- Step 6. The value of CapAll is returned to the point of the call to the function.
- Step 7. The value of [State] is set equal to the returned value of CapAll.

Although it looks complicated, the general function process is simple. The statement contains a function call. When the statement is executed, Access performs the function call, executes the function, returns a single value to the original statement, and completes that statement's execution. Study the steps in Figure 11-12 and trace their sequence until you understand the complete process.

Designing an Event Procedure

Whenever a user enters a new value or modifies an existing value in the State field in the frmCustomer form, Sarah wants Access to execute the CapAll function to ensure that all State field values appear in uppercase letters. After a user changes a State field value, the AfterUpdate event automatically occurs. You can set the AfterUpdate event property to run a macro, call a built-in Access function, or execute an event procedure. Because you want to call your user-defined function from within the event procedure, you'll set the AfterUpdate event property to [Event Procedure], and then add the VBA statements needed to use the CapAll function.

All event procedures are subroutines. Access automatically adds the Sub and End Sub statements to an event procedure. All you need to do is place the statements between the Sub and End Sub statements. Figure 11-13 shows the completed event procedure. The following text describes the parts of the procedure.

AfterUpdate event procedure for the State field   ◄   **Figure 11-13**

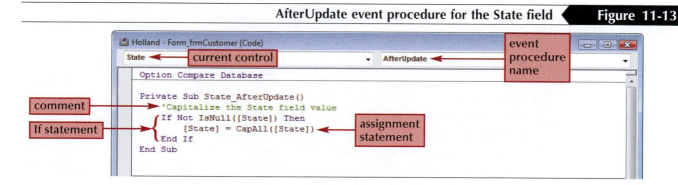

Access names each event procedure in a standard way: the name of the control, an underscore (_), and the event name. No parameters are passed to an event procedure, so Access places nothing in the parentheses following the name of the subroutine.

A user might delete an existing State field value, so that it contains no value, or becomes null. In this case, calling the function accomplishes nothing. The procedure is designed to call the CapAll function only when a user changes the State field to a value that is not null. The If statement screens out the null values. In its simplest form, an **If statement** executes one of two groups of statements based on a condition, similar to

Tip

If the name of the control contains spaces or special characters, Access substitutes underscores for them in the event procedure name.

common English usage. For example, consider the English statements, "If I work the night shift, then I'll earn extra spending money. Otherwise, I'll go to the movies, and I'll dip into my savings." In these sentences, the two groups of statements come before and after the "otherwise," depending on the condition, "if I work the night shift." The first group of statements consists of the clause "I'll earn extra spending money." This clause is called the **true-statement group** because it's what happens if the condition ("I work the night shift") is true. The second group of statements contains "I'll go to the movies, and I'll dip into my savings." This clause is called the **false-statement group** because it is what happens if the condition is false. VBA uses the keyword *If* to precede the condition. The keyword *Then* precedes the true-statement group and the keyword *Else* precedes the false-statement group. The general syntax of a VBA If statement is:

```
If condition Then
     true-statement group
[Else
     false-statement group]
End If
```

Access executes the true-statement group when the condition is true and the false-statement group when the condition is false. In this statement's syntax, the bracketed portions are optional. Therefore, you must omit the *Else* and its related false-statement group when you want Access to execute a group of statements only when the condition is true.

In Figure 11-13, the If statement uses the VBA **IsNull function**, which returns True when the State field value is null and False when it is not null. The *Not* in the If statement is the same logical operator you've used previously to negate an expression. So, Access executes the statement *[State] = CapAll([State])* only when the State field value is not null.

You are ready to make your changes to the frmCustomer form.

Tip

Notice that the State field name is enclosed in brackets, even though brackets are optional for field names and control names that do not contain spaces and special characters.

Adding an Event Procedure

To add an event procedure to the State field's AfterUpdate event property, you need to open the frmCustomer form in Design view.

Reference Window | **Adding an Event Procedure to a Form or Report**

- Open the form or report in Design view, select the control whose event property you want to set, open the property sheet for the control, and then click the Event tab in the property sheet.
- Click the desired event property box, click its Build button, click Code Builder in the Choose Builder dialog box, and then click the OK button.
- Enter the subroutine statements in the Code window.
- Compile the procedure, fix any statement errors, and then save the event procedure.

You can now add the event procedure to the frmCustomer form.

To add the event procedure to the frmCustomer form:

▶ **1.** If you took a break after the previous session, make sure that the Holland database is open and the Navigation Pane is open.

▶ **2.** Open the **frmCustomer** form in Design view.

3. Right-click the **State** text box to select it and to display the shortcut menu, click **Properties** to open the property sheet, and then if necessary click the **Event** tab in the property sheet. Access displays only the event properties in the property sheet. You need to set the AfterUpdate property for the State text box.

4. Click the **After Update** box, click the **Build** button [...] to the right of the After Update box to open the Choose Builder dialog box, click **Code Builder**, and then click the **OK** button. The Code window opens in the Visual Basic window. See Figure 11-14.

Starting a new event procedure in the Code window ◄ **Figure 11-14**

Trouble? If the Object list box does not display the State control, close the Visual Basic window, delete "[Event Procedure]" from the After Update box in the property sheet, click the State text box control on the form, and then repeat Step 4.

5. Enter the statements shown in Figure 11-15. Use the Tab key to indent the lines as shown in the figure, press the Enter key at the end of each line, and press the Backspace key to move one tab stop to the left. Compare your screen with Figure 11-15, and make any necessary corrections.

Completed event procedure ◄ **Figure 11-15**

```
Private Sub State_AfterUpdate()
    'Capitalize the State field value
    If Not IsNull([State]) Then
        [State] = CapAll([State])
    End If
End Sub
```

Trouble? If your event procedure contains errors, correct them by highlighting the errors and typing the corrections. Use the Backspace or Delete keys to delete characters.

Before saving the event procedure, you'll compile it.

Compiling Modules

The VBA programming language is not your native language, nor is it the computer's native language. Although you can learn VBA and become fluent in it, computers cannot understand or learn VBA. For a computer to understand the statements in your VBA modules, Access must translate the statements into a form that it can run. The process of translating modules from VBA to a form your computer understands is called **compilation**; you say that you **compile** the module when you translate it.

When you run a procedure for the first time, Access compiles it for you automatically and opens a dialog box only when it finds syntax errors in the procedure. If it finds an error, Access does not translate the procedure statements. If no errors are detected, Access translates the procedure and does not display a confirmation.

You also can compile a procedure at any time as you enter it by clicking the Compile <database name> command on the Debug menu in the Visual Basic window. In response, Access compiles the procedure and all other procedures in all modules in the database. It's best to compile and save your modules after you've made changes to them, to make sure they don't contain syntax errors. If you don't compile a procedure when you first create it or after you've changed it, Access will compile the procedure when the first user opens the form or report that uses the procedure, and the user could encounter a syntax error and be unable to use the form or report. You don't want users to experience these type of problems, so follow the sound strategy of compiling and fully testing all procedures.

You'll now compile the procedures in the Holland database and save the class module for the frmCustomer form.

To compile the procedures in the Holland database and save the class module:

▶ **1.** Click **Debug** on the menu bar, and then click **Compile Holland**. Access compiles all the modules in the Holland database. Because you have no syntax errors, Access translates the VBA statements and returns control to the Visual Basic window.

   Trouble? If Access identifies any errors in your code, correct the errors and repeat Step 1.

▶ **2.** Save your module changes, close the Visual Basic window, and then close the property sheet.

You have created the function and the event procedure and have set the event property. Next, you'll test the event procedure to make sure it works correctly.

Testing an Event Procedure

You need to display the frmCustomer form in Form view and test the State field's event procedure by entering a few different test State field values in the first record of the form. Moving the focus to another control on the form or to another record triggers the AfterUpdate event for the State field and executes your attached event procedure. Because the CapAll function is attached only to the frmCustomer form, the automatic capitalization of State field values is not in effect when you enter them in the tblCustomer table or in any other object in the Holland database.

To test the event procedure:

▶ **1.** Switch to Form view.

▶ **2.** Select the **State** field value (MI), type **mi** in the State text box, and then press the **Enter** key. Access executes the AfterUpdate event procedure for the State field and changes the State field value to "MI". See Figure 11-16.

frmCustomer form after executing the event procedure | Figure 11-16

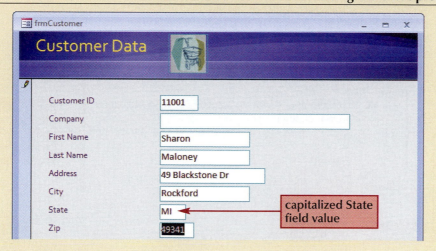

3. Repeat Step 2 three more times, entering **Mi**, then **mI**, and finally **MI** in the State text box. Access displays the correct value "MI" each time.

Sarah wants you to create a more complicated function for the Zip field in the frmCustomer form.

Adding a Second Procedure to a Class Module

Sarah has found that her staff makes frequent errors when entering Michigan zip codes, whose first two digits start 48 through 49, because they tend to transpose the first two digits. She asks you to create a procedure that will verify that Michigan zip codes are in the correct range when her staff updates the Zip field in the frmCustomer form. For this procedure, you will use an event procedure attached to the BeforeUpdate event for the frmCustomer form. The **BeforeUpdate event** occurs before changed data in a control or a record is updated. You'll use the form's BeforeUpdate event for this new procedure, because you want to find data-entry errors for Michigan zip codes and alert users to the errors before the database is updated.

Designing the Field Validation Procedure

Figure 11-17 shows the procedure that you will create to verify Michigan zip codes. You've already seen several of the statements in this procedure in your work with the CapAll function and with the form's Current event.

Figure 11-17

Zip validation procedure

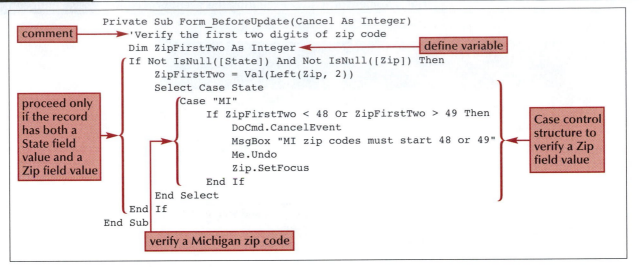

```
                    Private Sub Form_BeforeUpdate(Cancel As Integer)
comment                'Verify the first two digits of zip code
                       Dim ZipFirstTwo As Integer          ← define variable
                   If Not IsNull([State]) And Not IsNull([Zip]) Then
                           ZipFirstTwo = Val(Left(Zip, 2))
proceed only               Select Case State
if the record                  Case "MI"
has both a                         If ZipFirstTwo < 48 Or ZipFirstTwo > 49 Then
State field                            DoCmd.CancelEvent            Case control
value and a                            MsgBox "MI zip codes must start 48 or 49"   structure to
Zip field value                        Me.Undo                      verify a Zip
                                       Zip.SetFocus                 field value
                               End If
                           End Select
                   End If
               End Sub
                       verify a Michigan zip code
```

The Sub and End Sub statements begin and end the subroutine. As specified in the Sub statement, the subroutine executes when the form's BeforeUpdate event occurs. Within parentheses in the Sub statement, *Cancel As Integer* defines Cancel as a parameter with the Integer data type. VBA has data types that are different from the Access data types you've used to define table fields, but each Access data type is equivalent to one of the VBA data types. For example, the Access Number data type with an Integer field size is the same as the VBA Integer data type, and the Access Text data type is the same as the VBA String data type. Figure 11-18 shows the primary VBA data types.

Figure 11-18

Primary VBA data types

Data Type	Stores
Data Type	True/False values
Byte	Integer values from 0 to 255
Currency	Currency values from −922,337,203,685,477.5808 to 922,337,203,685,477.5807
Date	Date and time values from 1 January 100 to 31 December 9999
Decimal	Non-integer values with 0 to 28 decimal places
Double	Non-integer values from $-1.79769313486231*10^{308}$ to $-4.94065645841247*11^{-324}$ for negative values, from $4.94065645841247*11^{-324}$ to $1.79769313486232*10^{308}$ for positive values, and 0
Integer	Integer values from −32,768 to 32,767
Long	Integer values from −2,147,483,648 to 2,147,483,647
Object	Any object reference
Single	Non-integer values from $-3.402823*10^{38}$ to $-1.401298*11^{-45}$ for negative values, from $1.401298*11^{-45}$ to $3.402823*10^{38}$ for positive values, and 0
String	Text values up to 2 billion characters in length
Variant	Any numeric or string data type

When an event occurs, Access performs the default behavior for the event. For some events, such as the BeforeUpdate event, Access executes the event procedure or macro before performing the default behavior. Thus, if something is wrong and the default behavior should not occur, you can cancel the default behavior in the event procedure or macro. For this reason, Access automatically includes the Cancel parameter for the BeforeUpdate event.

The second procedure statement, which starts with a single quotation mark, is a comment. The third statement, *Dim ZipFirstTwo As Integer*, declares the Integer variable named ZipFirstTwo that the subroutine uses. A **variable** is a named location in computer memory that can contain a value. If you use a variable in a module, you must explicitly declare it in the Declarations section or in the procedure where the variable is used. You use the **Dim statement** to declare variables and their associated data types in a procedure. The subroutine will assign the first two digits of a zip code (the Zip field) to the ZipFirstTwo variable, and then will use the variable when verifying that a Michigan zip code begins in the correct range.

The procedure should not attempt to verify records that contain null field values for the State field and the Zip field. To screen out these conditions, the procedure uses the fourth procedure statement, *If Not IsNull([State]) And Not IsNull([Zip]) Then*, which pairs with the last *End If* statement. The If statement determines whether both the State and Zip fields are nonnull. If both conditions are true (both fields contain values), then Access executes the next statement in the procedure. If either condition is false, then Access executes the paired End If statement, and the following End Sub statement ends the procedure without the execution of any other statement.

The fifth procedure statement, *ZipFirstTwo = Val(Left(Zip, 2))*, uses two built-in VBA functions, the Val function and the Left function, to assign the first two digits of the Zip field value to the ZipFirstTwo variable. The **Left function** returns a string containing a specified number of characters from the left side of a specified string. In this case, the Left function returns the leftmost two characters of the Zip field value. The **Val function** returns the numbers contained in a specified string as a numeric value. In this case, the Val function returns the leftmost two characters of the Zip field value as an integer value.

You encountered the Case control structure previously in the frmCustomerContracts form's Current event procedure. For the BeforeUpdate event procedure, the *Select Case State* statement evaluates the State field value. For State field values equal to MI (Michigan zip codes), the next If statement is executed. For all other State field values, nothing further in the procedure is executed, Access performs the default behavior, and control returns back to the form for further processing. The procedure uses the Case control structure because although Sarah wants the procedure to verify the first two digits of only Michigan zip codes for now, she might want to expand the procedure in the future to verify the first two digits of zip codes for other states, as Belmont Landscapes expands its business.

Because valid Michigan zip codes start 48 through 49, invalid numeric values for the Zip field are less than 48 or are greater than 49. The next VBA statement, *If ZipFirstTwo < 48 Or ZipFirstTwo > 49 Then*, is true only for invalid Michigan zip codes. When the If statement is true, the next four statements are executed. When the If statement is false, nothing further in the procedure is executed, Access performs the default behavior, and control returns back to the form for further processing.

The first of the four VBA statements that execute for invalid Michigan zip codes is the DoCmd statement. The **DoCmd statement** executes an action in a procedure. The *DoCmd.CancelEvent* statement executes the CancelEvent action. The **CancelEvent action** cancels the event that caused the procedure or macro containing the action to execute. In this case, Access cancels the BeforeUpdate event and does not update the database with your changes to the current record. In addition, Access cancels subsequent events that would have occurred if the BeforeUpdate event had not been canceled. For example, because the form's BeforeUpdate event is triggered when you move to a different record, the following events are triggered when you move to a different record, in the order listed: BeforeUpdate event for the form, AfterUpdate event for the form, Exit event for the control with the focus, LostFocus event for the control with the focus, RecordExit event for the form, and Current event for the form. When the CancelEvent action executes, all these events are canceled and the focus remains with the record being edited.

The second of the four VBA statements that are executed for invalid Michigan zip codes is the MsgBox statement. The *MsgBox "MI zip codes must start 48 or 49"* statement displays its message in a message box that remains on the screen until the user clicks the OK button. The message box appears on top of the frmCustomer form so the user can view the changed field values in the current record.

For invalid Michigan zip codes, after the user clicks the OK button in the message box, the *Me.Undo* statement is executed. The **Me keyword** refers to the current object, in this case the frmCustomer form. **Undo** is a method that clears all changes made to the current record in the frmCustomer form, so that the field values in the record are as they were before the user made current changes. A **method** is an action that operates on specific objects or controls.

Finally, for invalid Michigan zip codes the *Zip.SetFocus* statement is executed. **SetFocus** is a method that moves the focus to the specified object or control. In this case, Access moves the focus to the Zip field in the current record in the frmCustomer form.

Adding a Second Event Procedure

After designing the procedure to verify Michigan zip codes, you can now add an event procedure for the frmCustomer form's BeforeUpdate event property. Access will execute the event procedure whenever field values in a record are entered or updated.

To add the event procedure for the frmCustomer form's BeforeUpdate event:

1. Switch to Design view.

2. Right-click the **form selector** to display the shortcut menu, and then click **Properties** to open the property sheet for the form.

3. If necessary, click the **Event** tab in the property sheet.

4. Click the **Before Update** box, click the **Before Update** arrow, click **[Event Procedure]**, and then click the **Build** button ⟦...⟧ to the right of the Before Update box. The Code window, which contains new Private Sub and End Sub statements, opens in the Visual Basic window.

   The Code window also contains the event procedure for the State control's After-Update property, which you entered earlier. Horizontal lines separate the Option Compare statement from the new procedure and from the AfterUpdate event procedure.

5. Press the **Tab** key, and then type the subroutine statements exactly as shown in Figure 11-19. Press the Enter key after you enter each statement, press the Tab key to indent lines as necessary, and press the Backspace key to move the insertion point one tab stop to the left. When you are finished, your screen should look like Figure 11-19.

Tip

As you enter statements for the procedure, remember that capitalization is important in all statements so that your code is readable and maintainable.

Event procedure for the frmCustomer form's BeforeUpdate event | **Figure 11-19**

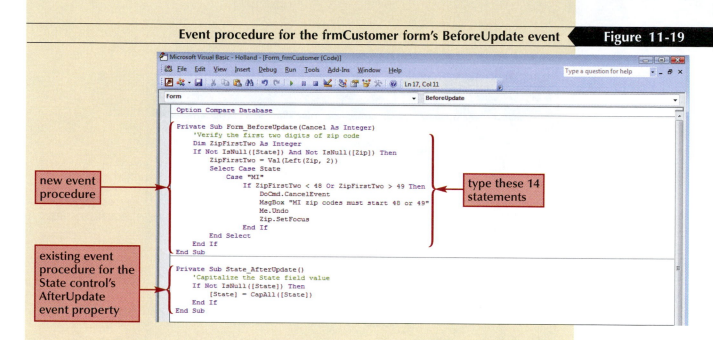

6. Click **Debug** on the menu bar, and then click **Compile Holland**. Access compiles all the modules in the Holland database.

   Trouble? If the editor finds an error, it highlights the error and opens a dialog box with a message describing the nature of the error. Click the OK button and then change the highlighted error by comparing your entries with those shown in Figure 11-19. Then repeat Step 6 to scan the statements for errors again and to compile the module.

7. Save your class module changes.

8. Close the Visual Basic window to return to the Form window, and then close the property sheet.

You can now test the event procedure. To do so, you'll switch to Form view for the frmCustomer form and test the form's BeforeUpdate event procedure by entering valid and invalid Zip field values.

To test the form's BeforeUpdate event procedure:

1. Switch to Form view. Access displays record 1 for Sharon Maloney. The first two digits of the Zip field value, 49, represent a valid Michigan zip code in the range that starts 48 or 49.

2. Select **49341** in the Zip text box, type **98765**, press the **Tab** key to move to the Phone text box, and then click the **Next record** navigation button ▶ to move to the next record. Access executes the BeforeUpdate event procedure for the frmCustomer form, determines that the Michigan zip code's first two digits are incorrect, and displays the message box you included in the procedure. See Figure 11-20.

Tip

After typing an invalid value in the Zip text box, pressing the Tab key to change the focus to the Phone text box does not trigger the form's BeforeUpdate event procedure. You must navigate to another record to trigger the form's BeforeUpdate event procedure.

Figure 11-20 | After the frmCustomer form's BeforeUpdate event procedure detects an error

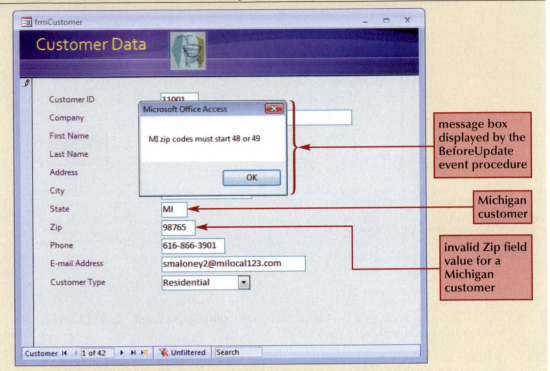

While the message box is open, the updated Zip field value of 98765 remains on screen for you to review.

▶ 3. Click the **OK** button. The message box closes, the Undo method changes the Zip field value to 49341, its original value, and the SetFocus method moves the focus to the Zip text box.

Next, you'll change the Zip field value to 49999, which is a valid Michigan zip code.

▶ 4. Change the Zip field value to **49999**, and then click the **Next record** navigation button ▶ to move to the next record. The form's BeforeUpdate event procedure verifies that the zip code is a valid value for a Michigan customer, and the focus moves to the Zip text box in the next record.

▶ 5. Click the **Previous record** navigation button ◀ to move to the first record, change the State field value to **TX**, change the Zip field value to **98765**, and then press the **Next record** navigation button ▶ to move to the next record. The form's BeforeUpdate event procedure checks zip codes only for Michigan, so the focus moves to the Zip text box in the next record.

Next, you'll change the first record's State field value to MI and the Zip field value to 49341, which are the original values for the record.

▶ 6. Click the **Previous record** navigation button ◀ to move to the first record, and then change the State field value to **MI** and the Zip field value to **49341**.

▶ 7. If you are not continuing on to the next session, close the Holland database, and then exit Access.

Sarah has one more procedure she wants you to create for the frmCustomer form, and then Lucia wants you to put the finishing touches on the Holland database user interface. You'll fulfill these requests in the next session.

Session 11.2 Quick Check | Review

1. The VBA _____ statement executes one of two groups of statements based on a condition.
2. What happens when you compile a module?
3. What is the purpose of the Dim statement?
4. The _____ function returns the numbers contained in a specified string as a numeric value.
5. What is the purpose of the DoCmd statement?
6. What is a method?

Session 11.3

Changing the Case of a Field Value

Sarah wants to make it easier for users to enter a company name when using the frmCustomer form, so she asks you to create a procedure that will automatically convert the case of letters entered in the Company field. This procedure will capitalize the first letter of each word in the field and change all other letters to lowercase. You'll use an event procedure attached to the AfterUpdate event for the Company field to perform this automatic conversion. For example, if a user enters "monroe sTate College" as the Company field value, the event procedure will correct the field value to "Monroe State College."

You'll use the StrConv function in the event procedure to perform the conversion. The **StrConv function** converts the letters in a string to all uppercase letters or to all lowercase letters, or converts the first letter of every word in the string to uppercase letters and all other letters to lowercase letters. The statement you'll use in the event procedure is: *Company = StrConv(Company, vbProperCase)*. The StrConv function's second argument, the **vbProperCase constant**, is a VBA constant that specifies the conversion of the first letter in every word in a string to uppercase letters and the conversion of all other letters to lowercase letters. Recall that the CapAll function you created earlier in this tutorial used the statement *CapAll = UCase(FValue)* to capitalize every character in a string. Instead, you could have used the statement *CapAll = StrConv(FValue, vbUpperCase)* to accomplish the same result.

Next, you'll create the AfterUpdate event procedure for the Company field in the frmCustomer form to perform the automatic conversion of entered and updated Company field values.

> **Tip**
>
> Other VBA constants you can use with the StrConv function are the **vbUpperCase constant**, which specifies the conversion of the string to all uppercase letters, and the **vbLowerCase constant**, which specifies the conversion of the string to all lowercase letters.

To add the event procedure for the Company field's AfterUpdate event:

1. If you took a break after the previous session, make sure that the Holland database is open, the Navigation Pane is open, and the frmCustomer form is open in Form view.

2. Switch to Design view.

3. Right-click the **Company** text box to display the shortcut menu, and then click **Properties** to open the property sheet for the control.

4. If necessary, click the **Event** tab in the property sheet.

▶ **5.** Click the **After Update** box, click the **After Update** arrow, click **[Event Procedure]**, and then click the **Build** button ⬚ to the right of the After Update box. The Code window, which contains new Private Sub and End Sub statements, opens in the Visual Basic window. The Code window also contains two other event procedures defined in the form's class module, one event procedure for the form's BeforeUpdate event, and the other event procedure for the State field's AfterUpdate event.

▶ **6.** Press the **Tab** key, and then type the subroutine statements exactly as shown in Figure 11-21.

Figure 11-21	Event procedure for the Company control's AfterUpdate event

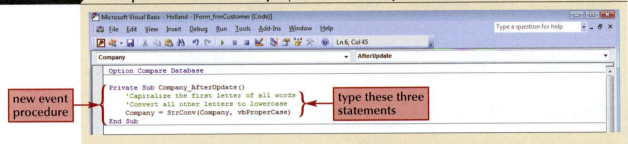

▶ **7.** Click **Debug** on the menu bar, click **Compile Holland**, save your class module changes, close the Visual Basic window, and then close the property sheet.

You can now test the event procedure. To do so, you'll view the frmCustomer form in Form view and test the Company field's event procedure by entering different Company field values.

To test the new event procedure:

▶ **1.** Switch to Form view, and then press the **Tab** key to move to the Company text box for the first record, for Sharon Maloney. This record does not display a Company field value.

You'll test the new event procedure by entering Company field values in record 1, making sure the field value is null when you finish testing.

▶ **2.** Type **test company name**, and then press the **Enter** key. Access executes the AfterUpdate event procedure for the Company field and changes the Company field value to "Test Company Name".

▶ **3.** Press the ↑ key to select the Company field value.

▶ **4.** Repeat Steps 2 and 3 two more times, entering **sECond test namE** (correctly changed to "Second Test Name"), and then entering **THIRD TEST NAME** (correctly changed to "Third Test Name").

▶ **5.** Press the ↑ key to select the Company field value, press the **Delete** key to remove the Company field value, and then close the form.

Hiding a Control and Changing a Control's Color

Sarah wants you to add a message to the frmContractsAndInvoices form that will remind her staff when a contract record should be considered for archiving and deletion from the tblContract table. Specifically, when the start date is prior to the year 2011, Sarah wants the StartDate field value displayed in red; all other StartDate field values should be displayed in black. She also wants to display a message to the right of the StartDate text box in red only when the contract is a candidate for archiving and deletion. The red font will help to draw attention to these contracts. See Figure 11-22.

Purge message and red StartDate field value in frmContractsAndInvoices form   Figure 11-22

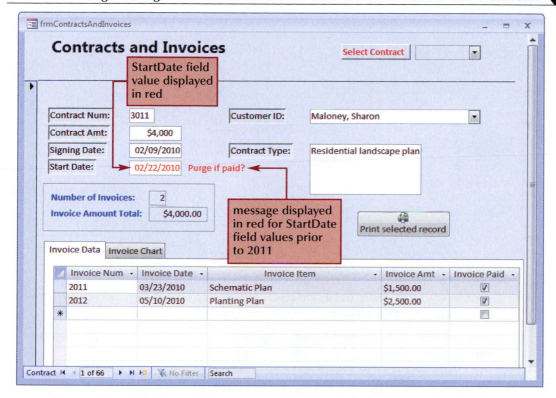

In the frmContractsAndInvoices form, you will add a label to the right of the StartDate text box that will display the text "Purge if paid?" in red. Because Sarah wants the text to appear only when the StartDate field has a value of less than 1/1/2011, you will change the label's Visible property during execution. You will also change the foreground color of the value in the StartDate text box to red when the StartDate field value is less than 1/1/2011 and to black for all other dates.

Because the change to the Visible property takes place during execution, you will add code to the Current event procedure in the frmContractsAndInvoices form. To set a property in a Visual Basic statement, you enter the object name followed by the property name, separating the two names with a period. For example, if the label name for the message is lblPurgeMsg, then the statement *[lblPurgeMsg].Visible = False* hides the label on the form.

First, you'll add a label to the frmContractsAndInvoices form that will display a message in red for values that have a StartDate field value of less than 1/1/2011. For all other dates, the label will be hidden.

To add the label to the frmContractsAndInvoices form:

▶ 1. Open the **frmContractsAndInvoices** form in Design view.

▶ 2. In the Controls group on the Design tab, click the **Label** button.

▶ 3. Position the pointer in the Detail section; when the center of the pointer's plus symbol is positioned two grid dots to the right of the StartDate text box and just below the top of the StartDate text box, click the mouse button.

▶ 4. Type **Purge if paid?** and then press the **Enter** key. The new label box appears in the form and displays the Error Checking Options button. See Figure 11-23.

| Figure 11-23 | Label box added to the form |

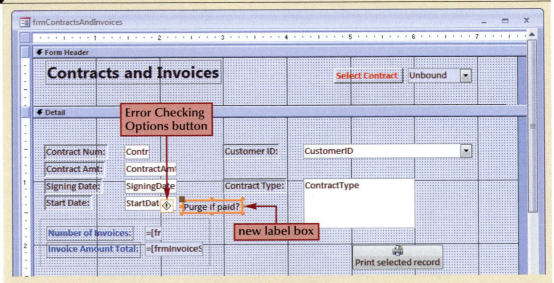

▶ 5. Position the pointer on the **Error Checking Options** button ⬦. The message, "This is a new label and is not associated with a control," appears. Because the new label should not be associated with a control, you'll choose to ignore this error.

▶ 6. Click the arrow on the **Error Checking Options** button ⬦, and then click **Ignore Error**. The Error Checking Options button disappears.

▶ 7. Hold down the **Shift** key, click the **StartDate** text box to select this control and the label box, right-click one of the selected controls, point to **Align**, and then click **Top** to align both controls on their top edges.

Trouble? If the Error Checking Options button appears, click the arrow on the Error Checking Options button, and then click Dismiss Error.

You'll now set the label's Name and ForeColor properties, and add the Current event procedure to the frmContractsAndInvoices form.

To set the label's properties and add the Current event procedure to the form:

▶ 1. Deselect all controls, right-click the **Purge if paid?** label to display the shortcut menu, and then click **Properties** to open the property sheet.

▶ 2. Click the **All** tab (if necessary), select the value in the **Name** box (if necessary), and then type **lblPurgeMsg**.

You can now set the ForeColor property for the label so that the message is displayed in red.

3. Click the **Fore Color** box, and then click the **Build** button [...] to the right of the Fore Color box. Access opens a color gallery.

4. Click the **Red** box (row 7, column 2 in the Standard Colors gallery), and then press the **Enter** key. Access sets the ForeColor property value to the code for red (255). Notice that Access changed the foreground (text) color of the Purge if paid? label to red.

You'll now enter the event procedure for the form's Current event. Access will execute this event procedure whenever the frmContractsAndInvoices form is opened or the focus moves from one record to another.

5. Click the **form selector**, scroll down the property sheet to the On Current box, click the **On Current** box, click the **On Current** arrow, click **[Event Procedure]**, and then click the **Build** button [...]. Access opens the Code window in the Visual Basic window, displaying the Sub and End Sub statements.

6. Press the **Tab** key, and then type the Sub procedure statements exactly as shown in Figure 11-24.

Current event procedure for the frmContractsAndInvoices form **Figure 11-24**

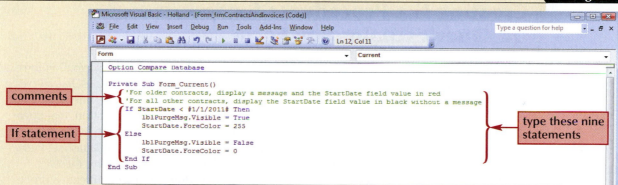

The form's Current procedure uses an If statement to determine whether the current value of the StartDate field is less than 1/1/2011. If the current value of the StartDate field is less than 1/1/2011, the procedure sets the lblPurgeMsg control's Visible property to True (which means the Purge if paid? message will appear in the frmContractsAndInvoices form), and it sets the StartDate control's ForeColor property to 255 (red). If the current value of the StartDate field is greater than or equal to 1/1/2011, the procedure sets the lblPurgeMsg control's Visible property to False, hiding the message in the form, and sets the StartDate control's ForeColor property to 0 (black).

7. Click **Debug** on the menu bar, and then click **Compile Holland**. Access compiles all the modules in the Holland database.

8. Save your class module changes, close the Visual Basic window, and then close the property sheet.

You'll now test the frmContractsAndInvoices form's Current event procedure.

To test the Current event procedure for the frmContractsAndInvoices form:

▶ 1. Switch to Form view. Access displays the first record for ContractNum 3011, whose start date is prior to 1/1/2011. The message "Purge if paid?" appears in red, as does the StartDate field value of 02/22/2010.

   Trouble? If Access displays a dialog box indicating a run-time error, Access could not execute the event procedure. Click the Debug button in the dialog box. Access displays the event procedure in the Code window and highlights the line containing the error. Check the statements carefully and make sure that they are exactly like those shown in Figure 11-24. Make the necessary changes, compile the module, save the module, and then close the Code window. Then repeat Step 1.

▶ 2. Click the **Last record** navigation button ▶| to display record 66 for ContractNum 3201, whose start date is after 1/1/2011. The Purge if paid? message does not appear, and the StartDate field value is displayed in black.

▶ 3. Close the form.

You have finished your work on the Current event procedure for the frmContractsAndInvoices form. Next, you'll create the necessary procedures for the command buttons on the frmQueriesDialogBox form.

Creating the Procedures for the frmQueriesDialogBox Form

Your last programming task is to complete the procedures for the frmQueriesDialogBox form. Lucia wants Access to highlight the first item in the list box when the frmQueriesDialogBox form first opens, by placing the focus on it. Next, when a user double-clicks a query name in the list box or selects a query name and then clicks the Preview command button, that query should open in Print Preview. Finally, when a user selects a query name in the list box and then clicks the Display command button, the selected query should open in Datasheet view. You'll create the three procedures for the frmQueriesDialogBox form to perform these processes. Figure 11-25 shows the names for the three procedures. You won't create a procedure for the Close command button because you used the Control Wizards tool in Tutorial 10 to attach a macro to close the form when you click the Close command button.

Figure 11-25 ▸ **frmQueriesDialogBox form's procedures**

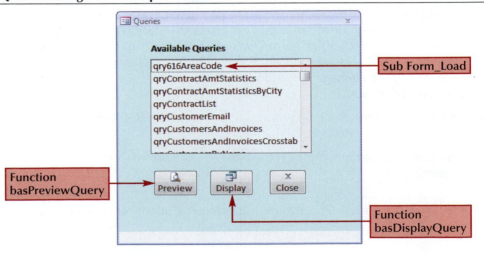

Coding the Load Event Procedure for the frmQueriesDialogBox Form

When a user opens the frmQueriesDialogBox form, Lucia wants Access to place the focus on the first query in the list box automatically. To accomplish this objective, you need to add VBA statements to the form's Load event. Figure 11-26 shows the code for the form's Load event.

Load event procedure for the frmQueriesDialogBox form   Figure 11-26

```
Private Sub Form_Load()
    'Move the focus to the list box and then to the first query in the list
    lstQueryList.SetFocus
    SendKeys "{Down}"
End Sub
```

The **Load event** occurs when Access opens a form. Anything you specify for this event will happen each time the form is opened. The statement *lstQueryList.SetFocus* moves the focus to lstQueryList, which is the name for the form's list box, but does not set the focus to any specific query name. The *SendKeys "{Down}"* statement sends the down arrow keystroke to the list box; Access responds to this statement by highlighting the first query in the list box. The end result of these statements is that when the user opens the dialog box, the first query is highlighted and has the focus.

Reusing Code from Other Sources | InSight

Creating your first few VBA procedures from scratch is a daunting task. To get started, you should take advantage of the available resources that discuss various ways of designing and programming commonly encountered situations. These resources include the Northwind database (a sample database available as one of the Access template databases), Access VBA books and periodicals, Web sites that provide sample code, and Access Help. These resources contain sample procedures and code segments, often with commentary about what the procedures and statements accomplish and why. However, when you create a procedure, you are responsible for knowing what it does, how it does it, when to use it, how to enhance it in the future, and how to fix it when problems occur. If you simply copy statement from another source without thoroughly understanding them, you won't be able to enhance or fix the procedure in the future. In addition, you might overlook better ways to accomplish the same thing—better because the procedure would run faster or would be easier to enhance. In some cases, the samples you find might be flawed, so that they won't work properly for you. The time you spend researching and completely understanding sample code will pay dividends in your learning experience to create VBA procedures.

You'll open the frmQueriesDialogBox form in Design view and create the Load event procedure.

To create the Load event procedure for the frmQueriesDialogBox form:

1. Open the **frmQueriesDialogBox** form in Design view.

2. Right-click the **form selector** to open the shortcut menu, and then click **Properties** to open the form's property sheet.

▶ **3.** Click the **Event** tab (if necessary), click the **On Load** box, click the **On Load** arrow, click **[Event Procedure]**, and then click the **Build** button ▣. Access opens the Code window in the Visual Basic window, displaying the Sub and End Sub statements for the Load event procedure.

▶ **4.** Press the **Tab** key, and then type the Sub procedure statements as shown in Figure 11-27.

Figure 11-27 | **Load event procedure entered in the Code window**

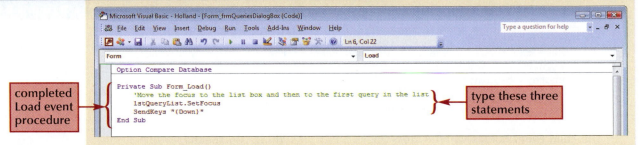

completed Load event procedure

type these three statements

The word "Private" in the first line of the subroutine definition indicates that the procedure can be used only in the class module for this form. Form_Load indicates that this subroutine is the event procedure for the form's Load event.

▶ **5.** Click **Debug** on the menu bar, click **Compile Holland**, and then save your module changes.

▶ **6.** Close the Visual Basic window, and then close the property sheet.

▶ **7.** Next, you'll test the procedure by opening the frmQueriesDialogBox form in Form view and verifying that the first query in the list box is selected.

▶ **8.** Switch to Form view. Notice that the first query in the list box is selected.

   Trouble? If the first query in the list box is not selected, you probably did not type the curly braces { } in the SendKeys statement. Switch to Design view, and then open the form's property sheet. Click the On Load box, click the Build button, and then correct the event procedure. Then repeat Steps 5 through 7.

You have finished your work with the Load event procedure for the frmQueriesDialogBox form. Next, you need to create the form's basPreviewQuery and basDisplayQuery procedures.

Coding the Procedures for the frmQueriesDialogBox Form

In the frmQueriesDialogBox form, double-clicking a query name in the list box or selecting a query name and then clicking the Preview command button must open that query in Print Preview. Selecting a query name in the list box and then clicking the Display command button must open that query in Datasheet view. Figure 11-28 shows the code you'll enter in procedures to perform these actions.

basPreviewQuery and basDisplayQuery functions for the form **Figure 11-28**

```
Private Function basPreviewQuery()
     'Open the selected query in Print Preview
     DoCmd.OpenQuery lstQueryList, acViewPreview
End Function

Private Function basDisplayQuery()
     'Open the selected query in Datasheet view
     DoCmd.OpenQuery lstQueryList, acViewNormal
End Function
```

The DoCmd statements in these two procedures run the OpenQuery action. The parameter choices for the OpenQuery action are the selected query in the lstQueryList list box and the view you'll use when opening the selected query. The query view choices are selected from these VBA constants: acViewPreview to open the query in Print Preview, acViewDesign to open the query in Design view, and acViewNormal to open the query in Datasheet view.

Next, you'll switch to Design view for the frmQueriesDialogBox form, create the two functions, and attach the functions to the appropriate control properties.

> **Tip**
>
> VBA constants, such as acViewPreview, acViewDesign, and acViewNormal, are pre-defined in Access, so you do not define them in a Dim statement as you do for variables you create.

To add the two functions to the frmQueriesDialogBox form:

▶ 1. Switch to Design view.

▶ 2. In the Tools group on the Design tab, click the **View Code** button 🔲 to open the Code window for the form's class module in the Visual Basic window.

▶ 3. Click the arrow on the **Insert Module** button 🔳 on the Standard toolbar, and then click **Procedure**. The Add Procedure dialog box opens. See Figure 11-29.

> **Tip**
>
> You can also press the F7 key to open the Code window.

Add Procedure dialog box **Figure 11-29**

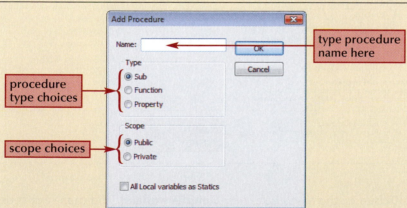

In the Add Procedure dialog box, you select the procedure type (sub, function, or property), and the procedure scope (public or private). You can also choose for all variables defined in the procedure to be static variables, which are variables that retain their values between executions of the procedure.

▶ 4. Type **basPreviewQuery** in the Name text box, click the **Function** option button, click the **Private** option button, and then click the **OK** button. Access displays the Function and End Function statements for the new basPreviewQuery procedure.

5. Press the **Tab** key, and then type the statements for the basPreviewQuery function exactly as shown in Figure 11-30.

| Figure 11-30 | basPreviewQuery function for the frmQueriesDialogBox form |

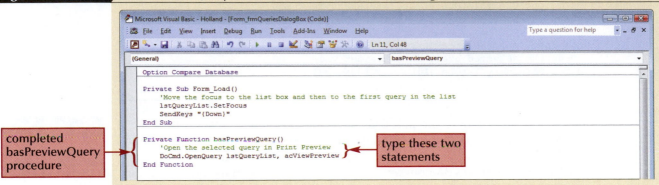

completed basPreviewQuery procedure

type these two statements

Now you'll enter the second function, basDisplayQuery, for opening the selected query in Datasheet view.

6. Click the **Insert Procedure** button on the Standard toolbar, type **basDisplayQuery** in the Name text box, click the **Function** option button, click the **Private** option button, and then click the **OK** button.

7. Press the **Tab** key, and then type the statements for the basDisplayQuery function exactly as shown in Figure 11-31.

| Figure 11-31 | basDisplayQuery function for the frmQueriesDialogBox form |

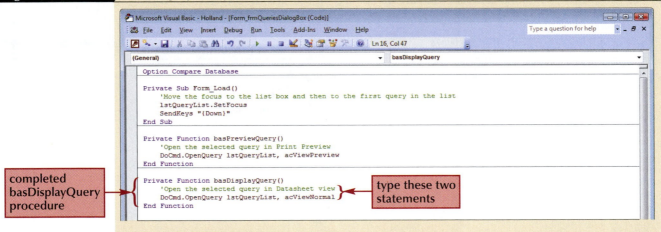

completed basDisplayQuery procedure

type these two statements

8. Click **Debug** on the menu bar, click **Compile Holland**, and then save your module changes.

9. Close the Visual Basic window.

Next, you'll attach the appropriate procedure to the correct properties for the form objects.

To specify the procedures for the event properties:

1. Right-click the form's list box (the box containing the word "Unbound") to open the shortcut menu, and then click **Properties** to open the property sheet.

2. Make sure the **Event** tab is selected, click the **On Dbl Click** box, and then type **=basPreviewQuery()**. This entry specifies that Access will execute the procedure for previewing a query whenever a user double-clicks a query name in the list box. See Figure 11-32.

Setting the OnDblClick event property for the list box | Figure 11-32

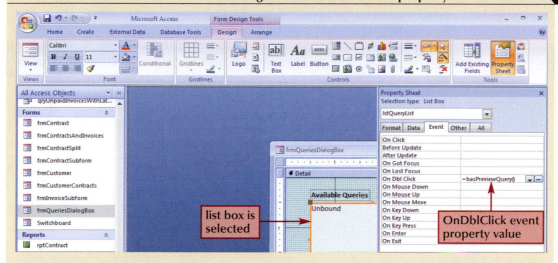

3. Click the form's **Preview** command button (the leftmost command button), click the property sheet's **On Click** box, and then type **=basPreviewQuery()**. This entry specifies that Access will execute the procedure for previewing a query whenever a user selects a query name and then clicks the Preview command button.

4. Click the form's **Display** command button (the middle command button), click the property sheet's **On Click** box, and then type **=basDisplayQuery()**. This entry specifies that Access will execute the procedure for opening the query datasheet whenever a user selects a query name and then clicks the Display command button.

5. Close the property sheet, and then save your form changes.

You'll now test the changes you made to the frmQueriesDialogBox form.

To test the changes to the frmQueriesDialogBox form:

1. Switch to Form view.

2. Double-click a few of the query names, in turn, in the list box to verify that the correct query opens in Print Preview, and close the Print Preview window each time to return to the dialog box in Form view.

3. Click a query name in the list box, click the **Preview** command button to verify that the correct query opens in Print Preview, and then close the Print Preview window to return to the dialog box in Form view.

4. Repeat Step 3 for several more query names in the form's list box.

5. Click a query name in the list box, click the **Display** command button to verify that the correct query datasheet opens, and then close the query to return to the dialog box in Form view.

▶ **6.** Repeat Step 5 for several more query names in the form's list box.

▶ **7.** Click the **Close** command button in the dialog box to close the form and return to the Access window.

▶ **8.** Close the Holland database, make a backup copy of the database, open the **Holland** database, compact and repair the database, close the database, and then exit Access.

Lucia stops by and views your results. She is very pleased with the VBA modifications to the forms. Next, she wants you to make access to the Holland database more secure, and she wants you to make the final enhancements to the database and the user interface. In the next tutorial, you'll complete your work with the Holland database.

Review | **Session 11.3 Quick Check**

1. What is a VBA constant?

2. You can use the UCase function or the _____ function to convert a string to all uppercase letters.

3. What does the Visible property determine?

4. What does the ForeColor property determine?

5. When does the Current event occur?

6. When does the Load event occur for an object?

Tutorial Summary | Review

In this tutorial, you worked with Visual Basic for Applications, the programming language for Microsoft Office programs. You executed, viewed, and modified an existing event procedure. You then created a new function to convert all characters in a field value to uppercase letters, tested it in the Immediate window, added an event procedure to a form to use the function, and then tested the event procedure after compiling the modules in the database. Next, you created event procedures to convert a field value to proper uppercase and lowercase letters and to show/hide a control and to change font colors based on a condition. Finally, you completed the frmQueriesDialogBox form by adding one event procedure and two functions to coordinate a list box selection with two command buttons.

Key Terms

AfterUpdate event
argument
assignment statement
BeforeUpdate event
calls
CancelEvent action
Case control structure
class module
Code window
coding
compilation
compile
control structure
Current event
debugging
Declarations section
Dim statement
DoCmd statement
End Function statement
End Sub statement
event-driven language
false-statement group

ForeColor property
function
Function procedure
Function statement
If statement
Immediate window
IsNull function
Left function
Load event
local procedure
logic error
Me keyword
method
module
object-oriented language
OnCurrent property
Option Compare
    statement
parameter
private procedure
public procedure
RGB function
scope

SetFocus
standard module
statement
StrConv function
string
Sub procedure
Sub statement
subroutine
true-statement group
UCase function
Undo
Val function
variable
VBA constant
vbLowerCase constant
vbProperCase constant
vbUpperCase constant
Visual Basic Editor (VBE,
    editor)
Visual Basic for
    Applications (VBA)
Visual Basic window

Practice | **Review Assignments**

Practice the skills you learned in the tutorial using the same case scenario.

Data File needed for the Review Assignments: Vendor.accdb (*cont. from Tutorial 10*)

Lucia asks you to continue your work with the user interface for the Vendor database. To help with this request, complete the following steps:

1. Open the **Vendor** database located in the Level.03\Review folder provided with your Data Files.
2. Create a procedure for the **frmCompaniesWithProducts** form to convert CompanyName field values to proper case—capitalize the first letter of each word, and convert all other letters to lowercase. Test the procedure, and then close the form.
3. Create a procedure for the **frmProductData** form to do the following:
   a. Display the Price field value in red when the value is greater than $1,000 and in black for other values.
   b. Display the message **high price** to the left of the Price text box in bold, red text. Display the message only when the Price field value is greater than $1,000. (*Hint*: Remove all controls from the control layout before resizing the Price label box and adding the label for the message.)
   c. Test the procedure, and then save and close the form.
4. Complete the **frmReportsDialogBox** form by doing the following:
   a. Create a Load event procedure that moves the focus to the first report name in the list box when the frmReportsDialogBox form opens.
   b. Create a **basPreviewReport** function to open a report in Print Preview.
   c. Attach the basPreviewReport function to the OnDblClick property for the list box on the frmReportsDialogBox form.
   d. Attach the basPreviewReport function to the OnClick property for the Preview command button on the frmReportsDialogBox form.
   e. Switch to Form view, and then test the form's procedures and functions. Save and close the form.
5. Close the Vendor database without exiting Access, make a backup copy of the database, open the **Vendor** database, compact and repair the database, close the database, and then exit Access.

Apply | **Case Problem 1**

Apply the skills you learned in the tutorial to work with the data contained in a database for a small music school.

Data File needed for this Case Problem: Portland.accdb (*cont. from Tutorial 10*)

Pine Hill Music School   Yuka Koyama wants you to continue your work with the user interface for the Portland database. To help Yuka with her request, complete the following steps:

1. Open the **Portland** database located in the Level.03\Case1 folder provided with your Data Files.
2. Create a procedure for the **frmContractsByTeacher** form to convert School field values to proper case—capitalize the first letter of each word, and convert all other letters to lowercase. Test the procedure, and then close the form.

 EXPLORE

3. Create a procedure for the **frmContract** form to do the following:
   a. Display the LessonType field value in bold, blue text when the value is "Voice" and in normal, black text for all other values. (*Hint*: Use the FontBold property.)
   b. Display the message **No instrument** to the right of the LessonType text box in bold, blue text only when the LessonType field value is "Voice".
   c. Test the procedure, and then save your form changes.

4. Complete the **frmQueriesDialogBox** by doing the following:

   a. Create a Load event procedure that moves the focus to the first query name in the list box when the frmQueriesDialogBox form opens.

   b. Create a **basPreviewQuery** function to open the selected query in the list box in Print Preview and a **basDisplayQuery** function to open the selected query in the list box in Datasheet view.

   c. Attach the basPreviewQuery function to the OnClick property for the Preview command button in the form.

   d. Attach the basDisplayQuery function to the OnClick property for the Display command button in the form and to the OnDblClick property for the form list box.

   e. Switch to Form view, and then test all the form's procedures and functions. Save and close the form.

5. Close the Portland database without exiting Access, make a backup copy of the database, open the **Portland** database, compact and repair the database, close the database, and then exit Access.

Apply | Case Problem 2

Apply what you learned in the tutorial to work with the data for a business in the health and fitness industry.

Data File needed for this Case Problem: Exercise.accdb (*cont. from Tutorial 10*)

Parkhurst Health & Fitness Center   Martha Parkhurst asks you to continue your work with the user interface for the Exercise database. To help Martha with her request, complete the following steps:

1. Open the **Exercise** database located in the Level.03\Case2 folder provided with your Data Files.

2. Use the Form tool to create a form named **frmMemberInfo** using the tblMember table as the source table. Create a procedure for the frmMemberInfo form to convert City field values to proper case—capitalize the first letter of each word, and convert all other letters to lowercase. Test the procedure.

3. Create a procedure to verify Phone field values in the frmMemberInfo form by doing the following:

   a. For a State field value of VA, the first three digits of the Phone field value must equal 703 or 804. If the Phone field value is invalid, display an appropriate message, cancel the event, undo the change, and move the focus to the Phone field.

   b. No special action is required for other Phone field values.

   c. Test the procedure, and then save your form changes.

⊕ **EXPLORE**   4. Create a procedure for the frmMemberInfo form to do the following:

   a. Display the word **Current** to the right of the MemberID text box in bold, magenta text only when the MembershipStatus field value is Active. Otherwise, display the word **Review** in bold, blue text. (*Hint:* Remove all controls from the control layout before resizing the MemberID text box and adding the label for the message. Use the Caption property in your VBA code, and make sure you enclose Caption property settings in quotation marks.)

   b. Test the modified form, and then save your form changes.

5. Close the Exercise database without exiting Access, make a backup copy of the database, open the **Exercise** database, compact and repair the database, close the database, and then exit Access.

Apply | **Case Problem 3**

Apply what you learned in the tutorial to modify the database for a recycling agency.

Data File needed for this Case Problem: Salina.accdb (*cont. from Tutorial 10*)

Rossi Recycling Group Mary and Tom Rossi want you to continue your work with the user interface for the Salina database. To help them with their request, complete the following steps:

1. Open the **Salina** database located in the Level.03\Case3 folder provided with your Data Files.

⊕ **EXPLORE**

2. Create a procedure for the **frmDonorDonations** form to do the following:
   a. Display the calculated field value (the donation total) in bold, black text when the value is greater than $500 and in regular, black text otherwise. (*Hint:* Use the FontBold property.)
   b. Display the message **Large donation** above the calculated field text box in bold, black text only when the calculated field value is greater than $500.
   c. Test the procedure, and then save your form design changes.

3. Complete the **frmQueriesDialogBox** form by doing the following:
   a. Create a Load event procedure that moves the focus to the first query name in the list box when the frmQueriesDialogBox form opens.
   b. Create a **basPreviewQuery** function to open the selected query in the list box in Print Preview and a **basDisplayQuery** function to open the selected query in the list box in Datasheet view.
   c. Attach the basPreviewQuery function to the OnClick property for the Preview command button in the form.
   d. Attach the basDisplayQuery function to the OnClick property for the Display command button in the form and to the OnDblClick property for the form list box.
   e. Switch to Form view, and then test the form's procedure and functions. Save and close the form.

4. Close the Salina database without exiting Access, make a backup copy of the database, open the **Salina** database, compact and repair the database, close the database, and then exit Access.

Apply	Case Problem 4

Apply what you learned in the tutorial to work with the data for a luxury property rental company.

Data File needed for this Case Problem: Rentals.accdb (*cont. from Tutorial 10*)

GEM Ultimate Vacations   Griffin and Emma MacElroy ask you to continue your work with the user interface for the Rentals database. To help them with their request, complete the following steps:

1. Open the **Rentals** database located in the Level.03\Case4 folder provided with your Data Files.

2. Create a procedure for the **frmGuestInfo** form to convert new Country field values to all uppercase letters. Test the procedure.

◆ EXPLORE

3. Add the message **Trips of a Lifetime!** to the frmGuestInfo form. Display the message in 14-point, bold, orange text and position it above and to the right of the GuestID text box. Display the message only when the GuestFirstName and GuestLastName field values equal your first and last names. (*Hint:* Make sure you enclose your first and last names in quotation marks in your VBA code.) Save your form changes, and then test the form.

4. Complete the **frmQueriesDialogBox** form by doing the following:
   a. Create a Load event procedure that moves the focus to the first query name in the list box when the frmQueriesDialogBox form opens.
   b. Create a **basDisplayQuery** function to open the selected query in Datasheet view.
   c. Attach the basDisplayQuery function to the OnDblClick property for the frmQueriesDialogBox form list box and to the OnClick property for the Display command button in the form.
   d. Switch to Form view, and then test all the form's procedure and functions. Save and close the form.

5. Complete the **frmReportsDialogBox** form by doing the following:
   a. Create a Load event procedure that moves the focus to the first report name in the list box when the frmReportsDialogBox form opens.
   b. Create a **basPreviewReport** function to open a report in Print Preview.
   c. Attach the basPreviewReport function to the OnDblClick property for the frmReportsDialogBox form list box and to the OnClick property for the Preview command button in the form.
   d. Switch to Form view, and then test the form's procedure and functions. Save and close the form.

6. Close the Rentals database without exiting Access, make a backup copy of the database, open the **Rentals** database, compact and repair the database, close the database, and then exit Access.

Challenge | **Case Problem 5**

Explore some new skills as you work with the data for an Internet service provider.

Data File needed for this Case Problem: Always.accdb (*cont. from Tutorial 10*)

Always Connected Everyday   Chris and Pat Dixon ask you to continue your work with the user interface for the Always database. To help them with their request, complete the following steps:

1. Open the **Always** database located in the Level.03\Case5 folder provided with your Data Files.

✦ EXPLORE
2. Modify the **frmAccessPlansAndCustomers** form by doing the following:
   a. Display the PlanMonthlyCost field value in bold, blue text when the value is greater than $50 and in regular, black text for all other values. (*Hint:* Use the FontBold property.)
   b. Display the message **Premium Customer** to the right of the PlanMonthlyCost text box in bold, blue text only when the PlanMonthlyCost field value is greater than $50.
   c. Test the modified form, and then save your form changes.

✦ EXPLORE
3. Modify the frmAccessPlansAndCustomers form by doing the following:
   a. To the right of the rectangle that encloses the Number of Customers calculated field, add a new calculated field that displays the product of the PlanMonthlyCost control value and Number of Customers calculated field value. Use the label **Monthly Income for Plan** and display the label and calculated field values in bold, blue text. Format the calculated field as Currency with two decimal places.
   b. Perform the Monthly Income for Plan calculation and display the label and calculated field value only when the Number of Customers calculated field value is not null.
   c. Test the modified form, and then save your form changes.
4. Close the Always database without exiting Access, make a backup copy of the database, open the **Always** database, compact and repair the database, close the database, and then exit Access.

Research | **Internet Assignments**

Use the Internet to find and work with data related to the topics presented in this tutorial.

The purpose of the Internet Assignments is to challenge you to find information on the Internet that you can use to work effectively with this software. The actual assignments are updated and maintained on the Course Technology Web site. Log on to the Internet and use your Web browser to go to the Student Online Companion for New Perspectives Office 2007 at **www.course.com/np/office2007**. Then navigate to the Internet Assignments for this tutorial.

Assess | **SAM Assessment and Training**

If you have a SAM user profile, you may have access to hands-on instruction, practice, and assessment of the skills covered in this tutorial. Log in to your SAM account (**http://sam2007.course.com**) to launch any assigned training activities or exams that relate to the skills covered in this tutorial.

Review | Quick Check Answers

Session 11.1

1. VBA statements respond to events that occur with the objects in a database.
2. a procedure that runs when a specific event occurs
3. A Function procedure performs operations, returns a value, accepts input values, and can be used in expressions. A Sub procedure performs operations and can accept input values, but does not return a value and cannot be used in expressions.
4. A standard module is a database object that is stored in memory with other database objects when you open a database. A class module is associated with a specific database object, such as a form or report.
5. scope
6. You use the Immediate window to test VBA procedures when you are coding them, without changing any data in the database.

Session 11.2

1. If
2. Access checks the modules in your database for syntax errors. If no syntax errors are found, Access translates the VBA code into a form that your computer understands.
3. to declare variables and their types
4. Val
5. executes an action in a procedure
6. an action that operates on specific objects or controls

Session 11.3

1. a predefined memory location that is initialized to a value that doesn't change
2. StrConv
3. whether Access displays a control
4. a control's foreground, or text, color
5. when the object is opened and every time the focus moves to another record
6. when the object is opened

Ending Data Files

Level.03 → Tutorial
Holland.accdb

Review
Vendor.accdb

Case1
Portland.accdb

Case2
Exercise.accdb

Case3
Salina.accdb

Case4
Rentals.accdb

Case5
Always.accdb

Objectives

Session 12.1
- Filter data in a table and a form
- Save a filter as a query and apply the saved query as a filter
- Create a subquery
- Create a multi-valued field

Session 12.2
- Create an Attachment field
- Use an AutoNumber field
- Save a database as a previous version
- Analyze a database's performance
- Link a database to a table in another database
- Use the Linked Table Manager
- Split a database
- Encrypt a database with a password
- Set database properties and startup options
- Create an ACCDE file

Managing and Securing a Database

Administering the Holland Database

Case | Belmont Landscapes

Lucia Perez and Sarah Fisher have planned training sessions for staff members to learn how to use the Holland database. These training sessions are scheduled to begin right after you finalize the Holland database. Your remaining work will address Lucia's interest with new Access 2007 features, such as multivalued fields and Attachment fields, and Sarah's concerns about database management, database security, and the database's overall performance. You'll also set database properties and startup options to complete the development of the Holland database.

Starting Data Files

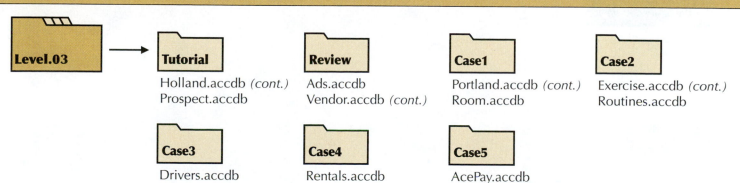

Level.03 →

Tutorial
Holland.accdb *(cont.)*
Prospect.accdb

Review
Ads.accdb
Vendor.accdb *(cont.)*

Case1
Portland.accdb *(cont.)*
Room.accdb

Case2
Exercise.accdb *(cont.)*
Routines.accdb

Case3
Drivers.accdb
Salina.accdb *(cont.)*

Case4
Rentals.accdb

Case5
AcePay.accdb
Always.accdb *(cont.)*

Session 12.1

Filtering Data

Sarah has two new filtering requests. She wants to see all contracts with May start dates using the tblContract table datasheet, and then she wants to view all residential customers in Rockford and Holland using the frmCustomer form.

Recall that a filter is a set of criteria you place on the records in an open form or datasheet to isolate a subset of the records temporarily. A filter is similar to a query, but it applies only to the open form or datasheet. If you want to use a filter at another time, you can save the filter as a query.

Four filter tools let you specify and apply filters in a form or datasheet: AutoFilter, Filter By Selection, Filter By Form, and Advanced Filter/Sort. With the first three tools, you specify the filter directly in the form or datasheet. An AutoFilter filters records that contain one of the selections displayed in a menu of values and context-sensitive choices for the selected field. Filter By Selection filters records that equal or contain (or do not equal or do not contain) a selected value in a field. Filter By Form filters records that match multiple selection criteria using the same Access logical and comparison operators used in queries. After applying one of these filter tools, you can use the Sort Ascending or Sort Descending buttons in the Sort & Filter group on the Home tab to rearrange the records, if necessary.

Advanced Filter/Sort lets you specify multiple selection criteria and specify a sort order for selected records in the Filter window, in the same way you specify record selection criteria and sort orders for a query in Design view.

Using an AutoFilter in a Table Datasheet

Although Sarah has used filters with a query datasheet and a form, she's never used a filter with a table datasheet. You'll show Sarah how to create a filter to display all contracts with May start dates in the tblContract table datasheet.

To filter records in the tblContract table datasheet:

1. Start Access, and then open the **Holland** database in the Level.03\Tutorial folder provided with your Data Files.

2. Open the Navigation Pane (if necessary), open the **tblContract** table in Datasheet view, and then close the Navigation Pane.

3. Click the **arrow** on the Start Date column heading to open the AutoFilter menu, point to **Date Filters** to open a submenu of context-sensitive options, and then point to **All Dates In Period** to open an additional submenu. See Figure 12-1.

Tip

In Tutorial 10, you set the database to use overlapping windows. You can resize the Table window and use the scroll bars to view the entire datasheet.

AutoFilter menu and submenus for a Date field ◄ Figure 12-1

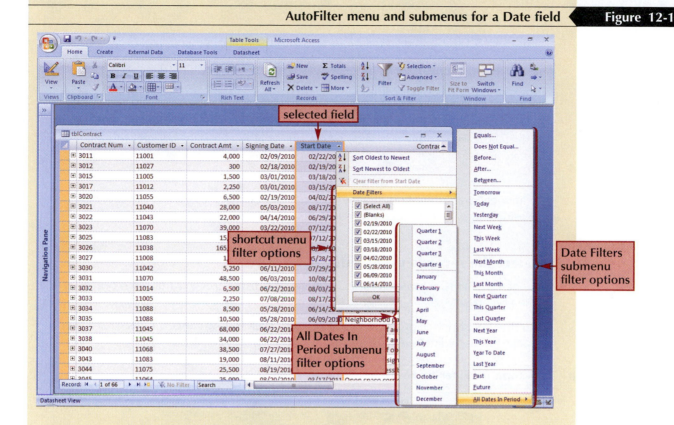

The shortcut menu displays all the values that appear in the Start Date column; you use the shortcut menu when you want to select specific values for the filter. The Date Filters submenu displays filter options that apply to a Date field, and the All Dates In Period submenu displays additional filter options for a Date field.

▶ **4.** In the All Dates In Period submenu, click **May**. Only the six records with May start dates are displayed in the recordset.

If you save a table with an applied filer, the filter is saved, and you can reapply the filter anytime you open the table datasheet.

▶ **5.** Save and close the table.

▶ **6.** Open the Navigation Pane, open the **tblContract** table datasheet to display all 66 records, and then click the **Toggle Filter** button (with the ScreenTip "Apply Filter") in the Sort & Filter group on the Home tab. Access applies the StartDate filter, displaying the six records with May start dates.

▶ **7.** Close the table.

Next, you'll use Filter By Form to produce the other results Sarah wants.

Filter By Form

You can use Filter By Form to display Sarah's information for residential customers in Holland and Rockford.

Reference Window | Selecting Records Using Filter By Form

- Open the form in Form view.
- In the Sort & Filter group on the Home tab, click the Advanced button, and then click Filter By Form.
- Enter a simple selection criterion or an And condition in the first form, using the text boxes for the appropriate fields.
- If there is an Or condition, click the Or tab and enter the Or condition in the second form. Continue to enter Or conditions on separate forms by using the Or tab.
- In the Sort & Filter group on the Home tab, click the Toggle Filter button (with the ScreenTip "Apply Filter").

To answer Sarah's question, the multiple selection criteria you will enter are: Holland *and* Residential *or* Rockford *and* Residential.

To select the records using Filter By Form:

▶ 1. Open the **frmCustomer** form in Form view to display record 1 of the 42 records in the recordset.

▶ 2. In the Sort & Filter group on the Home tab, click the **Advanced** button, and then click **Filter By Form**. Access displays a blank form. See Figure 12-2.

| Figure 12-2 | Blank form for Filter By Form |

Tip

For a criterion, you can select a value from the list of values in a text box, or you can use a comparison operator (such as <, >=, <>, and Like) and a value, similar to conditions you enter in the query design grid.

On this blank form, you specify multiple selection criteria by entering conditions in the text boxes for the fields in a record. If you enter criteria in more than one field, you create the equivalent of an And condition—Access selects any record that matches all criteria. To create an Or condition, you enter the criteria for the first part of the condition in the field on the first ("Look for") blank form, and then click the Or tab to display a new blank form. You enter the criteria for the second part of the condition on the second ("Or") blank form. Access selects any record that matches all criteria on the Look for form or all criteria on the Or form.

► **3.** Click the **City** text box, click the **City** arrow, and then click **Holland**. Access adds the criterion "Holland" to the City text box.

► **4.** Click the **CustomerType** arrow, and then click **Residential**. Access adds the criterion "Residential" to the CustomerType text box.

You specified the logical operator (And) for the condition "Holland" And "Residential". To add the rest of the criteria, you need to display the Or form.

► **5.** Click the **Or** tab to display a second blank form. The insertion point is in the text box for the CustomerType field.

► **6.** Click the **CustomerType** arrow, and then click **Residential**.

► **7.** Click the right side of the **City** text box to display the menu, click **Rockford**, and then click the **City** text box to deselect all values. The form now contains the second And condition: "Rockford" And "Residential". See Figure 12-3.

Tip

Notice that a third tab, also labeled "Or," is now available in case you need to specify another Or condition.

Completed Filter By Form | **Figure 12-3**

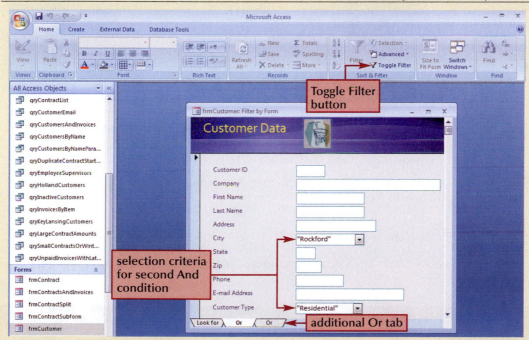

Combined with the Look for form, you now have the Or condition and the complete Filter By Form conditions.

► **8.** In the Sort & Filter group on the Home tab, click the **Toggle Filter** button (with the ScreenTip "Apply Filter"), and then click the **CustomerID** text box to deselect all values. Access applies the filter and displays the first record that matches the selection criteria (Sharon Maloney, a residential customer in Rockford). The Customer navigation bar at the bottom of the form shows that the filter selected six records. See Figure 12-4.

Figure 12-4 | **First record that matches the Filter By Form criteria**

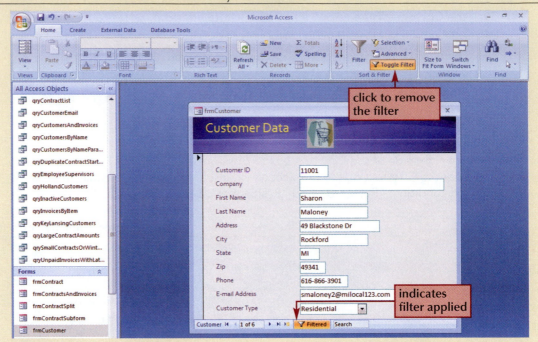

9. Navigate to record 3 to display the third record (Owen Hawes, a residential customer in Holland).

Now that you defined the filter, you can save it as a query, so that Sarah can easily view the information in the future.

Saving a Filter as a Query

When you save a filter as a query, you can reuse the filter in the future by opening the saved query.

Reference Window | Saving a Filter as a Query

- Create a filter using Filter By Selection, Filter By Form, or Advanced Filter/Sort.
- If you applied the filter using Filter By Form, click the Advanced button, and then click Filter By Form.
- In the Sort & Filter group on the Home tab, click the Advanced button, and then click Save As Query.
- Type the name for the query, and then press the Enter key.

Next, you'll save the filter as a query named qryHollandRockfordResidentialFilter.

To save the filter as a query:

1. In the Sort & Filter group on the Home tab, click the **Advanced** button, and then click **Filter By Form**. Access displays the form with the selection criteria.

2. In the Sort & Filter group on the Home tab, click the **Advanced** button, and then click **Save As Query**. The Save As Query dialog box opens.

3. Type **qryHollandRockfordResidentialFilter** in the Query Name text box, and then press the **Enter** key. Access saves the filter as a query in the Holland database and closes the dialog box.

   Now you can clear the selection criteria, close the Filter By Form window, and return to Form view.

4. In the Sort & Filter group on the Home tab, click the **Advanced** button, and then click **Clear Grid**. Access removes the selection criteria from the form.

5. Close the Filter By Form window to return to Form view for the frmCustomer form.

6. In the Sort & Filter group on the Home tab, click the **Toggle Filter** button (with the ScreenTip "Remove Filter"), click the **Advanced** button, and then click **Clear All Filters**. The Customer navigation bar shows that 42 records are available and the form has no filters.

   Next, you'll open the qryHollandRockfordResidentialFilter query in Design view. You'll leave the form open.

7. Open the **qryHollandRockfordResidentialFilter** query in Design view. In the design grid, the first And condition ("Holland" And "Residential") appears in the Criteria row, the second And condition ("Rockford" And "Residential") appears in the or row, and the Or condition combines the first And condition with the second And condition. See Figure 12-5.

> **Tip**
>
> If you apply a filter to a form and you close the form, Access automatically saves the filter with the form. If you don't want the filter saved with the form, you must clear all filters before closing the form.

Filter saved as a query in Design view | **Figure 12-5**

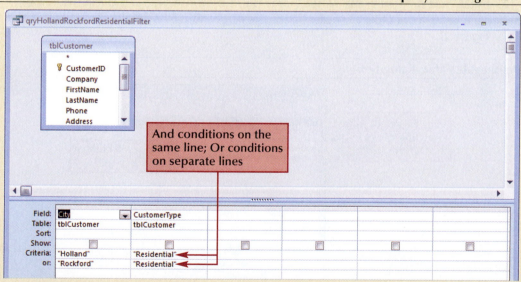

8. Run the query to display the six records that satisfy the selection criteria, close the query, and then close the form.

The next time Sarah wants to view the records selected by the filter, she can apply the qryHollandRockfordResidentialFilter query to the form. If she simply runs the query, she will see the selected records, but they will not be shown in the frmCustomer form. Instead, she can open the form and apply the saved query to select the records she wants to view in the form.

Applying a Filter Saved as a Query

To see how to apply a query as a filter to a form, you will open the frmCustomer form and apply the qryHollandRockfordResidentialFilter query as a filter.

Reference Window | **Applying a Filter Saved as a Query**

- Open the form to which you want to apply the filter.
- In the Sort & Filter group on the Home tab, click the Advanced button, and then click Filter By Form.
- In the Sort & Filter group on the Home tab, click the Advanced button, and then click Load from Query.
- In the Applicable Filter dialog box, click the query you want to apply as a filter, and then click the OK button.

Now you'll apply the qryHollandRockfordResidentialFilter query as a filter in the frmCustomer form.

To apply the filter saved as a query:

▶ **1.** Open the **frmCustomer** form in Form view.

▶ **2.** In the Sort & Filter group on the Home tab, click the **Advanced** button, and then click **Filter By Form**. Access displays the form with the selection criteria.

▶ **3.** In the Sort & Filter group on the Home tab, click the **Advanced** button, and then click **Load from Query**. Access opens the Applicable Filter dialog box. See Figure 12-6.

Figure 12-6 Applicable Filter dialog box

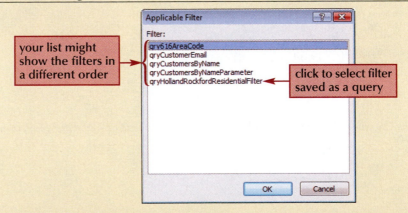

your list might show the filters in a different order

click to select filter saved as a query

▶ **4.** Click **qryHollandRockfordResidentialFilter** in the Filter list box, and then click the **OK** button. Access loads the saved query into the Filter By Form window.

▶ **5.** In the Sort & Filter group on the Home tab, click the **Toggle Filter** button. Access applies the filter and displays the first of six filtered records in the form.

▶ **6.** Click the **Advanced** button, click **Clear All Filters**, and then close the form.

Lucia wants to show you an alternative way to construct the filter you just applied by using a subquery.

Creating a Subquery

When you create a query using an SQL SELECT statement, you can place a second SELECT statement inside it; this second inner query is called a **subquery**. Access runs the subquery first, and then Access uses the results of the subquery to run the outer query.

Lucia will show you how to modify the qryHollandRockfordResidentialFilter query to use a subquery.

To view the qryHollandRockfordResidentialFilter query in SQL view:

▶ **1.** Open the **qryHollandRockfordResidentialFilter** query in Design view. In the design grid, the first And condition ("Holland" And "Residential") appears in the Criteria row, the second And condition ("Rockford" And "Residential") appears in the or row, and the Or condition combines the first And condition with the second And condition.

▶ **2.** Switch to SQL view, and then click an unused portion of the window to deselect the SQL SELECT statement. See Figure 12-7.

| SQL statement for the qryHollandRockfordResidentialFilter query | Figure 12-7 |

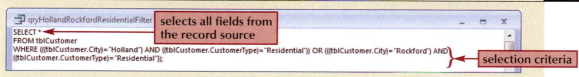

SELECT * FROM tblCustomer selects all fields from the tblCustomer table in the order in which they appear in the table. The WHERE clause specifies the selection criteria: records with a City field value of Holland and a CustomerType field value of Residential, or records with a City field value of Rockford and a CustomerType field value of Residential.

To modify the query to use a subquery, you'll retain the *SELECT * FROM tblCustomer* portion of the SQL statement to select all fields from the tblCustomer table in the order in which they appear in the table, and you'll use Figure 12-8 to change the selection criteria. The *WHERE CustomerType="Residential"* will select residential customers, and the *AND CustomerID IN* completes the outer query to select those records with CustomerID values that satisfy the subquery. The And logical operator specifies that records will be selected when both the CustomerType="Residential" and the CustomerID is among those selected by the subquery. *SELECT CustomerID FROM tblCustomer WHERE City="Holland" OR City="Rockford"* is the subquery, selecting CustomerID field values for Holland and Rockford customers. The subquery is enclosed in parentheses, and a semicolon terminates the entire SELECT statement.

| SQL SELECT statement using a subquery | Figure 12-8 |

```
SELECT *
FROM tblCustomer
WHERE CustomerType="Residential"
AND CustomerID IN
(SELECT CustomerID
FROM tblCustomer
WHERE City="Holland" OR City="Rockford");
```

Now you'll change the query to use a subquery.

To change the query to use a subquery:

▶ 1. Select the word **WHERE** and the text to the end of the statement (the semicolon), and then type the last five lines shown in Figure 12-8 to change the SQL SELECT statement to use a subquery. See Figure 12-9.

| Figure 12-9 | SQL statement using a subquery |

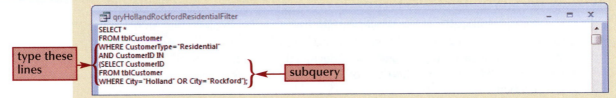

▶ 2. Save your query design changes, and then run the query. Access displays the same six records you viewed earlier before changing the query design to use a subquery.

▶ 3. Switch to Design view, and then click the first column's **Field** text box to deselect all values. The value in the CustomerType Criteria text box selects records for residential customers, and the value in the CustomerID Criteria box is a subquery that selects Holland and Rockford customers. See Figure 12-10.

| Figure 12-10 | Query using a subquery in the Design window |

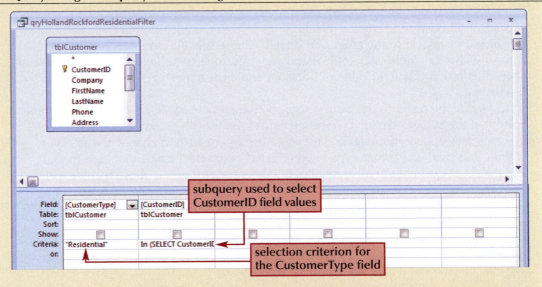

It's unclear from looking at the two columns in the design grid that all fields are displayed from the tblCustomer table.

▶ 4. In the Show/Hide group on the Design tab on the Ribbon, click the **Property Sheet** button to display the properties for the query. See Figure 12-11.

Properties for the query | Figure 12-11

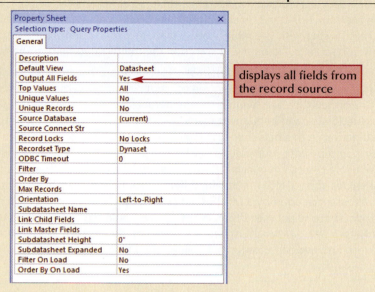

The Output All Fields property setting of Yes specifies that Access displays all fields from the record source, the tblCustomer table, without these fields being added to the design grid.

5. Close the property sheet, close the query, and then click the **Yes** button if you're asked to save changes to the query design.

Lucia has used previous versions of Access, attended an Access 2007 workshop, and wants to experiment with two new features of Access 2007: multivalued fields and Attachment fields.

Using Multivalued Fields

Sarah wants to keep track of the degrees, such as Associate, Bachelor, and Master, earned by employees. Because each employee can earn more than one degree, and each degree can be earned by more than one employee, there's a many-to-many relationship between employees and degrees. To implement this many-to-many relationship, you'd use the existing tblEmployee table, create a separate tblDegree table to store the Degree field values, and then create a third table to tie together the other two tables. Instead, with Access 2007, you can use a multivalued field. A **multivalued field** is a lookup field that allows you to store more than one value. Using a multivalued field, you can add a Degree field to the tblEmployee table and use the Lookup Wizard to enter the Degree field values and specify that you want to store multiple values in the Degree field. Sarah and her staff can then select one or more Degree field values from the list of degrees.

When you define a multivalued field in a table, Access does not actually store values in the field in that table. Instead, Access stores the values in hidden, system tables in a many-to-many relationship with the table. Access manages, manipulates, and displays the data to make it appear as if the data was stored in the multivalued field in the table.

Users with limited Access and database experience are the intended audience for multivalued fields, because understanding the concepts of many-to-many relationships and creating them are difficult for beginning or casual database users. Experienced database users avoid multivalued fields and implement many-to-many relationships in the traditional way you learned earlier in this book because they have total control over the data and are not limited as they would be with multivalued fields. One of the limitations of multivalued fields is that you can't sort records in queries, forms, and reports, except in special circumstances, based on the values stored in the multvalued field. Also, multivalued fields do not convert properly to a database managed by a DBMS such as SQL Server or Oracle. If you need to convert the Access database to another DBMS in the future, you'd have to change the multivalued field to many-to-many relationships, which is a change that's much more difficult at that point than if you had avoided using a multivalued field from the beginning.

Lucia wants to experiment with the multivalued field feature without modifying the existing tables and relationships, so you'll make a copy of the tblEmployee table and experiment with the copied version of the table.

To create a copy of the tblEmployee table:

1. In the Navigation Pane, right-click **tblEmployee** to open the shortcut menu, and then click **Copy**.

2. In the Clipboard group on the Home tab on the Ribbon, click the **Paste** button to open the Paste Table As dialog box, and then click the **Table Name** text box to deselect all values. See Figure 12-12.

| Figure 12-12 | Paste Table As dialog box |

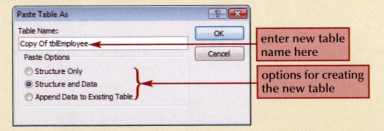

When you copy a table to create a new table, you can use the design of the table without copying its data (Structure Only), use the design and copy the data from the table (Structure and Data), or add the data to an existing table (Append Data to Existing Table).

You'll create the new table using the design and data from the tblEmployee table.

3. Change the name in the Table Name text box to **tblEmployeeCopy**, make sure the **Structure and Data** option button is selected, and then click the **OK** button. Access creates a new table named tblEmployeeCopy that contains the same structure and data as the tblEmployee table.

Now you can add the multivalued field in the tblEmployeeCopy table.

To add a multivalued field to the tblEmployeeCopy table:

▶ **1.** Open the **tblEmployeeCopy** table in Design view.

▶ **2.** Click the **Field Name** text box in the row below the SupervisorID field, type **Degree**, press the **Tab** key, click the **Data Type** arrow, and then click **Lookup Wizard**. The first Lookup Wizard dialog box opens.

   You'll type the Degree field values instead of obtaining them from a table or query.

▶ **3.** Click the **I will type in the values that I want** option button, and then click the **Next** button to open the second Lookup Wizard dialog box, in which you'll type the Degree field values.

▶ **4.** Click the **Col1** text box in the first row, type **Certificate**, press the **Tab** key, type **Associate**, press the **Tab** key, type **Bachelor**, press the **Tab** key, type **Master**, press the **Tab** key, and then type **Doctorate**. These are the five values that users can choose from for the Degree multivalued field. See Figure 12-13.

Values for the Degree multivalued field ◀ **Figure 12-13**

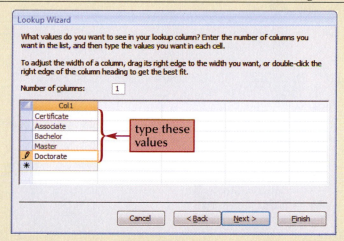

▶ **5.** Click the **Next** button to open the last Lookup Wizard dialog box, and then click the **Allow Multiple Values** check box to add a check mark to it. See Figure 12-14.

Specifying a multivalued field ◀ **Figure 12-14**

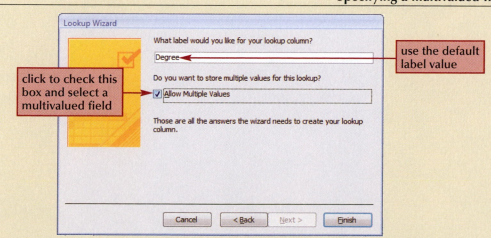

You'll accept the default label name of Degree for the field. When you click the Allow Multiple Values check box to place a check mark in it, you are specifying that you want the Degree field to be a multivalued field.

▶ 6. Click the **Finish** button to complete the definition of the Degree field as a lookup field that allows multiple values, or a multivalued field.

▶ 7. Click the **Lookup** tab in the Field Properties pane. The Degree field has its Row Source property set to the five values you typed in one of the Lookup Wizard dialog boxes, and the Allow Multiple Values property has been set to Yes. See Figure 12-15.

Figure 12-15 | **After defining the Degree field as a multivalued field**

Tip

If you forget to select the Allow Multiple Values check box when you use the Lookup Wizard, you can change to Design view and set the Allow Multiple Values property for the field to Yes to change the field to a multivalued field. If you need to add values in the future to the multivalued field, you can add them to the Row Source property.

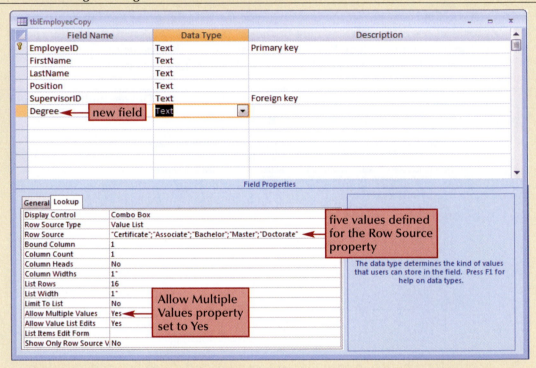

▶ 8. Save your table design changes, and then switch to Datasheet view.

▶ 9. Click the right side of the **Degree** text box for record 2 (Timothy Ering) to open the value list for the field. See Figure 12-16.

Value list for the Degree multivalued field   Figure 12-16

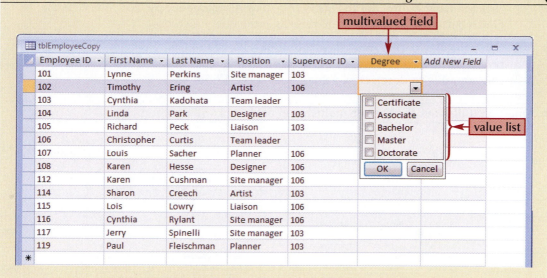

10. Click the **Associate** check box, and then click the **OK** button.

11. Repeat Steps 9 and 10 for record 4 (Linda Park), selecting **Associate**, **Bachelor**, and **Master**, and for record 5 (Richard Peck), selecting **Bachelor**, resize the Degree column to its best fit, and then click the **Degree** text box for record 5 to deselect all values. Records 2 (Timothy Ering) and 5 (Richard Peck) have one value selected for the Degree field, and record 4 (Linda Park) has three values selected for the Degree field. See Figure 12-17.

> **Tip**
>
> In the Sort & Filter group on the Home tab, the Ascending and Descending buttons are dimmed because you can't sort records based on multivalued fields.

After selecting values for the multivalued field   Figure 12-17

tblEmployeeCopy						
Employee ID ▾	First Name ▾	Last Name ▾	Position ▾	Supervisor ID ▾	Degree ▾	Add New
101	Lynne	Perkins	Site manager	103		
102	Timothy	Ering	Artist	106	Associate	
103	Cynthia	Kadohata	Team leader			
104	Linda	Park	Designer	103	Associate, Bachelor, Master	
105	Richard	Peck	Liaison	103	Bachelor	
106	Christopher	Curtis	Team leader			
107	Louis	Sacher	Planner	106		
108	Karen	Hesse	Designer	106		
112	Karen	Cushman	Site manager	106		
114	Sharon	Creech	Artist	103		
115	Lois	Lowry	Liaison	106		
116	Cynthia	Rylant	Site manager	106		
117	Jerry	Spinelli	Site manager	103		
119	Paul	Fleischman	Planner	103		

Lucia wants you to create queries to display all field values from the tblEmployeeCopy table to see how Access displays multivalued field values.

To create queries to display the Degree multivalued field:

1. Save and close the tblEmployeeCopy table, make sure the **tblEmployeeCopy** table is selected in the Navigation Pane, click the **Create** tab on the Ribbon, and in the Other group on the Create tab, click the **Query Wizard** button to open the New Query dialog box.

2. Make sure the **Simple Query Wizard** option is selected, click the **OK** button to open the Simple Query Wizard dialog box, select all fields from the tblEmployeeCopy table, click the **Next** button, set the query title to **qryEmployeeCopy**, and then click the **Finish** button. Access displays 16 records in the query recordset.

3. Close the Navigation Pane, drag the right edge of the Query window to the right so you can see all columns in the query, and then click the first row's Employee ID column value to deselect all values. See Figure 12-18.

| Figure 12-18 | Query that displays the Degree multivalued field |

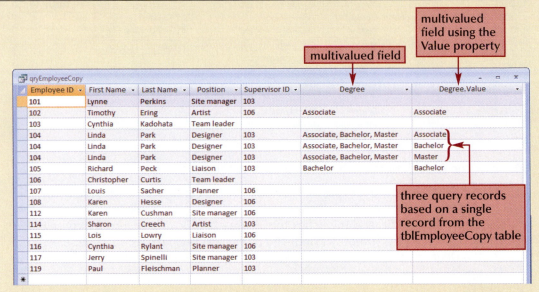

Trouble? The rightmost column heading on your screen might be the equivalent tblEmployeeCopy.Degree.Value instead of Degree.Value, indicating the Degree field in the tblEmployeeCopy table. This difference does not affect the contents of the column.

The six fields from the tblEmployeeCopy table are displayed in seven columns in the query recordset because the Degree field is displayed in two columns: the Degree column and the Degree.Value column. The Degree column displays field values exactly as they appear in the tblEmployeeCopy table; all values for the Degree multivalued field, such as those for Linda Park, are displayed in one row in the query. The Degree.Value column displays the Degree multivalued field in expanded form so that each value appears in a separate row in the query. *Degree.Value* identifies the Degree field and the Value property for the Degree field.

Tip

In queries that contain a multivalued field, you should display the field in a single column, not two, with values appearing as in the table or in expanded form. You can eliminate the extra column by deleting it, by clearing its Show check box in Design view, or by selecting just one of the two fields in the Simple Query Wizard.

4. Click the **Home** tab on the Ribbon, click the first row's **Degree** text box, notice that the Ascending and Descending buttons in the Sort & Filer group on the Ribbon are dimmed, and then click the first row's **Degree.Value** text box. The Ascending and Descending buttons are active and you can sort records in the query based on the values in the Degree.Value column.

Next, you'll review the query design.

5. Switch to Design view, and then drag down the bottom of the tblEmployeeCopy field list to show all values in the list. See Figure 12-19.

Design of the query containing the Degree multivalued field | Figure 12-19

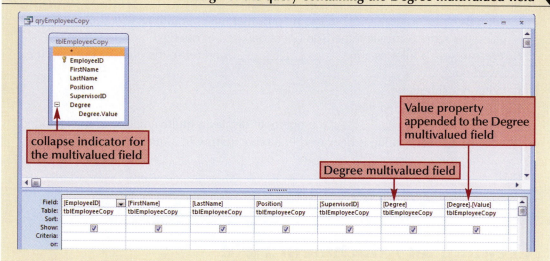

The Degree field in the tblEmployeeCopy field list has a collapse indicator to its left that you can click to hide the Degree.Value entry below it. The rightmost column in the design grid, [Degree].[Value], uses the Value property for the Degree field. Using the **Value property** with a multivalued field displays the multivalued field in expanded form so that each value is displayed in a separate row.

You'll delete the [Degree] column from the query design, retaining the [Degree].[Value] column and setting its Caption property, and then save the query with a new name.

▶ **6.** Right-click the **column selector bar** for the [Degree] column to highlight the column and open the shortcut menu, and then click **Cut**.

▶ **7.** Open the property sheet for the [Degree].[Value] column, set the Caption property to **Degree**, and then close the property sheet.

▶ **8.** Click the **Office Button** 🔘, point to **Save As**, click **Save Object As** to open the Save As dialog box, set the query name to **qryEmployeeCopyValue**, click the **OK** button, run the query, and then resize the Degree column to its best fit. Access displays 16 records in the query recordset.

▶ **9.** Save the query datasheet change and then close the query.

▶ **10.** Open the Navigation Pane, open the **qryEmployeeCopy** query in Design view, close the Navigation Pane, scroll to the right (if necessary), delete the **Degree.Value** column, save the query, and then run the query. Access displays the 14 records from the tblEmployeeCopy table and displays the Degree multivalued field values in one row.

▶ **11.** Close the query, and if you are not continuing on to the next session, close the Holland database, and then exit Access.

In the next session, Lucia wants you to experiment with Attachment fields using the tblEmployeeCopy table.

1. Filter By _____ filters records that match multiple selection criteria using the same Access comparison operators used in queries.
2. You can save a filter as a(n) _____ and reuse the filter by opening the saved object.
3. What is a subquery?
4. What is a multivalued field?
5. You use the _____ property to display a multivalued field in expanded form so that each value is displayed in a separate row in a query.

Session 12.2

Creating an Attachment Field

In addition to storing data such as text, numbers, and dates in a database, you can attach external files such as Excel workbooks, Word documents, and images, similar to how you attach external files to e-mail messages. You use the **Attachment data type** to attach one or more attachments to a table record. Access stores attachments in compressed form to minimize file size and maximize disk space usage.

Lucia wants you to add a field with the Attachment data type to the tblEmployeeCopy table.

To add a new field with the Attachment data type to the tblEmployeeCopy table:

▶ 1. If you took a break after the previous session, make sure that the Holland database is open.

▶ 2. Open the Navigation Pane (if necessary), open the **tblEmployeeCopy** table in Design view, and then close the Navigation Pane.

▶ 3. Click the **Field Name** text box for the row below the Degree field, type **AddedDocuments**, press the **Tab** key, type **at**, press the **Tab** key to select Attachment as the data type, press the **F6** key to switch to the Caption text box in the Field Properties pane, and then type **Added Documents**. You've completed adding the AddedDocuments field to the table. See Figure 12-20.

After adding the AddedDocuments field with the Attachment data type   Figure 12-20

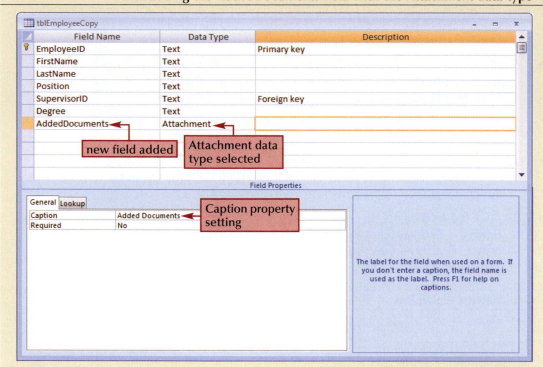

4. Save your table design changes, switch to Datasheet view, drag the right edge of the Table window to the right, resize the Added Documents column to its best fit, click the first row's **Employee ID** text box to deselect all values, and then save your datasheet format changes. See Figure 12-21.

Attachment field displayed in the table datasheet   Figure 12-21

Each AddedDocuments field value displays an attachment icon in the shape of a paper clip followed by a number in parentheses that indicates the number of files attached in that field for the record. You've not attached any files, so each record displays zero file attachments.

Lucia asks you to create a Word document, an Excel workbook, and a PowerPoint presentation, so she can experiment with attaching files in the Added Documents column.

5. Start Word, save the blank document that opens as **Perkins1** in the Level.03\Tutorial folder, exit Word, start Excel, save the blank workbook that opens as **Perkins2** in the Level.03\Tutorial folder, exit Excel, start PowerPoint, save the blank presentation that opens as **Perkins3** in the Level.03\Tutorial folder, and then exit PowerPoint.

6. Make sure the tblEmployeeCopy table is open in Datasheet view, right-click the first row's **AddedDocuments** text box to open the shortcut menu, and then click **Manage Attachments** to open the Attachments dialog box.

You'll add all three files you created as attachments to the first row's AddedDocuments text box.

7. Click the **Add** button to open the Choose File dialog box, navigate to the Level.03\Tutorial folder, click **Perkins1**, and then click the **Open** button to add the Perkins1.docx file to the Attachments dialog box.

8. Click the **Add** button to open the Choose File dialog box, click **Perkins2**, hold down the **Ctrl** key, click **Perkins3**, release the **Ctrl** key, and then click the **Open** button. The three files you've added now appear in the Attachments dialog box. See Figure 12-22.

| Figure 12-22 | Attachments dialog box |

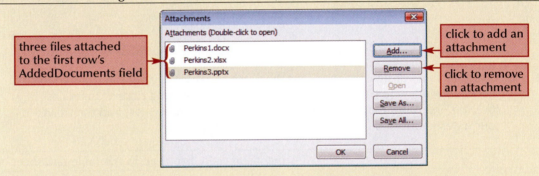

three files attached to the first row's AddedDocuments field

click to add an attachment

click to remove an attachment

9. Click the **OK** button to close the dialog box. The table datasheet now indicates that 3 files (the 3 in parentheses) are attached to the AddedDocuments field in the first record.

Next, you'll open one of the files attached in the first record, detach one of the attached files, and export an attached file.

To open, export, and detach files attached to a table field:

1. Right-click the first row's **AddedDocuments** text box to open the shortcut menu, and then click **Manage Attachments** to open the Attachments dialog box.

2. Click **Perkins2.xlsx** in the Attachments list, and then click the **Open** button. Excel starts and opens the Perkins2 workbook.

3. Exit Excel.

4. Click **Perkins1.docx** in the Attachments list, and then click the **Remove** button. Access removes the Perkins1 document from the Attachments list and detaches the Perkins1 document from the first row's AddedDocuments field.

Tip

The Perkins1 document remains in the Level.03\Tutorial folder because you don't delete a file when you detach it.

> **5.** Click **Perkins3.pptx** in the Attachments list, click the **Save As** button to open the Save Attachment dialog box, type **Perkins3 Export.pptx** in the File name text box, make sure the Level.03\Tutorial folder is the current destination folder, and then click the **Save** button. Access exports the Perkins3 presentation with the name Perkins3 Export and saves it in the Level.03\Tutorial folder.
>
> **6.** Click the **OK** button to close the Attachments dialog box. Because you removed the Perkins1 file from the first record, the Added Documents column for the first record now shows that there are two attachments.

Lucia wants you to add an AutoNumber field to the tblEmployeeCopy table.

Using an AutoNumber Field

When you create a table in Datasheet view, Access assigns the AutoNumber data type to the default ID primary key field because the AutoNumber data type automatically inserts a unique number in this field for every record in the table. Therefore, it can serve as the primary key for any table you create. When defining a field with the AutoNumber data type, you can specify sequential numbering or random numbering, either of which guarantees a unique field value for every record in the table.

You'll add an AutoNumber field to the tblEmployeeCopy table.

Tip

Read the Natural, Artificial, and Surrogate Keys section in the appendix titled "Relational Databases and Database Design" for more information about AutoNumber fields and primary keys.

To add an AutoNumber field to the tblEmployeeCopy table:

> **1.** Switch to Design view, right-click the **row selector** for the EmployeeID field to open the shortcut menu, and then click **Insert Rows**. Access adds a blank row above the EmployeeID row. You'll add the AutoNumber field to this new first row in the table design.
>
> **2.** Click the first row's **Field Name** text box, type **EmployeeNum**, press the **Tab** key, type **a**, press the **Tab** key to accept AutoNumber as the data type, press the **F6** key to switch to the Field Properties pane, press the **Tab** key three times to navigate to the Caption text box, and then type **Employee Num** in the Caption text box. You've finished adding the EmployeeNum field to the table. See Figure 12-23.

After adding the EmployeeNum field with the AutoNumber data type　　　**Figure 12-23**

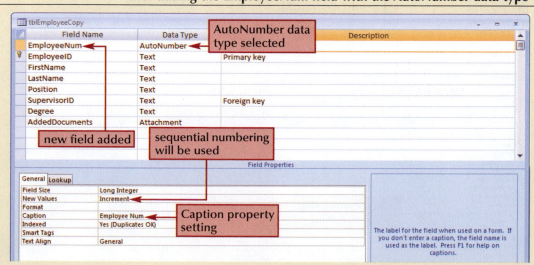

The default New Values property setting of Increment specifies that sequential numbering will be used for the AutoNumber field. The other New Values property value you can select is Random.

3. Click the **Field Name** text box for the EmployeeID field, save your table design changes, switch to Datasheet view, resize the first column to its best fit, and then click the first row's **Employee Num** text box to deselect all values. The new EmployeeNum field is displayed as the first column in the table, and Access automatically assigned unique sequential numbers to the EmployeeNum field for the 14 records in the table. See Figure 12-24.

Figure 12-24   AutoNumber field displayed in the table datasheet

Lucia wants to review the property settings for the Position field in the tblEmployeeCopy table.

4. Switch to Design view, and then click the **Field Name** text box for the Position field to display its properties. See Figure 12-25.

Figure 12-25   Property settings for the Position field

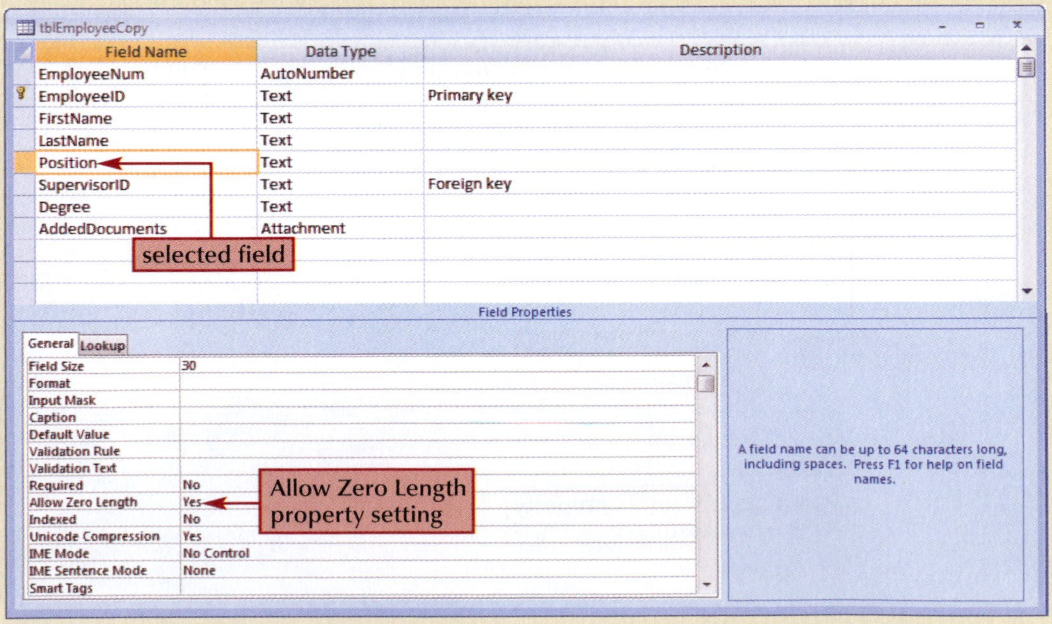

The Position field's Required property is set to No, which means field value entries are optional. The Allow Zero Length property is set to Yes, which is the default setting for Text fields and Memo fields. When its **Allow Zero Length property** is set to Yes, a field can store a zero length string value.

Setting the Allow Zero Length Property to No		InSight

For a Text or Memo field, there is a difference between how you specify a null field value and a zero length value and how Access interprets the two values. You specify a zero length value in a Text or a Memo field by typing two consecutive double quotation marks (""), and you specify a null value by entering no value. When you view a value for a Text or Memo field that has its Allow Zero Length property set to Yes, you can't determine if the field value has been set to null or has a zero length value because both field values look the same—the absence of a visible value.

However, Access treats the two values differently. If you run a query to display all records in the table that have a null value in the field using the IsNull function, only the records with a null field value appear in the query recordset; the records with a zero length value in the field do not appear. And if you change the query to display all records that have a nonnull value, the records with a zero length value in the field appear in the query recordset, which often raises questions by users about why those records are displayed. A typical user doesn't understand the distinction between a null value and a zero length value and doesn't need to make this distinction, so you should set the Allow Zero Length property to No for Text and Memo fields.

Sarah has a previous version of Access on her home computer and wonders if she can open the Holland database on that computer.

Saving an Access 2007 Database as a Previous Version

The default file format for databases you create in Access 2007 is Access 2007 with the .accdb filename extension. None of the previous versions of Access can open a database that has the Access 2007 file format. However, you can save an Access 2007 database to a format that is compatible with previous versions of Access—specifically, to a format that is compatible with Access 2000 or to a format that is compatible with Access 2002-2003; both have the .mdb filename extension. For people who don't have Access 2007 and have one of the previous versions of Access, saving the database to a previous version allows them to use the database. Unfortunately, when an Access 2007 database uses features such as multivalued and Attachment fields, you cannot save the database in a previous version.

To save an Access 2007 database as a previous version, you would follow these steps (note that you will not actually save the database now):

1. Make sure that the database you want to save is open and all database objects are closed, and that the database does not contain any multivalued, Attachment fields, or other features that are included only in Access 2007.

2. Click the Office Button, point to Save As, and then click Access 2002 - 2003 Database or click Access 2000 Database, depending on which file format you want to use.

3. In the Organize dialog box, navigate to the folder where you want to save the file, enter a name for the database in the File name text box, and then click the Save button.

Next, Lucia asks you to analyze the performance of the Holland database.

Analyzing Database Performance with the Performance Analyzer

Lucia wants the Holland database to respond as quickly as possible to user requests, such as running queries and opening reports. You'll use the Performance Analyzer to check the performance of the Holland database. The **Performance Analyzer** is an Access tool that you can use to optimize the performance of an Access database. You select the database objects you want to analyze for performance and run the Performance Analyzer, and then the Performance Analyzer lists three types of analysis results: recommendation, suggestion, and idea. Access can complete the recommendation and suggestion optimizations for you, but you must implement the idea optimizations. Analysis results include changes such as those related to the storage of fields and the creation of indexes and relationships.

Reference Window | **Using the Performance Analyzer**

- Start Access and open the database you want to analyze.
- In the Analyze group on the Database Tools tab on the Ribbon, click the Analyze Performance button.
- Select the object(s) you want to analyze, and then click the OK button.
- Select the analysis result(s) you want the Performance Analyzer to complete for you, and then click the Optimize button.
- Note the idea optimizations and perform those optimizations, as appropriate.
- Click the Close button.

You'll use the Performance Analyzer to optimize the performance of the Holland database.

To use the Performance Analyzer to optimize the performance of the Holland database:

▶ 1. Save and close the tblEmployeeCopy table.

▶ 2. Click the **Database Tools** tab on the Ribbon, and then in the Analyze group on the Database Tools tab, click the **Analyze Performance** button. The Performance Analyzer dialog box opens. See Figure 12-26.

Figure 12-26 ▶ Performance Analyzer dialog box

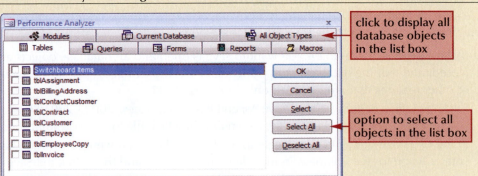

Lucia wants you to analyze every object in the Holland database.

   3. Click the **All Object Types** tab, and then click the **Select All** button. All objects in the Holland database appear in the list box, and all of them are now selected.

   4. Click the **OK** button. The Performance Analyzer analyzes all the objects in the Holland database and, after a few moments, displays its analysis results. See Figure 12-27.

Performance Analyzer analysis results   Figure 12-27

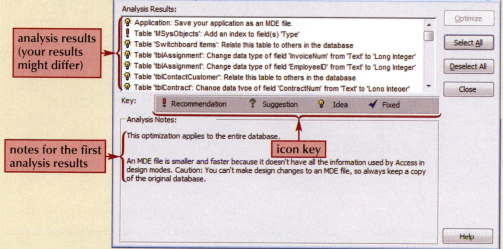

Trouble? The contents of the Analysis Results list box on your screen might be different from those shown in Figure 12-27, depending on how you've completed previous steps.

Most of the analysis results are in the idea category, which means that you have to implement them yourself. You should consider all idea analysis results, but more important now are the recommendation and suggestion analysis results, which the Performance Analyzer can complete for you automatically.

   5. Click several entries in the Analysis Results list box, and read each entry and its analysis notes.

You'll let the Performance Analyzer automatically create a relationship between the tblEmployee table and itself because the table has a one-to-many relationship based on the EmployeeID field as the primary key and the SupervisorID field as the foreign key.

   6. Scroll the Analysis Results list box as necessary, click the **Table 'tblEmployee': Relate to table 'tblEmployee'** analysis result (its icon is a green question mark) to select it, and then click the **Optimize** button. Access creates a relationship between the tblEmployee table and itself, and the icon for the selected analysis result changes to a blue check mark to indicate a "Fixed" status.

   7. Click the **Close** button to close the dialog box.

Next, you'll open the Relationships window to view the new relationship created by the Performance Analyzer.

To view the relationship created by the Performance Analyzer:

► 1. Click the **Database Tools** tab on the Ribbon, and then in the Show/Hide group on the Database Tools tab, click the **Relationships** button to open the Relationships window. See Figure 12-28.

Figure 12-28 tblEmployee table one-to-many relationship

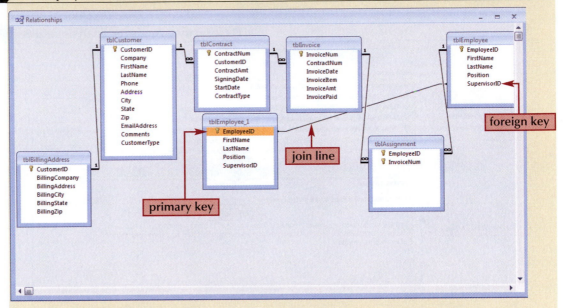

The Performance Analyzer added a second copy of the tblEmployee table (tblEmployee_1) and a join line between the tblEmployee and tblEmployee_1 tables to the Relationships window. The join line connects the primary table (tblEmployee_1) to the related table (tblEmployee) using the EmployeeID field as the primary key and the SupervisorID field as the foreign key. You'll use the Edit Relationships dialog box to view the join properties for the relationship.

► 2. Right-click the **join line** between the tblEmployee_1 and tblEmployee tables, and then click **Edit Relationship** on the shortcut menu to open the Edit Relationships dialog box. See Figure 12-29.

Figure 12-29 Edit Relationships dialog box for the new relationship

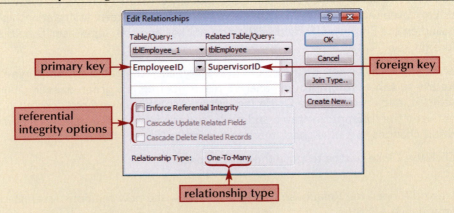

The referential integrity options are not selected, so you'll select them now for the new one-to-many relationship.

3. Click the **Enforce Referential Integrity** check box, click the **Cascade Update Related Fields** check box, and then click the **OK** button to close the dialog box.

4. Close the Relationships window.

Taylor Sico, marketing manager, has the responsibility at Belmont Landscapes for maintaining a separate database named Prospect in which she stores information about customers. Sarah wants to retrieve the data in the tblProspect table in the Prospect database from within the Holland database. To provide Sarah with access to this table, you'll create a link to the tblProspect table in the Holland database.

Linking Tables and Using the Linked Table Manager

You'll provide Sarah and other users of the Holland database with access to the tblProspect table by using a linked table in the Holland database. A **linked table** is a table that is stored in a file outside the open database and that can be updated from the open database. You can retrieve and update (add, change, and delete) records in a linked table, but you can't change its structure. From the Holland database, you'll be able to update the tblProspect table as a linked table, but you won't be able to change its structure. However, from the Prospect database, Taylor will be able to update the tblProspect table *and* change its structure. You can link a database to data stored in Excel worksheets, HTML documents, text files, other Access databases, and databases created by other DBMSs, such as SQL Server, Paradox, and dBASE. Although Access works faster with its own tables than it does with linked tables, you must use linked tables when you need access to data maintained in another Access database or by other programs.

Linking to a Table in Another Access Database | Reference Window

- Click the External Data tab on the Ribbon.
- In the Import group on the External Data tab, click the Access button (with the ScreenTip "Import Access database").
- Click the Link to the data source by creating a linked table option button.
- Click the Browse button, select the folder and file containing the linked data, and then click the Open button.
- Click the OK button, select the table(s) in the Link Tables dialog box, and then click the OK button.

You'll link to the tblProspect table in the Prospect database from the Holland database.

To link to the tblProspect table in the Prospect database:

1. Click the **External Data** tab on the Ribbon, and then in the Import group on the External Data tab, click the **Access** button (with the ScreenTip "Import Access database") to open the Get External Data - Access Database dialog box.

2. Click the **Link to the data source by creating a linked table** option button, and then click the **Browse** button to open the File Open dialog box.

3. Navigate to the Level.03\Tutorial folder, click **Prospect**, and then click the **Open** button to close the File Open dialog box and return to the Get External Data - Access Database dialog box. The path and file you selected now appears in the File name text box.

> **4.** Click the **OK** button. Access opens the Link Tables dialog box. See Figure 12-30.

Figure 12-30 | **Link Tables dialog box**

click to select this table in the Prospect database

> **5.** Click **tblProspect** in the Tables list box, and then click the **OK** button. The Link Tables dialog box closes, and you return to the Access window. A small blue arrow appears to the left of the tblProspect table icon in the Navigation Pane to identify the tblProspect table as a linked table.

Lucia informs Sarah that she'll be reorganizing the company network folders and might move the Prospect database to a different folder. Sarah asks if moving the Prospect database would cause a problem for the linked tblProspect table. You'll use the Linked Table Manager to show Sarah how to handle this situation. The **Linked Table Manager** is an Access tool you use to change the filename or disk location for linked tables in an Access database. When you use Access to link to data in another file, Access stores the file's location (drive, folder, and filename) in the database and uses the stored location to connect to the linked data. If you change the file's location, you can use the Linked Table Manager to change the stored file location, or **refresh the link**, in the Access database.

Next, you'll move the Prospect database to a different folder, and then you'll use the Linked Table Manager to refresh the link to the tblProspect table in the Holland database.

To move the Prospect database and refresh the link to the tblProspect table:

> **1.** Use Windows Explorer to move the **Prospect** database from the Level.03\Tutorial folder to the Level.03 folder.

> **2.** In Access, click the **Database Tools** tab on the Ribbon, and then in the Database Tools group on the Database Tools tab, click the **Linked Table Manager** button. The Linked Table Manager dialog box opens. See Figure 12-31.

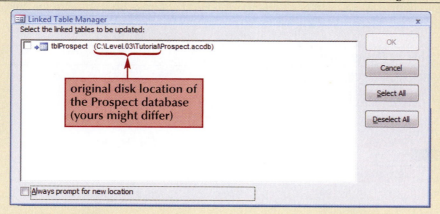

original disk location of the Prospect database (yours might differ)

The tblProspect table is the only linked table, so it's the only table listed in the list box. The Level.03\Tutorial folder provided with your Data Files, which is the original disk location of the Prospect database, is listed as the current disk location for the tblProspect table.

3. Click the **Select All** button, and then click the **OK** button. The Select New Location of tblProspect dialog box opens.

4. Navigate to the **Level.03** folder, click **Prospect** in the file list, and then click the **Open** button. A dialog box informs you that all selected linked tables were successfully refreshed.

5. Click the **OK** button to close the dialog box. The Linked Table Manager dialog box now displays the Level.03 folder as the current disk location of the linked tblProspect table.

6. Close the Linked Table Manager dialog box.

Next, you'll open the tblProspect table to show Sarah how she can update it as a linked table from the new disk location.

To update the tblProspect table and view its design in the Holland database:

1. Open the **tblProspect** table in Datasheet view. The tblProspect table datasheet displays four records.

   First, you'll add a new record to the tblProspect table.

2. Click the **New (blank) record** navigation button , type **12005** in the CustomerID column, press the **Tab** key, type **Gail** in the FirstName column, press the **Tab** key, type **Browning** in the LastName column, press the **Tab** key, type **6168881231** in the Phone column, press the **Tab** key, type **3200 Kent Cir** in the Address column, press the **Tab** key, type **Rockford** in the City column, press the **Tab** key, type **MI** in the State column, press the **Tab** key, type **49341** in the Zip column, and then press the **Tab** key twice.

   Next, you'll switch to Design view to show Sarah that she can't change the design of the tblProspect table from the Holland database.

3. Switch to Design view. A dialog box informs you that the tblProspect table is a linked table and has some properties that you cannot modify.

4. Click the **Yes** button to close the dialog box and switch to Design view. The CustomerID field is the current field, and the Help message in the Field Properties pane indicates that you can't change the Field Name property value for linked tables. See Figure 12-32.

Figure 12-32 **Linked table in Design view**

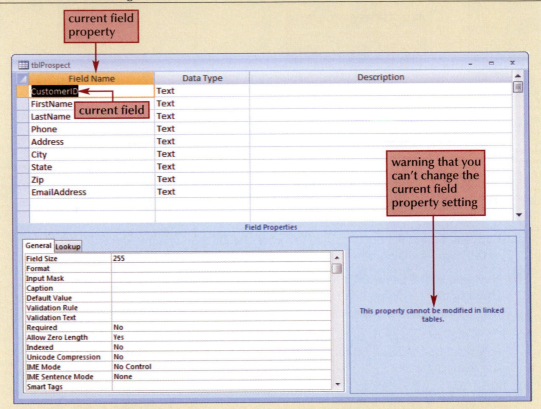

5. Press the **F6** key to highlight the Field Size property in the Field Properties pane. The Help message indicates that you can't change the Field Size property.

6. Press the **Tab** key to position the insertion point in the Format text box. The normal Help message for the Format property appears, so you can change this field property.

7. Close the table.

Now you'll open the Prospect database to show Sarah the new record in the tblProspect table that you added from the Holland database. Then you'll delete that record and view the table in Design view.

To update the tblProspect table and view its design in the Prospect database:

1. Start another instance of Access, and then open the **Prospect** database located in the Level.03 folder on the drive where you are storing your Data Files.

   Trouble? If the Security Warning is displayed below the Ribbon, click the Options button next to the Security Warning. In the dialog box that opens, click the "Enable this content" option button, and then click the OK button.

▶ 2. Open the Navigation Pane, open the **tblProspect** table datasheet, and then click the **row selector** for record 5. The record for Gail Browning, which you added to the tblProspect linked table in the Holland database, appears as record 5 in the tblProspect table in the Prospect database.

▶ 3. In the Records group on the Home tab, click the **Delete** button, and then click the **Yes** button to delete record 5.

▶ 4. Switch to Design view. Because the tblProspect table is not a linked table in the Prospect database, the Help message in the Field Properties pane does not warn you that you can't change the Field Name property. You can make any design changes you want to the tblProspect table in the Prospect database.

▶ 5. Close the tblProspect table, and then exit Access.

Sarah wants to know what would happen if she deletes the linked tblProspect table in the Holland database. You'll delete the linked tblProspect table in the Holland database to show her that Access deletes the link to the tblProspect table but does not delete the tblProspect table in the Prospect database.

To delete the linked tblProspect table in the Holland database:

▶ 1. Right-click **tblProspect** in the Navigation Pane to open the shortcut menu, and then click **Delete**. A dialog box asks you if you want to remove the link to the tblProspect table. See Figure 12-33.

Dialog box that opens when attempting to delete a linked table ◀ **Figure 12-33**

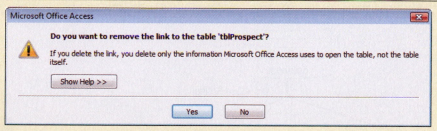

The dialog box confirms that you'll delete only the link to the tblProspect table, not the tblProspect table in the Prospect database.

▶ 2. Click the **Yes** button. Access deletes the link to the tblProspect table, and the tblProspect table no longer appears in the Navigation Pane for the Holland database.

Sarah now understands how to link to Taylor's tblProspect table and to other data if she needs to do so in the future.

Sarah wants to create several queries for the Holland database, but she doesn't want the user interface for other users to be cluttered with queries they won't need to use. She asks if there's a way for her to have a special user interface to access the data in the Holland database.

Using the Database Splitter

Users might want to customize their own versions of the user interface, while accessing the same central table data. The **Database Splitter** is an Access tool that splits an Access database into two files: one file contains the tables, and the other file contains the queries, forms, reports, and other database objects. Although a single master copy of the file containing the tables is stored and accessed, users can have their own copies of the other file and add their own queries, reports, and other objects to handle their processing needs. Each file created by the Database Splitter is an Access database. The database that contains the tables is called the **back-end database**; and the database that contains the other objects, including the user interface, is called the **front-end database**.

After you split a database, when users open a front-end database, the objects they open use data in the tables in the back-end database. Because the tables in the front-end database are linked tables that are stored in the back-end database, the front-end database contains the physical disk locations of the tables in the back-end database. You can move the front-end database to a different disk location without affecting the physical connections to the back-end database. However, if you move the back-end database to a different disk location, you'll need to use the Linked Table Manager to change the physical disk locations of the back-end database's tables in the front-end database.

People who develop databases and sell them to multiple companies usually split their databases. When a developer delivers a split database, the initial back-end database does not include the company's data, and the initial front-end database is complete as created by the developer. Companies use the front-end database to update their data in the back-end database, but they do not modify the front-end database in any way. Periodically, the database developer improves the front-end database by modifying and adding queries, reports, and other objects without changing the structure of the tables. In other words, the developer changes the front-end database, but does not change the back-end database. The developer gives its client companies replacement front-end databases, which continue to work with the back-end database that contains the company's data. This entire process is illustrated in Figure 12-34.

| Figure 12-34 | Split Access database |

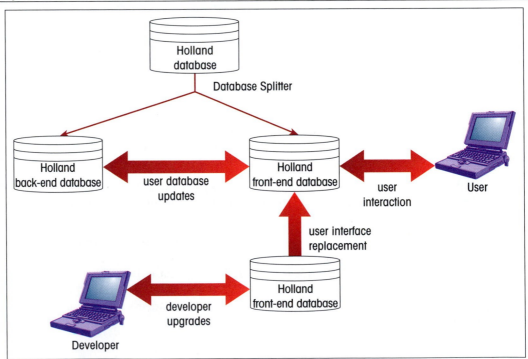

Splitting a database also lets you place the files on different computers. You can place the front-end database on each user's computer, and the back-end database on a network server that users access through their front-end databases; this arrangement distributes the workload across the network. Finally, as a company grows, it might need a more powerful database management system such as Oracle, Microsoft's SQL Server, IBM's DB2, or MySQL. You could retain the original Access front-end database and replace the Access back-end database with a new non-Access back-end database, which is an easier task than replacing all database objects.

Using the Database Splitter | Reference Window

- Make a backup copy of the database that you want to split.
- Start Access and open the database you want to split.
- Click the Database Tools tab on the Ribbon, and then in the Move Data group on the Database Tools tab, click the Access Database button.
- Click the Split Database button, select the drive and folder for the back-end database, type a name for the database in the File name text box, and then click the Split button.
- Click the OK button.

You'll use the Database Splitter to split the Holland database into two files. As a precaution, you'll make a backup copy of the database before you split the database.

To use the Database Splitter:

1. Close the Holland database without exiting Access, make a backup copy of the Holland database, and then open the **Holland** database.

2. Click the **Database Tools** tab on the Ribbon, and then in the Move Data group on the Database Tools tab, click the **Access Database** button. The Database Splitter dialog box opens. See Figure 12-35.

> **Tip**
>
> You should always make regular backups of databases, but it's especially important to make a backup before you make a significant database change such as splitting a database.

Database Splitter dialog box — Figure 12-35

3. Click the **Split Database** button. The Create Back-end Database dialog box opens. The back-end database will contain the tables from the Holland database. You'll use the default filename (Holland_be with the .accdb extension) for the back-end database.

4. Navigate to the **Level.03\Tutorial** folder, and then click the **Split** button. After a few moments, a dialog box informs you that the database was successfully split.

5. Click the **OK** button to close the dialog box and return to the Access window, and then scroll up to the top of the Navigation Pane, if necessary. See Figure 12-36.

Figure 12-36 ▶ **Linked tables in the Holland database**

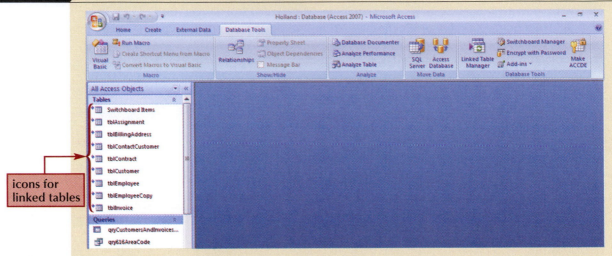

icons for
linked tables

Tip

You can use the linked tables as if they were stored in the Holland database, except you cannot change a table's design from the Holland database. You have to close the Holland database and open the Holland_be database to change a table's design.

Each table in the Holland database has an icon next to its name indicating that there's a link to that table in another file. The tables are no longer stored in the Holland database; they are stored in the Holland_be database file you just created with the Database Splitter.

6. Scroll down the Navigation Pane. The queries, forms, reports, macros, and modules you've created appear in the Navigation Pane and are still stored in the Holland database.

You'll close the Holland database and then open the Holland_be database to verify which objects are stored in the back-end database.

To verify the contents of the back-end database:

1. Close the Holland database without exiting Access, and then open the **Holland_be** database located in the Level.03\Tutorial folder.

2. In the Navigation Pane, click the **All Tables** button, and then click **Object Type** to display all objects in the Holland_be database by object type. The tables from the Holland database appear in the Navigation Pane with their usual icons, indicating the tables are now stored in the Holland_be database. No other objects exist in the Holland_be database.

3. Open the **tblInvoice** table in Design view. You can modify the design of the tables in the Holland_be database because they are stored in that database; they are not linked as they are in the Holland database.

4. Close the table, close the Holland_be database without exiting Access, and then open the **Holland** database.

Next, Lucia wants you to make access to the Holland database more secure.

Securing an Access Database

Security refers to the protection of a database against unauthorized access, either intentional or accidental. Access provides encryption and passwords as two of its security features.

Encryption translates the data in a database to a scrambled format that's indecipherable to a word processor or other program and stores it in an encrypted format. If unauthorized users attempt to bypass Access and get to the data directly, they will see only the encrypted version of the data. However, users accessing the data using Access will have no problem working with the data. When a user stores or modifies data in an encrypted database, Access will encrypt the data before updating the database. **Decrypting** a database reverses the encryption. Once you've encrypted a database, you can use Access to decrypt it. Before a user retrieves encrypted data using Access, the data will be decrypted and presented to the user in the normal format. If your encrypted database takes longer to respond to requests as it gets larger, you might consider decrypting it to improve its responsiveness.

To prevent access to a database by an unauthorized user through Access, you can assign a password to the database. A **password** is a string of characters assigned to a database that users must enter before they can open the database. As long as the password is known only to authorized users of the database, unauthorized access to the database is prevented. It's best if you use a password that's easily remembered by authorized users, but is not obvious and easily guessed by others.

Lucia wants to restrict access to the Holland database to authorized employees at Belmont Landscapes and also wants to prevent people from using other programs to access the data in the Holland database. Access provides a single option to encrypt a database and set a password at the same time.

Encrypting a Database and Setting a Password | Reference Window

- Start Access, click the Office Button, and then click Open.
- Select the drive and folder that contains the database, and then click the database.
- Click the Open arrow, and then click Open Exclusive.
- Click the Database Tools tab, and then in the Database Tools group on the Database Tools tab, click the Encrypt with Password button.
- Type the password in the Password text box, type the same password in the Verify text box, and then press the Enter key.

The way you usually open an Access database allows **shared access** of the database with others; that is, two or more users can open and use the same database at the same time. When you set a password for the Holland database, you need to open the database with exclusive access. When you open an Access database with **exclusive access**, you prevent other users from opening and using the database at the same time. You must open the database with exclusive access in order to set a password, so that you can guarantee that only one copy of the database is open when you set the password.

You'll now encrypt the Holland database and set the password for it to X81yK14.

To encrypt and set the password for the Holland database:

▸ **1.** Close the Holland database without exiting Access.

▸ **2.** Click the **Office Button** 🔘 , and then click **Open**. The Open dialog box opens.

▶ **3.** Navigate to the Level.03\Tutorial folder, click **Holland** in the list box (if necessary), and then click the **Open** arrow. See Figure 12-37.

Figure 12-37 **Opening a database with exclusive access**

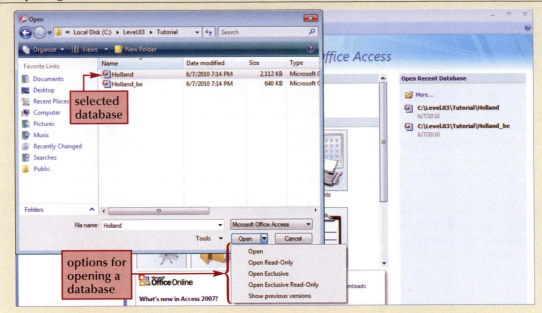

Clicking the Open option in the list opens the selected database with shared access for both reading and updating, whereas clicking the Open Read-Only option opens the selected database with shared access for reading only. **Reading** includes any database action that does not involve updating the database, such as running queries (but not action queries) and viewing table records. Actions that are prohibited when you open a database as read-only (because they involve updating the database) include changing the database design and updating table records. The other two open options in the Open list open the selected database with exclusive access for reading and updating (Open Exclusive) or for reading only (Open Exclusive Read-Only). The Show previous versions option displays previous versions of databases in the selection disk and folder location.

▶ **4.** Click **Open Exclusive**. The Holland database opens.

▶ **5.** Click the **Database Tools** tab on the Ribbon, and then in the Database Tools group on the Database Tools tab, click the **Encrypt with Password** button. The Set Database Password dialog box opens. See Figure 12-38.

Figure 12-38 **Set Database Password dialog box**

You must type the password twice: once in the Password text box, and again in the Verify text box. Passwords are case-sensitive, so you must type the same password in both text boxes. Because the password is stored in the database, you cannot open the database if you forget the password.

▶ **6.** Type **X81yK14** in the Password text box, press the **Tab** key, type **X81yK14** in the Verify text box, and then press the **Enter** key. The dialog box closes, and Access sets the Holland database password to X81yK14 and encrypts the database.

Trouble? If a dialog box opens, asking you to verify the new password by retyping it in the Verify box, click the OK button, type X81yK14 in the Verify text box, and then press the Enter key.

Next, you'll close and reopen the Holland database to verify that the password has been set. Then you'll unset, or remove, the password.

Unsetting a Database Password | Reference Window

- Start Access, click the Office Button, and then click Open.
- Select the drive and folder that contains the database, and then click the database.
- Click the Open arrow, and then click Open Exclusive.
- Click the Database Tools tab, and then in the Database Tools group on the Database Tools tab, click the Decrypt Database button.
- Type the password in the Password text box, and then press the Enter key.

Unsetting a password cancels the password protection for the database and also decrypts the database. After unsetting the password, you can encrypt the database again and set a new password.

To test and unset the password for the Holland database:

▶ **1.** Close the Holland database without exiting Access.

Because you'll be unsetting the password, you need to open the Holland database with exclusive access.

▶ **2.** Open the **Holland** database with exclusive access. The Password Required dialog box opens. See Figure 12-39.

Password Required dialog box | Figure 12-39

type password here

▶ **3.** Type **x81yk14** (all lowercase letters) in the text box, and then press the **Enter** key. A dialog box opens, warning you that you did not enter a valid password.

▶ **4.** Click the **OK** button, type **X81yK14** in the text box, and then press the **Enter** key. The Holland database opens.

You'll now unset the password. When you unset the password, you also decrypt the database.

▶ **5.** Click the **Database Tools** tab on the Ribbon, and then in the Database Tools group on the Database Tools tab, click the **Decrypt Database** button. The Unset Database Password dialog box opens. See Figure 12-40.

Figure 12-40 ▶ **Unset Database Password dialog box**

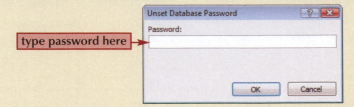

6. Type **X81yK14** in the Password text box, and then press the **Enter** key.

   The next time you open the Holland database, you won't be asked to enter a password because you've unset it.

Sarah is pleased with the changes you have made. As a final enhancement to the user interface, she asks you to set Access to open the Switchboard form automatically when a user opens the Holland database.

Setting the Database Properties and Startup Options

Tip

If you want to bypass the startup options that you set, press and hold down the Shift key when you open the database.

Access lets you specify certain actions, called **startup options**, that take place when a database opens. For example, you can specify the name that appears in the Access window title bar, prevent users from using the Navigation Pane, or specify a form that is automatically opened when you open a database.

Sarah wants users to be able to open the Holland database and have the Switchboard form open automatically. In this way, users won't need to use the Navigation Pane to access the Switchboard form.

Reference Window	**Setting the Database Properties and Startup Options**

- Open the database, click the Office Button, and then click the Access Options button.
- In the Access Options dialog box, click Current Database in the left section.
- Set the database properties and startup options, and then click the OK button. Most options will take effect the next time the database is opened.

You'll set the following database properties and startup options for the Holland database:

- The **Application Title property** specifies the name for the database that appears in the Access window title bar. You'll set the property to Holland Release 1.
- The **Display Form property** specifies the form that opens automatically when you open the database. You'll set the property to Switchboard. You must close and reopen the database for this property setting to take effect.
- The **Use Access Special Keys property** enables or disables the F11 key (show and hide the Navigation Pane), the Ctrl + G key combination (shows the Immediate window in the Visual Basic Editor) and the Alt + F11 key combination (starts the Visual Basic Editor). You'll disable this property because you don't want users to use the Navigation Pane or VBA. You must close and reopen the database for this property setting to take effect.

- The **Enable Layout View for this database property** shows or hides the Layout View button on the Access status bar and on shortcut menus. You'll disable this option.
- The **Enable design changes for tables in Datasheet view (for this database) property** allows you to change a table's design in Datasheet view. You'll disable this option.
- The **Display Navigation Pane property** controls whether the Navigation Pane is available in the Access window. You'll make the Navigation Pane unavailable to users because they'll navigate the database objects using the Switchboard form. You must close and reopen the database for this property setting to take effect.
- The **Allow Full Menus property** specifies whether all options are available on the Ribbon. You'll disable this property, which means only the Home tab is displayed on the Ribbon, limited options are available on the Home tab, and only the Close Database and Exit Access options are available when you click the Office Button. You must close and reopen the database for this property setting to take effect.
- The **Allow Default Shortcut Menus property** specifies whether shortcut menus are enabled or disabled. You'll disable shortcut menus. You must close and reopen the database for this property setting to take effect.
- The **Track name AutoCorrect info property** stores information about changes to the names of fields, controls, and objects, and the **Perform name AutoCorrect property** changes to control names and record source names in objects that depend upon the name changes tracked by the AutoCorrect feature. You'll disable both properties. You must close and reopen the database for these property settings to take effect.
- The **Enable error checking property** checks for design errors in forms and reports and alerts you to errors by displaying the Error Checking Options button. Clicking the Error Checking Options button allows you to fix the detected error. You'll disable this property. Unlike all the other properties, which appear on the Current Database page in the Access Options dialog box, the Enable error checking property appears on the Object Designers page in the Access Options dialog box.

Setting Database Properties and Startup Options | InSight

After you've developed and split a database and turned it over to your users, you've completed the design and creation of all fields and objects. Users don't need to change the design, so you should remove any Access property or feature that allows them to change the design. For this reason, you should and will disable the following properties: Use Access Special Keys, Enable Layout View for this database, Enable design changes for tables in Datasheet view, Allow Full Menus, Allow Default Shortcut Menus, Track name AutoCorrect info, Perform name AutoCorrect, and Enable error checking.

When your database design includes a Switchboard form, you want to display the Switchboard form when the database opens (set the Display Form property), and your users do not need the Navigation Pane (disable the Display Navigation Pane property).

Before you set the database properties and startup options, you'll set one of the basic properties that provide documentation about the Holland database. You'll also create a custom property to document the Holland database.

Reference Window | **Setting Database Documentation Properties**

- Open the database, click the Office Button, point to Manage, and then click Database Properties.
- Click the Custom tab.
- To set an existing property, scroll the Name list, click the property in the Name list, type the property setting in the Value text box, and then click the Add button.
- To create a new property, type the property name in the Name text box, select the data type in the Type list box, type the property value in the Value text box, and then click the Add button.
- Click the OK button.

Now you'll set the Checked by property and create a new property named Platform, which you'll use to document the operating system used on your computer.

To set the Checked by property and create the Platform property in the Holland database:

▶ 1. Click the **Office Button** , point to **Manage**, and then click **Database Properties** to open the Holland.accdb Properties dialog box.

▶ 2. Click the **Custom** tab, click **Checked by** in the Name list box, and then click the **Value** text box. See Figure 12-41.

Figure 12-41 ▸ **Setting a database property**

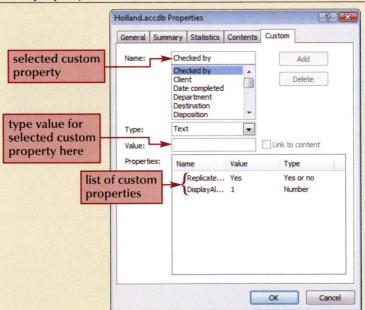

▶ 3. Type your full name in the Value text box, and then click the **Add** button. The Checked by property is added to the list of custom properties.

Next, you'll create the custom property named Platform.

▶ 4. Type **Platform** in the Name text box, type **Windows Vista** (or your operating system) in the Value text box, and then click the **Add** button to add the Platform custom property to the list of custom properties.

▶ 5. Click the **OK** button.

You can now finish developing the Holland database by setting the database properties and startup options.

To set the database properties and startup options in the Holland database:

▶ **1.** Click the **Office Button** 🔘, and then click the **Access Options** button to open the Access Options dialog box.

▶ **2.** In the left section of the dialog box, click **Current Database** to display the list of options for the current database. See Figure 12-42.

Options for the current database in the Access Options dialog box | Figure 12-42

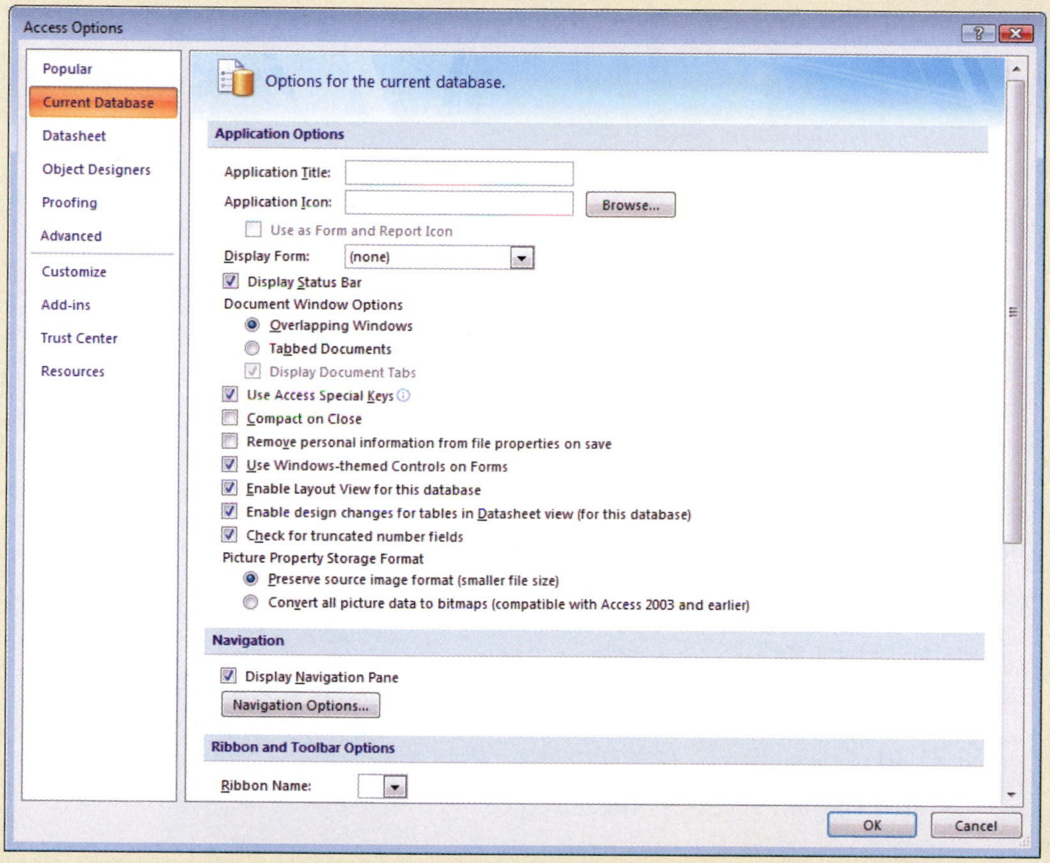

▶ **3.** Type **Holland Release 1** in the Application Title text box, click the **Display Form** arrow, and then click **Switchboard**.

▶ **4.** Scrolling as necessary, click the following check boxes to disable the properties: **Use Access Special Keys**, **Enable Layout View for this database**, **Enable design changes for tables in Datasheet view (for this database)**, **Display Navigation Pane**, **Allow Full Menus**, **Allow Default Shortcut Menus**, and **Track name AutoCorrect info**.

▶ **5.** In the left section of the dialog box, click **Object Designers** to display the list of options for creating and modifying database objects, and then scroll to the bottom of the dialog box. See Figure 12-43.

Figure 12-43 | **Error checking options in the Access Options dialog box**

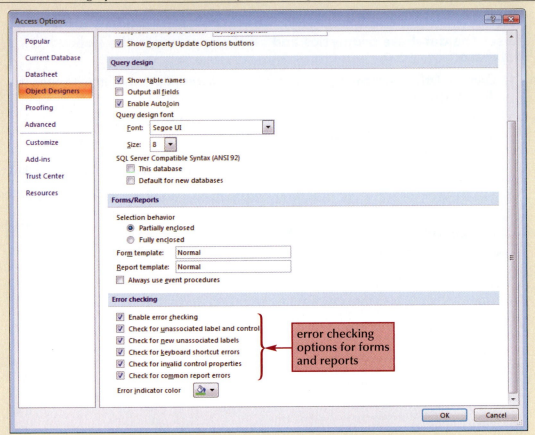

Tip

Unlike the other database properties, which apply only to the current database, the Enable error checking property applies to all databases.

6. If necessary, click the **Enable error checking** check box to clear it and disable all error checking options.

   Trouble? If the Error checking check box does not contain a check mark, continue on to the next step.

7. Click the **OK** button to close the Access Options dialog box. A dialog box informs you that you must close and reopen the Holland database for the options you selected to take effect.

8. Click the **OK** button to close the dialog box.

To test the database properties and startup options, you need to close and reopen the Holland database.

To test the database properties and startup options:

1. Close the Holland database without exiting Access.

2. Click the **Office Button** 🔘 , and then open the **Holland** database. See Figure 12-44.

Holland database user interface | Figure 12-44

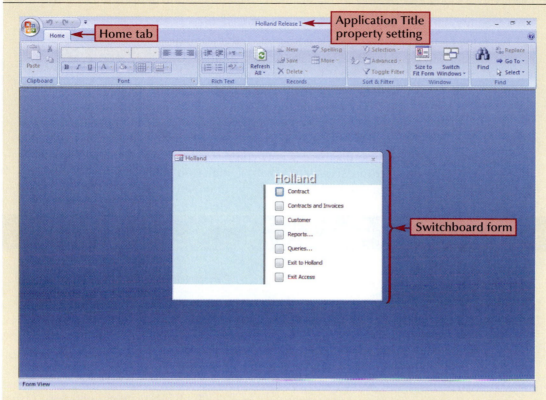

Access opens the Holland database, opens the Switchboard form, disables the Navigation Pane, displays a restricted Ribbon with only the Home tab, and displays Holland Release 1 in the Access title bar.

Now you can make one final test of the Holland database user interface.

3. Make one final pass through all the command button options to verify that all features work properly on the Holland database user interface.

4. Click the **Exit Access** command button on the switchboard as your last test to close the form, close the database, and exit Access.

Before completing your work with the Holland database, Sarah asks you to research another Access security feature—creating an ACCDE file.

Saving a Database as an ACCDE File

If a database contains VBA code, you can save an ACCDE file version of the database to prevent people from viewing or changing the VBA code. Saving an Access database as an **ACCDE file**, which has the .accde extension instead of the .accdb extension for a normal Access database, compiles all VBA modules, removes all editable VBA source code, and compacts the resulting database. The database and its VBA code continue to run as normal, but the VBA code can't be viewed or edited. Also, users can't view, modify, or create forms, reports, or modules in Design view, nor can they import or export forms, reports, or modules. Because an ACCDE file limits database design changes to tables and queries, saving a database as an ACCDE file is best suited to a front-end database. You should keep a backup copy of the complete front-end database in case you need to modify the database design. To save a database as an ACCDE file, follow these steps:

1. Open the database you want to save as an ACCDE file.
2. Click the Database Tools tab on the Ribbon, and then in the Database Tools group on the Database Tools tab, click the Make ACCDE button.
3. In the Save As dialog box, type the name for the file in the File name text box, navigate to the location where you want to store the file, and then click the Save button.

Because the Holland database has very few VBA modules, you won't save the Holland database as an ACCDE file.

Your work with the Holland database is now complete. Lucia and Sarah review the final user interface, security measures, and database management tools with the staff, and they agree that the database will fully satisfy the company's requirements.

Review | **Session 12.2 Quick Check**

1. Access stores attachments in _____ form to minimize file size and maximize disk space usage.
2. You can specify sequential numbering or random numbering for a(n) _____ field.
3. What is the Performance Analyzer?
4. When do you use the Linked Table Manager?
5. What is the Database Splitter?
6. _____ refers to the protection of a database against unauthorized access, either intentional or accidental.
7. What is a startup option?

Review | **Tutorial Summary**

In this tutorial, you finished your work with the Holland database by completing tasks related to new Access 2007 features, management, security, and overall performance. You filtered data in a table using an AutoFilter and in a form using Filter By Form, saved a filter as a query and applied the saved query as a filter, and created a subquery. You created a multivalued field and an Attachment field and used an AutoNumber field. You learned how to save a database as a previous version, used the Performance Analyzer to analyze the database's performance, used the Linked Table Manager to refresh the link to a table in another database after you changed its location, and used the Database Splitter. Finally, you secured the database by encrypting it and setting a database password, set database properties and startup options, and learned about saving a database as an ACCDE file.

Key Terms

ACCDE file
Advanced Filter/Sort
Allow Default Shortcut
 Menus property
Allow Full Menus property
Allow Zero Length prop-
 erty
Application Title property
Attachment data type
back-end database
Database Splitter
decrypting
Display Form property
Display Navigation Pane
 property

Enable design changes for
 tables in Datasheet
 view (for this database)
 property
Enable error checking
 property
Enable Layout View for
 this database property
encryption
exclusive access
front-end database
linked table
Linked Table Manager
multivalued field
password

Perform name AutoCorrect
 property
Performance Analyzer
reading
refresh the link
security
shared access
startup options
subquery
Track name AutoCorrect
 info property
Use Access Special Keys
 property
Value property

Practice	**Review Assignments**

Practice the skills you learned in the tutorial using the same case scenario.

Data Files needed for the Review Assignments: Ads.accdb and Vendor.accdb (cont. from Tutorial 11)

Lucia asks you to complete your work with the user interface for the Vendor database. To help with this request, complete the following steps:

1. Open the **Vendor** database located in the Level.03\Review folder provided with your Data Files.

2. Open the **tblProduct** table, use an AutoFilter to filter records using the Unit field for values of Square foot and Linear foot, and then save and close the table.

3. Use Filter By Form with the **frmCompaniesAndProducts** form to select all records in which the city is Grand Rapids or Kalamazoo and the initial contact date is before January 1, 2010. Apply the filter, save the filter as a query named **qryCityDateFilter**, clear all filters, and then close the form.

4. Create a query named **qryProductSubquery** that selects all fields from the tblProduct table for all products that weigh more than 100 pounds. Switch to SQL view, add a subquery that selects all products whose color is green, run the query, and then save and close the query.

5. Add a multivalued field to the end of the **tblInvoice** table, defining permitted values of **Courier**, **E-mail**, **Fax**, and **USPS**, and naming the field **Transmitted**. Save the table, and then add the following values to the field in the table datasheet: for record 11—E-mail and USPS, for record 16—Courier, and for record 17—Fax and USPS. Close the table.

6. Use the Simple Query Wizard to create a query named **qryInvoiceValue** that displays all fields from the tblInvoice table; for the Transmitted field, display only the version of the field that uses the Value property and change its Caption property setting to **Transmitted**. Save and close the query.

7. Add an Attachment field named **ProductFiles** to the end of the **tblProduct** table, using a Caption property setting of **Product Files**. Create two Excel workbooks named **First Last_1** and **First Last_2**, substituting your first name for *First* and your last name for *Last* and storing them in the Level.03\Review folder. Attach both workbooks to the ProductFiles field for record 5 in the tblProduct table, and then close the table.

8. Add an AutoNumber field named **ProductNum** to the beginning of the **tblProductSpecial** table, using a Caption property setting of **Product Num** and a New Values property setting of Random. Save and close the table.

9. Use the Performance Analyzer to analyze the entire Vendor database, but do not implement any of the analysis results. How many analysis results of the recommendation type did the Performance Analyzer find? Of the suggestion type? Of the idea type? Close the Performance Analyzer dialog box.

10. Link to the tblAd table in the Ads database located in the Level.03\Review folder. Use Windows Explorer to move the Ads database to the Level.03 folder, and then use the Linked Table Manager to refresh the link to the tblAd table. Open the tblAd table in Datasheet view, and then add a new record to the table: Ad Num **7**, Ad Date **9/13/2010**, Ad Cost **$227.60**, and Placed **Newspaper**.

11. Close the Vendor database without exiting Access, create a copy of the Vendor database in the Level.03\Review folder, and then rename the copy as **Sellers**. Open the **Vendor** database in the Level.03\Review folder, and then use the Database Splitter to split the Vendor database. Use the default name for the back-end database and store it in the Level.03\Review folder.

12. Encrypt the Vendor database and set the password to **k2Everest**.

13. Set the same database properties and startup options for the Vendor database that you set in Tutorial 12 for the Holland database, using a value of **Vendor for Belmont Landscapes** for the Application Title property.

14. Set the Client custom property to your school name, and then create a new custom property named **Course name**, setting its value to the name of the course for which you're using this book.

15. Compact and repair the Vendor database, close the Vendor database without exiting Access, make a backup copy of the database, open the **Vendor** database, test all the switchboard options, close the database, and then exit Access.

| Apply | | Case Problem 1 |

Apply the skills you learned in the tutorial to finalize the database for a small music school.

Data Files needed for this Case Problem: Portland.accdb (*cont. from Tutorial 11*) **and Room.accdb**

Pine Hill Music School Yuka Koyama wants you to complete your work with the user interface for the Portland database. To help Yuka with her request, complete the following steps:

1. Open the **Portland** database located in the Level.03\Case1 folder provided with your Data Files.

2. Open the **tblContract** table, use an AutoFilter to filter records using the LessonType field for values of Guitar, Piano, and Violin, and then save and close the table.

3. Use Filter By Form with the **frmStudentData** form to select all records in which the city is Cornelius or Portland and the gender is F. Apply the filter, save the filter as a query named **qryCityGenderFilter**, and then close the form.

⊕ **EXPLORE**

4. Make a copy of the qryInstrument query, naming it **qryInstrumentSubquery**. Switch to SQL view, add a subquery to the existing query that selects all students who play the guitar, run the query, and then save and close the query.

5. Add a multivalued field to the end of the **tblTeacher** table, defining permitted values of **Band**, **Group**, and **Solo**, and naming the field **LessonSize** with a Caption property value of **Lesson Size**. Save the table, and then add the following values to the field in the table datasheet: for record 1—Solo; for record 2—Solo; for record 3—Band and Group; for record 4—Band, Group, and Solo; and for record 5—Solo. Resize the Lesson Size column to its best fit, and then save and close the table.

6. Use the Simple Query Wizard to create a query named **qryTeacherMultivalued** that displays all fields from the tblTeacher table; for the LessonSize field, display only the version of the field that displays multiple values in a text box. Save and close the query.

7. Add an Attachment field named **PressRelease** to the end of the **tblTeacher** table, using a Caption property setting of **Press Release**. Create two Notepad documents named **Reese_1** and **Reese_2**, and store them in the Level.03\Case1 folder. Attach both documents to the PressRelease field for record 12 in the tblTeacher table, and then close the table.

8. Add an AutoNumber field named **SpecialNum** to the beginning of the **tblSpecialLesson** table, using a Caption property setting of **Special Num** and a New Values property setting of Increment. Specify the SpecialNum field as the primary key. Save and close the table.

9. Use the Performance Analyzer to analyze the entire Portland database. How many analysis results of the recommendation type did the Performance Analyzer find? Of the suggestion type? Of the idea type? Use the Performance Analyzer to implement any suggestion task, and perform any subsequent task(s) required due to implementing the suggestion(s). Close the Performance Analyzer dialog box.

10. Link to the tblRoom table in the Room database located in the Level.03\Case1 folder. Use Windows Explorer to move the Room database to the Level.03 folder, and then use the Linked Table Manager to refresh the link to the tblRoom table. Open the **tblRoom** table in Datasheet view, and then add a new record to the table: Room Num **2**, Rental Cost **$75**, and Room Type **Group**. Close the table.

11. Close the Portland database without exiting Access, create a copy of the Portland database in the Level.03\Case1 folder, and then rename the copy as **Oregon**. Open the **Portland** database in the Level.03\Case1 folder, and then use the Database Splitter to split the Portland database. Use the default name for the back-end database and store it in the Level.03\Case1 folder.

12. Encrypt the Portland database and set the password to **4Lhotse4**.

13. Set the same database properties and startup options for the Portland database that you set in Tutorial 12 for the Holland database, using a value of **Portland Final** for the Application Title property.

14. Set the Date completed custom property to today's date, and then create a new custom property named **My location**, setting its value to your home town or city.

15. Compact and repair the Portland database, close the Portland database without exiting Access, make a backup copy of the database, open the **Portland** database, test all the switchboard options, close the database, and then exit Access.

| Apply | | **Case Problem 2** |

Apply what you learned in the tutorial to finalize the database for a fitness center.

Data Files needed for this Case Problem: Exercise.accdb (*cont. from Tutorial 11*) and Routines.accdb

Parkhurst Health & Fitness Center   Martha Parkhurst asks you to complete your work with the user interface for the Exercise database. To help Martha with her request, complete the following steps:

1. Open the **Exercise** database located in the Level.03\Case2 folder provided with your Data Files.

2. Open the **tblMember** table, use an AutoFilter to filter records using the MembershipStatus field for values of Inactive and On Hold, and then save and close the table.

3. Use Filter By Form with the **frmMemberInfo** form to select all records in which the city is Ashland or Richmond and the membership status is Active. Apply the filter, save the filter as a query named **qryCityStatusFilter**, and then close the form. (*Hint*: You might need to increase the form width.)

⊕ EXPLORE 4. Make a copy of the qryMayMembers query, naming it **qryMayMembersSubquery**. Switch to SQL view, add a subquery to the existing query that selects all ProgramID field values that have a monthly fee of $25. Save and close the query.

5. Add an Attachment field named **MemberAttachment** to the end of the **tblMember** table, using a Caption property setting of **Member Attachment**. Create two Notepad documents named **Picard_1** and **Picard_2**, and store them in the Level.03\Case2 folder. Attach both documents to the MemberAttachment field for record 11 in the tblMember table, resize the Member Attachment column to its best fit, and then save and close the table.

6. Add an AutoNumber field named **MemberNum** to the beginning of the **tblSpecialMember** table, using a Caption property setting of **Member Num** and a New Values property setting of Random. Resize the Member Num column to its best fit, and then save and close the table.

7. Use the Performance Analyzer to analyze the entire Exercise database, but do not implement any of the analysis results. How many analysis results of the recommendation type did the Performance Analyzer find? Of the suggestion type? Of the idea type? Close the Performance Analyzer dialog box.

8. Link to the **tblRoutine** table in the **Routines** database located in the Level.03\Case2 folder. Use Windows Explorer to move the Routines database to the Level.03 folder, and then use the Linked Table Manager to refresh the link to the tblRoutine table. Open the **tblRoutine** table in Datasheet view, and then add a new record to the table: Routine ID **130**, and Routine Desc **Yoga**.

9. Close the Exercise database without exiting Access, create a copy of the Exercise database in the Level.03\Case2 folder, and then rename the copy as **GetInShape**. Open the **Exercise** database in the Level.03\Case2 folder, and then use the Database Splitter to split the Exercise database. Use the default name for the back-end database and store it in the Level.03\Case2 folder.

10. Encrypt the Exercise database and set the password to **10Annapurna01**.

11. Set the same database properties and startup options for the Exercise database that you set in Tutorial 12 for the Holland database, using a value of **Final Exercise** for the Application Title property.

12. Set the Owner custom property to your first and last name, and then create a new custom property named **Nickname**, setting its value to your nickname (or the version of your first name you use when introducing yourself).

13. Compact and repair the Exercise database, close the Exercise database without exiting Access, make a backup copy of the database, open the **Exercise** database, test all the switchboard options, close the database, and then exit Access.

| Apply | **Case Problem 3** |

Apply what you learned in the tutorial to finalize the database for a recycling agency.

Data Files needed for this Case Problem: Drivers.accdb and Salina.accdb (*cont. from Tutorial 11*)

Rossi Recycling Group   Mary and Tom Rossi want you to complete your work with the user interface for the Salina database. To help them with their request, complete the following steps:

1. Open the **Salina** database located in the Level.03\Case3 folder provided with your Data Files.

2. Open the **tblDonation** table, use an AutoFilter to filter records using the PickupRequired field for values of Yes, and then save and close the table.

3. Use Filter By Form with the **frmDonationInfo** form to select all records in which the agency ID is R15 or W22 and the donation description is Cash. Apply the filter, save the filter as a query named **qryAgencyDescFilter**, and then close the form.

✦ EXPLORE

4. Make a copy of the qryNetDonations query, naming it **qryNetDonationsSubquery**. Switch to SQL view, add a subquery to the existing query that selects all DonationID field values for which a pickup is required.

5. Add a multivalued field to the end of the **tblDonor** table, defining permitted values of **Donor**, **Driver**, **Speaker**, and **Volunteer**, and naming the field **DonorType** with a Caption property value of **Donor Type**. Save the table, and then add the following values to the field in the table datasheet: for record 1—Donor and Volunteer; for record 2—Donor and Driver; for record 3—Donor, Driver, Speaker, and Volunteer; and for record 4—Volunteer. Resize the Donor Type column to its best fit, and then save and close the table.

6. Create a query named **qryDonorValue** that displays all fields from the tblDonor table; for the DonorType field, display only the version of the field that uses the Value property and change its Caption property setting to **Donor Type**. Save and close the query.

7. Add an Attachment field named **AgencyFiles** to the end of the **tblAgency** table, using a Caption property setting of **Agency Files**. Create two Notepad documents named **Baker_1** and **Baker_2** and store them in the Level.03\Case3 folder. Attach both documents to the AgencyFiles field for record 3 in the tblAgency table, and then close the table.

8. Add an AutoNumber field named **DonationNum** to the beginning of the **tblSpecialDonation** table, using a Caption property setting of **Donation Num** and a New Values property setting of Increment. Specify the DonationNum field as the primary key. Save and close the table.

9. Use the Performance Analyzer to analyze the entire Salina database, but do not implement any of the analysis results. How many analysis results of the recommendation type did the Performance Analyzer find? Of the suggestion type? Of the idea type? Close the Performance Analyzer dialog box.

10. Link to the tblDriver table in the Drivers database located in the Level.03\Case3 folder. Use Windows Explorer to move the Drivers database to the Level.03 folder, and then use the Linked Table Manager to refresh the link to the tblDriver table.

11. Close the Salina database without exiting Access, create a copy of the Salina database in the Level.03\Case3 folder, and then rename the copy as **Kansas**. Open the **Salina** database in the Level.03\Case3 folder, and then use the Database Splitter to split the Salina database. Use the default name for the back-end database and store it in the Level.03\Case3 folder.

12. Encrypt the Salina database and set the password to **mT888T**.

13. Set the same database properties and startup options for the Salina database that you set in Tutorial 12 for the Holland database, using a value of **Salina Donations** for the Application Title property.

14. Set the Status custom property to **Salina version 1**, and then create a new custom property named **Milestone**, setting its value to **Completed**.

15. Compact and repair the Salina database, close the Salina database without exiting Access, make a backup copy of the database, open the **Salina** database, test all the switchboard options, close the database, and then exit Access.

Apply | Case Problem 4

Apply what you learned in the tutorial to finalize the database for a luxury property rental company.

Data File needed for this Case Problem: Rentals.accdb (*cont. from Tutorial 11*)

GEM Ultimate Vacations   Griffin and Emma MacElroy ask you to complete your work with the user interface for the Rentals database. To help them with their request, complete the following steps:

1. Open the **Rentals** database located in the Level.03\Case4 folder provided with your Data Files.

2. Open the **tblPersonnel** table, use an AutoFilter to filter records using the JobTitle field for values of Finance Manager and Staff Manager, and then save and close the table.

⊕ **EXPLORE**   3. Use Filter By Form with the **tblProperty** table to select all records in which the country is France or Italy and the property type is Villa. Apply the filter, save the filter as a query named **qryCountryPropertyFilter**, and then save and close the table. (*Hint*: You might have to close the Navigation Pane and widen the table before filtering.)

⊕ **EXPLORE**   4. Make a copy of the qryGuestData query, naming it **qryGuestDataSubquery**. Switch to SQL view, add a subquery to the existing query that selects all GuestID field values for guests from Chicago or Gary. Save and close the query.

5. Add an Attachment field named **AddedFiles** to the end of the **tblPersonnel** table, using a Caption property setting of **Added Files**. Create two Notepad documents named **Leary_1** and **Leary_2** and store them in the Level.03\Case4 folder. Attach both documents to the AddedFiles field for record 4 in the tblPersonnel table, and then close the table.

6. Add an AutoNumber field named **GuestNum** to the beginning of the **tblSelectedReservation** table, using a Caption property setting of **Guest Num** and a New Values property setting of Increment. Specify the GuestNum field as the primary key. Save and close the table.

7. Use the Performance Analyzer to analyze the entire Rentals database, but do not implement any of the analysis results. How many analysis results of the recommendation type did the Performance Analyzer find? Of the suggestion type? Of the idea type? Use the Performance Analyzer to implement any suggestion task, and perform any subsequent task(s) required due to implementing the suggestion(s). Close the Performance Analyzer dialog box.

8. Close the Rentals database without exiting Access, create a copy of the Rentals database in the Level.03\Case4 folder, and then rename the copy as **Illinois**. Open the **Rentals** database in the Level.03\Case4 folder, and then use the Database Splitter to split the Rentals database. Use the default name for the back-end database and store it in the Level.03\Case4 folder.

9. Encrypt the Rentals database and set the password to **9NangaParbat9**.

10. Set the same database properties and startup options for the Rentals database that you set in Tutorial 12 for the Holland database, using a value of **Rentals European** for the Application Title property.

11. Set the Language custom property to **English**, and then create a new custom property named **State completed**, setting its value to the full name of the state where you currently live.

12. Compact and repair the Rentals database, close the Rentals database without exiting Access, make a backup copy of the database, open the **Rentals** database, test all the switchboard options, close the database, and then exit Access.

| Apply | **Case Problem 5** |

Apply what you learned in the tutorial to finalize the database for an Internet service provider.

Data Files needed for this Case Problem: AcePay.accdb and Always.accdb (*cont. from Tutorial 11*)

Always Connected Everyday Chris and Pat Dixon ask you to complete your work with the user interface for the Always database. To help them with their request, complete the following steps:

1. Open the **Always** database located in the Level.03\Case5 folder provided with your Data Files.

2. Open the **tblServiceCall** table, use AutoFilter to filter records using the ServiceID field for values of 3 and 8, and then save and close the table.

3. Use Filter By Form with the **frmCustomer** form to select all records in which the city is Drayton and the access plan ID is 3 or 8. Apply the filter, save the filter as a query named **qryCityPlanFilter**, and then close the form.

⊕ **EXPLORE**

4. Make a copy of the qryCustomerNames query, naming it **qryCustomerNamesSubquery**. Switch to SQL view, add a subquery to the existing query that selects all CustomerAcctNum field values for customers in the cities of Blade or Brunson. Save and close the query.

5. Add a multivalued field to the end of the **tblServiceCall** table, defining permitted values of **Chet**, **Donna**, and **Kent**, and naming the field **ServiceName** with a Caption property value of **Service Name**. Save the table, and then add the following values to the field in the table datasheet: for record 10—Donna, for record 11—Chet and Kent, for record 12—Kent, and for record 13—Donna. Resize the Service Name column to its best fit, and then save and close the table.

6. Use the Simple Query Wizard to create a query named **qryServiceCallValue** that displays all fields from the tblServiceCall table; for the ServiceName field, display only the version of the field that uses the Value property. Resize the ServiceName.Value column to its best fit, and then save and close the query.

7. Add an AutoNumber field named **CustomerNum** to the beginning of the **tblSelectedCustomer** table, using a Caption property setting of **Customer Num** and a New Values property setting of Increment. Specify the CustomerNum field as the primary key. Resize the Customer Num column in the table datasheet to its best fit, and then save and close the table.

8. Use the Performance Analyzer to analyze the entire Always database, but do not implement any of the analysis results. How many analysis results of the recommendation type did the Performance Analyzer find? Of the suggestion type? Of the idea type? Close the Performance Analyzer dialog box.

9. Link to the tblPayment table in the AcePay database located in the Level.03\Case5 folder. Use Windows Explorer to move the AcePay database to the Level.03 folder, and then use the Linked Table Manager to refresh the link to the tblPayment table.

10. Close the Always database without exiting Access, create a copy of the Always database in the Level.03\Case5 folder, and then rename the copy as **Provider**. Open the **Always** database in the Level.03\Case5 folder, and then use the Database Splitter to split the Always database. Use the default name for the back-end database and store it in the Level.03\Case5 folder.

11. Encrypt the Always database and set the password to **3Kanchenjunga3**.

12. Set the same database properties and startup options for the Always database that you set in Tutorial 12 for the Holland database, using a value of **Always Internet Provider** for the Application Title property.

13. Compact and repair the Always database, close the Always database without exiting Access, make a backup copy of the database, open the **Always** database, test all the switchboard options, close the database, and then exit Access.

| Research | **Internet Assignments** |

Use the Internet to find and work with data related to the topics presented in this tutorial.

The purpose of the Internet Assignments is to challenge you to find information on the Internet that you can use to work effectively with this software. The actual assignments are updated and maintained on the Course Technology Web site. Log on to the Internet and use your Web browser to go to the Student Online Companion for New Perspectives Office 2007 at **www.course.com/np/office2007**. Then navigate to the Internet Assignments for this tutorial.

| Assess | **SAM Assessment and Training** |

If you have a SAM user profile, you may have access to hands-on instruction, practice, and assessment of the skills covered in this tutorial. Log in to your SAM account (**http://sam2007.course.com**) to launch any assigned training activities or exams that relate to the skills covered in this tutorial.

| Review | **Quick Check Answers** |

Session 12.1

1. Form
2. query
3. a second SQL SELECT statement inside another SELECT statement
4. a lookup field that allows you to store more than one value in a field
5. Value

Session 12.2

1. compressed
2. AutoNumber
3. an Access tool that you can use to optimize the performance of an Access database
4. to change the filename or disk location for linked tables in an Access database
5. an Access tool that splits an Access database into two files: one file contains the tables, and the other file contains the other database objects
6. security
7. an action that takes place when a database is opened

Ending Data Files

Level.03 →

Level.03
AcePay.accdb
Ads.accdb
Drivers.accdb
Prospect.accdb
Room.accdb
Routines.accdb

Tutorial
Holland.accdb
Holland_be.accdb
Perkins1.docx
Perkins2.xlsx
Perkins3.pptx
Perkins3 Export.pptx

Review
First Last_1.xlsx
First Last_2.xlsx
Sellers.accdb
Vendor.accdb
Vendor_be.accdb

Case1
Oregon.accdb
Portland.accdb
Portland_be.accdb
Reese_1.txt
Reese_2.txt

Case2
Exercise.accdb
Exercise_be.accdb
GetInShape.accdb
Picard_1.txt
Picard_2.txt

Case3
Baker_1.txt
Baker_2.txt
Kansas.accdb
Salina.accdb
Salina_be.accdb

Case4
Illinois.accdb
Leary_1.txt
Leary_2.txt
Rentals.accdb
Rentals_be.accdb

Case5
Always.accdb
Always_be.accdb
Provider.accdb

Reality Check

Throughout this book, you have learned how to use Access to develop and manage a database. The appendix at the end of this book, titled "Relational Databases and Database Design," includes additional content about designing tables, examining the keys used in those tables, creating entity-relationship diagrams to describe the tables and their relationships, and setting integrity constraints. In this Reality Check, you'll use a word processor or Access to design a database that will manage the data of your choice. You can choose any situation that interests you to complete this Reality Check. For example, you might design a database based on your work experience, your involvement with a club or program at your school, your participation or interest in sports or a hobby, or something that you need to organize in your personal life. Be sure to choose a situation that contains enough variation so that you can design at least six to eight tables that are related to each other with at least one many-to-many and at least one one-to-one relationship.

Note: Please be sure *not* to include any personal information of a sensitive nature in the database you design to be submitted to your instructor for this exercise. Later on, you can update the data in your database with such information for your own personal use.

1. Read the appendix titled "Relational Databases and Database Design," which appears at the end of this book.
2. Identify each entity (table) in the database that you are designing. Your database should have at least six to eight tables. For each table, list the fields and their attributes, such as data types, field sizes, and validation rules. Place the set of tables in third normal form and identify all primary, alternate, and foreign keys. You can document these tables using a word processor or by using Access. If you use a word processor for your design, make sure that your work clearly indicates each table and the fields it contains, the attributes for each field, and the keys. If you use Access for your design, create the tables by defining each table's fields and field attributes, specify the primary key for each table, and establish the table relationships in the Relationships window.
3. Draw an entity-relationship diagram showing the entities and the relationships between the entities. Your database should have at least one many-to-many relationship and at least one one-to-one relationship.
4. For each table in the database, represent the functional dependencies and determinants in a bubble diagram or by using the shorthand representation shown in the Appendix (that lists the determinant, followed by an arrow and the dependent fields).
5. Submit your completed database design to your instructor as requested.

Objectives

- Change field properties
- Add fields to a table
- Enter data in a table
- Create table relationships
- Create select, parameter, and crosstab queries
- Create a form using the Form Wizard
- Create calculated controls in a form
- Create a custom report
- Create macros
- Create a switchboard
- Set database properties and startup options

In this case you will use skills you learned in the following tutorials:

- Tutorials 1-10 and 12 (startup options only)

Enhancing an Investment Club Database

Case | Nest Egg Investment Club

Barbara and Neal Hennessey and some friends recently formed an investment club. Researching investment clubs on the Web, Barbara found the National Association of Investors Corporation (NAIC) site. Established in 1951, NAIC is a nonprofit organization founded to educate investment clubs and individual investors. Following guidelines recommended by NAIC, the club members chose Nest Egg as their club name, prepared and approved a partnership agreement and a set of bylaws, registered their club, obtained the club's tax ID, and established an online brokerage account to handle the club's investments.

The club decided to meet monthly and to set monthly dues at $200. The 15 permanent club members, each having one vote for all club matters, include 13 individuals and two couples for a total of 17 individuals. Each of the 15 members can contribute $200 monthly, a participation level of 1, or $400 monthly, a participation level of 2, but the participation level does not affect the voting rule of one vote per member.

The online brokerage account will track the club's investments, but Felicia Rodriquez, the club treasurer, has created a database to handle club accounting for monthly dues and for any future withdrawals. Felicia's database consists of two tables, tblMember and tblContribution. Figure 1 shows the structure of the tblMember table, which stores data about each club member. Each tblMember table record contains a member ID number and each member's first name, last name, address, phone, join date, and participation level (the Level field).

Starting Data Files

Dollars.jpg
NestEgg.accdb

Figure 1 | **Structure of the tblMember table**

Field Name	Data Type	Properties
MemberID	AutoNumber	Description: Primary key Caption: Member ID
FirstName	Text	Field Size: 15 Caption: First Name
LastName	Text	Field Size: 15 Caption: Last Name
Address	Text	Field Size: 32
Phone	Text	Field Size: 12
JoinDate	Date/Time	Format: mm/dd/yyyy Caption: Join Date
Level	Number	Description: Participation level used to determine the member's monthly dues Field Size: Byte Decimal Places: 0

Figure 2 shows the structure of the tblContribution table, which contains one record for each monthly dues payment. PaymentID is the table's primary key. MemberID is a foreign key in the tblContribution table, and the tblMember table will have a one-to-many relationship with the tblContribution table. The other fields in the tblContribution table are PaidDate and InvestmentAmt.

Figure 2 | **Structure of the tblContribution table**

Field Name	Data Type	Properties
PaymentID	AutoNumber	Description: Primary key Caption: Payment ID
MemberID	Number	Description: Foreign key Field Size: Long Integer Decimal Places: 0 Caption: Member ID
PaidDate	Date/Time	Format: mm/dd/yyyy Caption: Paid Date
InvestmentAmt	Currency	Decimal Places: 2 Caption: Investment Amt

Felicia wants to create special queries, forms, and reports in the database to help her manage club accounting. To help Felicia finish her work with the database, complete the following steps:

1. Make sure you have created your copy of the Access Data Files and that your computer can access them. Start Access, make sure the AddCases folder is a trusted folder, and then open the **NestEgg** database located in the AddCases folder.
2. Review the **tblMember** and **tblContribution** tables to become familiar with their structures and data. If you are unfamiliar with any property setting, use the Access Help system for an explanation of that property.

3. For the tblContribution table, specify PaymentID as the primary key and resize all datasheet columns to their best fit. For the tblMember table, add a validation rule for the Level field to store only values equal to 1 or 2, add an appropriate validation text message, and then add the following new Text fields between the Address and Phone fields: **City** (Field Size **24**), **StateProv** (Field Size **2** and Caption of **State/Prov**), and **PostalCode** (Field Size **10** and Caption of **Postal Code**).

4. Modify the first record in the tblMember table datasheet by entering your name, city, state or province (two-character postal abbreviation), postal code (zip code), and phone number; enter phone numbers in 987-654-3210 format. For the last four records, enter the same city, state or province, postal code, and phone area code but enter different phone numbers. Select a second city, state or province, postal code, and phone area code, and then enter these values in records 2-6, using five different phone numbers. Finally, select a third city, state or province, postal code, and phone area code, and then enter these values in records 7-11, using five different phone numbers. Resize all datasheet columns to their best fit.

5. Define a one-to-many relationship between the primary tblMember table and the related tblContribution table, using MemberID as the common field, enforcing referential integrity, and selecting the Cascade Update Related Fields option. Resize the tblMember field list so that all fields are visible, and then create and print the Relationships for NestEgg report but do not save it.

6. Export the tblMember table as an XML file named tblMember to the AddCases folder; do not create a separate XSD file. Save the export steps.

7. Create and save a query named **qryDistantMembers** that displays the FirstName, LastName, Address, City, StateProv, PostalCode, and Phone fields for all members not living in the same city where you live in ascending order by LastName. Print the query recordset in landscape orientation after testing and saving the query.

8. Create and save a query named **qryMarch17Contributions** that displays the FirstName, LastName, Phone, and InvestmentAmt fields for all contributions made on 3/17/2009 in ascending order by LastName. Print the query recordset after testing and saving the query.

9. Create and save a query named **qryInvestmentTotalsByMember** that displays each member's first name, last name, and total investment amount. For the calculated field, use the name **TotalInvested** and a Caption value of **Total Invested**. Sort in descending order by total investment amount, and resize all columns to best fit. Print the query recordset after testing and saving the query. Modify the query by deleting the FirstName and LastName fields, adding the PaidDate field as the first field in the query, sorting in ascending order by PaidDate (and not by the investment total), and then saving the query as **qryInvestmentTotalsByDate**. Print the query recordset.

10. Create and save a parameter query named **qryLevelParameter** that displays the FirstName, LastName, Phone, JoinDate, and Level fields in ascending order by LastName for a Level field value that the user enters. If the user doesn't enter a field value, select and display all records. After creating and saving the query, run the query and enter **1** as the Level field value. Print the query results.

EXPLORE 11. Create a crosstab query that uses PaidDate field values for the row headings, Level field values for the column headings, and the sum of the InvestmentAmt field as the summarized value. (*Hint:* Create a query named **qryInvestmentAmounts** that contains the three fields you need for the crosstab query.) Save the query as **qryInvestmentAmountsCrosstab**, resize the columns in the query recordset to their best fit, and then save and print the query recordset.

✦ **EXPLORE**   12. Use the Form Wizard to create a form containing a main form and a subform. Select all the fields from the tblMember table for the main form, and select all fields except MemberID from the tblContribution table for the subform. Use the Tabular layout and the Office style. Specify the title **frmContributionsByMember** for the main form and the title **frmContributionSubform** for the subform. Change the text in the main form's title control to **Contributions by Member**, and then resize the text box controls in the main form to reduce their widths to accommodate the longest value in the Address field. Change the AutoFormat of the subform to the Access 2007 style. Change the caption on the record navigation bar for the main form to **Member** and for the subform to **Contribution**. Print only the first main form record and its subform records.

✦ **EXPLORE**   13. Create a copy of the frmContributionsByMember form, and use **frmContributionsByMemberModified** as the new form's name. Modify the new form by adding a calculated control, as shown in Figure 3, that displays the sum of the InvestmentAmt field values that appear in the subform. Set the calculated control's Format property to Currency, set its ControlTip Text property to **Calculated total investment amount**, and set its Tab Stop property to No. Make sure the tab order in the main form is top-to-bottom and the tab order in the subform is left-to-right. Print only the first main form record and its subform records. (*Hint:* If the Form Footer section appears in the subform in your finished form, set its Visible property to No.)

| **Figure 3** | **Modified form** |

14. Create the custom Contributions by Date report shown in Figure 4. The report contains Page Header, Detail, PaidDate Footer, and Report Footer sections. Sort the detail records in ascending order by the PaidDate field, and then in ascending order by the LastName field. Hide duplicate values for the PaidDate field. Calculate and print totals of the InvestmentAmt field for each PaidDate field value and in grand total. The color used in the lines, title, and label controls is Dark Label Text in the Access Theme Colors gallery. Save the report as **rptContributionsByDate**. Print the report.

Figure 4   **Contributions by Date report**

Contributions by Date   Page 2 of 2

Paid Date	First Name	Last Name	Phone	Level	Investment Amt
04/21/2009	Kathy & Bob	Bakanas	406-555-2000	1	$200.00
	Francine	Barnes	905-555-8733	2	$400.00
	Kevin	Bioski	970-555-7811	1	$200.00
	Nancy	Ciriello	970-555-0744	1	$200.00
	Shawn	Erickson	905-555-3856	1	$200.00
	Thomas	Evensen	970-555-7144	2	$400.00
	Maureen	Heller	970-555-0101	1	$200.00
	Barbara & Neal	Hennessey	406-555-9786	2	$400.00
	Student	Name	512-555-6487	2	$400.00
	Lee	Nguyen	905-555-9033	1	$200.00
	Peter	O'Rourke	406-555-8631	1	$200.00
	Naomi	Ramos	970-555-8986	1	$200.00
	Felicia	Rodriguez	905-555-4848	1	$200.00
	Yonglei	Tao	406-555-3010	1	$200.00
	Marsha	Van Ry	406-555-7011	2	$400.00
					$4,000.00
					$11,000.00

15. Create a macro group named **mcrSwitchboardMacros** that contains macros to be used with the command buttons on the switchboard you'll create in the next step. The macros perform these actions:
    - Open the qryInvestmentAmounts query
    - Open the qryInvestmentTotalsByDate query
    - Open the qryInvestmentTotalsByMember query
    - Close the switchboard

16. Design and create a Switchboard form named **Switchboard**. Use Figure 5 and the following descriptions as a guide to create the switchboard.

Figure 5 NestEgg database switchboard

a. Change the database's window style to overlapping windows.

b. Use the Switchboard Manager to create the switchboard. Place the command buttons on the form; the command buttons should use the macros in the mcrSwitchboardMacros macro group as appropriate. Specify **Nest Egg Investment Club** as the main switchboard page name.

✦EXPLORE

c. Hide the default and shadow labels on the form. Add the label with the **Make your selection** text and add the Dollars.jpg picture located in the AddCases folder to the locations shown on the switchboard in Figure 5.

d. Resize the form, and then set form properties that are appropriate for a switchboard.

e. Test the command buttons on the main switchboard page to make sure that your switchboard items work correctly. If necessary, return to the Switchboard Manager and make any corrections.

17. Close the NestEgg database without exiting Access, make a backup copy of the database, open the **NestEgg** database, and then compact and repair the database.

18. Set the database properties for the **NestEgg** database so the Switchboard opens when the database is opened, to set startup options to disable features as appropriate for a database that uses a switchboard, and to change the Application Title property to **Nest Egg Investment Club**.

19. Close the database, and then exit Access.

Ending Data Files

NestEgg.accdb
tblMember.xml

Objectives

- Change field properties
- Create a new table
- Enter data in a table
- Create table relationships
- Create select, query wizard, parameter, and crosstab queries
- Create forms using wizards, and customize forms
- Create calculated controls in a form
- Create a custom report
- Create a dialog box form
- Create macros
- Create a switchboard
- Set database properties and startup options

In this case you will use skills you learned in the following tutorials:

- Tutorials 1-11 and 12 (startup options only)

Tracking Parking Permits and Violations

Case | Tophill College

Sandy Tatoian is the office manager in the Public Safety department at Tophill College. Among her responsibilities, Sandy coordinates issuing parking permits to staff, faculty, and students, and processing citations for on-campus parking violations. Reductions in the college budget have forced her department to reduce the number of part-time student workers. As a result, the department is experiencing an increase in the backlog for processing citations and parking permit requests. After discussing the problem with her supervisor, Sandy meets with Pat Davis, a database analyst in the college computer center.

Pat questions Sandy about her requirements and agrees to design a database to reduce her workload and to help her gain better control over her coordination responsibilities. Sandy explains that parking permits are issued to students, faculty, and staff for their vehicles. The permit is affixed to the windshield in the lower corner on the driver's side. Each parking permit request form includes the parking permit number, the vehicle license plate number, and the person's name. With each issued permit, a person receives a brochure that describes the campus parking regulations and the fines for parking violations.

The Public Safety department employs a patrol force that enforces the campus parking regulations. The patrol force issues citations for parking violations. Each citation includes the citation number, the date and time of the violation, and a description of the violation. For vehicles with permits, the citation includes the permit number and the license plate number. For vehicles without permits, the citation includes the license plate number but not the permit number. Sandy's staff also tracks payments for the fines levied with the citations.

Pat's initial database contains three tables: tblPermit, tblCitation, and tblPayment. Figure 6 shows the structure of the tblPermit table, which stores data about each parking permit issued to students, faculty, and staff. Each tblPermit table record contains a permit number, the vehicle license plate number, and the permit holder's name.

Starting Data Files

AddCases

NoPark.bmp
Tophill.accdb

Figure 6 Structure of the tblPermit table

Field Name	Data Type	Properties
PermitNum	Text	Description: Primary key; unique number issued to an individual's vehicle Field Size: 5 Caption: Permit Num
LicensePlateNum	Text	Description: License plate number of the vehicle issued the permit Field Size: 8 Caption: License Plate Num
OwnerFirst	Text	Description: Vehicle owner's first name Field Size: 15 Caption: Owner First
OwnerLast	Text	Description: Vehicle owner's last name Field Size: 15 Caption: Owner Last

Figure 7 shows the structure of the tblCitation table, which contains one record for each issued citation. Each tblCitation record contains the citation number, date, and time; the vehicle license plate number; the violation code; and the permit number, if a permit is visible on the front windshield.

Figure 7 Structure of the tblCitation table

Field Name	Data Type	Properties
CitationNum	Text	Description: Primary key; unique number assigned to a citation for a parking violation Field Size: 6 Caption: Citation Num
CitationDate	Date/Time	Description: Issue date for the citation Format: mm/dd/yyyy Caption: Citation Date
CitationTime	Date/Time	Description: Issue time for the citation Format: Medium Time Caption: Citation Time
PermitNum	Text	Description: Null if the vehicle has no visible permit Field Size: 5 Caption: Permit Num
LicensePlateNum	Text	Description: Vehicle license plate number Field Size: 8 Caption: License Plate Num
ViolationCode	Text	Description: Violation code for the parking infraction Field Size: 2 Caption: Violation Code

Figure 8 shows the structure of the tblPayment table, which contains one record for each parking violation payment. Each tblPayment record contains a unique payment ID, the payment amount and date, and the number of the citation to which the payment applies.

Figure 8 ▸ Structure of the tblPayment table

Field Name	Data Type	Properties
PaymentID	AutoNumber	Description: Primary key; unique number assigned to a parking violation payment Caption: Payment ID
PaymentAmt	Currency	Description: Amount paid Format: Currency Decimal Places: 2 Caption: Payment Amt
PaymentDate	Date/Time	Description: Payment date Format: mm/dd/yyyy Caption: Payment Date
CitationNum	Text	Description: Citation to which the payment applies Field Size: 6 Caption: Citation Num

Pat turns the completed database design over to Sandy, who wants to create special queries, forms, and reports in the database to help her manage parking permits and violations. To help Sandy finish her work with the database, complete the following steps:

1. Make sure you have created your copy of the Access Data Files and that your computer can access them. Start Access, make sure the AddCases folder is a trusted folder, and then open the **Tophill** database located in the AddCases folder.
2. Review the **tblPermit**, **tblCitation**, and **tblPayment** tables to become familiar with their structures and data and resize all columns to best fit the data they contain. If you are unfamiliar with any property setting, use the Access Help system for an explanation of that property.
3. The tblCitation table contains a two-character ViolationCode field. Design and create a new table to store the violation codes, descriptions, and fine amounts, using the field names **ViolationCode**, **ViolationDesc**, and **FineAmt**, making ViolationCode the primary key, and setting the Caption property and other field properties to appropriate values. Save the table as **tblViolation**, add the eight records shown in Figure 9 to the table, resize all datasheet columns to their best fit, and then print the tblViolation table recordset.

Figure 9 ▸ tblViolation table records

ViolationCode	ViolationDesc	FineAmt
BE	Improper Parking Building Entrance	$20
EM	Expired Meter	$15
HA	Improper Parking Handicapped Area	$75
OA	Improper Parking Other Areas	$20
RA	Improper Parking Reserved Area	$50
RD	Improper Parking Roadway	$15
SD	Improper Parking Service Drive	$17
WL	Improper Parking Walk/Lawn	$22

4. Modify the first record in the tblPermit table datasheet by entering your name in the Owner First and Owner Last columns.

5. Add all four tables to the Relationships window, make sure all fields are visible in the field lists, and then define the three one-to-many relationships. Enforce referential integrity, and select the Cascade Update Related Fields option for each relationship. Rearrange the field lists as appropriate so that join lines don't cross field lists, save your design, and then create and print the Relationships for Tophill report but do not save it.

6. Create and save a query named **qryCollegeCitations** that displays, in order, all fields from the tblCitation table, and the OwnerFirst and OwnerLast fields from the tblPermit table. Sort in ascending order by OwnerLast as the first sort field, OwnerFirst as the second sort field, CitationDate as the third sort field, and CitationTime as the fourth sort field. Print the query recordset in landscape orientation after testing and saving the query, but don't close the query.

7. Save the qryCollegeCitations query as **qryAllCitations**, and then modify the new query to use an outer join to include all records from the tblCitation table and the matching records from the tblPermit table. Print the query recordset in landscape orientation after testing and saving the query, and then close the query.

8. Export the data with formatting and layout in the qryAllCitations query to an Excel workbook in the AddCases folder. Save the export steps.

9. Create and save a query named **qryTotalPaymentsByDate** that displays the PaymentDate field and the sum of the PaymentAmt field from the tblPayment table. For the total field, use a Caption value of **Total Payments**. Sort the query in ascending order by PaymentDate. Resize all datasheet columns to their best fit, and then print the query recordset after testing and saving the query.

10. Create a find duplicates query based on the tblCitation table. Select LicensePlateNum as the field that might contain duplicates, and select all the other fields in the table as additional fields in the query recordset. Save the query as **qryVehiclesWithMultipleCitations**, and then view and print the query recordset.

11. Make a copy of the qryAllCitations query, save the copy as **qryAllCitationsParameter**, and then modify the new query to display records for a ViolationCode field value that the user enters. If the user doesn't enter a field value, select and display all records. After modifying and saving the query, run the query and enter **HA** as the ViolationCode field value. Print the query recordset in landscape orientation.

✦ EXPLORE 12. Make a copy of the qryAllCitations query, save the copy as **qryAllCitationsWithoutPermits**, and then modify the new query to display only those records that have a null PermitNum field value. After modifying and saving the query, run the query and print the query results in landscape orientation.

13. Create a crosstab query that uses the tblCitation table. Select the CitationDate field values for the row headings, ViolationCode field values for the column headings, and the count of the CitationNum field as the summarized value. Save the query as **qryCitationCrosstab**, use a Caption value of **Total Citations** for the Count Row Heading column, resize the columns in the query recordset to their best fit, print the query results, and then save and close the query.

⊕ EXPLORE

14. Create and save a query named **qryCitationsAndPayments** that displays, in order, all fields from the tblCitation table, and the PaymentID, PaymentAmt, and PaymentDate fields from the tblPayment table. Include all records from the tblCitation table and only the matching records from the tblPayment table. Sort in ascending order by CitationNum. Use the Totals row to add a count of the number of citations in the Citation Num column, a count of the number of payments in the Payment ID column, and a total of the payment amounts in the Payment Amt column. Print the query recordset in landscape orientation after testing and saving the query.

15. Use the Form Wizard to create a form containing the main form and subform shown in Figure 10. Select all the fields from the tblPermit table for the main form, and select the appropriate fields from the qryCitationsAndPayments query for the subform. Use the Tabular layout and the None style. Save the main form as **frmPermitsAndCitations** and the subform as **frmCitationsAndPaymentsSubform**. Change the text in the main form's title control to **Permits and Citations**. Change the caption on the record navigation bar for the main form to **Permit Num** and for the subform to **Citation**. Make sure the tab order in the main form is top-to-bottom and the tab order in the subform is left-to-right. Modify the form by adding the Total Payments calculated control that displays the total PaymentAmt field values from the subform. Print only main form record 29 and its subform records.

Figure 10 **Permits and Citations form**

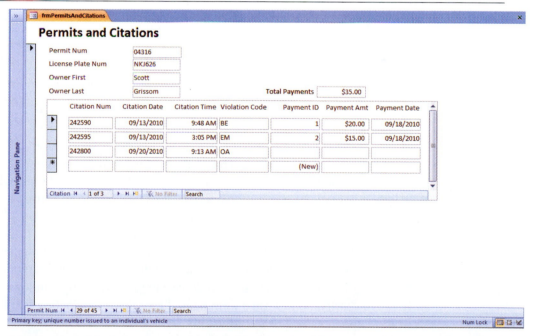

16. Create a blank form and add all fields from the tblCitation table to it, except for the ViolationCode field, in a Stacked layout. Add the ViolationCode field to the form as a combo box control that displays values from the tblViolation table. Display all three fields from the tblViolation table, sort the records in ascending order by ViolationCode, do not hide the key column, resize all columns to their best fit, store values in the ViolationCode field, and use the label **Violation Code**. Resize the text boxes and the combo box as appropriate for the displayed values. Save the form as **frmCitation**, and then print only the last form record.

17. Create the report shown in Figure 11, which is based on the qryCitationsAndPayments query, and save it as **rptCitationsAndPayments**. Use landscape orientation, and increase the report width to at least 9". Add the title, date, time, and picture (which is saved in the AddCases folder as NoPark.bmp) to the Report Header section. Print the first page of the report.

Figure 11   **Citations and Payments report**

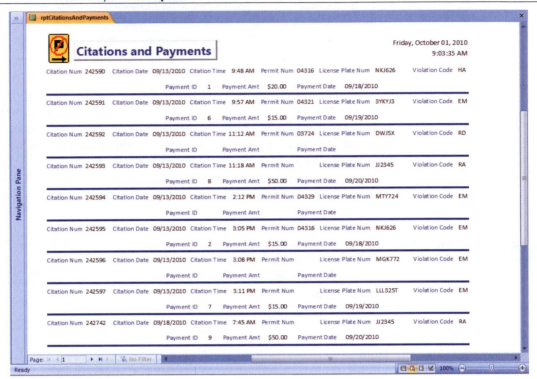

EXPLORE 18. Make a copy of the rptCitationsAndPayments report, and save the copy as **rptCitationsAndPaymentsModified**. Modify the new report to suppress the printing of the three controls that are based on the tblPayment table when the PaymentID control value is null. (*Hint:* Use the Detail section's Format event, and use assignment statements for all the labels and text boxes in the Detail section similar to *Me![control name].Visible = True/False*, where *Me* refers to the open form, and *True/False* means to select the appropriate property setting.) After modifying and saving the report, preview and print the first page of the report.

19. Change the database's window style to overlapping windows.

20. Design and create a form named **frmQueriesDialogBox** that has the following components and characteristics:

     a. The text **Queries** appears in the form's title bar.

     b. A list box (with a Name property value of **lstQueryList**) displays all the query names contained in the Tophill database, excluding those queries that start with a "~" character. To place the query names in the list box, use an SQL SELECT statement to retrieve the query names from the MSysObjects table, and display the queries in query name order. Delete the label attached to the list box, and then widen the list box to approximately 2.75".

     c. Use the heading **Available Queries**, formatted with 11-point, bold font, above the list box.

d. Two command buttons appear below the list box. The left command button displays the MS Access Query icon above the word **Display**, and the right command button displays the Close icon above the word **Close**. Double-clicking a query name has the same effect as selecting a query name in the list box and clicking the left command button. Both events cause Access to display the query datasheet for the selected query. Clicking the Close command button causes Access to close the dialog box.

e. Create a Load event procedure that moves the focus to the first query name in the list box when the frmQueriesDialogBox form opens.

f. Create a **basDisplayQuery** function to open the selected query in Datasheet view.

g. Attach the basDisplayQuery function to the OnDblClick property for the frmQueriesDialogBox form list box and to the OnClick property for the Display command button in the form.

h. Resize the form's Detail section in Design view, resize the form in Form view, and then set form properties that are appropriate for a dialog box.

i. Switch to Form view, and then test all the form options. Save and close the form.

21. Create a macro group named **mcrSwitchboardMacros** that contains macros to be used with two of the command buttons in the switchboard you'll create in the next step. The two macros perform these actions: close the switchboard, and close the switchboard and exit Access.

22. Design and create a switchboard form named **Switchboard**. Use Figure 12 and the following descriptions as a guide to create the switchboard:

Figure 12   **Tophill database switchboard**

a. Use the Switchboard Manager to create the switchboard. Place the command buttons on the form; the last two command buttons should use the macros in the mcrSwitchboardMacros macro group as appropriate. The first four command buttons should open the frmQueriesDialogBox form in edit mode; open the frmCitation form in edit mode, open the frmPermitsAndCitations form in edit mode, and open the rptCitationsAndPayments report. Specify **Tophill Database** as the main switchboard page name.

⊕ EXPLORE

b. Hide the default label and the shadow label on the form. Add a label above the command buttons, and add the NoPark.bmp picture located in the AddCases folder to the location shown on the switchboard in Figure 12.

⊕ **EXPLORE**

    c. Set the colors used in the form as shown in Figure 12. The background color for the form uses the Access Theme 1 color in the Access Theme Colors gallery. (*Hint:* Paste a copy of the green rectangle created by the Switchboard Manager into the Form Footer section and set the background color to make the Access Theme 1 color fill the rest of the dialog box.)

    d. Resize the switchboard in Form view, and then set form properties that are appropriate for a switchboard.

    e. Save the Switchboard form, and then test the command buttons on the main switchboard page to make sure that your switchboard items work correctly. If necessary, return to the Switchboard Manager and make any corrections.

23. Close the Tophill database without exiting Access, make a backup copy of the database, open the **Tophill** database, and then compact and repair the database.

24. Set the database properties for the **Tophill** database so the Switchboard opens when the database is opened, to set startup options to disable features as appropriate for a database that uses a switchboard, and change the Application Title property to **Tophill Database**.

25. Close the database, and then exit Access.

Ending Data Files

AddCases

qryAllCitations.xlsx
Tophill.accdb

Objectives

- Design a database and draw its entity-relationship diagram
- Create the tables and relationships for the database
- Create forms to maintain the database
- Design and enter test data for the database
- Create queries and reports from the database
- Design and create a switchboard
- Set database properties and startup options

In this case you will use skills you learned in the following tutorials:
- Tutorials 1-7, 9-11, 12 (startup options only), and the "Relational Databases and Database Design" appendix

Internship Program for West Bayside College

Case | West Bayside College

West Bayside College provides students in the central Florida area with opportunities for professional development and field study through its internship program, which is administered by the Office of Internships and Field Experience. Students complement their courses with a structured training experience provided by qualified professionals in selected fields. Internships are offered in many different areas, including law, counseling, government, administration, public relations, communications, health care, software engineering, and marketing.

The college recently hired Maria Senn as its new Internship Coordinator. She is eager to make information about the sponsoring agencies, potential internships, and current student interns more readily available to her office and to the students who qualify for the program. Maria's most ambitious project is to develop a database for the internship program to help meet these goals.

Instead of visually scanning all internship possibilities, Maria, her staff, and interested students will be able to use the new database to select internships of specific interest to them. The database will allow potential interns to view only the internships that meet the criteria they specify. Maria asks Robert Mendes, an information systems major working in the Office of Internships and Field Experience, to help her design and develop a database system for the internship program.

Maria first outlines the steps in the internship program process for Robert:

- Identify and document the available internships.
- Arrange for student intern placements.
- Assign and track student interns.

As the first step in the internship program process, Maria receives a letter or phone call from a potential sponsoring agency. After some discussions, a sponsoring agency proposes an internship possibility and fills out the Agency/Internship Information form shown in Figure 13.

Starting Data Files

AddCases

Intmatch.bmp
Inttrack.bmp

Figure 13   **Agency/Internship Information form**

AGENCY/INTERNSHIP INFORMATION

AGENCY INFORMATION

NAME OF AGENCY _____

DEPARTMENT _____

ADDRESS _____
Street

_____
City   State   Zip

CONTACT _____ PHONE _____

INTERNSHIP INFORMATION

TITLE _____

DESCRIPTION OF   _____
DUTIES   _____
                    _____

ORIENTATION &   _____
TRAINING   _____
                    _____

ACADEMIC   _____
BACKGROUND   _____
REQUIRED   _____

SUPERVISOR _____ PHONE _____

Office Use

Agency ID   _____
Internship ID   _____
Category   _____

Many agencies offer more than one type of internship possibility. For each possible internship, the agency fills out a separate form and assigns one person as the contact for all internship questions and problems. In addition, each internship lists a supervisor who will work with the student intern. The internship remains active until the agency notifies the Office of Internships and Field Experience that the internship is filled or no longer available.

Maria assigns a four-digit Agency ID to each new agency and a three-digit Internship ID to each new internship using sequential numbers. She also classifies each internship into a category that helps students identify internships that are related to their academic major or interests. For example, a student might be interested in health care, accounting, social service, or advertising.

A copy of each Agency/Internship Information form is placed in reference books in the Office of Internships and Field Experience. Students browse through these books to find internships that interest them. If an internship interests a student, the student copies the information about the internship and contacts the sponsoring agency directly to request an interview.

When a student gets an internship, the student and agency establish a Learning Contract, outlining the goals to be accomplished during the internship. The student then fills out the Student Internship form, shown in Figure 14, to provide basic personal information for the office files.

Figure 14   Student Internship form

STUDENT INTERNSHIP

NAME _____ SS# _____

ADDRESS _____
        Street

_____
        City   State   ZIP

PHONE _____   CLASS ____ Junior ____ Senior

MAJOR _____ GPA _____

Office Use

Internship ID   _____

Internship Term   ____ Fall ____ Spring ____ Summer

Internship Year   _____

Maria enters the Internship ID and year on the Student Internship form and checks the term for the internship. Next, a clerk enters information from the form into a word processor to prepare lists of current interns and internships, and then prints and places the form in a binder.

Maria and Robert determine that getting these two forms into an Access database is their first priority, and then they will work on creating several new reports. The first report, shown in Figure 15, lists all student interns alphabetically by last name for a selected term. In order to identify the student interns who should be included in the report, the system prompts the user for the term and year.

Figure 15   Student Interns report

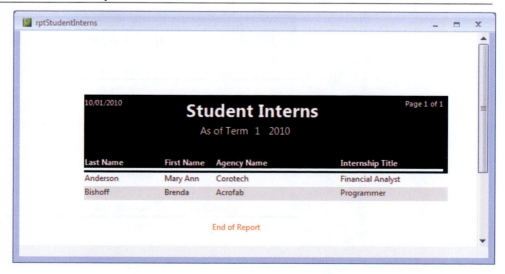

A second new report lists all agencies in the database alphabetically by agency name. Figure 16 shows the report.

Internship Agencies report

The Internships by Category report, shown in Figure 17, lists internships grouped by category. The staff will use this report when talking with students about the internship program.

Figure 17   Internships by Category report

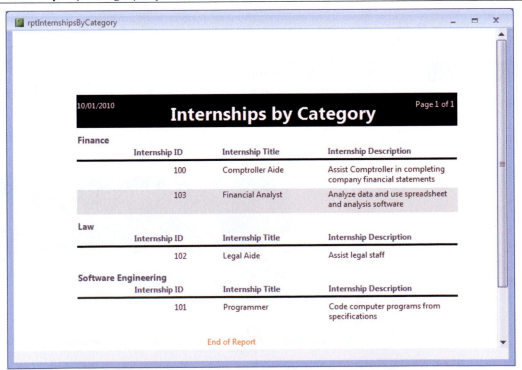

At the end of an internship, the intern's supervisor evaluates the intern's work experience, using an evaluation form mailed from the Office of Internships and Field Experience. Maria needs mailing labels addressed to the supervisor of each intern for the current term and year. The mailing labels should contain the supervisor's name on the first line; the agency name on the second line; the agency's street on the third line; and the agency's city, state, and zip code on the fourth line. Sort the labels by agency name.

To create the database, complete the following steps:

1. Read the appendix titled "Relational Databases and Database Design," which appears at the end of this book.

⊕ **EXPLORE**

2. Identify each entity (table) in the database for the internship system.

⊕ **EXPLORE**

3. Draw an entity-relationship diagram showing the entities and the relationships between the entities.

⊕ **EXPLORE**

4. Design the database for the internship system. For each table, list the fields and their attributes, such as data types, field sizes, and validation rules. Place the set of tables in third normal form and identify all primary, alternate, and foreign keys.

5. Make sure you have created your copy of the Access Data Files and that your computer can access them. Start Access, make sure the AddCases folder is a trusted folder, and then create the database using Access and name the database **Intern**. Be sure to define relationships between appropriate tables.

⊕ **EXPLORE**

6. Create and save forms to maintain data on agencies, internships, student interns, and any other table in your database structure. The forms should be used to view, add, edit, and delete records in the database.

7. Create test data for each table in the database and add the test data, using the forms you created in Step 6.

8. Create and save the **rptStudentInterns** report, the **rptInternshipAgencies** report, and the **rptInternshipsByCategory** report. The reports shown in Figures 15 through 17 are guides—improve them as you see fit. Then create the **rptMailingLabels** report to create mailing labels for agencies using a label of your choice.

9. Design, create, and save a form that a student can use to view internships for a selected category. Display one internship at a time on the screen. For each internship, display the category, internship ID, title, description of duties, orientation and training, academic background, agency name, department, agency address, contact name, and contact phone. Provide an option to print the current record displayed on the screen.

10. Design, create, and save a switchboard to coordinate the running of the internship system. (*Note:* The AddCases folder contains picture files named Intmatch.bmp and Inttrack.bmp that you can include on the switchboard if you want.)

11. Test all features of the internship system.

Ending Data Files

AddCases

Intern.accdb

Objectives

- Learn the characteristics of a table
- Learn about primary, candidate, alternate, composite, and foreign keys
- Study one-to-one, one-to-many, and many-to-many relationships
- Learn to describe tables and relationships with entity-relationship diagrams and with a shorthand method
- Study database integrity constraints for primary keys, referential integrity, and domains
- Learn about determinants, functional dependencies, anomalies, and normalization
- Understand the differences among natural, artificial, and surrogate keys
- Learn about naming conventions

Relational Databases and Database Design

Appendix

This appendix introduces you to the basics of database design. Before trying to master this material, be sure you understand the following concepts: data, information, field, field value, record, table, relational database, common field, database management system (DBMS), and relational database management system (RDBMS).

Starting Data Files

There are no starting Data Files needed for this appendix.

Tables

A relational database stores its data in tables. A **table** is a two-dimensional structure made up of rows and columns. The terms table, **record** (row), and **field** (column) are the popular names for the more formal terms **relation** (table), **tuple** (row), and **attribute** (column), as shown in Figure A-1.

Figure A-1 | **A table (relation) consisting of records and fields**

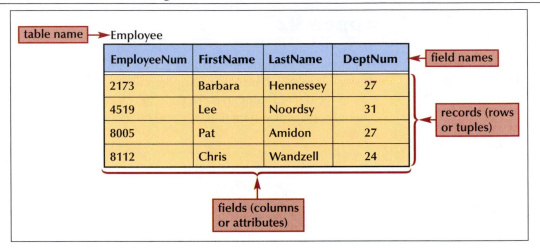

The Employee table shown in Figure A-1 is an example of a relational database table, a two-dimensional structure with the following characteristics:

- Each row is unique. Because no two rows are the same, you can easily locate and update specific data. For example, you can locate the row for EmployeeNum 8005 and change the FirstName value, Pat, the LastName value, Amidon, or the DeptNum value, 27.
- The order of the rows is unimportant. You can add or view rows in any order. For example, you can view the rows in LastName order instead of EmployeeNum order.
- Each table entry contains a single value. At the intersection of each row and column, you cannot have more than one value. For example, each row in Figure A-1 contains one EmployeeNum value, one FirstName value, one LastName value, and one DeptNum value.
- The order of the columns is unimportant. You can add or view columns in any order.
- Each column has a unique name called the **field name**. The field name allows you to access a specific column without needing to know its position within the table.
- The entries in a column are from the same domain. A **domain** is a set of values from which one or more columns (fields) draw their actual values. A domain can be broad, such as "all legitimate last names of people" for the LastName column, or narrow, such as "24, 27, or 31" for the DeptNum column. The domain of "all legitimate dates" could be shared by the BirthDate, StartDate, and TerminationDate columns in a company's employee table.
- Each row in a table describes, or shows the characteristics of, an entity. An **entity** is a person, place, object, event, or idea for which you want to store and process data. For example, EmployeeNum, FirstName, LastName, and DeptNum are characteristics of the employees of a company. The Employee table represents all the employee entities and their characteristics. That is, each row of the Employee table describes a different employee of the company using the characteristics of EmployeeNum, FirstName, LastName, and DeptNum. The Employee table includes only characteristics of employees. Other tables would exist for the company's other entities. For example, a Department table would describe the company's departments and a Position table would describe the company's job positions.

Knowing the characteristics of a table leads directly to a definition of a relational database. A **relational database** is a collection of tables (relations).

Note that this book uses singular table names, such as Employee and Department, but some people use plural table names, such as Employees and Departments. You can use either singular table names or plural table names, as long as you consistently use the style you choose.

Keys

Primary keys ensure that each row in a table is unique. A **primary key** is a column, or a collection of columns, whose values uniquely identify each row in a table. In addition to being *unique*, a primary key must be *minimal* (that is, contain no unnecessary extra columns) and must not change in value. For example, in Figure A-2 the State table contains one record per state and uses the StateAbbrev column as its primary key.

A table and its keys   Figure A-2

StateAbbrev	StateName	EnteredUnionOrder	StateBird	StatePopulation
CT	Connecticut	5	American robin	3,510,297
MI	Michigan	26	robin	10,120,860
SD	South Dakota	40	pheasant	775,933
TN	Tennessee	16	mockingbird	5,962,959
TX	Texas	28	mockingbird	22,859,968

primary key — StateAbbrev; alternate keys — StateName, EnteredUnionOrder; State table

Could any other column, or collection of columns, be the primary key of the State table?

- Could the StateBird column serve as the primary key? No, because the StateBird column does not have unique values (for example, the mockingbird is the state bird of more than one state).
- Could the StatePopulation column serve as the primary key? No, because the StatePopulation column values change periodically and are not guaranteed to be unique.
- Could the StateAbbrev and StateName columns together serve as the primary key? No, because the combination of these two columns is not minimal. Something less, such as the StateAbbrev column by itself, can serve as the primary key.
- Could the StateName column serve as the primary key? Yes, because the StateName column has unique values. In a similar way, you could select the EnteredUnionOrder column as the primary key for the State table. One column, or a collection of columns, that can serve as a primary key is called a **candidate key**. The candidate keys for the State table are the StateAbbrev column, the StateName column, and the EnteredUnionOrder column. You choose one of the candidate keys to be the primary key, and each remaining candidate key is called an **alternate key**. The StateAbbrev column is the State table's primary key in Figure A-2, so the StateName and EnteredUnionOrder columns become alternate keys in the table.

Figure A-3 shows a City table containing the fields StateAbbrev, CityName, and CityPopulation.

Figure A-3 ▸ **A table with a composite key**

What is the primary key for the City table? The values for the CityPopulation column periodically change and are not guaranteed to be unique, so the CityPopulation column cannot be the primary key. Because the values for each of the other two columns are not unique, the StateAbbrev column alone cannot be the primary key and neither can the CityName column (for example, there are two cities named Madison and two cities named Portland). The primary key is the combination of the StateAbbrev and CityName columns. Both columns together are needed to identify—uniquely and minimally—each row in the City table. A multiple-column primary key is called a **composite key** or a **concatenated key**.

The StateAbbrev column in the City table is also a foreign key. A **foreign key** is a column, or a collection of columns, in one table in which each column value must match the value of the primary key of some table or must be null. A **null** is the absence of a value in a particular table entry. A null value is not blank, nor zero, nor any other value. You give a null value to a column value when you do not know its value or when a value does not apply. As shown in Figure A-4, the values in the City table's StateAbbrev column match the values in the State table's StateAbbrev column. Thus, the StateAbbrev column, the primary key of the State table, is a foreign key in the City table. Although the field name StateAbbrev is the same in both tables, the names could be different. However, all experts use the same name for a field stored in two or more tables to broadcast clearly that they store similar values.

StateAbbrev as a primary key (State table) and a foreign key (City table) ◄ Figure A-4

primary key (State table)

State

StateAbbrev	StateName	EnteredUnionOrder	StateBird	StatePopulation
CT	Connecticut	5	American robin	3,510,297
MI	Michigan	26	robin	10,120,860
SD	South Dakota	40	pheasant	775,933
TN	Tennessee	16	mockingbird	5,962,959
TX	Texas	28	mockingbird	22,859,968

composite primary key (City table)

City

foreign key

StateAbbrev	CityName	CityPopulation
CT	Hartford	124,397
CT	Madison	18,812
CT	Portland	9,543
MI	Lansing	115,518
SD	Madison	6,223
SD	Pierre	14,052
TN	Nashville	549,110
TX	Austin	690,252
TX	Portland	16,219

A **nonkey field** is a field that is not part of the primary key. In the two tables shown in Figure A-4, all fields are nonkey fields except the StateAbbrev field in the State and City tables and the CityName field in the City table. *Key* is an ambiguous word because it can refer to a primary, candidate, alternate, or foreign key. When the word key appears alone, however, it means primary key and the definition for a nonkey field consequently makes sense.

Relationships

In a database, a table can be associated with another table in one of three ways: a one-to-many relationship, a many-to-many relationship, or a one-to-one relationship.

One-to-Many Relationship

The Department and Employee tables, shown in Figure A-5, have a one-to-many relationship. A **one-to-many relationship** (abbreviated **1:M** or **1:N**) exists between two tables when each row in the first table (sometimes called the **primary table**) matches many rows in the second table and each row in the second table (sometimes called the **related table**) matches at most one row in the first table. "Many" can mean zero rows, one row, or two or more rows. The DeptNum field, which is a foreign key in the Employee table and the primary key in the Department table, is the common field that ties together the rows of the two tables. Each department has many employees; and each employee works in exactly one department or hasn't been assigned to a department, if the DeptNum field value for that employee is null.

Figure A-5	A one-to-many relationship

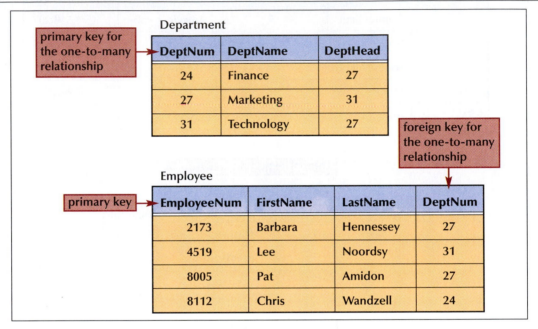

Many-to-Many Relationship

In Figure A-6, the Employee table (with the EmployeeNum field as its primary key) and the Position table (with the PositionID field as its primary key) have a many-to-many relationship. A **many-to-many relationship** (abbreviated as **M:N**) exists between two tables when each row in the first table matches many rows in the second table and each row in the second table matches many rows in the first table. In a relational database, you must use a third table (often called an **intersection table**, **junction table**, or **link table**) to serve as a bridge between the two many-to-many tables; the third table has the primary keys of the two many-to-many tables as its primary key. The original tables now each have a one-to-many relationship with the new table. The EmployeeNum and PositionID fields represent the primary key of the Employment table that is shown in Figure A-6. The EmployeeNum field, which is a foreign key in the Employment table and the primary key in the Employee table, is the common field that ties together the rows of the Employee and Employment tables. Likewise, the PositionID field is the common field for the Position and Employment tables. Each employee has served in many different positions within the company over time, and each position in the company has been filled by many different employees over time.

A many-to-many relationship   **Figure A-6**

primary key
(Position table)

Employee

primary key
(Employee
table)

EmployeeNum	FirstName	LastName	DeptNum
2173	Barbara	Hennessey	27
4519	Lee	Noordsy	31
8005	Pat	Amidon	27
8112	Chris	Wandzell	24

Position

PositionID	PositionDesc	PayGrade
1	Director	45
2	Manager	40
3	Analyst	30
4	Clerk	20

composite key of the
intersection table

foreign keys related
to the Employee and
Position tables

Employment

EmployeeNum	PositionID	StartDate	EndDate
2173	2	12/14/2008	
4519	1	04/23/2010	
4519	3	11/11/2004	04/22/2010
8005	3	06/05/2009	08/25/2010
8005	4	07/02/2007	06/04/2009
8112	1	12/15/2009	
8112	2	10/04/2008	12/14/2009

One-to-One Relationship

In Figure A-5, recall that there's a one-to-many relationship between the Department table (the primary table) and the Employee table (the related table). Each department has many employees, and each employee works in one department. The DeptNum field in the Employee table serves as a foreign key to connect records in that table to records with matching DeptNum field values in the Department table.

Furthermore, each department has a single employee who serves as the head of the department, and each employee either serves as the head of a department or simply works in a department without being the department head. Therefore, the Department and Employee tables not only have a one-to-many relationship, but these two tables also have a second relationship, a one-to-one relationship. A **one-to-one relationship** (abbreviated **1:1**) exists between two tables when each row in each table has at most one matching row in the other table. As shown in Figure A-7, each DeptHead field value in the Department table represents the employee number in the Employee table of the employee who heads the department. In other words, each DeptHead field value in the Department table matches exactly one EmployeeNum field value in the Employee table. At the same time, each EmployeeNum field value in the Employee table matches at most one DeptHead field value in the Department table—matching one DeptHead field value if the employee is a department head, or matching zero DeptHead field values if the employee is not a department head. For this one-to-one relationship, the EmployeeNum field in the Employee table and the DeptHead field in the Department table are the fields that link the two tables, with the DeptHead field serving as a foreign key in the Department table and the EmployeeNum field serving as a primary key in the Employee table.

Some database designers might use EmployeeNum instead of DeptHead as the field name for the foreign key in the Department table, because they both represent the employee number for the employees of the company. However, DeptHead better identifies the purpose of the field and would more commonly be used as the field name.

| Figure A-7 | A one-to-one relationship |

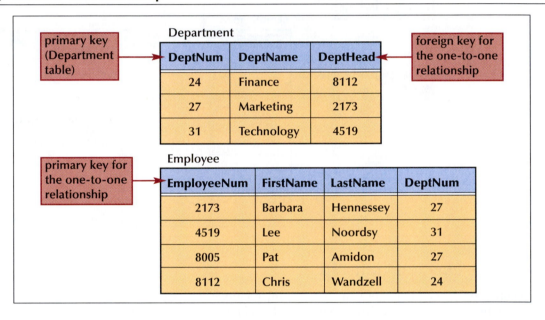

Entity Subtype

Suppose the company awards annual bonuses to a small number of employees who fill director positions in selected departments. As shown in Figure A-8, you could store the Bonus field in the Employee table, because a bonus is an attribute associated with employees. The Bonus field would contain either the amount of the employee's bonus (record 4 in the Employee table) or a null value for employees without bonuses (records 1 through 3 in the Employee table).

Bonus field added to the Employee table   Figure A-8

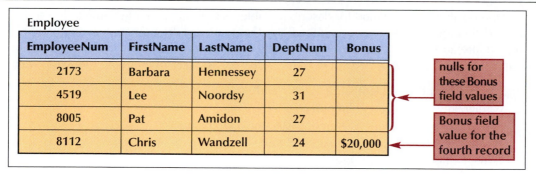

Figure A-9 shows an alternative approach, in which the Bonus field is placed in a separate table, the EmployeeBonus table. The EmployeeBonus table's primary key is the EmployeeNum field, and the table contains one row for each employee earning a bonus. Because some employees do not earn a bonus, the EmployeeBonus table has fewer rows than the Employee table. However, each row in the EmployeeBonus table has a matching row in the Employee table, with the EmployeeNum field serving as the common field; the EmployeeNum field is the primary key in the Employee table and is a foreign key in the EmployeeBonus table.

Storing bonus values in a separate table, an entity subtype   Figure A-9

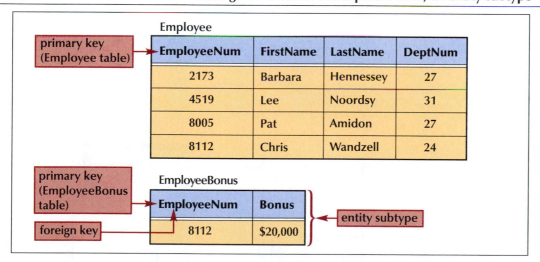

The EmployeeBonus table, in this situation, is called an **entity subtype**, a table whose primary key is a foreign key to a second table and whose fields are additional fields for the second table. Database designers create an entity subtype in two situations. In the first situation, some users might need access to all employee fields, including employee bonuses, while other employees might need access to all employee fields except bonuses. Because most database management systems allow you to control which tables a user can access, you can specify that some users can access both tables and that other users can access the Employee table but not the EmployeeBonus table, keeping the employee bonus information hidden from the latter group. In the second situation, you can create an entity subtype when a table has fields that could have nulls, as was the case for the Bonus field stored in the Employee table in Figure A-8. You should be aware that database experts are currently debating the validity of the use of nulls in relational databases, and many experts insist that you should never use nulls. This warning against nulls is partly based on the inconsistent way different RDBMSs treat nulls and partly due to the lack of a firm theoretical foundation for how to use nulls. In any case, entity subtypes are an alternative to the use of nulls.

Entity-Relationship Diagrams

A common shorthand method for describing tables is to write the table name followed by its fields in parentheses, underlining the fields that represent the primary key and identifying the foreign keys for a table immediately after the table. Using this method, the tables that appear in Figures A-5 through A-7 and Figure A-9 are described in the following way:

Department (<u>DeptNum</u>, DeptName, DeptHead)
    Foreign key: DeptHead to Employee table
Employee (<u>EmployeeNum</u>, FirstName, LastName, DeptNum)
    Foreign key: DeptNum to Department table
Position (<u>PositionID</u>, PositionDesc, PayGrade)
Employment (<u>EmployeeNum</u>, <u>PositionID</u>, StartDate, EndDate)
    Foreign key: EmployeeNum to Employee table
    Foreign key: PositionID to Position table
EmployeeBonus (<u>EmployeeNum</u>, Bonus)
    Foreign key: EmployeeNum to Employee table

Another popular way to describe tables *and their relationships* is with entity-relationship diagrams. An **entity-relationship diagram (ERD)** shows a database's entities and the relationships among the entities in a symbolic, visual way. In an entity-relationship diagram, an entity and a table are equivalent. Figure A-10 shows an entity-relationship diagram for the tables that appear in Figures A-5 through A-7 and Figure A-9.

Figure A-10	An entity-relationship diagram

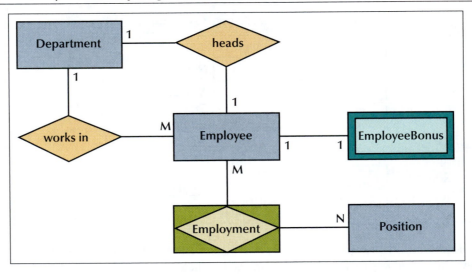

Entity-relationship diagrams have the following characteristics:

- Entities, or tables, appear in rectangles, and relationships appear in diamonds. The entity name appears inside the rectangle, and a verb describing the relationship appears inside the diamond. For example, the Employee rectangle is connected to the Department rectangle by the "works in" diamond and is read: "an employee works in a department."
- The 1 by the Department entity and the M by the Employee entity identify a one-to-many relationship between these two entities. In a similar manner, a many-to-many relationship exists between the Employee and Position entities and one-to-one relationships exist between the Department and Employee entities and between the Employee and EmployeeBonus entities.

- A diamond inside a rectangle defines a composite entity. A **composite entity** is a relationship that has the characteristics of an entity. For example, Employment connects the Employee and Position entities in a many-to-many relationship and acts as an entity by containing the StartDate and EndDate fields, along with the composite key of the EmployeeNum and PositionID fields.
- An entity subtype, for example, EmployeeBonus, appears in a double rectangle and is connected without an intervening diamond directly to its related entity, Employee.

You can also show fields in an ERD by placing each individual field in a bubble connected to its entity or relationship. However, typical ERDs have large numbers of entities and relationships, so including the fields might confuse rather than clarify the ERD.

Integrity Constraints

A database has **integrity** if its data follows certain rules; each rule is called an **integrity constraint**. The ideal is to have the DBMS enforce all integrity constraints. If a DBMS can enforce some integrity constraints but not others, the other integrity constraints must be enforced by other programs or by the people who use the DBMS. Integrity constraints can be divided into three groups: primary key constraints, foreign key constraints, and domain integrity constraints.

- One primary key constraint is inherent in the definition of a primary key, which says that the primary key must be unique. The **entity integrity constraint** says that the primary key cannot be null. For a composite key, none of the individual fields can be null. The uniqueness and nonnull properties of a primary key ensure that you can reference any data value in a database by supplying its table name, field name, and primary key value.
- Foreign keys provide the mechanism for forming a relationship between two tables, and referential integrity ensures that only valid relationships exist. **Referential integrity** is the constraint specifying that each nonnull foreign key value must match a primary key value in the primary table. Specifically, referential integrity means that you cannot add a row with an unmatched foreign key value. Referential integrity also means that you cannot change or delete the related primary key value and leave the foreign key orphaned. In some RDBMSs, if you try to change or delete a primary key value, you can specify one of these options: restricted, cascades, or nullifies. If you specify **restricted**, the DBMS updates or deletes the value only if there are no matching foreign key values. If you choose **cascades** and then change a primary key value, the DBMS changes the matching foreign key values to the new primary key value, or, if you delete a primary key value, the DBMS also deletes the matching foreign key rows. If you choose **nullifies** and then change or delete a primary key value, the DBMS sets all matching foreign key values to null.
- Recall that a domain is a set of values from which one or more fields draw their actual values. A **domain integrity constraint** is a rule you specify for a field. By choosing a data type for a field, you impose a constraint on the set of values allowed for the field. You can create specific validation rules for a field to limit its domain further. As you make a field's domain definition more precise, you exclude more and more unacceptable values for the field. For example, in the State table, shown in Figures A-2 and A-4, you could define the domain for the EnteredUnionOrder field to be a unique integer between 1 and 50 and the domain for the StateBird field to be any name containing 25 or fewer characters.

Dependencies and Determinants

Tables are related to other tables. Fields are also related to other fields. Consider the modified Employee table shown in Figure A-11. Its description is:

Employee (<u>EmployeeNum</u>, <u>PositionID</u>, LastName, PositionDesc, StartDate, HealthPlan, PlanDesc)

Figure A-11	A table combining fields from three tables

primary key

Employee

EmployeeNum	PositionID	LastName	PositionDesc	StartDate	HealthPlan	PlanDesc
2173	2	Hennessey	Manager	12/14/2008	B	Managed HMO
4519	1	Noordsy	Director	04/23/2010	A	Managed PPO
4519	3	Noordsy	Analyst	11/11/2004	A	Managed PPO
8005	3	Amidon	Analyst	06/05/2009	C	Health Savings
8005	4	Amidon	Clerk	07/02/2007	C	Health Savings
8112	1	Wandzell	Director	12/15/2009	A	Managed PPO
8112	2	Wandzell	Manager	10/04/2008	A	Managed PPO

The modified Employee table combines several fields from the Employee, Position, and Employment tables that appeared in Figure A-6. The EmployeeNum and LastName fields are from the Employee table. The PositionID and PositionDesc fields are from the Position table. The EmployeeNum, PositionID, and StartDate fields are from the Employment table. The HealthPlan and PlanDesc fields are new fields for the Employee table, whose primary key is now the combination of the EmployeeNum and PositionID fields.

In the Employee table, each field is related to other fields. To determine field relationships, you ask "Does a value for a particular field give me a single value for another field?" If the answer is Yes, then the two fields are related. For example, a value for the EmployeeNum field determines a single value for the LastName field, and a value for the LastName field depends on the value of the EmployeeNum field. In database discussions, the word functionally is used, as in: "EmployeeNum functionally determines LastName" and "LastName is functionally dependent on EmployeeNum." In this case, EmployeeNum is called a determinant. A **determinant** is a field, or a collection of fields, whose values determine the values of another field. A field is functionally dependent on another field (or a collection of fields) if that other field is a determinant for it.

You can graphically show a table's functional dependencies and determinants in a **bubble diagram**; a bubble diagram is also called a **data model diagram** and a **functional dependency diagram**. Figure A-12 shows the bubble diagram for the Employee table shown in Figure A-11.

A bubble diagram for the modified Employee table | **Figure A-12**

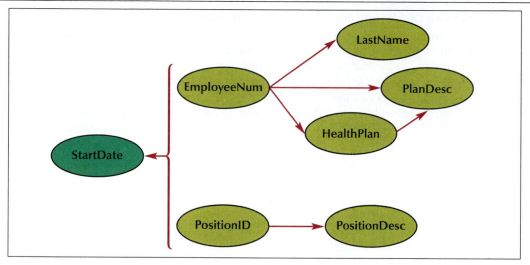

You can read the bubble diagram in Figure A-12 as follows:

- The EmployeeNum field is a determinant for the LastName, HealthPlan, and PlanDesc fields.
- The PositionID field is a determinant for the PositionDesc field.
- The StartDate field is functionally dependent on the EmployeeNum and PositionID fields together.
- The HealthPlan field is a determinant for the PlanDesc field.

Note that EmployeeNum and PositionID together is a determinant for the StartDate field and for all fields that depend on the EmployeeNum field alone and the PositionID field alone. Some experts include these additional fields and some don't. The previous list of determinants does not include these additional fields.

An alternative way to show determinants is to list the determinant, a right arrow, and then the dependent fields, separated by commas. Using this alternative, the determinants shown in Figure A-12 are:

EmployeeNum → LastName, HealthPlan, PlanDesc
PositionID → PositionDesc
EmployeeNum, PositionID → StartDate
HealthPlan → PlanDesc

Only the StartDate field is functionally dependent on the table's full primary key, the EmployeeNum and PositionID fields. The LastName, HealthPlan, and PlanDesc fields have partial dependencies because they are functionally dependent on the EmployeeNum field, which is part of the primary key. A **partial dependency** is a functional dependency on part of the primary key, instead of the entire primary key. Does another partial dependency exist in the Employee table? Yes, the PositionDesc field has a partial dependency on the PositionID field.

Because the EmployeeNum field is a determinant of both the HealthPlan and PlanDesc fields, and the HealthPlan field is a determinant of the PlanDesc field, the HealthPlan and PlanDesc fields have a transitive dependency. A **transitive dependency** is a functional dependency between two nonkey fields, which are both dependent on a third field.

How do you know which functional dependencies exist among a collection of fields, and how do you recognize partial and transitive dependencies? The answers lie with the questions you ask as you gather the requirements for a database application. For each field and entity, you must gain an accurate understanding of its meaning and relationships in the context of the application. **Semantic object modeling** is an entire area of study within the database field devoted to the meanings and relationships of data.

Anomalies

When you use a DBMS, you are more likely to get results you can trust if you create your tables carefully. For example, problems might occur with tables that have partial and transitive dependencies, whereas you won't have as much trouble if you ensure that your tables include only fields that are directly related to each other. Also, when you remove data redundancy from a table, you improve that table. **Data redundancy** occurs when you store the same data in more than one place.

The problems caused by data redundancy and by partial and transitive dependencies are called **anomalies** because they are undesirable irregularities of tables. Anomalies are of three types: insertion, deletion, and update.

To examine the effects of these anomalies, consider the modified Employee table that is shown again in Figure A-13.

Figure A-13 | **A table with insertion, deletion, and update anomalies**

primary key

Employee

EmployeeNum	PositionID	LastName	PositionDesc	StartDate	HealthPlan	PlanDesc
2173	2	Hennessey	Manager	12/14/2008	B	Managed HMO
4519	1	Noordsy	Director	04/23/2010	A	Managed PPO
4519	3	Noordsy	Analyst	11/11/2004	A	Managed PPO
8005	3	Amidon	Analyst	06/05/2009	C	Health Savings
8005	4	Amidon	Clerk	07/02/2007	C	Health Savings
8112	1	Wandzell	Director	12/15/2009	A	Managed PPO
8112	2	Wandzell	Manager	10/04/2008	A	Managed PPO

- An **insertion anomaly** occurs when you cannot add a record to a table because you do not know the entire primary key value. For example, you cannot add the new employee Cathy Corbett with an EmployeeNum of 3322 to the Employee table if you do not know her position in the company. Entity integrity prevents you from leaving any part of a primary key null. Because the PositionID field is part of the primary key, you cannot leave it null. To add the new employee, your only option is to make up a PositionID field value, until you determine the correct position. This solution misrepresents the facts and is unacceptable, if a better approach is available.

- A **deletion anomaly** occurs when you delete data from a table and unintentionally lose other critical data. For example, if you delete EmployeeNum 2173 because Hennessey is no longer an employee, you also lose the only instance of HealthPlan B in the database. Thus, you no longer know that HealthPlan B is the "Managed HMO" plan.

- An **update anomaly** occurs when you change one field value and either the DBMS must make more than one change to the database or else the database ends up containing inconsistent data. For example, if you change a LastName, HealthPlan, or PlanDesc field value for EmployeeNum 8005, the DBMS must change multiple rows of the Employee table. If the DBMS fails to change all the rows, the LastName, HealthPlan, or PlanDesc field now has different values in the database and is inconsistent.

Normalization

Database design is the process of determining the content and structure of data in a database in order to support some activity on behalf of a user or group of users. After you have determined the collection of fields users need to support an activity, you need to determine the precise tables needed for the collection of fields and then place those fields into the correct tables. Crucial to good database design is understanding the functional dependencies of all fields; recognizing the anomalies caused by data redundancy, partial dependencies, and transitive dependencies when they exist; and knowing how to eliminate the anomalies. Failure to eliminate anomalies leads to data redundancy and can cause data integrity and other problems as your database grows in size.

The process of identifying and eliminating anomalies is called **normalization**. Using normalization, you start with a collection of tables, apply sets of rules to eliminate anomalies, and produce a new collection of problem-free tables. The sets of rules are called **normal forms**. Of special interest for our purposes are the first three normal forms: first normal form, second normal form, and third normal form. First normal form improves the design of your tables, second normal form improves the first normal form design, and third normal form applies even more stringent rules to produce an even better design. Note that normal forms beyond third normal form exist; these higher normal forms can improve a database design in some situations but won't be covered in this section.

First Normal Form

Consider the Employee table shown in Figure A-14. For each employee, the table contains EmployeeNum, which is the primary key; the employee's first name, last name, health plan code and description; and the ID, description, pay grade, and start date of each position held by the employee. For example, Barbara Hennessey has held one position, while the other three employees have held two positions. Because each entry in a table must contain a single value, the structure shown in Figure A-14 does not meet the requirements for a table, or relation; therefore, it is called an **unnormalized relation**. The set of fields that includes the PositionID, PositionDesc, PayGrade, and StartDate fields, which can have more than one value, is called a **repeating group**.

Repeating group of data in an unnormalized Employee table — **Figure A-14**

Employee

EmployeeNum	PositionID	FirstName	LastName	PositionDesc	PayGrade	StartDate	HealthPlan	PlanDesc
2173	2	Barbara	Hennessey	Manager	40	12/14/2008	B	Managed HMO
4519	1 3	Lee	Noordsy	Director Analyst	45 30	04/23/2010 11/11/2004	A	Managed PPO
8005	3 4	Pat	Amidon	Analyst Clerk	30 20	06/05/2009 07/02/2007	C	Health Savings
8112	1 2	Chris	Wandzell	Director Manager	45 40	12/15/2009 10/04/2008	A	Managed PPO

First normal form addresses this repeating-group situation. A table is in **first normal form (1NF)** if it does not contain repeating groups. To remove a repeating group and convert to first normal form, you expand the primary key to include the primary key of the repeating group, forming a composite key. Performing the conversion step produces the 1NF table shown in Figure A-15.

Figure A-15   After conversion to 1NF

primary key

Employee

EmployeeNum	PositionID	FirstName	LastName	PositionDesc	PayGrade	StartDate	HealthPlan	PlanDesc
2173	2	Barbara	Hennessey	Manager	40	12/14/2008	B	Managed HMO
4519	1	Lee	Noordsy	Director	45	04/23/2010	A	Managed PPO
4519	3	Lee	Noordsy	Analyst	30	11/11/2004	A	Managed PPO
8005	3	Pat	Amidon	Analyst	30	06/05/2009	C	Health Savings
8005	4	Pat	Amidon	Clerk	20	07/02/2007	C	Health Savings
8112	1	Chris	Wandzell	Director	45	12/15/2009	A	Managed PPO
8112	2	Chris	Wandzell	Manager	40	10/04/2008	A	Managed PPO

The alternative way to describe the 1NF table is:

Employee (EmployeeNum, PositionID, FirstName, LastName, PositionDesc, PayGrade, StartDate, HealthPlan, PlanDesc)

The Employee table is now a true table and has a composite key. The table, however, suffers from insertion, deletion, and update anomalies. (As an exercise, find examples of the three anomalies in the table.) The EmployeeNum field is a determinant for the FirstName, LastName, HealthPlan, and PlanDesc fields, so partial dependencies exist in the Employee table. It is these partial dependencies that cause the anomalies in the Employee table, and second normal form addresses the partial-dependency problem.

Second Normal Form

A table in 1NF is in **second normal form (2NF)** if it does not contain any partial dependencies. To remove partial dependencies from a table and convert it to second normal form, you perform two steps. First, identify the functional dependencies for every field in the table. Second, if necessary, create new tables and place each field in a table, so that the field is functionally dependent on the entire primary key, not part of the primary key. If you need to create new tables, restrict them to ones with a primary key that is a subset of the original composite key. Note that partial dependencies occur only when you have a composite key; a table in first normal form with a single-field primary key is automatically in second normal form.

First, identifying the functional dependencies leads to the following determinants for the Employee table:

EmployeeNum → FirstName, LastName, HealthPlan, PlanDesc
PositionID → PositionDesc, PayGrade
EmployeeNum, PositionID → StartDate
HealthPlan → PlanDesc

The EmployeeNum field is a determinant for the FirstName, LastName, HealthPlan, and PlanDesc fields. The PositionID field is a determinant for the PositionDesc and PayGrade fields. The HealthPlan field is a determinant for the PlanDesc field. The composite key EmployeeNum and PositionID is a determinant for the StartDate field. Performing the second step in the conversion from first normal form to second form produces the three 2NF tables shown in Figure A-16.

After conversion to 2NF ◄ **Figure A-16**

Employee

primary key ►

EmployeeNum	FirstName	LastName	HealthPlan	PlanDesc
2173	Barbara	Hennessey	B	Managed HMO
4519	Lee	Noordsy	A	Managed PPO
8005	Pat	Amidon	C	Health Savings
8112	Chris	Wandzell	A	Managed PPO

Position

primary key ►

PositionID	PositionDesc	PayGrade
1	Director	45
2	Manager	40
3	Analyst	30
4	Clerk	20

primary key

Employment

EmployeeNum	PositionID	StartDate
2173	2	12/14/2008
4519	1	04/23/2010
4519	3	11/11/2004
8005	3	06/05/2009
8005	4	07/02/2007
8112	1	12/15/2009
8112	2	10/04/2008

The alternative way to describe the 2NF tables is:

Employee (EmployeeNum, FirstName, LastName, HealthPlan, PlanDesc)
Position (PositionID, PositionDesc, PayGrade)
Employment (EmployeeNum, PositionID, StartDate)
    Foreign key: EmployeeNum to Employee table
    Foreign key: PositionID to Position table

All three tables are in second normal form. Do anomalies still exist? The Position and Employment tables show no anomalies, but the Employee table suffers from anomalies caused by the transitive dependency between the HealthPlan and PlanDesc fields. (As an exercise, find examples of the three anomalies caused by the transitive dependency.) That is, the HealthPlan field is a determinant for the PlanDesc field, and the EmployeeNum field is a determinant for the HealthPlan and PlanDesc fields. Third normal form addresses the transitive-dependency problem.

Third Normal Form

A table in 2NF is in **third normal form (3NF)** if every determinant is a candidate key. This definition for 3NF is referred to as **Boyce-Codd normal form (BCNF)** and is an improvement over the original version of 3NF. What are the determinants in the Employee table? The EmployeeNum and HealthPlan fields are the determinants; however, the EmployeeNum field is a candidate key because it's the table's primary key, and the HealthPlan field is not a candidate key. Therefore, the Employee table is in second normal form, but it is not in third normal form.

To convert a table to third normal form, remove the fields that depend on the non-candidate-key determinant and place them into a new table with the determinant as the primary key. For the Employee table, the PlanDesc field depends on the HealthPlan field, which is a non-candidate-key determinant. Thus, you remove the PlanDesc field from the table, create a new HealthBenefits table, place the PlanDesc field in the HealthBenefits table, and then make the HealthPlan field the primary key of the HealthBenefits table. Note that only the PlanDesc field is removed from the Employee table; the HealthPlan field remains as a foreign key in the Employee table. Figure A-17 shows the database design for the four 3NF tables.

Figure A-17	After conversion to 3NF

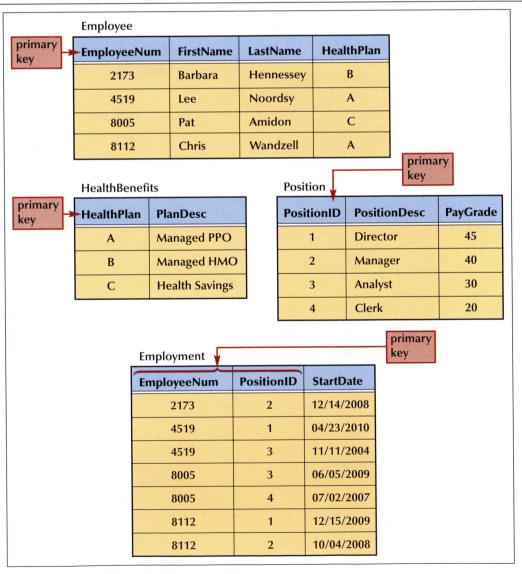

The alternative way to describe the 3NF relations is:

HealthBenefits (<u>HealthPlan</u>, PlanDesc)
Employee (<u>EmployeeNum</u>, FirstName, LastName, HealthPlan)
    Foreign key: HealthPlan to HealthBenefits table
Position (<u>PositionID</u>, PositionDesc, PayGrade)
Employment (<u>EmployeeNum</u>, <u>PositionID</u>, StartDate)
    Foreign key: EmployeeNum to Employee table
    Foreign key: PositionID to Position table

The four tables have no anomalies because you have eliminated all the data redundancy, partial dependencies, and transitive dependencies. Normalization provides the framework for eliminating anomalies and delivering an optimal database design, which you should always strive to achieve. You should be aware, however, that experts sometimes denormalize tables to improve database performance—specifically, to decrease the time it takes the database to respond to a user's commands and requests. Typically, when you denormalize tables, you combine separate tables into one table to reduce the need for the DBMS to join the separate tables to process queries and other informational requests. When you denormalize a table, you reintroduce redundancy to the table. At the same time, you reintroduce anomalies. Thus, improving performance exposes a database to potential integrity problems. Only database experts should denormalize tables, but even experts first complete the normalization of their tables.

Natural, Artificial, and Surrogate Keys

When you complete the design of a database, your tables should be in third normal form, free of anomalies and redundancy. Some tables, such as the State table (see Figure A-2), have obvious third normal form designs with obvious primary keys. The State table's description is:

State (<u>StateAbbrev</u>, StateName, EnteredUnionOrder, StateBird, StatePopulation)

Recall that the candidate keys for the State table are StateAbbrev, StateName, and EnteredUnionOrder. Choosing the StateAbbrev field as the State table's primary key makes the StateName and EnteredUnionOrder fields alternate keys. Primary keys such as the StateAbbrev field are sometimes called natural keys. A **natural key** (also called a **logical key** or an **intelligent key**) is a primary key that consists of a field, or a collection of fields, that is an inherent characteristic of the entity described by the table and that is visible to users. Other examples of natural keys are the ISBN (International Standard Book Number) for a book, the SSN (Social Security number) for a U.S. individual, the UPC (Universal Product Code) for a product, and the VIN (vehicle identification number) for a vehicle.

Is the PositionID field, which is the primary key for the Position table (see Figure A-17), a natural key? No, the PositionID field is not an inherent characteristic of a position. Instead, the PositionID field has been added to the Position table only as a way to identify each position uniquely. The PositionID field is an **artificial key**, which is a field that you add to a table to serve solely as the primary key and that is visible to users.

Another reason for using an artificial key arises in tables that allow duplicate records. Although relational database theory and most experts do not allow duplicate records in a table, consider a database that tracks donors and their donations. Figure A-18 shows a Donor table with an artificial key of DonorID and with the DonorFirstName and DonorLastName fields. Some cash donations are anonymous, which accounts for the fourth record in the Donor table. Figure A-18 also shows the Donation table with the DonorID field, a foreign key to the Donor table, and the DonationDate and DonationAmt fields.

Figure A-18 **Donor and Donation tables**

Donor

primary key →

DonorID	DonorFirstName	DonorLastName
1	Christina	Chang
2	Franco	Diaz
3	Angie	Diaz
4		Anonymous
5	Tracy	Burns

Donation

DonorID	DonationDate	DonationAmt
1	10/12/2010	$50.00
1	09/30/2011	$50.00
2	10/03/2011	$75.00
4	10/10/2011	$50.00
4	10/10/2011	$50.00
4	10/11/2011	$25.00
5	10/13/2011	$50.00

duplicate records

What is the primary key of the Donation table? No single field is unique, and neither is any combination of fields. For example, on 10/10/2011 two anonymous donors (DonorID value of 4) donated $50 each. You need to add an artificial key, DonationID for example, to the Donation table. The addition of the artificial key makes every record in the Donation table unique, as shown in Figure A-19.

Donation table after adding DonationID, an artificial key   Figure A-19

Donation

artificial key → DonationID	DonorID	DonationDate	DonationAmt
1	1	10/12/2010	$50.00
2	1	09/30/2011	$50.00
3	2	10/03/2011	$75.00
4	4	10/10/2011	$50.00
5	4	10/10/2011	$50.00
6	4	10/11/2011	$25.00
7	5	10/13/2011	$50.00

The descriptions of the Donor and Donation tables now are:

Donor (<u>DonorID</u>, DonorFirstName, DonorLastName)
Donation (<u>DonationID</u>, DonorID, DonationDate, DonationAmt)
   Foreign key: DonorID to Donor table

For another common situation, consider the 3NF tables you reviewed in the previous section (see Figure A-17) that have the following descriptions:

HealthBenefits (<u>HealthPlan</u>, PlanDesc)
Employee (<u>EmployeeNum</u>, FirstName, LastName, HealthPlan)
   Foreign key: HealthPlan to HealthBenefits table
Position (<u>PositionID</u>, PositionDesc, PayGrade)
Employment (<u>EmployeeNum</u>, <u>PositionID</u>, StartDate)
   Foreign key: EmployeeNum to Employee table
   Foreign key: PositionID to Position table

Recall that a primary key must be unique, must be minimal, and must not change in value. In theory, primary keys don't change in value. However, in practice, you might have to change EmployeeNum field values that you incorrectly entered in the Employment table. Further, if you need to change an EmployeeNum field value in the Employee table, the change must cascade to the EmployeeNum field values in the Employment table. Also, changes to a PositionID field value in the Position table must cascade to the Employment table. For these and other reasons, many experts add surrogate keys to their tables. A **surrogate key** (also called a **synthetic key**) is a system-generated primary key that is hidden from users. Usually you can use an automatic numbering data type, such as the Access AutoNumber data type, for a surrogate key. Figure A-20 shows the four tables with surrogate keys added to three of the four tables.

Figure A-20 ▷ Using surrogate keys

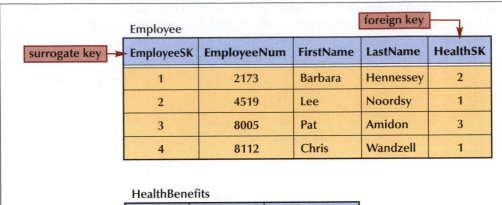

The HealthSK field replaces the HealthPlan field as a foreign key in the Employee table, and the EmployeeSK field replaces the EmployeeNum field in the Employment table. When you change an incorrectly entered EmployeeNum field value in the Employee table, you don't need to cascade the change to the Employment table. When you change an incorrectly entered HealthPlan field value in the HealthBenefits table, you don't have to cascade the change to the Employee table.

As you design a database, you should *not* consider the use of surrogate keys, and you should use an artificial key only for the rare table that has duplicate records. At the point when you implement a database, you might choose to use artificial and surrogate keys, but be aware that database experts debate their use and effectiveness. Some of the trade-offs between natural and surrogate keys that you need to consider are:

- Use surrogate keys to avoid cascading updates to foreign key values. Surrogate keys can also replace lengthier foreign keys when those foreign keys reference composite fields.
- You don't need a surrogate key for a table whose primary key is not used as a foreign key in another table, because cascading updates is not an issue.
- Tables with surrogate keys require more joins than do tables with natural keys. For example, if you need to know all employees with a HealthPlan field value of A, the surrogate key in Figure A-20 requires that you join the Employee and HealthBenefits tables to answer the question. Using natural keys as shown in Figure A-17, the HealthPlan field appears in the Employee table, so no join is necessary.
- Although surrogate keys are meant to be hidden from users, they cannot be hidden from users who create SQL statements and use other ad hoc tools.
- Because you need a unique index for the natural key and a unique index for the surrogate key, your database size is larger and index maintenance takes more time when you use a surrogate key. On the other hand, a foreign key using a surrogate key is usually smaller than a foreign key using a natural key, especially when the natural key is a composite key, so those indexes are smaller and faster to access for lookups and joins.

Microsoft Access Naming Conventions

In the early 1980s, Microsoft's Charles Simonyi introduced an identifier naming convention that became known as Hungarian notation. Microsoft and other companies use this naming convention for variable, control, and other object naming in Basic, Visual Basic, and other programming languages. When Access was introduced in the early 1990s, Stan Leszynski and Greg Reddick adapted Hungarian notation for Microsoft Access databases; their guidelines became known as the Leszynski/Reddick naming conventions. In recent years, the Leszynski naming conventions, the Reddick naming conventions, and other naming conventions have been published. Individuals and companies have created their own Access naming conventions, but many are based on the Leszynski/Reddick naming conventions, as are the naming conventions covered in this section.

An Access database can contain thousands of objects, fields, controls, and other items, and keeping track of their names and what they represent is a difficult task. Consequently, you should use naming conventions that identify the type and purpose of each item in an Access database. You can use naming conventions that identify items generally or very specifically.

For objects, include a prefix tag to identify the type of object, as shown in Figure A-21. In each example in Figure A-21, the final object name consists of a three-character tag prefixed to the base object name. The form name of frmEmployeesAndPositions, for example, consists of the frm tag and the EmployeesAndPositions base form name.

Figure A-21 **Object naming tags**

Object type	Tag	Example
Form	frm	frmEmployeesAndPositions
Macro	mcr	mcrCalculations
Module	bas	basCalculations
Query	qry	qryEmployee
Report	rpt	rptEmployeesAndPositions
Table	tbl	tblEmployee

The tags in Figure A-21 identify each object type in general. If you want to identify object types more specifically, you could expand Figure A-21 to include tags such as fsub for a subform, qxtb for a crosstab query, tlkp for a lookup table, rsub for a subreport, and so on.

For controls in forms and reports, a general naming convention uses lbl as a prefix tag for labels and ctl as a prefix tag for other types of controls. For more specific naming conventions for controls, you'd use a specific prefix tag for each type of control. Figure A-22 shows the prefix tag for some common controls in forms and reports.

Control naming tags ◄   Figure A-22

Control type	Tag
Check box	chk
Combo box	cbo
Command button	cmd
Image	img
Label	lbl
Line	lin
List box	lst
Option button	opt
PivotTable	pvt
Rectangle	shp
Subform/Subreport	sub
Text box	txt

Some database developers use a prefix tag for each field name to identify the field's data type (for example, dtm for Date/Time, num for Number, and chr for Text or Character), others use a prefix tag for each field name to identify in which table the field is located (for example, emp for the Employee table and pos for the Position table), and still others don't use a prefix tag for field names.

You might use suffix tags for controls that might otherwise have identical names. For example, if you have two text boxes in a form for calculated controls that display the average and the sum of the OrderAmt field, both could legitimately be named txtOrderAmt unless you used suffix tags to name them txtOrderAmtAvg and txtOrderAmtSum.

You should ensure that any name you use does not duplicate a property name or any keyword Access reserves for special purposes. In general, you can avoid property and keyword name conflicts by using two-word field, control, and object names. For example, use StudentName instead of Name, and use OrderDate instead of Date to avoid name conflicts.

All database developers avoid spaces in names, mainly because spaces are not allowed in server database management systems (DBMSs), such as SQL Server, Oracle, and DB2. If you are prototyping a Microsoft Access database that you'll migrate to one of these server DBMSs, or if future requirements might force a migration, you should restrict your Access identifier names so that they conform to the rules common to them all. Figure A-23 shows the identifier naming rules for Access, SQL Server, Oracle, and DB2.

Figure A-23 **Identifier naming rules for common database management systems**

Identifier naming rule	Access	SQL Server	Oracle	DB2
Maximum character length	64	30	30	30
Allowable characters	Letters, digits, space, and special characters, except for period (.), exclamation point (!), accent grave (`), and square brackets ([ ])	Letters, digits, dollar sign ($), underscore (_), number symbol (#), and at symbol (@)	Letters, digits, dollar sign ($), underscore (_), and number symbol (#)	Letters, digits, at symbol (@), dollar sign ($), underscore (_), and number symbol (#)
Special rules		No spaces; first character must be a letter or at symbol (@)	No spaces; first character must be a letter; stored in the database in uppercase	No spaces; first character must be a letter, at symbol (@), dollar sign ($), or number symbol (#); stored in the database in uppercase

Appendix Summary | Review

In this appendix, you learned about tables and their characteristics, keys (primary, candidate, alternate, composite, and foreign), relationships (one-to-many, many-to-many, one-to-one, and entity subtypes), entity-relationship diagrams, integrity constraints (entity, referential, and domain), dependencies and determinants, and anomalies. You also learned how to design a database using normalization to place all tables in third normal form. Finally, you learned about natural, artificial, and surrogate keys, and you examined naming conventions.

Key Terms

alternate key
anomalies
artificial key
attribute
Boyce-Codd normal
　　form (BCNF)
bubble diagram
candidate key
cascades
composite entity
composite key
concatenated key
data model diagram
data redundancy
database design
deletion anomaly
determinant
domain
domain integrity constraint
entity
entity integrity constraint
entity subtype

entity-relationship
　　diagram (ERD)
field
field name
first normal form (1NF)
foreign key
functional dependency
　　diagram
insertion anomaly
integrity
integrity constraint
intelligent key
intersection table
junction table
link table
logical key
many-to-many
　　relationship (M:N)
natural key
nonkey field
normal forms
normalization
null

nullifies
one-to-many
　　relationship (1:M or 1:N)
one-to-one relationship (1:1)
partial dependency
primary key
primary table
record
referential integrity
related table
relation
relational database
repeating group
restricted
second normal form (2NF)
semantic object modeling
surrogate key
synthetic key
table
third normal form (3NF)
transitive dependency
tuple
unnormalized relation
update anomaly

Practice | **Review Assignments**

1. What are the formal names for a table, for a row, and for a column? What are the popular names for a row and for a column?
2. What is a domain?
3. What is an entity?
4. What is the relationship between a primary key and a candidate key?
5. What is a composite key?
6. What is a foreign key?
7. Look for an example of a one-to-one relationship, an example of a one-to-many relationship, and an example of a many-to-many relationship in a newspaper, magazine, book, or everyday situation you encounter. For each one, name the entities and select the primary and foreign keys.
8. When do you use an entity subtype?
9. What is a composite entity in an entity-relationship diagram?
10. What is the entity integrity constraint?
11. What is referential integrity?
12. What does the cascades option, which is used with referential integrity, accomplish?
13. What are partial and transitive dependencies?
14. What three types of anomalies can be exhibited by a table, and what problems do they cause?
15. Figure A-24 shows the Employee, Position, and Employment tables with primary keys EmployeeNum, PositionID, and both EmployeeNum and PositionID, respectively. Which two integrity constraints do these tables violate and why?

Figure A-24

Employee

EmployeeNum	ClientName	LastName	HealthPlan
2173	Barbara	Hennessey	B
4519	Lee	Noordsy	A
8005	Pat	Amidon	C
8112	Chris	Wandzell	A

Position

PositionID	PositionDes	PayGrade
1	Director	45
2	Manager	40
3	Analyst	30
4	Clerk	20

Employment

EmployeeNum	PositionID	StartDate
2173	2	12/14/2008
4519	1	04/23/2010
4519		11/11/2004
8005	3	06/05/2009
8005	4	07/02/2007
8112	1	12/15/2009
9876	2	10/04/2008

16. The State and City tables, shown in Figure A-4, are described as follows:
    State (StateAbbrev, StateName, EnteredUnionOrder, StateBird,
          StatePopulation)
    City (StateAbbrev, CityName, CityPopulation)
          Foreign key: StateAbbrev to State table
    Add the field named CountyName for the county or counties in a state containing the
    city to this database, justify where you placed it (that is, in an existing table or in a
    new one), and draw the entity-relationship diagram for all the entities. Counties for
    some of the cities shown in Figure A-4 are Travis and Williamson counties for Austin
    TX; Hartford county for Hartford CT; Clinton, Eaton, and Ingham counties for Lansing
    MI; Davidson county for Nashville TN; Hughes county for Pierre SD; and Nueces and
    San Patricio counties for Portland TX.

17. Suppose you have a table for a dance studio. The fields are dancer's identification number, dancer's name, dancer's address, dancer's telephone number, class identification number, day that the class meets, time that the class meets, instructor name, and instructor identification number. Assume that each dancer takes one class, each class meets only once a week and has one instructor, and each instructor can teach more than one class. In what normal form is the table currently, given the following alternative description?

    Dancer (<u>DancerID</u>, DancerName, DancerAddr, DancerPhone, ClassID, ClassDay, ClassTime, InstrName, InstrID)

    Convert this relation to third normal form and represent the design using the alternative description method.

18. Store the following fields for a library database: AuthorCode, AuthorName, BookTitle, BorrowerAddress, BorrowerName, BorrowerCardNumber, CopiesOfBook, ISBN (International Standard Book Number), LoanDate, PublisherCode, PublisherName, and PublisherAddress. A one-to-many relationship exists between publishers and books. Many-to-many relationships exist between authors and books and between borrowers and books.

    a. Name the entities for the library database.

    b. Create the tables for the library database and describe them using the alternative method. Be sure the tables are in third normal form.

    c. Draw an entity-relationship diagram for the library database.

19. In the following database, which consists of the Department and Employee tables, add one record to the end of the Employee table that violates both the entity integrity constraint and the referential integrity constraint.

Figure A-25

Department

DeptID	DeptName	Location
M	Marketing	New York
R	Research	Houston
S	Sales	Chicago

Employee

EmployeeID	EmployeeName	DeptID
1111	Sue	R
2222	Pam	M
3333	Bob	S
4444	Chris	S
5555	Pat	R
6666	Meg	R

20. Consider the following table:

    Patient (PatientID, PatientName, BalanceOwed, DoctorID, DoctorName, ServiceCode, ServiceDesc, ServiceFee, ServiceDate)

    This is a table concerning data about patients of doctors at a clinic and the services the doctors perform for their patients. The following dependencies exist in the Patient table:

    PatientID → PatientName, BalanceOwed

    DoctorID → DoctorName

    ServiceCode → ServiceDesc, ServiceFee

    PatientID, DoctorID, ServiceCode → PatientName, BalanceOwed, DoctorName, ServiceDesc, ServiceFee, ServiceDate

    a. Based on the dependencies, convert the Patient table to first normal form.

    b. Next, convert the Patient table to third normal form.

21. Suppose you need to track data for mountain climbing expeditions. Each member of an expedition is called a climber, and one of the climbers is named to lead an expedition. Climbers can be members of many expeditions over time. The climbers in each expedition attempt to ascend one or more peaks by scaling one of the many faces of the peaks. The data you need to track includes the name of the expedition, the leader of the expedition, and comments about the expedition; the first name, last name, nationality, birth date, death date, and comments about each climber; the name, location, height, and comments about each peak; the name and comments about each face of a peak; comments about each climber for each expedition; and the highest height reached and the date for each ascent attempt by a climber on a face with commentary.

    a. Create the tables for the expedition database and describe them using the alternative method. Be sure the tables are in third normal form.

    b. Draw an entity-relationship diagram for the expedition database.

22. What is the difference among natural, artificial, and surrogate keys?

23. Why should you use naming conventions for the identifiers in a database?

Ending Data Files

There are no ending Data Files needed for this appendix.

Introduction to Microsoft Windows 7

This appendix introduces you to the new Microsoft Windows 7 operating system. In this appendix, you'll find a complete tutorial, "Exploring the Basics of Microsoft Windows 7," which covers fundamental Windows concepts and skills, including:

- Exploring the desktop and Start menu
- Running software programs and switching between them
- Navigating your computer using Windows Explorer and the Computer window
- Getting Help with Windows tasks

In addition, this appendix highlights some of the exciting advances in Windows 7, including the updated taskbar, the simplified Navigation pane, and the innovative library feature for easier file management.

This appendix also offers a preview of the new design elements you'll find in the upcoming Microsoft Windows 7 and Microsoft Office 2010 texts being produced by the *New Perspectives Series*:

- New *Visual Overviews* at the beginning of each session include colorful, enlarged screenshots with numerous callouts and key term definitions, giving you a comprehensive preview of the topics to be presented as well as a handy study guide.
- New *ProSkills boxes* provide guidance for how to use the software in real-world, professional situations, with relevant information on one or more of the following soft skills: decision making, problem solving, teamwork, verbal communication, and written communication.

OBJECTIVES

Session 1
- Start Windows 7 and tour the desktop
- Explore the Start menu
- Run software programs, switch between them, and close them
- Identify and use the controls in windows and dialog boxes

Session 2
- Navigate your computer using Windows Explorer and the Computer window
- Change the view of the items in your computer
- Get help with Windows 7 tasks
- Turn off Windows

Exploring the Basics of Microsoft Windows 7

Investigating the Windows 7 Operating System

Case | *Back to Work*

Back to Work is a nonprofit agency in Minneapolis, Minnesota, that helps people who want to develop skills for the contemporary workforce, such as retirees and parents who are returning to careers after raising a family. Back to Work creates customized plans for people preparing for full- or part-time work. Elena Varney, the director of the agency, coordinates training sessions on developing a wide range of computer skills.

Elena recently hired you to teach some introductory computer classes. Your first class on using the Microsoft Windows 7 operating system meets next week. To help you prepare for your class, Elena offers to walk you through the curriculum, from starting the computer and opening and closing programs to shutting down the computer. In this tutorial, you will start Windows 7 and practice some fundamental computer skills. Then, you'll learn how to navigate using the Computer window and Windows Explorer. Finally, you'll use the Windows 7 Help system and turn off Windows 7.

STARTING DATA FILES

There are no starting Data Files needed for this tutorial.

SESSION 1 VISUAL OVERVIEW

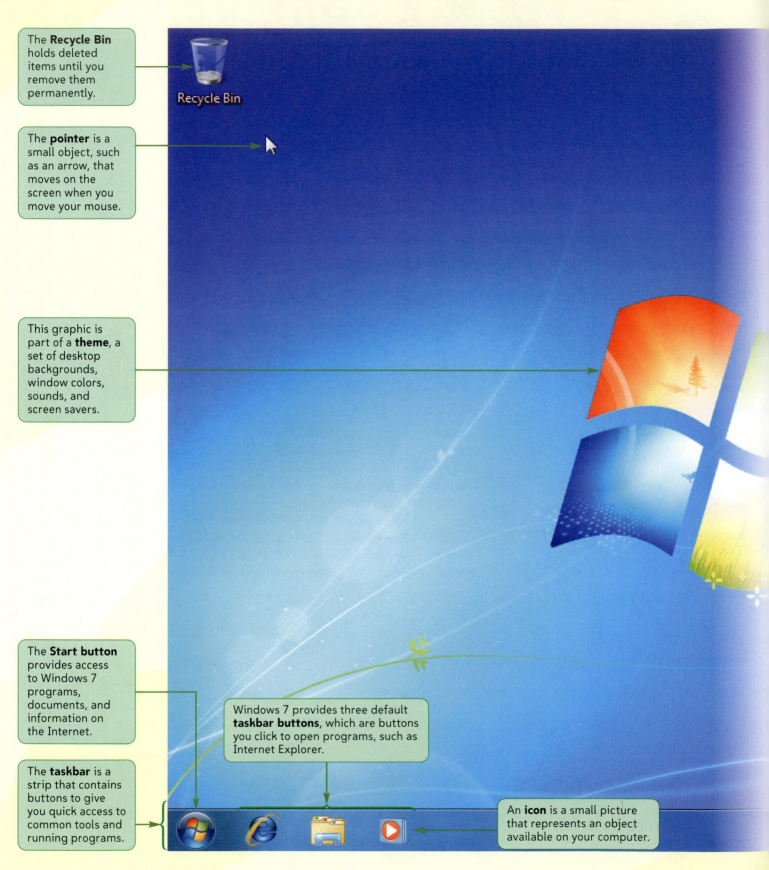

The **Recycle Bin** holds deleted items until you remove them permanently.

The **pointer** is a small object, such as an arrow, that moves on the screen when you move your mouse.

This graphic is part of a **theme**, a set of desktop backgrounds, window colors, sounds, and screen savers.

The **Start button** provides access to Windows 7 programs, documents, and information on the Internet.

Windows 7 provides three default **taskbar buttons**, which are buttons you click to open programs, such as Internet Explorer.

The **taskbar** is a strip that contains buttons to give you quick access to common tools and running programs.

An **icon** is a small picture that represents an object available on your computer.

Recycle Bin

THE WINDOWS 7 DESKTOP

The Windows 7 **desktop** is your workspace on the screen.

The **notification area** displays icons corresponding to services running in the background, such as an Internet connection.

The **Date/Time control** is an element that shows the current date and time and lets you set the clock.

11:19 AM
12/2/2013

Starting Windows 7

The **operating system** is software that manages and coordinates activities on the computer and helps the computer perform essential tasks, such as displaying information on the computer screen and saving data on disks. (The term *software* refers to the **programs**, or **applications**, that a computer uses to complete tasks.) Your computer uses the **Microsoft Windows 7** operating system—**Windows 7** for short. *Windows* is the name of the operating system, and *7* indicates the version you are using.

Much of the software created for the Windows 7 operating system shares the same look and works the same way. This similarity in design means that after you learn how to use one Windows 7 program, you are well on your way to understanding how to use others. Windows 7 allows you to use more than one program at a time, so you can easily switch between your word-processing program and your appointment book program, for example. It also makes it easy to access the **Internet**, a worldwide collection of computers connected to one another to enable communication.

Windows 7 starts automatically when you turn on your computer. After completing some necessary start-up tasks, Windows 7 displays a Welcome screen, which lists all the users for the computer. Before you start working with Windows 7, you might need to click your **user name** (a unique name that identifies you to Windows 7) and type a **password** (a confidential series of characters) before you can work with Windows 7. After you provide this information, the Windows 7 desktop appears.

To begin your review of Windows 7, Elena asks you to start Windows 7.

To start Windows 7:

▶ **1.** Turn on your computer. After a moment, Windows 7 starts and the Welcome screen appears.

Trouble? If you are asked to select an operating system, do not take action. Windows 7 should start automatically after a designated number of seconds. If it does not, ask your instructor or technical support person for help.

▶ **2.** On the Welcome screen, click your user name and enter your password, if necessary. The Windows 7 desktop appears, as shown in the Session 1 Visual Overview. Your desktop might look different.

Trouble? If your user name does not appear on the Welcome screen, first try pressing the Ctrl+Alt+Del keys to enter it. If necessary, ask your instructor or technical support person for further assistance.

Trouble? If you need to enter a user name and a password, type your assigned user name, press the Tab key, type your password, and then click the Continue button or press the Enter key to continue.

Trouble? If a blank screen or an animated design replaces the Windows 7 desktop, your computer might be set to use a **screen saver**, a program that causes a monitor to go blank or to display an animated design after a specified amount of idle time. Press any key or move your mouse to restore the Windows 7 desktop.

The Windows 7 desktop uses a **graphical user interface** (**GUI**, pronounced *gooey*), which uses graphics to represent items stored on your computer, such as programs and files. A computer **file** is a collection of related information; typical types of files include text documents, spreadsheets, digital pictures, and songs. Your computer displays files as icons, which are pictures of familiar objects, such as file folders and documents. Windows 7 gets its name from the rectangular work areas, called windows, that appear on your screen as you work, such as those shown in Figure 1.

| Figure 1 | Two windows open on the desktop |

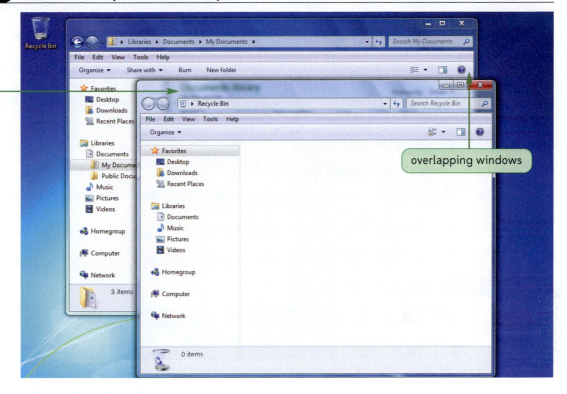

translucent color is characteristic of the Aero experience

overlapping windows

Windows 7 and the Aero Desktop Experience

Windows 7 provides themes, which are sets of desktop backgrounds, window colors, sounds, and screen savers that allow you to personalize the Aero desktop experience. The themes that take advantage of Aero's rich three-dimensional appearance are called Aero themes. You can use an Aero theme only if your computer hardware and version of Windows 7 support it. (The Microsoft Web site at *www.microsoft.com* provides detailed information about the requirements for using Aero themes.) Otherwise, your computer is set by default to use a desktop theme called Windows 7 Basic, which provides most of the same elements as the enhanced experience, including windows and icons, but not the same graphic effects. In this appendix, the figures show the Windows 7 Aero theme. If you are using Windows 7 Basic or a high contrast theme, the images on your screen will vary slightly from the figures and some features will not be available. (These are noted throughout the appendix.)

Touring the Windows 7 Desktop

In Windows terminology, the desktop is a workspace for projects and the tools that you need to manipulate your projects. When you first start a computer, it uses **default settings**, those Windows 7 has already set. The default desktop you see after you first install Windows 7, for example, displays a blue background with a four-color Windows logo. However, Microsoft designed Windows 7 so that you can easily change the appearance of the desktop. You can, for example, change images or add patterns and text to the desktop.

Interacting with the Desktop

To interact with the objects on your desktop, you use a **pointing device**. The most common type is called a **mouse**, so this book uses that term. If you are using a different pointing device, such as a trackball or touchpad, substitute that device whenever you see the term *mouse*.

You use a pointing device to move the mouse pointer over objects on the desktop, or to **point** to them. The pointer is usually shaped like an arrow, although it changes shape depending on the pointer's location on the screen and the tasks you are performing. As you move the mouse on a surface, such as a mouse pad, the pointer on the screen moves in a corresponding direction.

When you point to certain objects, such as the icons on the taskbar, a **ScreenTip** appears near the object to tell you the name or purpose of that object.

Elena suggests that you acquaint students with the desktop by viewing a couple of ScreenTips.

To view ScreenTips:

1. Use the mouse to point to the **Start** button ⊞ on the taskbar. After a few seconds, you see a ScreenTip identifying the button, as shown in Figure 2.

   Trouble? If you don't see the ScreenTip, make sure you are holding the mouse still for a few seconds.

Figure 2   Viewing a ScreenTip

2. Point to the time and date displayed at the right side of the taskbar. A ScreenTip showing today's date (or the date to which your computer's calendar is set) appears in a long format, such as Monday, December 2, 2013.

Clicking refers to pressing a mouse button and immediately releasing it. Clicking sends a signal to your computer that you want to perform an action on the object you click. In Windows 7, you perform most actions with the left mouse button. If you are told to click an object, position the pointer on that object and click the left mouse button, unless instructed otherwise.

When you click the Start button, the Start menu opens. A **menu** is a group or list of commands, and a **menu command** is text that you can click to complete tasks. If a right-pointing arrow follows a menu command, you can point to the command to open a **submenu**, which is a list of additional choices related to the command. The **Start menu** provides access to programs, documents, and much more.

To open the Start menu:

1. Point to the **Start** button ⊞ on the taskbar.

2. Click the left mouse button. The Start menu opens. An arrow ▶ points to the All Programs command on the Start menu, indicating that you can view additional choices by navigating to a submenu.

3. Click the **Start** button ⊞ on the taskbar to close the Start menu.

You need to select an item, or object, before you can work with it. To **select** an object in Windows 7, you usually point to and then click that object. Sometimes you can select menu commands simply by pointing to them. Windows 7 shows you which object is selected by highlighting it, usually by changing the object's color, putting a box around it, or making the object appear to be pushed in.

To select a menu command:

▶ **1.** Click the **Start** button 🔵 on the taskbar.

▶ **2.** Point to **All Programs** on the Start menu. The All Programs command is highlighted to indicate it is selected. After a short pause, the All Programs list opens. See Figure 3.

Figure 3   **All Programs list**

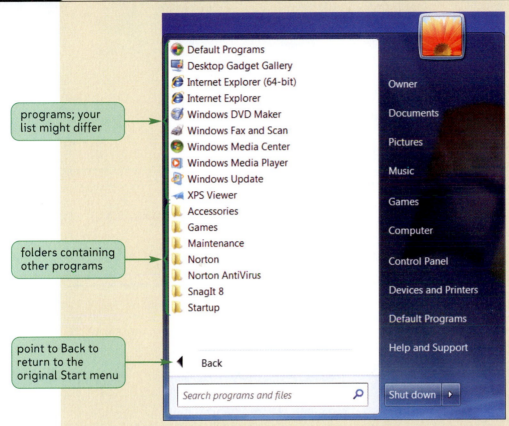

programs; your list might differ

folders containing other programs

point to Back to return to the original Start menu

▶ **3.** Click the **Start** button 🔵 on the taskbar to close the Start menu.

In addition to clicking an object to select it, you can double-click an object to open or start the item associated with it. For example, you can double-click a folder icon to open the folder and see its contents. (A **folder** is a container that helps to organize the contents of your computer, such as files and folders.) Or you can double-click a program icon to start the program. **Double-clicking** means clicking the left mouse button twice in quick succession.

Elena suggests that you have students practice double-clicking by opening the Recycle Bin. The Recycle Bin holds deleted items until you remove them permanently.

To view the contents of the Recycle Bin:

▶ **1.** Click the **desktop** to clear any selections, and then point to the **Recycle Bin** icon on the desktop. A ScreenTip appears that describes the Recycle Bin.

▶ **2.** Click the left mouse button twice quickly to double-click the **Recycle Bin** icon. The Recycle Bin window opens, as shown in Figure 4.

Figure 4   **Contents of the Recycle Bin**

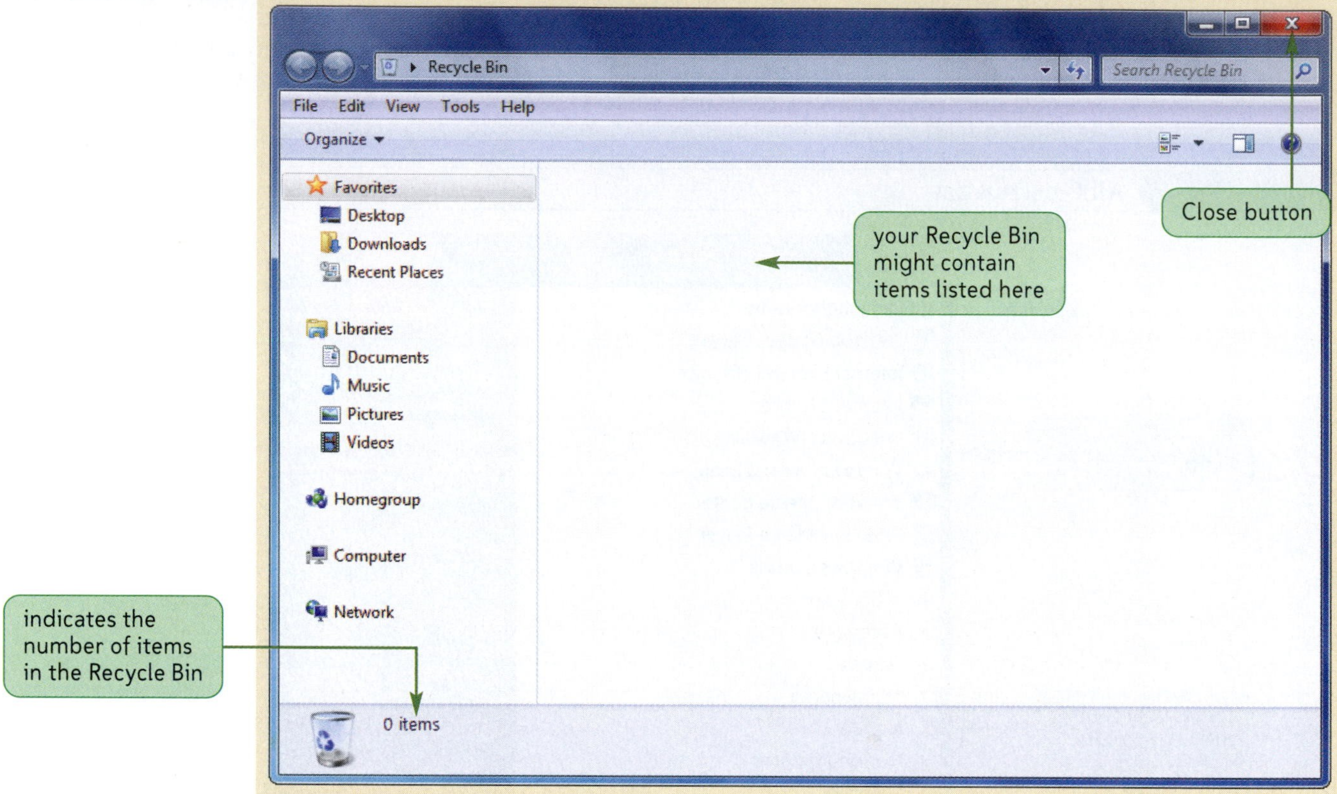

Trouble? If the Recycle Bin window does not open, and you see only the Recycle Bin name highlighted below the icon, you double-clicked too slowly. Double-click the icon again more quickly.

▶ **3.** Click the **Close** button ☒ in the upper-right corner of the Recycle Bin window.

You'll learn more about opening and closing windows later in this session.

Your mouse has more than one button. In addition to the left button, the mouse has a right button that you can use to perform certain actions in Windows 7. However, the term *clicking* continues to refer to the left button; clicking an object with the right button is called **right-clicking**.

In Windows 7, right-clicking selects an object and opens its **shortcut menu**, which lists actions you can take with that object. You can right-click practically any object—the Start button, a desktop icon, the taskbar, and even the desktop itself—to view commands associated with that object. Elena reminds you that you clicked the Start button with the left mouse button to open the Start menu. Now you can right-click the Start button to open the shortcut menu for the Start button.

To right-click an object:

▶ **1.** Position the pointer over the **Start** button 🟦 on the taskbar.

▶ **2.** Right-click the **Start** button 🟦 to open its shortcut menu. This menu offers a list of actions you can take with the Start button. See Figure 5.

Figure 5	Start button shortcut menu

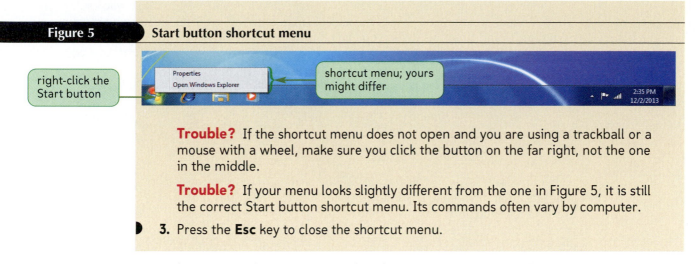

Trouble? If the shortcut menu does not open and you are using a trackball or a mouse with a wheel, make sure you click the button on the far right, not the one in the middle.

Trouble? If your menu looks slightly different from the one in Figure 5, it is still the correct Start button shortcut menu. Its commands often vary by computer.

3. Press the **Esc** key to close the shortcut menu.

After opening the Start menu and its shortcut menu, you're ready to explore its contents.

Exploring the Start Menu

Recall that the Start menu is the central point for accessing programs, documents, and other resources on your computer. The Start menu is organized into two **panes**, which are separate areas of a menu or window. Each pane lists items you can point to or click. See Figure 6.

Figure 6	Start menu

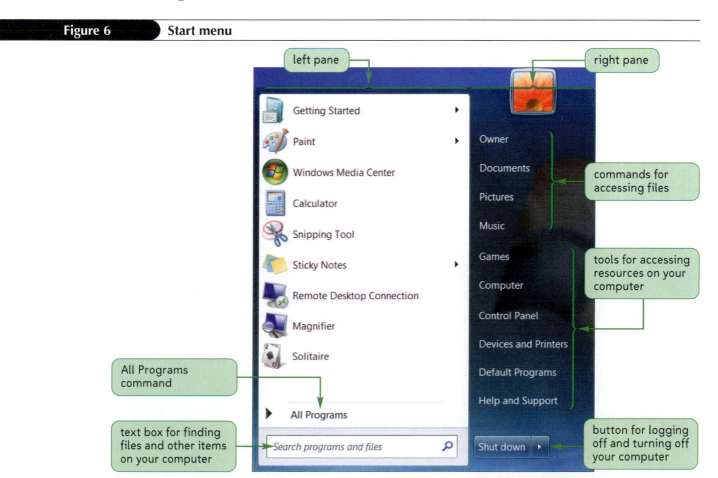

The left pane organizes programs for easy access. When you first install Windows 7, the left pane contains a short list of programs on your computer. After you use a program, Windows 7 adds it to this list so you can quickly find it the next time you want to use it. The Start menu can list only a certain number of programs—after that, the programs you have not opened recently are replaced by the programs you used last.

Near the bottom of the left pane is the All Programs command, which you have already used to display the All Programs list. The All Programs list provides access to the programs currently installed on your computer. You'll use the All Programs list shortly to start a program.

The **Search programs and files box** helps you quickly find anything stored on your computer, including programs, documents, pictures, music, videos, Web pages, and e-mail messages. When you want to use the Search programs and files box, you open the Start menu and type one or more words related to what you want to find. For example, if you want to find and play the Happy Birthday song stored on your computer, you could type *birthday* in the Search programs and files box. Windows 7 searches your computer for that song and displays it and any other search results in the Start menu, where you can click the song to play it.

From the right pane of the Start menu, you can access common locations and tools on your computer. For example, the **Computer window** is a tool that you use to view, organize, and access the programs, files, and drives on your computer.

From the bottom section of the right pane, you can open windows that help you effectively work with Windows 7, including the **Control Panel**, which contains special-ized tools that help you change the way Windows 7 looks and behaves, and **Help and Support**, which provides articles, video demonstrations, and steps for performing tasks in Windows 7. You also turn off your computer from the Start menu.

REFERENCE

Starting a Program

- Click the Start button on the taskbar, and then click the name of the program you want to start.

or

- Click the Start button on the taskbar, and then point to All Programs.
- If necessary, click the folder that contains the program you want to start.
- Click the name of the program you want to start.

Windows 7 includes an easy-to-use word-processing program called WordPad, which you can use to write a letter or report. To start WordPad, you open the Start menu and then navigate to the Accessories folder in the All Programs list.

To start the WordPad program from the Start menu:

1. Click the **Start** button 🔵 on the taskbar to open the Start menu.

2. Point to **All Programs**, and then click **Accessories**. The Accessories folder opens. See Figure 7.

   Trouble? If a different folder opens, point to Back to return to the initial Start menu, point to All Programs, and then click Accessories.

| **Figure 7** | **Accessories folder open on the Start menu** |

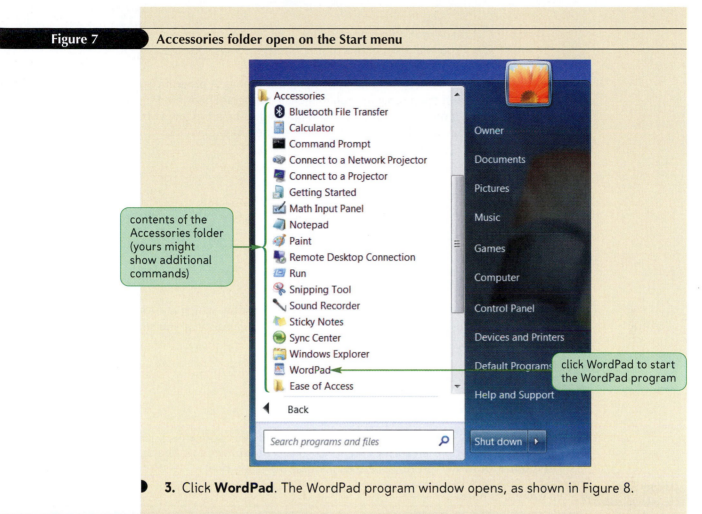

contents of the Accessories folder (yours might show additional commands)

click WordPad to start the WordPad program

3. Click **WordPad**. The WordPad program window opens, as shown in Figure 8.

| **Figure 8** | **WordPad program window** |

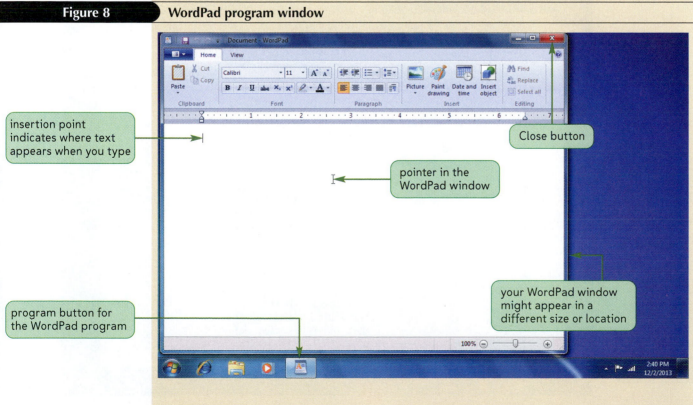

insertion point indicates where text appears when you type

Close button

pointer in the WordPad window

your WordPad window might appear in a different size or location

program button for the WordPad program

Trouble? If the WordPad program window fills the entire screen, continue with the next step. You will learn how to manipulate windows shortly.

When a program is started, it is said to be open or running. A **program button** appears on the taskbar for each open program. You can click a program button on the taskbar to switch between open programs. When you are finished using a program, you can click the Close button located in the upper-right corner of the program window to **exit**, or close, that program.

To exit the WordPad program:

▶ **1.** Click the **Close** button ❌ on the WordPad title bar. The WordPad program closes and you return to the desktop.

Running Multiple Programs

One of the most useful features of Windows 7 is **multitasking**, which allows you to work on more than one task at a time. To demonstrate, Elena suggests that you start WordPad and leave it running while you start the Paint program.

To run WordPad and Paint at the same time:

▶ **1.** Start WordPad again.

▶ **2.** Click the **Start** button ⊕ on the taskbar, point to **All Programs**, click **Accessories**, and then click **Paint**. The Paint program window opens, as shown in Figure 9. Now two programs are running at the same time.

Figure 9   Two programs open

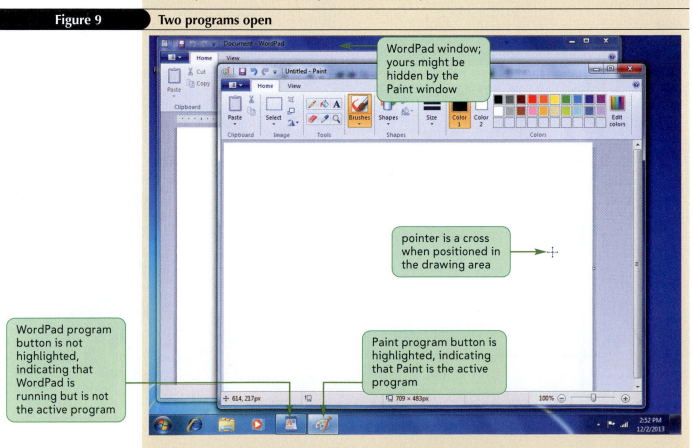

WordPad window; yours might be hidden by the Paint window

pointer is a cross when positioned in the drawing area

WordPad program button is not highlighted, indicating that WordPad is running but is not the active program

Paint program button is highlighted, indicating that Paint is the active program

Trouble? If the Paint program fills the entire screen, continue with the next set of steps. You will learn how to manipulate windows shortly.

The **active program** is the one you are working with—Windows 7 applies your next keystroke or command to the active program. Paint is the active program because it is the one you are currently using. The WordPad program button is still on the taskbar, indicating that WordPad is still running even if you can't see its program window.

Switching Between Programs

Because only one program is active at a time, you need to switch between programs if you want to work in one or the other. The easiest way to switch between programs is to use the program buttons on the taskbar.

To switch between WordPad and Paint:

1. Click the **WordPad** program button 🅰 on the taskbar. The WordPad program window moves to the front, and the WordPad program button appears highlighted, indicating that WordPad is the active program.

2. Click the **Paint** program button 🖌 on the taskbar to switch to the Paint program. The Paint program is again the active program.

You can also bypass the taskbar and use keyboard shortcuts to switch from one open window to another. A **keyboard shortcut** is a key or combination of keys that perform a command. If you are using an Aero theme, you can press and hold the Windows key and then press the Tab key to activate **Aero Flip 3D** (often shortened to *Flip 3D*), which displays all your open windows in a three-dimensional stack so you can see the windows from the side, the way you view the spine of a book. See Figure 10. To flip through the stack, you press the Tab key or scroll the wheel on your mouse while continuing to hold down the Windows button. When you release the Windows and Tab keys, you close Flip 3D and the window at the top of the stack becomes the active window.

Figure 10

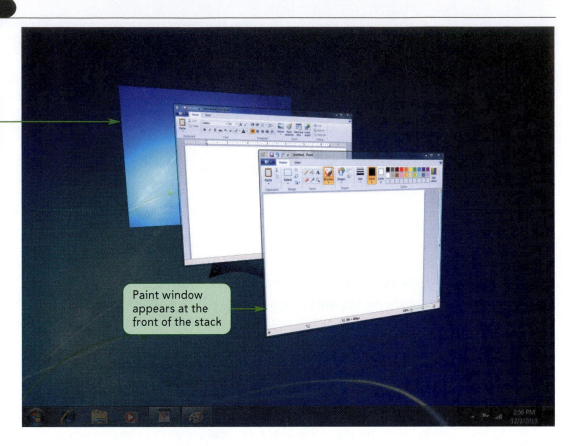

two windows and the desktop image are flipped and stacked

Paint window appears at the front of the stack

You can use another Aero keyboard shortcut called Windows Flip to switch from one window to another. When you hold down the Alt key and press the Tab key once, Windows Flip displays thumbnails (miniature versions) of your open windows. See Figure 1-11. The thumbnails display the exact contents of the open windows instead of generic icons so you can easily identify the windows. While continuing to hold down the Alt key, you can press the Tab key to select the thumbnail for the program you want; you release the Alt key to close Windows Flip.

Figure 11

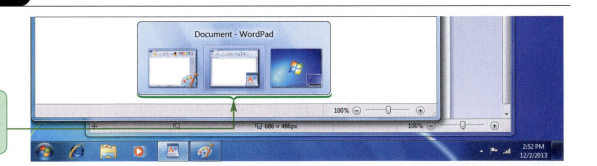

thumbnails of the Paint window, WordPad window, and desktop

To switch between program windows using Aero Flip 3D:

1. Press and hold the **Windows** key and then press the **Tab** key. Windows arranges the Paint and WordPad windows and the desktop in a stack, with the Paint window at the top of the stack.

Trouble? If a task switcher window displaying generic program icons opens when you press the Windows+Tab keys, you are not using an Aero theme. Click outside the task switcher window and then read, but do not perform, the remaining steps.

2. Press the **Tab** key to flip the WordPad window to the front of the stack. The Paint window moves to the back of the stack.

3. Press the **Tab** key to flip the desktop to the front of the stack, and then press the **Tab** key again to flip the Paint window to the front of the stack.

4. Release the **Windows** key to turn off Flip 3D and make Paint the active program.

In addition to using the taskbar to switch between open programs, you can close programs from the taskbar.

Closing Programs from the Taskbar

You should always close a program when you are finished using it. Each program uses computer resources, such as memory, so Windows 7 works more efficiently when only the programs you need are open. Elena reminds you that you've already closed an open program using the Close button on the title bar of the program window. You can also close a program, whether active or inactive, by using the shortcut menu associated with the program button on the taskbar.

To close WordPad and Paint using the program button shortcut menus:

1. Right-click the **Paint** program button 🖌 on the taskbar. The shortcut menu for the Paint program button opens. See Figure 12.

Figure 12	Program button shortcut menu

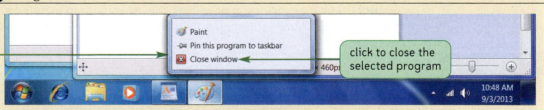

shortcut menu opens when you right-click a program button

click to close the selected program

2. Click **Close window** on the shortcut menu. The Paint program closes and its program button no longer appears on the taskbar.

Trouble? If a message appears asking if you want to save changes, click the Don't Save button.

3. Right-click the **WordPad** program button 🄰 on the taskbar, and then click **Close window** on the shortcut menu. The WordPad program closes, and its program button no longer appears on the taskbar.

PROSKILLS

Problem Solving: Working Efficiently on the Desktop

When you work with Windows and its programs, especially on a complicated project, you often start and run more than one program and open many windows. This can lead to two common problems that affect your productivity: having too many windows open can make it difficult to find the information you need, and running too many programs can slow the performance of your computer.

Deciding how many windows to open and how to arrange them on the desktop depends on your personal preference. Some people like to maximize all their open windows and use the taskbar to switch from one window to another. Other people like to size and arrange each window so it is visible on the desktop, even if that means having some small and overlapping windows. Keep in mind that a clean and organized desktop increases your productivity. Find an arrangement that works for you without cluttering your desktop.

If you find that your computer responds to your keystrokes and mouse actions more slowly than usual, you might have too many programs running at the same time. Closing the programs you are not using frees up system resources, which makes your computer faster and more responsive and can solve performance problems.

Using Windows and Dialog Boxes

When you run a program in Windows 7, the program appears in a **window**, a rectangular area of the screen that contains a program, text, or other data. A window also contains **controls**, which are graphical or textual objects you use to manipulate the window or use the program. Figure 13 describes the controls you see in most windows.

Figure 13	Window controls

Control	Description
Program menu button	Lists commands for common program tasks, such as creating, opening, and saving documents
Quick Access Toolbar	Contains buttons for performing tasks, such as saving a document
Ribbon	Provides access to the main set of commands organized by task into tabs and groups
Sizing button	Lets you enlarge, shrink, or close a window
Status bar	Displays information or messages about the task you are performing
Tab	Organizes commands on the Ribbon related to similar tasks
Title bar	Contains the window title and basic window control buttons
Window title	Identifies the program and document contained in the window
Workspace	Includes the part of the window where you manipulate your work—enter text, draw pictures, and set up calculations, for example
Zoom controls	Magnify or shrink the content displayed in the workspace

Elena suggests that you start WordPad and identify its window controls.

To look at the window controls in WordPad:

▶ **1.** Start WordPad. On your screen, identify the controls that are labeled in Figure 14.

Figure 14	WordPad window controls

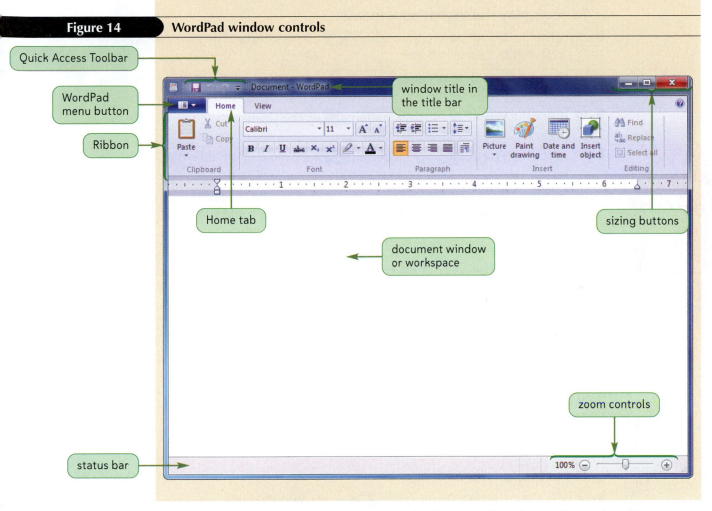

After you open a window, you can manipulate it by changing its size and position.

Manipulating Windows

In most windows, three buttons appear on the right side of the title bar. The first button is the Minimize button, which hides a window so that only its program button is visible on the taskbar. Depending on the status of the window, the middle button either maximizes the window or restores it to a predefined size. You are already familiar with the last button—the Close button. You can use the Minimize button when you want to temporarily hide a window but keep the program running.

To minimize the WordPad window:

▶ **1.** Click the **Minimize** button ▬ on the WordPad title bar. The WordPad window shrinks so that only the WordPad program button on the taskbar is visible.

Trouble? If the WordPad program window closed, you accidentally clicked the Close button ❌. Use the Start button ⊕ to start WordPad again, and then repeat Step 1. If you accidentally clicked the Maximize button ▢ or the Restore Down button ▢, repeat Step 1.

You can redisplay a minimized window by clicking the program's button on the task-bar. When you redisplay a window, it becomes the active window.

To redisplay the WordPad window:

▶ **1.** Click the **WordPad** program button 🖼 on the taskbar. The WordPad window is restored to its previous size.

The taskbar button provides another way to switch a window between its mini-mized and active states.

▶ **2.** Click the **WordPad** program button 🖼 on the taskbar again to minimize the window.

▶ **3.** Click the **WordPad** program button 🖼 once more to redisplay the window.

The Maximize button enlarges a window so that it fills the entire screen. Use maxi-mized windows when you need to see more of the program and your data.

To maximize the WordPad window:

▶ **1.** Click the **Maximize** button 🔲 on the WordPad title bar.

Trouble? If the window is already maximized, it fills the entire screen, and the Maximize button 🔲 does not appear. Instead, you see the Restore Down button 🗗. Skip this step.

The Restore Down button reduces the window so that it is smaller than the entire screen. This feature is useful if you want to see more than one window at a time, move the window to another location on the screen, or change the dimensions of the window.

To restore a window:

▶ **1.** Click the **Restore Down** button 🗗 on the WordPad title bar. After a window is restored, the Restore Down button 🗗 changes to the Maximize button 🔲.

You can use the mouse to move a window to a new position on the screen. When you click an object and then press and hold down the mouse button while moving the mouse, you are **dragging** the object. You can move objects on the screen by dragging them to a new location. If you want to move a window, you drag the window by its title bar. You cannot move a maximized window.

To drag the restored WordPad window to a new location:

▶ **1.** Position the mouse pointer on the WordPad title bar.

▶ **2.** Press and hold down the left mouse button, and then move the mouse up or down a little to drag the window. The window moves as you move the mouse.

3. Position the window anywhere on the desktop, and then release the left mouse button. The WordPad window stays in the new location.

4. Drag the WordPad window to the upper-left corner of the desktop.

   Trouble? If the WordPad window is maximized when you drag it near the upper part of the desktop, click the Restore Down button ▣ before performing the next steps.

You can also use the mouse to change the size of a window. When you point to an edge or corner of a window, the pointer changes to a double-headed arrow, similar to ↘. Use this resize pointer to drag an edge or corner of the window and change the size of the window.

To change the size of the WordPad window:

1. Position the pointer over the lower-right corner of the WordPad window. The pointer changes to ↘. See Figure 15.

Figure 15	Preparing to resize a window

2. Press and hold down the mouse button, and then drag the corner down and to the right.

3. Release the mouse button. Now the window is larger.

You can also use the resize pointer to drag any of the other three corners of the window to change its size. To change a window's size in any one direction, drag the left, right, top, or bottom window borders left, right, up, or down.

Using the Ribbon

Many Windows 7 programs use a Ribbon to organize the program's features and commands. The **Ribbon** is located at the top of the program window, immediately below the title bar, and is organized into tabs. Each **tab** contains commands that perform a variety of related tasks. For example, the Home tab has commands for tasks you perform frequently, such as changing the appearance of a document. You use the commands on the View tab to change your view of the WordPad window.

To select a command and perform an action, you use a button or other type of control on the Ribbon. Controls for related actions are organized on a tab in **groups**. For example, to enter bold text in a WordPad document, you click the Bold button in the Font group on the Home tab. Figure 16 shows examples of Ribbon controls.

Figure 16 | Examples of Ribbon controls

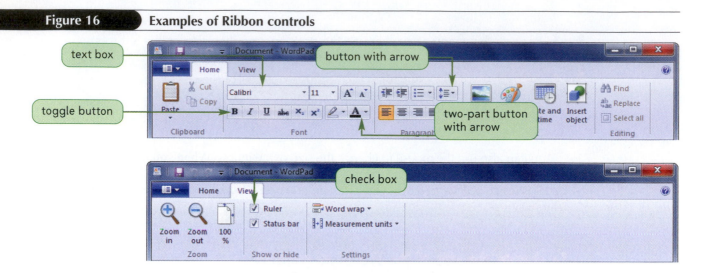

Figure 17 describes the Ribbon controls.

Figure 17 | Types of controls on the Ribbon

Control	How to Use	Example
Button with arrow	Click the button to display a menu of related commands.	
Check box	Click to insert a check mark and select the option, or click to remove the check mark and deselect the option.	
Text box	Click the text box and type an entry, or click the arrow button to select an item from the list.	
Toggle button	Click the button to turn on or apply a setting, and then click the button again to turn off the setting. When a toggle button is turned on, it is highlighted.	
Two-part button with arrow	If an arrow is displayed on a separate part of the button, click the arrow to display a menu of commands. Click the button itself to apply the current selection.	

Elena suggests exploring the buttons on the WordPad Ribbon by viewing their ScreenTips.

To determine the names and descriptions of the buttons on the WordPad Ribbon:

1. On the Home tab of the WordPad Ribbon, position the pointer over the **Bold** button B in the Font group to display its ScreenTip.

2. Move the pointer over each remaining button on the Home tab to display its name.

Most Windows 7 programs, including WordPad and Paint, include a **Quick Access Toolbar**, which is a row of buttons on the title bar that let you perform common tasks such as saving a file and undoing an action. You can display the name of each button on the Quick Access Toolbar in a ScreenTip by pointing to the button, just as you do for buttons on the Ribbon. You also can select a button on the Quick Access Toolbar or the Ribbon by clicking the button, which performs the associated command. One of the buttons you pointed to on the WordPad Ribbon is the Bold button, which you click to bold selected text. On the Quick Access Toolbar, you can click the Undo button to reverse the effects of your last action. Elena says you can see how both buttons work by typing some bold text, and then clicking the Undo button to remove that text.

To use buttons on the WordPad Ribbon and Quick Access Toolbar:

▶ **1.** Click the **Bold** button **B** in the Font group on the Home tab of the WordPad Ribbon. Now any text you type will appear as bold text.

▶ **2.** Type your full name in the WordPad window.

▶ **3.** Click the **Undo** button ⤺ on the Quick Access Toolbar. WordPad reverses your last action by removing your name from the WordPad window.

Using List Boxes

As you might guess from the name, a **list box** displays a list of available choices from which you can select one item. For example, to select a font size in WordPad, you use the Font size list box on the Home tab. A list box is helpful because it only includes options that are appropriate for your current task, such as selecting a font size. Some lists might not include every possible option, so you can type the option you want to select. In most cases, the right side of the list box includes an arrow. You can click the list box arrow to view all the options and then select one or type appropriate text.

Buttons can also have arrows. The arrow indicates that the button has more than one option. Rather than crowding the window with a lot of buttons, one for each possible option, including an arrow on a button organizes its options logically and compactly into a list. Ribbon tabs often include list boxes and buttons with arrows. For example, the Font size button list box on the Home tab includes an arrow. Elena suggests you select a different font size using the arrow on the Font size button list box.

To select a new font size in the Font size button list box:

▶ **1.** In the Font group on the Home tab, click the **Font size button arrow** 11 ▾.

▶ **2.** Click **18**. The Font size list closes, and the font size you selected appears in the list box.

▶ **3.** Type your full name to test the new font size, and then press the **Enter** key.

▶ **4.** Click the **Font size button arrow** 11 ▾ on the Home tab again, and then click **12**.

▶ **5.** Type your full name again to test this type size. Your name appears in 12-point font.

List boxes sometimes include a vertical scroll bar, which appears when the list of available options is too long or wide to fit in the list box. The scroll bar includes an up and down arrow and a scroll box that you use to scroll the list. Horizontal and vertical scroll bars are more common in windows and dialog boxes. You'll examine a typical dialog box next.

Working with Dialog Boxes

A **dialog box** is a special kind of window in which you enter or choose settings for how you want to perform a task. Dialog boxes can include tabs, option buttons, check boxes, and other controls to collect information about how you want to perform a task. Figure 18 displays examples of common dialog box controls.

Figure 18   **Examples of dialog box controls**

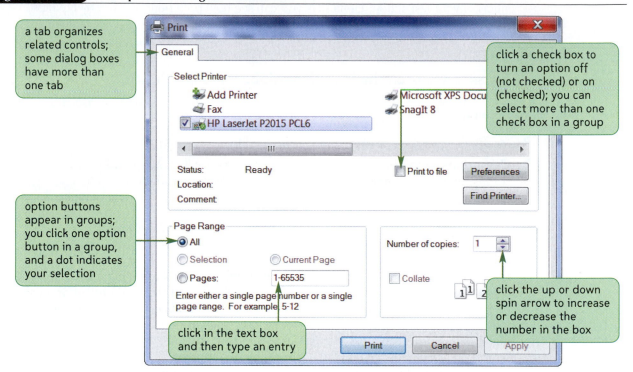

a tab organizes related controls; some dialog boxes have more than one tab

click a check box to turn an option off (not checked) or on (checked); you can select more than one check box in a group

option buttons appear in groups; you click one option button in a group, and a dot indicates your selection

click the up or down spin arrow to increase or decrease the number in the box

click in the text box and then type an entry

Besides using buttons on Ribbon tabs, you can also open dialog boxes by selecting a command on the WordPad button menu. The WordPad menu button appears in the upper-left corner of the WordPad window. You click the WordPad menu button to display a list of commands, such as Open, Save, and Print. To open a dialog box, such as the Print dialog box, you click the appropriate command, such as Print. If you point to certain commands on the WordPad button menu, a submenu appears listing related commands. A right-pointing arrow indicates that a command has a submenu. For example, when you point to the Print command, a submenu appears listing the Print, Quick print, and Print preview commands.

A good way to learn how dialog box controls work is to open a typical Windows 7 dialog box in WordPad, such as the Page Setup dialog box. You use this dialog box to determine how text appears on a page by specifying margins, page numbers, orientation, and other settings. Before selecting options in the Page Setup dialog box, you can switch to Print Preview using the WordPad menu button to see exactly how your selections affect the WordPad document containing two copies of your name.

To work with a typical Windows 7 dialog box:

▶ **1.** Click the **WordPad menu** button in the upper-left corner of the WordPad window, point to **Print**, and then click **Print preview**. The current document appears as it will when printed. Note that the page appears in portrait orientation, which is longer than it is wide. A page number might also appear at the bottom of the page. The Ribbon now contains only one tab—the Print preview tab.

▶ **2.** In the Print group on the Print preview tab, click the **Page setup** button. The Page Setup dialog box opens.

▶ **3.** Click the **Landscape** option button to change the orientation of the page.

▶ **4.** If a check mark appears in the Print Page Numbers check box, click the **Print Page Numbers** check box to remove the check mark. This means no page numbers will appear in the document.

▶ **5.** Click the **OK** button. WordPad accepts your changes and closes the Page Setup dialog box. Now the page appears in landscape orientation, so it is wider than it is long, and no page number appears at the bottom of the page.

Now that you're finished exploring dialog boxes, you can close Print Preview and exit WordPad. Besides using the Close button in the upper-right corner of the title bar, you can exit a program by clicking the program menu button and then clicking Exit.

To close Print Preview and exit WordPad:

▶ **1.** In the Close group on the Print preview tab, click the **Close print preview** button. The WordPad window appears in its original view, including the Home and View tabs.

▶ **2.** Click the **WordPad menu** button , and then click **Exit**. A WordPad dialog box opens asking if you want to save the document.

▶ **3.** Click the **Don't Save** button to close WordPad without saving the document.

In this session, you started Windows 7 and toured the desktop, learning how to interact with the items on the desktop and on the Start menu. You also started two Windows programs, manipulated windows, and learned how to select options from a Ribbon, toolbar, menu, and dialog box.

REVIEW

Session 1 Quick Check

1. What does the operating system do for your computer?
2. A(n) _____ is a confidential series of characters.
3. True or False. Your computer represents files with icons, which are pictures of familiar objects, such as file folders and documents.
4. What happens when you point to the Start button with a mouse? What happens when you click the Start button with the left mouse button?
5. In Windows 7, right-clicking selects an object and opens its _____.
6. When more than one window is open, the _____ appears on top of all other open windows.
7. Why should you close each program when you are finished using it?

SESSION 2 VISUAL OVERVIEW

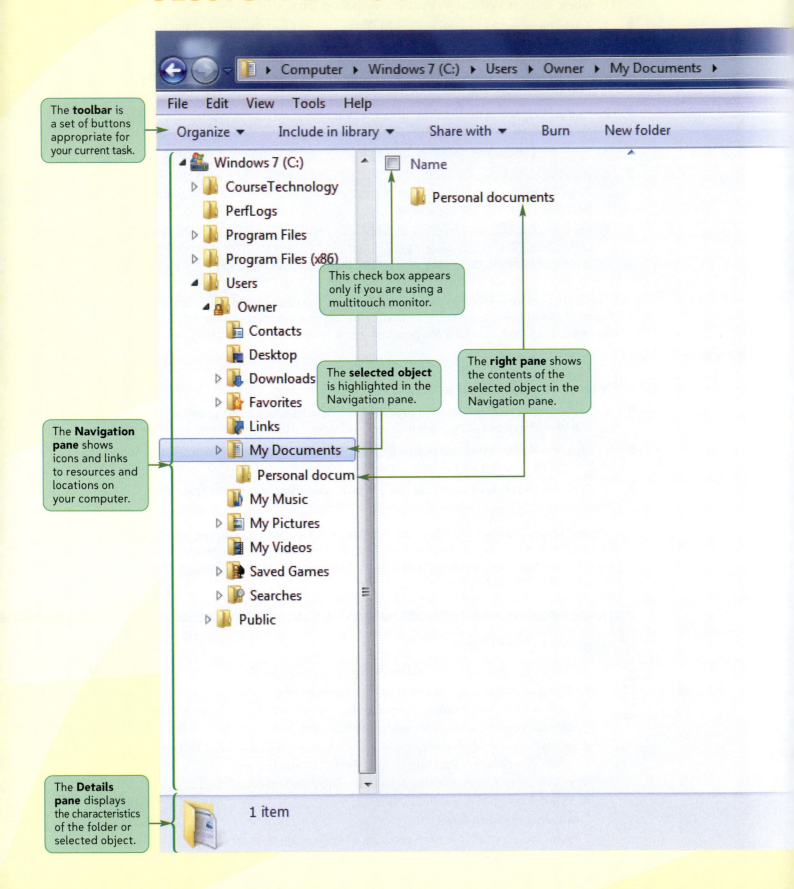

The **toolbar** is a set of buttons appropriate for your current task.

This check box appears only if you are using a multitouch monitor.

The **selected object** is highlighted in the Navigation pane.

The **right pane** shows the contents of the selected object in the Navigation pane.

The **Navigation pane** shows icons and links to resources and locations on your computer.

The **Details pane** displays the characteristics of the folder or selected object.

Computer ▶ Windows 7 (C:) ▶ Users ▶ Owner ▶ My Documents ▶

File   Edit   View   Tools   Help

Organize ▼   Include in library ▼   Share with ▼   Burn   New folder

Windows 7 (C:)
  CourseTechnology
  PerfLogs
  Program Files
  Program Files (x86)
  Users
    Owner
      Contacts
      Desktop
      Downloads
      Favorites
      Links
      My Documents
        Personal docum
      My Music
      My Pictures
      My Videos
      Saved Games
      Searches
    Public

Name

Personal documents

1 item

THE COMPUTER WINDOW

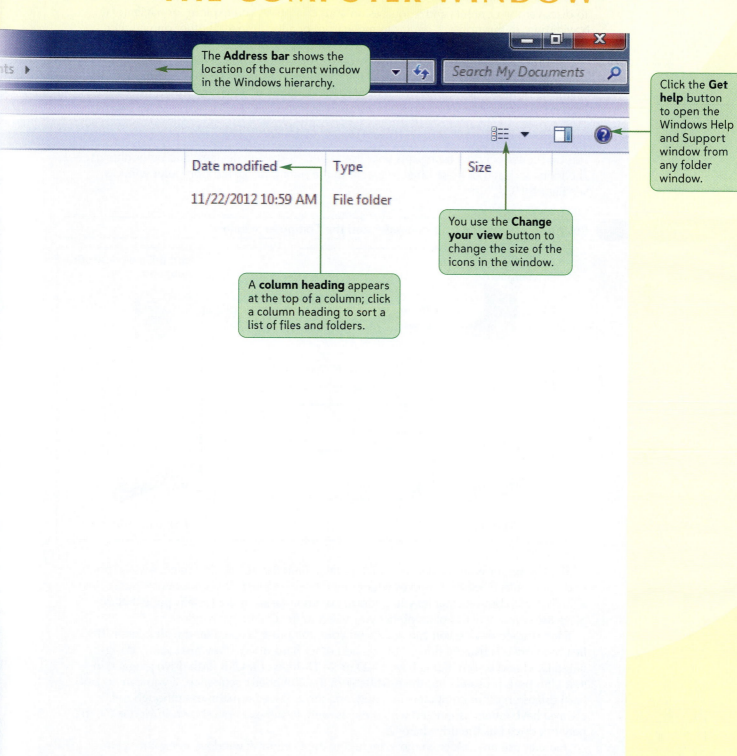

The **Address bar** shows the location of the current window in the Windows hierarchy.

Click the **Get help** button to open the Windows Help and Support window from any folder window.

You use the **Change your view** button to change the size of the icons in the window.

A **column heading** appears at the top of a column; click a column heading to sort a list of files and folders.

Date modified

11/22/2012 10:59 AM   File folder

Type

Size

Search My Documents

Exploring Your Computer

To discover the contents and resources on your computer, you explore, or navigate, it. **Navigating**, in this context, means to move from one location to another on your computer, such as from one window to another. Windows 7 provides two ways to navigate, view, and work with the contents and resources on your computer—the Computer window (shown in the Session 2 Visual Overview) and Windows Explorer. Both are examples of **folder windows**, which display the contents of your computer.

Navigating with the Computer Window

The Computer window represents your computer, its storage devices, and other objects. The icons for each of these objects appear in the right pane of the Computer window. See Figure 19.

Figure 19 | **Relationship between your computer and the Computer window**

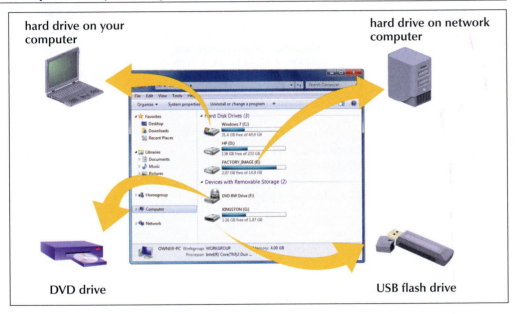

hard drive on your computer

hard drive on network computer

DVD drive

USB flash drive

The Computer window also has a left pane, called the Navigation pane, which shows icons and links to other resources your computer can access. This window also contains a toolbar with buttons that let you perform common tasks, and a Details pane that displays the characteristics of an object you select in the Computer window.

Each storage device you can access on your computer is associated with a letter. The first hard drive is usually drive C (if you add other hard drives, they are usually designated D, E, and so on). If you have a CD or DVD drive or a USB flash drive plugged in to a USB port, it usually has the next letter in the alphabetic sequence. If you can access hard drives on other computers in a network, those drives sometimes (although not always) have letters associated with them as well. In the example shown in Figure 19, the network drive has the drive letter Z.

You can use any folder window, including the Computer window, to explore your computer and organize your files. In this session, you explore the contents of your hard disk, which is assumed to be drive C. If you use a different drive on your computer, such as drive E, substitute its letter for C throughout this session.

Elena suggests you explore the Music library, which is a convenient location for storing your music files. (A **library** is a central place to view and organize files and folders stored anywhere that your computer can access, such as those on your hard disk, removable drives, and network.) Even if you store some music files on your hard disk and others on an external drive, such as a digital music player attached to your computer, they are all displayed in the Music library. Many digital music players use this location by default when you rip, download, play, and burn music.

The computer Elena provides for you has a multitouch monitor, which lets you interact with objects on the screen using your finger instead of a mouse. If you have a multitouch monitor, a feature in Windows 7 called Windows Touch lets you perform tasks such as selecting icons, opening folders, and starting programs using your finger as a pointing device. To make it easier to select objects and identify which ones are selected, Windows Touch displays a check box next to objects such as files and icons on the desktop and in folder windows. For example, you could touch the check box shown in Figure 20 to select all the folders in the Music library. If you are not using a multitouch monitor, these check boxes do not appear in your folder windows or on the desktop.

To explore the contents of your computer using the Computer window:

1. If you took a break after the previous session, make sure that your computer is on and Windows 7 is running.

2. Click the **Start** button on the taskbar, and then click **Computer** in the right pane of the Start menu. The Computer window opens.

3. In the Navigation pane, click the **Music** link. The right pane displays the contents of the Music library. See Figure 20.

| Figure 20 | Contents of the Music library |

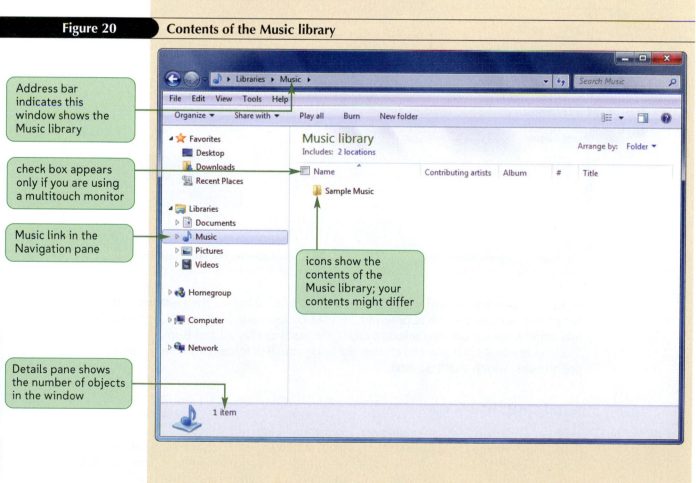

Address bar indicates this window shows the Music library

check box appears only if you are using a multitouch monitor

Music link in the Navigation pane

icons show the contents of the Music library; your contents might differ

Details pane shows the number of objects in the window

TIP

The Address bar displays your current location as a series of links separated by arrows. Click a folder name in the Address bar to display the contents of that folder.

Trouble? If your window looks different from Figure 20, you can still perform the rest of the steps. For example, your window might contain a different number of folders and files.

4. In the right pane, double-click the **Sample Music** icon to open the Sample Music folder. The right pane of the window shows the contents of the folder you double-clicked. You can learn more about the contents of a folder by selecting one or more of its files.

5. Click the first file listed in the Sample Music folder to select it. See Figure 21. (Your files might appear in a different order.)

| Figure 21 | Viewing files in a folder window |

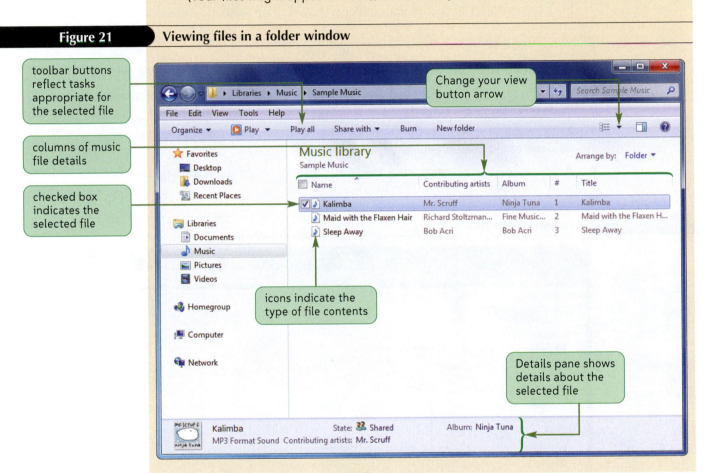

As you open folders and navigate with the Computer window, the contents of the toolbar change so that they are appropriate for your current task. In Figure 21, the toolbar lists actions to take with the selected music file, such as Play all and Burn.

Elena mentions that you can change the appearance of folder windows to suit your preferences, which you'll do next.

Changing the View

Windows 7 provides at least eight ways to view the contents of a folder—Extra Large Icons, Large Icons, Medium Icons, Small Icons, List, Details, Tiles, and Content. The default view is Details view, which displays a small icon and lists details about each file. The icon provides a visual cue about the file type. Although only Details view lists all file details, such as the contributing artists and album title for music files, you can see these details in any other view by pointing to an icon to display a ScreenTip.

To practice switching from one view to another, Elena says you can display the contents of the Sample Music folder in Tiles view. To do so, you'll use the Change your view button on the toolbar.

To view files in Tiles view:

1. In the Sample Music folder window, click the **Change your view button arrow** on the toolbar. See Figure 22.

   Trouble? If you click the Change your view button instead of the arrow, you cycle through the views. Click the Change your view button arrow , and then continue with Step 2.

Figure 22   **Preparing to change views**

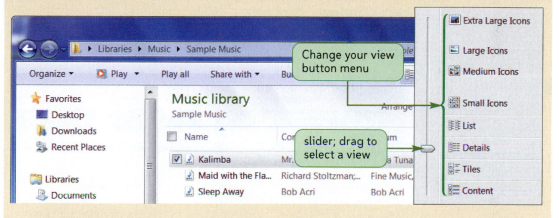

2. Click **Tiles**. The window shows the same files, but with larger icons than in Details view.

3. Click the **Change your view button arrow** on the toolbar, and then click Details to return to **Details** view.

No matter which view you use, you can sort the file list by filename or another detail, such as size, type, or date. If you're viewing music files, you can sort by details such as contributing artists or album title; and if you're viewing picture files, you can sort by details such as date taken or size. Sorting helps you find a particular file in a long file listing. For example, suppose you want to listen to a song on a certain album, but you can't remember the song title. You can sort the music file list in alphabetic order by album to find the song you want.

To sort the music file list by album:

1. Click the **Album** button at the top of the list of files. The up-pointing arrow in the upper-middle part of the Album button indicates that the files are sorted in ascending (A–Z) alphabetic order by album name.

2. Click the **Album** button again. The down-pointing arrow on the Album button indicates that the sort order is reversed, with the albums listed in descending (Z–A) alphabetic order.

3. Click the **Close** button to close the Sample Music window.

Now Elena says you can compare the Computer window to Windows Explorer, another navigation tool.

Navigating with Windows Explorer

Like the Computer window, Windows Explorer also lets you easily navigate the resources on your computer. All of the techniques you use with the Computer window apply to Windows Explorer—and vice versa. Both let you display and work with files and folders. The only difference is the initial view each tool provides. By default, when you open the Computer window, it shows the drives and devices on your computer. When you start Windows Explorer, it displays the Libraries folder, which lets you access resources such as documents, music, pictures, and videos.

Elena suggests you use both tools to navigate to folders people work with frequently. She also mentions that because people use Windows Explorer often, Windows 7 provides its button on the taskbar for easy access.

To start Windows Explorer:

▶ 1. Click the **Windows Explorer** button 📁 on the taskbar. The Windows Explorer window opens, displaying the contents of the Libraries folder, as shown in Figure 23.

Figure 23   Windows Explorer window

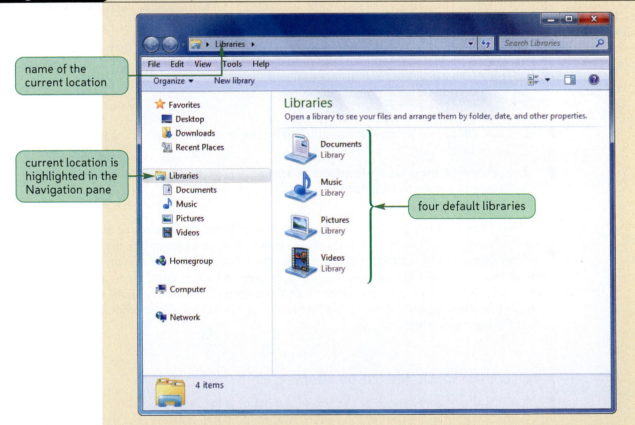

Trouble? If your Windows Explorer window looks slightly different from the one displayed in Figure 23, the configuration of your computer probably differs from the computer used in this figure.

Windows Explorer has the same tools and features you used in the Computer window: the Navigation pane, toolbar, Details pane, and file list in the right pane. The Navigation pane organizes resources into five categories: Favorites (for locations you access frequently), Libraries (for the Windows default libraries), Homegroup (for your shared home network, if any), Computer (for the drives and devices on your computer), and Network (for network locations your computer can access).

When you move the pointer into the Navigation pane, triangles appear next to some icons. An open triangle, or expand icon, ▷ indicates that a folder contains other folders that are not currently displayed in the Navigation pane. Click the triangle to expand the folder and display its subfolders. A filled triangle, or collapse icon, ◢ indicates the folder is expanded, and its subfolders are listed below the folder name. As you saw when working with the Computer window, you can click a folder in the Navigation pane to navigate directly to that folder and display its contents in the right pane.

INSIGHT

Exploring with the Navigation Pane

Using the Navigation pane to explore your computer usually involves clicking expand icons to expand objects and find the folder you want, and then clicking that folder to display its contents in the right pane. To display a list of all the folders on a drive, expand the Computer icon in the Navigation pane, and then expand the icon for the drive, such as Local Disk (C:). The folders list shows the hierarchy of folders on the drive, so you can use it to find and manage your files and folders.

Now you're ready to use the Navigation pane to find and open a folder people use often—the My Documents folder, which is a convenient place to store your documents and other work. The My Documents folder is stored in the Documents library by default.

To open the My Documents folder:

▶ **1.** If necessary, click the **expand** icon ▷ next to Libraries in the Navigation pane to display the four built-in library folders for Documents, Music, Pictures, and Videos. (Your computer might include additional library folders.)

   Trouble? If the expand icon ▷ does not appear next to Libraries in the Navigation pane, the Libraries folder is already expanded. Skip step 1.

▶ **2.** Click the **expand** icon ▷ next to Documents to display the folders in the Documents library. See Figure 24.

Figure 24   **Folders in the Documents library**

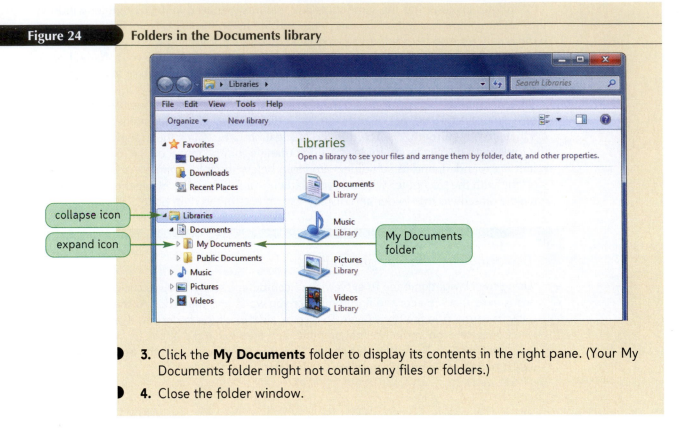

3. Click the **My Documents** folder to display its contents in the right pane. (Your My Documents folder might not contain any files or folders.)

4. Close the folder window.

Getting Help

Windows 7 Help and Support provides on-screen information about the program you are using. Help for the Windows 7 operating system is available by clicking the Start button and then clicking Help and Support on the Start menu.

When you start Help for Windows 7, a Windows Help and Support window opens, which gives you access to Help files stored on your computer as well as Help information stored on the Microsoft Web site. If you are not connected to the Web, you only have access to the Help files stored on your computer.

To start Windows 7 Help:

1. Click the **Start** button 🌀 on the taskbar.
2. Click **Help and Support** in the right pane of the Start menu. The home page of Windows Help and Support opens. See Figure 25. The contents of the home page differ depending on whether you are connected to the Internet.

Figure 25 ▶ **Windows Help and Support window**

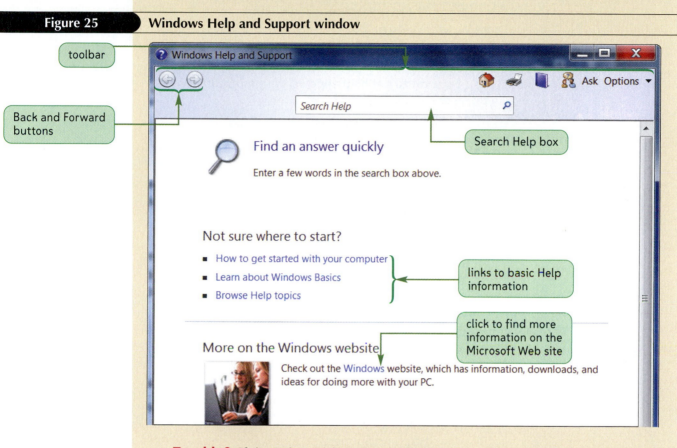

toolbar

Back and Forward buttons

Search Help box

links to basic Help information

click to find more information on the Microsoft Web site

Trouble? If the Help and Support window does not display the information you see in Figure 25, click the Help and Support home button 🏠 on the toolbar at the top of the window to view Help contents.

The home page in Windows Help and Support provides tools for finding answers and other information about Windows 7. To view popular topics, you click a link in the *Find an answer quickly* section of the Windows Help and Support home page. Click a topic to open an article providing detailed information about that topic or instructions for performing a task. You can also use the toolbar to navigate Windows Help and Support. For example, click the Help and Support home button to return to the home page. In addition to buttons providing quick access to pages in Windows Help and Support, you can use the Back button to return to the previous page you viewed. By doing so, you activate the Forward button, which you can click to go to the next page of those you've opened.

Viewing Windows Basics Topics

Windows Help and Support includes instructions on using Help itself. You can learn how to find a Help topic by using the *Learn about Windows Basics* link on the Windows Help and Support home page.

To view Windows Basics topics:

▶ 1. Click **Learn about Windows Basics**. A list of topics related to using Windows 7 appears in the Windows Help and Support window.

▶ 2. Scroll down to the *Help and support* heading, and then click **Getting help**. An article explaining how to get help appears, with the headings in the article listed in the *In this article* section on the right.

▶ 3. Click **Getting help with dialog boxes and windows**. The Windows Help and Support window scrolls to that heading in the article.

▶ 4. Click the **Back** button ⬅ on the toolbar. You return to the previous page you visited, which is the Windows Basics: all topics page. The Forward button is now active.

You can access the full complement of Help pages by using the Contents list.

Selecting a Topic from the Contents List

The Contents list logically organizes all of the topics in Windows Help and Support into topics and categories. In the Contents list, you can click a category to display the titles of related topics. Click a topic to get help about a particular task or feature. For example, you can use the Contents list to learn more about files and folders.

To find a Help topic using the Contents list:

▶ 1. Click the **Help and Support home** button 🔶 on the toolbar to return to the home page for Windows Help and Support.

▶ 2. Click the **Browse Help** button 📘 on the toolbar. A list of categories appears in the Windows Help and Support window.

▶ 3. Click **Files, folders, and libraries** to display the list of topics and other categories related to files, folders, and libraries.

▶ 4. Click the topic **Working with files and folders**. The Windows Help and Support window displays information about that topic.

▶ 5. In the first paragraph below the *Working with files and folders* heading, click the word **icons**, which is green by default. A ScreenTip shows the definition of *icons*.

▶ 6. Click a blank area of the Windows Help and Support window to close the ScreenTip.

Another Help tool is the Search Help box, a popular way to find answers to your Windows 7 questions.

Searching the Help Pages

If you can't find the topic you need by clicking a link or using the toolbar, or if you want to quickly find Help pages related to a particular topic, you can use the Search Help box. Elena provides a typical example. Suppose you want to know how to exit Windows 7, but you don't know if Windows refers to this as exiting, quitting, closing, or shutting down. You can search the Help pages to find just the right topic.

To search the Help pages for information on exiting Windows 7:

▶ **1.** Click in the Search Help box. A blinking insertion point appears.

▶ **2.** Type **shut down** and then press the **Enter** key. A list of Help pages containing the words *shut down* appears in the Windows Help and Support window. See Figure 26. (Your results might differ.)

Figure 26   **Search Help results**

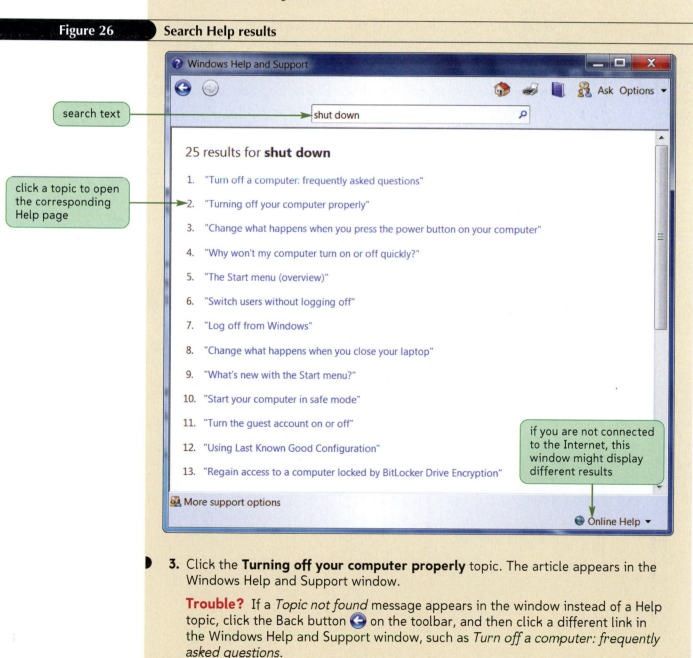

search text

click a topic to open the corresponding Help page

if you are not connected to the Internet, this window might display different results

Windows Help and Support

shut down

25 results for **shut down**

1. "Turn off a computer: frequently asked questions"
2. "Turning off your computer properly"
3. "Change what happens when you press the power button on your computer"
4. "Why won't my computer turn on or off quickly?"
5. "The Start menu (overview)"
6. "Switch users without logging off"
7. "Log off from Windows"
8. "Change what happens when you close your laptop"
9. "What's new with the Start menu?"
10. "Start your computer in safe mode"
11. "Turn the guest account on or off"
12. "Using Last Known Good Configuration"
13. "Regain access to a computer locked by BitLocker Drive Encryption"

More support options

Online Help ▼

▶ **3.** Click the **Turning off your computer properly** topic. The article appears in the Windows Help and Support window.

Trouble? If a *Topic not found* message appears in the window instead of a Help topic, click the Back button ◀ on the toolbar, and then click a different link in the Windows Help and Support window, such as *Turn off a computer: frequently asked questions.*

If this article did not answer your question, you could click the Ask button on the toolbar. Doing so opens a page listing other ways to get Help information.

▶ **4.** Click the **Close** button [X] on the title bar to close the Windows Help and Support window.

Now that you know how Windows 7 Help works, Elena reminds you to use it when you need to perform a new task or when you forget how to complete a procedure.

Turning Off Windows 7

You should always shut down Windows 7 before you turn off your computer. Doing so saves energy, preserves your data and settings, and makes sure your computer starts quickly the next time you use it.

You can turn off Windows 7 using the Shut down button at the bottom of the Start menu. When you click the Shut down button, your computer closes all open programs, including Windows itself, and then completely turns off your computer. For greater flexibility, you can click the arrow on the Shut down button to display a menu of shut down options, including Log off and Sleep. If you choose the Sleep option, Windows saves your work and then turns down the power to your monitor and computer. A light on the outside of your computer case blinks or turns yellow to indicate that the computer is sleeping. Because Windows saves your work, you do not need to close your programs or files before putting your computer to sleep. To wake a desktop computer, you press any key or move the mouse. To wake a notebook computer, you might need to press the hardware power button on your computer case instead. After you wake a computer, the screen looks exactly as it did when you turned off your computer.

> **TIP**
>
> Shutting down does not automatically save your work, so be sure to save your files before clicking the Shut down button.

To turn off Windows 7:

▶ **1.** Click the **Start** button 🟦 on the taskbar.

▶ **2.** Click **Shut down**. Windows 7 displays a message that it is shutting down, and then turns off your computer.

   Trouble? If you are supposed to log off rather than shut down, skip Step 2, click the More Options button [▶] instead, click Log off, and follow your school's logoff procedure.

PROSKILLS

Decision Making: Log Off, Sleep, or Shut Down?

If you are using a computer on the job, your organization probably has a policy about what to do when you're finished working on the computer. If it does not, deciding on the best approach depends on who uses the computer and how long it will be idle. Keep the following guidelines in mind as you make your decision:

- Log off: This command closes all programs and logs you off of Windows 7 but leaves the computer turned on. If another person might use your computer shortly, log off Windows to protect your data and prepare the computer for someone else to use.

- Sleep: By default, Windows 7 is set to sleep after 15–30 minutes of idle time, depending on whether you are using a notebook or desktop computer. Sleep is a low-power state in which Windows saves your work and then turns down the power to your monitor and computer. If you will be away from the computer for more than 15 minutes but less than a day, you can generally let the computer go to sleep on its own.

- Shut down: If your computer is plugged in to a power outlet and you don't plan to use the computer for more than a day, you save wear and tear on your electronic components and conserve energy by shutting down, which ends your Windows 7 session and turns off your computer off. You should also turn off the computer when it is susceptible to electrical damage, such as during a lightning storm, and when you need to install new hardware or disconnect the computer from a power source. If your notebook computer is running on battery power only and you don't plan to use it for more than a few hours, you should also turn it off to save your battery charge.

In this session, you learned how to start and close programs and how to use multiple programs at the same time. You learned how to work with windows and the controls they provide. Finally, you learned how to get help when you need it and how to turn off Windows 7. With Elena's help, you should feel comfortable with the basics of Windows 7 and be prepared to teach Back to Work clients the fundamentals of using this operating system.

Session 2 Quick Check

REVIEW

1. The left pane in a folder window is called the _____, which shows icons and links to other resources your computer can access.
2. True or False. The Music library is a convenient location that Windows provides for storing your music files.
3. Describe two ways to change the view in a folder window.
4. In the Windows Explorer window, what appears in the right pane when you click a folder icon in the left pane?
5. How can you view file details, such as size or date modified, in Large Icons view?
6. The _____ list logically organizes all of the topics in Windows Help and Support into books and pages.
7. How can you quickly find Help pages related to a particular topic in the Windows Help and Support window?
8. Describe what happens when you choose the Sleep option on the Shut down button menu.

Practice the skills you learned in the tutorial using the same case scenario.

PRACTICE

Review Assignments

There are no Data Files needed for the Review Assignments.

The day before your first class teaching Back to Work clients the basics of using Windows 7, Elena Varney offers to observe your tour of the operating system. You'll start working on the Windows 7 desktop, with no windows opened or minimized. Complete the following steps, recording your answers to any questions according to your instructor's preferences:

1. Start Windows 7 and log on, if necessary.
2. Use the mouse to point to each object on your desktop. Record the names and descriptions of each object as they appear in the ScreenTips.
3. Click the Start button. How many menu items or commands are on the Start menu?
4. Start WordPad. How many program buttons are now on the taskbar? (Don't count toolbar buttons, items in the notification area, or the three default taskbar buttons to the right of the Start button.)
5. Start Paint and maximize the Paint window. How many programs are running now?
6. Switch to WordPad. What are two visual cues that tell you that WordPad is the active program?
7. Close WordPad and then click the Restore Down button in the Paint window.
8. Open the Recycle Bin window. Record the number of items it contains. Drag the Recycle Bin window so that you can see it and the Paint window.
9. Close the Paint window from the taskbar. What command did you use?
10. Click the Organize button on the toolbar in the Recycle Bin window. Write down the commands on the menu. Point to Layout, and then click Menu bar to display the menu bar.
11. Use any menu on the Recycle Bin menu bar to open a dialog box. What steps did you perform? What dialog box did you open? For what do you think you use this dialog box? Click Cancel to close the dialog box. Close the Recycle Bin window.
12. Open a folder window, and then open the Public Documents folder from the Navigation pane. Explain how you navigated to this folder.
13. Open a folder in the Videos library and then describe its contents.
14. Change the view of the folder window. What view did you select? Describe the icon(s) in the folder window.
15. Close the folder window, and then open Windows Help and Support.
16. Use the *Learn about Windows Basics* link to learn something new about the Windows 7 desktop. What did you learn? How did you find this topic?
17. Return to the Home page, and then browse Help topics to find information about customizing your computer. How many topics are listed? (*Hint*: Don't include Help categories.) Use the Search Help box to find information about customizing your computer. How many topics are listed?
18. Close Help, and then close any other open windows.
19. Turn off Windows 7 by using the Sleep command, shutting down, or logging off.
20. Submit your answers to the preceding questions to your instructor, either in printed or electronic form, as requested.

Use your skills to explore the contents of a computer for a small electronics business.

APPLY

Case Problem 1

There are no Data Files needed for this Case Problem.

First Call Electronics   First Call Electronics is a small business in Atlanta, Georgia, that provides training and repair services for electronic devices, including computers, cell phones, cameras, and portable music players. Antoine Guillaume runs the training department and has hired you to conduct one-on-one training sessions with new computer users. You are preparing for a visit to a client who wants to determine the contents of his new Windows 7 computer, including sample media files and related programs already provided in folders or menus.

Some of the following steps instruct you to list the contents of windows. Refer to the instructions in the ProSkills exercise at the end of this tutorial if you want to print images of these windows instead. Complete the following steps:

1. Start Windows 7 and log on, if necessary.
2. Open a folder window.
3. List the names of the drives on the computer.
4. Click the Pictures link in the Navigation pane. Does the Pictures library contain any folders? If so, what are the names of the folders?
5. In the Navigation pane, expand the hard disk, such as Local Disk (C:), to display its contents. Navigate the folders on your computer to find the folder displayed in the Pictures library. Where is that folder located in the folder structure of your computer?
6. Open any folder in the Pictures library that contains images. View the files as Extra Large Icons.
7. Navigate to a folder that contains other types of media files, such as music, videos, or recorded TV. Point to a file to display the ScreenTip. What type of file did you select? What details are provided in the ScreenTip?
8. Use the Start menu to display the contents of the Accessories folder in the All Programs list, and then click Getting Started. Describe the contents of the Getting Started window.
9. Close all open windows, and then use the Start menu to open a program that you could use with DVDs. What program did you start?
10. Use the Start menu to open any program you might use with music or sound files. What program did you start?
11. Open Windows Help and Support, and then find and read topics that explain how to use a program you started in a previous step. Explain the purpose of one of the programs.
12. Close all open windows.
13. Submit your answers to the preceding questions to your instructor, either in printed or electronic form, as requested.

Work with Windows 7 on a computer for a catering business.

APPLY

Case Problem 2

There are no Data Files needed for this Case Problem.

East End Catering   After completing culinary school and working as a sous chef for restaurants in Santa Fe, New Mexico, Felicia Makos started a catering company called East End Catering that specializes in dishes that contain organic, locally grown ingredients. So that she can concentrate on cooking and marketing, she hired you to help her perform office tasks as her business grows. She asks you to start by teaching her the basics of using her computer, which runs Windows 7. She especially wants to know which programs are installed on her computer and what they do.

Some of the following steps instruct you to list the contents of windows and menus. Refer to the instructions in the ProSkills exercise at the end of this tutorial if you want to print images of these windows instead. Complete the following steps:

1. Open the Start menu and write down the programs listed in the left pane.
2. Start one of the programs in the left pane and then describe what it does. Close the program.
3. Open the Start menu, display the All Programs list, and then open the Accessories folder. Examine the list of programs in the Accessories folder and its subfolders, and then close the Start menu.

⊕ **EXPLORE**

4. Click the Start button, and then start typing the name of a program you noted in a previous step. Describe what happens.
5. Use Windows Help and Support to research one of the programs you examined in the previous step, such as Calculator or Notepad. Describe the purpose of the program and how to perform a task using that program.
6. Use the Search Help box in Windows Help and Support to list all the Help topics related to the program you researched in the previous step. How many topics are displayed in the results?

⊕ **EXPLORE**

7. Start the program you researched. Click the Help button on the program's menu bar, and then explore the Help topics. Open and read a Help topic in the program.
8. Find a similar topic in Windows Help and Support, and then read that topic. Compare these topics to the ones included in the Windows Help and Support window.
9. Close all open windows.
10. Submit your answers to the preceding questions to your instructor, either in printed or electronic form, as requested.

Extend what you've learned to customize folder windows.

CHALLENGE

Case Problem 3

There are no Data Files needed for this Case Problem.

Friedman Alternatives   Warren Friedman recently started his own small firm called Friedman Alternatives, which analyzes and recommends sources of alternative energy for various manufacturing businesses. Most of these businesses want to cut their expenses related to energy, and are interested in helping to conserve fuel and preserve the environment. Warren typically uses the Windows Explorer window to work with his files, but suspects he is not taking full advantage of its features. As his new special-projects employee, he asks you to show him around the Windows 7 folder windows and demonstrate how to customize their appearance. Complete the following steps:

1. Start Windows Explorer. Click the Organize button on the Windows Explorer toolbar, and write down any commands that seem related to changing the appearance of the window.

⊕ **EXPLORE**   2. Select a command that lays out the Windows Explorer window so that it displays a single pane for viewing files. What command did you select? Restore the window to its original condition.

3. Navigate to the Pictures library and display its contents. Double-click the Sample Pictures folder to open it. (If your computer does not contain a Sample Pictures folder, open any folder that displays pictures.) Display the icons using Large Icons view.

4. Change the view to Content view. Describe the differences between Large Icons and Content view.

⊕ **EXPLORE**   5. Click the Slide show button on the toolbar. Describe what happens, and then press the Esc key.

6. With the Details pane open, click a picture file. Describe the contents of the Details pane. Also identify the buttons on the toolbar.

⊕ **EXPLORE**   7. Repeatedly click the Change your view button to cycle from one view to another. Describe the changes in the window.

8. Display the window in Details view.

⊕ **EXPLORE**   9. On the Organize button menu, click Folder and search options to open the Folder Options dialog box. Select the option that shows all folders in the Navigation pane, and then click the OK button. Describe the changes in the Sample Pictures window.

⊕ **EXPLORE**   10. Open the Folder Options dialog box again, click the Restore Defaults button, and then click the OK button.

11. Open the Windows Help and Support window and search for information about folder options. Find a topic explaining how to show hidden files. Explain how to do so.

12. Close all open windows.

13. Submit the results of the preceding steps to your instructor, either in printed or electronic form, as requested.

Use the Internet to provide information to an import/export company.

RESEARCH

Case Problem 4

There are no Data Files needed for this Case Problem.

Majolica Imports   After moving from southern France to New York City, Marie and Bruno Tattinger decided to start a company that imports hand-painted French and Italian ceramics. Both Marie and Bruno travel frequently, and they use laptop computers running Windows 7 to manage their business when they are on the move. They have hired you as a consultant to help them use and maintain their computers. Marie asks you to help her research wireless networks so she can set up a wireless network at home and in their office. You suggest starting with Windows Help and Support, and then expanding to the Internet to search for the latest information. Complete the following steps:

1. In Windows Help and Support, find information about the hardware Marie needs to set up a wireless network.
2. Use the Ask button to visit the Microsoft Web site to obtain more information about wireless networks.
3. Choose a topic that describes how to set up a wireless network for a home or small office, and then read the topic thoroughly.
4. On the Microsoft Web site, search for information about adding a Bluetooth device to the network.
5. Write one to two pages for Marie and Bruno explaining what equipment they need to set up a wireless network and the steps they should perform. Also explain how they can add their Bluetooth mobile phones to the network.
6. Submit the results of the preceding steps to your instructor, either in printed or electronic form, as requested.

ENDING DATA FILES

There are no ending Data Files needed for this tutorial.

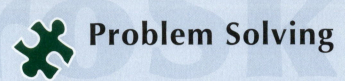

Problem Solving

Gathering Information to Solve Potential Computer Problems

When you solve problems, you work through a series of stages to gather information about the problem and its possible solutions. Problem solving in general involves the following tasks:

1. Recognize and define the problem.
2. Determine possible courses of action.
3. Collect information needed to evaluate alternative courses of action.
4. Evaluate each alternative's merits and drawbacks.
5. Select an alternative.
6. Implement the decision.
7. Monitor and evaluate performance to provide feedback and take corrective action.

If you are involved in solving a complex problem with many possible causes, you perform all seven steps in the process. If you are solving a simpler problem or have limited time to explore solutions, you can condense the steps. For example, you might recognize the problem in one step, determine possible actions, evaluate and select an alternative in the next step, and then implement and evaluate your decision in another step.

Recognize and Define the Problem

A problem is an obstacle that prevents you from reaching a goal. This definition is especially fitting for work with a computer. For example, suppose your goal is to create a report containing text and graphics, but you don't know which program to use. In this case, your lack of familiarity with the programs on your computer is an obstacle preventing you from reaching your goal of efficiently creating a report with text and graphics.

After identifying a simple problem such as which computer program to use, you can focus on solutions. Start by considering any possible solution. For example, start each program on your computer related to text and graphics and examine its features. Next, compare and evaluate those alternatives. Which programs help you meet your goal most effectively? Select the best solution and then try it, observing the results to make sure it actually solves the problem. Can you efficiently create the report with the program you selected? If not, try a different program until you find the best possible solution.

ProSkills

Anticipate Computer Problems

Even if you are familiar with some features of Windows 7 or regularly use your computer for certain tasks, such as accessing Web sites or exchanging e-mail, take some time to explore the basics of Windows 7 on your computer. To solve system problems that might occur later, you should capture and save images of your current desktop, the Start menu, and other resources on your computer. You can save these images for reference if you experience problems with your computer later or want to restore these settings.

To save screen images:

1. Start Paint, and then minimize the program window.
2. Open the window you want to preserve or arrange the desktop as you want it. If you want to capture a window, make sure that window is the active window.
3. Hold down the Alt key and press the Print Screen key. (The Print Screen key might be labeled *PrtScn* or something similar on your keyboard.) Pressing this key combination captures an image of the active window. To capture an image of everything shown on the screen, press the Print Screen key without holding down the Alt key.
4. Restore the Paint program window, and then press the Ctrl+V keys to paste the image in the Paint program window.
5. Click the Save button on the Quick Access Toolbar to open the Save As dialog box. By default, Paint saves images in the My Pictures folder in the Pictures library. Use the Navigation pane to navigate to a different folder, if necessary. Type a filename, and then press the Save button to save the screen image.
6. To print the screen images, click the Paint menu button, and then click Print to open the Print dialog box. Select your printer and other settings, and then click the Print button.
7. To open a new window for the next screen image, click the Paint menu button, and then click New.

Now you can explore Windows 7 on your computer and preserve screen images, which will help you solve computer problems:

1. Start Windows 7 and log on, if necessary.
2. Save and print images of your current desktop, the Start menu, the Computer window showing the drives on your computer, and your Documents folder.
3. Open a folder in the Documents library that you are likely to use often. Make sure the Navigation pane shows the location of this folder on your computer. Capture and save an image of this window.
4. To learn more about the programs that are included with Windows 7 and how they can help you solve problems, start at least two accessory programs that are new to you. Open a menu in each program, and then capture and save the image of each program window.
5. Using the Ribbon, toolbar, or menu bar in the new programs, find a dialog box in each program that you are likely to use. Capture and save images of the dialog boxes.

ProSkills

6. Explore both programs to determine how they might help you solve problems related to using your computer, completing your school work, or performing on the job.

7. Use Windows Help and Support to find information about a feature in one program that can help you solve problems. Choose an appropriate topic. Print an image of the Windows Help and Support window displaying information about this topic.

8. Close all open windows, and then shut down or log off Windows.

Glossary/Index

Note: Boldface entries include definitions.

Special Characters

* (asterisk), AC 167, AC 168
= (equal sign), AC 365
! (exclamation point), AC 167
- (hyphen), AC 167
(number sign), AC 167
+ (plus sign), AC 103
? (question mark), AC 167
"" (quotation marks), AC 455
[] (square brackets), AC 167

A

ACCDE file A special version of an Access database that runs as a normal database, but its VBA code can't be viewed or edited. Also, you can't view, modify, or create forms, reports, or modules in Design view, and you can't import or export forms, reports, or modules. The ACCDE file has an .accde extension instead of the usual .accdb extension. AC 647–648

Access. *See* Microsoft Office Access 2007

Access Options dialog box, AC 645–646

Access window. *See* Microsoft Access window

action An instruction to Access to perform an operation. AC 492–493
    adding to macros, AC 495–498
    adding to macros by dragging, AC 501–503
    arguments, AC 508–509

Action column A column in the Macro window in which you select the actions you want Access to perform. AC 496

action query A query that adds, changes, or deletes multiple table records at a time. AC 442

active program The program you are currently working with. WIN7 15

Add New Field column The datasheet column in Access in which you create a field for a table. AC 8

Address bar The bar at the top of a folder window that shows the location of the current window. WIN7 27, WIN7 29, WIN7 30
    exploring files and folders, FM 6

Advanced Filter/Sort A form and datasheet tool that lets you specify multiple selection criteria and specify a sort order for selected records in the Filter window, in the same way you specify record selection criteria and sort orders for a query in Design view. AC 606

Aero, WIN7 7

Aero Flip 3D (Flip 3D) A feature available in the Aero experience that displays all your open windows in a three-dimensional stack so you can see the windows from the side. WIN7 15

AfterUpdate event An event that occurs after changed data in a control or a record is updated. AC 561, AC 568

aggregate function A function that performs an arithmetic operation on selected records in a database. AC 137–141
    creating queries, AC 139–140
    record group calculations, AC 140–141
    Total row, AC 137–138

All Programs list, WIN7 9

All Tables The default group of objects in the Access Navigation Pane. AC 142

All Tables view The default view in the Navigation Pane in Access, which displays objects grouped according to the tables in the database. AC 33

Allow Default Shortcut Menus property A database property that specifies whether shortcut menus are enabled or disabled. AC 643

Allow Full Menus property A database property that specifies whether all options are available on the Ribbon. AC 643

Allow Zero Length property A property that allows you to store a zero length string value in a field when the property is set to Yes. AC 627

Alternate Fill/Back Color button The Access button that lets you change the alternating background colors of a datasheet. AC 124–125

alternate key A candidate key that was not chosen to be the primary key. AC A3

ampersand (&) operator A concatenation operator that joins text expressions. AC 211, AC 213

Anchor property A form control property that automatically resizes a control and places the control in the same relative position on the screen as the screen size and resolution change. AC 277–278

And logical operator The logical operator you use in a query when you want a record selected only if two or more conditions are met. AC 128, AC 129–130, AC 132

anomalies Undesirable irregularities of tables caused by data redundancy and by partial and transitive dependencies. Anomalies are of three types: insertion, deletion, and update. AC A14

Append Only property A field property for a Memo field that lets you edit the field value and, when set to Yes, causes Access to keep a historical record of all versions of the field value. You can view each version of the field value, along with a date and time stamp of when each version change occurred. AC 246

append query A query that adds selected fields in records from existing tables or queries to the end of another table. AC 442, AC 447–450

Applicable Filter dialog box, AC 612

application Software that a computer uses to complete tasks; also called a program. WIN7 6

application settings The most common program options. OFF 18

Application Title property A database property that specifies the name for a database that appears in the Access window title bar. AC 642

argument A value passed to a procedure and used in place of a parameter when the procedure is executed. AC 496, AC 569

Arguments column A column in the Macro window that displays the argument settings for an action. AC 496

artificial key A field that you add to a table to serve solely as the primary key and that is visible to users. AC A20–A21

assignment statement A statement that assigns the value of an expression to a field, control, or property. AC 566

asterisk (*), wildcard character, AC 167, AC 168

Attachment data type A data type used to attach one or more files to a table record. Access stores the attachments in compressed form to minimize file size and maximize disk space usage. AC 49, AC 622–625

Attachments dialog box, AC 624

attribute The formal term for a column in a relation (table). AC A2

AutoFilter An Access feature that enables you to quickly sort and display field values in various ways. AC 112
    filtering data, AC 209–211
    sorting data, AC 112–115
    table datasheets, AC 606–607

AutoFormat A predefined style that you can apply to a form or report. AC 156, AC 317
    changing in Layout view, AC 157–159

AutoNumber An Access data type that automatically assigns a unique number to a record. AC 10, AC 49, AC 625–627

Average function, AC 137

B

back-end database A database that contains the tables that are needed for an application. AC 636–637

background color, datasheet rows, changing, AC 124–125

backing up Making a copy of a database file to protect your database against loss or damage. AC 35

backup A duplicate copy of important files that you need. FM 5

BCNF. *See* Boyce-Codd normal form

Beep action, AC 493

BeforeUpdate event An event that occurs before changed data in a control or a record is updated. AC 561, AC 579

best fit Sizing a column so the column is just wide enough to display the longest visible value in the column, including the field name. AC 81

bound control A control that is connected, or bound, to a field in the database based on the record source, or the underlying table or query, and that is used to display and maintain a table field value. AC 283

bound form A form that has a table or query as its record source and is used for maintaining and displaying table data. AC 282

Boyce-Codd normal form (BCNF) A second normal form table is in Boyce-Codd normal form if every determinant is a candidate key. BCNF is also called third normal form in this book, although BCNF is an improvement over the original version of third normal form. AC A18

bubble diagram A diagram that graphically shows a table's functional dependencies and determinants. Also known as a data model diagram and a functional dependency diagram. AC A12

Task Reference

TASK	PAGE #	RECOMMENDED METHOD
Access, start	AC 5	Click 🪟, click All Programs, click Microsoft Office, click Microsoft Office Access 2007
Action, add by dragging	AC 501	*See* Reference Window: Creating an Action by Dragging
Action, add to macro	AC 497	In the Macro window, click the Action arrow, click the action
Aggregate functions, use in a datasheet	AC 138	Open table or query in Datasheet view, in Records group on Home tab click Totals button, click Total field row, click function
Aggregate functions, use in a query	AC 139	Display the query in Design view, click Totals button in the Show/Hide group on the Query Tools Design tab
Append query, create	AC 447	*See* Reference Window: Creating an Append Query
AutoFilter, use in a table or query datasheet	AC 209	Click arrow on column heading, click filter option
AutoFormat, change	AC 157	*See* Reference Window: Changing a Form's AutoFormat
Caption, change for a form's navigation bar	AC 411	Click the form selector, open the property sheet, type the value in the Navigation Caption text box, press Enter
Caption, change for a label	AC 292	*See* Reference Window: Changing a Label's Caption
Calculated field, add to a query	AC 133	*See* Reference Window: Using Expression Builder
Chart, edit with Microsoft Graph	AC 417	In Design view, right-click the chart's edge, point to Chart Object, click Open, make desired changes, click File, click Exit & Return
Chart, embed in a form	AC 414	*See* Reference Window: Embedding a Chart in a Form
Color, change an object's background	AC 318	Click the object, click the arrow for 🪣, click the desired color
Column, resize width in a datasheet	AC 12	Double-click ↔ on the right border of the column heading
Combo box, add to a form	AC 299	*See* Reference Window: Adding a Combo Box to Find Records
Command button, add to a form	AC 512	Click Design tab, make sure 🪄 is not selected, click Button tool in Controls group, position the pointer in the form, click the mouse button
Command button, add to a form using Control Wizards	AC 527	*See* Reference Window: Adding a Command Button to a Form Using Control Wizards
Compressed files, extract	FM 18	Right-click compressed folder, click Extract All, select location, click Extract
Compressed folder, create	FM 17	Right-click a blank area of a folder window, point to New, click Compressed (zipped) Folder
Computer window, open	WIN7 29	Click 🪟, click Computer
Control, anchor in a form	AC 277	In Layout view, select the control(s) to anchor, click Arrange tab, click Anchoring button in Position group, click option in gallery
Control, apply special effect	AC 317	Select the control, click the arrow for ▭, click the special effect
Control, delete	AC 289	Right-click the control, click Delete
Control, move in a form	AC 285	*See* Reference Window: Selecting and Moving Controls
Control, resize in a form	AC 289	*See* Reference Window: Resizing a Control
Control, select	AC 285	*See* Reference Window: Selecting and Moving Controls
Control layout, remove control from in a form	AC 276	In Layout view, click ✛, select the control, click Arrange tab, click Remove button in Control Layout Group

TASK	PAGE #	RECOMMENDED METHOD
Control tip property, set for a form control	AC 312	In Layout view, right-click the control, click Properties, click Other tab, type the tip in the ControlTip Text property, press Enter
Controls, align selected	AC 287	Right-click one of the selected controls, point to Align, click desired alignment
Crosstab query, create	AC 219	*See* Reference Window: Using the Crosstab Query Wizard
CSV file, import as an Access table	AC 395	*See* Reference Window: Importing a CSV File as an Access Table
Data, find	AC 166	*See* Reference Window: Finding Data in a Form or Datasheet
Data, group in a report	AC 356	*See* Reference Window: Sorting and Grouping Data in a Report
Data, sort in a report	AC 356	*See* Reference Window: Sorting and Grouping Data in a Report
Database, compact and repair	AC 34	*See* Reference Window: Compacting and Repairing a Database
Database, compact on close	AC 34	Click (icon), click Access Options, click Current Database, click Compact on Close
Database, compile	AC 578	Click Debug, click Compile *database name*
Database, create a blank	AC 6	Start Access, click Blank Database, type the database name, select the drive and folder, click OK, click Create
Database, decrypt	AC 641	*See* Reference Window: Unsetting a Database Password
Database, encrypt	AC 639	*See* Reference Window: Encrypting a Database and Setting a Password
Database, open	AC 20	*See* Reference Window: Opening a Database
Database, split	AC 637	*See* Reference Window: Using the Database Splitter
Database, save as a previous version	AC 627	Open the database to save and close all open objects, click (icon), point to Save As, click the desired Access format, enter the database name, click Save
Database, save as an ACCDE file	AC 647	Open the database, click Database Tools tab, click Make ACCDE button in Database Tools group, type database name, select the destination folder, click Save
Database documentation, set	AC 644	*See* Reference Window: Setting Database Documentation Properties
Database properties, set	AC 642	*See* Reference Window: Setting the Database Properties and Startup Options
Datasheet view for tables, switch to	AC 77	In the Views group on the Table Tools Design tab, click View button
Date and time, add to a report	AC 366	*See* Reference Window: Adding the Date and Time to a Report
Delete query, create	AC 450	*See* Reference Window: Creating a Delete Query
Design view, switch to	AC 65	In Views group on Home tab, click View button arrow, click Design View
Documenter, use	AC 267	*See* Reference Window: Using the Documenter
Duplicate values, hide	AC 363	*See* Reference Window: Hiding Duplicate Values in a Report
Event procedure, add	AC 576	*See* Reference Window: Adding an Event Procedure to a Form or Report
Event procedure, display an existing	AC 564	Open the property sheet for the control, click Event tab, click the event property box, click (icon)
Excel worksheet, link data from	AC 429	Click External Data tab, click Excel button in Import group, click Browse, select the workbook, click Open, click Link to the data source by creating a linked table, click OK, follow the steps in the Link Spreadsheet Wizard
Export steps, save	AC 407	Click Save export steps check box in Export dialog box, click Save Export

TASK	PAGE #	RECOMMENDED METHOD
Field, add to a form or report	AC 283	In Design view, click Add Existing Fields button in Tools group, click the record source, double-click the field
Field, add to a table	AC 63	*See* Reference Window: Adding a Field Between Two Existing Fields
Field, define in a table	AC 55	*See* Reference Window: Defining a Field in Design View
Field, delete from a table	AC 74	*See* Reference Window: Deleting a Field from a Table Structure
Field, move to a new location in a table	AC 78	Display the table in Design view, click the field's row selector, drag the field with the pointer
Field property change, update	AC 77	Click 🗒 ▾, select option for updating field property
File, attach to a record using an Attachment field	AC 624	Right-click the record's Attachment field, click Manage Attachments, click Add, select the file to attach, click Open, click OK
File, close	OFF 21	Click 🗐, click Close
File, copy	FM 14	*See* Reference Window: Copying a File or Folder
File, delete	FM 16	Right-click the file, click Delete
File, detach from a record's Attachment field	AC 624	Right-click the record's Attachment field, click Manage Attachments, select the file to detach, click Remove, click OK
File, export from a record's Attachment field	AC 624	Right-click the record's Attachment field, click Manage Attachments, select the file to export, click Save As, type the filename and choose the destination folder, click Save, click OK
File, move	FM 12	*See* Reference Window: Moving a File or Folder
File, open	OFF 22	*See* Reference Window: Opening an Existing File or Creating a New File
File, open from a record's Attachment field	AC 624	Right-click the record's Attachment field, click Manage Attachments, select the file to open, click Open
File, print	OFF 27	*See* Reference Window: Printing a File
File, rename	FM 16	Right-click the file, click Rename, type the new name, press Enter
File, save	OFF 18	*See* Reference Window: Saving a File
File, switch between open	OFF 5	Click the taskbar button for the file you want to make active
Files, compress	FM 17	Drag files into a compressed folder
Filter, apply to a form from a saved query	AC 612	*See* Reference Window: Applying a Filter Saved as a Query
Filter, save as a query	AC 610	*See* Reference Window: Saving a Filter as a Query
Filter By Form, use to select records	AC 608	*See* Reference Window: Selecting Records Using Filter By Form
Filter By Selection, activate	AC 116	*See* Reference Window: Using Filter By Selection
Find duplicates query, create	AC 226	*See* Reference Window: Using the Find Duplicates Query Wizard
Find unmatched query, create	AC 227	*See* Reference Window: Using the Find Unmatched Query Wizard
Folder, copy	FM 14	*See* Reference Window: Copying a File or Folder
Folder, create	FM 11	*See* Reference Window: Creating a Folder
Folder, move	FM 12	*See* Reference Window: Moving a File or Folder
Folder, rename	FM 16	Right-click the folder, click Rename, type the new name, press Enter
Folder, sort files in	WIN7 31	In a folder window, click a column heading (button)
Folder list, expand	WIN7 33	Click ▷
Folder or drive contents, view in Windows Explorer	FM 7–8	Click ▷

TASK	PAGE #	RECOMMENDED METHOD
Font size, select in WordPad	WIN7 23	In the Font group on the Home tab, click 11 ▾, type text
Form, create a custom	AC 282	*See* Reference Window: Creating a Form in Design View
Form, create using the Datasheet tool	AC 270	Select record source in Navigation Pane, click Create tab, click More Forms button in Forms group, click Datasheet
Form, create using the Multiple Items tool	AC 271	Select record source in Navigation Pane, click Create tab, click Multiple Items button in Forms group
Form, create using the Split Form tool	AC 273	Select record source in Navigation Pane, click Create tab, click Split Form button in Forms group
Form, select in Design view	AC 299	Click the form selector
Form Footer, add	AC 296	*See* Reference Window: Adding and Removing Form Header and Form Footer Sections
Form Footer, remove	AC 296	*See* Reference Window: Adding and Removing Form Header and Form Footer Sections
Form Header, add	AC 296	*See* Reference Window: Adding and Removing Form Header and Form Footer Sections
Form Header, remove	AC 296	*See* Reference Window: Adding and Removing Form Header and Form Footer Sections
Form Wizard, activate	AC 172	Click Create tab, click More Forms button in Forms group, click Form Wizard, choose the table or query for the form, select fields, click Next
Function, create	AC 569	Enter function statements in the Code window
Help, find topic in Windows 7	WIN7 35	Click 🪟, click Help and Support, click in the Search Help box, type a word or phrase, press Enter
Help, start in Windows 7	WIN7 34	*See* Reference box: Starting Windows Help and Support
Help task pane, use	OFF 24	*See* Reference Window: Getting Help
HTML document, export a query as	AC 391	*See* Reference Window: Exporting an Access Query to an HTML Document
Import steps, save	AC 402	Click Save import steps check box in Import dialog box, click Save Import
Index, create	AC 476	*See* Reference Window: Creating an Index
Index, view a table's existing	AC 474	*See* Reference Window: Viewing a Table's Existing Indexes
Input Mask Wizard, activate	AC 235	Click the field's Input Mask text box, click ⋯ , specify your choices in the Input Mask Wizard dialog boxes
Legend, add to PivotChart	AC 427	Click Design tab, click Legend button in Show/Hide group
Line, add to a form or report	AC 315	*See* Reference Window: Adding a Line to a Form or Report
Linked Table Manager, use	AC 632	*See* Reference Window: Using the Linked Table Manager
List box, add to a form	AC 518	*See* Reference Window: Adding a List Box to a Form
Lookup field, change to Text field	AC 265	Display the table in Design view, select the field, click the Lookup tab, set the Display Control property to Text Box
Lookup field, create	AC 231	Click the Data Type arrow, click Lookup Wizard, specify your choices in the Lookup Wizard dialog boxes
Macro, add to a macro group	AC 510	*See* Reference Window: Adding a Macro to a Macro Group
Macro, attach to a command button	AC 513	Open the property sheet for the command button, click the right side of the event property box, click the macro name

TASK	PAGE #	RECOMMENDED METHOD
Macro, create	AC 500	*See* Reference Window: Creating a Macro
Macro, run from the Macro window	AC 494	Click Design tab, click Run button in Tools group
Macro, run from the Navigation Pane	AC 494	Right-click the macro name in the Macros group, click Run
Macro, single step	AC 499	*See* Reference Window: Single Stepping a Macro
Macro group, create	AC 533	*See* Reference Window: Creating a Macro Group
Mailing labels, create	AC 373	*See* Reference Window: Creating Mailing Labels and Other Labels
Make-table query, create	AC 443	*See* Reference Window: Creating a Make-Table Query
Memo field, change properties of	AC 245	Display the table in Design view, select the memo field, click the Text Format property or click the Append Only property
Module, create	AC 568	*See* Reference Window: Creating a New Standard Module
Module, save	AC 572	Click 💾 on the Quick Access Toolbar, type macro name, press Enter
Multiple-column report, modify	AC 376	In Design view, click Page Setup tab, click Page Setup button, click the Columns tab, set the column options, click OK
Multivalued field, create in a table	AC 617	In Design view, enter the field name, choose the Lookup Wizard data type, select the method for looking up field values and choose the appropriate Lookup Wizard options, select the Allow Multiple Values check box, finish the Lookup Wizard
Music library, open	WIN7 29	In a folder window, click Music in the Navigation pane
My Documents folder, open	WIN7 32	In a folder window, click ▷ next to Libraries, click ▷ next to Documents, click My Documents
Object, open	AC 17	Double-click object in Navigation Pane
Object, save	AC 16	Click 💾, type the object name, click OK
Object dependencies, identify	AC 239	Click Database Tools tab, click Object Dependencies button in Show/Hide group, click the object, click ➕
Office program, start	OFF 3	*See* Reference Window: Starting Office Programs
Overlapping windows, change to	AC 517	Click 🔘, click Access Options, in the left section click Current Database, click the Overlapping Windows option button, click OK
Padding, change in a form control	AC 277	In Layout view, click the control, click Arrange tab, click Control Padding button, click the desired setting
Page numbers, add to a report	AC 368	*See* Reference Window: Adding Page Numbers to a Report
Parameter query, create	AC 215	*See* Reference Window: Creating a Parameter Query
Password, set a database	AC 639	*See* Reference Window: Encrypting a Database and Setting a Password
Password, unset a database	AC 641	*See* Reference Window: Unsetting a Database Password
Performance Analyzer, use	AC 628	*See* Reference Window: Using the Performance Analyzer
Picture, add to or change on a command button	AC 513	Open the property sheet for the command button, click the Picture box, click ▣, select the picture, click OK
Picture, insert in a form	AC 184	In Layout view, in Controls group on Form Layout Tools Format tab, click Logo button, select the picture file, click OK
Picture caption, add to a command button	AC 513	Open the property sheet for the command button, click the Caption box, press F2, type desired caption
Picture caption, change location of on a command button	AC 513	Open the property sheet for the command button, click the Picture Caption Arrangement arrow, click the desired location

TASK	PAGE #	RECOMMENDED METHOD
PivotChart, add to a table or query	AC 426	Open the table or query in Datasheet view, right-click the object tab, click PivotChart View, drag the fields from the Field List pane into the PivotChart
PivotTable, add a total field	AC 424	Click a detail field's column heading, click Design tab, click AutoCalc button in Tools group, click an aggregate option
PivotTable, add to a table or query	AC 422	Open the table or query in Datasheet view, right-click the object tab, click PivotTable View, drag the fields from the Field List pane into the PivotTable
PivotTable, show or hide details	AC 425	Click Design tab, click Show Details or Hide Details in Show/Hide group
Primary key, specify	AC 61	See Reference Window: Specifying a Primary Key in Design View
Procedure, test in the Immediate Window	AC 573	See Reference Window: Testing a Procedure in the Immediate Window
Print Preview, close in WordPad	WIN7 25	In the Close group on the Print preview tab, click Close print preview
Print Preview, open in WordPad	WIN7 25	Click [icon], point to Print, click Print preview
Program, close in Windows 7	WIN7 14	Click [icon]
Program, close inactive in Windows 7	WIN7 17	Right-click the program button on the taskbar, click Close window
Program, Office, exit	OFF 28	Click [icon] on the title bar
Program, start in Windows 7	WIN7 12	See Reference box: Starting a Program
Programs, Office, open	OFF 3	See Reference Window: Starting Office Programs
Programs, switch between open	OFF 5	Click the taskbar button for the program you want to make active
Property sheet, open	AC 136	Right-click the object or control, click Properties
Property sheet, open or close for a form or report control	AC 214	Select the control, click Design tab, click Property Sheet button in Show/Hide group
Query datasheet, sort	AC 114	See Reference Window: Sorting a Query Datasheet
Query, define	AC 120	Click Create tab, click Query Design button in Other group
Query, run	AC 121	Double-click query in Navigation Pane or, in Results group on Query Tools Design tab, click Run button
Query results, sort	AC 114	See Reference Window: Sorting a Query Datasheet
Record, add a new one	AC 16	In Records group on Home tab, click New button
Record, delete	AC 102	See Reference Window: Deleting a Record
Record, move to first	AC 23	Click [icon]
Record, move to last	AC 23	Click [icon]
Record, move to next	AC 23	Click [icon]
Record, move to previous	AC 23	Click [icon]
Records, print selected in a form	AC 171	Click [icon], point to Print, click Print, click Selected Record(s), click OK
Records, redisplay all after filter	AC 118	In Sort & Filter group on Home tab, click Toggle Filter button
Rectangle, add to a form or report	AC 316	See Reference Window: Adding a Rectangle to a Form or Report
Recycle Bin, open	WIN7 9	Double-click the Recycle Bin icon on the desktop
Report, create a custom	AC 353	See Reference Window: Creating a Blank Report in Layout View
Report, filter in Report view	AC 335	Right-click the value to filter, point to Text Filters, click filter option
Report, select and copy data in Report view	AC 337	Click the top of the selection, drag to the end of the selection, click Home tab, click [icon] in Clipboard group

TASK	PAGE #	RECOMMENDED METHOD
Report, print all	AC 32	*See* Reference Window: Printing a Report
Report, print specific pages of	AC 187–188	Click Print Preview tab, click Print button in Print group, click Pages, enter number of pages to print in From and To boxes, click OK
Report Wizard, activate	AC 177	Click Create tab, click Report Wizard button in Reports group, choose the table or query for the report, select fields, click Next
Saved export, run	AC 407	Click External Data tab, click Saved Exports button in Export group, click the saved export, click Run
Saved import, run	AC 402	Click External Data tab, click Saved Imports button in Import group, click the saved import, click Run
Self-join, create	AC 469	*See* Reference Window: Creating a Self-Join
Sort, specify ascending in datasheet	AC 113	Click column heading arrow, click Sort A to Z
Sort, specify descending in datasheet	AC 113	Click column heading arrow, click Sort Z to A
Spacing, change in a form control	AC 277	In Layout view, click the control, click Arrange tab, click Control Margins button in Control Layout group, click the desired setting
SQL statement, use for a list box	AC 523	Open the property sheet for the list box, right-click the Row Source box, click Zoom, enter the SQL statement, click OK
SQL statement, view	AC 521	*See* Reference Window: Viewing an SQL Statement for a Query
Start menu, open in Windows 7	WIN7 8	Click 🪟
Startup options, set for a database	AC 642	*See* Reference Window: Setting the Database Properties and Startup Options
Subform, open in a new window	AC 305	Right-click the subform, click Subform in New Window
Subform/Subreport Wizard, activate	AC 302	Make sure 🔧 is selected, click 📊, click in the grid at the upper-left corner for the subform/subreport
Switchboard Manager, activate	AC 537	Click Database Tools tab, click Switchboard Manager button in Database Tools group
Tab Control, add to a form	AC 409	Click Design tab, click Tab Control button in Controls group, click in the grid at the upper-left corner for the tab control
Tab order, change in a form	AC 313	In Design view, click Arrange tab, click Tab Order button in Control Layout group, drag the rows into the desired order, click OK
Tab Stop property, change for a form control	AC 312	In Layout view, right-click the control, click Properties, click Other tab, set the Tab Stop property
Tabbed documents, change to	AC 517	Click 🗄️, click Access Options, in the left section click Current Database, click Tabbed Documents option button, click OK
Table, analyze	AC 399	Select the table, click Database Tools tab, click Analyze Table button in Analyze group
Table, create in a database in Datasheet view	AC 8	*See* Reference Window: Creating a Table in Datasheet View
Table, link to in another Access database	AC 631	*See* Reference Window: Linking to a Table in Another Access Database
Table, open in a database	AC 17	Double-click table in Navigation Pane
Table, save in a database	AC 15	*See* Reference Window: Saving a Table

TASK	PAGE #	RECOMMENDED METHOD
Template, use an HTML	AC 392	Click the Export data with formatting and layout check box in the Export - HTML Document dialog box, click the Select a HTML Template check box, click Browse, select template, click OK
Title, add to a form or report	AC 296	In Controls group, click Title button, click and edit the title control, press Enter
Top values query, create	AC 229	*See* Reference Window: Creating a Top Values Query
Totals, calculating in a report	AC 343	In Layout view, click any value in the column to calculate, click Format tab, click Totals button in Grouping & Totals group, click Sum
Trusted folder, create	AC 246	Click [icon], click Access Options, click Trust Center, click Trust Center Settings, click Trusted Locations, click Add new location, click Browse, navigate to the desired folder, click OK four times
Update query, create	AC	*See* Reference Window: Creating an Update Query
Validation Rule property, set	AC 243	Display the table in Design view, select the field, enter the rule in the Validation Rule text box
Validation Text property, set	AC 241	Display the table in Design view, select the field, enter the text in the Validation Text text box
View, change in a folder window	WIN7 30	Click [icon], click the view to change to
Window, close	OFF 6	Click [icon] or click [icon]
Window, maximize	OFF 7	Click [icon] or click [icon]
Window, minimize	OFF 7	Click [icon] or click [icon]
Window, restore	OFF 7	Click [icon] or click [icon]
Windows, switch between using Aero Flip 3D	WIN7 16	Press and hold the Windows key and press Tab
Windows 7, log off	WIN7 39	Click [icon], point to [icon], click Log off
Windows 7, turn off	WIN7 39	Click [icon], click Shut down
Windows Explorer, open in Windows 7	WIN7 32	Click [icon] on the taskbar
Windows Explorer, start in Windows Vista	FM 7	Click [icon], click All Programs, click Accessories, click Windows Explorer
Workspace, zoom	OFF 8	*See* Reference Window: Zooming the Workspace
XML file, export an Access table to an	AC 404	*See* Reference Window: Exporting an Access Table as an XML File
XML file, import as a table	AC 400	*See* Reference Window: Importing an XML File as an Access Table